Admiralty Record®

Volume 7

PUBLISHED ADMIRALTY OPINIONS OF
THE SUPREME COURT OF THE UNITED STATES AND
THE UNITED STATES COURTS OF APPEALS ISSUED DURING
THE CALENDAR YEAR

2019

Cite as: 7 Adm. R. _____

REPORTED BY KIRK N. AURANDT, ESQ.
MEMBER OF THE BAR IN LOUISIANA AND PENNSYLVANIA

ADMIRALTY RECORD PUBLISHING COMPANY, L.L.C.
MANDEVILLE, LOUISIANA, U.S.A.

ISSN 2334-5411
ISBN 978-1-7337790-2-9

Admiralty record: published admiralty opinions of the
Supreme Court of the United States and the United
States Courts of Appeals issued during the calendar
year ... Mandeville, Louisiana, U.S.A.: Admiralty
Record Publishing Company, LLC, 2014-

    KF1104.A75
    ISSN: 2334-5411

https://lccn.loc.gov/2014200303

PREFACE

Volume 7—the seventh annual edition of the Admiralty Record®—reports the published admiralty opinions of the Supreme Court of the United States and the United States Courts of Appeals that were issued during the calendar year 2019. The opinions reported are the original majority, concurring, and dissenting opinions of the Court, with only minor changes in formatting to better suit a dual-column presentation. The pagination found in the Court's original opinion is indicated by the number contained inside of black brackets, *see, e.g.*, **[—15—]**. The pagination found in the official Reporter is indicated by the number contained inside of black braces, *see, e.g.*, **{–15–}**. Also, where applicable, I have added parallel citations to opinions reported in this Volume and in prior Volumes of the Admiralty Record®.

The decision to select an opinion to appear in Volume 7 of the Admiralty Record® was made solely by me following an examination of those opinions that each of the above-named courts designated for publication in 2019. Every effort has been made to ensure inclusion of all 2019 federal appellate court admiralty opinions that were designated for publication; however, to the extent that a relevant admiralty opinion has been inadvertently overlooked or otherwise mistakenly omitted, the error is regretted and is solely my own. A few opinions from appeals in civil cases that technically may not have fallen under a federal district court's admiralty or maritime jurisdiction have been reported if they touched upon admiralty matters, or were otherwise deemed to be of potential interest to the admiralty practitioner. Additionally, several opinions from criminal cases involving maritime crimes and civil cases arising under the Federal Employers' Liability Act have been included.

To assist the reader in locating those opinions from 2019 involving subject matters of interest, I have prepared an Index to the opinions. I have also prepared Tables of Authority, which supply page references to the cases, statutes, and rules cited in each opinion. Prior to relying upon any of the opinions reported herein, the reader is reminded to verify the current status of any particular case as valid precedent by checking the case with a reliable citator.

Additional copies of the Admiralty Record® may be ordered at www.admiraltyrecord.com. I hope that the Admiralty Record® will continue to be a valuable and ready reference source for not only the admiralty practitioner, but for anyone who is interested in reading the published admiralty opinions of the federal appellate courts.

KIRK N. AURANDT, ESQ.

This page intentionally left blank

TABLE OF CONTENTS [1]
(CASES ARRANGED CHRONOLOGICALLY BY COURT)

PAGE

---

[1] In 2019, there were no published admiralty opinions from the United States Court of Appeals for the Tenth Circuit.

This page intentionally left blank

Supreme Court of the United States

Supreme Court of the United States

No. 17-1104

AIR & LIQUID SYSTEMS CORP.
vs.
DEVRIES

On Writ of Certiorari to the United States Court of
Appeals for the Third Circuit

Decided: March 19, 2019

Citation: 586 U.S. ____, 139 S.Ct. 986, 7 Adm. R. 2 (2019).

KAVANAUGH, J., delivered the opinion of the Court in
which ROBERTS, C.J., and GINSBURG, BREYER,
SOTOMAYOR, and KAGAN, JJ., joined. GORSUCH,
J., filed a dissenting opinion, in which THOMAS and
ALITO, JJ., joined.

[—1—] {–990–} KAVANAUGH, J.: {–991–}

In maritime tort cases, we act as a common-law court, subject to any controlling statutes enacted by Congress. See *Exxon Shipping Co.* v. *Baker*, 554 U. S. 471, 507–508 (2008). This maritime tort case raises a question about the scope of a manufacturer's duty to warn. The manufacturers here produced equipment such as pumps, blowers, and turbines for three Navy ships. The equipment required asbestos insulation or asbestos parts in order to function as intended. When used on the ships, the equipment released asbestos fibers into the air. Two Navy veterans who were exposed to asbestos on the ships developed cancer and later died. The veterans' families sued the equipment manufacturers, claiming that the manufacturers were negligent in failing to warn of the dangers of asbestos.

The plaintiffs contend that a manufacturer has a duty to warn when the manufacturer's product requires incorpo- [—2—] ration of a part (here, asbestos) that the manufacturer knows is likely to make the integrated product dangerous for its intended uses. The manufacturers respond that they had no duty to warn because they did not themselves incorporate the asbestos into their equipment; rather, the Navy added the asbestos to the equipment after the equipment was already on board the ships.

We agree with the plaintiffs. In the maritime tort context, a product manufacturer has a duty to warn when (i) its product requires incorporation of a part, (ii) the manufacturer knows or has reason to know that the integrated product is likely to be dangerous for its intended uses, and (iii) the manufacturer has no reason to believe that the product's users will realize that danger. The District Court did not apply that test when granting summary judgment to the defendant manufacturers. Although we do not agree with all of the reasoning of the U. S. Court of Appeals for the Third Circuit, we affirm its judgment requiring the District Court to reconsider its prior grants of summary judgment to the defendant manufacturers.

I

Kenneth McAfee served in the U. S. Navy for more than 20 years. As relevant here, McAfee worked on the U. S. S. *Wanamassa* from 1977 to 1980 and then on the U. S. S. *Commodore* from 1982 to 1986. John DeVries served in the U. S. Navy from 1957 to 1960. He worked on the U.S. S. *Turner*.

Those ships were outfitted with equipment such as pumps, blowers, and turbines. That equipment required asbestos insulation or asbestos parts in order to function as intended. When used as intended, that equipment can cause the release of asbestos fibers into the air. If inhaled or ingested, those fibers may cause various illnesses.

Five businesses—Air and Liquid Systems, CBS, Foster Wheeler, Ingersoll Rand, and General Electric—produced [—3—] some of the equipment that was used on the ships. Although the equipment required asbestos insulation or asbestos parts in order to function as intended, those businesses did not always incorporate the asbestos into their products. Instead, the businesses delivered much of the equipment to the Navy without asbestos. The equipment was delivered in a condition known as "bare-metal." In those situations, the Navy later added the asbestos to the equipment.[1] {–992–}

McAfee and DeVries allege that their exposure to the asbestos caused them to develop cancer. They and their wives sued the equipment manufacturers in Pennsylvania state court. (McAfee and DeVries later died during the course of the ongoing litigation.) The plaintiffs did not sue the Navy because they apparently believed the Navy was immune. See *Feres* v. *United States*, 340 U. S. 135 (1950). The plaintiffs also could not recover much from the manufacturers of the asbestos insulation and asbestos parts because those manufacturers had gone bankrupt. As to the manufacturers of the equipment—such as the pumps, blowers, and turbines—the plaintiffs claimed that those manufacturers negligently failed to warn them of the dangers of asbestos in the integrated products. If the manufacturers had provided warnings, the workers on the ships presumably could have worn respiratory masks and thereby avoided the danger.

Invoking federal maritime jurisdiction, the manufacturers removed the cases to federal court. The manufacturers then moved for summary judgment on the ground that manufacturers should not be liable for harms caused by later-added third-party parts. That defense is known as the "bare-metal defense." [—4—]

The District Court granted the manufacturers' motions for summary judgment. The U. S. Court of Appeals for the Third Circuit vacated and remanded. *In re Asbestos Prods. Liability Litigation*, 873 F. 3d 232, 241, 5 Adm. R. 126, 132 (2017). The Third Circuit held that "a manufacturer of a bare-metal product may be held liable for a plaintiff 's injuries suffered from later-added asbestos-containing materials" if the manufacturer could foresee that the product would be used with the later-added asbestos-containing materials. *Id.*, at 240, 5 Adm. R. at 131.

---

[1] Sometimes, the equipment manufacturers themselves added the asbestos to the equipment. Even in those situations, however, the Navy later replaced the asbestos parts with third-party asbestos parts.

We granted certiorari to resolve a disagreement among the Courts of Appeals about the validity of the bare-metal defense under maritime law. 584 U. S. ___ (2018). Compare 873 F. 3d 232, 5 Adm. R. 126 (case below), with *Lindstrom* v. *A-C Prod. Liability Trust*, 424 F. 3d 488 (CA6 2005).

II

Article III of the Constitution grants the federal courts jurisdiction over maritime cases. Under 28 U. S. C. §1333, the federal courts have "original jurisdiction, exclusive of the courts of the States, of . . . [a]ny civil case of admiralty or maritime jurisdiction, saving to suitors in all cases all other remedies to which they are otherwise entitled."

When a federal court decides a maritime case, it acts as a federal "common law court," much as state courts do in state common-law cases. *Exxon Shipping Co.*, 554 U. S., at 507. Subject to direction from Congress, the federal courts fashion federal maritime law. See *id.*, at 508, n. 21; *Miles* v. *Apex Marine Corp.*, 498 U. S. 19, 27 (1990); *United States* v. *Reliable Transfer Co.*, 421 U. S. 397, 409 (1975); *Detroit Trust Co.* v. *The Thomas Barlum*, 293 U. S. 21, 42–44 (1934). In formulating federal maritime law, the federal courts may examine, among other sources, judicial opinions, legislation, treatises, and scholarly writings. See *Exxon Co., U. S. A.* v. *Sofec, Inc.*, 517 U. S. 830, 839 (1996); {–993–} *East River S. S. Corp.* v. *Transamerica* [—5—] *Delaval Inc.*, 476 U. S. 858, 864 (1986).

This is a maritime tort case. The plaintiffs allege that the defendant equipment manufacturers were negligent in failing to warn about the dangers of asbestos. "The general maritime law has recognized the tort of negligence for more than a century . . . ." *Norfolk Shipbuilding & Drydock Corp.* v. *Garris*, 532 U. S. 811, 820 (2001); see also *Kermarec* v. *Compagnie Generale Transatlantique*, 358 U. S. 625, 631–632 (1959). Maritime law has likewise recognized common-law principles of products liability for decades. See *East River S. S. Corp.*, 476 U. S., at 865.

In this negligence case, we must decide whether a manufacturer has a duty to warn when the manufacturer's product requires later incorporation of a dangerous part—here, asbestos—in order for the integrated product to function as intended.

We start with basic tort-law principles. Tort law imposes "a duty to exercise reasonable care" on those whose conduct presents a risk of harm to others. 1 Restatement (Third) of Torts: Liability for Physical and Emotional Harm §7, p. 77 (2005). For the manufacturer of a product, the general duty of care includes a duty to warn when the manufacturer "knows or has reason to know" that its product "is or is likely to be dangerous for the use for which it is supplied" and the manufacturer "has no reason to believe" that the product's users will realize that danger. 2 Restatement (Second) of Torts §388, p. 301 (1963–1964).

In tort cases, the federal and state courts have not reached consensus on how to apply that general tort-law "duty to warn" principle when the manufacturer's product requires later incorporation of a dangerous part in order for the integrated product to function as intended. Three approaches have emerged.

The first approach is the more plaintiff-friendly foreseeability rule that the Third Circuit adopted in this case: A **[—6—]** manufacturer may be liable when it was foreseeable that the manufacturer's product would be used with another product or part, even if the manufacturer's product did not require use or incorporation of that other product or part. See, *e.g.*, 873 F. 3d, at 240, 5 Adm. R. at 131; *Kochera* v. *Foster Wheeler, LLC*, 2015 WL 5584749, *4 (SD Ill., Sept. 23, 2015); *Chicano* v. *General Elec. Co.*, 2004 WL 2250990, *9 (ED Pa., Oct. 5, 2004); *McKenzie* v. *A. W. Chesterson Co.*, 277 Ore. App. 728, 749–750, 373 P. 3d 150, 162 (2016).

The second approach is the more defendant-friendly bare-metal defense that the manufacturers urge here: If a manufacturer did not itself make, sell, or distribute the part or incorporate the part into the product, the manufacturer is not liable for harm caused by the integrated product—even if the product required incorporation of the part and the manufacturer knew that the integrated product was likely to be dangerous for its intended uses. See, *e.g.*, *Lindstrom*, 424 F. 3d, at 492, 495–497; *Evans* v. *CBS Corp.*, 230 F. Supp. 3d 397, 403–405 (Del. 2017); *Cabasug* v. *Crane Co.*, 989 F. Supp. 2d 1027, 1041 (Haw. 2013).

The third approach falls between those two approaches. Under the third approach, foreseeability that the product may be used with another product or part that is likely to be dangerous is not enough to trigger a duty to warn. But a manufacturer does have a duty to warn when its product *requires* incorporation of a part and the manufacturer knows or has reason to know that the integrated product is likely to be dangerous for its intended **{–994–}** uses. Under that approach, the manufacturer may be liable even when the manufacturer does not itself incorporate the required part into the product. See, *e.g.*, *Quirin* v. *Lorillard Tobacco Co.*, 17 F. Supp. 3d 760, 769–770 (ND Ill. 2014); *In re New York City Asbestos Litigation*, 27 N. Y. 3d 765, 793–794, 59 N. E. 3d 458, 474 (2016); *May* v. *Air & Liquid Systems Corp.*, 446 Md. 1, 29, 129 A. 3d 984, 1000 (2015).

We conclude that the third approach is the most appro- **[—7—]** priate for this maritime tort context.

To begin, we agree with the manufacturers that a rule of mere foreseeability would sweep too broadly. See generally 1 Restatement (Third) of Torts: Liability for Physical and Emotional Harm §7, Comment *j*, at 82; 2 Restatement (Second) of Torts §395, Comment *j*, at 330. Many products can foreseeably be used in numerous ways with numerous other products and parts. Requiring a product manufacturer to imagine and warn about all of those possible uses—with massive liability looming for failure to correctly predict how its product might be used with other products or parts—would impose a difficult and costly burden on manufacturers, while simultaneously overwarning users. In light of that uncertainty and unfairness, we reject the foreseeability approach for this maritime context.

That said, we agree with the plaintiffs that the bare-metal defense ultimately goes too far in the other direction. In urging the bare-metal defense, the manufacturers contend that a business generally has "no duty" to "control the conduct of a third person as to prevent him from causing physical harm to another." *Id.*, §315, at 122. That is true, but it is also beside the point here. After all, when a manufacturer's product is dangerous in and of itself, the manufacturer "knows or has reason to know" that the product "is or is likely to be dangerous for the use for which it is supplied." *Id.*, §388, at 301. The same holds true, we conclude, when the manufacturer's product requires incorporation of a part that the manufacturer knows or has reason to know is likely to make the integrated product dangerous for its intended uses. As a matter of maritime tort law, we find no persuasive reason to distinguish those two similar situations for purposes of a manufacturer's duty to warn. See Restatement (Third)of Torts: Products Liability §2, Comment *i*, p. 30 (1997) ("[W]arnings also may be needed to inform users and [—8—] consumers of nonobvious and not generally known risks that unavoidably inhere in using or consuming the product").

Importantly, the product manufacturer will often be in a better position than the parts manufacturer to warn of the danger from the integrated product. See generally G. Calabresi, The Costs of Accidents 311–318 (1970). The product manufacturer knows the nature of the ultimate integrated product and is typically more aware of the risks associated with that integrated product. By contrast, a parts manufacturer may be aware only that its part could conceivably be used in any number of ways in any number of products. A parts manufacturer may not always be aware that its part will be used in a way that poses a risk of danger.[2]

To be sure, as the manufacturers correctly point out, issuing a warning costs time and money. But the burden usually is not significant. Manufacturers already {–995–} have a duty to warn of the dangers of their own products. That duty typically imposes a light burden on manufacturers. See, *e.g.*, *Davis* v. *Wyeth Labs., Inc.*, 399 F. 2d 121, 131 (CA9 1968); *Butler* v. *L. Sonneborn Sons, Inc.*, 296 F. 2d 623, 625–626 (CA2 1961); *Ross Labs.* v. *Thies*, 725 P. 2d 1076, 1079 (Alaska 1986); *Moran* v. *Faberge, Inc.*, 273 Md. 538, 543–544, 332 A. 2d 11, 15 (1975). Requiring a manufacturer to also warn when the manufacturer knows or has reason to know that a required later-added part is likely to make the integrated product dangerous for its intended uses should not meaningfully add to that burden.

The manufacturers also contend that requiring a warning even when they have not themselves incorporated the part into the product will lead to uncertainty about when product manufacturers must provide warnings. But the [—9—] manufacturers have not pointed to any substantial confusion in those jurisdictions that have adopted this approach. And the rule that we adopt here is tightly cabined. The rule does not require that manufacturers warn in cases of mere foreseeability. The rule requires that manufacturers warn only when their product *requires* a part in order for the integrated product to function as intended.

The manufacturers further assert that requiring a warning in these circumstances will lead to excessive warning of consumers. Again, however, we are not aware of substantial overwarning problems in those jurisdictions that have adopted this approach. And because the rule we adopt here applies only in certain narrow circumstances, it will not require a plethora of new warnings.

Requiring the product manufacturer to warn when its product requires incorporation of a part that makes the integrated product dangerous for its intended uses—and not just when the manufacturer itself incorporates the part into the product—is especially appropriate in the maritime context. Maritime law

---

[2] We do not rule out the possibility that, in certain circumstances, the parts manufacturer may also have a duty to warn.

has always recognized a "special solicitude for the welfare" of those who undertake to "venture upon hazardous and unpredictable sea voyages." *American Export Lines, Inc.* v. *Alvez*, 446 U. S. 274, 285 (1980) (internal quotation marks omitted). The plaintiffs in this case are the families of veterans who served in the U. S. Navy. Maritime law's longstanding solicitude for sailors reinforces our decision to require a warning in these circumstances. See *Yamaha Motor Corp., U. S. A.* v. *Calhoun*, 516 U. S. 199, 213 (1996); *Miles*, 498 U. S., at 36; *Moragne* v. *States Marine Lines, Inc.*, 398 U. S. 375, 387 (1970).

For those reasons, we conclude as follows: In the maritime tort context, a product manufacturer has a duty to warn when (i) its product requires incorporation of a part, (ii) the manufacturer knows or has reason to know that the integrated product is likely to be dangerous for its [—10—] intended uses, and (iii) the manufacturer has no reason to believe that the product's users will realize that danger. We do not purport to define the proper tort rule outside of the maritime context.

One final point for clarity: Courts have determined that this rule applies in certain related situations, including when: (i) a manufacturer directs that the part be incorporated, see, *e.g.*, *Bell* v. *Foster Wheeler Energy Corp.*, 2016 WL 5780104, *6–*7 (ED La., Oct. 4, 2016); (ii) a manufacturer itself makes the product with a part that the manufacturer knows will require replacement with a similar part, see, *e.g.*, *Chesher* v. *3M Co.*, 234 F. Supp. 3d 693,713–714 (S. C. 2017); {**-996-**} *Quirin*, 17 F. Supp. 3d, at 769–770; *May*, 446 Md., at 29, 129 A. 3d, at 1000; or (iii) a product would be useless without the part, see, *e.g.*, *In re New York City Asbestos Litigation*, 27 N. Y. 3d, at 793–794, 59 N. E. 3d, at 474. In all of those situations, courts have said that the product in effect requires the part in order for the integrated product to function as intended. We agree. The maritime tort rule we adopt today therefore encompasses those situations, so long as the manufacturer knows or has reason to know that the integrated product is likely to be dangerous for its intended uses, and the manufacturer has no reason to believe

that the product's users will realize that danger.

* * *

In the maritime tort context, we hold that a product manufacturer has a duty to warn when (i) its product requires incorporation of a part, (ii) the manufacturer knows or has reason to know that the integrated product is likely to be dangerous for its intended uses, and (iii) the manufacturer has no reason to believe that the product's users will realize that danger. The District Court should evaluate the evidence under that rule. Although we do not agree with all of the reasoning of the Third Circuit, we [—11—] affirm its judgment requiring the District Court to reconsider its prior grants of summary judgment to the defendant manufacturers.

It is so ordered.

(*Reporter's Note: Dissenting Opinion follows on p. 7*).

[—1—] {–996–} GORSUCH, J., with whom THOMAS and ALITO, JJ., join dissenting:

Decades ago, many of the defendants before us sold "bare metal" products to the Navy. Things like the turbines used to propel its ships. Did these manufacturers have to warn users about the dangers of asbestos that *someone else* later chose to add to or wrap around their products as insulation?

Start with a couple of things we can all agree on. First, everyone accepts that, under traditional tort principles, the manufacturers who actually supplied the later-added asbestos had to warn about its known dangers. Second, everyone agrees that the court of appeals erred when it came to analyzing the duties of the bare metal defendants. The court of appeals held that the bare metal manufacturers had a duty to warn because they could have "foreseen" the possibility that others would later use asbestos in conjunction with their products. Today, the Court rightly rejects this "foreseeability" standard, succinctly explaining that "[r]equiring a product manufacturer to imagine and warn about all of those possible uses—with massive liability looming for failure to correctly predict how its product [—2—] might be used with other products or parts—would impose a difficult and costly burden on manufacturers, while simultaneously overwarning users." *Ante*, at 7.

Our disagreement arises only in what comes next. Immediately after rejecting the court of appeals' approach, the Court proceeds to devise its own way of holding the bare metal manufacturers responsible for later-added asbestos. In the Court's judgment, the bare metal defendants had a duty to warn about the dangers of asbestos introduced by others so long as they (i) produced a product that "require[d] incorporation of" asbestos, (ii) "kn[ew] or ha[d] reason to know" that the "integrated product" would be dangerous, and (iii) had "no reason to believe" that users would realize that danger. *Ante*, at 9–10. The Court's new three-part standard surely represents an improvement over the court of appeals' unadorned "foreseeability" offering. But, respectfully, it seems to me to {–997–}

suffer from many of the same defects the Court itself has identified.

In the first place, neither of these standards enjoys meaningful roots in the common law. The common law has long taught that a manufacturer has no "duty to warn or instruct about another manufacturer's products, though those products might be used in connection with the manufacturer's own products." *Firestone Steel Prods. Co.* v. *Barajas*, 927 S. W. 2d 608, 616 (Tex. 1996). Instead, "the manufacturer's duty is restricted to warnings based on the characteristics of *the manufacturer's own product.*" *Powell* v. *Standard Brands Paint Co.*, 166 Cal. App. 3d 357, 364,212 Cal. Rptr. 395, 398 (1985).[1] It doesn't matter, either, [—3—] whether a manufacturer's product happens to be (or is designed to be) "integrated" with another's. Instead, it is black-letter law that the supplier of a product generally must warn about only those risks associated with the product itself, not those associated with the "products and systems into which [it later may be] integrated." Re-

---

[1] See also, *e.g.*, *Dreyer* v. *Exel Industries, S. A.*, 326 Fed. Appx. 353, 357–358 (CA6 2009); *Barnes* v. *Kerr Corp.*, 418 F. 3d 583, 590 (CA6 2005); *Reynolds* v. *Bridgestone/Firestone, Inc.*, 989 F. 2d 465, 472 (CA11 1993); *Baughman* v. *General Motors Corp.*, 780 F. 2d 1131, 1133 (CA4 1986); *In re Deep Vein Thrombosis*, 356 F. Supp. 2d 1055, 1068 (ND Cal. 2005); *Acoba* v. *General Tire, Inc.*, 92 Haw. 1, 18, 986 P. 2d [—3—] 288, 305 (1999); *Brown* v. *Drake-Willock Int'l, Ltd.*, 209 Mich. App. 136, 144–146, 530 N. W. 2d 510, 514–515 (1995); *Rastelli* v. *Goodyear Tire & Rubber Co.*, 79 N. Y. 2d 289, 297–298, 591 N. E. 2d 222, 225–226 (1992); *Walton* v. *Harnischfeger*, 796 S. W. 2d 225, 226 (Tex. App. 1990); *Toth* v. *Economy Forms Corp.*, 391 Pa. Super. 383, 388–389, 571 A. 2d 420, 423 (1990); *Mitchell* v. *Sky Climber, Inc.*, 396 Mass. 629, 631–632, 487 N. E. 2d 1374, 1376 (1986); *Johnson* v. *Jones-Blair Paint Co.*, 607 S. W. 2d 305, 306 (Tex. Civ. App. 1980); 63A Am. Jur. 2d, Products Liability §1027, p. 247 (2010); Behrens & Horn, Liability for Asbestos-Containing Connected or Replacement Parts Made by Third-Parties: Courts Are Properly Rejecting This Form of Guilt by Association, 37 Am. J. Trial Advocacy 489, 494–497 (2014).

statement (Third) of Torts: Products Liability §5, Comment *b*, p. 132 (1997).[2]

More than that, the traditional common law rule still makes the most sense today. The manufacturer of a product is in the best position to understand and warn users about its risks; in the language of law and economics, those who make products are generally the least-cost avoiders of their risks. By placing the duty to warn on a product's manufacturer, we force it to internalize the full cost of any injuries caused by inadequate warnings—and in that way ensure it is fully incentivized to provide adequate warnings. By contrast, we dilute the incentive of a manufacturer to warn about the dangers of its products when we require other people to share the duty to warn and its corresponding costs. See S. Shavell, Economic [—4—] Analysis of Accident Law 17 (1987); G. Calabresi, The Costs of Accidents 135, and n. 1 (1970); *Italia Societa per Azioni di Navigazione* v. *Oregon Stevedoring Co.*, 376 U. S. 315, 324 (1964).[3] {–998–}

The traditional common law rule better accords, too, with consumer expectations. A home chef who buys a butcher's knife may expect to read warnings about the dangers of knives but not about the dangers of under-cooked meat. Likewise, a purchaser of gasoline may expect to see warnings at the pump about its flammability but not about the dangers of recklessly driving a car. As the Court today recognizes, encouraging manufacturers to offer warnings about other people's products risks long, duplicative, fine print, and conflicting warnings that will leave consumers less sure about which to take seriously and more likely to disregard them all. In the words of the California Supreme Court, consumer welfare is not well "served by requiring manufacturers to warn about the dangerous propensities of products they do not design, make, or sell." *O'Neil* v. *Crane Co.*, 53 Cal. 4th 335, 343, 266 P. 3d 987, 991 (2012); see also *Cotton* v. *Buckeye Gas Prods. Co.*, 840 F. 2d 935, 938 (CADC 1988) ("The inclusion of each extra item dilutes the punch of every other item. Given short attention spans, items crowd each other [—5—] out; they get lost in fine print").

The traditional tort rule bears yet another virtue: It is simple to apply. The traditional rule affords manufacturers fair notice of their legal duties, lets injured consumers know whom to sue, and ensures courts will treat like cases alike. By contrast, when liability depends on the application of opaque or multifactor standards like the one proposed below or the one announced today, "equality of treatment" becomes harder to ensure across cases; "predictability is destroyed" for innovators, investors, and consumers alike; and "judicial courage is impaired" as the ability (and temptation) to fit the law to the case, rather than the case to the law, grows. Scalia, The Rule of Law as a Law of Rules, 56 U. Chi. L. Rev. 1175, 1182 (1989).

Just consider some of the uncertainties each part of the Court's new three-part test is sure to invite:

(i) When does a customer's side-by-side use of two products qualify as "incorporation" of the products? Does hanging asbestos on the outside of a boiler count, or must asbestos be placed inside a product? And when is incor-poration of a dangerous third-party

---

[2] See, *e.g.*, *Cipollone* v. *Yale Indus. Prods., Inc.*, 202 F. 3d 376, 379 (CA1 2000); *Crossfield* v. *Quality Control Equip. Co.*, 1 F. 3d 701, 703–704 (CA8 1993); *Childress* v. *Gresen Mfg. Co.*, 888 F. 2d 45, 48–49 (CA6 1989); *Koonce* v. *Quaker Safety Prods. & Mfg. Co.*, 798 F. 2d 700, 715 (CA5 1986).

[3] See also Restatement (Third) of Torts: Products Liability §5, Comment *a*, p. 131 (1997) ("If the component is not itself defective, it would be unjust and inefficient to impose liability solely on the ground" that others "utiliz[e] the component in a manner that renders the integrated product defective"); *Edwards* v. *Honeywell, Inc.*, 50 F. 3d 484, 490 (CA7 1995) (placing liability on a defendant who is not "in the best position to prevent a particular class of accidents" may "dilute the incentives of other potential defendants" who should be the first "line of defense"); *National Union Fire Ins. Co. of Pittsburgh* v. *Riggs Nat. Bank of Washington, D. C.*, 5 F. 3d 554, 557 (CADC 1993) (Silberman, J., concurring)("Placing liability with the least-cost avoider increases the incentive for that party to adopt preventive measures" that will "have the greatest marginal effect on preventing the loss").

product "required" as opposed to just optimal or preferred? What if a potential substitute existed, but it was less effective or more costly (surely alternatives to asbestos insulation have existed for a long time)? And what if the third-party product becomes less advantageous over time due to advancing technology (as asbestos did)? When does the defendant's duty to warn end?

(ii) What will qualify as an "integrated product"? In the past, we've suggested that a "product" is whatever assemblage of parts is "placed in the stream of commerce by the manufacturer," and we've stressed the importance of maintaining the "distinction between the components added to a product by a manufacturer [—6—] before the product's sale . . . and those items added" later by someone else. *Saratoga Fishing Co.* v. *J. M. Martinac & Co.*, 520 U. S. 875, 883–884 (1997). The Court's new standard blurs that distinction, but it is unclear how far it goes. The Court suggests a turbine and separately installed insulation may {–999–} now qualify as a single "integrated product." But what about other parts connected to the turbine? Does even the propeller qualify as part of the final "integrated product" too, so that its manufacturer also bears a duty to warn about the dangers of asbestos hung around the turbine? For that matter, why isn't the entire ship an "integrated product," with a corresponding duty for all the manufacturers who contributed parts to warn about the dangers of all the other parts? And when exactly is a manufacturer supposed to "know or have reason to know" that some supplement to its product has now made a resulting "integrated product" dangerous? How much cost and effort must manufacturers expend to discover and understand the risks associated with third-party products others may be "incorporating" with their products?

(iii) If a defendant reasonably expects that the manufacturer of a third-party product will comply with its own duty to warn, is that sufficient "reason to believe" that users will "realize" the danger to absolve the defendant of responsibility? Or does a defendant have to assume that the third-party manufacturer will behave negligently in rendering its own warnings? Or that users won't bother to read the warnings others offer? And what if the defendants here understood that the Navy itself would warn sailors about the need for proper handling of asbestos—did they still have to [—7—] provide their own warnings?[4]

Headscratchers like these are sure to enrich lawyers and entertain law students, but they also promise to leave everyone else wondering about their legal duties, rights, and liabilities.

Nor is this kind of uncertainty costless. Consider what might follow if the Court's standard were widely adopted in tort law. Would a company that sells smartphone cases have to warn about the risk of exposure to cell phone radiation? Would a car maker have to warn about the risks of improperly stored antifreeze? Would a manufacturer of flashlights have to warn about the risks associated with leaking batteries? Would a seller of hot dog buns have to warn about the health risks of consuming processed meat? Just the threat of litigation and liability would force many manufacturers of safe products to spend time and money educating themselves and writing warnings about the dangers of other people's more dangerous products. All this would, as well, threaten to leave consumers worse off. After all, when we effectively require manufacturers of safe products to subsidize those who make more dangerous items, we promise to raise the price and restrict the output of socially productive products. Tort law is supposed to be about aligning liability with responsibility, not

---

[4] See App. 40 (affidavit of retired Rear Admiral Roger B. Horne stating that "the Navy chose to control and make personnel aware of the hazards of asbestos exposures through . . . military specifications and personnel training").

mandating a social insurance policy in which everyone must pay for everyone else's mistakes.

Finally and relatedly, the Court's new standard implicates the same sort of fair notice problem that the court of appeals' standard did. Decades ago, the bare metal defendants produced their lawful products and provided all the warnings the law required. Now, they are at risk of [—8—] being held responsible retrospectively for failing to warn about other people's products. It is a duty they could not have anticipated then and one they cannot discharge now. They can only pay. Of course, that may be the {–1000–} point. In deviating from the traditional common law rule, the Court may be motivated by the unfortunate facts of this particular case, where the sailors' widows appear to have a limited prospect of recovery from the companies that supplied the asbestos (they've gone bankrupt) and from the Navy that allegedly directed the use of asbestos (it's likely immune under our precedents). *Ante*, at 3. The bare metal defendants may be among the only solvent potential defendants left. But how were they supposed to anticipate many decades ago the novel duty to warn placed on them today? People should be able to find the law in the books; they should not find the law coming upon them out of nowhere.

Still, there's a silver lining here. In announcing its new standard, the Court expressly states that it does "not purport to define the proper tort rule outside of the maritime context." *Ante*, at 10. Indeed, the Court acknowledges that it has created its new standard in part because of the "solicitude for sailors" that is a unique feature of our maritime jurisdiction. *Ante*, at 9. All of this means, of course, that nothing in today's opinion compels courts operating outside the maritime context to apply the test announced today. In other tort cases, courts remain free to use the more sensible and historically proven common law rule. And given that, "unlike state courts, we have little . . . experience in the development of new common-law rules of tort," *Saratoga*, 520

U. S., at 886 (Scalia, J., dissenting), that is a liberty they may be wise to exercise.[5]

---

[5] As the Court notes, some of the defendants sold the Navy products that were not "bare metal" but contained asbestos at the time of sale. *Ante*, at 3, n. 1. We can all agree that those defendants had a duty to [—9—] warn users about the known dangers of asbestos. And there's a colorable argument that their responsibility didn't end when the Navy, as part of routine upkeep, swapped out the original asbestos parts for replacements supplied by others. Under traditional tort principles, the seller of a defective, "unreasonably dangerous" product may be liable to an injured user if the product "is expected to and does reach the user . . . without substantial change in the condition in which it is sold." 2 Restatement (Second) of Torts §402A(1)(b), pp. 347–348 (1963–1964). And replacing worn-out parts every now and then with equivalently dangerous third-party parts may not qualify as a "substantial change" if the replacement part does "no more than perpetuate" problems latent in the original. *Sage* v. *Fairchild-Swearingen Corp.*, 70 N. Y. 2d 579, 584–587, 517 N. E. 2d 1304, 1306–1308 (1987); see, *e.g.*, *Whelan* v. *Armstrong Int'l Inc.*, 455 N. J. Super. 569, 597–598, 190 A. 3d 1090, 1106–1107 (App. Div. 2018). Of course, the defendants' original failure to warn might not be the legal cause of any harm if the use of the replacement part was unforeseeable, or if an intervening action severed the connection between the original sale and the injurious use. For example, if the replacement part itself posed the danger—or if, by the time the original part wore out, safer alternatives had become available. The Court's new standard, however, does not address these defendants separately, but focuses on the bare metal defendants.

Supreme Court of the United States

No. 17-949

STURGEON

vs.

FROST

On Writ of Certiorari to the United States Court of Appeals for the Ninth Circuit

Decided: March 26, 2019

Citation: 587 U.S. ___, 139 S.Ct. 1066, 7 Adm. R. 11 (2019).

KAGAN, J., delivered the opinion for a unanimous Court. SOTOMAYOR, J., filed a concurring opinion, in which GINSBURG, J., joined.

[—1—] {–1072–} KAGAN, J.:

This Court first encountered John Sturgeon's lawsuit three Terms ago. See *Sturgeon* v. *Frost*, 577 U. S. ___, 4 Adm. R. 2 (2016) (*Sturgeon I*). As we explained then, Sturgeon hunted moose along the Nation River in Alaska for some 40 years. See *id.*, at ___, 4 Adm. R. at 2 (slip op., at 1). He traveled by hovercraft, an amphibious vehicle able to glide over land and water alike. To reach his favorite hunting ground, he would pilot the craft over a stretch of the Nation River that flows through the Yukon-Charley Rivers National Preserve, a unit of the federal park system managed by the National Park Service. On one such trip, park rangers informed Sturgeon that a Park Service regulation prohibits the use of hovercrafts on rivers within any federal preserve or park. Sturgeon complied with their order to remove his hovercraft from the Yukon-Charley, thus "heading home without a moose." *Id.*, at ___, 4 Adm. R. at 4 (slip op., at 6). But soon afterward, Sturgeon sued the Park Service, seeking an injunction that would allow him to resume using his hovercraft on his accustomed route. The lower [—2—] courts denied him relief. This Court, though, thought there was more to be said. See *id.*, at ___–___, 4 Adm. R. at 8–9 (slip op., at 15–16).

As we put the matter then, Sturgeon's case raises the issue how much "Alaska is different" from the rest of the country—how much it is "the exception, not the rule." *Id.*, at

___–___, 4 Adm. R. at 7–8 (slip op., at 13–14). The rule, just as the rangers told Sturgeon, is that the Park Service may regulate boating and other activities on waters within national parks—and that it has banned the use of hovercrafts there. See 54 U. S. C. §100751(b); 36 CFR §2.17(e) (2018). But Sturgeon claims that Congress created an Alaska-specific exception {–1073–} to that broad authority when it enacted the Alaska National Interest Lands Conservation Act (ANILCA), 94 Stat. 2371, 16 U. S. C. §3101 *et seq.* In Alaska, Sturgeon argues, the Park Service has no power to regulate lands or waters that the Federal Government does not own; rather, the Service may regulate only what ANILCA calls "public land" (essentially, federally owned land) in national parks. And, Sturgeon continues, the Federal Government does not own the Nation River—so the Service cannot ban hovercrafts there. When we last faced that argument, we disagreed with the reason the lower courts gave to reject it. But we remanded the case for consideration of two remaining questions. First, does "the Nation River qualif[y] as 'public land' for purposes of ANILCA"? 577 U. S., at ___, 4 Adm. R. at 8 (slip op., at 15). Second, "even if the [Nation] is not 'public land,'" does the Park Service have authority to "regulate Sturgeon's activities" on the part of the river in the Yukon-Charley? *Id.*, at ___, 4 Adm. R. at 8–9 (slip op., at 16). Today, we take up those questions, and answer both "no." That means Sturgeon can again rev up his hovercraft in search of moose. [—3—]

I

A

We begin, as *Sturgeon I* did, with a slice of Alaskan history. The United States purchased Alaska from Russia in 1867. It thereby acquired "[i]n a single stroke" 365 million acres of land—an area more than twice the size of Texas. *Id.*, at ___, 4 Adm. R. at 2 (slip op., at 2). You might think that would be enough to go around. But in the years since, the Federal Government and Alaskans (including Alaska Natives) have alternately contested and resolved and contested and . . . so forth who should own and manage that bounty. We offer here a few highlights because they are the backdrop against which Congress enacted ANILCA. As we do so, you might catch a glimpse of some former-day John Sturgeons—who (for better or worse) sought greater independence from federal control and, in the process, helped to shape the current law.

For 90 years after buying Alaska, the Federal Government owned all its land. At first, those living in Alaska—a few settlers and some 30,000 Natives—were hardly aware of that fact. See E. Gruening, The State of Alaska 355 (1968). American citizens mocked the Alaska purchase as Secretary of State "Seward's Folly" and President Johnson's "Polar Bear Garden." They paid no attention to the new area, leading to an "era of total neglect." *Id.*, at 31. But as *Sturgeon I* recounted, the turn of the century brought "newfound recognition of Alaska's economic potential." 577 U. S., at ___, 4 Adm. R. at 2 (slip op., at 2). Opportunities to mine, trap, and fish attracted tens of thousands more settlers and sparked an emerging export economy. And partly because of that surge in commercial activity, the country's foremost conservationists—President Theodore Roosevelt and Gifford Pinchot, chief of the fledgling Forest Service—took unprecedented action to protect Alaska's natural resources. In particular, Roosevelt (and then President Taft) prevented settlers from logging or coal [—4—] mining on substantial acreage. See W. Borneman, Alaska: Saga of a Bold Land 240–241 (2003). Alaskans responded by burning Pinchot in effigy and, more creatively, organizing the "Cordova Coal Party"—a mass dumping of imported Canadian coal (instead of English tea) into the Pacific Ocean (instead of Boston Harbor). See *ibid.* The terms of future conflict were thus set: resource conservation vs. economic development, federal management vs. local control.

By the 1950s, Alaskans hankered for both statehood and land—and Congress {–1074–} decided to give them both. In pressing for statehood, Alaska's delegate to the House of Representatives lamented that Alaskans were no better than "tenants upon the estate of the national landlord"; and Alaska's Governor

(then a Presidential appointee) called on the country to "[e]nd American [c]olonialism." W. Everhart, The National Park Service 126–127 (1983) (Everhart). Ever more aware of Alaska's economic and strategic importance, Congress agreed the time for statehood had come. The 1958 Alaska Statehood Act, 72 Stat. 339, made Alaska the country's 49th State. And because the new State would need property—to propel private industry and create a tax base—the Statehood Act made a land grant too. Over the next 35 years, Alaska could select for itself 103 million acres of "vacant, unappropriated, and unreserved" federal land—an area totaling the size of California. §§6(a)–(b), 72 Stat. 340, as amended; see Everhart 127. And more: By incorporating the Submerged Lands Act of 1953, the Statehood Act gave Alaska "title to and ownership of the lands beneath navigable waters," such as the Nation River. 43 U. S. C. §1311; see §6(m), 72 Stat. 343. And a State's title to the lands beneath navigable waters brings with it regulatory authority over "navigation, fishing, and other public uses" of those waters. *United States* v. *Alaska*, 521 U. S. 1, 5 (1997). All told, the State thus emerged a formidable property holder. [—5—]

But the State's bonanza provoked land claims from Alaska Natives. Their ancestors had lived in the area for thousands of years, and they asserted aboriginal title to much of the property the State was now taking (and more besides). See Everhart 127. When their demands threatened to impede the trans-Alaska pipeline, Congress stepped in. The Alaska Native Claims Settlement Act of 1971 (ANCSA) extinguished the Natives' aboriginal claims. See 85 Stat. 688, as amended, 43 U. S. C. §1601 *et seq.* But it granted the Natives much in return. Under the law, corporations organized by groups of Alaska Natives could select for themselves 40 million acres of federal land—equivalent, when combined, to all of Pennsylvania. See §§1605, 1610–1615. So the Natives became large landowners too.

Yet one more land dispute loomed. In addition to settling the Natives' claims, ANCSA directed the Secretary of the Interior

(Secretary) to designate, subject to congressional approval, 80 million more acres of federal land for inclusion in the national park, forest, or wildlife systems. See §1616(d)(2). The Secretary dutifully made his selections, but Congress failed to ratify them within the five-year period ANCSA had set. Rather than let the designations lapse, President Carter invoked another federal law (the 1906 Antiquities Act) to proclaim most of the lands (totaling 56 million acres) national monuments, under the National Park Service's aegis. See 577 U. S., at ___, 4 Adm. R. at 3 (slip op., at 4). Many Alaskans balked. "[R]egard[ing] national parks as just one more example of federal interference," protesters demonstrated throughout the State and several thousand joined in the so-called Great Denali-McKinley Trespass. Everhart 129; see 577 U. S., at ___, 4 Adm. R. at 3 (slip op., at 4). "The goal of the trespass," as *Sturgeon I* explained, "was to break over 25 Park Service rules in a two-day period." *Ibid.*, 4 Adm. R. at 3. One especially eager participant played a modern-day Paul Revere, riding on horseback through the [—6—] crowd to deliver the message: "The Feds are coming! The Feds are coming!" *Ibid.*, 4 Adm. R. at 3 (internal quotation marks omitted).

And so they were—but not in quite the way President Carter had contemplated. Responding to the uproar his proclamation had set off, Congress enacted a third major {–1075–} piece of legislation allocating land in Alaska. We thus reach ANILCA, the statute principally in dispute in this case, in which Congress set aside extensive land for national parks and preserves—but on terms different from those governing such areas in the rest of the country.

B

Starting with the statement of purpose in its first section, ANILCA sought to "balance" two goals, often thought conflicting. 16 U. S. C. §3101(d). The Act was designed to "provide[] sufficient protection for the national interest in the scenic, natural, cultural and environmental values on the public lands in Alaska." *Ibid.* "[A]nd at the same time," the Act was framed to "provide[] adequate oppor-

tunity for satisfaction of the economic and social needs of the State of Alaska and its people." *Ibid.* So if, as you continue reading, you see some tension within the statute, you are not mistaken: It arises from Congress's twofold ambitions.

ANILCA set aside 104 million acres of federally owned land in Alaska for preservation purposes. See 577 U. S., at ___, 4 Adm. R. at 3 (slip op., at 5). In doing so, the Act rescinded President Carter's monument designations. But it brought into the national park, forest, or wildlife systems millions more acres than even ANCSA had contemplated. The park system's share of the newly withdrawn land (to be administered, as usual, by the Park Service) was nearly 44 million acres—an amount that more than doubled the system's prior (nationwide) size. See Everhart 132. With that land, ANILCA created ten new national parks, mon- [—7—] uments, and preserves—including the Yukon-Charley Preserve—and expanded three old ones. See §§410hh, 410hh–1. In line with the Park Service's usual terminology, ANILCA calls each such park or other area a "conservation system unit." §3102(4) ("The term . . . means any unit in Alaska of the National Park System"); see 54 U. S. C. §100102(6) (similar).

In sketching those units' boundary lines, Congress made an uncommon choice—to follow "topographic or natural features," rather than enclose only federally owned lands. §3103(b); see Brief for Respondents 24 (agreeing that "ANILCA [is] atypical in [this] respect"). In most parks outside Alaska, boundaries surround mainly federal property holdings. "[E]arly national parks were carved out of a larger public domain, in which virtually all land" was federally owned. Sax, Helpless Giants: The National Parks and the Regulation of Private Lands, 75 Mich. L. Rev. 239, 263 (1976); see Dept. of Interior, Nat. Park Serv., Statistical Abstract 87 (2017) (Table 9) (noting that only 2 of Yellowstone's 2.2 million acres are in non-federal hands). And even in more recently established parks, Congress has used gerrymandered borders to exclude most non-federal land. See Sax, Buying Scenery, 1980 Duke L. J. 709, 712, and n. 12. But Congress had no real way to do that in Alaska. Its prior cessions of property to the State and Alaska Natives had created a "confusing patchwork of ownership" all but impossible to draw one's way around. C. Naske & H. Slotnick, Alaska: A History 317 (3d ed. 2011). What's more, an Alaskan Senator noted, the United States might want to reacquire state or Native holdings in the same "natural areas" as reserved federal land; that could occur most handily if Congress drew boundaries, "wherever possible, to encompass" those holdings and authorized the Secretary to buy whatever lay inside. 126 Cong. Rec. 21882 (1980) (remarks of Sen. Stevens). The upshot was a vast set of so-called inhold- [—8—] ings—more than 18 million acres of state, Native, and private land—that wound up inside Alaskan {—1076—} system units. See 577 U. S., at ___–___, 4 Adm. R. at 3–4 (slip op., at 5–6).

Had Congress done nothing more, those inholdings could have become subject to many Park Service rules—the same kind of "restrictive federal regulations" Alaskans had protested in the years leading up to ANILCA (and further back too). *Id.*, at ___, 4 Adm. R. at 3 (slip op., at 4). That is because the Secretary, acting through the Director of the Park Service, has broad authority under the National Park Service Organic Act (Organic Act), 39 Stat. 535, to administer both lands and waters within all system units in the country. See 54 U. S. C. §§100751, 100501, 100102. The Secretary "shall prescribe such regulations as [he] considers necessary or proper for the use and management of System units." §100751(a). And he may, more specifically, issue regulations concerning "boating and other activities on or relating to water located within System units." §100751(b). Those statutory grants of power make no distinctions based on the ownership of either lands or waters (or lands beneath waters).[1] And although the Park Service has sometimes chosen not to regulate non-federally owned lands and waters, it has also imposed major

restrictions on their use. Rules about mining and solid-waste disposal, for example, apply to all lands within system units "whether federally or nonfederally owned." 36 CFR §6.2; see §9.2. And (of particular note here) the Park Service freely regulates activities on all navigable (and some other) waters "within [a park's] boundaries"—once more, "without regard to . . . ownership." §1.2(a)(3). So Alaska and its Natives had reason to worry about how [—9—] the Park Service would regulate their lands and waters within the new parks.

Congress thus acted, as even the Park Service agrees, to give the State and Natives "assurance that their [lands] wouldn't be treated just like" federally owned property. Tr. of Oral Arg. 50. (It is only—though this is quite a large "only"—the nature and extent of that assurance that is in dispute.) The key provision here is Section 103(c), which contains three sentences that may require some re-reading. We quote it first in one block; then provide some definitions; then go over it again a bit more slowly. But still, you should expect to return to this text as you proceed through this opinion.

Section 103(c) provides in full:

"Only those lands within the boundaries of any conservation system unit which are public lands (as such term is defined in this Act) shall be deemed to be included as a portion of such unit. No lands which, before, on, or after [the date of ANILCA's passage], are conveyed to the State, to any Native Corporation, or to any private party shall be subject to the regulations applicable solely to public lands within such units. If the State, a Native Corporation, or other owner desires to convey any such lands, the Secretary may acquire such lands in accordance with applicable law (including this Act), and any such lands shall become part of the unit, and be administered accordingly." §3103(c).

Now for the promised definitions. The term "land," as found in all three sentences,

---

[1] None of the parties here have questioned the constitutional validity of the above statutory grants as applied to inholdings, and we therefore do not address the issue. Cf. *Kleppe* v. *New Mexico*, 426 U. S. 529, 536– 541 (1976); *Kansas* v. *Colorado*, 206 U. S. 46, 88–89 (1907).

actually—and crucially for this case—"means lands, waters, and interests therein." §3102(1). The term "public lands," in the first two sentences, then {–1077–} means "lands" (including waters and interests therein) "the title to which is in the United States"— except for lands selected for future transfer to the State or [—10—] Native Corporations (under the Statehood Act or ANCSA). §3102(2), (3); see *supra*, at 4–5. "Public lands" are therefore most but not quite all lands (and again, waters and interests) that the Federal Government owns.

Finally, to recap. As explained in *Sturgeon I*, "Section 103(c) draws a distinction between 'public' and 'non-public' lands within the boundaries of conservation system units in Alaska." 577 U. S., at __, 4 Adm. R. at 8 (slip op., at 14). Section 103(c)'s first sentence makes clear that only public lands (again, defined as most federally owned lands, waters, and associated interests) would be considered part of a system unit (again, just meaning a national park, preserve, or similar area). By contrast, state, Native, or private lands would not be understood as part of such a unit, even though they in fact fall within its geographic boundaries. Section 103(c)'s second sentence then expressly exempts all those non-public lands (the inholdings) from certain regulations—though exactly which ones, as will soon become clear, is a matter of dispute. And last, Section 103(c)'s third sentence enables the Secretary to buy any inholdings. If he does, the lands (because now public) become part of the park, and may be administered in the usual way—*e.g.*, without the provision's regulatory exemption.

C

We can now return to John Sturgeon, on his way to a hunting ground alternatively dubbed "Moose Meadows" or "Sturgeon Fork." As recounted above, Sturgeon used to travel by hovercraft up a stretch of the Nation River that lies within the boundaries of the Yukon-Charley Preserve. See *supra*, at 1. Until one day, three park rangers approached Sturgeon while he was repairing his steering cable and told him he was violating a Park Service rule. According to the specified regulation, "[t]he operation or use of hovercraft is prohibited" on navigable (and some [—11—] other) waters "located within [a park's] boundaries," without any "regard to . . . ownership." 36 CFR §§2.17(e),1.2(a)(3); see *supra*, at 2. That regulation, issued under the Secretary's Organic Act authority, applies on its face to parks across the country. See *supra*, at 8 (describing Organic Act). And Sturgeon did not doubt that the Nation River is a navigable water. But Sturgeon protested that in Alaska (even though nowhere else) the rule could not be enforced on a waterway—like, he said, the Nation River—that is not owned by the Federal Government. And when his objection got nowhere with the rangers (or with the Secretary, to whom he later petitioned), Sturgeon stopped using his hovercraft—but also brought this lawsuit, based on ANILCA's Section 103(c).

In *Sturgeon I*, we rejected one ground for dismissing Sturgeon's case, but remanded for consideration of two further questions. The District Court and Court of Appeals for the Ninth Circuit had held that even assuming the Nation River is non-public land, the Park Service could enforce its hovercraft ban there. See 2013 WL 5888230 (Oct. 30, 2013); 768 F. 3d 1066, 2 Adm. R. 503 (2014). Those two courts interpreted Section 103(c) to limit only the Service's authority to impose Alaska-specific regulations on such lands—not its authority to apply nationwide regulations like the hovercraft rule. But we viewed that construction as "implausible." 577 U. S., at ___, 4 Adm. R. at 8 (slip op., at 15). ANILCA, we reasoned, "repeatedly recognizes that Alaska is different." *Id.*, at ___, 4 Adm. R. at 7 (slip op., at 13); see *id.*, at ___, 4 Adm. R. at 8 (slip op., at 14) (The Act "reflect[s] the simple truth that Alaska is {–1078–} often the exception, not the rule"). Yet the lower courts' reading would "prevent the Park Service from recognizing Alaska's unique conditions"—thus producing a "topsy-turvy" result. *Ibid.*, 4 Adm. R. at 8. Still, we thought two hurdles remained before Sturgeon could take his hovercraft out of storage. We asked the Court of Appeals to decide whether the Nation River "qualifies as 'public land' for purposes of [—12—] ANILCA," thus indisputably subjecting it to the Service's regulatory authority. *Id.*, at ___, 4 Adm. R. at 8 (slip op., at 15). And if the answer was "no," we asked the Ninth Circuit to address whether the Service, on some different theory from the one just dispatched, could still "regulate Sturgeon's activities on the Nation River." *Id.*, at ___, 4 Adm. R. at 8–9 (slip op., at 16).

The Ninth Circuit never got past the first question because it concluded that the Nation River is "public land[.]" See 872 F. 3d 927, 936, 5 Adm. R. 418, 424 (2017). The court explained that it was bound by three circuit decisions construing that term, when used in ANILCA's provisions about subsistence fishing, as including all navigable waters. *Id.*, at 933–934, 5 Adm. R. at 421–22. Accordingly, the court again rejected Sturgeon's challenge. *Id., at 936, 5 Adm. R. at 424.

And we again granted certiorari. 585 U. S. ___ (2018).

II

We first address whether, as the Ninth Circuit found, the Nation River is "public land" under ANILCA. As defined, once again, that term means (almost all) "lands, waters, and interests therein" the "title to which is in the United States." 16 U. S. C. §3102(1)–(3). If the Nation River comes within that definition, even Sturgeon agrees that the Park Service may enforce its hovercraft rule in the stretch traversing the Yukon-Charley. That is because the Organic Act authorizes the Park Service to regulate boating and similar activities in parks and other system units— and under ANILCA's Section 103(c) those units include all "public land" within their boundaries. 54 U. S. C. §100751(a)–(b); 16 U. S. C. §3103(c); see *supra*, at 8–10.

But the United States does not have "title" (as the just-quoted definition demands) to the Nation River in the ordinary sense. As the Park Service acknowledges, running waters cannot be owned—whether by a government or by a private party. See *FPC* v. *Niagara Mohawk Power* [—13—] *Corp.*, 347 U. S. 239, 247, n. 10 (1954); Brief for Respondents 33. In contrast, the lands beneath those waters— typically called submerged lands—can be

owned, and the water regulated on that basis. But that does not help the Park Service because, as noted earlier, the Submerged Lands Act gives each State "title to and ownership of the lands beneath [its] navigable waters." 43 U. S. C. §1311; see *supra*, at 4. That means Alaska, not the United States, has title to the lands beneath the Nation River.

So the Park Service argues instead that the United States has "title" to an "interest" in the Nation River, under what is called the reserved-water-rights doctrine. See Brief for Respondents 32–37. The canonical statement of that doctrine goes as follows: "[W]hen the Federal Government withdraws its land from the public domain and reserves it for a federal purpose, the Government, by implication, reserves appurtenant water then unappropriated to the extent needed to accomplish the purpose of the reservation." *Cappaert* v. *United States*, 426 U. S. 128, 138 (1976). For example, this Court decided that in reserving land for an Indian tribe, the Government impliedly reserved sufficient water from a nearby river to enable the {–1079–} tribe to farm the area. See *Winters* v. *United States*, 207 U. S. 564, 576 (1908). And similarly, we held that in creating a national monument to preserve a species of fish inhabiting an underground pool, the United States acquired an enforceable interest in preventing others from depleting the pool below the level needed for the fish to survive. See *Cappaert*, 426 U. S., at 147. According to the Park Service, the United States has an analogous interest in the Nation River and other navigable waters in Alaska's national parks. "Because th[e] purposes [of those parks] require that the waters within [them] be safeguarded against depletion and diversion," the Service contends, "Congress's reservations of park lands also reserved interests in appurtenant navigable waters." Brief for Respond- [—14—] ents 35.

That argument first raises the question whether it is even possible to hold "title," as ANILCA uses the term, to reserved water rights. 16 U. S. C. §3102(2). Those rights, as all parties agree, are "usufructuary" in nature, meaning that they are rights for the Government to use—whether by withdrawing or maintaining—certain waters it does not own. See *Niagara Mohawk Power Corp.*, 347 U. S., at 246; Brief for Petitioner 36; Brief for Respondents 36. The Park Service has found a couple of old cases suggesting that a person can hold "title" to such usufructuary interests. See *ibid.*; *Crum* v. *Mt. Shasta Power Corp.*, 220 Cal. 295, 307, 30 P. 2d 30, 36 (1934); *Radcliff's Ex'rs* v. *Mayor of Brooklyn*, 4 N. Y. 195, 196 (1850). But the more common understanding, recently noted in another ANILCA case, is that "reserved water rights are not the type of property interests to which title can be held"; rather, "the term 'title' applies" to "fee ownership of property" and (sometimes) to "possessory interests" in property like those granted by a lease. See *Totemoff* v. *State*, 905 P. 2d 954, 965 (Alaska 1995) (collecting cases); Brief for State of Idaho et al. as *Amici Curiae* 21–22 (same). And we see no evidence that the Congress enacting ANILCA meant to use the term in any less customary and more capacious sense.

But even assuming so, the Nation River itself would not thereby become "public land" in the way the Park Service argues. Under ANILCA's definition, the "public land" at issue would consist only of the Federal Government's specific "interest" in the River—that is, its reserved water right. §3102(1), (3). And that reserved right, by its nature, is limited. It does not give the Government plenary authority over the waterway to which it attaches. Rather, the interest merely enables the Government to take or maintain the specific "amount of water"—and "no more"—required to "fulfill the purpose of [its land] reservation." [—15—] *Cappaert*, 426 U. S., at 141. So, for example, in the cases described above, the Government could control only the volume of water necessary for the tribe to farm or the fish to survive. See *Winters*, 207 U. S., at 576–577; *Cappaert*, 426 U. S., at 141. And likewise here, the Government could protect "only th[e] amount of water" in the Nation River needed to "accomplish the purpose of the [Yukon Charley's] reservation." *Id.*, at 138, 141.

And whatever that volume, the Government's (purported) reserved right could not justify applying the hovercraft rule on the Nation River. That right, to use the Park Service's own phrase, would support a regulation preventing the "depletion or diversion" of waters in the River (up to the amount required to achieve the Yukon-Charley's purposes). Brief for Respondents 34–35. But the hovercraft rule does {–1080–} nothing of that kind. A hovercraft moves above the water, on a thin cushion of air produced by downward-directed fans; it does not "deplet[e]" or "diver[t]" any water. Nor has the Park Service explained the hovercraft rule as an effort to protect the Nation River from pollution or other similar harm. To the contrary, that rule is directed against the "sight or sound" of "motorized equipment" in remote locations—concerns not related to safeguarding the water. 48 Fed. Reg. 30258 (1983). So the Park Service's "public lands" argument runs aground: Even if the United States holds title to a reserved water right in the Nation River, that right (as opposed to title in the River itself) cannot prevent Sturgeon from wafting along the River's surface toward his preferred hunting ground.[2] [—16—]

III

We thus move on to the second question we posed in *Sturgeon I*, concerning the Park Service's power to regulate even non-public lands and waters within Alaska's system units (or, in our unofficial terminology, national parks). The Service principally relies on that sort of ownership-indifferent authority in defending its decision to expel Sturgeon's hovercraft from the Nation River. See Brief for

---

[2] As noted earlier, the Ninth Circuit has held in three cases—the so-called *Katie John* trilogy—that the term "public lands," when used in ANILCA's subsistence-fishing provisions, encompasses navigable waters like the Nation River. See *Alaska* v. *Babbitt*, 72 F. 3d 698 (1995); *John* v. *United States*, 247 F. 3d 1032 (2001) (en banc); *John* v. *United States*, 720 F. 3d 1214 (2013); *supra*, at 12. Those provisions are [—16—] not at issue in this case, and we therefore do not disturb the Ninth Circuit's holdings that the Park Service may regulate subsistence fishing on navigable waters. See generally Brief for State of Alaska as *Amicus Curiae* 29–35 (arguing that this case does not implicate those decisions); Brief for Ahtna, Inc., as *Amicus Curiae* 30–36 (same).

Respondents 16–18, 25–32. And we can see why. If Sturgeon lived in any other State, his suit would not have a prayer of success. As noted earlier, the Park Service has used its Organic Act authority to ban hovercrafts on navigable waters "located within [a national park's] boundaries" without any "regard to . . . ownership." 36 CFR §§2.17(e), 1.2(a)(3); see *supra,* at 10–11. And no one disputes that Sturgeon was driving his hovercraft on a stretch of the Nation River (a navigable water) inside the borders of the Yukon-Charley (a national park). So case closed. Except that Sturgeon lives in Alaska. And as we have said before, "Alaska is often the exception, not the rule." *Sturgeon I,* 577 U. S., at ___, 4 Adm. R. at 8 (slip op., at 14). Here, Section 103(c) of ANILCA makes it so. As explained below, that section provides that even when non-public lands—again, including waters—are geographically within a national park's boundaries, they may not be regulated as part of the park. And that means the Park Service's hovercraft regulation cannot apply there.[3] [—17—]

To understand why, first recall how Section 103(c) grew out of ANILCA's unusual method for drawing park boundaries. See *supra,* at 7–8. Those lines followed the area's "natural features," rather than (as customary) the Federal Government's property holdings. 16 U. S. C. §3103(b). The borders thus took in immense tracts owned by the State, Native Corporations, and private individuals. And as you might imagine, none of those parties was eager {–1081–} to have its lands newly regulated as national parks. To the contrary, all of them wanted to preserve the regulatory status quo—to prevent ANILCA's maps from subjecting their properties to the Park Service's rules. Hence arose Section 103(c). Cf. Tr. of Oral Arg. 50 (Solicitor General acknowledging that Section 103(c) responds to the State's and Native Corporations' "concern[s]" about the effects of "includ[ing

their lands] within the outer boundaries" of the new parks). Now might be a good time to review that provision, block quoted above. See *supra,* at 9. In broad brush strokes, *Sturgeon I* described it as follows: "Section 103(c) draws a distinction between 'public' and 'non-public' lands," including waters, "within the boundaries of [Alaska's] conservation system units." 577 U. S., at ___, 4 Adm. R. at 8 (slip op., at 14).

Section 103(c)'s first sentence sets out the essential distinction, relating to what qualifies as parkland. It provides, once again, that "[o]nly" the "public lands" (essentially, the federally owned lands) within any system unit's boundaries would be "deemed" a part of that unit. §3103(c). The non-public lands (everything else) were, by negative implication, "deemed" not a part of the unit— even though within the unit's geographic boundaries. The key word here is "deemed." That term is used in legal materials "[t]o treat (something) as if . . . it were really something else." Black's Law Dictionary 504 (10th ed. [—18—] 2014). Legislators (and other drafters) find the word "useful" when "it is necessary to establish a legal fiction," either by "'deeming' something to be what it is not" or by "'deeming' something not to be what it is." *Ibid.* (quoting G.C. Thornton, Legislative Drafting 99 (4th ed. 1996)). The fiction in Section 103(c) involves considering certain lands actually within the new national parks as instead without them. As a matter of geography, both public and non-public lands fall inside those parks' boundaries. But as a matter of law, only public lands would be viewed as doing so. All non-public lands (again, including waters) would be "deemed," abracadabra-style, outside Alaska's system units.[4]

---

[3] Because we see, for the reasons given below, no ambiguity as to Section 103(c)'s meaning, we cannot give deference to the Park Service's contrary construction. See *Chevron U. S. A. Inc. v. Natural Resources Defense Council, Inc.,* 467 U. S. 837, 842 (1984) ("If the intent [—17—] of Congress is clear, that is the end of the matter").

---

[4] Consistent with that approach, Congress left out non-public lands in calculating the acreage of every new or expanded system unit. Sections 201 and 202 of ANILCA, in describing those units, state the acreage of only their public lands. See, *e.g.,* §410hh(1) (providing that Aniakchak National Preserve would "contain[] approximately [367,000] acres of public lands"); §410hh–1(3) (providing that Denali National Park would grow "by the addition of an area containing approximately [2,426,000] acres of public land").

The effect of that exclusion, as Section 103(c)'s second sentence affirms, is to exempt non-public lands, including waters, from the Park Service's ordinary regulatory authority. Recall that the Organic Act pegs that authority to system units. See *supra,* at 8. The Service may issue rules thought "necessary or proper" for "System units." 54 U. S. C. §100751(a). And more pertinently here, the Service may prescribe rules about activities on "water located within System units." §100751(b). Absent Section 103(c), those grants of power enable the Service to administer even non-federally owned waters or lands inside national parks. See *supra,* at 8. But add Section 103(c), and the equation changes. Now, according to that section's first sentence, non-federally owned waters and lands inside system units (on a map) are declared outside them (for the [—19—] law). So those areas are no longer subject to the Service's power over "System units" and the "water located within" them. §100751(a), (b). Instead, only the federal property in system units is subject {–1082–} to the Service's authority.[5] And that is just what Section 103(c)'s second sentence pronounces, for waters and lands alike. Again, that sentence says that no state, Native, or private lands "shall be subject to the regulations applicable solely to public lands within [system] units." 16 U. S. C. §3103(c). The sentence thus

---

[5] At times, the Park Service has argued here that the Organic Act gives it authority to regulate waters outside system units, so long as doing so protects waters or lands inside them. See Brief for Respondents 28–32. If so, the argument goes, that authority would similarly permit the Service to regulate the non-federally owned waters that Section 103(c) has deemed outside Alaskan system units, if and when needed to conserve those units' federal waters or lands. But at other points in this litigation, the Service has all but disclaimed such out-of-the-park regulatory authority. See No. 14–1209, Tr. of Oral Arg. 58 (Jan. 20, 2016) ("The Park Service [has] consistently understood its authority to be regulating [within] the park's boundaries. It's never sought to enact a regulation outside of the park's boundaries"). We take no position on the question because it has no bearing on the hovercraft rule at issue here. That rule, by its express terms, applies only inside system units. See *supra,* at 10–11. It therefore does not raise any question relating to the existence or scope of the Service's authority over water outside system units.

expressly states the consequence of the statute's prior "deeming." The Service's rules will apply exclusively to public lands (meaning federally owned lands and waters) within system units. The rules cannot apply to any non-federal properties, even if a map would show they are within such a unit's boundaries. Geographic inholdings thus become regulatory outholdings, impervious to the Service's ordinary authority.[6] [—20—]

And for that reason, Section 103(c)'s third sentence provides a kind of escape hatch—for times when the Park Service believes regulation of the inholdings is needed. In that event, "the Secretary may acquire such lands" from "the State, a Native Corporation, or other owner." §3103(c). (As noted earlier, facilitating those acquisitions was one reason Congress put non-federal lands inside park boundaries in the first instance. See *supra,* at 7.) When the Secretary makes such a purchase, the newly federal land "become[s] part of the [system] unit." §3101(c). And the Park Service may then "administer[]" the land just as it does (in the second sentence's phrase) the other "public lands within such units." *Ibid.* In thus providing a way out of the Section's first two sentences, the third underlines what they are doing: insulating the state, Native, or private lands that ANILCA enclosed in national parks from new and unexpected regulation. In sum, those lands may be regulated only as they could have been before ANILCA's enactment, unless and until bought by the Federal Government.

The Park Service interprets Section 103(c) differently, relying wholly on its second sentence and mostly on the single word "solely" there. True enough, the Service acknowledges, that anxiety about how it

---

[6] Another provision of ANILCA reflects that result. Right after Sections 201 and 202 describe each new or expanded system unit by reference to how many acres of public land it contains, see n. 4, *supra,* Section 203 authorizes the Park Service to administer, under the Organic Act, the areas listed in "the foregoing sections." §410hh–2. In [—20—] other words, Section 203 of ANILCA ties the Service's regulatory authority to the statute's immediately preceding statements of *public-land* acreage.

would regulate inholdings was "really what drove [Section] 103(c)." Tr. of Oral Arg. 46; see *supra,* at 9, 17. But still, the Service argues, the Section's second sentence exempts those non-public lands from only "one particular class of Park Service regulations"—to wit, rules "'applicable *solely to public lands.'*" Brief for Respondents 30 (quoting and adding emphasis {–1083–} to §3103(c)). In other words, if a Park Service regulation on its face applies only ("solely") to public lands, [—21—] then the regulation shall not apply to a park's non-public lands. But if instead the regulation covers public and non-public lands alike, then the second sentence has nothing to say: The regulation can indeed cover both. See *ibid.* The Park Service labels that sentence a "tailored limitation" on its authority over inholdings. *Ibid.* And it concludes that the sentence has no bearing on the hovercraft rule, which expressly applies "without regard to . . . ownership." 36 CFR §1.2(a)(3).

But on the Park Service's view, Section 103(c)'s second sentence is a mere truism, not any kind of limitation (however "tailored"). Once again: It tells Alaskans, so the Park Service says, that rules applying only to public lands . . . will apply only to public lands. And that rules applying to both public and non-public lands . . . will apply to both. (Or, to say the same thing, but with approximate statutory definitions plugged in: It tells Alaskans that rules applying only to the Federal Government's lands . . . will apply only to the Federal Government's lands. And that rules applying to federal, state, Native, and private lands alike . . . will apply to them all.) In short, under the Park Service's reading, Section 103(c)'s second sentence does nothing but state the obvious. Its supposed exemption does not in fact exempt anyone from anything to which they would otherwise be subject. Remove the sentence from ANILCA and everything would be precisely the same. For it curtails none of the Service's ordinary regulatory authority over inholdings.[7] [—22—]

And more: The Park Service's reading of Section 103(c)'s second sentence also strips the first and third sentences of their core functions. Under the Service's approach, the first sentence's "deeming" has no point. There is no reason to pretend that inholdings are not part of a park if they can still be regulated as parklands. Nor is there a need to create a special legal fiction if the end result is to treat Alaskan inholdings no differently from those in the rest of the country. And similarly, the third sentence's acquisition option has far less utility if the Service has its full regulatory authority over lands the Federal Government does not own. Why cough up money to "administer[]" property as "part of the [system] unit" unless doing so makes a real difference, by removing a regulatory exemption otherwise in effect? The Service's reading effectively turns the whole of Section 103(c) into an inkblot.

And still more (if implicit in all the above): That construction would undermine ANILCA's grand bargain. Recall that ANILCA announced its Janus-faced nature in its statement of purpose, reflecting the century-long struggle over federal {–1084–} regulation of Alaska's resources. See *supra,* at 3–6. In that opening section, ANILCA spoke about safeguarding "natural, scenic, historic[,] recreational, and wildlife values." 16 U. S. C. §3101(a). Yet it insisted as well on "provid[ing] for" Alaska's (and its citizens') "economic and social needs." §3101(d). In keeping with the

---

[7] And just to pile on: Even taken as a truism, the Park Service's view of the second sentence misfires, because of the technical difference between "public lands" and federally owned lands in ANILCA. Recall that "public lands" is defined in the statute to mean most but not all federally owned lands: The term excludes those federal lands selected for future transfer to the State or Native Corporations. See §3102(3); *supra,* at 9–10. (That is why when we reframed the Park Service's argument just above, we noted that we were using "approximate" [—22—] statutory definitions.) But the Park Service's existing regulations apply, at a minimum, to *all* federally owned lands within a park's borders. See 36 CFR §1.2(a). That means there are no regulations "applicable solely to public lands" as defined in ANILCA. §3103(c). So when the Park Service argues that the second sentence exempts non-public lands from that single "class of [its] regulations," Brief for Respondents 18, 30, it is not even exempting those lands from obviously inapplicable regulations (as we assume in the text); instead, it is exempting them from a null set of rules.

statute's conservation goal, Congress reserved [—23—] huge tracts of land for national parks. But to protect Alaskans' economic well-being, it mitigated the consequences to non-federal owners whose land wound up in those new system units. See *supra*, at 17–20. Once again, even the Park Service acknowledges that Section 103(c) was supposed to provide an "assurance" that those owners would not be subject to all the regulatory constraints placed on neighboring federal properties. See Tr. of Oral Arg. 50; see *id.*, at 46–47; *supra*, at 9, 17, 20. But then the Service (head-spinningly) posits that it need only draft its regulations to cover both federal and non-federal lands in order to apply those rules to ANILCA's inholdings. On that view, limitations on the Service's authority are purely a matter of administrative grace, dependent on how narrowly (or broadly) the Service chooses to write its regulations. And ANILCA's carefully drawn balance is thrown off-kilter, as Alaskan, Native, and private inholdings are exposed to the full extent of the Service's regulatory authority.

The word "solely" in Section 103(c)'s second sentence does not support that kind of statute-gutting. We do not gainsay that the Park Service has identified a grammatically possible way of viewing that word's function: as pinpointing a narrow class of the Service's regulations (those "solely applicable to public lands").[8] But that reading, for all the reasons just stated, is "ultimately inconsistent" with the "text and context of the statute." *Sturgeon I*, 577 U. S., at ___, 4 Adm. R. at 7 (slip op., at 12). And a different understanding of "solely" instead aligns with that text and context. That word encapsulates Congress's view that the Park Service's regulations should apply "solely" to public lands (and not to state, Native, or private ones). See [—24—] *supra*, at 19, and n. 5. And the word serves to distinguish between the Park Service's rules and other regulations, both federal and state. Consider if Congress had exempted non-public lands in a system unit from regulations

"applicable to public lands" there (without the "solely").That language would apparently exempt those lands not just from park regulations but from a raft of others—*e.g.*, pollution regulations of the Environmental Protection Agency, water safety regulations of the Coast Guard, even employment regulations of Alaska itself. For those rules, too, apply to public lands inside national parks. By adding "solely," Congress made clear that the exemption granted was not from such generally applicable regulations. Instead, it was from rules applying only in national parks— *i.e.*, the newly looming Park Service rules. Congress thus ensured that inholdings would emerge from ANILCA not worse off— but also not better off—than before.[9] [—25—] {–1085–}

The legislative history (for those who consider it) confirms, with unusual clarity, all we have said so far. The Senate Report notes that state, Native, and private lands in the

---

[8] It is unfortunate for the Park Service's argument that the narrow class of regulations thus identified does not in fact exist. See n. 7, *supra*. But we put that point aside for the remainder of this paragraph.

[9] The Park Service points to one provision of ANILCA that (it says) contemplates application of its rules to inholdings; but as suggested in the text that provision really envisions other agencies' regulations. Section 1301(b)(7) requires the Service to create for each system unit a land management plan that includes (among other things) a description of "privately owned areas" within the unit, the activities carried out there, and the "methods (such as cooperative agreements and issuance or enforcement of regulations)" for limiting those activities if appropriate. 16 U. S. C. §3191(b)(7). Nothing in that section "directs the Park Service" itself to issue or enforce regulations, as the Service now argues. See Brief for Respondents 30–31. Instead, the Service satisfies all its obligations under the provision by reporting on the panoply of federal and state statutes and regulations that apply to any non-public land (whether or not in a park). And indeed, the Service's management plans have taken exactly that form. See, *e.g.*, Dept. of Interior, Nat. Park Serv., Kobuk Valley National Park: Land Protection Plan 123–124 (1986) (noting that "[w]hile [Park Service] regulations do not generally apply to private lands in the park (Section 103, ANILCA)," the regulations "that do apply" include those issued under "the Alaska Anadromous Fish Act, the Endangered Species Act, the Clean Water and Clean Air acts, and the Protection of Wetlands, to name a few"); Dept. of Interior, Nat. Park Serv., Noatak National Preserve: Land Protection [—25—] Plan 138–139, 142 (1986) (similar).

new Alaskan parks would be subject to "[f]ederal laws and regulations of general applicability," such as "the Clean Air Act, the Water Pollution Control Act, [and] U. S. Army Corps of Engineers wetlands regulations." S. Rep. No. 96–413, p. 303 (1980). But that would not be so of regulations applying only to parks. The Senate Report states:

> "Those private lands, and those public lands owned by the State of Alaska or a subordinate political entity, are not to be construed as subject to the management regulations which may be adopted to manage and administer any national conservation system unit which is adjacent to, or surrounds, the private or non-Federal public lands." *Ibid.*

The sponsor of Section 103(c) in the House of Representatives described that provision's effect in similar terms. The section was designed, he observed, to ensure that ANILCA's new boundary lines would "not in any way change the status" of the state, Native, and private lands placed within them. 125 Cong. Rec. 11158 (1979) (statement of Rep. Seiberling). Those lands, he continued, "are not parts of th[e system] unit and are not subject to regulations which are applied" by virtue of being "part of the unit." *Ibid.* In short, whatever the new map might suggest, they are not subject to regulation as parkland.

We thus arrive again at the conclusion that the Park Service may not prevent John Sturgeon from driving his hovercraft on the Nation River. We held in an earlier part of this opinion that the Nation is not public land. See *supra,* at 12–15. And here we hold that it cannot be regu- [—26—] lated as if it were. Park Service regulations—like the hovercraft rule—do not apply to non-public lands in Alaska even when those lands lie within national parks. Section 103(c) "deem[s]" those lands outside the parks and in so doing deprives the Service of regulatory authority.

IV

Yet the Park Service makes one last plea—for some kind of special rule relating to Alaskan navigable waters. Even suppose, the

argument runs, that those waters do not count as "public lands." And even assume that Section 103(c) strips the Service of power to regulate *most* non-public lands. Still, the Service avers—invoking "the overall statutory scheme"—that ANILCA must at least allow it to regulate navigable waters. Brief for Respondents 40; see *id.,* at 40–45; Tr. of Oral Arg. 42 (ANILCA's regulatory restrictions were "not about navigable waters"); *id.,* at 63–64 (similar). Here, the Service points to ANILCA's general statement of purpose, which lists (among many other things) the {–1086–} "protect[ion] and preserv[ation]" of "rivers." 16 U. S. C. §3101(b). Similarly, the Service notes that the statements of purpose associated with particular system units refer to "protect[ing]" named rivers there. *E.g.,* §410hh–1(1). And the Service highlights several statutory sections that in some way speak to its ability to regulate motorboating and fishing within the new units. See §§3121, 3170, 3201, 3203(b), 3204.[10] According to the [—27—] Service, all of those provisions show that "ANILCA preserves [its] authority to regulate conduct on navigable waters" in national parks. Brief for Respondents 42.

But ANILCA does not readily allow the decoupling of navigable waters from other non-federally owned areas in Alaskan national parks for regulatory (or, indeed, any other) purposes. Section 103(c), as we have described, speaks of "lands (as such term is defined in th[e] Act)." 16 U. S. C. §3103(c); see *supra,* at 9. The Act, in turn, defines "land" to mean "lands, waters, and interests therein." §3102(1)–(3); see *supra,* at 9. So according to an express definition, when ANILCA refers to

---

[10] The Park Service also points to a separate title of ANILCA, which raises issues outside the scope of this case. Title VI designates 26 named rivers in Alaska as "wild and scenic rivers," to be "administered by the Secretary" under the (nationwide) Wild and Scenic Rivers Act, 94 Stat. 2412–2413. According to the Service, those special designations (and associated management instructions) enable it to "administer the [specified] rivers pursuant to its general statutory authorities"—notwithstanding anything in Section 103(c). Brief for Respondents 42–43. But the Nation River, all agree, is not a "wild and scenic river." We may therefore leave for another day the interplay between Section [—27—] 103(c) and Title VI.

"lands," it means waters (including navigable waters) as well. And that kind of definition is "virtually conclusive." A. Scalia & B. Garner, Reading Law: The Interpretation of Legal Texts 228 (2012); see *ibid.* ("It is very rare that a defined meaning can be replaced" or altered). Save for some exceptional reason, we must read ANILCA as treating identically solid ground and flowing water. So if the Park Service were right that it could regulate the Nation River under its ordinary authorities, then it also could regulate the private fields and farms in the surrounding park. And more to the point, once Section 103(c) is understood to preclude the regulation of those landed properties, then the same result follows—"virtually conclusive[ly]"—for the river.

And nothing in the few aquatic provisions to which the Park Service points can flip that strong presumption, for none conflicts with reading Section 103(c)'s regulatory exemption to cover non-federal waters. The most substantive of those provisions, as just noted, contemplate some role for the Service in regulating motorboating and fishing. But contra the Park Service, those sections have effect under our interpretation because both activities can occur on federally owned (and thus fully regulable) non- [—28—] navigable waters. The other provisions the Service emphasizes are statements of purpose, which by their nature "cannot override [a statute's] operative language." *Id.*, at 220. And anyway, our construction leaves the Park Service with multiple tools to "protect" rivers in Alaskan national parks, as those statements anticipate. §3101(b); §410hh–1(1). The Park Service may at a minimum regulate the public lands flanking rivers. It may, additionally, enter into "cooperative agreements" with the State (which holds the rivers' submerged lands) to preserve the rivers themselves. §3181(j). It may similarly propose that state or other federal agencies with appropriate jurisdiction undertake needed regulatory action on those rivers. See §3191(b)(7); see also Kobuk Valley: Land Protection Plan, at 118, {–1087–} 121 (recommending that the Alaska Department of Natural Resources classify navigable parts of the Kobuk River for preservation efforts). And if all else fails, the Park Service may invoke Section 103(c)'s third

sentence to buy from Alaska the submerged lands of navigable waters—and then administer them as public lands. See §§3103(c), 3192; see also Kobuk Valley: Land Protection Plan, at 133 (proposing that if Alaska does not adequately protect the Kobuk River, the Park Service should "seek to acquire title to th[o]se state lands through exchange").

Those authorities, though falling short of the Service's usual power to administer navigable waters in system units, accord with ANILCA's "repeated[] recogni[tion] that Alaska is different." *Sturgeon I*, 577 U. S., at ___, 4 Adm. R. at 7 (slip op., at 13). ANILCA's broadly drawn parks include stretches of some of the State's most important rivers, such as the Yukon and Kuskokwim. See Brief for State of Alaska as *Amicus Curiae* 12. And rivers function as the roads of Alaska, to an extent unknown anyplace else in the country. Over three-quarters of Alaska's 300 communities live in regions unconnected to the State's road system. See *id.*, at 11. Residents of those areas include many of Alaska's [—29—] poorest citizens, who rely on rivers for access to necessities like food and fuel. See *id.*, at 11–12. Who knows?—maybe John Sturgeon could have found a comparable hunting ground that did not involve traveling by hovercraft through a national park. But some Alaskans have no such options. The State's extreme climate and rugged terrain make them dependent on rivers to reach a market, a hospital, or a home. So ANILCA recognized that when it came to navigable waters—just as to non-federal lands—in the new parks, Alaska should be "the exception, not the rule." *Sturgeon I*, 577 U. S., at ___, 4 Adm. R. at 8 (slip op., at 14). Which is to say, exempt from the Park Service's normal regulatory authority.

V

ANILCA, like much legislation, was a settlement. The statute set aside more than a hundred million acres of Alaska for conservation. In so doing, it enabled the Park Service to protect—if need be, through expansive regulation—"the national interest in the scenic, natural, cultural and environmental values on the public lands in Alaska."16 U. S. C. §3101(d). But public lands (and waters) was where it drew the line—or, at any rate, the legal one. ANILCA changed nothing for all the state, Native, and private lands (and waters) swept within the new parks' boundaries. Those lands, of course, remain subject to all the regulatory powers they were before, exercised by the EPA, Coast Guard, and the like. But they did not become subject to new regulation by the happenstance of ending up within a national park. In those areas, Section 103(c)makes clear, Park Service administration does not replace local control. For that reason, park rangers cannot enforce the Service's hovercraft rule on the Nation River. And John Sturgeon can once again drive his hovercraft up that river to Moose Meadows.

We accordingly reverse the judgment below and remand **[—30—]** the case for further proceedings consistent with this opinion.

It is so ordered.

(Reporter's Note: Concurring Opinion follows on p. 25).

[—1—] {–1087–} SOTOMAYOR, J., with whom GINSBURG, J., joins concurring:

Professors have long asked law students to interpret a hypothetical ordinance that prohibits bringing "a vehicle into the {–1088–} park."[1] The debate usually centers on what counts as a "vehicle." Is a moped forbidden? How about a baby stroller? In this case, we can all agree that John Sturgeon's hovercraft is a vehicle. But now we ask whether he has brought it "into the park"—and, if not, how a river's designation as "outside the park" will affect future attempts to regulate there.

The Court decides that the Nation River is not parkland, and I join the Court's opinion because it offers a cogent reading of §103(c) of the Alaska National Interest Lands Conservation Act (ANILCA), 94 Stat. 2371, 16 U. S. C. §3101 et seq. I write separately to emphasize the important regulatory pathways that the Court's decision leaves open for future exploration.

The Court holds only that the National Park Service may not regulate the Nation River as if it were within [—2—] Alaska's federal park system, not that the Service lacks all authority over the Nation River. A reading of ANILCA §103(c) that left the Service with no power whatsoever over navigable rivers in Alaska's parks would be untenable in light of ANILCA's other provisions, which state Congress' intent that the Service protect those very same rivers. Congress would not have set out this aim and simultaneously deprived the Service of all means to carry out the task.

Properly interpreted, ANILCA §103(c) cannot nullify Congress' purposes in enacting ANILCA. Even though the Service may not apply its ordinary park rules to nonpublic areas like the Nation River, two sources of Service authority over navigable rivers remain undisturbed by today's decision. First, as a default, the Service may well have authority to regulate out-of-park, nonpublic areas in the midst of parklands when doing so is necessary or proper to protect in-park, public areas—for instance, to ban pollution of the Nation River if necessary to preserve habitat on the riverbanks or to ban hovercraft use on that river if needed to protect adjacent public park areas. Nothing in ANILCA removes that power. Second, Congress most likely meant for the Service to retain power to regulate as parklands a particular subset of navigable rivers designated as "Wild and Scenic Rivers," although that particular authority does not, by its terms, apply to the Nation River.

Because the Court does not address these agency authorities, see ante, at 19, n. 5, 26–27, n. 10, I join its opinion. I also wish to emphasize, however, that the Court's opinion introduces limitations on—and thus could engender uncertainty regarding—the Service's authority over navigable rivers that run through Alaska's parks. If this is not what Congress intended, Congress should amend ANILCA to clarify the scope of the Service's authority. [—3—]

I

Since the National Park System's creation in 1872, it has grown to include over 400 historic and recreation areas encompassing over 84 million acres. 54 U. S. C. §100101(b)(1)(A); 83 Fed. Reg. 2065 (2018). These areas provide habitat for 247 threatened or endangered species and received more than 325 million visitors in 2016 alone. Id., at 2065–2066.

The task of protecting this vast park system principally falls to the Park Service. In the National Park Service Organic Act (Organic Act), 39 Stat. 535, Congress entrusted the Service with regulating to leave the parks "unimpaired for the enjoyment of future generations." 54 U. S. C. §100101(a). Congress empowered the agency to promulgate regulations "necessary {–1089–} or proper" for managing the Park System, including regulations "concerning boating and other activities on or relating to water located within [Park] System units." §§100751(a), (b). The Service has carried out this charge by enacting a wide range of regulations,

---

[1] See A. Scalia & B. Garner, Reading Law: The Interpretation of Legal Texts 36 (2012); Hart, Positivism and the Separation of Law and Morals, 71 Harv. L. Rev. 593, 607 (1958).

including the ban on hovercraft use at issue. See 36 CFR §2.17(e) (2018).

Wielding its Organic Act authority, the Service applies many park rules on federally owned lands and waters it administers, as well as navigable waters "within the boundaries of the National Park System." See 36 CFR §§1.2(a)(1), (3). The title to lands beneath navigable waters, even within national parks, typically belongs to the States.[2] Because park boundaries can encompass both federally and nonfederally owned lands and waters, this means that some nonfederally owned waters are subject to Service regulations—at least outside of Alaska. See *ante*, at 7–8. [—4—]

Against this backdrop, Congress enacted ANILCA. As the Court explains, ANILCA added millions of acres of federal land to the National Park System in Alaska and simultaneously swept around 18 million acres of nonfederally owned lands within the geographic boundary lines of the new Alaska parks. *Ante*, at 6–8; see also *Sturgeon* v. *Frost*, 577 U. S. ___, ___–___, 4 Adm. R. 2, 3–4 (2016) (slip op., at 5–6). In ANILCA, Congress directed the Service to manage Alaska's new and expanded parks "as new areas of the National Park System" under its Organic Act authority. 94 Stat. 2383, 16 U. S. C. §410hh–2.

ANILCA reflects Congress' expectation that the Service will manage Alaska's parks with a particular focus on rivers and river systems. For instance, the agency must "maintain unimpaired the water habitat" for salmon in Katmai National Monument, preserve "the natural environmental integrity and scenic beauty of . . . rivers" in Gates of the Arctic National Park, and "maintain the environmental integrity of the entire Charley River basin, including streams, lakes and other natural features."§§410hh(4)(a), (10); §410hh–1(2); see also §§410hh(1), (6),(7)(a), (8)(a); §410hh–1(1). Some provisions of ANILCA direct the Service to regulate boating

in Alaska's parklands. See, *e.g.,* §3170(a). Others command the Service to regulate fishing. See, *e.g.,* §3201. Together, these provisions make clear that Congress must have intended for the Park Service to have at least some authority over navigable waters within Alaska's parks.

And yet, ANILCA includes one provision that can be read to throw a wrench into that authority: §103(c). This provision says that "[o]nly those lands within the boundaries of any conservation system unit which are public lands (as such term is defined in this Act) shall be deemed to be included as a portion of such unit." 16 U. S. C. §3103(c). Section 103(c) then says that no state, native, or private lands "shall be subject to the regulations applica- [—5—] ble solely to public lands within such units," although the Secretary may acquire those lands and administer them as part of the unit. *Ibid.* ANILCA, in turn, defines "public lands" as nearly all "lands, waters, and interests therein" in which the United States has title. §§3102(1)–(3). Crucially, Alaska has title to the lands under its navigable waters. See n. 2, *supra.* If the Service's ordinary authority over navigable waters within park boundaries is diminished in Alaska relative to everywhere else in the United States, all agree that ANILCA §103(c) is the culprit. {–1090–}

II

Thus we arrive at the crux of this case: How, if at all, does ANILCA §103(c) circumscribe the Service's ordinary authority over navigable rivers within the geographic boundaries of national parks?

A

I agree with the Court that the Service may not treat every navigable river in Alaska as legally part of Alaska's parks merely because those (nonpublic) rivers flow within park boundaries. The majority ably explains why ANILCA's text leads to this outcome. See *ante*, at 16–20. According to ANILCA §103(c), navigable waters (at least apart from Wild and Scenic Rivers) must be treated as waters outside of park units for legal purposes. Thus

---

[2] Under the Submerged Lands Act of 1953, each State has "title to and ownership of the lands beneath [its] navigable waters." 43 U. S. C. §1311(a); see *ante,* at 4, 13.

they may not be "subject to the regulations applicable solely to public lands within such units." 16 U. S. C. §3103(c).[3] [—6—]

This principle is all that is required to resolve Sturgeon's case. The hovercraft rule applies only inside park boundaries. 36 CFR §1.2(a) ("regulations contained in this chapter apply to all persons entering, using, visiting, or otherwise within . . . [w]aters subject to the jurisdiction of the United States located within the boundaries of the National Park System"). The Nation River is, for legal purposes, outside of park boundaries. The hovercraft rule therefore does not apply on the Nation River.

B

Critically, although the Court decides today that the Service may not regulate the Nation River "as part of the park," *ante*, at 16, the Court does not hold that ANILCA §103(c) strips the Service of all authority to protect navigable waters in Alaska. For good reason. It would be absurd to think that Congress intended for the Service to preserve Alaska's rivers, but left it without any tools to do so.

Imagine if all Service regulations could apply in Alaska's parklands only up to the banks of navigable rivers, and the Service lacked any authority whatsoever over the rivers themselves. If Jane Smith were to stand

on the public bank of the Nation River, bag of trash in hand, Service rules could prohibit her from discarding the trash on the riverbank. See 36 CFR §2.14(a)(1). The rules also could bar her from intentionally disturbing wildlife breeding activities, §2.2(a)(2), making unreasonably loud noises, §2.12(a)(1)(ii), and introducing wildlife into the park ecosystem, §2.1(a)(2). But reading ANILCA §103(c) to bar any Park Service regulation of navigable waters would [—7—] permit Jane to evade those rules entirely if she were to wade into the river or paddle along the bank in a canoe. She could toss her trash bag in the water and amp up her speakers with impunity. Under this reading, the Park Service would be powerless to stop her. Jane's actions would likely harm flora {–1091–} and fauna on the banks of the river, which are public areas inside park boundaries. Jane's trash also could drift from a navigable (and thus out-of-park, nonpublic) stretch of the Nation River into a nonnavigable (and thus in-park, public) stretch of the same river.[4] So much for the Service's duty to maintain the "environmental integrity" of the Charley River basin "in its undeveloped natural condition," 16 U. S. C. §410hh(10).

How can the Service adequately protect Alaska's rivers if it cannot regulate? What is more, how can it maintain nearby park areas, such as riverbanks or nonnavigable park waters downstream, if it has no power to check the contamination of navigable waters? To achieve Congress' stated goals in creating Alaska's parks, the Service must have some authority to protect navigable rivers within those parks.[5] [—8—]

---

[3] Notably, the Park Service did not argue—nor does the Court's opinion address—whether navigable waters may qualify as "public lands" because the United States has title to some interest other than an interest in reserved water rights. See §§3102(1)–(3). In particular, the United States did not press the argument that the Federal Government functionally holds title to the requisite interest because of the navigational servitude. See, *e.g., Kaiser Aetna* v. *United States*, 444 U. S. 164, 177 (1979) ("The navigational servitude . . . gives rise to an authority in the Government to assure that [navigable] streams retain their capac- [—6—] ity to serve as continuous highways for the purpose of navigation in interstate commerce"); *United States* v. *Rands*, 389 U. S. 121, 123 (1967) ("This power to regulate navigation confers upon the United States a 'dominant servitude' "); 43 U. S. C. §1314 (providing that the United States retains the navigational servitude in navigable waters).

[4] The navigability of a river is determined "on a segment-by-segment basis." *PPL Montana, LLC* v. *Montana*, 565 U. S. 576, 593 (2012); see also *id.,* at 594.

[5] Even if the Service cannot regulate the rivers itself, the majority says that the agency can enter into "cooperative agreements" with Alaska to regulate the rivers, 16 U. S. C. §3181(j), propose that state or other federal agencies take action to protect the rivers, §3191(b)(7), or buy the submerged lands from Alaska and then regulate them, §§3103(c), 3192. See *ante*, at 28. But Congress made the Service directly responsible for protecting Alaska's parks and park resources. The Service cannot carry out its duty to "manag[e]" the

C

Thankfully, today's decision does not leave the Service without any authority over the Nation River and other rivers like it. Even though most navigable rivers in Alaska are not public parklands, Congress has left at least two avenues for the Service to achieve ANILCA's purposes. Neither is addressed by the Court's decision.

1

First, the Court expressly does not decide whether the Service may regulate navigable waters running through Alaska's parks as an adjunct to its authority over the parks themselves. See *ante*, 19, n. 5.[6] In my view, the Service likely retains power over navigable rivers that run through Alaska's parks when that power is necessary to protect Alaska's parklands.

The Service's default ability to regulate comes from the Organic Act. That Act gives the Service general authority to promulgate all regulations "necessary or proper" for managing park units, including power to regulate activities "on or *relating* to water located within [Park] System units." 54 U. S. C. §§100751(a), (b) (emphasis added). Nothing in the text of the Organic Act suggests that the Service is powerless over out-of-park areas in the midst of public parklands, like the Nation River.

This brings us back to Jane, this time canoeing down the Nation River with a gallon of toxic insecticide onboard. **[—9—]** If Jane

---

park areas, see §410hh, if it is estopped from promulgating necessary rules and regulations.

[6] The Court's interpretation prohibits the Service only from applying its usual, in-park rules to out-of-park areas. See, *e.g.*, *ante*, at 16 (nonpublic lands "may not be regulated as part of the park"); *ante*, at 18 (Section 103(c)'s exclusion "exempt[s] non-public lands . . . from the Park Service's ordinary regulatory authority"); *ante*, at 19 (the areas "are no longer subject to the Service's power over 'System units' and the 'water located within' them"); *ante*, at 22 (rejecting suggestion that inholdings can be "regulated as parklands"); *ante*, at 25 (the inholdings "are not subject to regulation as parkland").

spills the insecticide into the river, the effects will surely reach the riverbanks—public areas within the park's legal **{–1092–}** boundaries. An antipollution rule tailored to apply to the Nation River as it runs through the park thus could well be "necessary or proper" to manage the parklands on either side of the river, even though the river itself is not legally a part of the park. §100751(a). And if the pollution is likely to harm nonnavigable stretches of the river downstream—public waters that are "within" the park for legal purposes—the ban also could be authorized because it specifically concerns "activities . . . relating to water located within [Park] System units." §100751(b). Similar reasoning could justify a range of Service regulations, giving the Service substantial authority over navigable rivers inside geographic park boundaries in order to protect the parklands through which they flow.

Assuming that the Service has such authority over out-of-park areas pursuant to its Organic Act, nothing in ANILCA §103(c) takes it away. That section's first sentence explains that nonpublic lands are not part of Alaska's park units. See 16 U. S. C. §3103(c); *supra*, at 4–5. The second sentence then emphasizes that the Service cannot regulate nonpublic lands as if they were part of the park. Together, these sentences mean that the Service loses its authority to apply normal park rules to nonpublic lands, and instead can apply only those rules that it can justify by reference to the needs of other, public lands. For instance, the Service is unlikely to have power to apply rules against abandoning property, 36 CFR §2.22(a), or trespassing, §2.31(a)(1), to nonpublic lands amid parklands because doing so would have little or no impact on neighboring public areas within the legal boundaries of the park. But a Service regulation tailored to apply to nonparklands in order to protect sensitive surrounding parklands—like a rule against putting a toxic substance in the Nation River to stop harms to the riverbanks—would **[—10—]** present a different question. Such a regulation could be consistent with the Service's limited Organic Act authority over out-of-park areas, and it would not run afoul of ANILCA because it would not be applicable to public lands.

The Service's out-of-park authority is not at issue in this case given that the hovercraft regulation applies only within park boundaries, see *ante*, at 19, n. 5. Hovercraft can be unsightly, be loud, and disturb sensitive ecosystems within the park. See 48 Fed. Reg. 30258 (1983) ("The Service has determined that hovercraft should be prohibited because they provide virtually unlimited access to park areas and introduce a mechanical mode of transportation into locations where the intrusion of motorized equipment by sight or sound is generally inappropriate"). If the Service were to choose to apply its hovercraft ban to the Nation River, the agency could justify doing so in certain designated areas to protect a particular sensitivity in a surrounding (public) park area, including some habitats on the banks of the Nation River.

2

The Court also leaves open a second way for the Service to protect navigable rivers. Because the Nation River is not a designated Wild and Scenic River, the Court expressly does not decide the extent of the Service's power over such designated rivers. *Ante,* at 26–27, n. 10. If ANILCA §103(c) is to be harmonized with the remainder of the statute, the Service must possess authority to regulate fully, as parklands, at least that subset of rivers.[7] [—11—] {-1093-}

The Wild and Scenic Rivers Act, 16 U. S. §1271 *et seq.*, established a system of rivers

that "possess outstandingly remarkable scenic, recreational, geologic, fish and wildlife, historic, cultural, or other similar values." §1271. Congress created the system to "preserv[e]" designate drivers "in free-flowing condition." *Ibid.* Rivers can become part of the system if they are designated by an Act of Congress. §1273(a)(i).

ANILCA designated 26 Alaskan rivers as components of this system, more than doubling the mileage of the rivers in the system at the time. 16 U. S. C. §1274; S. Johnson & L. Comay, CRS Report for Congress, The National Wild and Scenic Rivers System: A Brief Overview 1 (2015); see §1281(c). ANILCA, in turn, expressly defines the Alaskan park system as including "any unit in Alaska of the . . . National Wild and Scenic Rivers Systems." §3102(4).

Although ANILCA §103(c) generally has the effect of removing navigable waters from the legal boundaries of Alaska's parks, Congress' highly specific definition of the Wild and Scenic Rivers as a portion of Alaska's park system overrides ANILCA §103(c)'s general carveout. "General language of a statutory provision . . . will not be held to apply to a matter specifically dealt with in another part of the same enactment." *D. Ginsberg & Sons, Inc.* v. *Popkin*, 285 U. S. 204, 208 (1932). To make sense of ANILCA §103(c) within the context of the rest of ANILCA, the Service should retain full authority to regulate the Wild and Scenic Rivers as parklands. [—12—]

* * *

One final note warrants mention. Although I join the Court's opinion, I recognize that today's decision creates uncertainty concerning the extent of Service authority over navigable waters in Alaska's parks. Courts ultimately may affirm some of the Service's authority over out-of-park areas and Wild and Scenic Rivers. But that authority may be more circumscribed than the special needs of the parks require. This would not only make it impossible for the Service to fulfill Congress' charge to preserve rivers, made plain in ANILCA itself, but also

---

[7] This authority would supplement, not replace, the Service's authority over out-of-park navigable rivers, because the Service's authority over the Wild and Scenic Rivers alone cannot explain all of ANILCA's express references to protecting Alaskan rivers. For instance, ANILCA states Congress' expectation that the Service will manage the Kobuk River in Kobuk Valley National Park. See 16 U. S. C. §410hh(6). That [—11—] portion of the river is not designated as a Wild and Scenic River, see §1274, but the Bureau of Land Management has found it to be navigable, see Dept. of Interior, Nat. Park Service, Kobuk Valley National Park: General Management Plan 65 (1987). The Service therefore must have another source of authority over the river if the statute's purpose provision is not to be deprived of meaning.

threaten the Service's ability to fulfill its broader duty to protect all of the parklands through which the rivers flow. See, *e.g.*, 16 U. S. C. §410hh(6) (Kobuk Valley National Park "shall be managed . . . [t]o maintain the environmental integrity of the natural features of the Kobuk River Valley, including the Kobuk, Salmon, and other rivers"). Many of Alaska's navigable rivers course directly through the heart of protected parks, monuments, and preserves. A decision that leaves the Service with no authority, or only highly constrained authority, over those rivers would undercut Congress' clear expectations in enacting ANILCA and could have exceedingly damaging consequences.

In light of the explicit instructions throughout ANILCA that the Service must regulate and protect rivers in Alaska, I am convinced that Congress intended the {–1094–} Service to possess meaningful authority over those rivers. If I am correct, Congress can and should clarify the broad scope of the Service's authority over Alaska's navigable waters.

Supreme Court of the United States

No. 17-1201

THACKER
vs.
TENNESSEE VALLEY AUTH.

On Writ of Certiorari to the United States Court of Appeals for the Eleventh Circuit

Decided: April 29, 2019

Citation: 587 U.S. ____, 139 S.Ct. 1435, 7 Adm. R. 31 (2019).

KAGAN, J., delivered the opinion for a unanimous Court.

[—1—] {–1437–} KAGAN, J.: {–1438–}

Federal law provides that the Tennessee Valley Authority (TVA), a Government-owned corporation supplying electric power to millions of Americans, "[m]ay sue and be sued in its corporate name." Tennessee Valley Authority Act of 1933 (TVA Act), 48 Stat. 60, 16 U. S. C. §831c(b). That provision serves to waive sovereign immunity from suit. Today, we consider how far the waiver goes. We reject the view, adopted below and pressed by the Government, that the TVA remains immune from all tort suits arising from its performance of so-called discretionary functions. The TVA's sue-and-be-sued clause is broad and {–1439–} contains no such limit. Under the clause—and consistent with our precedents construing similar ones—the TVA is subject to suits challenging any of its commercial activities. The law thus places the TVA in the same position as a private corporation supplying electricity. But the TVA might have immunity from suits contesting one of its governmental activities, of a kind not typically carried out by private parties. We remand this case for consideration of whether that limited immunity could apply here. **[—2—]**

I

Congress created the TVA—a "wholly owned public corporation of the United States"—in the throes of the Great Depression to promote the Tennessee Valley's economic development. *TVA* v. *Hill*, 437 U. S. 153, 157 (1978). In its early decades, the TVA focused on reforesting the countryside, improving farmers' fertilization practices, and building dams on the Tennessee River. See Brief for Respondent 3. The corporation also soon began constructing new power plants for the region. And over the years, as it completed other projects, the TVA devoted more and more of its efforts to producing and selling electric power. Today, the TVA operates around 60 power plants and provides electricity to more than nine million people in seven States. See *id.*, at 3–4. The rates it charges (along with the bonds it issues) bring in over $10 billion in annual revenues, making federal appropriations unnecessary. See *ibid.*; GAO, FY 2018 Financial Report of the United States Government 53 (GAO–19–294R, 2019).

As even that short description may suggest, the TVA is something of a hybrid, combining traditionally governmental functions with typically commercial ones. On the one hand, the TVA possesses powers and responsibilities reserved to sovereign actors. It may, for example, "exercise the right of eminent domain" and "condemn all property" necessary to carry out its goals. 16 U. S. C. §§831c(h), (i). Similarly, it may appoint employees as "law enforcement agents" with powers to investigate crimes and make arrests. §831c–3(a); see §831c–3(b)(2). But on the other hand, much of what the TVA does could be done—no, *is* done routinely—by non-governmental parties. Just as the TVA produces and sells electricity in its region, privately owned power companies (*e.g.,* Con Edison, Dominion Energy) do so in theirs. As to those commonplace commercial functions, the emphasis in the oft-used label "public corporation" rests heavily on the latter word. *Hill,* **[—3—]** 437 U. S., at 157.

In establishing this mixed entity, Congress decided (as it had for similar government businesses) that the TVA could "sue and be sued in its corporate name." §831c(b); see, *e.g.,* Reconstruction Finance Corporation Act, §4, 47 Stat. 6; Federal Home Loan Bank Act, §12, 47 Stat. 735. Without such a clause, the TVA (as an entity of the Federal Government) would have enjoyed sovereign immunity from suit. See *Loeffler* v. *Frank*, 486 U. S. 549, 554

(1988). By instead providing that the TVA could "be sued," Congress waived at least some of the corporation's immunity. (Just how much is the question here.) Slightly more than a decade after creating the TVA, Congress enacted the Federal Tort Claims Act of 1946 (FTCA), 28 U. S. C. §§1346(b), 2671 *et seq.*, to waive immunity from tort suits involving agencies across the Government. See §1346(b)(1) (waiving immunity from damages claims based on "the negligent or wrongful act or omission of any employee of the Government"). That statute carved out an exception for claims based on a federal employee's performance {–1440–} of a "discretionary function." §2680(a). But Congress specifically excluded from all the FTCA's provisions—including the discretionary function exception—"[a]ny claim arising from the activities of the [TVA]." §2680(*l*).

This case involves such a claim. See App. 22–33 (Complaint). One summer day, TVA employees embarked on work to replace a power line over the Tennessee River. When a cable they were using failed, the power line fell into the water. The TVA informed the Coast Guard, which announced that it was closing part of the river; and the TVA itself positioned two patrol boats near the downed line. But several hours later, just as the TVA workers began to raise the line, petitioner Gary Thacker drove his boat into the area at high speed. The boat and line collided, seriously injuring Thacker and killing a passenger. [—4—] Thacker sued for negligence, alleging that the TVA had failed to "exercise reasonable care" in "assembl[ing] and install[ing] power lines" and in "warning boaters" like him "of the hazards it created." *Id.*, at 31.

The TVA moved to dismiss the suit, claiming sovereign immunity. The District Court granted the motion. It reasoned that the TVA, no less than other government agencies, is entitled to immunity from any suit based on an employee's exercise of discretionary functions. See 188 F. Supp. 3d 1243, 1245 (ND Ala. 2016). And it thought that the TVA's actions surrounding the boating accident were discretionary because "they involve[d] some judgment and choice." *Ibid.* The Court of

Appeals for the Eleventh Circuit affirmed on the same ground. According to the circuit court, the TVA has immunity for discretionary functions even when they are part of the "TVA's commercial, power-generating activities." 868 F. 3d 979, 981, 5 Adm. R. 503, 504 (2017). In deciding whether a suit implicates those functions, the court explained that it "use[s] the same test that applies when the government invokes the discretionary-function exception to the [FTCA]." *Id.*, at 982, 5 Adm. R. at 504. And that test, the court agreed, foreclosed Thacker's suit because the challenged actions were "a matter of choice." *Ibid.*, 5 Adm. R. at 504–05 (internal quotation marks omitted).

We granted certiorari to decide whether the waiver of sovereign immunity in TVA's sue-and-be-sued clause is subject to a discretionary function exception, of the kind in the FTCA. 585 U. S. ___ (2018). We hold it is not.

II

Nothing in the statute establishing the TVA (again, the TVA Act for short) expressly recognizes immunity for discretionary functions. As noted above, that law provides simply that the TVA "[m]ay sue and be sued." 16 U. S. C. §831c(b); see *supra*, at 3. Such a sue-and-be-sued clause serves to waive sovereign immunity otherwise belonging [—5—] to an agency of the Federal Government. See *Loeffler*, 486 U. S., at 554. By the TVA Act's terms, that waiver is subject to "[e]xcept[ions] as "specifically provided in" the statute itself. §831c. But the TVA Act contains no exceptions relevant to tort claims, let alone one turning on whether the challenged conduct is discretionary.

Nor does the FTCA's exception for discretionary functions apply to the TVA. As described earlier, see *supra*, at 3, the FTCA retained the Federal Government's immunity from tort suits challenging discretionary conduct, even while allowing other tort claims to go forward. See 28 U. S. C. §§1346(b), 2680(a); *United States* v. *Gaubert*, 499 U. S. 315, 322–325 (1991) (describing the discretionary function exception's scope). But

Congress made clear {–1441–} that the FTCA does "not apply to[] [a]ny claim arising from the activities of the [TVA]." §2680(*l*). That means the FTCA's discretionary function provision has no relevance to this case. Even the Government concedes as much. It acknowledges that the FTCA's discretionary function exception "does not govern [Thacker's] suit." Brief for Respondent 15. Rather, it says, the TVA Act's sue-and-be-sued clause does so. See *id.*, at 6. And that is the very clause we have just described as containing no express exception for discretionary functions.

But that is not quite the end of the story because in *Federal Housing Administration* v. *Burr*, 309 U. S. 242 (1940), this Court recognized that a sue-and-be-sued clause might contain "implied exceptions." *Id.*, at 245. The Court in that case permitted a suit to proceed against a government entity (providing mortgage insurance) whose organic statute had a sue-and-be-sued clause much like the TVA Act's. And the Court made clear that in green-lighting the suit, it was doing what courts normally should. Sue-and-be-sued clauses, the Court explained, "should be liberally construed." *Ibid.*; see *FDIC* v. *Meyer*, 510 U. S. 471, 475 (1994) (similarly calling such clauses [—6—] "broad"). Those words "in their usual and ordinary sense," the Court noted, "embrace all civil process incident to the commencement or continuance of legal proceedings." *Burr*, 309 U. S., at 245–246. And Congress generally "intend[s] the full consequences of what it sa[ys]"—even if "inconvenient, costly, and inefficient." *Id.*, at 249 (quotation modified). But not quite always, the Court continued. And when not— when Congress meant to use the words "sue and be sued" in a more "narrow sense"—a court should recognize "an implied restriction." *Id.*, at 245. In particular, *Burr* stated, a court should take that route if one of the following circumstances is "clearly shown": either the "type[] of suit [at issue is] not consistent with the statutory or constitutional scheme" or the restriction is "necessary to avoid grave interference with the performance of a governmental function." *Ibid.*

Although the courts below never considered *Burr*, the Government tries to use its framework to defend their decisions. See Brief for Respondent 17–40. According to the Government, we should establish a limit on the TVA's sue-and-be-sued clause—like the one in the FTCA—for all suits challenging discretionary functions. That is for two reasons, tracking *Burr*'s statement of when to recognize an "implied exception" to a sue-and-be-sued clause. 309 U. S., at 245. First, the Government argues that allowing those suits would conflict with the "constitutional scheme"—more precisely, with "separation-of-powers principles"—by subjecting the TVA's discretionary conduct to "judicial second-guessing." Brief for Respondent 19, 21 (internal quotation marks omitted). Second, the Government maintains that permitting those suits would necessarily "interfere[] with important governmental functions." *Id.*, at 36; see *id.*, at 39–40; Tr. of Oral Arg. 39–41. We disagree.

At the outset, we balk at using *Burr* to provide a government entity excluded from the FTCA with a replica of that statute's discretionary function exception. Congress [—7—] made a considered decision *not* to apply the FTCA to the TVA (even as Congress applied that legislation to some other public corporations, see 28 U. S. C. §2679(a)). See *supra*, at 3, 5. The Government effectively asks us to negate that legislative choice. Or otherwise put, it asks us to let the FTCA in through the back door, when Congress has locked the {–1442–} front one. We have once before rejected such a maneuver. In *FDIC* v. *Meyer*, a plaintiff brought a constitutional tort claim against a government agency with another broad sue-and-be-sued clause. The agency claimed immunity, stressing that the claim would have fallen outside the FTCA's immunity waiver (which extends only to conventional torts). We dismissed the argument. "In essence," we observed, the "FDIC asks us to engraft" a part of the FTCA "onto [the agency's] sue-and-be-sued clause." 510 U. S., at 480. But that would mean doing what Congress had not. See *id.*, at 483. And so too here, if we were to bestow the FTCA's discretionary function exception on the TVA through the conduit of *Burr*. Indeed, the

Government's proposal would make the TVA's tort liability largely coextensive with that of all the agencies the FTCA governs. See Tr. of Oral Arg. 33–34. Far from acting to achieve such parity, Congress did everything possible to avoid it.

In any event, the Government is wrong to think that waiving the TVA's immunity from suits based on discretionary functions would offend the separation of powers. As this Court explained in *Burr*, the scope of immunity that federal corporations enjoy is up to Congress. That body "has full power to endow [such an entity] with the government's immunity from suit." 309 U. S., at 244. And equally, it has full power to "waive [that] immunity" and "subject[the entity] to the judicial process" to whatever extent it wishes. *Ibid.* When Congress takes the latter route—even when it goes so far as to waive the corporation's immunity for discretionary functions—its action [—8—] raises no separation of powers problems. The right governmental actor (Congress) is making a decision within its bailiwick (to waive immunity) that authorizes an appropriate body (a court) to render a legal judgment. Indeed, the Government itself conceded at oral argument that Congress, when creating a public corporation, may constitutionally waive its "immunity [for] discretionary functions." Tr. of Oral Arg. 37. But once that is acknowledged, the Government's argument from "separation-of-powers principles" collapses. Brief for Respondent 19. Those principles can offer no reason to limit a statutory waiver that even without any emendation complies with the constitutional scheme.

Finally, the Government overreaches when it says that all suits based on the TVA's discretionary conduct will "grave[ly] interfere[]" with "governmental function[s]." *Burr*, 309 U. S., at 245. That is so, at the least, because the discretionary acts of hybrid entities like the TVA may be not governmental but commercial in nature. And a suit challenging a commercial act will not "grave[ly]"—or, indeed, at all—interfere with the "governmental functions" *Burr* cared about protecting. The Government contests that point, arguing that this Court has not

meant to distinguish between the governmental and the commercial in construing sue-and-be-sued clauses. See Brief for Respondent 39–40. But both *Burr* and later decisions do so explicitly. *Burr* took as its "premise" that an agency "launched [with such a clause] into the commercial world" and "authorize[d] to engage" in "business transactions with the public" should have the same "amenab[ility] to judicial process [as] a private enterprise under like circumstances." 309 U. S., at 245. *Meyer* also made clear that such an agency "could not escape the liability a private enterprise would face in similar circumstances." 510 U. S., at 482; see *ibid.* ("[T]he liability of a private enterprise [is] a *floor* below which the agency's liability [may] [—9—] not fall"). And twice the {–1443–} Court held that the liability of the Postal Service (another sue-and-be-sued agency) should be "similar[] to [that of] other self-sustaining commercial ventures." *Franchise Tax Bd. of Cal.* v. *Postal Service*, 467 U. S. 512, 525 (1984); see *Loeffler*, 486 U. S., at 556. The point of those decisions, contra the Government, is that (barring special constitutional or statutory issues not present here) suits based on a public corporation's *commercial* activity may proceed as they would against a private company; only suits challenging the entity's *governmental* activity may run into an implied limit on its sue-and-be-sued clause.

Burr and its progeny thus require a far more refined analysis than the Government offers here. The reasons those decisions give to recognize a restriction on a sue-and-be-sued clause do not justify the wholesale incorporation of the discretionary function exception. As explained above, the "constitutional scheme" has nothing to say about lawsuits challenging a public corporation's discretionary activity—except to leave their fate to Congress. *Burr*, 309 U. S., at 245; see *supra*, at 8. For its part, Congress has not said in enacting sue-and-be-sued clauses that it wants to prohibit all such suits—quite the contrary. And no concern for "governmental functions" can immunize discretionary activities that are commercial in kind. *Burr*, 309 U. S., at 245; see *supra*, at 8–9. When the TVA or similar body operates in the marketplace as private companies do, it is as liable as they are for choices and judgments. The possibility of immunity arises only when a suit challenges governmental activities—the kinds of functions private parties typically do not perform. And even then, an entity with a sue-and-be-sued clause may receive immunity only if it is "clearly shown" that prohibiting the "type[] of suit [at issue] is necessary to avoid grave interference" with a governmental function's performance. *Burr*, 309 U. S., at 245. That is a high bar. But it is no [—10—] higher than appropriate given Congress's enactment of so broad an immunity waiver—which demands, as we have held, a "liberal construction." *Ibid.* (quotation modified).

III

All that remains is to decide this case in accord with what we have said so far. But as we often note at this point, "we are a court of review, not of first view." *Cutter* v. *Wilkinson*, 544 U. S. 709, 718, n. 7 (2005). In wrongly relying on the discretionary function exception, the courts below never addressed the issues we have found relevant in deciding whether this suit may go forward. Those courts should have the first chance to do so, as guided by the principles set out above and a few last remarks about applying them here.

As described earlier, the TVA sometimes resembles a government actor, sometimes a commercial one. See *supra*, at 2–3. Consider a few diverse examples. When the TVA exercises the power of eminent domain, taking landowners' property for public purposes, no one would confuse it for a private company. So too when the TVA exercises its law enforcement powers to arrest individuals. But in other operations—and over the years, a growing number—the TVA acts like any other company producing and supplying electric power. It is an accident of history, not a difference in function, that explains why most Tennesseans get their electricity from a public enterprise and most Virginians get theirs from a private one. Whatever their ownership structures, the two {–1444–} companies do basically the same things to deliver power to customers.

So to determine if the TVA has immunity here, the court on remand must first decide whether the conduct alleged to be negligent is governmental or commercial in nature. For the reasons given above, if the conduct is commercial—the kind of thing any power company might do—the TVA cannot invoke sovereign immunity. In that event, [—11—] the TVA's sue-and-be-sued clause renders it liable to the same extent as a private party. Only if the conduct at issue is governmental might the court decide that an implied limit on the clause bars the suit. But even assuming governmental activity, the court must find that prohibiting the "type[] of suit [at issue] is necessary to avoid grave interference" with that function's performance. *Burr*, 309 U. S., at 245. Unless it is, Congress's express statement that the TVA may "be sued" continues to demand that this suit go forward.

We accordingly reverse the judgment of the Court of Appeals and remand the case for further proceedings consistent with this opinion.

It is so ordered.

Supreme Court of the United States

No. 18-839

**PARKER DRILLING MANAGEMENT SERVS., LTD.
VS.
NEWTON**

On Writ of Certiorari to the United States Court of Appeals for the Ninth Circuit

Decided: June 10, 2019

Citation: 587 U.S. ____, 139 S.Ct. 1881, 7 Adm. R. 36 (2019).

THOMAS, J., delivered the opinion for a unanimous Court.

[—1—] {–1885–} THOMAS, J.: {–1886–}

The Outer Continental Shelf Lands Act (OCSLA), 67 Stat. 462, 43 U. S. C. §1331 *et seq.*, extends federal law to the subsoil and seabed of the Outer Continental Shelf and all attachments thereon (OCS). Under the OCSLA, all law on the OCS is federal law, administered by federal officials. The OCSLA denies States any interest in or jurisdiction over the OCS, and it deems the adjacent State's laws to be federal law "[t]o the extent that they are applicable and not inconsistent with" other federal law. §1333(a)(2)(A). The question before us is how to determine which state laws meet this requirement and therefore should be adopted as federal law. Applying familiar tools of statutory interpretation, we hold that where federal law addresses the relevant issue, state law is not adopted as surrogate federal law on the OCS.

I

Respondent Brian Newton worked for petitioner Parker Drilling Management Services on drilling platforms off the coast of California. Newton's 14-day shifts involved 12 **[—2—]** hours per day on duty and 12 hours per day on standby, during which he could not leave the platform. He was paid well above the California and federal minimum wages for his time on duty, but he was not paid for his standby time.

Newton filed a class action in California state court alleging violations of several California wage-and-hour laws and related state-law claims. Among other things, Newton claimed that California's minimum-wage and overtime laws required Parker to compensate him for the time he spent on standby. Parker removed the action to Federal District Court. The parties agreed that Parker's platforms were subject to the OCSLA. Their disagreement centered on whether the relevant California laws were "applicable and not inconsistent" with existing federal law and thus deemed to be the applicable federal law under the OCSLA. §1333(a)(2)(A).

The District Court applied Fifth Circuit precedent providing that under the OCSLA, "state law only applies to the extent it is necessary 'to fill a significant void or gap' in federal law." App. to Pet. for Cert. 51 (quoting *Continental Oil Co.* v. *London Steam-Ship Owners' Mut. Ins. Assn.*, 417 F. 2d 1030, 1036 (1969)). It determined that the Fair Labor Standards Act of 1938 (FLSA), 52 Stat. 1060, 29 U. S. C. §201 *et seq.*, constitutes a comprehensive federal wage-and-hour scheme and thus left no significant gap for state law to fill. Because all of Newton's claims relied on state law, the court granted Parker judgment on the pleadings.

The Ninth Circuit vacated and remanded. It first held that state law is "'applicable'" under the OCSLA whenever it "pertain[s] to the subject matter at hand." 881 F. 3d 1078, 1090, 6 Adm. R. 314, 321 amended and reh'g en banc denied, 888 F. 3d 1085 (2018). The court found that California wage-and-hour laws satisfied this standard and turned to "the determinative question in Newton's case": "whether Califor- **[—3—]** nia wage and hour laws are 'inconsistent with' existing federal law." 881 F. 3d, at 1093, 6 Adm. R. at 324. According to the Ninth Circuit, state laws are "inconsistent" with federal law under the OCSLA only "if they are mutually incompatible, incongruous, [or] inharmonious." *Ibid.*, 6 Adm. R. at 324 (internal quotation marks omitted). Applying that standard, the court determined that no inconsistency exists between the FLSA and California wage-and-hour law because the FLSA saving clause "explicitly permits more protective state wage and hour laws." *Id.*, at 1097, 6 Adm. R. at 327 (citing 29 U. S. C. §218(a)). Given the disagreement between the Fifth and Ninth Circuits, we granted {–1887–} certiorari. 586 U. S. ___ (2019).

II

Before the OCSLA, coastal States and the Federal Government disputed who had the right to lease submerged lands on the continental shelf. Some coastal States even asserted jurisdiction all the way to the outer edge of the shelf. See *Shell Oil Co.* v. *Iowa Dept. of Revenue*, 488 U. S. 19, 26 (1988). The disputes eventually reached this Court, which held in a series of decisions that the Federal Government has exclusive jurisdiction over the entire continental shelf. See *United States* v. *California*, 332 U. S. 19, 38–39 (1947); *United States* v. *Louisiana*, 339 U. S. 699, 705 (1950); *United States* v. *Texas*, 339 U. S. 707, 717–718 (1950).

After these decisions, Congress divided jurisdiction over the shelf. In 1953, Congress enacted the Submerged Lands Act, 67 Stat. 29, 43 U. S. C. §1301 *et seq.*, which ceded to the coastal States offshore lands within a specified distance of their coasts. A few months later, Congress passed the OCSLA, which affirmed that the Federal Government exercised exclusive control over the OCS, defined as "all submerged lands" beyond the lands reserved to the States up to the edge of the United States' jurisdiction and control. §1331(a). Specifically, the OCSLA declares that [—4—] "the subsoil and seabed of the [OCS] appertain to the United States and are subject to its jurisdiction, control, and power of disposition." §1332(1). The OCSLA then sets forth "detailed provisions for the exercise of exclusive jurisdiction in the area and for the leasing and development of the resources of the seabed." *United States* v. *Maine*, 420 U. S. 515, 527 (1975); see §§1334–1354.

Of primary relevance here, the OCSLA defines the body of law that governs the OCS. First, in §1333(a)(1), the OCSLA extends "[t]he Constitution and laws and civil and political jurisdiction of the United States" to the OCS. Section 1333(a)(1) provides that federal law applies "to the same extent as if the [OCS] were an area of exclusive Federal jurisdiction located within a State." Then, §1333(a)(2)(A) provides:

"To the extent that they are applicable and not inconsistent with this subchapter or with other Federal laws and regulations of the Secretary now in effect or hereafter adopted, the civil and criminal laws of each adjacent State, now in effect or hereafter adopted, amended, or repealed are declared to be the law of the United States for that portion of the subsoil and seabed of the outer Continental Shelf, and artificial islands and fixed structures erected thereon, which would be within the area of the State if its boundaries were extended seaward to the outer margin of the outer Continental Shelf . . . ."

Section 1333(a)(2)(A) also states that "[a]ll of such applicable laws shall be administered and enforced by the appropriate officers and courts of the United States." Finally, §1333(a)(3) emphasizes that "[t]he provisions of this section for adoption of State law as the law of the United States shall never be interpreted as a basis for claiming any interest in or jurisdiction on behalf of any State for any purpose over" the OCS. [—5—]

III.

A

The question in this case is how to interpret the OCSLA's command that state laws be adopted as federal law on the OCS "[t]o the extent that they are applicable {–1888–} and not inconsistent" with other federal law. §1333(a)(2)(A). Echoing the Ninth Circuit, Newton argues that state law is "applicable" on the OCS whenever it pertains to the subject matter at issue. Newton further argues that state law is only "inconsistent" with federal law if it is incompatible with the federal scheme. In essence, Newton's argument is that state law is "inconsistent" only if it would be pre-empted under our ordinary pre-emption principles.

Parker, on the other hand, argues that state law is not "applicable" on the OCS in the absence of a gap in federal law that needs to be filled. Moreover, Parker argues that state law can be "inconsistent" with federal law even if it is possible for a party to satisfy both sets of laws. Specifically, Parker contends that, although the FLSA normally accommodates more protective state wage-and-hour laws, such laws are inconsistent with the FLSA when adopting state law as surrogate federal law because federal law would then contain two different standards.

B

Although this is a close question of statutory interpretation, on the whole we find Parker's approach more persuasive because "'the words of a statute must be read in their context and with a view to their place in the overall statutory scheme.'" *Roberts* v. *Sea-Land Services, Inc.*, 566 U. S. 93, 101 (2012). That rule is particularly relevant here, as the terms "applicable" and "not inconsistent" are susceptible of interpretations that would deprive one term or the other of meaning. If Newton is right that "applicable" merely means relevant to the subject matter, then the [—6—] word adds nothing to the statute, for an irrelevant law would never be "applicable" in that sense. Cf. *Ransom* v. *FIA Card Services, N. A.*, 562 U. S. 61, 70 (2011) (declining to interpret the word "applicable" in such a way that Congress "could have omitted the term . . . altogether"). And if Parker is right that "applicable" means "necessary to fill a gap in federal law," it is hard to imagine circumstances in which "not inconsistent" would add anything to the statute, for a state law would rarely be inconsistent with a federal law that leaves a gap that needs to be filled. Moreover, when the OCSLA was enacted, the term "inconsistent" could mean either "incompatible," as Newton contends, or merely "inharmonious," as Parker argues. Webster's New International Dictionary 1259 (2d ed. 1953); see also Funk & Wagnalls New Standard Dictionary 1245 (1957) ("logically discrepant" or "disagreeing" and "discordant"); The New Century Dictionary 811 (1953) ("self-contradictory" or "at variance"); 5 Oxford English Dictionary 173 (1933) ("incongruous"

or "not agreeing in substance, spirit, or form"). In short, the two terms standing alone do not resolve the question before us. Particularly given their indeterminacy in isolation, the terms should be read together and interpreted in light of the entire statute. See *Star Athletica, L. L. C.* v. *Varsity Brands, Inc.*, 580 U. S. ___, ___ (2017) (slip op., at 6) ("'[I]nterpretation of a phrase of uncertain reach is not confined to a single sentence when the text of the whole statute gives instruction as to its meaning'").

Our pre-OCSLA decisions made clear that the Federal Government controlled the OCS in every respect, and the OCSLA reaffirmed the central role of federal law on the OCS. See *supra*, at 3–4. As discussed, the OCSLA gives the Federal Government complete "jurisdiction, control, and power of disposition" over the OCS, while giving the States no {–1889–} "interest in or jurisdiction" over it. §§1332(1), 1333(a)(3). The statute applies federal law to the OCS "to [—7—] the same extent as if the [OCS] were an area of exclusive Federal jurisdiction located within a State." §1333(a)(1). Accordingly, the only law on the OCS is federal law, and state laws are adopted as federal law only "[t]o the extent that they are applicable and not inconsistent with" federal law. §1333(a)(2)(A).

Taken together, these provisions convince us that state laws can be "applicable and not inconsistent" with federal law under §1333(a)(2)(A) only if federal law does not address the relevant issue. As we have said before, the OCSLA makes apparent "that federal law is 'exclusive' in its regulation of [the OCS], and that state law is adopted only as surrogate federal law." *Rodrigue* v. *Aetna Casualty & Surety Co.*, 395 U. S. 352, 357 (1969). The OCSLA extends all federal law to the OCS, and instead of also extending state law writ large, it borrows only certain state laws. These laws, in turn, are declared to be federal law and are administered by federal officials. Given the primacy of federal law on the OCS and the limited role of state law, it would make little sense to treat the OCS as a mere extension of the adjacent State, where state law applies unless it conflicts with federal law. See *PLIVA, Inc.* v. *Mensing*, 564

U. S. 604, 617–618 (2011). That type of pre-emption analysis is applicable only where the overlapping, dual jurisdiction of the Federal and State Governments makes it necessary to decide which law takes precedence. But the OCS is not, and never was, part of a State, so state law has never applied of its own force. Because federal law is the only law on the OCS, and there has never been overlapping state and federal jurisdiction there, the statute's reference to "not inconsistent" state laws does not present the ordinary question in pre-emption cases—*i.e.*, whether a conflict exists between federal and state law. Instead, the question is whether federal law has already addressed the relevant issue; if so, state law addressing the same issue would necessarily be **[—8—]** inconsistent with existing federal law and cannot be adopted as surrogate federal law. Put another way, to the extent federal law applies to a particular issue, state law is inapplicable.

C

Apart from §1333(a)(2)'s place in the overall statutory scheme, several other considerations support our interpretation, which accords with the standard long applied by the Fifth Circuit, see *Continental Oil*, 417 F. 2d, at 1036–1037. First, if Newton were correct that the choice-of-law question on the OCS is the same as it would be in an adjacent State, much of the OCSLA would be unnecessary. Second, our interpretation is consistent with the federal-enclave model—a model that the OCSLA expressly invokes— and the historical development of the statute. And third, the Court's precedents have treated the OCSLA in accord with our interpretation.

1

Under Newton's interpretation, state law would apply unless pre-empted by federal law, meaning that the OCS would be treated essentially the same as the adjacent State. See Tr. of Oral Arg. 49. But that interpretation would render much of the OCSLA unnecessary. For example, the statute would not have needed to adopt state law as federal law or say that federal law applies on the OCS as if it "were an area of exclusive Federal jurisdiction located within a State." §§1333(a)(1)–(2). It could have simply defined which State's law applied on the OCS and given federal {–1890–} officials and courts the authority to enforce the law. And the statute would not have needed to limit state laws on the OCS to those "applicable and not inconsistent" with federal law (as Newton understands those words), for irrelevant laws never apply and federal law is always "supreme," U. S. Const., Art. VI, cl. 2. Newton's **[—9—]** interpretation deprives much of the statute of any import, violating the "'cardinal principle' of interpretation that courts 'must give effect, if possible, to every clause and word of a statute.'" *Loughrin* v. *United States*, 573 U. S. 351, 358 (2014).

2

Further support for our interpretation comes from the statute's treatment of the OCS as "an area of exclusive Federal jurisdiction located within a State"—*i.e.*, as "an upland federal enclave." §1333(a)(1); *Rodrigue, supra*, at 366. It is a commonplace of statutory interpretation that "Congress legislates against the backdrop of existing law." *McQuiggin* v. *Perkins*, 569 U. S. 383, 398, n. 3 (2013). Generally, when an area in a State becomes a federal enclave, "only the [state] law in effect at the time of the transfer of jurisdiction continues in force" as surrogate federal law. *James Stewart & Co.* v. *Sadrakula*, 309 U. S. 94, 100 (1940). Existing state law typically does not continue in force, however, to the extent it conflicts with "federal policy." *Paul* v. *United States*, 371 U. S. 245, 269 (1963); see *Chicago, R. I. & P. R. Co.* v. *McGlinn*, 114 U. S. 542, 547 (1885). And going forward, state law presumptively does not apply to the enclave. See *Sadrakula, supra*, at 100; see also *Paul, supra*, at 268; *Pacific Coast Dairy, Inc.* v. *Department of Agriculture of Cal.*, 318 U. S. 285, 294 (1943). This approach ensures "that no area however small will be without a developed legal system for private rights," while simultaneously retaining the primacy of federal law and requiring future statutory changes to be made by Congress. *Sadrakula, supra*, at 100; *United*

States v. *Tax Comm'n of Miss.*, 412 U. S. 363, 370, n. 12 (1973).[1] [—10—]

The original version of the OCSLA both treated the OCS as a federal enclave and adopted only the "applicable and not inconsistent" laws of the adjacent State that were in effect as of the effective date of the Act. 43 U. S. C. §1333(a)(2) (1970 ed.); see §1333(a)(1) (1970 ed.) (deeming the OCS "an area of exclusive Federal jurisdiction located within a State"). This textual connection between the OCSLA and the federal enclave model suggests that, like the generally applicable enclave rule, the OCSLA sought to make all OCS law federal yet also "provide a sufficiently detailed legal framework to govern life" on the OCS. *Shell Oil*, 488 U. S., at 27. Once that framework was established, federal law (including previously adopted state law) provided a sufficient legal structure to accomplish that purpose, eliminating the need to adopt new state laws. The federal-state balance in a typical federal enclave is quite different than in a State, and that difference is all the more striking on the OCS, which {–1891–} was never under state control. The text and context of the OCSLA therefore suggest that state law is not adopted to govern the OCS where federal law is on point.

Although Congress later amended the OCSLA to adopt state law on an ongoing basis, this amendment only confirms the connection between the OCSLA and the federal enclave model. Beginning in 1825, when "federal statutory law punished only a few crimes committed on federal enclaves," Congress enacted several Assimilative Crimes Acts (ACAs) that "borrow[ed] state law to fill gaps in the federal criminal law" on enclaves. *Lewis* v. *United States*, 523 U. S. 155, 160 (1998); see 18 U. S. C. §13(a) (criminalizing "any act or omission which, although not made punishable by any enactment of Congress, would be punishable if committed or omitted within the jurisdiction of the" [—11—] relevant State or territory). Mirroring the general enclave rule discussed above, the first ACA was limited to state laws in existence when the Act was passed. *United States* v. *Sharpnack*, 355 U. S. 286, 291 (1958). Because of this limitation, the initial ACA "gradually lost much of its effectiveness in maintaining current conformity with state criminal laws," and Congress eventually provided for the adoption of the state laws in effect at the time of the crime. *Id.*, at 291–292. After this Court upheld this ongoing adoption of state criminal law against a nondelegation challenge, see *id.*, at 294, Congress amended the OCSLA to borrow state laws "'in effect or hereafter adopted, amended, or repealed.'" §19(f), 88 Stat. 2146. At the same time, Congress left unchanged the features of the OCSLA that we have emphasized above—*i.e.*, that the only law on the OCS is federal, and that state law is adopted only when it is "applicable and not inconsistent" with existing federal law. Thus, we do not understand the statutory amendment to alter our conclusion. If anything, this history reinforces that the OCS should be treated as an exclusive federal enclave, not an extension of a State, and that the OCSLA, like the ACAs, does not adopt state law "where there is no gap to fill." *Lewis, supra*, at 163.

3

Finally, our interpretation accords with the Court's precedents construing the OCSLA. We first interpreted the OCSLA's choice-of-law provision in *Rodrigue* v. *Aetna Casualty & Surety Co.*, where we considered whether suits brought by the families of men killed on OCS drilling rigs could proceed under only the federal Death on the High Seas Act or also under state law. 395 U. S., at 352–353. We emphasized that under the OCSLA, the body of law applicable to the OCS "was to be federal law of the United States, applying state law only as federal law and then only when not inconsistent with applicable federal law." [—12—] *Id.*, at 355–356. We explained that "federal law, because of its limited function in a federal system, might be inadequate to cope with the full range of potential legal prob-

---

[1] These general rules "may be qualified in accordance with agreements reached by the respective governments." *Sadrakula*, 309 U. S., at 99; see also *Paul*, 371 U. S., at 268 ("[A] State may not legislate with [—10—] respect to a federal enclave unless it reserved the right to do so when it gave its consent to the purchase by the United States").

lems," and that the OCSLA "supplemented gaps in the federal law with state law through the 'adoption of State law as the law of the United States.'" *Id.*, at 357 (quoting §1333(a)(3)). We reiterated that the statutory language makes it "evident" "that federal law is 'exclusive'" on the OCS and that "state law could be used to fill federal voids." *Id.*, at 357–358. After concluding that the Death on the High Seas Act did not apply to accidents on the OCS and thus left a gap related to wrongful deaths, we held that state law provided the rule of decision. We explained that "the inapplicability of the [federal Act] removes any {–1892–} obstacle to the application of state law by incorporation as federal law through" the OCSLA. *Id.*, at 366.

Two years later, in *Chevron Oil Co.* v. *Huson*, 404 U. S. 97 (1971), the Court again viewed the OCSLA as adopting state law to fill in federal-law gaps. In *Huson*, the question was whether federal admiralty law or a state statute governed a tort action arising from an injury that occurred on the OCS. *Id.*, at 98–99. Describing *Rodrigue*'s analysis, we explained that where "there exists a substantial 'gap' in federal law," "state law remedies are not 'inconsistent' with applicable federal law." 404 U. S., at 101. We highlighted that "state law was needed" as surrogate federal law because federal law alone did not provide "'a complete body of law,'" which is why "Congress specified that a comprehensive body of state law should be adopted by the federal courts in the absence of existing federal law." *Id.*, at 103–104. In other words, the OCSLA "made clear provision for filling in the 'gaps' in federal law." *Id.*, at 104. And because Congress had decided not to apply federal admiralty law on the OCS, leaving a gap on the relevant issue, we held that it was appropriate to "ab- [—13—] sor[b]" the state law as federal law. *Id.*, at 104, 109.

In *Gulf Offshore Co.* v. *Mobil Oil Corp.*, 453 U. S. 473 (1981), we once again emphasized that "[a]ll law applicable to the [OCS] is federal law" and that the "OCSLA borrows the 'applicable and not inconsistent' laws of the adjacent States" "to fill the substantial 'gaps' in the coverage of federal law." *Id.*, at 480. We noted that under the OCSLA, the Federal Government "retain[ed] exclusive . . . control of the administration of the [OCS]," and that state law is incorporated "to fill gaps in federal law." *Id.*, at 479–480, n. 7.

These precedents confirm our understanding of the OCSLA. Although none decided the precise question before us, much of our prior discussion of the OCSLA would make little sense if the statute essentially treated the OCS as an extension of the adjacent State. In *Rodrigue*, for example, there was no question that the state law at issue pertained to the subject matter or that the relevant federal law expressly preserved state laws regulating the same subject. See 395 U. S., at 355; 46 U. S. C. §767 (1964 ed.). Under Newton's interpretation, that should have ended the case. Yet the Court instead analyzed at length whether the federal law extended to the OCS. See 395 U. S., at 359–366. It would be odd for our decisions to focus so closely on the gap-filling role of state law under the OCSLA if, as Newton argues, the existence of a federal-law gap is irrelevant. Our consistent understanding of the OCSLA remains: All law on the OCS is federal, and state law serves a supporting role, to be adopted only where there is a gap in federal law's coverage.

In sum, the standard we adopt today is supported by the statute's text, structure, and history, as well as our precedents. Under that standard, if a federal law addresses the issue at hand, then state law is not adopted as federal law [—14—] on the OCS.[2] {–1893–}

IV

Applying this standard, some of Newton's present claims are readily resolvable. For instance, some of his claims are premised on the adoption of California law requiring

---

[2] Of course, it is conceivable that state law might be "inconsistent" with federal law for purposes of §1333(a)(2) even absent an on-point federal law. For example, federal law might contain a deliberate gap, making state law inconsistent with the federal scheme. Or, state law might be inconsistent with a federal law addressing a different issue. We do not foreclose these or other possible inconsistencies.

payment for all time that Newton spent on standby. See *Mendiola* v. *CPS Security Solutions, Inc.*, 60 Cal. 4th 833, 842, 340 P. 3d 355, 361 (2015); Cal. Lab. Code Ann. §510(a) (West 2011). But federal law already addresses this issue. See 29 CFR §785.23 (2018) ("An employee who resides on his employer's premises on a permanent basis or for extended periods of time is not considered as working all the time he is on the premises"); see also 29 U. S. C. §207(a). Therefore, this California law does not provide the rule of decision on the OCS, and to the extent Newton's OCS-based claims rely on that law, they necessarily fail.

Likewise, to the extent Newton's OCS-based claims rely on the adoption of the California minimum wage (currently $12), Cal. Lab. Code Ann. §1182.12(b) (West Supp. 2019), the FLSA already provides for a minimum wage, 29 U. S. C. §206(a)(1), so the California minimum wage does not apply. Newton points out that the FLSA sets a minimum wage of "*not less than* . . . $7.25 an hour," *ibid.* (emphasis added), and does not "excuse noncompliance with any Federal or State law . . . establishing a [higher] minimum wage," §218. But whatever the import of these provisions in an ordinary pre-emption case, they do not help Newton here, for the question under the OCSLA is [—15—] whether federal law addresses the minimum wage on the OCS. It does. Therefore, the California minimum wage is not adopted as federal law and does not apply on the OCS.

Newton's other claims were not analyzed by the Court of Appeals, and the parties have provided little briefing on those claims. Moreover, the Court of Appeals held that Newton should be given leave to amend his complaint. Because we cannot finally resolve whether Parker was entitled to judgment on the pleadings, we vacate the judgment of the Court of Appeals, and the case is remanded for further proceedings consistent with this opinion.

It is so ordered.

Supreme Court of the United States

No. 18-266

DUTRA GROUP
VS.
BATTERTON

On Writ of Certiorari to the United States Court of Appeals for the Ninth Circuit

Decided: June 24, 2019

Citation: 588 U.S. ____, 139 S.Ct. 2275, 7 Adm. R. 43 (2019).

ALITO, J., delivered the opinion of the Court in which ROBERTS, C.J., and THOMAS, KAGAN, GORSUCH, and KAVANAUGH, JJ., joined. GINSBURG, J., filed a dissenting opinion, in which BREYER and SOTOMAYOR, JJ., joined.

[—1—] {-2277-} ALITO, J.: {-2278-}

By granting federal courts jurisdiction over maritime and admiralty cases, the Constitution implicitly directs federal courts sitting in admiralty to proceed "in the manner of a common law court." *Exxon Shipping Co.* v. *Baker*, 554 U. S. 471, 489–490 (2008). Thus, where Congress has not prescribed specific rules, federal courts must develop the "amalgam of traditional common-law rules, modifications of those rules, and newly created rules" that forms the general maritime law. *East River S. S. Corp.* v. *Transamerica Delaval Inc.*, 476 U. S. 858, 864–865 (1986). But maritime law is no longer solely the province of the Federal Judiciary. "Congress and the States have legislated extensively in these areas." *Miles* v. *Apex Marine Corp.*, 498 U. S. 19, 27 (1990). When exercising its inherent common-law authority, "an admiralty court should look primarily to these legislative enactments for policy guidance." *Ibid.* We may depart from the policies found in the statutory scheme in discrete instances based on long-established history, see, *e.g.*, *Atlantic Sounding Co.* v. *Townsend*, 557 U. S. 404, 424–425 (2009), but we do so [—2—] cautiously in light of Congress's persistent pursuit of "uniformity in the exercise of admiralty jurisdiction." *Miles*, *supra*, at 26 (quoting *Moragne* v. *States Marine Lines, Inc.*, 398 U. S. 375, 401 (1970)).

This case asks whether a mariner may recover punitive damages on a claim that he was injured as a result of the unseaworthy condition of the vessel. We have twice confronted similar questions in the past several decades, and our holdings in both cases were based on the particular claims involved. In *Miles*, which concerned a wrongful-death claim under the general maritime law, we held that recovery was limited to pecuniary damages, which did not include loss of society. 498 U. S., at 23. And in *Atlantic Sounding*, after examining centuries of relevant case law, we held that punitive damages are not categorically barred as part of the award on the traditional maritime claim of maintenance and cure. 557 U. S., at 407. Here, because there is no historical basis for allowing punitive damages in unseaworthiness actions, and in order to promote uniformity with the way courts have applied parallel statutory causes of action, we hold that punitive damages remain unavailable in unseaworthiness actions.

I

In order to determine the remedies for unseaworthiness, we must consider both the heritage of the cause of action in the {-2279-} common law and its place in the modern statutory framework.

A

The seaman's right to recover damages for personal injury on a claim of unseaworthiness originates in the admiralty court decisions of the 19th century. At the time, "seamen led miserable lives." D. Robertson, S. Friedell, & M. Sturley, Admiralty and Maritime Law in the United States 163 (2d ed. 2008). Maritime law was largely judge- [—3—] made, and seamen were viewed as "emphatically the wards of the admiralty." *Harden* v. *Gordon*, 11 F. Cas. 480, 485 (No. 6,047) (CC Me. 1823). In that era, the primary responsibility for protecting seamen lay in the courts, which saw mariners as "peculiarly entitled to"—and particularly in need of—judicial protection "against the effects of the superior skill and shrewdness of masters and owners of ships."

Brown v. *Lull*, 4 F. Cas. 407, 409 (No. 2,018) (CC Mass. 1836) (Story, J.).[1]

Courts of admiralty saw it as their duty not to be "confined to the mere dry and positive rules of the common law" but to "act upon the enlarged and liberal jurisprudence of courts of equity; and, in short, so far as their powers extend[ed], they act[ed] as courts of equity." *Ibid.* This Court interpreted the Constitution's grant of admiralty jurisdiction to the Federal Judiciary as "the power to . . . dispose of [a case] as justice may require." *The Resolute*, 168 U. S. 437, 439 (1897).

Courts used this power to protect seamen from injury primarily through two causes of action. The first, maintenance and cure, has its roots in the medieval and renaissance law codes that form the ancient foundation of maritime common law.[2] The duty of maintenance and cure [—4—] requires a ship's master "to provide food, lodging, and medical services to a seaman injured while serving the ship." *Lewis* v. *Lewis & Clark Marine, Inc.*, 531 U. S. 438, 441 (2001). This duty, "which arises from the contract of employment, does not rest upon negligence or culpability on the part of the owner or master, nor is it restricted to those cases where the seaman's employment is the cause of the injury or illness." *Calmar S. S. Corp.* v. *Taylor*, 303 U. S. 525, 527 (1938) (citations omitted).

The second claim, unseaworthiness, is a much more recent development and grew out of causes of action unrelated to personal injury. In its earliest forms, an unseaworthiness claim gave sailors under contract to sail on a ship the right to collect their wages even if they had refused to {-2280-} board an unsafe vessel after discovering its condition. See, *e.g., Dixon* v. *The Cyrus*, 7 F. Cas. 755, 757 (No. 3,930) (Pa. 1789); *Rice* v. *The Polly & Kitty*, 20 F. Cas. 666, 667 (No. 11,754) (Pa. 1789). Similarly, unseaworthiness was a defense to criminal charges against seamen who refused to obey a ship master's orders. See, *e.g., United States* v. *Nye*, 27 F. Cas. 210, 211 (No. 15,906) (CC Mass. 1855); *United States* v. *Ashton*, 24 F. Cas. 873, 874–875 (No. 14,470) (CC Mass. 1834). A claim of unseaworthiness could also be asserted by a shipper to recover damages or by an insurer to deny coverage when the poor condition of the ship resulted in damage to or loss of the cargo. See *The Caledonia*, 157 U. S. 124, 132–136 (1895) (cataloging cases).

Only in the latter years of the 19th century did unseaworthiness begin a long and gradual evolution toward [—5—] remedying personal injury. Courts began to extend the cases about refusals to serve to allow recovery for mariners who were injured because of the unseaworthy condition of the vessel on which they had served.[3] These early cases were

---

[1] Riding circuit, Justice Story described mariners in markedly paternalistic terms:
"Seamen are a class of persons remarkable for their rashness, thoughtlessness and improvidence. They are generally necessitous, ignorant of the nature and extent of their own rights and privileges, and for the most part incapable of duly appreciating their value. They combine, in a singular manner, the apparent anomalies of gallantry, extravagance, profusion in expenditure, indifference to the future, credulity, which is easily won, and confidence, which is readily surprised." Brown, 4 F. Cas., at 409.
[2] A right resembling maintenance and cure appears in the Laws of Oleron, promulgated by Eleanor of Aquitaine around 1160, in the 13th-century Laws of Wisbuy, in the Laws of the Hanse Towns, published in 1597, and in the Marine Ordinances of Louis XIV, published in 1681. [—4—] See 30 F. Cas. 1169 (collecting sources). The relevant passages are the Laws of Oleron, Arts. VI and VII, 30 F. Cas., at 1174–1175; the Laws of Wisbuy, Arts. XVIII, XIX, and XXXIII, 30 F. Cas., at 1191–1192; the Laws of the Hanse Towns, Arts. XXXIX and XLV, 30 F. Cas., at 1200; the Marine Ordinances of Louis XIV, Tit. IV, Arts. XI and XII, 30 F. Cas., at 1209.

[3] Most of these cases allowed recovery for personal injury in "erroneous reliance" on certain passages in *Dixon* v. *The Cyrus*, 7 F. Cas. 755 (No. 3,930) (Pa. 1789). Tetreault, Seamen, Seaworthiness, and the Rights of Harbor Workers, 39 Cornell L. Q. 381, 390 (1954) (Tetreault). These cases misread *The Cyrus* as resting on an implied warranty of seaworthiness. Tetreault 390. But *The Cyrus* is more fairly read to turn on a theory of true implied condition. While a warranty would provide a basis for damages if the breach caused an injury, an implied condition would only allow the mariner to escape performance without surrendering the benefit of the contract. In other words, "[t]he manifest unseaworthiness of the vessel at the com-

sparse, and they generally allowed recovery only when a vessel's owner failed to exercise due diligence to ensure that the ship left port in a seaworthy condition. See, *e.g.*, *The Robert C. McQuillen*, 91 F. 685, 686–687 (Conn. 1899); *The Lizzie Frank*, 31 F. 477, 480 (SD Ala. 1887); *The Tammerlane*, 47 F. 822, 824 (ND Cal. 1891).

Unseaworthiness remained a suspect basis for personal injury claims until 1903, when, in dicta, this Court concluded that "the vessel and her owner are . . . liable to an indemnity for injuries received by seamen in consequence of the unseaworthiness of the ship." *The Osceola*, 189 U. S. 158, 175 (1903). Although this was the first recognition of unseaworthiness as a personal injury claim in this Court, we took pains to note that the claim was strictly cabined. *Ibid.* Some of the limitations on recovery were imported from the common law. The fellow-servant doctrine, in particular, prohibited recovery when an employee suffered an injury due to the negligent act of another employee without negligence on the part of the employer. *Ibid.*; see, *e.g.*, *The Sachem*, 42 F. 66 (EDNY 1890) (deny- [—6—] ing recovery based on fellow-servant doctrine). Because a claimant had to show that he was injured by some aspect of the ship's condition that rendered the vessel unseaworthy, a claim could not prevail based on "the negligence of the master, or any member of the crew."[4] {–2281–} *The Osceola*, *supra*, at 175; see also *The City of Alexandria*, 17 F. 390 (SDNY 1883) (no recovery based on negligence that does not render vessel unseaworthy). Instead, a seaman had to show

---

mencement of the voyage would excuse non-performance by the mariners but did not constitute a basis for damages." Tetreault 390.

[4] To be sure, in some instances the concept of "unseaworthiness" expanded to embrace conditions that resulted from the negligence of fellow servants, see, *e.g.*, *Carlisle Packing Co.* v. *Sandanger*, 259 U. S. 255, 259 (1922) (vessel was rendered unseaworthy when it left port with gasoline in a container labeled "coal oil"); see also G. Robinson, Handbook of Admiralty Law in the United States §37, p. 305–307 (1st ed. 1939) (collecting cases). But it was only after the passage of the Jones Act that negligence by a fellow mariner provided a reliable basis for recovery. See Part I–B, *infra*.

that the owner of the vessel had failed to exercise due diligence in ensuring the ship was in seaworthy condition. See generally *Dixon* v. *United States*, 219 F. 2d 10, 12–14 (CA2 1955) (Harlan, J.) (cataloging evolution of the claim).

B

In the early 20th century, then, under "the general maritime law . . . a vessel and her owner . . . were liable to an indemnity for injuries received by a seaman in consequence of the unseaworthiness of the ship and her appliances; but a seaman was not allowed to recover an indemnity for injuries sustained through the negligence of the master or any member of the crew." *Pacific S. S. Co.* v. *Peterson*, 278 U. S. 130, 134 (1928); see also *Plamals* v. *S. S. "Pinar Del Rio,"* 277 U. S. 151, 155 (1928) (vessel was not unseaworthy when mate negligently selected defective rope but sound rope was available on board). Because of these severe limitations on recovery, "the seaman's right to recover damages for injuries caused by unseaworthiness [—7—] of the ship was an obscure and relatively little used remedy." G. Gilmore & C. Black, The Law of Admiralty §6–38, p. 383 (2d ed. 1975) (Gilmore & Black).

Tremendous shifts in mariners' rights took place between 1920 and 1950. First, during and after the First World War, Congress enacted a series of laws regulating maritime liability culminating in the Merchant Marine Act of 1920, §33, 41 Stat. 1007 (Jones Act), which codified the rights of injured mariners and created new statutory claims that were freed from many of the common-law limitations on recovery. The Jones Act provides injured seamen with a cause of action and a right to a jury. 46 U. S. C. §30104. Rather than create a new structure of substantive rights, the Jones Act incorporated the rights provided to railway workers under the Federal Employers' Liability Act (FELA), 45 U. S. C. §51 *et seq.* 46 U. S. C. §30104. In the 30 years after the Jones Act's passage, "the Act was the vehicle for almost all seamen's personal injury and death actions." Gilmore & Black §6–20, at 327.

But the Jones Act was overtaken in the 1950s by the second fundamental change in personal injury maritime claims—and it was this Court, not Congress, that played the leading role. In a pair of decisions in the late 1940s, the Court transformed the old claim of unseaworthiness, which had demanded only due diligence by the vessel owner, into a strict-liability claim. In *Mahnich* v. *Southern S. S. Co.*, 321 U. S. 96 (1944), the Court stated that "the exercise of due diligence does not relieve the owner of his obligation" to provide a seaworthy ship and, in the same ruling, held that the fellow-servant doctrine did not provide a defense. *Id.*, at 100, 101. *Mahnich's* interpretation of the early cases may have been suspect, see Tetreault 397–398 (*Mahnich* rests on "startling misstatement" of relevant precedents), but its assertion triggered a sea-change in maritime personal injury. Less than two years later, we affirmed that the duty of seaworthiness [—8—] was "essentially a species of liability without fault . . . neither limited by conceptions of negligence nor contractual in character. It is a form of absolute duty owing to all within the range of its humanitarian policy." *Seas Shipping Co.* v. *Sieracki*, 328 U. S. 85, 94–95 (1946) (citations omitted). From *Mahnich* forward, "the decisions of this Court have undeviatingly reflected an understanding {–2282–} that the owner's duty to furnish a seaworthy ship is absolute and completely independent of his duty under the Jones Act to exercise reasonable care." *Mitchell* v. *Trawler Racer, Inc.*, 362 U. S. 539, 549 (1960). As a result of *Mahnich* and *Sieracki*, between the 1950s and 1970s "the unseaworthiness count [was] the essential basis for recovery with the Jones Act count preserved merely as a jury-getting device."[5] Gilmore & Black §6–20, at 327–328.

The shifts in plaintiff preferences between Jones Act and unseaworthiness claims were possible because of the significant overlap between the two causes of action. See *id.*, §6–

38, at 383. One leading treatise goes so far as to describe the two claims as "alternative 'grounds' of recovery for a single cause of action." 2 R. Force & M. Norris, The Law of Seamen §30:90, p. 30–369 (5th ed. 2003). The two claims are so similar that, immediately after the Jones Act's passage, we held that plaintiffs could not submit both to a jury. *Plamals, supra*, at 156–157 ("Seamen may invoke, at their election, the relief accorded by the old rules against the ship, or that provided by the new against the employer. But they may not have the benefit of both"). We no longer require such election. See *McAllister* v. *Magnolia Petroleum Co.*, 357 U. S. 221, 222, n. 2 (1958). But a plaintiff still cannot duplicate his recovery [—9—] by collecting full damages on both claims because, "whether or not the seaman's injuries were occasioned by the unseaworthiness of the vessel or by the negligence of the master or members of the crew, . . . there is but a single wrongful invasion of his primary right of bodily safety and but a single legal wrong." *Peterson*, 278 U. S., at 138; see also 2 Force, *supra*, §§26:73, 30:90.

II

Christopher Batterton worked as a deckhand and crew member on vessels owned and operated by the Dutra Group. According to Batterton's complaint, while working on a scow near Newport Beach, California, Batterton was injured when his hand was caught between a bulkhead and a hatch that blew open as a result of unventilated air accumulating and pressurizing within the compartment.

Batterton sued Dutra and asserted a variety of claims, including negligence, unseaworthiness, maintenance and cure, and unearned wages. He sought to recover general and punitive damages. Dutra moved to strike Batterton's claim for punitive damages, arguing that they are not available on claims for unseaworthiness. The District Court denied Dutra's motion, 2014 WL 12538172 (CD Cal., Dec. 15, 2014), but agreed to certify an interlocutory appeal on the question, 2015 WL 13752889 (CD Cal., Feb. 6, 2015).

---

[5] The decline of Jones Act claims was arrested, although not reversed, by our holding that some negligent actions on a vessel may create Jones Act liability without rendering the vessel unseaworthy. See *Usner* v. *Luckenbach Overseas Corp.*, 400 U. S. 494 (1971); see also 1B Benedict on Admiralty §23, p. 3–35 (7th rev. ed. 2018).

The Court of Appeals affirmed. 880 F. 3d 1089, 6 Adm. R. 308 (CA9 2018). Applying Circuit precedent, see *Evich* v. *Morris*, 819 F. 2d 256, 258–259 (CA9 1987), the Court of Appeals held that punitive damages are available for unseaworthiness claims. 880 F. 3d, at 1096, 6 Adm. R. at 313. This holding reaffirmed a division of authority between the Circuits. Compare *McBride* v. *Estis Well Serv., L. L. C.*, 768 F. 3d 382, 391, 2 Adm. R. 320, 326 (CA5 2014) (en banc) (punitive damages are not recoverable), and *Horsley* v. *Mobil Oil Corp.*, 15 F. 3d 200, 203 (CA1 1994) (same), with {–2283–} *Self* v. *Great Lakes Dredge &* [—10—] *Dock Co.*, 832 F. 2d 1540, 1550 (CA11 1987) ("Punitive damages should be available in cases where the shipowner willfully violated the duty to maintain a safe and seaworthy ship . . ."). We granted certiorari to resolve this division. 586 U. S. ___ (2018).

III

Our resolution of this question is governed by our decisions in *Miles* and *Atlantic Sounding*. *Miles* establishes that we "should look primarily to . . . legislative enactments for policy guidance," while recognizing that we "may supplement these statutory remedies where doing so would achieve the uniform vindication" of the policies served by the relevant statutes. 498 U. S., at 27. In *Atlantic Sounding*, we allowed recovery of punitive damages, but we justified our departure from the statutory remedial scheme based on the established history of awarding punitive damages for certain maritime torts, including maintenance and cure. 557 U. S., at 411–414 (discussing cases of piracy and maintenance and cure awarding damages with punitive components). We were explicit that our decision represented a gloss on *Miles* rather than a departure from it. *Atlantic Sounding*, *supra*, at 420 ("The reasoning of *Miles* remains sound"). And we recognized the importance of viewing each claim in its proper historical context. "'[R]emedies for negligence, unseaworthiness, and maintenance and cure have different origins and may on occasion call for application of slightly different principles and procedures.'" 557 U. S., at 423.

In accordance with these decisions, we consider here whether punitive damages have traditionally been awarded for claims of unseaworthiness and whether conformity with parallel statutory schemes would require such damages. Finally, we consider whether we are compelled on policy grounds to allow punitive damages for unseaworthiness claims. [—11—]

A

For claims of unseaworthiness, the overwhelming historical evidence suggests that punitive damages are not available. Batterton principally relies on two cases to establish that punitive damages were traditionally available for breach of the duty of seaworthiness. Upon close inspection, neither supports this argument.

The Rolph, 293 F. 269, 271 (ND Cal. 1923), involved a mate who brutally beat members of the crew, rendering one seaman blind and leaving another with impaired hearing. The central question in the case was not the form of damages, but rather whether the viciousness of the mate rendered the vessel unseaworthy. *The Rolph*, 299 F. 52, 54 (CA9 1924). The court concluded that the master, by staffing the vessel with such an unsuitable officer, had rendered it unseaworthy. *Id.*, at 55. To the extent the court described the basis for the damages awarded, it explained that the judgment was supported by testimony as to "the expectation of life and earnings of these men." 293 F., at 272. And the Court of Appeals discussed only the seamen's entitlement "to recover an indemnity" for their injuries. 299 F., at 56. These are discussions of compensatory damages—nowhere does the court speak in terms of an exemplary or punitive award.[6] {–2284–}

---

[6] Even if this case did involve a *sub silentio* punitive award, we share the Fifth Circuit's reluctance to "rely on one dust-covered case to establish that punitive damages were generally available in unseaworthiness cases." *McBride* v. *Estis Well Serv., L. L. C.*, 768 F. 3d 382, 397, 2 Adm. R. 320, 331 (2014) (Clement, J., concurring). Absent a clear historical pattern, *Miles* v. *Apex Marine Corp.*, 498 U. S. 19 (1990), commands us to

The Noddleburn, 28 F. 855, 857–858 (Ore. 1886), involved an injury to a British seaman serving on a British vessel and was decided under English law. The plaintiff in the case was injured when he fell to the deck after being [—12—] ordered aloft and stepping on an inadequately secured line. *Id.,* at 855. After the injury, the master neglected the man's wounds, thinking the injury a mere sprain. *Id.,* at 856. The leg failed to heal and the man had to insist on being discharged to a hospital, where he learned that he would be permanently disabled. *Ibid.* As damages, the court awarded him accrued wages, as well as $1,000 to compensate for the loss in future earnings from his disability and $500 for his pain and suffering. *Id.,* at 860. But these are purely compensatory awards—the only discussion of exemplary damages comes at the very close of the opinion, and it is clear that they were considered because of the master's failure to provide maintenance and cure. *Ibid.* (discussing additional award "in consideration of the neglect and indifference with which the libelant was treated by the master *after his injury*" (emphasis added)).

Finally, Batterton points to two other cases, *The City of Carlisle,* 39 F. 807 (Ore. 1889), and *The Troop,* 118 F. 769 (Wash. 1902). But these cases, like *The Noddleburn,* both involve maintenance and cure claims that rest on the willful failure of the master and mate to provide proper care for wounded sailors after they were injured. 39 F., at 812 ("master failed and neglected to procure or provide any medical aid or advice . . . and was contriving and intending to get rid of him as easily as possible"); 118 F.,at 771 (assessing damages based on provision of Laws of Oleron requiring maintenance). Batterton characterizes these as unseaworthiness actions on the theory that the seamen *could have* pursued that claim. But, because courts award damages for the claims a plaintiff actually pleads rather than those he could have brought, these cases are irrelevant.

The lack of punitive damages in traditional maritime law cases is practically dispositive.

By the time the claim of unseaworthiness evolved to remedy personal injury, punitive damages were a well-established part of the [—13—] common law. *Exxon Shipping,* 554 U. S., at 491. American courts had awarded punitive (or exemplary) damages from the Republic's earliest days. See, *e.g., Genay* v. *Norris,* 1 S. C. L. 6, 7 (1784); *Coryell* v. *Colbaugh,* 1 N. J. L. 77, 78 (1791). And yet, beyond the decisions discussed above, Batterton presents no decisions from the formative years of the personal injury unseaworthiness claim in which exemplary damages were awarded. From this we conclude that, unlike maintenance and cure, unseaworthiness did not traditionally allow recovery of punitive damages.

B

In light of this overwhelming historical evidence, we cannot sanction a novel remedy here unless it is required to maintain uniformity with Congress's clearly expressed policies. Therefore, we must consider the remedies typically recognized for Jones Act claims.

The Jones Act adopts the remedial provisions of FELA, and by the time of the Jones Act's passage, this Court and others had repeatedly interpreted the scope of damages available to FELA plaintiffs. These early decisions held that "[t]he damages recoverable [under FELA] are limited {–2285–} . . . strictly to the financial loss . . . sustained."[7] *American R. Co. of P. R.* v. *Didricksen,* 227 U. S. 145, 149 (1913); see also *Gulf, C. & S. F. R. Co.* v. *McGinnis,* 228 U. S. 173, 175 (1913) (FELA is construed "only to compensate . . . for the actual pecuniary loss resulting" from the worker's injury or death); *Michigan Central R. Co.* v. *Vreeland,* 227 U. S. 59, 68 (1913) (FELA imposes "a liability for the pecuniary [—14—] damage resulting to [the worker] and for that

---

seek conformity with the policy preferences the political branches have expressed in legislation.

---

[7] Treatises from the same period lend further support to the view that "in all actions under [FELA], an award of exemplary damages is not permitted." 2 M. Roberts, Federal Liabilities of Carriers §621, p. 1093 (1918); 1 *id.,* §417, at 708; 5 J. Berryman, Sutherland on Damages §1333, p. 5102 (4th ed. 1916) (FELA "provid[es] compensation for pecuniary loss or damage only").

only"). In one particularly illuminating case, in deciding whether a complaint alleged a claim under FELA or state law, the Court observed that if the complaint "were read as manifestly demanding exemplary damages, that would point to the state law." *Seaboard Air Line R. Co.* v. *Koennecke*, 239 U. S. 352, 354 (1915). And in the years since, Federal Courts of Appeals have unanimously held that punitive damages are not available under FELA. *Miller* v. *American President Lines, Ltd.*, 989 F. 2d 1450, 1457 (CA6 1993); *Wildman* v. *Burlington No. R. Co.*, 825 F. 2d 1392, 1395 (CA9 1987); *Kozar* v. *Chesapeake & Ohio R. Co.*, 449 F. 2d 1238, 1243 (CA6 1971).

Our early discussions of the Jones Act followed the same practices. We described the Act shortly after its passage as creating "an action for compensatory damages, on the ground of negligence."[8] *Peterson*, 278 U. S., at 135. And we have more recently observed that the Jones Act "limits recovery to pecuniary loss." *Miles*, 498 U. S., at 32. Looking to FELA and these decisions, the Federal Courts of Appeals have uniformly held that punitive damages are not available under the Jones Act. *McBride*, 768 F. 3d, at 388, 2 Adm. R. at 324 ("[N]o cases have awarded punitive damages under the Jones Act"); *Guevara* v. *Maritime Overseas Corp.*, 59 F. 3d 1496, 1507, n. 9 (CA5 1995) (en banc); *Horsley*, 15 F. 3d, at 203; *Miller, supra*, at 1457 ("Punitive damages are not . . . recoverable under the Jones Act"); *Kopczynski* v. *The Jacqueline*, 742 F. 2d 555, 560 (CA9 1984).

Batterton argues that these cases are either inapposite or wrong, but because of the absence of historical evidence to support punitive damages—evidence that was central to [—15—] our decision in *Atlantic Sounding*—we need not reopen this question of statutory interpretation. It is enough for us to note the general consensus that exists in the lower courts and to observe that the position of those courts conforms with the

discussion and holding in *Miles*. Adopting the rule urged by Batterton would be contrary to *Miles*'s command that federal courts should seek to promote a "uniform rule applicable to all actions" for the same injury, whether under the Jones Act or the general maritime law. 498 U. S., at 33.

C

To the extent Batterton argues that punitive damages are justified on policy grounds or as a regulatory measure, we are unpersuaded. In contemporary maritime {–2286–} law, our overriding objective is to pursue the policy expressed in congressional enactments, and because unseaworthiness in its current strict-liability form is our own invention and came after passage of the Jones Act, it would exceed our current role to introduce novel remedies contradictory to those Congress has provided in similar areas. See *id.*, at 36 (declining to create remedy "that goes well beyond the limits of Congress' ordered system of recovery"). We are particularly loath to impose more expansive liabilities on a claim governed by strict liability than Congress has imposed for comparable claims based in negligence. *Ibid.* And with the increased role that legislation has taken over the past century of maritime law, we think it wise to leave to the political branches the development of novel claims and remedies.

We are also wary to depart from the practice under the Jones Act because a claim of unseaworthiness—more than a claim for maintenance and cure—serves as a duplicate and substitute for a Jones Act claim. The duty of maintenance and cure requires the master to provide medical care and wages to an injured mariner in the period after [—16—] the injury has occurred. *Calmar S. S. Corp.*, 303 U. S., at 527–528. By contrast, both the Jones Act and unseaworthiness claims compensate for the injury itself and for the losses resulting from the injury. *Peterson, supra*, at 138. In such circumstances, we are particularly mindful of the rule that requires us to promote uniformity between maritime

---

[8] We also note that Congress declined to allow punitive damages when it enacted the Death on the High Seas Act. 46 U. S. C. §30303 (allowing "fair compensation for the pecuniary loss sustained" for a death on the high seas).

statutory law and maritime common law.[9] See *Miles, supra,* at 27. See also *Mobil Oil Corp.* v. *Higginbotham,* 436 U. S. 618, 625 (1978) (declining to recognize loss-of-society damages under general maritime law because that would "rewrit[e the] rules that Congress has affirmatively and specifically enacted").

Unlike a claim of maintenance and cure, which addresses a situation where the vessel owner and master have "just about every economic incentive to dump an injured seaman in a port and abandon him to his fate," in the unseaworthiness context the interests of the owner and mariner are more closely aligned. *McBride, supra,* at 394, n. 12, 2 Adm. R. at 329 n.12 (Clement, J., concurring). That is because there are signif- [—17—] icant economic incentives prompting owners to ensure that their vessels are seaworthy. Most obviously, an owner who puts an unseaworthy ship to sea stands to lose the ship and the cargo that it carries. And if a vessel's unseaworthiness threatens the crew or cargo, the owner risks losing the protection of his insurer (who may not cover losses incurred {-2287-} by the owner's negligence) and the work of the crew (who may refuse to serve on an unseaworthy vessel). In some instances,

the vessel owner may even face criminal penalties. See, *e.g.,* 46 U. S. C. §10908.

Allowing punitive damages on unseaworthiness claims would also create bizarre disparities in the law. First, due to our holding in *Miles,* which limited recovery to compensatory damages in wrongful-death actions, a mariner could make a claim for punitive damages if he was injured onboard a ship, but his estate would lose the right to seek punitive damages if he died from his injuries. Second, because unseaworthiness claims run against the owner of the vessel, the ship's owner could be liable for punitive damages while the master or operator of the ship—who has more control over onboard conditions and is best positioned to minimize potential risks—would not be liable for such damages under the Jones Act. See *Sieracki,* 328 U. S., at 100 (The duty of seaworthiness is "peculiarly and exclusively the obligation of the owner. It is one he cannot delegate").

Finally, because "[n]oncompensatory damages are not part of the civil-code tradition and thus unavailable in such countries," *Exxon Shipping,* 554 U. S., at 497, allowing punitive damages would place American shippers at a significant competitive disadvantage and would discourage foreign-owned vessels from employing American seamen. See Gotanda, Punitive Damages: A Comparative Analysis, 42 Colum. J. Transnat'l L. 391, 396, n. 24 (2004) (listing civil-law nations that restrict private plaintiffs to compensatory damages). This would frustrate another [—18—] "fundamental interest" served by federal maritime jurisdiction: "the protection of maritime commerce." *Norfolk Southern R. Co.* v. *James N. Kirby, Pty Ltd.,* 543 U. S. 14, 25 (2004) (internal quotation marks omitted; emphasis deleted).

Against this, Batterton points to the maritime doctrine that encourages special solicitude for the welfare of seamen. But that doctrine has its roots in the paternalistic approach taken toward mariners by 19th century courts. See, *e.g., Harden,* 11 F. Cas., at 485; *Brown,* 4 F. Cas., at 409. The doctrine has never been a commandment that

---

[9] The dissent, *post* at 9, and n. 7 (opinion of GINSBURG, J.), suggests that because of the existing differences between a Jones Act claim and an unseaworthiness claim, recognizing punitive damages would not be a cause of disparity. But, as the dissent acknowledges, much of the expanded reach of the modern unseaworthiness doctrine can be attributed to innovations made by this Court following the enactment of the Jones Act. See *post* at 8, and n. 6; *supra,* at 7–8. Although Batterton and the dissent would continue this evolution by recognizing damages previously unavailable, *Miles* dictates that such innovation is the prerogative of the political branches, our past expansion of the unseaworthiness doctrine notwithstanding.

Of course, *Miles* recognized that the general maritime law need not be static. For example, our decision in *Moragne* v. *States Marine Lines, Inc.,* 398 U. S. 375 (1970), smoothed a disjunction created by the imperfect alignment of statutory claims with past decisions limiting maritime claims for wrongful death. But when there is no disjunction—as here, where traditional remedies align with modern statutory remedies—we are unwilling to endorse doctrinal changes absent legislative changes.

maritime law must favor seamen whenever possible. Indeed, the doctrine's apex coincided with many of the harsh common-law limitations on recovery that were not set aside until the passage of the Jones Act. And, while sailors today face hardships not encountered by those who work on land, neither are they as isolated nor as dependent on the master as their predecessors from the age of sail. In light of these changes and of the roles now played by the Judiciary and the political branches in protecting sailors, the special solicitude to sailors has only a small role to play in contemporary maritime law. It is not sufficient to overcome the weight of authority indicating that punitive damages are unavailable.

IV

Punitive damages are not a traditional remedy for unseaworthiness. The rule of *Miles*—promoting uniformity in maritime law and deference to the policies expressed in the statutes governing maritime law—prevents us from recognizing a new entitlement to punitive damages where none previously existed. We hold that a plaintiff may not recover punitive damages on a claim of unseaworthiness. [—19—]

We reverse the judgment of the United States Court of Appeals for the Ninth Circuit and remand the case for further proceedings consistent with this opinion.

It is so ordered.

(Reporter's Note: Dissenting Opinion follows on p. 52).

[—1—] {–2287–} GINSBURG, J., with whom BREYER and SOTOMAYOR, JJ., join dissenting: {–2288–}

In *Exxon Shipping Co.* v. *Baker*, 554 U. S. 471 (2008), the Court recognized that punitive damages normally are available in maritime cases. *Id.*, at 489–490, 502, 508, n. 21. Relying on *Miles* v. *Apex Marine Corp.*, 498 U. S. 19 (1990), the Court today holds that unseaworthiness claims are an exception to that general rule. Respondent Christopher Batterton, defending the Ninth Circuit's decision in his favor, relies on the Court's more recent decision in *Atlantic Sounding Co.* v. *Townsend*, 557 U. S. 404 (2009). In my view, the Ninth Circuit correctly determined that *Atlantic Sounding* is the controlling precedent. See 880 F. 3d 1089, 1095–1096, 6 Adm. R. 308, 311–13 (2018) (case below). I would therefore affirm the judgment of the Court of Appeals, cogently explained in Senior Circuit Judge Kleinfeld's opinion.

I

Batterton was employed as a deckhand for petitioner The Dutra Group, a dredging and marine construction company. As Batterton worked on a Dutra vessel, fellow crew-members pumped pressurized air into a below-decks compartment. The build up of pressurized air blew open a hatch cover that crushed Batterton's hand, permanently disabling him. The accident could have been prevented, [—2—] Batterton alleges, by a valve to vent excess air from the compartment, something to hold the hatch cover open, or simply better warnings or supervision.

Batterton filed a civil action asserting one claim of negligence under the Jones Act[1] and two claims under general maritime law: one for breach of the duty to provide a seaworthy vessel and one for breach of the duty to provide maintenance and cure.[2] As to his unseaworthiness claim, Batterton sought punitive damages, alleging that Dutra's breach was wanton and willful.

Dutra moved to strike or dismiss Batterton's punitive damages request. The District Court denied the motion, 2014 WL 12538172, *2 (CD Cal. Dec. 15, 2014), and the Ninth Circuit, accepting an interlocutory appeal, affirmed, 880 F. 3d 1089, 6 Adm. R. 308. Longstanding Ninth Circuit precedent, the court observed, recognized the availability of punitive damages in seamen's actions for unseaworthiness. *Id.*, at 1091, 6 Adm. R. at 308 (citing *Evich* v. *Morris*, 819 F. 2d 256, 258 (1987)). *Miles*, 498 U. S., at 29–33, which held that loss-of-society damages are not available in survivors' actions for unseaworthiness resulting in a seaman's wrongful death, the court observed, did not undermine that precedent. 880 F. 3d, at 1093–1096, 6 Adm. R. at 310–13. "Whatever room might [have] be[en] left to support broadening *Miles* to cover punitive damages" sought by a seaman, the Ninth Circuit said, "was cut off by [—3—] [this] Court's decision in *Atlantic Sounding*," in which this Court, recognizing {–2289–} that "historically, punitive damages have been available and awarded in general maritime actions," held that such damages are available in seamen's suits for maintenance and cure. *Id.*, at 1095, 6 Adm. R. at 311. (quoting *Atlantic Sounding*, 557 U. S., at 407; alteration omitted). Punitive damages, the Ninth Circuit concluded, are similarly available when a seaman sues for unseaworthiness under general maritime law.

---

[1] The Jones Act provides: "A seaman injured in the course of employment or, if the seaman dies from the injury, the personal representative of the seaman[,] may elect to bring a civil action at law, with the right of trial by jury, against the employer. Laws of the United States regulating recovery for personal injury to, or death of, a railway employee apply to an action under this section." 46 U. S. C. §30104.

[2] "Maintenance and cure" is the right of "the seaman, ill or injured in the service of the ship without willful misbehavior on his part[to] wages to the end of the voyage and subsistence, lodging, and medical care to the point where the maximum cure attainable has been reached." 2 R. Force & M. Norris, The Law of Seamen §26:1, p. 26–4 (5th ed. 2003).

II

I turn now to an examination of *Miles* and *Atlantic Sounding* closer than the attention accorded those decisions by the Court.

Miles, decided in 1990, addressed this question: In a wrongful-death action premised on unseaworthiness, may a deceased seaman's parent recover damages for loss of society? 498 U. S., at 21. As the Court explained in *Miles*, historically, general maritime law did not recognize a cause of action for wrongful death. *Id.*, at 23 (citing *The Harrisburg*, 119 U. S. 199 (1886)). But since the late 19th century, every State had adopted a statutory wrongful-death cause of action. *Miles*, 498 U. S., at 23. And in two statutes, Congress had provided for wrongful-death recoveries in maritime cases. *Ibid.* First, the Jones Act, 46 U. S. C. §30104, provided a right of action for the survivor of a seaman killed in the course of his employment. Second, the Death on the High Seas Act (DOHSA), 46 U. S. C. §30301 *et seq.*, provided a right of action for the survivor of anyone killed "by wrongful act, neglect, or default . . . on the high seas." §30302; *Miles*, 498 U. S., at 24. But the Jones Act and DOHSA left some wrongful deaths at sea without a remedy. See *Miles*, 498 U. S., at 25–26.[3] To fill [—4—] gaps in this statutory regime, and in light of legislative abrogation of the common-law disallowance of wrongful-death claims, the Court in *Moragne* v. *States Marine Lines, Inc.*, 398 U. S. 375, 409 (1970), recognized a general maritime cause of action

---

[3] These were the unprovided-for cases: "First, in territorial waters, general maritime law allowed a remedy for unseaworthiness resulting in injury, but not for death. Second, DOHSA allowed a remedy for [—4—] death resulting from unseaworthiness on the high seas, but general maritime law did not allow such recovery for a similar death in territorial waters. Finally, . . . in those States whose statutes allowed a claim for wrongful death resulting from unseaworthiness, recovery was available for the death of a longshoreman due to unseaworthiness, but not for the death of a Jones Act seaman. This was because wrongful death actions under the Jones Act are limited to negligence, and the Jones Act pre-empts state law remedies for the death or injury of a seaman." *Miles* v. *Apex Marine Corp.*, 498 U. S. 19, 26 (1990) (citation omitted).

for the wrongful death of a longshoreman. See also *Miles*, 498 U. S., at 26–30 (claim for wrongful death is also available to seamen's survivors).

After recounting this history, the *Miles* Court addressed the damages relief available for maritime wrongful death. Because "Congress and the States ha[d] legislated extensively in" the field of maritime law, the Court stated, "admiralty court[s] should look primarily to these legislative enactments for policy guidance." *Id.*, at 27. Congress had expressly limited damages recoverable under DOHSA to "pecuniary loss" sustained by the decedent's survivor. *Id.*, at 31 (citing 46 U. S. C. App. §762, recodified at§30303). And the Jones Act adopted the substantive provisions of the Federal Employers Liability Act, 45 U. S. C. §51 *et seq.*, which the Court construed to confine wrongful-death damages to "pecuniary {–2290–} loss." *Miles*, 498 U. S., at 32. The *Miles* Court reasoned that loss-of-society damages were nonpecuniary, that such damages could not be recovered under DOHSA or the Jones Act, and that it would "be inconsistent with [the Court's] place in the constitutional scheme . . . to sanction more expansive remedies" under general maritime law. *Miles*, 498 U. S., [—5—] at 31–33.[4]

Some 19 years after *Miles*, in *Atlantic Sounding*, this Court held that punitive damages are available in actions for maintenance and cure under general maritime law. 557 U. S., at 408. *Atlantic Sounding*'s reasoning had four components. First, the Court observed, punitive damages had a long common-law pedigree. *Id.*, at 409–410. Second, the "general rule that punitive damages were available at common law

---

[4] The *Miles* Court relied on comparable reasoning in denying the deceased seaman's estate, which had brought a survival action, the right to recover future earnings. See *id.*, at 33–37. Under "the traditional maritime rule," "there [wa]s no survival of unseaworthiness claims." *Id.*, at 34. The Court declined to decide whether to recognize a general maritime survival right, however, because, even if such a right were recognized, it would not support recovery of lost future income. *Ibid.* This damages limitation followed from the Jones Act, DOHSA ,and most States' laws, which did not permit recovery of such damages. See *id.*, at 35–36.

extended to claims arising under federal maritime law." *Id.*, at 411; see *id.*, at 411–412. Third, "[n]othing in maritime law undermine[d] the applicability of this general rule in the maintenance and cure context," notwithstanding slim evidence that punitive damages were historically awarded in maintenance and cure actions. *Id.*, at 412; see *id.*, at 412–415, and n. 4. Finally, neither the Jones Act nor any other statute indicated that Congress sought to displace the presumption that remedies generally available under the common law are available for maritime claims. While the Jones Act armed seamen with a statutory action for negligence attributable to a vessel operator, that remedy, *Atlantic Sounding* noted, did not curtail preexisting maritime causes of action and remedies. *Id.*, at 415–418. The *Atlantic Sounding* Court rejected as "far too broad" the argument that the remedies available under general maritime law were confined to those available under the Jones Act or DOHSA. *Id.*, at 418–419. [—6—]

The *Atlantic Sounding* inquiries control this case. As in *Atlantic Sounding*, "both the general maritime cause of action"—here, unseaworthiness—"and the remedy (punitive damages) were well established before the passage of the Jones Act." 557 U. S., at 420; *Mitchell* v. *Trawler Racer, Inc.*, 362 U. S. 539, 544 (1960); *The Osceola*, 189 U. S. 158, 175 (1903). And, unlike the maritime wrongful-death action at issue in *Miles*, Batterton's claim of unseaworthiness resulting in personal injury was not created to fill gaps in a statutory scheme. See *Atlantic Sounding*, 557 U. S., at 420; *Miles*, 498 U. S., at 27, 36. The damages available for Batterton's unseaworthiness claim, *Atlantic Sounding* therefore signals, need not track those available under the Jones Act. See 557 U. S., at 424, n. 12.

III

Applying *Atlantic Sounding*'s test, see *supra*, at 5, punitive damages are not categorically barred in unseaworthiness actions. *Atlantic Sounding* itself answers the first two inquiries. See *supra*, at 5. "Punitive damages have long been an {–2291–} available

remedy at common law for wanton, willful, or outrageous conduct." 557 U. S., at 409; see *id.*, at 409–410. And "[t]he general rule that punitive damages [are] available at common law extended to claims arising under federal maritime law." *Id.*, at 411; see *id.*, at 411–412. As next explained, the third and fourth components of *Atlantic Sounding*'s test are also satisfied.

A

Atlantic Sounding asks, third, whether anything in maritime law "undermines the applicability [to the maritime action at issue] of th[e] general rule" that punitive damages are available under general maritime law. *Id.*, at 412. True, there is no evidence that courts awarded punitive damages for unseaworthiness before the mid-20th century. See *ante*, at 11–13. But neither is there [—7—] evidence that punitive damages were *unavailable* in unseaworthiness actions. Tr. of Oral Arg. 17.

Contrary to the Court's assertion, evidence of the availability of punitive damages for maintenance and cure was not "central to our decision in *Atlantic Sounding*." *Ante*, at 14–15. Far from it. "[A] search for cases in which punitive damages were awarded for the willful denial of maintenance and cure . . . yields very little." *Atlantic Sounding*, 557 U. S., at 430 (ALITO, J., dissenting). The Court in *Atlantic Sounding* invoked historical evidence about punitive damages in maintenance and cure actions, "strikingly slim" though it was, *id.*, at 431, only to underscore this point: Without a showing that punitive damages were unavailable, the generally applicable common-law rule allowing punitive damages should not be displaced. See *id.*, at 412–415 (majority opinion). Here, too, the absence of evidence that punitive damages were unavailable in unseaworthiness cases supports adherence to the general common-law rule permitting punitive damages.

B

Atlantic Sounding asks fourth: Has Congress "enacted legislation departing from th[e] common-law understanding" that punitive damages are generally available? See *id.*, at 415. Dutra contends that unseaworthiness claims and claims under the Jones Act are "simply two paths to compensation for the same injury." Brief for Petitioner 19–20 (emphasis deleted). Positing that punitive damages are unavailable under the Jones Act,[5] Dutra concludes they are likewise unavailable in unseaworthiness suits. *Id.*, at 17. See also *ante*, at 13–15. Dutra's argument is unavailing, for the Jones Act does not preclude the award of punitive damages in unseaworthiness cases. [—8—]

As noted, the Jones Act provides a cause of action for a seaman injured by his or her employer's negligence. 46 U. S. C. §30104. Congress passed the Act "primarily to overrule *The Osceola*, [189 U. S. 158,] in which this Court prohibited a seaman or his family from recovering for injuries or death suffered due to his employers' negligence." *Atlantic Sounding*, 557 U. S., at 415. The Jones Act was intended to "enlarge th[e] protection" afforded to seamen, "not to narrow it." *The Arizona* v. *Anelich*, 298 U. S. 110, 123 (1936). Accordingly, the Jones {–2292–} Act did not provide an "exclusive remedy" for seamen's injuries; instead, it "preserve[d]" and supplemented "common-law causes of action." *Atlantic Sounding*, 557 U. S., at 416–417. As *Miles* itself recognized, the Jones Act "d[id] not disturb seamen's general maritime claims for injuries resulting from unseaworthiness." 498 U. S., at 29.

When the Jones Act was enacted, unseaworthiness and negligence were "discrete concepts": Unseaworthiness related "to the structure of the ship and the adequacy of [its] equipment and furnishings," while negligence concerned "the direction and control of operations aboard ship." G. Gilmore & C. Black, Law of Admiralty §6–3, p. 277 (2d ed. 1975). Because these actions were distinct, it is improbable that, by enacting the Jones Act, Congress meant to limit the remedies available in unseaworthiness cases. Though unseaworthiness and Jones Act negligence

now "significant[ly] overlap," *ante*, at 8, that overlap resulted primarily from mid-20th-century judicial decisions expanding the scope of unseaworthiness liability. See *Mitchell*, 362 U. S., at 547–550.[6] Those decisions do not so [—9—] much as hint that Congress, in enacting the Jones Act, intended to cabin the relief available for unseaworthiness. Even today, unseaworthiness and Jones Act negligence are "not identical." 2 R. Force & M. Norris, The Law of Seamen §27:25, p. 27–61 (5th ed. 2003).[7] The persistent differences between unseaworthiness and Jones Act claims weigh against inserting into general maritime law damages limitations that may be applicable to Jones Act suits. See *supra*, at 7, n. 5.[8]

---

[5] This Court has not decided whether punitive damages are available under the Jones Act. See *Atlantic Sounding Co.* v. *Townsend*, 557 U. S. 404, 424, n. 12 (2009) (reserving the question).

[6] In particular, this Court held that a ship-owner's duty to provide a seaworthy vessel was "absolute," thereby rendering unseaworthiness a strict-liability tort. *Seas Shipping Co.* v. *Sieracki*, 328 U. S. 85, 94–95 (1946); *Mahnich* v. *Southern S. S. Co.*, 321 U. S. 96, 100–101 (1944); see 1B Benedict on Admiralty §23, pp. 3–12 to 3–16 (7th rev. ed. 2018). In addition, courts broadened the range of conditions that could render a [—9—] vessel unseaworthy. *Id.*, §23, at 3–16 to 3–19.

[7] Unseaworthiness is a strict-liability tort, *ante*, at 7–8; the Jones Act requires proof of negligence, *Lewis* v. *Lewis & Clark Marine, Inc.*, 531 U. S. 438, 441 (2001). Unseaworthiness claims run against the vessel's owner, *Mahnich*, 321 U. S., at 100; Jones Act claims are brought against the seaman's "employer," §30104. Injury caused by the negligent act or omission of a fit fellow crewmember may be actionable under the Jones Act but is not ground for an unseaworthiness suit. 1B Benedict on Admiralty §23, at 3–34 to 3–38; see *Usner* v. *Luckenbach Overseas Corp.*, 400 U. S. 494 (1971). And a vessel owner is liable for unseaworthiness only when the unseaworthy condition proximately caused the plaintiff's injury; under the Jones Act, a plaintiff can prevail upon showing the "slight[est]" causal connection between the defendant's conduct and the plaintiff's injury. 2 Force & Norris, The Law of Seamen §27:25, at 27–62 to 27–63. See also *id.*, §27:2, at 27–7, and n. 6 (the duty to provide a seaworthy vessel may run to "seamen" who do not qualify as such under the Jones Act).

[8] The Court recognizes "that the general maritime law need not be static," but would confine changes in that law to those needed to align it with statutory law. *Ante*, at 16, n. 9. As just stated, however, *supra*, at 8–9, the Jones Act was intended to augment, not to cabin, relief available to seamen.

The Court observes that a plaintiff may not recover twice for the same injury under the Jones Act and unseaworthiness. *Ante*, at 9. True enough. But the Court does not explain why a bar to double recovery of compensatory damages should affect the availability of a single award of punitive damages. Notably, punitive damages are not awarded to compensate the plaintiff; their office is to punish the defendant and deter misconduct. See {–2293–} *Exxon*, [—10—] 554 U. S., at 492; W. Keeton, D. Dobbs, R. Keeton, & D. Owen, Prosser and Keeton on Law of Torts §2, p. 9 (5th ed. 1984). There is thus no tension between preventing double recovery of compensatory damages and allowing the recovery, once, of punitive damages.

IV

Finally, the Court takes up policy arguments against the availability of punitive damages in unseaworthiness actions. *Ante*, at 15–18. The Court, however, has long recognized the general availability of punitive damages under maritime law. *E.g.*, *Atlantic Sounding*, 557 U. S., at 411–412; *Exxon*, 554 U. S., at 489–490; *The Amiable Nancy*, 3 Wheat. 546, 558 (1818).

Punitive damages serve to deter and punish "lawless misconduct." *Ibid.* The imperative of countering a "heightened threat of harm," *Exxon*, 554 U. S., at 490, is especially pressing with regard to sailors, who face unique "hazards in the ship's service," *Harden* v. *Gordon*, 11 F. Cas. 480, 483 (No. 6,047) (CC Me. 1823) (Story, J.). These dangers, more than paternalistic 19th-century attitudes towards sailors, see *ante*, at 18, account for the Court's "'special solicitude'" for "those who undertake to 'venture upon hazardous and unpredictable sea voyages.'" *Air & Liquid Systems Corp.* v. *DeVries*, 586 U. S. ___, ___, 7 Adm. R. 2, 6 (2019) (slip op., at 9) (quoting *American Export Lines, Inc.* v. *Alvez*, 446 U. S. 274, 285 (1980)).

Dutra and the Court warn that allowing punitive damages in unseaworthiness actions could impair maritime commerce. Brief for Petitioner 33–34; *ante*, at 17–18. But punitive damages have been available in maintenance and cure cases in all Circuits for the last decade, *Atlantic Sounding*, 557 U. S. 404, and in unseaworthiness cases in some Circuits for longer, see *Self* v. *Great Lakes Dredge & Dock Co.*, 832 F. 2d 1540, 1550 (CA11 1987); *Evich*, 819 F. 2d, at 258. No tidal wave has overwhelmed commerce [—11—] in those Circuits.

Permitting punitive damages for unseaworthiness, the Court further urges, would create "bizarre disparities." *Ante*, at 17. I see no "bizarre disparit[y]" in allowing an injured sailor to seek remedies unavailable to survivors of deceased seamen. See Keeton, *supra*, §127, at 949, 951 (state wrongful-death statutes frequently limit survivors' recoveries to pecuniary damages). Nor is it "bizarre" to permit recovery of punitive damages against a shipowner "for injuries due to unseaworthiness of the vessel." *The Arizona*, 298 U. S., at 120. Exposure to such damages helps to deter wrongdoing, particularly when malfeasance is "hard to detect." *Exxon*, 554 U. S., at 494. If there is any "bizarre disparit[y]," it is the one the Court today creates: Punitive damages are available for willful and wanton breach of the duty to provide maintenance and cure, but not for similarly culpable breaches of the duty to provide a seaworthy vessel.

* * *

For the reasons stated, I would affirm the Court of Appeals' judgment.

United States Court of Appeals for the First Circuit

United States Court of Appeals
for the First Circuit

No. 15-2377

UNITED STATES
vs.
AYBAR-ULLOA***

Appeal from the United States District Court for the
District of Puerto Rico

Decided: January 9, 2019

***Petition for rehearing en banc granted on Jan. 17, 2020.

Citation: 913 F.3d 47, 7 Adm. R. 58 (1st Cir. 2019).

Before **TORRUELLA, LYNCH,** and **BARRON,** Circuit Judges.

[—2—] {–49–} **BARRON,** Circuit Judge:

Johvanny Aybar-Ulloa ("Aybar") pleaded guilty in 2015 to two counts of drug trafficking in international waters while aboard a "stateless" vessel in violation of the Maritime Drug Law Enforcement Act ("MDLEA"), 46 U.S.C. §§ 70501-08. He now challenges those convictions on the ground that Congress lacks the authority under Article I, Section 8, Clause 10 of the United States Constitution to criminalize his conduct, given that he contends that the conduct for which he was convicted lacks any nexus to the United States. Aybar separately challenges the sentence that he received for those convictions. For the reasons that follow, we affirm the convictions but vacate the sentence.

I.

At the change of plea hearing, the government described, and Aybar does not dispute, the following events as having occurred on August 9, 2013. HMS *Lancaster*, a foreign warship, was on patrol in the Caribbean Sea and launched a helicopter that spotted a small vessel dead in the water. The vessel was located in international waters at the time and contained "numerous packages."

HMS *Lancaster* launched a small boat in order to conduct a right-of-visit approach. During this approach, Aybar and his co-defendant, who were aboard the vessel with the packages, claimed to be citizens of the Dominican Republic, although the vessel bore "no indicia of nationality." [—3—]

Law enforcement personnel aboard the small boat conducting the approach then determined that the vessel was "without nationality," as Aybar conceded to the District Court was true, and boarded it.[1] The men on board the vessel, including Aybar, were transferred to HMS *Lancaster* along with the packages that were taken from the vessel. {–50–}

A narcotics field test performed on board HMS *Lancaster* confirmed that the packages contained cocaine. At this point, Aybar was transferred to a United States Coast Guard vessel and transported to Puerto Rico, where he was held in custody by United States law enforcement.

On August 13, 2013, a federal grand jury in the District of Puerto Rico returned an indictment against Aybar. The indictment charged him under the MDLEA with conspiring to possess with intent to distribute cocaine on board a vessel subject to the jurisdiction of the United States, in violation of 46 U.S.C. § 70506(b) (count one), and aiding and abetting possession with intent to distribute cocaine on board a vessel subject to the jurisdiction of the United States, in violation of 46 U.S.C. §§ 70502(c)(1)(A), 70503(a)(1), 70504(b)(1), 70506(a), and 18 [—4—] U.S.C. § 2 (count two). A forfeiture allegation, under 46 U.S.C. § 70507, was also made against Aybar.

The MDLEA provides in part: "While on board a covered vessel, an individual may not knowingly or intentionally . . . manufacture or distribute, or possess with intent to manufacture or distribute, a controlled substance . . . ." 46 U.S.C. § 70503(a)(1). A "covered vessel" includes "a vessel subject to

---

[1] The government represented in a filing in the District Court that the law enforcement personnel were United States Coast Guard members who were embarked on HMS *Lancaster*. However, the government did not mention this allegation while describing the factual basis for the convictions at the change of plea hearing.

the jurisdiction of the United States." *Id.* § 70503(e)(1). A "vessel subject to the jurisdiction of the United States" is in turn defined to include "a vessel without nationality." *Id.* § 70502(c)(1)(A). And, as we mentioned, Aybar conceded below that he was on board a vessel "without nationality" at the time he was apprehended.

On October 2, 2014, Aybar filed a motion to dismiss the indictment for lack of jurisdiction. He argued that Congress lacked the power to criminalize his conduct, given the lack of what Aybar claimed to be any constitutionally sufficient nexus between his charged conduct and the United States, because Congress's power under Article I of the Constitution "[t]o define and punish Piracies and Felonies committed on the high Seas, and Offences against the Law of Nations," U.S. Const. art. I, § 8, cl. 10, did not extend to his conduct in such circumstances.

The government opposed Aybar's motion. The District Court denied Aybar's motion on December 22, 2014 and issued a nunc [—5—] pro tunc opinion and order on January 5, 2015. The District Court acknowledged that the vessel was not a "vessel of the United States" within the meaning of the MDLEA, 46 U.S.C. § 70503(e)(1); that Aybar was not a citizen of the United States; and that the other members of the crew were not either. But, the District Court reasoned, because "international law allows the United States 'to treat stateless vessels as if they were its own,'" it followed that "persons navigating the high seas aboard a vessel without nationality have effectively waived their rights to object to the exercise of jurisdiction over them by the United States." The District Court therefore concluded that Aybar's "as-applied constitutional challenge fails" because his vessel was stateless.

Following a change of plea hearing, Aybar entered a guilty plea to all charges on March 11, 2015. At that hearing, Aybar engaged in the following colloquy with the Magistrate Judge:

The Magistrate: Now, do you admit that in addition to the conspiracy you

actually and the other co-defendants possessed with the intent to distribute these substances, this cocaine?

Aybar: Yes, Your Honor.

The Magistrate: In the same circumstances on board this vessel without nationality and therefore subject to jurisdiction of the United States?

Aybar: Yes, Your Honor. [—6—] {–51–}

The District Court accepted Aybar's guilty plea, and the case proceeded to sentencing. A probation officer prepared a presentence report ("PSR") using the 2014 United States Sentencing Guidelines Manual. The PSR assigned Aybar a base offense level of thirty-eight under the United States Sentencing Guidelines. After receiving the PSR, Aybar filed an objection in which he argued that two levels should be subtracted from his offense level under § 3B1.2(b) of the Guidelines because he was a minor participant.

At sentencing, the District Court declined to reduce his offense level as Aybar had argued and sentenced Aybar to 135 months in prison. Aybar timely filed a notice appealing the judgment entered against him.

II.

In prior cases in our circuit that have presented constitutional challenges to MDLEA convictions not unlike the one that Aybar now makes to us, the defendant had either waived or forfeited the constitutional argument challenging the scope of Congress's power under Article I to criminalize conduct supposedly lacking a sufficient nexus to the United States. *See, e.g., United States v. Diaz-Doncel,* 811 F.3d 517, 4 Adm. R. 12 (1st Cir. 2016) (waived); *United States v. Nueci-Peña,* 711 F.3d 191 (1st Cir. 2013) [—7—] (forfeited).[2] But that is not the case here.

---

[2] We rejected a similar as-applied challenge to the constitutionality of the MDLEA under the Define and Punish Clause on plain error review in *Nueci-Peña. See* 711 F.3d at 196-98. In doing so, we noted that of all the circuits to have addressed the argument that this Clause "does not authorize

Aybar timely raised below the challenge that he now makes on appeal. And while Aybar did plead guilty to the offenses that underlie the convictions that he challenges on appeal, the government concedes that, in consequence of the Supreme Court's holding in *Class v. United States*, 138 S. Ct. 798 (2018), Aybar's guilty plea does not bar him from challenging Congress's constitutional power to criminalize his conduct pursuant to its Article I powers.

The government does separately argue that Aybar waived his right to bring this challenge because he conceded in the plea colloquy that the vessel he was on board was "without nationality"—which is one of the MDLEA's definitions for a "vessel subject to the jurisdiction of the United States." 46 U.S.C. § 70502(c)(1)(A). But, as we read the record, Aybar conceded only that his conduct fell within the MDLEA's scope and not that the MDLEA was a valid exercise of Congress's constitutional power under Article I insofar as it covered his conduct. [—8—]

Thus, we review de novo the district court's rejection of Aybar's constitutional challenge to Congress's power to criminalize the conduct for which he was convicted. *See United States v. Bravo*, 489 F.3d 1, 6 (1st Cir. 2007). Nevertheless, as we will explain, the particular constitutional challenge to Congress's power that Aybar develops fails because, although we have not had occasion directly to address it before, related precedent from our circuit precludes us from accepting the premise concerning international law on which his constitutional challenge to congressional power rests.

A.

Aybar contends that Congress exceeded its authority under Article I in criminalizing {–52–} his conduct under the MDLEA because Congress lacked the necessary power to criminalize such conduct under the Define and

Punish Clause. That Clause gives Congress the power "[t]o define and punish Piracies and Felonies committed on the high Seas, and Offences against the Law of Nations." U.S. Const. art. I, § 8, cl. 10. In responding to Aybar's constitutional challenge, the government does not identify any other source of constitutional authority pursuant to which Congress may criminalize Aybar's conduct. We thus focus here solely on the dispute between the parties regarding the scope of the power that the Define and Punish Clause affords Congress to criminalize Aybar's conduct. [—9—]

Aybar's constitutional challenge relies heavily on Judge Torruella's dissent in *United States v. Cardales-Luna*, 632 F.3d 731 (1st Cir. 2011).[3] Aybar first contends, by quoting Judge Torruella's dissent, that "piracy" under international law is only "robbery when committed upon the sea" and thus does not encompass drug trafficking. *Id.* at 745 (Torruella, J., dissenting). For that reason, he contends that Congress has no power to criminalize his conduct pursuant to the "Piracies" component of the Clause in question.

Aybar further contends, again by quoting the following portion of Judge Torruella's *Cardales-Luna* dissent, that the "'Law of Nations' is generally understood to be the eighteenth and nineteenth-century term for 'customary international law'" and that customary international law does not recognize drug trafficking as an offense against the law of nations. *Id.* at 745–47. Thus, Aybar contends, the "law of nations" component of the Clause at issue also does not give Congress the power to criminalize the conduct for which he was convicted. [—10—]

Congress to enact the MDLEA, which punishes conduct without a connection to the United States," at least one has squarely rejected that argument, and none has held otherwise. *Id.* at 198 (citing *United States v. Estupinan*, 453 F.3d 1336, 1338-39 (11th Cir. 2006)).

[3] The defendant in *Cardales-Luna* did not raise a constitutional challenge to Congress's power under Article I to regulate conduct aboard stateless vessels on the high seas absent any nexus between that conduct and the United States. 632 F.3d at 737. Judge Torruella nevertheless addressed this issue in his dissent because he concluded that this constitutional challenge implicated the court's subject matter jurisdiction. *Id.* The majority disagreed, however, and thus declined to address the issue sua sponte. *Id.*

Of course, Aybar recognizes that, even if these arguments are right, he still must show that Congress could not criminalize his conduct pursuant to its power to define and punish "Felonies" committed on the high seas. He acknowledges, as precedent compels him to do, that this portion of the Clause gives Congress an independent source of power to define and punish conduct on the high seas, separate and apart from the power that Congress has under the other portions of the Clause that we have just discussed. *See United States v. Smith*, 18 U.S. 153, 158–59 (1820).

In arguing that the portion of the Clause that empowers Congress to punish "Felonies" on the high seas does not permit Congress to criminalize his conduct, Aybar contends that Congress cannot define and punish his conduct as a "Felon[y]" within the meaning of Article I, Section 8, Clause 10, because there was no nexus between that conduct and the United States.[4] And Aybar bases that argument entirely on an assertion about the way that international {–53–} law—which he appears to treat as having been [—11—] invariant in the relevant respect from the Founding to the present—treats drug trafficking and a nation's power to prosecute it in circumstances like those involved here.

We note that, in advancing this argument about the content of international law, Aybar is less than clear in explaining the precise extent to which, in his view, international law reflects limits on national power that the Constitution incorporates in the portion of Article I that empowers Congress to define and punish "Felonies" committed on the high seas. But, be that as it may, it is at least clear that Aybar's constitutional contention with respect to the scope of Congress's power under

this part of Article I is necessarily premised on the underlying assertion that he makes about the content of international law as it relates to a nation's ability to criminalize conduct on the high seas where there is no more connection between that conduct and the United States than there is here. And so we now turn to a consideration of that international-law-based premise for his constitutional argument concerning Congress's power, for, unless we accept that premise, his constitutional challenge must fail.[5] [—12—]

B.

In asserting this premise, Aybar again relies heavily on the reasoning set forth in portions of Judge Torruella's dissent in *Cardales-Luna*. Aybar begins by quoting Judge Torruella's conclusion that, "under the international law doctrine of universal jurisdiction (UJ), a nation may prosecute certain serious offenses even though they have no nexus to its territory or its nationals, and no impact on its territory or its citizens." *Cardales-Luna*, 632 F.3d at 740. But, Aybar goes on to contend, once again by quoting Judge Torruella's dissent in *Cardales-Luna*, that "[o]ther than in the case of those limited crimes, there is no general authority to regulate purely foreign criminal conduct that does not have a demonstrable connection with the United States." *Id.* at 741. Aybar then ties up his constitutional argument by asserting (yet again by quoting Judge Torruella's dissent in *Cardales-Luna*) that, because "[d]rug trafficking is not recognized in customary international law as a universally cognizable offense," *id.* at 745, the MDLEA may not afford universal jurisdiction for drug trafficking as a "Felon[y]" within the meaning

---

[4] Specifically, Aybar asserts the following: He was "interdicted in a vessel in international waters"; "no offense occurred within the territorial jurisdiction of the United States"; his vessel neither departed from nor was bound for the United States; "there is no evidence that the cocaine aboard the vessel was intended for distribution" in the United States; he "did not commit any offense against a vessel of the United States"; and he was "located by and taken in custody aboard" a foreign warship.

[5] We note that the Supreme Court addressed Congress's constitutional power to define and punish piracies and felonies in a series of cases in the early nineteenth century. *See United States v. Furlong*, 18 U.S. (5 Wheat.) 184, 195-98 (1820); *Smith*, 18 U.S. (5 Wheat.) at 158-60; *United States v. Palmer*, 16 U.S. (3 Wheat.) 610, 630 (1818); *cf. United States v. Holmes*, 18 U.S. (5 Wheat.) 412 (1820); *United States v. Klintock*, 18 U.S. (5 Wheat.) [—12—] 144 (1820). But, Aybar makes no argument that these cases resolved his constitutional argument in his favor.

of Article I, Section 8, Clause 10 of the Constitution in a case in which the defendant's conduct did not have any more nexus to the United States than was present here. [—13—]

The problem for Aybar in advancing this argument is that, notwithstanding his contention that international law does not authorize the United States to prosecute conduct like his own due to what he claims to be the lack of any nexus between that conduct and the United States, we set forth a contrary view of international law in *United States v. Victoria*, 876 F.2d 1009 (1st Cir. 1989) (Breyer, J.). There, we considered a challenge to a conviction for possessing marijuana under a predecessor statute to the MDLEA based on conduct aboard a stateless vessel {—54—} that was captured off the coast of Colombia. *Id.* at 1009–10. And, in the course of rejecting that defendant's challenge to his drug conviction, we explained first that "international law . . . gives the United States . . . authority to treat stateless vessels as if they were its own." *Id.* at 1010 (second omission in original) (quoting *United States v. Smith*, 680 F.2d 255, 258 (1st Cir. 1982)). Then, on the basis of that understanding of international law's treatment of stateless vessels, we concluded: "Thus the United States, as a matter of international law, may prosecute drug offenders on stateless ships found on the high seas." *Id.*[6] [—14—]

To be sure, *Victoria* did not fully spell out why its conclusion that international law authorizes the United States to treat a stateless vessel as its own means that, as a matter of international law, the United States could prosecute a person on board such a vessel for a drug offense. *Victoria* nevertheless

made it clear that its ruling was definitive as to this point through its approving and extensive references to out-of-circuit precedents holding similarly and "explain[ing] in detail why this is so." *Id.* at 1011 (citing *United States v. Alvarez-Mena*, 765 F.2d 1259, 1265–66 (5th Cir. 1985); *United States v. Pinto-Mejia*, 720 F.2d 248, 260–61 (2d Cir. 1983); *United States v. Marino-Garcia*, 679 F.2d 1373, 1382–83 (11th Cir. 1982); *United States v. Rubies*, 612 F.2d 397, 402–03 (9th Cir. 1979); *United States v. Cortes*, 588 F.2d 106, 110 (5th Cir. 1979)).[7] [—15—]

We do recognize that *Victoria* did not consider a constitutional challenge to Congress's power under Article I, such as Aybar now makes to us. In *Victoria*, the defendant argued merely that the statute there at issue did not reach his conduct in light of the *Charming Betsy* canon, *see Murray v. The Schooner Charming Betsy*, 6 U.S. (2 Cranch) 64, 118 (1804) (reasoning that "an act of Congress ought never to be construed to violate the law of nations if any other possible construction remains"), given that he claimed that "international law would not permit the

---

[6] At oral argument, when asked why our holding in *Victoria* was not dispositive, Aybar's counsel responded that *Victoria* did not address the distinction between statelessness under the MDLEA and statelessness for the purposes of international law. But, while Aybar's brief asserts in a footnote that the MDLEA's definition of statelessness is broader than international law's, he does not develop any argument for distinguishing *Victoria* on [—14—] this basis. *See United States v. Zannino*, 895 F.2d 1, 17 (1st Cir. 1990).

---

[7] For this reason, we do not find significant the fact, not mentioned by the defendant here, that there was some evidence in *Victoria*—as there is not here—that the vessel in that case was potentially bound for the United States. *See* 876 F.2d at 1010. In fact, there is no indication in *Victoria* that the statute at issue made proof of such a tie between the defendant's conduct and the United States necessary to convict the defendant. Nor did we qualify our holding that "the United States, as a matter of international law, may prosecute drug offenders on stateless ships found on the high seas" in light of that evidence. *Id.* We also note that *Victoria*, in asserting the United States' broad authority under international law to prosecute persons who are not citizens of the United States for drug trafficking on a *stateless* vessel in international waters, made no reference to our decision the year before in *United States v. Robinson*, 843 F.2d 1, 3–4 (1st Cir. [—15—] 1988), in which we observed in dicta that there was a "forceful" argument to be made that international law would not justify the United States' prosecution of drug offenders on a *foreign-flagged* ship found on the high seas where there was no clear proof that the ship was bound for the United States and where the United States acted without the flag state's consent.

United States to convict him for possessing marijuana . . . so far from the United States." *Victoria*, 876 F.2d at 1010. But, even though our ruling in *Victoria* did not purport to address the constitutional {–55–} question of congressional power that Aybar now raises, its reasoning is no less dispositive as to the assertion about international law that supplies the premise for the constitutional argument that Aybar does make. Accordingly, because Aybar's constitutional challenge rests on an assertion about the content of international law that, as a panel, we are not free to accept in light of our prior precedent, we must reject his constitutional contention regarding [—16—] the scope of Congress's power. *See United States v. Wurie*, 867 F.3d 28, 34 (1st Cir. 2017) (explaining the law of the circuit rule). And, on that basis, we affirm his convictions.[8] [—17—]

---

[8] The dissent disputes the merits of *Victoria*'s holding as to international law, as well as the necessity of *Victoria* having resolved the *Charming Betsy* issue on the basis of that understanding of international law. *See* Diss. Op. 30–33. But, under the law of the circuit doctrine, what matters is simply whether *Victoria* did rely on that proposition for its holding that the *Charming Betsy* canon did not require a narrower construction of the MDLEA, and it is clear that *Victoria* did. In fact, in defending that view of international law, *Victoria* cited extensively to out-of-circuit precedent and included parentheticals in which those circuits set forth that very proposition of international law. *See Victoria*, 876 F.2d at 1011. We thus are not free to treat that aspect of the *Victoria* decision as mere dicta. We note, too, that other circuits, since *Victoria*, have continued to rule the same way. *See, e.g., United States v. Campbell*, 743 F.3d 802, 809–12, 2 Adm. R. 543, 547–50 (11th Cir. 2014); *United States v. Caicedo*, 47 F.3d 370, 372–73 (9th Cir. 1995); *United States v. Martinez-Hidalgo*, 993 F.2d 1052, 1056–57 (3d Cir. 1993).

The dissent also observes that *Smith*, 680 F.2d 255, a decision that predates *Victoria*, indicates that *Victoria*'s view of international law is mistaken. *See* Diss. Op. 31–32. The dissent further notes that *Victoria* relied on *Smith*. *See id.* However, as the dissent itself points out, *Victoria* did not cite the full passage from *Smith* that the dissent contends is at odds with *Victoria*'s assertion about international law. *See Victoria*, 876 F.2d at 1010. And, the particular part of that passage from *Smith* that *Victoria* did cite does not support the dissent's view. Nor does the dissent contend that it

There is, in addition to *Victoria*, another of our precedents that is at odds with Aybar's contention that international law of its own force requires there to be more of a nexus between a person charged with drug trafficking and the nation that wishes to criminally prosecute it than is present here. That precedent is *United States v. Cardales*, 168 F.3d 548 (1st Cir. 1999), which concerned the application of the MDLEA to drug smugglers on the high seas (there, on a foreign-flagged ship). *Id.* at 551–52.

In *Cardales*, the defendants argued that the Due Process Clause, rather than the Define and Punish Clause, "requires the government to prove a nexus between their criminal conduct and the United States in a prosecution for violating the MDLEA," 168 F.3d at 552, which is an argument that we rejected there, *id.* at 553, and that Aybar does not press here.[9] {–56–} Moreover, *Cardales*, unlike Aybar's case, involved a foreign-flagged vessel, *id.* at 552, and we noted that the flag nation had consented to the assertion of [—18—] jurisdiction by the United States, *id.*, which we identified as key to our holding

---

does. *See* Diss. Op. 31–32. In any event, we do not read even the full passage from *Smith* to support the dissent's view of it. *See* Diss. Op. 31. In that passage, *Smith* concludes that "[the United States] has the authority to treat stateless vessels as if they were its own," 680 F.2d at 258, and then follows that conclusion by emphasizing the circumstances of the case in front of it, stating that the United States "has [that] authority . . ., *particularly* when engaged in conduct affecting United States vessels and having an effect within the jurisdiction of the United States," *id.* (emphasis added). Read as a whole, therefore, the passage from *Smith* on which the dissent places much weight suggests that evidence of a nexus between the [—17—] conduct at issue and the United States is *not* necessary in order for the United States to exercise the authority that *Smith* recognizes.

[9] We note that Aybar's brief mentions that the warship that intercepted the stateless vessel on which he was aboard was a foreign one. That was not the case in either *Victoria* or *Cardales* (a point Aybar does not himself point out), but Aybar makes no argument as to why this difference should matter with respect to whether the exercise of United States jurisdiction over his conduct aboard the stateless vessel was consistent with international law. *See Zannino*, 895 F.2d at 17.

rejecting *Cardales*'s due process challenge on ground of a lack of any nexus.

But, apart from that aspect of our ruling, we also stated in *Cardales* that the application of the MDLEA in that case was consistent with the "protective principle" of international law, which permits a nation "to assert jurisdiction over a person whose conduct outside the nation's territory threatens the nation's security." *Id.* at 553 (quoting *Robinson*, 843 F.2d at 3). And, in so concluding, *Cardales* relied on a congressional finding in the MDLEA that "trafficking in controlled substances aboard vessels is a serious international problem and is universally condemned[, and] . . . presents a specific threat to the security . . . of the United States." *Id.* (alteration and omissions in original) (quoting 46 U.S.C. app. § 1902). *Cardales* then explained that "application of the MDLEA to the defendants is consistent with the protective principle of international law because Congress has determined that *all* drug trafficking aboard vessels threatens our nation's security." *Id.* (emphasis added).

There is no indication in this aspect of *Cardales*'s reasoning that its broad assertion regarding the United States' entitlement to assert protective jurisdiction, under international law, was limited only to cases in which the flag nation has consented to the United States' assertion of jurisdiction over a [—19—] vessel and those on board it. *See id.* at 553. Thus, the language on this point in *Cardales* is, like the language referenced in *Victoria* concerning international law that we have described above, directly contrary to Aybar's sole constitutional contention, given the assertion about international law on which his contention rests.

Moreover, Aybar makes no argument as to why, notwithstanding our conclusion to the contrary in *Cardales*, his conduct does not fall within the United States' *protective* jurisdiction. He instead contends only that his crime of drug trafficking is outside the United States' *universal* jurisdiction. He thus develops no argument for reconsidering our statement in *Cardales* concluding that the scope of protective jurisdiction encompasses conduct of the kind present here. *See Zannino*, 895 F.2d at 17.

III.

Aybar next argues that the District Court erroneously denied him a minor participant reduction under § 3B1.2(b) of the Sentencing Guidelines based on five factors that he contends show that he was a minor participant. That guideline provides that "[i]f the defendant was a minor participant in any criminal activity, decrease by 2 levels." U.S. Sentencing Guidelines Manual § 3B1.2(b) (2014). [—20—]

Application Note 3(C) of the November 2015 edition of the Sentencing Guidelines sets forth the five factors on which Aybar relies in challenging his sentence. U.S. Sentencing Guidelines Manual § 3B1.2, cmt. n.3(C) (2015). But, as the government points out, he was sentenced according to the November 2014 edition of the Guidelines in effect at the time of his October 21, 2015 sentencing, and the application note to the minor-role guideline in that edition did not include those specific factors. {–57–}

Nevertheless, Aybar did file a letter under Rule 28(j) calling our attention to our ruling in the companion case to this one, *United States v. Sarmiento-Palacios*, 885 F.3d 1, 6, 6 Adm. R. 8, 10–11 (1st Cir. 2018), which we decided after all briefing was complete in this case. *See* Fed. R. App. P. 28(j). *Sarmiento* held that Amendment 794 to the Sentencing Guidelines, which added the five factors to the application note, clarifies the Commission's original intent regarding § 3B1.2 and therefore that it does apply retroactively. *Id.*, 6 Adm. R. at 10–11. And, in *Sarmiento* we therefore vacated the sentence and remanded for resentencing, so that the District Court could have an opportunity to apply the new factors. *Id.*, 6 Adm. R. at 11.

The government argues that vacating the sentence and remanding for resentencing is not appropriate here, because, even under the factors set out in Amendment 794, Aybar would still have been denied the minor-role reduction. But the same argument was

[—21—] unsuccessful in *Sarmiento*, and we reject it for the same reasons that we did there:

> we think it prudent to leave that determination in the hands of the able district court judge. Accordingly, a remand is justified to allow the sentencing court the opportunity to consider the "Commission's current policy position[,] . . . [which] may have some influence on the judge's ultimate discretionary choice of sentence."

Id., 6 Adm. R. at 11 (alterations and omission in original) (quoting *United States v. Ahrendt*, 560 F.3d 69, 79 (1st Cir. 2009)).

IV.

We therefore ***affirm*** the convictions. But we ***vacate*** the District Court's sentence and ***remand*** for resentencing under the Commission's clarified guidance, as reflected in Amendment 794.***

- Separate Opinion Follows –

(Reporter's Note: Opinion joining in part and dissenting in part follows on p. 66).

(Reporter's Note: On January 20, 2020, the U.S. First Circuit ordered that this case be reheard en banc on Tuesday, May 5, 2020.)

[—22—] {–57–} **TORRUELLA,** Circuit Judge, joining in part and dissenting in part:

I join the majority with respect to Aybar's sentencing appeal in light of our recent decision in *Sarmiento-Palacios*, 885 F.3d at 6, 6 Adm. R. at 10–11. I respectfully dissent, however, from the majority's conclusion that our precedent requires us to affirm Aybar's conviction. As the majority notes, none of this Court's precedent directly considered a constitutional challenge to Congress's power to criminalize conduct pursuant to Article I, section 8, clause 10. Therefore, that precedent should not bind this panel. Moreover, the related but non-binding precedent upon which the majority relies diverges from international and constitutional law principles governing Congress' powers to criminalize the conduct in Aybar's case. These principles, as explained below, lead to the conclusion that the application of the MDLEA to Aybar was unconstitutional.

The majority correctly identifies that Aybar's conviction hinges on the provision of the Define and Punish clause which gives Congress the authority to define and punish "Felonies" on the high seas. *See Smith*, 18 U.S. at 159; U.S. Const. art. I, § 8, cl. 10. But as explained below, the majority's reliance and application of this court's precedent to the issues in Aybar's case is inapt.

The majority opinion relies to a great degree upon the rationale in *Cardales*, 168 F.3d at 553. *See* Maj. Op. 17–19. But, [—23—] as the majority in this case concedes, the facts and issues before the court in *Cardales* were quite different than those in the present case. The holding in *Cardales* relied only on the flag nation's consent in concluding that no nexus was required under the Due Process Clause. 168 F.3d at 553 ("[D]ue process does not require the government to prove a nexus between a defendant's criminal conduct and the United {–58–} States in a prosecution under the MDLEA *when the flag nation has consented* to the application of United States law to the defendants. . . . We therefore hold that when individuals engage in drug trafficking aboard a vessel, due process is satisfied *when the foreign nation in which the vessel is registered authorizes the application*

of United States law to the persons on board the vessel."(emphasis added)).[10] That holding is inapplicable to the case at hand, in which there is no such consent, and the majority's reliance on it is therefore erroneous. The *Cardales* defendants did not raise a challenge to Congress's constitutional authority to enact the MDLEA as applied to them, and, by arguing that due process required proof of a nexus between their conduct and the United States, *see id.* at 552–53, inherently accepted that the enacting authority had the constitutional power to create the law under which those due process rights arise. Not so in our case. [—24—]

Notably, the *Cardales* court discussed international law principles in dicta for the sole purpose of explaining why that court's application of the MDLEA to the facts in that case did not violate the precepts of due process. In its superfluous discussion of international law's protective principle, the *Cardales* court looked to a presumptuous Congressional statement that "trafficking in controlled substances aboard vessels is a serious international problem and . . . presents a specific threat to the security . . . of the United States." *Id.* (second alteration in original) (quoting 46 U.S.C. app. § 1902). The *Cardales* court leaned on this Congressional statement for support that "application of the MDLEA is consistent with the protective principle of international law." *Id.* (citing *United States v. Martinez-Hidalgo*, 993 F.2d 1052, 1056 (3d Cir. 1993)). The majority here leans almost as heavily on this statement. But, the accompanying parenthetical in *Cardales*, in expressing that the application of the MDLEA to drug trafficking on the high seas is not "fundamentally unfair," *id.* (quoting *Martinez-Hidalgo*, 993 F.2d at 1056), makes clear that the *Cardales* court's dicta regarding international law was used only to support its due process analysis. While the logic of *Cardales* may be persuasive to some, that case's conclusion is not binding to the as-applied constitutional challenge that Aybar raises here.

---

[10] Consent, after all, is the cornerstone of international law. *See generally The Paquete Habana*, 175 U.S. 677 (1900).

I pause for a moment to note that the Congressional statement relied upon by the *Cardales* court does not make an [—25—] application of the MDLEA to entirely foreign nationals and foreign conduct, with no nexus to the United States, consistent with the "protective principle" of international law. The protective principle of international law requires a showing that the regulated conduct has some nexus or effect on the prosecuting nation; the protective principle cannot be invoked simply through a blanket assertion that some disfavored conduct creates a "specific threat to the security" of that nation. *Id.* (quoting 46 U.S.C. app. § 1902). As I discussed in my dissent in *United States v. Angulo-Hernández*, some sort of actual cognizable threat to the nation is required under international law for an assertion of the protective principle. 576 F.3d 59, 61 (1st Cir. 2009) (Torruella, J., dissenting).

A broad grant of power to the executive branch to prosecute any and all vessels carrying illegal substances that are not in the United States' waters, are not headed for or departing from the United States, are not flying the United States' flag, and are not carrying United States nationals, is plainly inconsistent with international law. {–59–} *Id.* (citing Restatement (Third) of U.S. Foreign Relations Law § 402 cmt. f). Allowing a nation to make such a broad assertion under the guise of the protective principle with no substantial showing of a nexus to that nation would render the protective principle coterminous with the doctrine of universal jurisdiction. *Id.* And, while there may [—26—] be a global consensus about the negative effects of drug trafficking, it is not a universal crime—despite vigorous attempts by the United States at international law forums to make it one[11]—and cannot be prosecuted

under the "universality principle" of international law.

Having established that our precedent does not compel us to reject Aybar's as-applied constitutional challenge, I next address the constitutional limitations of Congress' ability to regulate Felonies on the high seas under the mandates of constitutional and international law. I am emphatically of the view that doing so requires us to hold that Congress' power under this clause is necessarily limited to instances where there is a nexus between the conduct underlying the felony and the United States. *See Cardales-Luna*, 632 F.3d at 739 (Torruella, J., dissenting); *Angulo-Hernández*, 576 F.3d at 62 (Torruella, J., dissenting); *cf. United States v. James-Robinson*, 515 F. Supp. 1340, 1346 (S.D. Fla. 1981) (holding that the court did not have subject matter jurisdiction because the defendant's conduct had no "effect whatsoever" on the U.S.); *United States v. Angola*, 514 F. [—27—] Supp. 933, 936 (S.D. Fla. 1981) (asserting that jurisdiction was valid under the protective principle because the ship was close enough to the U.S. to assume a "real, not an imaginary, potential for harm" to U.S. narcotics laws). Because Congress cannot grant the government the authority to prosecute conduct beyond that which the Define and Punish clause allows Congress to regulate, *see United States v. Furlong*, 18 U.S. (5 Wheat) 184, 196-97 (1820), and the Define and Punish clause does not give Congress the ability to regulate Felonies on the high seas having no nexus to the United States, Congress cannot create laws—such as the MDLEA—granting the government the authority to prosecute conduct by foreign individuals on the high seas that has no nexus to the United States. *See* Eugene Kontorovich, *Beyond the Article I Horizon: Congress's Enumerated Powers and Universal Jurisdiction over Drug Crimes*, 93 Minn. L. Rev. 1191, 1212 (2009). "[S]uch general jurisdiction over high seas offenses had never been suggested . . . [nor] intended," and if the Constitution did not explicitly forbid Congress from legislating against foreign conduct, it was "only because it was too silly for the Framers to have contemplated." *Id.* (citing Hon. John Marshall, Speech Delivered

---

[11] *See United States v. Bellaizac-Hurtado* 700 F.3d 1245, 1256 (11th Cir. 2012) ("The negotiators of the Rome Statute repeatedly referred to drug crimes as 'treaty crimes' only . . . [a]nd several delegates expressed the opinion that drug crimes had no place in a statute dealing with international crimes and should be addressed at the national level." (internal quotation marks and citation omitted)); *see also Cardales-Luna*, 632 F.3d at 745 (Torruella, J., dissenting).

in the House of Representatives, in 4 *The Papers of John Marshall*, 92-93, 96, 102 (Charles T. Cullen & Leslie Tobias eds., 1984)); *cf. Furlong*, 18 U.S. at 196-97. Just as Congress cannot create criminal laws regulating the conduct of foreign nationals [—28—] in foreign countries with no effect on the United States, *see United States v. Nippon Paper Industries Co., Ltd.*, 109 F.3d 1, 4–9 (1st Cir. 1997); Restatement (Third) of U.S. Foreign Relations Law § 402(1)(c), Congress cannot create laws regulating the conduct of foreign nationals on foreign {–60–} vessels over which the United States has no jurisdiction because those vessels are navigating on international waters, and there is no indication that they have either left from the United States or are headed thereto.

Early Supreme Court cases support the requirement of such a nexus. When first faced with the opportunity to determine the scope of Congress's ability to legislate extraterritorially, the Supreme Court held that, aside from universal jurisdiction crimes (that is, certain serious offenses recognized by international law that all nations may prosecute even without a nexus or impact to that nation's territory or citizens), there must be a nexus between the United States and the regulated conduct. *See United States v. Klintock*, 18 U.S. (5 Wheat) 144, 151–52 (1820). This principle has been continually upheld, *see United States v. Pizzarusso*, 388 F.2d 8, 10 (2d Cir. 1968) ("Acts done outside a jurisdiction, but intended to produce . . . detrimental effects *within it*, justify a state in punishing the cause of the harm." (emphasis added) (quoting *Strassheim v. Daily*, 221 U.S. 280, 285 (1911) (Holmes, J.))); *see also United States v.* [—29—] *Columba-Colella*, 604 F.2d 356, 358 (5th Cir. 1979) ("When an allegedly criminal act is performed by an alien on foreign soil[,] courts in the United States have long held that if jurisdiction is to be extended over that act, it must be supported by either the Protective or Objective territorial theory."), including in cases involving early interpretations of anti-drug trafficking laws similar to the MDLEA in situations involving stateless vessels. *See e.g., United States v. Smith*, 680 F.2d 255, 257-258 (1st Cir. 1982);

James-Robinson, 515 F. Supp. at 1346-1347; *Angola*, 514 F. Supp. at 935.

Here, Aybar was interdicted on a vessel in international waters, far from the United States. His vessel did not depart from the United States nor was there any evidence that it was bound for the United States. No concrete evidence suggests that the drugs aboard this specific vessel were intended for distribution in the United States. Aybar did not commit any offense against a vessel or citizen of the United States, or within the United States' territory. Save for the fact that he was intercepted by officers of the United States Coast Guard, who in fact were aboard a foreign vessel, there is absolutely nothing connecting Aybar to the United States. The United States nexus was *artificially* provided by the actions of the United States, a unique condition unheard of in the criminal law—in which it is the government that provides one of the elements of the crime that is charged. [—30—] Given this lack of nexus, the Felonies provision of the Define and Punish clause does not give Congress the authority to create laws criminalizing Aybar's conduct.

Because *Cardales* did not address the issues presented in this case, and constitutional and international law do not support the conclusion that the majority reaches, this Court need not and should not adopt the rationale in *Cardales* to reject Aybar's constitutional challenge. *See United States v. Irizarry-Colón*, 848 F.3d 61, 69 (1st Cir. 2017) (declaring that the district court was "led astray" by a prior panel's statement concerning an issue not before that prior panel); *see also Cohens v. Virginia*, 19 U.S. (6 Wheat) 264, 399 (1821) ("It is a maxim not to be disregarded, that general expressions, in every opinion, are to be taken in connection with the case in which those expressions are used. If they go beyond the case, they may be respected, but ought not to control the judgment in a subsequent suit when the very point is presented for decision."). The logical force of the *Cardales* dicta is insufficient to govern this Court's decision when the opposite {–61–} conclusion is consistent with constitutional and international law principles.

Nor does Aybar's admission that he was aboard a vessel without nationality provide a nexus to give the United States prescriptive jurisdiction to prosecute his conduct under its domestic laws. The majority points to *Victoria*, in which this [—31—] Court broadly stated that "as United States courts have interpreted international law, that law gives the 'United States . . . authority to treat stateless vessels as if they were its own." 876 F.2d at 1010 (quoting *Smith*, 680 F.2d at 248). *See* Maj. Op. 14. But, for the following reasons, this court should not rely too heavily on that statement.

First, in *Victoria*, there was evidence of a nexus between the conduct on the stateless vessel and the United States. 876 F.2d at 1010 (noting that "the Coast Guard found . . . navigational charts indicating a course for the . . . southern tip of Florida"). Therefore, the *Victoria* court did not need to consider whether the United States could in fact treat stateless vessels as its own when there was no nexus between the conduct at issue and the United States, for the charts provided evidence of a U.S. nexus. Second, the full quotation from *Smith*, only part of which the *Victoria* court cited,[12] itself actually supports the existence of a nexus requirement. *See Smith*, 680 F.2d at 258 (stating that the United States "has authority to treat stateless vessels as if they were its own, *particularly when engaged in conduct affecting United* [—32—] *States vessels and having an effect within the jurisdiction of the United States*" (emphasis added)).

Third, like in *Cardales*, the defendant in *Victoria* appealed his conviction on grounds not at issue here. The *Victoria* defendant partly based his argument on the *Charming Betsy* canon, in with the Supreme Court stated that "an act of Congress ought never to be construed to violate the law of nations if any other possible construction remains." *Murray v. The Schooner Charming Betsy*, 6 U.S. (2 Cranch) 64, 118 (1804). As the

majority recognizes, the defendant in *Victoria* asserted that Congress did not *intend* for the MDLEA to apply extraterritoriality, implicit in which is acceptance of Congress' authority to enact such a law. *See* 876 F.2d at 1010. Unlike the *Victoria* defendant, Aybar asserts that Congress did not have the *authority* under the Define and Punish clause to apply the MDLEA to regulate extraterritorial conduct having no nexus to the United States. Furthermore, the statement from *Victoria*, if read to foreclose any nexus requirement other than a defendant's presence aboard a stateless vessel, would run afoul of international law (and therefore the *Charming Betsy* cannon), which is clear that it allows countries to prescribe law extraterritorially only when there is some connection between the conduct and that country. *See* Restatement (Third) of U.S. Foreign Relations Law § 402. Therefore, the majority in this case [—33—] overstates the extent to which *Victoria* forecloses the argument that Aybar presents.

Before moving forward, I must fall on my own sword and recognize that I, like the *Victoria* court and the majority here, have made too broad an assertion. *See Sarmiento-Palacios*, 885 F.3d at 7, 6 Adm. R. at 12 (Torruella, J., concurring) ("And while the United States (like all nations) does have universal jurisdiction over stateless vessels . . . ."); *Cardales-Luna*, 632 F.3d at 747 ("These principles regarding [universal] jurisdiction {–62–} have been relaxed to include . . . stateless vessels."). But, "it is never too late to 'surrende[r] former views to a better considered position.'" *South Dakota v. Wayfair, Inc.*, 138 S. Ct. 2080, 2100 (2018) (Thomas, J., concurring) (quoting *McGrath v. Kristensen*, 340 U.S. 162, 178 (1950) (Jackson, J., concurring)). And, upon further reflection, I now realize that international law's allowance of any nation to prevent the operation of stateless vessels does not confer jurisdiction on that nation to prosecute the individuals aboard those vessels under that nation's domestic criminal codes.

It is widely accepted that international law confers the right of any nation to approach and "visit" a vessel if it is suspected that the vessel is stateless. *See* United Nations

---

[12] *Victoria*, 876 F.2d at 1010 ("[A]s United States courts have interpreted international law, that law gives the 'United States . . . authority to treat stateless vessels as if they were its own.'" (second alteration in the original) (quoting *Smith*, 680 F.2d at 258)).

Convention on the Law of the Sea [hereinafter "UNCLOS"] art. 110, Dec. 10, 1982, 1833 U.N.T.S. 397. But, international law distinguishes between a nation's authority to prescribe law [—34—] extraterritorially as to the conduct of foreign persons and its authority to interfere with the navigation of a vessel encountered on the high seas. Although stateless vessels enjoy no diplomatic protections and thus are subject to being stopped and boarded by any other nation's vessels, it does not follow that this "right to visit" confers jurisdiction on the boarding vessel's nation to prosecute the occupants of the stateless vessel—who continue to enjoy diplomatic protection from their nation—under the visiting nation's substantive criminal laws without some nexus between their conduct and the boarding nation. *See James-Robinson*, 515 F. Supp. at 1343 n.5 (explaining that the issue before the court was not whether the United States had jurisdiction over a stateless ship, but whether it had jurisdiction "over the foreign citizen crewmembers of such a stateless ship"); *see also* Ted L. McDorman, *Stateless Fishing Vessels, Int'l Law, and the U.N. High Seas Fisheries Conference*, 25 J. Mar. L & Com. 531, 540 (1994) (discussing the views of D. O'Connell, 2 *The Int'l Law of the Sea* 75 (Oxford University Press, Inc., 1984) and H. Meyers, *The Nationality of Ships* 318-321 (Martinus Nijhoff, 1967) (noting that individuals aboard stateless vessels "retain their nationality" and may thus be prosecuted by their home country under international law); *see, e.g.*, Robin R. Churchill & Alan V. Lowe, The Law of the Sea 172 (1988) (arguing that a vessel's "'statelessness' will not, of itself, entitle each and every State [—35—] to assert jurisdiction over [its occupants], for there is not in every case any recognized basis, such as nationality or territoriality, upon which jurisdiction can be asserted over them while they are on the high seas . . . . [T]here is a need for some jurisdictional nexus in order that a State may extend its laws to those on board a stateless ship and enforce the laws against them").

A review of customary international law reveals that in all instances for which a state may interfere with the right of passage of another vessel, aside from the universal jurisdiction crimes of piracy and slave trading, international law requires some independent nexus between the visiting state and the suspected basis for the interference. *See* UNCLOS at art. 110. For example, customary international law allows a State to board a foreign vessel on the high seas if the State has reason to believe that the foreign vessel is engaged in unauthorized broadcasting.[13] *Id.* at art. {—63—} 110(c). But that State may only prosecute those individuals engaged in that unauthorized broadcasting if that State has an independent basis for asserting jurisdiction over those individuals or that conduct. *See id.* at art. 109(3), [—36—] 110(1)(c). Similarly, while any nation may board and prevent navigation of a suspected stateless vessel under international law, that nation must have a nexus to the vessel's occupants or to those occupant's conduct to assert jurisdiction to prosecute those aboard the stateless vessel for a violation of its domestic laws—such as drug trafficking under the MDLEA. The application of that nation's domestic laws to a stateless vessel's occupants without a nexus unilaterally extends that nation's sovereignty over the high seas, in violation of customary international law. *See* UNCLOS at art. 89.

Moreover, allowing all nations to prosecute crewmembers aboard stateless vessels under that nation's own domestic laws simply because of their presence aboard that stateless vessel would convert the operation of a stateless vessel into a universal jurisdiction crime. "There are two premises underlying universal jurisdiction. The first involves the gravity of the crime. . . . The second involves the *locus delicti* (place of the act)." *Bellaizac-Hurtado*, 700 F.3d at 1260 (Barkett, J., concurring) (quoting Michael P. Scharf, *Application of Treaty-Based Universal Jurisdiction to Nationals of Non-Party States*, 35 New Eng. L. Rev. 363, 368-69 (2001)). But, piloting a stateless vessel is not of the same

---

[13] UNCLOS defines "unauthorized broadcasting" as "the transmission of sound radio or television broadcasts from a ship or installation on the high seas intended for reception by the general public contrary to international regulations, but excluding the transmission of distress calls." UNCLOS at art. 109(2).

heinous nature as those universal jurisdiction crimes (piracy, slavery and genocide) and has not been recognized as a universal crime under international law. *See* UNCLOS; Allyson [—37—] Bennett, *That Sinking Feeling: Stateless Ships, Universal Jurisdiction, and the Drug Trafficking Vessel Interdiction Act*, 37 Yale J. Int'l L. 433, 448-50 (2012) (explaining that universal crimes are those agreed upon by the international community to be "so heinous . . . that they offend the interest of all humanity," such as genocide, and noting that statelessness is not listed as a universal jurisdiction crime under UNCLOS). In fact, I have been unable to find any federal statute or regulation making piloting a stateless vessel a crime under the laws of the United States. Because being aboard a stateless vessel does not meet the substantive component (the gravity of the crime) of universal jurisdiction, and is not a universal crime, it follows that nations cannot apply their domestic laws to an individual simply by the fact that they are aboard a vessel without nationality.

Just as Congress cannot pass legislation "attempting to apply the criminal laws of the United States, with the Bolivian government's consent, to the conduct of Colombian nationals in Bolivia," *Cardales-Luna*, 632 F.3d at 741 (Torruella, J., dissenting), it cannot punish foreign nationals aboard foreign vessels. *See, e.g., Furlong*, 18 U.S. at 197-98; *Klintock*, 18 U.S. at 151. And, for the reasons explained in this dissent, the same must be true even if those foreign nationals were aboard stateless vessels. If any state can assert its own laws based purely on a vessel's statelessness, then it follows that a United States [—38—] citizen aboard a stateless vessel can be prosecuted under any foreign country's domestic laws even if the regulation of such conduct would be considered absurd in the United States. Common sense dictates that this is not and cannot be the case.

There is no denying that most circuits, including our own, have upheld the application of the MDLEA to the crews of stateless vessels. However, this Court has not yet directly addressed the exact constitutional {–64–} challenge Aybar has raised, and we need not be constrained by related but non-binding precedent. And because the Felonies provision of the Define and Punish clause requires that there be a nexus between the conduct and the United States to pass constitutional muster, and no such nexus has been shown here, Aybar's conviction must be overturned. For the foregoing reasons, I respectfully dissent.

United States Court of Appeals
for the First Circuit

No. 18-1225

PEÑA-GARCIA
VS.
DIRECTOR, OFFICE OF WORKERS' COMPENSATION
PROGRAMS

Petition for Review of a Final Order of the Benefits
Review Board

Decided: March 1, 2019

Citation: 917 F.3d 61, 7 Adm. R. 72 (1st Cir. 2019).

Before **HOWARD,** Chief Judge, **LYNCH** and **LIPEZ,**
Circuit Judges.

[—2—] {–62–} **LYNCH,** Circuit Judge:

This case raises the question of what is a "successful prosecution" in a claim for benefits under the Longshore and Harbor Workers' Compensation Act (LHWCA), so as to warrant an award of attorney's fees to a claimant. *See* 33 U.S.C. § 928.

After suffering a disabling back injury in 1994 while working for Calzadilla Construction Corporation (Calzadilla) in Puerto Rico, Luis Peña-Garcia (Peña) sought coverage for spinal surgery. Calzadilla's insurer, IMS Insurance Company of Puerto Rico (IMS), said it would pay for such surgery in Puerto Rico, where Peña's surgeon was willing and able to perform it. Peña rejected that and said the surgery must be at Beth Israel Spine Institute in New York. Peña then filed a claim for medical compensation for surgery in New York against Calzadilla and IMS under the LHWCA. 33 U.S.C. § 901 *et seq.*

An LHWCA administrative law judge (ALJ) determined that Calzadilla and IMS had never refused to pay for the surgery and rejected Peña's claim that it was necessary to perform his surgery in New York. Consequently, the ALJ later held that Peña was not entitled to attorney's fees and costs. The U.S. Department of Labor Benefits Review Board (the Board) affirmed the denial of attorney's fees and costs. Finding no error, we deny Peña's petition for review. [—3—]

I.

A. *Facts*

The pertinent facts are not disputed. At all relevant times, Peña lived and worked in Puerto Rico. Peña's back injury at Calzadilla left him totally and permanently disabled. Calzadilla and IMS accepted liability for Peña's injury and began paying him medical benefits even before he made the claim at issue here. {–63–}

On March 15, 2010, Peña saw an orthopedic surgeon, Dr. Luis Pio Sánchez-Caso (Dr. Sánchez), who recommended that Peña undergo a laminectomy decompression, a "complex spine reconstruction" surgery. Dr. Sánchez was willing and able to perform the surgery at San Pablo Hospital in Puerto Rico. Dr. Sánchez, though not board-certified, had post-graduate training in the area of orthopedic surgery, had performed spinal surgeries since 1998, and had previously performed the surgery that Peña needed in Puerto Rico. Peña could also obtain the rehabilitation he needed from two Health-South locations in Puerto Rico. The medical director of HealthSouth, Dr. Edward Ramos, was board-certified in physical medicine and in rehabilitation with a spinal cord injury medicine subspecialty.

Peña wanted instead to have the spinal surgery at Beth Israel Spine Institute in New York because it is "close to [his] family" and has "a record of being the best institution." In a [—4—] letter to Peña's attorney, dated April 13, 2010, IMS rejected that request and stated:

Please be advised that we can not cover your client's surgery outside of Puerto Rico. He has been examined and evaluated by a competent surgeon, Dr. S[á]nchez[-]Caso, who recommended the surgery in Puerto Rico, at the San Pablo Hospital.

Additionally, our decision is based on the fact that Mr. Peña and his immediate family continue to reside in Puerto Rico, and, Mr. Peña's recovery time will be approximately three months to one year and he will need considerable family assistance during his recovery. Under these circumstances, we must respectfully deny Mr. Peña's request to undergo his surgery outside Puerto Rico.

B. *Procedural History*

On October 13, 2010, Peña submitted a claim to the Director of the Office of Workers' Compensation Programs (the Director) against Calzadilla and IMS under the LHWCA, on the ground that IMS's refusal to pay for spinal surgery in New York violated the LHWCA's requirement that "[t]he employer shall furnish such medical, surgical, and other attendance or treatment . . . for such period as the nature of the injury or the process of recovery may require." 33 U.S.C. § 907(a). The Director referred the case to the Office of Administrative Law Judges. After the parties tried unsuccessfully to settle the matter, an ALJ held a hearing on September 17, 2015. At the hearing, IMS did not dispute that [—5—] Peña was entitled to medical benefits from Calzadilla due to his back injury, including for surgery in Puerto Rico.

On March 22, 2016, the ALJ ordered Calzadilla and IMS to "furnish to [Peña], such reasonable, appropriate, and necessary medical care and treatment as his back and neck injury which occurred on May 16, 1994, may require, including spinal surgery and post-surgery care such as rehabilitation." The ALJ's decision further stated that Calzadilla "will be liable only for the medical costs and incidental expenses associated with obtaining such care and treatment in Puerto Rico, regardless of where [Peña] chooses to obtain such care and treatment." Peña could, of course, have the surgery done in New York, but he would then be responsible for whatever additional expenses he incurred.

Peña's attorney then submitted a request to the ALJ for $60,515 in attorney's fees and $4,000 in fees for Peña's treating physician who had testified at the hearing. His argument was based on the assertion that Peña had successfully prosecuted the earlier claim before the ALJ, on the theory {—64—}

that his claim had been a victory because he had obtained what he called his right to choose to have the surgery in New York.

On August 3, 2016, the ALJ issued a supplemental decision and order denying the request for attorney's fees and costs. The ALJ stated that Peña had not obtained a "successful prosecution," which is required to recover attorney's fees and costs under the [—6—] LHWCA, because IMS "has been paying compensation to [Peña] prior to the hearing and has not refused to pay for [Peña's] surgery in Puerto Rico." The ALJ also noted that "[t]here is no evidence that [IMS] at any point . . . refused to cover any portion of [Peña's] surgery if it were performed outside Puerto Rico."[1] The ALJ added, "[h]ad [IMS] asserted that it would refuse to pay for *any portion* of [Peña's] surgery and rehabilitation if it were performed in New York, [Peña] would have been successful in litigating his case." The ALJ determined that Peña "did not gain any additional benefit above [and] beyond what he would have received had he not initiated this claim."

On September 2, 2016, Peña filed a petition for reconsideration on the issue of attorney's fees and costs. The ALJ denied the petition on October 5, 2016. Peña appealed the denial of attorney's fees and costs to the Board, which affirmed the ALJ's decision on September 13, 2017. The Board stated that Peña's self-proposed "'right to choose' to have the surgery in New York is not a 'victory' under the [LHWCA], because [the] employer's liability is limited to the cost of surgery and rehabilitation in Puerto Rico, which [the] employer had agreed to before the proceedings were initiated." The Board determined that Peña "did not obtain a tangible benefit that [the] employer had denied him." [—7—] On January 16, 2018, the Board denied Peña's motion for reconsideration. Peña then petitioned this court for review of the Board's decision.

---

[1] Peña did not challenge this finding before the Board.

II.

"This court reviews the [Board's] decision on legal issues de novo and determines whether the Board adhered to the 'substantial evidence' standard when it reviewed the ALJ's factual findings." *Bath Iron Works v. Brown*, 194 F.3d 1, 3 (1st Cir. 1999). "In reviewing for substantial evidence, we assess the record as a whole, and we will affirm so long as we are satisfied that the record contains 'such relevant evidence as a reasonable mind might accept as adequate to support a conclusion.'" *Bath Iron Works Corp. v. U.S. Dep't of Labor*, 336 F.3d 51, 56 (1st Cir. 2003) (quoting *Sprague v. Dir., Office of Workers' Comp. Programs, U.S. Dept. of Labor*, 688 F.2d 862, 865 (1st Cir. 1982)).

The LHWCA grants attorney's fees in two situations. 33 U.S.C. § 928(a)–(b). Under subsection (a) of the LHWCA's fee provision, attorney's fees "shall be awarded" to a claimant when the employer "declines to pay any compensation . . . on the ground that there is no liability" and the claimant "utilize[s] the services of an attorney at law in the successful prosecution of his claim." *Id.* § 928(a). Under subsection (b), if the employer accepts liability but the parties dispute the amount of "compensation" and the claimant "utilizes the services of an [—8—] attorney," the claimant "shall be awarded" attorney's fees if "compensation thereafter awarded is greater than the amount paid or tendered by the employer or carrier."[2] *Id.* § 928(b). {–65–}

The Board's decision is both correct and supported by substantial evidence. Peña makes an argument under subsection (a) that he obtained a "successful prosecution" because Calzadilla and IMS "raised a complete challenge to [his] request for treatment in New York." The argument is wrong. Subsection (a) is triggered only when the employer or insurance carrier denies liability

and refuses to pay the claimant "any compensation." *Id.* § 928(a). In fact, IMS was paying Peña some compensation in the form of medical benefits before this claim was initiated, calling into question whether subsection (a) applies at all. But we bypass that question to address the surgery compensation issue. The employer's actions here do not amount to a refusal to pay "any compensation." *See id.* There is no evidence that Calzadilla and IMS refused to cover the cost of the surgery in Puerto Rico.

Peña's argument under subsection (b) also fails. He mischaracterizes the ALJ's decision both as confirming his "right [—9—] to choose surgery/rehabilitation treatment in New York" and as an award of "additional compensation." Subsection (b) requires that Peña show that the "additional compensation" awarded after he filed his claim was "greater than the amount paid or tendered by the employer or carrier." *Id.* § 928(b). The LHWCA defines "compensation" as "money allowance payable to an employee or to his dependents as provided for in this chapter." *Id.* § 902(12); *see Dir., Office of Workers' Comp. Programs, U.S. Dep't of Labor v. Baca*, 927 F.2d 1122, 1124 (10th Cir. 1991) (noting that, under the LHWCA, "attorney['] s fees may only be awarded when the claimant has gained some economic benefit."). Peña was not awarded compensation greater than that tendered by his employer because there is no evidence that IMS refused to pay for surgery at the Puerto Rico cost, regardless of where Peña chose to have the surgery.

Peña's argument is also doomed by this court's decision in *Barker v. U.S. Dep't of Labor*, 138 F.3d 431 (1st Cir. 1998). In *Barker*, the petitioner argued that he was entitled to attorney's fees under subsection (b) because, "though he had not secured any additional benefits," he "was the prevailing party in the sense that the administrative proceedings confirmed his entitlement to LHWCA benefits." *Id.* at 438. *Barker* held that this argument "distorts the contours of subsection (b)" because under its plain meaning, entitlement to attorney's fees "turns on whether the [—10—] claimant succeeds in

---

[2] As to costs, the LHWCA provides that "[i]n cases where an attorney's fee is awarded against an employer or carrier there may be further assessed against such employer or carrier as costs, fees and mileage for necessary witnesses attending the hearing at the instance of claimant." 33 U.S.C. § 928(d).

securing *additional* compensation."[3]   *Id.* (emphasis added). Peña did not secure any additional compensation by filing his claim. The Board did not err in denying the request for attorney's fees and costs.

The petition for review, which is without merit, is *denied.*

---

[3] In *Barker*, we left open the question of "whether medical benefits are (or are not) subsumed within the phrase 'additional compensation'" in the LHWCA's attorney's fee provision. *Barker*, 138 F.3d at 439. As in *Barker*, we need not address that issue, because "[t]he record is bereft of any credible evidence indicating that . . . the petition brought about a payment that would not otherwise have occurred." *Id.*

United States Court of Appeals
for the First Circuit

No. 16-2089

UNITED STATES
VS.
DÁVILA-REYES

Appeal from the United States District Court for the District of Puerto Rico

Decided: September 3, 2019

Citation: 937 F.3d 57, 7 Adm. R. 76 (1st Cir. 2019).

Before **HOWARD**, Chief Judge, **LIPEZ** and **THOMPSON**, Circuit Judges.

[—3—] {–58–} LIPEZ, Circuit Judge:

These consolidated appeals arise from the U.S. Coast Guard's interdiction of a small speed boat in the western Caribbean Sea and the subsequent arrest and indictment of the three men on board the boat for drug trafficking under the Maritime {–59–} Drug Law Enforcement Act ("MDLEA"), 46 U.S.C. §§ 70501–70508. In a motion to dismiss the indictment, appellants José Reyes-Valdivia and Jeffri Dávila-Reyes challenged the constitutionality of the MDLEA. They argued that the statute, which in certain circumstances allows U.S. law enforcement to arrest foreign nationals for drug crimes committed in international waters, exceeds Congress's authority under Article I of the Constitution and violates the Due Process Clause. The district court denied the motion to dismiss. Both appellants then pleaded guilty pursuant to plea agreements in which each waived his right to appeal if sentenced in accordance with his agreement's sentencing recommendation provision.

On appeal, appellants renew their constitutional objections to their prosecution. However, their primary argument—that their vessel was not properly deemed stateless—founders on our governing precedent concerning the protective principle of international law. That principle, as applied by our court, permits prosecution under the MDLEA even of foreigners on foreign vessels. That precedent may only be reconsidered by the en banc court. We as a panel may not do so. Hence, we affirm both [—4—] appellants' convictions. Reyes-Valdivia also asserts sentencing error, but we find no abuse of discretion in the sentence imposed.

I.

We draw the following facts from appellants' change of plea colloquies and the uncontested portions of their Presentence Investigation Reports ("PSRs"). *See United States v. Vélez-Luciano*, 814 F.3d 553, 556 (1st Cir. 2016). While patrolling waters approximately 30 nautical miles southeast of San Andrés Island, Colombia,[1] U.S. Coast Guard officers observed a small vessel moving at a high rate of speed. When the occupants of the vessel became aware of the Coast Guard boat nearby, they began throwing packages and fuel barrels overboard. The Coast Guard officers approached the boat and began to question its occupants, the two appellants and a third co-defendant. The "master"[2] of the vessel "claimed Costa Rican nationality for the vessel," but did not provide any documentation of Costa Rican registry. The Coast Guard then contacted the government of Costa Rica, which neither confirmed nor denied the registry of the vessel. The Coast Guard [—5—] officers thus determined that, pursuant to § 70502(d)(1)(C) of the MDLEA,[3] the boat was "without nationality" and subject to U.S. jurisdiction, and they proceeded to board and search it. The officers did not find any contraband, but a chemical test found traces of cocaine. Based on that evidence, the

---

[1] San Andrés Island, although part of Colombia, is located off the coast of Nicaragua.

[2] The term "master" is synonymous with "captain." It is a legal term of art meaning "he [or she] to whom are committed the government, care, and direction of the vessel and cargo." *Kennerson v. Jane R., Inc.*, 274 F. Supp. 28, 30 (S.D. Tex. 1967). The government did not specify which of the three men the Coast Guard identified as the "master" of the vessel.

[3] This provision defines a "vessel without nationality" as one "aboard which the master or individual in charge makes a claim of registry and for which the claimed nation of registry does not affirmatively and unequivocally assert that the vessel is of its nationality." 46 U.S.C. § 70502(d)(1)(C).

Coast Guard detained the three men—all citizens of Costa Rica—and took them to the U.S. Naval Base at Guantánamo Bay, Cuba, and then eventually to Puerto Rico.

All three defendants were charged with two counts of trafficking cocaine in violation {–60–} of the MDLEA. Reyes-Valdivia and Dávila-Reyes moved to dismiss the indictment for lack of jurisdiction, arguing that the MDLEA, particularly § 70502(d)(1)(C), is unconstitutional. In their view, § 70502(d)(1)(C) exceeds Congress's authority under Article I of the Constitution, and it violates the Due Process Clause of the Fifth Amendment because it is unconstitutionally vague, subject to arbitrary enforcement, and criminalizes conduct that has no nexus with the United States. The district court denied the motion.

Reyes-Valdivia and Dávila-Reyes both subsequently agreed to plead guilty to one count of possession with intent to [—6—] distribute five or more kilograms of cocaine in violation of the MDLEA. *See* 46 U.S.C. § 70503(a)(1).[4] The plea agreements for both men calculated a total offense level of 27, based on a base offense level of 30 and a three-level deduction for acceptance of responsibility. *See* U.S.S.G. §§ 2D1.1(a); 3E1.1(a)–(b). The parties' recommended sentences depended on the court's eventual finding of the Criminal History Category ("CHC"), with the statutory minimum of 120 months' imprisonment to be recommended unless the court found CHC VI (the highest level) applicable. In a supplement to Reyes-Valdivia's plea agreement, the parties agreed to recommend a 57-month term if he qualified for the "safety valve" exception to the mandatory minimum. *See* 18 U.S.C. § 3553(f)(1)–(5); U.S.S.G. § 5C1.2.[5] Both men agreed to waive appellate review if sentenced in

accordance with the sentencing recommendation provisions.

The PSRs calculated the total base offense levels consistently with the plea agreements and assigned Reyes-Valdivia [—7—] a CHC of I and Dávila-Reyes a CHC of III, triggering the 120-month recommendation or, for Reyes-Valdivia, a 57-month term if he were found eligible for the safety valve. However, Reyes-Valdivia's PSR also concluded that he should be given a two-level enhancement for being the "captain" of the vessel. *See* U.S.S.G. § 2D1.1(b)(3)(C). After Reyes-Valdivia informally objected to the enhancement, the Probation Officer filed an addendum to the PSR stating that Reyes-Valdivia had told federal agents upon his arrival in Puerto Rico that he was the vessel's captain. Reyes-Valdivia then filed a written objection to the PSR in which he argued, inter alia, that the captain enhancement was inapplicable because he did not possess the "specialized skills" it required.

Consistent with the plea agreements, the parties jointly recommended a sentence of 120 months for Dávila-Reyes and a sentence of 57 months for Reyes-Valdivia. The court sentenced Dávila-Reyes to 120 months, but sentenced Reyes-Valdivia to 70 months based on its finding that both the safety valve and the captain enhancement applied. Reyes-Valdivia's motion for reconsideration was denied. Both Reyes-Valdivia and Dávila-Reyes then appealed.

II.

The government contends that Reyes-Valdivia and Dávila-Reyes each waived his right to appeal in two distinct ways: by the express appellate waiver provisions in their plea agreements and [—8—] by {–61–} entry of unconditional guilty pleas to drug trafficking in violation of the MDLEA. With respect to Reyes-Valdivia, the government is wrong in arguing that he is barred by his plea agreement. As described above, the district court declined to follow the parties' recommended term of 57 months and instead sentenced him to a 70-month term of imprisonment. Because Reyes-Valdivia's sentence

---

[4] The third defendant also pleaded guilty to this count and was sentenced to a 57-month term of imprisonment. He did not file an appeal.

[5] Section 3553(f) allows a court to disregard the mandatory minimum sentence for certain drug offenses when the defendant has met specified requirements, including having a limited criminal history and truthfully providing the government with all information about the offense.

exceeded the recommendation, the waiver provision plainly does not apply.[6]

Dávila-Reyes, however, received a 120-month sentence that aligns with the recommendation in his plea agreement. He argues that, despite the enforceable waiver, we should exercise our inherent authority to consider his claims to avoid "a miscarriage of justice." *United States v. Teeter*, 257 F.3d 14, 25–26 (1st Cir. 2001). He contends that his appeal raises "important questions of law and [of] first impression"—including the constitutionality of § 70502(d)(1)(C) of the MDLEA—and that preventing him from presenting that challenge would be unjust.

We agree that the constitutional issues Dávila-Reyes raises are significant and that the other factors allowing us to [—9—] exercise our discretion to disregard the appellate waiver also are present to the necessary degree. *See, e.g., United States v. Ortiz-Vega*, 860 F.3d 20, 27-28 (1st Cir. 2017). Particularly important is the lack of prejudice to the government, given Reyes-Valdivia's presentation of the same issues as Dávila-Reyes. *See id.* at 27. Indeed, if appellants request and obtain en banc reconsideration of the precedent that currently forecloses their constitutional claims, *see infra*, the potential for relief should not depend on the happenstance that the district court added an enhancement to Reyes-Valdivia's sentence. Thus, we exercise our discretion to decline to enforce Dávila-Reyes's appellate waiver.

Nor do appellants' guilty pleas foreclose their right to challenge the constitutionality of the MDLEA. The Supreme Court recently held in *Class v. United States* that "a guilty plea by itself" does not bar "a federal criminal defendant from challenging the constitu-

tionality of the statute of conviction on direct appeal." 138 S. Ct. 798, 803 (2018). In their briefing and oral argument, appellants present claims that are permissible under *Class*. Although they conceded through their guilty pleas that the MDLEA, by its terms, allows the government to prosecute them under U.S. law, they argue that Congress lacked authority to enact the applicable provisions. In other words, appellants accepted that their convictions were "proper" under the statute, but nonetheless unconstitutional. Such claims may proceed notwithstanding an [—10—] unconditional guilty plea. *See United States v. Aybar-Ulloa*, 913 F.3d 47, 51, 7 Adm. R. 58, 60 (1st Cir. 2019), petition for reh'g en banc filed, No. 15-2377 (Jan. 23, 2019); *cf. United States v. Miranda*, 780 F.3d 1185, 1194, 3 Adm. R. 676, 682 (D.C. Cir. 2015) (noting that Congress would want the "'[j]urisdiction of the United States with respect to a vessel,' [46] U.S.C. § 70504(a), to be insulated from waiver or forfeiture by a defendant" because "[t]he requirement aims to protect the interests of foreign nations, not merely the interests of the defendant"). {–62–}

III.

Appellants' primary constitutional challenge targets a section of the MDLEA that allows U.S. authorities to deem a vessel "without nationality"—i.e., "stateless"—when certain conditions are met. *See* 46 U.S.C. § 70502(d)(1). It is undisputed in this case that the "vessel without nationality" provision of the MDLEA was enacted pursuant to Congress's authority to "define and punish . . . Felonies committed on the high Seas" ("the Felonies Clause"). U.S. Const. art. I, § 8, cl. 10; *see United States v. Cruickshank*, 837 F.3d 1182, 1187, 4 Adm. R. 472, 472 (11th Cir. 2016) (stating that the MDLEA "was enacted under Congress's authority provided by the Felonies Clause"); *United States v. Matos-Luchi*, 627 F.3d 1, 3 (1st Cir. 2010) (stating that, in criminalizing drug trafficking in the MDLEA, Congress was "[i]nvoking its constitutional power" under the Felonies Clause). Appellants [—11—] argue that Congress's authority under the Felonies Clause is limited by the principles of

---

[6] The government contends that Reyes-Valdivia is nonetheless bound by the waiver provision because he failed to explain in his opening brief why it is inapplicable. However, it is apparent on the face of the plea agreement that Reyes-Valdivia was not sentenced in accordance with the sentencing recommendation provision, and he was not obligated to make that obvious point in his opening brief. *See United States v. Colón-Rosario*, 921 F.3d 306, 310-11 (1st Cir. 2019).

international law, and they maintain that, under that law, their vessel cannot be deemed stateless. Specifically, they contend that the definition of a stateless vessel relied upon by the government to support jurisdiction over their boat improperly disregards a master's verbal claim of nationality or registry based on mere inaction by the named country, i.e., its failure to confirm or deny "that the vessel is of its nationality." 46 U.S.C. § 70502(d)(1)(C). Thus, they say, their arrests and prosecution were unconstitutional.

Under our caselaw, however, appellants' prosecution does not depend on their vessel having been properly deemed stateless. Even if their challenge to the MDLEA's state-lessness definition were successful, appellants would still confront our precedent holding that the MDLEA is consistent with the "protective principle" of international law, which permits a nation "to assert jurisdiction over a person whose conduct outside the nation's territory threatens the nation's security." *United States v. Cardales*, 168 F.3d 548, 553 (1st Cir. 1999) (quoting *United States v. Robinson*, 843 F.2d 1, 3 (1st Cir. 1988) (Breyer, J.)).

In *Cardales*, we stated that the protective principle may be triggered in cases brought under the MDLEA "because Congress has determined that *all* drug trafficking aboard vessels threatens our nation's security." *Id.* (emphasis added). In so concluding, [—12—] we relied on a provision of the MDLEA stating, in pertinent part: "Congress finds and declares that [] trafficking in controlled substances aboard vessels is a serious international problem, is universally con-demned, and presents a specific threat to the security and societal well-being of the United States." 46 U.S.C. § 70501. Our court, albeit in mostly split panels, has subsequently accepted as governing precedent the view expressed in *Cardales* that the protective principle can be applied to drug trafficking in violation of the MDLEA. *See, e.g.*, *Aybar-Ulloa*, 913 F.3d at 56, 7 Adm. R. at 64 (majority opinion); *United States v. Vilches- Navarrete*, 523 F.3d 1, 21-22 (1st Cir. 2008) (separate opinion of Lynch and Howard, JJ.); *United States v. Bravo*, 489 F.3d 1, 7-8 (1st Cir. 2007); *but see, e.g.*, *Aybar-Ulloa*, 913 F.3d at 58-59, 7 Adm. R. at 66–67

(Torruella, J., joining in part and dissenting in part).[7] {–63–}

Significantly for the case before us, *Cardales* invoked the protective principle with respect to foreigners on a foreign vessel, initially spotted about 150 miles south of Puerto Rico. *See* 168 F.3d at 551. The captain of the boat, which was boarded by Coast Guard officers over the captain's objection, claimed it [—13—] was a Venezuelan vessel. *Id.* at 551-52. The Venezuelan government later confirmed that the vessel was registered there, and it authorized U.S. intervention. *Id.* at 552.

Although Venezuela's consent played a large role in the panel's rejection of the defendants' due process challenge to their prosecution, which was based on the lack of a nexus between their criminal conduct and the United States, *see id.* at 552-53, consent appeared to play no role in the panel's brief discussion of the protective principle as an alternative rationale for upholding U.S. jurisdiction over the defendants, *see id.* at 553. In a single paragraph, the panel described the principle and noted that Congress's specific finding of a security threat to the United States in § 70501 was "[c]onsistent with this principle." *Id.* As we observed in *Aybar-Ulloa*, "[t]here is no indication in this aspect of *Cardales*'s reasoning that its broad assertion regarding the United States' entitlement to assert protective jurisdiction, under inter-national law, was limited only to cases in which the flag nation has consented to the United States' assertion of jurisdiction over a vessel and those on board it." 913 F.3d at 56, 7 Adm. R. at 64. Rather, the *Cardales* panel seemingly treated the congressional dec-laration of a security threat as adequate on its own to support [—14—] protective jurisdiction

---

[7] Although our court discussed the protective principle at some length in *Robinson*, we ultimately sidestepped questions surrounding the principle's scope because the vessel's flag nation had consented to U.S. jurisdiction. *See* 843 F.2d at 3-4. We recognized in *Robinson*, however, that "any assertion of jurisdiction under the protective principle must be 'reasonable.'" *Id.* at 3 (citing Restatement (Revised) § 403; Brown, "Protective Jurisdiction," 34 Am. J. Int'l L. 112, 114 (1940)).

over the vessel under international law. *See id.*, 7 Adm. R. at 64.[8]

Accordingly, even if appellants' vessel possessed Costa Rican nationality, as they claim, appellants would nonetheless be subject to U.S. jurisdiction under our circuit's view of the protective principle. *See Vilches-Navarrete*, 523 F.3d at 5 (Honduran flagged vessel); *Cardales*, 168 F.3d at 552 (Venezuelan registry). Notwithstanding *Cardales* and the cases reiterating its approach, appellants urge us to reject the protective principle as a proper basis for U.S. jurisdiction over their vessel. That entreaty, however, can only be made to the en banc court. Based on our precedent, we must affirm appellants' convictions.

IV.

Reyes-Valdivia claims the district court committed procedural sentencing error when it applied a two-level enhancement based on his being the "captain" of the vessel. *See* U.S.S.G. § 2D1.1(b)(3)(C) (requiring a two-level enhancement if the defendant acted, inter alia, as a "pilot, copilot, captain, [or] navigator . . . aboard any craft or vessel carrying a [—15—] controlled substance"). He acknowledges that he stated at the time of his arrest that he was the captain, but he asserts that the evidence in fact shows that he shared the duties of steering the vessel with others. Reyes-Valdivia highlights the government's view, expressed at the sentencing hearing, that the enhancement should not apply "[g]iven the nature of the ship, and the fact that a captain of one of these boats could be one {–64–} person one minute and, literally, another person the other minute."

We review a district court's interpretation and application of a sentencing enhancement

de novo. *See United States v. Trinidad*, 839 F.3d 112, 114, 4 Adm. R. 25, 26 (1st Cir. 2016). The court's underlying factual findings may be undone only if clearly erroneous, *id.*, 4 Adm. R. at 26, and its judgment calls must be upheld absent an abuse of discretion, *United States v. Coleman*, 854 F.3d 81, 85 (1st Cir. 2017).

The transcript of the sentencing hearing makes plain that the district court understood the facts that prompted the government to conclude that the captain enhancement was unwarranted. The court acknowledged that Reyes-Valdivia may not have been the master of the vessel, and that he may have said he was the captain only to protect Dávila-Reyes (his cousin) from exposure to more severe punishment resulting from Dávila-Reyes's prior criminal activity. Nonetheless, Reyes-Valdivia not only reported being the captain, but, as his counsel noted at the [—16—] hearing, he admitted that "he did, in fact, steer along with the other co-[d]efendants in this case." On this record, we cannot conclude that the district court clearly erred in applying the enhancement. *See United States v. Cruz-Mendez*, 811 F.3d 1172, 1175-76, 4 Adm. R. 370, 371–72 (9th Cir. 2016) (joining other circuits, including the First Circuit, in construing the pilot/captain enhancement broadly to cover a defendant who shared piloting responsibilities); *cf. Trinidad*, 839 F.3d at 116, 4 Adm. R. at 27 (rejecting defendant's "contention that he did not act as a navigator because he was a subordinate to the other man on the vessel"); *United States v. Guerrero*, 114 F.3d 332, 346 (1st Cir. 1997) (rejecting defendant's argument that the enhancement "only applies to offense participants in a position of authority or command").

V.

We do not reach appellants' challenge to the constitutionality of the MDLEA definition of a "vessel without nationality." Under governing First Circuit precedent, the protective principle of international law permitted the United States to arrest and prosecute appellants even if, as they claim, their vessel possessed Costa Rican nationality.

---

[8] In a footnote, the *Cardales* panel observed that "[t]o the extent that international law requires a nexus to the United States, that nexus requirement is not overridden by the MDLEA, but instead is satisfied by the foreign flag nation's authorization to apply U.S. law to the defendants *and by the congressional finding that drug trafficking aboard vessels threatens the security of the United States.*" 168 F.3d at 553 n.2 (emphasis added).

Their argument seeking to change that precedent must be presented to the court en banc.

Accordingly, for the reasons given, we affirm the judgments of conviction and Reyes-Valdivia's sentence. [—17—]

So ordered.

–Concurring Opinion Follows–

(Reporter's Note: Concurring opinion follows on p. 82).

[—18—] {–64–} LIPEZ, Circuit Judge, concurring:

I write separately to explain why I believe our circuit's caselaw on the protective principle of international law is flawed and to urge my colleagues to reconsider that precedent en banc. The protective principle, as we have described it, permits prosecutions under the Maritime Drug Law Enforcement Act ("MDLEA") of foreigners on foreign vessels without any affirmative showing that the targeted drug trafficking impacts the United States or its citizens. That expansive reach of the principle far exceeds the traditional depiction of its scope as a proposition of international law. Indeed, such a broad view of U.S. jurisdiction over vessels is at odds with our obligation to respect every nation's authority over its own persons and vessels.

Harmonizing our view of the protective principle with international law would bring to the forefront appellants' challenge to the MDLEA's "vessel without nationality" provision. In other words, if we concluded that the protective principle does not justify application of the MDLEA to drug trafficking carried out by foreigners {–65–} on foreign vessels, absent a demonstrated nexus between the drug activity and U.S. security interests, we would need to address whether appellants' vessel was one "without nationality." That is so because the government has made no showing of such a nexus. Although I will not delve into the statutory issue here, I think it important to note that appellants **[—19—]** present a forceful argument that Congress exceeded its authority under Article I of the Constitution by expanding the definition of a stateless vessel beyond the bounds of international law. *See* 46 U.S.C. § 70502(d)(1).

Discussion

A close review of the cases in which we have considered the protective principle reveals that our court's approach to the doctrine rests on shaky footing. I describe that precedent below, explaining why its vulnerabilities warrant en banc reconsideration of our application of the principle, under the MDLEA, to drug trafficking aboard vessels in international waters.

A. The Protective Principle and the MDLEA

The "protective principle" is a long-recognized concept of international law that permits a nation to punish extraterritorial conduct that poses a risk to its security or other important state interests. *See, e.g., United States v. Robinson*, 843 F.2d 1, 3 (1st Cir. 1988). The current version of the applicable Restatement provision describes "Jurisdiction Based on the Protective Principle" as follows:

> International law recognizes a state's jurisdiction to prescribe law with respect to certain conduct outside its territory by persons not its nationals that is directed against the security of the state or against a limited class of other fundamental state interests, such as espionage, certain acts of terrorism, murder of government officials, counterfeiting of the state's seal or **[—20—]** currency, falsification of official documents, perjury before consular officials, and conspiracy to violate immigration or customs laws.

Restatement (Fourth) of Foreign Relations Law of the United States § 412 (2019).

The language of the MDLEA's declaration on drug trafficking, asserting that trafficking of controlled substances aboard vessels "presents a specific threat to the security and societal well-being of the United States," 46 U.S.C. § 70501,[9] tracks the Restatement provision, and it thus suggests a deliberate desire by Congress to bring drug trafficking within the protective principle. Significantly, the security risk as declared by Congress is not expressly limited to drug activity with a demonstrated impact on, or nexus to, the United States. Rather, the broadly worded statement would on its face include within its scope drug trafficking aboard a vessel halfway

---

[9] Section 70501 states, in pertinent part: "Congress finds and declares that [] trafficking in controlled substances aboard vessels is a serious international problem, is universally condemned, and presents a specific threat to the security and societal well-being of the United States."

around the world, without any showing that those drugs were headed toward the United States or would otherwise affect the United States or its citizens. *See United States v. Cardales*, 168 F.3d 548, 553 (1st Cir. 1999) [—21—] (noting Congress's finding that "*all* drug trafficking aboard vessels threatens our nation's security" (emphasis added)).[10] {—66—}

The other circuits have not taken a uniform stance on whether a direct nexus to the United States must be shown to trigger the protective principle with respect to drug trafficking. *Compare, e.g., United States v. Perlaza*, 439 F.3d 1149, 1162 (9th Cir. 2006) (rejecting "the notion that [the] 'protective principle' can be applied to 'prohibiting foreigners on foreign ships 500 miles offshore from possessing drugs that . . . might be bound for Canada, South America, or Zanzibar'" (quoting *Robinson*, 843 F.2d at 3) *with United States v. Gonzalez*, 776 F.2d 931, 939 (11th Cir. 1985) (stating that "[t]he protective principle does not require that there be proof of an actual or intended effect inside the United States" and concluding that "conduct may be forbidden if it has a potentially adverse effect and is generally recognized as a crime by nations that have reasonably developed legal systems").

The debate over the nexus requirement for drug trafficking in violation of the MDLEA could be framed as a debate over the types of crimes properly within the scope of the [—22—] protective principle. A Reporters' Note to the Restatement provision on protective jurisdiction observes that "no constituent element of the offense and *no actual or intended effect in the territory* of the regulating state need be shown." Restatement (Fourth) of Foreign Relations Law § 412 n.1 (emphasis added). However, the crimes the Restatement specifies in describing the protective principle—such as counterfeiting, espionage, and perjury before consular

officials—by their nature directly affect state interests wherever they occur. That is, the crimes traditionally associated with the protective principle are those that inherently include a "nexus" with the prosecuting country as an element. That category of crimes is small, and drug trafficking would not naturally fit within it. *See id.* cmts. a, b (describing the limited scope of the protective principle); Eugene Kontorovich, *Beyond the Article I Horizon: Congress's Enumerated Powers and Universal Jurisdiction Over Drug Crimes*, 93 Minn. L. Rev. 1191, 1229 (2009) (noting that the protective principle has been invoked to "allow[] a state to punish extra-territorially 'a limited class of offenses . . . directed against the security of the state or other offenses threatening the integrity of governmental functions'" (quoting Restatement (Third) of Foreign Relations Law § 402 cmt. f (1987)); *id.* at 1230 ("Commentators stress that the category of protective jurisdiction offenses is [—23—] quite small, and none suggest drug smuggling as one of [the offenses within it].").

Recognizing that drug trafficking does not fall within the category of crimes permissibly triggering the protective principle would not prevent the United States from criminalizing some controlled-substance activity aboard vessels outside its territorial jurisdiction. A different principle recognized under international law is arguably a better fit for drug-trafficking crimes, although that doctrine requires that a nexus be shown between the conduct and the prosecuting country. A Restatement provision titled "Jurisdiction Based on Effects" states: "International law recognizes a state's jurisdiction to prescribe law with respect to conduct that has a substantial effect within its territory." Restatement (Fourth) of Foreign Relations Law § 409 (2018). This jurisdictional principle allows nations to reach crimes other than those with a built-in nexus component— i.e., crimes like counterfeiting and espionage, which fall within the protective principle as traditionally understood—and would embrace drug trafficking that in fact "presents a specific threat to the security and {—67—} societal well-being of the United States." 46 U.S.C. § 70501. [—24—]

---

[10] Although we have acknowledged that the assertion of jurisdiction under the protective principle must be reasonable, *see Robinson*, 843 F.2d at 3, we did not discuss reasonableness in the post-*Robinson* cases adopting the protective principle and we have not defined the limits of "reasonable" protective principle jurisdiction.

B. The Protective Principle: First Circuit Precedent

1. *United States v. Robinson*

Only once has a panel majority of our court grappled with the international law implications of the protective principle. In that case, *Robinson*, the Coast Guard stopped a Panamanian ship about 500 nautical miles east of North Carolina, and boarding officers found a substantial quantity of marijuana in a fake fuel tank. 843 F.2d at 2. Writing for the panel, then-Judge Breyer noted that the appellants questioned the United States's justification for prosecuting drug crimes committed by foreigners on foreign vessels who "might be bound for Canada, South America, or Zanzibar." *Id.* at 3. He described as "forceful" appellants' argument that multiple courts had wrongly used international law principles to conclude that a predecessor statute to the MDLEA permitted such drug prosecutions in the absence of direct impact on the United States. *Id.*

In raising doubts about such a broad application of the protective principle, Judge Breyer pointed to a then-current provision of the Restatement of Foreign Relations Law that described the principle as "giv[ing] [a] state [the] power to prescribe law protecting *itself* from actions taken abroad that harm *it*." *Id.* (quoting Restatement (Revised) of Foreign Relations Law § 402(3)). The emphasis in that description is Judge Breyer's. He also quoted a comment to the same Restatement that similarly **[—25—]** depicts the "protective principle [as] 'based on the effect . . . [of an offshore] act *upon or in a state's territory*.'" *Id.* (quoting § 402(3), cmt. f) (second alteration in *Robinson*). Again, the emphasis is Judge Breyer's.

Robinson recognized the inherent tension that exists when a nation seeking to prosecute crime on the high seas must reconcile that objective with the bedrock principle of international law that "all nations have an equal and untrammeled right to navigate on the high seas." *United States v. Marino-Garcia*, 679 F.2d 1373, 1380 (11th Cir. 1982) (citing Convention on the High Seas, art. 2,

Apr. 29, 1958, 13 U.S.T. 2312, T.I.A.S. No. 5200); *see also id.* (noting that "international law generally prohibits any country from asserting jurisdiction over foreign vessels on the high seas," and that "vessels are normally considered within the exclusive jurisdiction of the country whose flag they fly"). Cognizant of the need to respect the sovereign interests of other nations, Congress has stated its intention "to stay within the boundaries of international law" when criminalizing maritime drug trafficking. *United States v. Matos-Luchi*, 627 F.3d 1, 11 (1st Cir. 2010) (Lipez, J., dissenting); *see also* S. Rep. 96-855 (1980), at 2 (reporting that the MDLEA's predecessor legislation, the Marijuana on the High Seas Act, would "give the Justice Department the maximum prosecutorial authority permitted under international law"); 125 Cong. Rec. 20,083 (1979) **[—26—]** (statement of Rep. Paul McCloskey) (explaining, in reference to the same law, that it authorizes prosecution "to the broadest extent possible under international law"). We also have acknowledged that deference to other nations' interests is a component of the MDLEA, observing that "Congress inserted the requirement that a vessel be subject to the jurisdiction of the United States . . . as a matter of diplomatic comity." *United States v. Vilches-Navarrete*, 523 F.3d 1, 22 (1st Cir. 2008) (separate opinion of Lynch & Howard, JJ.) (citing *United States v. Tinoco*, 304 F.3d 1088, 1108 (11th Cir. 2002)); *cf.* **{—68—}** *Jesner v. Arab Bank, PLC*, 138 S. Ct. 1386, 1417 (2018) (Gorsuch, J., concurring) ("[W]hen the framers gathered to write the Constitution they included among their chief priorities endowing the national government with sufficient power to ensure the country's compliance with the law of nations.").[11]

---

[11] To be sure, Congress in enacting the MDLEA apparently sought to expand U.S. jurisdiction over drug trafficking beyond what was contemplated by its predecessor statute, the Marijuana on the High Seas Act. *See* S. Rep. No. 99-530, at 15 (1986) (observing that "defendants in cases involving foreign or stateless vessel boardings and seizures have been relying heavily on international jurisdictional questions as legal technicalities to escape conviction"). Nonetheless, as described above, Congress has recognized that the United States must adhere to its responsibilities to the

The discussion in *Robinson* was subsequently described by the Ninth Circuit as having "called into question" the [—27—] "reasonableness of a broad reading of the 'protective principle.'" *Perlaza*, 439 F.3d at 1162 (citing *Robinson*, among other cases). The *Robinson* court ultimately sidestepped the questions surrounding the scope of the principle, however, because it found "another, different, but perfectly adequate basis in international law for the assertion of American jurisdiction." 843 F.2d at 4. The country of the vessel's nationality, Panama, had "*agreed* to permit the United States to apply its law on her ship," and the panel held that this acquiescence sufficed to support U.S. prosecution of persons on the vessel under U.S. drug laws. *Id.*

2. *United States v. Cardales*

Despite the questions about the scope of the protective principle raised in *Robinson*, and without addressing those issues, we held in *Cardales* that "application of the MDLEA to the defendants is consistent with the protective principle of international law." 168 F.3d at 553. As our panel opinion reports, the court in *Cardales* based that pronouncement on the congressional finding that drug trafficking aboard vessels "presents a specific threat to the security . . . of the United States," *id.* at 553 (quoting 46 U.S.C. § 70501), and we have accepted *Cardales*'s view of the protective principle as our governing precedent, *see, e.g., United States v. Aybar-Ulloa*, 913 F.3d 47, 56, 7 Adm. R. 58, 64 (1st Cir. 2019) (citing *Cardales*), *petition for reh'g* [—28—] *en banc filed*, No. 15-2377 (Jan. 23, 2019); *Vilches-Navarrete*, 523 F.3d at 22 (same) (separate opinion of Lynch & Howard, JJ.).

Whether *Cardales* deserves such acceptance, however, is debatable. In *Cardales*, we upheld the defendants' convictions by relying on the foreign government's consent to the application of U.S. law to both the vessel and the vessel's crew. *See Cardales*, 168 F.3d at 551-52 (describing the consent of Venezuela,

---

international community when prosecuting crimes on the high seas.

the country of registration). Unlike in *Robinson*, our discussion focused primarily on consent, and we only briefly addressed the protective principle. *See id.* at 553. We ultimately rejected the defendants' due process challenge to their prosecution under the MDLEA because "due process is satisfied when the foreign nation in which the vessel is registered authorizes the application of United States law to the persons on board the vessel." *Id.* We further explained:

> When the foreign flag nation consents to the application of United States law, jurisdiction attaches under the statutory requirements of the MDLEA without violation of due process or the principles of international law because the flag nation's consent eliminates any concern that the application of United States law may be arbitrary or fundamentally unfair. {–69–}

Id. Our one-paragraph consideration of the protective principle was offered as an additional basis for jurisdiction over the vessel's occupants. *Id.* [—29—]

The *Cardales* panel did not consider whether due process required a "domestic nexus requirement" in an MDLEA prosecution, but we concluded that the government need not "prove a nexus between a defendant's criminal conduct and the United States in a prosecution under the MDLEA when the flag nation has consented to the application of United States law to the defendants." *Id.* at 552-53. In a footnote, the panel observed that, even if international law required a nexus, the requirement was satisfied by Venezuela's consent *and* by Congress's "finding that drug trafficking aboard vessels threatens the security of the United States." *Id.* at 553 n.2 (referring to 46 U.S.C. § 70501).

Our extended discussion of the protective principle in *Robinson* suggests a concern that a broad view of its scope may transgress longstanding "limits [on] law enforcement on [the] high seas." *Robinson*, 843 F.2d at 3. Against that backdrop, the cursory treatment of the principle in *Cardales* and the expansive approach adopted there—applying the principle to cover even foreigners on foreign vessels—should give us pause.

3. The Need to Revisit *Cardales*

The questions concerning the proper scope of the protective principle that were bypassed in *Robinson* remain largely unaddressed by our court. Indeed, as the protective principle is depicted by the Restatement, *see supra*, the principle arguably does not apply to drug trafficking at all. As described above, [—30—] drug-trafficking offenses do not resemble the sorts of crimes typically associated with the principle—and the premise of "a specific threat to the security and societal well-being of the United States," 46 U.S.C. § 70501, is particularly inapt when there is no evidence that the drugs at issue would reach the United States or U.S. citizens. As Judge Torruella has observed, "drugs not destined for United States markets do not fall into the 'limited class of offenses . . . directed at the security of the State,' since that principle 'refers to the safety and integrity of the state apparatus itself (its "government functions" or "state interests"), not its overall physical and moral well-being.'" *United States v. Angulo-Hernández*, 576 F.3d 59, 61 (1st Cir. 2009) (Torruella, J., dissenting from the denial of en banc review) (quoting Kontorovich, *supra*, at 1229-31). Nor does it seem adequate, even if the protective principle can justify jurisdiction over foreign individuals involved in drug trafficking on foreign vessels, for Congress simply to invoke the principle with an unsubstantiated "blanket assertion" of a threat. *Aybar-Ulloa*, 913 F.3d at 58, 7 Adm. R. at 67 (Torruella, J., joining in part and dissenting in part) (discussing 46 U.S.C. § 70501).

Moreover, as Judge Torruella has emphasized, to accept the pronouncement in the MDLEA that *all* drug trafficking poses a security threat to the United States to justify reliance on the protective principle—without a "substantial showing of a nexus" [—31—] —"would render the protective principle coterminous with the doctrine of universal jurisdiction." *Id.* at 59, 7 Adm. R. at 67. The universal jurisdiction doctrine permits "a

nation [to] prosecute certain serious offenses even though they have no nexus to its territory or its nationals, and no impact on its territory or its citizens." *United States v. Cardales-Luna*, 632 F.3d 731, 740 (1st Cir. 2011) (Torruella, J., dissenting). However, few offenses qualify as universal jurisdiction crimes—only those considered "so serious and on such a scale that they can justly be regarded as an attack on the {–70–} international legal order." Kontorovich, *supra*, at 1224 n.228 (quoting Anne-Marie Slaughter, "Defining the Limits: *Universal Jurisdiction and National Courts,"* in *Universal Jurisdiction: National Courts and the Prosecution of Serious Crimes under International Law* 178-79 (Stephen Macedo ed., 2004)).

The Restatement of Foreign Relations Law identifies the crimes subject to universal jurisdiction as including "genocide, crimes against humanity, war crimes, certain acts of terrorism, piracy, the slave trade, and torture." Restatement (Fourth) of Foreign Relations Law § 413.[12] According to the Restatement, this [—32—] list is limited—covering only "the most serious offenses about which a consensus has arisen for the existence of universal jurisdiction"—because universal jurisdiction "departs from the more typical requirement of a specific connection between the state exercising jurisdiction and the person or conduct being regulated." *Id.* n.1; *see also United States v. Bellaizac-Hurtado*, 700 F.3d 1245, 1259 (11th Cir. 2012) (Barkett, J., specially concurring) (noting that the theories of jurisdiction other than "universality" "permit nations to exercise jurisdiction over offenses that implicate domestic interests— that is, offenses that occur within a nation's territory and those that occur outside the

---

[12] In full, section 413, titled "Universal Jurisdiction," provides:

International law recognizes a state's jurisdiction to prescribe law with respect to certain offenses of universal concern, such as genocide, crimes against humanity, war crimes, certain acts of terrorism, piracy, the slave trade, and torture, even if no specific [—32—] connection exists between the state and the persons or conduct being regulated.

territory *but have effects within it*" (emphasis added)). Our precedent on the MDLEA has identified "[n]o source of customary international law [that] has designated drug trafficking as being subject to universal jurisdiction." *Id.* at 1260-61.

To be sure, "a global consensus about the negative effects of drug trafficking" has developed over time, *Aybar-Ulloa*, 913 F.3d at 59, 7 Adm. R. at 67 (Torruella, J., joining in part and dissenting in part), and a close examination of international law norms in 2019 may suggest a different sensibility about the protective principle or universal jurisdiction than Judge Breyer intimated in *Robinson* [—33—] in 1988, *see* 843 F.2d at 3-4. Yet, it also may remain true that, "unlike genocide"—or crimes against humanity, torture, etc.—"the international community has addressed drug trafficking at the domestic, instead of international, level." *Bellaizac-Hurtado*, 700 F.3d at 1256 (Barkett, J., specially concurring).

Conclusion

Although appellants' challenge to their prosecution under the MDLEA founders on the First Circuit's current approach to the protective principle, there is a compelling argument that our approach is neither deeply considered nor faithful to the international law foundation on which it must rest. The need for our country to respect the sovereignty of other nations is reason enough to warrant careful reexamination of our precedent. The individual interests of defendants such as Reyes-Valdivia and Dávila-Reyes—citizens of Costa Rica plausibly claiming Costa Rican nationality for their vessel—reinforce the importance of revisiting caselaw that may erroneously allow their lengthy imprisonment for violating U.S. law. Hence, if appellants submit a petition for en banc rehearing, I urge my colleagues to grant it without hesitation or delay.

United States Court of Appeals
for the First Circuit

No. 18-2128

PEREZ-KUDZMA
VS.
UNITED STATES

Appeal from the United States District Court for the
District of Massachusetts

Decided: October 9, 2019

Citation: 940 F.3d 142, 7 Adm. R. 88 (1st Cir. 2019).

Before **THOMPSON, KAYATTA,** and **BARRON,** Circuit
Judges.

[—3—] {–143–} **BARRON,** Circuit Judge:

This appeal concerns a 2017 suit that challenges the federal government's decision, following the destruction wrought by Hurricane Maria, not to waive indefinitely the cabotage provision of the Jones Act for Puerto Rico. That provision, which applies to Puerto Rico, *see* 46 U.S.C. § 55101(a), prohibits foreign-flag vessels from transporting merchandise between United States coastwise points, *see id.* § 55102(b). The District Court dismissed the suit for failure to state a claim under Federal Rule of Civil Procedure 12(b)(6). We now find that the plaintiffs lack standing, and vacate and re-mand for dismissal on jurisdictional grounds.

I.

The chain of events that led to this lawsuit began when, following the damage that the hurricane inflicted on Puerto Rico, the Secretary of the United States Department of Homeland Security ("DHS") issued a ten-day waiver of the cabotage provision on September 28, 2017, *see id.* § 501, "to facilitate movement of all products {–144–} to be shipped from U.S. coastwise points to Puerto Rico." The waiver applied "to covered merchandise laded on board a vessel within the 10-day period of the waiver and delivered by October 18, 2017."[1] [—4—]

On October 2, 2017, Carmenelisa Perez-Kudzma, Vicente Perez Acevedo, Bixcia Noriega Acevedo, Carmen Gloria Acevedo Pagan, and Zulema Quinones Trabal (three of whom are residents of Massachusetts and one of whom is a resident of Puerto Rico) filed suit in the United States District Court for the District of Massachusetts. They named as the defendants the United States, President Donald J. Trump, and the Secretary of DHS.

The plaintiffs, each of whom owns real estate and/or personal property in Puerto Rico, contended that the defendants, by refusing to extend the waiver of the cabotage provision "until such time [as] Puerto Rico is deemed to have recovered from the catastrophe caused by Hurricane Maria," were in violation of the Equal Protection Clause, the Due Process Clause, and the Ninth Amendment of the federal Constitution, as well as what they describe as the public trust doctrine. The plaintiffs sought declaratory relief, as well as a temporary restraining order ("TRO") and preliminary injunction "requiring that [DHS] extend[] the Jones Act . . . [waiver] indefinitely."

The defendants opposed the plaintiffs' motion for a TRO and moved to dismiss the plaintiffs' claims under Rule 12(b)(6). [—5—] The District Court denied the plaintiffs' motion for a TRO on the ground that the plaintiffs could not show likelihood of success on the merits for their claims, and granted the defendants' motion to dismiss for failure to state a claim under Rule 12(b)(6). The plaintiffs then timely appealed.

---

[1] This waiver was the last in a series of waivers that DHS had issued relating to hurricanes that took place in September 2017. On September 8, 2017, in the wake of Hurricane Harvey and Hurricane Irma, the Secretary of DHS, at the request of the [—4—] Secretary of Defense and the Department of Energy, waived the cabotage provision for seven days to facilitate the movement of petroleum products into South Carolina, Georgia, Florida, and Puerto Rico. On September 11, 2017, at those same agencies' requests, the Secretary of DHS extended the waiver through September 22, 2017.

II.

Understanding the plaintiffs to be seeking ongoing injunctive relief, the defendants argue that the plaintiffs' claims must be dismissed on jurisdictional grounds, because they lack standing under Article III of the United States Constitution to bring them.[2] Because we are obliged to assure ourselves of our jurisdiction under the federal Constitution before we may proceed to the merits, *see Steel Co. v. Citizens for a Better Env't*, 523 U.S. 83, 94 (1998), we begin with this contention.

In order to bring a claim in federal court, a plaintiff must satisfy the strictures of Article III of the United States Constitution, which provides that federal courts have jurisdiction only over "Cases" or "Controversies." U.S. Const. art. III, § 2, cl. 1. To demonstrate that that there is a case or controversy, [—6—] a plaintiff must establish standing. And, to establish standing in that constitutional sense, "a plaintiff must {–145–} show (1) it has suffered an 'injury in fact' that is (a) concrete and particularized and (b) actual or imminent, not conjectural or hypothetical; (2) the injury is fairly traceable to the challenged action of the defendant; and (3) it is likely, as opposed to merely speculative, that the injury will be redressed by a favorable decision." *Friends of the Earth, Inc. v. Laidlaw Envtl. Servs. (TOC), Inc.*, 528 U.S. 167, 180-81 (2000); *see Spokeo, Inc. v. Robins*, 136 S. Ct. 1540, 1547 (2016), *as revised* (May 24, 2016) (citing *Lujan v. Defs. of Wildlife*, 504 U.S. 555, 560-61 (1992)).

The plaintiff "bears the burden of establishing these elements," *Spokeo, Inc.*, 136 S. Ct. at 1547, and must plead "sufficient factual matter to plausibly demonstrate [] standing to bring the action," *Gustavsen v. Alcon Labs., Inc.*, 903 F.3d 1, 7 (1st Cir. 2018) (quoting *Hochendoner v. Genzyme Corp.*, 823 F.3d 724, 731 (1st Cir. 2016)). The issue is one of law that we decide de novo. *See Katz v. Pershing, LLC*, 672 F.3d 64, 70 (1st Cir. 2012).

The plaintiffs' complaint alleges that the defendants' failure to extend indefinitely the waiver of the cabotage provision has "hindered" and will continue to "hinder[]": (1) the plaintiffs' "ability . . . to rebuild [their] family home[s] and contribute towards the reconstruction of roads, structures, [—7—] schools, buildings, monuments, and overall infrastructure of Puerto Rico"; (2) their "ability to . . . rebuild [their] properties in order to rent the same for income"; (3) their "present and future ability to engage" in certain professions (*e.g.*, "the practice of federal law in Puerto Rico," "real estate," "property management," and film production); and (4) their "ability to visit family members," "vacation," and "receive medical services" in Puerto Rico and on the mainland. In explaining the cause of this "hinder[ing]," the plaintiffs' complaint alleges that it will result from "slowdowns in the economy, [and in the] reconstruction of roads, infrastructure, schools, universities, hotels, and buildings since higher costs to rebuild will significantly delay the reconstruction of Puerto Rico due to higher costs in expenses resulted by the Jones Act."

Thus, the plaintiffs appear to predicate their standing on two interrelated contentions. First, they assert that the increased shipping costs that they attribute to the defendants' decision not to waive indefinitely the cabotage provision will, as a general matter, both increase the costs of rebuilding on the island and slow the island's economic recovery. Second, they assert that these general adverse consequences for Puerto Rico will in turn harm them specifically by "hindering" their ability to repair or to rebuild their property in Puerto Rico, pursue various economic opportunities through their businesses and [—8—] professions, or travel to and from Puerto Rico with the consequence that they will not be able to visit family and may even be unable to receive medical services.

But, the plaintiffs' complaint hardly describes the hindering in terms specific

---

[2] Insofar as the plaintiffs do not seek ongoing injunctive relief, their claims are moot, as they do not seek damages. *Horizon Bank & Tr. Co. v. Massachusetts*, 391 F.3d 48, 53 (1st Cir. 2004) (explaining that "a case is moot when the court cannot give any 'effectual relief' to the potentially prevailing party" (quoting *Church of Scientology of Cal. v. United States*, 506 U.S. 9, 12 (1992))).

enough to indicate that it will result from incrementally increased shipping costs attributable to the defendants' conduct rather than from the "multitude of other factors" that, post-hurricane, may bear on the costs of goods in Puerto Rico and the health of the economy there. *See Kauai Kunana Dairy Inc. v. United States*, No. CV. 09-00473 DAE-LEK, 2009 WL 4668744, at *5 (D. Haw. Dec. 8, 2009); *see also Warth v. Seldin*, 422 U.S. 490, 503-08 (1975) (finding that, despite an assumed increase in general housing costs due to the challenged government action, "[a]bsent the {–146–} necessary allegations of demonstrable, particularized injury, there can be no confidence" that the government caused a redressable injury). This concern is underscored by the plaintiffs' own recognition—as stated in their complaint—that millions in Puerto Rico are similarly hindered.

Compounding the problem, the plaintiffs set forth no facts that purport to establish the extent of the increase in shipping costs that may be attributed to the defendants' conduct or the particular ways in which the hindering of which they complain may be traced to such an increase rather than to the [—9—] impact on the island of the hurricane's unprecedented damage. Nor, on appeal, do the plaintiffs attempt to identify where in their complaint they do allege any such facts. Rather, in response to the defendants' challenge to their standing, they merely assert in conclusory fashion that they have "set forth concrete and particularized harms which were caused by violations of their legally protected interests."

We thus are left with a complaint that sets forth only a diffuse description of the asserted injuries and that omits any facts that explain how those injuries could be identified as resulting from increased shipping costs imposed by the Jones Act. As a result, we agree with the defendants that the plaintiffs have failed to set forth allegations in their complaint that are sufficient to establish their Article III standing.

III.

The judgment below is *vacated and remanded* for the claims to be dismissed on jurisdictional grounds. Each party shall bear their own costs.

United States Court of Appeals for the Second Circuit

United States Court of Appeals
for the Second Circuit

No. 16-1035

UNITED STATES
VS.
PRADO

Appeal from the United States District Court for the
Southern District of New York

Decided: August 5, 2019

Citation: 933 F.3d 121, 7 Adm. R. 92 (2d Cir. 2019).

Before **LEVAL, POOLER,** and **HALL,** Circuit Judges.

[—2—] {–125–} LEVAL, Circuit Judge:

Defendants Joaquin Alarcon Prado, Hector Valencia Bautista, and Luis Armando Valencia Bautista appeal from the judgment of the United States District Court for the Southern District of New York (Jed S. Rakoff, J.), [—3—] convicting them, on their pleas of guilty, of conspiracy to {–126–} distribute cocaine, and of possession of cocaine with intent to distribute, while on board a stateless vessel subject to the jurisdiction of the United States in violation of the Maritime Drug Law Enforcement Act, ("MDLEA" or "the Act"), 46 U.S.C. §§ 70501 et seq. The guilty pleas (and the judgments of conviction) are set aside because of the failure to follow Rule 11, Fed. R. Crim. P., in the guilty plea procedure. The indictment is dismissed because the government did not demonstrate that the vessel was subject to the jurisdiction of the United States.[1]

BACKGROUND

The district court conducted a hearing in part to determine whether the vessel on board which drugs were found was subject to the jurisdiction of the United States. The theory of the government was that the vessel was subject to the jurisdiction of the United States because it was without nationality, i.e., not registered in any nation. The government's evidence submitted at the hearing consisted entirely of the sworn complaint of Andres Mahecha, a [—4—] detective of the New York City Police Department on a task force of the United States Department of Homeland Security ("DHS"), supplemented by exhibits including a video and photographs taken by the Coast Guard showing the interception of the vessel.[2]

According to Mahecha's account, on June 19, 2015, officers of the United States Coast Guard patrolling the waters of the Pacific Ocean, off the coast of Central America, received a tip from Homeland Security that a Colombian drug cartel "was sending a go-fast carrying a large shipment of cocaine from Colombia towards Costa Rica." App'x 13. A "go-fast" is a small, rapid speed boat, which, because of its speed and low profile, is often used in drug trafficking.

Coast Guard officers in a reconnaissance plane spotted a small craft moving at high speed in international waters approximately 300 nautical miles off the border between Nicaragua and Costa Rica.[3] A Coast Guard [—5—] cutter then sped to the area and sent out a helicopter and an interceptor launch in pursuit of the go-fast. When the go-fast failed to stop after the firing of warning shots, the helicopter crew fired on the vessel and disabled its engines. As the go-fast came to a stop, one of its occupants was observed throwing bundles into the sea. Officers on the launch boarded the go-fast and there encountered the three defendants, the only persons aboard. They also found twelve

---

[1] The changing views of each member of the panel over time regarding the proper disposition of this case have substantially delayed the formation of a durable majority in favor of any particular disposition and required reassignment of authorship of the majority opinion.

[2] Mahecha does not purport to have witnessed the events described in his sworn statement. His description of the events is "based on [] participation in the investigation, [] conversations with other [unidentified] law enforcement agents, and [] review of documents obtained during the investigation." App'x 13.

[3] We use the term "officers" in reference to the Coast Guard personnel solely to signify their function in this episode as law enforcement officers, without reference to whether they held commissioned or enlisted rank in the Coast Guard.

bundles later determined to contain approximately 680 kilograms of cocaine. Mahecha's complaint states, "All three of the defendants claimed to be of Ecuadorian nationality. [] In response to questioning by members of the Boarding Team, none of the defendants claimed to be the master or individual in charge of the Go-Fast. ... The Boarding Team also {–127–} did not find any registration documents [i.e., documents indicating that it was registered as a vessel of any nation] onboard the Go-Fast." App'x 14. His affidavit adds that "[t]he Go-Fast was not flying any flag, nor did it have any signs of registry painted on the side of the vessel." *Id.*

According to the Government's memorandum of law filed in the district court, the boarding team removed the cocaine and defendants from the go-fast, and then set fire to the go-fast and sank it, concluding that it was a **[—6—]** navigation hazard. The defendants were arrested, transported to Guantanamo Bay in Cuba, and from there flown to New York to be charged and tried.

Affidavits submitted by defendants Hector Bautista and Javier Prado differ from Mahecha's account in a few respects. While Mahecha's affidavit stated that the go-fast was "not flying any flag," App'x 14, the defendants' affidavits asserted that the go-fast had an image of the Ecuadorian flag printed on the side of the vessel (which is corroborated by a video made by the Coast Guard boarding party that was attached to Mahecha's affidavit). There is no evidence that the officers inquired of the defendants as to the nationality or registration of the vessel, and both Javier Prado and Hector Bautista asserted in their affidavits that the officers did not make any such inquiry. Nor is there evidence (or a contention by the government) that the Coast Guard officers communicated with the registry of Ecuador or any other nation to determine whether the vessel was registered.

PROCEDURAL HISTORY

Following indictment, the defendants moved for various forms of relief, including dismissal of the indictment. The court conducted a hearing to **[—7—]** determine whether the vessel was stateless, at which point it received the evidence described above. On the basis of that evidence, the court concluded that the go-fast was stateless and therefore subject to the jurisdiction of the United States under 46 U.S.C. § 70502(c)(1)(A). Accordingly, it declined to dismiss the indictment. The defendants moved for reconsideration, but, while the motion was pending, they entered pleas of guilty. They were sentenced to 24 months of imprisonment and three years of supervised release. The defendants then brought these appeals.

DISCUSSION

Notwithstanding their having pleaded guilty, the defendants contend their convictions should be overturned, and the indictment dismissed, because the government failed to show that the go-fast was stateless and subject to the jurisdiction of the United States, as required by 46 U.S.C. § 70503(e)(1).

I. The Requirements of the MDLEA

The MDLEA, in Section 70503, captioned "Prohibited Acts," prohibits possession of a controlled substance with intent to distribute "even though ... committed outside the territorial jurisdiction of the United States," if the **[—8—]** prohibited act is committed aboard a "covered vessel." "Covered vessel" is defined to include three categories of vessels—one being a "vessel subject to the jurisdiction of the United States." The pertinent clauses are as follows:

(a) Prohibitions.—While *on board a covered vessel*, an individual may not knowingly or intentionally—

(1) manufacture or distribute, or possess with intent to manufacture or distribute, a controlled substance; ...

(b) Extension Beyond Territorial Jurisdiction.—Subsection (a) applies even though the act is committed outside the {–128–} territorial jurisdiction of the United States. ...

(e) Covered Vessel Defined.—In this section the term *"covered vessel"* means—

(1) a vessel of the United States or *a vessel subject to the jurisdiction of the United States*; or

(2) any other vessel if the individual is a citizen of the United States or a resident alien of the United States.

46 U.S.C. § 70503 (emphasis added).

Section 70502, captioned "Definitions," defines "vessel subject to the jurisdiction of the United States" to include a "vessel without nationality," as well as several other categories of vessels including, most prominently, vessels that are in, or entering, or have departed from, the waters of the United States, and, only if the foreign nation consents, vessels that are in the waters of a foreign nation or are registered in a foreign nation. *See id.* at [—9—] § 70502(c)(1). Whether a vessel is "without nationality" is addressed by § 70502(d) and can turn on the outcome of a "claim of nationality or registry."

(d) Vessel Without Nationality.—

(1) In general.— In this chapter, the term "vessel without nationality" includes—

(A) a vessel aboard which the master or individual in charge makes a claim of registry that is denied by the nation whose registry is claimed;

(B) a vessel aboard which the master or individual in charge fails, *on request of an officer of the United States* authorized to enforce applicable provisions of United States law, to make a claim of nationality or registry for that vessel; and

(C) a vessel aboard which the master or individual in charge makes a claim of registry and for which the claimed nation of registry does not affirmatively and unequivocally assert that the vessel is of its nationality.

(2) Response to claim of registry. — The response of a foreign nation to a claim of registry under paragraph (1)(A) or (C) may be made by radio, telephone, or similar oral or electronic means, and is proved conclusively by certification of the Secretary of State or the Secretary's designee.

(e) Claim of Nationality or Registry. — A claim of nationality or registry under this section includes only—

(1) possession on board the vessel and production of documents evidencing the vessel's nationality as provided in article 5 of the 1958 Convention on the High Seas;

(2) flying its nation's ensign or flag; or

(3) a verbal claim of nationality or registry by the master or individual in charge of the vessel.

Id. § 70502 (emphasis added). [—10—]

Section 70504, captioned "Jurisdiction and venue," of which part (a) was added to the MDLEA in 1996[4], provides:

(a) Jurisdiction. — Jurisdiction of the United States with respect to a vessel subject to this chapter is not an element of an offense. Jurisdictional issues arising under this chapter are preliminary questions of law to be determined solely by the trial judge. {–129–}

(b) Venue. — A person violating section 70503 or 70508 —

(1) shall be tried in the district in which such offense was committed; or

---

[4] Pub.L. No. 104-324, § 1138(a)(5), 110 Stat. 3901 (1996).

(2) if the offense was begun or committed upon the high seas, or elsewhere outside the jurisdiction of any particular State or district, may be tried in any district.

Section 70506(c) provides:

(c) Simple possession. —

(1) In general.— Any individual on a vessel subject to the jurisdiction of the United States who is found by the Secretary, after notice and an opportunity for a hearing, to have knowingly or intentionally possessed a controlled substance within the meaning of the Controlled Substances Act (21 U.S.C. 812) shall be liable to the United States for a civil penalty not to exceed $5,000 for each violation. The Secretary shall notify the individual in writing of the amount of the civil penalty.

Accordingly, to prosecute a criminal offense in violation of the MDLEA, the government must establish, as a "preliminary question of law to be determined by the court," that the vessel on which the offense was [—11—] committed was a covered vessel, which can be "a vessel subject to the jurisdiction of the United States." One way of proving that—the path undertaken by the government in this case—is by showing that the vessel was "without nationality" as defined in § 70502(d). That section offers three ways in which a vessel can be shown to be without nationality. These require that U.S. law enforcement officers take prescribed steps. If there is a "claim of nationality or registry," which can be asserted either by "possess[ing] on board the vessel and produc[ing] ... documents evidencing the vessel's nationality"; by "flying the nation's ensign or flag"; or by "a verbal claim of nationality or registry" by the "master or individual in charge." 46 U.S.C. § 70502(e), then the U.S. law enforcement officer can establish statelessness by seeking verification from the registry of the nation whose registry is claimed; if that registry office either "denies" registration or "does not affirmatively and unequivocally" confirm it, the vessel is deemed "without nationality." Alternatively, an officer of the United States may "request" of the master or person in charge to know whether there is a claim of nationality or registry, and if that person fails to make a claim of registry, then the vessel is deemed "without nationality." [—12—]

II. Whether the Government Showed the Vessel Was "Subject to the Jurisdiction of the United States"

Section 70504(a) imposes the obligation on the trial judge to determine, as a "preliminary question[] of law," whether the vessel in question was subject to the jurisdiction of the United States. As § 70504(a) requires that the trial judge make this determination as a preliminary matter, (i.e., prior to a jury trial), the defendants' motion to dismiss the indictment was superfluous in this respect. At the hearing on that question, the burden was on the government to show that the vessel was subject to the jurisdiction of the United States. *See, e.g., United States v. Perlaza*, 439 F.3d 1149, 1160 (9th Cir. 2006) ("For the Government to prosecute someone under the MDLEA, the Government must satisfy ... [the] 'statutory jurisdiction' requirement."); *United States v. Tinoco*, 304 F.3d 1088, 1114 (11th Cir. 2002) (same). If an indictment was premised on the vessel having been stateless and neither side offered any evidence on that subject, the court would have no basis for concluding that the vessel was subject to the jurisdiction of the United States and {–130–} would be compelled to dismiss the indictment.

The Coast Guard officers faced the question whether the prohibition of the Act applied on board the go-fast when they boarded it in international [—13—] waters and found a cargo of a controlled substance aboard. The crucial issue became whether the go-fast was registered in any nation. If it was registered, then the vessel was not a covered vessel that was "subject to the jurisdiction of the United States," and the prohibition set forth in MDLEA did not apply. If the vessel was not registered in any nation, then the MDLEA did apply and the defendants' conduct violated U.S. law. The detailed provisions of the statute, reviewed above, offered various ways for determining statelessness.

With respect to the making of a verbal claim of registration by the master (or individual in charge), the formulation of § 70502(e)(3), as to how a claim of registry is made, and that of § 70502(d)(1)(B), as to how a vessel's statelessness is shown, differ in an important respect. Under clause (e)(3), a verbal assertion of nationality by the master constitutes a claim, which is then tested by a U.S. officer's inquiry of the nation's registry authority. On the other hand, the absence of a master's claim of registration does not, by itself, establish absence of registration. It is only if "*on request*" of a duly authorized officer, the master "fail[s] to make a claim of nationality or registry," that statelessness is established. [—14—]

The Coast Guard boarding party's inattention to the terms of the statute virtually doomed the prosecution to failure at the investigation stage. If the go-fast was, in fact, not registered in any nation, its status as "subject to the jurisdiction of the United States" could easily have been demonstrated to the satisfaction of the MDLEA's standards if the boarding party had followed statutorily specified procedure. In the absence of indicia of registration such as flying a nation's flag, presenting registration papers, or a volunteered assertion of national registration by the master, the statute calls on the investigating officer to ask the master (or individual in charge) whether the vessel is registered in any nation. *See* 46 U.S.C. § 70502(d)(1)(B). If that request is made, and the master makes no claim of registry in response, that would establish that the vessel is a "vessel without nationality" and thus "subject to the jurisdiction of the United States." If, on the other hand, there is a claim of registry (such as an assertion of registry by the person in charge, the flying of a nation's flag, or the presence on board of documents indicating registry), it is then incumbent on the Coast Guard officers to communicate ("by radio, telephone, or similar oral or electronic means," *see id.* § 70502(d)(2)) with the registry office of the nation claimed to seek confirmation. *Id.* § 70502(d)(1)(c). [—15—]

Unless the registry office "affirmatively and unequivocally assert[s]" that the vessel is registered, its failure to do so conclusively establishes statelessness under the statute. *Id.*

The problem for the government in this prosecution was that the Coast Guard officers first failed to follow the procedures by which statelessness can be established, and then destroyed the vessel without having secured a vessel identification number (or other means of identifying the vessel), which made it impossible for the government to establish subsequently by other means that the vessel was without nationality.

The district court found that the vessel was subject to U.S. jurisdiction because the defendants, despite having "every reasonable opportunity, and every good reason, to make a claim of nationality," failed to do so. {–131–} *United States v. Prado*, 143 F. Supp. 3d 94, 99 (S.D.N.Y. 2015). That reasoning was not consistent with the statute. As explained above, failure to volunteer a claim of nationality does not suffice. Section 70502(d)(1)(B) makes clear that it is only if the master or person in charge fails "*on request* of an officer of the United [—16—] States" to make a claim that the failure establishes statelessness.[5] *Id.* (emphasis added).

That statutory distinction is only logical. The failure of the master of a vessel to state the vessel's nationality *when asked* supports a strong logical inference of statelessness. On the other hand, mere silence in the absence of a request for information supports no inference at all. In any event, the statute clearly provides that statelessness is established by the master's failure to assert a claim only when that failure is in response to a request.

---

[5] The government's evidence showed that none of the three defendants identified himself as the master. That did not prevent the officers from making the inquiry. They could have asked all three persons whether the vessel was registered, and if none responded, that would have shown a failure by whichever was in charge to make a claim.

The District Court further found that "the go–fast had minimal, if any, identifying features[,] [so that] [a]ttempting to trace the vessel back to any possible [registry] documents on land would ... have been a futile exercise, since there was no meaningful identifying information that could be provided to the Ecuadorian authorities." *Id.* at 99. There was, however, no evidentiary basis for the conclusion that the vessel had "no meaningful identifying information." Neither the Mahecha affidavit, nor any other evidence before [—17—] the court, showed that the vessel lacked a means of identification. It is a common practice in the manufacture of vessels to identify each newly built hull with a "hull identification number" or "HIN," akin to a VIN for vehicles. Such identification has been legally required by Coast Guard regulations for all boats built in the United States since at least 1983. Hull identification number display, 33 C.F.R. § 181.29 (1983). As with VINs, there is no requirement that such HINs be large or conspicuously displayed. *See id.* § 181.29(c) ("Each hull identification number must be carved, burned, stamped, embossed, molded, bonded or otherwise permanently affixed to the boat so that alteration, removal, or replacement would be obvious. If the number is on a separate plate, the plate must be fastened in such a manner that its removal would normally cause some scarring of or damage to the surrounding hull area. A hull identification number must not be attached to parts of the boat that are removable."). The government made no contention that the rules or practices in other countries are different. Neither the Mahecha affidavit, nor the grainy video made by the Coast Guard officers, nor any other evidence showed that the go-fast lacked an HIN. While the Mahecha affidavit stated that the go-fast had no "signs of registry painted on [—18—] the side of the vessel," App'x 14, it made no assertion demonstrating the absence of an HIN (or other means of identification).

The District Court also concluded that the display of the flag of Ecuador affixed to the side of the vessel, as shown on the Coast Guard's video, was not large or prominent enough to qualify as flying Ecuador's flag (which under § 70502(e)(2) qualifies as a claim of nationality). *Prado*, 143 F. Supp. 3d at 100–01. The court cited no authority for such a size or prominence requirement. We need not pass on the correctness of that ruling as a matter of law because nothing turns on it. Even if the go-fast was not flying the flag, that alone would be insufficient to establish {–132–} that it was stateless and subject to the jurisdiction of the United States. Under § 70502(c), the absence of a claim of registry does not establish that the vessel is "without nationality." To establish statelessness in the absence of a claim of registry, the United States officers must make a request of the master or person in charge for a claim of registry. And if a claim is made in any of the ways specified by the statute, the United States officers must seek verification from the claimed "nation of registry." 46 U.S.C. § 70502(d)(1)(C). [—19—]

Because of the Coast Guard's failure to follow statutorily prescribed steps that might have established statelessness at least to the satisfaction of the MDLEA's standards, followed by the Coast Guard's destruction of the vessel, it became virtually impossible for the government to demonstrate to the court in the statutorily mandated preliminary hearing that the vessel was subject to the jurisdiction of the United States and therefore that the MDLEA applied.

Because the evidence presented by the government to the court in support of the preliminary determination required by § 70504 was legally insufficient to support a finding that the go-fast was without nationality and subject to the jurisdiction of the United States, the District Court's finding that the go-fast was subject to the jurisdiction of United States must be vacated.

III. Did the government's failure to demonstrate that the vessel was without nationality mean that the court was without subject matter jurisdiction?

The government argues that its failure to prove the vessel was subject to the jurisdiction of the United States makes no difference because of the rule that a defendant's guilty plea waives all defects other than to the court's subject matter jurisdiction. Defendants respond that the rule cited by the [—20—] government does not apply because the government's failure to show that the vessel was "subject to the jurisdiction of the United States" *is* a defect as to the court's subject matter jurisdiction. Accordingly, they argue that the federal court lacked subject matter jurisdiction to hear the case, and their guilty pleas did not constitute a waiver of the defect. Although defendants did not make this contention until these appeals, they rely on the proposition that an "objection that a federal court lacks subject-matter jurisdiction may be raised by a party, or by a court on its own initiative, at any stage in the litigation, even after trial and the entry of judgment." *Arbaugh v. Y&H Corp.*, 546 U.S. 500, 506 (2006) (citations omitted). "Rule 12(h)(3) [Fed R. Crim. P.] instructs: 'Whenever it appears by suggestion of the parties or otherwise that the court lacks jurisdiction of the subject matter, the court shall dismiss the action.'" *Id.*

We reject the defendants' argument. Although the MDLEA's term, "a vessel subject to the jurisdiction of the United States," has caused confusion, we think it certain for numerous reasons that its function is not to confer subject matter jurisdiction on the federal courts, but rather to specify the reach of the statute beyond the customary borders of the United States. "Jurisdiction" is a chameleon word. The Supreme Court has described it as [—21—] having "many, too many, meanings." *Id.* at 510 (quoting *Steel Co. v. Citizens for Better Env't*, 523 U.S. 83, 90 (1998)). Among its possible meanings, the two here in contention are described in the language of legal scholarship as "judicial jurisdiction" (or "jurisdiction to adjudicate") and {–133–} "legislative jurisdiction" (or "jurisdiction to prescribe").

Judicial jurisdiction raises the question whether a case comes within the judicial power of the court, so that the court possesses the legal power to adjudicate the case. Legislative, or prescriptive, jurisdiction concerns itself with the reach of a nation's (or any political entity's) laws. With respect to conduct occurring outside of a nation's territory, it asks whether the nation possesses, or has exercised, legislative power over those acts.[6] The question [—22—] whether U.S. statutes reach foreign conduct arises relatively infrequently in the business of the U.S. courts. In contrast, jurisdiction to adjudicate, commonly referred to in the jurisprudence of the federal courts as "subject matter jurisdiction," is an issue that arises on a daily basis in the United States federal courts, because they are courts of limited jurisdiction and are charged with an "an independent obligation to ensure that they do not exceed the scope of their jurisdiction." *See Henderson ex rel. Henderson v. Shinseki*, 562 U.S. 428, 434 (2011). As the result of their daily preoccupation with the issues of subject matter jurisdiction, the federal courts have an instinctive inclination to assume that threshold statutory references to "jurisdiction" refer to their subject matter jurisdiction. As discussed below, in subpart 2, the Supreme Court has warned against indulging that

---

[6] Willis L. M. Reese, the reporter for the second conflict of laws restatement, defines "legislative jurisdiction" as "the power of a state to apply its law to create or affect legal interests." Willis L. M. Reese, Legislative Jurisdiction, 78 Colum. L. Rev. 1587, 1587 (1978). Judicial jurisdiction, on the other hand, is "the power of a state to try a case in its courts. *See generally* Donald Earl Childress III, "Jurisdiction, limits under international law," in Encyclopedia of Private International Law (Elgar 2017) (discussing the difference between jurisdiction to prescribe; jurisdiction to enforce; and jurisdiction to adjudicate, of which subject matter jurisdiction and personal jurisdiction are subcategories).
The Fourth Restatement of Foreign Relations Law makes a similar distinction, employing the term "jurisdiction to prescribe":
> The foreign relations law of the United States divides jurisdiction into three categories: [—22—]
> (a) jurisdiction to prescribe, i.e., the authority of a state to make law applicable to persons, property, or conduct;
> (b) jurisdiction to adjudicate, i.e., the authority of a state to apply law to persons or things, in particular through the processes of its courts or administrative tribunals; and
> (c) jurisdiction to enforce, i.e., the authority of a state to exercise its power to compel compliance with law."

See Restatement (Fourth) of Foreign Relations Law, § 401—*Categories of Jurisdiction* (2018).

inclination. [—23—]

A persuasive opinion of the First Circuit, *United States v. Gonzalez*, 311 F.3d 440 (1st Cir. 2002) (Boudin, J.), demonstrates that the MDLEA's reference poses the question whether its prohibition on drug possession extends to the vessel in question—not whether a prosecution under the statute falls within the subject matter jurisdiction of the federal courts. We agree. The factors that compel our agreement with *Gonzalez* are: (i) A general provision of United States law, 18 U.S.C. § 3231, which defines the subject matter jurisdiction of the federal courts in relation to criminal statutes, confers subject matter jurisdiction on the federal courts for such a prosecution. (ii) The Supreme Court, recognizing the many different senses of the word "jurisdiction," has repeatedly warned against construing provisions that limit a statute's coverage as references to subject matter jurisdiction unless that meaning was "clearly state[d]" in the statute. *See* {–134–} *Arbaugh*, 546 U.S. at 515-16. (iii) The natural meaning of the words of the statute, if they are read in context in the manner in which the various provisions and definitions fit together, make clear that the term "vessel subject to the United States" specifies the reach, or coverage, of the statute and does not in any way address the jurisdiction of the court. (iv) Interpreting the phrase as a limitation *on the court's jurisdiction*, [—24—] rather than *on the reach of the statute*, would give the prohibitory clauses a highly expansive and improbable meaning that would affront the sovereignty of other nations. (v) The numerous federal statutes that confer subject matter jurisdiction on federal courts uniformly express that concept through very different formulations. (vi) Perhaps most important, the terms "subject to the jurisdiction of the United States" and "vessel subject to the jurisdiction of the United States" appear repeatedly in the MDLEA and other provisions of the same Title 46 (which governs Shipping), in contexts where those phrases refer unmistakably to the reach of United States laws (as exercises of legislative jurisdiction) and not to the jurisdiction of the courts. (vii) The decisions of other courts that have treated the provision as a limitation on

court jurisdiction have either not recognized that it could have another meaning or have not recognized that the same phrase is used incompatibly with their interpretation repeatedly throughout title 46, as well as in a parallel provision of the very same MDLEA.

1. *The statutory law governing the subject matter jurisdiction of federal courts over federal criminal prosecutions.* The question whether the federal courts have subject matter jurisdiction over a prosecution of a criminal offense defined by [—25—] the statutes of the United States is simply and conclusively answered by 18 U.S.C. § 3231. It states in clear, unambiguous words, "The district courts of the United States have original jurisdiction ... of all offenses against the laws of the United States." If the indictment alleges an offense under U.S. criminal statutes, the courts of the United States have jurisdiction to adjudicate the claim. If the facts fail to show a violation, the court enters judgment for the defendant. It does not dismiss the case for lack of jurisdiction, leaving the case unadjudicated. *See United States v. Yousef*, 750 F.3d 254, 259 (2d Cir. 2014) ("Federal courts have subject-matter jurisdiction over federal criminal prosecutions by virtue of 18 U.S.C. § 3231, which vests the district courts with the power to hear 'all offenses against the laws of the United States.' "); *see also Lauritzen v. Larsen*, 345 U.S. 571, 575 (1953) (holding that because "[a] cause of action under [federal] law was asserted here, ... the [federal] court had power to determine whether it was or was not well founded in law and in fact"); *United States v. Williams*, 341 U.S. 58, 65 (1951) ("The District Court had jurisdiction of offenses against the laws of the United States. 18 U.S.C. § 3231 .... Hence, it had jurisdiction of the subject matter, to wit, an alleged violation of a federal conspiracy statute, and, of course, of the persons charged."); [—26—] *Lamar v. United States*, 240 U.S. 60, 65 (1916) (Holmes, J.) ("[N]othing can be clearer than that the district court ... acts equally within its jurisdiction whether it decides a man to be guilty or innocent under the criminal law, and whether its decision is right or wrong."); *United States v. Shellef*, 507 F.3d 82, 96 (2d Cir. 2007) ("The district court had jurisdiction

over the prosecution of Shellef and Rubenstein pursuant to 18 U.S.C. § 3231 because they were charged with violating federal criminal laws."). As the offense specified in § 70503 is undoubtedly an "offense under {–135–} the laws of the United States," § 3231 confers subject matter jurisdiction of prosecutions under § 70503 on the district courts.

To conclude that the district court nonetheless lacked jurisdiction of this prosecution of an offense under the laws of the United States, we would need to conclude that the MDLEA somehow displaced, superseded, or limited § 3231's express grant of jurisdiction. If it were the intention of the MDLEA to place limits on the federal courts' subject matter jurisdiction to adjudicate such a case notwithstanding their clear empowerment by § 3231 to do so, one would expect the limiting statute to say something to the effect of "notwithstanding § 3231," or "notwithstanding any other provision of law." [—27—] But there is not a word in the MDLEA to suggest that it conflicts with, limits, or supersedes § 3231's universal grant of subject matter jurisdiction to the federal courts over criminal offenses specified in federal statutes. *See Gonzalez*, 311 F.3d at 442 ("[U]nless Congress provided otherwise, subject matter jurisdiction existed in the present case [charging the defendant with criminal violation of § 70503] *because* [the defendant] was charged in district court under ... a federal criminal statute.").

2. *The Supreme Court's guidance for interpreting ambiguous statutory requirements instructs that such a requirement does not go to subject matter jurisdiction absent a "clear statement" to that effect.* The term "jurisdiction" can carry a variety of meanings; "In very general terms, 'jurisdiction' means something akin to 'authority over.'" *Gonzalez*, 311 F.3d at 443 (quoting BLACK'S LAW DICTIONARY 855 (7th ed. 1999)).

The Supreme Court has repeatedly addressed the problem that arises when a litigant advocates interpreting an ambiguous statutory requirement as a limitation on the subject matter jurisdiction of the federal courts. *See Henderson*, 562 U.S. 428; *Reed*

Elsevier, Inc. v. Muchnick, 559 U.S. 154 (2010); *Arbaugh*, 546 U.S. 500. In each of these cases, the Court insisted that statutory [—28—] limitations should not be understood to limit the subject matter jurisdiction of the courts unless that is the "clearly" stated intention of the statute. And in each of these cases, the Court concluded that the contested ambiguous usage did not refer to the subject matter jurisdiction of the federal courts. *See Arbaugh*, 546 U.S. at 515 (cautioning that ambiguous statutory requirements should not be interpreted as limiting the power to adjudicate unless "the Legislature *clearly states* that a threshold limitation on a statute's scope shall count as jurisdictional" (emphasis added)). The *Henderson* opinion re-emphasized *Arbaugh's* test, stating, "In *Arbaugh*, we applied a 'readily administrable bright line' rule .... [W]e look to see if there is any 'clear' indication that Congress wanted the rule to be 'jurisdictional.'" *Henderson*, 562 U.S. at 435-36. In *Reed Elsevier*, the Court summarized, "Our recent cases evince a marked desire to curtail ... drive-by jurisdictional rulings." *Reed Elsevier*, 559 U.S. at 161 (internal quotation marks omitted).

The Court has explained that its requirement of a clear statement is justified by the "unfairness and waste of judicial resources ... entailed in tying [a] requirement to subject– matter jurisdiction." *Arbaugh*, 546 U.S. at 515. When a statutory requirement is treated as an obstacle to the court's subject [—29—] matter jurisdiction, the court's jurisdiction may be challenged for the first time and new arguments raised long after the court has entered judgment. *See* {–136–} *id*. at 506. That is what the Supreme Court seeks to avoid, except where Congress has clearly stated a contrary intention.

3. *The words "vessel subject to the jurisdiction of the United States" specify how far the prohibitions reach into circumstances potentially conflicting with the sovereignty of other nations and make no apparent reference to the limited subject matter jurisdiction of the district courts.* The natural meaning of the statutory words, if read in context rather than in isolation, clearly specifies (and limits) the scope, reach, or coverage of the statutory

prohibition, without reference to the court's jurisdiction. Section 70503(a) make it a criminal offense to possess controlled substances (with intent to distribute) *if the possession occurs "on board a covered vessel"* (emphasis added). "Covered vessel[s]" include three categories: (i) a vessel of the United States; (ii) a vessel on which the individual who possesses the drugs with intent to distribute is a citizen or resident of the United States; (iii) a vessel subject to the jurisdiction of the United States. *See id.* at § 70503(e). "Vessel subject to the jurisdiction of the United States" is an umbrella term, which specifies categories of vessels that [—30—] are neither vessels of the United States nor vessels on which the person in possession of the drugs is a United States citizen or resident. This category is tailored to exercise Congressional regulatory authority in circumstances where the regulatory interest of the United States is clear, and to avoid exercising regulatory authority where doing so would cause conflict with the sovereignty of other nations. The category includes "vessels without nationality"; vessels that are in, or entering, or have departed from United States waters; and, only if the foreign nation consents to the enforcement of the United States law (or waives objection), vessels registered in a foreign nation, or in the waters of a foreign nation. *See id.* at § 70502(c)(1). The coverage therefore generally excludes non-U.S. vessels in the waters of another nation, and vessels registered in another nation, unless that nation consents or waives objection.

The MDLEA thus makes clear in what circumstances vessels are covered by the statute's prohibition. If the vessel falls outside the prescribed coverage, it is not a "covered vessel" and the prohibition specified in § 70503 does not apply to it. None of this in any way addresses the jurisdiction of the United States courts, which is normal, because (as demonstrated above) the [—31—] jurisdiction of the United States courts over "all offenses against the laws of the United States" is provided by another statute. *See* 18 U.S.C. § 3231. The function of the term "vessel subject to the jurisdiction of the United States" is to identify those vessels that fall

into one of the three categories of vessels that are "covered."

Specifying the circumstances in which a nation's laws apply extraterritorially typifies a legislature's exercise of *legislative jurisdiction* by defining the statute's reach.[7] The general subject of legislative jurisdiction encompasses at least three legislative concerns: (i) whether it is consistent with international law to so extend the reach of the nation's laws; (ii) whether doing so respects comity among nations, or would cause undesired friction with foreign nations; and, finally, (iii) exactly {–137–} how the extraterritorial reach of the statute is defined.[8] The relevant provisions of the MDLEA evince concern [—32—] for each of these. With respect to "vessel[s] subject to

---

[7] Restatement (Fourth) of Foreign Relations Law, *§ 401—Categories of Jurisdiction* (2018) (defining "jurisdiction to prescribe" as a state's authority "the authority of a state to make law applicable to persons, property, or conduct"); Willis L. M. Reese, Legislative Jurisdiction, 78 COLUM. L. REV. 1587, 1587 (1978) (describing "legislative jurisdiction" as "the power of the state to apply its law to create or affect legal interest").

[8] Courts have long assumed that Congress, in deciding whether and the extent to which it exercises extraterritorial prescriptive jurisdiction, bears in mind the potential for international discord that may arise from aggressive exercises of extraterritorial jurisdiction. Restatement (Fourth) of Foreign Relations Law, *§ 405—* [—32—] *Reasonableness in Interpretation*, cmt. a (2018) ("Reasonableness and prescriptive comity: In interpreting the geographic scope of federal law, courts seek to avoid unreasonable interference with the sovereign authority of other states. This principle of interpretation accounts for the legitimate sovereign interests of other nations."); *F. Hoffman-La Roche Ltd. v. Empagran. S.A*, 542 U.S. 155, 164 (2004) (assessing whether the extra-territorial exercise of prescriptive jurisdiction comports with "prescriptive comity"). *See also Murray v. Schooner Charming Betsy*, 2 Cranch 64, 118, 2 L.Ed. 208 (1804) ("[A]n act of congress ought never to be construed to violate the law of nations if any other possible construction remains."). Moreover, courts assume that Congress did not intend to exercise jurisdiction beyond the limits imposed by international law wherever and thus "will attempt to construe federal statutes to avoid conflicts with international law governing juris-diction to prescribe." *Id.* at *§ 406—Interpretation Consistent with International Law*, cmt. a.

the jurisdiction of the United States," the limits Congress imposed on the reach of the MDLEA to stateless vessels in international waters reflect concern for both international law and prescriptive comity. *See McCulloch v. Sociedad Nacional de Marineros de Honduras*, 372 U.S. 10, 21 (1963) (finding that the National Labor Relations Act does not apply to foreign-flagged vessels because of, *inter alia*, "the well-established rule of international law that the law of the flag state ordinarily governs the internal affairs of a ship" and "possibility of international discord" that would arise from the "concurrent application of the [NLRA] and the Honduran Labor Code"); *see also Lauritzen v. Larsen*, 345 U.S. 571, 577 (1953) ("While some [shipping laws] have been specific in application to foreign shipping and others in being confined to American shipping, many [—33—] give no evidence that Congress addressed itself to their foreign application and are in general terms which leave their application to be judicially determined from context and circumstance. By usage as old as the Nation, such statutes have been construed to apply only to areas and transactions in which American law would be considered operative under prevalent doctrines of international law.").

Congress here took pains to avoid interference with vessels regulated by other nations (absent the other nation's consent), such as by excluding from coverage vessels registered in other nations in international waters and vessels within the territorial waters of other nations, and by specifying the particular facts that can demonstrate that a vessel is without nationality and thus subject to the jurisdiction of the United States. In so doing, it specified the extent to which the law overcomes the "presumption against extraterritoriality," that U.S. laws are generally presumed to have only domestic effect unless Congress clearly manifests a contrary intention. *See Morrison v. Nat'l Australia Bank Ltd.*, 561 U.S. 247, 255 (2010) (holding that "[w]hen a statute gives no clear indication of an extraterritorial application, it has none"); *see also RJR Nabisco, Inc. v. European Cmty.*, 136 S. Ct. 2090, 2093 [—34—] (2016). The MDLEA specifies that

its substantive prohibition applies extraterritorially "even though the [prohibited] act is committed outside the territorial jurisdiction of the United States." 46 U.S.C. § 70503(b). Defining the extent of extraterritorial application {–138–} of a law is an exercise of prescriptive jurisdiction.

The Supreme Court has chastised us before for treating a question of the prescriptive reach of a U.S. statute as if it placed a limit on the subject matter jurisdiction of the federal courts. In *Morrison*, our court had dismissed for lack of subject matter jurisdiction a civil suit alleging violation of the antifraud provision of the Securities Exchange Act of 1934 because we concluded that the statute did not apply to the wholly foreign facts. *See Morrison*, 561 U.S. at 254. The Supreme Court corrected our reasoning, explaining that the extent of the statute's extraterritorial reach is not an issue related to the court's jurisdiction: "[T]o ask what conduct § 10(b) reaches is to ask what conduct § 10(b) prohibits, which is a merits question. Subject-matter jurisdiction, by contrast, refers to a tribunal's power to hear a case." *Id.* (internal quotation marks omitted). The point was also made by Judge Friendly in *Fogel v. Chestnutt*, 668 F.2d 100 (2d Cir. 1981): "[W]hen the plaintiff [—35—] bases his cause of action upon an act of Congress[,] [the jurisdiction of the court] cannot be defeated by a plea denying the merits of his claim." *Id.* at 106 (first alteration in original) (quoting *Fair v. Kohler Die & Specialty Co.*, 228 U.S. 22, 25 (1913) (Holmes, J.)). Similarly, the question posed by § 70503 whether its prohibition reaches the vessel on the high seas where the contraband cargo was found—is a question of prescriptive jurisdiction.

This is not to say that the MDLEA is devoid of potential confusions. In 1996, after many years of its prohibition on possession of controlled substances on vessels "subject to the jurisdiction of the United States," Congress added the provisions now identified as § 70504(a) that "[j]urisdiction of the United States ... is not an element of an offense," and that "[a]ll jurisdiction issues arising under this chapter are preliminary questions of law to be determined solely by the trial judge." 46

U.S.C. § 70504(a). As discussed further below, this amendment has misled some courts to reason that, if the vessel's status as "subject to the jurisdiction of the United States" is not an element *of the offense*, it must be a limitation on the court's subject matter jurisdiction. *See United States v. Miranda*, 780 F.3d 1185, [—36—] 1195, 3 Adm. R. 676, 683–84 (D.C. Cir, 2015); *United States v. Bustos-Useche*, 273 F.3d 622, 626 (5th Cir. 2001).

There are, however, strong reasons to reject that interpretation of the amendment. First, if Congress had intended this addition to change drastically the meaning of the prohibition on possession of narcotics on vessels subject to the jurisdiction of the United States, this would have been an oddly obscure and indirect way to go about saying something that would have been so easy to state in straightforward fashion.

The provisions of § 70504(a) were enacted a year after the Supreme Court decided in *United States v. Gaudin*, 515 U.S. 506, 522–23 (1995), that an "element of the offense" must be submitted to the jury. Presumably that is why Congress described the "jurisdiction of the United States" as "not an element of an offense" in prescribing that it "be determined solely by the trial judge." However, Congress's evident desire to exclude these issues from jury consideration did not amount to a congressional statement that they now involved the court's subject matter jurisdiction. Describing the issue as "not an element of an offense" is not to say that it is not an element of legislative jurisdiction--a so-called "jurisdictional element"—specifying what is needed [—37—] so that the reach of the statutory prohibition extends to conduct occurring outside the territorial borders. {–139–} There is a significant conceptual difference between provisions of a criminal statute that identify the offensive conduct prohibited and provisions that specify the conditions necessary for the statute to reach that conduct. The Supreme Court later explicitly recognized the difference in *Torres v. Lynch*, 136 S. Ct. 1619, 1630 (2016), noting the distinction between a statute's "jurisdictional element"—the portion of the statute "connect[ing] the law to one of

Congress's enumerated powers, thus establishing legislative authority"—and the "substantive elements," which "describe the evil Congress seeks to prevent."

It is true, as Judge Boudin observed in *Gonzalez*, 311 F.3d at 444, that by allocating "jurisdictional issues" to the judge, "Congress [] introduced a possible Sixth Amendment objection to the statute."[9] But as of 1996, the [—38—] Supreme Court had made no such ruling, and there is no reason to suppose that Congress believed it could not, consistent with the Constitution, give the court the sole authority to determine a jurisdictional element. There is likewise no reason to interpret the words of the statute to mean anything other than what they seem on their face to convey.

The MDLEA's legislative history contains no suggestion "that Congress had in mind the court's subject matter jurisdiction or that it

---

[9] Judge Boudin's concern came closer to realization in 2016, when the Supreme Court rendered decisions in *Torres* and *Taylor v. United States*, 136 S.Ct. 2074 (2016). In *Torres*, the Court asserted in dictum that jurisdictional elements, like offense elements, must be "proved to a jury beyond a reasonable doubt." *Torres*, 136 S.Ct. at 1630. (The assertion was dictum because it had no bearing on the Court's decision.) Then in *Taylor*, the Court stated, "[T]he Government in a Hobbs Act prosecution must prove beyond a reasonable doubt that the defendant engaged in conduct that satisfies the Act's commerce element, but the meaning of that element is a question of law." *Taylor*, 136 S.Ct. at 2080. This statement was also dictum, which had no effect on the judgment, as the government *had* proved the commerce element [—38—] beyond reasonable doubt in the jury trial, and the Court furthermore made no mention of whether the commerce element needed to be proved *to the jury*. Nonetheless, the Court's utterances in *Torres* and *Taylor* increase the likelihood that the Court will invalidate § 70504(a)'s provision that the jurisdiction of the United States be determined *solely* by the trial judge. In future prosecutions under § 70503 with respect to vessels "subject to the jurisdiction of the United States," trial courts might be well advised after making the preliminary determination required by § 70504(a) so that trial may proceed, to submit the issue of jurisdiction over the vessel to the jury notwithstanding the statutory word "solely."

meant to prevent a guilty plea from being given its normal effect." *Gonzalez*, 311 F.3d at 443. The conference report on the 1996 Coast Guard Authorization Act, by which what is now § 70504 was added, evidences an intent to strengthen the effectiveness of the MDLEA in combating drug trafficking on the high seas:

> The Conference substitute [for diverging Senate and House versions of the bill] establishes new law enforcement provisions which expand the Government's prosecutorial effectiveness in drug smuggling cases. Claims [—39—] of foreign registry must be "affirmatively and unequivocally" verified by the nation of registry to be valid. People arrested in these international situations would not be able to use as a defense that the U.S. was acting in violation of international law regarding recognition of registry at the time of the arrest. ... Jurisdictional issues would always be issues of law to be decided by the trial judge, not issues of fact to be decided by the jury.

142 Cong. Rec. H11485 § 1138 (Sept. 27, 1996). The President's signing statement similarly announces a goal to "strengthen {–140–} drug interdiction by clarifying U.S. jurisdiction over vessels in international waters." Presidential Statement on Signing the Coast Guard Authorization Act of 1996, 1996 PUB. PAPERS 1869 (Oct. 19, 1996). Interpreting the statutory reference to "jurisdiction of the United States" as meaning the subject matter jurisdiction of the federal courts, thus enabling defendants who had pleaded guilty to reopen the issue of statelessness long after their pleading guilty (at a time when the government might no longer be able to prove the necessary facts to establish jurisdiction), would weaken, not strengthen the Act's effectiveness in drug interdiction. The meaning of § 70503 did not change as a result of the addition of a requirement that the court decide jurisdiction as a matter of law. [—40—]

4. *Interpreting the phrase, "a vessel subject to the jurisdiction of the United States," as meaning a restriction on the jurisdiction of federal courts to hear a case (rather than as a limitation on the reach of the statute), would give the prohibitory terms of the statute a highly expansive, bizarre, unlikely meaning that would affront the sovereignty of other nations.* Interpreting the phrase, "vessel subject to the jurisdiction of the United States" as a limitation on the jurisdiction of the U.S. courts (rather than as a limitation on the reach of the statute), apart from the fact that it distorts the clear apparent meaning of the statute's words, causes bizarre distortions to the meaning of the statute that Congress is highly unlikely to have intended.

For example, the jurisdiction of the court to adjudicate the prosecution would turn on the government's ability to prove that the vessel was "covered" for one of the three categories of "covered vessel[s]," but not for the other two. Thus, if the prosecution is brought on the theory that the vessel is a "vessel of the United States" (because the vessel is "owned in any part by an individual who is a citizen of the United States," *see* 46 U.S.C. § 70502(b)(2)), or on the theory that the "individual [in possession of the drugs] is a citizen of the United States," *see id.* at §§ 70503(e)(1), (2), the court [—41—] would have jurisdiction regardless of whether the government proved the facts necessary for coverage. If the government failed to prove that the vessel was covered, the court would exercise jurisdiction and acquit the defendant. On the other hand, if the prosecution were premised on the vessel being "without nationality" (one of the categories of vessels that are "subject to the jurisdiction of the United States"), the failure of the government to prove that the vessel was unregistered would not result in acquittal, but would deprive the court of jurisdiction to enter a judgment of acquittal. There is no apparent reason why Congress would have wanted to make the jurisdiction of the court turn on satisfactory proof of coverage for one of the three categories of covered vessels, but not for the other two.

Interpreting "subject to the jurisdiction of the United States" as a limitation on the jurisdiction of the court, rather than on the reach of the statute, would have still more bizarre consequences for the meaning of the statute. If that phrase is a limit on the jurisdiction of the court, rather than on the reach of the statute, it would mean that the statute prohibits drug possession on foreign-registered vessels and on vessels in the waters of foreign nations, regardless of whether those nations consented. The United [—42—] States Coast Guard would be authorized to enforce violations by boarding such vessels in the waters of foreign nations, seizing the drugs, and arresting foreign nationals in {-141-} possession.[10] The only limitation on enforcement would be the unavailability of a court to impose criminal penalties. Passing a law purporting to criminalize drug possession by aliens on vessels registered in other nations or in the waters of other nations would create the very sort of affront to other nations that Congress clearly sought to avoid by the way it tailored the statute's coverage. The words of the statute show a clear intent of Congress's that the statute not apply in such circumstances that would affront the sovereignty of other nations. That intent is realized only if "vessel subject to the jurisdiction of the United States" is construed as a limitation on the reach of the statute. [—43—]

Finally, it would have been inexplicably strange for Congress to criminalize drug possession in those circumstances, only to deny the courts authority to adjudicate the prosecutions for the violations.

5. *The verbal formulations of statutes conferring subject matter jurisdiction on the*

---

[10] As Justice Breyer observed in *Kiobel v. Royal Dutch Petroleum Co.*, 569 U.S. 108 (2013) (concurring opinion), "a ship is like land, in that it falls within the jurisdiction of the nation whose flag it flies." *Id.* at 130 (citing *McCulloch v. Sociedad Nacional de Marineros de Honduras*, 371 U.S. 10, 20–21 (1963) (referring to "the well-established rule of international law that the law of the flag state ordinarily governs the internal affairs of a ship"); *United States v. Palmer*, 16 U.S. (3 Wheat) 610, 632 (1818) (describing piracy as an "offenc[e] against the nation under whose flag the vessel sails, and within whose particular jurisdiction all on board the vessel are"); Restatement (Third) of Foreign Relations Law of the United States § 502, cmt d (1986) ("The flag state has jurisdiction to prescribe with respect to any activity aboard the ship.")).

courts uniformly adopt a very different terminology. It is further instructive to compare the language of the MDLEA with the many acts of Congress that do confer subject matter jurisdiction on the federal courts. Section 3231, which confers subject matter jurisdiction in the federal courts in criminal cases, and the many statutes of Chapter 85 of the Judicial Code, Title 28, U.S. Code, that confer subject matter jurisdiction on the federal courts in civil cases, uniformly employ a forthright formulation, clearly stating, with tiny variations, "The district courts ... shall have ... jurisdiction of [a specified category of case]."[11] The MDLEA contains no such language. [—44—] {-142-} [—45—]

---

[11] *See, e.g.*, 28 U.S.C. § 1330 ("The district courts shall have original jurisdiction . . . of any nonjury civil action against a foreign state . . . ."); *id.* § 1331 ("The district courts shall have original jurisdiction of all civil actions arising under the Constitution, laws or treaties of the United States."); *id.* § 1332 ("The district courts shall have original jurisdiction of all civil actions where the matter in controversy exceeds the sum or value of $75,000, . . . and is between—citizens of different states . . . ."); *id.* § 1333 ("The district courts shall have original jurisdiction, exclusive of the courts of the states, of: (1) any civil case of admiralty or maritime jurisdiction . . . ."): *id.* § 1334 ("[T]he district courts shall have original jurisdiction of all cases under title 11 [bankruptcy cases and proceedings] . . . ."); *id.* § 1335 ("The district courts shall have [—44—] original jurisdiction of any civil action of interpleader or in the nature of interpleader . . . ."); *id.* at § 1336 ("Except as otherwise provided by Act of Congress, the district courts shall have jurisdiction of any civil action to enforce, in whole or in part, any order of the Surface Transportation Board . . . ."); *id.* § 1337 ("The district courts shall have original jurisdiction of any civil action or proceeding arisng under any Act of Congress regulating commerce or protecting trade and commerce against restraints and monopolies . . . ."); *id.* § 1338(a) ("The district courts shall have original jurisdiction of any civil action arising under any Act of Congress relating to patents . . . ."); *id.* § 1338(b) ("The district courts shall have original jurisdiction of any civil action asserting a claim of unfair competition when joined with a substantial and related claim under the copyright, patent, plant variety protection or trademark laws."): *id.* § 1339 ("The district courts shall have original jurisdiction of any civil action arising under any Act of Congress relating to the postal service."); *id.* § 1340 ("The district courts

The point is not merely that the MDLEA's formulation differs from that used by

shall have original jurisdiction of any civil action arising under any Act of Congress providing for internal revenue . . . ."); *id.* § 1343 ("The district courts shall have original jurisdiction of any civil action authorized by law to be commenced by any person . . . [t]o recover damages for injury to his person or property, or because of the deprivation of any right or privilege of a citizen of the United States, by any act done in furtherance of any conspiracy mentioned in section 1985 of Title 42 . . . ."); *id.* § 1344 ("The district courts shall have original jurisdiction of any civil action to recover possession of any office, except that of elector of President or Vice President, United States Senator, Representative in or delegate to Congress, or member of a state legislature, authorized by law to be commenced, where in it appears that the sole question touching the title to office arises out of denial of the right to vote, to any citizen offering to vote, on account of race, color or previous condition of servitude."); *id.* § 1345 ("Except as otherwise provided by Act of Congress, the district courts shall have original jurisdiction of all civil actions, suits or proceedings commenced by the United States, or by any agency or officer thereof expressly authorized to sue by Act of Congress."); *id.* § 1346(a) ("The district courts shall have original jurisdiction, concurrent with the United States Court of Federal Claims, of . . . [a]ny civil action against the United States for the recovery of any internal-revenue tax alleged to have been erroneously or illegally assessed or collected . . . ."); *id.* § 1346(d) ("The district courts shall not have jurisdiction under this section of any civil action or claim for a pension."); *id.* § 1346(f) ("The district courts shall have exclusive original jurisdiction of civil actions under section 2409a to quiet title to an estate or interest in real property in which an interest is claimed by the United States."); *id.* § 1347 ("The district courts shall have original jurisdiction of any civil action commenced by any tenant in common or joint tenant for the [—45—] partition of lands where the United States is one of the tenants in common or joint tenants."); *id.* § 1367 ("(a) Except as provided in subsections (b) and (c) or as expressly provided otherwise by Federal statute, in any civil action of which the district courts have original jurisdiction, the district courts shall have supplemental jurisdiction over all other claims that are so related to claims in the action within such original jurisdiction that they form part of the same case or controversy under Article III of the United States Constitution. Such supplemental jurisdiction shall include claims that involve the joinder or intervention of additional parties.").

Congress to confer jurisdiction on the federal courts. The MDLEA not only uses a very different formulation, but one which, on its face, contains neither a "clear statement" of intent to affect the jurisdiction on the federal courts, nor even a less-than-clear statement of such intent. If Congress had intended, either implicitly in enacting §§ 70502 and 70503, or in the 1996 amendment, to limit the subject matter jurisdiction of the federal courts, there is every reason to believe it would have used a formula that communicated the intended message. The proposition that the federal courts will have jurisdiction of a specified category of cases is so easy to state in clear, simple language, that it would be inexplicably astonishing if Congress, desiring to achieve that objective, had done such a bad job of stating it in the statutory language. [—46—]

6. *Other provisions of the MDLEA and of Title 46 use the formulation of § 70503 in circumstances that cannot refer to the subject matter jurisdiction of the federal courts.* Perhaps what most persuasively demonstrates that § 70503's use of the phrase "vessel subject to the jurisdiction of the United States" is not intended to confer subject matter jurisdiction on the federal courts is that other provisions of the MDLEA and Title 46 employ the same terminology referring to vessels and waters "subject to the jurisdiction of the United States" in a manner that cannot refer to the subject matter jurisdiction of the U.S. courts. Other statutes throughout {–143–} Title 46, the shipping title of the United States Code, use the phrase "subject to the jurisdiction of the United States" to refer to the waters where the provisions of United States laws will apply.[12] [—47—] [—48—] These pro-

---

[12] *See, e.g.,* 46 U.S.C. § 2101(49) (defining a "tank vessel" as one which "transfers oil or hazardous material in a port or place *subject to the jurisdiction of the United States*"); *id.* at § 2301 (stating that the chapter titled "Operation of Vessels Generally" "applies to a vessel operating on waters *subject to the jurisdiction of the United States* (including the territorial sea of the United States as described in Presidential Proclamation No. 5928 of December 27, 1988) and, for a vessel owned in the United States, on the high seas"); *id.* § 3715(a)(3) (providing that "[a] vessel may transfer oil or hazardous material in a port or *place subject to the jurisdiction of the United States,* when the

cargo has been transferred from another vessel on the navigable waters of the United States or in the marine environment, only if– . . . the delivering and the receiving vessel had on board at the time of transfer, a certificate of financial responsibility as would have been required under section 1016 of the Oil Pollution Act of 1990, had the transfer taken place in a place *subject to the jurisdiction of the United States*"); *id.* § 3716(a) (providing that "[a] vessel may not transfer cargo in a port or place *subject* [—47—] *to the jurisdiction of the United States* if, before arriving, the vessel has discharged tank washings containing oil or hazardous material in preparation for loading at that port or place in violation of the laws of the United States or in a manner or quantities inconsistent with a treaty to which the United States is a party"); *id.* § 4301(a) (providing that chapter titled "Recreational Vessels" "applies to a recreational vessel and associated equipment carried in the vessel on waters *subject to the jurisdiction of the United States* (including the territorial sea of the United States as described in Presidential Proclamation No. 5928 of December 27, 1988) and, for a vessel owned in the United States, on the high seas"); *id.* § 4304 (stating that "[t]he Secretary and the Secretary of the Treasury may authorize by joint regulations the importation of any nonconforming recreational vessel or associated equipment on conditions, including providing a bond, that will ensure that the recreational vessel or associated equipment will be brought into conformity with applicable safety regulations and standards of the Government before the vessel or equipment is operated on waters *subject to the jurisdiction of the United States*"); *id.* § 12115 (c) (providing that a vessel documented under the "Temporary endorsement for vessels procured outside the United States" section is "*subject to the jurisdiction and laws of the United States*"); *id.* § 70102 (directing the Secretary of the department in which the Coast Guard is operating, *see id.* § 70101 (5), to "conduct an assessment of vehicle types and United States facilities on or adjacent to the waters *subject to the jurisdiction of the United States* to identify those vessel types and United States facilities that pose a high risk of being involved in a transportation security incident"); *id.* § 70303(c)(7) (directing the Secretary to "require each owner or operator of a vessel or facility located within or adjacent to waters *subject to the jurisdiction of the United States* to implement any necessary interim security measures, including cargo security programs, to deter to the maximum extent practicable a transportation security incident until the security plan for that vessel or facility operator is approved"); *id.* § 70106(a)(1) (directing the Secretary to "establish deployable specialized forces

visions do not contemplate proceedings in the federal courts. Some of these references authorize the Secretary to prescribe regulations governing shipping in waters "subject to the jurisdiction of the United States." Their context clearly refers to the reach of U.S. law and not to the subject matter jurisdiction of the U.S. courts.

The most pertinent to our inquiry is another provision of this very statute. Section {–144–} 70506(c) of the MDLEA, enacted in 2010,[13] which, like § 70503(a), prohibits drug possession on "a vessel subject to the jurisdiction of the United States," applies in circumstances in which the federal courts will play no role whatsoever. Mere possession of a controlled substance (i.e., without intent to distribute) on "a vessel subject to the jurisdiction of the United States," is declared to be a "violation," to be enforced in administrative proceedings conducted by the Secretary. Thus, another section of the same statute employs the same phrase ("a vessel subject to the jurisdiction of the United States") in the same context (prohibiting drug possession on board the vessel), having no reference to the subject matter jurisdiction of the United States courts, as the proceedings it authorizes will [—49—] not be conducted in the United States courts. To accept the defendants' argument that "a vessel subject to the jurisdiction of the United States," as used in §§ 70502 and 70503, means a limitation on the subject matter jurisdiction of the federal district courts, one would need to construe these words as having a drastically different meaning from the same words used in the same context to define a less serious violation

of varying capabilities as are needed to safeguard the public and protect vessels, harbors, ports, facilities, and cargo in waters *subject to the jurisdiction of the United States* from destruction, loss or injury from crime, or sabotage due to terrorist activity"); *id.* § 70108(d) (describing chain of command "[d]uring a transportation security incident on or adjacent to waters *subject to the jurisdiction of the United States*"); *id.* § 70113(a) (directing the Secretary to "implement a system to collect, integrate, and analyze information concerning vessels operating on or bound for waters *subject to the jurisdiction of the United States*").
[13] Maritime Drug Law Enforcement Act, 46 U.S.C. § 70506(c), 124 Stat. 2905, 2923 (2010).

specified in § 70506. *See Sorenson v. Sec. of the Treasury of the U.S.*, 475 U.S. 851, 860 (1986) ("The normal rule of statutory construction assumes that identical words used in different parts of the same act are intended to have the same meaning." (internal quotation marks omitted)).

7. No prior court decisions have advanced persuasive arguments for construing this statute as a limitation of the jurisdiction of the federal courts.

While in a few instances courts have treated the MDLEA's reference to a "vessel subject to the jurisdiction of the United States" as a limitation on the subject matter jurisdiction of the federal courts, the majority of those decisions have simply assumed reflexively that a reference to "jurisdiction" means the subject matter jurisdiction of the court, without considering any possible alternative meaning. Only three opinions of Courts of Appeals, *Gonzalez*, 311 [—50—] F.3d 440, *Bustos-Useche*, 273 F.3d 622, and *Miranda*, 780 F.3d 1185, 3 Adm. R. 676, have confronted the question whether the reference was to the reach of the statute or to the jurisdiction of the court, and only *Bustos-Useche* and *Miranda* have reached the latter conclusion.

We turn to the decisions of the various Circuits that treat this language as referring to the subject matter jurisdiction of the court. The majority of opinions dealing with convictions for violation of the MDLEA have been, not surprisingly in view of its geographic situation, in the Eleventh Circuit. Defendants cite the Eleventh Circuit's decision in *United States v. De La Garza*, 516 F. 3d 1266 (11th Cir. 2008), as having concluded that the MDLEA's reference to "the jurisdiction of the United States" means the subject matter jurisdiction of the federal courts. This is incorrect. The *De La Garza* decision did not conclude that the phrase means "within the subject matter jurisdiction {-145-} of the United States courts." The *De La Garza* decision merely noted that the Circuit had previously, in *United States v. Tinoco*, 304 F.3d 1088, 1107 (11th Cir. 2002), "interpreted the 'on board a vessel subject to the

jurisdiction of the United States' portion of the MDLEA as a congressionally imposed limit on courts' subject matter jurisdiction." *De La Garza*, 516 F.3d at 1271. The *De La* [—51—] *Garza* opinion recognized in a footnote that the government was challenging *Tinoco*'s interpretation and was arguing that the statutory reference to "jurisdiction" "deals with the territorial jurisdiction of the United States and not the adjudicatory power of the federal courts." *Id.* at 1271–72 n.3. The court avoided deciding the question, concluding that it "need not decide the issue to resolve this appeal" because, regardless of which interpretation of "jurisdiction" was correct, it had been established in the district court proceedings that the vessel was subject to the jurisdiction of the United States. *Id.*

The previous *Tinoco* opinion had not interpreted the statutory phrase as referring to the subject matter jurisdiction of the courts; it had simply adopted that interpretation from prior rulings of the Eleventh Circuit in *United States v. Medina*, 90 F.3d 459 (11th Cir. 1996), and *United States v. Ayarza-Garcia*, 819 F.2d 1043 (11th Cir. 1987). *Medina* and *Ayarza-Garcia*, in turn, had simply assumed that the statutory reference to "jurisdiction" meant the subject matter jurisdiction of the federal courts without considering any alternative [—52—] meaning.[14] *See* {-146-} *Medina*, 90

_____

[14] Like *Medina* and *Ayarza-Garcia*, our court *assumed* in *United States v. Pinto-Mejia*, that the reference to "jurisdiction of the United States" in the predecessor to § 70503 meant the subject matter jurisdiction of the court. 720 F.3d 248 (2d Cir. 1983), *modified on denial of reh'g*, 728 F.2d 142 (1984). Venezuelan seamen were charged with possessing controlled substances with intent to distribute on a vessel subject to the jurisdiction of the United States on the high seas. *Id.* at 250. After moving unsuccessfully in the district court to suppress the fruits of the Coast Guard's search of their vessel, they pleaded guilty, subject to a stipulation reserving their right to appeal the denial of their suppression motion. *Id.* On appeal they argued that "the United States lack[ed] jurisdiction to prosecute them" because their vessel was not subject to the jurisdiction of the United States. *Id.* at 254–55. The government argued that their challenge to the jurisdiction of the United States should not be considered because it went beyond the issues preserved for appeal by the stipulation. We rejected the government's

argument, reasoning that "[a] question as to the court's jurisdiction ... may be raised at any time during the pendency of the proceedings." *Id.* at 255.

That decision cannot be counted as a holding on the question we consider here—whether the statute's reference to "a vessel subject to the jurisdiction of the United States" defines the reach of the statute or the subject matter jurisdiction of the court—because the court never considered the question. The government made no argument that the statutory reference to "jurisdiction" implicated the reach of the statute rather than the jurisdiction of the court, and the court simply assumed that it referred to subject matter jurisdiction. Furthermore, at the time of the decision, the Supreme Court had not yet uttered its admonishments (in the *Arbaugh* triad discussed above).

The meaning of the statutory invocation of "jurisdiction" arose again in our court shortly thereafter in a manner that has no influence on our decision because the court did not purport to resolve the confusion. In *United States v. Henriquez*, 731 F.2d 131 (2d Cir. 1983), the defendants, who had been apprehended by the Coast Guard in international waters, were indicted for possession of marijuana with intent to distribute on vessel that was unregistered and therefore subject to the jurisdiction of the United States. The defendants contended the vessel was registered in Honduras. On that ground, they had moved in the District Court for to dismiss the [—53—] indictment *for lack of subject matter jurisdiction.* "[B]oth counsel and [the district] court treated the question of statelessness as part of the issue of subject matter jurisdiction . . . ." *Id.* at 135. The district court found that the government had adequately demonstrated statelessness, and therefore denied the defendants' motion. The defendants then entered conditional guilty pleas, reserving the right to appeal "subject matter jurisdiction." They argued on appeal that the government's evidence failed to show that the vessel was stateless. The government argued that this issue was not preserved for appeal. Notwithstanding that all the participants in the district court including the government had treated the statutory reference to "jurisdiction" as a limitation on the court's subject matter jurisdiction, the government now argued on appeal that "it does not fall under the rubric 'subject matter jurisdiction,' but rather goes to the merits," *id.* at 135, so that the defendants' appellate attack on the district court's finding of statelessness was not within subject matter jurisdiction, which the defendants had reserved for appellate review. The government argued that our *Pinto-Mejia* decision had fallen "into the trap against which Judge Friendly warned in *Fogel v. Chestnutt*, 668 F. 2d

F.3d at 463; *Ayarza-Garcia*, 819 F.2d at 1048. The question, as seen by the court in all three cases, was whether a factual issue [—53—] *necessary to establish the subject matter jurisdiction of the court* should be decided by the court, or submitted to the jury as an element of the offense. *Ayarza-Garcia* and *Medina* had ruled that a factual issue necessary to the determination of the court's subject matter jurisdiction should be treated as an "element" of the crime and submitted to the jury. *Medina*, 90 F.3d at 463–64; [—54—] *Ayarza-Garcia*, 819 F.2d at 1048. Subsequent to those decisions, however, and prior to the *Tinoco* case, Congress amended the MDLEA by adding the provision of § 70504(a) that "[j]urisdiction of the United States ... *is not an element of an offense*," and that "[j]urisdictional issues ... are preliminary questions of law to be determined solely by the trial judge." 46 U.S.C. § 70504(a) (emphasis added). The *Tinoco* court viewed the intervening amendment of the statute as a Congressional rejection of *Medina*'s ruling that factual issues involved in the determination of the court's jurisdiction should go to the jury. *Tinoco* thus, while continuing to assume that "jurisdiction of the United States" referred to the subject matter jurisdiction of the United States courts, concluded that the issue was "*solely* one of subject matter jurisdiction for the court to decide, and not an element of the MDLEA substantive offense." *Tinoco*, 304 F.3d at 1112 (emphasis added).

100, 105-07 (2d Cir. 1981)]" that a failure to prove a claim means only that the claim fails and not that the court lacks subject matter jurisdiction. *Henriquez*, 731 F.2d at 135. While suggesting inferentially that the government may well be correct in arguing against *Pinto-Mejia*'s reading of the statute, *id.* ("[W]hether or not one agrees with the Government that the *Pinto-Mejia* panel fell into the trap, ..."), our court refrained from deciding whether the statutory reference to "jurisdiction" invokes the subject matter jurisdiction of the court. In view of the fact that both counsel and the court below had "treated the question of statelessness as part of the issue of subject matter jurisdiction," *id.*, the court expressed "no doubt that the issue of 'statelessness' was preserved for review" by the stipulation, and did not rule on the issue before us, *id.*

In sum, throughout the history of MDLEA litigation in the Eleventh Circuit, the court never decided whether the MDLEA's reference to "a vessel subject to the jurisdiction of the United States" refers to the reach of the United States statute or to the subject matter jurisdiction of the United States court to adjudicate the criminal prosecution. The Circuit's most recent case, [—55—] *De La Garza*, the only case in which the question was raised, explicitly left the issue unresolved.

In *Miranda*, 780 F.3d 1185, 3 Adm. R. 676, the District of Columbia Circuit did confront the meaning of the statutory phrase and concluded that it constitutes a limitation on the subject matter jurisdiction of the district courts. The opinion without doubt presents a dazzlingly imaginative array of arguments, but we find them unpersuasive. The {–147–} essential core of its reasoning begins with the justified perception that the interception of vessels on the high seas by United States law enforcement officers presents a risk of violations of international law and affronts to other nations. On that basis, the *Miranda* opinion assumes that that Congress must have wanted defendants who pleaded guilty to remain free thereafter to invoke jurisdiction-related objections to their convictions, so as to better protect the interests of foreign nations with respect to comity and international law and that Congress therefore must have intended the "jurisdiction of the United States" provision of § 70503 to mean the subject matter jurisdiction of the court, as that understanding would free defendants to raise these objections even long after the entry of judgment against them. *See id.* at 1194, 3 Adm. R. at 682 ("In that setting, it is eminently understandable [—56—] why Congress *would want* the '[j]urisdiction of the United States with respect to a vessel' to be insulated from waiver or forfeiture by a defendant, and *would also want* courts in every case— and at every level of review—to assure that the requirement is satis-fied."(emphasis added and internal citations omitted) (quoting 46 U.S.C. § 70504(a)).

The opinion cites no evidence in support of its speculation that Congress was concerned to free criminal defendants after pleading

guilty to raise for affronts to comity and international law. That proposition, further-more, is both far-fetched and inconsistent with explicit provisions of the MDLEA. Section 70505 specifies that a defendant "does not have standing to raise a claim of failure to comply with international law as a basis for a defense." It adds that "a failure to comply with international law does not divest a court of jurisdiction and is not a defense." 46 U.S.C. § 70505.[15] It is very difficult to reconcile the intentions *Miranda* attributes to Congress with the provisions Congress enacted. [—57—]

The government has no need, furthermore, to rely on defendant-drug traffickers to protect the Nation's interest in its foreign relations. The Departments of State and Justice are both parts of the executive branch. If a particular prosecution would cause undesirable friction with a foreign nation because of Coast Guard transgressions on another nation's maritime sovereignty, the government can simply drop the prosecution without need for the defendant to serve as a protesting ambassador, and without need for the court's approval to achieve a diplomatic objective. *Cf. Kiobel v. Royal Dutch Petroleum Co.*, 569 U.S. 108, 116 (2013) (reasoning that the unique role of the Executive branch in foreign relations should lead courts to be cautious in "impinging" on the Executive's management of foreign affairs); *United States v. Curtiss-Wright Export Corp.*, 299 U.S. 304, 320 (1936) (recognizing that the executive branch is the "sole organ of the federal government in the field of foreign relations").

A further serious flaw in the *Miranda* opinion's assessment is its unawareness that, as explained above in Part III(c) at page 50, the same shipping title of the United States Code repeatedly uses the phrase—"subject to the jurisdiction of the United States"—to mean *legislative* jurisdiction, [—58—] including a nearly identical usage in the MDLEA to prescribe a variant of the

---

[15] The provision of § 70505 that a failure to comply with national "does not divest the court of jurisdiction" demonstrates that, when Congress wanted to speak of the court's jurisdiction, it did so directly and clearly.

prohibited conduct where the reference cannot be to the subject matter jurisdiction of the federal court as the court will have no role in the prosecution. {–148–}

While quoting from the Supreme Court's *Arbaugh* opinion to the effect that "[i]f the Legislature clearly states that a threshold limitation on the statute's scope shall count as jurisdictional, then courts will be duly instructed," *Miranda*, 780 F.3d at 1192, 3 Adm. R. at 681 (quoting *Arbaugh*, 546 U.S. at 515–16), the *Miranda* opinion obscures the intended thrust of the *Arbaugh* triad, which is that threshold statutory requirements should be construed as limitations on subject matter jurisdiction *only* if that intention is "clearly stated" in the statute. Nor does it acknowledge that its justification for construing the statute as a limitation on the courts' subject matter jurisdiction is the very reason given by the Supreme Court for its admonishment not to interpret unclear coverage limitations in that manner—to wit, the uncertainty, waste, and lack of finality that result because this interpretation allows a dissatisfied party to reopen the issue long after the issuance of a final judgment. *See Arbaugh*, 546 U.S. at 515. [—59—]

Miranda argues that congressional intention to refer to subject matter jurisdiction is clearly stated, indeed "self-evident," because § 70504(a) groups references to "jurisdiction" together with the provision relating to venue, which "by nature speaks to the authority of the district court to hear a case." *Id.* at 1196, 3 Adm. R. at 684 (The "entire provision, including the references to 'jurisdiction' *self-evidently* concerned the authority of district courts, not the legislative authority of Congress." (emphasis added)). We respectfully disagree. If § 70504 were being construed in isolation, the argument would have more force. But the mere fact that § 70504's reference to jurisdiction is grouped with a provision for venue does not negate and alter the meaning of the jurisdictional provision it refers to in § 70503. The grouping in § 70504 makes perfect sense with regard to the MDLEA's grouping of subjects. Sections 70502 and 70503 specify the definition of the offense and the reach of the statute. Section

70504 turns to issues for trial, designating the proper district for trial and telling how issues are to be divided as between judge and jury. The grouping of issues in § 70504 furnishes no reason to interpret the language of §§ 70502 and 70503 as meaning anything other than what it appears on its face to say. [—60—]

Miranda further argues that "when Congress establishes a so-called 'jurisdictional element' addressing the reach of its legislative authority, Congress does not use the term 'jurisdiction' in the statute." *Id.* at 1195, 3 Adm. R. at 683. *Miranda* illustrates the proposition by referring to statutes criminalizing conduct when committed "by ... 'an officer, director, agent or employee ... with any Federal Reserve bank' " or making it unlawful to possess in a school zone a firearm "that has moved in or that otherwise affects interstate or foreign commerce." *Id.*, 3 Adm. R. at 683 (quoting 18 U.S.C. §§ 656, 922(q)(2)(A)). The opinion then asserts that the notion of a "jurisdictional element" is not an appropriate way to refer to a statutory term defining the reach of the statute but is rather a mere colloquialism used by lawyers and judges. *Id.*, 3 Adm. R. at 683. It is simply incorrect that the use of the word "jurisdiction" with reference to the reach of the statute is merely a colloquialism that Congress would not employ in a statute. As discussed above, the terms "legislative jurisdiction," "prescriptive jurisdiction," and "jurisdiction to prescribe" are well-recognized in legal scholarship, and in such documents as the American Law Institute's Restatement of Foreign Relations Law, especially with reference to the reach of the nation's laws beyond its territorial borders. *See* Reese, *supra* note 6, at [—61—] 1587; Childress, *supra* note 6. And Congress used "jurisdiction" numerous times in Title {–149–} 46 to refer to the reach of the U.S. law. Second, while *Miranda* is correct that most statutes set forth the jurisdictional elements by naming them, rather than referring to them as "jurisdictional," there is an obvious reason why § 70503 uses the term "subject to the jurisdiction of the United States," elsewhere enumerating the facts that define the reach of that jurisdiction. Unlike Congress's employment in other statutes of one-factor jurisdictional elements such as "by a Federal Reserve Bank," or "affect[ing] interstate commerce," the facts that may cause a vessel to be "subject to the jurisdiction of the United States" involve numerous complex alternatives, which are spelled out at length in § 70502 under "Definitions." To have included all those complexities in § 70503 together with the offense element would have been unwieldy and confusing.

A final illogic we find in *Miranda*'s arguments is that, while giving great importance to this altogether understandable use of a different approach to the identification of "jurisdictional elements" than in other statutes, *Miranda* dismisses without discussion the government's observation that the MDLEA formulation, if construed as conferring subject matter jurisdiction on the [—62—] courts, differs drastically from the virtual blueprint statutory formulation that is used again and again in the United States Code to confer subject matter jurisdiction on the federal courts. *Id.* at 1195, 3 Adm. R. at 683–84. (See discussion above at III(4)).

The reasoning of the Fifth Circuit in *Bustos-Useche*, 273 F.3d 622, was far simpler than in *Miranda*. As in our case and in *Miranda*, the defendant in *Bustos-Useche* had pleaded guilty without reservation to a violation of § 70503 in that he possessed controlled substances with intent to distribute on board a vessel subject to the jurisdiction of the United States. The vessel was alleged to be subject to the jurisdiction of the United States not because it was stateless but because Panama, the nation of registry, had given "express permission for the enforcement of United States laws on the vessel." *Id.* at 624. After the entry of judgment based on a guilty plea, the defendant argued on appeal that U.S. jurisdiction was not established because Panama's consent was given only after U.S. officers had seized the cocaine. Accordingly, he argued that he never possessed the cocaine at a time when the vessel was subject to the jurisdiction of the United States because the vessel did not become so subject until after he was no longer in possession. *Id.* at 625. [—63—]

The government argued that by pleading guilty without reservation, the defendant had waived the claim. The Fifth Circuit reasoned that whether the defendant had waived the claim turned on "whether the jurisdictional requirements of [the MDLEA] are merely substantive elements of the crime or prerequisites of the district court's subject matter jurisdiction." *Id.* at 626. Recognizing that the 1996 amendment provided that jurisdiction of the United States is not an element of the offense and is to be determined by the trial judge, the court concluded on that basis in a single sentence that the determination of jurisdiction of the United States "is a prerequisite to the court's jurisdiction" and that the defendant was "therefore not foreclosed from raising the issue on appeal." *Id.* The court nonetheless went on to affirm his conviction on the ground that Panama's consent, even delivered subsequent to the seizure of the cocaine, established the jurisdiction of the United States. *Id.* at 629.

As with *Miranda*, the *Bustos-Useche* court reached its conclusion that the statute's jurisdictional requirement was a limitation on the court's subject matter jurisdiction without awareness that § 70506(c) and Title 46 use the same language in {–150–} circumstances that unmistakably refer to the reach of the [—64—] statute and cannot mean to define the subject matter jurisdiction of the courts. The *Bustos-Useche* court, in 2001, furthermore, did not have the benefit of the Supreme Court's later admonition in the *Arbaugh* triad that statutory references to "jurisdiction" should not be interpreted as limitations on subject matter jurisdiction unless that intention was "clearly stated" in the statute. And, as discussed above, the fact that Congress did not regard the vessel's subjectivity to the reach of U.S. law as an offense element did not necessarily mean, as the court seemed to assume, that Congress considered this requirement as a limitation on the subject matter jurisdiction of the federal courts. At the time of the 1996 amendments, there was no judge-made law to the effect that Congress could not, consistent with the Sixth Amendment, withdraw a jurisdictional element from jury consideration.[16] In {–151–} our view, [—65—] [—66—] none of the

---

[16] Judge Pooler's concurring opinion expresses the view that the MDLEA "clearly states" a Congressional intent that the words, "a vessel subject to the jurisdiction of the United States" serve as a limitation on the subject matter jurisdiction of the federal courts. Concurring Op. at 3, 5. The only statutory text on which Judge Pooler relies as supporting her finding of such intention is § 70504(a), which says:

Jurisdiction of the United States with respect to a vessel subject to this chapter is not an element of an offense. Jurisdictional issues arising under this chapter are preliminary questions of law to be determined solely by the trial judge. [—65—]

Judge Pooler argues that Congress cannot have intended its use of the word "jurisdiction" as a so-called "jurisdictional element" referring to Congress's legislative jurisdiction (to define the reach of the statute), or provided that it was "to be determined solely by the trial judge," for two reasons: First, that would be "contrary to the clear statutory language" providing that "[j]urisdiction of the United States with respect to a vessel . . . is not an element of an offense,"and second, such an interpretation would "inject[] serious constitutional concerns into the statute," Concurring Op. at 7, because "the Fifth and Sixth Amendments 'require criminal convictions to rest upon a jury determination that the defendant is guilty of every element of the crime with which he is charged beyond a reasonable doubt.'" Concurring Op. at 9 (quoting *United States v. Gaudin*, 515 U. S. 506, 510 (1995)). Judge Pooler posits that there can be no such thing as a "'preliminary question of law' . . . that is not a question of subject matter jurisdiction or 'an element of an offense.'" Concurring Op. at 10 (quoting 46 U.S.C. § 70504(a)).

We find neither argument persuasive. Both fail for the same reason. Both arguments are based on law established by the Supreme Court many years after Congress enacted § 70504(a). Neither contemplates the law as it was in 1996. When Congress enacted § 70504(a), jurisdictional elements of criminal statutes relating to Congress's exercise of its legislative jurisdiction were widely regarded as different from the substantive elements of the criminal offense that defined the antisocial conduct being prohibited. At the time, there was no inconsistency between Congress prescribing what was called a "jurisdictional element" and asserting that the jurisdictional element is "not an element of an offense." Nor was it constitutionally objectionable to consign the jurisdictional element to the trial judge, rather than the jury.

Seventeen years later, such a distinction became problematic when the Supreme Court asserted in *United States v, Alleyne*, 570 U.S. 99, 103 (2013), and in *Torres v. Lynch*, 136 S. Ct. 1619, 1630 (2016), that any fact necessary to increase the penalty for an offense is necessarily deemed an offense element that must be submitted to the jury, and that jurisdictional elements must be proved to the jury just like the substantive elements of a crime. But in 1996, a statutory assertion that a jurisdictional element was "not an element of an offense" and was to be decided "solely by the trial judge" was neither an inconsistency nor a constitutional problem. In support of her argument, Judge Pooler contends her view is supported by the Supreme Court's holding in *United States v. Gaudin*, 515 US 506, 510 (1995), decided prior to the enactment of § 70504(a)) requiring submission of "every element of the crime" to the jury for determination beyond a reasonable doubt. The reliance is misplaced. The *Gaudin* ruling related to a substantive element of the crime charged [—66—] (the materiality of a false statement in a fraud prosecution)—not a jurisdictional element. *Gaudin*'s requirement of submission of "every element of the crime" to the jury did not address jurisdictional elements. That holding was perfectly compatible with the proposition that a jurisdictional element is "not an element of an offense" and may therefore be consigned solely to the trial judge.

Judge Pooler also offers a policy-based reason for her interpretation. Following views expressed by the D.C. Circuit in *Miranda*, she argues that, because of the risk of harm to international relations arising from arrests and seizures on foreign vessels outside the United States, the issue of the jurisdiction of the United States with respect to a vessel should be "insulated from waiver or forfeiture by a defendant" so that the courts "in every case—and at every level of review—[could] assure that the requirement is satisfied." Concurring Op. at 12–13 (quoting *Miranda*, 780 F.3d at 1194, 3 Adm. R. at 682). Judge Pooler attributes that intention to Congress. However, the reason she advances in support of her interpretation—preserving parties' ability to reopen judgments with respect to previously forfeited matters in subsequent appellate stages of the litigation—is precisely the reason given by the Supreme Court for *not* interpreting statutory limitations as limitations on the court's jurisdiction, absent a "clear statement" of such congressional intent. *See Arbaugh*, 546 U.S. at 515 (observing that "tying [a] requirement to subject-matter jurisdiction" results in "unfairness and waste of judicial resources"); Part III(2), *supra* opinions construing the MDLEA's juris-dictional requirements as a limitation on the subject matter jurisdiction of the federal courts refutes the [—67—] persuasive reasoning of *Gonzalez*, especially as supple-mented by the MDLEA's and Title 46's usages of the same words in provisions that cannot refer to the subject matter jurisdiction of the courts.

IV. Whether Defendants' Guilty Pleas Must Be Vacated Because of Deficiencies in the Plea Proceedings.

The final question before us is whether, even if the MDLEA's jurisdictional requirement pertains to the reach of the statute and not to the subject matter jurisdiction of the court, the defendants' guilty pleas nonetheless should not be treated as waivers of their claim that the jurisdiction of the United States was not shown, because the plea procedure did not adhere to the requirements of Fed. R. Crim. P. 11. The rule advocated by the government—that a guilty plea waives all defects except to the court's jurisdiction—applies only to valid guilty pleas, and the defendants' guilty pleas were defective.

Our court and others have ruled that a defective guilty plea will not necessarily be

---

(discussing *Arbaugh, Reed Elsevier,* and *Henderson*).

Judge Pooler attributes to Congress an intention to rely on defendants to protect the interests of foreign nations and thus guard against international friction by raising failures of proof that a vessel was within the jurisdiction of the United States even after having pled guilty. She fails, however, to acknowledge that the terms of the statute provide strong evidence that Congress's intention was the contrary. Section 70505 of the MDLEA specifies that a defendant "does not have standing to raise a claim of failure to comply with international law as a basis for a defense." It adds that "[a] failure to comply with international law does not divest a court of jurisdiction and is not a defense." 46 U.S.C. § 70505.

In short, we find nothing persuasive in Judge Pooler's argument that the language of section 70504(a) clearly states a congressional intent to limit the subject matter jurisdiction of the court, as required by the Supreme Court.

deemed to waive all objections to a conviction. For example, we ruled in *United States v. Gonzalez*, 420 F.3d 111, 131–34 (2d Cir. 2005), that two Rule 11 errors in the guilty plea proceeding—a violation of Rule 11(b)(1)(C), which requires the court to "inform the defendant of, and determine that the [—68—] defendant understands ... the right to a jury trial," {–152–} Fed. R. Crim. P. 11(b)(1)(C), in failing to tell the defendant of his right to have the jury determine drug quantity, and a violation of the obligation under Rule 11(b) (3) to determine that there was a "factual basis for the plea" with respect to drug quantity—required that the judgment of conviction be vacated and the defendant be permitted to withdraw his plea. In *United States v. Fisher*, 711 F.3d 460, 465 (4th Cir. 2013), the Fourth Circuit found a defendant's guilty plea invalid and permitted him to withdraw because of the reasonable probability that "impermissible government conduct" induced the defendant to plead guilty. *Id.* at 467–69. And in *United States v. Velazquez*, 855 F.3d 1021, 1039 (9th Cir. 2017), the Ninth Circuit vacated defendant's guilty plea on the ground that the district court had erroneously denied her motion to substitute counsel.

Notwithstanding the provision of Rule 11(h) that "a variance from the requirements of this rule is harmless error if it does not affect substantial rights," Fed. R. Crim. P. 11(h), we have found in several instances that deficiencies in the Rule 11 proceedings did affect substantial rights and therefore prevailed over the concept that a plea waives all defects. [—69—] Repeatedly, we have ruled that the court's failure to elicit a factual basis for the conviction would justify vacating the plea. *See, e.g., United States v. Culbertson*, 670 F.3d 183, 189-92 (2d Cir. 2012) (vacating defendant's plea of guilty to conspiracy to import cocaine and heroin for lack of sufficient factual basis as to drug quantity); *United States v. Adams*, 448 F.3d 492, 497-502 (2d Cir. 2006) (vacating defendant's conviction on a plea of guilty to conspiracy to import cocaine and heroin for lack of sufficient factual basis as to the requisite intent, drug quantity, and drug type); *Gonzalez*, 420 F.3d at 133; *United States v. Andrades*, 169 F.3d 131, 134-36 (2d Cir. 1999) (vacating defendant's conviction on a plea of guilty to conspiracy to distribute cocaine base for lack of sufficient factual basis as to "identity of defendant's coconspirators or other necessary facts"); *Montgomery v. United States*, 853 F.2d 83, 85-86 (2d Cir. 1988) (permitting defendant to withdraw plea of guilty to conspiracy to distribute heroin for lack of sufficient factual basis); *Godwin v. United States*, 687 F.2d 585, 590–91 (2d Cir. 1982) (finding that defendant's guilty plea was accepted without sufficient factual basis where defendant's statements at the plea proceeding "essentially [denied] the intent element of the offense," and the district court lacked "some basis" in the record "for doubting his account"). [—70—]

In this instance, we find that the plea proceedings departed from the requirements of Rule 11 in two significant related respects. Rule 11(b)(1)(G) requires that the court "must inform the defendant of, and determine that the defendant understands, ... the nature of each charge to which the defendant is pleading." Fed. R. Crim. P. 11(b)(1)(G). Rule 11(b)(3) requires the court to "determine that there is a factual basis for the plea."

The defendants could not be guilty of the offense unless the vessel on which they possessed drugs was "subject to the jurisdiction of the United States." The theory of the prosecution was that the vessel was subject to the jurisdiction of the United States because it was a "vessel without nationality." In advising the defendants of the nature of the charge, the court did inform them of aspects of the requirements of the charge, such as that they were accused of "conspiracy, that is to say an agreement between each defendant and at least one other person, to violate the Maritime Drug Law Enforcement Act by dealing in cocaine." App'x 388. But the court made no reference either to the requirement {–153–} that the vessel have been subject to the jurisdiction of the United States or to the crucial issue of its statelessness. Nor did the defendants demonstrate awareness in their allocutions of the crucial [—71—] significance of statelessness. Each of them acknowledged having agreed to transport cocaine on a boat that traveled the high seas, but none said anything about the boat's nationality or of its

being subject to the jurisdiction of the United States.

The court may have believed it was unnecessary to explain these issues in view of the fact that the defendants had moved through counsel to dismiss the indictment on the ground that statelessness had not been established. But Rule 11 does not allow the court to assume that a pleading defendant understands the charge because its nature has been the subject of discussion and argument by the defendant's counsel. A plea of guilty requires the personal participation of the defendant, and the court is obligated to inform the defendant of the nature of the charge.

In addition, the court failed to determine, as required by Rule 11(b)(3), that there was "a factual basis for the plea." In view of the probability, as a practical matter, that the defendants did understand from their attorneys that statelessness was an issue, this violation was even more problematic. In fact, as discussed at length in the early portions of this opinion, there was no factual basis for the plea, at least so far as could be demonstrated. Because of [—72—] the Coast Guard's failure to follow statutorily approved procedures for demonstrating the statelessness of the vessel and its subsequent destruction of the vessel, the government was unable to demonstrate that the vessel was stateless and therefore "subject to the jurisdiction of the United States," unless the defendants themselves supplied the missing information. The defendants never provided this information, and in fact, as defendants note, there was no mention of the issue of statelessness during the plea proceedings.

Rule 11(h) provides that "[a] variance from the requirements of this rule is harmless error if it does not affect substantial rights." Fed. R. Crim. P. 11(h). If the record had presented a convincing showing that the defendant understood the nature of the charges in pleading guilty, and sources other than the defendants' allocutions confirmed a factual basis for the plea, the violations of Rule 11 would perhaps not have affected substantial rights. But where the record provided no basis for a finding that the vessel was unregistered, or otherwise subject to the jurisdiction of the United States, the defendants' drug possession did not come within the reach of the MDLEA. They had not committed a criminal offense under the laws of the United States. There was no valid basis for their convictions. The deficiencies in the [—73—] Rule 11 procedure affected the defendants' substantial rights. Their guilty pleas and the judgments of conviction must be vacated.

VI. Disposition.

Section 70504(a) of the MDLEA requires the court to make a preliminary determination of jurisdictional issues. The import of this rule, although unstated, is that if the government fails to establish the jurisdictional element, such as by failing to show that the vessel was subject to the jurisdiction of the United States, the court should dismiss the indictment. In this case, for reasons explained above, the indictment should have been dismissed upon the government's failure to demonstrate at the pretrial hearing that the vessel was subject to the jurisdiction of the United States. The error was not cured by {–154–} the defendants' subsequent defective guilty pleas.

CONCLUSION

The judgments of conviction are hereby VACATED and the indictment is DISMISSED.

(Reporter's Note: Concurring Opinion follows on p. 117).

[—1—] {-154-} **POOLER**, Circuit Judge, concurring:

The Maritime Drug Law Enforcement Act (the "MDLEA") makes it illegal to engage in specified drug trafficking activity "[w]hile on board a covered vessel." 46 U.S.C. § 70503(a). The MDLEA defines the term "covered vessel" to mean "(1) a vessel of the United States or a vessel subject to the jurisdiction of the United States; or (2) any other vessel if the individual is a citizen of the United States or a resident alien of the United States." *Id.* § 70503(e). The terms "vessel of the United States" and "vessel subject to the jurisdiction of the United States" are, in turn, statutorily defined. *Id.* §§ 70502(b), (c).

The majority and I both agree that the government has failed to establish that Defendants-Appellants' "go-fast" was a "vessel subject to the jurisdiction of the United States." *Id.* § 70503(e). Moreover, we both agree that that failure requires vacatur of the judgments of conviction and dismissal of the indictment. We disagree, however, about why the government's failure in this regard demands that result.

Our disagreement centers on the following statutory command: "Jurisdiction of the United States with respect to a vessel subject to this chapter is not an element of an offense. Jurisdictional issues arising under this chapter are [—2—] preliminary questions of law to be determined solely by the trial judge." 46 U.S.C. § 70504(a). The majority concludes that neither this language nor the above-quoted jurisdictional language in Section 70503 imposes any limit on federal courts' subject-matter jurisdiction. The majority nevertheless holds that the government's failure of proof about whether the "go-fast" was "subject to the jurisdiction of the United States," 46 U.S.C. § 70503(e), means that the plea proceedings were deficient—because Defendants-Appellants' guilty pleas lacked a factual basis—and thus violated Rule 11 of the Federal Rules of Criminal Procedure.

If I agreed that the language in Section 70504(a) does not speak to federal courts' subject-matter jurisdiction, I would further agree with the majority regarding the inadequacy of the plea proceedings. However,

consistent with the majority of circuits to consider the issue, I would hold that the MDLEA imposes limits on federal courts' subject-matter jurisdiction. *See United States v. Miranda*, 780 F.3d 1185, 1192, 3 Adm. R. 676, 680–81 (D.C. Cir. 2015); *United States v. De La Garza*, 516 F.3d 1266, 1271 (11th Cir. 2008); *United States v. Bustos-Useche*, 273 F.3d 622, 626 (5th Cir. 2001). *But see United States v. González*, 311 F.3d 440, 443 (1st Cir. 2002). [—3—]

DISCUSSION

I. The Clear-Statement Rule

To determine whether statutory language imposes a limit on federal courts' subject-matter jurisdiction, we ask whether that language "clearly states" that the limitation at issue is "jurisdictional." *Reed Elsevier, Inc. v. Muchnick*, 559 U.S. 154, 163 (2010) (internal quotation marks omitted); *see also Henderson ex rel. Henderson v. Shinseki*, 562 U.S. 428, 435-36 (2011) ("[W]e look to see if there is any clear indication that Congress wanted the rule to be jurisdictional." (internal quotation marks omitted)). "If the Legislature clearly states that a threshold limitation on a statute's scope shall count {-155-} as jurisdictional, then courts and litigants will be duly instructed and will not be left to wrestle with the issue." *Arbaugh v. Y&H Corp.*, 546 U.S. 500, 515-16 (2006) (footnote omitted). "But when Congress does not rank a statutory limitation on coverage as jurisdictional, courts should treat the restriction as nonjurisdictional in character." *Id.* at 516.

Although the Supreme Court has described this rule as a "readily administrable bright line," *id.*, the line is not so bright that its application is always straightforward. Indeed, in determining whether a limitation "is one that is properly ranked as jurisdictional," we need not find "an express designation" [—4—] in order to find a clear statement. *Reed Elsevier*, 559 U.S. at 168; *see also Henderson*, 562 U.S. at 436 ("Congress, of course, need not use magic words in order to speak clearly on this point."). Rather, as with other efforts to divine legislative intent, courts must also examine, among other things, the "text and structure" of the particular statute to determine whether they clearly indicate Congress's intention to impose a limit on federal courts' subject-matter jurisdiction. *Reed Elsevier*, 559 U.S. at 162.

For instance, in *Arbaugh*, the Supreme Court held that Title VII's 15-employee numerosity requirement was not a jurisdictional limitation. 546 U.S. at 516. In so concluding, it observed that "the 15-employee threshold appears in a separate provision [from Title VII's jurisdiction-granting provision] that does not speak in jurisdictional terms or refer in any way to the jurisdiction of the district courts." *Id.* at 515 (internal quotation marks omitted). Likewise, in *Reed Elsevier*, the Court reasoned that the registration requirement in Section 411(a) of the Copyright Act, "like Title VII's numerosity requirement, is located in a provision separate from those granting federal courts subject-matter jurisdiction over those respective claims." 559 U.S. at 164. Similarly, in *Henderson*, the Supreme Court found it significant that Congress placed "the 120- day deadline for seeking [—5—] Veterans Court review" within "a subchapter entitled 'Procedure' " rather than the "subchapter entitled 'Organization and Jurisdiction,'" which the Court took as a signal that Congress "regarded the 120-day limit as a claim-processing rule." *Henderson*, 562 U.S. at 438-39.

Applying this rule to Section 70504(a), I find clear indication that Congress intended to impose limits on federal courts' jurisdiction. In other words, if alleged criminal conduct occurs on a vessel that is not subject to the jurisdiction of the United States, then any corresponding criminal charges are beyond federal courts' jurisdiction to entertain.

II. The MDLEA Limits Federal Courts' Jurisdiction

The strongest indication that Congress intended to limit federal courts' subject-matter jurisdiction is in the structure of the relevant statutory provision itself. *See Reed Elsevier*, 559 U.S. at 162. When it revised the MDLEA in 1996, Congress placed that

provision under a newly created section entitled "Jurisdiction and venue." 46 U.S.C. § 70504. By placing the relevant provision under that heading, Congress "provide[d] some indication of [its] intent." *See Henderson*, 562 U.S. at 440, 131 S.Ct. 1197; *see also Miranda*, 780 F.3d at 1196, 3 Adm. R. at 684 ("In other instances [—6—] in which Congress uses the term 'jurisdiction and venue,' the statute indisputably pertains to the jurisdiction of the courts.").[1] {—156—}

Moreover, that the MDLEA makes "[j]urisdictional issues ... preliminary questions of law to be determined solely by the trial judge," 46 U.S.C. § 70504(a), provides another strong indication that Congress meant to place a "threshold limitation on [the] statute's scope" that we should "count as jurisdictional." *Arbaugh*, 546 U.S. at 515. "The 'preliminary question' set out in § 70504(a) ... operates precisely in the nature of a condition on subject-matter jurisdiction: subject-matter jurisdiction presents a question of law for resolution by the court ...." *Miranda*, 780 F.3d at 1193, 3 Adm. R. at 681. Indeed, "courts have an obligation to determine whether subject-matter jurisdiction exists as a preliminary matter." *Id.*, 3 Adm. R. at 681 (internal quotation marks omitted); *see also Arbaugh*, 546 U.S. at 514.

Although this understanding of the reference to jurisdictional issues in Section 70504(a) is, admittedly, not without fault, the other possible [—7—] understandings of that term do not withstand scrutiny. Most significantly, if the concept of jurisdiction as it is employed in Section 70504(a) is meant to encompass the reach of the MDLEA—that is, the reach of Congress's legislative jurisdiction—rather than the federal courts' jurisdiction, it is necessarily transformed into a jurisdictional element of the offense. That

---

[1] The majority does not pause long on this point, concluding that Congress used the heading "Jurisdiction and venue" merely because the section "turns to issues for trial." I do not find such a facile explanation persuasive in light of the other instances in which Congress has used that heading in circumstances that clearly relate to a court's subject-matter jurisdiction. *E.g.*, 29 U.S.C. § 1370(c); 40 U.S.C. § 123(d).

interpretation is contrary to the clear statutory language and injects serious constitutional concerns into the statute.

Generally, when Congress is concerned with its own legislative power, it delineates the limits of that power in the definition of the crime it creates in what has become known as a "jurisdictional element." *See Gonzalez*, 311 F.3d at 446. That is because Congress "may enact only those criminal laws that are connected to one of its constitutionally enumerated powers." *Torres v. Lynch*, 136 S. Ct. 1619, 1624 (2016). "As a result, most federal offenses include, in addition to substantive elements, a jurisdictional one ...." *Id.* Jurisdictional elements include, for instance, requirements that a crime took place on "federal land," *see, e.g., United States v. Davis*, 726 F.3d 357, 362-67 (2d Cir. 2013), involved a "federally insured bank," *see, e.g., United States v. Schermerhorn*, 906 F.3d 66, 69-70 (2d Cir. 1990), or had an "effect on interstate commerce," *see, e.g., United States v. Farrish*, 122 F.3d [—8—] 146, 148-49 (2d Cir. 1997). So while substantive elements of a crime "relate to the harm or evil the law seeks to prevent," jurisdictional elements "tie[ ] the substantive offense ... to one of Congress's constitutional powers ..., thus spelling out the warrant for Congress to legislate." *Torres*, 136 S. Ct. at 1624 (internal quotation marks omitted). Nevertheless, proof of a jurisdictional element "is no different from proof of any other element of a federal crime." *Hugi v. United States*, 164 F.3d 378, 381 (7th Cir. 1999).

As noted above, the problem with treating the reference to jurisdiction in Section 70504(a) as an element of the offense is twofold. First, it contradicts the explicit language of the statute, which provides, "Jurisdiction of the United States with respect to a vessel subject to this chapter *is not an element of an offense.*" 46 U.S.C. § 70504(a) (emphasis added). I would adhere to that plain language.[2] [—9—] *See {–157-} United*

States v. Rowland, 826 F.3d 100, 108 (2d Cir. 2016) ("If the meaning is plain, the inquiry ends there.").

Second, and more significantly, even if we were content to disregard that clear instruction, construing the MDLEA's reference to jurisdiction as a jurisdictional element creates serious constitutional problems. That is because the Fifth and Sixth Amendments "require criminal convictions to rest upon a jury determination that the defendant is guilty of every element of the crime with which he is charged, beyond a reasonable doubt." *United States v. Gaudin*, 515 U.S. 506, 510 (1995); *see also Sullivan v. Louisiana*, 508 U.S. 275, 277-78 (1993) ("The prosecution bears the burden of proving all elements of the offense charged and must persuade the factfinder 'beyond a reasonable doubt' of the facts necessary to establish each of those elements." (citations omitted)). Jurisdictional elements are no different; they must be proven to a jury beyond a reasonable doubt.[3] *See, e.g., United States v. Parkes*, 497 F.3d 220, 229-30 (2d Cir. 2007). [—10—]

However, Section 70504(a) provides that "[j]urisdictional issues" are "to be determined

---

[2] Indeed, Congress appears to have added the disputed language in 1996 in response to the fact that the circuit courts of appeal that had explicitly decided the issue had treated the jurisdictional provisions of the MDLEA as creating a juris-

dictional element. *See United States v. Medina*, 90 F.3d 459, 464 (11th Cir. 1996); *United States v. Medjuck*, 48 F.3d 1107, 1110 (9th Cir. 1995); *United States v. Martinez-Hidalgo*, 993 F.2d 1052, 1057 (3d Cir. 1993); *United States v. Piedrahita-Santiago*, 931 F.2d 127, 129 (1st Cir. 1991); *cf.* H.R. Rep. 104-854, at 142 (1996) (Conf. Rep.), *as reprinted in* 1996 U.S.C.C.A.N. 4292, 4337 (noting that the 1996 enactment "establishes new law enforcement provisions which expand the Government's prosecutorial effectiveness in drug smuggling cases," including by [—9—] making "[j]urisdictional issues . . . issues of law to be decided by the trial judge, not issues of fact to be decided by the jury").

[3] Contrary to the majority's suggestion, the notion that jurisdictional elements must be proven to a jury beyond a reasonable doubt pre-dates Congress's 1996 revisions to the MDLEA, *see, e.g., United States v. DiSanto*, 86 F.3d 1238, 1246 (1st Cir. 1996); *United States v. Nukida*, 8 F.3d 665, 669-73 (9th Cir. 1993); *United States v. Medeiros*, 897 F.2d 13, 15 (1st Cir. 1990), though it was concededly not [—10—] universally accepted, *see, e.g., United States v. Calvi*, 830 F. Supp. 221, 222 n.1 (S.D.N.Y. 1993).

solely by the trial judge." 46 U.S.C. § 70504(a). If the term "[j]urisdictional issues" in fact refers to a jurisdictional element of the offense, taking those issues away from a jury's consideration almost certainly runs afoul of the above-described constitutional protections, which may well require striking Section 70504(a) as unconstitutional. I would construe the statute in a way that avoids this constitutional concern. *See Clark v. Martinez*, 543 U.S. 371, 380-82 (2005) (discussing the canon of constitutional avoidance, describing it as "a tool for choosing between competing plausible interpretations of a statutory text"); *United States v. Jin Fuey Moy*, 241 U.S. 394, 401 (1916) ("A statute must be construed, if fairly possible, so as to avoid not only the conclusion that it is unconstitutional, but also grave doubts upon that score.").

I also reject the notion that Congress instead permissibly created a "preliminary question[ ] of law," 46 U.S.C. § 70504(a), that is not a question of subject-matter jurisdiction or "an element of an offense," *id.*, but is still an **[—11—]** essential ingredient to a criminal conviction.[4] Indeed, a fact that {–158–} must be proven before a person can be convicted of a crime is precisely what an element of an offense *is. See Elements of Crime*, Black's Law Dictionary (11th ed. 2019) (defining the elements of a crime as "[t]he constituent parts of a crime ... that the prosecution must prove to sustain a conviction"). I thus regard the choice before us as a binary one. Congress's use of the term "vessel subject to the jurisdiction of the United States" in connection with criminal MDLEA violations that may be brought in federal court admits but two choices: the term "[j]urisdictional issues" either pertains to courts' subject-matter jurisdiction or refers to a jurisdictional element that must be submitted to a jury. The statutory text clearly precludes the latter. 46 U.S.C. § 70504(a).

Construing a statute to instead create a middle path that navigates between these two choices perilously dulls the line between "what conduct [a statute] prohibits," *Morrison v. Nat'l Austl. Bank Ltd.*, 561 U.S. 247, 254 (2010), and the "threshold limitation[s] on a statute's scope," *Arbaugh*, 546 U.S. at 515. To **[—12—]** dull that line is to venture down a dangerous path, the terminus of which is a rule that would allow criminal trials to become rife with "preliminary questions of law" on which a person's guilt hinges but which are decided solely by a judge. There is no room in our system of justice for such a rule. *Cf. Blakely v. Washington*, 542 U.S. 296, 305-08 (2004) (discussing the fundamental importance of the constitutional right to be tried by a jury).

Finally, as the District of Columbia Circuit has observed, "there are strong reasons"— grounded in international comity concerns rather than solicitude for defendants' rights— "to conclude that Congress intended the 'jurisdiction of the United States with respect to a vessel' to be non-waivable and non-forfeitable by a defendant and to be independently confirmed by courts regardless of whether it is raised." *Miranda*, 780 F.3d at 1193, 3 Adm. R. at 682. For instance, under the MDLEA, once the captain of a vessel makes a claim of nationality, the U.S. government must contact the nation whose protection is claimed and ask whether it asserts authority over the vessel. 46 U.S.C. §§ 70502(d)(2), (e). The statute also allows the government to exercise authority over "a vessel registered in a foreign nation if that nation has consented or waived objection to the enforcement of United States law by the United States." *Id.* § 70502(c)(1)(C). Similarly, the MDLEA **[—13—]** explicitly denies standing to defendants to raise objections based on international law but grants such standing to foreign nations.[5] *Id.* § 70505.

---

[4] The majority concludes that Defendants-Appellants' boat was not subject to the jurisdiction of the United States, and thus, their guilty pleas lacked a factual basis. In other words, "[t]he defendants could not be guilty of the offense unless the vessel on which they possessed drugs was 'subject to the jurisdiction of the United States.'"

[5] The majority claims to find support in 46 U.S.C. § 70505, which provides, inter alia, "A failure to comply with international law does not divest a court of jurisdiction and is not a defense to a proceeding under this chapter." This language, the majority concludes, "demonstrates that, when Congress wanted to speak of the court's jurisdiction, it did so directly and clearly." However, it is

With the understanding—rooted in the text of the MDLEA itself—that Congress was concerned about international relations, "it is eminently understandable why Congress would want the '[j]urisdiction of the United States with respect to a vessel' to be insulated from waiver or forfeiture by a defendant, {-159-} and would also want courts in every case—and at every level of review—to assure that the requirement is satisfied." *Miranda*, 780 F.3d at 1194, 3 Adm. R. at 682 (citation omitted).

The majority's most persuasive point is that 18 U.S.C. § 3231 grants district courts "original jurisdiction, exclusive of the courts of the States, of all offenses against the laws of the United States." 18 U.S.C. § 3231. Nevertheless, it does not necessarily follow that the MDLEA contains no limit on that seemingly blanket [—14—] grant of subject-matter jurisdiction. *Cf. Morales v. Trans World Airlines, Inc.*, 504 U.S. 374, 384 (1992) (observing that it is "a commonplace of statutory construction that the specific governs the general"). For instance, our Court has "jurisdiction of appeals from all final decisions of the district courts." 28 U.S.C. § 1291. However, when it comes to appeals from criminal sentences, our jurisdiction instead derives from 18 U.S.C. § 3742(a). *See United States v. Hotaling*, 634 F.3d 725, 728 (2d Cir. 2011). In contrast to Section 1291, "which grants broad appellate jurisdiction," Section 3742 "confers limited appellate jurisdiction." *United States v. Doe*, 93 F.3d 67, 67-68 (2d Cir. 1996).

The majority also observes that Title 46 of the United States Code repeatedly uses the phrase "vessel subject to the jurisdiction of the United States" in contexts that clearly do not refer to courts' subject-matter jurisdiction. That is true. However, I simply do not attach

---

at least equally compelling to read that language as demonstrating that the MDLEA *does* concern itself with the subject-matter jurisdiction of the federal courts—that is, absent Section 70505's express caveat, a failure to comply with international law might otherwise deprive federal courts of jurisdiction, the apparent blanket grant of subject-matter jurisdiction in 18 U.S.C. § 3231, discussed below, notwithstanding.

the same significance to that fact. There are numerous other instances where a particular phrase takes on jurisdictional significance in one statute but not others. Consider 18 U.S.C. § 3231, which grants federal district courts with "original jurisdiction, exclusive of the courts of the States, of all offenses against the laws of the United States." The phrase "offenses against the laws of the United States" carries obvious jurisdictional significance; [—15—] it defines the contours of Congress's grant of subject-matter jurisdiction to the federal courts. Yet a similar phrase is used throughout the United States Code in contexts that do not speak to courts' jurisdiction. *E.g.*, 18 U.S.C. § 3332(a) ("It shall be the duty of each such grand jury impaneled within any judicial district to inquire into *offenses against the criminal laws of the United States* alleged to have been committed within that district." (emphasis added)); 25 U.S.C. § 2802(c)(2) ("[T]he responsibilities of the Office of Justice Services in Indian country shall include ... in cooperation with appropriate Federal and tribal law enforcement agencies, the investigation of *offenses against criminal laws of the United States* ...." (emphasis added)). Similarly here, the fact that Congress used the phrase "vessel subject to the jurisdiction of the United States" throughout Title 46 does not "most persuasively demonstrate[]" much—aside from Congress's intent to import that phrase as a limitation on courts' subject-matter jurisdiction by using it in Section 70503 and referencing it in 70504(a).

CONCLUSION

I conclude with the following observation. The majority and I chart different courses but reach the same destination: the conclusion that Defendants-Appellants' convictions must be vacated and the indictment dismissed. Thus, in [—16—] this case, there is little practical consequence, if any, whether one understands the jurisdictional issues referenced in Section 70504(a) as referring to courts' subject-matter jurisdiction or only the reach of the MDLEA itself. I suspect the same will be true in most MDLEA cases.

Indeed, even if, as in this case, a criminal defendant pleads guilty, he or she can {–160–} still challenge on appeal whether the vessel on which he or she was apprehended was "subject to the jurisdiction of the United States." *See* 46 U.S.C. § 70503(e). If the vessel was not, as the majority concludes here, there will be no factual basis for the guilty plea, Fed. R. Crim. P. 11(b)(3), requiring that we vacate the judgment of conviction and dismiss the indictment. The only difference, as the majority observes, is that, if the issue is one of subject-matter jurisdiction, it can be raised for the first time on appeal. *E.g.*, *Yong Qin Luo v. Mikel*, 625 F.3d 772, 775 (2d Cir. 2010). But, even under the majority's interpretation, a district court is statutorily required in every case to determine "[j]urisdictional issues" as "preliminary questions." 46 U.S.C. § 70504(a). That determination, if not objected to, would be subject to the not-insurmountable requirements of plain error review should a defendant challenge it on appeal. *See* Fed. R. Crim. P. 52(b); *see also United States v. Garcia*, 587 F.3d 509, 515 (2d Cir. 2009). [—17—]

Because I agree with the disposition of this appeal, I concur in the judgment.

No. 17-2926

UNITED STATES

vs.

VAN DER END[1]

Appeal from the United States District Court for the Southern District of New York

Decided: November 14, 2019

Citation: 943 F.3d 98, 7 Adm. R. 123 (2d Cir. 2019).

Before **NEWMAN** and **POOLER**, Circuit Judges, and **COTE**, District Judge.[2]

[—3—] {–100–} POOLER, Circuit Judge:

Defendant-Appellant Stefan Van Der End appeals from a judgment of the United States District Court for the Southern District of New York (Richard J. Sullivan, J.), convicting him, after a plea of guilty, of engaging in drug trafficking activity, and {–101–} conspiring to do so, in violation of the Maritime Drug Law Enforcement Act (the "MDLEA"), 46 U.S.C. §§ 70501 et seq. Because Van Der End has waived his Confrontation Clause and jury trial right challenges to his conviction by pleading guilty, and because the Due Process Clause does not require a nexus between the United States and MDLEA violations that transpire on a vessel without nationality, we affirm the conviction.

BACKGROUND

I. Factual Background

Stefan Van Der End, a citizen of the Netherlands, was one of three foreign nationals on board the *Sunshine*, carrying more than 1,000 kilograms of cocaine from Grenada to Canada when it was stopped by the United States Coast Guard on May 23, 2016. Richard Dow, the master of the *Sunshine*, told the Coast Guard that the boat was registered in St. Vincent and the Grenadines ("SVG") and provided the vessel's registration information. The next morning, Coast Guard [—4—] officers boarded the boat—subject to the authority granted them by a treaty with SVG—and found more than 600 kilograms of cocaine below deck. The vessel began to sink after one of the crewmembers attempted to scuttle it, so the government was unable to recover all of the cocaine; however, the government subsequently learned that there were another 640 kilograms hidden on the *Sunshine*. Coast Guard officers detained Van Der End and the other members of the crew.

Coast Guard officers then inquired with SVG authorities about the *Sunshine*'s registration. SVG authorities disclosed that the *Sunshine*'s registration had expired on February 25, 2016, and that SVG did not consider the *Sunshine* to be subject to the SVG's jurisdiction. Van Der End and the other crewmembers who were on board the *Sunshine* were then brought to New York and subsequently arrested on June 3, 2016.

II. Procedural History

In an indictment filed on June 30, 2016, a grand jury indicted Van Der End and the other crewmembers with one count of manufacture and distribution, and possession with intent to manufacture and distribute, five kilograms and more of mixtures and substances containing a detectable amount of cocaine while aboard [—5—] a vessel subject to the jurisdiction of the United States in violation of the MDLEA, 46 U.S.C. §§ 70503(a)(1), 70504(b)(1), 70506(a); 18 U.S.C. §§ 3238 & 2; 21 U.S.C. § 960(b)(1)(B), and one count of conspiracy to engage in the above-described drug trafficking activity in violation of the MDLEA, 46 U.S.C. §§ 70503, 70506(b), 70504(b)(1); 18 U.S.C. § 3238; 21 U.S.C. § 960(b)(1)(B).[3]

On April 24, 2017, Van Der End filed a motion to dismiss the indictment for lack of

---

[1] The Clerk of the Court is directed to amend the caption as above.

[2] Denise Cote, United States District Court for the Southern District of New York, sitting by designation.

[3] The text of some of the MDLEA's provisions have since changed in ways that are immaterial for purposes of this appeal.

subject matter jurisdiction. He also challenged the constitutionality of the MDLEA as applied to him on due process grounds and raised a Sixth Amendment challenge to his prosecution based on the government's alleged forum shopping. The same day, the government filed a motion in limine in which it argued that the defendants should be precluded from arguing to a jury that the *Sunshine* was not subject to the jurisdiction of the United States.

At a May 4, 2017, hearing, the district court orally ruled in favor of the government {–102–} on all issues. The district court also ruled that it would permit the government to enter into evidence documents from the SVG government regarding ownership of the *Sunshine*. After the district court's rulings, Van Der [—6—] End stated that he intended to enter a guilty plea. The district court scheduled a plea hearing for that same afternoon, during which Van Der End pled guilty to both counts of the indictment without a plea agreement or otherwise reserving any rights to challenge his conviction on appeal. The district court later published an opinion and order formally announcing its ruling on subject matter jurisdiction, statelessness, and the other challenges to the indictment Van Der End and one of his codefendants had raised. *United States v. Suarez*, 16-cr-453 (RJS), 2017 WL 2417016, at *1 (S.D.N.Y. June 1, 2017).

On September 8, 2017, the district court sentenced Van Der End to 25 years of imprisonment and five years of supervised release, and entered judgment the same day. This appeal followed.

DISCUSSION

On appeal, Van Der End primarily argues that the district court erred by denying his motion to dismiss the indictment because (1) the government presented insufficient evidence that the *Sunshine* was a vessel subject to the jurisdiction of the United States, (2) the Fifth and Sixth Amendments required the district court to submit that question to a jury rather than decide it for itself, and (3) his conduct lacked the nexus to the United States that due process [—7—]

requires. In reviewing the denial of a motion to dismiss an indictment, we review the district court's findings of fact for clear error and its conclusions of law de novo. *United States v. Bout*, 731 F.3d 233, 237-38 (2d Cir. 2013).

I. Evidence of Statelessness

A. The MDLEA's Requirements

As presently drafted, the MDLEA makes it a federal crime to engage in certain specified drug trafficking activity "[w]hile on board a covered vessel." 46 U.S.C. § 70503(a). A "covered vessel" includes, as relevant here, "a vessel subject to the jurisdiction of the United States." *Id.* § 70503(e)(1). A vessel may be subject to the jurisdiction of the United States if, inter alia, it is "a vessel without nationality." *Id.* § 70502(c)(1)(A). For present purposes, a vessel is without nationality if "the master or individual in charge makes a claim of registry that is denied by the nation whose registry is claimed." *Id.* § 70502(d)(1)(A). A claim of registry may be made in one of three ways: "(1) possession on board the vessel and production of documents evidencing the vessel's nationality ...; (2) flying its nation's ensign or flag; or (3) a verbal claim of nationality or registry by the master or individual in charge of the vessel." *Id.* § 70502(e). "The response of a [—8—] foreign nation to a claim of registry ... is proved conclusively by certification of the Secretary of State or the Secretary's designee." *Id.* § 70502(d)(2).

"Jurisdiction of the United States with respect to a vessel subject to this chapter is not an element of an offense." *Id.* § 70504(a). Rather, "[j]urisdictional issues" that arise under MDLEA "are preliminary questions of law to be determined solely by the trial judge." *Id.* As we have recently explained, the function of MDLEA's jurisdictional language "is not to confer subject matter jurisdiction on the federal courts, but rather to specify the reach of the statute beyond the customary borders of the United States." *United States v. Prado*, 933 F.3d 121, 132, 7 Adm. R. 92, 98 (2d Cir. 2019). {–103–}

However, where there is no factual basis to find that the vessel on which a defendant was apprehended was a vessel subject to the jurisdiction of the United States, the defendant may still be permitted to raise that issue on appeal even after pleading guilty. That is because "a defective guilty plea will not necessarily be deemed to waive all objections to a conviction." *Id.* at 151, 7 Adm. R. at 114. And when the government's proof that a vessel was subject to the jurisdiction of the United States is lacking, a district court might run afoul of Federal Rule of Criminal Procedure 11(b)(1)(G), which "requires that the court must inform the defendant [—9—] of, and determine that the defendant understands, ... the nature of each charge to which the defendant is pleading," and 11(b)(3), which "requires the court to determine that there is a factual basis for the plea," rendering the defendant's guilty plea invalid. *Id.* at 152, 7 Adm. R. at 115 (alteration in original) (internal quotation marks omitted).

B. The *Sunshine* Was a Vessel Without Nationality

Van Der End argues that the government did not present sufficient evidence from which the district court could properly conclude that the *Sunshine* was a vessel without nationality. He argues that the district court's reliance on the State Department certification violated the Confrontation Clause because it amounted to a testimonial statement by a witness whom Van Der End did not have an opportunity to confront. This argument is without merit. Van Der End's guilty plea waived his right to raise that Sixth Amendment challenge to the evidence on which the government's prosecution relied. *Boykin v. Alabama*, 395 U.S. 238, 243 (1969) (observing that "the right to confront one's accusers" is among the "federal constitutional rights [that] are involved in a waiver that takes place when a plea of guilty is entered"); *United States v. Dhinsa*, 243 F.3d 635, 651 (2d Cir. 2001) ("[A] defendant who enters a plea of guilty waives his rights under [—10—] the Confrontation Clause."); *see also Class v. United States*, 138 S. Ct. 798, 803 (2018) (differentiating claims that call into question "the very power of the State to prosecute the

defendant" from constitutional claims "related to events (say, grand jury proceedings) that had occurred prior to the entry of the guilty plea" (internal quotation marks omitted)).

Moreover, we are satisfied that the evidence the government presented of the *Sunshine*'s statelessness sufficed. In *Prado*, we found problematic the "Coast Guard boarding party's inattention" to the MDLEA's procedures for establishing a vessel's statelessness. 933 F.3d at 130, 7 Adm. R. at 96. Most significantly, the government there relied on the fact that the master of the vessel did not make a verbal claim of nationality or registry; however, the government adduced no evidence that "an officer of the United States authorized to enforce applicable provisions of United States law," 46 U.S.C. § 70502(d)(2), had made such a request. *Id.* at 130 & n.5, 7 Adm. R. at 96 & n.5. And, because the Coast Guard had destroyed the vessel, "it became virtually impossible for the government to demonstrate to the court in the statutorily mandated preliminary hearing that the vessel was subject to the jurisdiction of the United States and therefore that the MDLEA applied." *Id.* at 132, 7 Adm. R. at 97. Further, at the defendants' plea allocution, the district court made "no reference either to the [—11—] requirement that the vessel have been subject to the jurisdiction of the United States or to the crucial issue of its statelessness," nor did the defendants "demonstrate awareness ... of the crucial significance of statelessness." *Id.* at 152-53, 7 Adm. R. at 115. Thus, neither through the Government's evidence nor {–104–} the defendants themselves, was there any "factual basis for the plea." *Id.* at 153, 7 Adm. R. at 116.

Here, however, the Coast Guard's investigation suffered none of the same defects. As explained above, Dow, the master of the *Sunshine*, claimed that the vessel was registered in SVG and provided the Coast Guard with SVG registration information. That sufficed to make a claim of registry. *See* 46 U.S.C. §§ 70502(e)(1), (e)(3). The Coast Guard then contacted SVG officials who "refuted the vessel's claimed nationality." App'x at 55. That established that the vessel was without nationality. *See* 46 U.S.C.

§ 70502(d)(1)(A). Finally, the government produced a certification from the United States Department of State that "proved conclusively" the response of the SVG government. *See id.* § 70502(d)(2).

In short, a MDLEA defendant does not automatically waive his or her ability to challenge the sufficiency of the government's evidence regarding whether a vessel is subject to the jurisdiction of the United States by pleading guilty. *See Prado*, 933 F.3d at 151-52, 7 Adm. R. at 114. However, that does not mean that a MDLEA [—12—] defendant who enters an unconditional guilty plea may still challenge all aspects of the government's evidence. We are satisfied here that there was a factual basis for Van Der End's guilty plea, such that he has waived his right to challenge the district court's determination that the vessel was subject to the jurisdiction of the United States.

II. Jury Trial Rights

Van Der End further argues that the district court was required to submit to a jury the question of whether the *Sunshine* was subject to the jurisdiction of the United States. This argument fails for much the same reason his Confrontation Clause argument fails. By pleading guilty, Van Der End waived his right to a jury trial. *McMann v. Richardson*, 397 U.S. 759, 766 (1970); *see also Class*, 138 S. Ct. at 804-05.

To be clear, we recently recognized that, if the issue were properly presented for appellate review, Section "70504(a)'s provision that the jurisdiction of the United States be determined *solely* by the trial judge" might be stricken as violative of a criminal defendant's right to a jury trial. *Prado*, 933 F.3d at 139 n.9, 7 Adm. R. at 103 n.9; *see also id.* at 157, 7 Adm. R. at 120 (Pooler, J., concurring in the judgment). We thus cautioned that district courts would be well advised "to submit the issue of jurisdiction over the [—13—] vessel to the jury notwithstanding the statutory word 'solely'"—"after making the preliminary determination required by § 70504(a) so that trial may proceed." *Id.* at 139 n.9, 7 Adm. R. at 103 n.9. But here, the district court had no

opportunity to submit the question to a jury because Van Der End pled guilty after the district court made the preliminary determination MDLEA requires.

III. Due Process

Finally, Van Der End argues that his prosecution violated the Due Process Clause because there was no nexus between the offense conduct and the United States. The government contends that no nexus is required because the *Sunshine* was a stateless vessel and, even if a nexus were required, there was a sufficient nexus here to satisfy due process.

As a threshold matter, we hold that Van Der End did not waive this challenge to his prosecution by pleading guilty. We have previously held that a criminal defendant who pleads guilty waives the argument "that the indictment to which he [or she] pled guilty failed to adequately allege a nexus between his [or her] alleged conduct and the United States, as required by the Due Process Clause of the Fifth Amendment before a criminal statute may apply extraterritorially." {—105—} *United States v. Yousef*, 750 F.3d 254, 256, 262 (2d Cir. 2014). [—14—] However, the Supreme Court has since clarified that a guilty plea does not "by itself bar[] a federal criminal defendant from challenging the constitutionality of the statute of conviction on direct appeal." *Class*, 138 S. Ct. at 803. Although criminal defendants cannot "contradict the terms of the indictment" to which they pled guilty "or written plea agreement[s]" pursuant to which they pled guilty, defendants may still raise constitutional challenges to the statute of conviction that "can be resolved without any need to venture beyond the record." *Id.* at 804 (internal quotation marks omitted). In other words, criminal defendants who have pled guilty may still "challenge the Government's power to criminalize [their] (admitted) conduct," "thereby call[ing] into question the Government's power to constitutionally prosecute" them. *Id.* at 805. Here, Van Der End raises precisely such a challenge. Whether the Due Process Clause requires MDLEA crimes committed on board a stateless vessel to have a nexus to the United States is a purely legal question on which the government's constitutional power to prosecute Van Der End turns.

Nevertheless, Van Der End's challenge fails on the merits. We have previously held that the MDLEA's predecessor statute did not, as a statutory matter, require a nexus. *United States v. Pinto-Mejia*, 720 F.2d 248, 261 (2d Cir. [—15—] 1983), *modified in part on denial of reh'g*, 728 F.2d 142 (2d Cir. 1984); *United States v. Henriquez*, 731 F.2d 131, 134 (2d Cir. 1984). We now hold that due process does not require that there be a nexus between the United States and MDLEA violations that transpire on a vessel without nationality.[4] To begin with, the MDLEA indisputably has extraterritorial application. 46 U.S.C. § 70503(b) ("Subsection (a) [which proscribes specified drug trafficking activity] applies even though the act is committed outside the territorial jurisdiction of the United States."). And "[w]here Congress expressly intends for a statute to apply extraterritorially, ... the burden is a heavy one for a defendant seeking to show that extraterritorial application of the statute violates due process." *United States v. Epskamp*, 832 F.3d 154, 168 (2d Cir. 2016) (internal quotation marks omitted).

Van Der End cannot meet that burden. Although we have adopted a "'sufficient nexus' test for determining whether the extraterritorial application of federal criminal law comported with constitutional due process," *id.*, MDLEA prosecutions involving stateless vessels do not present the same concerns that [—16—] are present in the extraterritorial application of typical criminal statutes. That is because stateless "vessels are international pariahs" that "subject themselves to the jurisdiction of all nations *solely* as a consequence of the vessel's status as stateless." *United States v. Caicedo*, 47 F.3d 370, 372 (9th Cir. 1995) (internal quotation marks omitted). "Because stateless vessels do not fall within the veil of another sovereign's territorial protection, all nations can treat

them as their own territory and subject them to their laws." *Id.* at 373. Thus, when a vessel is subject to the jurisdiction of another nation, a person trafficking drugs on board "would have a legitimate expectation that because he has subjected himself to the laws of one nation, other nations will not be entitled to exercise jurisdiction without some nexus." *Id.* at 372. The same is not {–106–} true when "a defendant attempts to avoid the law of *all* nations by travelling on a stateless vessel." *Id.* at 372-73.

The purpose of requiring a sufficient nexus with the United States is to prevent extraterritorial application of U.S. criminal laws from being "arbitrary or fundamentally unfair." *See Epskamp*, 832 F.3d at 168 (internal quotation marks omitted); *see also United States v. Ballestas*, 795 F.3d 138, 148, 3 Adm. R. 698, 703 (D.C. Cir. 2015) (same). That "ultimate question" of arbitrariness or unfairness, *Ballestas*, 795 F.3d at 148, 3 Adm. R. at 703 (internal quotation marks omitted), in turn, hinges in part on the notion of [—17—] "fair warning." *Epskamp*, 832 F.3d at 169. "The idea of fair warning is that no [person] shall be held criminally responsible for conduct which he [or she] could not reasonably understand to be proscribed." *United States v. Al Kassar*, 660 F.3d 108, 119 (2d Cir. 2011) (internal quotation marks omitted). "Fair warning does not require that the defendants understand that they could be subject to criminal prosecution *in the United States* so long as they would reasonably understand that their conduct was criminal and would subject them to prosecution somewhere." *Id.*

In other words, no nexus is required for the government to bring MDLEA prosecutions against persons who are trafficking drugs on board stateless vessels because such prosecutions are not arbitrary, since any nation may exercise jurisdiction over stateless vessels, and they are not unfair, since persons who traffic drugs may be charged with knowledge that such activity is illegal and may be prosecuted somewhere. On that score, we have little trouble concluding that those who participate in international drug trafficking activity are aware that such

---

[4] We need not, and do not, decide what the Due Process Clause may require before persons who are not on board a vessel without nationality may be prosecuted for violating the MDLEA.

conduct is illegal. *See* 46 U.S.C. § 70501 (congressional findings that "trafficking in controlled substances aboard vessels is a serious international [—18—] problem [and] is universally condemned"). In this context, that is all due process requires.

CONCLUSION

We have considered the remainder of Van Der End's arguments and find them to be without merit. For the foregoing reasons, we AFFIRM the judgment of the district court.

United States Court of Appeals
for the Second Circuit

No. 17-1956

UNITED STATES

vs.

CALDERON[1]

Appeal from the United States District Court for the
District of Connecticut

Decided: December 3, 2019

Citation: 944 F.3d 72, 7 Adm. R. 129 (2d Cir. 2019).

Before **KEARSE, POOLER,** and **LIVINGSTON,** Circuit
Judges.

[—3—] {–77–} **LIVINGSTON,** Circuit Judge:

Defendants-Appellants Brett C. Lillemoe
("Lillemoe") and Pablo Calderon
("Calderon") (together, "Defendants")
appeal {–78–} from their convictions for
conspiracy to commit wire and bank fraud, 18
U.S.C. § 1349, and wire fraud, 18 U.S.C.
§ 1343, following a jury trial in the United
States District Court for the District of
Connecticut (Hall, *J.*). The Defendants'
convictions arose from their involvement in a
scheme to defraud two financial institutions—
Deutsche Bank and CoBank—in connection
with an export guarantee program
administered by the United States Department of Agriculture ("USDA"). The Defendants falsified shipping documents and
presented these documents to the banks,
thereby facilitating the release of millions of
dollars in USDA-guaranteed loans to foreign
banks.

The Defendants argue that the
Government failed to produce sufficient
evidence at trial to support their convictions.
Specifically, they argue that the Government
failed to demonstrate that, in altering these
shipping documents, the [—4—] Defendants
made material misrepresentations that
deprived the banks of economically valuable
information, as required to support a
conviction for wire or bank fraud, or

conspiracy to commit those offenses. They also
argue that the district court erred in giving
the jury a "no ultimate harm" instruction, *see
infra* Part II.A, plainly erred in charging the
jury on the elements of bank fraud, 18 U.S.C.
§ 1344(2), and abused its discretion in giving
the jury a modified *Allen* charge, *see infra*
Part III. Finally, they assert that the district
court abused its discretion in ordering the
Defendants to pay over $18 million in
restitution pursuant to the Mandatory
Victims Restitution Act of 1996 ("MVRA"), 18
U.S.C. § 3663A.

We conclude that there was sufficient
evidence presented at trial to support the
jury's conclusion that the Defendants violated
the wire fraud and conspiracy statutes. We
also hold that the district court did not err in
giving the jury a "no ultimate harm"
instruction, did not plainly err in charging the
jury on the elements of bank fraud, and did
not abuse its discretion in giving a modified
Allen charge to the jury. Finally, however, we
conclude that the district court abused its
discretion in holding that the USDA was
entitled to a restitution amount of $18,501,353
under the MVRA because the Defendants did
not proximately cause financial losses
equating to that amount. Accordingly, for the
reasons given [—5—] herein, we reverse the
orders of restitution, vacate so much of the
judgments as order restitution, and remand
for the entry of amended judgments without
such orders.

BACKGROUND

I. Factual Background[2]

International business transactions involving the sale of physical goods are presently
carried out by use of unique documents and
contracts that serve to mitigate risk among
the geographically disparate parties. Such
transactions remain highly dependent upon
the compilation and presentation of certain
physical documents at different stages in the
sales process. Indeed, so crucial are the
documents underlying these sales that

---

[1] The Clerk of Court is respectfully directed to
amend the caption as set forth above.

[2] The factual background presented here is
derived from the parties' submissions and the
uncontroverted evidence presented at trial.

"international financial transactions" have long been said to "rest upon the accuracy of documents rather than on the condition of the goods they represent." *Banco Espanol de Credito v. State St. Bank & Tr. Co.*, 385 F.2d 230, 234 (1st Cir. 1967). The Defendants falsified bills of lading, one such category of shipping documents, so as to render {–79–} them compliant with contractual and regulatory requirements before their presentation to two U.S.- [—6—] based financial institutions.

A. Letters of Credit in International Sales

Understanding the Defendants' scheme requires a basic comprehension of the use of letters of credit in international sales, in this case sales of agricultural goods. "Originally devised to function in international trade, a letter of credit reduce[s] the risk of non-payment in cases where credit [is] extended to strangers in distant places." *Mago Int'l v. LHB AG*, 833 F.3d 270, 272, 4 Adm. R. 106, 107 (2d Cir. 2016) (internal quotation marks and citation omitted). As relevant here, the process begins with the contract for the sale of goods negotiated between a domestic exporter and a foreign importer. A typical contract at issue in this prosecution would be one for the sale of soybeans between an American exporter and a Russian importer.

To avoid the risk of nonpayment by the foreign importer, the American exporter bargains for and includes in the contract a term that requires payment by a confirmed and irrevocable letter of credit. The foreign importer then applies to an "issuing bank" (usually a foreign bank) to receive that letter of credit. The foreign-based bank then "issues" the letter of credit in favor of the American exporter, also referred to as the "beneficiary." The letter of credit itself constitutes an "irrevocable promise to pay the []beneficiary when the latter [—7—] presents certain documents . . . that conform with the terms of the credit." *Alaska Textile Co. v. Chase Manhattan Bank, N.A.*, 982 F.2d 813, 815 (2d Cir. 1992). At the same time, the domestic exporter often works with a domestic bank (also referred to as the "confirming" bank) and

assigns its right to payment on the letter of credit to that domestic bank in exchange for *immediate* payment of the contract price. The payment on the part of the confirming bank to the beneficiary triggers the issuing bank's obligation to reimburse the confirming bank. Thus, the domestic exporter receives immediate payment for the sale from the domestic bank, and the domestic bank is repaid over time and with interest by the foreign bank. The letter of credit thereby mitigates risk by assigning the rights and obligations of the original contract to financial institutions rather than individual importers and exporters. *Alaska Textile*, 982 F.2d at 815.

To obtain immediate payment of the contract price upon assigning its right to payment to a domestic bank, an exporter must compile a complete set of documents and present them to that confirming bank. Among the documents necessary to cause a bank to release funds in conformity with a letter of credit is the final contract of relevance here, the "bill of lading." The bill of lading is a contract between either the exporter or the importer and an international carrier [—8—] of goods, obligating the carrier to transport the goods to the importer's location or some other distant place. A bill of lading "records that a carrier has received goods from the party that wishes to ship them, states the terms of carriage, and serves as evidence of the contract for carriage." *Norfolk S. Ry. Co. v. James N. Kirby, Pty Ltd.*, 543 U.S. 14, 18–19 (2004).[3] The Defendants' presentation of {–80–} documents, including bills of lading, to

---

[3] According to the Defendants' expert, negotiable bills of lading allow for the flexibility of selling goods while they are in transit; non-negotiable bills do not. Regardless of whether a bill of lading is negotiable or non-negotiable, only an original bill of lading serves as a document of title; a copy of a bill of lading functions primarily as a receipt. Conversely, the Government's expert explained at trial that bills of lading are issued in sets that typically consist of three originals and any number of copies, which are referred to as "copies non-negotiable." In any event, the experts agree that a "copy non-negotiable" bill meaningfully differs from either a "negotiable" or "original" bill, and we need not decide which expert is correct in order to resolve the Defendants' sufficiency of the evidence challenge.

confirming banks for inspection in order to induce the banks to honor their obligations under various letters of credit provided the basis for the prosecutions here.

When a confirming bank examines documents submitted to it for the purpose of obtaining payment on a letter of credit, the confirming bank has two duties: (1) to determine whether these documents conform to the terms of the letter of credit; and (2) to respond if it finds any discrepancies. J.A. 893. The confirming bank never sees the goods at issue, only the documents (including the [—9—] bill of lading). J.A. 391. Because of this, it inspects the documents *rigorously* to determine that they comply *exactly* with the requirements of the letter of credit—for the documents are its only protection. *Id.*

Indeed, under the law of the majority of jurisdictions (including this one) if the documents provided by the seller to the confirming bank *did not* "strictly" comply with the requirements of the letter of credit, the issuing bank is entitled to refuse to honor the letter of credit, and the confirming bank is therefore unable to recover the money "assigned" to it by the seller. *See Voest-Alpine Int'l Corp. v. Chase Manhattan Bank, N.A.*, 707 F.2d 680, 683–85 (2d Cir. 1983); *see also Mago Int'l*, 833 F.3d at 272, 4 Adm. R. at 107 (noting that the "absolute duty" to honor the letter of credit "does not arise unless the terms of the letter have been complied with strictly" (internal quotation marks and citation omitted)). "This rule [of strict compliance] finds justification in the bank's role in the transaction being ministerial, and to require it to determine the substantiality of discrepancies would be inconsistent with its function." *Alaska Textile*, 982 F.2d at 816. If the documents were nonconforming but honored, an issuing bank could sue a confirming bank for "wrongful honor." *See, e.g., Bank of Cochin, Ltd. v. Mfrs. Hanover Tr. Co.*, 808 F.2d 209 (2d Cir. 1986) (dismissing on the ground of estoppel only because the issuing bank did not [—10—] comply with the requirements of the International Chamber of Commerce's Uniform Customs and Practice for Documentary Credits ("UCP"), Article 8,

calling for timely notice of discrepancies in the documents).

As the Defendants themselves note, in a letter of credit transaction "'[b]anks deal with documents and not with goods, services or performances to which the documents may relate.'" Br. Def.-Appellant Lillemoe at 5 (quoting Int'l Chamber of Commerce, *ICC Uniform Customs and Practice for Documentary Credits* art. 5 (2007)); *see also* S.A. 98. In sum, "because the credit engagement is concerned only with documents, . . . [t]here is no room for documents which are almost the same, or which will do just as well." *Alaska Textile*, 982 F.2d at 816 (internal quotation marks and citation omitted).

B. The GSM-102 Program and the Defendants' "Structured" Transactions

The GSM-102 program—which is administered by USDA's Foreign Agricultural Service on behalf of the Commodity Credit Corporation ("CCC"), the USDA entity that issues the credit guarantees—provides an incentive for United States banks {–81–} to participate in letters of credit export transactions with developing nations. As already made clear, the seller in such a transaction enjoys immediate payment for the sale, but the domestic bank must accept the risk that a foreign bank will default on its payment obligations, and in circumstances in which [—11—] redress may be difficult, if not impossible, to obtain. To encourage U.S.-based banks nevertheless to participate in such transactions, the CCC, through the GSM-102 program, *guarantees* the foreign bank's repayment to the domestic bank, generally covering ninety-eight percent of the foreign bank's obligation under the letter of credit. Every fiscal year, the USDA makes $5.5 billion available under the GSM-102 program.

The Defendants were not the exporters of agricultural goods, but instead participated in the GSM-102 program as financial intermediaries, creating "structured" or "third party" transactions. Essentially, the Defendants would pay a fee to "rent" or "purchase" program-eligible "trade flows," *i.e.*, the actual shipments of goods guaranteed by the GSM-102 program, from physical exporters and importers. Having secured the requisite "trade flow," the Defendants would arrange for letters of credit between foreign and domestic banks backed by the USDA guarantee. In exchange, they received fees from the foreign banks. In orchestrating these GSM-102 transactions, the Defendants were also responsible for the presentation of complying documents to the confirming (in this case the domestic) banks. *See* J.A. 1020 (Testimony of Lillemoe stating "[It's] not exactly a simple process . . . So my role is to put together a lot of different pieces and make [—12—] the transaction work . . . we describe it as sort of lining up the sun, the moon and the stars to align everything and put it all together").

C. Altering Bills of Lading and the "Cool Express" Transaction

Participating in the GSM-102 program as a financial intermediary is not itself illegal. The Defendants were convicted of wire fraud and conspiracy to commit wire and bank fraud for falsifying bills of lading before presenting them to two banks, Deutsche Bank and CoBank, in order to make the documents facially compliant with the terms of the relevant letters of credit and the requirements of the GSM-102 program. According to the evidence presented by the Government at trial, the Defendants applied for the GSM-102 program guarantees before acquiring the requisite "trade flow." They would then purchase shipping documents and arrange for letters of credit between foreign and domestic banks backed by this USDA guarantee. If the purchased documents failed to comply with the USDA's requirements as well as those provided for in the relevant letters of credit, the Defendants would simply falsify the documents to *make* them compliant. Of central importance are two types of alterations, which were explored at length in the trial described below: (1) the Defendants' redaction of the phrase "copy non-negotiable" and the stamping of the word "original" onto bills of lading; and (2) the Defendants' changing of certain bills of ladings' "on-board" [—13—] dates.

Finally, all of the counts of wire fraud on which the Defendants were convicted involved conduct relating to a GSM-102 transaction between CoBank and the International Industrial Bank located in Russia ("IIB"). The letter of credit for that transaction was issued by IIB, and the goods were shipped on a vessel called the "Cool Express." J.A. 1074, 1077. To facilitate this "Cool Express" transaction, Lillemoe "whited out" the word "copy non-negotiable" on some of the bills of lading {—82—} and placed an "original" stamp on them. J.A. 1092–94. These modified documents were forwarded to Calderon for his review before their submission to CoBank. J.A. 1093–94. Following the global financial crisis in 2007, IIB defaulted on its $6,000,000 in obligations to CoBank under the letter of credit. The USDA reimbursed the full amount available under the guarantee (ninety-eight percent of the loan value).[4]

II. Procedural History

On February 20, 2015, a grand jury returned a twenty-three-count indictment against Lillemoe, Calderon, and their associate, Sarah Zirbes. The Indictment charged Lillemoe with one count of conspiracy to commit bank fraud [—14—] and wire fraud, nineteen counts of wire fraud, one count of bank fraud, and one count of money laundering. It charged Calderon with one count of conspiracy to commit wire fraud and bank fraud, nineteen counts of wire fraud, one count of bank fraud, one count of money laundering, and one count of making a false statement. The Indictment alleged, in part, that Lillemoe and Calderon conspired to commit bank fraud and wire fraud by materially altering shipping documents.

A. The Trial

At trial, the Government offered a variety of evidence to demonstrate that the Defendants applied for guarantees under the GSM-102 program, purchased "trade flows" from third-parties that would *not* have been compliant with the terms of the program,

---

[4] The Defendants paid CoBank an upfront fee of three percent.

arranged letters of credit between foreign and domestic banks, falsified bills of lading, and then presented those altered documents to Deutsche Bank and CoBank, causing the banks to disburse funds to a U.S. exporter according to the terms of letters of credit associated with ten GSM-102 transactions. The Government introduced, *inter alia*, (a) the GSM–102 program files that contained the documents that were submitted to the American banks along with (b) the unaltered bills of lading that were provided to Lillemoe and [—15—] Calderon and the subsequently altered versions. The Government also introduced the testimony of CoBank representative Holly Womack, Deutsche Bank representative Rudolph Effing, USDA official John Doster, and Federal Bureau of Investigation Special Agent Steven West. The Government and the Defense introduced competing experts on letters of credit transactions, and Lillemoe testified in his own defense.[5] Because the significance of the Defendants' alterations of the bills of lading is the central issue on this appeal, we catalogue the evidence offered on this question below.

1. Stamping

The Government submitted evidence that the Defendants falsified bills of lading by redacting the word "copy non-negotiable" or "certified true copy" (usually via white out) and stamping the word "original" onto a number of them. The Defendants do not dispute that they modified the bills of lading in question nor that the respective letters of credit governing these altered bills of lading required presentation of a "copy of original on board . . . bill(s) of lading." J.A. 1851. Moreover, the Government presented evidence at trial that in order to submit a claim of loss to the GSM-102 program, a bank would need to submit a [—16—] *copy of an original* bill of lading. J.A. 1791. The Government also submitted evidence as to the Defendants' knowledge of this requirement. *See, e.g.* {–83–} J.A. 3617–18 (Email from Lillemoe stating "just checked with the bank financing the GSM deal. They need the copy of the [bill of lading] to state 'Original' in order to accept it"). CoBank representative Womack and Deutsche Bank representative Effing testified respectively at the Defendants' trial that they would not have accepted the Defendants' bills of lading (and therefore would not have released funds on the transactions) had they known that the Defendants had stamped the word "original" onto "copy non-negotiable" bills of lading. That is, if their banks "didn't have a copy of an original" they "wouldn't have paid the funds." J.A. 458. At trial, however, the Defense attempted to characterize the modifications to the bills of lading as insignificant, trivial changes that could not have affected the confirming banks' decisions as to whether to honor the letters of credit. Lillemoe testified that he stamped the word "original" in blue ink on the bills of lading in order to make it "easier for everybody." J.A. 1010. The Government and Defense also offered competing expert testimony as to the significance of the stamping activity.

2. Date Changes

The GSM-102 program guarantees also had restrictions limiting them to [—17—] shipments that occurred within specific date ranges. The Government introduced substantial evidence at trial demonstrating that Lillemoe and Calderon changed the "on-board" notation printed on three bills of lading associated with two GSM-102 transactions to state October 6, 2008, instead of October 5, 2008. J.A. 1057. The Defendants' alterations placed the shipments within an acceptable range. *See* 7 C.F.R. §§ 1493.20(d), 1493.60(f) (2012) (GSM-102 regulations stating that "date[s] of export prior to the date" of the guarantee application "are ineligible for . . . guarantee coverage" and defining a "date of export" as a bill of lading's "on board date"). Thus, the Government argued at trial that the Defendants altered dates on bills of lading to ensure each underlying transaction's eligibility for a GSM-102 guarantee. The parties contest neither that the relevant goods were aboard the ships on October 6th, nor that they were actually *shipped* on October 5th.

---

[5] The Defendants also introduced various character witnesses.

According to the Defense experts and Lillemoe, the "on-board" date on a bill of lading has a functional significance and can fall on *any date* that the goods are "on board" the ship. The Government presented a great deal of evidence, however, in support of its claim that the "on-board" date can *only* represent the date the goods are *actually* shipped, and that this understanding was shared by all **[—18—]** parties involved. For example, the Government's expert, Professor James Byrne, testified at trial:

> A. [The on-board date] is deemed to indicate the date that the goods are shipped. The date of shipment is extremely important in letter of credit practice. It is important to banks. It is important to applicants in most cases. And so the date which is given as the on board or loaded on board date is deemed to be the date of shipment or shipping. Shipping date. . . .
>
> Q. Can that be a range of dates?
>
> A. No. It is the date they are loaded on board.

J.A. 1246. USDA Official Doster, who was responsible for ensuring that "registrations were properly issued for the GSM-102 program," J.A. 522, also testified to that effect, as well as to that date's importance with regard to the USDA guarantee. J.A. 455, 526 ("Q: [D]oes the program ever guarantee [with respect to] shipments before the on board date? A: No"); *see also* J.A. 396 (defining "registration" as a record {–84–} reflecting "that the CCC has shipped that guarantee and received the fee and then they recorded that guarantee in their books as . . . a guarantor obligation on behalf of the CCC").[6] **[—19—]**

B. The Jury Verdict and Post-Trial Motions

On November 3, 2016, after hearing eighteen days of evidence, the jury began its deliberations. The jury deliberated for about a week, before stating that it had "concluded" deliberations, but informing the court that it was "deadlocked" on some counts. J.A. 1352. The court decided to give a modified *Allen* charge, which encouraged the jury to continue deliberating (discussed, *infra* Part III). After receiving the *Allen* charge, the jury returned a verdict of guilty for Lillemoe on Count One of conspiracy and Counts Two through Six of wire fraud, and it returned a verdict of guilty for Calderon on Count One of conspiracy and Count Six of wire fraud.[7] The Defendants were acquitted on the other counts of wire fraud, bank fraud, money laundering, and false statements. Following the guilty verdict, the district court sentenced Lillemoe to fifteen months' imprisonment to be followed by three years of supervised release, and it sentenced Calderon to five months' imprisonment. The Court also ordered forfeiture in the amount of $1,543,287.60 from Lillemoe and $63,509.97 from Calderon.

Lillemoe and Calderon each filed a motion for a judgment of acquittal **[—20—]** pursuant to Rule 29 of the Federal Rules of Criminal Procedure and a motion for a new trial pursuant to Rule 33. In an order dated March 16, 2017, the district court denied both motions. *United States v. Lillemoe*, 242 F. Supp. 3d 109, 115 (D. Conn. 2017). On September 11, 2017, the district court entered separate restitution orders as to both Defendants. *United States v. Lillemoe*, No. 15-CR-25 (JCH), 2017 WL 3977921, at *1 (D. Conn. Sept. 11, 2017). The district court held that the USDA was entitled to an order of restitution of $18,501,353 after reimbursing the banks in the GSM-102 program for various transactions with which the Defendants were involved. *Id*. The district court also ordered the Defendants to pay CoBank $305,743.33. *Id*. at *2. Each defendant filed timely notices of appeal from

---

[6] The Government also presented evidence at trial that the Defendants shaded blank "consignee" fields (which designate the receiving party of the goods) on six bills of lading, allegedly to make it less "obvious" that the consignee fields had been whited-out. J.A. 1018. The Defense offered evidence that the fields were whited-out to protect the confidentiality of the consignee. *See* J.A. 887–88. The Defendants were acquitted of all **[—19—]** of

the substantive counts of wire fraud that were connected to this "shading" activity.

[7] The jury acquitted Zirbes on all counts.

the judgment and the restitution order entered against him.

DISCUSSION

The Defendants raise a variety of challenges to their respective convictions and the ensuing restitution orders imposed by the district court. Many of these challenges relate to the Defendants' central contention that their alterations of the bills of lading were not and could not have been fraudulent. Ultimately, we reject that central contention. We do conclude, however, that the district court abused its discretion in fashioning the restitution orders at issue here. [—21—]

I.

The Defendants first challenge the sufficiency of the evidence underlying their convictions for wire fraud and conspiracy {–85–} to commit wire and bank fraud. The Defendants concede that they modified bills of lading in connection with various international transactions guaranteed by the GSM-102 program, but they argue that the Government failed to produce sufficient evidence at trial to support the jury's determination that this conduct satisfied the elements of wire or bank fraud (or conspiracy to commit the same). We disagree and find no reason to upset the jury's determination on this question.

We note at the outset that a defendant who challenges the sufficiency of the evidence to support his conviction "faces an uphill battle, and bears a very heavy burden." *United States v. Mi Sun Cho*, 713 F.3d 716, 720 (2d Cir. 2013) (internal quotation marks and citation omitted). In considering such a challenge, "[w]e must view the evidence in the light most favorable to the government, crediting every inference that could have been drawn in the government's favor, and deferring to the jury's assessment of witness credibility." *United States v. Baker*, 899 F.3d 123, 129 (2d Cir. 2018) (internal quotation marks and brackets omitted). "Although sufficiency review is *de novo*, we will uphold the judgment of [—22—] conviction if *any* rational trier of fact could have found the essential elements of the crime

beyond a reasonable doubt." *United States v. Martoma*, 894 F.3d 64, 72 (2d Cir. 2017) (internal quotation marks and brackets omitted).

The essential elements of wire fraud are "(1) a scheme to defraud, (2) money or property as the object of the scheme, and (3) use of . . . wires to further the scheme." *Fountain v. United States*, 357 F.3d 250, 255 (2d Cir. 2004) (internal quotation marks and brackets omitted). Similarly, the federal bank fraud statute criminalizes the "'knowing execution' of a scheme to 'defraud a financial institution.'" *United States v. Bouchard*, 828 F.3d 116, 124 (2d Cir. 2016) (quoting 18 U.S.C. § 1344) (brackets omitted). Thus, both wire fraud and bank fraud require the Government to prove that the defendant had an intent to deprive the victim of money or property. Moreover, to establish the existence of a scheme to defraud, the Government must prove the *materiality* of a defendant's false statements or misrepresentations. *United States v. Weaver*, 860 F.3d 90, 94 (2d Cir. 2017). The Defendants argue that (1) the Government failed to offer sufficient evidence as to the "materiality" of their alterations to the bills of lading; and (2) that the Government failed to present sufficient evidence that they intended to [—23—] deprive the victim banks of money or property. We take each of these arguments— and reject them—in turn.

A.

We first consider the Defendants' materiality claim. The wire and bank fraud statutes do not criminalize every deceitful act, however trivial. As noted above, to sustain a conviction under these statutes, the Government must prove that the defendant in question engaged in a deceptive course of conduct by making *material* misrepresentations. *Neder v. United States*, 527 U.S. 1, 4 (1999). "To be 'material' means to have probative weight, i.e., reasonably likely to influence the [bank] in making a determination required to be made." *United States v. Rigas*, 490 F.3d 208, 234 (2d Cir. 2007). As the Supreme Court has put it, a material misrepresentation has "a natural tendency to influence, or [is] capable of influencing, the decision of the decisionmaking body to which it [is] addressed." *Neder*, 527 U.S. at 16 (internal quotation marks and citation omitted). Where, as here, a "bank's discretion is limited by an agreement, we must look to the agreement to {–86–} determine what factors are relevant, and when a misstatement becomes material." *Rigas*, 490 F.3d at 235. All of these [—24—] specifications of the materiality inquiry target the same question: would the misrepresentation actually *matter* in a *meaningful way* to a rational decision-maker?

The Defendants argue that their alterations to the bills of lading could not have been material to the banks. They point to *United States v. Litvak*, 808 F.3d 160 (2d Cir. 2015), where we held that a defendant's admitted misstatements were not material to the Treasury Department because the Government had submitted *no* evidence demonstrating that these misstatements were capable of influencing a Treasury Department decision. *Id.* at 172. Instead, the evidence presented at trial established that the Treasury was "kept . . . away from making buy and sell decisions" and retained "no authority to tell investment managers which [security] to purchase or at what price to transact." *Id.* (internal quotation marks, brackets, and citation omitted). Similarly, in *Rigas*, we held that because there was no evidence that the Defendants' misstatements there would have influenced the banks' investment decisions as to what interest rate to charge, those misstatements were not material. 490 F.3d at 235.

The Defendants argue that the banks here, like the Treasury Department in *Litvak* and the banks in *Rigas*, retained limited discretion in rejecting the documents, and that the Government offered insufficient evidence that the [—25—] changes made to the bills of lading were capable of influencing the banks' decisions. Specifically, the Defendants first argue that the domestic banks' decisions as to whether to release the funds for these transactions were *not* discretionary *at all*, but were instead governed by the terms of the letters of credit, and contingent only on the

banks' being presented with evidence that the shipment was program compliant. Thus, because the bills of lading *appeared* to be compliant with the letters of credit and the GSM-102 program requirements, the argument goes, the banks had no discretion to reject them and any alterations were immaterial.

We reject this argument. As the court below described it, the Defendants essentially assert that "if the bank is presented with a document altered carefully enough," the bank lacks discretion to decline to honor the letter of credit and the misrepresentations therefore lack materiality. *Lillemoe*, 242 F. Supp. 3d at 117. In other words, under the Defendants' theory, the better the fraudster, the less likely he is to have committed fraud. We decline to reverse the jury's rejection of this argument, which would entail countenancing any and all falsifications of documents involved in these or similar transactions, as long as they were carried out with sufficient skill. [—26—]

The Defendants next argue that the bills of lading they provided fulfilled the obligations of the letters of credit prior to their altering them. Therefore, their theory goes, the Defendants *needlessly* modified the documents because, in any event, the bills of lading already fulfilled the function of the "required document[s]" even if they were altered in minor ways. Br. Def.-Appellant Lillemoe at 27. The Government offered substantial evidence at trial, however, that the banks could have and would have rejected the bills of lading had they not been altered or had the banks known of the specific alterations at issue. The relevant letters of credit clearly called for "copies of original" bills of lading, as did the GSM-102 program, *see, e.g.* J.A. 1851–54 (requiring a copy of an "original on board . . . bill(s) of lading"), 1791 (requiring "a true and correct copy" of "the negotiable . . . bill(s) of lading"), {–87–} and the program guarantees had restrictions limiting them to shipments that occurred within specific date ranges. J.A. 526.

Given these requirements, it is not surprising that CoBank representative Holly Womack and Deutsche Bank representative

Rudolph Effing testified that their respective banks would have declined to go through with the transactions at issue had they known about the specific alterations the Defendants made to the bills of lading. *See, e.g.* J.A. 458 (testimony of Womack that if the confirming bank [—27—] "didn't have a copy of an original on board, original bill of lading" it "wouldn't have paid the funds" because "we [wouldn't] have a complying set of documents so we wouldn't have an obligation under the [letter of credit] [from the] issuing bank"); J.A. 470 (testimony of Womack that she would not have accepted the unaltered bill of lading prior to the Defendants' date change because it would have made the document non-compliant and "[w]e wouldn't be able to file a claim [with the USDA] and be paid if the bank defaulted on the obligation"); J.A. 421 (testimony of Effing that "if any of the information that's on that document is not in compliance with the requirements on the program or letter of credit, then we just can't accept it"). After all, to submit a claim to the USDA, the banks had to submit these documents and certify that they were "true and correct copies of the originals that [they] received." J.A. 463. The testimony of USDA Official Doster, moreover, buttressed this testimony as to the materiality of the Defendants' changes, J.A. 548–49, as did the Government's expert, who testified as to the functional significance of the Defendants' changes. J.A. 1248–49. For example, to qualify for the already-secured USDA guarantee, the shipments involved had to have occurred on or after October 6, 2008. The Defendants' alterations implicated compliance with that requirement. [—28—]

Additionally, the Government produced several of the Defendants' *own* communications, which spoke to the materiality of the Defendants' changes. *See* J.A. 3616 (e-mail from Lillemoe stating that "we'll need a copy [of] the ORIGINAL [bill of lading]. We cannot execute with the 'Non-Negotiable' version"); J.A. 3617–18 (e-mail from Lillemoe stating "just checked with the bank financing the GSM deal. They need the copy of the [bill of lading] to state 'Original' in order to accept it."); J.A. 1907 (e-mail from Lillemoe stating "[f]or us we need [bills of lading] to state

'Original' and that are signed. We'll simply white out the 'Copy Non-Negotiable' on the signed copies and stamp 'Original' ourselves. So we're now OK on the [bills of lading]."); J.A. 2343 (e-mail from Lillemoe to Calderon describing a date change as "[n]ot my best work, but good enough for now"). These statements provide additional evidence that the confirming banks needed to receive copies of "original" bills of lading with specific "on-board" dates in order to honor their obligations under the letters of credit. They therefore provide further support for the conclusion that the banks could have and would have rejected nonconforming documents such as those at issue here, and that the discrepancies were material to the GSM-102 guarantees.

In sum, the Government produced a variety of testimonial and [—29—] documentary evidence demonstrating that the Defendants falsified documents in order to make them appear to be compliant with the terms of the governing letters of credit and the USDA program. The jury was also presented with substantial evidence that had the bank officials known about those specific types of alterations they would *not* have accepted those documents and therefore would not have entered into the transactions {–88–} at issue. We conclude, in light of the evidence described above and marshalled at trial, that the Government presented sufficient evidence for the jury to conclude that the Defendants' misstatements were material.

B.

The Defendants next argue that the Government failed to produce sufficient evidence to support the jury's conclusion that their scheme "contemplated some actual harm or injury to their victims," *United States v. Novak*, 443 F.3d 150, 156 (2d Cir. 2006) (emphasis, quotation marks, and citation omitted), a necessary element of their offenses of conviction. As we have often observed, for the purposes of satisfying the elements of mail, wire, or bank fraud, a victim can be deprived of "property" in the form of "intangible" interests such as the right to control the use of one's assets. *United States v.*

Carlo, 507 F.3d 799, 801–02 (2d Cir. [—30—] 2007). "[M]isrepresentations or non-disclosure of information" can support a conviction under the "right to control" theory if "those misrepresentations or nondisclosures can or do result in tangible economic harm." *United States v. Finazzo*, 850 F.3d 94, 111 (2d Cir. 2017). In particular, this Court has upheld convictions where misrepresentations "exposed the lender . . . to unexpected economic risk." *United States v. Binday*, 804 F.3d 558, 571 (2d Cir. 2015).

The Government produced a variety of evidence to support the jury's finding that the Defendants' falsifications exposed the confirming banks to severe economic risks across two dimensions. First, the Government produced evidence that the modifications to the bills of lading exposed the banks to risk of default or non-reimbursement from the *foreign* banks because these modifications sought to hide the true nature of the non-conforming documents. *See, e.g.,* J.A. 459 (CoBank representative Womack testifying that "we need to have [compliant] documents to have the issuing [letter of credit] . . . repay us"); J.A. 1249 (Government expert Professor Byrne stating that only the issuing bank can propose a change to the terms of a letter of credit). As recounted above, a confirming bank must determine if the presentation is compliant with the terms of a letter of credit, and it can reject non-compliant documents. This Circuit has [—31—] emphasized in the civil context that documents' compliance with the terms of a relevant letter of credit should generally be analyzed under a standard of "strict compliance," a standard followed by a majority of courts. *See Mago Int'l*, 833 F.3d at 272, 4 Adm. R. at 107. And the economic significance of the precise accuracy of the documents (including the bills of lading) was testified to at trial. *See, e.g.,* J.A. 405 (testimony of Deutsche Bank representative Effing, noting that accuracy is "[s]uper important. Because that's how we determine . . . whether all the [letter of credit's] terms and conditions are fulfilled").

The Defendants highlight that:

Our cases have drawn a fine line between schemes that do no more than cause their victims to enter into transactions they would otherwise avoid—which do not violate the mail or wire fraud statutes—and schemes that depend for their completion on a misrepresentation of an essential element of the bargain—which do violate the mail and wire fraud statutes.

Binday, 804 F.3d at 570 (quoting *United States v. Shellef*, 507 F.3d 82, 108 (2d Cir. 2007)). According to the Defendants, the victim banks got "what [they] bargained for" because they made "valid, 98%-guaranteed, interest-bearing loans to USDA-approved, {–89–} developing-world foreign banks." Br. Def.-Appellant Lillemoe at 24. But the Defendants ignore that the confirming banks did not receive "what they bargained for" because they bargained for a set of documents [—32—] that complied with the letters of credit and satisfied the USDA guarantee requirements.

Second, the modifications increased the risk that the USDA would decline to reimburse the banks in the event of a foreign bank's default. The evidence amply established that the Defendants falsified documents that were not in accordance with the governing GSM-102 regulations to make them guarantee-eligible. For example, the Government produced evidence at trial that, on three bill of lading copies associated with two GSM-102 transactions, the Defendants changed the printed "on-board" date of October 5, 2008, to October 6, 2008. For the transactions at issue to qualify for the already-secured USDA guarantee, the shipments involved had to have occurred on or after October 6, 2008. As noted above, several parties testified to the significance of this change at trial. For instance, USDA official Doster testified as follows:

A: When the [good] is loaded onto the vessel, a bill of lading is issued. And on that bill of lading is what's called a clean on board date. The clean on board date is the date that's stamped that is considered the date of the export.

Q: Is that an important date?

A: This is an important date. For one, it is important because it can determine ownership . . . The on board date . . . establishe[s] that ownership has passed. Our guarantee specifies the date range . . . [—33—] through which you may export. So the on board date on the bill of lading is the date you would look at to determine if the exporter is falling within the terms of the guarantee . . . .

Q: And does the program ever guarantee [with respect to] shipments before the on board date?

A: No. No.

J.A. 524; see also 7 C.F.R. §§ 1493.20(d), 1493.60(f) (2012) (GSM-102 regulations stating that "date[s] of export prior to the date" of the guarantee application "are ineligible for . . . guarantee coverage" and defining a "date of export" as a bill of lading's "on board date"). Doster's testimony was supported by that of the Government's expert, Professor James Byrne, who stated at trial that an "on board date" is "extremely important in letter of credit practice" and refers only to "the date [the goods] are loaded on board," and that he had "never" heard of the on-board date as being a "range" of dates. J.A. 1246–47. Similar testimony was also offered as to the significance of the Defendants' "stamping" activity on the banks' ability to obtain reimbursement from the USDA. See, e.g., J.A. 459. For example, the Government presented substantial evidence that in order to submit a claim of loss to the GSM-102 program, a bank would need to submit a copy of an original bill of lading. J.A. 1791.

The GSM–102 regulations in effect at the time provided that an assignee [—34—] could not be held liable for an exporter's misrepresentations of which the assignee lacked knowledge. See 7 C.F.R. § 1493.120(e) (2012). This provision, however, does not remotely suggest, as the Defendants would have it, that there was insufficient evidence that they contemplated any harm to the banks. As the district court noted, a confirming bank seeking indemnification pursuant to the GSM-102 program can rely on this provision only if "the assignee . . . has no knowledge." Lillemoe, 242 F. Supp. 3d at 119. Such a question could certainly have resulted in "protracted and costly litigation" as to whether the confirming {–90–} bank "had knowledge of the nature of the documents it had accepted." Id.; see also United States v. Frank, 156 F.3d 332, 335 (2d Cir. 1998) (finding intended harm proven where defendant waste disposers made misrepresentations to their customer that "could have subjected the [customer] to fines and to the loss of its environmental permit"). And the jury did not need to speculate as to the likelihood of such a dispute: USDA official Doster, who again, was responsible for ensuring that registrations were properly issued for the GSM-102 program, specifically testified that the Defendants' changes put the banks at risk of non-reimbursement. See J.A. 548; see also J.A. 2586.

The Government presented a great deal of evidence that the Defendants' [—35—] submission of falsified, non-compliant documents exposed the victim banks to the risk of "actual harm or injury" on multiple dimensions. We therefore decline to reverse the jury's determination that the Defendants' scheme contemplated economic harm.

II.

The Defendants next challenge two jury instructions issued by the district court, only one of which they objected to at trial. "[W]e review a properly preserved claim of error regarding jury instructions de novo," but we will reverse "only where, viewing the charge as a whole, there was a prejudicial error.'" United States v. Coplan, 703 F.3d 46, 87 (2d Cir. 2012) (internal quotation marks and citation omitted). If a defendant fails to object to a jury instruction at trial, however, a plain error standard of review applies on appeal. Fed. R. Crim. P. 30(d), 52(b). With these standards in hand, we consider and reject each of these challenges in turn.

A.

First, the Defendants challenge the district court's decision to give a "no ultimate harm" charge to the jury. A "no ultimate harm" instruction advises the jury that "where some immediate loss to the victim is contemplated by a [—36—] defendant, the fact that the defendant believes (rightly or wrongly) that he will 'ultimately' be able to work things out so that the victim suffers no loss is no excuse for the real and immediate loss contemplated to result from defendant's fraudulent conduct." *United States v. Rossomando*, 144 F.3d 197, 201 (2d Cir. 1998) (quoting 2 Leonard B. Sand *et al.*, *Modern Federal Jury Instructions* § 44.01 at 44-35). Such a charge is "proper where (1) there was sufficient factual predicate to necessitate the instruction, (2) the instruction required the jury to find intent to defraud to convict, and (3) there was no evidence that the instruction caused confusion." *United States v. Lange*, 834 F.3d 58, 79 (2d Cir. 2016). The district court declined to include a "no ultimate harm" charge in the preliminary jury instructions, but it changed course after the Defendants' attorneys made several references at trial to the fact that the banks were ultimately insulated against immediate financial loss by the USDA guarantees. *See, e.g.*, J.A. 501 (calling on witness to confirm that banks were "covered 101 percent on this deal").

The district court's "no ultimate harm" instruction satisfies all three of the above-mentioned factors. First and foremost, the Defendants' trial strategy, which focused on the fact that the banks were "ultimately" reimbursed for their losses by the USDA, *see* Br. Def.-Appellant Lillemoe at 42; Br. Def.-Appellant [—37—] Calderon at 52, created the "factual predicate" necessitating the charge. *Lange*, 834 F.3d at 79. The district court simply instructed the jurors that they should not acquit on the basis of the Defendants' asserted belief that things would all work out in the end—that the {-91-} USDA would, in any event, guarantee the transactions—if they nonetheless found that the Defendants intended to deceive the banks as to the economic risks involved *ex ante*. That instruction comports with our holding in

United States v. Ferguson, 676 F.3d 260 (2d Cir. 2011), where we upheld a "no ultimate harm" instruction that "ensured that jurors would not acquit if they found that the defendants knew the [transaction] was a sham but thought it beneficial for the stock price in the long run." *Id.* at 280. In *Ferguson*, we reasoned that "the immediate harm in such a scenario is the denial of an investor's right to control her assets by depriving her of the information necessary to make discretionary economic decisions," and that the absence of ultimate harm to the stock price did not vitiate that more immediate harm to victims. *Id.* (internal quotation marks and citation omitted). We reason similarly here.

The second and third factors are even more easily satisfied. The district court's instruction indisputably required the jury to find intent to defraud to convict. *See, e.g.*, J.A. 1310 ("A genuine belief that the scheme never exposed the [—38—] victim to loss or risk of loss in the first place would demonstrate a lack of fraudulent intent."). Finally, there was no evidence that the instruction caused confusion. *Cf. Rossomando*, 144 F.3d at 199, 203 (jury request that the court clarify its "no ultimate harm" instruction demonstrated "evident confusion" resulting from instruction). Given the foregoing analysis, we find no error in the district court's "no ultimate harm" instruction under the circumstances of this case.

B.

The Defendants also challenge—without having done so below—the district court's jury instructions regarding the elements of bank fraud. Because the Defendants did not object to this portion of the jury charge at trial, we review the district court's instructions for plain error here. *See* Fed. R. Crim. P. 52(b); *accord Johnson v. United States*, 520 U.S. 461, 466–67 (1997). Under the plain error standard:

[A]n appellate court may, in its discretion, correct an error not raised at trial only where the appellant demonstrates that (1) there is an error; (2) the error is clear or obvious, rather than subject to reasonable dispute; (3) the error affected the appellant's substantial rights, which in the ordinary case means it affected the outcome of the district court proceedings; and (4) the error seriously affects the fairness, integrity or public reputation of judicial proceedings.

United States v. Marcus, 560 U.S. 258, 262 (2010) (internal quotation marks and citation omitted); *see also United States v. Botti*, 711 F.3d 299, 308 (2d Cir. 2013). **[—39—]**

Under 18 U.S.C. § 1344, bank fraud is defined as the knowing execution of "a scheme or artifice—(1) to defraud a financial institution; or (2) to obtain any of the moneys, funds, credits, assets, securities, or other property owned by, or under the custody or control of, a financial institution, by means of false or fraudulent pretenses, representations, or promises." The district court instructed the jury on these elements, specifically explaining that the defendant must have "executed or attempted to execute the scheme with the *intent to obtain money or property from Deutsche Bank*." J.A. 1315 (emphasis added). With respect to that intent requirement, the court elaborated that "the Government must prove that the defendant you are considering executed or attempted to execute the scheme knowingly and willfully and with the intent to obtain money {–92–} or property owned by or under the custody or control of Deutsche Bank." J.A. 1316.

The Defendants argue that the district court should have instructed the jury that a bank fraud conviction requires a finding that the defendant "contemplated harm or injury to the victim." Br. Def.-Appellant Calderon at 58. In advancing this argument, the Defendants rely on Second Circuit precedent stating that "[t]he failure to instruct on an essential element of the offense generally constitutes plain error." *United States v. Javino*, 960 F.2d 1137, 1141 (2d Cir. 1992). In response, the **[—40—]** Government asserts that, even assuming Second Circuit precedent requires the instruction the Defendants' belatedly argue should have been provided, the Supreme Court's decision in *Loughrin v.*

United States has adopted a more limited construction of the elements of bank fraud. *See* 573 U.S. 351, 356 (2014) (holding that the Government need not prove that a defendant charged with § 1344(2) intended to defraud a bank); *see also United States v. Bouchard*, 828 F.3d 116, 124 (2d Cir. 2016). The parties dispute whether *Loughrin* affects the Second Circuit's preexisting interpretation of the bank fraud statute, *see United States v. Nkansah*, 699 F.3d 743, 748 (2d Cir. 2012) (holding that "intent to victimize a bank" is an element of bank fraud), and whether the Defendants' proposed instruction was required under either interpretation.

We need not wade into this debate. Even assuming *arguendo* that the district court erred in not including the Defendants' proposed instruction, the failure to include that instruction did not constitute plain error under the standard articulated above. Most obviously, the absence of the proposed instruction did not affect the Defendants' "substantial rights," Fed. R. Crim. P. 52(b), because the jury *acquitted* the Defendants on the substantive bank fraud charge, convicting them only of several substantive wire fraud charges and conspiracy to commit **[—41—]** wire fraud *and* bank fraud. Because we have already concluded that there was sufficient evidence to sustain the Defendants' convictions for wire fraud, *see supra* Part I, their convictions for conspiracy could have rested on those grounds alone. The bank fraud instructions therefore did not prejudice the Defendants. *See Ferguson*, 676 F.3d at 277. Moreover, given the district court's detailed instructions on the elements of bank fraud that tracked the language of the bank fraud statute, as well as the ambiguities regarding the elements of bank fraud in the caselaw described above, any error in the jury instructions was certainly not "clear or obvious." *Marcus*, 560 U.S. at 262. Finally, the Defendants have not explained how any alleged error in the jury instructions could have "seriously affect[ed] the fairness, integrity or public reputation of judicial proceedings." *Id.* Accordingly, we reject the Defendants' argument that the district court plainly erred in instructing the jury on the elements of bank fraud.

III.

The Defendants next argue that their convictions should be vacated because the district court issued an improper jury charge encouraging the jury to continue deliberating after reaching an apparent deadlock. A defining characteristic of a so-called *Allen* charge is that "it asks jurors to reexamine their own views and the [—42—] views of others." *Spears v. Greiner*, 459 F.3d 200, 204 n.3 (2d Cir. 2006). This Court reviews a district court's decision to give an *Allen* charge for abuse of discretion. *United States v. Vargas-Cordon*, 733 F.3d 366, 377 (2d Cir. 2013). {–93–}

During their deliberations, the jurors sent out two notes to the court indicating that they were struggling to reach a unanimous verdict on some of the counts charged in the indictment. After almost a full week, the jury announced via a third note to the court that it had "concluded [its] deliberations." J.A. 1352. After consulting with the jury foreman, the district court determined that the jury was still deadlocked on some counts and decided to give a modified *Allen* charge. The district court instructed the jury, *inter alia*, that:

> It is desirable for you to keep deliberating and to reach a verdict if you can conscientiously do so. However, under no circumstances should any juror abandon his or her conscientious judgment. It is understandable and quite common for jurors to disagree. . . .

> [T]here appears to be no reason to believe if the charge were to be submitted to another jury, that jury would be more intelligent, more impartial or more competent to decide it than you are. However, I stress to you, that your verdict must reflect the conscientious judgment of each juror. Under no circumstances should any jur[or] yield his or her conscientious judgment. Do not ever change your mind because the other jurors see things differently or just to get the case over with.

J.A. 1358. [—43—]

"An *Allen* charge is unconstitutional if it is coercive in the context and circumstances under which it is given." *United States v. Haynes*, 729 F.3d 178, 192 (2d Cir. 2013). Considering the "different factors" we have enumerated to determine an *Allen* charge's "coercive effect," *Vargas-Cordon*, 733 F.3d at 377, we are confident that the district court's carefully crafted *Allen* charge did not constitute reversible error. At the start, we recognize a distinction between "the original *Allen* charge," which conveys "the suggestion that jurors in the minority should reconsider their position," and the modern trend toward "'modified' *Allen* charges that do not contrast the majority and minority positions." *Spears*, 459 F.3d at 204 n.4. Neither the Government nor the Defendants contest that the district court gave a "modified" *Allen* charge, rather than the traditional *Allen* charge, in this case. A "modified" *Allen* charge is already a less explosive version of the "dynamite" *Allen* charge, and therefore carries with it a lesser threat of coercing jurors to abandon their conscientious beliefs. *Id.*

Moreover, the district court's *Allen* charge contained all of the safeguards, and none of the pitfalls, that we have previously recognized as relevant to an assessment of its propriety. For instance, "we generally expect that a trial judge using an *Allen*-type supplemental charge will . . . both urge jurors to try to [—44—] convince each other and remind jurors to adhere to their conscientiously held views." *United States v. McDonald*, 759 F.3d 220, 225 (2d Cir. 2014). The district court did just that: "repeatedly warn[ing] the jurors not to surrender their conscientiously held beliefs, which is an instruction we have previously held to mitigate greatly a charge's potential coercive effect." *Vargas-Cordon*, 733 F.3d at 378. Moreover, the district court did not inform the jury that it was *required* to reach an agreement; it did just the opposite. *See* J.A. 1358 ("[I]t is your right to fail to agree."). It thereby avoided the "incorrect and coercive" impression that "the only just result was a verdict." *Haynes*, 729 F.3d at 194; *see also id.* at 192–94 (holding that an *Allen* charge was impermissibly coercive where the court stated that it "believe[d]" that the jury would "arrive at a just verdict on Monday") (internal quotation marks omitted). {–94–}

The Defendants claim that the district court's *Allen* charge was improper because it failed to reinstruct the jury on the burden of proof. We note first that while the court did not mention the burden of proof specifically in its *Allen* charge, it did remind the jury to "follow all the instructions" it had "[previously] given," referencing the written jury instructions that the jury had on hand, which themselves recited the burden of proof. J.A. 1358. Moreover, this factor, on its [—45—] own, is not dispositive proof of coercion. *See Vargas-Cordon*, 733 F.3d at 377. The district court's *Allen* charge encouraged the members of the jury to continue deliberating on the deadlocked counts to see if a verdict could be reached without coercing them into abandoning their consciously held beliefs regarding the Defendants' guilt or innocence. As such, it resembles other *Allen* charges we have previously approved and its issuance was not an abuse of discretion.

IV.

Finally, the Defendants argue the district court acted improperly in ordering Lillemoe and Calderon to pay $18,807,096.33 in restitution with respect to five GSM-102 loans on which the Russian Bank, IIB, defaulted. This sum included $18,501,353 to be paid to the USDA, which had reimbursed CoBank and Deutsche Bank for 98% of their losses on these transactions, *see* 18 U.S.C. § 3664(j)(1) ("If a victim has received compensation from insurance or any other source with respect to a loss, the court shall order that restitution be paid to the person who provided or is obligated to provide the compensation."), and $304,743.33 to be paid to CoBank, which included $137,422 for losses associated with the transactions and $168,321.33 for costs and attorneys' fees incurred in connection with the investigation and prosecution of the case, *see id.* § 3663A(b)(4) (authorizing [—46—] reimbursement of "the victim for . . . expenses incurred during participation in the investigation or prosecution of the offense or

attendance at proceedings related to the offense").[8] We review a district court's order of restitution for abuse of discretion. *United States v. Pearson*, 570 F.3d 480, 486 (2d Cir. 2009). "A court abuses its discretion when it rests its decision on an error of law." *United States v. Archer*, 671 F.3d 149, 169 (2d Cir. 2011).

"The Mandatory Victims Restitution Act ('MVRA'), 18 U.S.C. § 3663A, is one of several federal statutes empowering courts to impose restitution obligations on criminal defendants." *United States v. Thompson*, 792 F.3d 273, 277 (2d Cir. 2015). Under the MVRA, in the case of an "offense resulting in . . . loss or destruction of property," the court shall "order restitution to each victim in the full amount of each victim's losses as determined by the court and without consideration of the economic circumstances of the defendant." *See* 18 U.S.C. §§ 3663A(b)(1), 3664(f)(1)(A). Where intended loss is incorporated to punish a culpable defendant, "restitution is designed to make the victim whole . . . and must therefore be based only on the actual loss caused by the scheme." *United States v.* [—47—] *Lacey*, 699 F.3d 710, 721 (2d Cir. 2012) (citation omitted).

The Defendants argue that the district court's order was improper because CoBank and Deutsche Bank do not qualify as "victims" under the Act.[9] A {–95–} "victim" for the purposes of the MVRA is "a person *directly and proximately harmed* as a result of the commission of an offense for which restitution may be ordered." 18 U.S.C. § 3663A(a)(2) (emphasis added). To qualify as a "victim," then, a party must have endured a financial loss that was "directly and proximately" *caused* by a defendant's fraud. *See United States v. Paul*, 634 F.3d 668, 676 (2d Cir. 2011) ("In determining the proper amount of restitution, a court must keep in mind that

---

[8] The Court also ordered forfeiture in the amount of $1,543,287.60 from Lillemoe and $63,509.97 from Calderon. The Defendants do not challenge the forfeiture amount.

[9] The Government bears the burden of establishing by a preponderance of the evidence that each individual it claims is entitled to restitution was actually a "victim." *Archer*, 671 F.3d at 173.

the loss must be the result of the fraud." (internal quotation marks, brackets, and citation omitted)).

"[P]roximate cause, as distinct from actual cause or cause in fact" (commonly labeled "but-for" causation) is a "flexible concept" that "defies easy summary." *Paroline v. United States*, 572 U.S. 434, 444 (2014) (internal quotation marks and citation omitted); *see also CSX Transp., Inc. v. McBride*, 564 U.S. 685, 701 (2011) (labeling proximate cause "a term notoriously confusing"). "Proximate [—48—] cause" is in essence a "shorthand for a concept: Injuries have countless causes, and not all should give rise to legal liability." *CSX Transp.*, 564 U.S. at 692. The central goal of a proximate cause requirement is to limit the defendant's liability to the kinds of harms he risked by his conduct, the idea being that if a resulting harm was too far outside the risks his conduct created, it would be unjust or impractical to impose liability. *See* Prosser & Keeton, The Law of Torts 281 (5th ed. 1984).

We have accordingly viewed the MVRA's proximate cause requirement as a "tool[]" to both "limit a person's responsibility for the consequences of that person's own acts" and to promote efficiency in the sentencing process. *United States v. Reifler*, 446 F.3d 65, 135 (2d Cir. 2006).[10] When interpreting the MVRA, we have clarified that "a misstatement or omission" is the "proximate cause" of an investment loss for the purposes of imposing restitution, "if the risk that caused the loss was within the zone of risk *concealed* by the misrepresentations and omissions alleged by a disappointed investor." *United States v. Marino*, 654 F.3d 310, 321 (2d Cir. 2011) (internal quotation marks and citation omitted). The [—49—] MVRA's proximate causation requirement is therefore "akin to the well-established requirement that there be 'loss causation' in securities-fraud cases and not merely transaction ('but-for') causation." *Archer*, 671 F.3d at 171 n.16; *see also Marino*, 654 F.3d at 321 (equating "proximate

causation" under the MVRA to "loss causation" in the securities context). And to establish loss causation, "a plaintiff must allege that the *subject* of the fraudulent statement or omission was the cause of the actual loss suffered." *Lentell v. Merrill Lynch & Co.*, 396 F.3d 161, 173 (2d Cir. 2005) (internal quotation marks, ellipses, and citation omitted).[11]

Given the above standard, we are confident that the banks do not qualify as {–96–} "victims" under the MVRA because the Defendants did not proximately cause their losses. As catalogued above, the Defendants fraudulently altered shipping documents in order to make them facially compliant with the relevant letters of credit. Their fraud concealed two risks from the domestic banks: (1) that the issuing (foreign) banks would refuse to honor the letters of credit on the ground that the domestic banks had failed to demand a valid, conforming presentation; [—50—] and (2) that the USDA would decline to reimburse the banks for their losses because the transactions were not compliant with the GSM-102 program requirements. *See supra* Part I.B. Neither of these risks even arguably materialized. Instead, the foreign banks defaulted on their obligations due to their financial inability to fulfill them following a global financial crisis. The fraudulent shipping documents had no bearing whatsoever on the foreign banks' potential to default in such circumstances, which is the risk that actually materialized here.

This case is thus distinct from those contexts where we have found that a defendant's fraud "proximately caused" an injury for purposes of the MVRA. To take one example, in *Paul*, the defendant artificially inflated the value of his stock holdings in

---

[10] The Supreme Court has indicated that the definition of "proximate cause" may vary depending on the statute in question. *See CSX Transp.*, 564 U.S. at 700 (recognizing a unique test for "proximate causation applicable in FELA suits").

[11] To take one example from the securities context, in *Citibank, N.A. v. K-H Corp.*, 968 F.2d 1489 (2d Cir. 1992), we dismissed a civil claim asserting violations of securities laws where the complaint alleged that a fraud "induced" the plaintiff to enter into a transaction but failed to allege facts supporting a "causal connection between the fraud alleged and the subsequent loss that it suffered." *Id.* at 1492, 1495.

order to secure a loan. 634 F.3d at 670. Once his scheme was discovered, the price of those holdings plummeted, and he was unable to repay his loans. *Id*. We concluded that the defendant's fraud "proximately caused" his lenders' losses (and that they were therefore "victims" under the MVRA entitled to restitution equaling the full amount of the loan) because his misrepresentations bore directly on "the making of the loans in the first instance," even if "market forces may have contributed to the decline in" the value of the [—51—] collateral. *Id*. at 677–78. Put differently, because Paul misrepresented his own creditworthiness, his financial inability to repay his loans was quite clearly within the zone of risk concealed by his fraud.[12]

Here, by contrast, the Defendants' misrepresentations were not even arguably related to CoBank's and Deutsche Bank's assessment of the foreign banks' *creditworthiness*. We can say this with complete certainty because *before* the Defendants presented the fraudulent documents to the confirming banks, the USDA and the banks had *pre-approved* the relevant foreign banks for participation in these transactions. This pre-approval process included the foreign banks' submission of three years of audited financial statements, and a "rigorous" independent analysis spearheaded by the USDA's Risk and Asset Management branch that could take "six or seven months" to complete. J.A. 595; *see also* S.A. 11 (the district court noting that the bank made its determination as to the foreign [—52—] banks' likelihood of default "before any of the altered documents were presented").

---

[12] Thus, if the Defendants here had, say, misrepresented the value of collateral held by the foreign banks and those banks had then defaulted on their loans, we would not hesitate to conclude that they "proximately caused" the banks' losses, even if the banks' ability to repay the loans was also affected by market forces. *Cf. United States v. Turk*, 626 F.3d 743, 748–51 (2d Cir. 2010) (affirming the district court's loss calculation as to the total value of a loan where the defendant lied to lenders as to whether they were secured creditors and never repaid them their principal).

The Government argues that the banks would not have gone through with the transactions without the Defendants' involvement, and therefore that the Defendants proximately caused the banks' losses on those transactions. This argument confuses "but-for" causation with proximate causation. To take one analogous example {–97–} from the securities context, in *Bennett v. United States Trust Co.*, 770 F.2d 308 (2d Cir. 1985), the plaintiffs "went to [a bank] with the idea of borrowing money to purchase public utility stock already in mind" when that bank misinformed them that the Federal Reserve's "margin rules" did not apply to their intended stock purchases. *Id*. at 313–14. The bank's error allowed the plaintiffs to borrow money to purchase the stock, but when the market value of the stock subsequently decreased, the plaintiffs were unable to repay their loans. *Id*. at 310. We held that even if the bank's misrepresentation regarding the margin requirements was a "but-for" cause of the plaintiffs' investment, the plaintiffs had still failed to plead loss causation because "the loss at issue was caused by the [plaintiffs'] own unwise investment decisions, not by [the bank's] misrepresentation." *Id*. at 314. Similarly, here, the Defendants presented [—53—] fraudulent documents to the confirming banks *after* those Banks had *already* decided to offer loans to the relevant foreign banks pursuant to comprehensive financial analyses conducted by the confirming banks and the USDA. That financial decision—to offer the foreign loans— was not influenced by the Defendants' misconduct.

The MVRA provides redress to the victims of fraud, but it does not supply a windfall for those who independently enter into risky financial enterprises through no fault of the fraudsters. As we stated in *Archer*: "[I]f a person gives the defendant his money to bet, knowing that the bet might lose, his later loss, for purposes of restitution, is, in this fundamental sense, caused not by the defendant accepting his money but by the outcome of the bet." 671 F.3d at 171. The domestic banks here made a bet that the foreign banks would be able to repay the relevant loans with interest, and their assessments as to the advisability of *that* bet were completely unrelated to the risks concealed by the Defendants' fraud. The banks therefore do not qualify as "victims" under the MVRA and the district court erred in finding to the contrary. Accordingly, neither the USDA nor the banks are entitled to any restitution for losses caused by participation in the transaction [—54—] or for expenses incurred during participation in the investigation, prosecution, or related proceedings. The entire restitution award must be reversed.

CONCLUSION

We have considered the parties' remaining arguments and find them to be without merit. For the foregoing reasons, we AFFIRM the district court's judgments of conviction but REVERSE the restitution orders. We REMAND the case with instructions that the judgments be amended to omit that portion stating that the defendant must pay restitution.

United States Court of Appeals
for the Second Circuit

No. 18-3236

ATLANTIC SPECIALTY INS. CO.
VS.
COASTAL ENVTL. GROUP INC.

Appeal from the United States District Court for the
Eastern District of New York

Decided: December 13, 2019

Citation: 945 F.3d 53, 7 Adm. R. 147 (2d Cir. 2019).

Before **KATZMANN**, Chief Judge, **CHIN** and **DRONEY**,
Circuit Judges.

[—4—] {–57–} DRONEY, Circuit Judge: {–58–}

Plaintiff-Appellant Atlantic Specialty Insurance Company ("Atlantic") appeals from a final judgment of the United States District Court for the Eastern District of New York (Azrack, *J.*). Atlantic brought that action after the April 2013 loss of the "MIKE B," a spud barge deployed to support a crane to repair Coney Island's Steeplechase Pier, which had been damaged by Hurricane Sandy in 2012. Atlantic had issued a maritime hull insurance policy to Defendant-Appellee Coastal Environmental Group Inc. ("Coastal") for coverage of the MIKE B, as well as related protection and indemnity insurance. Atlantic sought a declaratory judgment that the policy was void *ab initio* or, in the alternative, that the loss of the MIKE B and damage to the pier caused by the sinking vessel were not covered under the terms of the policy. Coastal counterclaimed for the amount it alleged it was owed under the policy. [—5—]

Judge Leonard D. Wexler of the United States District Court for the Eastern District of New York presided over the action and conducted a bench trial in October and November of 2017. However, Judge Wexler passed away in March 2018 prior to issuing findings of fact and conclusions of law. The case was transferred to Judge Joan M. Azrack, who, after no party requested the recall of any witness under Federal Rule of Civil Procedure 63, certified her familiarity with the record and issued her findings of fact and conclusions

of law in September 2018. *See Atl. Specialty Ins. Co. v. Coastal Envtl. Grp.*, 368 F. Supp. 3d 429 (E.D.N.Y. 2018). Judge Azrack found that the policy was not void and covered the losses, and entered judgment for Coastal.

On appeal, Atlantic asks us to vacate the district court's findings of fact and conclusions of law and enter a declaratory judgment in favor of Atlantic or, in the alternative, remand for a new trial. Atlantic argues, among other things, that this Court should review Judge Azrack's findings [—6—] of fact *de novo* due to her role as a successor judge, and that Judge Azrack erred by not recalling witnesses during her consideration of the record.

We hold that findings of fact made by a successor judge in the circumstances here are subject to the "clearly erroneous" standard of review contained in Federal Rule of Civil Procedure 52(a)(6), even where the successor judge rules based on a documentary record, and under that standard we find no basis to vacate the district court's judgment. We also conclude that Judge Azrack was not required to recall any witnesses because no party requested such a recall. Accordingly, we affirm the judgment of the district court.

I. BACKGROUND

A. Factual Background[1]

Coney Island's Steeplechase Pier is situated on the southern side of the island, extending into Lower New York Bay toward the Rockaways and the Atlantic Ocean. In 2012, the pier was substantially damaged by [—7—] Hurricane Sandy. The City of New York contracted with Triton Structural Concrete ("Triton") to repair the damage, and Triton in turn subcontracted with Coastal to actually perform the repairs.

To conduct the work, Coastal chartered the MIKE B, a spud barge, from Sterling Equipment, Inc. ("Sterling"). The MIKE B was to serve as a base for a crane to perform work on the pier. A spud barge {–59–} holds itself in

---

[1] The facts as recounted here are undisputed by the parties unless otherwise indicated.

place by lowering its spuds (in the case of the MIKE B, steel pipes measuring sixty-five feet in length) into the sea floor. The spuds are housed within spud wells, which serve as a sleeve around the spud and are welded to the barge's deck and the bottom of the barge. This structure prevents the barge from moving horizontally, while still allowing it to move up and down with the sea. The MIKE B had two spuds, which were located on its starboard side in aft and forward positions.

Coastal and Sterling signed an agreement (the "Charter Agreement") for the barge on March 28, 2013, for a charter period between April 7, 2013 and June 6, 2013. The Charter Agreement included an address of "1904 Surf [—8—] Avenue, Brooklyn[,] NY 11224" under the heading of "Job Site." Joint App'x 1409. Under the terms of the Charter Agreement, Coastal was obligated to secure both hull insurance, insuring against damage to or loss of the MIKE B, and protection and indemnity insurance covering third-party claims, including property damage. Coastal had a preexisting policy with Atlantic that covered other vessels for the period of January 2013 to January 2014; as a result, Coastal sought to add coverage of the MIKE B to this policy. The policy included a condition that "the vessel shall be confined to [the]: Coastal and Inland waters of the United States in and around Brooklyn, NY." Joint App'x 1445.

On Monday, April 1, 2013, Coastal's insurance broker, George Zerlanko of Global Indemnity Insurance Agency, Inc. ("Global"), emailed Dorothy Schmidt of All Risks, Ltd. ("All Risks") requesting that the MIKE B be added to the policy.[2] On Friday, April 5, 2013

at 2:17 p.m., Schmidt [—9—] emailed Mark Fairchild of Atlantic asking for a quote to add the MIKE B. Schmidt's email included the Charter Agreement as an attachment, including the job site address at 1904 Surf Avenue. At 3:36 p.m., less than ninety minutes later, Fairchild responded with a quote; in addition to the premiums for the additional coverages, the quote included a requirement that Coastal assume a higher deductible than that provided for in the Charter Agreement, but otherwise contained no conditions for the extension of coverage and did not request further information.[3] Three minutes later, Schmidt sent along Atlantic's quote to Zerlanko at Global; forty minutes after that, Zerlanko responded, indicating that Coastal would accept the quote, including the higher deductible. Finally, ten minutes later, at 4:27 [—10—] p.m., Schmidt forwarded the acceptance of the quote back to Fairchild at Atlantic, indicating that coverage should be bound.

Three days later, on Monday, April 8, an expert marine surveyor, Jason Meyerrose, conducted an in-water survey of the barge at Sterling's yard in Staten Island at Coastal's request, after which he prepared a survey titled "Preliminary Advices for Insurance Underwriting Purposes." Joint {–60–} App'x 1390. Meyerrose's survey declared the vessel's overall condition to be "fair for age and past services" and valued the vessel at $400,000.[4] Joint App'x 1391. The survey also stated that "the hull and equipment of the subject vessel are in satisfactory condition for operation in inland waters." Id. Meyerrose forwarded the survey to an employee of Coastal, Kristine Morehouse, later that day. In his cover email, Meyerrose indicated that Sterling needed to make some minor repairs before service, while

---

[2] All Risks is a "licensed insurance broker." Joint App'x 2438. Atlantic and Coastal dispute the nature of the relationship between All Risks and the parties. Atlantic [—9—] characterizes All Risks as "Coastal's insurance broker." Appellant Br. at 18. Coastal claims instead that All Risks was a "licensed agent with [International Marine Underwriters (IMU)]," and that Atlantic is "a writing company for IMU." Appellee Br. at 15 (quoting Joint App'x 835–36 (deposition testimony of Dorothy Schmidt)). We need not resolve whether Schmidt acted as Atlantic's agent because Atlantic bound coverage directly through its own employee, Mark Fairchild, as indicated in the text, *infra*.

---

[3] Specifically, Fairchild quoted a $10,000 deductible—to match that of the other vessels under Coastal's existing policy—while noting that the Charter Agreement called for no higher than a $5,000 deductible.

[4] The MIKE B had previously been surveyed by Meyerrose's father and partner at the firm, Rick Meyerrose, in 2012; at that point, Rick Meyerrose had valued the barge at $400,000, and Jason Meyerrose did not believe the value had changed in the subsequent year.

also [—11—] asking: "This barge will be working in protected waters at Coney Island correct, not on the Ocean / inlet side????" Joint App'x 1388–89. Morehouse responded a few minutes later by stating: "Yes that is correct it will be in protected waters at Coney Island, not in the Ocean." Joint App'x 1388. Morehouse subsequently forwarded the preliminary survey to Zerlanko at Global, who then forwarded it to Schmidt at All Risks, who passed it finally on to Fairchild at Atlantic. Morehouse's email and the subsequent communications all included Meyerrose's question, but none included Morehouse's response.

Coastal took possession of the MIKE B and towed it, first to a construction yard where a fifty-ton crane was installed, and then, on Thursday, April 11, to the job site at the pier. The barge was then "spudded" to the seabed to hold it in place next to the pier. That evening, Coastal's on- [—12—] site supervisor, Eric Gundersen, checked the weather forecast, which called for rain and one-foot seas.[5]

When he returned at 7:00 a.m. the next morning, Friday, April 12, Gundersen saw the waves were higher than forecasted, "2 to 4" feet and coming "from the ocean" to the south. Joint App'x 1242–43.[6] Gundersen testified that he promptly called Miller's Launch ("Miller"), a tug company with which Coastal had pre-arranged to have a tug available "within an hour at all times," to send over a tug. Joint App'x 1245.[7] The purpose of the

[—13—] standby tug was to tow the MIKE B away from the pier if warranted by sea conditions. Gundersen then boarded the barge, where he remained for "45 minutes to an hour" to inspect whether the waves were harming it and to ensure everything was "tied down"; Gundersen testified that the barge seemed to be in safe condition at that time but was starting to "mov[e] pretty good" as the seas continued to get rougher, and he called Miller again to check on the tug's status. Joint App'x 1244–46. Gundersen subsequently returned to the barge to further secure items on the deck, spending an {–61–} hour to an hour and a half on board; at that point he observed that one of the spuds appeared to have bent. By the time the tug finally arrived in the late morning, Gundersen had learned the aft spud well had failed and water was entering the barge.

That afternoon, Coastal deployed floating containment booms to protect against any oil spill from the then-listing barge; because the barge had already struck the pier, Miller also worked to anchor the barge to keep it from damaging the pier further. Coastal and Miller—and eventually the [—14—] crane manufacturer—also prepared to remove the crane from the barge's deck, with work continuing throughout the weekend. Coastal at that time informed Global that the barge was in trouble, and Global advised that Coastal should do whatever was in the "normal range to keep the barge afloat." Joint App'x 357–58. By Monday morning, April 15, the crane was removed; however, by Tuesday morning, April 16, because of the ongoing danger the barge posed to the pier and the high cost of the thus-far unsuccessful pumping effort, Coastal chose to allow the MIKE B to sink to the sea floor. By April 17, the barge was fully submerged and then, in June 2013, was removed for scrap purposes.

Atlantic sent a marine surveyor, Alan Colletti, to investigate the incident on Monday, April 15; he returned twice that

---

[5] Gundersen testified in a deposition, but not at trial. His deposition was admitted at the trial, however. Atlantic objected to the use of Gundersen's testimony below and continues to raise objections to it on appeal. For reasons discussed in more detail below, we find there was no error in the district court's consideration of Gundersen's testimony.

[6] Coastal's weather expert, Dr. Austin Dooley, testified that the waves would have been "4 to 6 feet" in the area of the pier on April 12, Joint App'x 1141, 1166, while Atlantic's expert, Trevor Bevens, testified that the waves would not have been more than two feet, Joint App'x 1177–78.

[7] There is additional testimony in the record that indicates the tug would be available within two hours, rather than one. Joint App'x 354. The record is unclear as to whether it was standard

operating procedure for Coastal to contract to have a tug available on such short notice, or if Coastal made such an arrangement specifically due to the MIKE B's location and associated operational conditions, including weather.

week, on April 16 and April 17, and submitted reports to Atlantic estimating the costs of repairs and evaluating the cause of the loss. In the interim, Atlantic wrote to Coastal on April 16 reserving its rights under the insurance policy for claims related to the MIKE B and did so again on April 25. [—15—]

On May 24, 2013, Atlantic wrote to Coastal declining coverage for the MIKE B. On October 17, 2013, Coastal requested payment of the $400,000 due under the policy for the loss of the barge, stating that the vessel's loss was "caused by perils of the seas." Joint App'x 1621–23. Atlantic again declined payment on February 3, 2014. On August 21, 2014, Coastal again wrote to Atlantic, this time also seeking payment under the policy's protection and indemnity coverage for damage to the pier and the costs of attempting to save the barge; Coastal also reiterated its claim related to the loss of the barge itself. All were denied by Atlantic. In total, Coastal claimed over $1.2 million under the policy.

B. Procedural Background

On December 19, 2014, Atlantic filed this action in the Eastern District of New York. An amended complaint was filed on December 30, 2014.[8] The complaint sought a declaratory judgment that the policy covering the MIKE [—16—] B was void *ab initio* or, in the alternative, that there was no coverage under the policy's terms.[9] As relevant here, Atlantic alleged that the policy was void due to the fact that Coastal had violated its admiralty law duty of *uberrimae fidei* (utmost good faith) by failing to disclose a material risk, and had breached either the express or implied warranties of seaworthiness. Alternatively, Atlantic alleged that the loss of the MIKE B was not due to a peril covered under the policy.

---

[8] References to the "complaint" in this opinion are to this amended complaint.

[9] Coastal and Sterling asserted counterclaims against Atlantic and cross claims against each other; Sterling also asserted a third-party claim against Global, and Global asserted a third-party claim against All Risks.

Judge Wexler presided over the case, including a bench trial conducted over seven days in October and November 2017. {—62—} The trial was limited to the question of whether Atlantic's declination of coverage was proper and, if not, the extent of damages owed by Atlantic to Coastal and/or Sterling under the policy. Resolution of other issues, such as potential damages owed by Coastal to Atlantic or the resolution of the third-party [—17—] and cross claims, was postponed. Though most witnesses presented live testimony, others did not appear in court despite attempts to subpoena them, and the court accepted their testimony from depositions in video or transcript form. Of particular relevance to this appeal, Gundersen, Coastal's on-site supervisor, apparently ignored two subpoenas for trial testimony, and Judge Wexler instead admitted Gundersen's deposition testimony into evidence. In March 2018, after conclusion of the trial but before he had issued a decision in the case, Judge Wexler passed away, and the case was reassigned to Judge Azrack in April 2018.

Upon taking over the case, Judge Azrack held a telephone conference with the parties on July 10, 2018, and one of its topics was whether any of the parties sought to recall witnesses under Federal Rule of Civil Procedure 63.[10] Atlantic's counsel suggested that the court "may wish to hear from" [—18—] Gundersen; however, when Judge Azrack asked why Gundersen would be likely to honor a third subpoena and appear on recall, Atlantic's counsel did not press his request for Gundersen to testify or seek to

---

[10] Rule 63 provides as follows:

If a judge conducting a hearing or trial is unable to proceed, any other judge may proceed upon certifying familiarity with the record and determining that the case may be completed without prejudice to the [—18—] parties. In a hearing or a nonjury trial, the successor judge must, at a party's request, recall any witness whose testimony is material and disputed and who is available to testify again without undue burden. The successor judge may also recall any other witness.

Fed. R. Civ. P. 63.

exclude Gundersen's deposition testimony.[11]
[—19—] {–63–}

---

[11] The full exchange between Judge Azrack and Atlantic's counsel (Attorney Carbin, misspelled as Corbin in the transcript) concerning the recall of witnesses is reproduced below:

MR. CORBIN [sic]: I note that your request was pursuant to Rule 63 and in particular, whether any of the parties thought that a trial witness should be recalled.
THE COURT: Right.
MR. CORBIN: And in that regard, I would suggest, your Honor, that from plaintiff's perspective, the only witness that your Honor may wish to hear from is a witness put forward by the defendant Coastal. He was their job superintendent for the job at the time of the casualty. In fact, he's an ex-employee, as I understand it. He was subpoenaed twice by the defendant Coastal and refused to honor either of those subpoenas. And over our objection, Judge Wexler accepted his deposition testimony to be read in. We had also objected to that testimony being read in because Mr. Gundersen, the name of the witness is Eric Gundersen. Mr. Gundersen had been previously convicted of attempted murder of a New York City Police Officer and had served time for that conviction. But as I said, when **[—19—]** he was twice subpoenaed by Coastal to appear and testify, he did not honor the subpoenas, did not appear in court and instead, Judge Wexler accepted some of hi[s] deposition testimony and I think the Court may be interested to hear from Mr. Gundersen directly rather than his deposition testimony.
THE COURT: But what makes you think Mr. Gundersen is going to appear now as opposed — since he didn't appear before?
MR. CORBIN: Fair question, your Honor. I do not know. I think it's a fair observation.
THE COURT: All right.
MR. CORBIN: I think the — rather than take his deposition testimony, I think the Court should have insisted on his appearance.
THE COURT: Okay, I understand but what you were referring to was the fact that he twice ignored subpoenas, correct?
MR. CORBIN: Yes.
THE COURT: Okay. All right. Anything else? Okay.

Joint App'x 2557–58.

On September 30, 2018, Judge Azrack issued her findings of fact and conclusions of law, stating that they were based on her "review of the record and the post-trial submissions." *Atl. Specialty Ins. Co.*, 368 F. Supp. 3d at 434. Judge Azrack found that Atlantic improperly denied coverage to Coastal under both the hull insurance policy for the loss of the MIKE B and the barge salvage costs, and the protection and indemnity policy for pier damage. Turning to damages, the court awarded Coastal the full $400,000 claimed **[—20—]** for the loss of the MIKE B; $394,725.13 for salvage costs (slightly less than the $400,000 Coastal sought for such costs); and the full $402,470.51 claimed for the damage to the pier. *Id.* at 449–53.

Atlantic timely appealed from Judge Azrack's findings of fact and conclusions of law, claiming error on a variety of legal, factual, and evidentiary grounds.

II. STANDARD OF REVIEW

On appeal from a bench trial, conclusions of law—as well as mixed questions of law and fact—are reviewed *de novo*, while findings of fact are reviewed for clear error. *See, e.g., Beck Chevrolet Co. v. Gen. Motors LLC*, 787 F.3d 663, 672 (2d Cir. 2015).[12] "Under the clear error standard, we 'may not **[—21—]** reverse [a finding] even though convinced that had [we] been sitting as the trier of fact, [we] would have weighed the evidence differently.'"

---

[12] Evidentiary decisions, meanwhile, are subject to the abuse of discretion standard, under which error occurs only where the district court "bases its ruling on an erroneous view of the law or on a clearly erroneous assessment of the evidence, or renders a decision that cannot be located within the range of permissible decisions." *United States v. Hendricks*, 921 F.3d 320, 328 n.37 (2d Cir. 2019) (citation and alterations omitted); *see also United States v. Apple, Inc.*, 791 F.3d 290, 313 (2d Cir. 2015) ("Following a bench trial, . . . [t]he district court's evidentiary rulings . . . are reviewed for abuse of discretion." (citations omitted)). Even where that standard is met, however, reversible error occurs only where an erroneous ruling "also affects a party's substantial rights." *Boyce v. Soundview Tech. Grp., Inc.*, 464 F.3d 376, 385 (2d Cir. 2006) (citation omitted).

Mobil Shipping & Transp. Co. v. Wonsild Liquid Carriers Ltd., 190 F.3d 64, 67 (2d Cir. 1999) (alterations in original) (quoting *Anderson v. City of Bessemer City*, 470 U.S. 564, 574 (1985)). "Rather, a finding is clearly erroneous only if 'although there is evidence to support it, the reviewing court on the entire evidence is left with the definite and firm conviction that a mistake has been committed.'" *Id.* at 67–68 (quoting *Anderson*, 470 U.S. at 573).

Atlantic argues that the particular circumstances of this case merit departure from that standard of review. Specifically, Atlantic contends that, because Judge Azrack was not present at trial, her factual "determinations are not entitled to deference" and should be reviewed *de novo*. Appellant Br. at 15. We disagree and hold that the factual findings of a successor judge who has certified her familiarity with the record in accordance with Federal Rule of Civil Procedure 63 are entitled to the same deference that would be due if the findings had been made by the district judge who presided over [—22—] the taking of the evidence, even when the successor judge relies entirely on a documentary record.

Such a conclusion is supported by the text of Rule 52(a)(6), which provides that "[f]indings of fact, *whether based on oral or other evidence*, must not be set aside unless clearly erroneous."[13] {–64–} Fed. R. Civ. P. 52(a)(6) (emphasis added). The Rule makes clear that a reviewing court shall not apply a more stringent standard than "clearly erroneous" to a finding of fact due to the form of evidence on which the factual finding is based. Instead, the deference to the factfinder embodied in Rule 52 "is the rule, not the exception." *Anderson*, 470 U.S. at 575. And, as the Supreme Court has stated, the rationale

for deference is not merely the trial court's superior ability to make credibility determinations; instead, the clear error standard takes into account the trial court's expertise in fact-finding as well as a concern over [—23—] the "huge cost" in judicial resources that a more searching review by appellate courts would entail for an only "negligibl[e]" improvement in accuracy. *Id.* at 574–75.

The drafting history of the Rule further supports our interpretation. Rule 52 was amended in 1985, with the addition of the phrase "whether based on oral or other evidence," in an effort to make explicit that deference was owed to a trial court's factual findings regardless of the form of evidence on which they were based. *See* Amendments to Rules, 105 F.R.D. 179, 204–05, 221–23 (1985); *see also* 9C Charles A. Wright & Arthur R. Miller, Federal Practice & Procedure § 2571 (3d ed. 2019) ("An amendment in 1985 made it clear that the standard for appellate review is the same for oral and documentary evidence."). Prior to the amendment, some courts of appeals had applied a lesser level of deference to factual findings where the "trial court's findings [did] not rest on demeanor evidence and evaluation of a witness' [sic] credibility." Amendments to Rules, 105 F.R.D. at 222 (Advisory Committee's Note) (citing, for example, *Marcum v. United States*, [—24—] 621 F.2d 142, 144–45 (5th Cir. 1980) (reviewing court more likely to find clear error where findings based on written evidence); and *Taylor v. Lombard*, 606 F.2d 371, 372 (2d Cir. 1979) (reviewing court "may make [its] own independent factual determination" based on written record)). However, as the Advisory Committee noted in explaining the amendment, deference to the district court's factual findings was based not only on the court's ability to weigh credibility, but also on a "public interest in the stability and judicial economy that would be promoted by recognizing that the trial court, not the appellate tribunal, should be the finder of the facts." *Id.* at 223. These objectives were determined to be sufficient bases for deferring to the district court's findings of fact regardless of the nature of the evidence, and the absence of credibility determinations on

---

[13] The Rule continues to provide that "the reviewing court must give due regard to the trial court's opportunity to judge the witnesses' credibility." Fed. R. Civ. P. 52(a)(6). As the Supreme Court has stated, however, this additional language "does not alter [the Rule's] clear command" that all factual findings, regardless of their evidentiary basis, are owed deference by the reviewing court. *Anderson*, 470 U.S. at 574.

documentary evidence was regarded as an insufficient reason for an appellate court to conduct a more searching review of factual findings based on such evidence.

As a result, since at least 1985 this Court has routinely applied the clear error standard in reviewing factual findings based on documentary [—25—] evidence, as well as those based on witness credibility. *See, e.g., Connors v. Conn. Gen. Life Ins. Co.*, 272 F.3d 127, 135 (2d Cir. 2001); *see also Koam Produce, Inc. v. DiMare Homestead, Inc.*, 329 F.3d 123, 126 (2d Cir. 2003). And while we have not previously had occasion to consider this approach where the factual findings are of a successor judge, we see no reason to depart from the clear directive of Rule 52 in these circumstances. A successor judge who has {–65–} certified his or her familiarity with the record and proceeds to make findings of fact based on that record conducts essentially the same analysis as a trial judge evaluating written or other documentary evidence. And the considerations that underlie deference to a district court's findings of fact—a recognition of the fact-finding expertise of the district court and concern over judicial stability and economy—apply with equal force to the findings of a successor judge.

Moreover, Rule 63, which governs the procedures to be followed by successor judges, provides an opportunity to recall witnesses to any litigant who believes that the credibility of a particular witness is material to the [—26—] accuracy of a successor judge's factual findings and that such credibility may be properly assessed only via new testimony. Rule 63 provides that, if any party so requests, the successor judge *"must ... recall any witness whose testimony is material and disputed,"* provided that witness *"is available to testify again without undue burden."* Fed. R. Civ. P. 63 (emphasis added). In addition, the Rule also provides that the successor judge has the discretion to recall any other witness. *Id.* Rule 63's mandatory and discretionary recall requirements are important tools to protect against an incomplete or inadequate record. As the D.C. Circuit has noted, Rule 63 seeks to "[b]alanc[e] efficiency and fairness." *Mergentime Corp. v.*

Wash. Metro. Area Transit Auth., 166 F.3d 1257, 1262 (D.C. Cir. 1999). While the recall provisions contribute to the completeness of the district court proceedings, once those requirements are satisfied, Rule 63 permits the successor judge to make factual findings and thus "complet[e] interrupted trials without causing 'unnecessary expense and delay.'" *Id.* (quoting Fed. R. Civ. P. 63 advisory committee's note to 1991 amendment). [—27—]

We find Atlantic's arguments to the contrary to be unavailing: their focus on Judge Azrack's determination that it was unnecessary to rehear the evidence as its basis for *de novo* review cannot be reconciled with the text of Rules 52 and 63, and they rest on the same reasoning rejected by the Supreme Court in *Anderson* and addressed by the 1985 amendment to Rule 52. Atlantic could have required the recall of any of the prior witnesses—including Gundersen—whose testimony it now claims Judge Azrack should not have relied upon, but it chose not to do so.[14]

For these reasons, we review Judge Azrack's factual findings for clear error, and will reverse them only if we are "left with the definite and firm conviction that a mistake has been committed." *Anderson*, 470 U.S. at 573. [—28—]

III. DISCUSSION

Turning to the merits of its appeal, Atlantic raises five primary grounds for error, in addition to challenging numerous evidentiary decisions made by Judges Wexler and Azrack. Atlantic's primary arguments are that Judge Azrack erred in finding that: (1) Coastal did not breach its duty of *uberrimae fidei*, and thus the policy was not void; (2) Atlantic failed to prove the MIKE B was unseaworthy; (3) the loss of the MIKE B was due to a "peril of the

---

[14] As discussed in more detail below, Atlantic failed to request the recall of the experts whose testimony it challenges, and its suggestion to the district court that it "may wish to hear from" Gundersen, Joint App'x 2557, likewise did not qualify as a request for a mandatory recall of a witness under Rule 63.

sea" and thus was covered by the policy; (4) Coastal was entitled to damages for contractual payments withheld by its contractor for repairs to the Steeplechase Pier; and (5) Coastal proved its damages {-66-} using only a summary spreadsheet of invoices, as well as unauthenticated invoices, as evidence. We address each claim in turn.

A. Coastal's Duty of *Uberrimae Fidei*

Atlantic first argues that Coastal breached its duty of *uberrimae fidei*, or utmost good faith, because "the risk Coastal presented to Atlantic ... was not the actual risk." Appellant Br. at 16. *Uberrimae fidei* is a doctrine in admiralty law that requires "the party seeking insurance ... to disclose all [—29—] circumstances known to it which materially affect the risk." *Fireman's Fund Ins. Co. v. Great Am. Ins. Co.*, 822 F.3d 620, 633, 4 Adm. R. 70, 77 (2d Cir. 2016) (quoting *Folksamerica Reinsurance Co. v. Clean Water of N.Y., Inc.*, 413 F.3d 307, 311 (2d Cir. 2005)). The doctrine "does not require the voiding of the contract unless the undisclosed facts were material and relied upon." *Id.* at 638, 4 Adm. R. at 81 (quoting *Puritan Ins. Co. v. Eagle S.S. Co. S.A.*, 779 F.2d 866, 871 (2d Cir. 1985)). "Further, a minute disclosure of every material circumstance is not required. The assured complies with the rule if he discloses sufficient to call the attention of the underwriter in such a way that, if the latter desires further information, he can ask for it." *Puritan*, 779 F.2d at 871 (alteration omitted). The materiality of the information and the underwriter's reliance on the information are distinct elements to be proven, *id.*, and the burden of proof is on the insurer to show that there was a breach of this duty, *see id.* at 872; *see also Contractors Realty Co. v. Ins. Co. of N. Am.*, 469 F. Supp. 1287, 1293–94 (S.D.N.Y. 1979). Finally, because the duty is imposed "so that the insurer can decide for itself ... whether to accept the risk," the duty to disclose [—30—] ceases once the insurer has accepted the risk by binding coverage. *Knight v. U.S. Fire Ins. Co.*, 804 F.2d 9, 14 (2d Cir. 1986).

Atlantic argues that Coastal breached this duty by failing to disclose two material facts:

first, that the barge would operate on the southern side of Coney Island facing the ocean, and, second, that the barge was "extensively corroded and deteriorated." Appellant Br. at 16. Because each of these issues is factual in nature, we apply the clearly erroneous standard of Rule 52(a)(6). *See Puritan*, 779 F.2d at 871 (applying clear error standard to factual findings bearing on breach of *uberrimae fidei*). In doing so, we find that the district court did not err in finding that Coastal did not breach that duty.

First, the district court did not clearly err in concluding that Coastal disclosed information concerning the actual location of the barge sufficient to comply with its duty. As the district court correctly noted, at the time Atlantic bound coverage, the policy covered operation of the barge in "[c]oastal and [i]nland waters of the United States in and around Brooklyn, [—31—] NY." Joint App'x 1445; *see also Atl. Specialty Ins. Co.*, 368 F. Supp. 3d at 437. This stated navigation limit encompassed the job site at the Steeplechase Pier. And Atlantic's Fairchild testified that upon receiving the Charter Agreement as part of Coastal's request for coverage, which included a Brooklyn address—1904 Surf Avenue—as the Job Site, he "looked at" the address only to confirm "it was within the navigation [limit] of the policy." Joint App'x 334. Because the record shows that Coastal disclosed the barge's operational location and Atlantic relied on this information only to confirm that the barge would be operated within the policy's navigational limits—and thus face the risks inherent in operating within those limits— Atlantic failed to prove a breach by Coastal of its duty of *uberrimae fidei* in regards to use of the barge at the Steeplechase Pier. {-67-}

Likewise, we are not persuaded by Atlantic's argument that Coastal violated its duty by failing to more fully disclose the condition of the barge. As an initial matter, Atlantic did not demonstrate that Coastal knew and did not disclose any material information concerning the MIKE B's condition [—32—] prior to the binding of coverage on April 5. Coastal obtained the preliminary survey conducted by Meyerrose only on Monday, April 8—three days after the date on which coverage was bound—and, in any event, that survey concluded that the barge's condition was "fair for age and past services" and the barge had recently been repaired. Joint App'x 1391. And though Atlantic cites to a number of "deficiencies" identified in Meyerrose's "On Hire Survey," which was based on his April 8 inspection, Coastal did not receive that survey until April 15.[15] Likewise, the statements of Coastal's employees cited by Atlantic as evidence of Coastal's knowledge of and failure to disclose material information about the barge's condition all were made after coverage was bound, with many being made only after the barge had already been exposed to and damaged by the high seas. We thus reject Atlantic's argument that the district court clearly erred in finding that [—33—] Coastal did not fail to disclose circumstances that materially affected the risk undertaken by Atlantic.

B. Seaworthiness of the MIKE B

Atlantic's second argument is that the district court clearly erred in concluding that Atlantic failed to prove that the MIKE B was unseaworthy. Atlantic first takes issue with the district court placing the burden of proof on it, the insurer, contending that Coastal instead bore the burden to prove that the MIKE B was seaworthy. Though this court has not previously held so explicitly, we agree with the consensus of authority that places that burden on the insurer. *See, e.g., Darien Bank v. Travelers Indem. Co.*, 654 F.2d 1015, 1021 (5th Cir. Unit B Aug. 1981); *Fed. Ins. Co. v. PGG Realty, LLC*, 538 F. Supp. 2d 680, 694 (S.D.N.Y. 2008); *Cont'l Ins. Co. v. Lone Eagle Shipping Ltd. (Liberia)*, 952 F. Supp. 1046, 1067 (S.D.N.Y. 1997) ("The burden is on the insurer to prove unseaworthiness."), *aff'd*, 134 F.3d 103 (2d Cir. 1998) (per curiam); *see also* 2 Thomas J. Schoenbaum, Admiralty & Maritime Law § 19:16 (6th ed. 2019) ("As a general rule, there is a presumption that the [—34—] vessel was seaworthy, so the burden

of proving unseaworthiness is on the insurer.").[16]

Turning to the district court's factual determinations concerning the seaworthiness of the MIKE B, we also review for clear error. *See Raphaely Int'l, Inc. v. Waterman S.S. Corp.*, 972 F.2d 498, 503 (2d Cir. 1992).[17] Judge Azrack made a {–68–} number of findings concerning the MIKE B's seaworthiness, ultimately crediting Coastal's and Sterling's experts' testimony over the expert testimony and evidence put forth by Atlantic. *Atl. Specialty Ins. Co.*, [—35—] 368 F. Supp. 3d at 446–47. Atlantic primarily disputes Judge Azrack's weighing of the evidence and her decision to credit Coastal's and Sterling's experts.

At the outset, we disagree with Atlantic's contention that, because Judge Azrack did not recall any witnesses under Rule 63, she was not entitled to weigh the evidence or credit one expert over another. As discussed above, no such restriction is found in the text of Rule 63, and the Rule is clear that a successor judge is obligated to recall a witness only when a party has so requested, with the decision to recall other witnesses left to the successor judge's discretion. Judge Azrack found that "[t]he parties have chosen not to

---

[15] We note also that Meyerrose did not mention in his April 15 On Hire Survey nor amended his preliminary survey to reflect that the barge was located on the ocean side of Coney Island.

[16] The district court concluded, in the alternative, that Coastal had proven by a preponderance of the evidence that the MIKE B was, in fact, seaworthy. *See Atl. Specialty Ins. Co.*, 368 F. Supp. 3d at 447.

[17] Earlier cases of this Court have suggested that a "conclusory finding of seaworthiness" may be entitled to slightly less deference on appeal, though even under that standard the finding is nevertheless "entitled to great weight and will ordinarily stand unless the lower court manifests an incorrect conception of the applicable law." *Mobil Shipping & Transp. Co.*, 190 F.3d at 67 (citing *In re Marine Sulphur Queen*, 460 F.2d 89, 97-98 (2d Cir. 1972)). As was pointed out in *Mobil Shipping*, however, more recent cases including *Raphaely* have adopted the clear error standard. *Id.* at 67–68. To the extent these standards are meaningfully different, we conclude, as the court did in *Mobil Shipping*, that we need not settle this question: as discussed below, the district court made extensive findings of fact concerning the seaworthiness of the barge, and we would defer to them under either standard.

recall any witnesses." *Atl. Specialty Ins. Co.*, 368 F. Supp. 3d at 434.

The record supports this finding: Atlantic did not request the recall of any of the experts or other witnesses, and its suggestion that Judge Azrack "may wish to hear from" Gundersen, Joint App'x 2557, without more, does not rise to the level of a recall request triggering the obligations of Rule 63. **[—36—]** Atlantic's reliance on *Mergentime Corp.*, therefore, is misplaced. There, the D.C. Circuit vacated a successor judge's decision because he failed to recall witnesses after the appealing party specifically requested that a damages expert be recalled and also offered to submit a list of other witnesses that should be recalled. *See* 166 F.3d at 1266. The court concluded that "the plain language of Rule 63 control[led]" in finding that the successor judge should have granted the appealing party's request. *Id.* We agree that the plain language of Rule 63 governs here as well, imposing an obligation to recall witnesses on a successor judge only after a party has so requested. After failing to request the recall of these witnesses below, then, Atlantic cannot now claim error on the basis of Rule 63.

We turn then to Atlantic's substantive arguments that the district court erred in finding that Coastal had not breached either the warranty of seaworthiness explicitly provided in the insurance policy or the warranty of seaworthiness implied under maritime law. Warranties of seaworthiness, whether express or implied, require a vessel to be able "adequately to **[—37—]** perform the particular services required of her on the voyage she undertakes." *GTS Indus. S.A. v. S/S "Havtjeld"*, 68 F.3d 1531, 1535 (2d Cir. 1995). While the warranty is "absolute"—i.e., "imposed regardless of fault" and irrespective of "the owner's knowledge of the alleged unseaworthy conditions"—the meaning of seaworthiness is "relative" and "varies with the vessel involved and the use for which the vessel is intended." *PGG Realty*, 538 F. Supp. 2d at 693; *see also* 2 Schoenbaum, *supra*, § 19:16 ("[T]he standard is not perfection but reasonableness.").

With this standard in mind, we find Atlantic's claim of unseaworthiness to be without merit. In concluding that Atlantic had failed to prove that the MIKE B was unseaworthy, Judge Azrack reasonably credited Meyerrose's testimony and the findings of his preliminary survey, which stated that the vessel was "in satisfactory condition for operation in inland waters," Joint App'x 1391, noting that Meyerrose was "the only qualified person[] to have **{–69–}** conducted a survey of the MIKE B before the incident," *Atl. Specialty Ins. Co.*, 368 F. Supp. 3d at 440. Similarly, Judge **[—38—]** Azrack's decision to credit Coastal's and Sterling's experts over Atlantic's concerning the condition of the barge and the cause of its loss is reasonably based on a comparison of the experts' qualifications and testimony. *See id.* at 441 (noting, for example, that Atlantic's expert Colletti had only limited experience with spud barges and finding material portions of his testimony to be "imprecise and not reliable").[18]

In addition to her conclusion concerning the barge's seaworthy condition, Judge Azrack found, and the record supports, that Coastal had in place an inclement weather plan to have a tug available on one- or two-hour notice to assist in lifting the MIKE B's spuds and moving the barge. Indeed, the record supports a finding that, had the tug arrived on time, the spud **[—39—]** may not have bent, as several hours passed between when Miller was first called and when the tug finally arrived, during which the spud bent and its well tore, causing the loss. To the extent it may bear on the MIKE B's seaworthiness, then, Coastal's contingency plan was reasonable under the circumstances reason-

---

[18] Atlantic contends also that Judge Wexler had already been "apparently persuaded" of the MIKE B's unseaworthiness when he barred Atlantic from showing further photos of the MIKE B's hull during trial. *See* Appellant Br. at 32–37. Based on this conclusion, Atlantic suggests it was error for Judge Azrack to find that Atlantic had not met its burden of proof. However, a review of the trial transcript compels only the conclusion that Judge Wexler, having already reviewed a number of photographs, found further testimony on potential holes in the barge to be cumulative and minimally probative. *See* Joint App'x 596.

ably known at the time; the fact that the tug took far longer to arrive than planned, coupled with the unanticipated severity of the weather and sea conditions, did not render the MIKE B unseaworthy.

Under the clear error standard applicable to determinations of seaworthiness, we reverse only where we are "left with the definite and firm conviction that a mistake has been committed." *Mobil Shipping & Transp. Co.*, 190 F.3d at 67–68. In light of the district court's extensive findings and their support in the record, we cannot find that any such mistake has been committed here.

C. Covered Peril

Atlantic's third claimed error concerns Judge Azrack's finding that Coastal had met its burden in proving that the loss of the MIKE B was **[—40—]** proximately caused by a peril of the sea as covered in the insurance policy.[19] A peril of the sea is a maritime insurance term, defined with reference to "those perils which are peculiar to the sea, and which are of an extraordinary nature or arise from irresistible force or overwhelming power." *R.T. Jones Lumber Co. v. Roen S.S. Co.*, 270 F.2d 456, 458 (2d Cir. 1959). Our cases have applied the term to "damage [] done by the fortuitous action of the sea," *N.Y., New Haven & Hartford R.R. Co. v. Gray*, 240 F.2d 460, 464 (2d Cir. 1957), and we have held the term includes "occasional visitations of the violence of nature, like great storms, even though these are no more than should be expected. ... Indeed, fortuitous actions of the sea much less {–70–} violent than storms have been held to be within its intended **[—41—]** coverage." *Cont'l Ins. Co. v. Hersent Offshore, Inc.*, 567 F.2d 533, 535 (2d Cir. 1977) (citation

---

[19] The Policy reads, in relevant part:

PERILS: Touching the Adventures and Perils which the Underwriters are contented to bear and take upon themselves, they are of the Seas . . . and of all other like Perils, Losses and Misfortunes that have or shall come to the Hurt, Detriment or Damage of the Vessel, or any part thereof . . . .

Joint App'x 1431.

omitted). For example, we have found high swells caused by a passing freighter to constitute a covered peril of the sea. *See Allen N. Spooner & Son, Inc. v. Conn. Fire Ins. Co.*, 314 F.2d 753, 756 (2d Cir. 1963), *cert. denied*, 375 U.S. 819. The determination of whether certain weather or sea conditions constitute a peril of the sea "is a fact-intensive inquiry which requires examination of the type of vessel, the location of the vessel, the expectability [sic] of the weather, as well as its severity." *Lone Eagle Shipping*, 952 F. Supp. at 1061; *see also Darien Bank*, 654 F.2d at 1020 ("[W]hether or not an occurrence constitutes an extraordinary risk so as to be a peril of the sea is not of itself an absolute and unvarying thing, but is dependent on the circumstances of the case and the character of the vessel insured." (citation omitted)).

In conducting this inquiry, Judge Azrack made detailed findings and concluded that Coastal had met its burden of showing that "wind and sea conditions had generated waves ... averaging 4 to 6 feet when the MIKE B **[—42—]** was lost" and that these conditions "were the proximate cause of the spud well tearing, initial ingress of water, and the loss of the MIKE B." *Atl. Specialty Ins. Co.*, 368 F. Supp. 3d at 447–48. Atlantic raises two sets of challenges to these findings. First, it raises evidentiary challenges, arguing that Judge Wexler should not have allowed the deposition testimony of Gundersen to be considered, that Judge Azrack should not have credited Gundersen's testimony, and that it was error for Judge Azrack to "refus[e]" to recall Gundersen. *See* Appellant Br. at 46–48. Second, Atlantic challenges Judge Azrack's ultimate conclusions, primarily arguing that Coastal did not prove the conditions were "extraordinary" and that it was the MIKE B's unseaworthiness instead that proximately caused the loss. *Id.* at 48–51.

We disagree with each argument. First, Judge Wexler's decision to consider Gundersen's testimony certainly was not an abuse of discretion. Federal Rule of Evidence 804 permits the admission of former testimony, including that "given as a witness at a ... lawful deposition," where the witness is unavailable to testify. Fed. R. Evid.

804(b)(1)(A). And, as relevant [—43—] here, a witness is considered unavailable where he or she is "absent from the trial ... and the statement's proponent has not been able, by process or other reasonable means, to procure ... the [witness]'s attendance." Fed. R. Evid. 804(a)(5). Given Gundersen's refusal to appear under subpoena and that the testimony was taken under oath during a deposition, the admission of the evidence instead appears to be a faithful application of Federal Rule of Evidence 804. Next, we do not find error in Judge Azrack's decision to credit Gundersen's testimony: the inconsistencies identified by Atlantic are at most minor, and in many cases—such as Gundersen's statements concerning the height of the seas on April 12—the credited testimony is supported by other evidence in the record.[20] And, lastly, we have already concluded that under Rule 63, Judge Azrack was under no obligation to [—44—] attempt {-71-} to recall Gundersen given Atlantic's lack of a specific request to do so.

Atlantic has likewise failed to demonstrate that Judge Azrack's factual findings concerning the presence of a peril of the sea and the cause of the barge's loss were clearly erroneous. As with the related inquiry into the MIKE B's seaworthiness, Judge Azrack reasonably credited Coastal's and Sterling's experts over Atlantic's on the condition of the barge and the cause of the spud well's tearing, finding that it was the unexpected sea conditions, not any inherent fragility of the barge, that caused the losses. And Judge Azrack's decision to credit Coastal's experts on weather and sea conditions over Atlantic's, due to the superior methodology and modeling relied on by the former, was similarly well reasoned. *See Atl. Specialty Ins. Co.*, 368 F. Supp. 3d at 442–43, 447–48. Taken together, then, the evidence in the record amply supports the district court's findings that the seas reached four to six feet, that such conditions were "fortuitous" in light of the barge's deployment, and that it was these conditions that caused the loss of the [—45—] barge. Accordingly, we do not find the district court's conclusion that the MIKE B was lost due to a covered peril under the policy to be clearly erroneous.[21] [22]

D. Damages

Atlantic's final two claims of error concern the calculation of damages undertaken by the district court. First, Atlantic contends that because the policy excludes "[a]ny liability assumed by the assured beyond that imposed by law," Joint App'x 1436—and thus excludes third-party contractual liabilities—it should not be responsible for payments withheld under the contract between Coastal and Triton.[23] Appellant Br. at 54–56. [—46—] Second, Atlantic challenges the inclusion of damages for barge salvage and pier damage that were substantiated at trial by "unauthenticated third party bills, records and unsupported summaries of sums Triton reportedly withheld under their contract." Appellant Br. at 56. We do not find either claim of error persuasive.

---

[20] Atlantic also argues that Judge Wexler should not have admitted Gundersen's testimony and Judge Azrack should not have credited it due to Gundersen's prior convictions for assault. *E.g.*, Appellant Br. at 47. Judge Azrack's exclusion of evidence of these prior convictions—none of which bears directly on Gundersen's truthfulness, and the latest of which occurred in 2003—was not an abuse of discretion. *See* Fed. R. Evid. 403, 609.

[21] The district court found in the alternative that the loss was caused by Gundersen's negligence in failing to properly account for the weather, which would be covered by the Policy's Inchmaree ("Additional Perils") clause. *See Atl. Specialty Ins. Co.*, 368 F. Supp. 3d at 448–49. Because we find no error with the district court's conclusion concerning the perils of the sea, we need not address this separate conclusion.

[22] Because we affirm the district court's conclusions that the policy was not void and that it covered the loss of the MIKE B, we reject Atlantic's claim for reimbursement of $238,750 it paid under a reservation of rights to a third party for removal of the MIKE B wreck.

[23] As recounted above, Triton was the prime contractor for the Steeplechase Pier project with the City of New York. Triton subcontracted with Coastal to undertake the pier [—46—] repairs. After the pier was further damaged by the MIKE B, Triton held back portions of its payments to Coastal under their subcontractor agreement to cover the costs Triton incurred to repair these further damages and to clean up related debris.

Regarding the claim that certain damages are not compensable under the policy by virtue of their being "contractual" in nature, Atlantic asks us to read into its policy terms that simply do not exist. The claimed damages do not arise out of a contractual dispute, but represent payments withheld specifically to compensate Triton for repairs necessitated by the MIKE B's collisions with the Steeplechase Pier. Atlantic's challenge to its liability for the repairs under the policy is, rather, a challenge to the form in which Coastal {-72-} paid for the repairs, not to the fact that such repairs are covered [—47—] under the policy. Under Atlantic's theory, it would apparently not avoid liability if Coastal had made the repairs itself, if Triton had simply sent an invoice requesting payment for the repairs, or if Triton had sued Coastal in tort for the costs of the repairs. Because the policy makes no distinction concerning the form of payment, we cannot agree with an argument that essentially implies such a term into the policy.

Similarly, we do not find persuasive Atlantic's arguments concerning Coastal's use and the court's admission of "un-authenticated third party bills, records and unsupported summaries of sums Triton reportedly withheld under their contract" to prove damages. Appellant Br. at 56. We find no abuse of discretion by the district court in admitting and crediting the challenged evidence. That evidence is a lengthy compilation of spreadsheets and supporting invoices prepared not for trial, but by Coastal's insurance adjuster for the purposes of submitting a claim under the policy, and it was sent to Atlantic in 2014. The district court correctly concluded that Atlantic failed to raise any credible reason to suspect the [—48—] documents were inauthentic or inaccurate. Moreover, even if Atlantic had done so, the documents, "taken together with all the circumstances," have the "distinctive characteristics" of the invoices Coastal propounds they are. Fed. R. Evid. 901(b)(4). And the district court rightly concluded that Rule 1006, which requires a party to be able to produce for examination the original documents underlying a summary chart prepared for trial, was inapplicable to these documents as they were prepared not for trial,

but for submission of the insurance claim in 2014.[24] *See* Fed. R. Evid. 1006. In sum, we do not find error in the district court's computation of Coastal's damages. [—49—]

IV. CONCLUSION

We have reviewed all of the remaining arguments raised by Atlantic on appeal and find them to be without merit. For the foregoing reasons, we **AFFIRM** the judgment of the district court.

---

[24] We note also that Atlantic had these documents in its possession as of 2014 and thus had ample time to seek discovery concerning their accuracy. Atlantic did produce evidence of inaccuracy concerning two invoices, and the district court excluded those from its calculation. *See Atl. Specialty Ins. Co.*, 368 F. Supp. 3d at 451. Given the substantial opportunity to evaluate the other invoices, Atlantic's failure to credibly call into question any of them supports the district court's rejection of Atlantic's challenge to their authenticity.

This page intentionally left blank

United States Court of Appeals for the Third Circuit

United States Court of Appeals
for the Third Circuit

No. 17-1519

BRYAN
vs.
UNITED STATES

Appeal from the District Court of the Virgin Islands
(Division of St. Croix)

Decided: January 18, 2019

Citation: 913 F.3d 356, 7 Adm. R. 162 (3d Cir. 2019).

Before **KRAUSE, ROTH,** and **FISHER,** Circuit Judges.

[—2—] {–357–} ROTH, Circuit Judge: {–358–}

In 2008, Carlyle Bryan, Julie Beberman, and Charles Francis (the travelers), residents of St. Croix in the U.S. Virgin Islands, embarked on a Caribbean cruise aboard the Adventure of the Seas. Their trip took them to a number of foreign ports before they returned to the United States. During their trip, U.S. Customs and Border Protection (CBP) officers searched their cabins on suspicion of drug-smuggling activity. Those searches yielded no contraband and prompted the three travelers to assert *Bivens* claims[1] against the officers for allegedly violating their Fourth Amendment rights. They also asserted tort claims against the United States government under the Federal Tort Claims Act (FTCA or the Act). The District Court of the Virgin Islands granted summary judgment in favor of the officers and the government. [—3—]

Because we conclude that the officers are entitled to qualified immunity and the United States government is shielded from liability under the FTCA's discretionary function exception, we will affirm.

---

[1] *Bivens* provides for private rights of action against federal officials for certain constitutional violations. *Bivens v. Six Unknown Named Agents of Federal Bureau of Narcotics*, 403 U.S. 388 (1971).

I.

The Cruise

The cruise lasted from August 31 to September 7, 2008. Beberman had booked two cabins for the three travelers: one for Bryan and herself, and a second for Francis. The cruise began in the United States. They sailed from San Juan, Puerto Rico, stopped at several foreign ports, including Antigua, Barbados, St. Lucia, and St. Maarten, proceeded to St. Thomas in the U.S. Virgin Islands, and returned to San Juan.

The travelers had to pass through a CBP checkpoint in San Juan before boarding the ship. Bryan and Beberman went through without incident. Francis's trip through the checkpoint was not so smooth. When a CBP officer asked Francis what his occupation was, he hesitated and then said "oil change." (Francis worked with automobiles and changed motor oil.) CBP officers then inspected Francis's bag. There was a very full canister of shaving powder in the bag. When a CBP officer opened the canister, the powder dispersed through the room and coated the officer. Bryan laughed. They contend now that the inspection of their cabins was in retaliation for Bryan's laughing at the CBP officer. The officers found nothing unlawful in Francis's bags. CBP Officer Baez made a notation in the Treasury Enforcement Communications System (TECS) database that Francis had appeared "disoriented and nervous" and that it took him some {–359–} time to state his employment, but that the examination of his bag did not uncover anything.[2]

The Creation of "Lookout" Entries by Officer Timothy Ogg (September 5, 2008)

CBP Officer Timothy Ogg, stationed in San Juan, was routinely assigned the task of reviewing passenger manifests for the Adventure of the Seas to identify passengers worthy of further scrutiny. Around September 1, he compared the names on the passenger manifest against the names on reports logged

---

[2] JA 8.

onto TECS. Both Bryan's and Francis's names yielded matches; both had TECS entries related to drug smuggling.

Officer Ogg found two entries on Bryan. The first, dated May 17, 2000, was authored by Immigration & Customs Enforcement (ICE) Agent Hillary Hodge. Referring to Bryan, the entry read: "Subject is associate[d] with suspected drug smugglers within the US Virgin Islands. Subject is also suspected of smuggling narcotics within the Virgin Islands. If encountered, conduct 100% exam . . . ."[3] Officer Ogg later testified that he [—4—] had previously worked with Agent Hodge and credited his entry in part because he regarded Hodge as an excellent worker. The second TECS entry, from 2004, referred to the prior entry, characterized Bryan as a "suspect in USVI drug smuggling," and encouraged agents to "document [his] co-travelers, employment and reason for travel."[4]

As for Francis, Officer Ogg uncovered two TECS reports from 2006 identifying Francis as the "Subject of [a Drug Enforcement Administration] indictment." The first report was authored while the Drug Enforcement Administration investigation was going on and characterized Francis as a "subject of current interest"; the second was authored after the investigation had ended and referred to him as a "Previous Suspect."[5] Both reports urged personnel to alert special agents if they encountered Francis.

According to Officer Ogg's subsequent deposition testimony, another factor aroused his suspicion: CBP officers had previously made narcotics seizures on the Adventure of the Seas on the same route. A number of islands along the route were known to be sources of narcotics smuggled into the United States. Officer Ogg characterized them as high-risk islands.

On September 5, primarily on the strength of the TECS records concerning Bryan and Francis, Officer Ogg created "lookout" entries for Bryan and Francis in the TECS database.

A "lookout" is a TECS entry that alerts CBP officers to specific passengers and recommends certain investigative steps when they are encountered. In the case of Bryan and Francis, the "lookout entries" noted their connection to "drug smuggling" and recommended, in the standard TECS shorthand (i.e., "100% exam"), that their cabins be inspected before their return to San Juan on September 7.[6]

Officer Ogg also entered a separate "lookout" for Beberman. Except for the co-travelers listed, the "lookout" entry for Beberman mirrored Bryan's. At his deposition, Officer Ogg gave two reasons for the Beberman "lookout." First, she was traveling with two individuals about whom there were independent TECS entries predicated on drug-smuggling concerns. Second, as a practical matter, Officer Ogg {–360–} stated that he had to enter a lookout for Beberman to ensure that Bryan and Francis did not use her to evade [—5—] detection and inspection by having her submit a single customs declaration form for the three of them, but in her name only.[7]

The St. Thomas Cabin Searches (September 6, 2008)

On the morning of September 6, 2008, after the travelers had returned to United States waters and had docked in St. Thomas, CBP Officers DeFelice, Demarais, Mazur, Santiago, and Torres (collectively, the St. Thomas Officers) inspected Bryan and Beberman's cabin, along with Francis's.

The cabin searches each lasted between five and ten minutes.[8] The St. Thomas

---

[3] JA 9.

[4] JA 9-10.

[5] JA 10.

[6] Id.

[7] Ogg testified at his deposition that passengers traveling together were allowed to submit a single customs declaration form without identifying every passenger. Because secondary inspections were triggered by the names included on declaration forms, Bryan and Francis could have attempted to evade detection by having Beberman submit a form in her name only. Officer Ogg explained that he had entered three separate "lookouts" to guard against that possibility.

[8] The cabin inspections differed in two respects: The occupants found themselves in different states

officers knocked on the cabin doors before opening them. The occupants were asked to get dressed without using the bathroom, and in at least partial view of the officers. They were then asked to leave their cabins and stand against a wall in the hallway. They waited in the hallway for between two and five minutes, while officers with a drug-sniffing dog inspected their cabins. Neither cabin search yielded any contraband; the St. Thomas Officers created TECS entries to that effect.[9]

II.

As a result of the searches, Beberman, Bryan, and Francis filed suit in the District Court for the Virgin Islands, asserting Fourth Amendment *Bivens* claims against Officer Ogg, who had recommended, but not participated in, the cabin searches and against the St. Thomas officers, who had executed the cabin searches. The travelers also asserted tort claims against the United States under the FTCA for invasion of privacy, false imprisonment, and intentional infliction of emotional distress. [—6—]

At the close of discovery, the officers and the United States moved for summary judgment. The District Court granted their motion on all claims.

As for the officers, the District Court reasoned that neither Officer Ogg's entry of "lookouts" nor the St. Thomas cabin searches violated the travelers' Fourth Amendment rights. Further, it held that the officers were entitled to qualified immunity because their conduct did not violate clearly established Fourth Amendment rights.

---

of undress (*i.e.*, Francis was naked, while Bryan and Beberman were partially clothed) and the occupants were observed to different extents while they dressed (*i.e.*, Bryan and Beberman dressed with their cabin door ajar and the officers outside, while Francis dressed in full view of the officers).

[9] On September 7, when the ship reached San Juan, a different set of CBP officers began to inspect the travelers' cabins but cut short the searches when they learned of the St. Thomas searches. The San Juan searches are not implicated in this appeal. The travelers voluntarily dismissed their *Bivens* claims against the San Juan officers.

As for the United States, the District Court held that the FTCA claims were barred by the Act's discretionary function exception.

We review the District Court's grant of summary judgment *de novo*, applying {–361–} the same decisional principle.[10] The District Court exercised subject matter jurisdiction under 28 U.S.C. §§ 1331 and 1346(b). We have appellate jurisdiction under 28 U.S.C. § 1291.

III.

The Fourth Amendment protects the public "against unreasonable searches and seizures."[11] Whether a search is reasonable turns on "all of the circumstances surrounding the search," including where the search took place.[12]

The search here took place at the border. The border serves a unique gate-keeping function. Our controlling Fourth Amendment precedent is attuned to that reality. The Supreme Court has stressed the border's role in protecting our territorial sovereignty, along with the need to curb the inflow of drugs at the border.[13] For those reasons, we extend the government special latitude at the border and strike "the Fourth Amendment balance between the interests of the Government and the privacy right of the individual" in the government's favor.[14] [—7—]

---

[10] Summary judgment should be granted when, "after drawing all reasonable inferences from the underlying facts in the light most favorable to the nonmoving party, the court concludes that there is no genuine issue of material fact to be resolved at trial and the moving party is entitled to judgment as a matter of law." *Petruzzi's IGA Supermarkets, Inc. v. Darling-Delaware Co.*, 998 F.2d 1224, 1230 (3d Cir. 1993).

[11] U.S. Const. amend. IV.

[12] *United States v. Montoya de Hernandez*, 473 U.S. 531, 537 (1985).

[13] *See Montoya*, 473 U.S. at 538 (highlighting a "longstanding concern for the protection of the integrity of the border. This concern is, if anything, heightened by the veritable national crisis in law enforcement caused by smuggling of illicit narcotics . . ..") (citation omitted); *see also Bradley v. United States*, 299 F.3d 197, 201-02 (3d Cir. 2002).

[14] *Montoya*, 473 U.S. at 539-40; *see also United States v. Hyde*, 37 F.3d 116, 119-20 (3d Cir. 1994).

In view of the government's interests, we "have long held that routine searches at our nation's borders are presumed to be reasonable under the Fourth Amendment."[15] Indeed, "[r]outine searches of the persons and effects of entrants are not subject to any requirement of reasonable suspicion, probable cause, or warrant . . .."[16] In contrast, "nonroutine searches . . . require reasonable suspicion."[17] This approach to border searches applies with equal force at "the functional equivalent" of the border,[18] such as a ship's first port of call in the United States.[19] Under this standard, the search here was a border search.

On September 4, 2008, a day before Officer Ogg entered "lookouts" for the travelers and two days before the cabin searches, we ruled for the first time on the constitutional propriety of border searches in the same context presented in this appeal—in remarkable coincidence, searches of cabins aboard the Adventure of the {–362–} Seas.[20] In *United States v. Whitted*, we acknowledged "the surprising dearth of authority" on whether a search of a cruise ship cabin at the border is a routine search requiring no suspicion, or a non-routine search requiring "reasonable suspicion" (*i.e.*, a "particularized and objective basis" to suspect criminal activity).[21] We held for the first time that because of a passenger's "high expectation of privacy" and the "level of intrusiveness," a search of a cruise ship cabin at the border is non-routine and requires reasonable suspicion.[22] We also held that unsubstantiated information from TECS can establish reasonable suspicion.[23]

IV.

In considering whether a government official is entitled to qualified immunity, a court can determine whether a constitutional right was violated or in the alternative, whether that right was clearly established.[24] Following that precedent, we will not opine as to whether there were underlying Fourth Amendment violations involved in the search here. We will instead determine whether the *Whitted* standard, that a search of a cabin on a cruise ship required reasonable suspicion, was clearly established when Officer Ogg included in his entry of "lookouts" in the TECS System that 100 % examination of the [—8—] three travelers, *i.e.*, examination of their cabins, was recommended and the next day when the St. Thomas officers searched the travelers' cabins.

The doctrine of qualified immunity shields government officials from *Bivens* claims and money damages, unless a plaintiff can establish that the official violated a statutory or constitutional right, and that the right was "clearly established at the time of the challenged conduct."[25] To be clearly established, a right's contours must be "sufficiently definite that any reasonable official in the defendant's shoes would have understood that he was violating it" and that "existing precedent . . . placed the statutory or constitutional question confronted by the official beyond debate."[26]

Further, as the Supreme Court recently reiterated, "clearly established law should not be defined at a high level of generality" but must instead "be particularized to the facts of the case."[27] The doctrine is designed to "give[] government officials breathing room to make reasonable but mistaken judgments by

---

[15] *Bradley*, 299 F.3d at 201 (citations omitted).

[16] *Montoya*, 473 U.S. at 538 (footnote omitted).

[17] *Bradley*, 299 F.3d at 204 n.8 (citation omitted).

[18] *Almeida-Sanchez v. United States*, 413 U.S. 266, 272-73 (1973).

[19] *United States v. Smith*, 273 F.3d 629, 633 n.8 (5th Cir. 2001) (citation omitted).

[20] *United States v. Whitted*, 541 F.3d 480 (3d Cir. 2008).

[21] *Whitted*, 541 F.3d at 486, 489.

[22] *Id.* at 489.

[23] *Id.* at 490.

---

[24] *Pearson v. Callahan*, 555 U.S. 223, 236 (2009).

[25] *Ashcroft v. al-Kidd*, 563 U.S. 731, 735 (2011) (citing *Harlow v. Fitzgerald*, 457 U.S. 800, 818 (1982)).

[26] *Plumhoff v. Rickard*, 134 S. Ct. 2012, 2023 (2014) (quoting *Ashcroft*, 563 U.S. at 741).

[27] *White v. Pauly*, 137 S. Ct. 548, 552 (2017) (per curiam) (citation omitted); *see also L.R. v. Sch. Dist. of Phila.*, 836 F.3d 235, 248 (3d Cir. 2016).

protect[ing] all but the plainly incompetent or those who knowingly violate the law."[28]

Supreme Court discussion of searches has emphasized the threats posed at borders and the government's compelling {–363–} interests in searches there.[29] Because the government's interest in preventing the entry of unwarranted persons and effects is at its zenith at the border,[30] Congress "has granted the Executive plenary authority to conduct routine searches and seizures at the border, without probable cause or a warrant . . . ."[31] Until September 4, 2008, there had been no ruling in the Third Circuit as to what constituted a "routine search." As for Officer Ogg, he was located in San Juan, Puerto Rico, in the First Circuit. There had not been any such ruling in the First Circuit, and the First Circuit courts would not be bound by *Whitted*, a Third Circuit case.

When such a ruling is made, a ruling which affects the procedures used in border searches, it is beyond belief that within two days the government could determine what was "reasonable suspicion" and what new policy was required to conform to the ruling, much less communicate that new policy to the CBP officers. We can only conclude that as of September 5, 2008, it was not clearly established in either the Third Circuit or the First Circuit that a search of a cruise ship cabin at the border had to be supported by [—9—] reasonable suspicion. Accordingly, under the circumstances that Officer Ogg confronted, he did not violate clearly established law by entering lookouts for the three passengers the day after we issued our decision in *Whitted*. He is entitled to qualified immunity.

We conclude that the same situation applies to the St. Thomas officers. On September 6, the *Whitted* standard was no more clearly established than it had been the day before. Moreover, if the St. Thomas officers had been aware of *Whitted*, they would have known that *Whitted* held that unsubstantiated information from TECS can establish reasonable suspicion.[32]

For these reasons, we conclude that the *Whitted* standard was not clearly established in the Third Circuit, or the First Circuit, on September 5 or 6. Within one or two days, neither Officer Ogg nor the St. Thomas officers could reasonably be expected to have learned of this development in our Fourth Amendment jurisprudence. At that time, it would not have been beyond debate that, absent reasonable suspicion, the Fourth Amendment prohibited the search of the travelers' cabins. For purposes of qualified immunity, a legal principle does not become "clearly established" the day we announce a decision, or even one or two days later.

This holding is informed by the overarching aim of the qualified immunity doctrine to insulate from civil liability "all but the plainly incompetent or those who knowingly violate the law,"[33] and the need to ensure that the relevant legal principle is framed with particularity[34] and settled "beyond debate."[35] We are, however, deciding only this case. For that reason, we decline to draw a bright line demarcating when a legal principle becomes "clearly established." We leave that exercise for another day.

Finally, the tort claims against the United States also fail because of the {–364–} FTCA's discretionary function exception. The FTCA provides a limited waiver of sovereign immunity in certain tort actions against the United States for money damages.[36] That waiver does not extend to various types of government conduct enumerated in 28 U.S.C. [—10—] § 2680, including "the exercise or performance or the failure to exercise or perform a discretionary function or duty . . .

---

[28] *City & Cty. of S.F. v. Sheehan*, 135 S. Ct. 1765, 1774 (2015) (citation omitted).

[29] *See, e.g., Montoya*, 473 U.S. at 539-40.

[30] *United States v. Flores-Montano*, 541 U.S. 149, 152-53 (2004).

[31] *Id.* at 153.

[32] 541 F.3d at 490.

[33] *White*, 137 S. Ct. at 552.

[34] *Id.*

[35] *Plumhoff*, 134 S. Ct. at 2023.

[36] 28 U.S.C. § 1346(b)(1).

whether or not the discretion involved be abused."[37]

The travelers do not dispute that Officer Ogg's entry of "lookouts" and the searches that followed were discretionary acts under the "discretionary function" exception.[38] Rather, they argue that the United States is not shielded from liability because the officers in this case, though exercising their discretion, violated "clearly established . . . constitutional rights of which a reasonable person would have known."[39]

Because, for the reasons set out above, the CBP officers did not violate clearly established constitutional rights, the FTCA claims also fail.

V.

For the reasons stated above, we will affirm the judgment of the District Court.

---

[37] 28 U.S.C. § 2680(a). Discretionary acts and omissions "involv[e] an element of judgment or choice." Conduct is non-discretionary only if a "federal statute, regulation, or policy specifically prescribes a course of action for an employee to follow" and the government "employee has no rightful option but to adhere to the directive." *United States v. Gaubert*, 499 U.S. 315, 322 (1991) (quoting *Berkovitz ex rel. Berkovitz v. United States*, 486 U.S. 531, 536 (1988)).

[38] Br. at 63-64.

[39] *Harlow*, 457 U.S. at 818.

United States Court of Appeals
for the Third Circuit

No. 17-3471

IN RE ASBESTOS PRODS. LIAB. LITIG. (NO. VI)

Appeal from the United States District Court for the
Eastern District of Pennsylvania

Decided: April 9, 2019

Citation: 921 F.3d 98, 7 Adm. R. 168 (3d Cir. 2019).

Before **SMITH**, Chief Judge, **McKEE**, and **FISHER**, Circuit Judges.

[—2—] {–100–} SMITH, Chief Judge: [—3—]

Decades after the filing of maritime asbestos injury cases in the Northern District of Ohio, the District Court for the Eastern District of Pennsylvania—which was by then presiding over a nationwide asbestos products multidistrict litigation {–101–} (MDL)—dismissed claims against numerous defendants for lack of personal jurisdiction. Unsurprisingly, the MDL Court's opinions regarding personal jurisdiction, which were subsequently applied to thousands of claims, have prompted multiple appeals, including two prior appeals to this Court. Now, for the third time, we address on appeal the MDL Court's personal jurisdiction rulings. Based on the unique history of the three consolidated cases now on appeal, we again conclude that dismissal for lack of personal jurisdiction was inappropriate. We will dismiss in part and reverse in part.

I.

A.

In the mid-1980s, merchant mariners filed thousands of lawsuits in the Northern District of Ohio against shipowners,[1] raising claims that the merchant mariners had been injured due to exposure to asbestos onboard ships. Northern District of [—4—] Ohio Judge Thomas Lambros[2] initially presided over the massive Ohio maritime asbestos docket (MARDOC) prior to the 1991 consolidation of the cases in an MDL in the Eastern District of Pennsylvania.

When they filed in the Northern District of Ohio, the merchant mariners relied on a theory of nationwide personal jurisdiction for maritime cases. In 1989, shipowners filed motions to dismiss for lack of personal jurisdiction, arguing that the nationwide theory of jurisdiction was improper and that they did not have sufficient ties to Ohio to justify the exercise of personal jurisdiction over them. In an oral ruling in October of 1989, Judge Lambros rejected the merchant mariners' theory of jurisdiction and ruled that the Northern District of Ohio lacked personal jurisdiction over a number of the shipowners.[3] Judge Lambros indicated, however, that he would be denying the motion to dismiss and issuing an order transferring the cases instead. Following Judge Lambros's ruling, defense counsel requested additional time to consult with his clients and determine whether the shipowners wanted to accept transfer or waive their personal jurisdiction defenses so that they could remain in the Northern District of Ohio. Counsel suggested that his clients may very well want to waive the defense: "It is conceivable, your Honor, in view of the fact that such motions to dismiss have been denied that some of [—5—] those defendants who filed motions will not care to be transferred and they wish to stay here, I don't know. I have to consult with them." App. 291.

The Northern District of Ohio followed up the next month with a hearing to address the shipowners' decisions as to whether they would waive the personal jurisdiction defense. Defense counsel advised Judge Lambros that

---

[1] Many shipowner defendants and multiple defense firms have been involved in this litigation. Unless otherwise indicated, when we describe actions taken by "defendants," "shipowners," and "defense counsel" in this Opinion, we are referring to appellees and their counsel at Thompson Hine LLP (previously Thompson, Hine & Flory).

[2] After over 27 years of distinguished service, Judge Lambros left the federal bench in 1995.

[3] The merchant mariners have since abandoned the nationwide contacts theory and do not appeal the MDL Court's ruling that there was not personal jurisdiction over defendants.

he did not yet have an answer because his clients wanted to know how Judge Lambros would rule on various issues prior to deciding whether they would consent to jurisdiction. *See, e.g.*, App. 362–63. Defense counsel explained that in his view "a lot of these people will stay once they know that information." App. 364. Counsel for the merchant {–102–} mariners objected to the shipowners' equivocation:

> And so [defense counsel] Mr. Murphy is saying well, he can't make a decision. And just like the old expression be careful what you ask for; you might get it. That's really what he has here. He says, 'Oh, Judge, we wanted to get out of here.' Then he says, 'Well, we want you to make a few more preliminary rulings before we decide whether we want to go or not.' I say get them out of here.

App. 373; *see also* App. 378. At the conclusion of the November hearing, the Northern District of Ohio directed the shipowners to simply file answers by the answer deadline if they intended to waive the personal jurisdiction objection, and, at the time, defense counsel accepted that procedure: [—6—]

> Judge Lambros: "What happens if in the management of these cases if we make the disclosure date the same date as the answer date, but if the position is that they are not leaving, they have to have their answers in on those dates?"
>
> ***
>
> Defense Counsel: "I see no problem with that, your Honor. Now that we have the information, we know what we have to do, that's no problem."

App. 401–02.[4]

_____

[4] *See also* App. 404 (Judge Lambros: "And unless of course the parties otherwise announce by January 5th, that then on January 6th or 7th these cases will be transferred. . . . But January 5th the answers have to be filed, and then we transfer then if those specific defendants don't answer and thus waive by the answer date, then the cases get transferred out."); App. 404–05 (Judge Lambros:

Judge Lambros issued MARDOC Orders No. 40 and 41, on November 22, 1989, and December 29, 1989, [—7—] respectively, reiterating the procedure announced at the November hearing and directing shipowners who wished to waive their personal jurisdiction defenses to file answers by January 5, 1990, in order to demonstrate waiver. *See* App. 416 (MARDOC 40: "Parties who, upon reconsideration of their motions to dismiss or transfer, wish to remain in this jurisdiction need only file answers to the complaints in accordance with the deadlines established below."); App. 419 (MARDOC 41: "Shipowner defendants, not subject to this transfer order, shall file answers by January 5, 1990."). MARDOC Order 41 expressly ordered transfer of the cases where there was no personal jurisdiction and identified the jurisdiction to which each case would be transferred. On December 29, 1989, shipowners filed a motion for interlocutory appeal and stay to challenge the Northern District of Ohio's authority to transfer the cases rather than dismissing them.

Before the Northern District of Ohio had ruled on the motion for interlocutory appeal and stay, all shipowners relevant to this consolidated appeal filed answers on January 5, 1990, in compliance with Judge Lambros's deadline. Yet shipowners asserted in those answers that they were filing under protest and continued to assert personal jurisdiction defenses. App. 1131; App. 1133–34; App. 1136. Other defendants did not file answers and were transferred out of the Northern District of Ohio.

After the shipowners filed their answers, the Northern District of Ohio proceeded as if they had waived their personal jurisdiction defenses. MARDOC Order 41, directing

_____

"In other words a transfer order goes on and we designate the particular jurisdictions to which it will be transferred, and that order will go into effect January 7th unless by January 5th those particular defendants choose to waive the in personam jurisdiction problem . . . Mr. Murphy: I don't perceive any difficulty. Special Master Martyn: Just for my understanding, so they will answer if they want to stay. [Judge Lambros]: That's right.").

{–103–} transfer of those cases where personal jurisdiction was lacking, was [—8—] never effectuated as to these shipowners.[5] Nor did the Northern District of Ohio rule on the motion for interlocutory appeal. Indeed, the cases progressed before Judge Lambros for over a year, with no additional motion practice challenging the Northern District of Ohio's jurisdiction or seeking transfer.[6]

B.

In 1991, authority over the maritime asbestos cases was transferred to the asbestos MDL in the Eastern District of Pennsylvania. Defendants opposed transfer to the MDL Court [—9—] but did not raise a personal jurisdiction defense in their opposition papers. After the creation of the MDL, the MARDOC cases were stayed. There is no dispute, however, that the shipowners consistently attempted to raise personal jurisdiction defenses in compliance with the MDL timelines.

In 2011, the cases at issue here were reactivated by Judge Robreno, who by then was presiding over the MDL in the Eastern District of Pennsylvania. In 2013 and 2014, the MDL Court issued two memorandum opinions concluding that a number of

shipowners were not subject to personal jurisdiction in Ohio and that the shipowners had not waived the defense. The MDL Court explained that the shipowners had preserved the defense by raising lack of personal jurisdiction before the Northern District of Ohio and again before the MDL Court on multiple occasions. Although shipowners filed answers in the Northern District of Ohio—a procedure Judge Lambros had ordered would indicate waiver—the MDL Court concluded that this did not result in waiver because "defendants did not intend to waive the defense." App. 53. The MDL Court noted that "defendants faced a Hobson's choice: they could either have agreed to a transfer of the cases to another jurisdiction (and thus lost the ability to assert cross-claims against manufacturer defendants), or they could have chosen to remain in the Northern District of Ohio and lost the defense of lack of personal jurisdiction." App. 54. Accordingly, the MDL Court held that "[b]y filing answers which clearly identified the defense, while at the same time seeking interlocutory review of Judge Lambros'[s] order, defendants preserved and did not waive the defense." App. 54 (internal citation omitted). The MDL Court subsequently [—10—] applied its prior memorandum opinions to the three merchant mariners relevant to this appeal and dismissed their claims against the shipowners for lack of personal jurisdiction. Merchant mariners Munnier, Schroeder, and Williams filed a timely notice of appeal.

II.

The District Court had jurisdiction under 28 U.S.C. §§ 1331 and 1333. We {–104–} have appellate jurisdiction under 28 U.S.C. § 1291.[7]

---

[5] There are indications in the record that other cases, in which an answer was not filed, were actually transferred. *See, e.g.*, App. 465–66 ("As a consequence of this Honorable Court's Order of December 10, 1989, *forum non conveniens* plagues plaintiffs, for each of the causes of action has been splintered, leaving part of the case here and part elsewhere."); App. 482.

[6] In February 1990, merchant mariners moved for transfer *in toto* of the cases such that they could all be tried in one jurisdiction. Defense counsel for the shipowners relevant to this appeal filed a brief opposing transfer and noting that some shipowners had waived their personal jurisdiction defenses in order to proceed in the Northern District of Ohio. Those waiver statements were not directly tied to any specific shipowner. Similarly, a group of cases was temporarily transferred to Michigan and defense counsel argued for retransfer back to the Northern District of Ohio, arguing in part that those shipowners had waived their personal jurisdiction defenses in Ohio. The cases now on appeal were not part of the Michigan group, as explained *infra*.

[7] The clerk's office *sua sponte* ordered the parties to brief whether the MDL Court's order was a final order such that this Court has jurisdiction to consider the appeal under 28 U.S.C. § 1291. Following a review of the parties' briefs, we have no doubt that the MDL Court's order was an appealable final order. *See Allegheny Int'l, Inc. v. Allegheny Ludlum Steel Corp.*, 920 F.2d 1127, 1131 (3d Cir. 1990) ("A district court's decision is final and appealable for purposes of § 1291 only when the decision ends the litigation on the merits and leaves nothing for the court to do but execute the judgment." (internal quotation marks omitted)).

See Brown Shoe Co. v. United States, 370 U.S. 294, 308–09 (1962). [—11—]

We must, nonetheless, dismiss Mr. Schroeder's appeal against Marine Transport Lines, Inc., because it is barred by res judicata. After the MDL Court dismissed Mr. Schroeder's claims, but before a final judgment had issued, Mr. Schroeder filed suit in South Carolina state court raising the same claims against Marine Transport Lines. After the state court dismissed similar cases brought by other plaintiffs because they were filed outside of the statute of limitations, Mr. Schroeder, apparently anticipating the state court's ruling, filed a motion to voluntarily dismiss his claims. The state court entered an order dismissing Mr. Schroeder's claims with prejudice.

This Court gives a judgment of a state court the same preclusive effect as would another court of that state. *Paramount Aviation Corp. v. Agusta*, 178 F.3d 132, 141 (3d Cir. 1999). In South Carolina, "[a] dismissal with prejudice acts as an adjudication on the merits and therefore precludes subsequent litigation just as if the action had been tried to a final adjudication." *Laughon v. O'Braitis*, 602 S.E.2d 108, 111 (S.C. Ct. App. 2004). Accordingly, the South Carolina dismissal with prejudice precludes Mr. Schroeder and his estate from pursuing claims against Marine Transport Lines. [—12—] We will therefore grant the motion

---

While the MDL Court indicated in its judgment that it was transferring the cases to the bankruptcy-only docket for plaintiffs to pursue claims against bankrupt defendants, there was clear "indicia of finality." In addition, the MDL Court elsewhere described the "transfer" to the bankruptcy docket as a "dismissal." *See, e.g., In re Asbestos Prods. Liability Litig.*, No. 2:02-md-875, Dkt. 4961 at 2 (directing plaintiffs to identify whether cases "can be [—11—] marked closed or *dismissed* to the 'bankruptcy only' docket" (emphasis added)); *see also Johnston v. Citizens Bank & Trust Co. of Flippin, Ark.*, 659 F.2d 865, 868 (8th Cir. 1981) (holding that a District Court judgment was a final judgment despite the fact that portions of the case were "transferred" to the Bankruptcy Court because it was clear that those portions of the case had actually been dismissed).

to dismiss Mr. Schroeder's appeal as to Marine Transport Lines.

III.

We review a District Court's decision as to the waiver of an affirmative defense for abuse of discretion. *Sharp v. Johnson*, 669 F.3d 144, 158 (3d Cir. 2012). "A court abuses its discretion when its decision rests upon a clearly erroneous finding of fact, an errant conclusion of law or an improper application of law to fact." *Id.* at 158 n.19 (internal quotation marks omitted). Here, the fundamental facts are not in dispute. Instead, the primary question at issue is whether the defendants' conduct amounted to waiver of the personal jurisdiction defense as a matter of law. We hold that the District Court's conclusion that there was no waiver was an improper application of law to fact that constitutes an abuse of discretion under this Court's precedent.

A.

Under Federal Rule of Civil Procedure 12(b)(2), defendants have the right to {–105–} move for dismissal for lack of personal jurisdiction, but that right is not unlimited. Rule 12(h) clarifies that the defense of lack of personal jurisdiction can be waived if a defendant fails to raise it in a timely fashion. Fed. R. Civ. P. 12(h). Precedent of the Supreme Court and this Court further holds that the right to assert a personal jurisdiction defense can be affirmatively and implicitly waived through conduct. *See, e.g., Ins. Corp. of Ireland, Ltd. v. Compagnie des Bauxites de Guinee*, 456 U.S. 694, 703 (1982) ("Because the requirement of personal jurisdiction represents [—13—] first of all an individual right, it can, like other such rights, be waived."); *Zelson v. Thomforde*, 412 F.2d 56, 59 (3d Cir. 1969) ("[P]ersonal jurisdiction may be conferred by consent of the parties, expressly or by failure to object." (citing *Petrowski v. Hawkeye Security Ins. Co.*, 350 U.S. 495, 496 (1956))).

Simply put, "[t]he actions of the defendant may amount to a legal submission to the jurisdiction of the court" even where a defendant has raised the defense. *Ins. Corp. of Ireland, Ltd.*, 456 U.S. at 704–05; *see also Yeldell v. Tutt*, 913 F.2d 533, 539 (8th Cir. 1990) ("Asserting a jurisdictional defect in the answer did not preserve the defense in perpetuity." (internal quotation marks omitted)). This aligns with the original purpose of Rule 12, which is to prevent "dilatory tactics" and "to expedite and simplify the pretrial phase of federal litigation" to facilitate adjudication on the merits. 5B C. Wright & A. Miller, *Fed. Prac. and Proc.* § 1342 (3d ed. 2004).

Thus, even where a party has met the technical requirements of Rule 12(h), that is not always sufficient to avoid waiver. *See Peterson v. Highland Music, Inc.*, 140 F.3d 1313, 1318 (9th Cir. 1998) ("Rule 12(h)(1) specifies the minimum steps that a party must take in order to preserve a defense."). A party's actions must also be consistent with the spirit of Rule 12 by diligently advancing its procedural objections. *See Yeldell*, 913 F.2d at 539 ("While the Tutts literally complied with Rule 12(h) by including the jurisdictional issue in their answer, they did not comply with the spirit of the rule, which is to expedite and simplify proceedings in the Federal Courts." (internal quotation marks omitted)). As this Court has explained, "a party is deemed to [—14—] have consented to personal jurisdiction if the party actually litigates the underlying merits or demonstrates a willingness to engage in extensive litigation in the forum." *In re Tex. E. Transmission Corp. PCB Contamination Ins. Coverage Litig.*, 15 F.3d 1230, 1236 (3d Cir. 1994). "In particular, where a party seeks affirmative relief from a court, it normally submits itself to the jurisdiction of the court with respect to the adjudication of claims arising from the same subject matter." *Bel-Ray Co. v. Chemrite (Pty) Ltd.*, 181 F.3d 435, 443 (3d Cir. 1999) (citing *Adam v. Saenger*, 303 U.S. 59, 67 (1938)).

B.

Here, there is no dispute that the shipowners timely filed a motion to dismiss for lack of personal jurisdiction in the Northern District of Ohio, in compliance with Rule 12.

The question is therefore whether the MDL Court abused its discretion when it concluded that the shipowners had not waived their personal jurisdiction defenses by subsequently consenting to, or acquiescing in, the jurisdiction of the Northern District of Ohio.

This Court has issued two non-precedential opinions in related cases where other merchant mariners appealed the MDL Court's orders dismissing maritime asbestos cases for lack of personal jurisdiction. {–106–} *See In re: Asbestos Prod. Liab. Litig. (No. VI) (Braun)*, 661 F. App'x 173 (3d Cir. 2016); *In re Asbestos Prod. Liab. Litig. (No. VI) (Blue)*, 721 F. App'x 111 (3d Cir. 2017).[8] In both cases, this Court reversed, concluding [—15—] that the shipowners had waived their personal jurisdiction defenses. Those appeals, however, involved cases that had been transferred from the Northern District of Ohio to Michigan, whereas the cases here had not been transferred. The panels relied on express statements by shipowners in the Michigan proceedings that they had waived their personal jurisdiction defenses in Ohio. We decline the merchant mariners' invitation to impute the shipowners' statements in *Braun* and *Blue* to defendants here.[9] There was no express waiver in the three cases before us.

The question, then, becomes whether the MDL Court abused its discretion when it concluded that the shipowners had not implicitly waived their personal jurisdiction defenses through their conduct in the Northern District of Ohio. We conclude that the facts and our precedent support a determination that there was implicit waiver. We hold, therefore, that the MDL Court's contrary ruling was an abuse of discretion.

First, the shipowners themselves introduced the possibility of waiver at the

---

[8] These dispositions were not opinions of the full Court and pursuant to I.O.P. 5.7 do not constitute binding precedent.

[9] We do note, however, that at the time defense counsel stated in the Michigan cases that the personal jurisdiction defense had previously been waived, nothing had transpired in those cases to indicate waiver apart from the conduct that had also taken place in the cases here.

October 1989 hearing by asking for additional time so they could choose whether to assent to transfer or waive their personal jurisdiction objections. Then, at the hearing the following month, the shipowners equivocated as to whether or not they intended to waive the [—16—] defense, and their counsel requested that Judge Lambros make additional rulings before his clients decided whether to waive jurisdiction. Generally, a party who requests affirmative relief and rulings from a court is considered to have waived the personal jurisdiction defense. *Bel-Ray Co.*, 181 F.3d at 443.

Second, the record is clear that the shipowners objected to transfer, and they stand by that objection on appeal. *See, e.g.,* Appellees' Br. at 39 ("Appellees declined either to waive their defenses or to assent to transfer."). Because Judge Lambros had already denied defendants' motions to dismiss and concluded that personal jurisdiction was absent, the shipowners were left with two options. They could waive their personal jurisdiction defenses and remain in the Northern District of Ohio, or they could submit to transfer to a court where personal jurisdiction existed. By objecting to transfer, the shipowners constructively opted to waive their personal jurisdiction defenses.

Third, we conclude that the shipowners unequivocally waived their personal jurisdiction defenses when they filed answers in the Northern District of Ohio. Generally, filing an answer in which lack of personal jurisdiction is identified as an affirmative defense would not constitute waiver. The circumstances of this case, however, require a different result. Judge Lambros and the parties expressly agreed that the shipowners could demonstrate waiver of the defense by filing an answer no later than January 5, 1990, and that shipowners not subject to personal jurisdiction who did not file an answer would be transferred to a court with personal jurisdiction {–107–} over them. App. 401–05. Defense counsel indicated an understanding of, and agreement to, this procedure. App. 402, [—17—] 405. Accordingly, when the shipowners then filed answers in compliance with the agreed-upon procedure, their actions were consistent with waiver, despite the fact that they purported to preserve the personal jurisdiction defense. Behavior that is consistent with waiver, and which indicates an intent to litigate the case on the merits, is sufficient to constitute waiver, regardless of whether the parties also express an intent to preserve the defense. *See Ins. Corp. of Ireland, Ltd.*, 456 U.S. at 704–05; *In re Tex. E. Transmission Corp. PCB Contamination Ins. Coverage Litig.*, 15 F.3d at 1236.

Further, to the extent the shipowners believed they had a basis for pursuing an interlocutory appeal regarding the validity of Judge Lambros's order denying dismissal and instead ordering transfer, they had already filed a motion to stay pending resolution of that appeal and could have relied on that motion or, if necessary, filed a petition for writ of mandamus. They were under no obligation to file answers in order to avoid immediate transfer or otherwise, as they were not bound by the scheduling orders of a court that did not have jurisdiction over them. *Cf. Ins. Corp. of Ireland*, 456 U.S. at 706 ("A defendant is always free to ignore the judicial proceedings, risk a default judgment, and then challenge that judgment on jurisdictional grounds in a collateral proceeding."). By filing pleadings responding to substantive allegations in the merchant mariners' complaints—after Judge Lambros had unequivocally ruled that he did not have jurisdiction—the shipowners chose to actively litigate their cases. The shipowners were fully aware that their conduct constituted waiver in the eyes of plaintiffs and Judge Lambros, and created an expectation of continued litigation on the [—18—] merits. *See In re Tex. E. Transmission Corp. PCB Contamination Ins. Coverage Litig.*, 15 F.3d at 1236; *see also Mobile Anesthesiologists Chicago, LLC v. Anesthesia Assocs. Houston Metroplex, P.A.*, 623 F.3d 440, 443 (7th Cir. 2010). We conclude the conduct here constitutes waiver.

Fourth, even if the shipowners had not waived their personal jurisdiction defenses by filing answers or through other conduct consistent with waiver, they subsequently forfeited the defense by failing to diligently pursue it in the Northern District of Ohio. *See*

United States v. Olano, 507 U.S. 725, 733 (1993) ("Whereas forfeiture is the failure to make the timely assertion of a right, waiver is the intentional relinquishment or abandonment of a known right." (internal quotation marks omitted)). As indicated by the ongoing proceedings, Judge Lambros must have believed that the shipowners had waived the defense because he continued to preside over the cases, despite his prior ruling that the Northern District of Ohio did not have personal jurisdiction, and he did not transfer the cases despite the fact that the defendants were clearly subject to MARDOC Order 41. If the shipowners had not intended to waive their defenses by filing answers and believed that the Northern District of Ohio continued to lack personal jurisdiction over them, they had an obligation to diligently pursue that defense rather than acquiesce in the ongoing Northern District of Ohio proceedings. *See In re Tex. E. Transmission Corp. PCB Contamination Ins. Coverage Litig.*, 15 F.3d at 1236. The shipowners' failure to do so constituted forfeiture. *See Hamilton v. Atlas Turner, Inc.*, 197 F.3d 58, 59 (2d Cir. 1999) ("We conclude that Atlas forfeited its defense of lack of personal jurisdiction by participating in [—19—] extensive pretrial proceedings {–108–} and forgoing numerous opportunities to move to dismiss during the four-year interval that followed its inclusion of the defense in its answer.").

Based on these grounds, it is clear that defendants both waived their personal jurisdiction defenses through their own affirmative conduct in the Northern District of Ohio and forfeited their personal jurisdiction defenses by subsequently failing to pursue them in that Court. It was an abuse of discretion for the MDL Court to conclude otherwise given the proceedings before Judge Lambros and the shipowners' undisputed conduct in the Northern District of Ohio.

Further, the MDL Court abused its discretion by applying incorrect legal standards. First, the MDL Court improperly concluded that the shipowners had preserved the personal jurisdiction defense simply by stating in their answers that they did not intend to waive it. The law is clear that words alone are insufficient to preserve a personal jurisdiction defense where conduct indicates waiver. And defendants can forfeit the defense even through conduct that is involuntary. *See Ins. Corp. of Ireland, Ltd.*, 456 U.S. at 704–05. Although the District Court accurately cited this law, it did not apply it correctly to the facts of this case.

Second, the MDL Court explained that the shipowners faced a "Hobson's choice" in deciding whether to answer and waive personal jurisdiction or agree to transfer, App. 54, and the MDL Court suggested that being forced to make a choice was somehow inappropriate. But defendants always face such a choice when a court lacks personal jurisdiction and rules in favor of transfer rather than dismissal. The shipowners did not [—20—] have the right to simultaneously maintain their personal jurisdiction defenses in the Northern District of Ohio and avoid transfer to a court with personal jurisdiction over them. To the extent the MDL Court concluded that a defendant should not be required to choose between waiver of the personal jurisdiction defense and transfer, that was legal error.

Based on the MDL Court's application of incorrect legal standards and its improper application of the waiver standard to the factual history of these cases, we will reverse.

C.

Notably, the Sixth Circuit has affirmed the MDL Court's order dismissing for lack of personal jurisdiction in an appeal by plaintiffs who share the same procedural history as the parties here. *See Kalama v. Matson Navigation Co.*, 875 F.3d 297, 5 Adm. R. 346 (6th Cir. 2017). Like the MDL Court, the Sixth Circuit concluded that Judge Lambros did not have the authority to institute a procedure whereby filing an answer would constitute waiver of the personal jurisdiction defense. We conclude that the Sixth Circuit's reasoning is not persuasive given both our precedent and what we understand to have transpired in Judge Lambros's courtroom. For that reason, we are constrained not to follow the Sixth Circuit's holdings.

The Sixth Circuit explained that the *Kalama* defendants did not waive their personal jurisdiction defenses by filing answers because Judge Lambros exceeded his authority by declaring that filing an answer would result in waiver: [—21—]

> Because the Federal Rules of Civil Procedure do not authorize a district court to strip a defendant of its right to assert an affirmative defense in an answer, it was not an abuse of discretion to determine that the ship-owner defendants could seek to preserve their personal-jurisdiction defense at that time. {–109–}

Id. at 305, 5 Adm. R. at 351. We disagree. While it would ordinarily be appropriate for a defendant to raise a personal jurisdiction defense in an answer and thereby preserve the defense, the procedural history of this case was anything but typical. Prior to the filing of answers, Judge Lambros had already ruled that he did not have personal jurisdiction over the shipowners. They could not continue to participate in the lawsuit and, simply by stating they were not waiving, preserve a defense that had already been ruled upon.

Thus, Judge Lambros did not "strip a defendant of its right to assert an affirmative defense in an answer." Instead, having already ruled that he did not have personal jurisdiction over the shipowners, he ruled that continuing to actively litigate the case by submitting an answer would indicate waiver and an intent to proceed in the Northern District of Ohio. That procedure was an exercise in case management that was entirely within Judge Lambros's discretion. *See United States v. Wecht*, 484 F.3d 194, 217 (3d Cir. 2007); *In re Fine Paper Antitrust Litig.*, 685 F.2d 810, 817 (3d Cir. 1982) ("We will not interfere with a trial court's control of its docket except upon the clearest showing that the procedures have resulted in actual and substantial prejudice to the complaining litigant." (internal quotation marks omitted)). [—22—]

The Sixth Circuit further explained that the MDL Court did not abuse its discretion by

concluding that there was no forfeiture because there was no concrete evidence of forfeiture: "On this record and absent concrete evidence that any specific ship-owner defendant had abandoned its personal-jurisdiction defense, it was not a clear error of judgment for the MDL court to reject the MARDOC plaintiffs' forfeiture argument." *Kalama*, 875 F.3d at 307, 5 Adm. R. at 353. As discussed above, we agree that there was no express waiver by the defendants here, but our precedent does not require concrete evidence or even an intent to waive or forfeit. Conduct consistent with waiver or forfeiture is enough. *See, e.g., In re Tex. E. Transmission Corp. PCB Contamination Ins. Coverage Litig.*, 15 F.3d at 1236; *Ins. Corp. of Ireland, Ltd.*, 456 U.S. at 704–05. Here, the shipowners objected to transfer, requested additional rulings from the Northern District of Ohio, complied with Judge Lambros's procedure for waiving their personal jurisdiction defenses, and continued to participate in the litigation for over a year after Judge Lambros unequivocally ruled that he did not have personal jurisdiction. That conduct establishes both waiver and forfeiture under this Circuit's jurisprudence. Accordingly, we must chart a different course than the Sixth Circuit followed in *Kalama*.

"While we are generally reluctant to create circuit splits, we do so where a compelling basis exists." *Parker v. Montgomery Cty. Corr. Facility/Bus. Office Manager*, 870 F.3d 144, 152 (3d Cir. 2017) (internal quotation marks omitted) (quoting *Karlo v. Pittsburgh Glass Works, LLC*, 849 F.3d 61, 75 n.7 (3d Cir. 2017)). To the extent our holding today creates a circuit split with the Sixth Circuit, it is compelled by [—23—] our own precedent. Yet even if we had discretion to depart from this Court's case law and reconcile our ruling with that of the Sixth Circuit, we would still conclude that the compelling interests of promoting adjudication on the merits and permitting the merchant mariners to have their day in court are sufficient to justify a circuit split in this instance. *See, e.g., Goldlawr, Inc. v. Heiman*, 369 U.S. 463, 466–67 (1962); *Schwilm v. Holbrook*, 661 F.2d 12, 16 (3d Cir. 1981); *Myers v. Am. Dental Ass'n*, 695 F.2d 716, 721 (3d Cir. 1982) ("[The Rule

12(h) waiver rule] reflects a strong policy against tardily {–110–} raising defenses that go not to the merits of the case but to the legal adequacy of the initial steps taken by the plaintiff in his litigation, namely his service of process on the defendant and his choice of forum for the action.").

IV.

For the reasons outlined above, we will grant shipowners' motion to dismiss Mr. Schroeder and his estate's appeal as to Marine Transports Lines, Inc. We will otherwise reverse the MDL Court's judgment and the orders granting the shipowners' motions to dismiss for lack of personal jurisdiction as they pertain to these merchant mariners. While the shipowner defendants did not expressly waive their personal jurisdiction defenses, their conduct in the Northern District of Ohio resulted in both waiver and forfeiture of those defenses. It was, therefore, an abuse of discretion for the MDL Court to dismiss for lack of personal jurisdiction. Barring any additional preliminary matters, these 30-year-old cases should at last proceed to adjudication on the merit.

(Reporter's Note: Dissenting Opinion follows on p. 177).

[—1—] {–110–} **FISHER,** Circuit Judge, dissenting:

Like buried treasure, the Appellant merchant mariners ask us to dig up court transcripts and interpret the meaning of off-the-cuff dialogue between counsel and the court that occurred more than three decades ago. However, the MDL Court already accomplished this task, and it did so according to the appropriate legal standards and within the bounds of reasonable factual interpretation. Because the record demonstrates that the MDL Court did not abuse its discretion in concluding that the shipowners preserved their personal jurisdiction defense, I would affirm.

I

After determining that the Northern District of Ohio did not have personal jurisdiction over certain defendants, Judge Lambros allowed defense counsel thirty days to consult with their clients regarding whether they would prefer to consent to jurisdiction in Ohio, or have their matter transferred to a court with jurisdiction.

At the hearing that followed, Special Master Martyn, who managed MARDOC, stated that the court would "assume transfer" if defendants' responses were not received by December 1, 1989. App. at 331. Special Master Martyn ordered that, if a party wished to waive jurisdiction, it must so "apprise the Court no later than Friday, December 1st, in writing." App. at 332. Later in the hearing, he reiterated that any defendant wishing to waive jurisdiction must affirmatively do so in writing. [—2—]

When Judge Lambros arrived at the hearing, defense counsel raised concerns about deciding whether to waive jurisdiction without additional information, such as the specific transferee courts and whether the cases would be consolidated. The court acknowledged defendants' interest in answers to these questions, but noted that it could not yet make a ruling. The judge then proposed that "the disclosure date [be] the same date as the answer date, but if the position is that they are not leaving, they have to have their

answers in on [January 5, 1990]." App. at 401-02. In response, a representative of defense counsel stated that he "saw no problem with that." App. at 402. To clarify Judge Lambros' position, Special Master Martyn asked, "[S]o they will answer if they want to stay[?] . . . And we will pull their name off the [transfer] list." App. at 405. Judge Lambros confirmed.

The next day, the court issued MARDOC Order No. 40, which required the merchant mariners to list the forum to which each case should be transferred and noted that "[p]arties who, upon reconsideration {–111–} of their motions to dismiss or transfer, wish to remain in this jurisdiction need only file answers to the complaints." App. at 416. One week before the deadline to file answers, Judge Lambros issued MARDOC Order No. 41, which identified the defendants and cases not in the court's jurisdiction and identified the jurisdictions to which the cases would be transferred.

The shipowners, who were named in MARDOC Order No. 41 and all represented by the same firm, filed answers on January 5. In Master Answer No. 1, they stated as an affirmative defense that "[t]he Court lacks personal jurisdiction due to insufficient contacts . . . ." App. at 1131. Master Answer No. 2 began with a preliminary statement specifically asserting that, by filing the answer, defendants were not waiving their personal jurisdiction defense: [—3—]

> In response to defendants' motion to dismiss for lack of personal jurisdiction, the Court has issued MARDOC Order Nos. 40 and 41 which transfer the numerous cases against defendant to multiple jurisdictions, up to and including thirteen separate districts around the nation. Each defendant maintains that the transfers are contrary to law. A motion to certify the order of transfer for interlocutory appeal has been filed on behalf of defendant, and in order to preserve the status quo pending appellate review of such order, defendant files its answer to the complaints as directed by MARDOC Order Nos. 40 and 41 under protest, so

that said cases will not be transferred automatically pursuant to MARDOC Order No. 40 prior to completion of appellate review. By filing its answer, defendant specifically does not waive its defense of lack of personal jurisdiction or waive its objections to the propriety of the transfers.

App. at 1133-34.

Over the next year, the court's only actions pertained to transferring cases. For instance, because MARDOC Order No. 41 would transfer the cases all over the United States and splinter cases across jurisdictions due to the numerous defendants in each action, the merchant mariners filed a motion to transfer *in toto*. Defendants, including the shipowners, objected, however, stating in part that:

> Several nonresident defendants, although not subject to the personal jurisdiction of this Court, nevertheless agreed to waive their personal jurisdiction defense as the quid pro quo to avoid [—4—] the expense of litigating these cases in as many as 13 different jurisdictions simultaneously, and to take advantage of the consolidated handling available in [the Northern District of Ohio].

App. at 474-75.

Though defendants' opposition noted that "several nonresident defendants" purposefully waived their personal jurisdiction defense, it did not identify who those defendants were. On appeal, the shipowners maintain that these statements "refer[] solely to nonresident defendants who were *not* clients of Thompson Hine and Flory, and are *not* Appellees here." Appellees' Br. at 17 (emphasis in original). Instead, they explain that these statements refer to defendants represented by other firms who informed the court that they would "just as soon be [in Ohio] as anywhere," filed motions consenting to the court's jurisdiction, and withdrew their motions to dismiss or transfer. *Id.* at 17-18.

The court ultimately denied the merchant mariners' Motion to Transfer *in Toto*. However, Judge Lambros never ruled on defendants' motion to certify interlocutory appeal of Order No. 41, nor did he transfer any cases pursuant to that Order, including those in which the defendants did not file answers. Instead, in January {–112–} of 1991, the court transferred forty-four cases, not including the shipowners' cases at issue here, to the Eastern District of Michigan, while the shipowners' cases (among others) remained on the Northern District of Ohio's docket. The Michigan cases were ultimately returned to Ohio, but it was not long before the Judicial Panel for Multidistrict Litigation transferred all asbestos cases, from jurisdictions across the United States, to the Eastern District of Pennsylvania for consolidated pre-trial proceedings.

There, the cases remained static for the next two [—5—] decades until Judge Robreno began presiding over MARDOC. At this time, the shipowners re-raised their motions to dismiss for lack of personal jurisdiction, which the MDL Court granted; the merchant mariners now appeal.

II

To reverse the lower court's ruling, we must conclude that the MDL Court abused its discretion in determining that the shipowners preserved their personal jurisdiction defense. *See Sharp v. Johnson*, 669 F.3d 144, 158 (3d Cir. 2012). Such an abuse occurs where the court's "decision rests upon a clearly erroneous finding of fact, an errant conclusion of law or an improper application of law to fact." *Id.* at 158 n.19 (internal quotations omitted).

The majority concludes "that the District Court's conclusion that there was no waiver was an improper application of law to fact that constitutes an abuse of discretion." Maj. Op. at § III. In reaching this holding, the majority also made a factual conclusion that "the shipowners were fully aware that [filing answers] constituted waiver in the eyes of the plaintiffs and Judge Lambros[] and created an expectation of continued litigation on the merits." Maj. Op. at § III(B). However, these conclusions overlook the significant deference afforded to the MDL Court's findings and incorporate arguments that were not raised by the merchant mariners on appeal.[1] [—6—]

A. The MDL Court Did Not Make Clearly Erroneous Finding of Fact.

Though the majority does not expressly state that the MDL Court made clearly erroneous findings of fact, it reaches different factual conclusions than the MDL Court to find that the shipowners waived their jurisdictional defense. In so doing, the majority applies a less deferential standard than that required. The "clearly erroneous" standard "does not envision an appellate court substituting its findings for that of the district court; rather it allows only an assessment of whether there is enough evidence on record to support such findings, regardless [of] whether different inferences could be drawn." *Leeper v. United States*, 756 F.2d 300, 308 (3d Cir. 1985); *see also Agathos v. Starlite Motel*, 977 F.2d 1500, 1504 (3d Cir. 1992) (highlighting that a finding of fact is only "clearly erroneous" if the record lacks sufficient evidence to support the court's factual conclusions).

First, the majority holds that the shipowners waived their jurisdiction defense by filing answers; however, those answers included clear and unequivocal statements preserving their jurisdictional defenses in {–113–} accordance with the Federal Rules of Civil Procedure and our law.

This Court has held that the Federal Rules of Civil Procedure permit "a defendant to answer to the merits in the same pleading in which he raises a jurisdictional defense

without waiving the jurisdictional defense." *Neifeld v. Steinberg*, 438 F.2d 423, 427 (3d Cir. 1971). In *Neifeld*, defendant filed an answer to plaintiff's claims asserting a lack of personal jurisdiction and—in the same pleading— raising a [—7—] counterclaim against plaintiff. *Id*. Plaintiff argued that, by filing a counterclaim, defendant submitted to the jurisdiction of the court. *Id*. at 425. On appeal, this Court noted that, though the Federal Rules do not explicitly authorize a party to couple a counterclaim and jurisdictional defense without waiving the jurisdictional defense, the language of Rule 12(b) does so implicitly. *Id*. at 427-28. This Court reasoned that, because Rule 12(b) permits a defendant to raise jurisdictional defenses by motion or answer, prohibiting the defendant from coupling his answer and counterclaim would invalidate the options expressly permitted by the Federal Rules, which the court cannot do. *Id*. at 428.

Relying on similar reasoning, the Sixth Circuit, reviewing cases from the same MDL Court as here, held that defendants did not waive personal jurisdiction by filing an answer, even in light of MARDOC Order No. 41. *Kalama v. Matson Navigation Co.*, 875 F.3d 297, 305, 5 Adm. R. 346, 351 (6th Cir. 2017). The *Kalama* Court reasoned that because the Rules "do not authorize a district court to strip a defendant of its right to assert an affirmative defense in an answer, it was not an abuse of discretion to determine that the ship-owner defendants could seek to preserve their jurisdictional defense at any time." *Id.*, 5 Adm. R. at 351. It further concluded that the defendants' preservation of their jurisdictional defense in Master Answer No. 2, the same Master Answer filed by the shipowners here, negated any inference that Judge Lambros' order was an "ultimatum" requiring all answers to be interpreted as a waiver. *Id.*, 5 Adm. R. at 351. Accordingly, the Sixth Circuit held that the MDL Court did not [—8—] abuse its discretion in granting the motion to dismiss.[2] *Id.* at 308, 5 Adm. R. at 353.

---

[1] Only where the lower court's "error is so 'plain' that manifest injustice would otherwise result" should an appellate court exercise its discretion to consider arguments that were not properly raised in the appellant's opening brief. *Gambino v Morris*, 134 F.3d 156, 169 (3d Cir. 1998). There is no evidence to suggest that the lower court committed an error so egregious [—6—] that a "manifest injustice" would occur if we did not consider these un-argued issues.

---

[2] The majority distinguishes its holding from *Kalama* by concluding that our Circuit's precedent demands a different result. However, the decisions cited by the majority are distinguishable from this

The merchant mariners argue, and the majority concludes, that the shipowners waived their jurisdictional defense by filing an answer in light of Judge Lambros' order. That reading, however, does not align with this Court's ruling in *Neifeld*, where we declined to permit a procedurally proper option—objecting to jurisdiction in the answer itself—to be taken away from a defendant. 438 F.2d at 428. Judge Lambros did not have the authority to order that filing an answer alone constituted waiver, because such an order would violate the Federal Rules.

Second, the majority "conclude[s] that the shipowners unequivocally waived their personal jurisdiction defenses when they filed answers in the Northern District of Ohio" because "Judge Lambros and the parties expressly agreed that the shipowners could demonstrate waiver of the defense by filing an answer." Maj. Op. at § III(B). To support its holding, the majority references Judge Lambros' statement that, "unless of course the parties otherwise announce" their intention to waive jurisdiction, the cases not under the court's jurisdiction "will be transferred." App. at 404. He went on to state that transfers would be effective on January 7 {–114–} or 8 "unless [the [—9—] defendants], by announcing to the court in the filing of [their] answers on January 5th," waived jurisdiction.[3] App. at 404.

To reverse the MDL Court's finding that filing an answer did not necessarily amount to a waiver, we must hold that this finding was a "clearly erroneous finding of fact," lacking support in the record. However neither Judge Lambros nor Special Master Martyn stated that a defendant could not both file an answer and preserve its jurisdictional defense. Instead, the court indicated that, to save defendants from having to make separate filings, defendants could inform the court of their desire to consent to its jurisdiction by filing answers. On the other hand, if a

case because, here, the shipowners did not actively litigate the merits of their cases. *Post* at § II(B).

[3] A reasonable interpretation of the phrase "by announcing" is that Judge Lambros expected answers to include an express waiver of jurisdiction, if that was the party's desire.

defendant did not file an answer, the court stated that it would assume that the party desired for its case to be transferred. These rulings leave room for a third option: to file an answer so that the case would not be automatically transferred, while also maintaining a jurisdictional defense and preserving the issue of dismissal for appellate review.[4] [—10—]

The language in the shipowners' Master Answer No. 2 unequivocally demonstrates the shipowners' intention to exercise this third option. For instance, the shipowners stated that "[e]ach defendant maintains that the transfers are contrary to law" and has filed a motion to certify the order of transfer for interlocutory appeal. App. at 1133. They further provided that "[b]y filing its answer, defendant specifically does not waive its defense of lack of personal jurisdiction or waive its objections to the propriety of the transfers." App. at 1133-34.

The MDL Court's factual findings were not "clearly erroneous" because the record contains sufficient evidence to support them. *See Agathos*, 977 F.2d at 1504. First, the district court could not have intended to remove defendants' right to preserve their personal jurisdiction defense when filing an answer because the Federal Rules of Civil Procedure expressly permit this action. Second, the hearing transcripts and the language in the shipowners' answers support the conclusion that filing an answer alone would not waive personal jurisdiction, reflecting the propriety of the MDL Court's factual conclusions.

[4] This option may have been particularly important as defendants did not receive notice of the intended transferee courts until December 29, though answers were due January 5. The majority states that the shipowners could have taken their chances with default judgment instead, but this suggestion imposes an unnecessary risk where the shipowners had the option to preserve their defense for appeal, as they did. *Cf. Neifeld*, 438 F.3d at 429 n.13 (finding no waiver where a defendant asserted a jurisdictional defense alongside a [—10—] compulsory counterclaim because the party had no alternative but to assert the claim in that filing or waive it).

B. The MDL Court Did Not Make a Misapplication of Law.

The MDL Court correctly noted that a party can waive its personal jurisdiction defense by participating in the litigation and taking advantage of the forum. App. at 51 (citing *Ins. Corp. of Ir., Ltd. v. Compagnie des Bauxites de Guinee*, 456 U.S. 694, 703 (1982)). Applying this law, the majority concludes that the shipowners implicitly waived their jurisdictional defense through both their active participation in [—11—] the litigation and their dilatoriness (or inactivity). However, we must defer to the MDL Court's factual findings when applying them to the law. {–115–}

The shipowners did not actively participate in litigation in the Northern District of Ohio. As the merchant mariners note, a party might waive its personal jurisdiction defense where it "actually litigates the underlying merits or demonstrates a willingness to engage in extensive litigation in the forum." Appellants' Br. at 19 (citing *In re Tex. E. Transmission Corp. PCB Contamination Ins. Coverage Litig.*, 15 F.3d 1230, 1236 (3d Cir. 1994)). In *Transmission Corp.*, we held that a party waived its personal jurisdiction defense by actively litigating the action, including pursuing counterclaims and moving for summary judgment. *Id.* Likewise, in *Bel-Ray*, we held that a party may waive its personal jurisdiction defense if it seeks affirmative relief from the court. *Bel-Ray Co. v. Chemrite Ltd.*, 181 F.3d 435, 443-44 (3d Cir. 1999). There, defendants actively litigated motions for summary judgment and enjoinment against arbitration, and then, only after the court denied summary judgment, did they file affidavits in support of their personal jurisdiction defense. *Id.* at 444. Because of this participation, we concluded that defendants submitted themselves to the court's jurisdiction. *Id.*

The majority concludes that the shipowners continued to actively litigate their cases in the Northern District of Ohio after filing their answers. However, the only activity reflected in the record pertains directly to the issue of jurisdiction and transfer. Participation related to jurisdictional issues does not reflect the merits-based litigation that this Court has required to find implicit waiver. *See Transmission Corp.*, 15 F.3d at 1236; *Bel-Ray*, 181 F.3d at 443. Unlike the parties in *Transmission Corp.* and *Bel-Ray*, the shipowners did not pursue counterclaims, seek summary judgment, move to [—12—] enjoin, or otherwise actively litigate the merits of the case. Instead, the shipowners' filings and participation reflect the complexity of this matter's jurisdictional issues, which ultimately led to the creation of an MDL.

On the other hand, the majority concludes that the shipowners forfeited their defense to personal jurisdiction because they "fail[ed] to diligently pursue it in the Northern District of Ohio." Maj. Op. at § III(B).[5] However, the record reflects that the case idled; the merchant mariners were not actively prosecuting these cases during this time period; and the shipowners were not delaying litigation or delinquent. *See Adams v. Trs. of the N.J. Brewery Emps.' Pension Tr. Fund*, 29 F.3d 863, 874-75 (3d Cir. 1994) (explaining that dilatoriness can be shown through "extensive or repeated delay or delinquency" or by a plaintiff's years-long failure to prosecute). Once Judge Robreno activated the cases against the shipowners, they filed renewed motions to dismiss for lack of personal jurisdiction and began pursuing the issue now before this Court. The shipowners' behavior reflects diligence, not dilatoriness.

III

The MDL Court rested its factual conclusions in the record and properly applied those facts to the correct legal standard. That its application of the law resulted in a different conclusion than the majority's does not reflect an "abuse of discretion," but the type of fair-minded disagreement upon which our judicial system is premised. Therefore, I respectfully dissent. I {–116–} would affirm the ruling of the District Court.

---

[5] On appeal, the merchant mariners did not argue that the shipowners forfeited their personal jurisdiction defense due to dilatoriness.

This page intentionally left blank

United States Court of Appeals for the Fourth Circuit

United States Court of Appeals
for the Fourth Circuit

No. 18-1695

MUHAMMAD

VS.

NORFOLK S. RY. CO.

Appeal from the United States District Court for the Eastern District of Virginia, at Norfolk

Decided: June 4, 2019

Citation: 925 F.3d 192, 7 Adm. R. 184 (4th Cir. 2019).

Before **NIEMEYER, KEENAN,** and **QUATTLEBAUM,** Circuit Judges.

[—2—] {–194–} NIEMEYER, Circuit Judge:

Kenneth Muhammad, a railroad employee, was injured while replacing railroad crossties on a bridge spanning navigable waters. When Muhammad filed a negligence claim against his employer under the Federal Employers' Liability Act ("FELA"), the district court granted the employer's motion to dismiss for lack of subject-matter jurisdiction. The court concluded that Muhammad was injured "upon navigable waters" and was engaged in "maritime employment" and therefore that the Longshore and Harbor Workers' Compensation Act ("LHWCA") provided the exclusive remedy for his claim. Because we conclude, however, that Muhammad's injury did not occur "upon navigable waters," as required by the LHWCA, we reverse and remand for further proceedings.

I

In May 2016, while Muhammad was employed by Norfolk Southern Railway Company as a carpenter in its "bridge and building" maintenance department, he performed maintenance work replacing railroad crossties on Norfolk Southern's South Branch Lift Bridge in Virginia. The Bridge crosses the Elizabeth River, which has been declared navigable by the U.S. Coast Guard, and the center span of the Bridge lifts upward to allow vessels to navigate under it. The train traffic crossing the Bridge primarily serves busi-

nesses to the west of the Elizabeth River, often traveling to the Portlock Railyard, which is landlocked and approximately a mile east of the River.

The work crew with whom Muhammad was working traveled to the South Branch Lift Bridge via truck, and their work never required the use of boats. While Muhammad [—3—] was working on the Bridge on May 19, a portion of the walkway on which he was walking collapsed. He was able to avoid falling into the River but sustained serious injuries that have prevented him from returning to work.

Muhammad then commenced this action against Norfolk Southern under the FELA, 45 U.S.C. § 51 *et seq.*, claiming that Norfolk Southern's negligence caused his injuries. Norfolk Southern filed a motion to dismiss Muhammad's action, claiming that "the court lack[ed] subject matter jurisdiction over [the] action and the LHWCA ha[d] exclusive jurisdiction." Granting the motion would benefit Norfolk Southern by limiting its damages exposure to the scheduled and specified amounts {–195–} provided by the LHWCA, which is a workers' compensation statute, as distinct from the unscheduled damages to which it was exposed by a negligence claim under the FELA.

The district court granted Norfolk Southern's motion and dismissed Muhammad's complaint. In doing so, the court held that "the LHWCA provides the exclusive remedy for [Muhammad's] claim" and that it therefore "[did] not have subject matter jurisdiction to proceed" on Muhammad's FELA action. In holding that the LHWCA applied exclusively to cover Muhammad's injuries, the court concluded that the circumstances of the incident satisfied both the "situs" requirement of the LHWCA that Muhammad's injury be "upon navigable waters" and the "status" requirement that he be engaged in "maritime employment." Relying on *LeMelle v. B. F. Diamond Construction Co.*, 674 F.2d 296 (4th Cir. 1982), the court concluded that the situs requirement includes work both "upon" and "over" navigable waters, reasoning that a bridge *over* navigable waters that allows ships to pass underneath it facilitates and aids the navigation of maritime [—4—] traffic. And relying on *Chesapeake & Ohio Railway Co. v. Schwalb*, 493 U.S. 40 (1989), the court concluded that Muhammad's work "constitute[d] maritime employment because repairing and rebuilding the [Bridge] [was] an essential and integral element of the loading or unloading process of the maritime traffic flowing under the Bridge." The court reasoned that the "Bridge lifts to permit passing vessels to navigate the Elizabeth River" and that Muhammad's "employment [was] essential when ensuring that the Bridge remain[ed] in safe, operating condition for maritime and commercial rail traffic to reach nearby loading facilities that rely on the South Branch of the Elizabeth River."

From the district court's order of dismissal dated June 13, 2018, Muhammad filed this appeal.

II

While Muhammad brought this action under the FELA based on allegations of Norfolk Southern's negligence, the district court concluded that Muhammad's action could only be brought under the LHWCA. It thus held that it did not have subject-matter jurisdiction and dismissed the action under Federal Rule of Civil Procedure 12(b)(1). This lack-of-jurisdiction conclusion was misplaced, however, as Muhammad's claim under the FELA indisputably invoked the district court's subject-matter jurisdiction under 45 U.S.C. § 56 (conferring jurisdiction on district courts for FELA claims) and 28 U.S.C. § 1331 (conferring jurisdiction on district courts for claims arising under the laws of the United States). [—5—]

To be sure, if Muhammad's injury was covered by the LHWCA, then that Act, as a workers' compensation law, would provide him with the exclusive remedy for his work-related injury. *See* 33 U.S.C. § 905(a) (providing that the employer's liability for covered injuries "shall be exclusive and in place of all other liability of such employer to the employee"); *In re CSX Transp., Inc.*, 151

F.3d 164, 171 (4th Cir. 1998) (holding that "LHWCA coverage is exclusive and preempts [the plaintiff] from pursuing an FELA claim"). The preemptive effect of the LHWCA would thus be an affirmative defense that Norfolk Southern could raise in response to Muhammad's complaint, but it would not deny the district court subject-matter jurisdiction over the complaint. *See Fisher v. Halliburton*, 667 F.3d 602, 609 (5th Cir. 2012) (noting that "the applicability of the LHWCA's exclusivity provision presents . . . an issue of preemption, not jurisdiction" {–196–} and that "Federal preemption is an affirmative defense that a defendant must plead and prove"); *cf.* 9 Lex K. Larson & Thomas A. Robinson, *Larson's Workers' Compensation Law* § 100.01 (2018) ("In a tort action by an employee to recover damages for a work-related injury, the employer has the burden of proving the affirmative defense that the plaintiff was an employee entitled only to workers' compensation").

Of course, had Muhammad filed his claim in the district court *under the LHWCA*, the district court would indeed have been required to dismiss it for lack of subject-matter jurisdiction. "An LHWCA claim must be filed with the Department of Labor where it is assigned to an administrative law judge whose decision is reviewed by the Benefits Review Board. Review by the courts is authorized through a petition for review, which may be filed only in the courts of appeals, not in the district court." *In re CSX Transp.*, [—6—] 151 F.3d at 171 (citing 33 U.S.C. §§ 910(a), 921(b), 921(c)); *see also Sidwell v. Express Container Servs., Inc.*, 71 F.3d 1134, 1136 (4th Cir. 1995) ("Congress legislated a 'status' requirement and a 'situs' requirement, both of which must be satisfied in order for the Board to have jurisdiction to award benefits"). But Muhammad did not assert an LHWCA claim here.

Accordingly, while the district court concluded erroneously that it lacked subject-matter jurisdiction, we will take the court's dismissal order to have concluded that Muhammad's FELA claim was barred because his injury was covered exclusively by the LHWCA, which preempted his FELA claim.

III

We now turn to the question of whether Norfolk Southern properly demonstrated to the district court that the LHWCA covered Muhammad's workplace injury.

The LHWCA makes employers liable for the payment of specified compensation to employees for certain injuries "arising out of and in the course of employment." 33 U.S.C. §§ 904, 902(2). For the LHWCA to apply, the employee must be a "person engaged in maritime employment," which is defined to include "any longshoreman or other person engaged in longshoring operations, and any harbor-worker including a ship repairman, shipbuilder, and ship-breaker." *Id.* § 902(3). Moreover, to be covered by the LHWCA, the employee's injury must "occur[] upon the navigable waters of the United States," which is defined to include "any adjoining pier, wharf, dry dock, terminal, [—7—] building way, marine railway,[1] or other adjoining area customarily used by an employer in loading, unloading, repairing, dismantling, or building a vessel." *Id.* § 903(a). Both the *status* of the employee ("engaged in maritime employment") and the *situs* of the injury ("upon the navigable waters of the United States") must be satisfied in order for the Act to apply.

The method for construing and applying the status and situs requirements is informed by Congress's 1972 amendments to the LHWCA. Prior to 1972, "the [LHWCA] applied only to injuries *occurring on navigable waters.* Longshoremen loading or unloading a ship were covered on the ship and the gangplank *but not shoreward,* even though they were performing the same functions whether on or off the ship." *Chesapeake & Ohio Ry. v. Schwalb,* 493 U.S. 40, 46 (1989) (emphasis added). In 1972, Congress obviated this anomaly by {–197–} amending the Act, inserting the parenthetical language in § 903(a) that expands the situs definition of "upon navigable waters" to include "any adjoining pier, wharf, dry dock, terminal,

building way, marine railway or other adjoining area customarily used by an employer in loading, unloading, repairing, dismantling, or building a vessel," 33 U.S.C. § 903(a), thereby "extend[ing] coverage to the area adjacent to the ship that is normally used for loading and unloading." *Schwalb,* 493 U.S. at 46. Recognizing that this "expansion of the definition of navigable waters to include rather large shoreside areas necessitated an affirmative description of the particular employees working in those areas who would be covered," Congress also [—8—] added the "maritime employment" requirement as part of the 1972 amendments in order to limit its expansion of the Act shoreside. *Herb's Welding, Inc. v. Gray,* 470 U.S. 414, 423 (1985). Thus, "[w]ith the 1972 amendments, the test for coverage . . . changed from a simple situs test to a test incorporating situs and status requirements." *Jonathan Corp. v. Brickhouse,* 142 F.3d 217, 220 (4th Cir. 1998).

In adding the status requirement, however, Congress did not narrow the overall coverage of the LHWCA, but instead only limited its shoreside expansion of the Act. *Dir., OWCP v. Perini N. River Assocs.,* 459 U.S. 297, 315 (1983). Thus, if an employee's injury would have been covered by the LHWCA prior to the 1972 amendments, the injury would still be covered by the Act following the 1972 amendments. *Id.* at 315, 325. Accordingly, when it is shown that an employee was injured "upon the actual navigable waters in the course of their employment"—*i.e.,* that the employee was injured working "on" navigable water and thus "traditionally covered" under the pre-1972 Act—the inquiry ends. *See id.* at 323, 325; *see also Zapata Haynie Corp. v. Barnard,* 933 F.2d 256, 259 (4th Cir. 1991) ("[T]he first question is whether Barnard would have fallen within the pre-1972 coverage of the Act. If so, the inquiry ends. If not, Barnard must satisfy both the status and situs requirements in order to be covered").

In this case, we conclude that the situs of Muhammad's injury on a railroad bridge over navigable waters would not satisfy the pre-1972 requirement that his injury occur "upon navigable waters." *See Schwalb,* 493 U.S. at 46 (noting that the pre-1972 situs test drew

---

[1] A marine railway is a patent slip or slipway for taking vessels in and out of the water.

the line between land and water at the ship's gangplank); *Nacirema Operating Co.* [—9—] *v. Johnson*, 396 U.S. 212, 215 (1969) ("[A] statute that covers injuries 'upon the navigable waters' would not cover injuries on a pier even though the pier, *like a bridge*, extends over navigable waters") (emphasis added)); *cf. Herb's Welding*, 470 U.S. at 420 ("Because until 1972 the LHWCA itself extended coverage only to accidents occurring on navigable waters, and because stationary rigs were considered to be islands, oil rig workers . . . were left to recover under state schemes" (citations omitted)).

Norfolk Southern cannot seriously contest the proposition that Muhammad's injury did not occur "upon navigable waters," as that term was consistently applied before 1972. It has pointed to no pre-1972 case where a court held that an employee working on a bridge *over* navigable waters was working *upon* navigable waters. The *Nacirema* Court made this distinction clear, observing that working on a pier, "like a bridge," would not be covered by a statute requiring that the employee work "upon navigable waters." 396 U.S. at 215. {–198–} To be sure, an employee working from a barge on navigable waters while constructing or maintaining a bridge would, under the pre-1972 standard, be on navigable waters, as that employee would then be physically working from a vessel on navigable waters. *See, e.g., Davis v. Dep't of Labor & Indus.*, 317 U.S. 249, 251 (1942). But Muhammad, who was working on a bridge itself and not from a barge or other vessel, would not have been covered by the LHWCA before 1972. We must therefore inquire as to whether the 1972 amendments expanded LHWCA coverage to the situs where Muhammad was injured.

The 1972 amendments to the LHWCA extended the situs of a covered injury to include "any adjoining pier, wharf, dry dock, terminal, building way, marine railway, or [—10—] other adjoining area customarily used by an employer in loading, unloading, repairing, dismantling, or building a vessel." 33 U.S.C. § 903(a). Because Muhammad's injury did not occur on a "pier, wharf, dry dock, terminal, building way [or] marine railway," our inquiry must focus on whether his injury occurred in an "other adjoining area." And in order for an "other adjoining area" to constitute a covered situs, "it must be a discrete shoreside structure or facility" that is "'customarily used by an employer in loading, unloading, repairing, dismantling, or building a vessel,' as the statute provides." *Sidwell v. Express Container Servs., Inc.*, 71 F.3d 1134, 1139–40 (4th Cir. 1995). Put differently:

> In extending the line of coverage landward, Congress . . . defined navigable waters to include certain land areas "adjoining" the navigable waters. The landward extension is a seamless annexation of land to navigable waters for purposes of LHWCA coverage. But the annexation does not include all adjacent land. *The statute extends "navigable waters" only to land relating to work on those waters*, specifically enumerating adjoining piers, wharfs, dry docks, terminals, building ways, and marine railways. These are facilities customarily used by longshoremen in loading and unloading ships and in repairing or building them. The link between the navigable waters and the land side facilities is thus established under the statute by (1) the contiguity of the land side facility and navigable water, and (2) the affinity of the land side facility to longshoremen's work on ships. . . . *The "other area" annexed to navigable waters by the Act must again be "adjoining" the water and must again be linked to the traditional longshoremen's work on the water*. The "other area" must be for the loading or unloading of cargo onto ships in navigable waters or for the "repairing, dismantling, or building" of those ships.

Jonathan Corp., 142 F.3d at 221 (emphasis added) (citations omitted); *see also Schwalb*, 493 U.S. at 46 (noting that the 1972 amendments "extended coverage to the area adjacent to the ship that is normally used for loading and unloading").

The undisputed facts in this case show that Muhammad was not injured on a facility contiguous to navigable waters that was customarily used for the loading, [—11—] unloading, repairing, dismantling, or building of a vessel—*i.e.*, a facility linked to traditional longshoremen's work on the water. Rather, the situs of Muhammad's injury was a railroad that was quite distinct from such a facility, and the location on the Bridge where Muhammad was injured was accessible only by land and was not contiguous to water.

While the Bridge's center span did lift to allow vessels to pass underneath it, a {–199–} land-based bridge's simple accommodation of ships is a far cry from a shoreside facility serving as "an integral or essential part of loading or unloading a vessel." *Schwalb*, 493 U.S. at 45. Norfolk Southern argues otherwise, asserting that a bridge allowing commercial navigation to travel underneath it provides a sufficient connection to "navigable waters" to support LHWCA coverage for injuries on that bridge. But the nexus to loading and unloading must not be so remote as to include any situs that is simply somehow *related* to navigable waters. Indeed, Norfolk Southern's argument would extend LHWCA coverage to injuries occurring on *every bridge* that allowed ships to pass under it. Congress clearly did not intend so broad a coverage. As the Supreme Court has noted, in enacting the 1972 amendments, Congress did not "seek to cover all those who breathe salt air. Its purpose was to cover those workers on the situs who are involved in the essential elements of loading and unloading." *Herb's Welding*, 470 U.S. at 423.

In reaching the contrary conclusion that the South Branch Lift Bridge was indeed a situs covered by the LHWCA, the district court relied principally on two cases, *LeMelle v. B. F. Diamond Construction Co.*, 674 F.2d 296 (4th Cir. 1982), and *Zapata Haynie* [—12—] *Corp. v. Barnard*, 933 F.2d 256 (4th Cir. 1991). Neither case, however, supports the district court's conclusion.

In *LeMelle*, we held that an employee injured while he was working to demolish and replace a bridge that crossed over the James

River, a navigable water in Virginia, was covered by the LHWCA. 674 F.2d at 297–98. The work there, however, was performed with the extensive use of boats, and the parties "agree[d] that the situs requirement for LeMelle's claim [was] satisfied." *Id.* at 297. Accordingly, in *LeMelle*, we only addressed the status requirement. Nonetheless, during the course of our discussion, we stated—what Norfolk Southern and the district court relied on heavily—that "bridge construction and demolition workers employed over navigable water were covered prior to the 1972 amendments" and cited three cases to support that statement. *See id.* at 298 (citing *Davis*, 317 U.S. 249; *Hardaway Contracting Co. v. O'Keeffe*, 414 F.2d 657 (5th Cir. 1968); and *Peter v. Arrien*, 325 F. Supp. 1361 (E.D. Pa. 1971)). In *Davis* and *Hardaway*, as was the case in *LeMelle* itself, the work involved the extensive use of barges, on which the employees' injuries occurred. *See Davis*, 317 U.S. at 251 (noting that "a tug, derrick barge, and a barge" were used in the project and that the employee fell from the barge and drowned); *Hardaway*, 414 F.2d at 660–61 (noting that the employee died while "transferring an oil drum from a small launch to a fixed barge"). And in *Peter*, instead of using barges, the contractor constructed a temporary causeway on the water "solely to provide access toward the middle of the river and it was to be dismantled as soon as the demolition was completed." 325 F. Supp. at 1364. Thus, our statement in *LeMelle*, which the district court took out of context, referred to bridge work performed [—13—] upon navigable waters insofar as the work was performed from barges, launches, and the like that were *actually on* navigable waters.

And in *Zapata*, the employee was working as an airplane pilot for a commercial fishing company, spotting fish from the air to aid commercial fishing boats. 933 F.2d at 257–58. Because we concluded that "fish spotting was traditionally an activity inherent to commercial fishing"—citing expert testimony that, "traditionally, crewmen would climb to the crow's nests of fishing vessels to spot fish"— we concluded that the employee performing that traditional {–200–} fishing function was covered by the LHWCA. *See id.* at 260. We reasoned that the employee's "duties required him to work over navigable waters at all times except for taking off and landing" and that he "was regularly engaged in the course of his duties over navigable waters and not merely *fortuitously* over water when his injury occurred." *Id.* at 259–60 (emphasis added).

Neither of these cases support the proposition that working on a land-accessed railroad bridge over navigable waters to replace railroad crossties qualifies as working on a situs covered by the LHWCA. Rather, the law is clear that, for a land-based situs to be covered under the Act, it must be a shoreside facility that is "an integral or essential part of loading or unloading a vessel"—a facility linked to traditional longshoremen's work on the water. *Schwalb*, 493 U.S. at 45; *Jonathan Corp.*, 142 F.3d at 222. The South Branch Lift Bridge is not such a facility.

Because Muhammad was not injured on a situs covered by the LHWCA, we need not reach the question of whether he was engaged in maritime employment. And since his injury was not covered by the LHWCA, the district court erred in dismissing his [—14—] FELA claim. The judgment of the district court is therefore reversed and the case remanded for further proceedings.

REVERSED AND REMANDED

This page intentionally left blank

United States Court of Appeals for the Fifth Circuit

United States Court of Appeals
for the Fifth Circuit

No. 18-30348

IN RE 4-K MARINE, L.L.C.

Appeal from the United States District Court for the
Eastern District of Louisiana

Decided: January 30, 2019

Citation: 914 F.3d 934, 7 Adm. R. 192 (5th Cir. 2019).

Before **WIENER, SOUTHWICK,** and **COSTA,** Circuit
Judges.

[—1—] {–936–} SOUTHWICK, Circuit Judge:

This is a maritime case involving an allision. The issue is whether the owner of the stationary, "innocent" vessel must be reimbursed for the medical expenses of an employee who fraudulently claimed his preexisting injuries had resulted from the allision. The district court said "no." We AFFIRM. [—2—]

FACTUAL AND PROCEDURAL BACKGROUND

In June 2015, the M/V TOMMY, a tug owned and operated by the claimant Enterprise Marine Services, LLC, was pushing a flotilla of barges on the lower Mississippi River. Its lead barge made contact with the M/V MISS ELIZABETH, a tug that along with its barges was essentially stationary and near the river's bank. That tug was owned by 4-K Marine and operated by Central Boat Rentals, Inc. ("CBR"). On board the M/V MISS ELIZABETH were the wheelman Prince McKinley and a deck hand named Justin Price. Both alleged they were injured in the allision.

CBR and 4-K Marine jointly filed a petition under the Shipowner's Limitation of Liability Act in the U.S. District Court for the Eastern District of Louisiana. *See* 46 U.S.C. § 30501, *et seq.* We will refer to the two petitioners as CBR. As required by Rule F of the Supplemental Rules for Admiralty or Maritime Claims, the district court issued a notice that all claimants respond. McKinley,

Price, and Enterprise {–937–} Marine all answered. A flurry of claims, cross-claims, and counter-claims followed with each of the crewmen, owners, and operators attempting to recover from one or more of the others.

Only one of those claims is at issue in this appeal, namely, CBR's counter-claim that Enterprise Marine reimburse it for amounts it paid to McKinley for medical expenses under its obligations as his Jones Act employer. CBR paid, and Enterprise Marine reimbursed, $23,485 in maintenance and $5,345.84 in cure to McKinley. CBR also agreed with a surgeon and a hospital to pay for a back surgery on behalf of McKinley, but Enterprise Marine refused to reimburse those expenses on the basis that McKinley's back condition was not the result of the allision.

After a bench trial, the district court found that McKinley's knee problems were caused by the accident. His back problems, though, predated the accident and were unaffected by the allision. The court also found that [—3—] McKinley fraudulently withheld "material issues about pre-existing medical conditions and medications both before and after the incident." Based on these findings, the district court held that CBR had no obligation to pay for McKinley's back surgery, and Enterprise Marine had no obligation to reimburse CBR.

Enterprise Marine sought the return of the amounts it had already reimbursed for maintenance and cure that were not related to McKinley's knee problem. The district court refused to grant that relief on the grounds that each party was a sophisticated maritime company, knowledgeable about its obligations and its defenses. Enterprise Marine's failure to make a reasonable investigation earlier in the process meant it would not now be allowed to recoup unnecessary reimbursements to CBR. CBR timely appealed, and there is no cross-appeal.

DISCUSSION

In this appeal from a judgment entered after a bench trial, we review the district court's conclusions of law *de novo* and its factual findings for clear error. *Lewis v.*

Ascension Par. Sch. Bd., 806 F.3d 344, 353 (5th Cir. 2015). CBR argues that maritime principles as well as a contract between the parties compel Enterprise Marine to reimburse McKinley's back surgery regardless of the employee's fraud.[1] [—4—]

I. Maritime principles concerning reimbursement

If a seaman "becomes ill or suffers an injury while in the service of a vessel," regardless of which party is to blame, his Jones Act employer owes him "an absolute, non-delegable duty" to pay "a 'per diem living allowance for food and lodging,'" which is called "maintenance," as well as "payment for medical, therapeutic, and hospital expenses," which is called "cure." *Bertram v. Freeport McMoran, Inc.*, 35 F.3d 1008, 1011–13 (5th Cir. 1994) {–938–} (citations omitted); *see also Armstrong v. Trico Marine, Inc.*, 923 F.2d 55, 58 n.2 (5th Cir. 1991). If a third-party "partially or wholly caused the seaman's injury," the employer can recover the maintenance and cure payments from it. *Bertram*, 35 F.3d at 1013.

Enterprise Marine withheld reimbursement of the costs of McKinley's back surgery after reviewing his medical history and concluding his injury was not caused by the allision. McKinley's treating physician,

---

[1] CBR also briefed an equitable estoppel argument on appeal but did not raise the issue in the district court until a post-trial memorandum. The district court ignored the issue in its opinion and judgment. "If an argument is not raised to such a degree that the district court has an opportunity to rule on it, we will not address it on appeal." *F.D.I.C. v. Mijalis*, 15 F.3d 1314, 1327 (5th Cir. 1994). Regardless, CBR's argument fails on the merits. CBR had to demonstrate "justifiable reliance" on Enterprise Marine's "conduct or word." *Johnson v. Seacor Marine Corp.*, 404 F.3d 871, 878 (5th Cir. 2005). CBR admits, however, that Enterprise Marine "balked at paying for the surgery" in the "Fall of 2016" and that the surgery did not occur until February 2017. CBR could not have justifiably relied on [—4—] Enterprise Marine's other representations it alleges communicated a willingness to pay for the back surgery.

though, believed his back injury was due to the incident.

A seaman's entitlement to maintenance and cure applies only to injuries "suffered [or] . . . aggravated or [that] become manifest while he [is] 'in the service of the vessel.'" 1 THOMAS J. SCHOENBAUM, ADMIRALTY AND MARITIME LAW § 6:30 (6th ed. 2018). The district court found the allision did not cause or aggravate McKinley's back injury. CBR does not dispute this. A third-party must reimburse only where its negligence "caused or contributed to the *need* for maintenance and cure." *Bertram*, 35 F.3d at 1014 (emphasis added) (citation omitted). Because McKinley's back condition did not result from the allision, Enterprise Marine did nothing that "caused or contributed to [a] need [—5—] for maintenance and cure" for that particular medical problem. *Id.* That means it did not owe reimbursement to CBR for McKinley's back surgery.

We acknowledge that CBR identifies practical problems it faced in deciding whether to cover its employee's medical expenses. Decisions about maintenance and cure had to be made early, well before this bench trial. CBR was presented with what initially appeared to be a plausible claim for cure. A Jones Act employer who "unreasonably rejects [a maintenance and cure] claim" becomes liable for compensatory damages, and employers who have "not only been unreasonable but ha[ve] been more egregiously at fault," are liable for punitive damages and attorney's fees. *Morales v. Garijak, Inc.*, 829 F.2d 1355, 1358 (5th Cir. 1987); *see also Atlantic Sounding Co., Inc. v. Townsend*, 557 U.S. 404, 424 (2009).

Practical problems notwithstanding, maritime law makes Enterprise Marine liable only for such injuries as it causes. CBR did have options. "Upon receiving a claim for maintenance and cure, the [employer] need not immediately commence payments; he is entitled to investigate and require corroboration of the claim." *Morales*, 829 F.2d at 1358. The employer becomes liable for compensatory damages only if it "*unreasonably* rejects the claim" after an investigation. *Id.* (emphasis added). Punitive damages and attorney's fees are assessed only for behavior that is *egregious*. Accordingly, CBR could have refused to pay for McKinley's back surgery so long as it had a reasonable factual or legal basis. We do not minimize the uncertainties of such decisions, but the law at least provides a means to deal with them. CBR also had the right to deny payment of maintenance and cure where the employee "intentionally misrepresent[ed] or conceal[ed] material medical facts, the disclosure of which [was] plainly desired" by the employer. *McCorpen v. Cent. Gulf S.S. Corp.*, 396 F.2d 547, 549 (5th Cir. 1968). [—6—]

This holding does not, as CBR asserts, compromise the law's concern for injured seamen nor does it "place a burden on an innocent employer to conduct an investigation and possibly assert a . . . defense as a condition to later receiving reimbursement from a third party." The seaman's right to maintenance and cure is balanced with his employer's interests by {–939–} allowing the employer to investigate and reasonably withhold payment. *Morales*, 829 F.2d at 1358. There is no reason the balance should be different when the mechanisms of maintenance and cure make a third-party tortfeasor the ultimate entity responsible for any *required* payment. Indeed, in those circumstances these rules arguably are all the more justified.

II. *Contractual obligations to reimburse*

CBR also argues that it is entitled to be reimbursed because of an agreement between the parties. The existence of a maritime contract and its terms are questions of fact we review for clear error. *See One Beacon Ins. Co. v. Crowley Marine Servs., Inc.*, 648 F.3d 258, 262–64 (5th Cir. 2011). On the other hand, "interpretation of [those] terms is a matter of law that we review *de novo.*" *Id.* at 262.

Enterprise Marine concedes there was an agreement regarding reimbursement for maintenance and cure. The agreement arose from a conference in April 2016 among counsel for each party and a claims adjuster. At the time of the meeting, though, doubts about the cause of McKinley's back problems were at most inchoate. It is not clear when Enterprise Marine began to question the veracity of McKinley's back complaints, but an independent medical examination in July 2016 concluded the injuries were preexisting.

No written contract fully embodies these parties' agreement, but both sides reference an email CBR's counsel sent to Enterprise Marine. CBR says the email "outline[s] the agreement reached between the parties" while [—7—] Enterprise Marine characterizes it as "a memorandum . . . setting out the steps which would be taken for submitting reimbursement requests to Enterprise [Marine]" through a third-party claims adjuster. The email does not address either party's obligations if any medical expenses were found to be for injuries unrelated to the allision. The operative language in the email simply states:

> As discussed in the meeting [between CBR and Enterprise Marine], maintenance and cure checks will be issued directly from [CBR] . . . every two weeks. [The adjuster of McKinley's claims] will request reimbursement from Enterprise [Marine] . . . every sixty days.
>
> [The adjuster] will have [McKinley] send all medical invoicing directly to [the adjuster] . . . . Medical invoicing of [McKinley] will be audited by [the adjuster] and forwarded to [CBR] for payment. [The adjuster] will request reimbursement for medicals from Enterprise [Marine] . . . . [The adjuster] will also request reimbursement from Enterprise [Marine] for [CBR's] past maintenance and cure payments.

CBR claims that contractual terms not mentioned in the email were established at the meeting, but the evidence contains few details. There was testimony that the email "was a recitation of the meeting." The claims adjuster who was at the meeting testified that there were no "limitations given to [him] about not paying for certain items." The adjuster stated specifically that Enterprise Marine's attorney did not mention limits on reimbursement. Enterprise Marine quotes the adjuster's testimony that the purpose of the email "was to summarize the process of how maintenance and cure would be issued . . . and reimbursed by Enterprise" Marine. The district court made note of the email and the testimony about the meeting, but it did not make findings about the agreement's details.

Even with the adjuster's testimony that the agreement contained no "limitations" about payments, we see no concession at {–940–} that time by Enterprise Marine that it would make these payments even if it were later determined [—8—] that the medical expenses were unrelated to injuries arising from the allision. The district court gave short shrift to the agreement, which is indicative of a finding that the agreement simply did not cover a situation in which it later became clear that the seaman's claims were fraudulent. We see no error.

AFFIRMED.

United States Court of Appeals
for the Fifth Circuit

No. 18-30652

LATIOLAIS
VS.
HUNTINGTON INGALLS, INC.***

Appeal from the United States District Court for the
Eastern District of Louisiana

Decided: March 11, 2019

***Petition for rehearing en banc granted on May 8, 2019.

Citation: 918 F.3d 406, 7 Adm. R. 196 (5th Cir. 2019).

Before **JONES**, **HAYNES**, and **OLDHAM**, Circuit Judges.

[—1—] {–407–} JONES, Circuit Judge:

Like several actions before it, this case involves a Plaintiff who was exposed to asbestos at the Avondale shipyard and eventually contracted mesothelioma. The Defendant removed the case to federal court pursuant to 28 U.S.C. § 1442(a)(1), the "federal officer removal statute," but the district court remanded to state court. Constrained by a welter of conflicting precedent, we must affirm. [—2—]

BACKGROUND

During the 1960s and 1970s, the United States Navy contracted with the Defendant Avondale[1] to build and refurbish naval vessels. Most of the contracts in the 1960s required asbestos for thermal insulation. According to Avondale's expert, a marine engineer and naval historian, the contracts obligated Avondale "to comply with government plans and specifications, and the federal government had the right to and did exercise supervision over the process to ensure such compliance." Importantly, however, a Navy ship inspector who worked at Avondale during the 1960s testified that he and his colleagues "neither monitored nor enforced safety regulations" and "on the job safety during the construction of vessels for the United States government was the responsibility of Avondale Shipyards' safety department."

The Plaintiff, James Latiolais, formerly a machinist aboard the *USS TAPPA-HANNOCK*, was exposed to asbestos while his ship underwent refurbishing at Avondale for several months. During the refurbishing process, Latiolais spent most of each day on the ship. In 2017, Latiolais was {–408–} diagnosed with mesothelioma. He died in October, 2017.[2]

Latiolais sued Avondale in Louisiana state court for causing him to contract mesothelioma. He asserts, *inter alia*, that Avondale negligently failed to warn him about asbestos hazards and failed to provide adequate safety equipment. He did not allege strict liability claims against Avondale.

Avondale removed the case to federal court under 28 U.S.C. § 1442(a)(1). Latiolais sought remand, however, and the district court granted the motion. [—3—] It ruled in relevant part that because Avondale had not met the "causal nexus" requirement for officer removal, *i.e.* had not shown that the United States or any of its officials exercised any control over Avondale's safety practices, removal under this statute was improper. Avondale timely appealed.

STANDARD OF REVIEW

Although an order remanding a case to state court is not generally reviewable, "an order remanding a case to the State court from which it was removed pursuant to section 1442 or 1443 of this title shall be reviewable by appeal or otherwise." 28 U.S.C. § 1447(d). "We review the district court's remand order de novo without a thumb on the remand side of the scale." *Legendre v. Huntington Ingalls, Inc.*, 885 F.3d 398, 400, 6

---

[1] The Defendant Huntington Ingalls was formerly known by many names including Northrop Grumman Shipbuilding and Avondale Industries. Because the parties refer to the Defendant as Avondale, the court does the same.

[2] Although Latiolais died shortly after filing his petition in Louisiana state court, no party argues that his death affects any issue in this appeal.

Adm. R. 193, 193 (5th Cir. 2018) (quotation marks omitted).

DISCUSSION

On appeal, Avondale makes three arguments as to why officer removal is proper. First, as amended in 2011, the removal statute now requires only that a federal directive "relates to"—but not necessarily has a causal relationship to—the Plaintiffs' injuries. Second, Avondale asserts that it has satisfied the causal nexus requirement by showing "that its relationship with Mr. Latiolais derived solely from its work for the federal government." Third, Avondale seeks to avoid precedents of this court contrary to the foregoing propositions. Unfortunately, the failure of the third argument dooms the others. [—4—]

I. The "relating to" language

The federal officer removal statute was amended in 2011 to broaden the basis for removal to federal court of claims brought against officers or agents of the federal government and those working under its direction. Thus, the statute states that an action filed in state court may be removed to federal court by: "[t]he United States or any agency thereof or any officer (or any person acting under that officer) of the United States or of any agency thereof, in an official or individual capacity, *for or relating to* any act under color of such office." 28 U.S.C. § 1442(a)(1) (emphasis added).

The Supreme Court has observed more than once that when the term "relating to" appears in a statute, it implies broad and comprehensive coverage. *See, e.g., Morales v. Grans World Airlines, Inc.*, 504 U.S. 374, 383, 112 S. Ct. 2031, 2037 (1992) ("The ordinary meaning of these words is a broad one—'to stand in some relation; to have bearing or concern; to pertain; refer; to bring into association with or connection with.'") (quoting BLACK'S LAW DICT. 1158 (5th ed. 1979)); *see also Shaw v. Delta Air Lines, Inc.*, 463 U.S. 85, 96-98, 103 S. Ct. 2890, 2899-2900 (1983). From the text alone, enhanced by the Supreme Court's understanding of its {–409–}

language, Avondale's argument has considerable appeal. Avondale's work, after all, clearly related to the federal government's directive to employ asbestos insulation. Under the "relating to" test, Avondale would preserve a federal venue.

In this court, however, what's past is prologue. Before the amendment, Section 1442 authorized removal of a suit against a federal officer, or person acting under a federal officer, only when the suit was *"for* any act under color of such office." 28 U.S.C. § 1442(a)(1) (1996) (emphasis added). To successfully remove a case under the earlier version, this court held, quite reasonably, that a defendant must show that it is a person within the meaning of the statute, that it has a colorable federal defense, that it acted pursuant to a federal [—5—] officer's directions and that a causal nexus exists between its actions under color of federal office and the plaintiff's claims. *Winters v. Diamond Shamrock Chem. Co.*, 149 F.3d 387, 398-400 (5th Cir. 1998). Further, under the causal nexus test, "mere federal involvement does not satisfy the causal nexus requirement; instead, the defendant must show that its actions taken pursuant to the government's direction or control caused the plaintiff's specific injuries." *Savoie v. Huntington Ingalls, Inc.*, 817 F.3d 457, 462, 4 Adm. R. 225, 227 (5th Cir. 2016).

This court applied to the post-2011 amended statute the "causal nexus" test articulated for the prior statute. *Bartel v. Alcoa S.S. Co., Inc.*, 805 F.3d 169, 172, 3 Adm. R. 422, 422–23 (5th Cir. 2015). In *Bartel*, the court quoted the post-2011 statute but adopted the same causal nexus test that predates the new statute. *Id.* at 172, 174-75, 3 Adm. R. at 422, 424–25. Three years later, when Avondale raised the same textual argument that it makes now, the court held that *Bartel*'s status as precedent precluded one panel from overruling the former decision. *Legendre v. Huntington Ingalls, Inc.*, 885 F.3d 398, 403, 6 Adm. R. 193, 196–97 (5th Cir. 2018). Although this court's precedents on the interpretation of Section 1442(a)(1) have proliferated since *Bartel*, the reasoning of *Legendre* continues to control our work.

It is true that in *Zeringue*, a case decided after *Bartel* but before *Legendre*, this court appeared to relax the causal nexus standard in light of the post-2011 "relating to" language, but reliance on that case is not appropriate. *Zeringue v. Crane Company*, 846 F.3d 785, 793, 5 Adm. R. 193, 197 (5th Cir. 2017). *Zeringue* explained that the addition of the phrase "relating to" in the removal statute "broadens the scope of the statute as the ordinary meaning of [relating to] is a broad one," but "[i]t remains, however, that the causal nexus inquiry must . . . be tailored to fit the facts of each case." *Id.*, 5 Adm. R. at 197 (quotation marks omitted). Although these statements appear to give effect to the post-2011 "relating to" language, *Zeringue* ruled only on the propriety of removing a strict liability claim under this statute and specifically declined to consider a negligence-[—6—] based failure to warn claim. Before *Zeringue,* however, in a case brought against Avondale, this court had decided that claims for negligent exposure to asbestos could not be removed pursuant to *Bartel. Savoie,* 817 F.3d at 463, 4 Adm. R. at 228.

In a case with similar facts to this one, the *Savoie* court relied on *Bartel* and found no causal nexus between Avondale's conduct and government requirements. Even though the government contracts required Avondale to build ships with asbestos, "the government had no control over the shipyard's safety procedures" and "the Navy neither imposed any special safety requirements on the shipyard nor prevented the shipyard from imposing its own safety procedures." *Id.,* 4 Adm. R. at 228. Accordingly, "the government's directions to the shipyard via the contract specifications did not {–410–} cause the alleged negligence, and those claims do not support removal." *Id.,* 4 Adm. R. at 228.

In contrast, the *Savoie* plaintiff's strict liability claims were held to support removal,[3] and the court explained that, "[u]nlike claims based on negligence, those based on strict

liability do not turn on discretionary decisions made by the shipyard." *Id.* at 465, 4 Adm. R. at 229. "Thus, it is the government's detailed specifications, which the shipyard was contractually obligated to follow, that required the use of asbestos that allegedly caused [the Plaintiff's] death. This is enough to show a causal nexus between the . . . strict liability claims and the shipyard's actions under the color of federal authority." *Id.* at 465-66, 4 Adm. R. at 230.[4]

The dichotomy between *Zeringue* and *Savoie* was adhered to by *Legendre*, where the plaintiffs sued Avondale for the plaintiff's asbestos [—7—] disease based on the theory of negligent failure to warn, not strict liability. *Legendre*, 885 F.3d at 399, 6 Adm. R. at 193. *Legendre* explained that "in *Zeringue*, we recognized that the 2011 amendment shifted the causal nexus calculus" but "[i]mportantly, in *Zeringue*, we explicitly reaffirmed *Bartel*." *Id.* at 401-02, 6 Adm. R. at 195. *Legendre* also relied on *Savoie. Id.* at 401, 6 Adm. R. at 194–95.

All of these cases post-date the 2011 amendment to Section 1442(a)(1), and all continue to cite *Bartel,* while drawing a distinction for removal purposes between claims for negligence (not removable) and strict liability (removable) pursuant to the causal nexus test. We are bound by this series of cases.

II. The Causal Nexus Test

Avondale attempts to demonstrate that even under the causal nexus test used in our case law, removal may be sustained. This contention is not persuasive.

Avondale's evidence has not changed since *Legendre*. Although the government contractually required Avondale to use asbestos in refurbishing the Navy vessels,

---

[3] The court concluded that removal was proper because "removal of the entire case is appropriate so long as a single claim satisfies the federal officer removal statute." *Savoie,* 817 F.3d at 463, 4 Adm. R. at 228.

---

[4] Mere use of asbestos is a strict liability claim, whereas failure to warn is a negligence claim. *See Savoie,* 817 F.3d at 465, 4 Adm. R. at 229 ("The strict liability claims rest on the mere use of asbestos . . . [u]nlike claims based on negligence, those based on strict liability do not turn on discretionary decisions made by the shipyard.").

Avondale once again "makes no showing that it was not free to adopt the safety measures the plaintiffs now allege would have prevented their injuries." *Legendre*, 885 F.3d at 403, 6 Adm. R. at 196 (quotation marks omitted). From all appearances, Navy vessel inspectors at Avondale "neither monitored nor enforced safety regulations" and "on the job safety during the construction of vessels for the United States government was the responsibility of Avondale Shipyards' safety department." Avondale points to nothing to rebut this evidence. As the district court concluded, "[b]ased on the evidence produced by both parties, there is nothing to suggest that the Navy, in its official authority, issued any orders, specifications, or directives relating to safety procedures." Accordingly, Avondale has not shown a causal nexus under analogous exposure facts. [—8—]

Avondale alleges instead that it has satisfied the causal nexus requirement because "its relationship with Mr. Latiolais derived solely from its work for the federal government." Avondale contends that in the *Bartel* line of cases, the plaintiffs were former employees (or their family members) who sued the employer defendants, whereas Latiolais, a Navy man, was never {–411–} employed by Avondale, and Avondale's contact with him occurred solely because of its contracts with the federal government. In other words, Avondale's contention is that because its contact with Latiolais was solely due to its government work on the Navy ship on which Latiolais served, officer removal is proper.

This contention might have prevailed but for the discussions in our other cases. Avondale relies on three pre-*Bartel* Supreme Court cases and *Zeringue* for its proposition. *See Maryland v. Soper*, 270 U.S. 9, 46 S. Ct. 185 (1926); *Willingham v. Morgan*, 395 U.S. 402, 89 S. Ct. 1813 (1969); *Jefferson County v. Acker*, 527 U.S. 423, 119 S. Ct. 2069 (1999). To be sure, those cases contain statements suggesting that removal is proper if the defendant's relationship with the plaintiff is derived solely from the defendant's official federal duties. For example, *Willingham* ruled:

In a civil suit of this nature, we think it was sufficient for petitioners to have shown that their relationship to respondent derived solely from their official duties . . . In this case, once petitioners had shown that their only contact with respondent occurred inside the penitentiary, while they were performing their duties, we believe that they had demonstrated the required 'causal connection.'

Willingham, 395 U.S. at 409; 89 S. Ct. at 1817 (footnote omitted). Further, in *Zeringue*, this court quoted *Willingham*, noting that "'it [is] *sufficient*' for a federal officer in a civil suit to establish the requisite causal connection by showing that the officer's 'relationship to [the plaintiff] derived solely from [the [—9—] officer's] official duties.'" *Zeringue*, 846 F.3d at 793, 5 Adm. R. at 197 (quoting *Willingham*, 395 U.S. at 409, 89 S. Ct. at 1817) (alterations and emphasis in *Zeringue*). Indeed, the *Zeringue* court reasoned pursuant to this rule that the defendant had met the causal nexus requirement because its "relationship with [the plaintiff] derives solely from its official authority to provide parts to the Navy, and that official authority *relates to* [the defendant's] allegedly improper actions, namely its use of asbestos." *Zeringue*, 846 F.3d at 793-94, 5 Adm. R. at 197–98 (emphasis in original).

Whatever force could be derived from these statements in *Zeringue*, however, was weakened by its assurance that "[o]ur recent holding in *Bartel* . . . is not to the contrary." *Id.* at 794, 5 Adm. R. at 198. *Zeringue* continued that in *Bartel*, the charged conduct of failure to warn of the dangers of asbestos "was private conduct that implicated no federal interest. Because the very purpose of the causal nexus requirement is to ensure that removal only arises when a federal interest in the matter exists, an extension of § 1442 to allow those defendants to remove would have stretched the causal nexus requirement to the point of irrelevance." *Id.* at 794, 5 Adm. R. at 198 (quotation marks omitted). One year later, *Legendre* quoted *Zeringue* for these same propositions. *Legendre*, 885 F.3d at 402, 6 Adm. R. at 195.

Legendre added, "[i]mportantly, in *Zeringue* we explicitly reaffirmed *Bartel*. We described the charged conduct in *Bartel* as failing to warn, train, and adopt safety procedures regarding asbestos. These actions we explained, were private conduct that implicated no federal interests." *Id.* at 402, 6 Adm. R. at 195 (citations and quotation marks omitted). Accordingly, the *Bartel* defendants did not meet the causal nexus requirement. *Id.*, 6 Adm. R. at 195.

Because Latiolais's claims are the same failure to warn claims that both *Zeringue* and *Legendre* held implicated no federal interests, we cannot hold that this case meets the causal nexus requirement. [—10—] {–412–}

III. The rule of orderliness and need to reconsider *Bartel* en banc

Avondale argues that *Legendre* misapplied the rule of orderliness vis-a-vis *Bartel* and that *Bartel* should not control this case "because it did not meaningfully consider or address the effect of the 2011 amendment." *Legendre* explained that, "[t]his court adheres to a rule of orderliness, under which a panel may not overturn a controlling precedent absent an intervening change in law, such as by a statutory amendment, or the Supreme Court, or our en banc court." *Legendre*, 885 F.3d at 403, 6 Adm. R. at 196 (quotation marks omitted). "The 2011 amendment was, of course, not 'intervening'; *Bartel* was decided after the change and quoted the new 'relating to' language. *Bartel*'s articulation of the causal nexus standard, and its requirement that the claimed negligence conflict with a federal directive, was integral to the result. We are therefore bound by the *Bartel* standard." *Id.*, 6 Adm. R. at 196. Avondale cites no case in which this court bypassed the rule of orderliness because a later panel found unconvincing the earlier panel's statutory interpretation. This appeal is accordingly governed by *Bartel* and *Legendre*.

Nevertheless, *Bartel* should be reconsidered en banc in order to align our precedent with the statute's evolution. As discussed above, "[b]efore 2011, § 1442 allowed the removal of a state suit against a federal

officer, or person acting under a federal officer, only when the state suit was 'for any act under color of such office.'" *Zeringue*, 846 F.3d at 793, 5 Adm. R. at 197. In 2011, however, Congress amended the statute "to allow the removal of a state suit 'for *or relating to* any act under color of such office.'" *Id.*, 5 Adm. R. at 197. Thus, Congress specifically added the words "relating to" into § 1442. Those words have meaning, and the meaning is plainly broader than that of the predecessor provision.

Bartel's causal nexus standard simply does not give effect to the words "relating to." This case exemplifies the problem. Avondale refurbished vessels using asbestos insulation as directed by the Navy. Because Avondale ran its [—11—] own safety department free of Navy directives, however, any alleged failure by Avondale to warn its employees or others about asbestos is not an act under color of federal office, so Avondale is not being sued "for" a federal act. However, Avondale's failure to warn about asbestos certainly "relates to" its federal act of building the ships. Applying the post-2011 statutory language would change the outcome of this appeal and would authorize removal of many more cases than the causal nexus test permits.

Finally, *Legendre* explained that "although we are bound by precedent, we note that other circuits have read the 2011 amendments to eliminate the old 'causal nexus' requirement." *Id.* at 403, 6 Adm. R. at 197. The Third and Fourth Circuits shifted their jurisprudence away from the causal nexus test and now require only a "connection" or "association." Specifically, the Third Circuit, after discussing the addition of the phrase "relating to," held "it is sufficient for there to be a 'connection' or 'association' between the act in question and the federal office." *In re Commonwealth's Motion to Appoint Counsel Against or Directed to Defender Association of Philadelphia*, 790 F.3d 457, 471 (3d Cir. 2015). The Fourth Circuit agreed that the addition of "relating to" "broaden[ed] the universe of acts that enable federal removal such that there need only be a *connection or association* between the act in question and the federal office." *Sawyer v. Foster Wheeler LLC*, 860 F.3d 249,

258, 5 Adm. R. 167, 172 (4th Cir. 2017) (emphasis in original) (quotation marks and internal citation {–413–} omitted).[5] Federal courts should be in harmony concerning the interpretation of statutes governing essential procedures like removal. This court is out of step with Congress and our sister circuits. [—12—]

CONCLUSION

For the foregoing reasons, but in hopes that our precedents will be reordered, the remand order of the district court must be **AFFIRMED**.

(Reporter's Note: Dissenting Opinion follows on p. 202).

(Reporter's Note: Rehearing en banc granted on May 8, 2019. See, 923 F.3d 427, 7 Adm. R. 256 (5th Cir. 2019) (reh'g en banc granted)).

---

[5] The Eleventh Circuit has also considered the "relating to" language, but the court's position is less clear. *See Caver v. Central Alabama Electric Coop.*, 845 F.3d 1135, 1144-45 & n.8 (11th Cir. 2017) (citing the Third Circuit's "connection or association" language but applying a "causal connection" test).

[—13—] {–413–} **HAYNES,** Circuit Judge, dissenting:

I respectfully dissent from the court's decision to extend *Bartel v. Alcoa Steamship Co.*, 805 F.3d 169, 3 Adm. R. 422 (5th Cir. 2015), to the facts of this case. I agree that we are bound by the legal standard that *Bartel* and progeny established. But even under that standard, Avondale should prevail on the jurisdictional issue.

The core fact that distinguishes this case from *Bartel* is that Latiolais was a member of the Navy. He was subject to Avondale's actions exclusively because the Navy assigned him to the *USS TAPPAHANNOCK*. The Navy alone, not Avondale, could control Latiolais's actions.

Our case law, including *Bartel*, has never addressed such a situation.[1] Though we are bound to apply the standard that *Bartel* uses—the causal nexus test—the result is not predetermined.

Latiolais's status as a Navy man and Avondale's status as a contractor for the Navy satisfies the causal nexus test. The Supreme Court has held that the causal nexus test is satisfied when defendants "have shown that their relationship to [a plaintiff] derived solely from their official duties." *Willingham v. Morgan*, 395 U.S. 402, 409 (1969). Latiolais had no relationship with Avondale other than through its contract to refurbish the *USS TAPPAHANNOCK*. Their relationship is therefore "derived solely" from Avondale's official duties.

The majority opinion seems to agree with this point, noting that *Willingham* "suggest[s] that removal is proper" based on that test, but it reasons that our decision in *Zeringue v. Crane Co.*, 846 F.3d 785, 5 Adm. R. 193 (5th Cir. 2017), forbids it. *Zeringue* does not prohibit removal. *Zeringue* does say that [—14—] negligence claims like those in *Bartel* involve "private conduct that implicated no federal interest." *Zeringue*, 846 F.3d at 794, 5

Adm. R. at 198. But that statement must be read in light of the facts of *Bartel*, which involved an employee of a private, federal contractor suing the contractor. There, the relationship involves private conduct because it centers on a private contractor directing the work of its private employees—a relationship that would exist independent of federal involvement. But here, the relationship is not wholly private. Both Avondale and Latiolais were at the ship at the direction of the federal government and neither could control the other's behavior. The treatment of federal workers by a contractor for the federal government implicates a "federal interest." *Id.*, 5 Adm. R. at 198.

Other circuits have reached the same result based on nearly identical facts. *See* {–414–} *Ruppel v. CBS Corp.*, 701 F.3d 1176, 1179, 1181 (7th Cir. 2012) (concluding that a Navy man satisfied the causal nexus test against for his negligence claim against contractor that "manufactured, sold, distributed, or installed" turbines with asbestos under the direction of the navy); *Bennett v. MIS Corp.*, 607 F.3d 1076, 1088, 1091 (6th Cir. 2010) (concluding the causal nexus test was satisfied for FAA employees against a company that remediated mold at their work site). I would follow these cases and conclude that the district court had jurisdiction; therefore, I respectfully dissent.

(Reporter's Note: Rehearing en banc granted on May 8, 2019. See, 923 F.3d 427, 7 Adm. R. 256 (5th Cir. 2019) (reh'g en banc granted)).

---

[1] Because this case differs significantly from the *Bartel* line of cases, it is not a good vehicle to take the underlying issue en banc even assuming arguendo that the *Bartel* line of cases are wrong.

United States Court of Appeals
for the Fifth Circuit

No. 18-30147

BP EXPLORATION & PROD., INC.
VS.
CLAIMANT ID 100217946

Appeal from the United States District Court for the
Eastern District of Louisiana

Decided: March 18, 2019

Citation: 919 F.3d 258, 7 Adm. R. 203 (5th Cir. 2019).

Before WIENER, DENNIS, and OWEN, Circuit Judges.

[—1—] {–260–} PER CURIAM:

This is an appeal from an award to Claimant ID 100217946 (Claimant) under the Settlement Program established following the *Deepwater Horizon* oil spill. The Claims Administrator concluded that the non-profit Claimant is entitled to compensation of nearly $15 million. An Appeal Panel within the Settlement Program affirmed, and the district court denied discretionary review. BP appeals, arguing that two donations were improperly counted by the Claims Administrator and the district court was required to review the award. We affirm the district court's judgment. [—2—]

I

In April 2010, an explosion on the *Deepwater Horizon*, a mobile offshore drilling unit leased by BP Exploration & Production, Inc., BP America Production Company, and BP, P.L.C. (collectively, BP), caused the discharge of millions of gallons of oil into the Gulf of Mexico.[1] Two years later, BP entered into the "*Deepwater Horizon* Economic and Property Damages Settlement Agreement" with a class of individuals and entities allegedly injured by the *Deepwater Horizon* oil spill. The Settlement Agreement created the Settlement Program under which claims for settlement benefits are reviewed by the

---

[1] *Ctr. for Biological Diversity, Inc. v. BP Am. Prod. Co.*, 704 F.3d 413, 418, 1 Adm. R. 193, 193 (5th Cir. 2013).

Claims Administrator, whose decisions may be appealed to an Appeal Panel.

Businesses seeking settlement benefits as compensation for economic losses "must establish that their loss was due to or resulting from the Deepwater Horizon Incident" by meeting the applicable "causation requirement[]." The Settlement Agreement imposes different causation requirements on businesses located in different geographic "zones." Businesses located in Zone A are not required to establish causation unless they fall into one of the agreed-upon exceptions. Claimant is located in Zone A and is not one of the agreed-upon exceptions, so it was not required to establish causation.

Once causation is established or inferred, claimants must prove an economic loss using the methodology in Exhibit 4C. Under Step 1 of the formula, claimants compare their Variable Profit in the Compensation Period— a consecutive three-month period between May and December 2010—to their Variable Profit during a Benchmark Period of the claimant's choosing. The Variable Profit is calculated by considering the total monthly revenue over [—3—] the period and subtracting the corresponding variable expenses over the same time period, including "Variable Costs," variable portions of salaries, and other expenses. If the Claimant has less Variable Profit in the Compensation Period than in the Benchmark period, it is entitled to compensation for that difference. Under Step 2 of the compensation formula, claimants are also compensated for incremental profits the claimant might have expected to generate in 2010 in the absence of the spill, based on the claimant's revenue trend before the spill. Claimants may also be entitled to a Risk Transfer Premium (RTP) {–261–} depending on where the business is located. The amount of the risk transfer premium is based on the total Step 1 and Step 2 Compensation multiplied by a variable found in Exhibit 15 of the Settlement Agreement, the RTP Chart.

Claimant is a non-profit organization that solicits donations for its own programming and distributes grants to other non-profit organizations. Claimant submitted a Business

Economic Loss (BEL) Claim to the Settlement Program. The Claims Administrator determined that Claimant was eligible for $5,814,307.79 at Step 1 Compensation by comparing its Variable Profit in August through October 2010 with the same period in 2009. The Claims Administrator then determined that Claimant was entitled to an RTP of 1.5 times the amount of its losses, which was $8,721,461.69. In addition, the Claims Administrator awarded $7,062.50 of Claimant Accounting support as reimbursement for expenses that Claimant incurred in the claims process. All told, the Claims Administrator awarded $14,542,831.98 to Claimant.

BP appealed the award to a three-member Appeal Panel. It argued that two large donations received by Claimant totaling $8.9 million were improperly included in the economic loss calculation, which resulted in an excessive award. The first donation was an unsecured non-negotiable promissory note for $5,913,491.66 to be paid in eight equal annual installments [—4—] beginning June 30, 2010, with interest accruing on the unpaid balance. The other donation at issue was a $3,000,000 pledge to be paid over ten years in annual installments of $300,000, with a check for the first $300,000 attached to the pledge. BP argued there were four issues with the inclusion of these donations in the economic loss calculation: (1) The donations were not "revenue," (2) even if the payments were revenue, Claimant could only treat those payments that were actually received in 2009 as revenue for 2009, (3) if the entire $8.9 million could be properly treated as revenue, the Settlement Program failed to match the donations with corresponding distributions that Claimant granted to other non-profits that should be treated as expenses, and (4) awards made to entities that maintained funds with Claimant should offset Claimant's award to avoid impermissible double recovery.

BP requested that an en banc Appeal Panel review the award to "promote and maintain uniformity and consistency of the Appeal Panel decisions," contending that an Appeal Panel in another case involving a non-profit had ruled differently than the Claims Administrator. The Appeal Panel initially indicated that it would consider the appeal en banc. Before rendering a decision, the Appeal Panel decided not to address the issue en banc. An Appeal Panel then reviewed the decision de novo and rejected each of BP's arguments.

BP then requested discretionary review in the district court. BP repeated its arguments with one exception. It did not argue that the award should be offset by awards to other non-profits to whom it had made grants to prevent double recovery. The district court denied discretionary review. BP appeals the denial of discretionary review. [—5—]

II

We review the district court's denial of discretionary review for abuse of discretion.[2] It is generally an abuse of discretion not to review a decision that "actually contradicted or misapplied the Settlement Agreement, or had the clear {—262—} potential to" do so.[3] However, we have been careful to note that it is "wrong to suggest that the district court must grant review of all claims that raise a question about the proper interpretation of the Settlement Agreement."[4] It is not an abuse of discretion to deny a request for review that "involve[s] no pressing question of how the Settlement Agreement should be interpreted or implemented, but simply raise[s] the correctness of a discretionary administrative decision in the facts of a single

---

[2] *Claimant ID 100212278 v. BP Expl. & Prod., Inc.*, 848 F.3d 407, 410, 5 Adm. R. 202, 203 (5th Cir. 2017) (citing *Holmes Motors, Inc. v. BP Expl. & Prod.*, 829 F.3d 313, 315, 4 Adm. R. 263, 263 (5th Cir. 2016)).

[3] *Id.*, 5 Adm. R. at 203 (quoting *Holmes Motors*, 829 F.3d at 315, 4 Adm. R. at 263) (internal quotations omitted).

[4] *Id.*, 5 Adm. R. at 203 (quoting *Holmes Motors*, 829 F.3d at 316, 4 Adm. R. at 264) (internal quotations omitted); *see also In re Deepwater Horizon*, 785 F.3d 986, 999, 3 Adm. R. 341, 350 (5th Cir. 2015) ("We do not intend any part of this opinion to turn the district court's discretionary review into a mandatory review. To do so would frustrate the clear purpose of the Settlement Agreement to curtail litigation.").

claimant's case."[5] It may also be an abuse of discretion to deny a request for review that raises a recurring issue on which the Appeal Panels are split if "the resolution of the question will substantially impact the administration of the Agreement."[6]

BP argues that the district court abused its discretion by failing (1) to resolve a recurring issue on which the Appeal Panels are split, and (2) to review an Appeal Panel's decision that contradicts the Settlement Agreement. We address each argument.

A

BP argues that the treatment of grant-making entities like Claimant is "a recurring and important issue in administering the Settlement [—6—] [Agreement]." It reasons that the award is significant because of (1) the amount involved, (2) the "unusually lengthy" analysis of the Appeal Panel, (3) the Panel's reliance on contested characterization of precedent, (4) Claimant's admission that donors play a role in determining how grants are made, and (5) the threat of double-recovery. BP additionally maintains that there is a "split" among the Appeal Panels.

BP points to a decision of an Appeal Panel that excluded from "revenue" funds received by a non-profit that were immediately distributed to other non-profit affiliates. In that appeal, the claimant challenged the Claims Administrator's decision to exclude a state-grant from revenue because the Claims Administrator found the funds were a "pass-through" grant in which the state granted money to claimant and claimant distributed an identical amount to its affiliates. The Appeal Panel upheld the exclusion.

"For [a] ruling to create a conflict with the one now before us, it must have involved substantially identical claimants relying on

substantially identical documentation."[7] The one award identified by BP does not show a split among the Appeal Panels. In that case, the receipt of funds coupled with an exactly matching distribution in the same month supported the Claims Administrator's decision to treat the funds as pass-through and not revenue. Here, BP has not shown that Claimant is engaged in the same type of dollar-for-dollar distribution. Claimant does not dispute that it grants a large percentage of funds it receives to other entities. However, {–263–} Claimant contests the characterization of its funding as merely a pass-through, and the Appeal Panel agreed. The question of what particular percentage of funds that a charity passes through will give rise to the characterization of the donations [—7—] as pass-throughs instead of revenue is a difficult one. But, we cannot say that the Appeal Panels are split. The Appeal Panel here explicitly rejected BP's argument that Claimant is primarily a pass-through organization because a large part of its donations are passed through and donors are involved in the ultimate decision about where donated funds are spent. Rather than reflecting a split that must be resolved by the district court, the Appeal Panel's decision reflects that the Panels are conscious of factual differences that may distinguish claimants.[8]

Nor can we agree with BP's argument that the size of the award requires appellate review. While any multi-million dollar award is "significant" in the ordinary sense, the size of the award alone does not make the issue significant enough to require district court review.[9] Further, the "unusually lengthy"

---

[5] *Claimant ID 100212278*, 848 F.3d at 410, 5 Adm. R. at 203 (quoting *In re Deepwater Horizon*, 641 F. App'x 405, 410 (5th Cir. 2016)) (alterations in original).

[6] *Id.*, 5 Adm. R. at 203 (quoting *In re Deepwater Horizon*, 632 F. App'x 199, 203-04 (5th Cir. 2015)).

[7] *Claimant ID 100128765 v. BP Expl. & Prod., Inc.*, 709 F. App'x 771, 773 (5th Cir. 2017) (per curiam).

[8] *See Claimant ID 100190818 v. BP Expl. & Prod., Inc.*, 718 F. App'x 220, 222 (5th Cir. 2018); *Claimant ID 100051301 v. BP Expl. & Prod., Inc.*, 694 F. App'x 236, 240 (5th Cir. 2017) ("[T]he fact that Appeal Panels have reached different conclusions for this issue depending on the circumstances of each case does not represent the type of Appeal Panel split that would require the district court's review.").

[9] *See In re Deepwater Horizon*, 785 F.3d 1003, 1021, 3 Adm. R. 325, 338 (5th Cir. 2015) ("*Non-*

decision of the Appeal Panel is not a reason to doubt the Panel—it is an indication that the Panel thoroughly considered all of BP's arguments and assessed the documentation provided by Claimant to apply the Settlement Agreement. Finally, BP did not argue to the district court that it should have addressed the specter of double recovery, so BP cannot rely on that argument to show that the district court abused its discretion.[10] [—8—]

B

BP also argues that the district court abused its discretion because the award is contrary to the terms of the Settlement Agreement. BP argues three ways in which the award is contrary to "economic reality": (1) The donations at issue are not "revenue," (2) if the donations are revenue, the Appeal Panel did not properly match expenses to revenue in the month earned, and (3) if the donations are revenue, the entire $8.9 million should not be recorded in 2009.

1

BP's contention that the $8.9 million donations are not "revenue" is contrary to this court's *Non-Profit Decision*.[11] In that case, we were confronted with the argument that donations and grants to non-profits did not qualify as "revenue" for purposes of Exhibit 4C's compensation formula.[12] We recognized that "modern nonprofits are commercial entities that seek to generate cash surpluses," and held that {–264–} revenue includes donations and grants to non-profits.[13] We also addressed the work that non-profits do to raise funds, and noted that non-profits must

do significant work to solicit donations and grants "to keep their doors open."[14] We rejected BP's narrow view of the work that non-profits perform to "earn their revenue" and upheld the Claims Administrator's reading of the Settlement Agreement that non-profit donations and grants are typically "revenue" under Exhibit 4C.[15]

While acknowledging our *Non-Profit Decision*, BP nevertheless argues that these particular $8.9 million donations are not revenue. It insists that the donations are not made to Claimant, but that Claimant merely acts as a "'fiduciary' for the ultimate beneficiaries." BP likens Claimant to Western [—9—] Union, arguing that none of the funds belong to Claimant and must be distributed according to the wishes of the donors. The basis of this argument is that Claimant solicits donations for placement in donor-advised funds, where the donor expresses how the donations are to be spent. Despite the fact that the Internal Revenue Code requires all charitable donations in donor-advised funds to be exclusively the funds of the non-profit,[16] BP argues that Claimant is ultimately subject to the will of donors and therefore those donations cannot be considered Claimant's revenue. The Appeal Panel disagreed and focused on the aspects of Claimant's operations that cannot be considered pass-through, such as the workshops it conducts, the series of lectures and performances it presents, and the funding of a police perception survey which was used in undertaking police reform in Claimant's community. The Appeal Panel held that the contested donations were unrestricted donations made to Claimant, and thus fall squarely within the definition of "revenue" we set forth in *Non-Profit Decision*.[17]

BP argues that this factual determination was error and urges us to remand to the district court for evidentiary hearings to determine whether the particular donations were of donor-advised funds. However, the district court did not abuse its discretion by

---

Profit Decision") ("[D]enying this award because of its size would open the floodgates to a flurry of challenges to nonprofit awards, undermining the aims of the [settlement program].")

[10] *In re Deepwater Horizon*, 814 F.3d 748, 752, 4 Adm. R. 196, 198 (5th Cir. 2016) (citing *Cent. Sw. Tex. Dev., L.L.C. v. JPMorgan Chase Bank, Nat'l Ass'n*, 780 F.3d 296, 300-01 (5th Cir. 2015)) ("Claimants did not make this argument in their memorandum in support of their motion before the district court, and it is accordingly forfeited.").

[11] 785 F.3d 1003, 3 Adm. R. 325 (5th Cir. 2015).

[12] *Id.* at 1012, 3 Adm. R. at 330.

[13] *Id.*, 3 Adm. R. at 330.

[14] *Id.* at 1013, 3 Adm. R. at 331.

[15] *Id.*, 3 Adm. R. at 331.

[16] *See* 26 U.S.C. § 170(f)(18).

[17] 785 F.3d 1003, 3 Adm. R. 325 (5th Cir. 2015).

deferring to the Claims Administrator's discretionary administrative decision regarding the documentation required to substantiate a BEL claim.[18] The Settlement Agreement contemplates that the Claims Administrator will review supporting documentation to process claims. The district court's decision to defer to the Claims Administrator's **[—10—]** substantiation requirements and factual finding that the two donations at issue were unrestricted grants was not an abuse of discretion.

2

BP also argues that, even if the donations are revenue, the Claims Administrator did not properly match the $8.9 million donations with expenses. In BP's view, Claimant gave some or all of the donations at issue to other non-profits and those grants should be considered "Variable Expenses" that must be matched to the month in which the donations were received. The Claims Administrator determined the expenses of the claim were "not sufficiently matched" and applied "Policy {–265–} 495" to match the expenses. Policy 495 was created by the Claims Administrator and approved by the district court in response to a decision of this court.[19] We first held in *Deepwater Horizon I*[20] that the Settlement Agreement should be interpreted "in accordance with economic reality" and remanded for the district court to determine whether the agreement required the Claims Administrator to "match" profits and losses.[21] In "matched" profit and loss statements, costs follow revenue—which is registered when generated or received—and this provides a clear picture of net income.[22] In "unmatched" profit and loss statements, revenue is registered when generated or received, and costs are registered when incurred.[23] We noted that unmatched profit and loss statements can "make it appear as if a claimant has suffered damages that he, **[—11—]** in fact, did not suffer."[24] Policy 495 was created to address the problem of unmatched revenues.[25]

This court approved of a portion of Policy 495 in our *Policy 495 Decision*.[26] Policy 495 had five different formulas for matching revenue with expenses, and we upheld only the Annual Variable Margin Methodology (AVMM).[27] "The AVMM requires the Claims Administrator to match all unmatched profit and loss statements."[28] We held the other methodologies were impermissible because they required the Claims Administrator to "move, smooth, or otherwise reallocate revenue for claimants," contrary to the express terms of the Settlement Agreement that gives each claimant the right to choose its own Compensation Period.[29] We had assumed that "process[ing] claims in accordance with economic reality" would comport with the text of the Settlement Agreement, but recognized that will not always be true.[30] Accordingly, when the text of the Settlement Agreement conflicts with economic reality, the text controls.[31]

The Claims Administrator applied the AVMM to Claimant's claims and matched the unmatched profit and loss statements. BP is not satisfied with that methodology in this case because, in its view, real matching would correlate any distributions from the $8.9 million donations back to the month in which the donations were generated. It argues, without support, that the Claims Administrator did not undertake the first step

---

[18] *See Claimant ID 100212278 v. BP Expl. & Prod., Inc.*, 848 F.3d 407, 410, 5 Adm. R. 202, 203 (5th Cir. 2017) (quoting *In re Deepwater Horizon*, 641 F. App'x 405, 410 (5th Cir. 2016)) (alterations in original).

[19] *See In Re Deepwater Horizon*, 858 F.3d 298, 300-01, 5 Adm. R. 259, 259 (5th Cir. 2017) ("*Policy 495 Decision*").

[20] 732 F.3d 326, 1 Adm. R. 287 (5th Cir. 2013) ("*Deepwater Horizon I*").

[21] *Id.* at 339, 1 Adm. R. at 296.

[22] *Policy 495 Decision*, 858 F.3d at 301, 5 Adm. R. at 259.

[23] *Id.*, 5 Adm. R. at 259.

[24] *Id.*, 5 Adm. R. at 259.

[25] *Id.* at 301-02, 5 Adm. R. at 260.

[26] *Id.* at 301, 5 Adm. R. at 259.

[27] *Id.* at 300-01, 5 Adm. R. at 259.

[28] *Id.* at 302, 5 Adm. R. at 260.

[29] *Id.* at 303, 5 Adm. R. at 261.

[30] *See id.* at 304, 5 Adm. R. at 262 (quoting *Deepwater Horizon I*, 732 F.3d 326, 339, 1 Adm. R. 287, 296 (5th Cir. 2013)).

[31] *Id.*, 5 Adm. R. at 262.

of making line-by-line corrections to a claimant's records. BP has not identified any errors that [—12—] should have been corrected, except for its blanket assertion that the $8.9 million was donated for the express purpose of granting those funds to other organizations.

Policy 495 and the AVMM recognize that the Settlement Agreement does not mandate that BEL claimants keep profit and loss statements under any particular basis, so the Claims Administrator "will {–266–} analyze the P&Ls under the basis . . . of accounting used by the claimant in the normal course of business." The Claims Administrator analyzed Claimant's profit and loss statements under its usual accounting method, found that such statements were not sufficiently matched, and then applied the AVMM to match them. The Appeal Panel upheld the application of the AVMM. Claimant maintains that it properly attributes expenses to the months in which it distributes funds and that the donations to which BP objects were not tied to any planned or accrued distribution. BP's objection is limited to the individual factual determination of a specific claimant, and denying review was not an abuse of discretion.[32]

3

Finally, BP argues that the entire $8.9 million should not be recorded as revenue in 2009. In BP's view, because Claimant did not receive the entire amount in cash in 2009, Claimant should have recorded its donations in the years in which it received cash payments. Claimant records the entire value of unconditional promises to give in the year of the pledge, discounted to present value, in accordance with Generally Accepted Accounting Principles (GAAP), and its auditors approved of this method. BP seeks to reallocate [—13—] revenue to a different time period. We disapproved of such a practice in

the *Policy 495 Decision*.[33] Requiring the Claims Administrator to take the revenue, properly allocated under Claimant's normal accounting procedures that follow GAAP, and reallocate them to the month in which Claimant received the cash payment would deprive "claimant [of] the right to choose his or her Compensation Period."[34] The Appeal Panel's decision to apply the Claimant's usual accounting procedure did not contradict the Settlement Agreement. Accordingly, the district court did not abuse its discretion in denying review.

* * *

For the foregoing reasons, we AFFIRM the judgment of the district court.

---

[32] *See Claimant ID 100236236 v. BP Expl. & Prod., Inc.*, 699 F. App'x 308, 310-11 (5th Cir. 2017) (citing *In re Deepwater (Sexton)*, 641 F. App'x 405, 410 (5th Cir. 2016)); *Claimant ID 100051301 v. BP Expl. & Prod., Inc.*, 694 F. App'x 236, 240 (5th Cir. 2017).

[33] 858 F.3d 298, 304, 5 Adm. R. 259, 262 (5th Cir. 2017).

[34] *Id.*, 5 Adm. R. at 261–62.

United States Court of Appeals
for the Fifth Circuit

No. 18-30394

BP EXPLORATION & PROD., INC.
VS.
CLAIMANT ID 100281817

Appeal from the United States District Court for the
Eastern District of Louisiana

Decided: March 20, 2019

Citation: 919 F.3d 284, 7 Adm. R. 209 (5th Cir. 2019).

Before **JONES, HAYNES,** and **OLDHAM,** Circuit
Judges.

[—1—] {–285–} OLDHAM, Circuit Judge: {–286–}

An NBA player named David West negotiated a contract with the New Orleans Hornets before the Deepwater Horizon oil spill. He received every penny specified in that contract both before and after the spill. Still, the Claims Administrator for the Deepwater Horizon Economic and Property Damages Settlement Agreement awarded West almost $1.5 million in "lost" earnings. The Settlement Appeal Panel affirmed, and the district court denied discretionary review. We reverse.

I.

The Deepwater Horizon oil rig exploded on April 20, 2010. At that time, David West played professional basketball for the New Orleans Hornets (now [—2—] known as the New Orleans Pelicans). He was four years into a five-year contract. That contract paid West a total of $45 million. But it was "front-loaded," meaning West's annual salary decreased every year of the contract—including from 2009 to 2010. West received all $45 million owed to him under the contract.

Still, he submitted an "Individual Economic Loss Claim" under the Deepwater Horizon Economic and Property Damages Settlement Agreement ("Settlement").[1] These claims can

be submitted only by individuals "who seek compensation for lost earnings from employment *due to or resulting from the [Deepwater Horizon] Spill*." Settlement Agreement Ex. 8A at 1 (emphasis added). And the Individual Economic Loss Claim form states, on its very first page, that it covers only "individuals who have experienced income losses *caused by the Spill*." Individual Economic Loss Claim Form 1 (emphasis added). It also required West to certify "that the information provided in [his] Claim Form [was] true and accurate to the best of [his] knowledge." *Id.* at 15. Based on that attestation, the Claims Administrator used West's tax forms to calculate his "lost earnings." The Claims Administrator determined West was entitled to $1,412,673.06. BP contested that determination because West "lost" nothing—he received all the money promised by the front-loaded terms of his pre-spill contract.

BP first sought reversal before the Appeal Panel. It argued West was not entitled to any award under the Agreement because (1) Individual Economic Loss Claimants can recover only if they experienced a loss caused by the spill, and (2) West cannot satisfy the Settlement's attestation [—3—] requirements. The Appeal Panel affirmed West's award. It concluded West established causation because his employer—the Hornets—benefited from presumed causation under the Settlement. It therefore held West needed nothing more to claim "lost" earnings.

BP asked the district court to review the award decision. But the court denied discretionary review without explanation. BP timely appealed. {–287–}

---

[1] In previous cases, we have discussed the Deepwater Horizon oil spill and resulting

settlement at great length. *See, e.g., In re Deepwater Horizon (Deepwater Horizon III),* 744 F.3d 370, 2 Adm. R. 183 (5th Cir. 2014); *In re Deepwater Horizon (Deepwater Horizon II),* 739 F.3d 790, 2 Adm. R. 140 (5th Cir. 2014); *In re Deepwater Horizon (Deepwater Horizon I),* 732 F.3d 326, 1 Adm. R. 287 (5th Cir. 2013). We therefore need not recount that history here.

II.

Our review is for abuse of discretion. *Holmes Motors, Inc. v. BP Expl. & Prod., Inc.*, 829 F.3d 313, 315, 4 Adm. R. 263, 263 (5th Cir. 2016). The district court abuses its discretion when "the decision not reviewed by the district court actually contradicted or misapplied the Settlement Agreement, or had the clear potential to contradict or misapply the Settlement Agreement." *Ibid.*, 4 Adm. R. at 263 (quotation omitted). It's likewise "an abuse of discretion to deny a request for review that raises a recurring issue on which the Appeal Panels are split if the resolution of the question will substantially impact the administration of the Agreement." *Claimant ID 100212278 v. BP Expl. & Prod., Inc.*, 848 F.3d 407, 410, 5 Adm. R. 202, 203 (5th Cir. 2017) (per curiam) (quotation omitted). In contrast, denying "a request for review that involve[s] no pressing question of how the Settlement Agreement should be interpreted or implemented, but simply raise[s] the correctness of a discretionary administrative decision in the facts of a single claimant's case," does not amount to an abuse of discretion. *Ibid.*, 5 Adm. R. at 203 (quotation omitted) (alterations in original).

That said, the Settlement Agreement is a contract. The proper interpretation of it "is a question of law." *In re Deepwater Horizon (Deepwater Horizon I)*, 732 F.3d 326, 345, 1 Adm. R. 287, 301 (5th Cir. 2013). And making "an error of law constitutes an abuse of discretion." *In re Deepwater Horizon*, 785 F.3d 986, 999, 3 Adm. R. 341, 349 (5th Cir. 2015). Accordingly, when the district court is "presented with purely [—4—] legal questions of contract interpretation," our review is *de novo. In re Deepwater Horizon*, 785 F.3d 1003, 1011, 3 Adm. R. 325, 329 (5th Cir. 2015).

A.

We start with the contractual provisions governing West's claim. West submitted a specific type of claim—an "Individual Economic Loss Claim." It is defined to include a claim brought by an individual described in Exhibit 8A. Exhibit 8A, in turn, provides the following description for Individual Economic Loss Claims:

> Individual economic loss claims are claims by **Individuals**, who shall be defined as (i) Natural Persons who (a) satisfy (or whose employers satisfy) the Class Definition and (b) whose *losses* are not excluded from the Class and (ii) who seek compensation for *lost earnings* from employment *due to or resulting from* the [Deepwater Horizon oil spill] . . . .

Settlement Agreement Ex. 8A at 1 (emphases added). The claim form that West submitted similarly stated: "The Individual Economic Loss Claim is for individuals who have experienced *income losses caused by the Spill*." Individual Economic Loss Claim Form 1 (emphasis added). Thus, these types of claims may be brought only by individuals who experienced losses and seek compensation for lost earnings caused by the oil spill. We've previously interpreted the Agreement as allowing "proof of loss as a substitute for proof of causation." *In re Deepwater (Deepwater Horizon III)*, 744 F.3d 370, 375, 2 Adm. R. 183, 185 (5th Cir. 2014). But what do "loss" and "lost earnings" mean?

They are undefined in the Settlement, so we look to their plain meaning. *See BP Expl. & Prod., Inc. v. Claimant ID 100094497*, 910 F.3d 797, 801, 6 Adm. R. 273, 275 (5th Cir. 2018). "Loss" typically means "the disappearance or diminution of value . . . in an unexpected or relatively unpredictable way." *Loss*, BLACK'S LAW DICTIONARY (10th ed. 2014); *see also Economic Loss*, BLACK'S LAW DICTIONARY (10th ed. 2014) (explaining "economic loss" means "monetary loss such as lost wages or lost profits" and usually "refers to a type of damages [—5—] recoverable {–288–} in a lawsuit"). And "lost earnings" refers to "[w]ages, salary, or other income that a person could have earned if he or she had not lost a job, suffered a disabling injury, or died." *Earnings*, BLACK'S LAW DICTIONARY (10th ed. 2014). These definitions suggest "loss" or "lost earnings" are unexpected diminutions in wages or other income that could otherwise support a claim for civil damages.

West argues these plain meanings of "loss" and "lost earnings" do not apply. Instead, he says, his "loss" is proved by the seven-step mathematical equation that appears in Exhibit 8A. But that puts the cart before the horse. Only claimants who suffer unexpected damages can submit an Individual Economic Loss Claim; then they use Exhibit 8A's equation to determine the value of that claim. The defined terms in the seven-step equation make that clear. "**Claimant Lost Earnings**" is defined as "[t]he claimant's **Expected Earnings** from all **Claiming Jobs** minus the claimant's **Actual Earnings** from all **Claiming Jobs** during the **Compensation Period**, minus any **Offsetting Earnings**." Settlement Agreement Ex. 8A at 4. "**Expected Earnings**" refers to the "[c]laimant's earnings in the **Compensation Period** in the **Claiming Job** *that would have been expected in the absence of the [Deepwater Horizon] Spill*." *Id.* at 5 (emphasis added). West expected to earn in the absence of the spill precisely what he did earn after it. He therefore did not suffer unexpected damages, and Exhibit 8A does not apply to him.[2] [—6—]

This interpretation comports not only with the Agreement's text, but also with our

_____

[2] Because West's expected earnings equal his actual earnings based on Exhibit 8A's definitions, West ignores them. (Indeed, he does not even include the Agreement's definition of "Expected Earnings" in his brief.) He instead implies "Expected Earnings" is defined in Exhibit 8A as a calculation based on what he earned in previous time periods, not what his five-year contract provided. And applying that "definition," West's expected earnings would be higher than his actual earnings. But we cannot focus exclusively on Exhibit 8A's calculations and ignore its list of defined terms and accompanying definitions. Instead, we must read the Agreement's provisions "as a whole," *Claimant ID 100094497*, 910 F.3d at 801, 6 Adm. R. at 275, and harmonize the Agreement—giving effect to all its terms "without rendering any of them [—6—] meaningless or superfluous," *Chembulk Trading LLC v. Chemex Ltd.*, 393 F.3d 550, 555 (5th Cir. 2004). The fact that the definition of "Expected Earnings" cannot be squared with the calculation as applied to West's claim further illustrates the compensation formula does not apply to him. It applies only to eligible individuals—those who suffered unexpected damages.

precedent. As we explained in *Deepwater Horizon I*, when interpreting the Agreement, we must give "some weight" to "what damages recoverable in civil litigation actually are." 732 F.3d at 339, 1 Adm. R. at 296. And in civil litigation, the plaintiff can recover damages only after suffering actual losses. *See Lewis v. Casey*, 518 U.S. 343, 349 (1996) (explaining the court's role is limited to "provid[ing] relief to claimants, in individual or class actions, who have suffered, or will imminently suffer, actual harm").

B.

West did not suffer actual and unexpected "losses" or damages. In 2010, he earned exactly what he was entitled to receive under his contract. The fact that West received less money in 2010 than in 2009 does not mean he "lost" anything or was "damaged" in any way. It means only he agreed to a front-loaded contract. And he did so many years before the Deepwater Horizon catastrophe.

The decision to give money to West "actually contradicted or misapplied the {–289–} Settlement Agreement." *Holmes Motors*, 829 F.3d at 315, 4 Adm. R. at 263 (quotation omitted). Our holding to that effect answers a "purely legal question[] of contract interpretation." *In re Deepwater Horizon*, 785 F.3d at 1011, 3 Adm. R. at 329. Accordingly, "remand is unnecessary." *Aransas Project v. Shaw*, 775 F.3d 641, 658 (5th Cir. 2014) (per curiam); *cf. United States v. Douglas*, 696 F. App'x 666, 669 (5th Cir. 2017) (per curiam) ("In certain circumstances, however, the appellate court may determine that remand of a particular case is unnecessary and instead, simply reverse and render."); *United States v. Hernandez-* [—7—] *Guevara*, 162 F.3d 863, 878 (5th Cir. 1998) ("[W]e need not waste judicial resources by remanding for what undoubtedly would be a rote resentencing.").

The judgment of the district court is REVERSED.

(Reporter's Note: Concurring and Dissenting Opinion follows on p. 212).

[—8—] {–289–} HAYNES, Circuit Judge, concurring and dissenting:

I concur in the portion of the judgment reversing the district court's denial of review and the determination by the majority opinion that the particular sums awarded, which rely upon the contractual losses, reflect a "loss" that was not caused by the oil spill. However, I would stop there and remand the case to the district court.

As the majority opinion explains, the question before us is whether the district court abused its discretion in not reviewing the Appeal Panel's decision because there was an erroneous interpretation of the Settlement Agreement impacting the settlement as a whole. *Holmes Motors, Inc. v. BP Expl. & Prod.*, 829 F.3d 313, 315, 4 Adm. R. 263, 263 (5th Cir. 2016). We answer that "yes." The remedy, then, is to send it back to the district court to review the case consistent with our analysis. *BP Expl. & Prod. Inc. v. Claimant ID 100094497*, 910 F.3d 797, 803, 6 Adm. R. 273, 276–77 (5th Cir. 2018) (remanding to the district court even though the majority opinion (in the face of a dissenting opinion) decided a legal question); *see also In re Deepwater Horizon*, 632 F. App'x 199, 204 (5th Cir. 2015) (per curiam) (remanding where district court refused to review issues that would arise repeatedly); *cf. Claimant ID 100227611 v. BP Expl. & Prod.*, No. 18-30396, 2018 U.S. App. LEXIS 33357, at *6 (5th Cir. Nov. 28, 2018) (per curiam) (declining to overturn the refusal of discretionary review[1] when the case involved a decision on "the facts of a single claimant's case"); *see generally* [—9—] *Sanchez v. Young Cty.*, 866 F.3d 274, 279 (5th Cir. 2017) (per curiam) ("In deference to the trial court's responsibility to review the record in the first instance, we vacate and remand . . . ."). Yet the majority opinion does not.

Would a remand be based upon a mere technicality and, in turn, be a waste of time here because it is a purely legal question? No.

There are additional factual questions here. The question of whether the particular contractual "loss" approved by the Claims Administrator is fundable under the Settlement Agreement is, perhaps, a pure legal question. But West raises arguments concerning losses beyond the "do the math" arguments we rejected. If I {–290–} were a factfinder, I would be unpersuaded by his arguments. But, as appellate judges, we are not factfinders in this case. Accordingly, we should remand to the district court to review and make any necessary determinations in the first instance (or, in turn, remand for factual investigation by the Claims Administrator), including determination of whether arguments were properly raised or forfeited.

The decision not to remand ignores the reality of how these Settlement Agreement cases proceed and the history of this specific case. Throughout the proceedings below, the question was whether the Claims Administrator, Appeals Panel, and District Court can or should "pierce the veil" of the claimant's application which, on its face, undeniably demonstrated a loss. At each stage, West successfully argued, "No, there should be no piercing," meaning he had no reason to provide evidence of any other theory of recovery; the whole point was that the document to which he attested stands as is. He prevailed repeatedly on that theory as numerous others had and still do. We have now, for the first time, found a case that we only theorized about in earlier decisions, the "implausible" causation case ("implausible" being a nice way of putting it here). *See In re Deepwater Horizon*, 744 F.3d 370, 377–78, 2 Adm. R. 183, 187 (5th Cir. [—10—] 2014). But that case specifically stated: "The claims administrator, parties, and *district court* can resolve real examples of implausible claims as they resolve other questions that arise in the

---

[1] While the legal question may be reviewed "de novo," even a "legal error" should not cause us to reverse a denial of discretionary review that involves just a single claim or does not negate relevant portions of the Settlement Agreement. In other words, whether a legal error is made is not discretionary but whether to grant discretionary review of a legal error is discretionary. Here, however, the district court's failure to address this glaring legal error involves the very heart of the Settlement Agreement, so denial of review was an abuse of discretion.

handling of specific claims." *Id.*, 2 Adm. R. at 187 (emphasis added). Nothing in that opinion suggested making the Fifth Circuit the factfinder.

Indeed, BP has stipulated that causation arguments are preserved in this context. The stipulation states: "BP and Class counsel further agree that, for any Deepwater Horizon Court-Supervised Settlement Program appeal, request for discretionary review, *or appeal to the Fifth Circuit Court* in which the attestation issue is raised, the Claimant will be deemed to have preserved, and not waived, any argument that BP is estopped from challenging the attestation . . . , as well as *any other appropriate argument and / or objection relevant to the question of causation.*" (emphasis added). BP acknowledged that stipulation in its briefing to the Appeals Panel in this very case: "Pursuant to the stipulation entered into between BP and the Class . . . , BP is preserving [the attestation requirement] issue for further review but does not brief it further herein." BP's footnote to that statement suggests that it did not expect West to address this argument. This case is thus not one of the "mine-run" of forfeiture or waiver cases where a litigant should have raised an issue sooner but failed to do so.[2]

Finally, perhaps for the above reasons, BP did not request that we "reverse and render." It only asked for a remand: "For the foregoing reasons, the district court's denial of discretionary review should be reversed and [—11—] remanded." "[A] party is bound by, or limited to, the relief it seeks on appeal." *Whitehead v. Food Max, Inc.*, 163 F.3d 265, 270 (5th Cir. 1998); *see also Holloway v. Purvis*, 680 F. App'x 282, 286 (5th Cir. 2017) ("[O]ur precedent states that parties are limited to the relief requested in their briefs.") Thus, we must remand, not render. {–291–}

In sum, our usual course is to remand to the district court to resolve outstanding factual issues and failing to do so on this procedural history is particularly inappropriate. Our precedent also requires that we not grant more relief than requested by rendering when only remand was sought. I would reverse and remand to the district court. Because the majority opinion leaves out this important step, I respectfully dissent from that portion of the opinion and resulting judgment.

---

[2] Indeed, the entire record on appeal is very thinly developed beyond BP citing to articles about the contract in question, and West not denying the fact of the contract but arguing its irrelevance. BP itself put into evidence the article West relies upon to show that he had a potential for a future lucrative contract. Thus, the thin record provides some support for West's argument.

United States Court of Appeals
for the Fifth Circuit

No. 18-30835

BP EXPLORATION & PROD., INC.
vs.
CLAIMANT ID 100141850

Appeal from the United States District Court for the
Eastern District of Louisiana

Decided: March 26, 2019

Citation: 919 F.3d 887, 7 Adm. R. 214 (5th Cir. 2019).

Before **HIGGINBOTHAM**, **ELROD**, and **DUNCAN**, Circuit Judges.

[—1—] {–887–} PER CURIAM: {–888–}

This case presents another appeal arising out of the *Deepwater Horizon* disaster and the resulting BP Deepwater Horizon Economic and Property Damages Settlement (Settlement Agreement). Here, BP contends that Claimant was not entitled to the $65 million award it received pursuant to the Settlement Agreement because it did not suffer a loss that was caused by the oil spill despite submitting a claim form certifying that it did. Because the district court did not abuse its discretion in declining discretionary review, we AFFIRM. [—2—]

I.

Claimant is a manufacturer of electrical transformers and other industrial products. In November 2012, it filed a Business Economic Loss Claim Form (Claim Form) pursuant to the Settlement Agreement. The Claim Form explains that Business Economic Loss (BEL) Claims are for businesses "that assert economic loss due to the Spill," and instructs claimants to "submit certain Supporting Documentation to prove [their claims]." The Claim Form also requires claimants to certify under penalty of perjury that the information provided is "true and accurate" and that the supporting documents are "true, accurate, and complete." Prior decisions of this court have referred to this certification as the "attestation." *E.g.*, *In re Deepwater Horizon*

(*Deepwater Horizon III*), 744 F.3d 370, 376–77, 2 Adm. R. 183, 186 (5th Cir. 2014).

As a class member located in economic loss Zone D, Claimant also had to satisfy one of the causation tests set out in Exhibit 4B to the Settlement Agreement to recover on its economic loss claim. The parties do not dispute that Claimant satisfied one of these tests: the V-shaped revenue pattern test.

After reviewing the Claim Form, the Claims Administrator awarded Claimant $65 million. BP appealed to a three-member Appeal Panel, arguing *inter alia* that "the claim does not comply with the attestation requirement as recognized in" this court's opinion in *Deepwater Horizon III*. BP also noted the following in its recitation of the facts: (1) due to the economic recession and regulatory changes, Claimant's revenue decreased significantly from 2007 to 2009 and increased in 2010; and (2) in 2009, Claimant entered into an unfavorable take-and-pay contract which required it to purchase more steel than it needed at above-market prices. While BP did not brief the issue fully before the Appeal Panel due to a stipulation by the parties, its briefs on appeal make clear that it believes these facts prove that Claimant did not suffer any [—3—] post-spill "loss" that was "caused by" the oil spill despite filing a certified Claim Form indicating that it had.

The Appeal Panel unanimously ruled in favor of Claimant. Rejecting BP's attestation argument, the Panel emphasized that "[t]his position has been rejected by every {–889–} Panel that has considered it and it will be rejected here as well," although the issue was preserved for appeal. It further noted that the information BP provided regarding market factors that affected Claimant's business was not "material to the assessment of this appeal." BP sought discretionary review by the district court,[1] which the district court denied. BP now appeals.

---

[1] BP's request for discretionary review raised two additional issues separate from its attestation argument. However, BP does not mention these issues in its briefs on appeal, so they are forfeited. *Norris v. Causey*, 869 F.3d 360, 373 n.10 (5th Cir.

II.

We review the district court's denial of discretionary review for an abuse of discretion. *Claimant ID 100250022 v. BP Expl. & Prod., Inc.*, 847 F.3d 167, 169, 5 Adm. R. 199, 200 (5th Cir. 2017). The district court abuses its discretion if the underlying Appeal Panel decision not reviewed by the district court "actually contradicted or misapplied the Settlement Agreement, or had the clear potential to contradict or misapply the Settlement Agreement." *Id.*, 5 Adm. R. at 200 (quoting *Holmes Motors, Inc. v. BP Expl. & Prod., Inc.*, 829 F.3d 313, 315, 4 Adm. R. 263, 263 (5th Cir. 2016)). It is also an abuse of discretion to deny a request for review that "raises a recurring issue on which the Appeal Panels are split if 'the resolution of the question will substantially impact the administration of the Agreement.'" *Claimant ID 100212278 v. BP Expl. & Prod., Inc.*, 848 F.3d 407, 410, 5 Adm. R. 202, 203 (5th Cir. 2017) (quoting *In re Deepwater Horizon*, 632 F. App'x 199, 203–04 (5th Cir. 2015)). [—4—]

III.

BP contends that the district court erred in denying discretionary review for two reasons: (1) Claimant did not suffer a post-spill "loss," a "threshold requirement" separate from the Exhibit 4C loss compensation formula; and (2) Claimant's attestation that its loss was "due to the Spill" was not made in good faith. We will address each in turn.

A.

Beginning with BP's arguments regarding post-spill loss, BP believes that financial data submitted by Claimant demonstrates that Claimant did not suffer a loss after the oil spill. Specifically, BP points out that Claimant experienced a "dramatic drop in revenues" between 2007 and 2009, and that from May to December 2010 its "revenues actually *increased* . . . compared to the same months in 2009." Citing evidence it presented to the Appeal Panel, BP offers several market-

related explanations for this revenue decline: regulatory changes, the significant impact of the 2008 economic recession on the electrical transformer industry, and an unfavorable take-and-pay contract that Claimant entered into in 2009. BP insists that these facts prove that Claimant did not suffer any lost profits after the spill.

As the Appeal Panel correctly concluded, none of this information is material to the question on appeal. We indicated as much in our *Policy 495 Opinion*, where we rejected BP's argument in favor of using industry-specific calculation methodologies to determine the compensation owed under the Settlement Agreement. *In re Deepwater Horizon (Policy 495 Opinion)*, 858 F.3d 298, 303, 5 Adm. R. 259, 261 (5th Cir. 2017). There, acknowledging that the accounting methods in some industries may result in higher awards, we held that the Claims Administrator may not reallocate a claimant's revenue to "ensur[e] that damages are awarded to those who have suffered real losses"—to do so would not comport with the plain language of the Settlement {–890–} Agreement, which gives [—5—] each claimant the right to choose its Compensation Period. *Id.* at 303–04, 5 Adm. R. at 261–62. Significantly, we emphasized that a claimant who "did not suffer economic losses pursuant to tort principles" may still have "suffer[ed] economic losses pursuant to the Settlement Agreement." *Id.* at 303, 5 Adm. R. at 261. Thus, under the *Policy 495 Opinion*, it is the loss compensation formula set out in Exhibit 4C of the Settlement Agreement—and not BP's definition or the plain meaning of "loss"—that determines whether a claimant has suffered a post-spill loss. Because BP's arguments regarding Claimant's lack of loss rely on financial information and market factors not considered in that loss compensation formula, BP has not demonstrated that Claimant did not suffer a post-spill loss. The district court accordingly did not err in denying discretionary review on this basis.

B.

BP next contends that Claimant's attestation in its Claim Form that its loss was

---

2017) (failure to adequately brief an issue constitutes forfeiture).

"due to the Spill" was implausible and made in bad faith, and that the district court erred by declining to address this implausibility issue. BP's argument on this point relies on the same evidence it presented in support of its "loss" point of error: that any loss Claimant suffered resulted from market factors such as the recession and an unfavorable contract, not the oil spill. BP cites our decision in *Deepwater Horizon III* as requiring the Claims Administrator and district court to investigate "suspicious forms" and "resolve real examples of implausible claims" that arise during the claims process.

In *Deepwater Horizon III*, we explained that "[c]ausation for BEL claims is primarily addressed in Exhibit 4B to the Settlement Agreement," which "provides for the use of proof of loss as a substitute for proof of causation." 744 F.3d at 375, 2 Adm. R. at 185. As BP points out, however, we also emphasized that at the claim submission stage, proof of causation is made by the claimant's "certification on the document that the claimant was injured by the *Deepwater Horizon* [—6—] disaster." *Id.* at 376, 2 Adm. R. at 186. Thus, a claimant need not provide evidence that its economic loss was caused by the oil spill, as BP made a "contractual concession" to limit the causation inquiry in processing claims. *Id.* at 376–77, 2 Adm. R. at 186.

Relevant here, we then provided an example to illustrate that a claimant may be entitled to an award under the Settlement Agreement even if its economic losses may have resulted in part from an alternative cause: Three accountants were partners in a small firm in a region affected by the spill. Shortly after the spill, one of the partners took medical leave. Although at least some of the resulting decrease in profits may have been due to the partner's leave, the Settlement Agreement permits payment of the firm's claim without regard for this alternative cause. *Id.* at 377, 2 Adm. R. at 187. As we explained:

> These are business loss claims. . . . [W]hy one year is less or more profitable than another [is a] question[] often

rigorously analyzed by highly-paid consultants, who may still reach mistaken conclusions. There may be multiple causes for a loss. . . . The difficulties of a claimant's providing evidentiary support and the claims administrator's investigating the existence and degree of nexus between the loss and the disaster in the Gulf could be overwhelming.

Id. at 377, 2 Adm. R. at 186–87. Thus, to facilitate efficient resolution of claims, the Settlement Agreement substitutes "a formal assertion of the causal nexus" for the in-depth causation analysis required in a typical business economic loss case. *Id.*, 2 Adm. R. at 187.

BP appears to agree that the above framework controls the resolution of BEL claims under the Settlement Agreement, {–891–} but it insists that the evidence it presented warrants an investigation into the plausibility of Claimant's causation attestation. Our *Deepwater Horizon III* opinion forecloses any categorical duty on the part of the Claims Administrator "to ensure that implausible claims are adequately scrutinized such that those lacking a causal nexus are rejected." *Id.* at 378, 2 Adm. R. at 187; *see also In re Deepwater Horizon* (*Deepwater Horizon IV*), 753 F.3d 509, 513, 2 Adm. R. 217, 218 (5th Cir. 2014) (concluding that the Claims [—7—] Administrator does not have an "additional duty . . . to ensure that every claim contains a direct causal nexus to BP's conduct"). And the Claims Administrator's October 2012 policy statement, which BP did not object to, clarifies that the Claims Administrator will not evaluate potential alternative causes for a claimant's losses. *Deepwater Horizon III*, 744 F.3d at 378, 2 Adm. R. at 187.

Here, Claimant satisfied the causation formula set out in Exhibit 4B of the Settlement Agreement and formally attested to the fact that its losses were caused by the oil spill. While the evidence BP presents may indicate additional, market-related causes for Claimant's loss, the existence of these alternative causes does not eliminate the possibility that the oil spill contributed to cause Claimant's loss, nor does it preclude Claimant from recovering under the Settlement Agreement. In our view, Claimant's case is akin to the accountant example, where alternative causes may exist, but determining the loss attributable to those alternative causes versus that attributable to the oil spill would require the kind of "rigorous analysis" that the Settlement Agreement was intended to avoid.

To be sure, our *Deepwater Horizon III* opinion acknowledges that "[s]uspicious forms [will] be subject to investigation" and suggests that district courts "resolve real examples of implausible claims." *Id.* at 377–78, 2 Adm. R. at 186–87. But we do not believe this case presents such a claim. This does not foreclose the possibility that in some other case—where, for example, the Claimant's attestation plainly gives rise to suspicion or BP has presented credible evidence of a sole, superseding cause for a claimant's loss—an investigation into the plausibility of the attestation may be warranted. Here, however, because BP has not demonstrated that Claimant's attestation is implausible, the district court did not err in denying discretionary review. [—8—]

IV.

For the reasons described, we AFFIRM the judgment of the district court.

United States Court of Appeals
for the Fifth Circuit

No. 18-20115

ENI US OPERATING CO.

VS.

TRANSOCEAN OFFSHORE DEEPWATER DRILLING,
INC.

Appeal from the United States District Court for the
Southern District of Texas

Decided: March 28, 2019

Citation: 919 F.3d 931, 7 Adm. R. 218 (5th Cir. 2019).

Before **CLEMENT, OWEN,** and **HO,** Circuit Judges.

[—1—] {–933–} CLEMENT, Circuit Judge:

Eni and Transocean are both companies in the oil-drilling business. They formed a contract about drilling for oil. Their relationship soured. Both sued for breaches of that contract. After a bench trial, Eni suffered a resounding loss on all issues: The district court rejected its claims surrounding Transocean's maintenance of its equipment, found that Eni had wrongly repudiated the contract, and awarded damages to Transocean. Eni asks us to undo all of this. Save for the repudiation ruling, we find Eni's arguments meritorious. The district court's judgment is vacated in part and affirmed in part. [—2—]

I.

In 2008, when oil prices were high, Eni—a multinational oil company—sought to conduct new exploratory drilling in the Gulf of Mexico. It circulated a request for a drilling vessel. Transocean—the largest offshore driller in the Gulf—responded. The parties soon entered into a contract. Transocean agreed to provide *Deepwater Pathfinder* to Eni for its drilling operations and to operate it on Eni's behalf. In exchange, Eni agreed to pay for the right to use the rig for five years.

Before commencing drilling operations in 2010, the *Pathfinder* went into a shipyard for maintenance. During this time, Transocean installed a previously used blowout preventer[1] salvaged from the sea floor. Though old and initially bent, Transocean successfully refurbished it, and eventually it was certified for use. By February 2011, the *Pathfinder*'s maintenance was complete, and it set out to drill Eni's first well. {–934–}

Almost immediately thereafter, problems began to bubble up on the *Pathfinder*. Most notably, the blowout preventer kept malfunctioning—requiring Transocean to suspend drilling on numerous occasions. These problems persisted throughout the contract's duration. From 2011 to 2014, maintenance and repairs resulted in the *Pathfinder* being inoperable for 19% of the time. Nonetheless, during that same time, the *Pathfinder* successfully operated on numerous wells for Eni, including one in excess of 10,000 feet underwater.

In early September 2014, the *Pathfinder*'s drawworks malfunctioned, but were soon fixed. Also in September, a loop current damaged one of the two MUX cables that connect the blowout preventer to its redundant yellow and [—3—] blue control pods. It is against federal regulation to drill wells unless both control pods are fully operational. *See* 30 C.F.R. § 250.442(b). Thankfully, when the cable was damaged, the *Pathfinder* was not drilling. Eni had long before grown tired of the *Pathfinder*'s equipment problems, so it seized upon these two occurrences to sever the contract. On October 13, Eni sent a letter terminating the contract immediately, and by October 25, Eni's men had fully evacuated the *Pathfinder*.

About a year before this point, Eni had sued Transocean arguing both breach of contract and breach of warranty. Both claims were anchored in what Eni believed was Transocean's failure to upkeep its equipment in accordance with the contract and with industry standards. Once Eni sent the October 13 letter in 2014, Transocean filed a

---

[1] The blowout preventer is the most important piece of safety equipment on an oil rig. It attaches to the well and seals it off in case of a spill. It was the failure of the blowout preventer that caused the *Deepwater Horizon* catastrophe.

counterclaim, arguing that the October 13 letter was not a valid termination because it did not comply with the contract's specific procedures. In Transocean's view, the letter was a repudiation and should be treated as a total breach.

After a 10-day bench trial, the district court issued findings of fact and conclusions of law. It rejected Eni's breach-of-contract and breach-of-warranty claims. It held that Transocean had not breached any contractual requirements related to the maintenance of its equipment and that the warranty claims were barred by the contract's indemnity provision. As to Transocean's counterclaim, the district court held that Eni did not follow the contract's specific termination procedures. It therefore agreed with Transocean that the October 13 letter was indeed a repudiation, not a termination. It awarded damages to Transocean on its counterclaim. Eni timely appealed, challenging all the district court's conclusions.

II.

After a bench trial, findings of fact are reviewed for clear error while conclusions of law and mixed questions of law and fact are reviewed de novo. [—4—] *In Re Luhr Bros., Inc.*, 325 F.3d 681, 684 (5th Cir. 2003). A finding of fact is clearly erroneous if, after reviewing all the evidence, the court "is left with the definitive and firm conviction that a mistake has been committed." *Flint Hills Res. LP v. Jag Energy, Inc.*, 559 F.3d 373, 375 (5th Cir. 2009) (quotation omitted).

III.

In Eni's eyes, the district court got nothing right. It wrongly rejected its breach-of-contract and breach-of-warranty claims, incorrectly found it liable on Transocean's breach-of-contract claim, and used an improper methodology to calculate Transocean's damages. We will address each argument in turn, beginning with Eni's breach-of-contract claim. {–935–}

A.

Under § 501(b)(1) of the contract, Transocean needed to "employ commercially reasonable efforts to perform all work and operations . . . in conformity with the requirements of the Contract and good oilfield practice." Eni claimed that Transocean materially breached this contractual obligation by not adequately maintaining and repairing important equipment on the *Pathfinder*, most importantly the blowout preventer. The district court rejected this claim, finding that Transocean complied with § 501(b)(1).

Eni argues that the district court's ultimate conclusion must be set aside because the court only conducted half of the relevant analysis necessary for that conclusion. Section 501(b)(1) requires that Transocean use commercially reasonable efforts to do two things: (1) conform with the contract's requirements; and (2) conform with good oilfield practice. These are separate inquiries. The district court, however, only meaningfully addressed the first one. On the good-oilfield-practice requirement, the court simply noted that the term was undefined. It never specifically examined Transocean's practices to determine if they met that standard. Despite its failure to engage with the [—5—] relevant evidence, the court still concluded that Transocean used good oilfield practice. This, Eni says, was legal error. On its account, the district court needed to lay out the many subsidiary factual findings that would have been necessary to reach the ultimate factual conclusion that Transocean used commercially reasonable efforts to comply with good oilfield practice throughout the contract's life.[2]

We start with the basics. After a bench trial, a district court must make factual findings. Federal Rule of Civil Procedure 52(a) makes that clear. The question before us is how detailed those factual findings need to be.

---

[2] For example, after the *Pathfinder* left port in 2011, it experienced many equipment problems, most notably with the blowout preventer. Yet the district court's order does not mention any equipment failures occurring in 2011. This lapse is just one example; Eni gives many others.

Is the district court required to make subsidiary findings? Or can it announce only its ultimate factual conclusion? We long ago answered that question: Rule 52(a) compels a district court to lay out enough subsidiary findings to allow us to understand "the basis of the trial court's decision." *Gulf King Shrimp Co. v. Wirtz*, 407 F.2d 508, 515 (5th Cir. 1969). Put differently, "the findings . . . must be sufficiently detailed to give us a clear understanding of the analytical process by which [the] ultimate findings were reached and to assure us that the trial court took care in ascertaining the facts." *Golf City, Inc. v. Wilson Sporting Goods, Co.*, 555 F.2d 426, 433 (5th Cir. 1977).[3] When the district court fails to do this, remand for additional fact finding is proper. *See, e.g., Redditt v. Miss. Extended Care Ctrs., Inc.*, 718 F.2d 1381, 1386–87 (5th Cir. 1983) [—6—] (remanding for additional fact finding on the issue of pretext in a discrimination case).

This basis-of-decision approach encourages district courts to lay out their factual findings as skillfully as possible. *See Golf City, Inc.*, 555 F.2d at 433 (noting that "every effort should be made to render {–936–} [fact finding] as adequate as it humanly can be" (quotation omitted)); *Hydrospace-Challenger, Inc. v. Tracor/MAS, Inc.*, 520 F.2d 1030, 1033 (5th Cir. 1975) ("Statements conclusory in nature are to be eschewed in favor of statements of the preliminary and basic facts on which the District Court relied." (quotation omitted)). The more complex the case, the more important the task of articulating detailed factual findings becomes. *Chandler v. City of Dall.*, 958 F.2d 85, 90 (5th Cir. 1992) (per curiam).

Regardless of the basis-of-decision approach's many benefits, an alternative rule has crept into our precedent—a rule that

Transocean would like us to adopt. We have, at times, said that if "a trial judge fails to make a specific finding on a particular fact, the reviewing court may assume that the court impliedly made a finding consistent with its general holding so long as the implied finding is supported by the evidence." *Becker v. Tidewater, Inc.*, 586 F.3d 358, 371 n.9 (5th Cir. 2009) (quotation omitted). This implicit-finding rule seems to have originated—over the dissent of Judge Godbold—in *Gilbert v. Sterrett*, 509 F.2d 1389, 1393 (5th Cir. 1975). In that case, Judge Godbold astutely recognized that the majority's implicit-finding rule was inconsistent with *Gulf King Shrimp Co.*'s basis-of-decision approach. *Id.* at 1397–98 (Godbold, J., dissenting). We agree. The former transforms this court into the factfinder by supplying the subsidiary facts necessary to support the general holding; the latter cabins this court to its appellate role of reviewing the district court's factual reasoning. [—7—]

In any event, as *Gilbert* was decided after *Gulf King Shrimp Co.*, the rule of orderliness mandates that the basis-of-decision approach be retained, and the implicit-finding rule jettisoned.[4] *See Mercado v. Lynch*, 823 F.3d 276, 279 (5th Cir. 2016) ("Under our rule of orderliness, one panel of our court may not overturn another panel's decision, absent an intervening change in the law, such as by a statutory amendment, or the Supreme Court, or our *en banc* court." (quotation omitted)). We now vindicate Judge Godbold and set our jurisprudence back on course: Under Rule 52(a), implicit findings will not automatically be inferred to support a conclusory ultimate finding. The district court must lay out enough subsidiary findings to allow us to

---

[3] *See also McCuller v. Nautical Ventures, LLC*, 434 F. App'x 408, 416 (5th Cir. 2011) (per curiam) ("[T]he findings of fact must include as much of the subsidiary facts as is necessary to disclose to the reviewing court the steps by which the trial court reached its ultimate conclusion on each factual issue." (alteration in original) (quoting Charles Alan Wright & Arthur R. Miller, Federal Practice & Procedure § 2579 (3d ed. 2008))).

[4] Not only did *Gilbert* violate the rule of orderliness by creating the implicit-finding rule, it also contravened a Supreme Court case directly on point. *See Kelley v. Everglades Draining Dist.*, 319 U.S. 415, 420 (1943) (explaining that under Rule 52(a), "there must be findings, in such detail and exactness as the nature of the case permits, of subsidiary facts on which the ultimate conclusion [on the relevant issue] can rationally be predicated" and that "it is not the function of this court to search the record and analyze the evidence in order to supply findings which the trial court failed to make").

glean "a clear understanding of the analytical process by which [the] ultimate findings were reached and to assure us that the trial court took care in ascertaining the facts." *Golf City, Inc.*, 555 F.2d at 433.

With the proper test in hand, we must vacate the district court's judgment and remand the case for more factual findings. The district court's order contains two sentences in two separate sections that make the ultimate factual conclusion on the good-oilfield-practice issue. Yet these conclusory statements are unsupported by the factual analysis they follow, leaving us to speculate as to whether the district court sufficiently grappled with the facts relevant to the good-oilfield-practice issue.

The first relevant section of the order is entitled "Eni's Breach of Contract Claim." The only factual analysis in that section {–937–} states that the [—8—] parties' contract clearly contemplates equipment failures, time for repairs and replacements, and potential downtime. The court also found that Transocean initiated corrective actions within 30 days of Eni's written notices of equipment problems. For these reasons, the district court concluded that "Transocean employed commercially reasonable efforts to perform under the Contract."[5] But it does not follow that simply because the contract contemplates equipment failures and time for repairs, Transocean must have followed good oilfield practice. To make that determination, the court would have needed to ask why the equipment failed and whether the repairs were done properly. It did not do so. Neither did it grapple with the extensive expert testimony concerning whether the *Pathfinder*'s non-productive time is a good indication of whether Transocean followed good oilfield practice. And the fact that Transocean responded to Eni's written notices

---

[5] Eni suggests that this is not actually a finding on the good-oilfield-practice issue. We disagree. The requirement to conform with good oilfield practice is stated in the contract. So "using commercially reasonable efforts to perform under the Contract," when read in context, includes a finding that Transocean complied with good oilfield practice.

is only one small piece of the good-oilfield-practice puzzle.

The district court's other conclusory statement is equally unsupported by the discussion it follows. In the section entitled "Eni's Sole Remedy is Termination," the district court held that the sole-termination provisions are enforceable, noted that the parties are sophisticated, and then simply proclaimed that "Eni did not prove that . . . Transocean failed to 'employ commercially reasonable efforts to perform all work and operations [] in conformity with the requirements of the Contract and good oilfield practice.'" Again, there is no indication that the district court considered the relevant evidence necessary to make this conclusion. [—9—]

Of course, had the district court elsewhere in the order made factual findings related to this issue, those could buttress the conclusory statements. Alas, no other factual findings can be found. Not only does the district court's order not discuss any other relevant facts; it omits a critical time period in its entirety. The findings of fact do not discuss anything from the day the *Pathfinder* left the shipyard in 2011 until the blowout preventer's annulars failed testing in early 2013, even though many problems that Eni complains of occurred during that missing time period.

It is the district court—which heard all the evidence and is most familiar with the case—that should make the subsidiary factual findings in the first instance. *See Redditt*, 718 F.2d at 1386 ("It is not the function of this Court to make credibility choices and findings of fact."). But for the reasons above, it is impossible for us to ascertain whether the district court performed this important function. We would simply be guessing as to the factual basis for the district court's conclusion. *See Chandler*, 958 F.2d at 89 (noting that the court "cannot review bare conclusions" and that the court "cannot be left to second-guess the factual basis for the district court's conclusion" (quotation omitted)).

Accordingly, we vacate the district court's judgment as to Eni's breach-of-contract claim for failing to comply with Rule 52(a) and remand the claim to the district court to make additional factual findings on the good-oilfield-practice issue. *See Redditt*, 718 F.2d at 1387. Importantly, we do not hold that the district court's ultimate conclusion that Transocean used good oilfield practice was clearly erroneous. {–938–} The district court is free to make that conclusion again (or not) on remand. We hold only that the district court must give us a clear indication of the basis of its decision on this issue.[6] [—10—]

B.

The district court held that Eni's breach-of-warranty claims were barred as a matter of law by § 910(a) of the contract. That provision states that the parties shall "indemnify, hold harmless and defend" each other "from and against any and all claims, demands, causes of action, damages, judgments and awards of any kind or character, without limit and without regard to the cause or causes thereof, including but not limited to claims, demands, and causes of action arising out of . . . breach of representation or warranty (express or implied) . . . or any other theory of legal liability."

Eni argues that § 910(a) is not the general indemnification clause the district court made it out to be—it is a definitional provision. We agree. The section clearly states that it is defining the term "be responsible for and hold harmless and indemnify" found in §§ 901–09. It then defines that term using the above language. So the district court needed to turn to §§ 901–09 to see if any of those provisions

created a relevant indemnification because § 910(a), by itself, could not defeat Eni's claims.

Transocean does not quarrel with Eni's interpretation of § 910(a). Instead, it directs our attention to § 909, which provides that the parties will indemnify each other for "special, indirect, or consequential damages resulting from or arising out of" the contract. This provision, Transocean claims, encompasses the damages that Eni seeks on its warranty claims.

Transocean's argument is unpersuasive. Section 909 is a limitation on the type of damages allowed. It says nothing about what type of claims can be brought. While § 909 could limit the type of damages Eni would receive if it [—11—] successfully proves its breach-of-warranty claims, it does not stop Eni from bringing breach-of-warranty claims in the first place. Transocean points to no other contractual provision (and we could not find one) that would preclude as a matter of law Eni's breach-of-warranty claims.

Thus, we vacate the district court's warranty holding and remand for a new trial on this issue to determine whether Transocean made any expressed or implied warranties and whether Transocean breached those warranties.

C.

We now turn to Transocean's breach-of-contract counterclaim, which centers around Eni's attempt to get out of the contract.

On October 13, 2014, Eni sent a letter to Transocean purporting to terminate the contract effective on that date. The letter stated that the termination was based on §§ 203(c)(1) and 1305(c). Those provisions, respectively, allow Eni to terminate the contract if (1) Transocean failed to "initiate the correction of any material non-conformity {–939–} with [the] Contract within thirty (30) days of having received written notice thereof from [Eni]," or (2) Eni had a good-faith belief that Transocean had taken any action violating a relevant law or regulation.

---

[6] As an alternative argument, Transocean asks us to uphold the district court's rejection of Eni's breach-of-contract claim because § 203(c)(1) of the contract states that Eni's "sole and exclusive" remedy for "any material nonconformity" with the contract is [—10—] termination. Eni's claim that Transocean did not follow good oilfield practice would be a material nonconformity, so Transocean posits that § 203(c)(1) forbids Eni from suing for damages on this claim. The district court did not address this argument; it noted only that § 203(c)(1) is enforceable. We decline to address Transocean's argument in the first instance.

The letter alleged that the failure of the drawworks constituted a material non-conformity within the meaning of § 203(c)(1).[7] As for § 1305(c), it claimed that the *Pathfinder* had violated 30 C.F.R. § 250.442(b), which mandates that a blowout preventer must have two operable control pods attached to it when drilling. Eni claimed that this requirement had been violated when the MUX cable connecting one control pod to the blowout preventer was damaged. [—12—]

The district court held that the letter did not establish proper termination under either provision. Because of this, it treated the letter as a repudiation that materially breached the contract since it unequivocally demonstrated a refusal to perform. On appeal, Eni argues that it properly terminated the contract under both provisions.[8]

i.

The district court held that Eni could not terminate under § 203(c)(1) based on the drawworks' failure because Transocean had initiated corrective action, completed repairs, and successfully used the drawworks by October 10, 2014—three days before Eni sent its letter.

Eni now argues that while the letter clearly singles out the malfunctioning drawworks as the reason for termination, it was really terminating for all the past problems with the blowout preventer. On its account, to "initiate

a correction" means that Transocean was required to successfully fix the blowout preventer. Eni points to the blowout preventer's repeated failures as evidence that Transocean never did this. There are two problems with Eni's position.

The first one being that the letter says nothing about the blowout preventer. Indeed, Eni's own Vice President of Operations testified that the reason for the termination was the failure of the drawworks—not the past problems with the blowout preventer. It was perfectly reasonable for the district court to read the letter for what it said. [—13—]

The second one being that Eni misunderstands what it means to "initiate a correction." Nothing in § 203(c)(1)'s text requires Transocean to fix a problem with finality on the first go; nothing stops it from using more convenient, short-term fixes; and nothing gives any indication that a repair's effectiveness is the measure for when termination is proper.[9] Eni's attempt to redefine "to initiate a correction" in a way that would cover the above circumstances is irreconcilable with ordinary English. Section 203(c)(1) is clear: It allows for termination only if Transocean took no action to fix the problem—or in the contractual {–940–} words, "failed to initiate a correction." The end.

It appears that even Eni understands this. It sought to modify the contract in 2014 to allow for termination if Transocean failed to "diligently pursue [a correction] to completion." This revision would not have been needed if Eni really thought that § 203(c)(1) already required such diligence.

In the end, Eni admits that after receiving each written notice about the blowout preventer, Transocean initiated a repair job. That fact—even in a counterfactual world where termination was based on the blowout preventer's problems—is enough to defeat Eni's argument under § 203(c)(1). Moreover, Transocean's repairs on the blowout preventer were not as shoddy has Eni makes them seem.

---

[7] Eni alleges that the failure of the drawworks is a non-conformity with the contract because § 509 requires Transocean to keep its well-control equipment in "good condition."

[8] For the first time, Eni also argues that termination was proper under general maritime law. It cites to a 100-year-old case for the proposition that a maritime contract contains an implied right to terminate the contract based on concern over the crew's safety. *See The W.J. Keyser*, 56 F. 731, 734 (5th Cir. 1893). But "arguments not raised before the district court are waived and will not be considered on appeal unless the party can demonstrate 'extraordinary circumstances.'" *AG Acceptance Corp. v. Veigel*, 564 F.3d 695, 700 (5th Cir. 2009). Eni has not argued that any extraordinary circumstances exist. The argument is waived.

[9] Eni does not allege any bad faith on Transocean's part in fixing the blowout preventer.

Before each drill, the blowout preventer was certified by third-party experts hired by Eni and found to be fully functional.

ii.

Section 1305(c) allows for termination when Eni has a good-faith belief that Transocean materially violated a relevant law or regulation, provided certain procedures are observed: (1) Eni must advise Transocean in writing of the violation; (2) the parties must meet within 10 days; (3) Transocean must [—14—] fail to provide Eni with evidence within 30 days that reasonably demonstrates that it did not run afoul of the law; (4) Eni must still believe in good faith that Transocean did violate the law; and (5) Eni must send a written notice of termination.

The district court held that Eni did not correctly terminate under § 1305(c) for three reasons: (1) Eni did not meet § 1305(c)'s notice requirements; (2) Transocean provided Eni with evidence reasonably demonstrating that it did not violate 30 C.F.R. § 250.442(b); and (3) Transocean did not actually violate 30 C.F.R. § 250.442(b). We find it unnecessary to address the last two points; the first point is sufficient to uphold the district court's decision.

Section 1305(c) requires two written documents—an initial notice advising Transocean of a violation and a final termination notice. But Eni only sent one written document, namely the October 13 letter. That letter is a final termination notice. It states that termination was effective immediately. No initial violation notice was sent. Thus, Eni did not comply with § 1305(c)'s dual-writing requirement.

Despite the letter's plain meaning, Eni now dubs the letter as a notice of "its intention to terminate." But even if it could be classified as the initial notice, termination would still be improper under § 1305(c), because then Eni would not have sent a final written notice of termination after the 30-day review period.

Eni's response to this fact is simple. It claims that it never had to send a second letter. It insists that on November 12—30 days after the first notice was sent—it had a unilateral right to terminate the contract and that the court should treat the initial "notice of termination" also as a premature final termination that became operative on November 12. This argument contorts the dual-writing requirement into a single-writing requirement. The letter [—15—] cannot operate as an initial notice and a final notice at the same time. The parties bargained for a dual-writing requirement, and Eni cannot now wiggle out of it. Eni did not properly terminate under § 1305(c).

iii.

We affirm the district court's judgment on Transocean's breach-of-contract claim because Eni did not properly terminate the contract under § 203(c)(1) or § 1305(c). Therefore, the October 13 letter {–941–} was rightly treated as a repudiation that materially breached the contract.

D.

Lastly, we turn to damages. The district court awarded $160,526,322.10 to Transocean on its breach-of-contract claim. "A district court's damages award is a finding of fact, which this court reviews for clear error. The conclusions of law underlying the award are reviewed *de novo.*" *Jauch v. Nautical Servs., Inc.,* 470 F.3d 207, 213 (5th Cir. 2006) (per curiam). Eni argues that the award must be vacated for two reasons—one factual; one legal.

First, Eni argues that the district court failed to meaningfully assess whether Transocean was ready, willing, and able to perform under the contract—a finding that is necessary before damages can be awarded after a material breach. 15 WILLISTON ON CONTRACTS § 47:1 (4th ed.). While admitting that the court did make an explicit finding on this issue, Eni complains the finding is conclusory, with no meaningful reasoning or explanation to back it up.

This argument must be rejected. The district court did, in fact, make other factual findings supporting its conclusion. As the court noted, just before Eni sent the termination letter, Eni and Transocean attempted to negotiate a new deal for the *Pathfinder* for four more years of drilling in Ghana. That deal fell through because the Ghanaian Government did not give them permission. And immediately after Eni sent the October 13 letter, Transocean began to [—16—] remarket the *Pathfinder*. These factual findings, supported by the record, demonstrate that Transocean was ready to continue drilling operations—or at the very least, would not have totally failed to perform. *See* RESTATEMENT (SECOND) OF CONTRACTS § 254 cmt. a (stating that a breaching party's "duty to pay damages is discharged if it subsequently appears that there would have been a total failure of performance by the injured party"). Thus, the district court's factual conclusion that Transocean was ready, willing, and able to perform under the contract was not clearly erroneous.

Next, Eni argues that the district court committed legal error in calculating the expectation damages. Expectation damages attempt to give the nonbreaching party the benefit of the bargain by placing him "in as good a position as he would have been in had the contract been performed." *Id.* § 344 cmt. a; *see also Hoffman v. L & M Arts*, 838 F.3d 568, 584 (5th Cir. 2016).

Had Eni not breached the contract, Transocean would have been entitled to monthly payments from Eni. The amount of each payment would depend on what the *Pathfinder* did during each month. For example, if the *Pathfinder* was drilling, the full Operating Rate would apply; if it was being repaired, the Repair Rate would kick in, and if Eni failed to give any instructions to Transocean, the Standby Rate would take effect. The district court selected the Standby Rate as the applicable rate for the remainder of the contract. It did so because after Eni repudiated the contract and evacuated the *Pathfinder* on October 25, 2014, Eni never issued any further instructions.

We cannot approve of this analysis. That is because it looks to what Eni actually *did* after termination, when the operative question is what Eni *would* have done in a non-breach world. *See* 24 WILLISTON ON CONTRACTS § 64.3 (4th ed.) (noting that expectation damages ae "designed to secure for that party the benefit of the bargain that he or she made"). Had Eni not repudiated the contract, Eni would have likely continued to issue instructions to Transocean. [—17—] The district court should have attempted to determine, in the hypothetical non-breach world, how many days {–942–} the *Pathfinder* would have spent at each applicable rate. Possibly relevant to this inquiry is the *Pathfinder*'s past performance, any testimony on how the *Pathfinder*'s machinery would have operated going forward, and any evidence suggesting what Eni's plans for the *Pathfinder* would have been. What is clear, though, is applying the Standby Rate simply because Eni never issued any instructions after repudiation missed the mark.

Accordingly, we vacate the damages award and remand with instructions to recalculate the damages using the correct methodology.

* * *

The district court's judgment is VACATED in part and AFFIRMED in part. This case is REMANDED to the district court for proceedings consistent with this opinion.

United States Court of Appeals
for the Fifth Circuit

No. 18-30844

BP EXPLORATION & PROD., INC.
vs.
CLAIMANT ID 100261922

Appeal from the United States District Court for the
Eastern District of Louisiana

Decided: March 28, 2019

Citation: 919 F.3d 942, 7 Adm. R. 226 (5th Cir. 2019).

Before **HIGGINBOTHAM**, **ELROD**, and **DUNCAN**, Circuit Judges.

[—1—] {–944–} **ELROD**, Circuit Judge:

In this *Deepwater Horizon* appeal, BP challenges the $2 million award Claimant received pursuant to the Economic and Property Damages Settlement (Settlement Agreement). Because the district court properly denied discretionary review, we AFFIRM.

I.

Claimant, an Alabama-based manufacturer of commercial signs, submitted a claim to the Settlement Program in November 2013. While processing the claim, the Claims Administrator requested additional information from Claimant on several occasions, including information [—2—] pertaining to a $900,000 "Research & Development" expense that Claimant classified as a "variable" cost on its profit and loss statements. Claimant complied, explaining the purpose of the R&D effort and listing the types of costs included, and provided a month-by-month breakout demonstrating that the costs had been incurred periodically between February 2010 and June 2011.

During this exchange, the Claims Administrator rejected Claimant's claim twice, and Claimant requested re-review each time. In its explanation of the second denial, the Claims Administrator noted that it had adjusted Claimant's accounting data to record the R&D costs in the months in which they were incurred rather than as a lump sum in June 2011. Finally, after a third review of the claim, the Claims Administrator determined that Claimant was entitled to approximately $2 million under the Settlement Agreement. This time, the Claims Administrator's analysis did not include the adjustments to the R&D expense.

BP appealed the award to an Appeal Panel on three grounds: (1) Claimant's {–945–} attestation on its claim form that the oil spill caused its losses was implausible; (2) the Claims Administrator improperly characterized the R&D expense as "variable" rather than "fixed"; and (3) the Claims Administrator erroneously omitted its adjustments that "matched" the R&D costs to the months in which they were incurred.[1] The Appeal Panel declined to consider the attestation issue but noted that it was preserved for further review. On the fixed vs. variable costs issue, the Appeal Panel affirmed the Claims Administrator's classification of the R&D expense as a variable cost. Finally, turning to the matching issue, the Appeal Panel found the issue [—3—] mooted because, even if it was error to omit the R&D expense adjustments, the correct value would be closer to the $2 million award amount than BP's final proposal of $0. Thus, the Appeal Panel denied the appeal.

BP next sought discretionary review in the district court, raising the same issues it raised before the Appeal Panel. The district court denied review in June 2018, and BP now appeals.

II.

This court reviews the district court's denial of discretionary review for an abuse of discretion. *Holmes Motors, Inc. v. BP Expl. & Prod., Inc.*, 829 F.3d 313, 315, 4 Adm. R. 263, 263 (5th Cir. 2016). The district court abuses its discretion if it declines to review a decision that "actually contradicted or misapplied the

---

[1] BP raised a fourth argument regarding whether Claimant qualifies as a defense contractor under the Settlement Agreement, but "appellate counsel has chosen not to renew that argument" before this court."

Settlement Agreement, or had the clear potential to contradict or misapply the Settlement Agreement." *Id.*, 4 Adm. R. at 263 (quoting *In re Deepwater Horizon*, 641 F. App'x 405, 409–10 (5th Cir. 2016)). It is also an abuse of discretion to deny a request for review that "raises a recurring issue on which the Appeal Panels are split if 'the resolution of the question will substantially impact the administration of the Agreement.'" *BP Expl. & Prod., Inc. v. Claimant ID 100094497*, 910 F.3d 797, 800, 6 Adm. R. 273, 274 (5th Cir. 2018) (*Texas Gulf Seafood*) (quoting *Claimant ID 100212278 v. BP Expl. & Prod., Inc.*, 848 F.3d 407, 410, 5 Adm. R. 202, 203 (5th Cir. 2017)). In contrast, the district court does not abuse its discretion if it denies a request for review that "involve[s] no pressing question of how the Settlement Agreement should be interpreted and implemented, but simply raise[s] the correctness of a discretionary administrative decision in the facts of a single claimant's case." *Id.*, 6 Adm. R. at 274 (alterations in original) (quoting *Claimant ID 100212278*, 848 F.3d at 410, 5 Adm. R. at 203).

III.

BP contends that the district court abused its discretion because the Claims Administrator: (1) failed to investigate Claimant's implausible attestation that the oil spill caused its losses; (2) improperly classified [—4—] Claimant's R&D expense as variable rather than fixed; and (3) erred by omitting its previous matching adjustments to the R&D expense.

A.

BP's attestation argument is familiar—BP has raised the same issue in several other appeals currently pending in this court. Here, BP argues that "[t]here is no logical connection" between Claimant's sign manufacturing business and the oil spill, so the Appeal Panel should have remanded the claim to the Claims Administrator for "further investigation."

Although our opinion in *Deepwater Horizon III* forecloses any categorical duty on the part

of the Claims Administrator {–946–} "to ensure that implausible claims are adequately scrutinized," BP is correct that that opinion also acknowledges that "[s]uspicious forms [will] be subject to investigation" and suggests that the Claims Administrator should "resolve real examples of implausible claims" as they arise during the claims process. *In re Deepwater Horizon*, 744 F.3d 370, 377–78, 2 Adm. R. 183, 186–87 (5th Cir. 2014) (*Deepwater Horizon III*). However, the only argument BP offers to demonstrate that Claimant's attestation is implausible is that "[it is] not clear how the fortunes of a sign manufacturer 160 miles inland were tied to an oil spill." BP does not identify any other possible causes of Claimant's loss, nor does it rely on any evidence or authority to demonstrate that Claimant's losses could not have been caused at least in part by the *Deepwater Horizon* disaster. Accordingly, BP has not established that Claimant's causation attestation is implausible.[2] The district court therefore properly denied discretionary review. [—5—]

B.

Regarding the fixed vs. variable costs issue, BP insists that classifying Claimant's R&D expense as variable artificially inflated Claimant's award. Conceding that R&D costs are not on the list of fixed and variable expenses in Exhibit 4D, BP nonetheless insists that the Claims Administrator's classification violated the Settlement Agreement. BP further suggests that the Claims Administrator did not make "any reasoned choice" on the R&D expense because it simply "did not notice [Claimant's] wrong classification." According to BP, the Appeal Panel erred by declining to correct this omission and instead deferring to the Claims Administrator's classification.

Our recent opinion in *Texas Gulf Seafood* clarified the proper approach for Claims

---

[2] Even if BP had made such a showing, the Claims Administrator appears to have closely scrutinized the causation issue in its review of the claim: the Claims Administrator twice requested additional documentation demonstrating that Claimant's losses were caused by the spill.

Administrators and Appeal Panels in classifying a claimant's expenses as fixed or variable. There, resolving an Appeal Panel split, we held that "the Settlement Agreement requires claims administrators to use their independent judgment and classify expenses as 'fixed' or 'variable' according to their substantive nature, rather than rational basis review of the claimants' own descriptions." *Texas Gulf Seafood*, 910 F.3d at 802, 6 Adm. R. at 276. We further held that "Appeal Panels, too, are bound by the substantive nature of the expense claims under the Settlement Agreement rather than the claimants' inaccurate characterizations." *Id.*, 6 Adm. R. at 276. Because the Appeal Panel had deferred to the claimant's "rational basis" for classifying certain expenses as "supplies"— a category listed as a fixed cost in Exhibit 4D—we vacated the award and remanded for proper classification of the expenses. *Id.* at 800, 803, 6 Adm. R. at 274, 276–77.

Although the Claims Administrator and Appeal Panel in this case did not have the benefit of *Texas Gulf Seafood* when they reviewed Claimant's claim, we believe their analyses comport with our holdings in that case. We note first that this is not a case in which the Claims Administrator applied a particular classification simply because the label the Claimant assigned to that [—6—] expense was included on one of the lists in Exhibit 4D. *Cf. BP Expl. & Prod., Inc. v. Claimant ID 100185315*, 2019 WL 597598, at *2 (5th Cir. Feb. 8, 2019) (vacating and remanding where Appeal Panel "agreed with the claimant's argument that its Management Fee expense was properly classified as a fixed cost because 'fees' are included as a fixed cost in [Exhibit 4D]"). As BP admits, {–947–} R&D expenses are not listed on Exhibit 4D, so the Claims Administrator had to follow Policy 361 and "use discretion to apply the classification that best conform[ed] to delineations made by the Parties." The record indicates that the Claims Administrator did so—it requested additional information from Claimant about the R&D expense, including the "nature of the expenses recorded," and Claimant responded with a substantive description. Engaging in this kind of independent analysis is all that *Texas Gulf Seafood* requires.

While BP complains that the Appeal Panel applied an abuse of discretion standard in reviewing the Claims Administrator's classification, the Appeal Panel expressly considered the substantive nature of the R&D expense. It first listed the purpose of the expense and the types of costs included. Then, it explained the basis for its conclusion that the Claims Administrator's variable classification was correct: "[T]he expenses involved are those relating to the development of operational aspects of 'the sign,' i.e. a particular project." Importantly, the Appeal Panel did not merely defer to the label that Claimant assigned to the expense. Thus, on this record, we cannot conclude that the Appeal Panel's analysis ran afoul of *Texas Gulf Seafood*.

BP makes much of its argument that, regardless of the analyses undertaken by the Claims Administrator and Appeal Panel, applying a variable classification to the R&D expense was substantively inaccurate. Even if this were true, it "simply raise[s] the correctness of a discretionary administrative decision in the facts of a single claimant's case" and therefore does not warrant discretionary review. *Texas Gulf Seafood*, 910 F.3d at 800, 6 Adm. R. at 274 [—7—] (alteration in original). The district court did not abuse its discretion in denying review on this issue.

C.

In its third issue, BP complains that the Claims Administrator's "inexplicable deletion" of the matching adjustments it had previously made to the R&D expense resulted in a larger award than Claimant was entitled to under the Settlement Agreement. But in its calculation notes in support of Claimant's award, the Claims Administrator confirmed that its review had been conducted according to this court's and the district court's instructions regarding matching under Policy 495. In any event, even if the Claims Administrator erred in omitting the adjustments, the error bears only on the processing of Claimant's claim and does not "raise[] a recurring issue on which the Appeal Panels are split" or "involve [a] pressing question of how the Settlement Agreement should be interpreted." *Id.*, 6 Adm. R. at 274. As a result, the district court did not err in declining to grant discretionary review.

IV.

For the reasons described, BP has not demonstrated that discretionary review was appropriate in this case. We therefore AFFIRM the district court's judgment.

United States Court of Appeals
for the Fifth Circuit

No. 18-30375

BP EXPLORATION & PROD., INC.
VS.
CLAIMANT ID I OO246928

Appeal from the United States District Court for the
Eastern District of Louisiana

Decided: March 29, 2019

Citation: 920 F.3d 209, 7 Adm. R. 230 (5th Cir. 2019).

Before **COSTA,** Circuit Judge.

[—1—] {–210–} ORDER:

Claimant ID 100246928—a/k/a the Tampa Bay Buccaneers—asks this court to seal the courtroom where the team will argue its appeal on April 1. It also wants to bar public access to the recording of the argument that this court routinely makes available on its website. The team's motion is DENIED.

Until recently, this court filed *Deepwater Horizon* appeals under seal when they were first docketed. Even under that sealing order, however, the court ultimately unsealed many cases and the vast majority of appeals were argued in a public courtroom. Reflecting this determination that most BP cases did not warrant full sealing, an en banc order issued last month vacating the court's prior sealing order. As is the situation for other cases, parties in *Deepwater Horizon* cases must now justify sealing. The default is public access. **[—2—]** After that order issued, the Buccaneers succeeded in keeping the record and briefs sealed based on its concerns that the amount of revenue it receives from the NFL—a focus of this appeal—is proprietary.

But its request to seal the courtroom goes too far—by a longshot. "The right to public access 'serves to promote trustworthiness of the judicial process, to curb judicial abuses, and to provide the public with a more complete understanding of the judicial system, including a better perception of its fairness.'" *United States v. Holy Land Found. for Relief & Dev.*, 624 F.3d 685, 690 (5th Cir. 2010)

(quoting *Littlejohn v. BIC Corp.*, 851 F.2d 673, 682 (3d Cir. 1988)). Public confidence in the courts is the issue: How can the public know that courts are deciding cases fairly and impartially if it doesn't know what is being decided? *In re Hearst Newspapers, L.L.C.*, 641 F.3d 168, 179 (5th Cir. 2011) (discussing the need for "openness" of court proceedings in the criminal context); **{–211–}** *In re High Sulfur Content Gasoline Prods. Liab. Litig.*, 517 F.3d 220, 230 (5th Cir. 2008) (noting same interest for attorney's fee dispute in civil case). Sealing a record undermines that interest, but shutting the courthouse door poses an even greater threat to public confidence in the justice system. "Open trials assure the public that procedural rights are respected, and that justice is afforded equally. Closed trials breed suspicion of prejudice and arbitrariness, which in turn spawns disrespect for law." *Richmond Newspapers, Inc. v. Virginia*, 448 U.S. 555, 595 (1980) (Brennan, J., concurring).

The team cites three reasons it believes override this strong interest in transparency. None of them comes close to doing so.

It first says that the briefs discuss confidential financial data, which would "likely" come up at oral argument. But that type of proprietary information is present in all these BP cases—a claimant has to submit profit **[—3—]** and loss statements to get paid. Yet lawyers have argued these cases in open court multiple times during recent argument weeks without disclosing confidential revenue amounts. The judges have the data at their fingertips, so there is no need for a lawyer to mention the actual numbers.

Next the team contends that keeping the courtroom open would "gratify [BP's] private spite," "promote public scandal," and "harm [the team's] competitive standing." *See Nixon v. Warner Commc'ns, Inc.*, 435 U.S. 589, 598 (1978) (noting these potential interests in judicial secrecy). It recites an aside from BP's brief stating that the public would be "surprised to learn that a professional football team has claimed spill-related losses." Maybe so. But public "surprise" at a football team's seeking money from an oil-spill settlement is not in the same universe as the types of scandal or spite that warrant closing the courthouse door. *See, e.g., id.* (mentioning these concerns in the context of "the painful and sometimes disgusting details of a divorce case" (quotation omitted)). Cases are heard in courtrooms every day addressing matters so much more sensitive than this dispute— workplace harassment, sex crimes, or child abuse to name just a few. Even in those cases the courtroom typically remains open to the public.

The Buccaneers' final justification is an expectation of secrecy the team says it had throughout the claim process. Under the classwide agreement, settlement program proceedings are confidential. But confidentiality agreements entered into by private parties, even if approved by the district court, do not bind this court. *Baxter Intern., Inc. v. Abbott Labs.*, 297 F.3d 544, 545–46 (7th Cir. 2002) (stating that notwithstanding prior confidentiality agreements, "any claim of secrecy must be reviewed independently in [the appellate] court"). Indeed, the standard letter that is sent to parties in this court states: [—4—]

> Our court has a strong presumption of public access to our court's records, and the court scrutinizes any request by a party to seal . . . . Counsel moving to seal matters must explain in particularity the necessity for sealing in our court. Counsel do not satisfy this burden by simply stating that the originating court sealed the matter, as the circumstances that justified sealing in the originating court may have changed or may not apply in an appellate proceeding.

And there is a more fundamental reason that a sealing agreement by the parties should not bind a court. It is the *public* that has the right of access, so private litigants should not be able to contract that right away. Most litigants have no incentive to protect the public's right of access. Both sides may want confidentiality. Even when only one party does, the other may {–212–} be able to extract a concession by agreeing to a sealing request (this type of tradeoff is common in settlement

agreements). That is why it is for judges, not litigants, to decide whether the justification for sealing overcomes the right of access.

At the end of the day, because this court has maintained confidential treatment of its financial statements, the Buccaneers' request for sealing the oral argument is based on nothing more than a desire to keep secret that it filed a *Deepwater Horizon* claim. The court will leave it to others to guess why the team is so concerned about public disclosure of its claim when numerous other BP claimants in the appeals inundating our court are not. Just three months into this year, at least ten *Deepwater Horizon* decisions naming the claimants have issued. Among them is one from another of Tampa Bay's professional sports franchises, the NHL's Lightning. *See Claimant ID 100248748 v. BP Expl. & Prod., Inc.*, 2019 WL 1306302 (5th Cir. Mar. 20, 2019). The court is unable to discern any reason for keeping secret the oil-spill claim of a football team when the claim of a hockey team (and of course those of numerous other businesses) is a public matter. [—5—]

As is its right, Claimant ID 100246928 has used the federal courts in its attempt to obtain millions of dollars it believes BP owes because of the oil spill. But it should not able to benefit from this public resource while treating it like a private tribunal when there is no good reason to do so. On Monday, the public will be able to access the courtroom it pays for.

_____
[Signature]
GREGG J. COSTA
UNITED STATES CIRCUIT JUDGE

United States Court of Appeals
for the Fifth Circuit

No. 18-30644

BP EXPLORATION & PROD., INC.
vs.
CLAIMANT ID 100166533

Appeal from the United States District Court for the
Eastern District of Louisiana

Decided: April 8, 2019

Citation: 920 F.3d 314, 7 Adm. R. 232 (5th Cir. 2019).

Before **STEWART,** Chief Judge, and **DAVIS** and
ELROD, Circuit Judges.

[—1—] {–315–} **ELROD,** Circuit Judge: {–316–}

This *Deepwater Horizon* case involves the fixed vs. variable cost issue that has arisen frequently in appeals of claims submitted pursuant to BP's Economic and Property Damages Settlement Agreement (Settlement Agreement). Because the reviews conducted by the Claims Administrator and Appeal Panel were consistent with our recent decision in *Texas Gulf Seafood*, and because BP's arguments regarding the substantive accuracy of the "fixed" classification only raise the correctness of a fact-dependent decision in a single claimant's case, we AFFIRM the district court's judgment. [—2—]

I.

The claimant here, Ordes Services LLC (Ordes), is an electrical contractor that provides installation, maintenance, and repair services in southeast Louisiana. Ordes submitted a claim pursuant to the Settlement Agreement in March 2013. Relevant here, in the profit-and-loss statements Ordes submitted with its claim, Ordes recorded an expense labeled "Management Fee." The Claims Administrator requested additional information about this expense during the processing of Ordes's claim.

In October 2017, the Claims Administrator determined that Ordes was entitled to $2.1 million under the Settlement Agreement. In calculating the award, the Claims Admin-

istrator classified Ordes's Management Fee as a "fixed" cost rather than a "variable" cost under the Settlement Agreement.[1] BP appealed to a three-member Appeal Panel, challenging the Claims Administrator's treatment of the Management Fee. The Appeal Panel concluded that the Claims Administrator had properly categorized the expense as fixed and affirmed Ordes's award. The district court denied BP's request for discretionary review. [—3—]

II.

This court reviews the district court's denial of discretionary review for an abuse of discretion. *Holmes Motors, Inc. v. BP Expl. & Prod., Inc.*, 829 F.3d 313, 315, 4 Adm. R. 263, 263 (5th Cir. 2016). The district court abuses its discretion if the decision it declined to review "actually contradicted or misapplied the Settlement Agreement, or had the clear potential to contradict or misapply the Settlement Agreement." *Id.*, 4 Adm. R. at 263 (quoting *In re Deepwater Horizon*, 641 F. App'x 405, 409–10 (5th Cir. 2016)). It is also an abuse of discretion to deny a request for review that "raises a recurring issue on which the Appeal Panels are split if 'the resolution of

---

[1] We explained the significance of the fixed vs. variable cost classification in *Texas Gulf Seafood*:

Variable Profit is central to calculating damages in a [Business Economic Loss] Claim. Step 1 Compensation is determined by calculating "the difference in Variable Profit between the 2010 Compensation Period selected by the claimant and the Variable Profit over the comparable months of the Benchmark Period." Variable Profit, in turn, is defined as the sum of monthly revenue over the Benchmark Period minus variable costs identified in Exhibit 4D, among others. Thus, whether a cost is defined as "variable" (and factored into Variable Profit calculations) or "fixed" (and excluded from such calculations) can significantly alter the size of an award.

BP Expl. & Prod., Inc. v. Claimant ID 100094497 (Texas Gulf Seafood), 910 F.3d 797, 799, 6 Adm. R. 273, 273 (5th Cir. 2018). Exhibit 4D to the Settlement Agreement, which contains a list of expenses the parties have designated as either fixed or variable, lists "Fees" as a fixed cost.

the question will substantially impact the administration of the Agreement.'" *BP Expl. & Prod., Inc. v. Claimant ID 100094497* (*Texas Gulf Seafood*), 910 F.3d 797, 800, 6 Adm. R. 273, 274 (5th Cir. 2018) {–317–} (quoting *Claimant ID 100212278 v. BP Expl. & Prod., Inc.*, 848 F.3d 407, 410, 5 Adm. R. 202, 203 (5th Cir. 2017)). In contrast, the district court does not abuse its discretion if it denies a request for review that "involve[s] no pressing question of how the Settlement Agreement should be interpreted and implemented, but simply raise[s] the correctness of a discretionary administrative decision in the facts of a single claimant's case." *Id.*, 6 Adm. R. at 274 (alterations in original) (quoting *Claimant ID 100212278*, 848 F.3d at 410, 5 Adm. R. at 203).

III.

On appeal, BP contends that the district court's denial of discretionary review was an abuse of discretion for two reasons: (1) the district court failed to resolve an Appeal Panel split regarding the proper approach to classifying fixed vs. variable expenses; and (2) classifying the Management Fee as "fixed" was substantively incorrect.

A.

We recently resolved the Appeal Panel split that BP complains of in our decision in *Texas Gulf Seafood*. There, we set out the proper approach for [—4—] Claims Administrators and Appeal Panels in classifying fixed vs. variable costs under the Settlement Agreement:

> [T]his court holds that the Settlement Agreement requires claims administrators to use their independent judgment and classify expenses as "fixed" or "variable" according to their substantive nature, rather than rational basis review of the claimants' own descriptions. Appeal Panels, too, are bound by the substantive nature of the expense claims under the Settlement Agreement rather than the claimants' inaccurate characterizations.

Id. at 802, 6 Adm. R. at 276. Because the Appeal Panel relied on the claimant's "rational basis" for classifying the disputed expense as fixed rather than conducting an independent review, we vacated the claimant's award and remanded the case for re-classification of the expense. *Id.* at 802–03, 6 Adm. R. at 276–77.

In a subsequent unpublished case, we applied *Texas Gulf Seafood*'s holdings to a set of facts similar to this case: the Claims Administrator and Appeal Panel classified an expense the claimant labeled "Management Fee" as fixed rather than variable, and the district court denied BP's request for discretionary review. *BP Expl. & Prod., Inc. v. Claimant ID 100185315*, 2019 WL 507598, at *1 (5th Cir. Feb. 8, 2019). On appeal, we vacated the claimant's award because the Appeal Panel "did not address the substantive nature of the expense" and instead found that the Management Fee was a fixed expense because Exhibit 4D lists "fees" as a fixed cost. *Id.* at *2. Consequently, because the Appeal Panel improperly "focus[ed] on the label given to the expense," we remanded for proper classification. *Id.* at *2–3.

BP contends that, given the factual similarity, our decision in *Claimant ID 100185315* controls here. We disagree. While the expense at issue resembles the disputed expense in that case, the Claims Administrator and Appeal Panel here engaged in the kind of independent, substantive analyses that *Texas Gulf Seafood* requires. [—5—]

Beginning with the Claims Administrator, it included the following calculation note with its documentation in support of Ordes's award:

> DWH Accountant further noted the Claimant recorded expenses to account 'Management Fee Expense'. Per the Claimant's attorney, the Claimant is in contract with Ordes Electric, Inc. Ordes Electric, Inc. provides management services to the Claimant, including {–318–} providing office and warehouse space, insurance coverage, office per-

sonnel, equipment, supplies, utilities, telephone services, etc. The expense is calculated based on sales of the combined companies (Ordes Services, LLC and Ordes Electric, Inc.), and the Claimant pays the percentage portion of the management service expenses equal to its portion of the combined sales . . . . There are no shared revenues between the companies . . . . As such, DWH Accountant classified the account as 'Fees – Fixed'.

The Claims Administrator therefore expressly considered the substantive nature of the Management Fee: it examined the types of costs included as well as the fact that the amount is calculated based on Ordes's sales. Significantly, the Claims Administrator did not merely defer to Ordes's label for the expense, nor did it rely only on whether that label was listed as a fixed cost in Exhibit 4D of the Settlement Agreement. This demonstrates an exercise of independent judgment on the part of the Claims Administrator consistent with *Texas Gulf Seafood*.

In its decision affirming the Claims Administrator's award, the Appeal Panel stated the following:

> This Appeal Panel has conducted a de novo review of the record in this matter. That review and the nature of the charges included in the "Management Fee Expense" account (See Exhibit 4D[] of the Settlement Agreement[)] compel this Appeal Panel to unanimously conclude that the [Settlement Program]'s professional staff properly categorized the expense as fixed.

Thus, the Appeal Panel did not defer to the claimant's "Management Fee" label as prohibited by *Texas Gulf Seafood*—instead, it conducted its own de novo [—6—] review of the expense classification. Importantly, the Appeal Panel specifically stated that it had considered "the nature of the charges included" in the Management Fee before concluding that it was properly categorized as fixed. It did not, as in *Claimant ID 100185315*, affirm the "fixed" classification merely because "fees" are listed as fixed on Exhibit 4D. Accordingly, the Appeal Panel's decision comports with *Texas Gulf Seafood* as well, so the district court did not abuse its discretion in denying discretionary review.

B.

BP separately asserts that classification of the Management Fee as "fixed" was substantively incorrect and that this error alone warranted discretionary review. Because the Management Fee fluctuates depending on Ordes's sales, the argument goes, it should properly be classified as a "variable" cost under the definition set out in *Texas Gulf Seafood*. *See* 910 F.3d at 802 n.2, 6 Adm. R. at 276 n.2.

Even if BP is correct that Ordes's Management Fee is a variable cost, an inaccurate expense classification "simply raise[s] the correctness of a discretionary administrative decision in the facts of a single claimant's case." *Id.* at 800, 6 Adm. R. at 274 (alteration in original); *see also Claimant ID 100250022 v. BP Expl. & Prod., Inc.*, 847 F.3d 167, 170, 5 Adm. R. 199, 200 (5th Cir. 2017) ("In reaching our decision that the district court did not abuse its discretion in denying discretionary review . . . , we need not examine whether the [Settlement Program] was actually correct . . . ."). Therefore, the district court did not err in declining to grant discretionary review to determine whether the Claims Administrator and Appeal Panel accurately classified the Management Fee expense.

IV.

Because BP has not identified any issue requiring discretionary review in this case, {–319–} we AFFIRM the judgment of the district court.

United States Court of Appeals
for the Fifth Circuit

No. 18-30268

CLAIMANT ID 100081155
vs.
BP EXPLORATION & PROD., INC.

Appeal from the United States District Court for the
Eastern District of Louisiana

Decided: April 9, 2019
Revised: April 18, 2019

Citation: 920 F.3d 925, 7 Adm. R. 235 (5th Cir. 2019).

Before **REAVLEY**, **ELROD**, and **WILLETT**, Circuit Judges.

[—1—] {–926–} ELROD, Circuit Judge: {–927–}

JME Management, Inc. (JME)—a vacation rental business affected by the 2010 BP oil spill—filed five claims for compensation with the Settlement Program. The Settlement Program determined that JME was a "failed business" under the meaning of the Settlement Agreement and calculated JME's compensation according to the Failed Business Economic Loss framework. The district court granted discretionary review and agreed that JME was a failed business under the Settlement Agreement. Because the [—2—] district court incorrectly interpreted the Settlement Agreement, we VACATE and REMAND.

I.

A.

Following the Deepwater Horizon oil spill in 2010, BP negotiated and agreed to the Settlement Agreement with a proposed class of individuals and entities. The Settlement Agreement created a framework whereby class members can submit claims to the Claims Administrator and receive payment for approved claims. Under the Settlement Agreement, there are two frameworks for calculating the compensation available to businesses that suffered economic losses resulting from the oil spill. Class members can submit claims under the Business Economic Loss ("BEL") framework or, where applicable, the Failed Business Economic Loss ("FBEL") framework.

Under the BEL framework, claimants are generally compensated for lost profit and lost profit growth, multiplied by a "Risk Transfer Premium" which accounts for unknown and future risks and injuries. By contrast, the FBEL framework uses a business's past earnings to calculate compensation and does not offer a Risk Transfer Premium. The FBEL compensation is calculated by subtracting the "Liquidation Value" from the pre-spill "Total Enterprise Value." A failed business with negative earnings before interest, tax, depreciation, and amortization (EBITDA) for the twelve-month period prior to May 1, 2010, is categorically ineligible for compensation. Moreover, because of the Risk Transfer Premium, businesses that bring claims under the BEL framework are generally entitled to a greater recovery than they would be under the FBEL framework.

The Settlement Agreement defines a failed business as: [—3—]

[A] business Entity that commenced operations prior to November 1, 2008 and that, subsequent to May 1, 2010 but prior to December 31, 2011, either (i) ceased operations and wound down, or (ii) entered bankruptcy, or (iii) otherwise initiated or completed a liquidation of substantially all of its assets, as more fully described in Exhibit 6.

Exhibit 6 explains the additional documentation requirements for an FBEL claim. A Claims Administrator determines whether a claimant is an ongoing or failed business and how much compensation is due, and the claimant may request reconsideration of these decisions. Either BP or the claimant may appeal a final decision to the Appeal Panel. The district court retains the discretion to review the Settlement Program's determinations to ensure that the Claims Administrator and the Appeal Panel correctly interpreted and applied the Settlement Agreement.

B.

JME was in the short-term vacation rental business at the time of the oil spill in 2010. In June 2011, JME entered into an agreement with Gulf Blue Vacations Inc. (Gulf Blue), a company founded by JME's sole owner with the members of his {–928–} family, and sold substantially all of its assets to Gulf Blue in exchange for $800,000.

Subsequently, in May 2013, JME submitted five claims to the Settlement Agreement Claims Administrator, calculating the value of its claims using the BEL framework.[1] However, the Claims Administrator classified and evaluated all five of JME's claims under the FBEL framework. Under the FBEL framework, the Claims Administrator determined that JME was [—4—] entitled to $0 for three locations and denied compensation altogether for two locations. JME requested reconsideration by the Claims Administrator, seeking valuation under the BEL framework. However, the Claims Administrator determined that JME's claims were properly evaluated under the FBEL framework, and the Appeal Panel affirmed. The district court granted discretionary review after consolidating JME's five claims and affirmed the Appeal Panel's decision. JME appealed to this court, arguing that it was not a failed business under the meaning of the Settlement Agreement.

II.

JME and BP disagree about the applicable standard of review. In JME's view, we should review the district court's decision *de novo* as this appeal turns on the interpretation of the Settlement Agreement. *See In re Deepwater Horizon*, 785 F.3d 1003, 1011, 3 Adm. R. 325, 329 (5th Cir. 2015) ("The interpretation of a settlement agreement is a question of contract law that this Court reviews de novo."). BP, on the other hand, argues that we should review only for an abuse of discretion because, in its

view, the district court did not render an interpretation but merely applied the Settlement Agreement to JME's case. Here, however, JME has raised interpretative issues, which we review *de novo*.

Alternatively, citing to an unpublished case, BP argues that this court has applied the abuse-of-discretion standard when the district court granted discretionary review but affirmed the denial of claim. *See BP Expl. & Prod., Inc. v. Claimant ID 100169608*, 682 F. App'x 256, 258–59 (5th Cir. 2017). But this case does not stand for the proposition that BP puts forth. In *Claimant ID 100169608*, we observed that "[w]e have not yet directly addressed whether the abuse of discretion standard of review varies depending on whether the district court granted or denied a request of review" and declined to resolve the issue because the parties did not brief the issue and the claimant would have [—5—] lost under either standard. *Id.* at 259 n.3. In any event, we also observed that "'[t]he standard of review is effectively de novo' when the district court is presented with purely legal questions of contract interpretation.'" *Id.* at 259 (quoting *Claimant ID 100197593 v. BP Expl. & Prod., Inc.*, 666 F. App'x 358, 360 (5th Cir. 2016); *see also United States v. Delgado-Nunez*, 295, F.3d 494, 496 (5th Cir. 2002) ("[A]buse of discretion review of purely legal questions . . . is effectively *de novo* because '[a] district court by definition abuses its discretion when it makes an error of law.'" (quoting *Koon v. United States*, 518 U.S. 81, 100 (1996)). Thus, we will review the interpretative issues *de novo*.

III.

We now turn to JME's argument that the district court misinterpreted the {–929–} Settlement Agreement's definitions of a "failed business." The Settlement Agreement defines a failed business in three ways:

[A] business Entity that commenced operations prior to November 1, 2008 and that, subsequent to May 1, 2010 but prior to December 31, 2011, either (i) ceased operations and wound down, or (ii) entered bankruptcy, or (iii) otherwise

---

[1] Although the record does not clearly show the exact amount that JME claimed for all five locations, it appears that the total amount claimed would have easily exceeded $1 million after accounting for the Risk Transfer Premium.

initiated or completed a liquidation of substantially all of its assets, as more fully described in Exhibit 6.

Because JME has never entered bankruptcy, it would qualify as a failed business only if it either "ceased operations and wound down" or "otherwise initiated a liquidation of substantially all of its assets, as more fully described in Exhibit 6." The district court concluded that the Settlement Program correctly classified JME as a failed business because JME "ceased operations after it sold its assets to another entity." JME challenges, and BP defends, the district court's conclusion under both definitions. We hold that the district court's conclusion was erroneous under both the first and third definitions. [—6—]

A.

The district court's interpretation of the first definition of a failed business was erroneous.

Under the first definition in the Settlement Agreement, an entity is a failed business if it "ceased operations and wound down." The conjunction "and" that separates the phrases "ceased operations" and "wound down" is crucial to interpreting the first definition. "[I]f there are two elements in the construction," then the conjunction "and" generally "entails an express or implied *both* before the first element." Antonin Scalia & Bryan A. Garner, *Reading Law: The Interpretation of Legal Texts*, 117 (2012). For example, under "the well-known constitutional phrase *cruel and unusual punishments*, the *and* signals that cruelty or unusualness alone does not run afoul of the clause: The punishment must meet both standards to fall within the constitutional prohibition." *Id.* at 116; *see also Musacchio v. United States*, 136 S. Ct. 709, 714 (2016) ("The parties agree that [the district court's jury instruction] was erroneous: By using the conjunction 'and' . . . the instruction required the Government to prove an *additional* element." (emphasis added)); *Matador Petroleum Corp. v. St. Paul Surplus Lines Ins. Co.*, 174 F.3d 653, 657 (5th Cir. 1999) ("The endorsement's use of the

conjunction 'and' indicates that, to obtain coverage, the insured must satisfy the requirements of *both* the seven-day notice provision *and* the thirty-day reporting provision." (emphasis added)). Likewise, under the Settlement Agreement, having ceased operations or having wound down alone does not render an entity a failed business. It must have *both* ceased operations *and* wound down to be a failed business.

Winding down is commonly defined as a process through which a corporation "collect[s] [its] assets, dispose[s] of any assets that will not be distributed in kind to shareholders, discharge[s] or make[s] provision to [—7—] discharge its liabilities, . . . and settle[s] the business and its affairs." 30 Fletcher, Corporations § 137:1 (5th ed. 2016). It is an act of "draw[ing] or bring[ing]" a corporate existence "to a close." *Wind, New Oxford American Dictionary* (3d ed. 2010). "For convenience in winding [down], the corporate existence is usually continued either *indefinitely* or for some period limited by law in order to dispose of the corporation's assets and pay creditors." Cox & Hazen, {–930–} 4 Treatise on the Law of Corporations § 26:1 (3d ed. 2010) (emphasis added).

In interpreting the phrase "wound down," JME argues that the Settlement Agreement requires an entity to have completed winding down by December 31, 2011 to satisfy the "wound down" element. We disagree. As BP notes, the Settlement Agreement does not require that a business "completely" or "fully" have wound down. Moreover, JME's interpretation of "wound down" would require an entity to complete winding down within less than a two-year period. Because winding down is typically a process that could take place over a substantial—or perhaps indefinite—period of time as the business brings its existence to a gradual close, JME's interpretation would thus render the first definition a narrow eye of a needle that only few entities can pass through. The better reading of the first definition of a failed business is to see, first, whether the business ceased operations, and, second, whether it set into motion a process to bring its corporate existence to a close by collecting its assets, disposing of its assets, discharging its liabilities, and taking other actions necessary to conclude the business. *See* Fletcher, Corporations § 137:1.

Although the district court correctly concluded that JME "ceased operations" by transferring almost all of its assets to another corporate entity, *see Claimant ID 100262194 v. BP Expl. & Prod., Inc.*, 745 F. App'x 539, 540 (5th Cir. 2018) (observing that a business ceased operations when it merged [—8—] into a new LLC),[2] the district court's order reveals that the district court did not see "wound down" as an additional element under the first definition of a failed business as it failed to analyze whether JME also wound down. Accordingly, the district court's interpretation of the first definition was erroneous.

B.

Next, the district court also misinterpreted the third definition of a failed business. Under the third definition, an entity is considered a failed business if it "otherwise initiated or completed a liquidation of substantially all of its assets, as more fully described in Exhibit 6." Here, JME and BP mainly disagree about the meaning of the word "liquidation." JME argues that "liquidation" as used in the Settlement Agreement means the sale of

assets for the purpose of paying off debts and liabilities. Because it has not sold its assets to pay off its debt, JME contends that it did not "initiate[] or complete[] a liquidation of substantially all of its assets." On the other hand, BP interprets "liquidation" to mean simply disposing of assets. Under BP's interpretation, because JME disposed of its assets by selling them to Gulf Blue, it liquidated substantially all {–931–} of its assets, thus qualifying as a failed business. [—9—]

JME's interpretation is more persuasive given, and more consistent with, the word's common usage and place in the Settlement Agreement. "Under admiralty law, a contract 'should be read as a whole and its words given their plain meaning unless the provision is ambiguous.'" *Holmes Motors, Inc. v. BP Expl. & Prod. Inc.*, 829 F.3d 313, 315, 4 Adm. R. 263, 264 (5th Cir. 2016) (quoting *Breaux v. Halliburton Energy Servs.*, 562 F.3d 358, 364 (5th Cir. 2009)).

As a threshold matter, dictionaries heavily favor JME's interpretation. "Dictionaries . . . are helpful resources in ascertaining a term's generally prevailing meaning." *In re Katrina Canal Breaches Litig.*, 495 F.3d 191, 210 (5th Cir. 2007). Black's Law Dictionary defines "liquidation" as "[t]he act or process of converting assets into cash, *esp. to settle debts*," which is consistent with JME's interpretation. *Liquidation, Black's Law Dictionary* (10th ed. 2010) (emphasis added). The sense divider "esp." (for especially) "denot[es] the most common usage [and] suggests that other usages, although acceptable, might not be common or ordinary." *Taniguchi v. Kan. Pac. Saipan, Ltd.*, 566 U.S. 560, 568 (2012) (holding that the ordinary meaning of "interpreter" is one who orally translates, not one who translates writing). Many other dictionaries also favor JME as they list JME's definition as the primary definition and BP's as the tertiary or quaternary definition. *See* Blue Br. at 28 (cataloguing dictionaries); *see also Liquidation, Merriam-Webster's Collegiate Dictionary* (Deluxe ed. 1998) ("1a. (1) to determine by agreement or by litigation the precise amount of (indebtedness, damages, or

---

[2] BP argues that *Claimant ID 100262194 v. BP Expl. & Prod., Inc.*, 745 F. App'x 539, 540 (5th Cir. 2018), warrants a summary affirmance because the facts are similar and yet we upheld the conclusion that the business that ceased operations was a failed business without inquiring whether it also wound down. One crucial difference that BP forgets is that *Claimant ID 100262194* came to this court after the district court *denied* discretionary review, thus triggering the abuse-of-discretion standard. *See Claimant ID 100212278 v. BP Expl. & Prod., Inc.*, 848 F.3d 407, 410, 5 Adm. R. 202, 203 (5th Cir. 2017) ("It is not an abuse of discretion to deny a request to review that . . . simply raise[s] the correctness of a discretionary administrative decision in the facts of a single claimant's case." (alteration in original) (quoting *In re Deepwater Horizon*, 641 F. App'x 405, 410 (5th Cir. 2016)). Here, the district court *granted* discretionary review, and we are reviewing the district court's interpretation of the Settlement Agreement *de novo*. Thus, *Claimant ID 100262194*, 745 F. App'x at 540, is not dispositive.

account) . . . ; 4. to convert (assets) into cash"). These dictionaries, therefore, suggest that the prevailing meaning of "liquidation" is sale of assets to pay off debts.

Contextual clues also support JME's interpretation in two ways. *Cf.* Scalia & Garner, *Reading Law* at 69 ("Words are to be understood in their ordinary, everyday meanings—unless the context indicates that they bear a [—10—] technical sense."). First, the two preceding definitions of a failed business provide a hint about how to construe the third definition. *See In re Deepwater Horizon*, 745 F.3d 157, 172, 2 Adm. R. 171, 180 (5th Cir. 2014) (applying *noscitur a sociis*—"words grouped in a list should be given related meaning"). The first two definitions define a failed business as one that either ceased operations and wound up or entered bankruptcy. BP's interpretation that a failed business includes any entity that has sold substantially all of its assets for any reason, even if the entity was simply seeking to reinvest its assets elsewhere, does not fit this list neatly. JME's interpretation of "liquidation" fits the two preceding definitions better as it naturally points to an entity that has found it necessary to sell substantially all of its assets to settle its debts although it may not have left the market or entered bankruptcy.

Second, Exhibit 6 shows that the Settlement Agreement generally contemplates "liquidation" in connection with debt. *See Envtl. Def. v. Duke Energy Corp.*, 549 U.S. 561, 574 (2007) (discussing the "natural presumption that identical words used in different parts of the same act are intended to have the same meaning" although context may ultimately dictate when the meanings diverge (quoting *Atl. Cleaners & Dryers, Inc. v. United States*, 286 U.S. 427, 433 (1932))). The third definition defines a failed business as one that "otherwise initiated or completed a liquidation of substantially all of its assets, *as more fully described* {–932–} *in Exhibit 6*." Exhibit 6 requires a claimant to provide an affidavit certifying that "[n]o bankruptcy filing, asset liquidation, or debt restructuring had been initiated" and thus employs the word "liquidation" in connection with debt. If the claimant has not filed for bankruptcy, Exhibit 6 further requires the claimant to provide "documentation reflecting the company's entry into the liquidation process." The claimant must also provide "[e]vidence of any asset sales, . . . and evidence of any [—11—] payments of liquidation proceeds in satisfaction of debt and/or other creditor obligations." Exhibit 6 employs the word "liquidation" in connection with debt, and it should be interpreted consistently throughout the Settlement Agreement. In sum, given the word's generally prevailing meaning, its place in the Settlement Agreement, and its usage throughout Exhibit 6, we hold that an entity must have "initiated or completed a liquidation of substantially all of its assets" to settle its debts to be a failed business under the third definition.

BP argues that this court has already interpreted the word "liquidation" as simply disposing of assets in *In re Deepwater Horizon*, 857 F.3d 247, 250, 5 Adm. R. 246, 247 (5th Cir. 2017) (*Crystal Seafood*). This is not an accurate description of our holding in that case which only opined on fact issues. *See id.*, 5 Adm. R. at 247. *Crystal Seafood* involved BP's motion for claw-back after a claimant had been awarded compensation based on the claimant's misrepresentation that it did not liquidate substantially all of its assets. *Id.* at 249, 5 Adm. R. at 246. It appears that neither BP nor the claimant raised an argument before this court about how the word "liquidation" should be interpreted; instead, the appeal turned on whether the claimant had raised a genuine issue of fact sufficient to survive summary judgment by contradicting its own previous sworn statement. *Id.* at 250, 5 Adm. R. at 247. We held that this was insufficient. *Id.*, 5 Adm. R. at 247. Thus, we reject BP's mischaracterization of our holding in *Crystal Seafood*.

IV.

Because the district court analyzed JME's claims under an erroneous interpretation of the first and third definitions of a failed business, we VACATE and REMAND.

United States Court of Appeals
for the Fifth Circuit

No. 17-20550

LLOYD'S SYNDICATE 457
vs.
FLOATEC, L.L.C.

Appeal from the United States District Court for the
Southern District of Texas

Decided: April 17, 2019

Citation: 921 F.3d 508, 7 Adm. R. 240 (5th Cir. 2019).

Before **SMITH, DUNCAN,** and **ENGELHARDT,** Circuit
Judges.

[—1—] {–510–} **DUNCAN,** Circuit Judge:

This case concerns a disputed siting of Big Foot in the Gulf of Mexico. We refer to a floating oil-drilling platform that rests on four massive columns—hence the name "Big Foot"—moored by steel tendons to the ocean floor. Chevron, which operates and co-owns Big Foot, contracted with FloaTEC to engineer the tendons. During installation in 2015, several tendons failed, causing Chevron huge losses. Big Foot was insured by various Lloyd's of London syndicates (collectively, "Underwriters") through a policy issued to Chevron. To cover the tendon mishap, Underwriters paid Chevron over $500 million and then went looking to recoup that money. Among others, [—2—] Underwriters sued FloaTEC. Underwriters claimed that, having paid Chevron's losses under the policy, they were subrogated to Chevron's right to sue FloaTEC for damages caused by the tendon failures.

Eventually the case landed in federal district court and FloaTEC moved to dismiss. FloaTEC argued that it qualified as an "Other Assured" under Underwriters' policy and that the policy waives subrogation against "Other Assureds"—hence Underwriters' subrogation-based claims {–511–} should fail. Underwriters responded in two ways. First, they argued that the subrogation issue should be decided by an arbitrator, not the district court, by virtue of the broad arbitration clause in Chevron's contract with FloaTEC. Second,

Underwriters argued that, in any event, FloaTEC was not an "Other Assured" under a proper reading of the policy.

The district court sided with FloaTEC on both points. It decided the arbitration clause did not apply because Underwriters were not a party to the Chevron/FloaTEC contract. It then decided FloaTEC did qualify as an "Other Assured" under the policy, thus enabling FloaTEC to raise the subrogation waiver. The court dismissed Underwriters' claims with prejudice.

Underwriters appeal both issues. We affirm.

I.

A.

Big Foot is a major deepwater oil drilling project in the Gulf of Mexico off the Louisiana coast. It is located on the Outer Continental Shelf in the Walker Ridge Area, Block 29, about 225 miles south of New Orleans. The project is operated by Chevron, which co-owns it with Statoil Gulf of Mexico LLC and Marubeni Oil & Gas (USA) Inc. As part of the project, in 2015, Chevron began to build and install an "extended tension-leg platform" that would be anchored to the seafloor almost a mile below. This is a photo of the platform in transit to Walker Ridge: [—3—]

The platform would be kept stationary by sixteen steel tendons attached to pilings driven into the seafloor. These tendons were critical to the floating platform's stability.

Chevron contracted with FloaTEC to provide engineering services in connection with Big Foot, including the design and installation of the tendons. We will refer to the Chevron/FloaTEC agreement as the "Chevron/FloaTEC Contract" or simply the "Contract." The Contract required FloaTEC to maintain specific kinds of insurance related to the performance {–512–} of its duties on the project. The Contract also included a broad arbitration clause, empowering a chosen arbitrator or arbitrators to "rule on objections concerning jurisdiction, including the existence or validity of this arbitration clause and existence or the validity of this Contract[.]"

Big Foot was insured by Underwriters through an Offshore Construction Project Policy with Chevron. We will refer to this Underwriters/Chevron agreement as the "Underwriters/Chevron Policy" or [—4—] simply as the "Policy." The Policy was written on a "WELCAR 2001" form, a standard construction risk policy developed for the offshore energy market at Lloyd's in the late 1990s. *See, e.g.,* Tim Taylor, *Offshore Energy Construction Insurance: Allocation of Risk Issues*, 87 TUL. L. REV. 1165, 1170 (2013) ("Taylor"). Risks covered by the Policy included physical loss or damage to Big Foot incurred during the project's design and engineering. The Policy included a clause stating that Underwriters agreed to "waive rights of subrogation" against any "Principal Assureds" or "Other Assureds." "Other Assureds" were defined in a separate section of the Policy to include "[a]ny" other companies with whom Chevron had "entered into written contract(s) in connection with the [Big Foot] Project."

In mid-2015, before the platform's stabilizing tendons had been installed, nine of the sixteen tendons detached from their supporting buoys and plummeted to the seafloor. An investigation revealed that the bolts holding the tendons to the buoys had come loose. Chevron rejected the remaining seven tendons and had them sent back to shore. The failure of the tendons and the resulting delay to Big Foot caused Chevron huge losses. As a result, Underwriters paid Chevron over $500 million under the Policy.

B.

Seeking to recoup those payments, Underwriters filed a lawsuit in a Texas state court in May 2016, naming as defendants various contractors connected to Big Foot, including FloaTEC. Underwriters alleged FloaTEC had negligently designed and manufactured the tendons and attachment bolts and had therefore caused the damages to Big Foot. Prior to service of process, claims against all defendants except FloaTEC were dropped. FloaTEC removed the case to federal court.

Underwriters then filed an amended complaint, adding the claim that FloaTEC breached its contract with Chevron. Underwriters' claims against [—5—] FloaTEC were all based on subrogation—meaning Underwriters sought to stand in Chevron's shoes by virtue of having paid Chevron's losses under the Policy. *See* LA. CIV. CODE art. 1825 (subrogation is "the substitution of one person to the rights of another" and "may be conventional or legal"); *id.* art. 1827 ("conventional" subrogation occurs when "[a]n obligee who receives performance from a third person . . . subrogate[s] that person to the rights of the obligee, even without the obligor's consent"); *see also, e.g., Old Repub. Life Ins. Co. v. Transwood, Inc.*, 2016-0552 (La. App. 1 Cir. 6/2/17); 222 So.3d 995, 1005 (explaining that, "[u]nder Louisiana law, although an insurer which pays claims on behalf of an insured is not entitled to legal subrogation, it may still be entitled to conventional subrogation if appropriately provided in the contract of insurance") (citing *Watters v. State Dep't of Transp. & Devel.*, 33,870 (La. App. 2 Cir. 9/27/00); 768 So.2d 733, 737).

FloaTEC moved to dismiss for failure to state a claim and, alternatively, to compel arbitration if the court found Underwriters had stated a claim. FloaTEC's argument for dismissal hinged on three clauses in {–513–} the Underwriters/Chevron Policy. The first clause, entitled "Subrogation," states:

Underwriters shall be subrogated to all rights which the Assured may have against any person or other entity, *other than Principal Assureds and Other Assureds*, in respect of any claim or payment made under the Policy (emphasis added).

The second clause, entitled "Waiver of Subrogation," states:

Underwriters agree to waive rights of subrogation against any Principal Assured(s) and/or *Other Assured*(s) including drilling contractors and/or their sub-contractors (emphasis added).

Finally, the third clause defines "Other Assureds" to include:

[a]ny other company, firm, person, or party . . . with whom [various entities including Chevron] have entered into written contract(s) in connection with the [Big Foot] Project." [—6—]

FloaTEC argued that it qualified as an "Other Assured" and that Underwriters' claims were therefore barred by the Policy's subrogation waiver. Underwriters opposed FloaTEC's motion, arguing (1) FloaTEC was not an "Other Assured" under the Policy, and (2) FloaTEC had waived any right to arbitration by moving to dismiss.

The district court agreed with FloaTEC that it was an "Other Assured" under the Policy and that Underwriters' claims were thus barred by the subrogation waiver. The court therefore dismissed Underwriters' claims with prejudice for failure to state a claim.[1] Underwriters appeal.

---

[1] In the order dismissing FloaTEC, the district court also denied a motion to dismiss or to compel arbitration filed by another defendant, American Global Maritime, Inc., which had been added by Underwriters' amended complaint. The court subsequently granted Underwriters' motion for partial final judgment under Federal Rule of Civil Procedure 54(b), allowing Underwriters to appeal the dismissal of its claims against FloaTEC. *See, e.g., Johnson v. Ocwen Loan Servicing, LLC*, 916 F.3d 505, 507 (5th Cir. 2019).

II.

We review *de novo* a dismissal for failure to state a claim, asking whether the plaintiff "fail[ed] to allege any set of facts in support of his claim which would entitle him to relief." *Taylor v. Books A Million, Inc.*, 296 F.3d 376, 378 (5th Cir. 2002). We also review *de novo* a district court's interpretation of a contract. *Greenwood 950, LLC v. Chesapeake Louisiana, LP*, 683 F.3d 666, 668 (5th Cir. 2012); *Steel Warehouse Co. v. Abalone Shipping Ltd. of Nicosai*, 141 F.3d 234, 236–37 (5th Cir. 1998).

III.

Underwriters' appeal requires us to consider two related issues. First, we must decide whether the district court improperly disregarded the arbitration clause in the Chevron/FloaTEC Contract when it ruled, as an initial matter, on FloaTEC's motion to dismiss. If we decide that the district court properly considered FloaTEC's motion to dismiss before any arbitrability [—7—] issue, then, second, we must decide whether the court's ruling on the motion to dismiss was correct. We consider each issue in turn.

A.

Underwriters argue that the Contract's delegation clause required the district court to send their claims to arbitration instead of ruling on FloaTEC's motion to dismiss. That clause, Underwriters assert, "clearly and unmistakably" delegates to the arbitrator all "gateway arbitrability issues," including whether the Policy's subrogation {–514–} waiver bars their claims. *See, e.g., Petrofac, Inc. v. DynMcDermott Petroleum Oper. Co.*, 687 F.3d 671, 675 (5th Cir. 2012) (parties must "'clearly and unmistakably provide'" that they have agreed to "arbitrate arbitrability") (quoting *AT&T Techs., Inc. v. Commc'ns Workers of Am.*, 475 U.S. 643, 649 (1986)).[2]

---

[2] As already explained, the delegation clause provides that "[t]he . . . arbitrators have the power to rule on objections concerning jurisdiction, including the existence or validity of this Contract." Given our resolution of this issue, we need not determine whether Underwriters are correct that

According to Underwriters, the clause prohibited the court from ruling on FloaTEC's motion to dismiss because "a valid delegation clause requires the court to refer a claim to arbitration to allow the arbitrator to decide gateway arbitrability issues." *Kubala v. Supreme Prod. Servs., Inc.*, 830 F.3d 199 (5th Cir. 2016) (citing *Rent-A-Ctr., W., Inc. v. Jackson*, 561 U.S. 63, 68–69 (2010)). By ruling on that motion, say Underwriters, the court let FloaTEC "game the system"—that is, "seek[ ] a decision on the merits while keeping the arbitration option as a backup plan in case the effort fails." *In re Mirant*, 613 F.3d 584, 590 (5th Cir. 2010).

Underwriters misread our precedent. To assess whether a claim must be arbitrated, we follow a two-step analysis. At step one, "the court must **[—8—]** determine 'whether the parties entered into *any arbitration agreement at all.*'" *IQ Prod. Co. v. WD-40 Co.*, 871 F.3d 344, 348 (5th Cir. 2017) (quoting *Kubala*, 830 F.3d at 201). "This first step is a question of contract formation only—did the parties form a valid agreement to arbitrate some set of claims." *Id.* (citing *Kubala*, 830 F.3d at 201–02). This inquiry is for the court: "Where the very existence of any [arbitration] agreement is disputed, it is for the *courts* to decide at the outset whether an agreement was reached[.]" *Will-Drill Res., Inc. v. Samson Res. Co.*, 352 F.3d 211, 218 (5th Cir. 2003) (emphasis added); *see also, e.g., DK Joint Venture 1 v. Weyand*, 649 F.3d 310, 317 (5th Cir. 2011) ("[It] is for the courts and not the arbitrator to decide in the first instance . . . whether the parties entered into an arbitration agreement in the first place."). Only if we answer "yes" at the first step do we proceed to the second. At step two, we engage in a "limited" inquiry: "[W]hether the [parties'] agreement contains a valid delegation clause." *IQ Prod.*, 871 F.3d at 348 (citing *Kubala*, 830 F.3d at 202). We ask only whether there is "'clear and unmistakable' evidence" that the parties

the clause "clearly and unmistakably" delegates arbitrability to the arbitrator. *Cf., e.g., Petrofac*, 687 F.3d at 675 (explaining that "the express adoption of [American Arbitration Association] rules presents clear and unmistakable evidence that the parties agreed to arbitrate arbitrability").

intended to arbitrate. *Id.*[3] If so, a "motion to compel arbitration should be granted in almost all cases." *Id.* (quoting *Kubala*, 830 F.3d at 202). **{–515–}**

Underwriters skip the first step of the analysis. They would compel arbitration of their claims against FloaTEC based on the Contract's delegation clause. But that is step two. Underwriters must first contend with the step one **[—9—]** question, which is whether they "form[ed] a valid [arbitration] agreement" with FloaTEC to begin with. *IQ Prod.*, 871 F.3d at 348. FloaTEC denies this strenuously: It points out that Underwriters are not parties to the Contract and, moreover, that the only agreement Underwriters are parties to (the Underwriters/Chevron Policy) bars subrogation against "Other Assureds" like FloaTEC. *See infra* III.B. Hence FloaTEC moved to dismiss Underwriters' claims, which are based entirely on subrogation.

The district court correctly treated this subrogation issue as a step one inquiry because it goes to whether any arbitration agreement exists between Underwriters and FloaTEC. If the Policy bars Underwriters from stepping into Chevron's shoes and benefitting from the Contract's delegation clause, then Underwriters and FloaTEC never "entered into *any arbitration agreement at all.*" *IQ Prod.*, 871 F.3d 344, 348. We have consistently treated attacks on an arbitration agreement's existence as step one matters for courts, not arbitrators. *See, e.g., Will-Drill*, 352 F.3d at 216 & nn. 26–28 (treating as a step one

---

[3] Along with other circuits, we previously recognized a narrow exception to this rule when "a claim of arbitrability is 'wholly groundless.'" *IQ Prod.*, 871 F.3d at 349 (quoting *InterDigital Commc'ns, LLC v. Int'l Trade Comm'n*, 718 F.3d 1336, 1346–47 (Fed. Cir. 2013), *vacated as moot by LG Electronics, Inc. v. InterDigital Commc'ns, LLC*, 572 U.S. 1056 (2014)). This "wholly groundless" exception was recently abrogated by the Supreme Court in *Henry Schein, Inc. v. Archer & White Sales, Inc.*, 139 S. Ct. 524 (2019). That development leaves intact the remainder of our two-part framework for assessing a claim's arbitrability. More to the point, *Schein*'s abrogation of the wholly groundless exception has no impact on this case since it altered step two of our framework, and here we apply only step one.

inquiry cases where "the parties resisting arbitration attack the existence of the entire agreement, not the arbitration clause specifically"). For example, we have followed sister circuit cases that "refus[ed] to order arbitration of disputes where one party claims that it is not bound by the arbitration agreement . . . because it was not an original party to the agreement." *Id.* at 216 (discussing *Chastain v. Robinson-Humphrey Co.*, 957 F.2d 851 (11th Cir. 1992); *Joseph Co. v. Mich. Sugar Co.*, 803 F.2d 396 (8th Cir. 1986)). The subrogation issue here falls into the same category: FloaTEC argues that the Policy's subrogation bar means Underwriters cannot step into the Chevron/FloaTEC Contract containing the arbitration agreement. By deciding FloaTEC's motion to dismiss at the outset, the district court properly resolved [—10—] that contract-formation issue, which is "for the courts and not the arbitrator to decide in the first instance." *DK Joint Venture 1*, 649 F.3d at 317.[4]

Underwriters cannot avoid this outcome by calling the subrogation issue a "merits-based affirmative defense" to its claims against FloaTEC. That again ignores that we have two contracts here, not one. If we were dealing with a disagreement between Chevron and FloaTEC concerning FloaTEC's engineering of Big Foot's tendons, we might have a "merits-based" issue that would presumably have to be arbitrated under the Contract. We have nothing like that here, however. FloaTEC

argues Underwriters were not parties to the Contract *at all* and so could not invoke the Contract's delegation provision in the first place. This is not a dispute about the "merits" {-516-} of Underwriters' claims; it is "a simpler type of dispute which, we have held, is for the courts and not the arbitrator to decide in the first instance: a dispute over whether the parties entered into any arbitration agreement in the first place." *Id.*[5] [—11—]

For the same reason, Underwriters are wrong that FloaTEC "gamed the system by asking the district court to first determine the merits" and, if that failed, asking "to send the case to mandatory arbitration" for a second bite at the apple. As explained, FloaTEC's motion to dismiss did not ask the court to "determine the merits" of Underwriters' claims; it asked the court to rule that Underwriters could not be subrogated to Chevron's rights. And FloaTEC asked for arbitration *only if* the court ruled that Underwriters *were* subrogated to Chevron's rights. By making these alternative requests, FloaTEC was not "gaming the system"—it was covering its bases. *Cf. Mirant*, 613 F.3d at 590–91 (a party "game[d] the system" when it "did not initially present its motion to compel arbitration . . . as an alternative to its motion to dismiss," but instead litigated the merits extensively before moving to compel arbitration).

---

[4] The parties submitted post-argument briefs addressing the impact, if any, of the Supreme Court's recent decisions in *Schein*, 139 S. Ct. 524, and *New Prime, Inc. v. Oliveira*, 139 S. Ct. 532 (2019). Neither decision bears on the issues before us. *Schein* simply rejected the "wholly groundless" exception to arbitrability delegations. 139 S. Ct. at 529. It did not change—to the contrary, it reaffirmed—the rule that courts must first decide whether an arbitration agreement exists at all. *See id.* at 530 ("To be sure, before referring a dispute to an arbitrator, the court determines whether a valid arbitration agreement exists."). Similarly, *Oliveira* decided only that "a court should decide for itself whether [the Federal Arbitration Act's] 'contracts of employment' exclusion applies before ordering arbitration," 139 S. Ct. at 537, but said nothing about how a court should determine whether any arbitration agreement exists to begin with.

[5] Underwriters urge that arbitration is "strongly favored" and should be granted unless the pertinent arbitration clause is "not susceptible of an interpretation" that would cover the dispute. *See, e.g., Sedco, Inc. v. Petroleos Mexicanos Mexican Nat. Oil Co. (Pemex)*, 767 F.2d 1140, 1145 (5th Cir. 1985), *as modified by Freudensprung v. Offshore Tech. Servs., Inc.*, 379 F.3d 327 (5th Cir. 2004). We do not question those principles, but they have no bearing here. We are not interpreting an arbitration clause; we are deciding whether an arbitration clause exists between the relevant parties. The "strong federal policy favoring arbitration," we have held, "'does not apply to the determination of whether there is a valid agreement to arbitrate between the parties.'" *Will-Drill*, 352 F.3d at 214 (quoting *Fleetwood Enters. Inc. v. Gaskamp*, 280 F.3d 1069, 1073 (5th Cir. 2002)).

In sum, we conclude the district court correctly ruled on FloaTEC's motion to dismiss before addressing any issue concerning the arbitrability of Underwriters' claims.[6]

B.

We turn to Underwriters' argument that the district court erred by dismissing its claims against FloaTEC. The district court reasoned that FloaTEC qualified as an "Other Assured," as defined in the Policy, because FloaTEC "entered into a written contract" with Chevron "in connection with the [Big Foot project]." The court therefore concluded that Underwriters' subrogated claims were barred, because in the Policy Underwriters "agree[d] to waive rights of subrogation against any . . . Other Assured(s)." [—12—]

On appeal, Underwriters contend the district court misread the Policy. They focus, not on the definition of "Other Assured," but on a distinct clause entitled "Special Conditions for Other Assureds," which provides as follows (we present the three sentences of the clause separately for easier reading):

[1] The interest of the Other Assured(s) shall be covered throughout the entire Policy Period for their direct participation in the venture, unless specific contract(s) contain provisions to the contrary.

[2] The rights of any Assured under this insurance shall only be exercised through the Principal Assureds.

[3] Where the benefits of this insurance have been passed to an Assured by contract, {—517—} the benefits passed to that Assured shall be no greater than such contract allows and in no case greater than the benefits provided under the insuring agree-

ments, terms[,] conditions[,] and exclusions in the Policy (brackets added).

The definition of "Other Assured," argue Underwriters, must be read in light of these Special Conditions. Specifically, they say the clause's first and third sentences require consulting the Chevron/FloaTEC Contract to see whether Chevron is obligated to provide insurance coverage to FloaTEC under the Policy. If not, Underwriters argue that FloaTEC cannot qualify as an "Other Assured" and so cannot invoke the Policy's subrogation waiver. Moreover, Underwriters contend that by defining "Other Assured" in isolation, the district court rendered the Special Conditions clause meaningless. They argue that, "[i]f possession of a written contract [with Chevron] alone was sufficient to qualify for full coverage under the [Policy], there would be no need for the Special Conditions provision."

To resolve this issue, we apply Louisiana law[7] governing contract interpretation. *See generally* LA. CIV. CODE, bk. III, tit. IV, ch. 13; *id.* arts. [—13—] 2045–2057; *see also, e.g., In re Katrina Canal Breaches Litig.*, 495 F.3d 191, 206–08 (5th Cir. 2007) (discussing Louisiana law principles for interpreting insurance contracts). Under Louisiana law, "[t]he role of the judiciary in interpreting insurance contracts is to ascertain the common intent of the insured and insurer as reflected by the words in the policy." *Peterson v. Schimek*, 98-1712 (La. 3/2/99); 729 So. 2d 1024, 1028; *see also* LA. CIV. CODE art. 2045 (contractual interpretation is "the determination of the common intent of the parties"). "Words and phrases used in an insurance policy are to be construed using

---

[6] Given our resolution of this threshold issue, we need not consider FloaTEC's alternative argument that Underwriters waived their right to argue for arbitration now by opposing arbitration below.

[7] As the district court correctly found, Louisiana law applies under the Outer Continental Shelf Lands Act. *See* 43 U.S.C. § 1333(a). Congress has "adopt[ed] as surrogate [—13—] federal law the 'civil and criminal laws of each adjacent State'" to govern disputes on the Outer Continental Shelf. *Petrobras Am., Inc. v. Vicinay Cadenas, S.A.*, 815 F.3d 211, 215, 4 Adm. R. 199, 200 (5th Cir.), *order clarified on reh'g*, 829 F.3d 770 (5th Cir. 2016) (quoting 43 U.S.C. § 1333(a)(2)(A)). Parties cannot alter this rule by choosing another state's law in their contract. *Id.*, 4 Adm. R. at 200–01.

their plain, ordinary and generally prevailing meaning, unless the words have acquired a technical meaning." *Cadwallader v. Allstate Ins. Co.*, 2002-1637 (La. 6/27/03); 848 So. 2d 577, 580 (citing La. Civ. Code art. 2047). Insurance policies should be construed holistically, meaning that "one policy provision is not to be construed separately at the expense of disregarding other policy provisions." *Louisiana Ins. Guar. Ass'n v. Interstate Fire & Cas. Co.*, 93-0911 (La. 1/14/94); 630 So. 2d 759, 763; *see also* La. Civ. Code art. 2050 (contractual provisions must be interpreted "in light of the other provisions" to give each "the meaning suggested by the contract as a whole"). "The rules of construction do not authorize . . . the exercise of inventive powers to create an ambiguity where none exists or the making of a new contract when the terms express with sufficient clearness the parties' intent." *Cadwallader*, 848 So. 2d at 580; *see also* La. Civ. Code art. 2046 (when words are "clear and explicit and lead to no absurd consequences, no further interpretation may be made in search of the parties' intent"). On the other hand, "[i]f after applying the other general rules of construction an ambiguity remains, the ambiguous contractual [—14—] provision is to be construed against the drafter, or, as originating in the insurance context, in favor of the insured." *Louisiana Ins. Guar. Ass'n*, 630 So. 2d at 764; *see also* {–518–} *Katrina Canal Breaches Litig.*, 495 F.3d at 207 (same). Under this "rule of strict construction," ambiguous clauses are "construed against the insurer and in favor of coverage" and "equivocal provisions seeking to narrow an insurer's obligation are strictly construed against the insurer." *Bonin v. Westport Ins. Corp.*, 2005-0886 (La. 5/17/06); 930 So.2d 906, 911 (citations omitted).

Applying these principles to the insurance contract at issue, we reject Underwriters' arguments that the district court misread its terms. To the contrary, the court correctly found FloaTEC to be an "Other Assured" under the Policy and thus correctly concluded that Underwriters' claims against FloaTEC are barred by the Policy's subrogation waiver.

First, the "plain . . . meaning" of the Policy qualifies FloaTEC as an "Other Assured." *Cadwallader*, 848 So. 2d at 580. It is uncontested that FloaTEC contracted with Chevron to provide engineering services for Big Foot. This makes FloaTEC an "Other Assured" under the Policy's text because it "entered into [a] written contract[]" with Chevron "in connection with the [Big Foot] project." The Policy places no additional conditions on the status of an "Other Assured." *See, e.g., AGIP Petroleum Co., Inc. v. Gulf Island Fabrication, Inc.*, 920 F. Supp. 1318, 1325–26 (S.D. Tex. 1996) (construing materially identical definition of "other assured" and concluding this "clear and unambiguous language . . . [was] intended to include contractors . . . who entered into agreements with [the principal Assured] concerning the [project]"). FloaTEC therefore qualifies under the Policy as an "Other Assured" against whom Underwriters "agree[d] to waive rights of subrogation," as the district court correctly found. No further analysis was required in the face of that plain language. *See* La. Civ. Code art. 2046 ("no further interpretation [—15—] may be made in search of the parties' intent" when a contract's words are "clear and explicit and lead to no absurd consequences").

Tellingly, Underwriters' arguments are not directed to the text of the "Other Assured" definition or the subrogation waiver. Instead, they rely on cases allegedly standing for the proposition that an "Other Assured" must be entitled to insurance coverage from a Principal Assured. *See, e.g., WH Holdings, LLC v. Ace Am. Ins. Co.*, 481 F. App'x 894 (5th Cir. 2012); *Edwards v. Brambles Equip. Servs., Inc.*, 75 F. App'x 929 (5th Cir. 2003). But "[n]one of th[ose] cases," the district court cogently observed, "supports a general proposition that, always and everywhere, Other Assured status is determined by reference to the contract between a Principal Assured and a putative Other Assured." To the contrary, in those cases the issue turned—as it does here—on the specific policy definition in play.

The policies in Underwriters' cases limit an "insured" to entities a principal is obligated to insure. *See WH Holdings,* 481 F. App'x at 895 (defining "insured" to include "any party in interest *which the insured is responsible to insure*"); *Edwards,* 75 F. App'x at 932 (involving a policy that "extend[ed] coverage to 'any person or organization you [the main policyholder] are *required by written contract to include as an insured*'") (emphases added). Here, the pertinent definition is materially different: "Other Assured" means an entity with whom a principal Assured has "entered into written contract(s) in connection with the [Big Foot] Project." That definition does not require that the principal Assured *also* be obligated to provide coverage to the entity, and we cannot blue-pencil that extra clause into the Contract. "[I]t is too obvious for argument that courts will not add words to a contract for the purpose of {–519–} ascertaining the true intent of the parties." *Ross v. Zuntz,* 36 La. Ann. 888, 894 (La. 1884); *see also Sims v. Mulhearn Funeral Home, Inc.,* 2007-0054 (La. 5/22/07); 956 So. 2d 583, 589 (explaining "[c]ourts lack the authority to alter [—16—] the terms of insurance contracts under the guise of contractual interpretation when the policy's provisions are couched in unambiguous terms").

Second, we disagree with Underwriters that the Special Conditions clause somehow alters or qualifies the Policy's otherwise unambiguous definition of "Other Assured." Nothing in the Special Conditions clause purports to modify that definition. To the contrary, the clause assumes that its conditions apply only to entities that already *are* "Other Assureds." Nor does the clause purport to modify the Policy's subrogation waiver, which unambiguously "waive[s] rights of subrogation against . . . Other Assured[s]." Reading the Special Conditions clause to strip an otherwise-qualified entity of "Other Assured" status, as Underwriters urge us to do, would be an impermissible "exercise of inventive powers to create an ambiguity where none exists." *Cadwallader,* 848 So. 2d at 580. We lack authority to do that. *See* LA. CIV. CODE art. 2046; *Sims,* 956 So. 2d at 589.

Even if we possessed that revisionary authority—and could pretend the Special Conditions clause somehow modifies the definition of "Other Assured"—that would not help Underwriters. We would then be left with an insurance contract ambiguous on what constitutes an "Other Assured," and ambiguous on how the subrogation waiver applies. But it is bedrock law that ambiguous insurance provisions are read *against* the insurer and in favor of coverage. *LeBlanc v. Aysenne,* 2005-0297 (La. 1/19/06); 921 So.2d 85, 89 (explaining "[i]f there is an ambiguity in a[n] [insurance] policy, then that ambiguity should be construed in favor of the insured and against the insurer") (citing *Pareti v. Sentry Indemnity Co.,* 536 So.2d 417, 420 (La. 1988); *accord Bonin,* 930 So.2d at 911; *Carrier v. Reliance Ins. Co.,* 1999-2573 (La. 4/11/00); 759 So. 2d 37, 43; *Louisiana Ins. Guar. Ass'n,* 630 So. 2d at 764. Moreover, when "subrogation is disputed," then the intent to subrogate "must be shown by clear proof . . . that unquestionably implies it." *A. Copeland Enter., Inc. v.* [—17—] *Slidell Mem'l Hosp.,* 94-2011 (La. 6/30/95); 657 So.2d 1292, 1298 (citing 5 LA. CIV. L. TREATISE, LAW OF OBLIGATIONS § 11.22 (1992)). Far from "clear proof" of an intent to subrogate, here the Policy's plain text shows intent to *bar* subrogation against a putative "Other Assured" like FloaTEC and does not even hint that the Special Conditions clause tempers that bar.

If there were any doubt on this point, the record shows that Underwriters and Chevron knew exactly how to limit "Other Assured" status in the Policy. The parties struck through a provision in the Special Conditions section that made conformity with certain "Quality Assurance/Quality Control system(s)" a *"condition precedent . . . to benefit from the Other Assureds status"* (emphasis added).[8] If

---

[8] The stricken clause appears in the record as follows:

~~It is a condition precedent for any party identified in Other Assureds definition clause iii. and iv. above to benefit from the Other Assureds status under the Policy that they perform their operations according to Quality Assurance/Quality Control system(s) which comply with the Quality Assurance/Quality Control provisions passed on by the Principal Assureds through each and every written contract awarded within the~~

Underwriters {–520–} and Chevron wanted to impose a similar condition precedent for required Policy coverage (or anything else), a template was thus readily available: The parties could have inserted a provision making Chevron's obligation to extend Policy coverage a "condition precedent" to an entity's ability to benefit from "Other Assured" status or from the subrogation waiver. They did not, and we cannot do it for them.

We also reject Underwriters' argument that allowing FloaTEC to benefit from the subrogation waiver as an "Other Assured" renders the Special Conditions clause "meaningless." To be sure, we must read an insurance [—18—] contract to give every provision meaning. LA. CIV. CODE art. 2050; *see, e.g., Arias-Benn v. State Farm Fire & Cas. Ins. Co.*, 495 F.3d 228, 231 (5th Cir. 2007) (under Louisiana law, "[a]n insurance contract is to be construed as a whole"). But, even on the district court's straightforward reading of "Other Assured" (requiring an "Other Assured" only to have a Big Foot contract with Chevron), the Special Conditions clause would still play a role in the parties' contractual relationships. For instance, the first sentence of the Special Conditions clause permits Chevron to limit a contractor's Policy coverage through a "provision" in a "specific contract." Suppose Chevron did that in its contract with FloaTEC (as appears to be the case)[9]: That

---

~~scope of insured works as scheduled under the Policy.~~

See, e.g., Taylor, *supra,* at 1181 (explaining that this provision, which was "designed to limit access to the policy for contractors" who failed to comply with agreed quality control procedures, "has not been a popular clause and is now frequently deleted"). The parties also struck a similar clause from the Policy's subrogation waiver. That clause would have made conformity with the same quality control provisions a "condition precedent to [Other Assureds] benefiting from the [Policy's] automatic waiver of subrogation."

[9] As the district court explained, the Chevron/FloaTEC Contract requires FloaTEC to maintain specific insurance covering certain project risks, such as workers' compensation and employer's liability insurance, commercial general liability insurance, and automobile, watercraft, and aircraft insurance. The Contract further provides

---

limitation might come into play should *FloaTEC* seek affirmative recovery under the Policy *against Underwriters* (which, of course, is not the scenario we have here). The second Special Conditions sentence would also play a role in this scenario: FloaTEC would have to "exercise[ ]" whatever "rights" it has under the Policy "through the Principal Assureds," like Chevron. And the third Special Conditions sentence would insure that any recovery FloaTEC sought under the Policy "shall be no greater than such contract [with Chevron] allows." {–521–}

This reading harmonizes the "Other Assured" definition and the Special Conditions clause. The definition concerns a party's *status* as an "Other Assured," whereas the clause concerns the *extent* to which an "Other Assured" [—19—] may claim Policy coverage. By arguing that a party has "Other Assured" status only insofar as it has coverage, Underwriters conflate status and extent of coverage. But the Policy does not. As the district court cogently explained, "the Policy definition of an Other Assured . . . plainly does not require the contract between [Chevron] and [FloaTEC] to address the subject of insurance[.]" Moreover, under the rules of contract interpretation, we should avoid an interpretation of the Special Conditions clause that overrides the plain language of the "Other Assured" definition. *See, e.g., Clovelly Oil Co., LLC v. Midstates Petroleum Co., LLC*, 2012-2055 (La. 3/19/13); 112 So.3d 187, 195 (courts should "interpret contract provisions 'so as to avoid neutralizing or ignoring any of them or treating them as surplusage'") (quoting *John Bailey Contractor, Inc. v. State Dept. of Transp. & Devel.*, 439 So.2d 1055,

---

that, to the extent of FloaTEC's liabilities, this required insurance "is primary with respect to all insureds . . . and that no other insurance carried by [Chevron] will be considered as contributory insurance for any loss." We need not decide to what extent these provisions limit FloaTEC's interests under the Policy because, as explained, FloaTEC is not seeking recovery under the Policy. Rather, it is seeking only to raise the subrogation waiver against Underwriters' claims. It is enough to say, with the district court, that these insurance requirements in the Chevron/FloaTEC Contract "have nothing to do with [FloaTEC's] Other Assured status" under the Policy.

1058 (La. 1983)) (citing LA. CIV. CODE art. 2050).

Finally, another reason for rejecting Underwriters' counter-textual reading of the Policy (and for accepting the district court's textual reading) is that Underwriters' reading collides with the "anti-subrogation" rule. Under this "fundamental principle of insurance law[,]" "[a]n insurer cannot by way of subrogation recover against its insured *or an additional assured* any part of its payment for a risk covered by the policy." *Peavey v. M/V ANPA*, 971 F.2d 1168, 1177 (5th Cir. 1992) (citing, *inter alia, Dow Chemical Co. v. M/V Roberta Taylor*, 815 F.2d 1037, 1043 (5th Cir. 1987)) (emphasis added).[10] Importantly, the rule applies even when the additional assured is not covered under the [—20—] policy for the specific risk at issue. *See, e.g., Dow Chemical Co.*, 815 F.2d at 1044–45 (discussing *Marathon Oil Co. v. Mid-Continent Underwriters*, 786 F.2d 1301, 1302 (5th Cir. 1986); *Wiley v. Offshore Painting Contractors, Inc.*, 711 F.2d 602 (5th Cir.), *on reh'g*, 716 F.2d 256 (5th Cir. 1983)). Our key decision is *Marathon Oil*, in which Judge Rubin explained:

> [W]hen underwriters issue a policy covering an additional assured and waiving 'all subrogation' rights against it, they cannot recoup from the additional assured any portion of the sums they have paid to settle a risk covered by the policy, *even on the theory that the recoupment is based on the additional assured's exposure for risks not covered by the policy.*

---

[10] *See also, e.g., Shelter Mut. Ins. Co. v. State Farm Mut. Auto. Ins. Co.*, 2007-0163 (La. App. 1 Cir. 7/18/08); 993 So.2d 236, 240 (observing "[i]t is well settled [under Louisiana law] that an insurer cannot be subrogated against its own insured") (citations omitted); 16 COUCH ON INS. § 224:12 ("Pursuant to the antisubrogation rule, an insurer is not entitled to subrogation against persons or entities named in the policy as insureds, *or who are additional insureds under the terms of the policy.*") (citing, *inter alia, Olinkraft, Inc. v. Anco Insulation, Inc.*, 376 So.2d 1301 (La. App. 2 Cir. 1979) (emphasis added).

786 F.2d at 1302 (emphasis added); *see also AGIP*, 920 F. Supp. at 1329 (*Marathon Oil* "determined . . . that waiver of subrogation is not co-extensive with, but is broader than, coverage under the insurance policy"); *and see, e.g., Lanasse v. Travelers Ins. Co.*, 450 F.2d 580 (5th Cir. 1971) (op. of Brown, C.J.) (underwriters could not recover against additional assured "in the face of the explicit policy provision waiving subrogation" even though the "additional assured . . . cannot claim the affirmative benefit of the [policy] coverage"). {–522–}

Underwriters' awkward yoking of "Other Assured" status to the Special Conditions clause would bring their suit perilously close to the anti-subrogation danger zone. Recall Underwriters' theory: Despite the Policy definition, they say FloaTEC is not an "Other Assured" (and thus can be sued via subrogation) solely because the Contract withholds full Policy coverage from FloaTEC. This is precisely the forbidden scenario laid out in Judge Rubin's *Marathon Oil* opinion: (1) Underwriters would "recoup from [an] additional assured [*i.e.*, FloaTEC] sums they have paid to settle a risk covered by the policy"; (2) the Policy "waiv[es] . . . subrogation" against an "additional assured"; and (3) Underwriters rely "on the theory that the recoupment is based on [FloaTEC's] exposure for risks not covered by the [P]olicy." *Marathon* [—21—] *Oil*, 786 F.2d at 1302 (brackets added). Thus FloaTEC, understandably, urges us to rule that the anti-subrogation principle bars Underwriters' suit as a matter of public policy. *See, e.g., Peavey*, 971 F.2d at 1177 (describing anti-subrogation rule as based on "public policy"). But we need not go that far. It is enough to say that avoiding conflict with the anti-subrogation rule provides yet another reason—over and above the textual and contextual reasons already discussed—to give the Policy definition of "Other Assured" the straightforward reading the district court did. *See, e.g., In re Katrina Canal Breaches Litig.*, 2010-1823 (La. 5/10/11); 63 So.3d 955, 963 (assessing whether certain insurance provisions "violate public policy"); *Peterson*, 729 So.2d at 1031 (explaining that insurance contracts should be construed to "give[ ] effect to the long-standing public policy of this State").

IV.

To sum up, we conclude that the district court properly ruled on FloaTEC's motion to dismiss Underwriters' claims before considering arbitrability. We also conclude that the district court correctly found FloaTEC was an "Other Assured" under the Policy and could thus invoke the subrogation waiver. We therefore affirm the district court's judgment dismissing Underwriters' claims with prejudice.

AFFIRMED.

United States Court of Appeals
for the Fifth Circuit

No. 18-30008

GRAHAM
VS.
BP EXPLORATION & PROD., INC.

Appeal from the United States District Court for the
Eastern District of Louisiana

Decided: April 29, 2019

Citation: 922 F.3d 660, 7 Adm. R. 251 (5th Cir. 2019).

Before **ELROD**, **WILLETT**, and **DUNCAN**, Circuit
Judges.

[—3—] {–663–} DUNCAN, Circuit Judge: [—4—]
{–664–}

“This case presents another in the line of cases related to the Deepwater Horizon oil spill.” *In re Deepwater Horizon (Barrera)*, 907 F.3d 232, 233, 6 Adm. R. 270, 270 (5th Cir. 2018). The more than eight hundred appellants, who assert various contract and tort claims arising out of the oil clean-up, are divided into two groups: the "Lindsay Appellants" and the "D'Amico Appellants." Both groups separately appeal their with-prejudice dismissals for failure to follow the district court's order requiring they file individual complaints. The district court unquestionably had authority to issue the order as a sensible means of managing multi-district litigation we have described as "epic." *In re Deepwater Horizon (Seacor Holdings)*, 819 F.3d 190, 197, 4 Adm. R. 248, 252 (5th Cir. 2016). And the district court unquestionably has authority to dismiss parties' claims with prejudice for disobeying its docket management orders. At the same time, however, to justify wielding dismissal-with-prejudice as a sanction, our precedents demand "a clear record of delay or contumacious conduct." *Barrera*, 907 F.3d at 235, 6 Adm. R. at 271 (internal quotations omitted). We fail to find that clear record as to one of the two groups before us, the D'Amico Appellants.

We therefore affirm the district court's judgment as to the Lindsay Appellants. As to the D'Amico Appellants, however, we reverse and remand.

I.

A.

As part of its herculean efforts overseeing MDL 2179, the district court created eight "pleading bundles" for various categories of cases and claims. *See, e.g., Ctr. for Biological Diversity, Inc. v. BP Am. Prod. Co.*, 704 F.3d 413, 419, 1 Adm. R. 193, 194 (5th Cir. 2013) (explaining court's use of "'pleading bundles' into . . . which claims of similar nature would be placed for the purpose of filing a master complaint, answers, and any Rule 12 motions"). The two sets of claims we address in this appeal fall into the "B3" bundle, which "include[s] all claims related to post-explosion Clean-Up, Medical Monitoring, and Post-April 20 [—5—] Personal Injury Claims." As with other categories, claims in the B3 bundle were initially managed through a "master complaint," which plaintiffs could join simply by filing a "short form joinder." *See, e.g., In re Deepwater Horizon*, 745 F.3d 157, 162, 2 Adm. R. 171, 172 (5th Cir. 2014) (discussing use of master complaint for "pleading bundle 'C'" concerning government claims). Alternatively, plaintiffs who filed individual B3-type lawsuits were deemed part of the B3 bundle, even if they had not filed short-form joinders. {–665–}

On February 22, 2017, the district court issued pretrial order 63 ("PTO 63"), dismissing the B3 master complaint and conveying additional instructions to B3 plaintiffs. First, any B3 plaintiff who had filed an individual complaint—defined as "a single-plaintiff complaint without class allegations"—was instructed to complete a sworn statement, which was to be filed and served in the individual lawsuit by April 12, 2017. Failure to do so would result in a complaint being "dismissed with prejudice without further notice." Second, any B3 plaintiff who had only filed a short-form joinder, or was "part of a complaint with more than one plaintiff or a class action," was instructed to file and serve an individual lawsuit, also by April 12, 2017. Failure to do so would similarly result in claims being "dismissed with prejudice without further notice." Finally, the order explained that this second category does not include "complaints that contain related parties, such as a husband and wife or co-owners of a business"—those would instead be considered "individual complaints" under the first category.

B.

The Lindsay Appellants comprise hundreds of workers hired by Plant Performance Services, LLP and its parent corporation (collectively, "P2S") to perform clean-up work in the aftermath of the oil spill. After being allegedly "fired . . . through no fault of their own," the Lindsay Appellants filed two multi-plaintiff lawsuits against P2S in Florida, with over eight hundred [—6—] plaintiffs in total. They also asserted "a third party beneficiary theory" against various BP entities, who had contracted with P2S to provide clean-up services. These two cases were transferred to MDL 2179 in April and May 2013 based on the claims asserted against BP.

On the April 12, 2017 deadline set by PTO 63, the Lindsay Appellants filed motions for relief from PTO 63. The district court denied relief, but "granted [the Lindsay Appellants] an extension up to and including May 3, 2017 to comply with PTO 63." The Lindsay Appellants, however, submitted no additional filings by the extended deadline. Per the district court's instruction, BP provided the court a list of plaintiffs BP understood to have complied with PTO 63. The Lindsay Appellants did not appear on that list, and the court dismissed their claims with prejudice on July 18, 2017. They filed post-judgment motions under Federal Rules of Civil Procedure 59(e) and 60, claiming that P2S—the main target of their lawsuit—was not "a party to the MDL" and that based on communications with the Plaintiffs' Steering Committee ("PSC"), they believed their claims were not part of the B3 bundle. The district court denied those motions, and the Lindsay Appellants sought our review.

C.

The D'Amico Appellants are a group of seventeen people who allege personal injuries from exposure to the spilled oil and the chemicals used along the Gulf Coast to disperse that oil. They originally brought two suits in the Eastern District of Louisiana and one in the Northern District of Florida. The Florida case was transferred to MDL 2179 in May 2013. After issuance of PTO 63, the D'Amico Appellants sought advice from the PSC on how it applied to their claims. After conferring with the PSC, they believed that their three lawsuits qualified as "individual lawsuits" under the order and that they were thus required only to file sworn statements. They filed the required statements [—7—] before the April 12, 2017 deadline. Subsequently, the D'Amico Appellants appeared on BP's {–666–} court-ordered list of plaintiffs with deficient submissions. On July 18, 2017, the district court dismissed the D'Amico Appellants' claims with prejudice for failing to file individual lawsuits. In subsequent Rule 59(e) motions, the D'Amico Appellants claimed their failure to comply with PTO 63 was unintentional because they believed their previous filings qualified as individual lawsuits. The district court denied those motions, and the D'Amico Appellants sought our review.

II.

"We review matters concerning docket management for an abuse of discretion," affording a district court "special deference . . . in the context of an MDL." *Barrera*, 907 F.3d at 234–35, 6 Adm. R. at 271 (citing *In re Asbestos Prod. Liab. Litig. (No. VI)*, 718 F.3d 236, 243 (3d Cir. 2013); *In re Fannie Mae Sec. Litig.*, 552 F.3d 814, 822 (D.C. Cir. 2009)). Yet, because "[a] dismissal with prejudice 'is an extreme sanction that deprives the litigant of the opportunity to pursue his claim,' . . . this [c]ourt has limited the district court's discretion in dismissing cases with prejudice." *Berry v. CIGNA/RSI–CIGNA*, 975 F.2d 1188, 1191 (5th Cir. 1992) (quoting *Callip v. Harris Cty. Child Welfare Dep't*, 757 F.2d 1513, 1519 (5th Cir. 1985)) (cleaned up); *see also Price v. McGlathery*, 792 F.2d 472, 474 (5th Cir. 1986).

We will therefore affirm dismissals-with-prejudice for violations of docket management orders "only on a showing of 'a clear record of delay or contumacious conduct by the plaintiff . . . , and where lesser sanctions would not serve the best interests of justice.'" *Sealed Appellant v. Sealed Appellee*, 452 F.3d 415, 417 (5th Cir. 2006) (quoting *Rogers v. Kroger Co.*, 669 F.2d 317, 320 (5th Cir. 1982)) (cleaned up); *see also Barrera*, 907 F.3d at 235, 6 Adm. R. at 271. [—8—]

III.

A.

We first address the Lindsay Appellants' arguments. They contest the dismissal of their claims on three grounds: (1) that the record fails to clearly show "delay or contumacious conduct"; (2) that they did not have adequate notice that dismissal with prejudice was a possible sanction; and (3) that dismissal with prejudice effectively denies them access to the courts guaranteed by the Florida Constitution. We address each argument in turn.

First, contrary to the Lindsay Appellants' claim, we find that the record clearly shows contumacious conduct under our precedents, justifying dismissal-with-prejudice. We are guided by our recent decision in *Barrera*, 907 F.3d 232, 6 Adm. R. 270, affirming dismissal-with-prejudice of over 1,500 claims for failure to comply with a similar *Deepwater Horizon* pretrial order. As in *Barrera*, the pretrial order here warned plaintiffs that non-compliance would result in "dismissal of their claims with prejudice without further notice." *Id.* at 234, 6 Adm. R. at 270 (addressing PTO 60). As in *Barrera*, the Lindsay Appellants received extra time to comply with the order's deadline. *See id.*, 6 Adm. R. at 270 (noting district court granted "a fourteen-day extension"). Finally, despite the extension, as in *Barrera* the Lindsay Appellants failed to file anything by the new deadline. *See id.*, 6 Adm. R. at 270 (observing that plaintiffs "did not properly file their declarations by the [extended] deadline"). Indeed, the *Barrera* plaintiffs at least asked for a second extension and tried to explain why they could not comply with the filing requirements (albeit

without supporting evidence). *See id.*, 6 Adm. R. at 270. The Lindsay Appellants, by contrast, did nothing. "Contumacious" means "[a] willful disobedience of a court order." BLACK'S LAW DICTIONARY at 358 (10th ed. 2014). [—9—] That is evident from this record, justifying the district court's dismissal-with-prejudice {–667–} sanction.[1]

Second, we reject the Lindsay Appellants' argument that they lacked notice that dismissal-with-prejudice was on the table. PTO 63 explicitly warned that non-compliant plaintiffs would "face dismissal of their claims with prejudice without further notice." And the Lindsay Appellants were given an extension specifically to comply with the order. In similar circumstances, we have found it "unclear what lesser sanctions could have been appropriate following the district court's warnings and second chances." *Barrera*, 907 F.3d at 236, 6 Adm. R. at 272. We reach the same conclusion here. "Any sanction other than dismissal would not achieve the desired effect of PTO [63], and would further delay the district court's efforts to adjudicate the MDL expeditiously." *Id.*, 6 Adm. R. at 272 (citing *In re Asbestos*, 718 F.3d at 248).

Finally, we are unpersuaded by the Lindsay Appellants' invocation of the Florida Constitution's access-to-courts guarantee. *See* FLA. CONST. Art. I, § 21 (guaranteeing "[t]he

---

[1] Any differences between this case and *Barrera* are superficial. For example, the *Barrera* plaintiffs had three chances—rather than the Lindsay Appellants' two—to comply with the order. *Id.* at 234, 6 Adm. R. at 270. But the prior dismissals under PTO 60 in *Barrera* should have alerted the Lindsay Appellants that these management orders must be taken seriously. *See id.*, 6 Adm. R. at 270 (noting district court dismissed claims under PTO 60 on December 16, 2016); *see also, e.g., In re Deepwater Horizon (Perez)*, 713 F. App'x 360, 363 (5th Cir.), *reh'g denied* (Apr. 12, 2018), *cert. denied sub nom. Perez v. BP, P.L.C.*, 139 S. Ct. 231 (2018) (upholding similar dismissals in December 2016). Also, unlike the *Barrera* plaintiffs, the Lindsay Appellants claimed to be confused about whether the order applied to their claims. But any confusion was dissipated by the court's extension, which expressly told them they were "to comply with PTO 63."

courts shall be open to every person for redress of any injury, and justice shall be administered without sale, denial or delay"). This argument was not raised before the district court and is therefore "waived and cannot be raised for the first time on appeal." *In re Deepwater Horizon*, 857 F.3d 246, 251, 5 Adm. R. 246, 247–48 (5th Cir. 2017) (quoting *LeMaire v. La. Dep't of Transp. & Dev.*, 480 F.3d 383, 387 (5th Cir. 2007)). Moreover, even indulging the dubious [—10—] proposition that the Florida Constitution applies here, the Lindsay Appellants direct us to no authority suggesting that a dismissal-with-prejudice sanction categorically denies access to courts under the Florida Constitution. *Cf., e.g., Kinney v. R.H. Halt Assoc., Inc.*, 927 So. 2d 920, 921 (Fla. Dist. Ct. App. 2006) (dismissal-with-prejudice for non-compliance with court orders appropriate if court makes "explicit findings of willful or flagrant disregard").

B.

We turn to the D'Amico Appellants' arguments. Like the Lindsay Appellants, they contend the record shows no contumacious conduct in their failure to comply with PTO 63. To the contrary, they claim to have made a good-faith effort to comply, emphasizing they sought guidance from the PSC and then, based on that advice, timely filed sworn statements instead of individual lawsuits. Consequently, the D'Amico Appellants urge that a lesser sanction would better serve the interests of justice and that dismissal-with-prejudice was inappropriate. We agree.

We do not find the "clear record of delay or contumacious conduct" by the D'Amico Appellants required to justify a dismissal-with-prejudice sanction. *Barrera*, 907 F.3d at 235, 6 Adm. R. at 271. Confused about whether their three existing complaints were "individual lawsuits" under PTO 63, the D'Amico Appellants queried the PSC and were advised only to file sworn statements. This was a {–668–} mistake, as the D'Amico Appellants concede. But based on this flawed understanding of PTO 63, the D'Amico Appellants then timely filed and served sworn statements before the April 12, 2017 deadline. None of this makes those filings any less

mistaken under PTO 63, but it does show an absence of willful conduct. And BP points to nothing in the record to dispel that impression. There is a critical difference between trying but failing, on the one hand, and simply not trying, on the other. Because the record shows the former, we conclude that the D'Amico Appellants did not engage in delay or contumacious [—11—] conduct sufficient to support dismissal-with-prejudice. *Barrera*, 907 F.3d at 235, 6 Adm. R. at 271; *cf., e.g., Moore v. CITGO Ref. & Chems. Co., L.P.*, 735 F.3d 309, 316 (5th Cir. 2013) (dismissal proper where discovery order violation showed "blatant disregard for the judicial process . . . [that] constitutes willful and contumacious conduct").

None of the factors we relied on in *Barrera* to find contumaciousness is present here. The D'Amico Appellants did not receive an extension to comply with PTO 63 and then blow it off: To the contrary, they timely filed sworn statements before the original deadline. *Cf. Barrera*, 907 F.3d at 235, 6 Adm. R. at 271 ("Despite receiving a fourteen-day extension with an explicit warning that no further extensions of time would be granted, Plaintiffs did not comply with PTO 60."). Furthermore, even after their claims were dismissed, they sought leave to re-file individual lawsuits. *Cf. id.* at 236, 6 Adm. R. at 272 (observing that, "aside from a few untimely individuals, Plaintiffs *never* filed sworn declarations that complied with PTO 60"). Finally, the D'Amico Appellants corroborated their claim that they misunderstood PTO 63 with documentation. *Cf. id.* at 235, 6 Adm. R. at 271 (noting that, despite show cause order, "Plaintiffs still did not submit any documentation or other evidence . . . corroborating their explanation for the delay"). In short, unlike the Lindsay Appellants, the record does not clearly show the D'Amico Appellants' contumacious conduct.

We find BP's arguments to the contrary unpersuasive. For instance, BP relies on *Perez*, 713 F. App'x 360, which upheld dismissal of numerous claims for failure to follow a similar order. *Perez*, of course, is unpublished and therefore non-binding. *See* 5th Cir. R. 47.5.4. That aside, the decision is distinguishable. Unlike the D'Amico Appellants, the *Perez* plaintiffs were "given numerous opportunities"—including an extension of time—to "file single-plaintiff complaints," and yet failed to do so. 713 F. App'x at 362. Also distinguishable is *Nottingham v. Warden, Bill Clements Unit*, 837 F.3d 438 [—12—] (5th Cir. 2016). There, the plaintiff repeatedly defied a court's order to verify his suspicious *in forma pauperis* motion despite multiple warnings threatening dismissal-with-prejudice. *Id.* at 439–41. The district court finally dismissed his case pursuant to express statutory authority. *Id.* at 441; *see* 28 U.S.C. § 1915(e)(2)(A) (providing court "shall dismiss" case if it "determines that . . . the allegation of poverty [in an IFP motion] is untrue"). This case does not involve the obnoxious defiance of a court order in *Nottingham*.

Finally, we reject BP's waiver argument. Specifically, BP argues the D'Amico Appellants failed to object to PTO 63 when issued and, further, failed to raise their current arguments post-judgment. We disagree. When PTO 63 was issued, the D'Amico Appellants had no reason to object—they tried to *comply* with the order—and they objected in post-judgment motions after their lawsuits were dismissed. As for those post-judgment motions, it is true they did not deploy the magic words "contumacious conduct." But that is immaterial. The D'Amico Appellants {–669–} argued they "did not [act] with any intent to disobey [the district c]ourt's order, [to] circumvent the rules, or to unduly delay this matter" and urged their failure to file individual lawsuits was an "inadvertent mistake." This was enough to preserve the argument that dismissal-with-prejudice was unwarranted. *See, e.g., Keelan v. Majesco Software, Inc.*, 407 F.3d 332, 340 (5th Cir. 2005) (to avoid waiver, "[a]n argument must be raised to such a degree that the district court has an opportunity to rule on it").

IV.

We AFFIRM the district court's judgment dismissing the Lindsay Appellants' claims, but we REVERSE the district court's judgment dismissing the D'Amico Appellants' lawsuits and REMAND for further proceedings consistent with this opinion.

AFFIRMED IN PART; REVERSED AND REMANDED IN PART

United States Court of Appeals
for the Fifth Circuit

No. 18-30652

LATIOLAIS
vs.
HUNTINGTON INGALLS, INC.

On Petition for Rehearing En Banc
(Opinion March 11, 2019, 5 Cir. 2019, 918 F.3d 406,
7 Adm. R. 196)

Decided: May 8, 2019

Citation: 923 F.3d 427, 7 Adm. R. 256 (5th Cir. 2019) (reh'g
en banc granted).

Before **STEWART**, Chief Judge, **JONES**, **SMITH**,
DENNIS, **OWEN**, **ELROD**, **SOUTHWICK**, **HAYNES**,
GRAVES, **HIGGINSON**, **COSTA**, **WILLETT**, **HO**,
DUNCAN, and **OLDHAM**, Circuit Judges.[1]

[—1—] {–427–} BY THE COURT:

A member of the court having requested a poll on the petition for rehearing en banc, and a majority of the circuit judges in regular active service and not disqualified having voted in favor, [—2—]

IT IS ORDERED that this cause shall be reheard by the court en banc with oral argument on a date hereafter to be fixed. The Clerk will specify a briefing schedule for the filing of supplemental briefs.

---

[1] Judge Engelhardt is recused and did not participate in this decision.

United States Court of Appeals
for the Fifth Circuit

No. 18-20248

CARMONA
VS.
LEO SHIP MANAGEMENT, INC.

Appeal from the United States District Court for the
Southern District of Texas

Decided: May 10, 2019

Citation: 924 F.3d 190, 7 Adm. R. 257 (5th Cir. 2019).

Before **HIGGINBOTHAM**, **SMITH**, and **HIGGINSON**,
Circuit Judges.

[—1—] {–192–} **SMITH**, Circuit Judge:

Jose Carmona was injured while unloading cargo from a vessel docked outside Houston. He sued Leo Ship Management, Inc. ("LSM"), a foreign corporation that managed the ship. Noting that LSM had no control over the ship's ports of call, the district court dismissed for want of personal jurisdiction, holding that the company did not purposely avail itself of the privilege of conducting activities in Texas. We affirm in part, vacate in part, and remand. [—2—]

I.

As a stevedore, Carmona was tasked with unloading cargo from the M/V Komatsushima Star in April 2014. While he was rigging a bundle of pipes in the ship's hold, the pipes fell and injured his ankle and lower leg.

LSM is a Philippine corporation with its principal place of business in Manila. None of its employees, officers, shareholders, or directors has ever resided in Texas, and the company does not own or rent property in the state. LSM solicits no business in Texas and has never contracted with a Texas resident to render performance there.

In 2009, LSM contracted with the owners of the M/V Komatsushima Star to serve as the ship manager. In that capacity, LSM supplied and supervised the crew and arranged for necessary repairs and maintenance to ensure compliance with the laws "of the places where [the vessel] trades." The contract was freely terminable with two months' notice. Under the agreement, LSM did not have an ownership interest in the ship and could not direct where it traveled, what it carried, or for whom it worked. Rather, the charterer or subcharterer possessed the sole authority to set the ship's course. Nonetheless, the agreement required the ship's owners and LSM "to maintain close communication with each other and [to] share relevant information regarding [the] ship's schedule" and "port information." In fact, LSM had advance notice that the ship would be docking in Texas to discharge the pipes.

Although a third party had loaded the pipes aboard the ship outside the United States, Carmona sued LSM in state court, claiming negligence under general maritime law and the Longshore and Harbor Workers' Compensation Act ("LHWCA"). See 33 U.S.C. §§ 905(b), 933. Specifically, {–193–} he alleged that LSM breached its duty to (1) stow the pipes properly; (2) minimize hazards associated with falling pipes; (3) take precautions to protect workers; [—3—] (4) provide a safe work environment; (5) turn over the vessel in a safe condition for discharging cargo; (6) warn of hidden dangers; and (7) intervene. After removing to federal court, LSM moved to dismiss for lack of personal jurisdiction. See FED. R. CIV. P. 12(b)(2).

The district court granted the motion, finding that LSM did not purposely avail itself of the benefits and protections of Texas. The court reasoned that because LSM had no control over the itinerary, any contact with the state was "merely fortuitous or random." This appeal followed.

II.

We review a ruling on personal jurisdiction de novo. Sangha v. Navig8 ShipManagement Private Ltd., 882 F.3d 96, 101, 6 Adm. R. 182, 184 (5th Cir. 2018). Where, as here, the district court dismissed "without conducting an evidentiary hearing, the plaintiff bears the burden of establishing only a prima facie case of personal jurisdiction." *Id.*, 6 Adm. R. at 184. "We accept the plaintiff's uncontroverted, nonconclusional factual allegations as true and resolve all controverted allegations in the plaintiff's favor." *Panda Brandywine Corp. v. Potomac Elec. Power Co.*, 253 F.3d 865, 868 (5th Cir. 2001) (per curiam).

There is personal jurisdiction if the forum state's long-arm statute extends to the nonresident defendant and the exercise of jurisdiction comports with due process. *Sangha*, 882 F.3d at 101, 6 Adm. R. at 184. Because Texas's long-arm statute is coextensive with the Due Process Clause of the Fourteenth Amendment, the two inquiries merge. *Id.*, 6 Adm. R. at 184. Though "[p]ersonal jurisdiction can be general or specific," this case implicates only the latter. *See Seiferth v. Helicopteros Atuneros, Inc.*, 472 F.3d 266, 271 (5th Cir. 2006). In evaluating whether due process permits the exercise of specific jurisdiction, we consider

> (1) whether the defendant has minimum contacts with the forum state, i.e., whether it purposely directed its {—4—} activities toward the forum state or purposefully availed itself of the privileges of conducting activities there; (2) whether the plaintiff's cause of action arises out of or results from the defendant's forum-related contacts; and (3) whether the exercise of personal jurisdiction is fair and reasonable.

Id. (citation omitted). If the plaintiff establishes the first two prongs, the burden shifts to the defendant to make a "compelling case" that the assertion of jurisdiction is not fair or reasonable.[1]

A.

For there to be minimum contacts, a defendant must have "purposefully availed himself of the benefits and protections of the forum state"[2] "such that he should reasonably

anticipate being haled into court there."[3] That requirement is the "constitutional touchstone" of personal jurisdiction. *Burger King*, 471 U.S. at 474. It "ensures that a defendant will not be haled into a jurisdiction {–194–} solely as a result of random, fortuitous, or attenuated contacts, or of the unilateral activity of another party or a third person." *Id.* at 475 (internal quotation marks and citations omitted). That is, the plaintiff cannot supply "the only link between the defendant and the forum." *Walden v. Fiore*, 571 U.S. 277, 285 (2014). Rather, jurisdiction is proper only where the "defendant *himself*" made deliberate contact with the forum. *Id.* at 284 (quoting *Burger King*, 471 U.S. at 475).

The parties do not dispute that LSM made contacts with the forum when [—5—] the vessel, containing its employees, docked outside Houston.[4] Instead, they disagree as to (1) whether a defendant's contacts with a forum and the purposefulness of those contacts are independent inquiries and (2) if so, whether LSM's presence in Texas was purposeful.

1.

According to Carmona, knowing and voluntary entry into a forum state, coupled with commission of a tort inside that state, is sufficient to support specific jurisdiction, irrespective of whether the defendant purposely availed itself of the privilege of conducting activities there. Carmona posits that purposeful availment is analytically useful only in "effects" cases in which a defendant's *out-of-state* conduct inflicted injury within the forum. He suggests that in such cases, purposeful availment operates as a "conceptual tool" for determining whether the defendant's contacts with the forum "are such that he should reasonably anticipate" litigation there. *Burger King*, 471 U.S. at 474 (quoting *World-Wide Volkswagen*, 444 U.S. at

---

[1] *Sangha*, 882 F.3d at 102, 6 Adm. R. at 185 (quoting *Burger King Corp. v. Rudzewicz*, 471 U.S. 462, 477 (1985)); *see also Seiferth*, 472 F.3d at 271.

[2] *Moncrief Oil Int'l Inc. v. OAO Gazprom*, 481 F.3d 309, 311 (5th Cir. 2007).

[3] *Burger King*, 471 U.S. at 474 (quoting *World-Wide Volkswagen Corp. v. Woodson*, 444 U.S. 286, 297 (1980)).

[4] *See Trois v. Apple Tree Auction Ctr., Inc.*, 882 F.3d 485, 490 (5th Cir. 2018) ("A defendant may be subject to personal jurisdiction because of the activities of its agent within the forum state . . . .").

297). But Carmona urges that where, as here, the tortious act both occurred and caused injury within the forum, the court need not independently consider whether the conduct was purposefully directed at the forum state or whether the defendant purposefully availed itself of the forum state's protections.

In most cases, the defendant's commission of a tort while physically present in a state will readily confer specific jurisdiction.[5] "Generally, the commission of an intentional tort in a forum state is a purposeful act that will satisfy the purposeful availment prong . . . ." 16 JAMES WM. MOORE ET AL., [—6—] MOORE'S FEDERAL PRACTICE § 108.42[3][a], at 108-70 (3d ed. 2019). Nonetheless, while recognizing that a defendant's physical entry into a forum "is certainly a relevant contact,"[6] the Supreme Court has never held that such presence is dispositive in the "minimum contacts" analysis.[7] Instead, the Court has stressed that "where the defendant *deliberately* has engaged in significant activities within a State, . . . he manifestly has availed himself of the privilege of conducting business there." *Id.* at 475–76 (emphasis added) (cleaned up).

Purposeful availment is a constitutional prerequisite for jurisdiction, regardless of where the tortious conduct occurred. In {–195–} *Elkhart Engineering Corp. v. Dornier Werke*, 343 F.2d 861 (5th Cir. 1965), the plaintiff sued a German corporation for crashing his plane during a demonstration in Alabama. Beyond the requirement that the defendant have "minimum contacts . . . with the forum," we recognized "the additional element that in every case . . . there must be 'some act by which the defendant purposefully avails itself of the privilege of conducting activities within the forum State, thus invoking the benefits and protections of its

laws.'" *Id.* at 866 (quoting *Hanson v. Denckla*, 357 U.S. 235, 253 (1958)). Because the defendant "*voluntarily* entered [the] state and invoked the protections of its laws," personal jurisdiction extended to "any tortious acts committed while there." *Id.* at 868 (emphasis added).

Similarly, in *Jones v. Petty-Ray Geophysical Geosource, Inc.*, 954 F.2d 1061 (5th Cir. 1992), we explained that a nonresident defendant's activities, "whether direct acts *in* the forum or conduct outside the forum, must justify a [—7—] conclusion that the defendant should reasonably anticipate being called into court there." *Id.* at 1068 (emphasis added). As the "constitutional touchstone" of personal jurisdiction, purposeful availment is an essential element even where the defendant committed a tort within the forum state. *Burger King*, 471 U.S. at 474.

In an effort to show otherwise, Carmona cites *Burnham v. Superior Court of California*, 495 U.S. 604, 611 (1990) (plurality opinion), for the proposition that a defendant's physical presence in the forum—"no matter how fleeting"—is sufficient to trigger personal jurisdiction. But *Burnham* is inapposite for two reasons. First, it concerned "tag" or "transient jurisdiction," whereby personal jurisdiction is established by serving process on a nonresident defendant while it is physically present in the forum state. *Id.* at 610. The Court never addressed whether personal jurisdiction might exist over an *absent* non-resident that had previously committed a tort in the forum.[8] Second, because the defendant "voluntarily and knowingly" entered the forum, the Court had no occasion to consider whether physical presence alone permits the exercise of jurisdiction.[9]

---

[5] We are aware of no example—and LSM has cited none—in which a court lacked jurisdiction under those circumstances.

[6] *Walden*, 571 U.S. at 285.

[7] *See Burger King*, 471 U.S. at 476 (noting that "territorial presence" often will only *enhance* a potential defendant's affiliation with a State and reinforce the reasonable foreseeability of suit there") (emphasis added).

[8] *See Burnham*, 495 U.S. at 621 (plurality opinion) (observing that traditional principles of jurisdiction have treated "physically present defendants" and "absent [defendants] . . . quite differently").

[9] *See id.* at 640 (Brennan, J., concurring) ("[A]s a rule the exercise of personal jurisdiction over a defendant based on his *voluntary* presence in the forum will satisfy the requirements of due process" (emphasis added)).

Invoking *Moncrief Oil*, Carmona yet insists that "[w]hen a nonresident defendant commits a tort within the state . . . [,] that tortious conduct amounts [—8—] to sufficient minimum contacts with the state" to allow the assertion of jurisdiction.[10] But nothing in that statement abrogates the constitutional requirement that a defendant deliberately make those contacts. Indeed, we began our analysis in *Moncrief Oil* by pronouncing that a defendant must "purposefully . . . establish[] minimum contacts with the forum state."[11] And one of the corporate {–196–} defendants had done so.[12]

In sum, a defendant's contacts with a forum and the purposefulness of those contacts are distinct—though often overlapping—inquiries. Although tortious conduct within a forum ensures the existence of contacts, *see Moncrief Oil*, 481 F.3d at 314, it does not always guarantee that such contacts were deliberate. Accordingly, LSM is subject to jurisdiction only if it has purposely directed its activities to the forum state or purposely availed itself of its protections.

2.

LSM purposely availed itself of Texas when its employees voluntarily entered the jurisdiction aboard the vessel. Although LSM had no control over the vessel's course, the ship management agreement contemplated that the [—9—] ship would travel to locations throughout the world.[13] Moreover, the contract required the ship's owners "to maintain close communication with" LSM, "shar[ing] relevant information regarding [the] ship's schedule" and "port information." Notably, LSM received actual notice that the ship would be departing for Texas. Especially considering that the contract was freely terminable with two months' notice, LSM was hardly compelled to travel to Texas against its will. Rather, it made a deliberate choice to keep its employees aboard a ship bound for Texas. LSM thus purposely availed itself of the benefits and protections of the forum state because it reasonably should have anticipated being haled into court for torts committed there. *See Burger King*, 471 U.S. at 474.

LSM misconstrues *Asarco, Inc. v. Glenara, Ltd.*, 912 F.2d 784 (5th Cir. 1990), in asserting that there is no purposeful availment where a ship manager does not control the itinerary. There, the plaintiffs sued both the owner and the manager of a ship to recover damages for cargo lost at sea when the vessel sank in the Pacific Ocean. Although no tortious conduct occurred in the forum state, the plaintiffs claimed specific jurisdiction because the defendants had allegedly contracted to deliver cargo there, "and their failure to do so . . . [had given] rise to this cause of action." *Id.* at 786.

We disagreed. In light of the "uncontroverted evidence negating the existence of any such contract," the defendants did not establish minimum contacts. *Id.* "[T]he fact that the vessel [had] set sail for a Louisiana port d[id] not imply an agreement by either defendant to deliver cargo there" because the [—10—] vessel had "sailed only on orders from its charterers." *Id.* Consequently, "[s]pecific jurisdiction d[id] not lie" where "neither [the owner] nor [the manager had] purposefully directed the cargo to Louisiana." *Id.* at 787.

---

[10] *Moncrief Oil*, 481 F.3d at 314 (second alteration in original) (quoting *Guidry v. U.S. Tobacco Co.*, 188 F.3d 619, 628 (5th Cir. 1999)).

[11] *See id.* at 311 (cleaned up). The other cases Carmona raises all recite that same test *ad nauseum. See Streber v. Hunter*, 221 F.3d 701, 718 (5th Cir. 2000); *Guidry*, 188 F.3d at 625; *D.J. Invs., Inc. v. Metzeler Motorcycle Tire Agent Gregg, Inc.*, 754 F.2d 542, 545 & n.1 (5th Cir. 1985).

[12] *See Moncrief Oil*, 481 F.3d at 313–14 (noting that the corporation's vice-chairman visited Texas to speak at an energy summit); *see also Streber*, 221 F.3d at 718 (holding that the defendant "'purposefully availed' himself of Texas laws when he gave tax advice that he knew would be received by a Texas client"); *Guidry*, 188 F.3d at 630 (finding that the defendants' "alleged intentional and negligent tortious actions were knowingly initiated and aimed at" residents of the forum state); *D.J. Invs.*, 754 F.2d at 548 (concluding that the defendants "engaged in purposeful activity which was directed at Texas").

---

[13] For instance, the contract authorized LSM to incur necessary expenditures to ensure compliance with the "laws . . . of the places where [the vessel] trades."

This case is plainly distinguishable from *Asarco* in that LSM engaged in purportedly tortious conduct while present in the forum state. Unlike the litigants in *Asarco*, the parties do not contest that LSM made {–197–} forum contacts that gave rise to at least some of Carmona's claims. *Asarco* thus sheds little light on the question whether LSM purposely availed itself of Texas by allowing its agents to enter the forum and allegedly commit a tort therein. Additionally, the fact that LSM did not seek to abrogate its contract despite knowing that the ship was en route to Texas "impl[ies] an agreement . . . to deliver cargo there." *Id.* at 786. Hence, even under *Asarco*, LSM purposely directed its activities at the forum state or purposely availed itself of that state's benefits and protections.

LSM's reliance on *Nuovo Pignone, SpA v. STORMAN ASIA M/V*, 310 F.3d 374 (5th Cir. 2002),[14] is similarly unavailing. There, the defendant agreed to supply a safe vessel for the transportation of a reactor from Italy to Louisiana. While the reactor was being unloaded in Louisiana, the onboard crane failed, causing the reactor to fall. *Id.* at 377. We found personal jurisdiction because the contract had specified Louisiana as the destination. *Id.* at 379. Considering the defendant "reasonably should have anticipated that its failure to meet its contractual obligations might subject it to suit there," we held that the defendant could "[]not now claim that its contact with Louisiana was merely fortuitous, random, or attenuated." *Id.* We noted the outcome would be different, however, if Louisiana were not the intended destination but [—11—] unexpected circumstances such as "bad weather" forced the ship to dock there. *Id.* at 379 n.2. "In that case, [the defendant] could not have reasonably foreseen being haled into a Louisiana court." *Id.*[15]

That by far is not the situation here. The location of the vessel was the product of neither compulsion nor surprise. Instead, with full knowledge of the intended destination, LSM deliberately permitted its employees to enter Texas. It may not now escape liability resulting from its considered commercial decision.

B.

For specific jurisdiction, Carmona's claims still must stem from LSM's contacts with Texas. *See id.* at 381–82. "A plaintiff bringing multiple claims that arise out of different forum contacts of the defendant must establish specific jurisdiction for each claim." *Seiferth*, 472 F.3d at 274. Carmona alleges that LSM breached its duty under general maritime law and the LHWCA to (1) stow the pipes properly; (2) minimize cargo hazards; (3) take precautions to protect workers; (4) provide a safe work environment; (5) turn over the vessel in a safe condition for discharging activities; (6) warn of hidden dangers; and (7) intervene.

LSM concedes that most of Carmona's claims result from its conduct in Texas after the ship's arrival there. But it maintains that Carmona adduced no evidence showing that LSM's alleged failure to minimize cargo hazards or to take safety precautions occurred in Texas. Not so: Carmona averred that while the ship was docked in Texas, LSM's crewmember had inspected the pipe bundles but failed to ensure that they were properly stacked for discharge. [—12—] When viewed in Carmona's favor, such allegations are sufficient to establish that those two claims arise out of LSM's forum contacts. {–198–}

Nevertheless, LSM presented undisputed evidence that a third party had stowed the pipes aboard the ship while it was outside the United States. Unlike Carmona's other allegations, the claim that the pipes were improperly stowed does not stem from LSM's activities in Texas. Instead, the alleged tortious conduct occurred outside the United States at the hands of a third party. As a result, the district court correctly dismissed,

---

[14] *Nuovo Pignone* was abrogated on grounds not relevant here by *Water Splash, Inc. v. Menon*, 137 S. Ct. 1504 (2017).

[15] The defendant at issue, Fagioli, never was physically present in the forum—an important distinction *vis-à-vis* LSM.

for want of personal jurisdiction, the claim of failure to load the pipes properly.[16]

C.

Finally, we ask whether the exercise of personal jurisdiction accords "with traditional notions of fair play and substantial justice." *Sangha*, 882 F.3d at 101, 6 Adm. R. at 184 (cleaned up). Because the district court did not reach that question, we remand for it to decide that prong. *See Seiferth*, 472 F.3d at 276.

The dismissal, for want of personal jurisdiction, of the claim that LSM negligently stowed the pipes is AFFIRMED. Dismissal of the remaining claims is VACATED and REMANDED for proceedings as needed. We express no view on what decisions the district court should make on remand or on what matters it may consider.

---

[16] Carmona suggests that because he has raised only one *type* of claim—i.e., negligence—the court need not analyze specific jurisdiction on a claim-by-claim basis. But it matters not that Carmona's allegations all sound in negligence; the court must separately consider specific jurisdiction for each claim that arises from different forum contacts. *See Seiferth*, 472 F.3d at 274.

United States Court of Appeals
for the Fifth Circuit

No. 17-41198

GOWDY
vs.
MARINE SPILL RESPONSE CORP.

Appeal from the United States District Court for the
Southern District of Texas

Decided: May 23, 2019

Citation: 925 F.3d 200, 7 Adm. R. 263 (5th Cir. 2019).

Before **KING**, **HIGGINSON**, and **COSTA**, Circuit Judges.

[—1—] {–202–} HIGGINSON, Circuit Judge:

This personal injury Jones Act case presents two issues. The first is whether the district court erred by failing to act on an allegation that the defendant-appellee provoked the plaintiff-appellant's attorney to withdraw. The second is whether the district court erroneously granted summary judgment to the defendant-appellee because the plaintiff-appellant lacked expert medical evidence of causation. On the first issue, we affirm. On the second, we reverse and remand. [—2—]

BACKGROUND

Plaintiff-Appellant James Earlton Gowdy sued Defendant-Appellee Marine Spill Response Corporation (MSRC) for unseaworthiness and Jones Act negligence. Gowdy alleged that he, while employed as a seaman aboard one of MSRC's vessels, injured his left foot when he stepped off the last rung of a ladder that was dangerously raised four feet off the floor. He also claimed that there was clutter beneath the ladder that required him to jump off to the left. There were no witnesses to the incident.

Represented by attorney Matthew Shaffer, Gowdy filed a complaint in the United States District Court for the Southern District of Texas. Less than three months into the litigation, Shaffer moved to withdraw as counsel, citing "irreconcilable differences over issues related to . . . the management of this litigation." Gowdy opposed the motion. After a hearing, the district court permitted Shaffer to withdraw. Gowdy alleged that counsel for MSRC caused Shaffer's withdrawal by providing Shaffer with "false and misleading information about another person with a similar name." Specifically, Gowdy averred that MSRC's counsel sent Shaffer certain documents from a Mississippi criminal case against someone named James *Edward* Gowdy. According to Gowdy, Shaffer pointed at MSRC's counsel at the conclusion of the hearing on the motion to withdraw and said, "Here's the guy who sent us all this false information about you." {–203–} Following Shaffer's withdrawal, Gowdy proceeded (and remains) pro se.

MSRC eventually moved for summary judgment. The motion was filed electronically on July 31, 2017. Three hours later, a "Motion to Oppose Summary Judgment" from Gowdy was electronically entered on the docket. It had been postmarked July 29, 2017. With due acknowledgement of Gowdy's pro se status, the district court construed that filing as Gowdy's response to [—3—] MSRC's motion or, alternatively, a cross-motion for summary judgment. We will do the same.

MSRC's motion began by describing Gowdy's pre-incident medical history of diabetes and chronic kidney disease, as was revealed both in Gowdy's deposition and also in the deposition of his long-time treating physician, Dr. Chad Clause. Dr. Clause's records reflected that Gowdy had been receiving treatment for pressure ulcers on his left foot for about two-and-a-half years preceding the ladder incident. The records also indicated that Gowdy went to see Dr. Clause about four days after the ladder incident. Dr. Clause's notes from that appointment stated, "On boat, hit foot, painful, red."

During the deposition, Dr. Clause described that appointment as concerning "an injury" that was "something additional to what we were doing at that time." Dr. Clause also characterized that injury as a "trauma." The day after Gowdy's appointment with Dr.

Clause, a CT scan revealed fractures in Gowdy's left foot.

Dr. Clause's records described Gowdy's foot as having developed "Charcot changes," which Dr. Clause described as a "breakdown of certain areas of the foot." According to Dr. Clause, Charcot is typically experienced by patients with diabetes and it can be triggered by "any kind of trauma to the foot." As Dr. Clause laid out the timeline in this case, "From the trauma when he had an injury at work, . . . that's when we ended up treating the fracture. And from the fracture . . . after that is when he developed the Charcot." According to Dr. Clause, "the Charcot never arose until after . . . he had the fracture."

A month after the incident, Dr. Clause performed foot surgery on Gowdy. Two months after that, Gowdy underwent a second surgery to correct [—4—] complications from the first. Due to continuing problems, Gowdy's foot was later amputated.

MSRC's motion for summary judgment highlighted testimony from Dr. Charles Bain, its designated biomechanical expert. Dr. Bain explained that he had examined the depositions of Gowdy and Dr. Clause along with medical records from the seven medical facilities that had treated Gowdy. He also reviewed photographs of the accident site. Based on that evidence, Dr. Bain opined that Gowdy's foot injury "would not have occurred by Mr. Gowdy stepping off the bottom rung of the ladder." He specified:

> Based on the various imaging studies' reports, Mr. Gowdy sustained either a high energy impact to his left mid foot or a crush injury. This type of injury would not occur by stepping off the bottom (fourth) welded rung on the wall of the engine room. Stepping off this rung can be made in a controlled manner. Even coming off the bottom rung in an uncontrolled manner is unlikely to yield the loading necessary to cause Mr. Gowdy's injuries. Mr. Gowdy has described jumping off the bottom rung. Had he done this and landed solely on his left foot, it is unlikely to see his

injury pattern considering the low energy involved with this maneuver.

Dr. Bain concluded, "[I]t is likely that Mr. Gowdy's fractures and joint disruptions in his left foot developed insidiously over {–204–} time and were not the result of a one-time loading event."

MSRC's motion for summary judgment argued that Gowdy's failure to designate an expert of his own was "fatal to his claim" because a Jones Act plaintiff bears the burden of proving causation by medical expert testimony.

Gowdy's opposition highlighted Dr. Clause's observation that the Charcot changes had occurred in his left foot only *after* the ladder incident. Gowdy also cited three exam summaries from post-incident medical visits indicating that Gowdy's left foot evinced Charcot changes while his right foot had no deformity. He argued, "It is something anyone can understand; you [—5—] cannot step off a 48 inch high ladder rung to a metal floor and expect to not get injured."

After a hearing, the district court orally granted MSRC's motion "because [Mr. Gowdy did] not have an expert to testify to the jury on the issue of medical causation." A written order followed, which stated that Gowdy's evidence was insufficient to create a genuine dispute of material fact as to whether the damage to his left foot was caused by MSRC's negligence.

With liberal construction, Gowdy's brief on appeal presents two issues for our review: (1) whether the district court erred by granting Shaffer's motion to withdraw and failing to investigate allegations that MSRC provoked the withdrawal, and (2) whether the district court erred in granting summary judgment to MSRC.

DISCUSSION

I. Withdrawal of Counsel

a. Standard of Review

"An attorney may withdraw from representation only upon leave of the court and a showing of good cause and reasonable notice to the client." *Matter of Wynn*, 889 F.2d 644, 646 (5th Cir. 1989). The matter of attorney withdrawal is "entrusted to the sound discretion of the court and will be overturned on appeal only for an abuse of that discretion." *Id.* (quotation omitted).

b. Analysis

Gowdy suggests that the district court erroneously permitted his former counsel, Shaffer, to withdraw. Gowdy also argues that the district court should have investigated his allegations that MSRC was involved in the withdrawal. Both arguments fail.

First, all evidence in the record indicates that Gowdy's attorney made a showing of good cause and provided reasonable notice to his client. Shaffer's [—6—] motion to withdraw described "irreconcilable differences over issues related to . . . the management of [the] litigation" and certified that he had conferred with his client on the matter. No evidence calls the veracity of those statements into question or suggests an alternative set of facts. Shaffer also noted accurately that withdrawal would not materially prejudice Gowdy because the litigation was in its early stages.

Second, the district court took procedural care in resolving Shaffer's withdrawal motion. The court prudently held a hearing on the motion, at which time Gowdy had the opportunity to present his opposition.

Finally, Gowdy's own description of the conduct that the district court allegedly failed to investigate indicates that the district court was not required to do so. Gowdy's theory is that MSRC's counsel provided Shaffer with information that Shaffer knew to be about a different person. Gowdy does not explain, nor does common sense, why information identifiably about a person unrelated to a case would cause an attorney to withdraw. {–205–}

In sum, we affirm the decision to grant Shaffer's motion to withdraw and discern no error in the district court's handling of this issue.

II. Summary Judgment

a. Standard of Review

We review a grant of summary judgment de novo, applying the same standards as the district court. *Austin v. Kroger Texas, L.P.*, 864 F.3d 326, 328 (5th Cir. 2017). Summary judgment is appropriate "if the movant shows that there is no genuine dispute as to any material fact and the movant is entitled to judgment as a matter of law." Fed R. Civ. P. 56(a). "A genuine issue of material fact exists when the evidence is such that a reasonable jury could return a verdict for the non-moving party." *Austin*, 864 F.3d at 328 (quotation omitted). "All evidence is viewed in the light most favorable to the nonmoving [—7—] party and all reasonable inferences are drawn in that party's favor." *Id.* at 328-29.

"A seaman is entitled to recovery under the Jones Act . . . if his employer's negligence is the cause, in whole or in part, of his injury." *Randle v. Crosby Tugs, L.L.C.*, 911 F.3d 280, 283, 6 Adm. R. 279, 280 (5th Cir. 2018) (quoting *Gautreaux v. Scurlock Marine, Inc.*, 107 F.3d 331, 335 (5th Cir. 1997) (en banc)). "The standard of causation in Jones Act cases is not demanding." *Johnson v. Cenac Towing, Inc.*, 544 F.3d 296, 302 (5th Cir. 2008). Indeed, a claim under the Jones Act requires only that employer negligence "played *any part, even the slightest*, in producing the injury." *Id.* (citing *Chisholm v. Sabine Towing & Transp. Co., Inc.*, 679 F.3d 60, 62 (5th Cir. 1982)).

"Unseaworthiness is a claim under general maritime law based on the vessel owner's duty to ensure that the vessel is reasonably fit to be at sea." *Beech v. Hercules Drilling Co., L.L.C.*, 691 F.3d 566, 570 (5th Cir. 2012). (quotation omitted). "There is a more demanding standard of causation in an unseaworthiness claim than in a Jones Act negligence claim." *Johnson v. Offshore Express, Inc.*, 845 F.2d 1347, 1354 (5th Cir. 1988). An unseaworthiness claim requires proximate causation, and "a plaintiff must prove that the unseaworthy condition played a substantial part in bringing about or actually causing the injury and that the injury was either a direct result or a reasonably probable consequence of the unseaworthiness." *Id.*

b. Analysis

At issue is whether the district court erred by ruling as a matter of law that Gowdy was required to produce expert medical evidence of causation.[1] The [—8—] well-settled "general rule" about expert testimony is that it is unnecessary when jurors, as people "of common understanding," are "as capable of comprehending the primary facts and of drawing correct conclusions from them as are witnesses possessed of special or peculiar training, experience, or observation in respect of the subject under investigation." *Salem v. U.S. Lines Co.*, 370 U.S. 31, 35 (1962) (quotation omitted). For that reason, in "many if not most" cases, expert testimony is not needed because "jurors are generally entitled to draw their own inferences from the evidence." {–206–} *Huffman v. Union Pac. R.R.*, 675 F.3d 412, 419 (5th Cir. 2012) (discussing causation under the Federal Employers Liability Act (FELA)); *cf. Brown v. Parker Drilling Offshore Corp.*, 410 F.3d 166, 178 (5th Cir. 2005) ("Jones Act cases follow cases under the FELA.").

However, "when conclusions as to the evidence cannot be reached based on the everyday experiences of jurors," expert testimony is needed. *Huffman*, 675 F.3d at 419. Put differently, expert evidence is "often

required" where "the nexus between the injury and the alleged cause would not be obvious to the lay juror." *Wills v. Amerada Hess Corp.*, 379 F.3d 32, 46 (2d Cir. 2004) (citing *Moody v. Maine Cent. R.R. Co.*, 823 F.2d 693, 695 (1st Cir. 1987)).

i. Negligence

This court has had relatively few opportunities to opine about when expert medical testimony is needed to survive summary judgment in a Jones Act negligence case. We have not required expert testimony as always necessary to prove Jones Act causation. *See Naquin v. Elevating Boats, L.L.C.*, 744 F.3d 927, 931 n.65, 2 Adm. R. 200, 208 n.65 (5th Cir. 2014) (despite no expert medical testimony on Jones Act plaintiff's claim for mental anguish damages, finding that the claim [—9—] "was supported by the testimony of his wife, his visits to doctors and social workers, and his prescription use of an anti-depressant drug following the accident"). Rather, we follow the general rule that expert testimony is unnecessary when lay fact-finders are capable of understanding causation.[2] Because that inquiry is highly context-dependent, we are guided by example.

---

[1] Gowdy's argument that MSRC committed fraud on the district court by failing to tell Dr. Bain about the 48-inch distance between the ladder rung and the floor is without merit. Dr. Bain testified that he examined photos from the accident scene, which, Gowdy concedes, [—8—] displayed the 48-inch space. Aside from Gowdy's bald assertions, there is no evidence suggesting that MSRC withheld or falsified information when communicating with Dr. Bain.

[2] MSRC cites *Johnson v. Horizon Offshore Contractors, Inc.*, No. CIV.A. 06-10689, 2008 WL 916256, at *4 (E.D. La. Mar. 31, 2008) (quoting *Mayhew v. Bell S.S. Co.*, 917 F.2d 961 (6th Cir. 1990)) for the proposition that "a medical expert must be able to articulate that there is more than a mere possibility that a causal relationship exists between the defendant's negligence and the injury for which the plaintiff seeks damages." MSRC has misapplied that quote. In *Mayhew*, a Jones Act plaintiff appealed his favorable jury verdict, claiming inadequate damages. 917 F.2d at 962. Specifically, Mayhew argued that the district court erred in excluding portions of his treating physician's testimony that the district court had deemed speculative. *Id.* Affirming, the Sixth Circuit held, "Although a Jones Act plaintiff need not present medical evidence that the defendant's negligence was *the* proximate cause of the injury, we believe that a medical expert must be able to articulate that there is more than a mere possibility that a causal relationship exists between the defendant's negligence and the injury for which the plaintiff seeks damages." *Id.* at 963. The Sixth Circuit assumed the existence of a medical expert and explained how that medical expert could

In toxic tort cases, expert testimony is often required. For instance, in *Seaman v. Seacor Marine L.L.C.*, this court determined that the plaintiff needed expert testimony to rebut the defense expert's opinion that second-hand smoke, rather than hazardous chemicals, caused the plaintiff's cancer. 326 F. App'x 721, 729 (5th Cir. 2009). The court reasoned that lay fact-finders lack the requisite scientific knowledge about harm-causing levels of exposure to chemicals. *Id.* at 723. Similarly, in *Wills v. Amerada Hess Corporation*, the Second Circuit explained that expert testimony was needed on the question of whether exposure to toxic chemicals caused squamous cell carcinoma because that causal link was "sufficiently beyond the knowledge of the lay juror." 379 F.3d 32, 46 (2d Cir. 2004) (Sotomayor, J.). The court observed that it had "never [—10—] held that a Jones Act plaintiff can survive summary judgment in a toxic tort case without admissible {–207–} expert testimony on the issue of causation." *Id.*

Expert testimony has also been required in cumulative trauma cases. For example, in *Myers v. Illinois Central Railroad Company*, "neither [the plaintiff] nor his physicians could point to a specific injury or moment that brought on the problems with his knee, elbow, and back and neck." 629 F.3d 639, 643 (7th Cir. 2010).[3] Instead, the plaintiff claimed that the injuries were "the product of years of working for the Railroad." *Id.* The Seventh Circuit applied the rule that "unless the connection between the negligence and the injury is a kind that would be obvious to laymen, expert testimony is required." *Id.* at 642. The court observed that cumulative trauma injuries "can be caused by a myriad of factors, none of which is obvious or certain" and therefore, most often, expert testimony is required. *Id.* at 643 (citing *Brooks v. Union Pacific Railroad Co.*, 620 F.3d 896, 899–900 (8th Cir. 2010) (expert needed for degenerative disk disease); *Granfield v. CSX Transp., Inc.*, 597 F.3d 474, 484–487 (1st Cir. 2010) (expert needed for epicondylitis); *Moody v. Maine Cent. R.R. Co.*, 823 F.2d 693, 696 (1st Cir. 1987) (expert testimony needed for emotional trauma)).

By contrast, expert testimony is not required in cases where the nature of the injury can be understood by lay fact-finders based on ordinary knowledge and experience. In *Tufariello v. Long Island Rail Road Co.*, the Second Circuit gave two examples: "a broken leg from being struck by an automobile" and "hearing loss [from] repeated exposure to noise so loud that it causes physical pain or ear-ringing." 458 F.3d 80, 89 (2d Cir. 2006) (citing *Simpson v. Northeast Ill. Regional Commuter R.R. Corp.*, 957 F.Supp. 136, 138 (N.D. Ill. 1997) for [—11—] the first example); *see also Myers*, 629 F.3d at 643 ("[W]hen a plaintiff suffers from a broken leg or a gash when hit by a vehicle, he doesn't need to produce expert testimony.").

That an injury is acute does not necessarily bring it into the realm of ordinarily cognizable cases. In *Brooks v. Union Pacific Railroad Co.*, the Eighth Circuit confronted facts resembling but slightly differing from the instant case, and the difference is instructive. 620 F.3d at 897. The plaintiff, Robert Brooks, sued Union Pacific Railroad Company (Union Pacific) under the FELA to recover damages for a back injury he claimed to have suffered during an acute traumatic event at work. *Id.* Unlike Gowdy, who identified the exact four-foot-high step that allegedly caused his injury, Brooks stated only that he experienced acute pain "while working underneath a locomotive" on a particular date; he could not "point to a specific incident that injured him." *Id.* at 897, 899. During litigation, Brooks never designated an expert witness, but he did produce medical records and offer an affidavit from his treating physician, who gave a medical opinion that "Brooks's work for Union Pacific caused or contributed to [his] injury." *Id.* at 898 (quotation marks omitted). Union Pacific designated an expert who produced a report stating that Brooks had no specific injury correlated with his employment. *Id.* Then, Union Pacific moved for summary judgment, which the court granted. *Id.* Brooks appealed. *Id.*

---

testify; the court did not have occasion to opine on what should happen if a plaintiff has no medical expert.

[3] This was a FELA case but, as mentioned above, Jones Act cases follow cases under the FELA. *Brown*, 410 F.3d at 178.

The Eighth Circuit held that "[b]ecause the type of injury Brooks suffered had no obvious origin, expert testimony [was] necessary {–208–} to establish even that small quantum of causation required by FELA." *Id.* at 899 (internal quotation marks and citation omitted). In other words, the link between any negligence associated with conditions underneath a locomotive and acutely injuring one's back was deemed to be not "obvious to laymen." *Id.* [—12—]

Whereas it is reasonable to assume that the average lay fact-finder lacks understanding of the physical risks attendant to general working conditions under a locomotive as in *Brooks*, the danger implicated by stepping down from a four-foot-tall ladder rung falls within ordinary understanding. Stepping down from a high ladder rung and fracturing one's foot is closer to breaking one's leg after being hit by a car than to developing cancer after years of toxic tort exposure or experiencing a back injury explicable only by general working conditions underneath a train. The causal link in this case can be understood by jurors based on everyday knowledge and experience.

The only remaining wrinkle is whether a layperson's ability to understand the injury's causal link to the ladder step changes in light of Dr. Bain's expert opinion that Gowdy's step down from the ladder did not cause the injury. When an expert casts doubt on something that is normally obvious, does the thing cease to be obvious?

Our caselaw indicates no. "Juries are often asked to make difficult decisions and, even when expert evidence is available to assist them, they are not bound to follow the experts. The jury may discredit expert testimony and base its decision on its collective judgment and experience." *Moore v. Johns-Manville Sales Corp.*, 781 F.2d 1061, 1064–65 (5th Cir. 1986); *cf. Western Air Lines, Inc. v. Criswell*, 472 U.S. 400, 423 (1985) (explaining that jurors may attach "little weight" to expert testimony they find "unpersuasive").

In this case, a jury could find Dr. Bain's declaration unconvincing. Dr. Bain stated that

Gowdy "sustained either a *high energy* impact to his left mid foot or a crush injury" but that his "injury would not [have] occur[ed] by stepping off the [ladder]" because even if Gowdy had jumped off the ladder "and landed solely on his left foot, it is unlikely to see his injury pattern considering the *low energy* involved with this maneuver." He asserted both that Gowdy's [—13—] injury "would not occur" from the ladder step and also that it would have been "unlikely" to occur from the ladder step. And he commented that "Mr. Gowdy's Charcot . . . pre-dated the alleged event," whereas Dr. Clause's records reflected otherwise.

We emphasize that for Jones Act negligence, proximate causation is not required. As long as the employer's negligence "played any part, even the slightest, in producing the injury," liability attaches. *Gautreaux*, 107 F.3d at 335.

The district court erred in determining that Gowdy's Jones Act negligence claim could not survive summary judgment. Gowdy's simple argument that "[i]t is something anyone can understand; you cannot step off a 48 inch high ladder rung to a metal floor and expect to not get injured" was enough to create a fact issue as to Jones Act negligence, whether or not it ultimately proves convincing.

ii. Unseaworthiness

"Jones Act negligence and unseaworthiness are two separate and distinct claims." *Chisholm v. Sabine Towing & Transp. Co., Inc.*, 679 F.2d 60, 62 (5th Cir. 1982). For Jones Act negligence, the "[d]efendant must bear responsibility if his negligence played any part, even the slightest, in producing the injury." *Id.* "The standard of {–209–} causation for unseaworthiness is a more demanding one and requires proof of proximate cause." *Id.*

In this case, the district court's opinion asserted that a plaintiff's unseaworthiness claim will fail if his Jones Act negligence claim fails. Because the unseaworthiness causation inquiry differs only in degree, not in kind, from Jones Act causation, *see Johnson*, 845 F.2d at 1354 (explaining proximate causation as requiring that the unseaworthy condition "played a substantial part in bringing about or actually causing the injury and that the injury was [—14—] either a direct result or a reasonably probable consequence of the unseaworthiness"), we reverse summary judgment on Gowdy's unseaworthiness claim as well.

CONCLUSION

Because the district court properly handled Shaffer's motion to withdraw, we AFFIRM that ruling. We REVERSE and REMAND for further proceedings on Gowdy's negligence and unseaworthiness claims.

United States Court of Appeals
for the Fifth Circuit

No. 16-30984

STEMCOR USA INC.
VS.
CIA SIDERURGICA DO PARA COSIPAR

On Petition for Rehearing

Decided: June 25, 2019

Citation: 927 F.3d 906, 7 Adm. R. 270 (5th Cir. 2019).

Before **HIGGINBOTHAM**, **GRAVES**, and **HIGGINSON**, Circuit Judges.

[—2—] {–907–} **GRAVES**, Circuit Judge:

On second rehearing of this matter, we certified to the Louisiana Supreme Court the question of whether a suit seeking to compel arbitration is an "action for a money judgment" under Louisiana's non-resident attachment statute, La. Code Civ. Proc. art. 3542. *See Stemcor USA Inc. v. Cia Siderurgica do Para Cosipar*, 740 F. App'x 70 (5th Cir. 2018). The Louisiana Supreme Court having now provided its answer, we conclude that Louisiana's non-resident attachment statute allows for attachment {–908–} in aid of arbitration. Thus, we grant rehearing, withdraw our prior opinion, 895 F.3d 375, 6 Adm. R. 214 (5th Cir. 2018), and substitute the following. We also VACATE the judgment of the district court and REMAND.

I

This is a dispute between two creditors, each of which attached the same pig iron owned by America Metals Trading L.L.P. ("AMT"). Plaintiff–Appellant Daewoo International Corp. ("Daewoo") is a South Korean trading company. In May 2012, Daewoo entered into a series of contracts with AMT for the purchase of pig iron, to be delivered in New Orleans. The sale contracts contained arbitration clauses. Although Daewoo made payments under the contracts, AMT never shipped the pig iron. Thyssenkrupp Mannex GMBH ("TKM") is a German company. Between June 2010 and February 2011, TKM entered into six

contracts to purchase pig iron from AMT. AMT never delivered. In response to the breach of contract, TKM and AMT negotiated a settlement, which required AMT to make quarterly payments to TKM. AMT did not pay. [—3—]

Daewoo sued AMT in the Eastern District of Louisiana, seeking an order compelling arbitration and an attachment of the pig iron on board a ship then-anchored in New Orleans. Daewoo invoked both maritime attachment and the Louisiana non-resident attachment statute, which allows attachments in aid of any "action for a money judgment." La. Code Civ. Proc. art. 3542. Citing both types of attachment, the district court granted Daewoo its attachment. Intervenor-Appellee TKM later attached the same pig iron in Louisiana state court and intervened in Daewoo's federal action arguing that maritime jurisdiction was improper and Louisiana's non-resident attachment statute was in-applicable.

The district court agreed with TKM and vacated Daewoo's attachment. *See Stemcor USA, Inc. v. Am. Metals Trading, LLP*, 199 F. Supp. 3d 1102 (E.D. La. 2016). Specifically, the district court found that because Daewoo's underlying suit sought to compel arbitration, it was not an "action for a money judgment." Thus, the district court found that Daewoo could not receive a non-resident attachment writ. After Daewoo's writ was dissolved, TKM's state court attachment became first in time and the district court transferred proceeds from the parties' agreed sale of the pig iron to state court. Daewoo appealed the district court's conclusion that its Louisiana non-resident attachment writ was invalid. This court heard oral arguments, rendered a decision and reconsidered this matter on rehearing. *See Stemcor USA Inc. v. Cia Siderurgica do Para Cosipar*, 870 F.3d 370, 5 Adm. R. 306 (5th Cir. 2017), *opinion withdrawn and superseded on reh'g*, 895 F.3d 375, 6 Adm. R. 214 (5th Cir. 2018).

On second rehearing of this matter, we certified to the Louisiana Supreme Court the question of whether a suit seeking to compel arbitration is an "action for a money judgment" under Louisiana's non-resident attachment statute, La. Code Civ. Proc. art. 3542. *See Stemcor USA Inc. v. Cia Siderurgica [—4—] do Para Cosipar*, 740 F. App'x 70 (5th Cir. 2018). The Louisiana Supreme Court has now answered. *See Stemcor USA Inc. v. Cia Siderurgica do Para Cosipar*, --- So.3d ----, 2018-CQ-1728, 2019 WL 2041826, (La. May 8, 2019).

II

The district court found federal subject matter jurisdiction under the Convention on the Recognition and Enforcement of Foreign Arbitral Awards (the "Convention"). We agree. {–909–}

For a federal court to have jurisdiction under the Convention, two requirements must be met: (1) there must be an arbitration agreement or award that falls under the Convention, and (2) the dispute must relate to that arbitration agreement. These requirements flow from the text of two sections of the Convention. The explicit jurisdictional provision is Section 203, which gives federal courts jurisdiction over all "action[s] or proceeding[s] falling under the Convention." 9 U.S.C. § 203. "An arbitration agreement or arbitral award arising out of a legal relationship, whether contractual or not, which is considered as commercial, including a transaction, contract, or agreement described in section 2 of this title, falls under the Convention." 9 U.S.C. § 202. Accordingly, the first step for determining jurisdiction is deciding whether the "arbitration agreement or award . . . falls under the Convention." *Id.*

The next step, derived from Section 203, is to ask whether the "action or proceeding"—as opposed to the arbitration agreement or award—falls under the Convention. The Convention's removal statute offers guidance on what "falling under" means because "[g]enerally, the removal jurisdiction of the federal district courts extends to cases over which they have original jurisdiction." *Francisco v. Stolt Achievement MT*, 293 F.3d 270, 272 (5th Cir. 2002). Section 205 of the Convention allows for removal whenever "the subject [—5—] matter of an action or

proceeding pending in a State court relates to an arbitration agreement or award falling under the Convention." 9 U.S.C. § 205. We have read "relates to" to mean "has some connection, has some relation, [or] has some reference" to. *Acosta v. Master Maint. & Constr. Inc.*, 452 F.3d 373, 378–79 (5th Cir. 2006). And reading "falling under" to mean "relates to" makes sense grammatically. "Fall" means "to come within the limits, scope, or jurisdiction of something." Merriam-Webster's Collegiate Dictionary 418 (10th ed. 2002). Accordingly, the second step of the jurisdictional question is asking whether the "action or proceeding" "relates to" a covered arbitration agreement or award. *See Fred Parks, Inc. v. Total Compagnie*, 981 F.2d 1255, 1992 WL 386999, at *1–2 (5th Cir. 1992) (unpublished) (treating the question of original and removal jurisdiction under the Convention as identical).

This two-step jurisdictional inquiry is consistent with case law interpreting the Convention. *See, e.g., BP Expl. Libya Ltd. v. ExxonMobil Libya Ltd.*, 689 F.3d 481, 487 & n.4 (5th Cir. 2012) (finding jurisdiction where there was a covered arbitration agreement and the suit sought appointment of arbitrators); *Borden, Inc. v. Meiji Milk Prods. Co.*, 919 F.2d 822, 826 (2d Cir. 1990) (holding that jurisdiction over preliminary injunction in aid of covered arbitration was proper because the remedy sought did not try to "bypass arbitration"); *Sunkyong Eng'g & Const. Co. v. Born, Inc.*, 149 F.3d 1174, 1998 WL 413537, at *5 (5th Cir. 1998) (unpublished) ("The FAA grants the United States district courts original federal question jurisdiction over arbitral awards and agreements to arbitrate that fall within the Convention."); *Venconsul N.V. v. Tim Int'l. N.V.*, 03Civ.5387(LTS)(MHD), 2003 WL 21804833, at *3 (S.D.N.Y. Aug. 6, 2003) ("*Borden* has been interpreted as recognizing a court's power to entertain requests for provisional remedies in aid of arbitration even where the request for remedies does not accompany a motion to compel arbitration or [—6—] to confirm an award.").

Both jurisdictional requirements are met here. First, Daewoo's arbitration agreements with AMT are covered by the Convention. For an arbitration agreement to be covered by the Convention, four requirements {–910–} must be met: (1) there must be an agreement in writing to arbitrate the dispute; (2) the agreement must provide for arbitration in the territory of a Convention signatory; (3) the agreement to arbitrate must arise out of a commercial legal relationship; and (4) at least one party to the agreement must not be an American citizen. *See Freudensprung v. Offshore Tech. Servs., Inc.*, 379 F.3d 327, 339 (5th Cir. 2004); *Sunkyong*, 149 F.3d 1174, 1998 WL 413537, at *5; *Sedco, Inc. v. Petroleos Mexicanos Mexican Nat'l Oil Co. (Pemex)*, 767 F.2d 1140, 1144–45 (5th Cir. 1985). All four requirements are met here:

- There is an agreement in writing to arbitrate Daewoo and AMT's dispute.

- That agreement provides for arbitration in New York, and the United States is a signatory to the Convention.

- The agreement arises out of a commercial relationship between Daewoo and AMT.

- Both Daewoo and AMT are not American citizens.

Second, this suit is related to the AMT arbitration agreements because Daewoo seeks an attachment to facilitate the arbitration provided for in the AMT agreements. *See Borden*, 919 F.2d at 826 ("[T]he desire for speedy decisions in arbitration is entirely consistent with a desire to make as effective as possible recovery upon awards, after they have been made, which is what provisional remedies do." (internal quotation marks and citation omitted)). Our decision in *E.A.S.T., Inc. of Stamford v. M/V Alaia*, 876 F.2d 1168 (5th Cir. 1989), strongly counsels towards recognizing subject matter jurisdiction based on the Convention to issue provisional remedies in aid of arbitration. The court in *E.A.S.T.*, albeit in the context of a maritime attachment, found [—7—] that the "the arrest of a vessel prior to arbitration is not inconsistent with the Convention." *Id.* at 1173.

And the court noted that the Convention "does not expressly forbid pre-arbitration attachment" and that pre-arbitration attachment "may 'serve[] . . . as a security device in aid of arbitration.'" *Id.* (alteration in original) (quoting *Atlas Chartering Servs., Inc. v. World Trade Grp., Inc.*, 453 F. Supp. 861, 863 (S.D.N.Y. 1978)).

Indeed, *E.A.S.T.*'s reasoning mirrors the reasoning of courts that have found subject matter jurisdiction under the Convention to order state-law provisional remedies. Like the court in *E.A.S.T.*, those courts reason that "nothing in the Convention divests federal courts of jurisdiction to issue provisional remedies . . . such as an attachment, when appropriate in international arbitrations." *Bahrain Telecomms. Co. v. Discoverytel, Inc.*, 476 F. Supp. 2d 176, 181 (D. Conn. 2007); *see also China Nat'l Metal Prods. Imp./Exp. Co. v. Apex Dig., Inc.*, 155 F. Supp. 2d 1174, 1180 (C.D. Cal. 2001) ("Rather than conflicting with the parties' agreement to arbitrate, provisional remedies such as attachment reinforce arbitration agreements by ensuring that assets from which an arbitration award would be satisfied are secured while arbitration is pending."). *E.A.S.T.* therefore strongly suggests that this court recognizes jurisdiction under the Convention to issue state-law preliminary remedies in aid of arbitration.[1] [—8—] {–911–}

---

[1] And there are compelling reasons against reading jurisdiction under Section 203 as narrowly limited to the three remedies expressly allowed by the Convention (compelling arbitration and appointing arbitrators in Section 206 and confirming awards in Section 207). Namely,

[n]othing in § 206 or § 207 limits the subject matter jurisdiction of federal courts. These sections merely identify the remedies that federal courts may grant, and do not speak in jurisdictional terms or refer in any way to the jurisdiction of the district courts. . . . To grant the remedies provided in those sections, the Court must first determine that it has jurisdiction . . . . [—8—]

Treating §§ 206 and 207 as jurisdictional provisions confuses the subject matter jurisdiction of federal courts with their remedial authority. Although jurisdiction is

Applying *E.A.S.T.* and the cases that follow it, the Convention grants jurisdiction over Daewoo's request for an attachment. Like the plaintiff in *E.A.S.T.*, Daewoo sought to attach the pig iron in order to facilitate arbitration and increase its chance of recovering on any award. Because Daewoo sought attachment to bring about a covered arbitration—that is, because Daewoo's suit related to a covered arbitration agreement—this court has subject matter jurisdiction.[2]

III

The parties dispute whether Louisiana's non-resident attachment statute allows for attachment in aid of arbitration. The district court held that it does not.

As stated previously, we certified to the Louisiana Supreme Court the question of whether a suit seeking to compel arbitration is an "action for a money judgment" under Louisiana's non-resident attachment statute, La. [—9—] Code Civ. Proc. art. 3542. *See Stemcor USA Inc. v. Cia Siderurgica do Para Cosipar*, 740 F. App'x 70 (5th Cir. 2018). The Louisiana Supreme Court accepted the

certified question and answered: "Louisiana Code of Civil Procedure article 3542 allows for attachment in aid of arbitration if the origin of the underlying arbitration claim is one pursuing money damages and the arbitral party has satisfied the statutory requirements necessary to obtain a writ of attachment." *See Stemcor USA Inc. v. Cia Siderurgica do Para Cosipar*, --- So.3d ----, 2018-CQ-1728, 2019 WL 2041826, *1 (La. May 8, 2019).

Louisiana's attachment statute provides that "[a] writ of attachment may be obtained in any action for a money judgment, whether against a resident or a nonresident, regardless of the nature, character, or origin of the claim, whether it is for a certain or uncertain amount, and whether it is liquidated or unliquidated." La. Code Civ. Proc. art. 3542. The underlying action seeking to compel arbitration here is clearly an "action for a money judgment" under Louisiana's non-resident attachment statute. See La. Code Civ. Proc. art. 3542. Daewoo has made it clear from the outset that it would be pursuing a money judgment. The "nature, character, or origin of the claim" just happens to be arbitration. La. Code Civ. Proc. art. 3542. Thus, we conclude that the district court erred in finding that the Louisiana non-resident attachment {–912–} statute was not available to Daewoo.

IV

For the above reasons, we VACATE and REMAND.

---

a word of many . . . meanings, there is a difference between the two. The nature of the relief available after jurisdiction attaches is, of course, different from the question whether there is jurisdiction to adjudicate the controversy . . . . The breadth or narrowness of the relief which may be granted under federal law . . . is a distinct question from whether the court has jurisdiction over the parties and the subject matter. Any error in granting or designing relief does not go to the jurisdiction of the court.

CRT Capital Grp. v. SLS Capital, S.A., 63 F. Supp. 3d 367, 374–75 (S.D.N.Y. 2014) (internal quotations marks, citations, and alterations omitted). Simply put, the question of what remedies are available in a Convention suit is distinct from the question of jurisdiction.

[2] We asked the parties to brief whether this court has personal jurisdiction under quasi in rem principles. We are satisfied that we have personal jurisdiction. *See Republic Nat'l Bank of Miami v. United States*, 506 U.S. 80, 88–89 (1992); *Nassau Realty Co., Inc. v. Brown*, 332 So. 2d 206, 210 (La. 1976).

United States Court of Appeals
for the Fifth Circuit

No. 17-30727

LAKE EUGENIE LAND & DEV., INC.
VS.
BP EXPLORATION & PROD., INC.

Appeal from the United States District Court for the
Eastern District of Louisiana

Decided: June 26, 2019

Citation: 928 F.3d 394, 7 Adm. R. 274 (5th Cir. 2019).

Before **GRAVES** and **OLDHAM**, Circuit Judges.*

* Judge Edith Brown Clement was a member of the
panel that heard oral argument. She has since recused
and has not participated in this decision. This case is
being decided by a quorum. *See* 28 U.S.C. § 46(d).

[—2—] {–396–} OLDHAM, Circuit Judge:

We've twice before explained how to "match" revenues and expenses under the Deepwater Horizon Class Action Settlement Agreement. The question presented is whether the district court deviated from our mandate. It did.

I.

On April 20, 2010, Deepwater Horizon exploded and began leaking oil into the Gulf of Mexico. Two years later, the district court simultaneously certified a class of plaintiffs and approved a class action Settlement Agreement. We ultimately affirmed the district court's decision. *See In re Deepwater Horizon*, 739 F.3d 790, 796, 821, 2 Adm. R. 140, 141, 162 (5th Cir. 2014).

The "settlement" settled little. To the contrary, it sparked vehement disputes over its terms and the amounts claimants were entitled to recover. The Settlement Agreement establishes a Court Supervised Settlement Program ("CSSP"): A Claims Administrator oversees third-party accountants who process individual claims in the first instance. *See* DEEPWATER HORIZON ECONOMIC AND PROPERTY DAMAGES SETTLEMENT AGREEMENT § 4.3.2. Either party can appeal an initial claim determination to a three-person Claims Administration Panel. *Id.* §§ 4.3.4, 5.11.4, 6.1.2.3, 6.1.2.4. At the back end, the district court has discretion to review any disputes over the settlement's implementation—including claim determinations. *Id.* §§ 4.3.2, 4.3.4, 4.4.7, 6.6. From there, either party can appeal to us. *See In re Deepwater Horizon (Matching Decision)*, 732 F.3d 326, 332 n.3, 1 Adm. R. 287, 289 n.3 (5th Cir. 2013) ("Based on its use throughout the Settlement, the term 'the Court' appears to refer to the district [—3—] court. . . . However, the parties clearly intended a broader interpretation of the term—one that retained their right to appeal to this court—as shown by BP's appeal and Class Counsel's failure to object."). And while the district court's review is discretionary, *see* SETTLEMENT AGREEMENT § 6.6, ours apparently {–397–} is not, *see Matching Decision*, 732 F.3d at 332 n.3, 1 Adm. R. at 289 n.3 (finding jurisdiction under the collateral order doctrine).

Underlying this elaborate apparatus are myriad claims for money. This appeal involves only one—a "Business Economic Loss" ("BEL") claim. BEL claims provide compensation for the difference between a business's *actual* profits during a three-month period after the oil spill and its *expected* profits over that same period. Expected profits are calculated based on actual profits during a "comparable" period before the spill. SETTLEMENT AGREEMENT Ex. 4C at 1–2. The claimant provides the comparators by designating a post-spill Compensation Period—"three or more consecutive months between May and December 2010"—and a pre-spill Benchmark Period—those same months in 2009, averaged over 2008–2009, or averaged over 2007–2009. *Id.* at 2–3. In relevant part, the Claims Administrator then determines the variable profits for both periods and subtracts the Compensation Period profits from the Benchmark Period profits. *Id.* at 3.

The parties' disputes over this seemingly simple formula have generated an entire body of federal common law in this Circuit. At the risk of adding still more pages to the corpus, we briefly recount the bare essentials here.

In the beginning, the Claims Administrator announced "he would typically consider both revenue and expenses in the period in which those revenues and expenses were recorded" no matter how the claimant recorded them; he "would not typically re-allocate such revenues or expenses to different periods." *Matching Decision*, 732 F.3d at 330–31, 1 Adm. R. at 288 (quotations omitted). BP objected that this approach would give some claimants inflated awards simply [—4—] because they recorded associated revenues and expenses at different times. *Id.* at 331, 1 Adm. R. at 289. It argued the Settlement Agreement required the Claims Administrator to reallocate or "match" a business's expenses to any associated revenues when calculating profits for the Benchmark Period and the Compensation Period. The district court disagreed. *Ibid.*, 1 Adm. R. at 289.

In the *Matching Decision*, we reversed in part and vacated in part. Insofar as the Claims Administrator asserted the power to disaggregate revenues and expenses that a claimant had *already matched*, we instructed the district court to "make certain that this is not occurring." *Id.* at 335, 1 Adm. R. at 293. With respect to those claimants who did *not* match their expenses to revenues, we suggested the Settlement Agreement might require the Claims Administrator to match those claims as well. *Id.* at 336–38, 1 Adm. R. at 293–95. But we ultimately elected not to decide "whether a matching principle should apply to all claims." *Id.* at 339, 1 Adm. R. at 296. Instead, we directed the district court to address that question in the first instance after "develop[ing] a more complete factual record." *Ibid.*, 1 Adm. R. at 296.

On remand, the district court did just that. After revisiting the Settlement Agreement's language, the court concluded "that the provision for subtracting corresponding variable expenses requires that revenue must be matched with the variable expenses incurred by a claimant in conducting its business, and that does not necessarily coincide with when revenue and variable expenses are recorded." *In re Oil Spill by the Oil Rig "Deepwater Horizon" in the Gulf of Mexico*, No. MDL 2179, 2013 WL 10767663, at

*3 (E.D. La. Dec. 24, 2013). It then instructed the Claims Administrator to develop a policy implementing that view. *Ibid.*

The result was Policy 495. In it, the Claims Administrator established different methods for correcting unmatched financial statements. Policy 495 at 3–4. First, it {–398–} created an "Annual Variable Margin Methodology ("AVMM")—the default method for any claims that were insufficiently matched. *Id.* at B1– [—5—] B6. Second, it created Industry-Specific Methodologies ("ISMs") for claimants working in construction, agriculture, education, and professional services. *Id.* at C1–F13.

On appeal, we upheld the AVMM but rejected the ISMs. *In re Deepwater Horizon (Policy 495 Decision)*, 858 F.3d 298, 304, 5 Adm. R. 259, 262 (5th Cir. 2017). The AVMM appropriately required the Claims Administrator to "ensure that costs are registered in the same month as corresponding revenue, regardless of when those costs were incurred." *Id.* at 302, 5 Adm. R. at 260. The ISMs, however, went too far by requiring "smooth[ing]" profits in addition to "matching" revenues and expenses. *Id.* at 303, 5 Adm. R. at 261. Accordingly, we held "that all claimants—including those engaged in construction, agriculture, education, and professional services—shall, on remand, be subject to the AVMM." *Id.* at 304, 5 Adm. R. at 262. Our decretal language reiterated the point: "For the reasons set out above, we AFFIRM as to the AVMM, REVERSE as to the ISMs, and REMAND for further proceedings consistent with this opinion." *Ibid.*, 5 Adm. R. at 262.

On remand, the district court issued orders to implement our decision. In them, it instructed the Claims Administrator to "apply the AVMM to [all Business Economic Loss] claims." But it also said, "the Claims Administrator shall not reallocate revenues, except for the purpose of correcting errors." A later order said "that revenue shall not be reallocated, restated, smoothed, or moved unless done to correct an error." BP appealed, believing these orders deviated from our instructions to apply the AVMM.

II.

We agree with BP. The district court's orders are inconsistent with our mandate in the *Policy 495 Decision*. We first explain the mandate rule. Then we explain the district court's violation of it. **[—6—]**

A.

The mandate rule is a subspecies of the law-of-the-case doctrine: When a court decides a question, it usually decides it once and for all "subsequent stages in the same case." *Arizona v. California*, 460 U.S. 605, 618 (1983). This doctrine operates on a horizonal plane—constricting a later panel vis-à-vis an earlier panel of the same court. BRYAN A. GARNER ET AL., THE LAW OF JUDICIAL PRECEDENT 442 (2016). It also operates on a vertical plane—constricting a lower court vis-à-vis a higher court. *Ibid.*; *see Himely v. Rose*, 9 U.S. (5 Cranch) 313, 316–17 (1809). The vertical variant is what we call the "mandate rule," and it's the kind at issue here. We review *de novo* a district court's compliance with our mandate. *Ball v. LeBlanc*, 881 F.3d 346, 350–51 (5th Cir. 2018).

The first step is figuring out what our mandate said. After all, "a mandate is controlling [only] as to matters within its compass." *Sprague v. Ticonic Nat'l Bank*, 307 U.S. 161, 168 (1939). This inquiry includes consulting "[t]he opinion delivered by this court at the time of rendering its decree." *In re Sanford Fork & Tool Co.*, 160 U.S. 247, 256 (1895). The parties agree our *Policy 495 Decision* was clear: We told the district court to apply the AVMM, but not the ISMs. 858 F.3d at 304, 5 Adm. R. at 262. We did so because the Settlement Agreement permits "matching" a particular claimant's expenses to revenue, *id.* at 303, 5 Adm. R. at 261, but not "smoothing" profits across time using industry-wide methodologies, *id.* at 304, 5 Adm. R. at 262. **{–399–}**

Let's start with "matching." The AVMM is designed to address "[in]sufficient 'matching' of revenue and expenses." Policy 495 at 3. That usually consists of moving *expenses* to match revenue. *See Policy 495 Decision*, 858 F.3d at 302, 5 Adm. R. at 260 (matching requires "ensur[ing] that costs are registered in the same month as corresponding revenue, regardless of when those costs were incurred"). But Policy 495 may permit moving *revenue* where necessary to achieve matching: **[—7—]**

> Contemporaneous P&Ls submitted by the claimant will be restated if [the Claims Administrator identifies] either an error . . . or a mismatch of revenue and variable expenses which can be explained and supported by appropriate documentation. If matching issues remain after such restatements, revenue and/or variable expenses will be allocated [based on the applicable methodology, here AVMM].

Policy 495 at 7 (footnote omitted). And the AVMM itself provides that if the Claims Administrator "identif[ies] an error[] in how the claimant has accounted for revenue or expenses, correcting entries will be made to the P&Ls to *restate revenue and expense to the appropriate month.*" *Id.* at B1–B2 (emphasis added). The bottom line is the AVMM requires moving "revenues and/or variable expenses" to ensure they are matched. The appellees now concede this point. *See* Red Br. 9 ("[T]he Program Accountants also retained discretion to move . . . or otherwise re-allocate revenues" under the AVMM.).

"Smoothing" is different. It starts by matching expenses and revenues, as the AVMM does. Then the ISMs "go a significant step farther." *Policy 495 Decision*, 858 F.3d at 303, 5 Adm. R. at 261. They require the Claims Administrator to reallocate or "smooth" otherwise-lumpy *profits*, using industry-specific formulas on an industry-wide basis. For example, in the *Policy 495 Decision*, we described a hypothetical farmer who received his entire annual profit on a single day when he took his crops to market. *See ibid.*, 5 Adm. R. at 261. The agriculture-specific "ISM would spread [that profit] across the crop season" for all farmers. *Ibid.*, 5 Adm. R. at 261. By doing so, it would prohibit the hypothetical farmer from picking a compensation period with lumpy profits in the benchmark year and little or no profits in the post-spill year. *See, e.g.*, Policy 495 at D1–D6 (Agriculture ISM).

We rejected such smoothing. We recognized it "may well be a fairer alternative," but "it is inconsistent with the plain text of the Settlement Agreement." *Policy 495 Decision*, 858 F.3d at 303, 5 Adm. R. at 261. That plain text gives the individual claimant—there the farmer—"the right to choose his or her [—8—] compensation period." *Id.* at 304, 5 Adm. R. at 261–62. The ISMs undermined that right by treating all farmers alike and then "smoothing" their profits on an industry-wide basis. By contrast, we blessed the AVMM because it respected each individual's choice of compensation period, matched expenses and revenues for that chosen period, and thus ensured each individual claim would be processed "in accordance with economic reality." *Matching Decision*, 732 F.3d at 339, 1 Adm. R. at 296; *see Policy 495 Decision*, 858 F.3d at 302–03, 5 Adm. R. at 260–61.

Therefore, neither the *Matching Decision* nor the *Policy 495 Decision* broadly prohibited the movement of revenue. To the contrary, our latter decision affirmed the AVMM, which expressly *requires* moving "revenue and/or variable expenses" where necessary to ensure matching. We simply held once the Claims Administrator is satisfied that revenues and expenses for a particular claimant are properly matched, he cannot take the additional {–400–} step of "smoothing" the claimant's profits using an industry-wide formula.[1]

---

[1] This accords with our holdings in other cases that the Settlement Agreement compensates only those who suffered actual losses. *See, e.g.*, *BP Explor. & Prod., Inc. v. Claimant ID 100281817*, 919 F.3d 284, 288, 7 Adm. R. 209, 210–11 (5th Cir. 2019); *Matching Decision*, 732 F.3d at 343, 1 Adm. R. at 299 ("[T]he district court had no authority to approve the settlement of a class that included members that had not sustained losses at all, or had sustained losses unrelated to the oil spill . . . ."). Matching and the AVMM help ensure only claimants with losses from the spill are allowed to invoke the machinery of the federal courts to get paid. The prohibition on industry-wide smoothing also furthers that goal by ensuring claims are processed based on the economic realities of the individual claimant.

B.

The next question is whether the district court deviated from that mandate. *See Stewart v. Salamon*, 97 U.S. 361, 362 (1878). It did.

In its first order, the court instructed the Claims Administrator to "apply the AVMM." But it also said "not [to] reallocate revenues, except for the purpose of correcting errors." A subsequent order said something similar: The Claims Administrator should apply the AVMM, "except that revenue shall not [—9—] be reallocated, restated, smoothed, or moved unless done to correct an error." The district court refused to reconsider the orders after BP challenged them.

Both parties agree these orders are inconsistent with the AVMM. The appellees even distinguish them from the "original" AVMM. Red Br. 23. But the AVMM admits of no sequels or substitutes. There is only one. We affirmed it in the *Policy 495 Decision*. The AVMM affirmed by this Court permits the Claims Administrator to move "revenue and/or variable expenses" not only "to correct an error" but also to correct any "matching issues."

We REVERSE and REMAND for further proceedings consistent with this opinion.

United States Court of Appeals
for the Fifth Circuit

No. 17-20599

APACHE DEEPWATER, L.L.C.

vs.

W&T OFFSHORE, INC.

Appeal from the United States District Court for the
Southern District of Texas

Decided: July 16, 2019

Citation: 930 F.3d 647, 7 Adm. R. 278 (5th Cir. 2019).

Before HIGGINBOTHAM, GRAVES, and WILLETT,
Circuit Judges.

[—1—] {–650–} HIGGINBOTHAM, Circuit Judge:

This dispute arises from a successful plugging and abandonment operation of three offshore oil and gas wells in the Mississippi Canyon area of the Gulf of Mexico. Apache Deepwater, LLC performed the operation and seeks payment from its non-operator partner, W&T Offshore, Inc. A jury awarded $43.2 million to Apache for W&T's breach of the Joint Operating Agreement. W&T challenges the district court's application of the Louisiana Civil Code and interpretation of the contract. Alternatively, W&T contends that it is entitled to an offset in damages because of Apache's bad faith. Finding no error, we affirm. [—2—]

I.

In May 1999, Apache and W&T's predecessors entered into a Joint Operating Agreement ("JOA") that governed the operation of three offshore deepwater oil and gas wells (the "Wells") in the Mississippi Canyon area of the Gulf of Mexico. This dispute arises from operator Apache's plugging and abandonment ("P&A") of the Wells.

In 2012, Apache attempted to P&A the Wells with an intervention vessel called *Uncle John* with the consent of W&T, but that operation was unsuccessful. Following that failure, Apache contracted to use a different intervention vessel, the *Helix-534* ("*Helix*").

An internal figure by Apache estimated that the cost to P&A the Wells with the *Helix* was approximately $56,350,000. In June 2014, W&T contacted Apache to set up a status conference in July discussing the P&A operation, confirming that W&T knew "that the *Helix 534* is contracted for the project." At that meeting, W&T learned that Apache proposed using two drilling rigs for the project instead of the *Helix*, the *Ocean Onyx* ("*Onyx*") and *Ensco-8505* ("*Ensco*").

W&T and Apache offered to the jury competing explanations for the switch from the *Helix* to the *Onyx* and *Ensco* drilling rigs. By W&T's telling, Apache's decision to use the *Onyx* and *Ensco* was a simple matter of cost: W&T contends that Apache entered into a contract for the two drilling rigs for the purpose of drilling new deepwater wells, but abandoned that project in 2014 and was left with exorbitant stacking costs for the idle rigs (approximately $1,000,000 per day). W&T asserts that Apache's decision to use the rigs instead of the *Helix* was an attempt to recoup on the costs of contracting for the {–651–} unused rigs because Apache had been unsuccessful in unloading the rigs onto another operator. Prior to the July meeting, Apache prepared estimates for the use of the rigs which totaled between $81 and $104 million. W&T points to an internal presentation in which Apache was weighing the costs of using the [—3—] *Helix* against the rigs and determining that with the stacking costs Apache was paying for the idle rigs, the use of the rigs would be cheaper because the cost would be split with W&T. Apache cancelled the *Helix* contract. W&T claims that although Apache purported to rely on written evaluations explaining the technical reasons the rigs were necessary (including that the *Helix* no longer complied with government regulations), Apache refused to provide those analyses to W&T.

Apache rejects W&T's economic explanation and argues that the *Helix* was not a safe option after the *Deepwater Horizon* spill and the government regulators would not have approved the *Helix* for the P&A operations. Apache put on evidence that it had discussed the risks of using the *Helix* with

W&T, and demonstrated that technical difficulties posed by the Wells would make the "open water" operations of the *Helix* environmentally risky, that the Wells were "high risk," and that the drilling rigs were able to conduct the P&A operations with safeguards mitigating the risk of oil spills. Apache also claimed that the federal Bureau of Safety and Environmental Enforcement ("BSEE") advised Apache that it was no longer approving the type of open-water operations that *Helix* would need to perform to complete the P&A task. In Apache's version, W&T began "actively resisting" the P&A plan using the rigs because the *Helix* operation would be far cheaper for W&T and W&T was disregarding the environmental risk.[1] Apache argued to the jury that W&T ignored the fact that *Helix* would have had operational issues that would have [—4—] increased the costs of the operation past the initial estimates and that the use of the rigs was "reasonably necessary."

Amid their dispute over the appropriate intervention vessel, Apache sought W&T's approval for use of the rigs through an Authorizations for Expenditure ("AFE"), but W&T decided not to approve the use of the rigs,[2] and rejected two other requests for AFEs. Apache decided to use the rigs for the P&A and the work was successfully completed in February 2015 for a total cost of $139,900,000. Apache billed W&T for its

contractual 49% share, or $68,570,000. W&T decided to pay $24,860,640, which represented 49% of the estimate for use of the *Helix*, contending that "Apache's insistence on using a drilling rig unnecessarily and unreasonably increased the costs of this work," and determining that it was not obligated to pay the full billed amount because it had not approved the AFEs. {–652–}

Apache sued for breach of contract in Texas state court in December 2014 and the case was removed by W&T in January 2015. Prior to trial, W&T moved for summary judgment on Apache's breach of contract claim, arguing that the JOA was unambiguous in requiring the operator (Apache) to obtain an approved AFE before expending over $200,000. The parties' argument turned on the reading of two provisions in the JOA: § 6.2 governing authorizations for expenditures and § 18.4 governing abandonment operations required by the government:

6.2. Authorization for Expenditure: The Operator shall not make any single expenditure or undertake any activity or [—5—] operation costing Two Hundred Thousand Dollars ($200,000) or more, unless an AFE has either (1) been included in a proposal for an activity or operation and is approved by the Participating Parties through their Election to participate in the activity or operation, or (2) received the approval of the Parties as a General Matter. When executed by a party, an AFE grants the Operator the authority to commit or expend funds on the activity or operation in accordance with this Agreement for the account of the Participating Parties. . . .

18.4. Abandonment Operations Requirement by Governmental Authority: The Operator shall conduct the abandonment and removal of any well, Production System or Facilities required by a governmental authority, and the Costs, risks and net proceeds will be shared by the Participating Parties in such well, Production System or

---

[1] Apache points to an internal e-mail from W&T's vice president Cliff Williams in which he wrote: "I'd like to determine options should we not agree with operators plan and believe we can perform well abandonments cheaper. Can we non-consent and take over abandonment operations with Apache obligated to pay their share of estimated abandonment costs?"

[2] In its response, W&T stated: "We believe Apache, as a prudent operator, has an obligation to conduct the operation in a cost effective and safe manner in compliance with all governmental regulations. We do not understand why Apache continues to advocate the use of the Ensco 8505 rig when it is clear that an intervention vessel could safely perform the abandonment work at a much lower cost. . . . We do not believe W&T should be obligated to pay the additional charges arising from the use of the Ensco rig when other less expensive options are available."

Facilities according to their Participating Interest Share.

The district court denied W&T's motion for summary judgment and determined that the interaction of the provisions in the JOA was ambiguous, creating an issue of fact as to the "parties' intent on the applicability of § 6.2 to a government-mandated plugging and abandonment operation governed by § 18.4." The case proceeded to trial and the jury made five findings:

(1) Did W&T fail to comply with the Contract by failing to pay its proportionate share of the costs to plug and abandon the MC 674 wells? **Yes.**

(2) What sum of money, if any, would compensate Apache for W&T's failure to pay its proportionate share of costs to plug and abandon the MC 674 wells? **$43,214,515.83.**

(3) Was Apache required to obtain W&T's approval under Section 6.2 of the Contract before Apache plugged and abandoned the MC 674 wells as required under Section 18.4 of the Contract? **No.** [—6—]

(4) Did Apache act in bad faith, thereby causing W&T to not comply with the contract? **Yes.**

(5) By what amount, if any, should the amount you found in response to Jury Question No. 2 be offset? **$17,000,000.**

Following trial, the court entered its order and final judgment, determining that the jury's "bad faith" finding in Question 4 did not preclude Apache's recovery for breach of contract under Louisiana law and holding that W&T was not entitled to an offset under Louisiana law. The district court also denied W&T's motion for a new trial or remittitur and renewed motion for judgment as a matter of law. This appeal followed.

II.

This court reviews the denial of a Rule 50(b) renewed motion for judgment {–653–} as a matter of law de novo, "but our standard of review with respect to a jury verdict is especially deferential."[3] A party is only entitled to judgment as a matter of law on an issue where no reasonable jury would have had a legally sufficient evidentiary basis to find otherwise.[4] In evaluating the evidence, this court "credit[s] the non-moving party's evidence and disregard[s] all evidence favorable to the moving party that the jury is not required to believe."[5] This court also has jurisdiction "to hear an appeal of the district court's legal conclusions in denying summary judgment, but only if it is sufficiently preserved in a Rule 50 motion."[6]

"A district court's resolution of a motion for new trial is reviewed for abuse of discretion, and '[t]he district court abuses its discretion by denying a [—7—] new trial only when there is an "absolute absence of evidence to support the jury's verdict."'"[7] "A motion for a new trial or to amend a judgment cannot be used to raise arguments which could, and should, have been made before the judgment issued."[8] "To the extent that a Rule 59(e) ruling was a reconsideration of a question of law, . . . the standard of review is de novo."[9]

---

[3] Olibas v. Barclay, 838 F.3d 442, 448 (5th Cir. 2016) (quoting Evans v. Ford Motor Co., 484 F.3d 329, 334 (5th Cir. 2007)) (internal quotation marks omitted).

[4] FED. R. CIV. P. 50(a)(1).

[5] Janvey v. Romero, 817 F.3d 184, 187 (5th Cir. 2016) (quoting Abraham v. Alpha Chi Omega, 708 F.3d 614, 620 (5th Cir. 2013)) (internal quotation marks omitted).

[6] Feld Motor Sports, Inc. v. Traxxas, L.P., 861 F.3d 591, 596 (5th Cir. 2017).

[7] McCaig v. Wells Fargo Bank (Tex.), N.A., 788 F.3d 463, 472 (5th Cir. 2015) (quoting Wellogix, Inc. v. Accenture, L.L.P., 716 F.3d 867, 881 (5th Cir. 2013)).

[8] Garriot v. NCsoft Corp., 661 F.3d 243, 248 (5th Cir. 2011) (citation omitted) (internal quotation marks omitted).

[9] Hoffman v. L&M Arts, 838 F.3d 568, 581 (5th Cir. 2016) (internal quotation marks, citations, and alterations omitted). The parties dispute whether the district court's denial of W&T's Rule 59 motion involved a pure question of law, with W&T arguing

III.

W&T contends that the plain language of Louisiana Civil Code Article 2003 dictates that the jury's bad faith finding bars Apache's recovery for breach of contract. Article 2003 states that

An obligee may not recover damages when his own bad faith has caused the obligor's failure to perform or when, at the time of the contract, he has concealed from the obligor facts that he knew or should have known would cause a failure.

If the obligee's negligence contributes to the obligor's failure to perform, the damages are reduced in proportion to that negligence.[10]

In answering the fourth question on the verdict form, the jury found that "Apache act[ed] in bad faith thereby causing W&T to not comply with the contract."

The district court denied W&T's motion for judgment as a matter of law, concluding that it was bound by the Louisiana Supreme Court's decision in [—8—] *Lamar Contractors, Inc. v. Kacco, Inc.*[11] The district court determined that, under *Lamar*, Article 2003's bad faith damages bar is only implicated where the obligor has established {–654–} that the obligee failed to perform a contractual obligation that caused the obligor's failure to perform. In other words, to avoid liability pursuant to Article 2003's bad faith bar, W&T would have to show that Apache failed in its performance of the contract and that failure caused W&T's breach. Because the jury did not find that Apache had breached any obligation under the contract,[12] the district

court reasoned that it was required to set aside the jury's finding on Question 4—that Apache's bad faith caused W&T's failure to perform—meaning Apache was not barred from recovery under Article 2003.

W&T disputes the district court's reading of and reliance on *Lamar*, arguing that (1) *Lamar* is not binding on this court because it is not *jurisprudence constante* and this court must instead follow the plain language of Article 2003, which contains no language limiting Article 2003's application to situations where the obligee has breached; (2) *Lamar*'s holding is limited to Article 2003's negligence clause; and (3) application of *Lamar* is contrary to public policy.

In diversity cases where this court must apply Louisiana substantive law,[13] "we look to the final decisions of the Louisiana Supreme Court."[14] In the absence of a final decision by the state's supreme court, we make an *Erie* guess, which requires us to "employ Louisiana's civilian methodology, whereby we [—9—] first examine primary sources of law: the constitution, codes, and statutes."[15] Even caselaw rising to the level of *jurisprudence constante* is "secondary law in Louisiana"[16] and, accordingly, we are not strictly bound by the decisions of Louisiana's intermediate appellate courts.[17] So, it is only when the Louisiana Supreme Court has not made a

---

that it did and Apache suggesting that W&T's motion merely criticized the evidence presented at trial. The Rule 59 motion and district court's ruling is discussed below in Section III.

[10] La. Civ. Code art. 2003.

[11] 189 So. 3d 394 (La. 2016).

[12] The district court noted that the jury considered and rejected that Apache had breached. For example, had the jury answered Question 3 in the affirmative, that would have amounted to a

finding that Apache had breached an obligation under the contract. Question 3 asked whether Apache was required to obtain W&T's approval under § 6.2 before completing the P&A as required by § 18.4, which the jury answered in the negative.

[13] *Erie R.R. Co. v. Tompkins*, 304 U.S. 64, 78 (1938).

[14] *In re Katrina Canal Breaches Litig.*, 495 F.3d 191, 206 (5th Cir. 2007).

[15] *Id.* at 206 (quoting *Am Int'l Specialty Lines Ins. Co. v. Canal Indem. Co.*, 352 F.3d 254, 260 (5th Cir. 2003)).

[16] *Prytania Park Hotel, Ltd. v. Gen. Star Indem. Co.*, 179 F.3d 169 (5th Cir. 1999).

[17] *In re Katrina*, 495 F.3d at 206 ("Thus, although we will not disregard the decisions of Louisiana's intermediate courts unless we are convinced that the Louisiana Supreme Court would decide otherwise, we are not strictly bound by them.") (citing *Am Int'l Specialty Lines*, 352 F.3d at 261).

determinative decision that this court must make an *Erie* guess, employing Louisiana's civilian methodology.[18]

The parties dispute whether *Lamar* speaks definitively on the issue of whether Article 2003 bars recovery of damages only when the obligee has been found in breach. In *Lamar*, the Louisiana Supreme Court considered a trial court's decision to reduce breach of contract damages awarded to a general contractor, Lamar, after finding that Lamar had contributed to the {–655–} subcontractor's failure to perform.[19] The obligation imposed by Article 2003 is "correlative to the general duty imposed by [Article] 1983, which requires 'contracts must be performed in good faith.'"[20] However, the court warned that the duty of good faith is not to be considered in isolation, and that it is circumscribed by the obligations imposed by the contract.[21] The court noted that "[a]lthough we have not had occasion to consider [Article] 2003 since its [—10—] enactment in 1985, jurisprudence interpreting the predecessor article . . . emphasized that the obligor must establish that the obligee breached the contract, thereby making it more difficult for the obligor to perform its obligation."[22] It concluded: "[A]n obligor cannot establish an obligee has contributed to the obligor's failure to perform unless the obligor can prove the obligee itself failed to perform duties owed under the contract. Stated in other words, Kacco must demonstrate that Lamar failed to perform its obligations under the contract, which in turn

contributed to Kacco's breach of the contract."[23] The question of the obligee's bad faith does not become relevant until there is a determination that the obligee failed to perform a contractual obligation that in turn caused the obligor's failure to perform.[24] For Article 2003 to apply as a damages bar, there must be an antecedent determination of breach.

While W&T urges that the Louisiana Supreme Court's reading was limited to the second sentence of Article 2003—the negligence prong—the *Lamar* court drew no such limitation.[25] The reasoning of *Lamar* did not depend on the relationship between bad faith and negligence. W&T offers no principled reason why the Louisiana Supreme Court would have chosen not to recognize a requirement of breach had the obligee in that case acted in bad faith, rather than negligently. Indeed, we find no distinction in *Lamar*. Because *Lamar* is controlling here, the district court correctly concluded that the good-faith inquiry in Article 2003 is limited to situations where the obligee has [—11—] breached.[26] The jury did not find that Apache breached so Article 2003 does not bar Apache's entitlement to damages as a matter of law.

IV.

W&T also contends that the case never should have gone before a jury because W&T

---

[18] *Boyett v. Redland Ins. Co.*, 741 F.3d 604, 607 (5th Cir. 2014); *see also Moore v. State Farm Fire & Cas. Co.*, 556 F.3d 264, 269–70 (5th Cir. 2009) ("To determine Louisiana law, we look to the final decisions of the Louisiana Supreme Court. In the absence of a final decision by the Louisiana Supreme Court, we must make an *Erie* guess . . . . When faced with unsettled questions of Louisiana law we adhere to Louisiana's civilian decision-making process.").

[19] *Lamar*, 189 So. 3d at 395–97.

[20] *Id.* (citing La. Civ. Code art. 1983) (internal alteration omitted).

[21] *Id.* at 398.

[22] *Id.* (referring to its decisions in *Board of Levee Com'rs of Orleans Levee Dist. v. Hulse*, 120 So. 589, 590 (La. 1929) and *Favrot v. Favrot*, 68 So. 3d 1099, 1109 (La. Ct. App. 2011)).

[23] *Id.*

[24] *Id.* at 399 (summarizing the intermediate appellate court's conclusion in *Favrot* that "the question of a party's good or bad faith does not become relevant until there has been a determination that the party failed to perform an obligation under the contract").

[25] *Id.*

[26] W&T suggests as a last resort that this court may certify the question to the Louisiana Supreme Court. Because we conclude that the Louisiana Supreme Court resolved this issue in *Lamar*, certification is unnecessary here. *Cf. Janvey v. Golf Channel, Inc.*, 792 F.3d 539, 547 (5th Cir. 2015) ("Given . . . that this is a question of state law that no on-point precedent from the Supreme Court of Texas has resolved, that the Supreme Court of Texas is the final arbiter of Texas's law . . . we believe it is best to certify the question at issue.").

did not breach the contract as a matter of law. Section 6.2 of the JOA provides that the operator "shall not make {–656–} any single expenditure or undertake any activity or operation costing Two Hundred Thousand Dollars ($200,000 or more), unless an AFE [is approved]." W&T reads that provision in conjunction with Exhibit C, governing accounting, which provides that "[a]cceptable reasons for non-payment or short payment . . . are as follows: . . . when an AFE is not approved." Together, W&T argues, those provisions unambiguously resolve the issue of whether W&T breached. Because W&T as the non-operator decided not to approve any AFE, it contends that it was entitled to short the payment (and pay its share of the *Helix* P&A estimate) without being found in breach of the JOA. W&T emphasizes that Section 6.2 does not contain an explicit exception for government-mandated operations undertaken pursuant to Section 18.4 and suggests that AFE approval was required even for operations performed under that Section. W&T points out that the parties understood how to make an exception to Section 6.2 and did so in a separate instance, exempting the operator from obtaining AFE approval in the event of a safety-threatening emergency.[27] [—12—]

Apache disputes W&T's reading of the contract, arguing that under Section 18.4, which covers government-mandated P&A operations, Apache was required to undertake its P&A of the Wells as the operator and was authorized to do so without obtaining an AFE from W&T pursuant to Section 6.2. Section 18.4 provides that

> The Operator shall conduct the abandonment and removal of any well, Production System or Facilities required by a governmental authority, and the Costs, risks and net proceeds will be shared by the Participating Parties in

such well, Production System or Facilities according to their Participating Interest Share.

Apache asserts that this provision contemplates cost-sharing between the parties and does not incorporate Section 6.2's AFE process. Apache stresses that requiring a Section 6.2 AFE for a government-mandated P&A operation would lead to an absurd result because the non-operator could essentially holdup an operator from completing a P&A required by federal law to avoid sharing the costs.

The district court denied W&T's motion for summary judgment, concluding that the interplay between Section 6.2 and Section 18.4 was ambiguous, leaving a material question of fact as to the parties' intent. In answering Question Three, the jury found that Apache was not required to obtain W&T's approval through an AFE before conducting the P&A as required by Section 18.4[28]

Whether contract language is ambiguous under Louisiana law is a question of law.[29] Under Louisiana law, "[w]hen the words of a contract are clear and explicit and lead to no absurd consequences, no further [—13—] interpretation may be made in search of the parties' intent."[30] "[I]f a court finds the contract to be unambiguous, it may construe the intent from the face of the document— without considering {–657–} extrinsic evidence—and enter judgment as a matter of law."[31] If the court determines that there is an ambiguity, the question of intent is an issue of fact.[32] "Louisiana courts will not interpret a contract in a way that leads to unreasonable consequences or inequitable or

---

[27] "Notwithstanding the foregoing, in the event of an emergency which poses a threat to life, safety, property, or the environment, the Operator is empowered to immediately make such expenditures for the Joint Account as, in its opinion as a reasonable and prudent Operator, are necessary to deal with the emergency."

[28] "Was Apache required to obtain W&T's approval under Section 6.2 of the Contract before Apache plugged and abandoned the MC-674 wells as required under Section 18.4 of the Contract?"

[29] *Cadwallader v. Allstate Ins. Co.*, 848 So. 2d 577, 580 (La. 2003).

[30] La. Civ. Code art. 2046.

[31] *Preston Law Firm, L.L.C. v. Mariner Health Care Mgmt Co.*, 622 F.3d 384, 392 (5th Cir. 2010) (internal citation omitted).

[32] *Gebreyesus v. F.C. Schaffer & Assocs., Inc.*, 204 F.3d 639, 643 (5th Cir. 2000).

absurd results even when the words used in the contract are fairly explicit."[33]

Applying Section 6.2's expenditure provision to a government-mandated P&A undertaken pursuant to Section 18.4 would lead to an absurd consequence: namely a situation where a non-operator is empowered to hold an operator hostage, preventing the operator from completing a legally required P&A, in order to extract a better bargain or avoid cost-sharing altogether. The oddity of that result is compounded by the fact that Section 18.4 has its own cost-sharing provision,[34] making the idea that the operator was required to obtain an AFE to complete the P&A less tenable. In light of that absurd consequence, the district court correctly concluded that the jury needed to resolve the question of the parties' intent.[35] We agree therefore that [—14—] the question of whether Section 6.2's expenditure requirement applies to government-mandated P&A undertaken pursuant to Section 18.4— which itself mandates cost-sharing—is ambiguous and was properly put to the jury.

W&T's response to the absurdity concern is unavailing. It suggests that if the parties fail to agree on costs through the AFE process, the government can simply conduct the P&A operation itself and charge the operator and non-operator later.[36] W&T does not dispute that federal law required the P&A operation of the Wells—rather it reads the Section 6.2 AFE requirement to apply to government-mandated P&A operations and urges that Apache, having failed to obtain an AFE from W&T, could have decided not to comply with federal regulations and allow the government to P&A the Wells itself. Allowing Apache to evade its obligations under federal law to P&A the Wells is contrary to its duty to conduct all operations as would a prudent operator.[37] W&T's proposed answer to the troubling consequences of its reading is no solution at all. {–658–}

V.

Finally, W&T claims that even if Apache was not barred from recovering damages, W&T is entitled to an offset based on Jury Question No. 5 and that the damages award of $43,214,515.83 should be reduced by $17 million. As to the legal basis for the offset, W&T points to "the basic law of damages" in Louisiana set out in La. Civ. Code art. 1995 that damages cannot place the obligee in a better position than it would have been in if the contract had been fulfilled. W&T posits that the jury determined that a $17 million offset was [—15—] appropriate to account for the savings that Apache enjoyed by not incurring the stacking costs for the rigs. In its view, the jury credited testimony that Apache would have incurred stacking costs between $29.5 million and $36.4 million and adopted the $17 million figure as a reasonable determination of Apache's windfall. The district court denied W&T's motion for entry of judgment and motion for a new trial, concluding that W&T was not entitled to an offset on the basis of Question 5. Specifically, the district court determined that Questions 2

---

[33] *Tex. E. Transmission Corp. v. Amerada Hess Corp.*, 145 F.3d 737, 742 (5th Cir. 1998); *see also* La. Civ. Code art. 2046 ("When the words of a contract are clear and explicit and lead to no absurd consequences, no further interpretation may be made in search of the parties' intent.").

[34] "The Operator shall conduct the abandonment and removal of any well, Production System or Facilities required by a governmental authority, and the *Costs, risks and net proceeds will be shared* by the Participating Parties in such well, Production System or Facilities according to their Participating Interest Share."

[35] La. Civ. Code art. 2046 ("When the words of a contract are clear and explicit and lead to no absurd consequences, no further interpretation may be made in search of the parties' intent."); *Stewart Enters., Inc. v. RSUI Indem. Co., Inc.*, 614 F.3d 117 (5th Cir. 2010) (holding that the most straightforward reading of the contract would lead to an absurd result that "could not have been intended by the parties").

---

[36] "If parties cannot agree about costs and thus fail to P&A wells, the government can arrange for the P&A, deem the bond the working interest owners were required to provide forfeited to the amount that would cover P&A costs, and charge the working interest owners for any excess costs."

[37] "The Operator shall conduct all operations in a good and workmanlike manner, as would a prudent operator under the same or similar circumstances."

and 5 were *not* linked, and offset was unavailable as an affirmative defense under any of W&T's theories.

Article 1995 provides that "[d]amages are measured by the loss sustained by the obligee and the profit of which he has been deprived."[38] "The measure of damages for a breach of contract is the sum that will place plaintiff in the same position as if the obligation had been fulfilled."[39] On Question 2, the jury was instructed in accordance with Article 1995 to calculate "an amount that is fair compensation for those damages." The court then explained to the jury:

> Damages are measured by the loss sustained by the non-breaching party. These are called compensatory damages. The damages amount is the amount that will place Apache in the position it would have been in if the parties' contract had been properly performed. The damages include the amount a party owed under the contract.

The jury was instructed to determine the actual loss sustained without reference to Question 5. W&T's own closing argument emphasized this understanding, encouraging the jury in calculating an amount for Question 2 to subtract the amount of savings W&T attributed to Apache's avoiding the [—16—] stacking costs by using the rigs.[40] W&T's offset argument on appeal ignores the fact that the jury instructions with respect to Question 2 tracked the language of Article 1995. The two cases W&T relies on do not offer a theory entitling W&T to offset. In *Evangeline Parish School Bd. v. Energy Contracting Servs., Inc.*, the Louisiana appellate court considered a damages award in favor of an obligee to an energy-savings services contract.[41] The court reaffirmed the general principle of Article 1995 that "[d]amages for obligor's failure to perform are measured by the loss sustained by the obligee and the profit of which he has been deprived" and remanded, noting that the experts failed to calculate the amount overcharged and the {-659-} appellate court was therefore "unable to make such a determination from the record."[42] There is no lack of clarity in the record here—W&T simply disputes the jury's rejection of its stacking costs theory. In *Swoboda v. SMT Prop., LLC*, the Louisiana appellate court considered the damages award in a contract dispute involving the construction of a residential home.[43] In accordance with Article 1995, the court "consider[ed] the benefit to plaintiffs in maintaining ownership and possession of the adjacent lot [and] conclude[ed] that plaintiffs [we]re not entitled to reimbursement."[44] Again, W&T ignores that the jury was instructed in accordance with Article 1995 and explicitly calculated the actual loss sustained by Apache. W&T's stacking costs theory was rejected by the jury and it has offered no legal theory to support upsetting that verdict. [—17—]

W&T posits two additional legal bases to support an offset in Apache's damages award. First, W&T suggests that Article 2323, governing comparative fault, provides an independent legal basis for a reduction. Article 2323 applies in tort cases; the Civil Code provides its own rule governing comparative fault in contract cases—Article 2003—that we have already determined does not aid W&T here.[45] W&T also claims the doctrine of compensation under Article 1893 gives independent grounds for an offset.[46] As

---

[38] La. Civ. Code art. 1995.

[39] *Gloria's Ranch LLC v. Tauren Exploration, Inc.*, 252 So. 3d 431, 445–46 (La. 2018) (internal citation and quotation marks omitted).

[40] "Number two is the damage issue. We believe that if you get to that issue, and you believe that somehow damages should be awarded in this case, they say it is 43.2 million. We think they benefited anywhere . . . between 29 to 36 million. So we believe you should subtract that from any damage amount you decide to award in the case."

[41] 617 So. 2d 1259 (La. App. 3d. 1993).

[42] *Id.* at 1267.

[43] 975 So. 2d 691 (La. App. 2008).

[44] *Id.* at 695.

[45] *See Justiss Oil Co. v. Oil Country Tubular Corp.*, 216 So. 3d 346, 356–57 (La. Ct. App.), *writ denied*, 227 So. 3d 830 (La. 2017) (quoting *Hanover Ins. Co. v. Plaquemines Parish Gov't*, No. 12–1680, 2015 WL 4167745, at *5–6 (E.D. La. July 9, 2015).

[46] Article 1893 provides that "Compensation takes place by operation of law when two persons

the district court correctly noted, W&T "previously admitted neither [compensation or unjust enrichment] could be the basis of the jury's finding, as that was not the nature of the evidence presented to the jury." In its post-verdict briefing, W&T conceded that Article 1893 did *not* apply, because "the jury was not instructed on the specific requirements of the traditional doctrine of offset or setoff, which requires debts owed by both parties being offset against each other." Neither comparative fault nor compensation provide a basis for a reduction in the damages award here.

Finally, W&T offers a last-ditch argument that the jury award was clearly excessive because of Apache's savings on the stacking costs. The district court did not abuse its discretion in denying W&T's motion for a new trial or remittitur. We agree with the district court the damages award was supported by substantial evidence. The jury logically awarded the precise amount that W&T shorted by making a partial payment after the P&A operation. Such an award was not excessive or "contrary to right reason"— rather, it reflects that [—18—] the jury's consideration of the evidence led it to reject W&T's assertion that Apache enjoyed a windfall by avoiding the stacking costs.[47] {–660–}

VI.

For the foregoing reasons, the judgment of the district court is affirmed.

---

owe to each other sums of money or quantities of fungible things identical in kind, and these sums or quantities are liquidated and presently due. In such a case, compensation extinguishes both obligations to the extent of the lesser amount." La. Civ. Code art. 1893.

[47] *Laxton v. Gap, Inc.*, 333 F.3d 572, 586 (5th Cir. 2003) ("When a damage award is merely excessive or so large as to appear contrary to right reason, remittitur is the appropriate remedy.").

United States Court of Appeals
for the Fifth Circuit

No. 18-60542

WOOD GROUP PROD. SERVS.
vs.
DIRECTOR, OFFICE OF WORKERS' COMPENSATION
PROGRAMS

Petition for Review of an Order of the Benefits
Review Board

Decided: July 22, 2019

Citation: 930 F.3d 733, 7 Adm. R. 287 (5th Cir. 2019).

Before CLEMENT, DUNCAN, and OLDHAM, Circuit
Judges.

[—1—] {–734–} DUNCAN, Circuit Judge: {–735–}

Luigi Malta was injured while unloading a vessel on a fixed platform in the territorial waters of Louisiana. Malta made a claim against his employer, Wood Group Production Services (Wood Group), under the Longshore and Harbor Workers' Compensation Act. To enjoy coverage under the Act, a claimant must show both that he was in a place covered by the Act (situs) and that he was engaged in maritime employment (status). The Benefits Review Board concluded that because Malta—who spent 25 to 35 percent of his working hours loading/unloading vessels—was injured while unloading a [—2—] vessel on a platform customarily used for that task, Malta satisfied both the situs and status requirements. We deny Wood Group's petition for review.[1]

I.

Wood Group, which staffs personnel for clients in the oil and gas industry,[2] employed Malta as a warehouseman for the Black Bay Central Facility (Central Facility), a fixed platform located in the territorial waters of

Louisiana.[3] Central Facility provides support services for oil and gas production occurring at various satellite production platforms in the Helis Black Bay Field. Twenty-two workers, including Malta, lived, worked, and slept at Central Facility, which comprises four separate platforms, connected by catwalks. A warehouse sits on one of these platforms, and in it the workers stored supplies and tools necessary for their sustenance and operations. Three cranes, located at various parts of Central Facility, assisted the workers as they loaded and unloaded these supplies from vessels, which often came from Venice, Louisiana. When workers on the satellite platforms required tools for their operations, the necessary items were taken from the warehouse and loaded onto vessels by crane. The vessels then travelled to the satellite platforms with these supplies.

Malta worked twelve hours each day—from sunup to sundown—seven days per week at Central Facility (and then he would rest shoreside for seven days). He never worked on any of the satellite platforms. His primary duties included ordering, receiving, and maintaining all supplies and equipment at the Central Facility warehouse. It is undisputed that, although not listed [—3—] among his official job duties, a significant portion of Malta's "hitch" (shift), was dedicated to loading and unloading vessels arriving at and leaving from Central Facility. Wood Group's project manager, Ray Pitre, testified that this was a "big part" of Malta's job. And Malta testified that he spent roughly 25 to 35 percent of each hitch loading and unloading vessels.

Malta explained that he regularly would load/unload all sorts of things into/from the vessels: "It can be anywhere from piping to big valves, compressors, drinking water supplies, various items, nothing in particular everyday. It's just whenever we order and something is needed, [I] pull it off the work barge or the water barge." Pitre similarly testified that Malta would unload "a various assortment of things from rags to repair parts to nitrogen

---

[1] Wood Group's insurer—Authorized Group Self-Insurer Signal Mutual Indemnity Association, Ltd. c/o Coastal Risk Services, LLC—is also a petitioner.

[2] Here, Wood Group was a contractor for Helis Oil and Gas Company.

[3] Two photographs of Central Facility appear at the end of our opinion.

cylinders to valves and phalanges . . . [because] the oil industry uses just a vast assortment of {–736–} supplies." During a typical 12-hour hitch, if a group of workers on a "satellite platform needed additional supplies and equipment," Malta "would help load the field boat." This required Malta, "depending on exactly what it was [and] how big it was, [to] put it on a basket, and send it down to the boat and then off to the respective platform or field operator." Malta testified that there was "no difference" between his duties and those of "a dock worker loading and unloading" vessels in Venice.

Malta was injured when unloading a boat owned by a third party. He received a call seeking help to offload something coming up from the boats (which had come from one of the satellite platforms). Malta did not go onto the vessel to retrieve the item. Rather, it was "sent up to [him] via crane" while he was standing on the platform in front of the warehouse. As the basket was coming up, he "grabbed the tag line, pulled it in[,] and as the basket collapsed," Malta saw that the item was a CO2 cannister—which had been mistakenly marked as empty. While Malta was removing the cannister from the cargo basket, it exploded, and he was injured. [—4—]

Malta made a claim for benefits against Wood Group under the Longshore and Harbor Workers' Compensation Act (LHWCA or Act), 33 U.S.C. § 901, *et. seq.* By way of background, the Act "provides compensation for the death or disability of any person engaged in 'maritime employment,'" under certain conditions. *Herb's Welding, Inc. v. Gray,* 470 U.S. 414, 415 (1985). Wood Group contested Malta's claim for benefits. None of the facts was disputed, and the only question was whether Malta was qualified to recover under the Act. After a hearing, an Administrative Law Judge (ALJ) initially ruled against Malta, concluding "that [because] the fixed platform on which [Malta] worked" was not covered under the Act, there was no jurisdiction to consider his claim. In light of this holding, the ALJ did not initially decide whether Malta enjoyed maritime status under § 902 of the Act.

The Benefits Review Board (Board) reversed the ALJ's decision, concluding the ALJ misapplied this court's precedent and the plain language of the statute. It held that Malta's "injury occurred on a covered situs" and remanded the case so that the ALJ could address Malta's status.

On remand, once again, none of the facts was in dispute. The only question was whether Malta enjoyed maritime status. The ALJ found that, because Malta "loaded or unloaded the cargo from a ship or vessel, he was performing a traditional maritime activity" and satisfied "the status requirement of the Act." Wood Group appealed to the Board, which affirmed the ALJ's decision.

Having exhausted its options before the Department of Labor, Wood Group filed a petition for review with this court, arguing that Malta cannot recover under the Act because he lacks status and his injury did not occur on [—5—] a covered situs. Both Malta and the Director of the Office of Worker's Compensation Programs[4] filed briefs defending the Board's decision.

II.

If "the facts are not in dispute"—as is true of this appeal—then whether a worker is covered under the Act presents a "pure question of law" that "is an issue of statutory construction and legislative intent." {–737–} *New Orleans Depot Servs., Inc. v. DOWCP (Zepeda),* 718 F.3d 384, 387, 1 Adm. R. 228, 229 (5th Cir. 2013) (quoting *DOWCP v. Perini N. River Assocs.,* 459 U.S. 297, 300, 305 (1983)). Accordingly, we review the Board's decision de novo. *Id.,* 1 Adm. R. at 229.

III.

Wood Group contends the Board erred by reversing the ALJ's initial decision holding that Malta's injury failed to satisfy the Act's situs requirement. The current form of the

---

[4] "The Director is a party to the litigation of disputed claims under the Act at all stages of the litigation." *Munguia v. Chevron U.S.A. Inc.,* 999 F.2d 808, 810 n.1 (5th Cir. 1993).

situs requirement—found at § 903—says a claimant is eligible for benefits

> only if the disability or death results from an injury occurring upon the navigable waters of the United States (including any adjoining pier, wharf, dry dock, terminal, building way, marine railway, or other adjoining area customarily used by an employer in loading, unloading, repairing, dismantling, or building a vessel).

33 U.S.C. § 903(a). Congress has tinkered with the situs requirement. "Prior to 1972, the Act applied only to injuries occurring on navigable waters. Longshoremen loading or unloading a ship were covered on the ship and the gangplank but not shoreward, even though they were performing the same functions whether on or off the ship." *Chesapeake & Ohio Ry. Co. v. Schwalb*, 493 U.S. 40, 46 (1989). The Supreme Court has said that the current version of the situs requirement, which should be "liberally construed," covers "all those [—6—] on the situs involved in the essential or integral elements of the loading or unloading process." *Id.* The Supreme Court has defined loading and unloading a vessel to mean "taking cargo out of the hold, moving it away from the ship's side, and carrying it immediately to a storage or holding area." *Ne. Marine Terminal Co. v. Caputo*, 432 U.S. 249, 266–67 (1977).

It is undisputed that Central Facility does not meet the definition of "navigable waters" or any of the structures enumerated in this section ("pier, wharf, dry dock, terminal, building way, marine railway"). So, under the language of the statute, Malta can recover only if his injury occurred on an "other adjoining area customarily used by an employer in loading [and] unloading a vessel." § 903(a).

This court has said that, "[t]o qualify as an 'other adjoining area,' the situs must be located in proximity to navigable waters (i.e., possess a geographical nexus) and have a maritime nexus—here, 'customarily used by an employer in loading . . . a vessel.'" *Coastal Prod. Servs. Inc. v. Hudson*, 555 F.3d 426, 432

(5th Cir. 2009) (quoting § 903(a)). These two factors have been described as the geographic and functional components of the situs test. *See Zepeda*, 718 F.3d at 389, 1 Adm. R. at 231 (explaining that "'other adjoining area' must satisfy two distinct situs components: (1) a geographic component (the area must adjoin navigable waters) and (2) a functional component (the area must be 'customarily used by an employer in loading [or] unloading . . . a vessel'")). "To satisfy the situs inquiry's functional prong, the site of the injury need not be 'exclusively' or 'predominantly' used for unloading—only customarily." *BPU Mgmt., Inc./Sherwin Alumina Co. v. DOWCP (Martin)*, 732 F.3d 457, 461, 1 Adm. R. 326, 328 (5th Cir. 2013). And the court looks to "the general purpose of the area rather than requiring 'every square inch of an area' to be used for a maritime activity." *Id.*, 1 Adm. R. at 328.

It is undisputed that Central Facility—situated in the territorial waters of Louisiana—has a geographical nexus to navigable waters. So the situs [—7—] question boils down to whether Central Facility, or at least the part of it where Malta was injured, {–738–} meets the functional component of the test—*i.e.*, whether it is "customarily used" in loading and unloading vessels.

Wood Group offers two reasons to support its position that Malta's injury does not satisfy the situs requirement: (a) the purpose of Central Facility was oil and gas production, and so it did not have a maritime purpose; and (b) the items Malta loaded/unloaded were not maritime cargo.

The Board rejected Wood Group's argument and compared the platform where Malta was injured to an offshore dock, emphasizing the plain language of the statute:

> In a case like this one in which claimant is injured in an area that is customarily used for loading and unloading vessels, it follows that the requisite relationship with maritime commerce is established for purposes of the functional component of the situs test, and any further inquiry

into whether there is an independent connection to maritime commerce is superfluous.

But, despite the plain language of the statute, Wood Group contends—and the ALJ initially agreed—that the Board's situs reasoning conflicts with this court's precedent as illuminated by Wood Group's two arguments. We address, and reject, each argument in turn.

A.

Wood Group first contends that Central Facility cannot satisfy the situs requirement because it did not have a "maritime purpose." The text of the Act does not expressly include any "maritime purpose" requirement. So, to support its position, Wood Group relies principally on this court's opinion in *Thibodeaux v. Grasso Production Management, Inc.*, 370 F.3d 486 (5th Cir. 2004). In that case, Randall Thibodeaux worked as "a pumper/gauger" on "a fixed oil and gas production platform," and, "[a]s part of his duties," he "monitored gauges both on the platform and on nearby wells." *Id.* at 487. [—8—] Thibodeaux's injury occurred after he noticed an oil leak five feet below the deck of the platform. Because a small wooden platform under the deck offered a better vantage to view the leak, he jumped down onto the wooden platform. The wood gave way, Thibodeaux fell into the marsh, and a nail stabbed his hand. *Id.* at 488. Describing the mishap, the court noted that "[t]he accident did not occur on the portion of the platform used to dock the two vessels." *Id.*

After Thibodeaux made a claim under the Act, the "sole issue" before the court was "whether a fixed oil production platform built on pilings over marsh and water inaccessible from land constitutes either a 'pier' or an 'other adjoining area' within the meaning of § 903(a)." *Id.* (footnote omitted). The court decided that "[t]he maritime nature of the LHWCA imparts a meaning to § 903(a)'s enumerated terms that goes beyond their use in ordinary language." *Id.* at 490–91. And, "when viewed together in the context of the LHWCA, a connection to maritime commerce

becomes the unifying thread connecting the listed structures" in the Act—*i.e.*, "pier, wharf, dry dock, terminal, building way, marine railway." *Id.* at 491 (discussing § 903(a)). So, the court reasoned, "in light of the statute's origin and aim, it would be incongruous to extend it to cover accidents on structures serving no maritime purpose." *Id.* Because the "work commonly performed on oil production platforms is not maritime in nature," and because "to be a pier within the meaning of the LHWCA a structure must have some maritime purpose," the court held that the oil production platform where Thibodeaux worked did not meet that standard. *Id.* at 493. The court bolstered this reasoning by noting that Supreme {—739—} Court precedent "considered fixed oil production platforms to be islands." *See id.* at 492 (discussing *Herb's Welding*, 470 U.S. at 422 n.6; *Rodrigue v. Aetna Casualty & Surety Co.*, 395 U.S. 352, 360 (1969)). And, islands, of course, are not covered under the Act. *See id.* [—9—]

The *Thibodeaux* court also considered whether the platform was an "other adjoining area" under the Act. *Id.* at 494. Even construing the term "area" broadly to include not just the wooden platform but also the production platform, the court determined that the oil production platform was not "the site of significant maritime activity." *Id.* Thus, the court denied Thibodeaux's claim because the injury did not occur on a covered situs.

Wood Group contends that if even an enumerated structure (*e.g.*, a pier as discussed in *Thibodeaux*) requires a "maritime purpose" then, *a fortiori*, an "other adjoining area" like Central Facility must also have a "maritime purpose" to qualify as a covered situs. Wood Group disagrees with the Board's characterization of the Central Facility platform as an "offshore dock." Because Central Facility is a fixed platform with the purpose of finding and producing oil—like the fixed oil production platform in *Thibodeaux*—Wood Group argues Central Facility does not have a maritime purpose. Thus, according to Wood Group, Malta's injury cannot satisfy the statutory situs requirement.

In response, Malta and the Director emphasize the features of Central Facility that differ from the fixed platform discussed in *Thibodeaux*. Specifically, Malta points out that, as evidenced by the pictures in the record, Central Facility is not a standalone fixed platform. It is a facility designed as a central hub to support a multitude of smaller platforms in and around the oilfield. Central Facility comprises four platforms and includes a safe harbor designed to allow for loading and unloading vessels in rough seas. Third-party vessels service the surrounding facilities, including a vessel that travels daily between Central Facility and Venice, Louisiana. Importantly, Central Facility is equipped with three cranes and a fulltime crane operator who works with the dedicated warehousemen (including Malta) to load and unload vessels throughout the day. [—10—]

Moreover, Malta and the Director contend the Board was correct when it determined that the plain language of the Act is dispositive here. Although this court has said that "the mere act of loading, unloading, moving, or transporting something is not enough"—because, of course, these activities can occur in non-maritime contexts—loading/unloading is maritime when "undertaken with respect to a ship or vessel." *Martin,* 732 F.3d at 462, 1 Adm. R. at 328.

We are not persuaded by Wood Group's argument that the purpose of the structure where the injury occurred is the Alpha and Omega of the situs inquiry, regardless of whether the platform is customarily used for loading/unloading vessels. This does not comport with either the plain text of the statute or the Supreme Court's command to construe the Act liberally. *See Schwalb*, 493 U.S. at 46; *see also Estate of Cowart v. Nicklos Drilling Co.,* 505 U.S. 469, 475 (1992) ("[W]hen a statute speaks with clarity to an issue judicial inquiry into the statute's meaning, in all but the most extraordinary circumstance, is finished."). Here, it is undisputed that significant unloading occurred on the dock where Malta was injured. Indeed, Malta was injured while unloading a boat. And Wood Group's argument overlooks significant nuance in

Thibodeaux, which expressly noted that "[t]he {—740—} accident did not occur on the portion of the platform used to dock the two vessels." 370 F.3d at 488. The *Thibodeaux* court observed that minor maritime activity occurring in specific areas of the fixed platform—where the injury did not occur—did not transform the entire platform into a covered situs. It does not follow from this unobjectionable proposition, however, that an injury should evade coverage if it occurs on a specific portion of a platform where loading/unloading *does* occur merely because the general purpose of the entire platform is dedicated to another task. Wood Group's heavy reliance on *Thibodeaux* is misplaced. [—11—]

B.

The second piece of Wood Group's situs argument is that the Board erred by finding that the nature of the items Malta loaded and unloaded was "irrelevant" to determining whether an "other adjoining area" satisfies the functional component of the situs inquiry. Wood Group's argument is that, to meet the situs requirement, the cargo being loaded/unloaded from a vessel must be "product to be delivered into the stream of commerce."[5]

---

[5] Wood Group contends that "[c]rucial in determining whether an item constitutes 'cargo,' is pinpointing the exact point at which the item in question 'moves from the stream of maritime commerce and longshoring operations to . . . its ultimate destination." (quoting *McKenzie v. Crowley Am. Transp., Inc.*, 36 BRBS 41, 2002 WL 937755 at *5 (April 3, 2002)). Wood Group supports this contention by citing numerous trucking cases that limit recovery under the Act for truckers picking up stored cargo. Wood Group contends that these cases stand for the proposition that when items have reached their ultimate destination in the stream of commerce, they cease being "cargo." According to Wood Group, the items initially shipped to the warehouse at Central Facility had reached their final destination and were no longer cargo, even when later shipped to the satellite platforms. Wood Group misreads these cases, which do not graft a maritime cargo requirement onto the text of the statute. Instead, they detail when coverage under the Act applies (or does not apply) to truckers involved (or not) in loading and unloading a vessel. *See, e.g., id.* at *6 ("In this case, claimant drove a truck not to move cargo as part of

According to Wood Group, the items Malta loaded/unloaded were not maritime "cargo" under its definition because the vessels were loaded with supplies used by the workers on the platforms with the purpose to produce oil and gas. The language of the statute's situs requirement does not use the word "cargo." But Wood Group contends that the Board's reasoning conflicts with several opinions of this court that at least implicitly read a maritime cargo requirement into the Act.

Wood Group looks for support in *Coastal Production Services Inc. v. Hudson*, 555 F.3d at 428. In *Hudson*, a fixed platform with living quarters was connected to a sunken storage barge by pipes and a walkway. *Id.* The platform collected oil via pipeline from surrounding satellite wells, processed that oil, and then transferred it into the sunken barge. Vessels would then dock at the [—12—] barge to be loaded with oil. *Id.* While on the fixed platform (not on the barge where the loading occurred), Terry Hudson was injured when a saltwater disposal pump he was fixing exploded. *Id.* at 429. The question for the court was whether the situs requirement was satisfied even though Hudson was injured on the fixed platform. Wood Group points to a line from *Hudson* that notes the "[v]essels were not loaded or unloaded directly from the [fixed] platform, *at least not with cargo*." 555 F.3d at 434 (emphasis added). Wood Group argues that, from this line of text, the court should conclude that, although *something* was being loaded and unloaded from the fixed platform, whatever {–741–} it was apparently was not "cargo" as Wood Group defines that term. As a result, whatever loading/unloading activity was occurring on the fixed platform was insufficient to render it a covered situs under the Act.

Even assuming the *Hudson* court meant to freight that one stray line of text with such meaning, the court held that the platform was a covered situs under the Act on other grounds, and so the language was dicta. Under the plain language of the statute, coverage extends to an area "customarily used

by an employer in loading [or] unloading . . . a vessel." *Zepeda*, 718 F.3d at 389, 1 Adm. R. at 231. When the plain language of the statute is clear, as it is here, that ends our inquiry. *See Cowart*, 505 U.S. at 475. In any event, we do not read *Hudson* to add anything to the statute, including a maritime cargo requirement.

Wood Group also looks to this court's decision in *Martin* to support its position. 732 F.3d at 459, 1 Adm. R. at 326. David Martin was injured in an "underground transport tunnel." *Id.*, 1 Adm. R. at 326. The court held that the tunnel did not meet the situs requirement because the tunnel was not "'customarily used' for unloading vessels." *Id.* at 461, 1 Adm. R. at 328. In arriving at this conclusion, the *Martin* court reiterated this court's analysis that "the primary purpose of . . . loading and unloading [is] to get cargo on or off the [vessel]." *Id.* at 462, 1 Adm. R. at 328. The facility where Martin worked processed bauxite (a clayey rock that is the chief commercial ore of [—13—] aluminum), and some of the bauxite, which was delivered to the facility by ship, would go through the underground tunnel where Martin was injured. But the bauxite would enter the tunnel only after it "[sat] in a long-term storage stockpile, migrate[d] to the bottom of its respective ore pile, [was] specifically selected . . . for production, [was] crushed in the screw feeder, and [was] finally transported towards the metal-extraction facility." *Id.* at 464, 1 Adm. R. at 330. The court concluded that the "[o]re at this stage is clearly no longer being 'unloaded' from a vessel in any sense of the word." *Id.*, 1 Adm. R. at 330.

Wood Group argues that *Martin* shows the nature of the items being unloaded matters when determining whether a structure serves a maritime purpose. According to Wood Group, the bauxite ceased being "cargo" before it arrived at the underground tunnel, and because Martin was unloading something other than maritime cargo, he was ineligible for coverage under the Act. But Wood Group reads too much into *Martin*, which addressed the express term "unloading" in the statute. § 903(a). The court explained that the long process the bauxite took before entering the

a loading process, but to start it on its overland journey.").

tunnel was not "unloading." And "the fact that surface-level storage buildings are connected to the unloading process [did] not automatically render everything above and below the buildings [including underground transport tunnels] a part of the unloading process." 732 F.3d at 461–62, 1 Adm. R. at 328. Whether the bauxite was "cargo" was irrelevant.

Nor does this court's opinion in *Munguia v. Chevron U.S.A. Inc.*[6] offer refuge to Wood Group's position. Noel Munguia, a pumper-gauger, was injured while working on a fixed well platform. 999 F.2d at 809. The court listed Munguia's duties as follows: "He loaded onto [a] boat the tools and equipment [—14—] he would need for the day and then navigated the boat to and from the various platforms. At each platform he {—742—} unloaded the tools and equipment needed to do the work required at that platform." *Id.* at 812. The court noted that his duties "involved little or no loading and unloading of boats." *Id.* And the court downplayed the loading/unloading that the claimant performed: "Because the transfer of small amounts of supplies between tank batteries by Munguia and his fellow roustabouts . . . [furthered] the non-maritime-related purpose of servicing and maintaining the fixed platform wells, the mere fact that Munguia may have loaded and unloaded them onto his skiff cannot confer coverage." *Id.* at 813. The court further explained that "[a]ny contact Munguia may have had with cargo was fleeting, unrelated to maritime commerce, and usually at a time by which these supplies no longer possessed the properties normally associated with 'cargo.'" *Id.*

Wood Group contends this language adds a maritime cargo requirement to the Act, but *Munguia*, like *Martin*, merely glosses the Act's express terms "loading and unloading." According to *Munguia*, if a claimant unloads nothing more than personal gear from a boat in furtherance of pursuits not customarily

thought of as maritime commerce, that claimant has failed to satisfy the loading/unloading requirement because he has performed "little or no loading and unloading of boats." Moreover, the facts of *Munguia* are distinguishable from Malta's case in important respects. First, it is undisputed that Malta spent at least 25 percent of his hitch unloading vessels. But the rare loading/unloading Munguia performed applied only to his own personal gear. And although Wood Group attempts to characterize the items Malta unloaded as his own personal tools and equipment, Malta used a crane to unload vessels containing tools and supplies for the use of 22 men on multiple satellite production platforms throughout the oilfield. [—15—]

Wood Group again looks to *Thibodeaux* for support. When finding the Act did not extend to Thibodeaux, this court explained that, "[a]lthough personal gear and occasionally supplies [were] unloaded at docking areas on the platform, the purpose of the platform is to further drilling for oil and gas, which is not a maritime purpose."[7] 370 F.3d at 494. Wood Group reads this analysis as grafting a maritime cargo requirement onto the plain language of the statute. But, again, Thibodeaux's accident did not occur on the part of the platform where the loading/unloading occurred, and those activities were limited in any event. Under the Act, the nature of the items loaded and unloaded is not determinative. Rather, coverage under the Act extends to "all those on the situs involved in the essential or integral elements of the loading or unloading process." *Schwalb*, 493 U.S. at 46. And Malta, unlike Thibodeaux, was injured while unloading a boat on a platform used to load and unload boats. So, the cases are distinguishable and coverage extends to Malta.

In sum, because the Board correctly applied the plain language of the Act,[8] we

---

[6] The court in *Munguia* was asked to decide whether the claimant satisfied the *status* requirement of the Act, not the *situs* requirement. But because Wood Group contends the nature of the cargo is relevant to both the situs and status inquiries, we address Wood Group's argument here.

[7] Like the platform in *Thibodeaux*, oil is not shipped directly from Central Facility.

[8] The Board, Malta, and the Director view this court's opinion in *Gilliam v. Wiley N. Jackson Co.* as settling the proposition that the use to which cargo will be put after its unloading is irrelevant to the question of coverage under the Act. 659 F.2d 54

{–743–} affirm its conclusion that Malta met the situs requirement. [—16—]

IV.

Wood Group also challenges the Board's conclusion that Malta meets the Act's maritime status requirement. That requirement—located at § 902—is satisfied by

> any person engaged in maritime employment, including any longshore-man or other person engaged in longshoring operations, and any harbor-worker including a ship repairman, shipbuilder, and ship-breaker.

§ 902(3). The Supreme Court has characterized the requirement as "an occupational test that focuses on loading and unloading." *P. C. Pfeiffer Co. v. Ford*, 444 U.S. 69, 80 (1979); *see Schwalb*, 493 U.S. at 46 ("[Section] 903(a) extended coverage to the area adjacent to the ship that is normally used for loading and unloading, but restricted the covered activity within that area to maritime employment.").

This court has explained that "[a]n employee may qualify for maritime status based on either (1) the nature of the activity in which he is engaged at the time of the injury or (2) the nature of his employment as a whole." *Hudson*, 555 F.3d at 439. A claimant will satisfy the status requirement if he spends at least some time loading or unloading ships, and this court has expressly ruled that this time need not be "substantial." *Boudloche v. Howard Trucking Co.*, 632 F.2d 1346, 1347 (5th Cir. 1980) (holding that a worker who only spent 2.5 to 5 percent of his

---

(5th Cir. 1981). There the court held that the Act covered a worker injured while unloading a vessel even though the pilings unloaded from the supply barge were used in the construction of a bridge at the site of the unloading. *Id.* at 55. To avoid the force of this case and its holding, Wood Group argues that it is no longer good law after the Supreme Court's holding in *DOWCP v. Perini North River Associates*, 459 U.S. 297 (1983), and this court's later decision in *Fontenot v. AWI, Inc.*, 923 F.2d 1127 (5th Cir. 1991). In light of our holding that the Board correctly applied the plain language of the statute, we need not address this issue.

time loading and unloading was covered under the Act); *see also Caputo*, 432 U.S. at 273; *Hudson*, 555 F.3d at 440 (concluding claimant was covered even though he spent less than 10 percent of his time in maritime activities). But if a claimant "was not injured on actual navigable waters at the time of the injury, then the employee is engaged in 'maritime employment' only if his work is directly connected to the commerce carried on by a ship or vessel." *Fontenot*, 923 F.2d at 1130. [—17—]

The undisputed record shows that Malta—who spent 25 to 35 percent of his hitches loading/unloading vessels—was injured while unloading a vessel. This seems, on its face, to satisfy the maritime status requirement. And, indeed, the Board affirmed the ALJ's ruling that Malta satisfied the status requirement, reasoning that Malta was covered "based on both his overall job, a portion of which involved loading and unloading vessels, and the covered employment duties he was performing at the moment of injury."

Wood Group contends that the Board reversibly erred because the purpose of Malta's employment was not maritime in nature as his loading/unloading did not "enable a ship to engage in maritime employment."[9] *See Trotti & Thompson v. Crawford*, 631 F.2d 1214, 1221 n.16 (5th Cir. 1980). Wood Group explains that the "sole purpose" of Malta's work on Central Facility was oil and gas exploration and production. And all the items he loaded/unloaded were intended solely for that purpose. {–744–} So Malta's loading/unloading was "incidental to non-maritime work" and cannot constitute maritime employment as required by the status requirement.

---

[9] Wood Group also contends that Malta lacks maritime status because his loading/unloading was not connected to maritime commerce. To advance this position, Wood Group again relies on the "maritime cargo" argument we rejected when determining that Malta satisfied the situs requirement. Because no cargo requirement appears in the language of § 902(3), we similarly reject Wood Group's maritime cargo argument in the context of Malta's status.

Wood Group supports this argument with discussions of three Board opinions. But we conclude that none of these opinions is helpful to Wood Group. In *Smith v. Labor Finders*, Lee Smith worked as a "beach-walker"—gathering oil residue and pollutants after an oil spill from the beaches of an island dedicated as a wildlife preserve. Each day, Smith would load his tools and supplies into a boat and ride for 30-45 minutes to/from the mainland. After Smith gathered the oil and pollutants, another crew would then bag and load [—18—] them into a boat. Smith was injured after his trailer crashed into another trailer when returning to the transport boat. The Board denied Smith's claim for recovery under the Act after concluding that Smith's "work duties were not in furtherance of 'maritime commerce' because [Smith's] purposes in cleaning up the island were to protect the wildlife preserve." No. BRB No. 12-0035, 2012 WL 4523618, at *4 (DOL Ben. Rev. Bd. Sept. 11, 2012). Wood Group contends that Malta's case is similar because the purpose of his work was oil and gas production. But this argument overlooks the fact that the Board found it relevant that Smith "did not routinely participate in the loading/unloading of the collected oil onto vessels." *Id.* at *5. Plus, Smith was injured on a trailer, and he was not engaged in loading/unloading a vessel at the time of his injury. The facts of Malta's case are clearly distinguishable. So it is unclear how this case shows that the loading/unloading Malta performed could be "incidental to non-maritime work."[10]

In *Hough v. Vimas Painting Co., Inc.*, the claimant vacuumed up and disposed of debris that accumulated from the cleaning of a bridge. The vacuum deposited the debris into a machine on a barge. The Board found it significant that "the debris was merely collected and stored on the barge until the end of the bridge cleaning project; the vacuumed debris did not 'enable' the barge to 'engage in maritime commerce.'" No. BRB No. 10-0534, 2011 WL 2174854, at *7 (DOL Ben. Rev. Bd. May 24, 2011). And the Board found that "[n]either the vacuumed debris nor claimant's role in vacuuming the debris was integral to [—19—] any maritime purpose." *Id.* The Board concluded that, "[b]ecause claimant's work was neither maritime in nature nor integral to maritime commerce, . . . claimant's vacuuming of debris from the bridge does not constitute 'loading' as that term relates to coverage under the Act." *Id.* Wood Group similarly contends that Malta's work was not integral to maritime commerce. But there is a great deal of daylight between the facts of Malta's case and those of *Hough*. For one thing, the ALJ found that the claimant grew sick while working on the bridge, not the barge. And, for another, vacuuming debris from a bridge onto a vessel is quite different from the loading/unloading activities that Malta undertook. Ultimately, the Board's analysis was geared to determining whether the vacuuming could be considered "loading" a vessel as that term is understood in the Act. There is no dispute that Malta was loading/unloading vessels at the time of the injury. {—745—}

In the third case, *Bazenore v. Hardaway Constructors, Inc.*, the claimant was injured while working in a construction yard cutting poles with a chainsaw. The Board noted that "claimant's work essentially facilitated the sale of construction materials to a nonmaritime customer, and as such did not in any way further maritime commerce." No. BRB no. 83-2842, 1987 WL 107407, at *2 (DOL Ben. Rev. Bd. June 18, 1987). This fact "support[ed] the administrative law judge's determination that any connection to the ship-loading, ship-construction, and harbor-maintenance processes was too attenuated to afford coverage." *Id.* Because cutting poles for nonmaritime customers in a construction yard differs significantly from the loading/unloading occurring here, *Bazenore* is inapposite.

---

[10] Wood Group also directs us to another decision by the Board that relied heavily on *Smith*'s analysis, *Miller v. CH2M Hill Alaska, Inc.*, Ben. Rev. Bd No. 13-0069, 2013 WL 6057071 (DOL Ben. Rev. Bd. Sept. 25, 2013). There the Board explained that "there is no significant distinction to be drawn between this case and *Smith*." *Id.* at *6. Because there is "no significant distinction" between these cases, the reasons for concluding that *Smith* is unhelpful to Wood Group apply equally to *Miller*.

At bottom, because Malta's injury occurred when he was loading/unloading a vessel, and because he regularly loaded/unloaded vessels, the status requirement is satisfied. The cases Wood Group relies on offer no [—20—] real support for the contention that Malta's employment takes him outside the ambit of the statute.

The petition for review is DENIED.

[—21—] {–746–}

United States Court of Appeals
for the Fifth Circuit

No. 18-30243

IN RE DEEPWATER HORIZON

Appeal from the United States District Court for the
Eastern District of Louisiana

Decided: August 13, 2019

Citation: 934 F.3d 434, 7 Adm. R. 297 (5th Cir. 2019).

Before **KING, ELROD,** and **ENGELHARDT,** Circuit
Judges.

[—5—] {–438–} PER CURIAM:

Following the *Deepwater Horizon* disaster, Halliburton Energy Services, Inc. and Transocean Holdings, L.L.C. each entered into a punitive damages settlement agreement with a class of claimants who alleged that they were harmed by the oil spill. In these consolidated appeals, a group of menhaden fishermen challenge the denial of their claims pursuant to those settlements. Because the magistrate judge properly affirmed the denial of the claims and the district court properly declined review, we AFFIRM. [—6—]

I.

Appellants are commercial menhaden fishermen (the Fishermen) who allegedly suffered economic loss due to the *Deepwater Horizon* oil spill. The Fishermen did not file separate lawsuits against BP or any of the other entities involved in the spill. However, they fell within the class definition in the class-action portion of the B1 Master Complaint filed in the *Deepwater Horizon* MDL.[1] The B1 Master Complaint {–439–}

sought compensatory and punitive damages on behalf of the B1 plaintiffs and class members.

The familiar *Deepwater Horizon* Economic and Property Damages Settlement (E&P Settlement) eventually resolved the majority of the claims asserted in the B1 Master Complaint. However, the terms of that agreement specifically excluded the Fishermen. Instead, the Fishermen entered into settlement agreements with the Appellees, Halliburton Energy Services, Inc. (HESI) and Transocean Holdings, L.L.C. (Transocean). These class settlement agreements (the HESI Settlements) created a fund to distribute among the claimants for punitive damages arising out of the oil spill, and the parties agree that the Fishermen fit within the class definition set out in the settlements.[2] The HESI Settlements also include a provision limiting the claimants' rights [—7—] to appeal to this court. The HESI Settlements were entered into and filed with the district court on September 2, 2014 (HESI) and May 29, 2015 (Transocean).[3]

While these settlements were awaiting district court approval, the district court issued Pretrial Order 60 (PTO 60) on March 29, 2016, which applied to all claims in the B1 pleading bundle. Foreseeing "no further administrative or procedural benefit to maintaining" the B1 Master Complaint, PTO 60 first dismissed that complaint. It then instructed "[p]laintiffs [who] did not file an individual lawsuit, but instead filed a [short-form joinder] and/or were part of a complaint with more than one plaintiff" to file an individual lawsuit with the district court by May 2, 2016. PTO 60 warned that plaintiffs who failed to comply would "have their claims

---

[1] As we explained in *Graham*, the district court divided the claims against BP, Transocean, and the other entities into pleading bundles for ease of administration. *In re Deepwater Horizon* (*Graham*), 922 F.3d 660, 664, 7 Adm. R. 251, 251 (5th Cir. 2019). The B1 Master Complaint asserted claims on behalf of plaintiffs in the B1 pleading bundle, which encompassed claims for "non-governmental economic loss and property damages." The class-action portion of the complaint defined the class as

follows: "All individuals and entities residing or owning property in the United States who claim economic losses, or damages to their occupations, businesses, and/or property as a result of the April 20, 2010 explosions and fire aboard, and sinking of, the Deepwater Horizon, and the resulting Spill."

[2] The terms of the two HESI Settlements are substantially the same for purposes of this appeal, except where otherwise indicated.

[3] The HESI Settlement was amended on September 2, 2015.

deemed dismissed with prejudice without further notice."

On April 12, 2016, the district court preliminarily approved the HESI Settlements, and notice of their terms was given to class members, including the Fishermen. The April 12, 2016 order, *inter alia*, set deadlines for objecting to (September 23, 2016) and opting out of (October 16, 2016) the proposed settlements and scheduled a fairness hearing to be held on October 20, 2016. A few weeks later, on May 2, 2016, the deadline to comply with PTO 60 expired. The Fishermen did not file individual lawsuits, nor did they seek relief from PTO 60 or additional time to comply. On June 7, 2016, the district court issued a show cause order to B1 plaintiffs who had failed to comply with PTO 60. The Fishermen did not respond to the order. Thereafter, on July 14, 2016, the district court found that "[a]ll remaining Plaintiffs in the B1 bundle . . . [were] deemed noncompliant with PTO 60" and dismissed their claims with prejudice. [—8—] Order Re: Compliance with PTO 60 at 5, *In re Oil Spill by the Oil Rig "Deepwater Horizon" in the Gulf of Mex. on Apr. 20, 2010*, No. 2:10-md-2179-CJB-JCW (E.D. La. July 14, 2016), ECF No. 20996.

After the issuance of the June 7, 2016 show cause order but before the June 28, {–440–} 2016 deadline to respond, the Claims Administrator for the HESI Settlements filed a proposed Distribution Model on June 13, 2016 detailing how claims would be processed under the agreements. The Distribution Model specified that commercial fishermen, including menhaden fishermen, would be required to provide "proof of [their] timely preservation of [their] rights to a claim for damages by compliance with [PTO 60]." Both the Distribution Model and the attached Claim Form warned that claims would be assigned a value of $0 if the claimant had failed to comply with PTO 60. Although other class members filed objections to the Distribution Model on the ground that it improperly required claimants to comply with PTO 60, the Fishermen did not object. Nor did the Fishermen attend the "fairness hearing" that the district court held in November 2016 to address objections to the Distribution Model.

On February 15, 2017, the district court gave its final approval of the HESI Settlements and the Claims Administrator's Distribution Model. In its approval order, the district court declined to comment on the propriety of the Claims Administrator's interpretation of the HESI Settlements as requiring compliance with PTO 60. Instead, the district court observed that "[t]his objection [was] most properly considered in an appeal to [the district court] after claim determinations [were] concluded." On February 14, 2018, a year after the district court issued the approval order, the Fishermen filed a Federal Rule of Civil Procedure 60(b) motion for relief from that order, arguing that the Distribution Model was contrary to the terms of the HESI Settlements and [—9—] that they had not received adequate notice of PTO 60 or its applicability to their claims. The district court denied the motion.

The Fishermen submitted claims pursuant to the HESI Settlements, but the Claims Administrator denied them because the Fishermen had failed to comply with PTO 60. The Fishermen then appealed to the district court, which had referred "all appeals of claim determinations by the HESI/Transocean settlements claims administrator" to the magistrate judge pursuant to an agreement between the parties. The magistrate judge affirmed the denial, holding that requiring the Fishermen to comply with PTO 60 was consistent with the terms of the HESI Settlements and "the general maritime law precept that a claimant may obtain punitive damages only if that claimant has underlying compensatory damages."

The Fishermen objected to the magistrate judge's determination, complaining that his reliance on PTO 60 was contrary to the terms of the HESI Settlements and violated their due process rights. The district court overruled the objection on the ground that the claimants had waived their right to appeal the magistrate judge's determination to any other court, including the Fifth Circuit. The Fishermen then appealed to this court.

II.

As an initial matter, we address the Fishermen's pending motion to take judicial notice of the docket and complaint in *Bruhmuller v. BP Exploration & Production Inc.* Complaint, *Bruhmuller v. BP Expl. & Prod. Inc.*, No. 2:13-CV-97 (E.D. La. Jan. 18, 2013), ECF No. 1. We may take judicial notice of prior court proceedings as matters of public record. *ITT Rayonier Inc. v. United States*, 651 F.2d 343, 345 n.2 (5th Cir. 1981) ("A court may . . . take judicial notice of its own records or of those of inferior courts."). We GRANT the motion, and we have considered these materials in our review of the case. [—10—] {–441–}

III.

The Fishermen raise four issues on appeal: (1) whether this appeal is barred by the appeal waiver in the HESI Settlements; (2) whether the magistrate judge erred in affirming the denial of their claims; (3) whether the district court erred by declining to review the magistrate judge's decision; and (4) whether the district court erred in denying their Rule 60(b) motion.

A.

The appeal waiver in the HESI Settlement reads as follows:

> [T]he Claims Administrator shall establish rules for appealing the determinations of the Claims Administrator to the [district] Court. The [district] Court's decision on any such appeal involving the amount of any payment to any individual claimant (other than a determination that a claimant is not entitled to any payment due to a failure to meet the class definition) shall be final and binding, and there shall be no appeal to any other court including the U.S. Court of Appeals for the Fifth Circuit.

The Transocean Settlement contains a similar provision, but it omits the exception in parentheses.

The Fishermen argue that this appeal waiver does not foreclose our review because their appeal does not "involv[e] the amount of any payment to any individual claimant" under the HESI Settlements—instead, the Claims Administrator determined that they were not eligible to recover at all. Alternatively, they argue that their appeal fits within the parenthetical exception for "a determination that a claimant is not entitled to any payment due to a failure to meet the class definition." The Appellees respond that "the Claims Administrator's decision was that Appellants are entitled to receive $0, a clear determination as to 'the amount of payment to any individual claimant.'" [—11—]

We have enforced appeal waivers in settlement agreements in prior unpublished cases. *See Hill v. Schilling*, 495 F. App'x 480, 487–88 (5th Cir. 2012); *Campbell Harrison & Dagley, L.L.P. v. Hill*, 582 F. App'x 522, 523–24 (5th Cir. 2014). And in the context of the *Deepwater Horizon* settlements specifically, we have indicated that we would enforce an express waiver of the right to appeal from the district court's claim determinations. *In re Deepwater Horizon*, 785 F.3d 986, 997, 3 Adm. R. 341, 348 (5th Cir. 2015). But because we conclude that the Fishermen cannot prevail on the merits, we need not determine whether the appeal waiver in the HESI Settlements bars their appeal. *See United States v. Story*, 439 F.3d 226, 230 (5th Cir. 2006) ("[A]ppeal waivers . . . do not deprive us of jurisdiction.").

B.

We turn next to the issue of whether the magistrate judge erred in affirming the denial of the Fishermen's claims. We conclude that the magistrate judge's decision was correct.

Under maritime law, a plaintiff's recovery of punitive damages is tied to his or her underlying compensatory damages claim. *See Exxon Shipping Co. v Baker*, 554 U.S. 471, 506–07 (2008). It is unsurprising, then, that the HESI Settlements contemplated that claimants would need to "establish a claim for commercial fishing loss" to recover punitive damages. The Distribution Model set out three methods by which claimants could establish a compensatory damages claim: (1) by filing a claim pursuant to the E&P Settlement; (2) by filing proof of a separate settlement with BP that did not release the claimant's punitive {–442–} damages claims; or (3) by filing an individual lawsuit as required by PTO 60. As we explained, the Fishermen were excluded from the E&P Settlement, and they do not argue here that they entered into a separate compensatory damages settlement with BP. Consequently, to establish a [—12—] compensatory damages claim upon which to predicate their recovery of punitive damages under the HESI Settlements, the Fishermen had to comply with PTO 60.

The Fishermen acknowledge that they received notice of this obligation to comply with PTO 60 at the latest when the Claims Administrator filed the Distribution Model in the district court on June 13, 2016. At that time, although the deadline to comply with PTO 60 had passed, the district court's show cause order was in effect, and the deadline to respond—June 28, 2016—was two weeks away. The Fishermen did not respond to the show cause order, nor did they attempt *at any point* to file individual lawsuits or seek additional time to comply with PTO 60, although the district court had granted extensions to other parties.

The circumstances of this case are quite similar to those in our recent decision in *Barrera*. *In re Deepwater Horizon (Barrera)*, 907 F.3d 232, 6 Adm. R. 270 (5th Cir. 2018). There, although the plaintiff-fishermen received notice of PTO 60, they failed to comply, arguing that they were unable to file individual lawsuits because they were working offshore. *Id.* at 234, 6 Adm. R. at 270. The district court dismissed their claims with prejudice, and we affirmed, observing that the plaintiffs had a "number of opportunities . . . to either comply with PTO 60 [or] explain why they could not do so." *Id.* at 235–37, 6 Adm. R. at 271–72. As in *Barrera*, the Fishermen here knew of their obligation to comply with PTO 60 but still failed to file individual lawsuits. And unlike in *Barrera*, the Fishermen did not attempt to comply with PTO 60 at any point throughout these proceedings. The magistrate

judge therefore correctly affirmed the denial of their claims.

Despite the above, the Fishermen challenge the magistrate judge's decision on several grounds: (1) requiring compliance with PTO 60 was contrary to the terms of the HESI Settlements; (2) PTO 60 did not apply to the [—13—] Fishermen; and (3) requiring compliance with PTO 60 violated the Fishermen's due process rights. Each of these arguments is unavailing.

1.

The Fishermen first contend that requiring compliance with PTO 60 was contrary to the terms of the HESI Settlements, arguing that the settlements deem any claimant who fits within the class definition to have standing. Thus, they maintain that they did not need to make a separate showing of standing by filing individual lawsuits to preserve their compensatory damages claims. According to the Fishermen, this was a "contractual concession" by the Appellees similar to BP's contractual concession that proof of causation was not required under the E&P Settlement. *See In re Deepwater Horizon (Bon Secour Fisheries)*, 744 F.3d 370, 377, 2 Adm. R. 183, 186 (5th Cir. 2014). The Fishermen also emphasize that "the law is not settled in this circuit" as to whether they have standing, but the HESI Settlements nonetheless expressly include them in the class definition. They argue that the HESI Settlements would not have included claimants whose standing is unclear in the class definition if a separate showing of standing was required—instead, a claimant is entitled to recover under the HESI Settlements merely by proving that he is a member of the class.

"The interpretation of a settlement agreement is a question of contract law that this [c]ourt reviews de novo." {–443–} *In re Deepwater Horizon*, 785 F.3d 1003, 1011, 3 Adm. R. 325, 329 (5th Cir. 2015). The primary provision of the HESI Settlements on which the Fishermen rely to deem standing is the class *description* found in Section 3: "It is the intent of the Parties to capture within the New Class definition all potential claimants

. . . who may have valid maritime law standing to make a Punitive Damages Claim under general maritime law against [Appellees.]" However, the class *definition* in Section 4 does not include any language [—14—] regarding standing. Nor does the quoted language from the class description unequivocally deem standing for class members as the Fishermen contend. Instead, the class description provision demonstrates that the parties recognized that the class definition encompasses claimants whose standing is uncertain under existing law, without saying anything about whether a separate showing of maritime standing is required for recovery under the settlements. At best, this provision is silent as to whether class members must separately prove standing.

Helpfully, the class description in Section 3 is not the only provision in the HESI Settlements that sheds light on whether claimants were deemed to have standing such that compliance with PTO 60 was unnecessary. First, the HESI Settlements contain the statement that "this [settlement agreement] shall be interpreted in accord with general maritime law." As we discussed above, maritime law links a plaintiff's recovery of punitive damages to his or her underlying compensatory damages claim. *See Exxon Shipping Co.*, 554 U.S. at 506–07.

In addition, as we also noted above, the section of the HESI Settlements providing for the creation of the Distribution Model by the Claims Administrator, Section 8, contains the following provision: "The plan for distribution of payments to the New Class recommended by the Claims Administrator may, at his/her discretion, include . . . a standard to establish a claim for commercial fishing loss." This expressly recognizes that claimants may be required to demonstrate that they have a claim for loss—in other words, a claim seeking compensatory damages—in order to proceed under the HESI Settlements. By requiring compliance with PTO 60 as one possible way to establish such a claim, the Claims Administrator was exercising the discretion afforded him under this provision. [—15—]

Finally, in Section 19, the HESI Settlements contain a series of provisions stipulating that the parties will seek certain orders from the district court to effectuate the settlements. One of those provisions requires the parties to obtain an order that:

> Adopt[s] the interpretation as to the scope of *Robins Dry Dock* in the [district court's] Order and Reasons [As to Motions to Dismiss the B1 Master Complaint] . . . by finding that the New Class as defined and described in sections 3 and 4 includes all potential claimants who have standing to bring claims under general maritime law as interpreted by *Robins Dry Dock v. Flint*, 275 U.S. 203 (1927), *State of Louisiana ex. Rel. Guste v. M/V Testbank*, 752 F.2d 1019 (5th Cir. 1985), and their progeny[.]

Thus, the parties specifically bargained for an order by the district court limiting the class of claimants who could recover under the HESI Settlements to "claimants *who have standing to bring claims under general maritime law*" as interpreted by the two named cases and their progeny.

Robins Dry Dock stands for the proposition that a plaintiff who sustains only economic loss unaccompanied by personal injury or property damage generally {–444–} does not have standing to recover damages under maritime law. *See Robins Dry Dock & Repair Co. v. Flint*, 275 U.S. 303, 309 (1927); *Wiltz v. Bayer CropScience, Ltd. P'ship*, 645 F.3d 690, 695–96 (5th Cir. 2011). In *M/V Testbank*, we noted that "[a] substantial argument can be made that commercial fishermen possess a proprietary interest in fish in waters they normally harvest sufficient to allow recovery for their loss." *State of La. ex rel. Guste v. M/V Testbank*, 752 F.2d 1019, 1027 n.10 (5th Cir. 1985). But we declined to decide whether commercial fishermen were an exception to the *Robins Dry Dock* rule. *Id.*

The district court order referenced in the provision—the order on the motions to dismiss the B1 complaint—interpreted these two cases, in [—16—] conjunction with the district court's decision in *M/V Testbank*, as creating an exception to *Robins Dry Dock* to allow commercial fishermen to sue for mere economic loss arising out of the *Deepwater Horizon* oil spill. Order and Reasons Granting in Part, Denying in Part, Defendants' Motions to Dismiss the B1 Master Complaint at 19–20, *In re Oil Spill by the Oil Rig "Deepwater Horizon" in the Gulf of Mex. on Apr. 20, 2010,* No. 2:10-md-2179-CJB-JCW (E.D. La. Aug. 26, 2011), ECF No. 3830. In light of this interpretation, we read the above-quoted provision to indicate that for the purposes of the HESI Settlements, the Fishermen are not barred from recovery by *Robins Dry Dock* even though we have not affirmatively established that they would have standing under that rule. However, this provision does not purport to eliminate standing issues unrelated to *Robins Dry Dock*, especially the fundamental requirement that a plaintiff has suffered injury in fact. *See Lujan v. Defs. of Wildlife*, 504 U.S. 555, 560 (1992).

Thus, this case is distinguishable from *Bon Secour Fisheries* in that the settlement at issue there—the familiar E&P Settlement—set out express causation requirements that departed from the proof of causation a claimant would have been required to provide under general tort law. 744 F.3d at 375–77, 2 Adm. R. at 184–87. Here, the HESI Settlements contemplate that the class encompasses only claimants "who *have* standing to bring claims *under general maritime law*"—suggesting that claimants must make the same showing of standing to recover under the settlements as they would under maritime law, subject to the district court's interpretation of *Robins Dry Dock* and *M/V Testbank*. Unlike in *Bon Secour Fisheries*, the Appellees did not "contractually concede" standing under the HESI Settlements.

For the reasons described, we hold that requiring the Fishermen to establish underlying compensatory damages claims by complying with PTO [—17—] 60—in other words, requiring them to have standing to recover punitive damages under maritime law—was not contrary to the terms of the HESI Settlements.

2.

The Fishermen next argue that PTO 60 did not apply to them. Specifically, they contend that the district court's conclusion that PTO 60 applied to unnamed class members in class action suits was incorrect because PTO 60 only mentions "mass joinder" plaintiffs, and class actions are distinct from mass joinder suits. Although the Fishermen acknowledge that we affirmed the district court's dismissal of class action claims under PTO 60 in *Perez*, they "make a good-faith assertion that the *Perez* ruling was incorrect and should be reconsidered." *See In re Deepwater Horizon (Perez)*, 713 F. App'x 360 (5th Cir. 2018). {–445–}

We review the district court's docket management decisions for an abuse of discretion, affording "special deference" to a district court administering an MDL. *Barrera*, 907 F.3d at 234–35, 6 Adm. R. at 271. In *Perez*, the appellants, who had filed a series of class action suits in the BP MDL, challenged the district court's decision that they were required to comply with PTO 60 and file single-plaintiff lawsuits instead. 713 F. App'x at 362. Observing that PTO 60 applied to class actions, we affirmed the district court's dismissal of the appellants' class action claims with prejudice. *Id.* The Supreme Court denied the appellants' petition for a writ of certiorari. *Perez v. B.P., P.L.C.*, No. 18-59, 139 S. Ct. 231 (Oct. 1, 2018). We see no reason to revisit *Perez* here: The district court did not err in applying PTO 60 to unnamed class members.

3.

The Fishermen's third basis for challenging the magistrate judge's decision is that requiring them to comply with PTO 60 violated their due [—18—] process rights. Their core argument in this regard is that they "did not have constitutionally adequate notice that they had to comply [with PTO 60] in order to receive compensation under the [HESI Settlements]." Whether a claimant's due process rights were violated is a question of law that this court reviews de novo. *See Simi Inv. Co. v. Harris Cty.*, 236 F.3d 240, 249 (5th Cir. 2000).

On this issue, the Fishermen first point to the district court's decision to excuse noncompliance with PTO 60 for certain claimants due to a "notice gap." They also contend that the terms of PTO 60, the terms of the HESI Settlements, and the notices of those settlements sent to class members did not adequately inform them that compliance with PTO 60 was a prerequisite to recovery under the settlements. Finally, while the Fishermen acknowledge that the Distribution Model put them on notice of the requirement to file individual lawsuits, they emphasize that the Distribution Model was not filed until after the deadline to comply with PTO 60 had expired.

The Fishermen's "notice gap" argument analogizes their situation to that of Zat's Restaurant, a claimant that the district court excused from compliance with PTO 60 because it had not received notice of that order. As addressed above, we reject this argument because, unlike Zat's, the Fishermen did not attempt to comply with PTO 60 once they *did* receive notice of it. In fact, we observe that the Fishermen had numerous opportunities to comply with, object to, or otherwise challenge the PTO 60 compliance requirement before their claims were denied by the Claims Administrator, but they failed to do so. First, the Fishermen had an opportunity to respond to the district court's show cause order with respect to PTO 60 *after* they unequivocally received notice via the Distribution Model that failure to comply with PTO 60 would bar their claims under the HESI Settlements. Second, the Fishermen had an opportunity to [—19—] object to the Distribution Model itself based on the PTO 60 compliance requirement. Third, the Fishermen had an opportunity to participate in a fairness hearing before the district court to challenge the Distribution Model based on the PTO 60 compliance requirement. Fourth, the Fishermen had an opportunity to appeal the district court's order approving the HESI Settlements and Distribution Model based on the PTO 60 compliance requirement.

Given the above, we cannot conclude that the Fishermen did not receive adequate notice or an opportunity to be heard on the PTO 60 compliance issue. *See* {–446–} *Barrera*, 907 F.3d at 236, 6 Adm. R. at 272 (affirming dismissal of plaintiffs' claims for failure to comply with PTO 60 "[g]iven the number of opportunities the district court gave Plaintiffs to either comply with PTO 60 [or] explain why they could not do so"). Requiring compliance with PTO 60 to recover under the HESI Settlements did not violate the Fishermen's due process rights.

None of the Fishermen's arguments convince us that the magistrate judge's decision to affirm the denial of their claims was incorrect. We therefore hold that the magistrate judge did not err in applying PTO 60 to the Fishermen's claims under the HESI Settlements.

C.

The Fishermen also complain that the district court erred in declining to review their objections to the magistrate judge's decision. First, they note that the district court's order referring matters to the magistrate judge (the Referral Order) only delegated "questions regarding the amount of payments." This is not correct. The Referral Order, which the parties agreed to, referred "all appeals of claim determinations by the HESI/Transocean settlements claims administrator" to the magistrate judge. Thus, the Fishermen's appeal from [—20—] the denial of their claims was within the scope of the Referral Order and was properly reviewed by the magistrate judge.

Second, the Fishermen point to the district court's statement in its order approving the HESI Settlements that objections to the PTO 60 compliance requirement were "most properly considered in an appeal to [the district court] after claim determinations [were] concluded." In the Fishermen's view, this statement reserved the PTO 60 compliance issue for the district court's review, so it should not have been delegated to the magistrate judge. However, the Fishermen cite no authority for the proposition that this determination was not delegable to the magistrate judge. On the contrary, that is precisely what the parties agreed to in the

Referral Order, which the district court issued *after* the approval order in which it expressed that it would consider the PTO 60 compliance issue at a later time. Thus, as the magistrate judge recognized, his decision in this case *was* the promised consideration of the PTO 60 compliance issue at a later stage of the proceedings. That the Fishermen disagree with the magistrate judge's decision on that issue does not permit them to circumvent the Referral Order that they bargained for.

D.

Finally, the Fishermen contend that the district court erred in denying their Rule 60(b) motion, which they filed a year after the district court issued the order approving the Distribution Model. This court reviews a district court's denial of a Rule 60(b) motion for an abuse of discretion. *Lowry Dev., L.L.C. v. Groves & Assocs. Ins., Inc.*, 690 F.3d 382, 385 (5th Cir. 2012). As the Fishermen explain, their Rule 60(b) motion raised the same arguments that they raised in their appeal of the magistrate judge's decision affirming the denial of their claims. Because we conclude that the magistrate judge's [—21—] decision was correct, we hold that the district court did not err in denying the Fishermen's Rule 60(b) motion for the same reasons.

IV.

We recognize that, in the unique facts of this case, our holding leads to an unfortunate result for the Fishermen, who were unnamed, unrepresented class members for much of these proceedings—the record is not clear as to when they became represented. {–447–} As a result, as even the Appellees recognized at oral argument, affirming the denial of the Fishermen's claims may appear unduly harsh. However, we are bound by our precedent, by the plain language of the HESI Settlements, and by the deferential standard of review applicable to several of the issues in this case. Under those standards, the magistrate judge correctly affirmed the denial of the Fishermen's claims, the district court did not err in declining to review the magistrate judge's decision, and the district court did not err in denying the Fishermen's Rule 60(b) motion. We must therefore AFFIRM the district court's judgment.

United States Court of Appeals
for the Fifth Circuit

No. 18-30776

JONES
vs.
UNITED STATES

Appeal from the United States District Court for the
Eastern District of Louisiana

Decided: August 28, 2019

Citation: 936 F.3d 318, 7 Adm. R. 305 (5th Cir. 2019).

Before **KING**, **SMITH**, and **WILLETT**, Circuit Judges.

[—1—] {–320–} **WILLETT**, Circuit Judge:

Wilfred Jones fell while making his duty rounds aboard the M/V CAPE KNOX, injuring his arm. He alleges that grease on the deck caused him to slip. He sued the ship's owner—the United States—for negligence under the Jones Act and unseaworthiness under general maritime law. The district court granted summary judgment against Jones because he had no evidence that grease caused his fall.

On appeal, causation evidence remains scant. The Jones Act causation standard is lower than at common law. But it still requires some evidence. Plus, the district court had more than the usual summary-judgment discretion since this would be a bench trial. We AFFIRM the judgment. [—2—]

I

Jones was an engineer aboard the CAPE KNOX. The United States owns the CAPE KNOX, and Keystone Shipping Company operates it. While making his rounds as duty officer, Jones entered the emergency diesel generator room. As he lifted his left foot over the hatch's nine-inch threshold, his right foot slipped. He fell against the carbon dioxide bottles inside the emergency diesel generator room. He did not see what caused him to slip. It was after dark, but Jones had a flashlight with him. He did not see grease on the deck or on his shoes at the time. In a "Report of Illness" the next day, Jones wrote "as I was completing duty round I lost balance and fell into the CO2 bottles in the EDG room causing me to fall on my right forearm."

At his deposition, Jones testified he believed he slipped on grease on the deck. The CAPE KNOX had cables above the weather decks that were greased regularly. That grease often dropped onto the deck. An overhang covers the deck outside the emergency diesel generator room, but {–321–} grease can be tracked or spread across a deck. The deck outside the emergency diesel generator room had a nonskid coating. Jones admitted that it was only "some time after" his fall that he realized he had slipped on grease. He looked into the matter after realizing the seriousness of his injury.

Jones sued the United States and Keystone. He asserted a negligence claim under the Jones Act, 46 U.S.C. § 30104, via the Suits in Admiralty Act, 46 U.S.C. § 30903 (waiving sovereign immunity); an unseaworthiness claim under general maritime law; and a claim for maintenance and cure under general maritime law. The district court granted summary judgment to the United States, and Jones appealed. On appeal he argues only the negligence and unseaworthiness claims. [—3—]

II

The summary-judgment standard marks our course. The everyday standard is familiar but applies uniquely in bench-trial cases. So we lay it out from harbor to anchorage.

A

"We review grants of summary judgment *de novo*."[1] Summary judgment is proper if "there is no genuine dispute as to any material fact and the movant is entitled to judgment as a matter of law."[2] "[A] party seeking summary judgment always bears the initial responsibility of . . . demonstrat[ing] the absence of a genuine issue of material

---

[1] *Cal-Dive Int'l, Inc. v. Seabright Ins. Co.*, 627 F.3d 110, 113 (5th Cir. 2010).

[2] Fed. R. Civ. P. 56(a).

fact."[3] Once the moving party does so, the nonmoving party must "go beyond the pleadings and . . . designate specific facts showing that there is a genuine issue for trial."[4] An issue is "genuine" if "the evidence is such that a reasonable [factfinder] could return a verdict for the nonmoving party."[5] "A non-movant will not avoid summary judgment by presenting 'speculation, improbable inferences, or unsubstantiated assertions.'"[6] "Rule 56 'mandates the entry of summary judgment . . . against a party who fails to make a showing sufficient to establish the existence of an element essential to that party's case, and on which that party will bear the burden of proof at trial.'"[7]

Under 46 U.S.C. § 30903(b), an admiralty action against the United States as shipowner must be tried to the court. We have held that "[i]n a non- [—4—] jury case, such as this one, 'a district court has somewhat greater discretion to consider what weight it will accord the evidence.'"[8] "When deciding a motion for summary judgment prior to a bench trial, the district court 'has the limited discretion to decide that the same evidence, presented to him or her as a trier of fact in a plenary {–322–} trial, could not possibly lead to a different result.'"[9]

B

Jones seeks to recover for his injuries based on employer negligence. Under 46 U.S.C. § 30104, "[a] seaman injured in the course of employment . . . may elect to bring a civil action at law . . . against the employer." Here

Jones's employer, Keystone, acted as agent for the shipowner, the United States. So the United States is liable for Keystone's negligence.[10]

Some elements of Jones Act negligence follow the common law. In *Gautreaux v. Scurlock Marine, Inc.*, we recognized that the employer's duty of care "retains the usual and familiar definition of ordinary prudence."[11] But the Jones Act causation standard is lighter than at common law. "A seaman is entitled to recovery under the Jones Act . . . if his employer's negligence is the cause, in whole or in part, of his injury."[12] The plaintiff can show causation if "employer negligence played any part, even the slightest, in producing the injury."[13] This standard is identical to that of the Federal Employers' Liability Act, 45 U.S.C. § 51, so "FELA case law applies to Jones Act cases."[14] [—5—]

Jones contends there was grease in many places on the ship's deck, and this was the most likely cause of his fall. He also contends that the district court prematurely decided witnesses' credibility and incorrectly burdened him with immediately investigating the accident. The United States responds that Jones has no evidence for the causation element of his claim. Jones did not see himself slip on grease or see grease on his shoes. And neither Jones nor any other witness saw grease outside the emergency diesel generator room.

We hold that Jones did not have enough causation evidence to survive summary judgment. "[S]peculation" cannot defeat summary judgment on a required element of the claim.[15] We of course follow the Supreme

---

[3] *Celotex Corp. v. Catrett*, 477 U.S. 317, 323 (1986) (internal quotation marks omitted).

[4] *Id.* at 324 (internal quotation marks omitted).

[5] *Anderson v. Liberty Lobby, Inc.*, 477 U.S. 242, 248 (1986).

[6] *Lawrence v. Fed. Home Loan Mortg. Corp.*, 808 F.3d 670, 673 (5th Cir. 2015) (quoting *Likens v. Hartford Life & Accident Ins. Co.*, 688 F.3d 197, 202 (5th Cir. 2012)).

[7] *Little v. Liquid Air Corp.*, 37 F.3d 1069, 1075 (5th Cir. 1994) (en banc) (per curiam) (quoting *Celotex*, 477 U.S. at 322).

[8] *Johnson v. Diversicare Afton Oaks, LLC*, 597 F.3d 673, 676 (5th Cir. 2010) (quoting *In re Placid Oil Co.*, 932 F.2d 394, 397 (5th Cir. 1991)).

[9] *Id.* (quoting *Placid Oil*, 932 F.2d at 398).

---

[10] *See Randle v. Crosby Tugs, L.L.C.*, 911 F.3d 280, 284, 6 Adm. R. 279, 281 (5th Cir. 2018) (holding shipowner is liable for injuries inflicted by its agents).

[11] 107 F.3d 331, 335 (5th Cir. 1997) (en banc).

[12] *Id.*

[13] *Id.* (quoting *Ferguson v. Moore–McCormack Lines, Inc.*, 352 U.S. 521, 523 (1957)).

[14] *Beech v. Hercules Drilling Co.*, 691 F.3d 566, 570 (5th Cir. 2012).

[15] *Lawrence*, 808 F.3d at 673 (quoting *Likens*, 688 F.3d at 202).

Court's instruction that "entirely circum-stantial" evidence can prove a Jones Act claim.[16] But grease elsewhere on the ship's deck at various times is not "probative" circumstantial evidence that can withstand summary judgment.[17] If Jones returned to the hatch that night or the next morning and saw grease where he slipped, things might be different.[18] But Jones never saw grease in the spot where he slipped, even when he later investigated his fall. As we explained in *Huffman v. Union Pacific Railroad*, some evidence {–323–} must complete "[t]he path from worker injury to employer liability."[19] Evidence that other parts of the ship were slippery at other times does not do so.[20] [—6—]

The causation standard for Jones Act negligence is "slight[]," well below the common-law standard.[21] But it is not no standard at all. In *Huffman* we reversed a jury verdict because the employee only had evidence that his work could cause musculoskeletal disorders, not that it caused his particular injury (osteoarthritis).[22]

And most contrary decisions are distinguishable. The Supreme Court normally presumes that a jury should decide causation for Jones Act and FELA claims.[23] But, by

statute, admiralty actions against the United States as shipowner are tried to the court.[24] And in bench-trial cases the district court has greater discretion to grant summary judgment. The judge may "decide that the same evidence, presented to him or her as a trier of fact in a plenary trial, could not possibly lead to a different result."[25] This resolves any remaining doubt about the sufficiency of Jones's summary-judgment evidence.

Jones's other arguments lack force. He says the district court prematurely decided credibility because it relied on the United States's affidavits about the CAPE KNOX's deck condition but not Jones's expert affidavit. But Jones's expert simply cited Jones's deposition for the fact that "there was grease and oil on the deck" and concluded this most likely caused Jones to slip. His opinion is conclusory on this point, and "unsubstantiated assertions" cannot defeat summary judg-ment.[26] Choosing not to rely on this evidence was not a credibility determination. Jones's argument that negligence [—7—] plaintiffs are not obligated to conduct a full immediate investigation also misses the mark. The district court did not fault Jones's investigation or lack thereof. It simply held that no summary-judgment evidence, however it might have been developed, reached the fact of whether Jones slipped on grease.

C

Jones also seeks to recover for unseaworthiness. "Unseaworthiness is a claim under general maritime law 'based on the vessel owner's duty to ensure that the vessel is reasonably fit to be at sea.'"[27] A deck slippery from grease may render a vessel unseaworthy.[28] To recover, Jones must also

---

[16] *Rogers v. Mo. Pac. R.R. Co.*, 352 U.S. 500, 508 (1957) (reinstating plaintiff's jury verdict in FELA case).

[17] *Huffman v. Union Pacific R.R.*, 675 F.3d 412, 425 (5th Cir. 2012) (granting judgment as a matter of law on causation element of FELA claim).

[18] *Cf. Colburn v. Bunge Towing, Inc.*, 883 F.2d 372, 374 (5th Cir. 1989) (affirming liability verdict based in part on testimony that deck was "slippery as ice").

[19] 675 F.3d at 426.

[20] *Cf. Jackson v. OMI Corp.*, 245 F.3d 525, 527 (5th Cir. 2001) (noting absence of evidence that "oil or other slippery substances were present in the area of the doorway").

[21] *Gautreaux*, 107 F.3d at 335 (quoting *Ferguson*, 352 U.S. at 523).

[22] 675 F.3d at 426.

[23] *E.g.*, *Rogers*, 352 U.S. at 507–10 ("Congress . . . was particularly concerned that the issues whether there was employer fault and whether that fault played any part in the injury . . . should be decided by the jury whenever fair-minded men could reach these conclusions on the evidence.").

[24] 46 U.S.C. § 30903(b).

[25] *Johnson*, 597 F.3d at 676 (quoting *Placid Oil*, 932 F.2d at 398).

[26] *Lawrence*, 808 F.3d at 673 (quoting *Likens*, 688 F.3d at 202).

[27] *Beech*, 691 F.3d at 570 (quoting *Lewis v. Lewis & Clark Marine, Inc.*, 531 U.S. 438, 441 (2001)).

[28] *See, e.g.*, *Davis v. Hill Eng'g, Inc.*, 549 F.2d 314, 330 (5th Cir. 1977) (affirming finding that

prove "a causal connection between {–324–} his injury and the breach of duty that rendered the vessel unseaworthy."[29] "The standard of causation for unseaworthiness is a more demanding one [than the Jones Act] and requires proof of proximate cause."[30] "[P]roximate cause" means that "the unseaworthy condition played a substantial part in bringing about or actually causing the injury and that the injury was either a direct result or a reasonably probable consequence of the unseaworthiness."[31]

Jones alleges that grease on the deck made the CAPE KNOX unseaworthy. But to recover he must show that this condition caused his injury.[32] He did not show this under the lighter Jones Act standard and cannot do so here either.[33] [—8—]

III

We AFFIRM the judgment.

---

slippery deck breached duty of seaworthiness), *overruled on other grounds by Gautreaux*, 107 F.3d at 331.

[29] *Jackson*, 245 F.3d at 527.

[30] *Chisholm v. Sabine Towing & Transp. Co.*, 679 F.2d 60, 62 (5th Cir. 1982).

[31] *Brister v. A.W.I., Inc.*, 946 F.2d 350, 355 (5th Cir. 1991) (quoting *Johnson v. Offshore Express, Inc.*, 845 F.2d 1347, 1354 (5th Cir. 1988)).

[32] *See Jackson*, 245 F.3d at 527.

[33] *See Chisholm*, 679 F.2d at 62 (explaining that the unseaworthiness causation standard is "more demanding").

United States Court of Appeals
for the Fifth Circuit

No. 18-60004

MAYS

vs.

DIRECTOR, OFFICE OF WORKERS' COMPENSATION PROGRAMS

Petition for Review of an Order of the Benefits Review Board

Decided: September 11, 2019

Citation: 938 F.3d 637, 7 Adm. R. 309 (5th Cir. 2019).

Before **HIGGINBOTHAM, ELROD,** and **HO,** Circuit Judges.

[—1—] {–639–} **HIGGINBOTHAM,** Circuit Judge:

Tom Mays and his former employer, Huntington Ingalls, Inc. ("Avondale"), cross-petition for review of an order of the Benefits Review Board denying Mays's motion for modification of his Longshore and Harbor Workers' Compensation Act benefits. We affirm. [—2—]

I.

This case arises from nearly three decades of administrative and state-court litigation. In the spring of 1991, Tom Mays was employed by Avondale as a welder at its shipyard in Avondale, Louisiana. Avondale contracted with International Marine & Industrial Applicators, Inc. ("IMIA" or "International Marine") for cleaning and sandblasting services on a Naval vessel. Under the companies' agreement, IMIA employees would work at Avondale's facility for up to ninety days, during which time they would continue to be supervised and insured by IMIA. Although Avondale reserved the right to remove IMIA employees from its shipyard, only IMIA could fire them. At the end of the sandblasting job, Avondale was to pay IMIA a fixed lump sum, out of which IMIA would compensate its own workers.

John Gliott was one of the IMIA employees placed on temporary work duty at the Avondale shipyard. On March 18, 1991, Gliott kicked Mays in the head, fracturing Mays's cheekbone and injuring his eye. Mays was treated for his injuries, underwent surgery, and saw several psychiatrists to address a resulting psychological condition. Avondale voluntarily paid Mays {–640–} $5,514.68 in disability and medical benefits for a five-month period, after which it requested that he return to work. Mays did not return, and instead filed a claim for workers' compensation benefits under the Longshore and Harbor Workers' Compensation Act ("the Act").[1] The Office of Administrative Law Judges ("ALJ") initially denied Mays's claims for medical benefits and wage indemnity, but reversed its position as to medical benefits upon remand from the Benefits Review Board ("BRB" or "Board"). Avondale appealed, and the Board affirmed. [—3—]

Meanwhile, Mays had filed suit against Gliott and IMIA in Louisiana state court. In January of 2000, Mays accepted a settlement of $60,000 from Gliott and IMIA without Avondale's approval. As part of the settlement agreement, Mays agreed to "dismiss all claims in the Longshoremen and Harbor Workers Compensation matter against Avondale." Following the settlement, Avondale sought relief against Mays under Section 33(g) of the Act, which requires an injured employee to obtain his employer's approval before accepting a third-party tort settlement for less than the value of his workers' compensation benefits.[2] If the employee fails to obtain employer approval of such a settlement, "all rights to compensation and medical benefits . . . shall be terminated."[3]

Avondale argued that because it had not approved Mays's settlement with Gliott and IMIA, it was no longer liable for his medical expenses pursuant to Section 33(g). At the same time, Mays filed a request for modification of his workers' compensation award, providing new documentation showing that his injuries were more extensive than previously recognized.[4] The ALJ denied

---

[1] 33 U.S.C. § 901 *et seq.*

[2] 33 U.S.C. § 933(g).

[3] *Id.* § 933(g)(2).

[4] Section 22 of the Act "provides two avenues for modification of a prior judgment: (1) a change in

Avondale's request because the $60,000 settlement exceeded the value of the workers' compensation benefits Mays had received up to that point, rendering Section 33(g) inapplicable. However, the ALJ granted Avondale relief under Section 33(f) of the Act, which entitles an employer to credit its liability for medical benefits against the net settlement amount.[5] Finally, the ALJ denied Mays's request for modification as untimely. [—4—]

On appeal, the Board affirmed the ALJ's grant of Section 33(f) relief but found that Mays's modification action was not time-barred. The Board remanded the case with instructions to determine whether Mays was entitled to any further periods of disability compensation and, if so, whether his lifetime compensation benefits would become subject to forfeiture under Section 33(g).

Mays withdrew his request for modification in 2006 but reinstated it several years later, this time arguing that a mistake of fact had been made in the earlier proceedings. Mays claimed that he had never entered into a third-party settlement because Gliott was a borrowed servant of Avondale, not a third-party employee of IMIA. Because Longshore Act compensation is the exclusive remedy for an employee injured by a person "in the same employ," neither Section 33(f)'s setoff provision nor Section 933(g)'s forfeiture provision would apply if Gliott were determined to be Avondale's borrowed servant.[6] {–641–}

In July of 2016, the ALJ rejected Mays's mistake-of-fact argument and found that Gliott was not a borrowed servant. However, the ALJ also found that Mays was entitled to additional disability compensation of $335,012.08.[7] Had the inquiry ended there,

Mays's compensation would have been modified upward by this amount. However, per the Board's earlier instruction, the ALJ next considered the interaction between the hypothetical increase in compensation and Mays's settlement with Gliott and IMIA. Before the hypothetical increase, Mays's workers' compensation was less than his recovery under the settlement. However, with the increase, Mays's compensation would far exceed his recovery under the settlement, and this change would trigger Section 33(g) of the Act. Because Avondale had not [—5—] approved the settlement and Gliott was not an Avondale employee, Mays would forfeit his benefits under the Act. In short, if the ALJ were to make the hypothetical increase in benefits, it would also have to cancel those benefits under Section 33(g)—resulting in no change for Mays. Thus, the ALJ denied the modification.

In affirming this decision, the Benefits Review Board stated that because the request for modification was denied, the status quo ante remained in place: "The result of the denial of [Mays's] motion for modification is that the administrative law judge's prior award of medical benefits to claimant and offset to employer of the net amount of the third-party settlement pursuant to Section 33(f) remain in effect." The Board denied both parties' motions for reconsideration. Mays and Avondale now cross-petition for review of the Board's affirmance. Mays objects to the Board's findings on Gliott's employment status, while Avondale challenges the Board's denial of Section 33(g) relief.

II.

A.

Our review of BRB decisions is limited. We inquire only whether the Board "correctly concluded that the ALJ's order was 'supported by substantial evidence on the record as a whole and is in accordance with the law.'"[8]

---

conditions, or (2) a mistake in a determination of fact by the ALJ." *Island Operating Co., Inc. v. Dir., OWCP*, 738 F.3d 663, 667, 1 Adm. R. 337, 338 (5th Cir. 2013); *see* 33 U.S.C. § 922.

[5] *See* 33 U.S.C. § 933(f).

[6] *Id.* § 933(i); *see Gaudet v. Exxon Corp.*, 562 F.2d 351, 354 & n.4 (5th Cir. 1977).

[7] Because of a technical error, the ALJ initially found that Mays was entitled to an additional

$502,518.13. It corrected that figure downward on reconsideration.

[8] *Avondale Indus., Inc. v. Dir., OWCP*, 977 F.2d 186, 189 (5th Cir. 1992) (quoting *Odom Constr. Co. v. United States Dep't of Labor*, 622 F.2d 110, 115

Evidence is substantial if "a reasonable mind might accept [it] as adequate to support a conclusion."⁹ "The substantial evidence standard is less demanding than that of preponderance of the evidence, and the ALJ's decision need not constitute [—6—] the sole inference that can be drawn from the facts."¹⁰ To the contrary, the ALJ "is exclusively entitled to assess both the weight of the evidence and the credibility of witnesses," and neither the Court nor the Board may substitute its judgment for that of the ALJ.¹¹

B.

We consider the nine *Ruiz* factors to determine whether an employee is a borrowed servant: {–642–}

(1) Who has control over the employee and the work he is performing, beyond mere suggestion of details or cooperation?
(2) Whose work is being performed?
(3) Was there an agreement, understanding, or meeting of the minds between the original and the borrowing employer?
(4) Did the employee acquiesce in the new work situation?
(5) Did the original employer terminate his relationship with the employee?
(6) Who furnished tools and place for performance?
(7) Was the new employment over a considerable length of time?
(8) Who had the right to discharge the employee?
(9) Who had the obligation to pay the employee?¹²

Although no single one of these factors is decisive, the first is the most critical.¹³ As we have stated, "[t]he central question in borrowed servant cases [—7—] is whether someone has the power to control and direct another person in the performance of his work."¹⁴

C.

In general, the Longshore and Harbor Workers' Compensation Act "allows injured workers, without forgoing compensation under the Act, to pursue claims against third parties for their injuries."¹⁵ However, Sections 33(f) and 33(g) of the Act place limits on this right. Section 33(f) provides in relevant part:

If the person entitled to compensation institutes proceedings [against a third-party tortfeasor] the employer shall be required to pay as compensation under this chapter a sum equal to the excess of the amount which the Secretary determines is payable on account of such injury or death over the net amount recovered against such third person.

In other words, when an injured worker successfully sues a third party, the worker's employer is entitled to reduce the benefits it would otherwise owe under the Act by the amount the worker recovers from the third party.¹⁶

In addition, Section 33(g) imposes duties on the worker-plaintiff himself. Under Section 33(g)(1), an injured worker must obtain his employer's written approval before accepting a settlement from a third-party tortfeasor for

---

(5th Cir. 1980)); *see Ceres Gulf, Inc. v. Dir., OWCP*, 683 F.3d 225, 228 (5th Cir. 2012).

⁹ *Avondale*, 977 F.2d at 189 (quoting *Diamond M Drilling Co. v. Marshall*, 577 F.2d 1003, 1006 (5th Cir. 1978)).

¹⁰ *Id.*

¹¹ *Bis Salamis, Inc. v. Dir., OWCP*, 819 F.3d 116, 126, 4 Adm. R. 209, 215–16 (5th Cir. 2016) (quoting *Ceres Gulf*, 683 F.3d at 228); *see Ingalls Shipbuilding, Inc. v. Dir., OWCP*, 991 F.2d 163, 165 (5th Cir. 1993).

¹² *Gaudet*, 562 F.2d at 355 (citing *Ruiz v. Shell Oil Co.*, 413 F.2d 310, 312–13 (5th Cir. 1969)).

¹³ *See Hall v. Diamond M Co.*, 732 F.2d 1246, 1249 (5th Cir. 1984) (per curiam).

¹⁴ *Hebron v. Union Oil Co. of Cal.*, 634 F.2d 245, 247 (5th Cir. Unit A Jan. 1981) (per curiam) (citing *Gaudet*, 562 F.2d at 355).

¹⁵ *Estate of Cowart v. Nicklos Drilling Co.*, 505 U.S. 469, 471 (1992).

¹⁶ *See Jackson v. Land & Offshore Servs., Inc.*, 855 F.2d 244, 246 (5th Cir. 1988) (per curiam) (noting that the employer's "right to set-off the amount of the settlement against future payments" furthers the statutory goal of "protect[ing] the compensation scheme from costs that should be borne by third party tortfeasors").

any "amount less than the compensation to which the [employee] would be entitled under" the Act.[17] If the employee fails to obtain that prior approval, "all future [—8—] benefits including medical benefits are forfeited."[18] Where an employee obtains a court judgment against a third party or accepts a settlement for *more* than the compensation due under the Act, his duty to his employer is less onerous. In such cases, Section 33(g)(2) requires only that the employer receive notice, {–643–} not register its approval.[19] Together, these provisions of Section 33(g) are "designed to ensure that the employer's rights are protected . . . and to prevent the claimant from unilaterally bargaining away funds to which the employer or its carrier might be entitled under" the Act.[20]

III.

Mays contends that the Benefits Review Board erred by concluding that Gliott was an independent contractor employed by IMIA rather than a borrowed servant of Avondale. Specifically, Mays challenges the Board's analysis of the *Ruiz* factors and its conclusions as to Avondale's purported judicial admissions regarding Gliott's employment status and the relevance of certain Board precedent.

A.

The ALJ found that eight of the nine *Ruiz* factors weighed against borrowed servant status, and one factor was neutral. The Board affirmed, concluding that while the evidence may not have been as overwhelming as the ALJ suggested, "at least five of the nine factors favor the finding that . . . Gliott is a 'third party' and not [Avondale's] borrowed employee." We find no genuine issue as to any of the facts concerning the *Ruiz* factors.[21]

Therefore, the only [—9—] question for this Court is whether the BRB erred as a matter of law in finding that Gliott was an independent contractor.[22]

Regarding the first and most important *Ruiz* factor, the ALJ and BRB agreed that IMIA retained control over Gliott and his work at the Avondale shipyard. The primary evidence for this conclusion was the testimony of IMIA's president that his on-site foremen were in charge of all tasks to be performed by IMIA employees. Mays now argues that the control factor favors borrowed servant status for four reasons. First, "[c]ontrary to the [ALJ's] conclusion, the control factor does not require micromanagement." Second, Avondale inspected the work of the IMIA employees to ensure it was up to Avondale's standards—a power Mays describes as "the essence of control." Third, Avondale, not IMIA, conducted the investigation of the Mays-Gliott altercation. Finally, ultimate direction over IMIA's tasks came from Avondale: "IMIA did not simply appear one day at the Avondale site and begin working where it wanted, doing whatever it wanted." Therefore, "[a]ny orders Gliott received from his supervisors were in direct response to IMIA's orders from Avondale." Avondale counters that "[t]here is absolutely no evidence in the record that anyone from Avondale had control over Mr. Gliott's work in any manner." Furthermore, Mays himself testified that he and Gliott had two separate foremen, indicating that IMIA never relinquished control over Gliott's employment.[23]

We agree with the administrative courts below that the first factor weighs in favor of independent contractor status. As we have long noted, "a careful distinction must be made 'between authoritative direction and control, and mere suggestion {–644–} as to details or the necessary co-operation, where the [—10—] work furnished is part of a larger

---

[17] 33 U.S.C. § 933(g)(1).

[18] *Cowart*, 505 U.S. at 471.

[19] *See* 33 U.S.C. § 933(g)(2).

[20] *Parfait v. Dir., OWCP*, 903 F.3d 505, 509, 6 Adm. R. 252, 254 (5th Cir. 2018).

[21] *See Kiff v. Travelers Ins. Co.*, 402 F.2d 129, 131 (5th Cir. 1968) (noting that where the relevant facts are undisputed, the borrowed servant determination is a question of law to be decided by the court).

[22] *See Gaudet*, 562 F.2d at 358–59.

[23] *See Capps v. N.L. Baroid-NL Indus., Inc.*, 784 F.2d 615, 616, 618 (5th Cir. 1986) (considering "direct supervision" by an agent of the purported borrowing employer as a factor supporting borrowed servant status).

undertaking.'"[24] "'Co-operation,' as distinguished from 'subordination,' is not enough to create an employment relationship."[25] Here, the facts indicate that although Avondale monitored the sandblasting project it had hired IMIA to complete, Avondale did not direct the actions of IMIA employees during the course of their daily work. Some degree of oversight is a necessary component of any contract relationship; it is never the case that an independent contractor "simply appear[s]" at a job site and does "whatever it want[s]." Avondale's quality checks and general site management are readily distinguished from the conduct of a borrowing employer, who gives direct orders to its borrowed servant.[26]

Next, we disagree with the ALJ and BRB's conclusion that the second *Ruiz* factor—whose work is being performed—is neutral. Instead, we conclude that the second factor weighs in favor of borrowed servant status. It is true that unlike the labor pool companies that feature in many borrowed servant cases, IMIA did have a substantial business function independent of its work with Avondale.[27] However, the discrete tasks IMIA completed at the Avondale shipyard were crucial to Avondale's ship-expansion contract with the United States Navy. In analogous cases, the Court has consistently held that a worker assisting with a company's central task is functionally an employee of the company, even if his payroll employer is a separate entity. In *Melancon*, for example, we held that a welder whose work assisted the borrowing employer with "an essential, although only incidental, aspect of [its] business" was [—11—] properly categorized as a borrowed servant.[28] More-

over, at least one court adjudicating a separate dispute involving the same corporate parties has concluded that the tasks IMIA employees performed at the Avondale shipyard were ultimately part of Avondale's work.[29]

Next, although the ALJ considered the third *Ruiz* factor neutral, the Board found that "there was no agreement between the two employers that Gliott would become [Avondale's] servant." We agree with the ALJ and hold that the third *Ruiz* factor is neutral. Given that discovery took place more than two decades after the underlying altercation, it is unsurprising that Avondale was unable to produce the Master Service Agreement between itself and IMIA. Lacking the Agreement or the testimony of the executives who arranged it, the Court cannot credit the inferences urged by either side.[30] {–645–}

The fourth *Ruiz* factor considers whether the employee acquiesced in his new work situation.[31] The ALJ and the Board concluded that Gliott did not acquiesce to becoming Avondale's borrowed servant because the Avondale job lasted only a few months, during which IMIA maintained control over Gliott's tools, equipment, and wages. As Mays points out, however, the administrative courts applied an incorrect legal standard. The question is not whether Mays agreed to become Avondale's employee but whether he "was aware of his work [—12—] conditions and chose to continue working in them."[32] It is clear from the facts presented that Gliott

---

[24] *Ruiz*, 413 F.2d at 313 (quoting *Standard Oil Co. v. Anderson*, 212 U.S. 215, 222 (1909)).

[25] *Id.* (quoting *Anderson*, 212 U.S. at 226).

[26] *See, e.g., Melancon v. Amoco Prod. Co.*, 834 F.2d 1238, 1245 (5th Cir. 1988); *Hebron*, 634 F.2d at 247.

[27] *See, e.g., Capps*, 784 F.2d at 616 (according borrowed servant status to a worker whose nominal employer was "a company specializing in the supplying of general laborers to companies in need of temporary help").

[28] *Melancon*, 834 F.2d at 1245; *see also Lemaire v. Danos & Curole Marine Contractors, Inc.*, 265 F.3d 1059, at *2, *5 (5th Cir. 2001) (unpublished) (per curiam) (describing a situation in which

workers' nominal employers "were under contract with Texaco to provide employees to operate Texaco platforms offshore" as exemplifying "the nature of the 'borrowed employee'" relationship).

[29] *Musa v. Litton-Avondale Indus., Inc.*, 10-627 (La. App. 5 Cir. 3/29/11), 63 So. 3d 243, 247.

[30] Given the age of the document and the many corporate transitions that have happened in the years since it was executed, the Court declines Mays's request to draw an adverse inference against Avondale for failing to produce the Agreement.

[31] *Gaudet*, 562 F.2d at 355 (citing *Ruiz*, 413 F.2d at 312–13).

[32] *Brown v. Union Oil Co. of Cal.*, 984 F.2d 674, 678 (5th Cir. 1993) (per curiam) (citing *Melancon*, 834 F.2d at 1246).

was aware of his working conditions at the Avondale site and voluntarily continued to work there.[33] The fourth *Ruiz* factor therefore supports borrowed servant status.

However, the fifth factor—whether the original employer terminated his relationship with the employee—clearly supports independent contractor status. The ALJ and the Board agreed "that [IMIA] continued to employ [Gliott], provided for his Longshore insurance, paid his wages, provided him with his tools and equipment for work, and supervised him on a daily basis." Moreover, Gliott moved with IMIA to its next job when the contract at Avondale was finished. Of course, the fifth *Ruiz* factor does not "require[] a lending employer to completely sever his relationship with the employee" before the employee may be considered a borrowed servant.[34] However, it does require that the lending employer "cease[] *control* in its relationship" with the employee.[35] Here, IMIA retained control over all the most important aspects of Gliott's employment: his pay, his performance, his supplies, and his insurance.

The sixth factor—who furnished the tools and place of performance—likewise indicates that Gliott was an independent contractor, not an Avondale employee. The ALJ found that "International Marine provided the scaffolding and [Gliott's] tools of work, while [Avondale] provided the ship and shipyard on which he worked." Contrary to the Board's conclusion, however, this bifurcation of duties between IMIA and Avondale does not render the sixth [—13—] factor neutral. In this case, the tools provided by IMIA were essential to Gliott's task, while the location of the work was merely incidental. The facts are readily distinguished from *Melancon*, which Mays cites for the proposition that the company at

whose site the work takes place should generally be considered the true employer. In *Melancon*, the worker was required to be on the borrower's premises because operation of the premises—an oil drilling platform—was the very job to be performed.[36] In this case, by contrast, "[i]f the ship had been on International Marine's premises, [Gliott's] work and tools would be the same." {–646–}

As to the seventh factor, the ALJ found that Gliott's employment was not "over a considerable length of time"[37] because "the job in question lasted no more than 90 days after which Gliott moved with International Marine to its next job." The Board considered this factor neutral, noting that while "a lengthy period of employment tends to support a finding that the worker is a borrowed employee . . . a laborer employed for only one day may be a borrowed servant" under the right set of facts.[38] Although scattershot findings abound, the case law provides little guidance on how to categorize Gliott's ninety-day term at Avondale. In *Brown*, for instance, a thirty-day period of employment was considered neutral,[39] while in *Melancon* a seven-year term weighed in favor of borrowed servant status.[40] In another case, we noted that "it is debatable whether approximately a year and a half is a 'considerable' length of time."[41] Given these precedents, we hold there is substantial evidence to support the ALJ's conclusion that Gliott's 90-day term should lead to a neutral finding on the seventh *Ruiz* factor. [—14—]

The eighth factor asks which company—the nominal employer or the purported borrowing employer—had the right to discharge the employee. Testimony before the ALJ established that while Avondale could not terminate Gliott's employment, it did have the right to remove him from its property for inappropriate conduct. The ALJ concluded that this factor favored independent

---

[33] *See Fontenot v. Mobil Oil Expl. & Producing Se., Inc.*, 997 F.2d 881, at *3 (5th Cir. 1993) (per curiam) (citing *Capps*, 784 F.2d at 617) ("[T]his court considers [a worker's] acceptance of a job that regularly sent him to temporary work places as acquiescence to each of those employment situations.").

[34] *Capps*, 784 F.2d at 617.

[35] *Melancon*, 834 F.2d at 1246 (emphasis added).

[36] *See Melancon*, 834 F.2d at 1241.

[37] *Gaudet*, 562 F.2d at 355.

[38] *See Capps*, 784 F.2d at 618.

[39] 984 F.2d at 679.

[40] 834 F.2d at 1246.

[41] *U.S. Fire Ins. Co. v. Miller*, 381 F.3d 385, 390 (5th Cir. 2004).

contractor status, but the Board found the opposite. We agree with the Board. As Mays argues, "the proper focus when considering who has the right to discharge the employee" is whether the purported borrower "had the right to terminate [the worker's] services with *itself*," not his employment with the lending employer.[42] Avondale does not contest that it could remove Gliott from working on its premises. Therefore, Avondale had the right to "discharge" Gliott within the meaning of the eighth *Ruiz* factor.[43]

Finally, we agree with the ALJ and the Board that the ninth factor—who had the obligation to pay the employee—weighs in favor of independent contractor status. The ALJ found that Avondale "paid [IMIA] a lump sum" upon completion of the contract, and IMIA paid its own employees out of that sum. Avondale never made direct payments to Gliott and had no obligation to do so. Citing *Capps* and *Melancon*, Mays contends that "[w]here the lending employer receives the funds to pay the employee from the borrowing employer, the borrowing employer, in essence, has paid the employee."[44] This is not an entirely accurate representation of our case law. Although a payment to a nominal employer may sometimes constitute an indirect payment to the borrowed servant, that is not always the case. Mays's interpretation would swallow any analysis of this factor; after all, a contractor can always trace his payment in wages back to another employer. Typically, the distinguishing [—15—] factor is the basis on which the purported borrower makes its payments. In both *Capps* and *Melancon*, the borrower paid the nominal employer based on the {–647–} number of hours the borrowed servant worked, and then the nominal employer paid the borrowed servant a percentage of that payment.[45] Here, by contrast, "[t]he amount International Marine received . . . was not

connected to the hours worked" by Gliott or any other IMIA employee.

In sum, four of the nine *Ruiz* factors, including the most important factor of control, indicate that Gliott was not Avondale's borrowed servant. Three factors weigh in favor of borrowed servant status, while the remaining two are neutral. Given this calculus, we affirm the Board's conclusion "that the ALJ's order was supported by substantial evidence on the record as a whole and is in accordance with the law."[46]

B.

Mays raises two further challenges to the Board's borrowed servant analysis. First, citing *Nicholson v. Securitas Security Services USA, Inc.*, he argues that Avondale is estopped by prior admissions from denying that Gliott was its borrowed servant.[47] In support, Mays points to various statements made by Avondale agents in which Gliott was described as an "employee" of Avondale. For example, in a witness report submitted shortly after Mays's injury, an Avondale employee described the incident as an "altercation between two employees." Later, Avondale appeared to admit in a discovery response that Mays and Gliott were "co-employees," though later in the same document Avondale expressly denied that Gliott was a borrowed employee. For its part, Avondale characterizes these statements as "inadvertent use[s]" of the [—16—] term "employee" and directs the Court to numerous discovery documents in which Avondale denied that Gliott was its employee or borrowed servant.

Avondale is correct that none of the statements to which Mays points constitutes a judicial admission. "A judicial admission is a formal concession in the pleadings or stipulations by a party or counsel that is

---

[42] *Capps*, 784 F.2d at 618 (emphasis added); *see Hebron*, 634 F.2d at 247–48.

[43] *See, e.g., Melancon*, 834 F.2d at 1246.

[44] *See Capps*, 784 F.2d at 618; *Melancon*, 834 F.2d at 1246.

[45] *See Capps*, 784 F.2d at 618; *Melancon*, 834 F.2d at 1246.

[46] *Avondale*, 977 F.2d at 189.

[47] *See Nicholson*, 830 F.3d 186, 189 (5th Cir. 2016) ("[T]he 'right to control test' is not implicated when there is an admission by a defendant of employment." (internal quotation marks omitted)).

binding on the party making them."[48] A statement made during the course of a lawsuit—even a statement made in a pleading filed with the court—should be considered a judicial admission only "if it was made intentionally as a waiver, releasing the opponent from proof of fact."[49] An *evidentiary* admission, by contrast, "is 'merely a statement of assertion or concession made for some independent purpose,' and it may be controverted or explained by the party who made it."[50]

Avondale's admissions were of the latter variety. The evidence shows that although Avondale agents occasionally referred to Gliott as an employee, such statements were never made in a context indicating intentional waiver. To the contrary, when specifically asked during discovery, Avondale denied that Gliott was a borrowed employee. *Nicholson* does not dictate a different result. There, the employer had averred that Nicholson was its employee in an employment contract and in its answer, and conceded the point in its briefing to the Court.[51] Unlike here, there {-648-} were no inconsistent discovery materials or denials of Nicholson's employment status.[52] Considering the full context of the litigation, the ALJ properly concluded that the statements made by Avondale [—17—] agents regarding Gliott's employment were not judicial admissions of borrowed servant status.

C.

Next, Mays argues that the Board erred by failing to follow its own precedent on borrowed servant liability. In Mays's view, the Board's 2010 opinion in *Phillips v. PMB Safety & Regulatory, Inc.* "controls in this case."[53] In *Phillips*, the claimant was injured in an attack by a coworker aboard a Chevron oil rig. Although the attacker and the claimant were nominally employed by separate sub-contractors, the BRB concluded that Chevron was liable for the claimant's injuries under the Longshore Act because both workers were Chevron's borrowed servants.[54] Mays claims that *Phillips*'s liability finding controls here because he and Gliott, like the workers in *Phillips*, labored in a confined environment and were both doing work for the same company. Avondale counters that *Phillips* provides no guidance because it does not examine the *Ruiz* factors. Rather, the primary issue in *Phillips* was whether the claimant was acting within the scope of his employment at the time of his injury.

Avondale is correct. Although factual similarities exist between *Phillips* and the present case, *Phillips*'s legal conclusion is not controlling. At no point in *Phillips* does the BRB mention *Ruiz*. In fact, both *Phillips* itself and the Fifth Circuit case upon which it relies assume the prior establishment of borrowed servant status.[55] Only after the *Ruiz* analysis has been conducted and resolved in favor of borrowed servant status does *Phillips* become relevant. [—18—] Because the *Ruiz* analysis in this case weighs in favor of independent contractor status, *Philips* does not apply.

IV.

On cross-appeal, Avondale argues that the Board erred in its conclusion as to the form of Section 33 relief to which Avondale is entitled. Section 33(f) entitles an employer to credit "against his compensation payments . . . any amount received by [an] employee by way of settlement with a third party tortfeasor."[56]

---

[48] *Martinez v. Bally's La., Inc.*, 244 F.3d 474, 476 (5th Cir. 2001).

[49] *Id.*; *see Dartez v. Owens-Ill., Inc.*, 910 F.2d 1291, 1294 (5th Cir. 1990).

[50] *Martinez*, 244 F.3d at 476–477 (quoting *McNamara v. Miller*, 269 F.2d 511, 515 (D.C. Cir. 1959)).

[51] *Nicholson*, 830 F.3d at 189.

[52] *See Heritage Bank v. Redcom Labs., Inc.*, 250 F.3d 319, 329 (5th Cir. 2001) ("To qualify as a judicial admission, [a] statement must be," among other things, "deliberate, clear, and unequivocal . . . ."); *Dartez*, 910 F.2d at 1294 ("Procedural context may . . . prevent the use as admissions of statements made by a party . . . .").

[53] *See Phillips*, 44 BRBS 1 (2010 BRB).

[54] *Id.* at 5.

[55] *Phillips*, 44 BRBS at 5; *see Perron v. Bell Maint. & Fabricators, Inc.*, 970 F.2d 1409, 1410 (5th Cir. 1992).

[56] *Petroleum Helicopters, Inc. v. Collier*, 784 F.2d 644, 646 (5th Cir. 1986) (citing 33 U.S.C. § 933(f)).

Section 33(g) contemplates even more significant relief for the employer. Where an employee fails to obtain his employer's approval before accepting a third-party tort settlement for less than the value of his longshore benefits, the employer is completely excused from all statutory obligations to the employee.[57]

In 2003, the Board affirmed the ALJ's grant of Section 33(f) relief to Avondale based on Mays's $60,000 settlement with Gliott and IMIA. In 2016, the ALJ found that Mays was entitled to additional disability compensation of more than three hundred thousand dollars. However, because {–649–} that additional award would far exceed Mays's earlier, unapproved settlement with Gliott and IMIA, Section 33(g) would mandate forfeiture of the additional award. In other words, it would be a wash. Accordingly, the ALJ denied Mays's request for modification. In affirming the ALJ's decision, the Board noted that "the administrative law judge's prior . . . offset to employer of the net amount of the third-party settlement pursuant to Section 33(f) remain[s] in effect."

Avondale now argues that the Board "should have affirmed the lower Court's ruling based on Section 33(g), which was the basis of the lower Court's decision." To be clear, Avondale does not argue that the Board made an error [—19—] of law; it argues that the Board "fail[ed] to consider the findings . . . of the Administrative Law Judge whereby [Section] 33(g) was invoked." But Avondale misunderstands the ALJ's decision: it did not modify Mays's benefits and then apply a Section 33(g) forfeiture to the modified amount. Rather, the ALJ determined that modification was not required, because any upwards modification would trigger, and be cancelled out by, a Section 33(g) forfeiture. Thus, the Section 33(f) relief awarded by the ALJ remains in effect, and the unmodified compensation award stands following this appeal.

V.

We find no error in the Board's conclusion that the ALJ's decision below was supported by substantial evidence and in accordance with the law. The Order of the Benefits Review Board is therefore affirmed.

---

[57] 33 U.S.C. § 933(g)(2); *see Cowart*, 505 U.S. at 471.

United States Court of Appeals
for the Fifth Circuit

No. 18-30908

CLAIMANT ID 100235033
VS.
BP EXPLORATION & PROD., INC.

Appeal from the United States District Court for the
Eastern District of Louisiana

Decided: October 29, 2019

Citation: 941 F.3d 801, 7 Adm. R. 318 (5th Cir. 2019).

Before **OWEN**, Chief Judge, and **SOUTHWICK** and
HIGGINSON, Circuit Judges.

[—1—] {–802–} **HIGGINSON**, Circuit Judge:

As our court and the public well know, the Deepwater Horizon oil spill in 2010 led to a massive settlement between BP and class action plaintiffs. The Economic and Property Damages Class Action Settlement Agreement adopted streamlined procedures for processing claims in the hopes of speedily granting relief and concluding litigation. To that end, one innovation of the Settlement Agreement was to simplify the inquiry into causation—the process of determining whether and to what extent the oil spill caused a given claimant's asserted injury. *See In re Deepwater Horizon*, 753 F.3d 509, 2 Adm. R. 217 (5th Cir. 2014); *In* [—2—] *re Deepwater Horizon*, 744 F.3d 370, 2 Adm. R. 183 (5th Cir. 2014); *In re Deepwater Horizon*, 732 F.3d 326, 1 Adm. R. 287 (5th Cir. 2013). This simplification reduced much of the scrutiny that might be devoted to causation in an ordinary tort case. In some instances, this has meant an award might go to a claimant who, in conventional litigation, would have failed to establish causation for one reason or another. This altered causation inquiry furthered a fundamental goal: avoiding the "overwhelming" administrative burden that would follow if we treated every Deepwater Horizon claimant with the scrutiny that confronts the typical tort plaintiff. *In re Deepwater Horizon*, 744 F.3d at 377, 2 Adm. R. at 187. It likewise made it possible to encompass the extensive but diffuse effects of the environmental catastrophe and region-alized economic crisis that was the Deepwater Horizon disaster, which might otherwise have seemed too attenuated under ordinary causation analysis.

The questions in the present appeal stem from that reduced causation inquiry: whether a claimant's alleged unlawful conduct wholly or partially disqualifies it from the Settlement Program and, if so, what evidence is adequate to show that the {–803–} claimant engaged in such conduct. Common sense would seem to furnish answers. Surely bank robbers could not file a Deepwater Horizon claim on the ground that the oil spill left banks along the Gulf Coast with less cash to grab. Just as surely, the mere allegation of wrongdoing, without more, should not disqualify a claimant from recovering its damages.

And yet, simple as these questions may seem, the parties have been unable to give us clear answers that are rooted in the Settlement Agreement or other law. Given that, and given the recurrence of the issues this appeal implicates, we reverse the district court's decision to decline discretionary review and remand for further proceedings. [—3—]

I

The Claimant describes itself as "a Florida company that provided back office support to clients," such as voicemail, fax, and tech support. According to BP, the Claimant is no longer in business, though the record does not make the current status of the company entirely clear.

The Claimant submitted a Business Economic Loss (BEL) claim as a Zone C claimant in July 2013.

In 2011, the Claimant featured in a report by the majority staff of the U.S. Senate Committee on Commerce, Science, and Transportation, *Unauthorized Charges on Telephone Bills*.[1] The report concerned the problem of "cramming": unauthorized charges

---

[1] STAFF OF S. COMM. ON COMMERCE, SCI., & TRANSP., 112TH CONG., UNAUTHORIZED CHARGES ON TELEPHONE BILLS (2011), *accessible at* https://ecfsapi.fcc.gov/file/7021859847.pdf.

to telephone users by third-party vendors— that is, by companies other than the provider of the phone service. The report described the scope of the problem, as well as enforcement efforts by the Federal Trade Commission (FTC) and various state attorneys general. The Committee's investigation initially focused on the then-largest companies providing landline phone service, AT&T, Qwest, and Verizon, and eventually expanded to include the Claimant, among others. Though couched in suggestive language, the Committee's report made damning allegations against the Claimant. For instance, the report alleged that the Claimant and other companies were "each part of complex enterprises that are engaged in cramming and designed to conceal their true activities and structure from the public and telephone companies."

Enforcement actions by the FTC followed. AT&T, which appeared in the report, agreed to pay $105 million to settle cramming charges.[2] The Claimant [—4—] points to another substantial settlement by numerous corporate and individual defendants.[3] The Claimant notes that, by contrast, the FTC "closed its inquiry" into the Claimant in 2013 without a penalty or settlement.[4]

In December 2013, the Claimant and associated entities and individuals entered into a settlement agreement with the Florida {–804–} Attorney General, labeled an "Assurance of Voluntary Compliance" (AVC) by that office. The AVC had the following disclaimer:

---

[2] Press Release, Federal Trade Commission, AT&T to Pay $80 Million to FTC for Consumer Refunds in Mobile Cramming Case (Oct. 8, 2014), https://www.ftc.gov/news- [—4—] events/press-releases/2014/10/att-pay-80-million-ftc-consumer-refunds-mobile-cramming-case.

[3] Press Release, Federal Trade Commission, FTC Wraps up Major Phone Cramming Case as Remaining Defendants Settle Charges (June 23, 2017), https://www.ftc.gov/news-events/press-releases/2017/06/ftc-wraps-major-phone-cramming-case-remaining-defendants-settle. None of these defendants seems to have appeared in the Senate report.

[4] The parties did not supply any FTC documentation explaining the agency's declination.

[T]his AVC does not constitute a finding of law or fact, or any evidence supporting any such finding of law or fact by any court or agency that Respondents have engaged in any act or practice declared unlawful by any laws, rules, or regulations of the State of Florida or as might apply or be applied in Florida. Respondents deny any liability or violation of law and enter into this AVC without any admission of liability. The parties intend that this AVC shall not be used as evidence against Respondents in any action or proceeding other than in an action or proceedings brought by the Attorney General to enforce its terms.

The AVC briefly described the Claimant's billing practices and noted that it and its associates had already refunded or credited customers $2 million. The AVC provided that the Claimant would pay an additional $165,447 in restitution to various consumers and government entities. The AVC also enjoined the Claimant from enrolling any Florida customers in "services billable to Florida landline or mobile telephone bills" or causing any charges to appear on Florida telephone bills. [—5—]

As noted, the Claimant submitted a BEL claim to the Court-Supervised Settlement Program in 2013. In April 2015, the Claims Administrator issued a "Notice of Request for Document Verification" to the Claimant concerning the Florida settlement. The notice directed the Claimant to

Provide a breakout of the revenues and corresponding expenses reported on the 2007, 2008, 2009, 2010, and 2011 profit and loss statements that are applicable to the terms in the settlement agreement reached with the Florida Attorney General's office related to unauthorized charges billed by the claimant to its clients.

In June,[5] the Claimant submitted a spreadsheet of "revenue and corresponding expenses refunded to Claimant's Customers, by month and year, according to the settlement agreement reached with the Florida Attorney General's office."[6]

In December 2015, the Claims Administrator notified the Claimant that its claim had been flagged for review by the Fraud, Waste, or Abuse (FWA) Department, and it gave the Claimant the option to withdraw.[7] In February 2016, the Claims Administrator notified the Claimant that an investigation had been opened. That October, the Claims Administrator informed the Claimant that its claim had been denied. The FWA review had "revealed clear and compelling evidence" that the claim contained "false, misleading, forged, or fabricated documents, information, or statements." The Claims Administrator explained that the Claimant's allegedly lost {–805–} revenues were [—6—] "derived primarily, if not solely from Cramming, an illegal activity." The Claims Administrator ruled that "such damages are not cognizable under the terms of the Settlement Agreement, nor allowed as a matter of public policy," though it did not mention any particular law or Settlement Agreement provision. As evidence, the Claims Administrator cited the Senate report on cramming.

The Claimant sought reconsideration, challenging the Senate report's contents as "unsubstantiated and unproven charges" and not the work of a "law enforcement agency." The Claimant professed full cooperation with the FTC and represented that the FTC's investigation "found no wrongdoing" and closed without charges or a settlement. The Claimant also enclosed a "white paper" from the law firm of Skadden Arps that described the Claimant's legitimate business practices and critiqued the Senate report.

In August 2017, the Claims Administrator again denied the Claimant's claim. The denial notice added no new reasoning but noted that a new reviewer had made the decision.

In December 2017, however, the Claims Administrator informed the Claimant that the initial "Notice of FWA Claim Denial" had been "overturned" and the claim "referred for continued processing." It did not say why.

But on January 9, 2018, the Claims Administrator again denied the Claimant's claim. The notice, now more equivocal, explained that the Claimant's revenues "relate[d,] at least in part, to cramming" from 2007 to 2011. It no longer mentioned the FWA review, and no reference to any evidence or to any provision of the Settlement Agreement appeared in the notice. The Claimant again requested reconsideration, protesting the dearth of evidence and pointing to the outcome of the FTC's investigation as exculpatory. In February 2018, the Settlement Program again denied the claim, the fourth time it did so, providing precisely the same explanation as the previous denial. [—7—] The Claimant appealed, addressing the Senate report, FTC investigation, and settlement with the Florida Attorney General.

In May 2018, the Appeal Panel affirmed the denial. It recounted the Senate report's discussion of cramming and its allegations as to the Claimant's business structure. It acknowledged that the FTC's investigation closed without an enforcement action. It also noted the Florida Attorney General settlement's avowal that it was not a finding or admission of illegal conduct. The Appeal

---

[5] The Claims Administrator had to send the notice twice, because the Claimant did not respond the first time.

[6] In its brief, BP asserted that the Claimant never responded. That was wrong and rebutted by the record, as counsel for BP acknowledged at oral argument. *See Claimant ID 100235033 v. BP Explor. & Prod., Inc.* (5th Cir. May 1, 2019) (No. 18-30908), http://www.ca5.uscourts.gov/OralArgRecordings/18/18-30908_5-1-2019.mp3.

[7] The district court had appointed former FBI Director Louis Freeh as Special Master in July 2013 to investigate fraud and abuse in the Settlement Program, to develop anti-fraud and anti-corruption protocols, and to initiate actions to "claw back" ill-gotten payments from the Settlement Program. *See In re Oil Spill by the Oil Rig "Deepwater Horizon" in the Gulf of Mexico, on April 20, 2010*, 2015 WL 12724047, at *1–3 (E.D. La. Feb. 26, 2015).

Panel then fell back on the "[m]ore important[]" Senate report, concluding that its "findings . . . establish that [the C]laimant was guilty of illegal activity and the ill gotten gains from these activities are represented in [the Claimant's] financials which form the basis of this claim." Because the Claimant's recovery "would be based, at least in part, on the company's illegal conduct," the Appeal Panel affirmed the denial of the claim.

The Claimant timely but unsuccessfully sought discretionary review from the district court, bringing this appeal to our court.

II

We review the district court's denial of discretionary review for abuse of discretion. *Holmes Motors, Inc. v. BP Explor. & Prod., Inc.*, 829 F.3d 313, 315, 4 Adm. R. 263, 263 (5th Cir. 2016). We typically consider "whether the decision not reviewed by the district court actually contradicted or misapplied the Settlement Agreement, or had the clear potential to contradict or misapply the Settlement Agreement." *Id.*, 4 Adm. R. at 263 (quotation omitted). "[M]aking an error of law constitutes {–806–} an abuse of discretion." *BP Explor. & Prod., Inc. v. Claimant ID 100281817*, 919 F.3d 284, 287, 7 Adm. R. 209, 210 (5th Cir. 2019) (quotation omitted). That said, the district court is not obligated to review all cases raising "a question about the proper interpretation of the Settlement Agreement." *Holmes Motors*, 829 F.3d at 316, 4 Adm. R. at 264. It is not an abuse of discretion to deny review if the appeal simply raises "the [—8—] correctness of a discretionary administrative decision" in a claimant's unique case. *Claimant ID 100212278 v. BP Explor. & Prod., Inc.*, 848 F.3d 407, 410, 5 Adm. R. 202, 203 (5th Cir. 2017) (quotation omitted). It may be an abuse, however, if the district court "den[ies] a request for review that raises a recurring issue on which the Appeal Panels are split if 'the resolution of the question will substantially impact the administration of the Agreement.'" *Id.*, 5 Adm. R. at 203 (quoting *In*

re Deepwater Horizon, 632 F. App'x 199, 203–04 (5th Cir. 2015)).[8]

III

The Claimant and BP disagree both on the factual question specific to this case—whether disqualifying illegal conduct by the Claimant was adequately shown—and on the legal rules for disqualifying claimants due to illegal activity. Had this appeal simply presented the first of these two disputes, we would not likely reverse the district court's denial of discretionary review.[9] But the parties have not been able to articulate rules, rooted either in [—9—] the Settlement Agreement or in some other source of law, that explain why the Claimant should be disqualified from

---

[8] We have found that a denial of discretionary review was an abuse of discretion in varying circumstances. *See, e.g., BP Explor. & Prod., Inc. v. Claimant ID 100281817*, 919 F.3d 284, 287–89, 7 Adm. R. 209, 209–11 (5th Cir. 2019) (reversing denial where award contradicted Settlement Agreement's text, though not in any apparently recurring manner); *BP Explor. & Prod., Inc. v. Claimant ID 100094497*, 910 F.3d 797, 800–03, 6 Adm. R. 273, 274–77 (5th Cir. 2018) (reversing denial and supplying new test for distinguishing "fixed" from "variable" expenses, because issue frequently recurred and appeal panel misapplied Settlement Agreement); *BP Explor. & Prod., Inc. v. Claimant ID 100301594*, --- F. App'x ---, 2019 WL 2477212, at *1 (5th Cir. June 12, 2019) (reversing denial because intervening Fifth Circuit decision "squarely contradict[ed]" appeal panel decision); *BP Explor. & Prod., Inc. v. Claimant ID 100195328*, 766 F. App'x 141, 145–46 (5th Cir. 2019) (reversing denial due to misapplication of Settlement Agreement by Claims Administrator in policy document, where recurrence was suggested because "several examples of the application of this Policy appear to exist").

[9] We consistently affirm denials of review in cases questioning only the correctness of the Claims Administrator's decision on the facts of the case. *See, e.g., Claimant ID 100154392 v. BP Explor. & Prod., Inc.*, --- F. App'x ---, 2019 WL 2866494 (5th Cir. July 2, 2019); *BP Explor. & Prod., Inc. v. Claimant ID 100157225*, --- F. App'x ---, 2019 WL 2719916 (5th Cir. June 28, 2019); *Claimant ID 100324302 v. BP Explor. & Prod., Inc.*, --- F. App'x ---, 2019 WL 2323647 (5th Cir. May 30, 2019); *BP Explor. & Prod., Inc. v. Claimant ID 100283067*, --- F. App'x ---, 2019 WL 2144391 (5th Cir. May 15, 2019).

recovery—or why it should not—when its revenues derived "at least in part" from illegal activity. Nor has BP been able to explain the evidentiary threshold for such disqualification, if the law indeed requires it. Due to that void at the base of the parties' arguments, and to a split among appeal panels in the resolution of comparable cases, we conclude that the district court's denial of review was an abuse of discretion.

A

We begin with a brief review of the causation inquiry that claimants must satisfy in order to obtain an award from the Settlement Program. The Claimant is from Zone C and is not part of an industry that the Settlement Agreement excuses from demonstrating causation.[10] Accordingly, it {–807–} must satisfy one of several revenue-based causation tests set out in Exhibit 4B of the Settlement Agreement.[11] These tests compare a claimant's financial performance before and after the spill, thereby ensuring "a temporal relationship to the spill." *In re Deepwater Horizon*, 858 F.3d 298, 301, 5 Adm. R. 259, 259 (5th Cir. 2017). This temporal relationship supplements the geographic relationship established by a claimant's residence in a zone near the spill. "Causation is, in all other respects, presumed." *Id.*, 5 Adm. R. at 259.

We approved this approach to causation in a series of decisions concerning Exhibit 4B early in the life of the Settlement Program. *See In re Deepwater Horizon*, 753 F.3d 509, 2 Adm. R. 217 (5th Cir. 2014); *In re Deepwater Horizon*, 744 F.3d 370, 2 Adm. R. 183 (5th Cir. 2014); *In re Deepwater Horizon*, 732 F.3d 326, 1 Adm. R. 287 (5th Cir. 2013). [—10—] The question in these cases was whether the

Settlement Agreement's method of assessing causation satisfied the traceability component of Article III's standing requirements. *See* 744 F.3d at 375–78, 2 Adm. R. at 184–88; *id.* at 383–84, 2 Adm. R. at 192–94 (Clement, J., dissenting).

As explained in the second of these decisions, the Settlement Agreement established that, if a claimant met the geographic and temporal requirements, "traceability between [BP's] conduct and a claimant's injury would be satisfied . . . by a certification on the document that the claimant was injured by the *Deepwater Horizon* disaster." 744 F.3d at 376, 2 Adm. R. at 186. The certification, done under penalty of perjury, was that one's losses were "*due to the spill.*" *Id.*, 2 Adm. R. at 186. This combination of geography, timing, and attestation would permit the parties to avoid "the claims administrator's investigating the existence and degree of nexus between [every] loss and the disaster in the Gulf," sure to be an "overwhelming" administrative burden. *Id.* at 377, 2 Adm. R. at 187. As to cases lacking an apparent causal nexus, we acknowledged that no "specific provision in the Settlement Agreement" seemed to address such cases. *Id.* at 378, 2 Adm. R. at 187. Accordingly, it was left to the Claims Administrator, parties, and district court to "resolve real examples of implausible claims" in the same way they might resolve any other factual question. *Id.*, 2 Adm. R. at 187.

In the third of these decisions, we considered BP's argument that "there are certain claimants who, while they meet every explicit evidentiary standard in Exhibit 4B, should be denied recovery by the Claims Administrator if their claim lacks an actual causal nexus to the *Deepwater Horizon* disaster." 753 F.3d at 514, 2 Adm. R. at 219. We rejected BP's argument, explaining that "Exhibit 4B explicitly contains no requirement that the Claims Administrator perform an additional calculation or take an additional step to ensure that each paid claim has a direct causal nexus to BP's conduct." *Id.* at 513, 2 Adm. R. at 219. [—11—]

---

[10] For instance, charter fishing businesses and seafood wholesalers were excused from showing causation. *See* Ex. 4B at 1, *Deepwater Horizon Economic and Property Damages Settlement Agreement As Amended on May 2, 2012, In re Oil Spill by the Oil Rig "Deepwater Horizon" in the Gulf of Mexico, on April 20, 2010*, No. 2:10-md-2179 (E.D. La. May 3, 2012), ECF No. 6430-9. ECF LAED 2:10-md-2179, 6430-10, 2.

[11] ECF LAED 2:10-md-2179, 6430-10, 2–6.

Alongside this parsimonious approach to causation, the district court developed and we approved a framework to address fraud in the Settlement Program. *See In re Deepwater Horizon*, 643 F. App'x 377, 379 (5th Cir. 2016). Following an external investigation into a particular conflict of interest, a court-appointed special master developed anti-fraud and anti-corruption protocols for the Settlement Program. *In re Oil Spill*, 2015 WL 12724047, at *2–3. The special master was also empowered to bring actions to recover funds paid on false or fraudulent claims. *E.g.,* {–808–} *In re Deepwater Horizon*, 857 F.3d 246, 249–52, 5 Adm. R. 246, 246–49 (5th Cir. 2017); *In re Deepwater Horizon*, 643 F. App'x at 379. The special master's "clawback" actions were not based on any particular provision of the Settlement Agreement. Rather, they proceeded from the district court's inherent power to enforce settlement agreements and to sanction litigation misconduct. *In re Deepwater Horizon*, 643 F. App'x at 380–81. We have adjudicated the special master's clawback motions as common-law fraud claims arising under general maritime law. *See In re Deepwater Horizon*, 857 F.3d at 249, 5 Adm. R. at 246. Thus, though not a creation of the Settlement Agreement, the special master has played a substantial part in the administration of the Settlement Program.

B

Before taking up the parties' answers to the questions raised in this appeal, we examine a set of appeal panel decisions to see whether they have split on recurring issues with a substantial impact on the Settlement Program. Between them, the parties brought twelve decisions to our attention. Six, though perhaps superficially similar, address different problems.[12] The other [—12—] six

decisions, however, indicate that those panels would likely have reached a different conclusion had they handled the Claimant's case.

The most divergent decision is APD 2018-964, which concerned a Louisiana attorney convicted in 2011 of conspiracy to commit fraud. He was suspended from practicing law in October 2011, a year and a half after the spill, and sentenced to jail time. The lawyer contended that the spill caused his revenue to decline and that the cessation of his law practice in October 2011 was a "factor outside his control" preventing the recovery of his revenues in the post-spill period.[13] The Claims Administrator apparently accepted this argument and determined that he was eligible for an award. BP appealed. As understood by the Appeal Panel, "BP suggest[ed] that [the lawyer] is somehow foreclosed from receiving an award because he would then be profiting from his own wrongdoing." The Appeal Panel rejected BP's argument, in strong terms as "complete nonsense," viewing it as "an alternative causation argument which is not sanctioned by the Settlement Agreement or allowed by the [Fifth Circuit]."

Five decisions seem to find a middle ground: unlawful conduct may cause disqualification—or at least a reduced

potential disqualifying effect [—12—] if pre-spill conduct is shown to be unlawful. The Claimant also cites APD 2017-3975, but that decision addressed the possibility of fraudulent entries in records submitted to the Settlement Program, also a different matter. Similarly, APD 2016-417 concerned a claimant whose former employer had been investigated by the Florida Attorney General and reached a settlement. The decision considered her obligation to report the investigation, again a different issue.

---

[12] Two decisions identified by the Claimant, Appeal Panel Decision (APD) 2016-122 and APD 2016-82, said that allegations by BP against claimants must be supported by record evidence, but these decisions concerned dissimilar situations. Two other decisions, APD 2015-1274 and APD 2014-591, concerned alternative causes of claimants' post-spill revenue declines. That is a different matter than we confront here: the

[13] Under one of Exhibit 4B's revenue-based causation tests, a claimant may show a post-spill revenue decline and then one of several "factors outside the control of the claimant that prevented the recovery of revenues in 2011." Those factors include, for instance, the entry of a competitor or the bankruptcy of a significant customer. ECF LAED 2:10-md-2179, 6430-10, 4. *See Claimant ID 100128765 v. BP Explor. & Prod., Inc.*, 709 F. App'x 771, 772–73 (5th Cir. 2017).

award—but only if it is adequately established. In APD 2016-948, the claimant, a Key West hotel that experienced a hazardous {–809–} carbon monoxide leak, closed for a period of months, and the State [—13—] Attorney for Monroe County, Florida investigated the hotel for negligence. The State Attorney did not pursue charges, concluding that the episode did not indicate the "conscious intent to harm" or the "gross and flagrant negligence" that might warrant them. BP argued that "well-established judicial precedent and holdings in prior Appeal Panel Decisions prohibit a Claimant from profiting from its own illegal conduct." Noting the State Attorney's decision not to file charges, the Appeal Panel rejected BP's argument and affirmed the hotel's award.

In APD 2016-704, the claimant, a Florida dentist, was investigated by the state's Medicaid Fraud Control Unit. The dentist had been erroneously using a billing code for "conscious sedation," which requires a permit the dentist did not have. The dentist reached a settlement agreement with the Florida Attorney General under which he corrected the billing error, paid back funds, and otherwise experienced no sanction. The State Board of Dentistry dismissed its pending complaint against the dentist, also without sanction. Appealing the dentist's award, BP argued that his claim should be barred "by the doctrine forbidding compensation based on illegal activities" or at least reduced to not compensate "illegal profit streams." Finding that BP's accusations had "no merit," the Appeal Panel affirmed the award.

In APD 2015-1535, the claimant, an Alabama appliance retailer, was the subject of local news reports, civil suits, and government investigations concerning its alleged failure to issue customer refunds. BP argued that these activities mandated an FWA review. The Appeal Panel disagreed. The issues with customers had been resolved; the civil suits were actually about unrelated matters; and all investigations had been closed without indictments or criminal charges against the claimant. The panel ruled that "BP's contentions are nothing short of speculation without support in the record." [—14—]

In APD 2015-1434, the claimant, a Louisiana provider of "home nursing and health care services," and its parent company were sued by the U.S. Department of Justice under the False Claims Act.[14] The suit settled, with the Justice Department acknowledging that the allegations were "unproven" and that there was no "determination of liability." BP argued that the claim should be referred for FWA review "to determine (1) whether the entire claim is barred by the doctrine which prohibits profiting from illegal activity; and (2) if not entirely barred, what reductions must be made to remove revenue generated by illegal activity." The Appeal Panel affirmed the claimant's award and rejected BP's argument, ruling that settlement of the litigation "without an admission or determination of wrongdoing is, and should be, of no moment to the Claims Administrator in this case." APD 2015-1526 concerned another subsidiary of the same parent company, so that panel affirmed for the same reasons given in APD 2015-1434.

Like the present case, these five decisions involved government investigations that ended either without charge, in the cases of the Key West hotel and the Alabama appliance retailer; with a settlement, in the cases of the home-nursing companies; or both, in the case of the Florida dentist. The panel handling each decision concluded that the record did not show {–810–} evidence of wrongdoing sufficient to disqualify the claimant. Each rejected arguments from BP substantially similar to the ones that BP advances here.

BP contends that there is no panel split; the record of the Claimant's wrongdoing here simply is stronger than in these other cases. To be sure, each set of facts is unique to some degree, but comparison still is reasonable. The Claimant persuasively argues that the Senate report is not a conclusive, [—15—] reliable work by a law enforcement agency and so should not be taken as evidence of

---

[14] The Justice Department had alleged that the companies were "participating in a scheme to defraud the Medicare System" by, for instance, "billing for ineligible services and unnecessary care."

wrongdoing. The FTC's decision to decline enforcement situates the Claimant similarly to the Key West hotel and the Alabama retailer. Likewise, the Claimant's settlement agreement with the Florida Attorney General, disclaiming any admission or finding of wrongdoing, resembles the agreements reached by the Florida dentist and the home-nursing companies. BP does not argue expressly that the cumulative effect of the Senate report and Florida Attorney General investigation are enough to establish wrongdoing, but if it did, such an argument would run counter to the decisions in the Florida dentist's case and the Alabama retailer's case, where multiple government entities each scrutinized the claimant and then declined to act.

Consequently, we find a three-way split among appeal panels on the significance of wrongdoing: (1) not disqualifying, even if conclusively demonstrated, as in the case of the Louisiana lawyer; (2) perhaps disqualifying but only if adequately demonstrated, as in the five decisions just discussed; and (3) disqualifying even if just alleged, as in the present appeal.

C

We still might affirm the district court's denial of discretionary review if the treatment of the Claimant's appeal were simply a one-off determination under a settled framework of law. No such framework seems to exist, however, and the parties have neither agreed nor persuaded us what that framework ought to be.

The Claimant's view is that, because it fully satisfied the causation requirements of the Settlement Agreement, BP's allegations of illegality cannot prevent it receiving an award. Though that might decide this appeal if we agreed with the Claimant about the strength of BP's evidence, the Claimant's view does not help us resolve cases of claimants with better-demonstrated or obvious wrongdoing. At oral argument, the Claimant [—16—] suggested that a "wholly illegal enterprise" would clearly be disqualified from recovery but did not identify a source of law

for that rule.[15] Such a rule also would not help to decide whether, if only a portion of the claimant's activity is proven unlawful, partial or full disqualification should result.

BP's view is that, "[a]s a matter of law, parties cannot be awarded compensation for illegal activity," basing this principle on cases applying "the doctrine of unclean hands." A point in BP's favor is that the district court previously entertained the possibility that the unclean-hands doctrine might disqualify a claimant involved in illegal conduct. *See In re Oil Spill*, 2015 WL 12724047, at *2–3.[16] But the district court ultimately concluded that the claim at issue {–811–} was legitimate and untainted by misconduct, *id.*, so the case did not require the court to say precisely how and to what extent misconduct might disqualify a claimant.

Otherwise, BP does not identify applicable caselaw to support its invocation of the unclean-hands doctrine. The Settlement Agreement is a contract governed by maritime law. *Holmes Motors*, 829 F.3d at 315, 4 Adm. R. at 264. BP has put forward no authority showing that unclean hands, an equitable doctrine, applies when a party seeks relief under a contract.[17] Contrary authority exists,

---

[15] *Claimant ID 100235033 v. BP Explor. & Prod., Inc.* (5th Cir. May 1, 2019) (No. 18-30908).

[16] Attorneys that had represented claimants went to work for the Settlement Program but then received payments from the lawyers to whom they had referred their clients. 2015 WL 12724047 at *1–2. When this came to light, the district court appointed the aforementioned special master. ECF EDLA 2:10-md-02170, 10564. Among the attorneys involved was Jon Andry, and the Andry Law Firm had itself filed a BEL claim. 2015 WL 12724047 at *3. Following the special master's initial report, the district court ordered the firm to show cause why the court should not adopt the special master's recommendation "disallowing the Andry Law Firm's claim under the Unclean Hands Doctrine." ECF EDLA 2:10-md-02170, 11288, 3.

[17] BP cites five cases, none by this court and none dealing with analogous situations. First, BP cites *Ashwood v. Patterson*, 49 So.2d 848 (Fla. 1951), in which a husband killed his wife and then killed himself, leaving the court with the question of who owned their property. *Id.* at 849. Second, BP cites *Kulla v. E.F Hutton & Co., Inc.*, 426 So.2d 1055 (Fla. App. 1983), [—17—] in which Kulla sued

[—17—] and it is cause to doubt BP's theory. *See Bagby Elevator Co. v. Schindler Elevator Corp.*, 609 F.3d 768, 774 (5th Cir. 2010) (explaining, in case governed by Texas law, that "the affirmative defense of unclean hands is available only in equity"); *Western Sys., Inc. v. Ulloa*, 958 F.2d 864, 869 n.7 (9th Cir. 1992) (ruling that unclean hands "could not be used to bar a suit for damages for breach of contract").[18] Applications in the maritime context reflect this distinction between legal and equitable relief. *Compare Dziennik v. Sealift, Inc.*, 2013 WL 5502916, at *8–9 (E.D.N.Y. Sept. 30, 2013) (entertaining unclean-hands doctrine in maritime case as argument against defendant's invocation of

laches), *with CMA CGM S.A. v. AZAP Motors, Inc.*, 2015 WL 9601157, at *7 (E.D. Va. Nov. 25, 2015), *report and recommendation adopted by* 2016 WL 50926 (E.D. Va. Jan. 4, 2016) (rejecting application of unclean hands to purely contractual claims in maritime context). [—18—]

These cases comport with our decisions applying the unclean-hands doctrine. *See* {–812–} *State of Israel v. Motor Vessel Nili*, 435 F.2d 242, 248–49 (5th Cir. 1970) (applying unclean-hands doctrine to mortgagee of vessel, seeking foreclosure, in priority dispute with maritime lienholders); *see also Meis v. Sanitas Service Corp.*, 511 F.2d 655, 657–58 (5th Cir. 1975) (considering unclean-hands argument in suit for equitable rescission of corporate merger agreement); *N.Y. Football Giants, Inc. v. L.A. Chargers Football Club, Inc.*, 291 F.2d 471, 473–74 (5th Cir. 1961) (rejecting equitable remedy of specific performance due to plaintiff's unclean hands).[19]

BP's reliance on the unclean-hands doctrine has the added problem that the inequitable conduct of the party at issue ordinarily must bear a direct relationship to the proceeding in which the doctrine is invoked. "The maxim of unclean hands is not applied where plaintiff's misconduct is not directly related to the merits of the controversy between the parties." *Mitchell Bros. Film Grp. v. Cinema Adult Theater*, 604 F.2d 852, 863 (5th Cir. 1979) (citing *Keystone Driller Co. v. Gen. Excavator Co.*, 290 U.S. 240, 245 (1933)). "The alleged wrongdoing of

---

Hutton for giving him a bad stock tip and Hutton argued in response that Kulla had himself "actively participated" in the fraud scheme. *Id.* at 1056–57. Third, BP cites *Guillie v. Comprehensive Addiction Programs, Inc.*, 735 So.2d 775 (La. App. 1999), in which a man with alcohol and gambling problems argued he was misdiagnosed during a hospitalization and the failure to diagnose his bipolar disorder was the cause of his later troubles (most notably, being fired after stealing from his employer). *Id.* at 776–79. Fourth, BP cites *Allvend, Inc. v Payphone Communications Co., Inc.*, 804 So.2d 27 (La. App. 2001), in which a payphone company surreptitiously surveilled a competitor and then brought trumped-up unfair trade practices and other claims. *Id.* at 28–34. Fifth, and finally, BP cites *R.M.S. Titanic, Inc. v. Wrecked and Abandoned Vessel*, 742 F. Supp. 2d 784 (E.D. Va. 2010), in which the entity that had found and recovered artifacts from the wreck of the Titanic sought a "salvage award" for its efforts and the district court considered whether it had engaged in "disqualifying salvor misconduct." *Id.* at 788, 803–04. The last of these at least is a maritime case, but it dealt with too-different an issue to guide us on the unclean-hands doctrine's application here.

[18] The Claimant brings three germane, unpublished district court decisions to our attention. *See Nautilus Neurosci., Inc. v. Fares*, 2013 WL 6501692, at *4 (S.D.N.Y. Dec. 11, 2013) ("[T]he doctrine is not a defense to [a] breach of contract claim for money damages."); *Royal Palm Properties, LLC v. Premier Estate Properties, Inc.*, 2010 WL 3941745, at *2 (S.D. Fla. Oct. 6, 2010) ("[T]he unclean hands doctrine traditionally only applies to equitable remedies and does not bar a plaintiff from recovering damages."); *S.E.C. v. Eberhard*, 2006 WL 17640, at *3 (S.D.N.Y. Jan. 3, 2006) ("Unclean hands can only be asserted with respect to equitable—not legal—claims.").

[19] Decisions of other circuit courts in the maritime context do not give us reason to think that the unclean-hands doctrine applies outside of claims for equitable relief. *See, e.g., Inst. of Cetacean Research v. Sea Shepherd Conservation Soc'y*, 725 F.3d 940, 947, 1 Adm. R. 406, 410 (9th Cir. 2013) (considering doctrine's implications in ruling on preliminary injunction); *Columbus-America Discovery Grp. V. Atlantic Mut. Ins. Co.*, 56 F.3d 556, 569–70 (4th Cir. 1995) (considering but rejecting unclean-hands argument against equitable award for salvor of shipwreck); *Williams v. Jones*, 11 F.3d 247, 256–58 (1st Cir. 1993) (ruling, in suit seeking writ to enforce award under Longshore and Harbor Workers' Compensation Act, that employer could raise unclean-hands defense in Department of Labor administrative proceedings).

the plaintiff does not bar relief unless the defendant can show that he has personally been injured by the plaintiff's conduct." *Id.* For instance, in a suit seeking rescission of a merger due to pre-merger misrepresentations, the plaintiff's alleged post-merger misbehavior was held not to bar his suit. *Meis*, 511 F.2d at 657–58. "After all, 'Equity does not demand that its suitors [—19—] shall have led blameless lives.'" *Id.* at 658 (quoting *Loughran v. Loughran*, 292 U.S. 216, 229 (1934)). By contrast, in a priority dispute regarding a vessel, a mortgagee was held to have unclean hands because it delayed foreclosing on the vessel and the competing liens arose only during that delay. *See Motor Vessel Nili*, 435 F.2d at 249. Similarly, in a suit for specific performance of a contract negotiated in secret, the plaintiff's unclean hands barred its claim because the secrecy was for nefarious purposes. *See N.Y. Football Giants*, 291 F.2d at 474. BP cannot show that direct relationship here, nor could it in the other appeal panel decisions from which the present one split.

We do not decide here the legal standards that should apply to claimants alleged to have engaged in unlawful conduct, and we do not rule out alternate sources of law that might shape those standards but have not been discussed here.[20] We certainly {–813–} do not say that the Claimant must prevail on remand. The parties' briefing to us focused more on the Claimant's history and on the existence of panel splits than on the legal regime that should govern disqualification due to illegal conduct. The latter issue thus has not received the full adversarial treatment it deserves. It is for the district court to consider and decide in the first instance. [—20—]

VI

For the foregoing reasons, we REVERSE the denial of discretionary review and REMAND for proceedings consistent with this opinion.

---

[20] There is, for instance, a long history in admiralty law of courts invalidating contractual provisions or adopting contractual interpretations based on public policy. *See, e.g., Bisso v. Inland Waterways Corp.*, 349 U.S. 85, 90–91 (1955) (invalidating exculpatory clause in towing contract); *Dow Chem. Co. v. M/V Roberta Tabor*, 815 F.2d 1037, 1045 n.7 (5th Cir. 1987) (following *Bisso*); *Fireman's Fund Am. Ins. Co. v. Boston Harbor Marina, Inc.*, 406 F.2d 917, 920–21 (1st Cir. 1969) (suggesting invalidation of exculpatory clause in vessel storage contract); *cf. Harden v. Gordon*, 11 F. Cas. 480, 483 (C.C.D. Me. 1823) (Story, J.) (interpreting maritime contract of employment to require care for ill or injured seamen, based *inter alia* on "the great public policy of preserving this important class of citizens for the commercial service and maritime defence of the nation"). If the Settlement Agreement were read to compensate the loss of revenues from unlawful activity, the involvement of federal courts in enforcing the Agreement might well raise substantial public policy concerns.

United States Court of Appeals
for the Fifth Circuit

No. 18-10801

UNITED STATES
vs.
$4,480,466.16 IN FUNDS SEIZED

Appeal from the United States District Court for the
Northern District of Texas

ON PETITION FOR PANEL REHEARING

Decided: November 5, 2019

Citation: 942 F.3d 655, 7 Adm. R. 328 (5th Cir. 2019).

Before **ELROD**, **WILLETT**, and **DUNCAN**, Circuit Judges.

[—1—] {–656–} DUNCAN, Circuit Judge:

The petition for panel rehearing is DENIED. We withdraw the previous opinion issued August 22, 2019, 936 F.3d 233, and substitute the following:

We address whether a claimant in a civil forfeiture proceeding may counterclaim for constitutional tort damages against the United States. The district court held a claimant may never file counterclaims of any kind. It adopted the First Circuit's reasoning that, because a forfeiture is an *in rem* [—2—] proceeding against property, there is no "claim" against a claimant that he may "counter." Although this reasoning has been adopted by several district courts and recently by the Sixth Circuit, we find it unpersuasive and decline to adopt it. We nonetheless affirm the district court's judgment dismissing the counterclaims for a different reason. The counterclaims here seek damages based on alleged Fourth and Fifth Amendment violations arising from the property seizure. The United States has not waived sovereign immunity for either claim. We therefore affirm the district court's judgment on the alternative {–657–} ground that the counterclaims are barred by sovereign immunity.

I.

Appellant Retail Ready Career Center ("RRCC") was a private school in Texas offering a six-week "boot camp style" course to train students as Heating, Ventilation, and Air Conditioning ("HVAC") technicians.[1] According to RRCC, "[m]ost" students were "veterans who pa[id] for the course using their earned GI Bill benefit," but "courses were open to other participants" as well. In 2017, the United States Department of Veterans Affairs ("VA") began investigating whether RRCC had falsely claimed to be in compliance with the "85-15" rule. This rule prohibits the VA from approving a veteran's enrollment in a course "for any period during which more than 85 percent of the students enrolled in the course are having all or part of their tuition, fees or other charges paid for them by the educational institution or by VA[.]" 38 C.F.R. § 21.4201. The rule's purpose is to "minimize the risk that veterans' benefits will be wasted on educational programs of little value . . . and to prevent charlatans from grabbing the veterans' education money." *Cleland v. Nat'l Coll. of Bus.*, 435 U.S. 213, 219 (1978) (cleaned up). [—3—]

In September 2017, federal warrants were issued to seize the money in RRCC's bank accounts—amounting to over $4.6 million—as the alleged proceeds of federal law violations. *See* FED. R. CIV. P., SUPPLEMENTAL RULE ("SUPP. RULE") G(3)(b) ("the court—on finding probable cause—must issue a warrant" to seize movable property not in government control).[2] In October 2017, the government filed a complaint *in rem* seeking forfeiture of the funds under various fraud and conspiracy statutes.[3] After receiving notice of the

---

[1] We draw these facts primarily from RRCC's verified claim, which we accept as true for purposes of reviewing the district court's grant of a motion to dismiss. *See Masel v. Villareal*, 924 F.3d 734, 743 (5th Cir. 2019).

[2] The government also seized other property not relevant to this appeal, including over $100,000 from five other bank accounts; real property located in Dallas, Texas; and seven luxury vehicles.

[3] *See, e.g.*, 18 U.S.C. § 981(a)(1)(C) (providing "[a]ny property, real or personal, which constitutes or is derived from proceeds traceable to a violation of [certain federal laws]" is "subject to forfeiture to

forfeiture action, RRCC filed a verified claim to the seized property. *See* 18 U.S.C. § 983(a)(4)(A) (providing that "[a]ny person claiming an interest in the seized property may file a claim asserting such person's interest in the property"); SUPP. RULE G(5)(a) (setting out claim requirements). In its verified claim, RRCC alleged that the seizure occurred without prior notice or hearing; caused "an immediate and devastating effect on RRCC's business"; and forced RRCC to "close the school," dismiss employees without pay, and fly students home lest they be "stranded in Texas." RRCC also included two "constitutional counterclaims," which alleged the seizure violated the Fourth and Fifth Amendments and sought "damages to compensate [RRCC] for the destruction of its business."

The government moved to dismiss RRCC's counterclaims under Federal Rule of Civil Procedure 12(b)(6). Relying principally {–658–} on the First Circuit's [—4—] decision in *United States v. One Lot of U.S. Currency ($68,000)*, 927 F.2d 30 (1st Cir. 1991) ("*$68,000*"), the government argued that "claimants in civil-forfeiture cases may not file counterclaims against the United States, as they are merely claimants, not the party against which the suit is directed." The district court noted the parties had not cited "any binding Fifth Circuit authority" on this question, but found "persuasive" the First Circuit's reasoning in *$68,000*, which had been followed by several district courts from other circuits.[4] The

district court therefore granted the government's motion to dismiss RRCC's counterclaims, "hold[ing] that, as a claimant in an *in rem* civil forfeiture action, RRCC cannot bring a counterclaim."

Meanwhile, the government struggled to state an adequate claim against RRCC's funds under the forfeiture rules. The district court dismissed the government's first amended complaint, finding its allegations insufficiently specific. The second amended complaint met the same fate. *See, e.g., United States v. $4,480,466.16 In Funds Seized*, 2018 WL 4096340, at *3 (N.D. Tex. Aug. 28, 2018) (ruling allegations in second amended complaint were "insufficient to comply with Supp[lemental] R[ule] G(2)'s requirement that the complaint must 'state sufficiently detailed facts to support a reasonable belief that the government will be able to meet its burden of proof at trial'"); SUPP. RULE G(2)(f). The parties continue to litigate that issue below.[5] [—5—]

The issues before us on appeal concern only the fate of RRCC's counterclaims. On June 12, 2018, the district court entered a final judgment dismissing RRCC's counterclaims under Federal Rule of Civil Procedure 54(b), which RRCC timely appealed. We have jurisdiction to review that Rule 54(b) judgment. *See New Amsterdam Cas. Co. v. United States*, 272 F.2d 754, 756 (5th Cir. 1959) (dismissal of counterclaim, when plaintiff's claim is still pending, is non-

---

the United States"); *id.* § 981(a)(1)(D) (providing "[a]ny property, real or personal, which represents or is traceable to the gross receipts obtained, directly or indirectly, from a violation of [federal fraud statutes]" is "subject to forfeiture to the United States"); *id.* § 982(a)(3) (providing a court shall order that a person convicted of a federal fraud offense forfeit to the United States any property "which represents or is traceable to the gross receipts obtained, directly or indirectly, as a result of such violation").

[4] *See United States v. 8 Luxury Vehicles*, 88 F.Supp.3d 1332, 1337 (M.D. Fla. 2015); *United States v. Funds from Fifth Third Bank Account # 0065006695*, 2013 WL 5914101, at *12 (E.D. Mich. Nov. 4, 2013); *United States v. $22,832.00 in U.S. Currency*, 2013 WL 4012712, at *4 (N.D. Ohio Aug. 6, 2013); *United States v. $43,725.00 in U.S.*

Currency, 2009 WL 347475 at *1 (D.S.C. Feb. 3, 2009); *United States v. 1866.75 Board Feet*, 2008 WL 839792, at *3 (E.D. Va. Mar. 25, 2008); *United States v. Assorted Comput. Equip.*, 2004 WL 784493, at *2 (W.D. Tenn. Jan. 9, 2004).

[5] Following RRCC's appeal in this case, the government filed its third amended complaint, in response to which RRCC moved for dismissal and summary judgment. The district court has not ruled on those motions. Instead, the district court granted the government's motion to stay the forfeiture action for 120 days during the pendency of a [—5—] related, ongoing criminal investigation. The stay expired June 6, 2019, at which point the government moved to extend the stay for an additional 120 days. That motion is pending before the district court.

appealable "absent a certificate under Rule 54(b)").

II.

We review the district court's judgment dismissing RRCC's counterclaims *de novo*, "'accepting all well-pleaded facts [in RRCC's counterclaims] as true and viewing those facts in the light most favorable to [RRCC].'" *SGK Props., LLC v. U.S. Bank Nat'l Ass'n*, 881 F.3d 933, 943 (5th Cir. 2018) (quoting *Stokes v. Gann*, 498 F.3d 483, 484 (5th Cir. 2007)). We may affirm the district court's judgment "on any basis supported by the record." *Total Gas & Power North Am., Inc. v. FERC*, 859 F.3d 325, 332 (5th Cir. 2017) (citing *Taylor v. City of Shreveport*, 798 F.3d 276, 279 (5th Cir. 2015); {–659–} *EEOC v. Simbaki, Ltd.*, 767 F.3d 475, 481 (5th Cir. 2014)); *see also Lee v. Kemna*, 534 U.S. 362, 391 (2002) ("[I]t is well settled that an appellate tribunal may affirm a trial court's judgment on any ground supported by the record.").

III.

We decline to endorse the district court's ruling that claimants in *in rem* civil forfeiture proceedings are barred, always and everywhere, from filing counterclaims. As we explain below, that broad holding relies on dubious reasoning in a First Circuit opinion that overlooks the procedural rights of claimants in *in rem* forfeiture actions and that conflicts with longstanding [—6—] practice in *in rem* admiralty cases. Nonetheless, we affirm the district court's judgment on the narrower ground that RRCC's constitutional damages claims are barred by sovereign immunity.

A.

The district court relied heavily on the First Circuit's decision in *$68,000*, which concerned an *in rem* forfeiture action against a cocaine-tainted Lincoln Town Car. 927 F.2d at 31–32. The claimant, Castiello, sought to retrieve a "portable telephone" from the car by "fil[ing] what he termed a 'counterclaim' for [its] return." *Id.* at 34. The First Circuit identified multiple flaws in Castiello's

position. For instance, the court pointed out that, because the forfeiture warrant did not even encompass the telephone, Castiello's "personal property claim had no place in th[e] action." *Id.* at 35.[6] But the court also laid down this broader reason for rejecting Castiello's "counterclaim":

> By definition, a counterclaim is a turn-the-tables response directed by one party ("A") at another party ("B") in circumstances where "B" has earlier lodged a claim in the same proceeding against "A." A forfeiture action is *in rem*, not *in personam*. The property is the defendant. Since no civil claim was filed by the government against Castiello—indeed, rather than being dragooned into the case as a *defendant*, he intervened as a *claimant*—there was no "claim" to "counter." Thus, Castiello's self-styled counterclaim was a nullity, and the court below appropriately ignored it. [—7—]

$68,000, 927 F.2d at 34. This citationless half-paragraph furnished the sole rationale for the district court's holding below that "a claimant in an *in rem* civil forfeiture action . . . cannot bring a counterclaim."

We readily grasp why the district court disposed of RRCC's counterclaims on this basis. As the court pointed out, the First Circuit's musing in *$68,000* has metastasized to several district courts, and also recently to the Sixth Circuit. *See Zappone v. United States*, 870 F.3d 551, 561 (6th Cir. 2017) (stating that owner in civil forfeiture action may "intervene" but "may not assert counterclaims against the United States")

---

[6] Had the warrant included the telephone, the court stated it was "at least arguable" that Castiello could "replevy" it "within the contours of the government's forfeiture action." *Id.* at 34 n.7 (citing *United States v. Castro*, 883 F.2d 1018 (11th Cir. 1989); *Goodman v. Lane*, 48 F.2d 32 (8th Cir. 1931)). The court also pointed out that, regardless, Castiello remained free to retrieve the phone "administratively, by a motion in [his] underlying criminal case, or by bringing an independent civil action." *Id.* at 35 (cleaned up) (citing 19 U.S.C. § 1618; FED. R. CRIM. P. 41(e); *United States v. Wilson*, 540 F.2d 1100, 1104 (D.C. Cir. 1976)).

(citing *$68,000*). And the district court had no binding authority from our court, because we have never squarely addressed the issue. We do so now. Examining the issue as one of first impression, {–660–} we respectfully reject the First Circuit's broad rationale for barring counterclaims in *in rem* civil forfeiture proceedings.

First, the fact that a forfeiture proceeding is "*in rem*, not *in personam*" does not determine a claimant's rights in the proceeding. The forfeiture rules allow a claimant to take numerous actions respecting the seized property, even though the proceeding is "*in rem*." To begin with, a claimant may "file a claim" to protect his interests in the property.[7] He may also file: (1) an answer to the government's complaint, SUPP. RULE G(5)(b); (2) a Rule 12 motion, *id.*; (3) objections to government interrogatories, SUPP. RULE G(6)(b); (4) a motion to suppress use of the seized property as evidence, SUPP. RULE G(8)(a); and (5) a motion raising a defense under the Excessive Fines Clause of the Eighth Amendment, SUPP. RULE G(8)(e); *see also* 18 U.S.C. § 983(g) (claimant may file [—8—] a "petition" to "determine whether the forfeiture was constitutionally excessive"). And the civil forfeiture statute lets claimants do other things, such as: (1) raise and prove an "innocent owner" defense, 18 U.S.C. § 983(d); (2) move to set aside the forfeiture for lack of notice, *id.* § 983(e); and (3) seek immediate release of seized property, *id.* § 983(f).[8] The point being: If a claimant can do all this in *in rem* forfeiture proceedings, it cannot be that he is barred from filing counterclaims simply because forfeitures are "*in rem* and not *in personam*."

Thus, contrary to the First Circuit's view in *$68,000*, the answer to this puzzle does not lie in the brute fact that, in a forfeiture proceeding, "[t]he property is the defendant." 927 F.2d at 34. That truism begs the question what *other* actors in the proceeding (besides the property itself) may assert rights arising out of the forfeiture. *See, e.g., United States v. All Funds In Account Nos. 747.034/278, 747.009/278, & 747.714/278 Banco Espanol de Credito, Spain*, 295 F.3d 23, 25 (D.C. Cir. 2002) (observing that "[c]ivil forfeiture actions are brought against property, not people," but that "[t]he owner of the property may intervene to protect his interest"). The multiple procedural options given claimants by the civil forfeiture rules sit uneasily with the notion that a claimant can never bring counterclaims in those proceedings.

Second, the reasoning in *$68,000* overlooks the rules governing intervenors. Rule 24 allows intervention of right to "anyone" who, *inter alia*, "claims an interest relating to the property . . . that is the subject of the action." FED. R. CIV. P. 24(a)(2). That sounds quite like the position of a claimant in a [—9—] forfeiture proceeding; indeed, the forfeiture rules treat a claimant in precisely those terms. *See* 18 U.S.C. § 983(a)(4)(A) (allowing "any person claiming an interest in the seized property" to file a claim); SUPP. RULE G(5)(a)(i) (allowing "[a] person who asserts an interest in the defendant property" to contest the forfeiture). Moreover, our {–661–} cases have described "claimants" in forfeiture proceedings as "intervenors."[9] In *$68,000* itself, the First

---

[7] *See* 18 U.S.C. § 983(a)(4)(A) (providing "any person claiming an interest in the seized property may file a claim asserting such person's interest in the property in the manner set forth in the Supplemental Rules"); SUPP. RULE G(5)(a)(i) (providing "[a] person who asserts an interest in the defendant property may contest the forfeiture by filing a claim in the court where the action is pending").

[8] *See generally* Stefan D. Cassella, *The Civil Asset Forfeiture Reform Act of 2000: Expanded Government Forfeiture Authority and Strict Deadlines Imposed on All Parties*, 27 J. Legis. 97, 97, 125–151 (2001) ("Casella") (summarizing "comprehensive revision" to forfeiture procedures enacted by Civil Asset Forfeiture Reform Act of 2000 ("CAFRA"), Pub. L. 106-185, 117 Stat. 202 (2000)).

[9] *See, e.g., United States v. An Article of Drug Consisting of 4,680 Pails*, 725 F.2d 976, 981 (5th Cir. 1981) (observing, "[a]fter seizure pursuant to a warrant for arrest *in rem*, Pfizer intervened as claimant and filed an answer"); *United States v. 110 Bars of Silver*, 508 F.2d 799, 801 (5th Cir. 1975) (per curiam) ("This forfeiture proceeding stems from intervenor's conviction for melting down United States coins[.]"); *Westfall Oldsmobile, Inc. v. United States*, 243 F.2d 409, 411 (5th Cir.

Circuit said Castiello "intervened as a claimant." 927 F.2d at 34. Likewise here, the government described RRCC as "an intervening party." The kinship between "claimants" and "intervenors" does not support a blanket rule barring claimants' counterclaims in forfeiture proceedings. Quite the opposite. As we have explained, "[u]nder federal law, an intervenor of right 'is treated as he were an original party and has equal standing with the original parties.'" *Brown v. Demco*, 792 F.2d 478, 480–81 (5th Cir. 1986) (quoting *Donovan v. Oil, Chem., and Atomic Workers Int'l Union*, 718 F.2d 1341, 1350 (5th Cir. 1983)); *see also* 7C WRIGHT & MILLER, FED. PRAC. & PROC. § 1920 (3d ed.) (explaining an intervenor "has equal standing with the original parties" and "is entitled to litigate fully on the merits once intervention has been granted") (citing *Gilbert v. Johnson*, 601 F.2d 761, 768 (5th Cir. 1979) (Rubin, J., specially concurring)).[10] [—10—]

Third and finally, adopting the First Circuit's reasoning in *$68,000* would conflict with practice in admiralty cases, which have long entertained counterclaims (or their equivalents) in *in rem* proceedings. *See, e.g., Superior Derrick Services, LLC v. LONESTAR 203*, 547 F. App'x. 432, 437 (5th Cir. 2013)

1957) (describing owner contesting automobile forfeiture as "claimant-intervenor").

[10] To be sure, the Supplemental Rules applicable to forfeiture actions do not expressly provide that a claimant may file counterclaims. But "[t]he Federal Rules of Civil Procedure also apply to [in rem forfeiture] proceedings except to the extent that they are inconsistent with these Supplemental Rules." SUPP. RULE A(2). We discern nothing in the Supplemental Rules inconsistent with the general proposition that claimants may file counterclaims in forfeiture proceedings. Relatedly, one district court has suggested that Rule 13(d) implicitly [—10—] bars claimants in forfeiture proceedings from counterclaiming against the United States. *See United States v. 8 Luxury Vehicles*, 88 F.Supp.3d at 1334–1335, 1337 (M.D. Fla. 2015). We disagree. Rule 13 merely confirms that allowing counterclaims does not "expand" any waivers of sovereign immunity by the United States. *See* FED. R. CIV. P. 13(d) ("These rules do not expand the right to assert a counterclaim—or to claim a credit—against the United States or a United States officer or agency."). We address sovereign immunity *infra*.

(unpublished) (discussing merits of counterclaim asserted in *in rem* proceeding); *Incas & Monterey Printing and Packaging, Ltd. v. M/V Sang Jin*, 747 F.2d 958, 963–964 & n.16 (5th Cir. 1984) (considering counterclaims by time-charterer of seized vessel in *in rem* action); *Treasure Salvors, Inc. v. Unidentified Wrecked and Abandoned Sailing Vessel*, 569 F.2d 330, 335 (5th Cir. 1978) (considering United States' claims when it "intervened in plaintiffs' in rem action as a party defendant and filed a counterclaim asserting a property right in the res"); *Ellis Diesel Sales & Serv., Inc. v. M/V On Strike*, 488 F.2d 1095 (5th Cir. 1973) (per curiam) (considering *in rem* action in which "[d]efendant filed a counterclaim alleging damages negligently caused to the vessel")[11]; *see also, e.g.,* {–662–} *Compania Naviera Vascongada v. United States*, 354 F.2d 935, 940 (5th Cir. 1966) (addressing merits of "libel" and "cross-libel" in [—11—] *in rem* proceeding)[12]; *and see, e.g.,* THOMAS J.

---

[11] *See also, e.g., Puerto Rico Ports Auth. v. Barge Katy-B, O.N. 606665*, 427 F.3d 93, 99, 100 (1st Cir. 2005) (noting intervenor's counterclaim for damages in *in rem* proceeding); *Hawkspere Shipping Co., Ltd. v. Intamex, S.A.*, 330 F.3d 225, 230 (4th Cir. 2003) (considering counterclaim by claimants in *in rem* proceeding for wrongful arrest of vessel); *Bradford Marine, Inc. v. M/V Sea Falcon*, 64 F.3d 585, 586–587 (11th Cir. 1995) (reviewing attorney's fees awarded on a counterclaim in an *in rem* action); *Teyseer Cement Co. v. Halla Maritime Corp.*, 794 F.2d 472, 478 (9th Cir. 1986) (considering whether counterclaim by intervenor in *in rem* proceeding waived personal jurisdiction); *Ocean Ship Supply, Ltd. v. MV Leah*, 729 F.2d 971, 973 (4th Cir. 1984) (considering counterclaim for wrongful seizure and damages incurred therein); *Koch Fuels, Inc. v. Cargo of 13,000 Barrels of No. 2 Oil*, 704 F.2d 1038, 1039 (8th Cir. 1983) (reviewing district court's decision to sever counterclaims in an *in rem* action for trial by jury).

[12] The older admiralty term "cross-libel" is equivalent to "counterclaim": "With the merger of law and admiralty in 1966, admiralty's classic and ancient phraseology of libels and cross-libels was replaced with the more mundane terminology of claims and *counterclaims*[.]" *Titan Nav., Inc. v. Timsco, Inc.*, 808 F.2d 400, 403 (5th Cir. 1987) (emphasis added); *see also* 3A BENEDICT ON ADMIRALTY § 306 (2019) ("Rule 13, Federal Rules of Civil Procedure which treats of counterclaims and cross-claims is the modern counterpart of the old

SCHOENBAUM, 2 ADMIRALTY & MAR. LAW § 21:6 (6th ed. 2018) ("SCHOENBAUM") (explaining that a claimant must prove "demonstrable bad faith or malice" to succeed on a wrongful seizure counterclaim).

Moreover, the modern procedural rules applicable to admiralty and maritime claims plainly foresee counterclaims in *in rem* and *quasi in rem* proceedings. For instance, Supplemental Rule E(7)—which applies to "actions *in rem* and *quasi in rem*"—sets forth the circumstances under which a plaintiff must furnish "security" for damages demanded in a "counterclaim." *See* SUPP. RULE E(7)(a), (b)[13]; *id.*, advisory committee notes (2000) (explaining that "[s]ubdivision (7)(a) is amended to make it clear that a plaintiff need give security to meet a counterclaim only when the counterclaim is asserted by a [—12—] person who has given security to respond in damages in the original action").[14] Given those textual cues in the

---

admiralty cross-libels. While the nomenclature has changed the admiralty practice has basically remained the same.").

[13] Supplemental Rule E(7) provides as follows:

(7) Security on Counterclaim.

(a) When a person who has given security for damages in the original action asserts a counterclaim that arises from the transaction or occurrence that is the subject of the original action, a plaintiff for whose benefit the security has been given must give security for damages demanded in the counterclaim unless the court, for cause shown, directs otherwise. Proceedings on the original claim must be stayed until this security is given unless the court directs otherwise.

(b) The plaintiff is required to give security under Rule E(7)(a) when the United States or its corporate instrumentality counterclaims and would have been required to give security to respond in damages if a private party but is relieved by law from giving security.

[14] *See also, e.g., Transportes Caribe, S.A. v. M/V Trader*, 860 F.2d 637 (5th Cir. 1988) (affirming district court's order to post

Supplemental Rules, it would seem anomalous to say that counterclaims are always out-of-bounds in *in rem* {–663–} proceedings. And yet the First Circuit's rule would bar counterclaims in forfeiture actions precisely *because* they are "*in rem*, not *in personam*" proceedings. *$68,000*, 927 F.2d at 34. That overbroad proposition clashes with venerable admiralty practice and modern maritime rules, and we decline to endorse it.

In sum, we respectfully decline to adopt the reasoning in *$68,000* that, because "the property is the defendant" in a forfeiture proceeding, a claimant with interests in that property may never file a counterclaim. If RRCC's counterclaims are to be dismissed, it must be for a different reason.[15]

---

countersecurity under Rule E); *Titan Nav.*, 808 F.2d at 402–03 & n.2 (discussing development of Supplemental Rule E(7)); *Seaboard & Carribean Transp. Corp. v. Hafen-Dampfschiffahrt A.G. Hapag-Hadac Seebader-Dienst*, 329 F.2d 538, 539–541 (5th Cir. 1964) (applying Rule E precursor, Admiralty Rule 50, to a "cross-libelant" in a "libel *in rem*" proceeding); *and see also* SCHOENBAUM § 21:6 (explaining that "[s]ubsection 7 of [Supplemental Rule E] contemplates the filing of a counterclaim against the party initiating the seizure"); 4 BENEDICT ON ADMIRALTY § 2.23 (2019) (illustrating how a court may consider "whether or not a counterclaim has merit for the purposes of determining whether or not a counterclaimant is entitled to countersecurity" under Rule E(7)).

[15] In addition to rejecting its reasoning, we note that *$68,000* addressed a scenario quite different from ours. As the First Circuit observed, the forfeiture warrant in that case did not encompass the property that was the subject of the claimant's "counterclaim." *See* 927 F.2d at 34 n.7 ("This is not a case where the claimant seeks the return of the same property which the government seeks to forfeit."). Had the warrant included the property, the First Circuit acknowledged, the claimant might have sought to "replevy" the property in the forfeiture action. *Id.* The Sixth Circuit's decision in *Zappone*—the only circuit case to have adopted the First Circuit's reasoning—is also procedurally distinguishable. That case affirmed the dismissal of untimely "counterclaims" asserting *Bivens* claims against IRS agents who seized property in a forfeiture action. 870 F.3d at 554. But the IRS agents were not even parties in the forfeiture proceeding, making a "counterclaim" against them particularly tenuous.

B.

We affirm the district court's judgment on a narrower ground. *See, e.g., AT&T, Inc. v. United States*, 629 F.3d 505, 510 (5th Cir. 2011) ("[i]t is well **[—13—]** settled" that a court of appeals may affirm "on any ground supported by the record") (citation omitted). On appeal, the government argues in the alternative that the United States has not waived its sovereign immunity with respect to the particular claims asserted in RRCC's counterclaims—damages claims for violations of the Fourth and Fifth Amendments—and that those claims are therefore barred. We agree.

"It is axiomatic that the United States may not be sued without its consent and that the existence of consent is a prerequisite for jurisdiction." *United States v. Mitchell*, 463 U.S. 206, 212 (1983) (citing *United States v. Sherwood*, 312 U.S. 584, 586 (1941); 14 WRIGHT, MILLER & COOPER, FED. PRAC. & PROC. § 3654); *see also, e.g., In re Supreme Beef Processors, Inc.*, 468 F.3d 248, 251–52 (5th Cir. 2006) (en banc) ("The Constitution contemplates that, except as authorized by Congress, the federal government and its agencies are immune from suit.") (citing *Hercules, Inc. v. United States*, 516 U.S. 417, 422 (1996)). A waiver of sovereign immunity "cannot be implied but must be unequivocally expressed," and any waiver "will be strictly construed, in terms of its scope, in favor of the sovereign." *Doe v. United States*, 853 F.3d 792, 796 (5th Cir. 2017) (quoting *United States v. Mitchell*, 445 U.S. 535, 538 (1980); *Lane v. Peña*, 518 U.S. 187, 192 (1996)) (internal quotation marks omitted). The government argues that RRCC has identified no statute unequivocally waiving the United States' immunity for the damages claims in RRCC's counterclaims. Specifically, RRCC seeks damages arising from the "unreasonable seizure" of its bank accounts in violation of the Fourth Amendment and from the lack of "notice and hearing" in violation of the Fifth Amendment's Due Process Clause. The government is correct. **{–664–}**

In its reply brief, RRCC attempts to identify the required waiver in 28 U.S.C.

§ 2680(c). In that provision, Congress "rewaived" the United States' sovereign immunity under the Federal Tort Claims Act ("FTCA") for certain **[—14—]** property damages claims arising out of forfeitures.[16] *See, e.g., Smoke Shop, LLC v. United States*, 761 F.3d 779, 782 (7th Cir. 2014) (explaining that in the 2000 CAFRA reforms Congress "'rewaived' the government's immunity" under the FTCA "for tort actions stemming from law-enforcement detentions of property" under specific circumstances); *Foster v. United States*, 522 F.3d 1071, 1075 (9th Cir. 2008) (explaining that "CAFRA . . . restored the

---

[16] Section 2680(c) provides, in relevant part, that the FTCA immunity waiver applies "to any claim based on the injury or loss of goods, merchandise, or other property, while in the possession of any officer of customs or excise or any other law enforcement officer, if—

(1) the property was seized for the purpose of forfeiture under any provision of Federal law providing for the forfeiture of property other than as a sentence imposed upon conviction of a criminal offense;

(2) the interest of the claimant was not forfeited;

(3) the interest of the claimant was not remitted or mitigated (if the property was subject to forfeiture); and

(4) the claimant was not convicted of a crime for which the interest of the claimant in the property was subject to forfeiture under a Federal criminal forfeiture law."

28 U.S.C. § 2680(c)(1)–(4). The subsection cross-references 28 U.S.C. § 1346(b), which in relevant part provides that federal district courts have exclusive jurisdiction over post-January 1, 1945 money damages claims against the United States for

injury or loss of property, or personal injury or death caused by the negligent or wrongful act or omission of any employee of the Government while acting within the scope of his office or employment, under circumstances where the United States, if a private person, would be liable to the claimant in accordance with the law of the place where the act or omission occurred.

Id. § 1346(b)(1).

waiver of sovereign immunity—or 're-waived' sovereign immunity—with respect to certain forfeiture-related seizures"). What RRCC overlooks, however, is that the FTCA's immunity waiver does not extend to "constitutional torts" like the Fourth and Fifth Amendment damages claims pled in RRCC's counterclaims. We have squarely recognized that "[c]onstitutional torts . . . do not provide a proper predicate for an FTCA claim." *Spotts v. United States*, 613 F.3d 559, 565 n.3 (5th Cir. 2010) (citing *FDIC v. Meyer*, 510 U.S. 471, 478 (1994)); *see also,* [—15—] *e.g.,* *Coleman v. United States*, 912 F.3d 824, 835 (5th Cir. 2019) (the "source of substantive liability under the FTCA" must be the "law of the State" and not federal law) (citing *Meyer*, 510 U.S. at 478); *Sanchez v. Rowe*, 870 F.2d 291, 295 (5th Cir. 1989) (explaining "the FTCA does not provide a cause of action for constitutional torts" because "by definition constitutional torts are not based on state law") (cleaned up). Thus, the FTCA waiver does not encompass the constitutional damages claims in RRCC's counterclaims, and the district court therefore lacked jurisdiction over them.[17] {–665–}

---

[17] We do not decide whether RRCC could bring valid FTCA claims as counterclaims in a civil forfeiture proceeding. *See, e.g., Life Partners Inc. v. United States*, 650 F.3d 1026, 1029–1030 (5th Cir. 2011) (discussing administrative exhaustion requirements which are "a prerequisite to suit under the FTCA") (citing 28 U.S.C. § 2675(a); *McAfee v. 5th Circuit Judges*, 884 F.2d 221, 222–23 (5th Cir. 1989)). We decide only that the specific claims asserted in RRCC's counterclaims fall outside the CAFRA re-waiver and are therefore barred by sovereign immunity. Additionally, we note that neither the Tucker Act nor its companion, the Little Tucker Act, waive sovereign immunity over RRCC's claims. The Tucker Act provides a judicial avenue for "any claim against the United States founded . . . upon the Constitution." 28 U.S.C. § 1491(a)(1); *see also United States v. Bormes*, 568 U.S. 6, 11 (2012) (discussing Tucker Act). The waiver in the Tucker Act, however, "has been limited to apply only to the Takings Clause . . . because only that clause contemplates payment by the federal government." *Rothe Dev. Corp. v. U.S. Dept. of Defense*, 194 F.3d 622, 625 (5th Cir. 1999). Here, RRCC does not invoke the Tucker Act, and its Fifth Amendment claims are premised on an alleged due process violation, not the Takings Clause. *See, e.g., Bellamy v. United States*, 7 Cl. Ct.

RRCC also argues that the United States waives sovereign immunity simply by "initiat[ing] an *in rem* proceeding." RRCC cites no authority supporting that grandiose proposition. It points only admiralty cases allowing a limited cross-libel against the United States when the United States sues another vessel for collision damages. *See United States v. The Thekla*, 266 U.S. 328 (1924); *United States v. The Paquete Habana*, 189 U.S. 453 (1903); *The Siren*, 74 U.S. 152 (1868); *see also, e.g., United States v. Shaw*, 309 U.S. 495, [—16—] 502–03 (1940) (explaining that, in such cases, "it is necessary to determine the cross-libel as well as the original libel to reach a conclusion as to liability for the collision").[18] But RRCC directs us to no authority supporting the proposition that this distinct admiralty rule waives the United States' sovereign immunity whenever it institutes a civil forfeiture proceeding. Nor does RRCC direct us to any unambiguous statutory waiver of the United States' immunity under such circumstances.[19] As we have already explained, Congress did enact an unambiguous immunity waiver with respect to forfeiture proceedings, *see* 28 U.S.C. § 2680(c)(1)–(4), but it has no application here.

Finally, RRCC claims we cannot reach sovereign immunity for two reasons. First,

---

720, 723 (1985) (explaining claims court "has no jurisdiction over claims based upon the Due Process and Equal Protection guarantees of the Fifth Amendment, because these constitutional provisions do not obligate the Federal Government to pay money damages" (quoting *Carruth v. United States*, 224 Ct. Cl. 422, 445 (1980) (cleaned up)).

[18] *See also generally* 2 AM. JUR. 2d ADMIRALTY § 44 ("Whenever the United States sues for damage inflicted on its vessel or cargo, it impliedly waives its exemption from admiralty jurisdiction as to cross libels or counterclaims arising from the same transaction.") (citing *The Thekla*, 266 U.S. 328; *The Western Maid*, 257 U.S. 419 (1922)).

[19] RRCC incorrectly points to the immunity waiver in 46 U.S.C. § 30903(a), but that statute also pertains only to certain admiralty claims involving the United States. *See, e.g., MS Tabea Schiffahrtsgesellschaft MBH & Co. KG v. United States*, 636 F.3d 161, 165 n.1 (5th Cir. 2011) (explaining that "[t]he Suits in Admiralty Act (SAA) . . . provides the appropriate waiver for maritime tort claims against the United States") (citing 46 U.S.C. § 30903).

RRCC points out the government did not raise the issue below. That is irrelevant: Whether the United States' sovereign immunity has been waived is a question of subject matter jurisdiction we can address for the first time on appeal. *See, e.g., Lewis v. Hunt*, 492 F.3d 565, 568 (5th Cir. 2007) (appellate court may consider United States' sovereign immunity *sua sponte*, "[a]lthough the parties and the district court did not raise [it]"); *Bodin v. Vagshenian*, 462 F.3d 481, 484 (5th Cir. 2006) (lack of waiver of United States' sovereign immunity under FTCA "deprives federal courts of subject matter jurisdiction"). Second, RRCC claims that addressing sovereign immunity would convert a without-prejudice dismissal below into a with-prejudice [—17—] dismissal on appeal, which would be inappropriate without a cross-appeal. *See, e.g.,* {–666–} *Jennings v. Stephens*, 135 S. Ct. 793, 798 (2015) (explaining "an appellee who does not cross-appeal may not 'attack the [district court's] decree with a view either to enlarging his own rights thereunder or of lessening the rights of his adversary'") (quoting *United States v. American Railway Express Co.*, 265 U.S. 425, 435 (1924)). RRCC is again mistaken. Claims barred by sovereign immunity are dismissed without prejudice, not with prejudice. *See, e.g., Warnock v. Pecos Cty., Tex.*, 88 F.3d 341, 343 (5th Cir. 1996) (explaining that "[b]ecause sovereign immunity deprives the court of jurisdiction, the claims barred by sovereign immunity can be dismissed only under Rule 12(b)(1) and not with prejudice"); *see also, e.g., United States v. Texas Tech Univ.*, 171 F.3d 279, 285 n.9 (5th Cir. 1999) (same, citing *Warnock*); 9 WRIGHT & MILLER, FED. PRAC. & PROC. § 2373 (because dismissal for lack of jurisdiction does not reach merits, claim "must be considered to have been dismissed without prejudice."). Thus, we may, and do, rule that RRCC's counterclaims are barred by sovereign immunity.[20]

---

[20] Because we resolve the appeal on sovereign immunity grounds, we do not address the government's argument that RRCC's damages counterclaims are barred by 28 U.S.C. § 2465(b)(2)(A). Part of a provision addressing government liability for costs, fees, and interest when a claimant prevails in a forfeiture proceeding, § 2465(b)(2)(A) provides that "[t]he United States

IV.

Congress has provided various remedies for claimants like RRCC who assert that the United States has wrongfully seized their property in forfeiture proceedings. *See, e.g., United States v. Khan*, 497 F.3d 204, 208 (2nd Cir. 2007) (by reforming the forfeiture laws in CAFRA, "Congress was reacting to public outcry over the government's too-zealous pursuit of civil and criminal [—18—] forfeitures"). Under certain circumstances, claimants who "substantially prevail[ ]" in a forfeiture action may recover attorneys' fees, costs, and interest. *See* 28 U.S.C. § 2465(b)(1)(A)–(C). In some cases, they may sue the United States for property damages under the FTCA. *See* 28 U.S.C. § 2680(c)(1)–(4). What claimants may not do, however, is sue the United States for constitutional torts arising out of the property seizure. Congress has not waived the United States' sovereign immunity for damages claims of that nature. Because RRCC's counterclaims sought precisely those kinds of damages, we hold its counterclaims are barred by sovereign immunity.

AFFIRMED

---

shall not be required to disgorge the value of any intangible benefits nor make any other payments to the claimant not specifically authorized by this subsection." 28 U.S.C. § 2465(b)(2)(A).

United States Court of Appeals
for the Fifth Circuit

No. 18-31203

BARRIOS

vs.

CENTAUR, L.L.C.

Appeal from the United States District Court for the
Eastern District of Louisiana

Decided: November 11, 2019

Citation: 942 F.3d 670, 7 Adm. R. 337 (5th Cir. 2019).

Before **JONES, SMITH,** and **HAYNES,** Circuit Judges.

[—1—] {–672–} SMITH, Circuit Judge: {–673–}

Devin Barrios—an employee of Centaur, L.L.C. ("Centaur")—was injured while offloading a generator from a crew boat to a barge. The crew boat was owned and operated by River Ventures, L.L.C. ("River Ventures"); the barge was leased by Centaur. Barrios sued River Ventures and Centaur for [—2—] vessel negligence under general maritime law and the Jones Act. River Ventures crossclaimed against Centaur for contractual indemnity. The district court granted summary judgment to Centaur, and River Ventures appeals. We reverse and remand.

I.

Before Barrios's accident, non-party United Bulk Terminals Davant, LLC ("UBT"), executed a Master Service Contract (the "MSC") with Centaur, a small marine construction company. The MSC added Centaur to UBT's approved vendor list for work at its dock facility adjoining the Mississippi River (the "Davant Facility").

The MSC contained two provisions relevant to this appeal. The first imposed on Centaur an obligation to indemnify UBT and its contractors:

CONTRACTOR SHALL RELEASE, DEFEND, INDEMNIFY AND HOLD UBT GROUP (DEFINED AS UBT AND UBT'S OTHER CONTRACTORS AND SUBCONTRACTORS OF ANY TIER . . .) HARMLESS FROM AND AGAINST ANY AND ALL CLAIMS . . . BROUGHT BY ANY PERSON, PARTY OR ENTITY IN RESPECT OF PERSONAL OR BODILY INJURY TO, SICKNESS, DISEASE OR DEATH OF ANY MEMBER OF CONTRACTOR GROUP (DEFINED AS CONTRACTOR GROUP . . . *REGARDLESS OF CAUSE OR FAULT*, AND EVEN IF CAUSED IN WHOLE OR IN PART BY THE SOLE, JOINT OR CONCURRENT NEGLIGENCE OR FAULT OF ANY MEMBERS OF THE UBT GROUP OR THE UNSEAWORTHINESS OF ANY VESSELS OWNED, OPERATED OR OTHERWISE UNDER THE CONTROL OF ANY MEMBER OF UBT GROUP.

The second required Centaur to obtain insurance covering those same parties:

Prior to Contractor commencing Work hereunder for UBT, Contractor shall, but only to the extent of the liabilities assumed by Contractor in this Agreement, obtain from each of its insurers a waiver of subrogation in favor of each of the "UBT Group" . . . and, with the exception of Workers' Compensation Coverage . . . and the [—3—] Hull Insurance . . . name each of the UBT Group as additional insured to each insurance policy . . . , but only to the extent of the liabilities assumed by Contractor in this Agreement. . . . Contractor shall ensure that any endorsement naming the UBT Group as additional insureds shall not exclude from coverage the sole negligence of the insureds. Contractor shall be responsible for payment of all deductibles, premiums, retentions and payment for all expenditures incurred under any sue and labor provision.

The MSC governed future project-specific work orders between the parties. {–674–}

Centaur and UBT executed several work orders for projects at the Davant Facility. One—for which Centaur submitted a proposal in October 2015—required installation of a concrete containment rail at one of the facility's docks. The dock was principally used to load and offload ships carrying "dry bulk materials," including coal and petroleum coke. The containment rail was necessary to prevent those materials from spilling both onto the dock and into the river.

Centaur's proposal indicated that, at an increased cost, both a barge and a tug boat would be required to complete the project. UBT accepted the proposal and issued a purchase order in November 2015. That purchase order and the MSC, in tandem, formed the contract at issue (the "Dock Contract").

To perform the work, Centaur chartered barge DB-582, which was equipped with a crane. Because DB-582 was a "dumb" barge that couldn't self-navigate, it was moved up and down the river using a tugboat and winch. The Centaur crew used the barge to perform some construction work on the dock, including "drilling holes, cutting rebar, and pouring forms." It also used the barge to store items, pack and unpack tools, hold safety meetings, take breaks, and eat lunch.

Because the dock was most easily accessed by boat, UBT contracted with River Ventures for a crewed vessel—the M/V TROOPER—to transport [—4—] Centaur's employees from the parking area to their worksite. Centaur also used the crew boat to ferry tools and equipment in addition to its employees.

On the day of the incident, Barrios and other Centaur employees were transporting a portable generator on the crew boat. While attempting to offload the generator, the M/V TROOPER began to separate from DB-582. That movement caused Barrios to fall into the river, where the generator hit him in the head, severely injuring him.

Barrios sued River Ventures and Centaur, alleging, *inter alia*, vessel negligence under general maritime law and the Jones Act.[1]

River Ventures—averring that it was a third-party beneficiary of the Dock Contract—cross-claimed against Centaur for contractual indemnity and additional assured status under its insurance policies.

Centaur moved for summary judgment on River Ventures's crossclaim, averring that the Dock Contract was nonmaritime and that its indemnity provision was therefore void under Louisiana law. To determine whether the contract was maritime, the court considered whether "(1) the work Centaur was performing for UBT involve[d] maritime commerce, (2) it involved work from a vessel, and (3) the contract provided or the parties expected that a vessel would play a substantial role in completing the contract."

Applying that test, the court held that the Dock Contract was a "land-based construction contract" governed by Louisiana law. It granted summary judgment because the Louisiana Construction Anti-Indemnity Statute ("LCAIS") "applie[d] to prohibit the indemnity and insurance provisions."

River Ventures filed a notice of interlocutory appeal challenging the [—5—] summary judgment, averring that this court had jurisdiction under 28 U.S.C. § 1292(a)(3) because its claims against Centaur arose in an "admiralty case" and determined the "rights and liabilities" between the parties. Centaur moved to dismiss that appeal for {–675–} lack of jurisdiction, maintaining that the appeal "should not go forward until a Final Judgment is entered by the District Court." A panel of this court determined that Centaur's motion should be carried with the case.

While the interlocutory appeal was pending, Barrios's underlying tort claims proceeded to a bench trial. The court ruled for Barrios, holding that River Ventures was liable and that Centaur wasn't liable because Barrios wasn't a Jones Act seaman. The court then entered final judgment.

River Ventures appealed, reasserting its intent to seek review of the summary judgment. It also filed a notice of appeal of the bench-trial findings, but it voluntarily

---

[1] The Jones Act, 46 U.S.C. § 30104, provides a cause of action for seamen against their employer if they are "injured in the course of employment."

dismissed that appeal after settling with Barrios. River Ventures's crossclaim against Centaur is the only claim remaining on appeal.

II.

"[W]e have a constitutional obligation to satisfy ourselves that subject matter jurisdiction is proper before we engage the merits of an appeal." *Ziegler v. Champion Mortg. Co.*, 913 F.2d 228, 229 (5th Cir. 1990). Therefore, we first consider Centaur's motion to dismiss the appeal.

We need not decide, however, whether we have jurisdiction under § 1292(a)(3). That is because after final judgment was entered, River Ventures filed a renewed notice of appeal related to its indemnity and insurance claims. Because we have jurisdiction over River Ventures's appeal under 28 U.S.C. § 1291, Centaur's motion to dismiss for lack of jurisdiction is denied as moot. [—6—]

III.

The indemnity dispute presents issues with which this court is familiar. It boils down to what law governs. If federal maritime law controls, then the Dock Contract's indemnity provision is enforceable. *See Hoda v. Rowan Cos., Inc.*, 419 F.3d 379, 380 (5th Cir. 2005). If Louisiana law applies, then the LCAIS voids the indemnity provision as against public policy. *See* LA. STAT. ANN. § 9:2780.1. So the question is whether the Dock Contract is maritime. But before we can resolve that, we must identify the proper test for making that determination, a task that has vexed this court for decades.

A.

From 1990 to 2018, we applied the six-factor test announced in *Davis & Sons, Inc. v. Gulf Oil Corp.*, 919 F.2d 313, 316 (5th Cir. 1990), to determine whether a contract was maritime:

1) what does the specific work order in effect at the time of injury provide? 2) what work did the crew assigned under the work order actually do? 3) was the crew assigned to work aboard a vessel in navigable waters; 4) to what extent did the work being done relate to the mission of that vessel? 5) what was the principal work of the injured worker? and 6) what work was the injured worker actually doing at the time of injury?

Though *Davis & Sons* was intended to provide clear criteria for courts to apply, the test proved unwieldy in practice, with "final result[s] [often] turn[ing] on a minute parsing of the facts." *Hoda*, 419 F.3d at 380.

Fourteen years after *Davis & Sons*, the Supreme Court erected a guide-post in *Norfolk Southern Railway Co. v. Kirby*, 543 U.S. 14 (2004). The Court considered whether a money-damages claim arising from a train derailment fell within its admiralty jurisdiction. The cargo destroyed in the derailment {–676–} was completing the second, land-based leg of its journey from Australia to [—7—] Alabama. The first leg had transported the cargo by boat from Australia to Georgia. The two legs of the trip had separate but co-extensive bills of lading.

To determine whether the bills of lading were maritime, the Court noted that it could not merely "look to whether a ship or other vessel was involved in the dispute" or "to the place of the contract's formation or performance." *Id.* at 23–24. Geography couldn't be controlling because "the shore [was] now an artificial place to draw a line." *Id.* at 25. Instead, "the answer depends upon the nature and character of the contract, and the true criterion is whether it has reference to maritime service or maritime transactions." *Id.* at 24 (cleaned up).[2] That approach vindicated the fundamental interest under-girding maritime jurisdiction: "the protection of maritime *commerce*." *Id.* at 25.

Applying those principles, the Court held that the bills of lading were maritime "because their *primary objective* [was] to

---

[2] The Court rejected the "spatial approach," on which several of the factors in *Davis & Sons* were based. *Kirby*, 543 U.S. at 23–24.

accomplish the transportation of goods by sea from Australia to the eastern coast of the United States." *Id.* at 24 (emphasis added). "[S]o long as a bill of lading requires *substantial* carriage of goods by sea, its purpose is to effectuate maritime commerce— and thus it is a maritime contract." *Id.* at 27 (emphasis added). That some of the performance was land-based did "not alter the essentially maritime nature of the contracts." *Id.* at 24.

In *In re Larry Doiron, Inc.*, 879 F.3d 568, 6 Adm. R. 160 (5th Cir.) (en banc), *cert. denied*, 138 S. Ct. 2033 (2018), we sought to remedy the infirmities of *Davis & Sons* and harmonize our law with *Kirby*. We considered whether a "work order . . . to perform 'flow-back' services on a gas well in navigable waters" was a maritime contract. *Id.* at 570, 6 Adm. R. at 160. The work didn't require vessels, and neither [—8—] party expected to use them. A crane barge was engaged only after the workers "determined that some heavy equipment was needed to complete the job." *Id.*, 6 Adm. R. at 160. A worker was injured when he was struck by the crane.

In a unanimous opinion, we adopted a two-question test—centering the inquiry "on the contract and the expectations of the parties," *id.* at 576, 6 Adm. R. at 166—to determine whether a contract was maritime:

> First, is the contract one to provide services to facilitate the drilling or production of oil and gas on navigable waters? . . . Second, if the answer to the above question is "yes," does the contract provide or do the parties expect that a vessel will play a substantial role in the completion of the contract?

Id., 6 Adm. R. at 165. That standard jettisoned the irrelevant prongs of *Davis & Sons* and made clear that "contract rather than tort principles" control when determining whether a *contract* is maritime.[3]

Applying the new test, we held that the contract was nonmaritime because "[t]he {–677–} use of the vessel to lift the equipment was an insubstantial part of the job and not work the parties expected to be performed." *Id.* at 577, 6 Adm. R. at 167. The crew had involved a vessel only after it had "encountered an unexpected problem that required a vessel and a crane to lift equipment needed to resolve [it]." *Id.*, 6 Adm. R. at 166–67. Even though the vessel's involvement was *important*, it wasn't *substantial* because its use didn't comport with the parties' expectations.

Since *Doiron*, we've had only one occasion to apply its standard: *Crescent Energy Services, L.L.C. v. Carrizo Oil & Gas, Inc.*, 896 F.3d 350, 6 Adm. R. 224 (5th Cir.), *cert. denied*, 139 S. Ct. 642 (2018). There, the contract involved the plugging and [—9—] abandonment of three offshore oil wells on small fixed platforms. *Id.* at 352, 6 Adm. R. at 224. About half the job involved "wireline work."[4] To complete the task, Crescent charted three vessels: a crane barge, a tug boat, and a cargo barge. A Crescent employee's leg was severely injured when a piece of pipe struck him while he was sitting on one of the fixed platforms.

Crescent's insurers, attempting to limit *Doiron*'s reach, made two contentions. First, the insurers posited—relying primarily on circuit caselaw stating that work performed on fixed offshore platforms is nonmaritime— that *Doiron*'s first prong wasn't satisfied because "the plugging and abandoning work did not occur on 'navigable waters.'" *Id.* at 356, 6 Adm. R. at 228. Second, and relatedly, they averred "that *Doiron* must be read in

---

[3] *Doiron*, 879 F.3d at 576–77, 6 Adm. R. at 165–67. When announcing the test, we recognized that we dealt "only with determining the maritime or nonmaritime nature of contracts involving the exploration, drilling, and production of oil and gas."

Id. at 577 n.52, 6 Adm. R. at 166 n.52. We noted, however, that we expected the standard to be "helpful in determining whether a [non-oil-and-gas] contract is maritime" if that "activity . . . involves maritime commerce and work from a vessel." *Id.*, 6 Adm. R. at 166 n.52.

[4] *Crescent*, 896 F.3d at 361, 6 Adm. R. at 231. "A 'wireline' is a continuous cable used to perform various subsurface functions in a well, including the lowering and raising of various tools, instruments, and other devices." *Roberts v. Cardinal Servs., Inc.*, 266 F.3d 368, 371 (5th Cir. 2001).

conjunction with other law," specifically precedents classifying activities as either maritime or not. *Id.* at 357, 6 Adm. R. at 228.

We rejected both theories, affirming that, for analyzing whether a contract was maritime, "*Doiron* now control[led] that endeavor." *Id.* at 358, 6 Adm. R. at 229. Because the wells at issue "were located within the territorial inland waters of Louisiana and . . . the vessels involved . . . were able to navigate to them," the contract "was to facilitate the drilling or production of oil and gas on navigable waters." *Id.* at 357, 6 Adm. R. at 228. And because the "contract anticipated the constant and substantial use of multiple vessels," it was maritime. *Id.* at 361, 6 Adm. R. at 232.

Outside of the instant case, only one district court that we know of has applied *Doiron* to a non-oil-and-gas contract. In *Lightering LLC v. Teichman Group, LLC*, 328 F. Supp. 3d 625, 627–29 (S.D. Tex. 2018), the court considered whether a contract for wharfage, storage, and other dockside services was maritime. In determining how to apply *Doiron* outside the oil-and-gas sector, [—10—] the court first observed that "*Kirby* state[d] that for a contract to be maritime, its principal objective must be maritime commerce." *Id.* at 636. *Doiron*, the court inferred, "applie[d] *Kirby* to interpret a 'principal objective.'" *Id.*

Based on that, the court determined that *Doiron*'s first factor—*i.e.*, "is the activity at issue oil and gas?"—was a substitute for *Kirby*'s broader question whether a contract involved maritime commerce and work from a vessel. *Id.* "Under *Doiron* and *Kirby*, determining whether a contract is maritime requires three steps: (1) [T]he activity must be maritime commerce; (2) the activity must involve work from a vessel; and (3) the contract must provide or the parties must expect that a vessel will play a substantial role in completing the contract." *Id.* at 637.

Though the analysis is seemingly clear-cut, applying that test—and especially the first prong—was far from straightforward. {–678–} As the court recognized, the caselaw doesn't

clearly define the boundaries of "maritime commerce." *Id.* As a result, "most courts resort to a case-by-case approach, relying heavily on precedent." *Id.* Utilizing that precedent-focused method, the court determined that the contract's wharfage and dockside services were subsumed within a wide range of land-based activities that facilitate maritime commerce but that aren't, themselves, maritime commerce. *See id.* at 637–38. As a result, the contract was "[nonmaritime] in nature and character."[5]

B.

The parties agree that *Kirby*, *Doiron*, and their progeny govern, but they read those authorities differently.[6] Their primary disagreement centers on [—11—] how to apply *Doiron*'s first prong outside the oil-and-gas context. River Ventures avers that "this Court should apply a test that the contract be performed or facilitate operations on navigable waters and that the contract provide or the parties expect that a vessel will play a substantial role in the completion of the contract."[7] Centaur counters that *Lightering*

---

[5] *Lightering*, 328 F. Supp. 3d at 643. Therefore, the court dismissed the case for want of 28 U.S.C. § 1333 admiralty jurisdiction. *Id.*

[6] That isn't unreasonable: "Our cases do not draw clean lines between maritime and nonmaritime contracts," *Kirby*, 543 U.S. at 23, and, indeed, they "have long been confusing [—11—] and difficult to apply," *Doiron*, 879 F.3d at 571, 6 Adm. R. at 161.

[7] Centaur posits that River Ventures is estopped from asserting the test for which it now advocates because it "initially agreed with the test applied by the district court." Centaur points to River Ventures's opposition to summary judgment, in which it stated that "as applied to this case, critical determinations for this Court to make are: (1) whether the work Centaur was performing for UBT involved maritime commerce and (2) whether it involved substantial work from a vessel." Because River Ventures stated that "maritime commerce" was an important consideration, Centaur suggests that it cannot be allowed to propose a new test eliminating that requirement on appeal.

Judicial estoppel is an equitable doctrine that prevents a party from gaining an advantage by asserting contradictory positions in different

sets forth the proper test. The district court accepted Centaur's position and applied *Lightering*.

River Ventures has the better of the argument: *Doiron* should apply essentially as written. For non-oil-and-gas contracts, *Doiron* would ask whether (1) the contract is "one to provide services to facilitate [activity] on navigable waters," and (2) if so, whether "the contract provide[s] or . . . the parties expect that a vessel will play a substantial role in the completion of the contract." *Doiron*, 879 F.3d at 576, 6 Adm. R. at 165. That test is preferable for two reasons: [—12—] (1) *Doiron* was meant to streamline the inquiry regarding whether a contract is maritime; {–679–} and (2) *Doiron*'s rule, even applied to non-oil-and-gas contracts, is consistent with *Kirby*.

In *Doiron*, the en banc court clarified that its test was intended to simplify the is-this-contract-maritime inquiry, not complicate it. To do that, we abrogated a significant portion of *Davis & Sons*'s six-factor standard. Chief among those factors that *Doiron* jettisoned was the second, which required courts "to parse the precise facts related to the services performed under the contract and determine whether those services were inherently maritime." *Id.* at 573, 6 Adm. R. at 163. That was true even for mixed-services contracts where *none* of the services were inherently maritime. *Id.*, 6 Adm. R. at 163.

That inquiry, *Doiron* held, was irrelevant to whether a contract was maritime because it didn't focus on whether the contract required "substantial work to be performed from a vessel." *Id.* at 573, 576–77, 6 Adm. R. at 163, 165–67. To the extent that the *Davis & Sons* factors remained relevant, they were so only as they helped to explain the "scope of the contract" or "the extent to which the parties expect[ed] vessels to be involved in the work." *Id.* at 577, 6 Adm. R. at 166. *Doiron*'s method, in contrast to *Davis & Sons*, ensures that courts aren't determining whether some "service work has a more or less salty flavor than other service work when neither type is inherently salty." *Id.*, 6 Adm. R. at 166.

Centaur's position would turn *Doiron* on its head and effectively return courts to *Davis & Sons*'s precedent-laden trudge. *Lightering* recognized as much.[8] But *Doiron* and *Crescent* made clear, and for good reason, that we should be out of that business. "[R]egardless of what other Fifth Circuit [—13—] caselaw there may be, nothing in such caselaw detracts from the clarity of our 2018 en banc decision in *Doiron*."[9]

Centaur contends that applying *Doiron* outside the oil-and-gas context would run afoul of *Kirby*'s command that the "principal

---

proceedings. *See New Hampshire v. Maine*, 532 U.S. 742, 749 (2001). Judicial estoppel has two elements: "First, the estopped party's position must be clearly inconsistent with its previous one, and second, that party must have convinced the court to accept that previous position." *Gabarick v. Laurin Mar. (Am.) Inc.*, 753 F.3d 550, 553, 2 Adm. R. 228, 229 (5th Cir. 2014) (quotation marks omitted). "[T]he rule is intended to prevent improper use of judicial machinery" and is therefore within the court's discretion to apply. *Maine*, 532 U.S. at 750 (quotation marks omitted).

Contrary to Centaur's assertion, neither prong of *Gabarick*'s test is satisfied. First, River Ventures advances essentially the same position on appeal as it did in the district court: that *Doiron*'s two-prong test applied. Furthermore, the quote on which Centaur relies must be considered in its appropriate context. Only a few pages earlier in its motion, River Ventures advanced that *Doiron* established a two-part test, and it quoted that test. Second, the district court refused to apply *Doiron*'s two-part test and instead applied *Lightering*.

---

[8] *See Lightering*, 328 F. Supp. 3d at 637 ("Though the rule from *Kirby* seems simple in theory, its application proves to be complicated. Thus, most courts resort to a case-by-case approach, relying heavily on precedent." (cleaned up)).

[9] *Crescent*, 896 F.3d at 359, 6 Adm. R. at 230. *Crescent*'s rejection of precedent-based arguments was critically important to its outcome because this court's precedent had long held that wireline work was nonmaritime even when performed from a vessel. *See, e.g., Domingue v. Ocean Drilling & Expl. Co.*, 923 F.2d 393, 398 (5th Cir. 1991); *Thurmond v. Delta Well Surveyors*, 836 F.2d 952, 956 (5th Cir. 1988). Moreover, *Lightering*'s analysis didn't consider *Crescent*. That is understandable, given that *Lightering* was issued only two days later.

objective" of the contract must be maritime commerce. That is so because *Doiron* established its two-part test only after it "emphasiz[ed] the importance of first determining whether the activity is 'commercial maritime activity.'"[10] *Doiron*'s first prong, Centaur posits, merely provides "a short-cut for deciding whether a contract's principal objective is maritime commerce, but only for oil and gas contracts." "Outside the oil and gas context, the test first requires the court to ask whether the activity involves maritime commerce and work from a vessel." *Lightering*, 328 F. Supp. 3d at 637 (quotation marks omitted). But Centaur's position, though somewhat supported by language in the caselaw, doesn't adequately grapple with *Kirby*, *Doiron*, or *Crescent*.

In *Doiron*, 879 F.3d at 576, 6 Adm. R. at 166, we found "strong support in *Kirby*" for our two-prong test. Several passages provide those buoys. First, *Kirby* states that "[t]o {–680–} ascertain whether a contract is a maritime one, . . . the answer depends upon the nature and character of the contract, and the true criterion is whether it has reference to maritime service or maritime transactions." *Kirby*, 543 U.S. at 23–24 (cleaned up). Next, *Kirby* instructs that "[m]aritime commerce has evolved . . . and is often inseparable from some land-based obligations." *Id.* [—14—] at 25. And finally, *Kirby* declares that "[c]onceptually, so long as a bill of lading requires *substantial* carriage of goods by sea, its purpose is to effectuate maritime commerce—and thus it is a maritime contract."[11]

Those statements are entirely consistent with *Doiron*'s standard as applied to *any mixed-services contract*. *Doiron*'s first prong—though requiring some nexus to the traditional maritime predicate of activity on navigable waters[12]—doesn't exclude non-sea-based obligations. And *Doiron*'s second prong clarifies that cursory or unexpected vessel involvement, even if important, isn't enough; the involvement must be *substantial*. In that sense, *both prongs* of *Doiron* stand in for *Kirby*'s requirement that the "principal objective" of the contract be maritime commerce.[13]

In short, *Doiron*'s two-part test applies as written to all mixed-services contracts. To be maritime, a contract (1) must be for services to facilitate activity on navigable waters and (2) must provide, or the parties must expect, that a vessel will play a substantial role in the completion of the contract. [—15—]

IV.

Having fashioned the appropriate test— and because "the interpretation of a maritime contract is a question of law"—we now apply it. *See Int'l Marine, L.L.C. v. Integrity Fisheries Inc.*, 860 F.3d 754, 759, 5 Adm. R. 277, 279 (5th Cir. 2017).

---

[10] Centaur seizes on one paragraph in *Doiron*, 879 F.3d at 575, 6 Adm. R. at 165, which begins "[o]ur cases have long held that the drilling and production of oil and gas on navigable waters from a vessel is commercial maritime activity."

[11] *Kirby*, 543 U.S. at 27 (emphasis added). The *Doiron* en banc court found particular support for its rule in that statement. *See Doiron*, 879 F.3d at 576, 6 Adm. R. at 166.

[12] "In general, a contract relating to a ship in its use as such, or to commerce or navigation on navigable waters, or to transportation by sea or to maritime employment is subject to maritime law and the case is one of admiralty jurisdiction, whether the contract is to be performed on land or water." 1 BENEDICT ON ADMIRALTY § 182 (Joshua S. Force & Steven F. Friedell eds., 2019); *accord Gulf Coast Shell & Aggregate LP v. Newlin*, 623 F.3d 235, 240 (5th Cir. 2010); *J.A.R., Inc. v. M/V Lady Lucille*, 963 F.2d 96, 98 (5th Cir. 1992).

[13] For that reason, applying Doiron to non-oil-and-gas contracts won't cause the sea change that Centaur fears. For example, contracts for the sale of vessels would presumably remain nonmaritime. *See, e.g., Newlin*, 623 F.3d at 240; *Jones v. One Fifty Foot Gulfstar Motor Sailing Yacht, Hull No. 01*, 625 F.2d 44, 47 (5th Cir. 1980). As would contracts to build ships when the construction doesn't require vessels. *See, e.g., E. River S.S. Corp. v. Transamerica Delaval, Inc.*, 476 U.S. 858, 872 n.7 (1986); *Thames Towboat Co. v. The Schooner "Francis McDonald"*, 254 U.S. 242, 243 (1920); *Jones*, 625 F.2d at 47. So too would contracts for wharfage that don't relate to a specific vessel. *See, e.g., Lightering*, 328 F. Supp. 3d at 638 (collecting cases).

1.

The Dock Contract easily satisfies *Doiron*'s first prong. It called for Centaur to install a concrete containment rail at one of the Davant Facility's docks. That dock extended into the Mississippi River, a waterway on which both DB-582 and the M/V TROOPER were navigated. The dock was used to load and offload ships carrying dry bulk materials. And the containment rail was meant to prevent those materials—principally coal and petroleum coke—from {–681–} spilling onto the dock or into the river, which would result in adverse effects to both commerce and the environment. Collectively, those facts establish that the Dock Contract required services to be performed to facilitate the loading, offloading, and transportation of coal and petroleum coke via vessels on navigable waters. That some services were also performed on the dock, which was affixed to the land, isn't dispositive.[14]

2.

When considering whether there was substantial involvement of a vessel, "[w]e must remember that the contracting parties' expectations are central." *Crescent*, 896 F.3d at 359, 6 Adm. R. at 231. "When work is performed in part on a vessel and in part on a platform or on land, we should consider not only time spent on the vessel but also the relative importance and value of the vessel-based work to completing the contract." *Doiron*, 879 F.3d at 576 n.47, 6 Adm. R. at 165 n.47. *Doiron* [—16—] suggests that a rule of thumb similar to the thirty-percent guideline in Jones Act cases might be useful. *Id.*, 6 Adm. R. at 165–66 n.47.[15] But that "would not include transportation to and from the job site."[16] Even significant vessel involvement

isn't enough if that involvement was unexpected. *Crescent*, 896 F.3d at 359–60, 6 Adm. R. at 231.

Based on that standard, *Doiron*'s second prong is likewise satisfied. The Dock Contract makes clear that the parties expected DB-582 to play a significant role in the completion of the work. Centaur's project proposal indicated that the "[p]rice is significantly higher due to having [a] crane barge on site to mix the concrete and pour it for the concrete containment rail." It also stated that a "[t]ug boat will . . . need to be present to shift the barge as needed." Far from being "an insubstantial part of the job and not work the parties expected to be performed," *Doiron*, 879 F.3d at 577, 6 Adm. R. at 167, the proposal shows that the parties expected the barge to play a critically important role.

Moreover, Taylor Roy, Centaur's lead project manager, admitted that "at the end of the day, Centaur could not have done the job properly without [the] crane barge." That differs materially from *Doiron*, where the vessel was used only after the "crew encountered an unexpected problem." *Id.*, 6 Adm. R. at 166–67. Instead, like the situation in *Crescent*, the parties here recognized that DB-582 provided a necessary work platform, an essential storage space for equipment and tools, and a flexible area for other endeavors related to the construction work. *See Crescent*, 896 F.3d at 361, 6 Adm. R. at 231–32.

The district court's findings of fact show that the parties' expectations about the use of the barge were borne out. Just as the proposal indicated, [—17—] Centaur's crew used DB-582 to perform construction work for the containment rail, including "drilling holes, cutting rebar, and pouring forms." The crew also used the barge for several activities related to the construction, including storing and packing tools, holding safety meetings, taking breaks, and eating lunch. That Centaur's workers may have worked on the

---

[14] *See Kirby*, 543 U.S. at 27 ("Its character as a maritime contract is not defeated simply because it also provides for some land carriage.").

[15] But that "figure . . . serves as no more than a guideline established by years of experience, and departure from it will certainly be justified in appropriate cases." *Chandris, Inc. v. Latsis*, 515 U.S. 347, 371 (1995).

[16] *Doiron*, 879 F.3d at 576 n.47, 6 Adm. R. at 165–66 n.47. River Ventures's contentions regard-

---

ing the involvement of its crew boat to reach the worksite are irrelevant.

dock a majority of the time {–682–} doesn't alter that conclusion.[17]

* * * *

In sum, the district court misapplied *Doiron* and erroneously concluded that the Dock Contract was nonmaritime. Because federal maritime law applies, the LCAIS does not. The summary judgment is REVERSED and REMANDED. We place no limitation on the matters that the district court may consider, as appropriate and in its discretion, on remand.

---

[17] *See Crescent,* 896 F.3d at 359, 6 Adm. R. at 230 ("*Doiron* did not hold that to be a maritime contract, the parties must have contemplated that a vessel will be used for a majority of the work.").

United States Court of Appeals
for the Fifth Circuit

No. 18-60662

INTERNATIONAL-MATEX TANK TERMINALS
vs.
DIRECTOR, OFFICE OF WORKERS' COMPENSATION
PROGRAMS

Petition for Review of an Order of the Benefits
Review Board

Decided: November 25, 2019

Citation: 943 F.3d 278, 7 Adm. R. 346 (5th Cir. 2019).

Before **KING**, **HIGGINSON**, and **DUNCAN**, Circuit
Judges.

[—1—] {–280–} DUNCAN, Circuit Judge: {–281–}

Respondent Dwayne Victorian was an
assistant shift foreman at an oil-and-gas
storage facility ("Facility"[1]) on the
Mississippi River owned by Petitioner
International-Matex Tank Terminals
("IMTT").[2] While at work, Victorian was
injured and disabled. Victorian filed a claim
with the Department of Labor under the
Longshore and Harbor Workers' Compensation Act ("Act"), 33 U.S.C. § 901 *et seq.*,
which, under certain circumstances, [—2—]
compels employers to compensate employees
who become temporarily disabled while on the
job. The administrative law judge ("ALJ")
found that Victorian fulfilled the Act's
requirements, in part because: (1) Victorian's
injury occurred at a marine "terminal," one of
the enumerated areas covered by the Act; (2)
at the time of his injury, Victorian was
engaged in maritime employment; (3)
Victorian had not reached "maximum medical
improvement" when he filed his claim; and (4)
Victorian had made adequate efforts to locate
alternative employment. The Benefits Review
Board ("Board") affirmed the ALJ's findings.
We will deny IMTT's petition for review.

_____

[1] In its own literature, IMTT calls the Facility a
"marine terminal." We avoid that term because the
parties dispute whether the Facility is a "terminal"
for purposes of the legal issues presented in this
appeal.

[2] IMTT's insurer, Zurich American Insurance
Company, is also a petitioner.

I.

A.

The Facility, one of ten owned by IMTT,
lies on the west bank of the Mississippi River
in Gretna, Louisiana. It exists primarily to
store oil products: its sixty storage tanks have
a combined capacity of 2.3 million barrels. The
Facility's operations are centered on the
Mississippi River. Although the Facility is
accessible by railroad and commercial truck,
all the product stored at the Facility departs it
by ship, and most arrives by ship, too. The
Facility's dock can accommodate four barges
at once and is used by barges every day.

Facility employees occasionally heat oil to
make it easier to pump. They also sometimes
engage in "sparging," a process by which fuel
is created from diesel and oil. The resultant
fuel is consumed by ships that dock at the
Facility.

B.

At the time of his injury, Victorian was an
assistant shift foreman. Typically, during a
vessel's loading or unloading, the assistant
foreman monitors the rate at which product
flows from ship to tank or vice versa in order
to ensure the correct amount is transferred.
Sometimes, this can be done from an office
and does not require the assistant foreman to
be in the yard. But [—3—] increased
workload, crew absences, {–282–} and other
circumstances often require the assistant
foreman to work in the yard. For instance, the
assistant foreman must sometimes act as a
"pumper," checking pipes and manifolds in the
yard to ensure product flows correctly. He
must also help "blow out"[3] the pipes that
connect tanks to each other and to vessels.

Victorian participated in all these tasks,
assisting in loading and unloading product
from vessels daily. Even when working from
the office, he went to the yard and the dock
every day and occasionally had to board
vessels.

_____

[3] "Blowing out" is a process by which air is
pumped through a pipeline to force oil products out
of it.

C.

Like all other team members, Victorian also assisted with tank-to-tank transfers. On June 25, 2014, Victorian assisted with a transfer from Tank 123 to Tank 107. During the transfer, Victorian was pulling an air hose up a staircase to reach an elevated platform near Tank 107, in order to blow out a pipeline. He prepared to throw the hose "to get [it] nearer" the pipeline he was blowing out. The hose "apparently became hooked on the bottom step," such that when Victorian attempted to throw it, the hose "jerked him back in the opposite direction from where he was throwing the hose." Victorian "immediately felt pain in his 'neck and upper extremity'" but finished his shift.

D.

The next day, Victorian visited Elmwood Industrial Medical Center in Metairie, Louisiana, complaining of pain in his left shoulder, scapula, and lower neck. Over the following weeks, Victorian returned several times to Elmwood, complaining of more pain. He was diagnosed with cervical radiculopathy, and on July 29, 2014, his physician noted he had "no work capacity." [—4—]

On September 8, 2014, Victorian was referred to a neurosurgeon, Lucien Miranne. Dr. Miranne diagnosed Victorian with disc herniation and recommended an electromyogram and medication. Based on the effectiveness of the electromyogram, Dr. Miranne "deferred any surgical consideration" and recommended nonsurgical treatment instead. At IMTT's behest, Dr. Karen J. Ortenberg examined Victorian on December 15, 2015, and opined that he was a good candidate for cervical fusion. She also opined that if Victorian did not want to pursue surgery, he had reached maximum medical improvement ("MMI").4

On August 12, 2016, after months of fruitless nonsurgical treatment, Dr. Miranne recommended Victorian undergo a cervical discectomy and fusion. Victorian told Dr. Miranne he intended to undergo the surgery. Victorian's brief states that he has undergone the procedure and is now recovering.

E.

Stacie A. Nunez, an IMTT rehabilitation counselor, submitted a vocational rehabilitation report for Victorian on February 29, 2016. Nunez reviewed Victorian's medical records and work history and developed a list of jobs near Victorian's residence that would be compatible with his medical condition, education, and experience. With the help of his wife, Victorian applied to many {–283–} jobs, both online and in person, but he received no offers.

F.

Victorian made a claim for benefits under the Act against IMTT, which IMTT contested. In a lengthy and detailed order, the ALJ concluded that [—5—] Victorian stated a valid claim under the Act and rejected IMTT's objections. The ALJ also found that Victorian had not yet reached MMI and was temporarily totally disabled. The ALJ ordered IMTT to pay Victorian compensation for temporary total disability starting from July 30, 2014.

IMTT appealed to the Board, arguing among other things that: (1) Victorian's injury did not occur on an Act-covered "situs," *see* 33 U.S.C. § 903(a); (2) at the time of his injury, Victorian was not "engaged in maritime employment," *id.* § 902(3); (3) the ALJ's finding that Victorian had not reached MMI was not supported by substantial evidence; and (4) the ALJ's finding that Victorian had adequately sought alternate employment was not supported by substantial evidence.

The Board rejected these arguments (and others not before us) and affirmed the ALJ's order. As relevant here, the Board held that

---

4 After an employee reaches MMI, his injury is deemed "permanent," and he may become eligible for federal vocational rehabilitation. *La. Ins. Guar. Ass'n v. Abbott*, 40 F.3d 122, 126 (5th Cir. 1994) (citations omitted). At that point, the otherwise-liable employer can stop compensating him for his

disability. *Id.* It would thus reduce IMTT's liability for Victorian to have already reached MMI.

the Facility is a "terminal" within the Act's ambit and that Victorian's "job duties as an assistant shift foreman" rendered him a maritime employee. The Board affirmed the ALJ's factual findings that Victorian had not met MMI and that he had exercised due diligence in seeking alternate employment.

IMTT timely petitioned for review. The Director of the Office of Worker's Compensation Programs joins Victorian in defending the Board's decision. *See Wood Grp. Prod. Servs. v. Malta*, 930 F.3d 733, 736 n.4, 7 Adm. R. 287, 288 n.4 (5th Cir. 2019) ("The Director is a party to the litigation of disputed claims under the Act at all stages of the litigation." (citation omitted)). We have jurisdiction under 33 U.S.C. § 921(c). **[—6—]**

II.

Where the facts are not in dispute, we review *de novo* the Board's legal conclusion that a worker is covered under the Act. *Wood Grp.*, 930 F.3d at 736–37, 7 Adm. R. at 288 (citing *New Orleans Depot Servs., Inc. v. Zepeda*, 718 F.3d 384, 387, 1 Adm. R. 228, 229 (5th Cir. 2013) (en banc)). We must also ensure the Board's decision treated as "conclusive" the ALJ's findings of fact, so long as they were "supported by substantial evidence in the record considered as a whole." 33 U.S.C. § 921(b)(3); *see also Port Cooper/T. Smith Stevedoring Co. v. Hunter*, 227 F.3d 285, 287 (5th Cir. 2000) (same). In reviewing the ALJ's fact findings, neither the Board nor this panel may "substitute [its] judgment for that of the ALJ" or "reweigh or reappraise the evidence." *Hunter*, 227 F.3d at 287 (cleaned up).

III.

"[T]he Act 'provides compensation for the death or disability of any person engaged in maritime employment,' under certain conditions." *Wood Grp.*, 930 F.3d at 736, 7 Adm. R. at 288 (cleaned up) (quoting *Herb's Welding v. Gray*, 470 U.S. 414, 415 (1985)). In its petition, IMTT contends the Board erred in affirming the ALJ's decisions that (1) Victorian's injury occurred on a maritime situs; (2) Victorian was engaged in maritime

employment; (3) Victorian had not reached MMI; and (4) Victorian adequately sought alternative employment. We address each argument in turn.

A.

The Act applies only to claimants injured "on a maritime situs." {–284–} *Coastal Prod. Servs., Inc. v. Hudson*, 555 F.3d 426, 431 (5th Cir. 2009). This means that a claimant's injury must have

> occurr[ed] upon the navigable waters of the United States (including any adjoining pier, wharf, dry dock, terminal, building way, marine railway, or other adjoining area customarily used by an employer in loading, unloading, repairing, dismantling, or building a vessel). **[—7—]**

33 U.S.C. § 903(a). Our cases have conceptualized the situs requirement as having two components: geographic and functional. *Wood Grp.*, 930 F.3d at 737, 7 Adm. R. at 289 (citations omitted).

To satisfy the geographic component—*i.e.*, that the area of injury be "adjoining" navigable waters—the area must "border on" or "be contiguous with" navigable waters. *Zepeda*, 718 F.3d at 393–94, 1 Adm. R. at 235. To satisfy the functional component, our precedent requires a more complicated analysis. If the area of injury is putatively one enumerated under § 903(a)—a "pier, wharf, dry dock, terminal, building way, [or] marine railway"—then we ask whether that area has "some maritime purpose." *Thibodeaux v. Grasso Production Management, Inc.*, 370 F.3d 486, 493 (5th Cir. 2004); *see also Wood Grp.*, 930 F.3d at 738–40, 7 Adm. R. at 290–91 (discussing *Thibodeaux*). If, on the other hand, the area is not one of the enumerated places but instead an "other adjoining area," we ask whether that area is "customarily used by an employer in loading, unloading, repairing, dismantling, or building a vessel." 33 U.S.C. § 903(a); *see also Zepeda*, 718 F.3d at 389, 1 Adm. R. at 231; *Wood Grp.*, 930 F.3d at 739–40, 7 Adm. R. at 290–92.

We agree with the Board's conclusion—and with its affirmance of the ALJ's findings—that Victorian fulfills the Act's situs requirement because the Facility (1) adjoins navigable waters (meeting the geographic component) and (2) qualifies as a "terminal" under § 903(a) and serves the maritime purpose of loading and unloading vessels (meeting the functional component).[5]

1.

We first consider the determination that the Facility adjoins navigable waters and therefore satisfies the geographic component of the situs test.

The ALJ correctly relied on our holding in *Zepeda* that to satisfy this [—8—] component, the putative situs must "border on" or "be contiguous with navigable waters." *See Zepeda*, 718 F.3d at 392, 1 Adm. R. at 235. The ALJ found that the Facility, "although large in size, is situated along the navigable waters of the Mississippi River." It also found that the Facility's activities center on its dock and that it is a "discrete shoreside facility." The Board affirmed, holding that the Facility was a "contiguous" area that "adjoin[ed] the water."

We find no error in these determinations. Both the Board and the ALJ inquired, as our precedent requires, whether the Facility borders on or is contiguous with navigable waters. *See id.*, 1 Adm. R. at 235. As the Board properly concluded, the ALJ's finding that the Facility borders the Mississippi River is supported by substantial evidence, including aerial photographs of the Facility and ample testimony regarding its dock and physical connections to the river.

IMTT does not dispute that the Facility as a whole adjoins the river but argues that the particular platform on which Victorian was injured is too far from the river to fulfill the

geographic component. We disagree. "It is the parcel of land {–285–} underlying the employer's facility that must adjoin navigable waters, not the particular part of that parcel upon which a claimant is injured." *Zepeda*, 718 F.3d at 392, 1 Adm. R. at 233–34; *cf. BPU*, 732 F.3d at 461, 1 Adm. R. at 328 (focusing on "the general purpose of the area rather than requiring 'every square inch of an area' to be used for a maritime activity" (quoting *Hudson*, 555 F.3d at 435)). The only case on which IMTT relies to support this argument, *Zepeda*, does not help its position, as no part of the facility at issue there adjoined navigable waters. *See* 718 F.3d at 394, 1 Adm. R. at 235 ("[T]here is no dispute that the Chef Yard . . . did not adjoin navigable waters.").

2.

We next consider the determination that the Facility satisfies the functional component of the situs requirement because the Facility is a [—9—] "terminal" under § 903(a) that had "some maritime purpose."

a.

The Act does not define "terminal," and, as the ALJ correctly noted, neither have we. For guidance, the ALJ looked to an OSHA regulation, Webster's Dictionary, and a definition invoked by the Supreme Court.

The pertinent OSHA regulation defines a "marine terminal" as

> wharves, bulkheads, quays, piers, docks and other berthing locations and adjacent storage or adjacent areas and structures associated with the primary movement of cargo or materials from vessel to shore or shore to vessel including structures which are devoted to receiving, handling, holding, consolidating and loading or delivery of waterborne shipments or passengers.

29 C.F.R. § 1917.2. The regulation further explains that "[t]he term does not include production or manufacturing areas nor does the term include storage facilities directly associated with those production or

---

[5] The ALJ held alternatively that the Facility is an "other adjoining area customarily used by an employer in loading [and] unloading . . . a vessel." Like the Board, we conclude the Facility is a "terminal" and therefore will not review the ALJ's alternative holding.

manufacturing areas." *Id*. The dictionary the ALJ cited defines "terminal" as "'[o]f, relating to, situated at, or forming an end or boundary,' 'relating to or occurring at the end of a section or series,' 'either end of a transportation line, as a railroad.'" *See* WEBSTER'S II NEW RIVERSIDE UNIVERSITY DICTIONARY 1194 (1988). Finally, the ALJ also relied on a state commission's definition of "marine terminal" which the Supreme Court cited as "useful":

> an area which includes piers, which is used primarily for the moving, warehousing, distributing or packing of waterborne freight or freight to or from such piers, and which, inclusive of such piers, is under common ownership or control.

Ne. Marine Terminal Co. v. Caputo, 432 U.S. 249, 268 n.30 (1977) (citation omitted).

Applying these definitions, the ALJ concluded that the Facility is a "terminal" under the Act. The ALJ relied on testimony that all the product stored at the Facility departs it by ship and that most arrives by ship, too. The **{—10—}** ALJ also cited testimony that the Facility's dock is used by barges every day and that several barges dock there. The ALJ further considered that IMTT itself refers to the Facility as a "terminal." The Board affirmed. Specifically, the Board held that the definitions relied on by the ALJ "describe[d] both the physical attributes of the area and the maritime purpose of the docks, pipelines and storage tanks at employer's Gretna facility, which is to move waterborne shipments from vessel to shore and product from shore to vessel."

We find no error in this analysis. Like the Board, we conclude that the definitions **{—286—}** of "marine terminal" on which the ALJ relied are pertinent. The Act employs the undefined word "terminal" as a "maritime term of art," and therefore we must give the term its "established" meaning in the maritime industry. *McDermott Int'l, Inc. v. Wilander*, 498 U.S. 337, 342 (1991). The definition relied on in *Caputo* was, as the Supreme Court explained, a "useful indicator[]

of the terminology used by the industry." 432 U.S. at 268 n.30. Similarly, the OSHA definition—found in Part 1917 of the Department of Labor regulations concerning "marine terminals"—provides relevant evidence of established industry usage of the term. *See generally* 29 C.F.R. § 1917.1(a) (providing "[t]he regulations of this part apply to employment within a marine terminal as defined in § 1917.2"). Of particular relevance here, the definition "includ[es] structures which are devoted to receiving, handling, *holding, consolidating* and loading or delivery of waterborne shipments." *Id*. § 1917.2 (emphases added); *accord Caputo*, 432 U.S. at 268 n.30 (a terminal is an area "used primarily for the moving, *warehousing*, distributing or *packing* of waterborne freight" (emphases added)).[6] **[—11—]**

Moreover, as the Board concluded, substantial evidence supported the ALJ's finding that the Facility falls comfortably within these definitions of "terminal." In particular, the ALJ relied on undisputed testimony that the Facility "receives" oil products, "consolidates and/or mixes product, stores product, and transports or loads product out of the facility." The ALJ also relied on undisputed testimony that the Facility has a number of "adjacent" structures that are "devoted to receiving, handling, holding, consolidating and loading or delivery of waterborne shipments." In addition, while IMTT's label for the Facility—a "marine terminal"—is not dispositive, the ALJ reasonably found that it provides some evidence that the Facility meets the industry definition of a "terminal."

For its part, IMTT offers no alternative definition of "terminal." Instead, it argues that in defining the term, the ALJ should not have relied on a dictionary definition or an OSHA regulation but should instead have taken the "functional approach" mandated by our decision in *Thibodeaux*. IMTT misreads our precedent. Our "functional approach" does not inform the inquiry whether a particular locale falls within one of § 903(a)'s enumerated

---

[6] We find less helpful Webster's generic definition of "terminal," given that "terminal" as used in the Act is a maritime term of art.

terms. Instead, it asks the subsequent and distinct question whether a particular locale has a "maritime purpose." *See Thibodeaux*, 370 F.3d at 488–89 ("functional approach" requires that putative situs also "serve a maritime purpose" (citations omitted)).

IMTT also attacks head-on the conclusion that the Facility meets the definition of a "terminal." In IMTT's view, the Facility should instead be characterized as either a "storage" facility, or perhaps—pointing to its heating and sparging processes—a "manufacturing" facility. Emphasizing these aspects of the Facility, IMTT argues that the Facility "is not just the end of a transportation line for vessels" and therefore not a "terminal." This argument, [—12—] however, ignores the OSHA and *Caputo* definitions, which include not only structures used for loading and unloading vessels but also those used for "receiving, handling, holding, consolidating," and "warehousing" products. *See* 29 C.F.R. § 1917.2; *Caputo*, 432 U.S. at 268 n.30. Indeed, only lines later in its {—287—} brief, IMTT admits that the Facility is "engaged in loading, unloading, [and] storage." Similarly, the Facility's heating and sparging procedures do not convert it into a "manufacturing facility," as IMTT contends. If anything, these procedures reinforce its characterization as a shipping terminal: the fuel it blends is used to power the vessels that dock at the Facility, and the Facility heats oil in part to make it easier to load and unload from vessels.[7]

Finally, IMTT argues that because the Facility is "mixed-use," the Board should have analyzed it as an "other adjoining area" instead of a "terminal." But IMTT cites no cases suggesting a "mixed-use" facility cannot be a "terminal" but can constitute only an "other adjoining area." And, as discussed above, the OSHA and *Caputo* definitions make clear that the term "marine terminal" can encompass facilities with several functions.

b.

We also agree with the Board that the ALJ's finding that the Facility has "some maritime purpose" was supported by substantial evidence.

The Board identified the relevant legal standard, namely that an enumerated situs is marked not only by its physical characteristics but also by its "maritime purpose." *Thibodeaux*, 370 F.3d at 488–89. As already explained, [—13—] this is the "functional approach" to the situs inquiry. *Id*. The Board also correctly noted that not "every square inch of an area" must be used for maritime activity. *Hudson*, 555 F.3d at 435.

We affirm the Board's holding that substantial evidence supported the ALJ's finding that the Facility has "some maritime purpose." *See Thibodeaux*, 370 F.3d at 488–89. The Board pointed to the "[s]ubstantial evidence of record" supporting "the finding that the Gretna facility ships and receives the overwhelming majority of its liquid bulk product from vessels at a dock on its property, and has 60 storage tanks for the liquid bulk product that is unloaded directly from ship to tanks and stored there." This finding rests on the unrefuted testimony of multiple IMTT employees. Moreover, as we have recently reaffirmed, the "maritime purpose" test is fulfilled by evidence that the putative situs is used for loading or unloading vessels. *See Expeditors & Prod. Serv. Co., Inc. v. Spain*, No. 18-60895, Slip Op. at 3 (5th Cir. Nov. 4, 2019), *as revised* Nov. 5, 2019 (citing *Thibodeaux*, 370 F.3d at 488–89).

The Board also correctly rejected IMTT's "misguided" argument that because some "manufacturing"—blending and sparging[8]—

---

[7] For similar reasons, we reject IMTT's argument that the Facility's non-shipping structures—like its "guard shack," "office building," and "product testing facilities"—somehow strip the Facility of its terminal status. This argument again ignores the OSHA and *Caputo* definitions, both of which show that a "marine terminal" encompasses facilities that do more than simply load and unload cargo. *See* 29 C.F.R. § 1917.2 (term includes structures devoted to "handling, holding, [and] consolidating" cargo); *Caputo*, 432 U.S. at 268 n.30 (term includes structures used for "warehousing, distributing or packing" cargo).

[8] We assume only for the sake of argument that "blending and sparging" are properly considered "manufacturing" processes.

occurred at Gretna Terminal, it lacked maritime purpose. The Board correctly noted that not "every square inch of an area" must be used for maritime activity. *Hudson*, 555 F.3d at 435. Based on substantial evidence, the ALJ found that no tanks are dedicated solely to these processes and that all sixty of the Facility's {–288–} tanks are customarily used to load and unload vessels. As we have held more than once before, a covered situs "need not be used exclusively or even primarily for maritime purposes, as long as it is customarily used for significant maritime activity." *Hudson*, 555 F.3d at 432; *see also BPU*, 732 F.3d at 461, 1 Adm. R. at 328 ("[T]he site [—14—] of the injury need not be 'exclusively' or 'predominantly' used for unloading—only customarily." (citation omitted)).

B.

We turn next to the Board's conclusion that Victorian fulfills the Act's status requirement. As explained above, the status requirement means that Victorian must have been "engaged in maritime employment" at the time of his injury. 33 U.S.C. § 902(3).

The ALJ found that Victorian's "employment as a whole was an integral part of the loading and unloading operations at the Gretna terminal." The ALJ supported this conclusion by reasoning that Victorian's

> activities of opening and closing valves which directed the flow of product into specific tanks, monitoring and lighting-up the pipelines, reading the gauges on tanks, and communicating with the dockmen to assist in the smooth transfer of product from the moored vessels into the tanks, were all integral parts of the loading and unloading process at the terminal and were one step in the direct chain of unloading or loading vessels.

The ALJ concluded that "[u]ndoubtedly, none of the product would be loaded or unloaded on vessels without [Victorian] performing his duties in the tank yard." The Board affirmed the ALJ, concluding substantial evidence showed that Victorian's "job duties were

integral to the loading and unloading process" and that Victorian therefore satisfied the status requirement.

We find no error in the Board's analysis. The Board correctly noted that a worker is "engaged in maritime employment" under § 902(3) if he is loading or unloading a vessel at the time of injury or if his employment as a whole entails loading or unloading vessels. *Hudson*, 555 F.3d at 439. To meet the latter criterion, the worker need not spend a "substantial" amount of time loading or unloading. *Boudloche v. Howard Trucking Co.*, 632 F.2d 1346, 1347 (5th Cir. 1980); *see also id.* (worker covered despite spending only 2.5 to 5 [—15—] percent of his time loading and unloading); *Hudson*, 555 F.3d at 440 (worker covered despite spending only 10 percent of his time in maritime activities). Instead, as the Board wrote, the worker need only spend "some" time doing maritime work. *Caputo*, 432 U.S. at 273.

The Board also correctly concluded that substantial evidence supported the ALJ's findings on Victorian's maritime status. Victorian was tasked with monitoring and effecting the flow of oil products, opening and closing manifolds to direct flow, and communicating with other team members to ensure vessels were loaded and unloaded properly. He visited the dock and assisted with loading and unloading every day. IMTT fails to explain why this does not constitute substantial evidence supporting the ALJ's maritime status finding.

Finally, to support its position that Victorian lacks maritime status, IMTT leans heavily on Judge Clement's concurrence in *Zepeda*, 718 F.3d at 394, 1 Adm. R. at 236 (Clement, J., concurring). Even if that concurrence were circuit law (it is not), that would not help IMTT. To determine maritime status, Judge Clement's *Zepeda* concurrence asked whether the employee engages in "the type of customary maritime work that a dockworker or longshoreman would have {–289–} to perform in order to successfully transfer cargo between ship and land transportation." *Id.*, 1 Adm. R. at 237. Contrary to IMTT's argument, however, the

ALJ found that Victorian's "employment as a whole[] was an integral part of the loading and unloading operations at the Gretna terminal."

In sum, we affirm the Board's determination that Victorian had maritime status under the Act.

C.

We next consider the Board's affirmance of the ALJ's finding that Victorian had not reached MMI, which IMTT argues was not supported by substantial evidence. [—16—]

As the Board correctly observed, MMI "is reached when an injury has received the maximum benefit of treatment such that the patient's condition will not improve." *Gulf Best Elec., Inc. v. Methe*, 396 F.3d 601, 605 (5th Cir. 2004). But "[i]f a physician determines that further treatment should be undertaken, then . . . further medical improvement is possible until such treatment has been completed—even if, in retrospect, it turns out not to have been effective." *La. Ins. Guar. Ass'n v. Abbott*, 40 F.3d 122, 126 (5th Cir. 1994). The Board was obligated to defer to the ALJ's finding unless it was not supported by substantial evidence. *Hunter*, 227 F.3d at 287.

We agree with the Board that the ALJ's finding was supported by substantial evidence. The ALJ scoured Victorian's medical records with extraordinary care. The record shows that although Dr. Miranne initially recommended nonsurgical treatment for Victorian's back, it eventually became clear that Victorian's physical rehabilitation was ineffective and that surgery would have made "further medical improvement . . . possible." *Abbott*, 40 F.3d 126. Both Drs. Miranne and Ortenberg recommended the surgery, evidence that they had "determine[d] that further treatment should be undertaken." *Id.* The record also reflects that on August 12, 2016, Victorian told Dr. Miranne he intended to undergo the surgery.

IMTT contends that Victorian achieved MMI on December 15, 2015, when Dr. Ortenberg opined that if Victorian chose not to pursue surgery, then he had achieved MMI. IMTT points to record evidence suggesting that Victorian did not pursue surgery immediately after it was recommended to him by Dr. Ortenberg, choosing instead a more conservative course of treatment. IMTT further argues that the "mere expression of a desire to undergo surgery does not automatically render a claimant temporarily and totally disabled." IMTT contends that because Victorian would have achieved MMI and could [—17—] have returned to some form of work if he chose not to pursue the recommended surgery, the Board's reading of the Act "would allow a claimant to live in a [perpetual] state of temporary disability" and that "it is the actual surgical procedure and subsequent recovery itself that would render a claimant temporarily disabled"

IMTT's argument is unconvincing. There may be a point after which a claimant's unreasonable delay in electing further treatment leads to de facto MMI. The Director suggests as much, and the Act allows the ALJ or the Secretary of Labor to suspend payment if a claimant "unreasonably refuses to submit to medical or surgical treatment . . . unless the circumstances justified the refusal." *Methe*, 396 F.3d at 604 (quoting 33 U.S.C. § 907(d)(4)). But IMTT has not articulated where that point may be, identified any evidence that Victorian's delay was unreasonable, or supplied legal authority that Victorian bears the burden of proving his delay was reasonable. {—290—}

Instead, IMTT seems to suggest that to avoid slipping into MMI, Victorian had an affirmative duty immediately to undergo every kind of treatment available. Again, IMTT cites no authority for this proposition, which is contrary to our precedent. *See Methe* 396 F.3d at 605 (MMI reached only when "an injury has received the maximum benefit of treatment such that the patient's condition will not improve."); *Abbott*, 40 F.3d at 126 (MMI not reached "[i]f a physician determines that further treatment should be undertaken").

D.

Finally, we turn to the Board's affirmance of the ALJ's finding that Victorian reasonably sought alternative employment.

Victorian claims "temporary total" disability, one of the types of disability for which the Act mandates varying compensation levels. *See* [—18—] *generally* 33 U.S.C. § 908.[9] To establish temporary total disability, a claimant must "demonstrate" that his injury has rendered him "unable to perform his former longshore employment tasks." *Abbott*, 40 F.3d at 127. The employer can respond by "establish[ing] that the employee is capable of performing other realistically available jobs." *Id.* If the employer succeeds on that showing, the claimant's disability remains total (rather than becoming "partial") only if he "demonstrates that he diligently tried and was unable to secure such employment." *Roger's Terminal*, 784 F.2d at 691.

Here, it is undisputed that Victorian established a prima facie case and that IMTT responded adequately by providing Victorian a list of suitable alternative jobs. IMTT does not contest that Victorian applied for those jobs but claims he was not diligent in trying to secure alternative employment. We disagree.

The ALJ identified a trove of evidence demonstrating Victorian's efforts to find alternative employment. This includes a "job application log" Victorian created, detailing several applications he had submitted. The ALJ also identified testimony from both Victorian and his wife that Victorian applied for several other positions online. Victorian's wife testified further that she and her daughter had on separate occasions driven Victorian to workplaces to apply for other jobs.

IMTT responds that the ALJ disregarded testimony from Stacie Nunez that some employers listed in the labor market survey she conducted had not [—19—] received applications from Victorian. Elsewhere, IMTT claims that the ALJ was wrong to find Victorian credible because while he had testified that a particular employer did not respond to his application, he had in fact "received a letter" from the employer "informing him that he was no longer being considered for the position." These arguments do little to offset the substantial evidence on which the ALJ relied. The ALJ acknowledged Nunez's testimony and analyzed it at length. Even assuming Victorian conflated one employer's rejection with another's non-response, it would hardly be grounds to impeach the rest of his testimony. And even if we found merit in these arguments, to accept them now would be to inappropriately "reweigh" {–291–} and "reappraise the evidence." *Hunter*, 227 F.3d at 287 (cleaned up).

* * *

The petition for review is DENIED.

---

[9] Among these types are "total permanent, permanent partial, temporary total, and temporary partial disabilities." *Roger's Terminal & Shipping Corp. v. Smith*, 784 F.2d 687, 690 (5th Cir. 1986). The Act does not define these terms. *New Orleans (Gulfwide) Stevedores v. Turner*, 661 F.2d 1031, 1037 (5th Cir. 1981). But "[i]t is settled law that the degree of disability is determined not only on the basis of physical condition but also on factors such as age, education, employment history, rehabilitative potential, and the availability of work that the claimant can do." *Smith*, 784 F.2d at 691 (cleaned up).

United States Court of Appeals
for the Fifth Circuit

No. 19-60067

EXCEL MODULAR SCAFFOLD & LEASING CO.
VS.
OCCUPATIONAL SAFETY & HEALTH REVIEW
COMM'N

Petition for Review of an Order of the Occupational
Safety and Health Review Commission

Decided: November 26, 2019

Citation: 943 F.3d 748, 7 Adm. R. 355 (5th Cir. 2019).

Before **WIENER, HIGGINSON,** and **HO,** Circuit Judges.

[—1—] {–751–} **HIGGINSON,** Circuit Judge:

On September 12, 2016, an employee of Excel Modular Scaffold & Leasing Company ("Excel") was killed when a scaffold he was constructing collapsed into Galveston Bay in Texas City, Texas. In the aftermath of this tragedy, the Occupational Safety and Health Administration ("OSHA") conducted an investigation into the incident and issued Excel a number of safety citations. One of those citations charged Excel {–752–} with a "serious" violation of 29 C.F.R. § 1926.106(d), a regulation which required Excel to ensure the presence of a "lifesaving skiff" at all jobsites where employees were required to work over water. Excel contested the issuance of the citation and the resulting [—2—] penalty, but it was upheld by an Administrative Law Judge ("ALJ"). The ALJ's decision became a final order when the Occupational Safety and Health Review Commission ("the Commission") declined to conduct further review. For the reasons explained below, we deny Excel's petition for review.

I.

Excel manufactures scaffolds and provides scaffold construction and dismantling services to companies in the refining industry. In 2015, Marathon Refinery hired Excel to build a series of scaffolds beneath three docks on Galveston Bay. The scaffolding system was comprised of "hanging scaffolds," which were constructed by attaching a horizontal bar to hanging vertical legs that were connected to I-beams under the docks. The project required Excel's employees to work both above and below the docks, and the water surrounding the docks was approximately eighteen feet deep.

On September 12, 2016, Luis Gonzalez was a member of an Excel crew working on the construction of a scaffold bay beneath one of Marathon's three docks. At the time, all crew members, including Gonzalez, were wearing safety harnesses with lanyards and personal flotation devices. While he worked, Gonzalez connected his lanyard to the vertical leg of one of the scaffold systems. As he attempted to attach the vertical leg to the existing scaffold bay, the leg became detached and fell into the water, dragging Gonzalez along with it. Two other members of the crew jumped into the water in an attempt to save Gonzalez, but they were unable to retrieve him. Tragically, by the time rescue personnel arrived, it was too late to save him, and Coast Guard divers recovered his body later that day.

After the incident, OSHA commenced an investigation into the fatality and the conditions at the jobsite. The Secretary of Labor ("the Secretary") issued Excel four safety citations. Only one of the citations is at issue in this [—3—] appeal.[1] That citation charged Excel with a "serious" violation of 29 C.F.R. § 1926.106(d), which requires employers to ensure that "[a]t least one lifesaving skiff" is made "immediately available at locations where employees are working over or adjacent to water." *Id.* A lifesaving skiff is a small boat located close enough to a jobsite that it can attempt to rescue someone who falls into the water within three or four minutes. The Secretary classified Excel's violation of the regulation as "serious," and proposed that Excel pay a penalty of $12,675.

---

[1] The other three citations were subsequently dismissed. The Secretary voluntarily withdrew two of the citations before the ALJ issued her decision, and one was dismissed by the ALJ in her order, which was affirmed by the Commission.

Excel contested the citation by submitting a Notice of Contest form along with an answer containing twenty-five affirmative defenses, including "impossibility/infeasibility of compliance." A two-day hearing was scheduled to begin on March 19, 2018 before an ALJ. A month before the hearing, the parties filed a joint Prehearing Statement with the ALJ. The Prehearing Statement stipulated that Excel violated the regulation requiring a skiff and informed the ALJ that the following two "issues of fact" were the only ones that "remain[ed] to be litigated" with respect to that citation: {–753–}

1. Whether failing to have a lifesaving skiff immediately available exposed [Excel's] employees to a substantial probability of death or serious injury under the facts and circumstances of this case; and

2. Whether the proposed penalty is appropriate.

The Prehearing Statement made no reference to Excel's earlier contention that compliance with the regulation was either impossible or infeasible.

At the beginning of the hearing, the ALJ sought to further clarify the issues in dispute. She asked counsel for Excel to explain the nature of the company's stipulation regarding the lifesaving skiff citation. Excel's lawyer [—4—] explained that the company stipulated that it "did not comply with the standard," but continued to "challenge the serious type of the violation classification." The ALJ asked once again whether Excel was "only challenging the classification," and Excel responded that it was challenging "[t]he classification and, of course, that goes along with that, the penalty amount." Throughout this exchange, Excel omitted any reference to the infeasibility or impossibility defense.

During the hearing, Excel introduced testimony from employees who explained that, given the layout of the docks at the Marathon Refinery, it would have been difficult for a boat to navigate under the dock where Gonzalez fell. The Secretary did not object to the introduction of this testimony.

After the hearing, the parties submitted post-hearing briefs. In Excel's brief, the company argued that the testimony introduced during the hearing established that compliance with the lifesaving skiff regulation "was infeasible because a skiff could not have been deployed and successfully navigated underneath Dock 34 to rescue Luis Gonzalez." Excel further argued that, in the event the ALJ disagreed with the company's defense, the citation's classification of the violation should be reduced to "other than serious."

The ALJ issued a decision and order on October 26, 2018. The order held that Excel had abandoned the defense of infeasibility by failing to preserve the defense in the parties' joint Prehearing Statement. As a result, the ALJ disregarded the section of Excel's post-hearing brief pertaining to the infeasibility defense. In the alternative, the ALJ held that the evidence submitted during the hearing failed to establish by a preponderance of the evidence that it would have been infeasible for Excel to comply with the lifesaving skiff regulation, in part because the evidence established that partial compliance with the regulation was possible. After reviewing the evidence [—5—] presented at the hearing, the ALJ concluded that Excel's violation of the citation was "serious," and imposed the Secretary's proposed penalty.

Excel filed a petition for discretionary review with the Commission on October 19, 2018. When the Commission declined to direct the case for review, the ALJ's order became the final order of the Commission on November 27, 2018. See 29 U.S.C. § 661(j); 29 C.F.R. § 220.90(d).

II.

We have jurisdiction over this appeal under 29 U.S.C. § 660(a). Though the ALJ's order became final only when the Commission declined to conduct discretionary review, we apply the same standard of review to the final decision here as we would if the Commission had directly issued its own decision. *See MICA Corp. v. OSHRC*, 295 F.3d 447, 449 (5th Cir. 2002) (applying the same standard of review in such a situation). We review the ALJ's findings of fact under the substantial evidence {–754–} standard. *Id.* We will affirm the ALJ's findings of fact as long as they are "supported by substantial evidence [in] the record considered as a whole even if this court could justifiably reach a different result de novo." *Id.* "Substantial evidence is 'such relevant evidence as a reasonable mind might accept as adequate to support a conclusion.'" *Chao v. OSHRC*, 401 F.3d 355, 362 (5th Cir. 2005) (quoting *Consolo v. Fed. Mar. Comm'n*, 383 U.S. 607, 619–20 (1966)).

We will overturn the ALJ's legal conclusions only if they are "arbitrary, capricious, an abuse of discretion, or otherwise not in accordance with law." 5 U.S.C. § 706(a); *Chao*, 401 F.3d at 367. The ALJ's determination that Excel waived its affirmative defense of infeasibility is a legal conclusion that we review for an abuse of discretion. *See Davis v. Fort Bend Cty.*, 765 F.3d 480, 487 n.1 (5th Cir. 2014). [—6—]

III.

First, Excel argues that it was error for the ALJ to conclude that Excel waived the affirmative defense of infeasibility. Excel insists that it provided the Secretary with ample notice of the defense in its answer to the complaint, and argues that the testimony elicited during the hearing clearly established the company's intent to pursue the defense to contest the Secretary's issuance of the lifesaving skiff citation.

When presiding over a hearing involving a violation of a safety regulation, an ALJ is permitted to first conduct a prehearing conference with the parties to discuss "settlement, stipulation of facts, or any other matter that may expedite the hearing." 29 C.F.R. § 2200.51(b). The same regulation provides that the ALJ may utilize the "prehearing procedures set forth in Federal Rule of Civil Procedure 16," *id.*, which in turn permits a judge to schedule a pretrial conference to "formulate[] and simplify[] the

issues, . . . eliminat[e] frivolous claims or defenses," and issue a pretrial order.[2] Fed. R. Civ. P. 16(c)–(d). A pretrial or prehearing order "controls the course of the trial." *Trinity Carton Co. v. Falstaff Brewing Corp.*, 767 F.2d 184, 192 n.13 (5th Cir. 1985). "Because of the importance of the pre-trial order in achieving efficacy and expeditiousness upon trial in the district court, appellate courts are hesitant to interfere with the court's discretion in creating, enforcing, and modifying such orders." *Flannery v. Carroll*, 676 F.2d 126, 129 (5th Cir. 1982) (citations omitted). [—7—]

We have previously held that a party's failure to include an affirmative defense in a pretrial order constitutes a waiver of that defense—even if the defense was included in other pleadings. *See Flannery*, 676 F.2d at 129 ("If a claim or issue is omitted from the [pretrial] order, it is waived." (citing cases)); *Pacific Indem. Co. v. Broward County*, 465 F.2d 99, 103–04 (5th Cir. 1972) ("The failure to indicate in the pre-trial order that an issue remains to be resolved at trial usually precludes the offer of proof on the issue at trial—to the detriment of the party who has the burden to prove the issue.") (citing *Shell v. Strong*, 151 F.2d 909 (10th Cir. 1945)). In this case, {–755–} the joint Prehearing Statement that Excel and the Secretary submitted to the ALJ omitted any reference to Excel's affirmative defense of infeasibility. Though it is undisputed that Excel previously included this defense in its answer to the citation, "[i]t is a well-settled rule that a joint pretrial order signed by both parties supersedes all pleadings and governs the issue and evidence to be presented at trial." *Elvis Presley Enters., Inc. v. Capece*, 141 F.3d 188, 206 (5th Cir.

---

[2] Though Federal Rule of Civil Procedure 16 uses the term "trial" instead of "hearing," the Commission has noted that "[t]he purpose of Rule 16 appears to be identical with that of Commission Rule 51." *Duquesne Light Co.*, 8 BNA OSHC 1218, at *3 (No. 78-5034 1980). As such, the Commission refers to "trials" and "hearings" interchangeably, observing that "[p]rehearing procedures that aid in the early formulation of issues benefit all parties during trial preparation and result in the more efficient use of Commission resources at both the hearing and review stages." *Id.*

1998) (quoting *McGehee v. Certainteed Corp.*, 101 F.3d 1078, 1080 (5th Cir. 1996)).

On the first day of the hearing, the ALJ spoke with Excel's counsel in an effort to clarify the meaning of the parties' stipulations and the Prehearing Statement. This exchange provided Excel with an additional chance to explain that the company continued to pursue the affirmative defense of infeasibility, notwithstanding its failure to include the defense in the Prehearing Statement. Despite this opportunity, however, Excel failed to mention the infeasibility defense during the conversation, reporting to the ALJ that the *only* issues that remained to be litigated were the classification of the citation and the resulting penalty. "Each party has an affirmative duty to allege at the pretrial conference all factual and legal bases upon which the party wishes to litigate the case." *Trinity Carton*, 767 F.2d at 192 n.13. In light of Excel's repeated failure to preserve the affirmative defense of infeasibility, it was not an abuse [—8—] of discretion for the ALJ to conclude that Excel waived the defense. *See, e.g., Flannery*, 676 F.2d at 129–30 ("Unless the court has abused its discretion, its rulings concerning the [pretrial] order will not be disturbed on appeal." (citation omitted)); *Hodges v. United States*, 597 F.2d 1014, 1017 (5th Cir. 1979).[3]

Excel acknowledges that it did not include the defense of infeasibility in its Prehearing Statement, but it argues that the Secretary implicitly consented to the defense by failing to object at the hearing to the introduction of testimony that was relevant to that defense. As a result, Excel argues that the Secretary could not have been prejudiced or surprised by Excel's attempt to pursue the infeasibility defense in its post-hearing brief. While it is true that parties may consent to trial of an issue that was not preserved, consent occurs "only when the parties squarely recognized that they were trying an issue not raised in the pleadings." *Armstrong Steel Erectors, Inc.*, 17 BNA OSHC 1385, at *2 (No. 92-262 1995) (citation omitted). More importantly, "[f]ailure to object to evidence relevant to the unpleaded issue" does *not* indicate consent "if the evidence is also relevant to a pleaded issue." *Id.* (citation omitted); *see also Int'l Harvester Credit Corp. v. E. Coast Truck*, 547 F.2d 888, 890 (5th Cir. 1977) ("[T]he introduction of evidence relevant to an issue already in the case may not be used to show consent to trial of a new issue absent a clear indication that the [—9—] {–756–} party who introduced the evidence was attempting to raise a new issue." (citations omitted)).

Here, Excel points to testimony from the hearing suggesting that it would have been difficult to navigate a skiff beneath Marathon's docks. This same testimony, however, was also relied upon by Excel to support its argument that the citation's classification should be reduced to "other than serious." Because the proffered testimony was used by Excel to support its other claims, it was not an abuse of discretion for the ALJ to conclude that it would have been prejudicial to the Secretary to allow Excel to pursue the infeasibility defense.[4] *See Ingraham v. United*

---

[3] In its reply brief, Excel cites *Rathborne Land Co. v. Ascent Energy, Inc.*, 610 F.3d 249 (5th Cir. 2010), where we held that a trial court "not only has the right but the duty to relieve a party from a pretrial stipulation where necessary to avoid manifest injustice . . . or where there is substantial evidence contrary to the stipulation." *Id.* at 262–63 (quoting *Coastal States Mktg., Inc. v. Hunt*, 694 F.2d 1358, 1369 (5th Cir. 1983)). The ALJ's decision to hold Excel to its Prehearing Statement did not lead to manifest injustice. Above all, even if Excel had not waived the infeasibility defense, the evidence presented at the hearing would not have been sufficient to establish the company's entitlement to the defense. *See also Coastal States*, 649 F.3d at 1369–70 (declining to find an abuse of discretion where the court was unable to find "substantial evidence contradicting the stipulations").

[4] Excel also argues that the Secretary's failure to file a motion to strike Excel's affirmative defense of infeasibility demonstrated that the Secretary implicitly consented to Excel's reliance on the defense. Excel notes, by contrast, that the Secretary *did* move to strike the affirmative defense Excel advanced with respect to a different citation. This argument is misplaced, however. As the Secretary notes, the decision to "address a *different* affirmative defense as to a *separate* citation item is simply irrelevant to the question whether the Secretary knew that the infeasibility defense was at issue." Put differently, the fact that

States, 808 F.2d 1075, 1079 (5th Cir. 1987) ("A defendant should not be permitted to 'lie behind a log' and ambush a plaintiff with an unexpected defense." (quoting *Bettes v. Stonewall Ins. Co.*, 480 F.2d 92 (5th Cir. 1973))).

IV.

We also agree with the ALJ's alternative basis for dismissing Excel's infeasibility defense. In a footnote, the ALJ held that Excel had failed to establish by a preponderance of the evidence that it was infeasible for the company to comply with § 1926.106(d). Thus, even if Excel had not abandoned [—10—] the infeasibility defense, the ALJ held that Excel had not met its burden of proving that it was entitled to the defense on the merits.

To prove infeasibility, an employer must show by a preponderance of the evidence that "(1) literal compliance with the terms of the cited standard was infeasible under the existing circumstances and (2) an alternative protective measure was used or there was no feasible alternative measure." *Westvaco Corp.*, 16 BNA OSHC 1374, at *6 (No. 90-1341 1993). Because infeasibility is an affirmative defense, Excel bore the burden of producing sufficient evidence to meet each prong of the test. *See Ace Sheeting & Repair Co. v. OSHRC*, 555 F.2d 439, 441 (5th Cir. 1977); *A.J. McNulty & Co. v. Sec'y of Labor*, 283 F.3d 328, 334 (D.C. Cir. 2002) (holding that an employer must prove each prong of the test to establish the infeasibility defense).

An employer is not entitled to an infeasibility defense if it would have been possible to partially comply with the standard. *See Cleveland Consol. Inc. v. OSHRC*, 649 F.2d 1160, 1167 (5th Cir. 1981) (observing that OSHA "requires limited compliance where it furnishes some protection, even if

the ALJ chose not to infer from these arguments that the Secretary consented to the infeasibility defense was not an abuse of discretion. *Cf. Johnson v. Mississippi*, 606 F.2d 635, 638 (5th Cir. 1979) ("The 'abuse of discretion' standard of review contemplates an area in which the district court can act either way, exercising its own discretion, without reversal.").

exact compliance is not possible"); *Walker Towning Corp.*, 14 BNA OSHC 2072, at *4 (No. 87-1359 1991) ("[E]ven when an employer cannot fully comply with the literal terms of a standard, it must nevertheless comply to the extent that compliance is feasible."). Excel presented evidence during the hearing to suggest it would have been difficult for a lifesaving skiff to navigate beneath Dock 34, but the evidence also suggested that a {–757–} lifesaving skiff could have navigated around *other* areas of the same jobsite.[5] Even if this evidence [—11—] demonstrates that Excel could have only partially complied with the lifesaving-skiff regulation, the evidence established that limited compliance with the regulation could have provided protections to other members of the crew.[6] Therefore, the ALJ did not err in concluding that Excel's infeasibility defense failed on the merits.

V.

Finally, Excel argues that the ALJ improperly affirmed the Secretary's classification of Excel's violation of the lifesaving skiff regulation as "serious." Under the Occupational Safety and Health Act, violations of a safety regulation are considered "serious" if "there is a substantial probability that death or serious physical harm could result." 29 U.S.C. § 666(k). "A violation may be determined to be serious where, although the accident itself is merely possible . . . there

[5] Indeed, Excel itself acknowledges that "a skiff rescue might have been feasible at another location under different circumstances," but argues that that fact "does not defeat the defense's applicability." To the contrary, however, we endorsed the ALJ's view in *Peterson Bros. Steel Erection Co. v. Reich*, 26 F.3d 573 (5th Cir. 1994), where we held that it was not an abuse of discretion for the Commission to conclude that an employer was not entitled to [—11—] an impossibility defense when the evidence established that it would have been feasible for the employer to partially comply with a regulation. *Id.* at 579.

[6] It is not immediately clear that Excel's proffered evidence demonstrates that complete compliance with the regulation was impossible. If anything, this evidence established that the lack of a skiff did not cause Gonzalez's death, not that Excel was unable to place a skiff near the jobsite.

is a substantial probability of serious injury if it does occur." *E. Tex. Motor Freight, Inc. v. OSHRC*, 671 F.2d 845, 849 (5th Cir. 1982) (internal quotation marks omitted).

Excel's arguments for alteration of the classification rest on its insistence that the absence of a skiff was not a substantial cause of Gonzalez's death. This focus is misplaced. As the ALJ held, the purpose of OSHA's safety regulations is "preventative, not reactionary." *Sanderson Farms, Inc. v. Perez*, 811 F.3d 730, 737 (5th Cir. 2016). Therefore, the question is not whether compliance with the standard would have prevented the *particular* tragedy here, but, instead, whether failure to comply with the regulation exposed employees to [—12—] accidents where there was "a substantial probability of death or serious injury." *See, e.g., Boh Bros. Constr. Co.*, 24 BNA OSHC 1067, at *9 (No. 09-1072, 2013) (affirming issuance of a "serious" citation for violation of the lifesaving skiff standard where the absence of a skiff exposed employees "to water-related hazards such as hypothermia and drowning"). *Cf. Champlin Petroleum Co. v. OSHRC*, 593 F.2d 637, 642 (5th Cir. 1979) ("Because OSHA is designed to encourage abatement of hazardous conditions themselves . . . rather than to fix blame after the fact for a particular injury, a citation is supported by evidence which shows the preventability of the Generic hazard, if not this particular instance." (citation omitted)). Indeed, *Brennan v. OSHRC*, 494 F.2d 460 (8th Cir. 1974), a case upon which Excel relies, perfectly encapsulates this point, holding that the requisite inquiry focuses on "the general hazard" at issue, not the "foreseeability of the incident as it actually occurred." *Id.* at 463.

The ALJ's conclusion that the absence of a skiff exposed Excel's employees to a substantial probability of death or serious injury is amply supported by the record. For at least a year, Excel crew members {–758–} worked at the Galveston Bay jobsite without a skiff. Excel crew members worked above and below the dock, using ladders to move between the areas of the scaffolding system. The top of the dock was thirty feet from the water, and the water around the docks was eighteen feet deep, with conditions ranging from calm to choppy. The ALJ also found that there was no evidence that it would have been difficult to navigate a skiff "if an employee fell from the dock or the ladder into an area of the water that was not underneath the dock"—a proposition Excel does not refute. Given these circumstances, there was substantial evidence to support the ALJ's conclusion that the absence of a skiff exposed Excel's employees to a substantial probability of death or serious injury. [—13—]

VI.

For the foregoing reasons, the petition for review is DENIED.

United States Court of Appeals for the Sixth Circuit

United States Court of Appeals
for the Sixth Circuit

No. 18-3615

DIMOND RIGGING CO.
vs.
BDP INT'L, INC.

Appeal from the United States District Court for the
Northern District of Ohio at Cleveland

Decided: January 25, 2019

Citation: 914 F.3d 435, 7 Adm. R. 362 (6th Cir. 2019).

Before **BOGGS**, **KETHLEDGE**, and **NALBANDIAN**, Circuit Judges.

[—1—] {–438–} BOGGS, Circuit Judge:

Appellant Dimond Rigging Company, LLC ("Dimond"), appeals from a district-court judgment dismissing its suit against Appellees BDP International, Inc. ("BDP") and Logitrans International, LLC ("Logitrans") because Dimond's suit was not **[—2—]** timely filed within the one-year statute of limitations set forth in the Carriage of Goods by Sea Act ("COGSA"). We affirm the district court's judgment.

I. FACTUAL BACKGROUND

Dimond was hired by a Chinese auto manufacturer to "rig, dismantle, wash, and pack," and ultimately ship several tons of used automotive assembly-line equipment to China (the "Equipment"). Dimond lacked experience in international shipment. *Dimond Rigging Co., LLC v. BDP Int'l, Inc.*, 320 F. Supp. 3d 947, 948 (N.D. Ohio 2018). Dimond alleged that it received an "unsolicited call" from BDP offering to "assume and perform . . . each and every aspect of the shipment." *Ibid*. Dimond hired BDP to ship the Equipment. Dimond asserted that BDP did not disclose that it was not a licensed Ocean Transport Intermediary ("OTI") by the Federal Maritime Commission. *Ibid*.

In May 2011, BDP informed Dimond that it had obtained a ship and sent a booking note to Dimond that included proposed terms and conditions of the shipment. At that time, the

Equipment had not been completely dismantled and weighed. *Id.* at 948–49. Between May and October 2011, Dimond completed these tasks and prepared a "preliminary and estimated packing list" for BDP. BDP allegedly provided the preliminary packing list when it obtained quotes from third-party contractors who would load the Equipment. *Id.* at 949.

In October 2011, BDP notified Dimond that the first ship it had booked was no longer available. Dimond asserted that BDP had "without Dimond's knowledge, consent or approval" hired Logitrans to "perform some, or all of BDP's freight forwarding duties including locating/booking or providing a ship; acting in the capacity as the NVOCC carrier for the shipment . . . and negotiating loading services . . . ." Dimond alleged that BDP misrepresented {–439–} that Logitrans was a Non-Vessel Operating Common Carrier[1] ("NVOCC").

BDP and Logitrans hired the *Gisele Scan*, operated by Scan-Trans, Inc. ("Scan-Trans"), to transport the Equipment from the Port of Cleveland to Xingang, China. BDP prepared a new **[—3—]** Booking Note and Bill of Lading for the transportation of the Equipment aboard the *Gisele Scan*.[2] *Dimond Rigging Co.*, 320 F. Supp. 3d at 949. The Booking Note identified Dimond[3] as the Merchant,[4]

---

[1] A non-vessel operating common carrier "consolidate[s] cargo from numerous shippers into larger groups for shipment by an ocean carrier." *Prima U.S. Inc. v. Panalpina, Inc.*, 223 F.3d 126, 129 (2d Cir. 2000). The NVOCC, rather than the ship that transports the cargo, "issues a bill of lading to each shipper." *Ibid*.

[2] A bill of lading is a contract for the transportation of goods. It "records that a carrier has received goods from the party that wishes to ship them, states the terms of carriage, and serves as evidence of the contract for carriage." *Norfolk S. Ry. Co. v. Kirby*, 543 U.S. 14, 18–19 (2004).

[3] The Bill of Lading lists "Absolute Rigging and Millwrights" as the Merchant. Dimond appears in various cases as Dimond Rigging Company, LLC d/b/a Absolute Rigging and Millwrights. *See Federal Marine Terminals, Inc. v. Dimond Rigging Co., LLC*, No. 1:13-cv-01329, 2014 WL 4809427 (N.D. Ohio Sept. 26, 2014).

Logitrans as the Carrier, Scan-Trans as the Agent-Shipbrokers, and BDP as the Merchant's Representative. *Ibid.*

The Booking Note incorporated the Bill of Lading. The following terms in the Bill of Lading are of particular relevance.

(a) In case the Contract evidenced by this Bill of Lading is subject to the Carriage of Goods by Sea Act of the United States of America, 1936 ("U.S. COGSA"), then the provisions stated in said Act shall govern before loading and after discharge and throughout the entire time the cargo is in the Carrier's custody and in which event freight shall be payable on the cargo coming into the Carrier's custody.

The Bill of Lading also contained a "Himalaya Clause."[5]

(a) It is hereby expressly agreed that no servant or agent of the Carrier (which for the purpose of this Clause includes every independent contractor from time to time employed by the Carrier) shall in any circumstances whatsoever be under any liability whatsoever to the Merchant under this contract of carriage for any loss, damage or delay of whatsoever kind arising or resulting directly or indirectly from any act, neglect or

default on his part while acting in the course of or in connection with his employment. [—4—]

(b) Without prejudice to the generality of the foregoing provisions in this Clause, every exemption from liability, limitation, condition and liberty herein contained and every right, defence and {–440–} immunity of whatsoever nature applicable to the Carrier or to which the Carrier is entitled, shall also be available and shall extend to protect every such servant and agent of the Carrier as aforesaid.

Both Logitrans and Dimond signed the Booking Note.

Dimond alleged that it was not informed about a pre-load inspection meeting and that Logitrans and BDP did not attend the meeting either. This, Dimond asserted, led to delays and increased costs, because the *Gisele Scan* was not able to take on all the Equipment, and the stevedores would not load all the Equipment because it was not included in their quote. *Dimond Rigging*, 320 F. Supp. 3d at 949–50. Ultimately, the *Gisele Scan* departed, leaving behind approximately 34 pieces of equipment. It arrived in China in March 2012.

As a result of these shipping difficulties, Dimond became involved in multiple lawsuits, including suits with its Chinese customer and the stevedores. *Id.* at 950. Dimond filed a Complaint against BDP in the Northern District of Ohio on July 11, 2013, alleging Breach of Fiduciary Duty, Unjust Enrichment, and Fraud. *Ibid.* Dimond never served BDP with the Complaint and, when the summons expired, the district court dismissed the Complaint without prejudice. *Ibid.* On August 9, 2017, Dimond filed a Motion to Amend and Praecipe for Issuance of Amended Summons for its 2013 suit against BDP. The district court denied the Motion. Dimond filed a five-count Complaint against BDP and Logitrans on October 2, 2017, asserting claims for: (1) breach of fiduciary duty; (2) fraudulent non-disclosure; (3) intentional fraud; (4) breach of

---

[4] The Bill of Lading defines "Merchant" to include "the charterer, shipper, the receiver, the consignor, the consignee, the holder of the Bill of Lading, the owner of the cargo and any person entitled to possession of the cargo."

[5] A "Himalaya Clause" is a clause that imposes liability limitations. *See Kirby*, 543 U.S. at 20 & n.2. The name originates from an English case, *Adler v. Dickinson (The Himalaya)*, [1955] 1 Q.B. 158, [1954] 2 Lloyd's List L. Rep. 267, in which personal-injury claims were brought against the master and boatswain of the *Himalaya*. The *Himalaya*'s owners had included "customary exculpatory clauses" protecting them from liability for negligent injury to passengers. *See* Joseph C. Sweeney, *Crossing the Himalayas: Exculpatory Clauses in Global Transport*. Norfolk Southern Railway Co. v. James N. Kirby, Pty Ltd., *125 S. Ct. 385, 2004 AMC 2705 (2004)*, 36 J. Mar. L. & Com. 155, 161 (2005).

agreement, failure to perform and illegality of contract; and (5) unjust enrichment.

II. PROCEDURAL HISTORY

BDP filed a Motion to Dismiss, asserting that Dimond had failed to state a claim upon which relief could be granted because the statute of limitations on Dimond's claims had run. Logitrans was served on November 27, 2017. Logitrans's president sent Dimond's counsel a letter on December 19, 2017, denying liability and responding to Dimond's complaint. Logitrans did not file a copy of the letter with the court. Dimond filed a Request for an Entry of Default pursuant to Fed. R. Civ. P. 55(a) on December 29, 2017. Logitrans retained counsel and filed a **[—5—]** Memorandum opposing Dimond's Request on January 3, 2018. The district court denied Dimond's Request for Entry of Default and ordered Logitrans to file an amended answer. Logitrans then filed a Motion to Dismiss, asserting the same defense that BDP used— that the statute of limitations had run.

The district court granted the Motions to Dismiss. It explained that, because bills of lading are "maritime contracts, governed by federal maritime law[,]" COGSA governed Dimond's claims. *Dimond Rigging*, 320 F. Supp. 3d at 952–53. Because COGSA has a one-year statute of limitations for cargo claims in contract or tort that begins to run after the goods have been delivered, or on the date the goods should have been delivered, the district court concluded that Dimond should have filed its claims in May 2013, one year after the goods were released to Dimond's customer. Because it did not, the district court concluded that Dimond's claims were outside the statute of limitations. *Id.* at 953. In reaching this conclusion, the district court substantially relied on *Federal Marine Terminals, Inc. v. Dimond Rigging Co., LLC*, No. 1:13-cv-01329, 2014 WL 4809427 (N.D. Ohio Sept. 26, 2014), a related case in which the same district court (albeit by a different judge) had already {–441–} determined that, through the Bill of Lading, COGSA governed the shipment of the Equipment, and the Himalaya Clause extended COGSA to independent contractors. *Dimond Rigging*, 320 F. Supp. 3d at 950. The

district court also rejected Dimond's arguments that BDP and Logitrans should be estopped from benefiting from COGSA's one-year statute of limitations because they allegedly did not comply with certain licensing requirements. The district court explained that, because COGSA does not include licensure requirements, Dimond failed to sufficiently allege that BDP and Logitrans were in violation of COGSA. *Id.* at 953–54.

Dimond appealed the district court's order granting the Motions to Dismiss. It also asserts that the district court should have entered a default against Logitrans.

III. ANALYSIS

A. Standard of Review

We review a district court's dismissal of claims pursuant to Fed. R. Civ. P. 12(b)(6) de novo. *Marks v. Newcourt Credit Grp., Inc.*, 342 F.3d 444, 451 (6th Cir. 2003). In reviewing the **[—6—]** motion, the court accepts all factual allegations in the complaint as true, construed in the light most favorable to the plaintiff. *See Hall v. Callahan*, 727 F.3d 450, 453 (6th Cir. 2013). "Dismissal of a complaint because it is barred by the statute of limitations is proper when 'the statement of the claim affirmatively shows that the plaintiff can prove *no* set of facts that would entitle him to relief.'" *Gibson v. Am. Bankers Ins. Co.*, 289 F.3d 943, 946 (6th Cir. 2002) (emphasis in original) (quoting *Duncan v. Leeds*, 742 F.2d 989, 991 (6th Cir. 1984)).

B. COGSA

The primary issues in this case are whether COGSA controls, and whether BDP and Logitrans are "carriers" within the meaning of COGSA. If so, then Dimond should have filed its claim within one year after delivery, or the date when the goods should have been delivered.[6] *See* 46 U.S.C. § 30701

---

[6] Dimond argues that it "was not a party to the contract of carriage with the ship/carrier directly, or via any authorized agent . . . ." The district court rejected this argument because Dimond is listed as a party on the bill of lading. *Dimond Rigging Co., LLC v. BDP Int'l, Inc.*, 320 F. Supp. 3d 947, 952 n.1

(Notes § 3(6)). The Equipment arrived in China on March 21, 2012 and was released to Dimond's customer on May 17, 2012. *Dimond Rigging*, 320 F. Supp. 3d at 953. Accordingly, if COGSA applies, Dimond should have filed its claims against BDP and Logitrans by May 17, 2013, *ibid.*; 46 U.S.C. § 30701 (Notes § 3(6)), and the district court correctly granted Appellees' Motions to Dismiss.

1. Does COGSA Control the Bill of Lading?

Dimond argues that this is not a maritime dispute, but instead is about "breaches of contractual agreements, breaches of fiduciary duties, and outright fraud," which do not create maritime jurisdiction. In determining whether this is a maritime dispute, the "answer 'depends upon . . . the nature and character of the contract' and the true criterion is whether it has 'reference to maritime service or maritime transactions.'" *Norfolk S. Ry. Co. v. Kirby*, 543 U.S. 14, 24 (2004) (quoting *North Pac. S.S. Co. v. Hall Bros. Marine Ry. & Shipbuilding Co.*, 249 U.S. 119, 125 (1919)). This case arises from a contract to transport used manufacturing equipment by sea from the {–442–} United States to China. It is plainly a maritime transaction. [—7—] Dimond's argument is without basis. "When a contract is a maritime one, and the dispute is not inherently local, federal law controls the contract interpretation." *Id.* at 22–23.

Dimond points out that the Bill of Lading and Rider contain multiple choice-of-law options, including Hague-Visby,[7] COGSA, and English law. Dimond does not, however, argue that we should apply Hague-Visby or English law, or submit the matter to arbitration in London. Instead, Dimond suggests that these options render the Bill of Lading ambiguous

and unenforceable.[8] Dimond maintains that the true reason COGSA does not apply is because BDP and Logitrans were not in compliance with federal statutes and regulations concerning shipping, and therefore the court should apply Ohio law to assess whether Dimond's claims were timely filed. BDP and Logitrans argue that the Bill of Lading, coupled with Dimond's allegations, demonstrate that COGSA does apply, and urge us to affirm the district court's ruling. Even assuming that COGSA does not apply, BDP and Logitrans maintain that Dimond's claims are not timely under the applicable state statutes of limitations.

COGSA applies "to all contracts for carriage of goods by sea to or from ports of the United States in foreign trade." 46 U.S.C. § 30701 (Notes § 13); *see Fortis Corp. Ins., S.A. v. Viken Ship Mgmt. AS*, 597 F.3d 784, 787 (6th Cir. 2010). "[E]very bill of lading or similar document of title which is evidence of a contract for the carriage of goods by sea from ports of the United States, in foreign trade, shall contain a statement that it shall have effect subject to the provisions of this [Act]." 46 U.S.C. § 30701 (Notes § 13).

United States courts must apply COGSA if the statute so requires. *See Acciai Speciali Terni USA v. M/V BERANE*, 182 F. Supp. 2d 503, 506 (D. Md. 2002) ("United States courts

---

(N.D. Ohio 2018). Dimond *signed* the Bill of Lading. We agree with the district court.

[7] Hague-Visby refers to the 1924 International Convention for the Unification of Certain Rules of Law Relating to Bills of Lading, which was subsequently modified by the Hague-Visby Amendments of 1968. *See Royal Ins. Co. of Am. v. Orient Overseas Container Line Ltd.*, 525 F.3d 409, 413 (6th Cir. 2008).

[8] Dimond also suggests that an amended bill of lading, issued when the *Gisele Scan* stopped in Denmark, that covers the remainder of the shipment from Denmark to China supersedes the Bill of Lading. We considered a related question in *Royal Ins. Co.*, 525 F.3d at 418–20. There we held that an "intermediary stop" pursuant to a maritime contract that uses multiple modes of transportation with an ultimate destination in the United States does not "prevent the application of COGSA liability rules as a matter of federal common law." *Id.* at 420. Under *Royal Ins. Co.*, we conclude that the stop in Denmark, even one that resulted in an amended Bill of Lading (Dimond asserts that this was due to damage to the cargo from a storm), does not bar the application of COGSA because this is a contract for carriage of goods by sea *from* a port of the United States. *See* 46 U.S.C. § 30701 (Notes § 13). Further, the Denmark Bill of Lading includes an identical COGSA clause to the original Bill of Lading.

[—8—] must apply COGSA, when its terms so require, regardless [of] where bills of lading were issued or whence carriage began."); *Farrell Lines Inc. v. Columbus Cello-Poly Corp.*, 32 F. Supp. 2d 118, 128 (S.D.N.Y. 1997) ("Courts must apply COGSA, when its terms so require, no matter where the bill of lading was issued."). By the statute's own terms, COGSA applies to contracts of carriage[9] {—443—} of goods to or from United States ports in foreign trade. *See* 46 U.S.C. § 30701 (Notes § 13) ("[COGSA] shall apply to all contracts for carriage of goods by sea to or from ports of the United States in foreign trade."); *Royal Ins. Co. of Am. v. Orient Overseas Container Line Ltd.*, 525 F.3d 409, 416 (6th Cir. 2008) (listing cases). Because the Bill of Lading is a contract to transport goods in foreign trade from a United States port (Cleveland) to a foreign port (China), COGSA applies.[10]

---

[9] Under COGSA:

The term "contract of carriage" applies only to contracts of carriage covered by a bill of lading or any similar document of title, insofar as such document relates to the carriage of goods by sea, including any bill of lading or any similar document as aforesaid issued under or pursuant to a charter party from the moment at which such bill of lading or similar document of title regulates the relations between a carrier and a holder of the same.

46 U.S.C. § 30701 (Notes § 1(b)).

[10] Dimond asserts that we must attempt to "determine what law—maritime or state or federal common law—governs the various stages of sea and overland portions of the intermodal transport." The district court concluded that Dimond made separate arrangements to transport the Equipment from its plant to Cleveland, and that the Chinese customer was responsible for transport from the port of arrival, Xingang, to wherever it needed to go. *See Dimond Rigging Co.*, 320 F. Supp. 3d at 952–53. Dimond's Complaint asserts that it hired BDP to handle shipping the Equipment to China. Dimond's brief states that it moved the Equipment to Cleveland by truck and rail and notified BDP that it was doing so.

Even if Dimond were to have made arrangements with BDP to cover the overland transportation, we observe that in *Kirby*, 543 U.S. at 27, the Supreme Court resolved the question of how federal courts must determine whether a

2. *Are BDP and Logitrans Carriers?*

The question remains whether BDP and Logitrans are "carriers" within the meaning of COGSA, and so may fairly invoke its one-year statute of limitations. The Bill of Lading lists Logitrans as the carrier. Dimond acknowledges this, then reiterates that COGSA cannot apply [—9—] because it was a non-party to the contract (that it signed) and BDP and Logitrans "are not agents of the vessel or the carrier." Dimond asserts that this is not a suit "between Dimond and the actual carrier," the *Gisele Scan*, but "between Dimond and two companies that represented themselves as licensed carriers." Dimond insists that because Logitrans and BDP are not in compliance with various maritime licensing statutes and regulations, they cannot be carriers.[11]

BDP argues that because Dimond characterized it as a carrier, freight forwarder, or NVOCC in the Complaint, assuming all allegations are true, it is covered by the COGSA statute of limitations. BDP asserts that COGSA applies "even where a party's role is uncertain, based on how the parties to a contract of carriage represent themselves or are viewed by the other parties to the contract." The cases BDP cites for this

---

contract for maritime and land transport is a maritime contract. The Court explained that "so long as a bill of lading requires substantial carriage of goods by sea, its purpose is to effectuate maritime commerce—and thus it is a maritime contract." *Ibid.* Even if it provides for *some* overland transport, it is still a maritime contract as long as the case is not inherently local. *Ibid.* The Bill of Lading requires transport from the port of Cleveland to Xingang. It does not refer to any other ground transportation. We have already concluded that, contrary to Dimond's assertions, this is obviously a maritime dispute.

[11] Dimond insists that "the carrier clearly states that Dimond is NOT and was not the shipper in this case." It supports this proposition by citing the Denmark Bill of Lading, which expressly identifies Dimond (there d/b/a as Absolute Rigging and Millwrights, *see supra* note 3), as the shipper. The other Bill of Lading, which identifies Dimond as the "Merchant," states that that term includes shippers. *See supra* note 4. We fail to understand how Dimond can squarely make this argument in light of the evidence it cites.

proposition are not authoritative: one is unpublished, and all are from district courts that are not within this circuit. Logitrans maintains that because it was the Carrier on the Bill of Lading, and based {–444–} on its role, it was a "carrier" within the meaning of COGSA. Both BDP and Logitrans assert that, in any event, the statute of limitations applies through the Himalaya Clause.

The district court observed that *Federal Marine Terminals*, 2014 WL 4809427, at *3, had found that the Bill of Lading's Himalaya Clause included contractors who were not even listed on the Bill of Lading. *Dimond Rigging*, 320 F. Supp. 3d at 953. Applying this reasoning, the district court concluded that, "regardless of their specific roles in the transaction," both Logitrans and BDP were subject to COGSA. *Ibid.* It did not make any findings regarding whether BDP and Logitrans were "carriers." *Ibid.* The problem with this approach is that it ignored the fact that COGSA's one-year statute of limitations does not apply to *every* party in the transaction. Specifically: "[T]he *carrier and the ship* shall be discharged from all liability in respect of loss or damage unless suit is brought within one year after delivery of the goods or the date when the goods should have been delivered[.]" 46 U.S.C. § 30701 (Notes § 3(6)) (emphasis added). Parties may extend COGSA by "adding provisions to bills of lading extending the COGSA [—10—] regime to any and all agents or independent contractors who participate in the shipment of goods under a particular contract." *Fortis Corp.*, 597 F.3d at 792 (citing *Kirby*, 543 U.S. at 30–31). In other words, COGSA permits the use of Himalaya Clauses to limit parties' liability. *Ibid.* But merely because a Bill of Lading contains a Himalaya Clause does not mean that the Clause covers *every* entity or individual involved in a transaction.

We first consider whether Logitrans and BDP are carriers within the meaning of COGSA. *See Sabah Shipyard v. M/V Harbel Tapper*, 178 F.3d 400, 404 (5th Cir. 1999) (explaining that COGSA liability limits only apply to carriers); *Shonac Corp. v. Maersk, Inc.*, 159 F. Supp. 2d 1020, 1025 (S.D. Ohio 2001) (discussing carriers). A "carrier" under

COGSA means "the owner, manager, charterer, agent, or master of a vessel." 46 U.S.C. § 30701; *see also id.* (Notes § 1(a)) ("The term 'carrier' includes the owner or the charterer who enters into a contract of carriage with a shipper."). "COGSA provides that 'carriers' are subject to certain statutory 'responsibilities and liabilities,' and in turn they are provided with certain 'rights and immunities,' such as [a] one-year statute of limitations . . . ." *Fortis Corp.*, 597 F.3d at 787. An NVOCC, as noted, *supra*, consolidates cargo from various shippers and issues a bill of lading. *Prima U.S. Inc. v. Panalpina, Inc.*, 223 F.3d 126, 129 (2d Cir. 2000) (explaining that NVOCCs are carriers under COGSA). A freight forwarder[12] "facilitates the movement of cargo to the ocean vessel." *Ibid.* "Freight forwarders generally make arrangements for the movement of cargo at the request of clients . . . . a freight forwarder does *not* issue a bill of lading, and is therefore not liable to a shipper for anything that occurs to the goods being shipped." *Ibid.* (emphasis in original) (citing *United States v. Am. Union Trans.*, 327 U.S. 437, 442–43 (1946)).

In *Fortis Corp.*, 597 F.3d at 789, we considered whether a ship's manager was a carrier under COGSA. We focused on the plain language of COGSA in concluding that the manager was not a carrier. *Id.* at 789–92. *See also* {–445–} *Shonac Corp.*, 159 F. Supp. 2d at 1026 (discussing the "plain language" approach for assessing whether a party is a carrier). Under this approach, a [—11—] court considers whether a party satisfies the statutory definition.[13] *See Sabah Shipyard*,

---

[12] BDP asserts in its brief that it "was and is a licensed NVOCC." The record contains a copy of BDP's Ocean Transportation Intermediary ("OTI") License. The License states that BDP is authorized to provide freight-forwarding services.

[13] In *Shonac Corp. v. Maersk, Inc.*, 159 F. Supp. 2d 1020, 1026 (S.D. Ohio 2001), the district court identified a second approach, set forth in *Zima Corp. v. M.V. Roman Pazinski*, 493 F. Supp. 268, 273 (S.D.N.Y. 1980). Under this approach, a party may be determined to be a carrier through a four-factor test: (1) how the party's obligation is expressed in documents pertaining to the agreement; (2) the history of dealings between the parties; (3) whether the party issued a bill of lading; and (4) how the party charged the shipper.

178 F.3d at 405. This is an assessment of *function*, rather than *form*. *Prima U.S. Inc.*, 223 F.3d at 130 n.1 (explaining that a party calling itself a freight forwarder that performed carrier functions would be a carrier). The key inquiry is what the party did. If it issued a bill of lading, then it is usually a "carrier" under COGSA. *See id.* at 129; *Sabah Shipyard*, 178 F.3d at 405; *Shonac Corp.*, 159 F. Supp. 2d at 1026. It is not dispositive that the party hired a third party to actually carry the goods. *See Sabah Shipyard*, 178 F.3d at 405; *Shonac Corp.*, 159 F. Supp. 2d at 1026.

We turn to the Complaint and the Bill of Lading. Because this is an appeal from a Motion to Dismiss, we must construe Dimond's factual allegations as true. *See Hall*, 727 F.3d at 453. Dimond alleged that BDP represented that BDP would handle all aspects of the shipment including, *inter alia*, providing a ship, dispatching the shipments, handling export documents, and preparing bills of lading. Dimond asserted that BDP had "subcontracted its shipping/freight forwarding services/obligations" to Logitrans. BDP apparently obtained one ship for Dimond and provided a booking note, but the first ship became unavailable. BDP also allegedly made all the arrangements for the stevedores to load the ship. Dimond alleges that after the original ship was no longer available, BDP notified it that Logitrans would be involved in shipping the Equipment, and that BDP and Logitrans ultimately selected the *Gisele Scan*. BDP issued the Bill of Lading, which identified Logitrans as the "carrier" to Dimond.

Assuming Dimond's allegations about Appellees' roles are true, BDP appears to have engaged in some freight-forwarding services, such as securing the ship, handling export documents, and making arrangements for stevedores to load the Equipment. *See Prima U.S. Inc.*, 223 F.3d at 129. BDP was not

Ibid.; *see also Sabah Shipyard v. M/V Harbel Tapper*, 178 F.3d 400, 405 n.2 (5th Cir. 1999). In *Fortis Corp. Ins., S.A. v. Viken Ship Mgmt. AS*, 597 F.3d 784, 789 (6th Cir. 2010), we focused on the language of the statute instead of a multi-factor test.

responsible for transporting the Equipment to the Port of Cleveland—Dimond asserts that it handled that. BDP, however, issued the Bill of Lading, which is a service provided by a carrier. *Ibid.*; *Sabah Shipyard*, 178 F.3d at 405; *Shonac Corp.*, 159 F. [—12—] Supp. 2d at 1026. Logitrans was also involved in securing the ship. It is listed as the "carrier" on the Bill of Lading. Dimond also refers to Logitrans as the "carrier" in its briefs.

Sabah Shipyard is illustrative in resolving whether BDP and Logitrans are "carriers" under COGSA. In that case, Sabah had to ship some equipment to Malaysia. 178 F.3d at 403. IMB won the bid to transport the equipment. IMB's agent, Intermarine, issued a bill of lading. After some of the equipment slid into the Singapore harbor, Sabah filed suit seeking damages under COGSA. The district court found that the defendants were liable for negligence but did not apply a COGSA limit on liability because it held that IMB {–446–} and Intermarine were forwarders, not carriers. *Ibid.* The Fifth Circuit concluded that the district court erred when it determined that IMB and Intermarine were not carriers within the meaning of COGSA. *Id.* at 406. The Fifth Circuit explained that "[t]o determine whether a party is a COGSA carrier, we have followed COGSA's plain language, focusing on whether the party entered into a contract of carriage with a shipper." *Id.* at 405. Because IMB and Intermarine entered into a contract of carriage—namely, they "agreed to carry Sabah's goods by sea, and they issued a bill of lading[,]" they were carriers. *Ibid.*

BDP entered into a contract of carriage with Dimond because it took on the responsibility of transporting the Equipment by sea. BDP issued the Bill of Lading. *Dimond Rigging*, 320 F. Supp. 3d at 949. BDP is a carrier. *See Sabah Shipyard*, 178 F.3d at 405; *Bunge Edible Oil Corp. v. M/Vs Torm Rask & Fort Steele*, 949 F.2d 786, 788–89 (5th Cir. 1992) (explaining that charterer of vessel who enters into contract of carriage with shipper is a carrier); *Nitram, Inc. v. Cretan Life*, 599 F.2d 1359, 1370 (5th Cir. 1979) (concluding that party that entered into a contract of carriage covered by a bill of lading is a carrier within COGSA's definition). Logitrans also entered into a contract of carriage with Dimond. It signed the Bill of Lading and is identified as the "carrier." Accordingly, Logitrans is also a carrier. *See Bunge Edible Oil Corp.*, 949 F.2d at 788; *Nitram, Inc.*, 599 F.2d at 1370. Because we conclude that BDP and Logitrans are "carriers" within the meaning of COGSA, there is no need to address the Himalaya Clause.

Dimond argues that equitable estoppel should bar BDP and Logitrans from benefiting from COGSA's one-year statute of limitations because BDP and Logitrans were not in [—13—] compliance with COGSA. Dimond maintains that we should apply equitable estoppel to "refuse to validate Defendant's wrongful conduct in this case through a Motion to Dismiss on limitations grounds arising from a statute with which they did not comply." Dimond offers a list of various federal shipping laws and regulations that it asserts BDP and Logitrans have violated and argues that because they misrepresented their status as licensed entities, they should not be allowed to use COGSA as a defense. Dimond has not identified *any* portion of COGSA that the Appellees have allegedly not complied with.

The district court ruled that there was no basis to apply equitable estoppel because COGSA does not include licensure provisions. *Dimond Rigging*, 320 F. Supp. 3d at 953–54. To be sure, COGSA does not supersede rights and obligations set forth in other federal statutes. *See* 46 U.S.C. § 30701 (Notes §§ 8, 12). COGSA establishes "particularized duties and obligations upon, and grants stated immunities" to carriers. *Robert C. Herd & Co. v. Krawill Mach. Corp.*, 359 U.S. 297, 301 (1959). We explained in *Fortis Corp.*, 597 F.3d at 789, that COGSA "was drafted to address the belief that carriers used their superior bargaining power against shippers when contracting for the carriage of goods, and could often dictate the terms of bills of lading to exempt themselves from any liability." Nonetheless, the district court was quite correct that COGSA does not concern itself with licensing.

Dimond's complaint does not allege that BDP and Logitrans represented that they were in compliance with COGSA. For Dimond to estop BDP and Logitrans from using COGSA as a defense, it would have to show that it detrimentally relied on such representations. *See Thomas v. Miller*, 489 F.3d 293, 302 (2007) (setting {–447–} out elements of equitable estoppel); *see also Oxford Shipping Co., Ltd. v. N.H. Trading Corp.*, 697 F.2d 1, 3–4 (1st Cir. 1982) (equitable estoppel claim under COGSA). It has not done so.

Dimond also maintains that the Bill of Lading is an illegal contract because, as unlicensed entities, BDP and Logitrans could not issue an enforceable Bill of Lading, although Dimond suggests that BDP might be a licensed freight forwarder. BDP and Logitrans dispute the accuracy of Dimond's licensing arguments. BDP asserts that the record below shows that it has been a licensed Ocean Transport Intermediary under the Federal Maritime Commission [—14—] ("FMC") since 1999.[14] Logitrans maintains that it is not required to have a license because it is a "vessel/cargo/charter broker." Appellees also insist that licensure is irrelevant to the application of COGSA and the lack of a license does not void a contract. As noted above, the district court only ruled that COGSA does not contain licensing requirements. It did not take judicial notice of BDP's license or make any findings on that issue.

Dimond points to FMC regulations concerning licensing, particularly 46 C.F.R. § 515.3, which provides: "Except as otherwise provided in this part, no person in the United States may act as an ocean transport intermediary unless that person holds a valid license issued by the Commission." Dimond insists that FMC regulations, specifically *id.* § 515.2(h)(5) and (k)(4), prohibit an unlicensed person (Logitrans) or a licensed freight-forwarder (BDP) from issuing a legally-enforceable bill of lading. Subsection (h) in that regulation defines "[f]reight forwarding

---

[14] Dimond argues that BDP only obtained a license in 2013, *after* the events at issue.

services," which "refers to the dispatching of shipments on behalf of others" to facilitate shipments by a common carrier, "which may include, but are not limited to . . . [p]reparing and/or processing common carrier bills of lading or other shipping documents." *Id.* § 515.2(h)(5). Subsection (k)(4) states that NVOCC services "may include . . . [i]ssuing bills of lading or other shipping documents." *Id.* (k)(4). This definitional regulation may identify what certain services within the regulations *are* or *include*, but it does not contain any language establishing, as Dimond argues, that BDP could not issue a legally-enforceable bill of lading.

Assuming, for the sake of argument, that an unlicensed entity issued the Bill of Lading, we briefly consider whether an unlicensed entity may make a valid contract. The parties dispute whether *Adams Express Co. v. Darden*, 286 F. 61 (6th Cir. 1923), supports the argument that an unlicensed entity may create a valid and enforceable contact. In *Adams Express*, the shipper arranged for a carrier to transport six horses. In violation of the Interstate Commerce Act, the carrier misrepresented the horses' value to pay lower tariff rates. *Id.* at 62–63. The carrier was negligent and the car containing the horses wrecked, killing five horses. The shipper sued and was awarded the value of the horses. The carrier appealed, arguing that because it violated the Act, the shipping contract was void. *Id.* at 63. We explained that whether the contract was void and unenforceable depended on the public policy of the United States. *Id.* at 65. The **[—15—]** statute penalized the carrier's practices (and would have penalized the shipper as well), but it "never declared the contract of carriage unenforceable . . . ." *Ibid.* We offered the following analysis: "[W]hen a statute imposes specific penalties for its violation, where the act is not malum in se, and the purpose of the statute can be accomplished without declaring contracts in violation thereof illegal, the inference is that it was not the {–448–} legislative intent to render such contracts illegal and unenforceable." *Ibid.* Applying this principle, we concluded that "Congress presumably believed" that it was better to permit suit to hold a carrier liable for the value of the items

destroyed by its negligence, even if the carrier had violated the Act and was subject to the penalties. *Ibid.*

Dimond argues that *Adams Express* cannot apply because there are no penalties in the Shipping Act for operating without a license and operating without a license is malum in se.[15] As to the first point, whatever the Act may say, FMC regulations pursuant to the Act do, in fact, impose civil penalties for operating without a license. *See* 46 C.F.R. § 515.1(b) (civil penalty that does not exceed $9,000 per violation, unless said violation was knowing or willful, in which case penalty may not exceed $45,000 per violation). Dimond's insistence that *only* licensed entities may operate is further undermined by FMC regulations that permit operations without a license. *See, e.g., id.* § 515.4(c) (common carriers or their agents may perform freight-forwarding services without a license with respect to cargo carried under carrier's own bill of lading).

The FMC regulatory scheme surrounding licensing emphasizes experience and character, but also financial dependability, and compliance with other federal statutes and regulations. *See id.* § 515.11. The bond requirements ensure that claims against an OTI may be adequately compensated in the event that a complaint is filed with the FMC— although this is *not* the sole remedy. *See id.* § 515.23. It does not appear that the purpose of these regulations may only be accomplished by voiding a bill of lading issued by an unlicensed party in violation of the **[—16—]** regulations. As Dimond has not offered *any* authority within the Shipping Act or its regulations that states that such a bill of lading is unenforceable, we reject these arguments.

---

[15] Operating without a license is an act that is purely prohibited by statute, rather than inherently wrong in and of itself. *Compare malum in se*, Black's Law Dictionary (8th ed. 2004) ("A crime or act that is inherently immoral, such as murder, arson, or rape."), *with malum prohibitum, id.* ("An act that is a crime merely because it is prohibited by statute, although the act itself is not necessarily immoral.").

The Bill of Lading is a contract of carriage, subject to COGSA. BDP and Logitrans are carriers as the term is defined in COGSA. We reject Dimond's arguments that the Appellees should be estopped from using the one-year statute of limitations as a defense, and that BDP could not issue a legally enforceable Bill of Lading. Accordingly, we do not need to address whether state statutes of limitations would bar Dimond's action even if COGSA did not apply. The district court did not err in concluding that COGSA's one-year statute of limitations barred Dimond's suits.

C. Default

Dimond asserts that the district court should have entered a default against Logitrans because it did not answer Dimond's Complaint. Within the time permitted to respond, Logitrans's President sent Dimond a letter that answered the gist of the Complaint. Logitrans, however, failed to file any responsive pleading with the court. After Dimond asked the district court to enter a default on December 29, 2017, Logitrans filed a memorandum opposing the entry of default on January 3, 2018. The district court denied Dimond's request for default and ordered Logitrans to file an amended answer by January 16. Logitrans filed its motion to dismiss by the deadline. {–449–}

An order that denies a motion for a default is not immediately appealable. *McNutt v. Cardox Corp.*, 329 F.2d 107, 108 (6th Cir. 1964). Dimond appealed from the final judgment of the district court, which would include all prior interlocutory orders and rulings that were not reviewable until the final judgment. *See Tetro v. Elliott Popham Pontiac, Oldsmobile, Buick & GMC Trucks, Inc.*, 173 F.3d 988, 993 (6th Cir. 1999) ("[A]n appeal from a final judgment generally brings up all prior interlocutory orders and rulings that were not reviewable until the entry of a final judgment."). The district court dismissed Dimond's case, and therefore the denial of the motion of default is reviewable along with the order of dismissal. Because Dimond has appealed from the entry of a final judgment, the court has jurisdiction over this issue on appeal. *Ibid.* [—17—]

Logitrans argues that Dimond has waived this issue on appeal because it did not identify this issue in the "issues presented for review" section of its brief.[16] Federal Rule of Appellate Procedure 28(a)(5) states that the appellant's brief "*must* contain . . . a statement of the issues presented for review . . . ." (Emphasis added). Applying this rule, we have concluded that when an appellant does not comply by listing *all* the issues presented for review in the statement of issues, the appellant waives that argument. *See United States v. Calvetti*, 836 F.3d 654, 664 (6th Cir. 2016); *United States v. Honeycutt*, 816 F.3d 362, 370 (6th Cir. 2016), *rev'd on other grounds by* 137 S. Ct. 1626 (2017); *Barrett v. Detroit Heading, LLC*, 311 F. App'x 779, 796 (6th Cir. 2009). Because Dimond did not include its claim that the district court should have granted it a default against Logitrans in its statement of issues, it is waived.

The judgment of the district court is AFFIRMED.

---

[16] Dimond offers no response to this argument in its Reply Brief.

United States Court of Appeals
for the Sixth Circuit

No. 18-1421

MAGER
vs.
WISCONSIN CENT. LTD.

Appeal from the United States District Court for the
Western District of Michigan at Marquette

Decided: May 15, 2019

Citation: 924 F.3d 831, 7 Adm. R. 372 (6th Cir. 2019).

Before GUY, SUTTON, and NALBANDIAN, Circuit
Judges.

[—1—] {–833–} GUY, Circuit Judge: {–834–}

Peter Mager sought to recover damages under the Federal Employer's Liability Act (FELA), 45 U.S.C. § 51, *et seq.*, for injuries he allegedly [—2—] sustained while employed by Wisconsin Central Ltd. (WCL) as a trackman at a railway yard near Marquette, Michigan. Mager appeals the dismissal of his complaint with prejudice, which was ordered as a sanction primarily for his and his attorney's conduct at a court-ordered independent medical examination. Reviewing the dismissal for abuse of discretion, we affirm.

I.

Mager alleged that he was seriously and permanently injured on July 29, 2013, when he slipped on hydraulic oil that had leaked onto the rear deck of a truck where he was working. Mager filed suit in June 2016, was deposed in June 2017, and was sent notice that defendant had scheduled an independent medical examination (IME) in early August 2017. Plaintiff's counsel, James T. Foley, objected to the IME because the examiner's office was in Appleton, Wisconsin—a substantial drive from where Mager lived in the Upper Peninsula of Michigan. That prompted WCL, through its counsel Mary O'Donnell, to move both for an order compelling the IME pursuant to Rule 35(a) of the Federal Rules of Civil Procedure and to delay the third-party mediation scheduled for late August 2017. At a hearing on the motion on September 27, counsel reached an agreement at the magistrate judge's urging. Namely, it was agreed that Mager would submit to the IME, that WCL would pay his mileage, and that a settlement conference would be scheduled with the court in lieu of mediation. A new Case Management Order was promptly entered on September 28, 2017.

Once the IME was rescheduled, Mager was asked to complete a five-page written questionnaire prior to the appointment. That questionnaire—which is in the record—inquired into Mager's complaints, medical history, medications, prior evaluations, and how and where his injury occurred. When Foley objected to the questionnaire as unnecessary in light of plaintiff's recent deposition, O'Donnell brought the matter before the magistrate judge by way of a conference call. O'Donnell asked that Mager be required to either complete the questionnaire or be interviewed by a doctor's assistant. The magistrate judge "determined that background information was necessary for the IME." Accordingly, a Rule 35 Order was entered the next day expressly directing Mager to "appear at the IME on October 20, 2017 at 10:00 a.m. C.S.T., {–835–} *for an interview by a physician assistant and for Dr. Revord to conduct an IME.* The interview and exam shall not exceed three (3) hours." (Emphasis added.) No other conditions were specified. [—3—]

Mager appeared for the IME as directed and was joined there by his attorney James Foley, who not only remained present throughout the appointment but also surreptitiously made an audio recording of the visit. Later, Foley conceded that he did so without prior notice to defense counsel; stated that he regularly attended IMEs with other clients; and explained that he had determined ahead of time that one-party-consent recording is legal in Wisconsin. As a result of that recording, however, there can be no dispute that Mager himself repeatedly declined to answer relevant questions about his condition, his medications, and how the injury occurred.

An unofficial transcript of the recording[1] reflects that although Mager provided some identifying information to the receptionist upon arrival, he and Foley did not allow his driver's license to be copied. An assistant then escorted Mager and Foley to an exam room, where she attempted to conduct an interview. Mager was asked what problems or concerns he wanted to have addressed—one of the questions highlighted on the questionnaire—but Mager would not do so and said he had already answered questions about his problems during his deposition. Foley interjected that Mager was there to be evaluated at defendant's request and not to have any problems addressed. The assistant explained that the doctor still wanted some of the questions answered, but Mager replied that he was sure that they had all of his medical records. Finally, Mager declined to list the medications he was taking, again referring the assistant to the deposition transcript that he had brought with him. That concluded the assistant's attempt to interview Mager.

Forewarned, Dr. Revord introduced himself to Mager and Foley; confirmed that Mager did not want to answer any questions; indicated that he had reviewed Mager's records; and took the copy of Mager's deposition when it was offered. During that exchange, Foley also stated that Mager was "not trying to be an obstructionist" but did not want to "rehash" his deposition testimony. Dr. Revord explained that he was there to see Mager, listen to his story, and write a report evaluating his condition and what had caused it. Dr. Revord tried to ask about how the injury occurred and about Mager's physical problems, but Mager referred him to the deposition [—4—] for those answers. The full exchange was as follows:

---

[1] In fairly contentious briefing, WCL's counsel impugns the transcript because it was made by an unidentified individual in Foley's office. Despite having received a copy of the recording, however, WCL does not suggest that the transcript is inaccurate in any way. Indeed, WCL relies on that very transcript as proof of deliberate violation of the Rule 35 Order.

[Dr. Revord]: . . . Now I was a little confused. You're talking in the summons of oil and slipping in the back of a truck but on your, when you filled out the injury report that day, you were saying you were walking to the front door of the truck and your legs gave way.

[Peter Mager]: Everything is in the deposition there.

DR: Got it.

PM: We went over all the, all the stuff.

DR: Got it.

PM: I'm not trying to give you a hard time.

DR: I understand.

PM: All the information should be there. {–836–}

DR: I think you are smart to listen to your attorney. If your attorney, if my attorney told me to dye my hair red, I'd dye my hair red. You know, so if your attorney has told you not to …

[FOLEY]: You're assuming I told him that.

DR: to answer specific questions.

JTF: That might be his own, his own line of thinking.

DR: He had told me, we had been told, eh, that . . . Well is it, let me ask you, is it your idea not to fill out the form?

JTF: That's not relevant doc.

PM: I'm complying with the Order. They told me I had to come down here and be examined by you.

DR: Very good. Ok I will go with the history in the chart and what you said when you filled out the initial report.

(inaudible)

Ok great. Do you want to tell me what problems you are having or would you rather I just look at your deposition?

PM: It's all in the deposition.

Mager then complied as Dr. Revord conducted a physical examination. Lastly, Dr. Revord asked Mager what medications he was currently taking, but Mager declined to answer and responded that it was all in his deposition and medical records. That concluded the IME. [—5—]

Dr. Revord prepared a six-page report the same day, which noted Mager's refusals to answer questions, relied on a review of Mager's medical and other records, and concluded—in short—that Mager presented with a "volitional" tremor, had no significant pathology in his lumbar region, required no further treatment, and was asserting contradictory claims about how the injury occurred. The report added that Mager's deposition "did not contain the answers to the questions [Dr. Revord] was asking him." The deposition itself is not part of the district court record.[2]

Ten days later, WCL moved to dismiss the complaint pursuant to Rule 37(b)(2)(A)(v) of the Federal Rules of Civil Procedure because Mager had violated the "spirit and letter" of the Rule 35 Order. WCL also argued that it had been denied the opportunity to object to Foley's presence or to have the magistrate judge consider whether to allow Foley's presence as a condition of the IME. Plaintiff's response to the motion was filed one day late—at 1:30 a.m. on November 15—and revealed the audio recording. Defendant replied on November 21.

A hearing was held on November 28, 2017, which also was the date set for the agreed settlement conference. That conference was cancelled, however, because Foley had failed to send a "confidential settlement letter" to the magistrate judge as directed by the Case Management Order. Although the magistrate judge indicated his intention to impose monetary sanctions on counsel for that failure, an order to that effect was not entered prior to the dismissal.

Next, the magistrate judge asked Foley about his and his client's conduct at the IME. Foley insisted that Mager had complied by appearing to be interviewed; stated that he was present at Mager's request; and explained that both his presence and the recording were in response to concerns that the IME might be used as a "de facto deposition." O'Donnell countered that the circumstances showed intentional defiance of the court's order. On December 28, 2017, the magistrate judge issued a report {–837–} and recommendation setting forth the facts, addressing the relevant factors, and concluding that dismissal was warranted because of the "flagrant and repeated misconduct exhibited by Plaintiff and his attorney." Over plaintiff's objections, the district court adopted the R&R and dismissed the complaint with prejudice on [—6—] March 9, 2018. Plaintiff appealed, and, notably, he is no longer represented by Foley.

II.

The decision to dismiss a complaint for failure to comply with a discovery obligation or other court order is reviewed for abuse of discretion. *Nat'l Hockey League v. Metro. Hockey Club, Inc.*, 427 U.S. 639, 642 (1976) (per curiam); *see also Knoll v. Am. Tel. & Tel. Co.*, 176 F.3d 359, 363 (6th Cir. 1999); *Harmon v. CSX Transp., Inc.*, 110 F.3d 364, 366 (6th Cir. 1997).

Rule 37(b) specifically authorizes the imposition of sanctions for failure to comply with a Rule 35 Order, or for failing to obey a scheduling or other pretrial order under Rule 16(f)(1)(C) of the Federal Rules of Civil Procedure. Under Rule 37(b)(2)(A), "a district court may sanction parties who fail to comply with its orders in a variety of ways, including dismissal of the lawsuit." *Bass v. Jostens, Inc.*,

---

[2] Dr. Revord's report also commented that although Mager had refused to provide identification, "claimant appears to be the same individual . . . [in] photographs provided to me." Nothing in the record suggests otherwise.

71 F.3d 237, 241 (6th Cir. 1995). Four factors are to be considered in determining whether dismissal is an appropriate sanction for failure to comply with a discovery obligation or other court order:

> (1) whether the party's failure is due to willfulness, bad faith, or fault; (2) whether the adversary was prejudiced by the dismissed party's conduct; (3) whether the dismissed party was warned that failure to cooperate could lead to dismissal; and (4) whether less drastic sanctions were imposed or considered before dismissal was ordered.

United States v. Reyes, 307 F.3d 451, 458 (6th Cir. 2002) (quoting *Knoll*, 176 F.3d at 363). "Although no one factor is dispositive, dismissal is proper if the record demonstrates delay or contumacious conduct." *Id.*; *see also Harmon*, 110 F.3d at 366-67. "Contumacious conduct refers to behavior that is perverse in resisting authority and stubbornly disobedient." *Carpenter v. City of Flint*, 723 F.3d 700, 705 (6th Cir. 2013) (citation and internal quotation marks omitted).[3] [—7—]

A. Willfulness, Bad Faith, or Fault

To show that a party's failure to comply was motivated by bad faith, willfulness, or fault, the conduct "must display either an intent to thwart judicial proceedings or a reckless disregard for the effect of [his] conduct on those proceedings." *Carpenter*, 723 F.3d at 705 (alteration in original) (quoting *Wu v. T.W. Wang, Inc.*, 420 F.3d 641, 643 (6th Cir. 2005)). This court has expressed reluctance to uphold a dismissal "merely to discipline an errant attorney" to the detriment of an innocent client. *Knoll*, 176 F.3d at 363 (citation omitted); *see also Mulbah v. Detroit Bd. of Educ.*, 261 F.3d 586, 590 (6th Cir. 2001). Thus, notwithstanding the Supreme

Court's declaration that dismissal of a plaintiff's complaint based on his attorney's unexcused conduct would *not* impose an undue penalty on the client in *Link v. Wabash R.R. Co.*, 370 U.S. 626, 633-34 (1962), this court {-838-} has instructed that "[d]ismissal is usually inappropriate where the neglect is solely the fault of the attorney," *Carpenter*, 723 F.3d at 704 (alteration in original and citation omitted).

Here, although there were some failures that were attributable solely to counsel, the magistrate judge expressly found that "Plaintiff and his attorney acted in bad faith and willfully violated the [Rule 35] discovery order" that "required Plaintiff to submit to an interview." Because that finding is supported by the record, it was not an abuse of discretion to find this factor weighs in favor of dismissal.

Late or Missing Filings. The magistrate judge identified two instances of failure to comply with a scheduling or pretrial order: (1) the tardy filing of the response to the motion to dismiss; and (2) the failure to submit the confidential settlement letter to the magistrate judge. Submission of a settlement letter was expressly required by court order. The failure to submit the letter caused the cancellation of the settlement conference on the day it was scheduled to occur, and the magistrate judge indicated his intention to impose sanctions at the time.

Violation of Rule 35 Order. A court "may order a party whose mental or physical condition . . . is in controversy to submit to a physical or mental examination by a suitably licensed or certified examiner." Fed. R. Civ. P. 35(a)(1). The order is to be "made only on a motion for good cause," and "must specify the time, place, manner, conditions, and scope of the [—8—] examination, as well as the person or persons who will perform it." Fed. R. Civ. P. 35(a)(2)(A), (B). There is no dispute that Mager's physical condition was in controversy. Both the extent and cause of his injuries were contested and central to his claim, and counsel agreed that he would submit to the examination on the condition that defendant pay his mileage. Plaintiff relies on email correspondence to suggest that it was defense

---

[3] When Rule 37(b) applies, there is no need to rely on the court's inherent powers or on Rule 41(b)'s authorization to dismiss for failure "to prosecute or to comply with these rules or a court order." Fed. R. Civ. P. 41(b); *see also Societe Internationale Pour Participations Industrielles Et Commerciales, S.A. v. Rogers*, 357 U.S. 197, 207 (1958).

counsel who asked that the questionnaire be completed. Be that as it may, what matters is that, as the magistrate judge found, the order requiring Mager to submit to an interview "was the result of a telephone conference in which Plaintiff's counsel discussed his concerns with allowing an interview." In other words, notwithstanding Foley's objections and concerns, Mager was expressly ordered to submit to an interview as part of the IME.

Mager cannot credibly claim either that he was unaware of the obligation or that he complied with it by sitting for the interview but declining to answer questions regarding his condition, his current medications, or how his injury occurred. Foley represented that he and Mager had discussed their concerns about the interview, and Foley denied that he told Mager what to do. The fact is, Mager arrived for the IME with a copy of his deposition transcript and his attorney in tow, and then proceeded to repeatedly deflect questions by stating that the answers could be found in his deposition or prior medical records. Now that he is no longer represented by Foley, plaintiff asserts that it "was unreasonable for the court to conclude that he did anything other than follow the instructions of his attorney when he attended the IME." But Mager cannot escape the consequences of his own actions by laying blame on the advice of counsel. The actions that Mager took with the support of Foley were deliberate and calculated to circumvent the order requiring him to submit to an interview as part of the IME.

Counsel's Presence and Secret Recording. Although not a violation of the Rule 35 Order itself, the magistrate judge found that Foley's unexpected attendance at and surreptitious recording of the IME "show[ed] bad faith and a lack of respect {–839–} for the integrity of the legal profession." Plaintiff's new counsel concedes that Foley "should have discussed his desire to attend and record the IME with opposing counsel and, if necessary, raised the issue with the court prior to the IME." Admitting that Foley's conduct should not be condoned, plaintiff argues that Mager had no way of knowing that it was improper. But Mager's hands are not so clean. **[—9—]**

Foley and Mager were concerned that the examiner was a defense-side expert who may try to elicit information adverse to their case—*i.e.*, the "de facto" deposition argument—and "discussed the advantages of audio-taping the entire IME event." (Pl's Br., p. 17.) There is no reason to doubt that Mager knew Foley was secretly recording the visit on a hidden cell phone, which was deceitful even if not actually illegal in Wisconsin. That recording, in turn, shows that Foley's presence provided support to Mager and furthered the concerted and deliberate effort to thwart the court-ordered interview and avoid questions they did not want to have to answer. Plaintiff's new counsel acknowledges that "[e]ven in state courts where attorneys often attend and videotape an IME, it is most often done with notice to opposing counsel." (Reply Br., p. 5.) It should also go without saying, that, even then, the recording would be done in the open.

Failure to Request Conditions. These actions were found to be particularly egregious because plaintiff's counsel knew or should have known that "federal courts generally do not allow a third-party to be present during an IME or to have an IME recorded unless the party has established a special need or good cause." Plaintiff does not dispute that this is the general rule, although this court has not had occasion to address the parameters of the trial court's discretion to grant or deny such a request. *See, e.g.*, *Elder v. Harrison Twp.*, No. 10-cv-13144, 2014 WL 6668696, at *3-5 (E.D. Mich. Nov. 24, 2014) (finding inherently adversarial nature was not sufficient reason); *Lahar v. Oakland Cty.*, No. 05-72920, 2006 WL 2269340, at *7-8 (E.D. Mich. Aug. 8, 2006) (finding interest in assuring accuracy was insufficient reason); *but see Gohl v. Livonia Pub. Schs.*, No. 12-cv-15199, 2015 WL 1469749, at *2-5 (E.D. Mich. Mar. 30, 2015) (allowing parental presence for exam of children with cognitive deficiencies but finding no good cause for it to be recorded).

Nor is there reason to think the state courts would condone what happened here. *See, e.g.*, *Metro. Prop. & Cas. v. Overstreet*, 103 S.W.3d 31, 39 (Ky. 2003) (Kentucky's similar rule allows third persons to attend where there is good cause, although an attorney's presence is "most likely to be problematic because of the potential to unfairly disrupt the examination"). Indeed, even though Michigan law provides a statutory right to have counsel present during an [—10—] IME, that condition would be included in the order. *See* Mich. Ct. R. 2.311 (order "may provide that the attorney for the person to be examined may be present at the examination").[4]

It was not an abuse of discretion to find that the concerted actions of plaintiff and his attorney displayed an intent to thwart {–840–} the judicial proceedings, or at least a reckless disregard for the effect of that conduct on the proceedings. Nor is this a case in which the dismissal was merely to discipline an attorney "to the detriment of an innocent client." *Knoll,* 176 F.3d at 363. This factor weighs in favor of dismissal.

B. Prejudice to the Adversary

As noted earlier, plaintiff conceded that prejudice resulted from the cancellation of the settlement conference on the day it was scheduled to occur. The magistrate judge also found that WCL was prejudiced because Mager and Foley failed to comply with the order requiring him to submit to an interview as part of the IME. Plaintiff argues that there was no prejudice because the refusals did not prevent Dr. Revord from preparing his report and providing an opinion based on a physical examination and review of the prior medical records. In fact, the report did not identify the conditions that Mager claimed were disabling, describe the manner of the injury, or list the medications he was taking at the time. Nor

---

[4] Plaintiff's new counsel wisely abandoned reliance on Wright & Miller, which observes that "the norm in federal court is that counsel will not be allowed to attend unless good cause is presented to justify that." 8B Charles Alan Wright & Arthur R. Miller, *Federal Practice and Procedure* § 2236 at 496 (3d ed. 2010). That same passage also explains that concerns about overreaching or abusive behavior during an IME "can be minimized in other ways, particularly by excluding from evidence any statements made by the party to the doctor relating to nonmedical matters." *Id.*

did Dr. Revord believe the deposition answered the questions he was asking. Plaintiff counters that Dr. Revord did not insist on answers, but Dr. Revord was not wrong in believing that it was not his place to do so. The magistrate judge found that WCL was prevented "from receiving an expert report with all the medical information that the physician was seeking." Although the report was favorable to the defense, it was arguably incomplete and potentially subject to impeachment. Plaintiff has not shown it was clear error to conclude that the deliberate circumvention of the Rule 35 Order prejudiced the ability of the defense to rely on the IME report. [—11—]

C. Prior Warning

The magistrate judge recognized that plaintiff was not expressly warned that failure to comply with the Rule 35 Order could lead to dismissal, although WCL's motion provided some notice that dismissal was a possibility. *See Reyes,* 307 F.3d at 458. When "a plaintiff has not been given notice that dismissal is contemplated, a district court should impose a penalty short of dismissal unless the derelict party has engaged in bad faith or contumacious conduct." *Harmon,* 110 F.3d at 367 (internal quotation marks omitted) (quoting *Harris v. Callwood,* 844 F.2d 1254, 1256 (6th Cir. 1988)). As is discussed at length above, the record supports the conclusion that plaintiff and his attorney deliberately disobeyed the Rule 35 Order through the calculated refusals to answer questions during the IME. As such, the lack of a prior warning would not prevent dismissal of the complaint as a first sanction.

D. Alternative Sanctions

The fourth factor asks whether less drastic sanctions were imposed or considered before dismissal was ordered. They were. The magistrate judge explained that he "considered lesser sanctions, such as imposing costs for the IME, striking Plaintiff's own expert witnesses, and/or striking Plaintiff's claim for permanent disability" but found that "[n]one of these sanctions would reflect the seriousness of the conduct in this case." This consideration also supports the decision to dismiss the complaint pursuant to Rule 37(b)(2)(A)(v).

AFFIRMED.

(Reporter's Note: Concurring Opinion follows on p. 379).

[—12—] {–840–} **SUTTON**, Circuit Judge, concurring:

I join Judge Guy's well-reasoned opinion in full. I write separately to emphasize the propriety of holding parties accountable for their lawyers' actions. {–841–}

Our system of representative litigation makes the parties principals, the lawyers agents. *See* Restatement (Third) of Agency § 1.01 reporter's note c (Am. Law Inst. 2006); Restatement (Third) of the Law Governing Lawyers § 26 cmt. b (Am. Law Inst. 2000); William A. Gregory, *The Law of Agency and Partnership* § 21 (3d ed. 2001). Under tried and true agency principles, parties become bound by the actions of lawyers taken with actual or apparent authority. Restatement (Third) of Agency §§ 2.01–.03; Restatement (Third) of the Law Governing Lawyers §§ 26–27. That understanding has deep roots, centuries-deep roots, in the common law. The thirteenth-century jurist Henry de Bracton wrote that "the attorney represents the person of his lord in almost all matters." 4 Bracton, *On the Laws and Customs of England* 85 (George E. Woodbine ed., Samuel E. Thorne trans., 1977). By Justice Oliver Wendell Holmes' time, the idea had become cliché, the well-worn adage being that the "act of the attorney is the act of his client." Oliver Wendell Holmes, Jr., *Agency*, 5 Harv. L. Rev. 1, 7–8 (1891) (quotation omitted).

This representative ideal pervades every aspect of our modern legal system. We stylize our cases as contests of "Plaintiff v. Defendant" even though the combatants who appear behind the lectern are lawyers, not parties. We write that "plaintiff argues so-and-so," full well knowing that the client often hasn't the foggiest about the obscure arguments his lawyer just submitted on his behalf. The concept even suffuses our vocabulary. The word attorney means one who is attorned—in other words, a person appointed to act for another. 1 *Oxford English Dictionary* 772 (2d ed. 1989). Trying to pry apart a lawyer's representational actions from those of his client is like trying to separate Mark Twain from Samuel Clemens.

One implication of this foundational principle is that parties must be held accountable for their attorneys' misconduct. That's why there is "certainly no merit to the contention that [—13—] dismissal of petitioner's claim because of his counsel's unexcused conduct imposes an unjust penalty on the client. Petitioner voluntarily chose this attorney as his representative in the action, and he cannot now avoid the consequences of the acts or omissions of this freely selected agent." *Link v. Wabash R.R. Co.*, 370 U.S. 626, 633–34 (1962). "Any other notion," the Court added, "would be wholly inconsistent with our system of representative litigation, in which each party is deemed bound by the acts of his lawyer-agent and is considered to have notice of all facts, notice of which can be charged upon the attorney." *Id.* at 634 (quotation omitted). In the past fifty years, the Court has hammered the point over and over. *See Maples v. Thomas*, 565 U.S. 266, 280–81 (2012); *Pioneer Inv. Servs. Co. v. Brunswick Assocs.*, 507 U.S. 380, 396–37 (1993); *Irwin v. Dep't of Veterans Affairs*, 498 U.S. 89, 92–93 (1990); *United States v. Boyle*, 469 U.S. 241, 249–50 (1985).

Even so, our circuit remains queasy about *Link*'s iron-clad logic in sanction cases like this one. Reasoning that dismissal with prejudice unfairly punishes a plaintiff for his lawyer's misdeeds, we have "expressed an extreme reluctance to uphold the dismissal of a case merely to discipline a party's attorney." *Mulbah v. Detroit Bd. of Educ.*, 261 F.3d 586, 590 (6th Cir. 2001); *see also Patterson v. Grand Blanc Twp.*, 760 F.2d 686, 688 (6th Cir. 1985) (per curiam). So it is that "[d]ismissal is usually inappropriate where the neglect is solely the fault of the attorney." {–842–} *Carpenter v. City of Flint*, 723 F.3d 700, 704 (6th Cir. 2013) (quotation omitted).

This sentiment is unfair to the defendant, is inconsistent with other areas of the law, and may do more harm than good for the party it tries to help: the plaintiff. Why should a defendant be made to endure abuses by a plaintiff's lawyer just because the plaintiff was unaware? That is not the way we usually think about it. *See Link*, 370 U.S. at 634 n.10. Our anxiety about harming blameless plaintiffs also breaks sharply from our usual practices. When a plaintiff loses his case because his lawyer filed the complaint outside the statute of limitations, we rarely pause to ask whether the client was responsible for the delay. *See, e.g., Rocheleau v. Elder Living Constr., LLC*, 814 F.3d 398, 400–01 (6th Cir. 2016). In that situation, we treat the lawyer's actions as those of his client, no matter how steep the cost.

The law already marks a deeply grooved path for addressing the grievances of clients bilked out of good claims by bad lawyers. It's called a malpractice lawsuit. *See Link*, 370 U.S. [—14—] at 634 n.10; *Inman v. Am. Home Furniture Placement, Inc.*, 120 F.3d 117, 119 (8th Cir. 1997). A dismissal with prejudice predicated on lawyer misconduct would provide powerful ammunition for a client in a malpractice proceeding. *See* Restatement (Third) of the Law Governing Lawyers § 53 cmt. b. By departing from our traditional rules of agency to protect plaintiffs, we may do just the opposite. If we make party misconduct a near precondition in every dismissal, we unduly complicate the inevitable malpractice action by giving the lawyer a ready defense: My client behaved just as badly as I did. *See Carpenter*, 723 F.3d at 704.

Left to my own devices, I would take a different tack. While a party's conduct may enter the equation in determining whether to dismiss the case with prejudice as a sanction, we should not make it a near precondition for doing so.

United States Court of Appeals for the Seventh Circuit

United States Court of Appeals
for the Seventh Circuit

No. 17-3602

KOPPLIN
vs.
WISCONSIN CENT. LTD.

Appeal from the United States District Court for the
Eastern District of Wisconsin

Decided: February 1, 2019

Citation: 914 F.3d 1099, 7 Adm. R. 382 (7th Cir. 2019).

Before **SYKES, BARRETT,** and **ST. EVE,** Circuit
Judges.

[—1—] {–1101–} SYKES, Circuit Judge:

Jeffery Kopplin brought two claims
against the Wisconsin Central railroad
under the Federal Employers' Liability
Act ("FELA"), 45 U.S.C. §§ 51 *et seq.* Both rest
on the same allegation: that Kopplin injured
his elbow in an effort to operate a broken
railroad switch while employed by Wisconsin
Central. The district court entered summary
judgment for the railroad in part because
Kopplin **[—2—]** could not prove that the
broken switch caused his injury. While the
parties raise several other questions, that
alone is sufficient to affirm.

I. Background

Prior to his injury, Kopplin worked for
Wisconsin Central as a train conductor. On
January 24, 2014, he pulled a train into the
Fond du Lac yard. To bring the train onto the
correct track, Kopplin had to get out and
"throw" a switch, which involves pulling a
handle to correctly align the tracks. The
weather that morning was severe, with below-
freezing temperatures and 20- to 30-mile-per-
hour winds. As a result ice and snow had built
up inside the switch's mechanisms. Kopplin
tried to remove the ice and snow with a simple
broom—the only tool Wisconsin Central had
provided—but after straining himself for
several minutes, the switch would not budge.

Kopplin claims that this effort was the
initial cause of a long-term elbow disability,
though the evidence is less than clear. A video
of the incident shows no immediate signs of
injury. And Kopplin never mentioned any pain
symptoms to his coworkers until two hours
later—time in which he continued to perform
other physical tasks.

After his physician diagnosed him with
medial and lateral epicondylitis, Kopplin took
time off work to receive treatment. Among
other things, he received an effective pain-
relief injection in February. By **{–1102–}** April
the injury had fully healed. But in August the
pain suddenly reemerged when Kopplin tried
to drive a riding lawnmower one-handed while
holding his son. After that his career as a
conductor was effectively over. **[—3—]**

Kopplin then brought two related FELA
claims against Wisconsin Central, both
alleging that the railroad was responsible for
the broken switch and the injury it allegedly
caused. The first is a run-of-the-mill
negligence claim. The second is a negligence
per se claim premised on Wisconsin Central's
alleged failure to comply with 49 C.F.R.
§ 213.135, the regulation that sets national
standards for switches. Kopplin's sole
causation expert was Dr. Etienne Mejia, who
testified by deposition that the pain-relief
injection Kopplin received often provides only
temporary relief, which could explain the
pain's reemergence. However, Dr. Mejia
conceded that he never investigated whether
something other than the January 24 incident
could have caused the initial injury. In fact, he
testified that he knew so little about Kopplin's
job that it would be mere speculation to say
throwing a switch even *could* cause the elbow
injury. Moreover, he admitted that he did not
investigate whether Kopplin's other physical
activities—say, riding a lawnmower in a
dangerous fashion—could have caused the
renewed elbow problems in August.

For two months after the deposition,
Kopplin made no attempt to supplement Dr.
Mejia's testimony. But after Wisconsin
Central moved for summary judgment,
Kopplin attached to his response a new
affidavit by Dr. Mejia. The contents of that
affidavit were markedly different than the
deposition testimony. Dr. Mejia definitively

stated that the January 24 incident caused the elbow injury, explaining that the nature of the injury was so clear that there was no need to even consider other potential causes. In the end, Kopplin's effort to bolster his causation evidence was in vain. The judge refused to consider the affidavit because it contradicted sworn deposition testimony. And without the affidavit, [—4—] she found Dr. Mejia's testimony unreliable under *Daubert v. Merrell Dow Pharmaceuticals, Inc.*, 509 U.S. 579 (1993). As a result, Kopplin had no causation evidence at all.

The judge addressed several other questions, including the extent to which regulations promulgated under the Federal Railroad Safety Act define the standard of care for FELA actions and the extent to which 49 C.F.R. § 213.5(a) imposes a notice requirement for negligence per se claims. Because the failure to prove causation is fatal to both FELA claims, *see Walden v. Ill. Cent. Gulf R.R.*, 975 F.2d 361, 364 (7th Cir. 1992), we need not reach those issues here.

II. Discussion

We review a summary judgment de novo, asking whether the movant has shown "that there is no genuine dispute as to any material fact." *Hansen v. Fincantieri Marine Grp., LLC*, 763 F.3d 832, 836 (7th Cir. 2014) (quotation marks omitted). We review the exclusion of the affidavit "for abuse of discretion, giving the trial judge much deference." *Buckner v. Sam's Club, Inc.*, 75 F.3d 290, 292 (7th Cir. 1996). Finally, "we review *de novo* a district court's application of the *Daubert* framework. If the district court properly adhered to the *Daubert* framework, then we review its decision to exclude (or not to exclude) expert testimony for abuse of discretion." *C.W. ex rel. Wood v. Textron, Inc.*, 807 F.3d 827, 835 (7th Cir. 2015) (citations omitted).

We start with the admissibility of Dr. Mejia's affidavit. As the judge explained, a party may not "create an issue {–1103–} of fact by submitting an affidavit whose conclusions contradict prior deposition or other sworn testimony." *Buckner*, 75 F.3d at 292. The affidavit here contradicts Dr. Mejia's

testimony in [—5—] at least two ways. First, Dr. Mejia was asked at his deposition whether "there could be other various causes of this type of condition" besides the January 24 incident. He answered unequivocally, "Yes." But then in his affidavit, Dr. Mejia wrote that there was no need to consider other causes because "[t]he etiology and diagnosis [were] clear" that "the patient suffered from left traumatic medial epicondylitis as a result of the injury of January 24, 2014." That clearly contradicts his original statement that other causes could be at play.

Second, Dr. Mejia was asked at his deposition whether throwing a switch "seem[ed] like the kind of activity that could lead to the tendinosis," and he answered, "It would be speculation on my part … ." That admission is squarely at odds with his affidavit's definitive conclusion that Kopplin injured his elbow throwing the switch. *See id.* at 293 (excluding a supplemental affidavit's detailed description of a fact when the affiant had disclaimed knowledge of that same fact at her deposition).

To be sure, we have carved out several exceptions to the general rule barring contradictory supplemental affidavits. None apply here. For instance, we've said that a party may offer an affidavit in response to a summary-judgment motion "to clarify ambiguous or confusing testimony." *Bank of Ill. v. Allied Signal Safety Restraint Sys.*, 75 F.3d 1162, 1171 (7th Cir. 1996). Yet nothing about Dr. Mejia's deposition testimony was ambiguous or confusing: without qualification, he said that other factors could have caused this condition. Similarly, while we have held that an affidavit may contradict sworn deposition testimony if "it is based on newly discovered evidence," *id.* at 1172, even Kopplin concedes [—6—] that Dr. Mejia received all of the materials supporting his affidavit before his deposition. Finally, a new affidavit may be appropriate if the earlier testimony was "the result of a memory lapse." *Cook v. O'Neill*, 803 F.3d 296, 298 (7th Cir. 2015). Kopplin argues that this exception applies because Dr. Mejia did not have the full medical record at his fingertips during the deposition itself. But nothing in Dr. Mejia's responses indicates that he was struggling to recall what those records said. To the contrary, his responses were direct and honest admissions that he never considered certain issues at all.

Even if the affidavit were perfectly consistent with Dr. Mejia's prior statements, a larger problem remains. In essence the affidavit sets forth a brand new expert opinion on a topic beyond the scope of anything in Dr. Mejia's prior disclosures. In his original expert report, Dr. Mejia discussed Kopplin's treatment history and prognosis but never explained how the switch actually caused the disability. The issue surfaced for the first time—at least to any meaningful degree—in the affidavit itself. By then, the time had long passed to disclose a new report on a previously unexplored topic: Kopplin attached it as an exhibit to his summary-judgment response on June 27, 2017, months after the district court's December 30, 2016 deadline for Kopplin's expert reports. See FED. R. CIV. P. 26(a)(2)(D) ("A party must make [expert] disclosures at the time and in the sequence that the court orders.").

Without the affidavit the *Daubert* analysis is relatively straightforward. Under *Daubert* the court considers "whether the expert is proposing to testify to (1) scientific knowledge that (2) will assist the trier of fact to understand [—7—] or determine a fact in issue." 509 U.S. at 592. The ultimate question is {–1104–} whether the expert's approach is scientifically valid, which requires a careful examination of its "evidentiary relevance and reliability." *Id.* at 594–95. The focus is on the expert's methodology, not his ultimate conclusions. *See id.* at 595.

Both relevance and reliability are problems here. As to reliability, the judge identified a number of causation questions that Dr. Mejia conceded he never considered. Each concession significantly undermined the validity of his methods. The most troubling were his admissions that he never considered whether factors other than the switch could have caused the initial injury in January, nor whether other factors could have caused the renewed symptoms in August. The judge

found this unacceptable, and that was not an abuse of discretion. *See Brown v. Burlington N. Santa Fe Ry. Co.*, 765 F.3d 765, 773–74, 2 Adm. R. 457, 462–63 (7th Cir. 2014) (faulting an expert's differential etiology not just for failing to "rule in" the alleged cause but also for failing to "rule out" other potential causes).

As to relevance, only one of the opinions Dr. Mejia gave at his deposition is even probative of causation: his testimony that the pain may have resurfaced in August because the pain-relief injection Kopplin received often wears off. That is, Dr. Mejia had one theory for how the January injury could have had long-term effects. Even that is a partial theory because he admitted that he did not know whether throwing the switch could have caused the January injury in the first place. He testified that it would be "speculation" to say one way or another. Because Dr. Mejia's opinion is only [—8—] marginally relevant, there is little reason to think that his testimony would be helpful to the trier of fact.

Kopplin has two final objections. First, he argues that even without the affidavit and despite all the problems with Dr. Mejia's deposition testimony, he should prevail because the injury's origin is obvious. It is true that we do not require expert testimony when causation is so clear that "a layperson can understand what caused the injury." *Myers v. Ill. Cent. R.R. Co.*, 629 F.3d 639, 643 (7th Cir. 2010). For example, a pedestrian hit by a truck would generally not need an expert to prove the cause of his broken leg. *See id.* But this case is much different. There are several steps between Kopplin's effort to fix the switch and his long-term disability, and none is clear. For instance, take the fact that the injury resurfaced when Kopplin attempted to hold his son while riding a lawnmower. To put it mildly, we are skeptical that the average layperson knows whether operating heavy machinery one-handed can contribute to medial and lateral epicondylitis. And because it would not be obvious to a layperson, expert testimony was indeed necessary.

Second, Kopplin insists that his claims should survive because Wisconsin Central's expert Dr. Jan Bax noted in a report that "Mr.

Kopplin sustained a work-related strain to his left-elbow on January 14." But that one stray line does very little work. To start, the report never says that the broken switch caused the injury. It says only that the injury was "work-related," which could refer to a number of different things. The report also oddly says the injury began on January 14, ten days *before* Kopplin operated the broken switch. Moreover, Dr. Bax faces many of the same problems as Dr. Mejia—namely, that there is no evidence he consid- **[—9—]** ered whether other factors may have caused the injury. In fact, there is no evidence at all that Dr. Bax's testimony would have been admissible under *Daubert*. Perhaps the greatest flaw is that he never said a word about the reemergence of the injury in August. One way or another, Kopplin still needs admissible expert testimony that the January 24 {–1105–} incident caused a long-term disability. That report is not it.

As mentioned, causation is a necessary element of every FELA claim. *See Walden*, 975 F.2d at 364. So Kopplin's failure to present reliable expert testimony on that issue is fatal.

AFFIRMED.

United States Court of Appeals
for the Seventh Circuit

No. 17-2429

RUARK

vs.

UNION PAC. R.R. CO.

Appeal from the United States District Court for the Southern District of Illinois

Decided: February 20, 2019

Citation: 916 F.3d 619, 7 Adm. R. 386 (7th Cir. 2019).

Before **FLAUM, ROVNER,** and **SCUDDER,** Circuit Judges.

[—1—] {–623–} ROVNER, Circuit Judge:

The Federal Employers Liability Act (FELA), 45 U.S.C. §§ 51-60, was enacted more than a hundred years ago to compensate railroad employees for injuries they receive on the job. Ruark was an employee of the Union Pacific Railroad when a hydraulic rail drill malfunctioned and sprayed him with hot oil. He sought relief under FELA using the legal doctrine of "res ipsa loquitur," a doctrine that asks a finder of fact to infer liability when (as the Latin is often [—2—] translated) "the thing speaks for itself." Because of the burden-shifting nature of the doctrine, it requires some baseline conditions—namely that the defendant was in control of the instrumentality that caused the injury and that the plaintiff was not also negligent. The district court found that these conditions were not met and thus the jury should not be instructed that they could assume that "the matter spoke for itself" under the doctrine. We agree and find that the district court did not abuse its discretion by refusing to grant Ruark a continuance before trial. We affirm on both points.

I.

On September 22, 2013, Ruark was working as a machine operator on rail maintenance on the Union Pacific Railroad using a hydraulic rail drill to drill holes into the rails. To use the drill, the operator clamps it in place on the rail and then uses a lever to start the drill. When the drill is finished, the operator pushes the lever {–624–} back to stop the drill and retract the bit, and then unclamps it from the rail. The drill is powered by hydraulics which requires that it connect to machinery by hoses carrying fluid. Ruark began working at six o'clock in the morning and was involved in hooking the drill up to the hydraulic lines before the work began. He used the drill throughout the day, attaching it to the rail, pushing the lever to start the drilling, pushing the lever to stop the drill and retract it, and then detaching it from the rail. Ruark used the machine to drill five or six holes that day, including the last one, and had not noticed any leaking hydraulic fluid or other malfunction. As he drilled the last hole, Ruark reached down to retract the drill bit out of the hole and turn the drill off when [—3—] he heard a "boom."[1] Hot fluid sprayed over him, including in his eyes. Ruark jerked upward, twisted, and stumbled backward. After Ruark informed his supervisor that the drill had exploded, the supervisor gave him napkins to wipe off the oil and Ruark declined further medical attention. The supervisor sent him home to clean up and told him to return to work the next day and report how he was feeling. Ruark returned to work the following day, but did not participate in much of the work, because, as he stated at his deposition, "it hurt too bad." Ruark's Short App. at 88. Ruark went home that evening and made an appointment to see his regular nurse practitioner the next day. The form he completed at her office stated that he was experiencing "sinus and stomach problems." Ruark's Short App. at 125. Ruark did not return to work after September 23 and was pulled out of service a few days later because he had been convicted of a felony unrelated to the workplace accident. On October 2, Ruark completed an accident report form based on the September 22 incident. On March 13, 2014, Ruark filed suit under FELA claiming injuries from the incident with the rail drill.

---

[1] Because this is an appeal from a grant of judgment as a matter of law pursuant to Fed. R. Civ. P. 50(a)(1), we note the facts in the light most favorable to the party against whom judgment has been entered—in this case, Ruark. *Equal Employment Opportunity Comm'n v. Costco Wholesale Corp.*, 903 F.3d 618, 621 (7th Cir. 2018).

Ruark began a prison sentence a short while later (on June 28, 2016), a fact we note because it interrupted Ruark's representation and trial preparation. Two months into Ruark's incarceration (the end of August, 2016), his first set of lawyers moved to withdraw, asserting that it was impossible to [—4—] represent him in this tort matter while he was incarcerated. His new counsel took over a few months later (early December, 2016) and the district court scheduled a pretrial conference for the end of February. At that conference, the judge denied a pending motion for a continuance, reasoning that the case had been pending for almost three years, Ruark had been well represented by his initial counsel, he had been given a normal scheduling order, and the fact of his incarceration was not cause to reopen exhausted deadlines and allow Ruark to begin the discovery process anew. Despite the denial, the district court judge did permit some planned discovery to continue. He allowed Ruark's counsel to take his client's trial testimony by video deposition and to depose Ruark's treating physician. He also stated that he would consider a new motion to reopen discovery once a trial date was set and the new counsel became more familiar with the case. Ruark's lawyer, however, did not pursue that option. The trial began on June 13, 2017. Ruark proceeded on a theory of negligence based on res ipsa loquitur. Once the district court determined that the plaintiff had not met the requirements for use of the doctrine, it granted Union Pacific's {–625–} motion for judgment as a matter of law, on June 14, 2017, a ruling which we review de novo. *Martin v. Milwaukee Cty.*, 904 F.3d 544, 550 (7th Cir. 2018). Judgment as a matter of law is proper if "a reasonable jury would not have a legally sufficient evidentiary basis to find for the party on that issue." *Id.* (quoting Fed. R. Civ. P. 50(a)(1)). We review the district court's decision to deny the motions for a continuance and to reopen discovery for an abuse of discretion. [—5—]

II.

A. Judgment as a matter of law on the FELA claim.

This case involves an interplay between FELA and the doctrine of res ipsa loquitur. While FELA provides the cause of action under federal statute for injuries received while in the employ of the railroad, the plaintiff here, Ruark, went about hoping to prove that liability by using the doctrine of res ipsa loquitur. Res ipsa loquitur describes not a substantive claim, but a manner of proceeding on that claim. As we will describe in more detail below, it is "a shortcut to a negligence claim." *Blasius v. Angel Auto., Inc.*, 839 F.3d 639, 649 (7th Cir. 2016) (citing *Maroules v. Jumbo, Inc.*, 452 F.3d 639, 642 (7th Cir. 2006)). Thus whether Ruark could proceed below depended on whether he had met the prerequisites for a res ipsa claim. In short, FELA provides the substantive framework for Ruark's claim but the evidentiary theory under which he opted to proceed is that rail drills do not, in the ordinary course of events, spray oil on their users. As we will discuss, the cost of admission to this plaintiff-friendly, burden-shifting doctrine requires a plaintiff to make some significant preliminary showings.

As for FELA, it may be true, as Ruark argues, that FELA requires a lower threshold for submitting matters to the jury. FELA is a remedial statute, lowering the burden of proof so that an employee might meet it if "employer negligence played any part, even the slightest, in producing the injury." *Rogers v. Missouri Pac. R.R.*, 352 U.S. 500, 506 (1957); *Brown v. Burlington N. Santa Fe Ry. Co.*, 765 F.3d 765, 771, 2 Adm. R. 457, 460 (7th Cir. 2014). [—6—]

This lowered threshold, however, does not mean that an employer is responsible for any injury that occurs in the course of employment. As the Supreme Court explained:

That FELA is to be liberally construed, however, does not mean that it is a workers' compensation statute. We have insisted that FELA does not make the employer the insurer of the safety of his employees while they are on duty. The basis of his liability is his negligence, not the fact that injuries occur.

Consol. Rail Corp. v. Gottshall, 512 U.S. 532, 543–44, 114 S. Ct. 2396, 2404 (1994) (internal citations omitted).

Ruark, therefore, is correct that a FELA case should go to a jury if even the slightest of facts support a finding of negligence. As the plaintiff has established in the multitude of FELA cases it has set forth in its brief (none of which, we note however, is a claim brought on the theory of res ipsa loquitur), the amount of evidence required to submit a FELA case to the jury is "scarcely more substantial than pigeon bone broth." Ruark Brief at 11 (citing *Green v. CSX Transp., Inc.*, 414 F.3d 758, 766 (7th Cir. 2005)). But, "[a]s light as this burden is, the plaintiff must still present some evidence of negligence ... specifically, the plaintiff must offer evidence creating a genuine issue of fact {–626–} on the common law elements of negligence, including duty, breach, foreseeability, and causation." *Green*, 414 F.3d at 766. *See also Tennant v. Peoria & P. U. Ry. Co.*, 321 U.S. 29, 32, 64 S. Ct. 409, 411 (1944) ("[p]etitioner [is] required to present probative facts from which the negligence and the causal relation could reasonably be inferred."). A FELA plaintiff "is not impervious to summary judgment. If the plaintiff presents no evidence whatsoever to support the inference of [—7—] negligence, the railroad's summary judgment motion is properly granted." *Lisek v. Norfolk & W. Ry. Co.*, 30 F.3d 823, 832 (7th Cir. 1994). And if the plaintiff opts to proceed on a doctrine that the injury speaks for itself, as opposed to some other theory of liability, he must meet the requirements to proceed on that theory, just as he would have been required to offer evidence creating a genuine issue of fact on duty, breach, foreseeability, and causation if Ruark's theory of the case had been an ordinary negligence claim. *See Green*, 414 F.3d at 766. In this case, Ruark's theory of the case is that Union Pacific's negligence should be inferred under the doctrine of res ipsa loquitur, and so we turn now to the requirements for the evidence he was required to offer to present his case to a jury.

Ordinarily negligence may not be inferred from the mere fact that an injury occurred, but the doctrine of res ipsa loquitur recognizes that "in some situations an occurrence is so unusual that, absent a reasonable justification, the person in control of the situation should be held responsible." *Maroules*, 452 F.3d at 642. The doctrine of res ipsa loquitur permits an inference of liability on the part of the defendant if the plaintiff can demonstrate that certain conditions existed making it likely that the defendant was responsible for the injury. The doctrine means "the matter speaks for itself" and thus, as the Supreme Court explained,

> When a thing which causes injury, without fault of the injured person, is shown to be under the exclusive control of the defendant, and the injury is such, as in the ordinary course of things, does not occur if the one having such control uses proper care, it affords reasonable evidence, [—8—] in the absence of an explanation, that the injury arose from the defendant's want of care.

Jesionowski v. Boston & M.R.R., 329 U.S. 452, 456, 67 S. Ct. 401, 403 (1947) (citing *San Juan Light & Transit Co. v. Requena*, 224 U.S. 89, 98–99, 32 S. Ct. 399, 401 (1912)). And because courts are fond of enumerated lists, we often state the prerequisites for a res ipsa claim as follows: (1) The injury must be one that does not ordinarily occur absent negligence; (2) the injury must have been caused by some agency or instrumentality in the exclusive control of the defendant; and (3) the injury must not have been due to any contribution or voluntary activity on the part of the plaintiff. *Robinson v. Burlington N. R.R. Co.*, 131 F.3d 648, 652 (7th Cir. 1997) (citing *Stillman v. Norfolk & W. Ry*, 811 F.2d 834, 836–37 (4th Cir. 1987)).

Once the plaintiff has met the prerequisites listed above, the reward is high. She is entitled to have the court instruct the jury that it may draw an inference of negligence. That is not to say that the jury would be compelled to find negligence—just that the facts of the occurrence warrant such an inference. *Jesionowski*, 329 U.S. at 457, 67 S. Ct. at 404 (citing *Sweeney v. Errving*, 228 U.S. 233, 240, 33 S. Ct. 416, 418 (1913)).

A plaintiff may use the doctrine of res ipsa loquitur in a FELA case. *See Robinson*, 131 F.3d at 652. And in this case, the last two factors in the list are the {–627–} ones at play—that is whether the Railroad had exclusive control of the drill or not, and whether any of Ruark's injuries could be attributed to his own actions. And these factors are, of course, really two sides of the same coin. In order for a plaintiff to show that the defendant was responsible for the accident, he must preclude other possible causes of the injury—including his own contribution. *See Jesionowski*, 329 U.S. at 454, 67 S. Ct. at 402. [—9—]

In this case, the key question, therefore, was whether Ruark's injury was caused by some agency or instrumentality in the exclusive control of the Railroad. The district court concluded that there was no question that the drill was not in the exclusive control of the Railroad, and we agree. As Ruark testified, he was touching and using the drill when the hydraulic fluid came squirting out. He was involved in hooking the rail drill to the hydraulic lines on the machine that day, and he used the rail drill to drill at least four or five holes. The drill was operating properly when he first began using it and worked without incident throughout the day up until the time of the accident. In fact, at the hearing on Union Pacific's motion for judgment as a matter of law, Ruark's counsel admitted that he had partial control over the drill.

Court: We know that he—at least he was, in part, in control of this drill, correct?

Ruark's counsel: Correct.

As the district court concluded, "in light of the plaintiff's testimony about the control that he had in this case, hooking up the hoses, hooking up the hoses to the drill, hooking up the drill to the rail, pulling the lever in and

out, turning the drill on and off, I find res ipsa loquitur does not apply." R. 110 at 28. We agree.

Ruark attempts to nudge the control factor in Ruark's favor in two ways. First, Ruark claims that the requirement of "exclusive control" is not as exclusive as the phrase might suggest. Second, he argues that Union Pacific had a "non-delegable duty to maintain its equipment in safe working order and to provide Ruark with a safe place in which to work and safe equipment." Ruark Brief at 21. [—10—]

Turning to exclusive control first, Ruark argues that the doctrine is applicable even where there is some evidence that the "plaintiff's participation in the employer's activity might have produced the accident." Ruark Brief at 6. For this proposition, Ruark cites *Colmenares Vivas v. Sun Alliance. Ins. Co.*, 807 F.2d 1102 (1st Cir. 1986). In *Colmenares Vivas*, the plaintiffs were injured when an airport escalator handrail malfunctioned causing them to tumble down the stairs. The court had to decide whether the doctrine of res ipsa loquitur could be applied where the Ports Authority of Puerto Rico owned and maintained the airport but contracted with Westinghouse to maintain the escalator. *Id.* at 1105-06. In deciding that res ipsa loquitur could be applied in the case against the airport authority, the court used the following language, on which Ruark relies:

> Thus, res ipsa loquitur applies even if the defendant shares responsibility with another, or if the defendant is responsible for the instrumentality even though someone else had physical control over it. ... It follows that a defendant charged with a nondelegable duty of care to maintain an instrumentality in a safe condition effectively has exclusive control over it for the purposes of applying res ipsa loquitur.

Colmenares Vivas, 807 F.2d at 1106 (internal citations omitted). But in *Colmenares Vivas*, the court was deciding which of two potential tort feasors (in a non-FELA case) effectively had control over the escalator. {–628–} There was no question that the injured parties themselves had no control over the escalator. *Id.* at 1107. In this case, in contrast, the question is whether the plaintiff may have contributed to the accident, and the [—11—] Supreme Court and this court have been clear that one cannot employ the doctrine of res ipsa loquitur where there is a possibility of negligence on the part of the injured plaintiff. *Robinson*, 131 F.3d at 653–54. The injury must have occurred "without fault of the injured person." *Jesionowski*, 329 U.S. at 456–57, 67 S. Ct. at 403-04 (1947).

Ruark is correct that a court can still give an instruction on res ipsa loquitur when the plaintiff's allegedly negligent acts are "part of the employer's general activity." *Robinson*, 131 F.3d at 655, n. 6. But this is only true if a jury can first eliminate the possibility that the plaintiff's activity contributed to the injury. *Jesionowski*, 329 U.S. at 456–57, 67 S. Ct. at 403–04; *Robinson*, 131 F.3d at 653–54. What matters is whether the injured person participated in the operations in a manner that contributed to the accident—not merely whether he participated in the operations of the injuring instrumentality. *Jesionowski*, 329 U.S. at 457, 67 S. Ct. at 404. *Robinson*, 131 F.3d at 655 & n.6. *See also Potthast v. Metro-N. R.R. Co.*, 400 F.3d 143, 151 (2d Cir. 2005) ("It is this consideration of *inappropriate* interaction, rather than whether there ever was or was not *any* interaction involving the plaintiff and the instrumentality of the injury, that constitutes the salient criterion.") (emphasis in original).

And so, for example, if a jury concludes that an injured brakeman's activities—throwing a switch and giving a signal—did not contribute to the accident where he was thrown from a rail car and killed, the defendant railroad qualifies as the exclusive controller of the factors which caused the injury. *Jesionowski*, 329 U.S. at 458, 67 S. Ct. at 404. The jury may then proceed on a res ipsa loquitur instruction, inferring negligence on the part of the railroad. *Id.* In contrast, a railroad employee who is not riding in the proper position while [—12—] switching railcars may have contributed to her own

injuries and thus is not entitled to a res ipsa instruction. *See Robinson*, 131 F. 3d at 655. Nor is a railroad worker plaintiff entitled to such an instruction if he made the decision to attempt to free a jammed forklift load by pulling on it while standing beneath it. *Stillman*, 811 F.2d at 837. *See also McGinnis v. Consolidated Rail Corp.*, Nos. 96-2571, 97–1009, 1997 WL 457530, at *3 (4th Cir. Aug. 12, 1997) (railroad worker who lost his balance and grabbed a coupler which then crushed his hand could not recover on a res ipsa loquitur theory because of his contribution to or voluntary activity in the accident); *Mandrgoc v. Patapsco & Back Rivers R.R. Co.*, No. 95-3123, 1996 WL 477253, at *5 (4th Cir. Aug. 23, 1996) (an employee had partial control of the instrumentality of injury because he operated the switch and elected to jump from the car in anticipation of the derailment); *Santa Maria v. Metro-North Commuter R.R.*, 81 F.3d 265, 272 (2d Cir. 1996) (holding res ipsa loquitur instruction was inappropriate because employee had partial control over a cot, supplied by the Railroad, which collapsed while the employee was sleeping on it).

Ruark argues that there was "no evidence that Plaintiff operated the drill in any negligent manner." Ruark Reply Brief at 3. This is, of course, correct, but it misunderstands the relationship between the second and third requirements of a res ipsa loquitur claim and the plaintiff's burden. Recall that the doctrine of res ipsa loquitur shifts the burden to the defendant and allows a jury to infer negligence. This is not the usual way our legal {–629–} system proceeds and places a heavy thumb on the plaintiff's side of the scale. Before that thumb can be placed, the doctrine requires that a plaintiff make a significant showing that he can eliminate other possible explanations for the injury— aside from the employer's negligence. The [—13—] prerequisites, therefore, are "rigidly defined." *Jesionowski*, 329 U.S. at 456, 67 S. Ct. at 403. One of those prerequisites is that "the defendant must have exclusive control of all the things used in an operation which might probably have caused injury." *Jesionowski*, 329 U.S. at 456, 67 S. Ct. at 403. If the employer is not in control of the instrumentality of the injury then there is a greater chance that the person or thing that is, in fact, in control of that instrumentality caused the injury. Because Ruark controlled the drill and its set up, his actions could have been the cause of his injury. That is not to say that they were. Ruark is correct that there is no evidence that he operated the drill negligently. There need not be. But without a demonstration that Union Pacific had control of the instrumentality of the injury, we cannot employ a doctrine that assumes Union Pacific's negligence by mere fact of the accident itself. As the Supreme Court put it:

> there can be no application of the doctrine of res ipsa loquitur if other causes than the negligence of the defendant, its agents or servants, might have produced the accident[.] [T]he plaintiff … has the burden to exclude the operation of such causes by a fair preponderance of the evidence before the rule can be applied. This is so because if there are other causes than the negligence of the defendant that might have caused the accident, the defendant cannot be said to be in exclusive control—one of the prerequisites to the application of the rule here invoked.

Jesionowski, 329 U.S. at 454, 67 S. Ct. at 402 (1947).

Here the district court concluded that "it isn't just that the plaintiff had some role, but that he was in control of this tool, [—14—] this instrumentality, and … more so than the railroad." R. 110 at 29. And thus the court concluded that Ruark had not presented sufficient evidence that the Railroad controlled the drill in order to meet the prerequisites for a res ipsa loquitur instruction. R. 110 at 24. We agree.

Ruark's brief also states, without argument, that "Union Pacific has a non-delegable duty to maintain its equipment in safe working order and to provide Ruark with a safe place in which to work and safe equipment." Ruark Brief at 21. This seems to be just another way of saying that a jury can infer negligence by an employer any time an accident occurs. If this position were true, then in every FELA case, the railroad would be assumed to have complete control over everything in the workplace regardless of the plaintiff's contributory negligence, and every FELA case would warrant a res ipsa loquitur instruction. We know, however, that is not so. *See, e.g., Robinson*, 131 F. 3d at 654; *Stillman*, 811 F.2d at 837; *Santa Maria*, 81 F.3d at 272; *McGinnis*, 1997 WL 457530, at *3; *Mandrgoc*, 1996 WL 477253, at *5.

Ruark failed to meet the prerequisites for a res ipsa loquitur instruction, and because this was his sole theory of the case, the district court correctly granted Union Pacific's motion for judgment as a matter of law.

B. The denial of a request for a continuance.

As Ruark's FELA case ambled along, so too did the criminal claims against him in his unrelated criminal case. After he was incarcerated in that matter, {–630–} his lawyers moved to withdraw, claiming it was impossible to represent him under the [—15—] circumstances. (R. 41, R. 43, R. 39 at ¶ 7, R. 42 at ¶ 6).[2] Once Ruark's new counsel first appeared in the case, the judge set a pretrial conference for two months later. Sixteen days before that conference, Ruark's counsel first requested to continue the conference and trial. He did not expressly request that the court reopen discovery, but he noted that he wanted to take statements or depositions of multiple individuals and wished to hire an economist. The Railroad argued that all of those individuals had been disclosed and were known to the plaintiff since 2014 and could have been deposed in a timely manner. The district court denied the motion.

---

[2] Ruark's brief states that, "[t]he district judge seemed to begrudge that Ruark was serving a sentence on an unrelated issue … ." Ruark Brief at 24. It is worth noting that the district court did not seem particularly concerned about the logistical problems of deposing Ruark in prison, noting that the judge had been involved in a similar case where a plaintiff who was in prison needed to be deposed. R. 109 at 12.

Ruark argues that the district court abused its discretion by denying the motion to continue. A district court, however, must have a wide berth to manage caseloads and dockets and therefore "[a] district court's exercise of its discretion in scheduling trials and granting or denying continuances is 'almost standardless.'" *United States v. Egwaoje*, 335 F.3d 579, 587–88 (7th Cir. 2003) (citing *United States v. Moya-Gomez*, 860 F.2d 706, 742 (7th Cir. 1988)). *See also, Flint v. City of Belvidere*, 791 F.3d 764, 768 (7th Cir. 2015). And in this case, the district court judge managed his discretion reasonably. As explanation for denying the motion for the continuance at the February 6 pretrial conference, the judge noted that Ruark had a normal scheduling order, competent former counsel, and that the trial had already been continued two or three times [—16—] previously. Moreover, he did not deny definitively Ruark's motion for a continuance, but rather he denied it for the time being, encouraging Ruark's counsel to file such a motion if it became necessary later in the proceedings:

> ... as you get more familiar with your case, I am open to you filing a motion to—[a] formal motion to continue that trial date, setting out the kind of things you talked about, which defendant can respond to, and I'll rule on that motion, you know, and see if you come up with anything that might convince me.

R. 109 at 15-16. Additionally, on February 22, 2017, the district court entered a formal written order that stated "[u]pon a trial date being set, Plaintiff is granted leave to file a formal motion to continue, if appropriate." R. 58.

Loss of counsel is not a per se reason that a district court might reopen discovery. Like other factors it is one of many that a court might consider in exercising its broad discretion to grant or deny a continuance. *See, e.g., Egwaoje*, 335 F.3d at 588 (considering plaintiff's knowledge of the trial schedule, his repeated requests for a speedy trial, multiple rescheduling after the plaintiff fired counsel, likelihood of prejudice, complexity of case, diligent use of trial preparation time, and inconvenience and burden to the court and parties); *Washington v. Sherwin Real Estate, Inc.*, 694 F.2d 1081, 1085–86, 1088–89 (7th Cir. 1982) (affirming the denial of continuance where the plaintiffs' lawyer withdrew on the day of trial, the case had been pending for three years, and the district court permissibly concluded that "no further delay could be tolerated."). In this case, however, the judge recognized that the change of counsel might be a hindrance to preparation {–631–} and advised [—17—] Ruark's counsel that he would keep an open mind in considering a new motion to continue.

Plaintiff's counsel, however, never filed a motion to continue the June trial date or to reopen discovery, and instead proceeded to trial. Even if the judge had erred (and for the reasons asserted above, we find that he was well within his discretion), Ruark cannot show any prejudice from the district court's ruling. He knew the identities of the individuals he wanted to interview, but he appears to have abandoned any attempt to interview them or reopen discovery.

III.

In short, we conclude that the district court correctly entered judgment as a matter of law for the Railroad as Ruark failed to satisfy the prerequisites for the theory of negligence under which he pursued the case—res ipsa loquitur. The district court did not abuse its discretion in refusing to grant a motion for a continuance. We therefore AFFIRM the judgment in all respects.

No. 18-3149

SELECTSUN GMBH

vs.

PORTER, INC.

Appeal from the United States District Court for the
Northern District of Indiana, Fort Wayne Division

Decided: June 25, 2019

Citation: 928 F.3d 550, 7 Adm. R. 393 (7th Cir. 2019).

Before **HAMILTON, BARRETT,** and **SCUDDER,** Circuit
Judges.

[—1—] {–551–} SCUDDER, Circuit Judge:

Contractual disputes can be messy and
present many tangled knots. A year ago
in a similar contractual dispute under
Indiana law we observed that sometimes the
harder questions can be avoided where the
evidentiary record shows that the plaintiff
"failed to prove its damages with anything
close to reasonable certainty." *Entertainment
USA, Inc. v. Moorehead Communications, Inc.*,
897 F.3d 786, 797 (7th Cir. 2018). This same
observation and evidentiary [—2—] shortcoming resolves this appeal and leads us to
affirm the district court's judgment against
SelectSun GmbH in this contract and
warranty dispute over whether the exhaust
system on a $1 million yacht manufactured by
Porter, Inc. complied with particular
regulatory requirements imposed by the
European Union.

I

A

Porter is an Indiana company that
manufactures boats under the Formula and
Thunderbird trade names. At the center of
this dispute is a 40-foot Formula yacht custom
manufactured by Porter for a German
businessman and boat enthusiast, Erich
Schwaiger. Only a general understanding of
how the sale and underlying contract came
about is necessary here.

In September 2012, Schwaiger attended a
boat show in Friedrichshafen, Germany, and
met Alfred Zurhausen, the owner of Poker-
Run-Boats, one of Porter's international
dealers of Formula boats. Impressed with a
Formula display model, Schwaiger expressed
interest in ordering a Formula yacht with
supercharged engines and high-end
accessories and furnishings. Shortly thereafter Zurhausen met Schwaiger in Munich to
discuss these options and pricing in more
detail. Those discussions culminated in
Schwaiger, through one of his companies,
executing a contract with Poker-Run-Boats on
October 1, 2012. The yacht and a custom-built
lift cost Schwaiger approximately $1 million.
Porter, as the manufacturer, was not a party
to the contract. The only parties were Poker-
Run-Boats and (following a substitution)
Schwaiger's company, SelectSun. [—3—]

By its terms, the contract required the boat
to be "CE certified," meaning authorized for
operation in the European Union. Porter did
not manufacture the boat to meet this
specification, and the reason seems to be
because of communications {–552–} during the
ordering process that Porter had with one of
its domestic dealers, International Nautic.
Based in Florida, International Nautic had
worked with Poker-Run-Boats (the German
dealer) to receive Schwaiger's order and, in
turn, to transmit that order to Porter. The
order conveyed by International Nautic called
for the yacht to come with a switchable
exhaust system, one that would allow the
operator to choose to divert exhaust either
above or below the water line. Exhaust
diversion above the water line results in a
boat operating with more noise. EU
regulations, however, require exhaust
expulsion below the water line. Porter caught
this conflict and explained to International
Nautic that the boat could not be both
equipped with the switchable exhaust system
specified in the original order and CE
certified. In the end, and following dialogue on
the issue, International Nautic authorized
Porter to proceed with manufacturing the boat
with the originally designed exhaust system.
Apparently Schwaiger knew nothing of
International Nautic's decision and therefore
believed the yacht would come CE certified.

Schwaiger took delivery of the yacht in Germany in May 2013. He used the boat throughout much of the 2013 season in Europe. (It is not clear whether he did so believing the boat was CE certified or knowing that it was not.) During these first few months, Porter covered a series of minor warranty repairs at no charge to Schwaiger. By the end of August, however, Schwaiger appeared fed up with the yacht, complaining to Poker-Run-Boats of problems with the boat's engines, steer- [—4—] ing column, exterior gel coating, and interior furnishings. Rather than seek repairs, Schwaiger returned the yacht to Poker-Run-Boats with instructions to sell it. When the boat did not immediately sell, Schwaiger resorted to litigation.

B

In January 2014, Schwaiger's company SelectSun, the party to the contract with the German dealer Poker-Run-Boats, filed a complaint against Porter in federal court in New York. SelectSun amended its complaint a month later to add International Nautic, Porter's Florida dealer, as a defendant. On Porter's motion, the district court in New York then transferred venue to the Northern District of Indiana, where Porter is headquartered.

SelectSun's claims against International Nautic ended in a default judgment. This resulted from International Nautic shuttering its business in January 2015, and from there forward failing to participate in the litigation. Equally noteworthy is that Porter's German dealer, Poker-Run-Boats, ceased operations sometime after this litigation commenced. These developments left SelectSun with claims only against Porter as the manufacturer of the yacht.

Summary judgment resulted in a partial ruling in Porter's favor and SelectSun proceeding to trial on three particular claims. First, and recognizing that Porter did not sign the October 2012 contract, SelectSun nonetheless sought to hold Porter liable for breach of contract under a theory of agency based on apparent authority. Second,

SelectSun highlighted the damage to the yacht that Schwaiger experienced during the 2013 season, as well as the absence of the boat being CE certified, as part of alleging that Porter had breached express and [—5—] implied warranties and likewise violated the Magnuson-Moss Warranty Act, 15 U.S.C. §§ 2301, *et seq.* Third, SelectSun advanced a claim of unjust enrichment. In its amended complaint, SelectSun sought damages for the full purchase price of the yacht, the cost of the lift, and related financing costs—a total exceeding $1,000,000. {–553–}

A four-day bench trial followed in the district court. SelectSun focused much of its evidence on matters of contract formation and, in particular, the facts pertinent to determining whether Porter could be held to the contract terms under agency principles of apparent authority. The trial court, for example, heard substantial testimony about Schwaiger's direct and indirect interactions with Porter personnel, other indications that Poker-Run-Boats (Porter's German dealer) and International Nautic (Porter's Florida-based dealer) acted with Porter's authority, and Schwaiger's expectations that the yacht would come CE certified.

As for damages, and in keeping with the award sought in its amended complaint, SelectSun (and by extension Schwaiger) approached trial in an all-or-nothing manner: it sought to recover either over $1 million (reflecting the full purchase price of the boat, the cost of the lift, and financing costs) or $0— nothing in between. Put differently, SelectSun, despite offering expert testimony about the cause of particular damage to the yacht, did not approach trial with a plan B to recover the specific costs associated with the damage the boat experienced during the 2013 season. Even more specifically, SelectSun offered no evidence of the value of the yacht at the time of trial, the costs to repair various items like the cracked gel coating and damaged appliances, or the cost to render the yacht CE certified. [—6—]

For its part, Porter approached trial by offering evidence to explain why it did not manufacture the yacht to be CE certified. So, too, did Porter offer competing expert testimony to show that the damage the yacht sustained during the 2013 season was the product of misuse by Schwaiger. Porter also offered testimony that the yacht's exhaust system could be modified to be compliant with the requirements for CE certification for an estimated $2,000.

The district court entered judgment for Porter on each of SelectSun's claims. In a thorough opinion, Chief Judge Springmann determined that SelectSun's breach of contract claims failed because Porter neither was a party to the October 2012 contract nor could be bound to its terms by a theory of apparent authority. On the latter point, the district court reasoned that the course of dealing between the parties "would not cause a reasonable person, much less a sophisticated businessperson, to believe that Zurhausen was an agent of Porter." As to SelectSun's breach of warranty claims, the district court emphasized that Schwaiger's all-or-nothing approach to damages—insisting on recovering the full purchase price of the boat instead of the more discrete repair costs—left him outside of the scope of relief available under Indiana law. Finally, the district court rejected the unjust enrichment claim based on the finding that Porter received no benefit at SelectSun's (or Schwaiger's) expense.

Before concluding the case, and as part of quantifying the amount of the default judgment against International Nautic, the district court invited SelectSun to "provid[e] evidence estimating the cost to replace the exhaust system to bring the Boat into compliance with EU standards." SelectSun responded not by supplying a cost estimate to bring the vessel {—7—} into compliance with EU regulations, but instead by summarily positing that it is "impossible to assess cost of repair for this Boat," because "this Boat cannot be made CE compliant and is a total loss."

II

On appeal SelectSun devotes substantial effort to challenging the district court's determination that Poker-Run-Boats {–554–}

and International Nautic did not act with the apparent authority requisite to bind Porter to the October 2012 contract for the yacht. In much the same way, SelectSun spills meaningful ink arguing that it offered ample evidence to prove that Porter breached its express and implied warranties by failing to manufacture the watercraft to be CE certified. Along the way, in advancing both contentions, however, SelectSun devotes little to no attention to explaining what we see as a plain failure of proof under Indiana law—establishing damages to a reasonable certainty—that independently defeats both its breach of warranty and breach of contract claims against Porter. It is on this alternative ground that we affirm the district court's judgment in Porter's favor. *See Continental Ins. Co. v. M/V ORSULA*, 354 F.3d 603, 606 (7th Cir. 2003) (explaining that "[w]e may affirm a district court's judgment on alternate grounds found in the record").

Similar circumstances presented themselves in *Entertainment USA, Inc.* There we confronted a contract dispute under Indiana law regarding a customer referral agreement between a cell phone wholesaler, Entertainment USA, and Moorehead Communications, an agent for wireless service provider Verizon. *See* 897 F.3d at 789–90. The agreement required Moorehead to pay Entertainment USA a certain amount each time {—8—} its referrals resulted in a new activation of a cell phone contract. *See id.* After Moorehead stopped paying, Entertainment USA filed suit but then in the ensuing litigation, including ultimately at trial, never developed evidence (in the form of a traditional damages calculation or otherwise) of what Moorehead had paid and still owed in light of the precise breach at issue and terms and conditions of the governing agreement. Entertainment USA, the trial record showed, "presented a damages calculation [that] aligned with its broad theories of liability, but it did not present an estimate or evidence that could, with reasonable effort, be disaggregated and recalculated in accordance with the district court's much narrower bases for finding liability." *Id.* at 791. The evidentiary shortcoming left the district court without a reliable evidentiary basis from which to measure and assess damages. *See id.*

The failing mattered—and indeed proved dispositive—because, under Indiana law, a breach of contract claim requires showing the existence of a contract, the defendant's breach, and damages. *See id.* at 793 (quoting *Old Nat'l Bank v. Kelly*, 31 N.E.3d 522, 531 (Ind. Ct. App. 2015)). The burden for establishing damages fell squarely on Entertainment USA, and the company was required to do so with evidence at trial "proving with reasonable certainty the damages which he incurred." *See id.* (quoting *Indiana Bell Tel. Co. v. O'Bryan*, 408 N.E.2d 178, 183 (Ind. Ct. App. 1980)). But "Entertainment USA's presentation of damages fell well short" of the evidentiary threshold—despite the district court's offering multiple opportunities to do so, the company never presented an estimate of damages that aligned with Moorehead's actual liability. *See id.* at 794. And because this failure of proof on damages was fatal, we stopped short on appeal of wading into the merits of Entertainment USA's challenge to the finding of a [—9—] breach of contract, emphasizing that "[i]t is not always necessary to march through this entire process if a single issue proves to be dispositive." *Id.* (quoting *Lesch v. Crown Cork & Seal Co.*, 282 F.3d 467, 473 (7th Cir. 2002)).

We chart the same course here. Substantial complexity accompanies SelectSun's challenges to the district court's rulings. Take, for example, the apparent authority question and, specifically, {–555–} whether the trial evidence showed that Porter was bound to the October 2012 contract by virtue of particular actions the company took to allow Schwaiger to reasonably believe that the German dealer (Poker-Run-Boats) was Porter's agent. *See Rogers v. Sigma Chi Int'l Fraternity*, 9 N.E.3d 755, 764 (Ind. Ct. App. 2014) (delineating the parameters of apparent authority). The district court answered the question not only by analyzing the particulars of phone calls between the parties, Formula's marketing materials, and other aspects of the transaction, but also by making the related legal determination that only events before the contract signing date were relevant. While the district court's conclusion that no apparent authority existed has much to support it in the record, SelectSun has lodged a detailed, multipronged challenge to that conclusion on appeal, including by contending the court committed legal error by limiting its focus to interactions before the execution of the contract. The parties' briefing on these factual and legal issues is extensive.

All of this is avoidable, though, because regardless of the answers we would come to, the evidence presented by SelectSun at trial falls well short of its burden in proving damages on either its breach of warranty or breach of contract claims. The governing principles under Indiana law are straightfor- [—10—] ward. Indiana warranty law required SelectSun to present evidence of damages as to the cost of repairing the boat, replacing it, or proving its fair market value. *See Irmscher Suppliers, Inc. v. Schuler*, 909 N.E.2d 1040, 1050 (Ind. Ct. App. 2009). Likewise, Indiana contract law compelled SelectSun to offer at trial a reasonable calculation of damages resulting from the breach that was "supported by evidence in the record" and not "the mere basis of conjecture or speculation." *R & R Real Estate, Co., LLC v. C & N Armstrong Farms, Ltd.*, 854 N.E.2d 365, 370–71 (Ind. Ct. App. 2006).

Yet recall how SelectSun approached damages at trial, taking the position that the only appropriate award was not to recover specific necessary repairs to the yacht, but instead to return the vessel's purchase price as well as the financing costs and the cost of the lift—totaling approximately $1 million. SelectSun, in short, insisted the yacht was worth $0—literally worthless, not even retaining scrap value—absent the CE certificate called for by the contract.

There is more. At trial a Porter representative testified that the yacht's exhaust system could have been made compliant with EU regulations for an estimated $2,000. The district court credited this testimony as part of finding that any warranty damages would not exceed that estimate, and having presented no contrary estimate, SelectSun had no evidentiary ground to stand on to challenge the finding as clearly erroneous.

On this evidentiary record, we conclude that SelectSun did not meet its burden of proving damages to a reasonable certainty on either its breach of contract or warranty claims. Not only did SelectSun decline to present affirmative evidence as to the cost of specific damage or the current value of the boat, [—11—] it failed to rebut Porter's evidence that the boat could be made CE compliant for only $2,000. While Indiana law affords some flexibility in proving damages, a plaintiff must come forward with an estimate rooted in evidence and demonstrated to a reasonable certainty. *See Stoneburner v. Fletcher*, 408 N.E.2d 545, 550–51 (Ind. Ct. App. 1980); *see also Indiana Bell Tel. Co.*, 408 N.E.2d at 183 (explaining "the party asserting the breach has the burden of proving with reasonable certainty the damages which he incurred"). {–556–} Against this standard and on this factual record, SelectSun failed to carry its burden in demanding a return of the yacht's entire purchase price.

III

A failure of proof likewise plagued SelectSun's claim of unjust enrichment. Under Indiana law, SelectSun needed to show that it conferred a benefit upon Porter, expected payment in return, and yet received none— yielding an unjust result. *See Neibert v. Perdomo*, 54 N.E.3d 1046, 1051 (Ind. Ct. App. 2016). The district court found that the trial evidence demonstrated that this case was a poor fit for recovery on a theory of unjust enrichment. Porter received no benefit, much less unjust enrichment, by receiving partial payment for the yacht it manufactured and then delivered to Schwaiger. Nor did Porter bear any responsibility for, or receive any benefit from, the financing costs or price of the boat lift. We cannot say these conclusions reflect any error of fact or law.

For these reasons, we AFFIRM.

United States Court of Appeals
for the Seventh Circuit

No. 19-1187

GUERRERO
VS.
BNSF RY. CO.

Appeal from the United States District Court for the
Central District of Illinois

Decided: July 17, 2019

Citation: 929 F.3d 926, 7 Adm. R. 398 (7th Cir. 2019).

Before **WOOD**, Chief Judge, and **BAUER** and **EASTERBROOK**, Circuit Judges.

[—1—] {–927–} **WOOD**, Chief Judge:

Behind the legal question we must resolve in this case is a sad story: as Celso Guerrero was trying to drive to his job at BNSF Railway through a snowstorm early one morning, his car skidded, it collided with a snowplow, and he was killed. His widow, Rita Guerrero, who appears on [—2—] her own behalf and as administrator of her late husband's estate, is seeking compensatory money damages from BNSF. (Our references in this opinion to Guerrero refer to Celso Guerrero, unless the context requires otherwise.) The district court concluded that Guerrero was not acting within the scope of his employment when the fatal accident occurred, and thus the Federal Employer's Liability Act (FELA) does not apply to the case. In our view, the question of work status is a close one, but it is one that we need not resolve. No jury could find that BNSF was negligent in any action it took or failed to take with respect to Guerrero, and so on that ground we affirm the district court's judgment.

I

We take our account of the undisputed facts from the district court's opinion, recognizing that this case was resolved through a motion for summary judgment, and so (as the district court also did), we accept the facts in the light most favorable to the opponent of the motion, Guerrero. {–928–}

Celso Guerrero was a machine operator for BNSF. His normal schedule required him to work from Monday through Friday, but he was subject to possible overtime work at other times. His primary duty was track repair, but he was also expected to perform other tasks as needed, including snow removal. On Saturday, January 31, 2015, Guerrero received a telephone call around 6:00 p.m. from Nick Burwell, the BNSF Roadmaster in charge of track maintenance for the Galesburg, Illinois, railyard and surrounding area. Burwell told Guerrero that a significant snowstorm was expected, and so he was looking for employees to clear snow from the tracks starting the next morning at 7:00 a.m. at the Galesburg facility. In mak- [—3—] ing these calls, Burwell followed a union seniority list. Guerrero was not required to accept this work opportunity, but he did. From that point onward, we can assume that BNSF was relying on him to show up at the assigned time, and he at a minimum would have had to notify the company if he no longer wanted to accept the extra work.

Driving his personal vehicle, Guerrero left his home in Kewanee, Illinois (about 40 miles northeast of Galesburg) at 5:00 a.m. on February 1. The predicted snowstorm was underway, and it was snowing hard as Guerrero drove along Illinois Route 34. The National Weather Service documented at least four, but likely closer to eight, inches of snow cover along his route. *Interactive Snow Information, Modeled Snow Depth for 2015 February 1, 12:00 UTC*, THE NATIONAL WEATHER SERVICE'S NATIONAL OPERATIONAL HYDRAULIC REMOTE SENSING CENTER, https://www.nohrsc.noaa.gov/interactive/html/map.html (Physical Element "Snow Depth"; Date "February 1, 2015, 12:00 UTC"; City, ST "Galesburg, IL"). While heading southbound, near Oneida, his car slid on the roadway, spun across the median, and collided with a snowplow being operated by the Illinois Department of Transportation (IDOT); the plow was in the northbound lane. Guerrero was severely injured and died the next day in the hospital. Illinois State Trooper Carrie Worsfold responded to the collision. Commenting that "I was the plow, it felt like," she recalled that the road was completely covered with snow—maybe three inches or more.

II

Rita Guerrero, suing in her own right and for Guerrero's Estate, filed this action under the FELA, 45 U.S.C. §§ 51–59. Asserting that her husband was killed while he was on duty [—4—] and acting within the scope of his employment, she sought compensatory damages. BNSF took issue with her assertion that Guerrero was on duty at the time of his injury; it contended that he was merely commuting to work, as he did for his normal shift every day, and that commuting falls outside the scope of employment in this situation. BNSF argued in the alternative that no trier of fact could find that BNSF was negligent either by act or omission, and that this was an independent reason for judgment in its favor. On BNSF's motion for summary judgment, the district court ruled that Guerrero's fatal injury occurred at a time when he was not acting within the scope of his employment. The FELA thus did not apply—a conclusion to which the judge attached jurisdictional significance. Without addressing BNSF's negligence argument, the judge granted summary judgment in BNSF's favor, presumably with prejudice, since the judgment document does not specify otherwise and makes no mention of a jurisdictional ground for dismissal. See FED. R. CIV. P. 41(b); *Swanigan v. City of Chicago*, 775 F.3d 953, 959 n.2 (7th Cir. 2015). Guerrero has appealed. {–929–}

III

Although the parties spend most of their time arguing over the district court's finding about scope of employment, we have much less to say about that, and more to say about BNSF's alternate, negligence-based argument. The reason is simple: it appears to us that there are disputed issues of material fact on the former point that would preclude summary judgment, but there are no such issues on the latter point. [—5—]

A

Before turning to the merits, we need to say a word about jurisdiction. Citing *Caillouette v. Balt. & Ohio Chicago Terminal R. Co.*, 705 F.2d 243, 245–46 (7th Cir. 1983), the district court held that the answer to the question whether the FELA covers Guerrero's claims—here, the answer to the question whether Guerrero was within the scope of his employment when the accident occurred—"implicates the Court's subject matter jurisdiction." It is true that the *Caillouette* court's discussion of FELA coverage appears in a section headed "Subject Matter Jurisdiction." But saying so does not make it so. All the court actually held in *Caillouette* was that the injured rail worker was indeed acting within the scope of his employment when he walked across a rail yard, and it affirmed a jury verdict in the worker's favor.

Quite a bit of water has gone under the bridge since 1983, when *Caillouette* characterized a question relating to the scope of coverage under a statute as one affecting the district court's subject-matter jurisdiction. In *Arbaugh v. Y & H Corp.*, 546 U.S. 500 (2006), the Supreme Court endeavored to clarify the difference between "federal-court 'subject-matter' jurisdiction over a controversy; and the essential ingredients of a federal claim for relief." *Id.* at 503. In that case, it held that the provision in Title VII of the Civil Rights Act limiting its coverage to employers having 15 or more employees does not affect subject-matter jurisdiction. Instead, it simply "delineates a substantive ingredient of a Title VII claim for relief." *Id.* Later decisions from the Supreme Court have made clear that this was not a mere quirk of Title VII law. Over and over, the Court has stressed the difference between the fundamental power to ad- [—6—] judicate a claim (*i.e.* something affecting subject-matter jurisdiction) and lesser restrictions, including claim-processing rules and ingredients of a claim. *See, e.g., Fort Bend Cnty., Texas v. Davis*, 139 S. Ct. 1843 (2019) (administrative charge-filing requirement under Title VII is a mandatory, but non-jurisdictional, prerequisite to suit); *Morrison v. National Australia Bank Ltd.*, 561 U.S. 247 (2010) (extent of extraterritorial reach of securities statute relates to scope of statute, not subject-matter jurisdiction); *Reed Elsevier, Inc. v. Muchnick*, 559 U.S. 154 (2010) (Copyright Act's registration requirement is precondition to suit, but does not affect subject-matter jurisdiction).

The import of those cases is unmistakable: unless Congress has unambiguously said in a statute that a particular limitation affects the district court's subject-matter jurisdiction, a limitation on the right to recover (such as number of employees, or extraterritorial reach, or scope of employment) describes an element of the case. Nothing in the FELA compels the conclusion that the merits of a claim and subject-matter jurisdiction are conflated for its purposes. The question before us is thus only whether Guerrero has alleged enough to survive summary judgment on the scope-of-employment issue. BNSF {–930–} properly preserved this point in the district court, and so the fact that it would be too late now to inject that issue into the case is of no moment.

B

The federal reporters are littered with cases examining whether the FELA applies to an employee injured while he or she is commuting to or from work. Often the answer is no: courts generally hold that the employee is on her own during the commute and does not report to work until she has reached her place of employment. Some cases, however, slip [—7—] into a gray area. For example, employment status is often contested where a commuter is injured while traveling to or from work on the same railway that employs her, using a pass issued by the employer. Nonetheless, those cases usually find that the travel is outside the scope of employment. We have noted that those commuters "are excluded from [FELA] coverage for two reasons—they are not required to commute on their employer's trains, and while commuting, they are in no greater danger than any other member of the commuting public." *Caillouette*, 705 F.2d at 246 (citing *Sassaman v. Pennsylvania R.*, 144 F.2d 950, 953 (3d Cir. 1944)); *Metropolitan Coal Co. v. Johnson*, 265 F.2d 173, 178 (1st Cir. 1959). A second group

of borderline cases includes those in which an employee has just clocked out, or not yet clocked in, but is traversing the work site on her way to or from her assigned post when she is injured. Those cases typically uphold FELA coverage, because "traversing the work site ... is a necessary incident of the day's work." *Id.* (citing *Erie Railroad Co. v. Winfield*, 244 U.S. 170, 173 (1917). Relying on the former line of cases, the district court found that Guerrero's accident occurred while he was on his way to work, far from his worksite, as he drove his personal vehicle on a public highway and faced dangers identical to the rest of the commuting public.

But the situation is more complex than that. With respect to the last point, evidence in the record (for example, Trooper Worsfold's testimony that she was "the plow," implying that she was the first to drive on the newly fallen snow) indicated that members of the commuting public were not out and about— they were waiting out the storm until IDOT could clear the roads and render them passable. Guerrero's commitment to BNSF thus distinguished him from the general population. In addition, Guerrero was not heading to work for his [—8—] normal job, which as we noted ran from Monday through Friday. He had accepted a special assignment, and once he accepted it, BNSF was relying on him to show up. Guerrero notes that the union contract to which he was subject provides that "the time of an employee who is called after release from duty to report for work will begin *at the time called* and will end at the time he returns to designated point at headquarters." (Emphasis added.) Burwell called Guerrero at 6:00 p.m. on January 31 and obtained Guerrero's agreement to be at the Galesburg facility by 7:00 a.m. the next morning. Recognizing the adverse conditions caused by the snow, Guerrero budgeted a full two hours to drive the 40 miles between his home and the railyard. In addition, the record shows that Burwell later approved a settlement for Guerrero's wages from the 6:00 p.m. telephone call until the planned time of arrival the next morning. Although BNSF insists that Burwell erred in doing so, a jury would not be required to accept that explanation. Taking that fact favorably to Guerrero, it is evidence that he was not commuting, but instead was "on the clock" and working on {–931–} the special assignment at the time of the crash.

We set forth these competing views of the record to show why the question of scope of employment is not a straightforward one. It is a question of fact for the jury in an FELA case. *See Wilson v. Chicago, Milwaukee, St. Paul, and Pac. R.R. Co.*, 841 F.2d 1347, 1353–54 (7th Cir. 1988). Rather than wrestle it to the ground to see if summary judgment was nonetheless correct on this ground, we prefer to move to BNSF's alternate argument: whether a trier of fact could find that it was negligent, even under the generous FELA standard, on this record. [—9—]

C

Because the district court did not reach the negligence argument, Guerrero understandably said nothing about it in his opening brief. But BNSF properly raised the issue before the district court, and it followed up in its responsive brief in this court. Guerrero then had an opportunity to address negligence in his reply brief. We may affirm on any ground supported by the record, *see Isby v. Brown*, 856 F.3d 508, 529 (7th Cir. 2017), and so this argument is properly before us.

Guerrero argues that there is ample evidence that would support a jury finding of negligence, and so we begin with his examples. He asserts that BNSF had a non-delegable duty to provide a reasonably safe place to work, and that this duty extended to "places remote from railroad premises." Reply Br. at 8. But the cases to which he refers for that proposition do not go so far as to impose on BNSF the duty to keep snowy state highways plowed and safe. Instead, they cover private places specifically known to, if not chosen by, the employer such as snow-covered employee motel parking lots (*Duffield v. Marra, Inc.*, 166 Ill. App. 3d 754 (1988)), snow-, ice-, and debris-covered premises of a customer (*Howes v. Baker*, 16 Ill. App. 3d 39 (1973)), and an off-site defective stairwell at a training facility (*Mills v. CSX Transp., Inc.*, 300 S.W. 3d 627 (Tenn. 2009). Guerrero also suggests that BNSF was negligent when, acting through Burwell, it asked Guerrero to show up at 7:00 a.m. the morning after a bad storm. Burwell, he contends, should have paid more attention to the weather forecast, or he should have had Guerrero show up at 10:00 p.m. the night before and given him a hotel room, or he should have cancelled the work request in the middle of the night when it turned out that the storm was as severe as it was. [—10—]

We grant that Burwell could have gone the extra mile and taken one or more of those steps, but that fact does not demonstrate that BNSF was negligent when Burwell did not do so. As BNSF points out in its brief, Kewanee and Galesburg are in the upper Midwest, where snow is hardly an unusual phenomenon. (One estimate shows an average annual snowfall for Galesburg of 23 inches. *See Climate Galesburg – Illinois*, U.S. CLIMATE DATA, https://www.usclimatedata.com/climate/galesburg/illinois/united-states/usil0439 (last visited July 12, 2019).) Guerrero had lived in Kewanee for more than 35 years, and so it is impossible that he was a novice driving in snow. BNSF did not instruct him when to leave his house to start the drive to Galesburg. Even assuming, as we have, that he was "on the clock" from the time of Burwell's call, he had some discretion in deciding how to carry out his promise to show up at the railyard.

Note in this connection that we are *not* relying on the voluntary nature of Guerrero's initial decision to accept the assignment. From the time he said "yes" forward, we can assume that he was obliged {–932–} to show up. But we cannot ignore the fact that the reason Burwell needed the extra help was the snowstorm, and nothing but the snowstorm. Nor can we ignore the fact that BNSF had no control over IDOT's efforts to plow the roads. In fact, Trooper Worsfold's testimony, estimating that the road was covered by about three inches of snow as she was driving to reach the accident site, might suggest that the roads had been plowed, even if new snow had already started accumulating.

A decision that BNSF was negligent merely by asking Guerrero to drive while it was still dark (as it would have been on January 31 to February 1 between 6:00 p.m. and 7:00 a.m., [—11—] since sunset was about 5:15 p.m. and sunrise about 7:10 a.m., *see Sunrise & Sunset for Galesburg, IL,* OLD FARMER'S ALMANAC, https://www.almanac.com/astronomy/sun-rise and-set/IL/Galesburg/2015-02-01# (last visited July 12, 2019)) would have far-reaching implications. Taken to the extreme, it would mean that employers in snowy (or rainy, or icy) regions would be negligent whenever they required their employees to drive in bad weather. Even under the liberal negligence standards that apply in FELA cases, *Consol. Rail Corp. v. Gottshall*, 512 U.S. 532, 543 (1994), that is too much. As the Supreme Court itself recognized in *Gottshall*:

> "[t]hat FELA is to be liberally construed, however, does not mean that it is a workers' compensation statute. We have insisted that FELA does not make the employer the insurer of the safety of his employees while they are on duty. The basis of his liability is his negligence, not the fact that injuries occur.

Id. (quotations and citations omitted).

In the end, all that BNSF asked Guerrero to do was to come in and help out with the task of clearing snow from the tracks. Its failure, if one can call it that, to micro-manage exactly when Guerrero left his house, which route he took from Kewanee to Galesburg, and how he handled his car in the snow, cannot be characterized as negligence. Even in the railyard (that is, on the employer's premises and at the place of employment), workers have some discretion in how they carry out their jobs. So too here.

No one doubts that Mrs. Guerrero suffered a terrible personal loss when her husband lost his life as he tried to get to work. And no one here is saying that Guerrero was at fault for [—12—] the accident. It may have been caused by a sudden gust of wind, or a patch of black ice that was invisible under the snow, or any of a number of other external factors. But by the same token, this record shows that the only action BNSF took was to ask Guerrero to come to work under conditions known to both of them. We cannot pin a finding of negligence on such a slender reed.

The judgment of the district court granting summary judgment in favor of BNSF is AFFIRMED.

United States Court of Appeals
for the Seventh Circuit

No. 18-2068

ABERNATHY

vs.

EASTERN ILL. R.R. CO.

Appeal from the United States District Court for the Central District of Illinois

Decided: October 16, 2019

Citation: 940 F.3d 982, 7 Adm. R. 403 (7th Cir. 2019).

Before **KANNE, SYKES,** and **HAMILTON,** Circuit Judges.

[—1—] {–985–} **HAMILTON,** Circuit Judge: {–986–}

laintiff Marvin Abernathy was injured while working for defendant Eastern Illinois Railroad Company. He sued under the Federal Employers' Liability Act (FELA), 45 U.S.C. § 51 et seq., alleging that the Railroad negligently failed to provide reasonably safe working conditions by failing to provide appropriate equipment for the job he was doing when he was hurt. [—2—]

A jury awarded Abernathy $525,000 in damages. The Railroad moved for judgment as a matter of law or a new trial. The district court denied both requests, and the Railroad has appealed, raising a host of issues. Abernathy has filed a cross-appeal asserting that the district court erred by not awarding him sufficient costs to cover his expert witness fees. We affirm Judge Myerscough's decisions in all respects.

I. *Facts*

Abernathy worked as a track inspector for the Eastern Illinois Railroad Company. His duties included replacing and repairing railroad ties. On September 13, 2012, the Railroad sent Abernathy and another employee, Richard Probus, to repair a railroad crossing about six or seven miles away from the Railroad's yard in Charleston, Illinois. Abernathy was in charge of the job. The repair required him and Probus to transport six ties from the yard to the crossing.

In 2012, the Railroad had a "tie crane," a vehicle that runs on the railroad tracks and is well-suited to transporting railroad ties, but it had been out of commission for years. Abernathy and Probus had only two options for transporting the ties: a backhoe or a pickup truck, either of which would need to travel on public roads rather than railroad tracks. Abernathy chose to use the backhoe. He testified that he had never used the pickup truck to haul ties before, but that he had used the backhoe for similar jobs numerous times, although not on public roads and not with this heavy a load. Abernathy and Probus loaded four ties into the bucket of the backhoe and two across the top of the bucket, resting on the arms of the machine. Abernathy testified that when the bucket is rolled back, it locks the resting ties into place. Abernathy drove the [—3—] backhoe along a public highway. Probus followed in the pickup, which was loaded with tools needed to install the ties.

Abernathy drove in low gear, but he started to experience "road bounce." He started braking, and two ties fell out of the backhoe's bucket. Abernathy stopped on the shoulder of the road and tried to lift the ties back into the bucket. In lifting a tie, he injured his back. He also smashed a finger between the tie he was holding and another tie in the bucket. Despite the accident, Abernathy and Probus were able to finish reloading the ties, and they resumed their trip and finished the repair job. Abernathy remained in pain for the rest of the day.

The following morning, Abernathy reported the injury to Tim Allen, the general manager of the Railroad. Allen told him "to take it easy" and "be on light duty" for a while. Abernathy worked through the pain on lighter duty for the next year but was unable to return to his regular work. The Railroad terminated his employment in February 2014. He eventually had physical therapy, epidural injections, and then surgery in 2016. After the surgery, he continued to experience pain in his back and legs. At the time of trial, his surgeon {–987–} had still not cleared him for any type of work.

II. *The Trial*

Abernathy sued the Railroad under the FELA, 45 U.S.C § 51, alleging that it had been negligent in failing to provide an operable tie crane and requiring him to use the backhoe, which was inadequate for his assigned task of transporting the ties. The trial lasted three days. Abernathy testified and called three other lay witnesses: his wife Carrie Abernathy, Richard Probus, and Lowell McElwee, a Railroad engineer who worked with Abernathy. [—4—]

Probus testified that on the day of Abernathy's injury, they could not have used the pickup truck to transport the ties because they needed the pickup truck to transport the other equipment needed to install the ties. Probus also testified that the Railroad had acquired an operable tie crane after Abernathy's accident. Probus explained that the tie crane was now being used to transport ties and that manual lifts of ties were not necessary with the new machine. He stated that the availability of the tie crane makes his job safer.

Abernathy testified that when the Railroad's tie crane had been operational, he used it regularly. He explained that the tie crane was the preferred method for moving ties because it did not require manual lifting or traveling on public roads. He also testified that before his 2012 injury, he had repeatedly asked the Railroad to replace the tie crane.

Abernathy also presented the depositions of Doctors Renu Bajaj, James Kohlman, and Thomas Lee. Dr. Lee, Abernathy's surgeon, offered testimony relevant to damages and causation. He testified that he did not expect Abernathy to regain the level of functionality he had prior to his accident. He also testified that Abernathy certainly would not be able to return to work involving heavy manual labor. Dr. Lee also said that, to a reasonable degree of medical certainty, Abernathy's symptoms were caused or aggravated by the lifting accident in September 2012.

The Railroad called four witnesses: general manager Tim Allen; Everett Fletcher; Gayle Garrett, the office secretary for the Railroad; and Kendall Mulvaney, the superintendent of R&R Contractors, testifying as an expert witness in railroad repair and maintenance. The Railroad defended on the theory [—5—] that a backhoe is a generally accepted method for transporting ties in the rail repair industry.

After the close of Abernathy's case-in-chief, the Railroad moved for judgment as a matter of law under Federal Rule of Civil Procedure 50(a), which the court denied. The Railroad renewed its motion under Rule 50(b) at the close of all evidence and prior to the verdict, and the court again denied it.

The jury found that the Railroad was negligent and that its negligence contributed to Abernathy's injuries. The jury calculated Abernathy's total damages to be $750,000. However, the jury found that Abernathy was also at fault for thirty percent of the total fault, which meant the jury awarded a net verdict of $525,000. The district court denied the Railroad's post-trial motions for judgment as a matter of law or a new trial. The district court also awarded costs to Abernathy as the prevailing party but rejected his request to include as costs $3,800 in witness fees paid to Doctors Lee and Bajaj. The Railroad has appealed the judgment against it, and Abernathy has cross-appealed the denial of his request for expert witness fees as part of his costs.

III. *Legal Analysis*

We take up the issues on appeal in three groups. First, we address the Railroad's {–988–} arguments for judgment as a matter of law on the theory that Abernathy's evidence was insufficient. Second, we address the Railroad's arguments that the district court abused its discretion in admitting certain evidence at trial. Third, we address Abernathy's cross-appeal on the award of costs. [—6—]

A. *Judgment as a Matter of Law*

The FELA provides a federal remedy for railroad employees who are injured on the job. To prove a claim under the FELA, a plaintiff must prove "the traditional common law elements of negligence, including foreseeability, duty, breach, and causation." *Fulk v. Illinois Central Railroad Co.*, 22 F.3d 120, 124 (7th Cir. 1994). However, "[b]ecause it is meant to offer broad remedial relief to railroad workers, a plaintiff's burden when suing under the FELA is significantly lighter than in an ordinary negligence case." *Holbrook v. Norfolk Southern Railway Co.*, 414 F.3d 739, 741–42 (7th Cir. 2005); *see also Harbin v. Burlington Northern Railroad Co.*, 921 F.2d 129, 131 (7th Cir. 1990) ("It is well established that the quantum of evidence required to establish liability in an FELA case is much less than in an ordinary negligence action."). A railroad-employer is liable where "employer negligence played any part, even the slightest, in producing the injury." *Rogers v. Missouri Pacific Railroad Co.*, 352 U.S. 500, 506 (1957).

The Railroad challenges the sufficiency of evidence as to all elements of negligence. We consider duty and breach together, and foreseeability and causation separately. "This Court reviews sufficiency of the evidence challenges *de novo*, viewing the evidence in the light most favorable to the nonmoving party and drawing all inferences in [his] favor." *Crompton v. BNSF Railway Co.*, 745 F.3d 292, 295, 2 Adm. R. 452, 454 (7th Cir. 2014). We "will overturn a jury verdict 'only when there is a complete absence of probative facts to support the conclusion reached.'" *Id.* at 295–96, 2 Adm. R. at 454, quoting *Lavender v. Kurn*, 327 U.S. 645, 653 (1946). Here, probative evidence supported the jury's verdict that Abernathy established each element of negligence. [—7—] The district court did not err in declining to overturn the jury's verdict.

1. *Duty & Breach*

The Railroad had a duty to provide Abernathy a reasonably safe working environment. *See Crompton*, 745 F.3d at 296,

2 Adm. R. at 454. The Railroad points out correctly that it "could have provided a reasonably safe workplace notwithstanding the fact that safer workplace alternatives exist." *Taylor v. Illinois Central Railroad Co.*, 8 F.3d 584, 586 (7th Cir. 1993). The Railroad argues that Abernathy produced no evidence that the equipment available to haul ties (the backhoe and pickup truck) and the way in which he was trained to perform a manual lift were unsafe. Instead, Abernathy produced evidence pertaining to the absence of the tie crane. The tie crane evidence, the Railroad argues, showed only that there was a safer alternative to the backhoe and pickup, which is not sufficient to establish negligence. *See Darrough v. CSX Transportation Inc.*, 321 F.3d 674, 676 (7th Cir. 2003) (railroad does not have duty to provide the safest working environment).

The Railroad's argument relies on the faulty premise that evidence of safer alternatives can never even be relevant to whether an employer exercised reasonable care. When a railroad assigns an employee a task using a particular method and the employee is injured while executing the task, evidence of a safer alternative method is relevant to whether the method provided was reasonable. *See* {–989–} *Stone v. New York, Chicago & St. Louis Railroad Co.*, 344 U.S. 407, 409 (1953) (plaintiff was injured pulling ties using the method his supervisor instructed him to use; evidence of three alternative methods for pulling ties was relevant to whether railroad was negligent). Based on all the evidence presented, the jury could reasonably [—8—] have found that it was not reasonably safe to assign Abernathy to replace the ties without an operable tie crane.

The Railroad's argument as to the safety of a manual lift is similarly flawed. Abernathy did not argue that under all circumstances, the Railroad is negligent if it requires an employee to perform a manual lift. He argued that the Railroad was negligent where it could have provided employees with equipment that prevented the need for impromptu manual lifts on public roads but chose not to repair or replace this equipment.

The Railroad's reliance on *Walker v. Northeast Regional Commuter Railroad*, 225 F.3d 895 (7th Cir. 2000), is thus misplaced. In *Walker*, we affirmed summary judgment for a railroad in an FELA case for injuries from performing a manual lift. Plaintiff Walker worked as a machinist in a repair shop. He injured his back lifting a replacement blade for a machine that cut metal. *Id*. at 896. The blade weighed about 140 pounds, and Walker lifted it with one other employee. *Id*. A crane and a forklift were available to the men but could not be used to assist in the lift because of the configuration of the shop. Walker argued that his employer was negligent in requiring him to lift more than fifty pounds and "in configuring the shop in such a way as to prohibit the use of mechanical lifting aids." *Id*. at 898.

Walker is distinguishable. First, Walker actually made an explicit argument that his employer's demand that he lift more than fifty pounds was sufficient by itself to support a finding of negligence. In rejecting this argument, we contrasted the case with those in which plaintiffs "showed the availability of alternative methods and safeguards that would ensure employee safety" and found telling that Walker [—9—] produced no evidence that he or any other machinists "had complained about problems in changing the blade on other occasions." *Id*. In this case, Abernathy offered evidence of safer alternatives and prior employee complaints about the lack of an operable tie crane. As to the second argument about the shop configuration, Walker presented no evidence that the manual lift in his case was not reasonably safe given the circumstances, and in fact he "testified that he and [his co-lifter] assumed that they could pick up the blade" with no problem. *Id*. at 899.

Here, however, Abernathy offered evidence that the tie crane was the appropriate equipment to use for the job he was performing with a backhoe on the day he was injured. Allen's testimony on cross-examination and Probus's testimony allowed the jury to find that the pickup truck was not an adequate alternative. Abernathy and Probus both testified that an operable tie

crane made their work safer. Abernathy explained that the tie crane allowed employees to avoid manual lifts and traveling on public roads. The jury could reasonably have found that the Railroad did not provide Abernathy with equipment appropriate for the task he was assigned and that his working environment was not reasonably safe.

2. *Foreseeability*

Abernathy was required to show that it was foreseeable to the Railroad that transporting ties using a backhoe or pickup as opposed to a tie crane "would or might result in a mishap and injury." {–990–} *CSX Transportation, Inc. v. McBride*, 564 U.S. 685, 703 (2011), quoting *Gallick v. Baltimore and Ohio Railroad Co.*, 372 U.S. 108, 118, n.7 (1963). To establish foreseeability, "a plaintiff must show that the employer had actual or constructive notice" of potential harm. *Holbrook v. Norfolk Southern* [—10—] *Railway Co.*, 414 F.3d 739, 742 (7th Cir. 2005). The railroad may be liable "even if 'the *extent* of the [injury] or the *manner* in which it occurred' was not 'probable' or 'foreseeable.'" *McBride*, 564 U.S. at 703–04, quoting *Gallick*, 372 U.S. at 120–21 & n.8 (alteration in *McBride*; emphasis added here). The Railroad argues that Abernathy failed to prove negligence because he failed to show that his injury was foreseeable. The Railroad argues that it could not have known that Abernathy would use the backhoe or that doing so would result in dropped ties. The backhoe, the Railroad points out, had been used to transport ties without incident on multiple prior occasions and there was no defect in the machine that caused the tie to fall. Further, as the Railroad's expert, Mulvaney, testified, a backhoe was an accepted method in the railroad repair injury for transporting ties. From these facts, the Railroad contends there was insufficient proof of foreseeability.

The Railroad's argument misunderstands what the FELA requires. Abernathy does not need to show that the Railroad could have foreseen the particular consequences of its negligence. He needed to show only that "a particular condition"—here, the absence of appropriate equipment—"would or *might* result in" any type of "mishap and injury." *McBride*, 564 U.S. at 703, quoting *Gallick*, 372 U.S. at 118 n. 7 (emphasis added here); *see Gallick*, 372 U.S. at 118–20 (potential harm was foreseeable where railroad had allowed stagnant pool of filthy water to remain near worksite and employee was bitten by an insect, which led to infection and ultimately amputation of both legs). Abernathy needed to show only "circumstances which a reasonable person would foresee as creating a potential for harm." *McGinn v. Burlington Northern Railroad Co.*, 102 F.3d 295, 300 (7th Cir. 1996). [—11—]

The evidence here supported a finding that a reasonable person in the Railroad's position could have foreseen that transporting ties in a backhoe or pickup could lead to injury. The Railroad knew that its tie crane had not been operational since 2008. Abernathy offered evidence that he had repeatedly asked the Railroad to repair or replace it. Abernathy and Probus both testified that the tie crane was safer to use in hauling ties, in part because it prevented employees from having to lift ties manually and travel on public roads.

3. *Causation*

In support of judgment as a matter of law, and now on appeal, the Railroad argued that even if it was negligent in failing to provide a tie crane, Abernathy failed to prove that the alleged negligence caused his injuries. Abernathy's manual lift, the Railroad contends, caused his injuries, and this lift was an act subsequent to and independent of any safety issues that arose because the tie crane was not available.

The Railroad's argument conflicts with the liberal causation standard under the FELA. "Juries in such cases are properly instructed that a defendant railroad 'caused or contributed to' a railroad worker's injury 'if [the railroad's] negligence played a part—no matter how small—in bringing about the injury." *McBride*, 564 U.S. at 705; *see also* {–991–} *Harbin v. Burlington Northern Railroad Co.*, 921 F.2d 129, 131 (7th Cir. 1990), quoting *Rogers v. Missouri Pacific Railroad Co.*, 352 U.S. 500, 506 (1957) ("For under the FELA, 'the test of a jury case is simply whether the proofs justify with reason the conclusion that employer negligence played *any part, even in the slightest*, in producing the injury….") (emphasis in *Harbin*). "The FELA vests the jury with broad discretion to engage in common [—12—] sense inferences regarding issues of causation and fault." *Crompton v. BNSF Railway Co.*, 745 F.3d 292, 296, 2 Adm. R. 452, 454 (7th Cir. 2014).

There was sufficient evidence here that the Railroad's negligence played a part in bringing about Abernathy's injury. Abernathy had to use the backhoe on a public roadway to transport the ties because the Railroad had not repaired or replaced its tie crane, which had been out of service for years. Vibrations caused a tie to fall off the backhoe and onto the public roadway that Abernathy was forced to use because of the absence of a tie crane. Abernathy had to remove the tie, which was obstructing the public road, and he had to do it quickly. He had no option other than to lift the tie manually back into the backhoe, which injured his back. A reasonable jury could infer that the Railroad's negligence played some part in causing Abernathy's injury. The district court correctly denied the Railroad's motion for judgment as a matter of law.

B. *New Trial Motion Based on Evidentiary Rulings*

The Railroad also argues that the district judge erred in three decisions to admit evidence, contending that each is sufficient to warrant a new trial. We review the denial of a new trial motion for an abuse of discretion. *See, e.g., Johnson v. General Board of Pension & Health Benefits of United Methodist Church*, 733 F.3d 722, 730 (7th Cir. 2013); *Kossman v. Northeast Illinois Regional Commuter Railroad*, 211 F.3d 1031, 1036 (7th Cir. 2000). We find no abuse of discretion in any of the challenged evidentiary rulings.

1. *Testimony of Timothy Allen*

First, the Railroad objects to a line of cross-examination of its general manager, Timothy Allen, regarding his own use of a company pickup truck to transport railroad ties. The [—13—] Railroad argues that Allen's use of the truck was so dissimilar from the way Abernathy might have used the truck on the day he was injured as to make the evidence irrelevant.

Again, Abernathy had to prove that the Railroad did not provide a reasonably safe method for transporting railroad ties. *See Brown v. Western Railway of Alabama*, 338 U.S. 294, 297–98 (1949). The Railroad argued that the pickup truck was a reasonably safe and available way for Abernathy to do his job. Allen testified that he thought Abernathy should have used the pickup truck rather than using the backhoe to haul ties on a public road.

During cross-examination, Allen acknowledged that on one occasion, he had used the same pickup to take 20 to 25 rejected railroad ties to a friend. Allen admitted that, assuming each tie weighed just 140 pounds, hauling 20 ties would have meant the pickup truck was carrying 2,800 pounds.[1] The pickup truck was rated to haul only 1,500 pounds. When asked about this discrepancy, Allen said he had not been aware that he had been operating the pickup truck at almost double its load capacity. {–992–} Probus later testified that he and Abernathy chose not to use the pickup on the day of Abernathy's injury because they could not use it to haul both the ties and the tools needed for the job.

Judge Myerscough acted well within her discretion in allowing this line of cross-examination. Evidence is relevant if it has any tendency to make the existence of any fact that is of consequence to the determination of the action more probable [—14—] or less probable than it would be without the evidence. Fed. R. Evid. 401. The testimony about Allen's previous use of the pickup satisfied this definition. It was relevant for the jury to know that when Allen testified that the pickup truck was a reasonably safe alternative method available to Abernathy—a

key point for the Railroad's defense—he was not familiar with the pickup's hauling capacity. That rebuttal was especially relevant given Probus's testimony that he and Abernathy chose not to use the pickup in part because of the truck's load limit.

2. *Testimony about ADM*

Second, the Railroad objects to the admission of evidence regarding the financial ties of its expert witness, Kevin Mulvaney, to the Railroad's parent company, the agribusiness giant Archer Daniels Midland Company ("ADM"). Before trial, the district court had granted the Railroad's unopposed motion in limine barring mention of its relationship to ADM. At trial, the court reversed that ruling after Abernathy's counsel explained that they had not known before trial that Mulvaney would testify. The district court let Abernathy's counsel ask Mulvaney whether ADM was the largest customer of his employer. He answered "yes." In response to the next question, Mulvaney said he did not know whether ADM was the Railroad's parent company.

The court did not abuse its discretion in allowing these questions. Bias is a "permissible and established basis of impeachment." *United States v. Abel*, 469 U.S. 45, 50 (1984) (holding that government's evidence as to a defense witness's bias was properly admitted). Bias is the "quintessentially appropriate topic for cross examination." *Bachenski v. Malnati*, 11 F.3d 1371, 1375 (7th Cir. 1993). We have held repeatedly that [—15—] parties should be granted reasonable latitude in cross-examining witnesses for bias. *See, e.g., United States v. Manske*, 186 F.3d 770, 777 (7th Cir. 1999), citing *United States v. Frankenthal*, 582 F.2d 1102, 1106 (7th Cir. 1978).

The information involving ADM did not become relevant to bias until Mulvaney took the stand. In choosing to call an expert witness with economic ties to ADM, the Railroad made its parent-subsidiary relationship with ADM relevant to show potential bias on the part of Mulvaney. The

---

[1] The jury heard conflicting testimony regarding the weight of railroad ties. For purposes of this line of questioning, it was assumed that the average railroad tie weighs 140 pounds.

district court did not abuse its discretion by allowing this evidence of arguable bias.

3. *The Tie Crane Evidence*

The Railroad's third evidentiary challenge is to admission of evidence regarding the tie crane. The Railroad argues on appeal, as it did at trial, that this evidence is not relevant to whether the available methods of transporting ties when Abernathy was injured (i.e., the backhoe and the pickup truck) were reasonably safe. The Railroad also contends that this evidence confused the jury because it implied that the Railroad had a duty to employ the safest methods available, instead of just reasonably safe methods. The Railroad is particularly critical of the court's admission of evidence that it bought a new tie crane after Abernathy's injury. (The Railroad's {–993–} briefs on appeal do not cite Federal Rule of Evidence 407, which addresses evidence of subsequent remedial measures, but its arguments invoke that rule's rationale.)

As explained above, the Railroad is right that an employer can provide a reasonably safe workplace even if safer workplace alternatives exist, and evidence of a safer alternative is not conclusive evidence of negligence. *See Taylor v. Illinois* [—16—] *Central Railroad Co.*, 8 F.3d 584, 586 (7th Cir. 1993) ("proof of a safer alternative is not necessarily proof of negligence"). Nevertheless, evidence of safer alternative methods is still relevant to show that the available methods were not reasonably safe. *See Stone v. New York Central & St. Louis Railroad Co.*, 344 U.S. 407, 409 (1953). Such evidence is relevant to show industry standards and to establish whether a given method is reasonably safe relative to alternatives. *See Rogers v. Missouri Pacific Railroad Co.*, 352 U.S. 500, 503 (1957) (reinstating jury verdict for injured employee in light of evidence of safer alternative method). Thus, evidence of the tie crane was relevant to the issues of duty and breach, and specifically to determine whether the methods the Railroad made available to Abernathy were in fact reasonably safe. The jury was permitted to make inferences from evidence presented on an alternative method, the tie crane. That does

not mean the jury applied an incorrect standard (requiring the safest possible workplace). The jury instructions stated correctly that the applicable standard is that the "FELA requires defendant to exercise reasonable care to provide a reasonably safe workplace."

The evidence that a new tie crane was purchased after Abernathy's injury was also admissible. Rule 407 generally prevents admission of evidence of subsequent remedial measures to prove fault, but the rule and our precedents expressly permit this evidence if, among other reasons, "the feasibility of the remedial measure" is contested. *See, e.g., Ross v. Black & Decker Inc.*, 977 F.2d 1178, 1184–85 (7th Cir. 1992) (affirming admission of subsequent remedial measures where defendant disputed feasibility).

In this case, the Railroad chose to contest the feasibility of both purchasing a new tie crane and fixing the old one. At trial [—17—] and in deposition testimony, the Railroad's witnesses offered several reasons why the Railroad chose not to make a tie crane available in the four years or so between the original tie crane's breakdown and Abernathy's injury. These reasons included that the cost of repairing the original tie crane or buying a new one was prohibitively high, that the original tie crane was not used enough to justify the expense, and that the Railroad was concerned that any money spent would be wasted because Abernathy would misuse the machine so that it would soon break down again.

We can assume that if the Railroad had chosen to stipulate before trial to the feasibility of making a tie crane available to Abernathy, he would not have been allowed to present evidence of the post-injury purchase of a new tie crane. *See Ross*, 977 F.2d at 1185. But the Railroad could not both dispute feasibility and block Abernathy from introducing contrary evidence to show that it would have been feasible to replace the equipment. If the Railroad was concerned that the jury might use this evidence to infer negligence improperly, it also could have requested a limiting jury instruction. It did not. *See Trytko v. Hubbell, Inc.*, 28 F.3d 715, 725 (7th Cir. 1994), citing *United States v. Murzyn*, 631 F.2d 525, 531 (7th Cir. 1980). {–994–} The district court did not err by admitting this evidence.

C. *Plaintiff's Bill of Costs*

Following trial, Abernathy filed a bill of costs. The only point of controversy is his claim for $3,800 for fees paid to his treating physicians for their depositions. The Railroad objected to these costs on the ground that 28 U.S.C. § 1821(b) limits witness fees to forty dollars per day unless some other provision of law provides for a higher rate. The district court [—18—] agreed with the Railroad and limited the witness fees in the bill of cost to forty dollars per witness per day.

We review the district court's award of costs for an abuse of discretion. *See Halasa v. ITT Educational Services, Inc.*, 690 F.3d 844, 852 (7th Cir. 2012); *Stanley v. Cottrell, Inc.*, 784 F.3d 454, 464 (8th Cir. 2015). However, we review legal questions related to the cost award de novo. *See Central States, Southwest Areas Pension Fund v. White*, 258 F.3d 636, 640 (7th Cir. 2001) (standard of appellate review is *de novo* on a question of law in interpreting a statute); *see also Stanley*, 784 F.3d at 464.

Both doctors' video depositions were sought by Abernathy himself, and he presented them as evidence at trial. He contends that Federal Rules of Civil Procedure 26(b)(4)(E)(i) and 54(d)(1) work together to supersede the forty-dollar-per-day limit of § 1821 and allow him, as the prevailing party, to recover the entire "reasonable fee" he paid his expert witnesses for their depositions.

We affirm the district court's denial of the higher witness fees. Abernathy's argument is contrary to the Supreme Court's interpretation of the interaction between these rules set forth in *Crawford Fitting Co. v. J. T. Gibbons, Inc.*, 482 U.S. 437 (1987), and is not supported by Seventh Circuit precedent. The district court properly limited the witness fees the Railroad must pay to forty dollars per witness per day.

In *Halasa*, we affirmed the district court's ruling that the prevailing defendant could be reimbursed for fees related to the deposition of an expert witness in excess of forty dollars per day under Rule 26(b)(4)(E)(i). We held that the "reasonable fee" requirement in Rule 26(b)(4)(E)(i) can, in certain cases, supersede the specific payment schedule in § 1821(b). 690 F.3d [—19—] at 852. However, the district court decision in that case was based on the fact that the deposition of that expert witness, though initially paid for by the defendant, had been taken by the plaintiff. *Halasa v. ITT Educational Services, Inc.*, 2012 WL 639520, at *2 (S.D. Ind. Feb. 27, 2012) ("Federal Rule of Civil Procedure 26(b)(4)(E)(i) provides that the party who deposes an expert witness—which in this case was Halasa—shall 'pay the expert a reasonable fee for time spent.'"). The defendant in *Halasa* had not insisted that plaintiff pay its witness at the time of the deposition, as it could have under Rule 26(b)(4)(E)(i). Instead, the defendant had paid its own witness his usual expert fee for time spent on the deposition the plaintiff had taken. The defendant waited until its final bill of costs to request that payment under Rule 26(b)(4)(E)(i).

Thus, because the defendant in *Halasa* was the prevailing party and because plaintiff, as the party who had sought the deposition of the defendant's expert, had an obligation under the Rule 26(b)(4)(E)(i) to pay the costs of that deposition, the district court was permitted to order that the defendant be awarded the amount of reasonable witness fees it actually paid, regardless of the fee limits set forth in 28 U.S.C. § 1821(b). Here, however, Abernathy {–995–} is not asking that the costs of the depositions be reimbursed under Rule 26(b)(4)(E)(i). He instead seeks to have the costs of deposing his own expert witnesses reimbursed under Rule 54(d)(1) alone, a question that was not addressed in *Halasa*.

This case is much closer to the Supreme Court's decision in *Crawford Fitting*, which rejected Abernathy's interpretation of these rules. The issue in *Crawford Fitting* was whether a party could be reimbursed under Rule 54(d)(1) for the higher expert fees it had paid to have its own expert witness testify

[—20—] at trial. 482 U.S. at 438–39. The Court rejected that claim, holding that "when a prevailing party seeks reimbursement for fees paid to its own expert witnesses, a federal court is bound by the limit of § 1821(b), absent contract or explicit statutory authority to the contrary." *Id.* at 439. The Court found that the rule and statute did not conflict, and that while Rule 54(d)(1) permits prevailing parties to recover costs, § 1821(b) places a limit on the amount that can be recovered. *Id.* at 444–45.

Abernathy argues that we should distinguish *Crawford Fitting* and instead follow and extend the reasoning of the Eighth Circuit in *Stanley v. Cottrell, Inc.*, 784 F.3d 454, 464–65 (8th Cir. 2015), which allowed Cottrell, the prevailing party, to recover the full expert witness fees it actually paid to Stanley under Rule 26(b)(4)(E)(i) during discovery to take the deposition of Stanley's expert witness. Whether *Stanley* was correct or not on its own facts, its reasoning does not extend to the case before us, where the prevailing party seeks to recover full expert fees for the depositions of his own expert witnesses. This is *Crawford Fitting*, except that we address here expert depositions rather than expert trial testimony. It would be a mistake to limit *Crawford Fitting* on that basis. If we held that prevailing parties could recover under Rule 54(d) the full costs of deposing their own expert witnesses before trial, but not of calling those expert witnesses to testify live at trial, *see Crawford Fitting*, we would create an incentive for parties to offer expert depositions at trial in lieu of live expert testimony. Nothing in the text or logic of the rules calls for such a perverse incentive, and we see no persuasive reason to distinguish this case from *Crawford Fitting*.

The judgment of the district court and its award of costs are AFFIRMED.

This page intentionally left blank

United States Court of Appeals for the Eighth Circuit

United States Court of Appeals
for the Eighth Circuit

No. 18-2297

BRYANT

vs.

JEFFREY SAND CO.

Appeal from the United States District Court for the
Eastern District of Arkansas - Little Rock

Decided: March 18, 2019

Citation: 919 F.3d 520, 7 Adm. R. 414 (8th Cir. 2019).

Before **BENTON, MELLOY,** and **KELLY,** Circuit Judges.

[—1—] {–524–} **KELLY,** Circuit Judge:

After trial, a jury awarded Adrian Bryant nominal compensatory damages and $250,000 in punitive damages for his claim of hostile work environment against his former employer, Jeffrey Sand Company. The district court[1] denied Jeffrey Sand's [—2—] post-trial motions and granted Bryant's motion for attorney's fees. Jeffrey Sand appeals, and we affirm.

I

We recite the facts ascertained at trial, viewed in the light most favorable to the jury's verdict. *Morse v. S. Union Co.*, 174 F.3d 917, 920 (8th Cir. 1999). Bryant worked from 2009 to 2013 for Jeffrey Sand as a deckhand on the *Cora*, a barge that dredges sand from the Arkansas River. During this period, Bryant's co-workers on the *Cora* were the foreman, Jerry Skaggs; the pumper, Donald Lambert; and another deckhand, Chad Bateman. Bryant was the only black employee on the barge.

The evidence at trial revealed that Skaggs, Bryant's direct supervisor, engaged in a pattern of racially-motivated abuse. Skaggs taunted Bryant with racial slurs, calling him "nigger," "Kunte Kinte," "spear chucker,"

---

[1] The Honorable Brian S. Miller, Chief Judge, United States District Court for the Eastern District of Arkansas.

"monkey," "bitch," "porch monkey," and "boy," among other names. On at least some occasions, he uttered these epithets in the presence of other employees. Skaggs would give Bryant difficult tasks that he would not assign to the *Cora*'s white employees. Lambert testified that "a number of times," Skaggs would "get up in [Bryant's] face and use his chest {–525–} to push [Bryant] around trying to get [Bryant] to fight him."

Bryant complained to his plant manager, Ken Bolton, twice and to the then-president of the company, Joe Wickliffe, four times regarding Skaggs's behavior. He testified that he received no response to his complaints. Bolton testified that, in response to a complaint from Bryant on May 4, 2012, he sent another employee, Randy Marshall, to the *Cora* for a few days in an attempt to corroborate Bryant's allegation that Skaggs was using racial slurs. After Marshall reported back that he had not heard any slurs, Bolton did no further investigation. Bolton did not attempt to interview Bryant or any other employees. Jeffrey Sand has no written anti-harassment or anti-discrimination policy and no human resources personnel. [—3—]

Bryant testified that the harassment persisted and that he continued to make complaints after May 2012. He testified about a particular incident on August 7, 2012, when Skaggs made him paint rails in the hot sun and would not allow him to come into the air-conditioned part of the barge or to access water. When Bryant attempted to get out of the sun and told Skaggs that he felt ill, Skaggs responded, "[G]o out there and paint those rails like I told your black ass to," and sent him back outside. Bryant felt lightheaded and experienced chest pains, so he went to Lambert for help. Lambert measured Bryant's blood pressure, which was very high, and convinced Skaggs to call an ambulance. It was later determined that Bryant had suffered a heart attack, and he did not return to work for two weeks.

On January 30, 2013, Clay McGeorge, then the sales director (and now the president) of Jeffrey Sand, received an anonymous email stating: "Hi Clay I want to remain anonymous but I would like to inform you about the racist comments I've overheard the foreman on dredge *Cora* make." McGeorge alerted Wickliffe and Bolton to the email and Bolton interviewed several employees. Lambert corroborated that Skaggs had made racist comments toward Bryant, but Bolton discounted Lambert as merely a disgruntled employee. Several other employees told Bolton that they had heard second-hand about Skaggs using racial slurs. Bateman, the other deckhand, later admitted that he had authored the anonymous email. He testified that he had not heard Skaggs make racist comments personally, but had heard Bryant complaining about it and believed Bryant's accusations. Bolton did not interview Bryant as part of his investigation. The company took no disciplinary action against Skaggs.

Jeffrey Sand fired Bryant shortly after the investigation into the email, purportedly for absenteeism. Bryant brought this suit under 42 U.S.C. § 1981 on July 13, 2016, alleging a racially hostile work environment and retaliatory termination. The district court granted summary judgment in favor of Jeffrey Sand on the retaliation claim but allowed the hostile-work-environment claim to proceed to trial. The jury found in Bryant's favor and awarded him $1.00 in compensatory damages [—4—] and $250,000 in punitive damages. The district court denied Jeffrey Sand's post-trial motions for judgment as a matter of law and to amend the award of punitive damages. It also granted Bryant's motion for $64,432.50 in attorney's fees and $1,028.15 in costs. Jeffrey Sand appeals.

II

Jeffrey Sand argues it was entitled to judgment as a matter of law because there was insufficient evidence to charge punitive damages to the jury and because Bryant's claim is time-barred. We review the district court's denial of Jeffrey Sand's {–526–} motion de novo, viewing the facts in the light most favorable to Bryant and drawing all reasonable inferences in his favor. *Weitz Co. v. MacKenzie House, LLC*, 665 F.3d 970, 974 (8th Cir. 2012). Judgment as a matter of law is proper if "a party has been fully heard on an

issue and there is no legally sufficient evidentiary basis for a reasonable jury to find for that party on that issue." *Id.* (quoting Fed. R. Civ. P. 50(a)(1)).

Under either Title VII or § 1981, an award of punitive damages requires the plaintiff to show that his employer engaged in a discriminatory practice with "malice" or "reckless indifference" to his federally protected rights. 42 U.S.C. § 1981a(b)(1); *Kim v. Nash Finch Co.*, 123 F.3d 1046, 1063 (8th Cir. 1997). This standard may be satisfied when an employer exhibits reckless indifference toward discriminatory actions taken by those serving in a managerial capacity, *MacGregor v. Mallinckrodt, Inc.*, 373 F.3d 923, 931 (8th Cir. 2004), or when a supervisor's "sufficiently abusive" behavior manifests malice, *Ogden v. Wax Works, Inc.*, 214 F.3d 999, 1009–10 (8th Cir. 2000) (quoting *Kimbrough v. Loma Linda Dev., Inc.*, 183 F.3d 782, 785 (8th Cir. 1999)).

The award of punitive damages is supported by the record. Bryant repeatedly complained to supervisors that his manager, Skaggs, was using racial slurs. Those [—5—] supervisors never interviewed Bryant in response to his complaints, even though Skaggs's comments evidenced a "clear intent" to discriminate against Bryant based on race. *MacGregor*, 373 F.3d at 932. Even when another employee corroborated Bryant's allegations, the company did not take any action to discipline Skaggs or prevent further harassment. Jeffrey Sand also lacked any formal or informal policy prohibiting workplace discrimination. The jury could have reasonably concluded from these facts that Jeffrey Sand exhibited reckless indifference to Bryant's rights. *See Williams v. ConAgra Poultry Co.*, 378 F.3d 790, 796 (8th Cir. 2004) ("[W]hen the victim of harassment repeatedly complains to various supervisors of harassment and the harassment is not stopped, a submissible case on punitive damages has been made.").

We also conclude that Bryant's § 1981 claim was timely under the applicable four-year statute of limitations. *See Jones v. R.R. Donnelley & Sons Co.*, 541 U.S. 369, 383–85

(2004) (explaining that federal statute of limitations in 28 U.S.C. § 1658 applies to such claims). "[U]nder federal law one act of the hostile work environment must occur . . . within the § 1981 statute of limitations period. If that requirement is met, a party may then recover for all illegal acts that made up the hostile work environment." *Madison v. IBP, Inc.*, 330 F.3d 1051, 1061 (8th Cir. 2003). The continuing violation rule applies to punitive, as well as compensatory, damages. *See id.* at 1060–61.[2] Thus, in order for Bryant's claim to be timely, at least one act of the [—6—] hostile work environment must have occurred after July 13, 2012—four years before Bryant filed his complaint. {–527–}

Several witnesses testified that Skaggs's abuse continued into the limitations period and that Jeffrey Sand was on notice of that abuse. Bryant suffered a heart attack in August 2012 after Skaggs forced him to work in the hot sun without access to water, even after Bryant told Skaggs that he felt ill. The jury readily could have inferred—from Skaggs's own words—that this abuse was motivated by racial animus. Jeffrey Sand was on notice of Skaggs's abuse from Bryant's earlier complaints but was alerted again to the issue in January 2013 when another employee sent an anonymous email asserting that he overheard the abuse. The jury reasonably could have concluded that the company's response to this complaint was inadequate and evidenced a reckless disregard for Bryant's protected rights continuing well into the limitations period. We accordingly find no error in the district court's denial of Jeffrey Sand's motion for judgment as a matter of law.

---

[2] Jeffrey Sand argues that *Kline v. City of Kansas City, Missouri, Fire Department*, 175 F.3d 660 (8th Cir. 1999), stands for the proposition that damages in a continuing violation case are limited to those within the statute-of-limitations period. That is incorrect, as *Madison* makes clear. *Kline* was effectively overruled by the Supreme Court's decision in *National Railroad Passenger Corp. v. Morgan*, 536 U.S. 101, 122 (2002), which held that a hostile-work-environment claim is not time-barred so long as at least one act of the continuing violation falls within the limitations period.

III

Jeffrey Sand also argues that the jury's award of $250,000 in punitive damages violates due process because it is excessive and disproportionate to the nominal compensatory damages award. We review the constitutionality of the punitive damages award de novo. *Cooper Indus., Inc. v. Leatherman Tool Grp., Inc.*, 532 U.S. 424, 436 (2001).

"Juries have considerable flexibility in determining the level of punitive damages." *Ondrisek v. Hoffman*, 698 F.3d 1020, 1028 (8th Cir. 2012). An award of punitive damages nonetheless violates due process when it is so "grossly excessive" or "arbitrary" that the defendant failed to receive fair notice of the severity of the penalty that might be imposed. *State Farm Mut. Auto. Ins. Co. v. Campbell*, 538 U.S. 408, 416–17 (2003); *see BMW of N. Am., Inc. v. Gore*, 517 U.S. 559, 574 (1996). [—7—] The Supreme Court has identified three factors that guide our inquiry: "(1) the degree of reprehensibility of the defendant's misconduct; (2) the disparity between the actual or potential harm suffered by the plaintiff and the punitive damages award; and (3) the difference between the punitive damages awarded by the jury and the civil penalties authorized or imposed in comparable cases." *State Farm*, 538 U.S. at 418.

The degree of a party's reprehensibility is the "most important" factor in our analysis. *Id.* at 419 (quoting *Gore*, 517 U.S. at 575); *Bowles v. Osmose Utilities Servs., Inc.*, 443 F.3d 671, 675 (8th Cir. 2006). We must consider whether:

the harm caused was physical as opposed to economic; the tortious conduct evinced an indifference to or a reckless disregard of the health or safety of others; the target of the conduct had financial vulnerability; the conduct involved repeated actions or was an isolated incident; and the harm was the result of intentional malice, trickery, or deceit, or mere accident.

State Farm, 538 U.S. at 419. Citing these factors, the district court opined that Jeffrey Sand's conduct was "clearly . . . reprehensible." Skaggs's abuse was repeated, not isolated, and involved both verbal racist insults and physical altercations. His actions were not accidental but intentionally malicious. Jeffrey Sand failed to meaningfully investigate repeated complaints from Bryant and other employees. The district court also concluded that Bryant was financially vulnerable because he had a criminal record and so could not easily find another job. {–528–}

We agree that these facts, viewed in Bryant's favor, show that Jeffrey Sand's actions were "so reprehensible as to warrant the imposition of further sanctions to achieve punishment or deterrence." Id. The company argues that its response to Bryant's complaints was more fulsome than in other cases where we have upheld sizeable punitive damage awards. See, e.g., Henderson v. Simmons Foods, Inc., 217 F.3d 612, 619 (8th Cir. 2000) (affirming award of $100,000 in punitive damages where employer only half-heartedly responded to plaintiff's numerous complaints of [—8—] sexual harassment); Blackmon v. Pinkerton Sec. & Investigative Servs., 182 F.3d 629, 636–37 (8th Cir. 1999) (reinstating jury's $100,000 punitive damages award where employee was sexually harassed by her supervisors, company failed to investigate her complaints or take remedial action, and company engaged in retaliation). We disagree. Jeffrey Sand's indifference to Bryant's complaints was no less egregious than the meager efforts of the employers in Henderson and Blackmon. In particular, Skaggs's verbal and physical abuse went unchecked even after another employee corroborated Bryant's allegations, and even after Skaggs placed Bryant at risk of serious injury. These circumstances are at least as repugnant as those in Williams, where the plaintiff received $600,000 in punitive damages after his supervisor regularly swore at him, used racist language, and treated him differently than white employees. See 378 F.3d at 798–99.

The next guidepost for our consideration is proportionality. While punitive damage awards are ordinarily within a single-digit multiple of the compensatory damage award, this ratio's usefulness diminishes when the jury awards only nominal damages. The Supreme Court has "consistently rejected the notion that the constitutional line is marked by a simple mathematical formula" comparing compensatory and punitive damages. Gore, 517 U.S. at 582. "Punitive damages may withstand constitutional scrutiny when only nominal or a small amount of compensatory damages have been assigned, even though the ratio between the two will necessarily be large." JCB, Inc. v. Union Planters Bank, NA, 539 F.3d 862, 876 (8th Cir. 2008).

As in prior cases addressing nominal damages, we decline to place undue weight on the mathematical ratio between compensatory and punitive damages. See, e.g., Haynes v. Stephenson, 588 F.3d 1152, 1158 (8th Cir. 2009). The "general goal" of the proportionality factor is to ensure that punitive damages are "proportional to the actual injury suffered." Arizona v. ASARCO LLC, 773 F.3d 1050, 1056 (9th Cir. 2014) (en banc). The higher award of punitive damages is justified in this case [—9—] because "a particularly egregious act has resulted in only a small amount of economic damages" and "the monetary value of noneconomic harm might have been difficult to determine." Gore, 517 U.S. at 582. The jury may not have been able to easily quantify the monetary value of Bryant's injuries. But that does not mean the indignities he suffered were insubstantial, or that a punitive damages award of $250,000 is unreasonable. See id. at 583 ("[A] general concern of reasonableness properly enters into the constitutional calculus." (cleaned up) (quoting TXO Prod. Corp. v. All. Res. Corp., 509 U.S. 443, 458 (1993))).

The final factor for consideration is how the award compares to penalties authorized for similar misconduct. Jeffrey Sand emphasizes that, had Bryant brought his hostile-work-environment claim under Title VII, any award of punitive damages would be statutorily capped at $50,000 {–529–} because the company has fewer than 101 employees. 42

U.S.C. § 1981a(b)(3)(A). But Bryant brought his claim under § 1981, so Jeffrey Sand was on fair notice that the jury's award could exceed the Title VII cap. *See Williams*, 378 F.3d at 798–99 (declining to find any "constitutionally required ratio between § 1981 damages awards and the Title VII cap"). Considering the egregiousness of Jeffrey Sand's conduct, the company should have been aware that the trial could result in a substantial monetary award if the jury concluded that one was "necessary to deter future misconduct." *Gore*, 517 U.S. at 584. We conclude that the jury's punitive damages award was constitutionally sound.

IV

Finally, Jeffrey Sand argues that the district court erred in awarding Bryant attorney's fees. A prevailing party in a § 1981 action may be awarded a reasonable attorney's fee. 42 U.S.C. § 1988(b). "Attorney's fees are within the broad discretion of the district court and will not be reversed absent an abuse of discretion." *Hanig v. Lee*, 415 F.3d 822, 825 (8th Cir. 2005). To calculate attorney's fees, courts typically begin by using the lodestar method, which multiplies the number of hours reasonably **[—10—]** expended by reasonable hourly rates. *Brewington v. Keener*, 902 F.3d 796, 805 (8th Cir. 2018). "When determining reasonable hourly rates, district courts may rely on their own experience and knowledge of prevailing market rates." *Hanig*, 415 F.3d at 825.

Jeffrey Sand does not dispute that Bryant was the prevailing party at trial and that the hours expended by Bryant's counsel were reasonable. Instead, it argues only that the district court erroneously accepted the lodestar rate of $350 per hour based solely on Bryant's counsel's representation that he had been awarded fees at this rate in similar recent cases. Jeffrey Sand argues that the district court should have demanded a sworn affidavit attesting that this was his counsel's "normal" hourly rate.

The law imposes no such requirement. Bryant's counsel averred that his requested rate was "reasonable and commensurate" with his qualifications and extensive experience. He supported that statement by providing a list of recent fee awards he had obtained, including one from only a few months prior in which the same district court had concluded his $350 rate was reasonable. Jeffrey Sand has produced no evidence undermining the reasonableness of the rate. The district court's decision to accept the rate as reasonable, in light of its own experience and knowledge, was not an abuse of discretion.

Accordingly, we affirm the judgment of the district court.

United States Court of Appeals
for the Eighth Circuit

No. 18-2143

DAKOTA, MINN. & E. R.R. CORP. & SOO LINE
R.R. CO.
vs.
INGRAM BARGE CO.

Appeal from the United States District Court for the
Northern District of Iowa - Dubuque

Decided: March 21, 2019

Citation: 918 F.3d 967, 7 Adm. R. 419 (8th Cir. 2019).

Before **BENTON, MELLOY,** and **KELLY,** Circuit Judges.

[—1—] {–969–} **KELLY,** Circuit Judge:

The M/V Aubrey B. Harwell Jr. (the *Harwell*), a towboat operated by Ingram {–970–} Barge Company, was pushing empty barges up the Mississippi River when the barges struck the Sabula Railroad Bridge, owned by Dakota, Minnesota & Eastern Railroad Corporation (DM&E). DM&E sued Ingram for damages. Following a bench trial, [—2—] the district court entered judgment in favor of DM&E for the full amount sought.[1] Ingram appeals. Because we conclude that the district court committed an error of law, we vacate the judgment and remand for further proceedings.

I

The Secretary of War authorized the construction of the Sabula Railroad Bridge in 1880. To allow river traffic to pass, a portion of the Bridge rotates 90 degrees on a central pivot, producing two 154-foot-wide channels on either side. Protection piers extend north and south from the center of the Bridge; when the Bridge is in its open position, the Bridge's tracks rest above the piers separating the two

channels. Northbound traffic ordinarily uses the east channel, and southbound traffic ordinarily uses the west channel. The typical barge arrangement on this portion of the river is approximately 105 feet wide, leaving under 25 feet of clearance on either side. Unsurprisingly, barge operators are sometimes unsuccessful at avoiding contact between their modern-sized tows and the centenarian Bridge. *See generally I&M Rail Link, LLC v. Northstar Nav., Inc.*, 198 F.3d 1012 (7th Cir. 2000) (discussing a May 5, 1997, allision with the Bridge).

On June 17, 1996, the United States Coast Guard issued an Order to Alter pursuant to the Truman-Hobbs Act, 33 U.S.C. §§ 511 et seq. The Order to Alter declared the Bridge to be an "unreasonable obstruction to the free navigation of the Upper Mississippi River" and directed the then-owner to reconstruct the Bridge to expand the horizontal clearance to at least 300 feet, approximately double its current [—3—] width. Neither DM&E nor any prior owner of the Bridge took any action to complete such reconstruction.

On April 24, 2015, the *Harwell* was traveling north on the Mississippi River. Hershey Dampier was steering under the supervision of pilot Tommy Hinton. Dampier was on his first trip as a licensed steersman but had traveled under the Bridge many times during his twelve years as a deckhand. He discussed the procedure for passing through the Bridge with Hinton prior to their approach. Because the wind was blowing from east to west, Hinton advised Dampier to keep the barges pointed to the right side of the eastern channel. About 300 or 400 feet from the Bridge, Dampier realized that the barges were too close to the protection pier on the left side. Dampier attempted to correct by steering further to the east but the barges allided with the protection pier, causing damage to the wooden structure and a maintenance platform. Dampier was not disciplined for the incident, and he has since piloted through the Bridge more than a dozen times without incident. DM&E's staff concluded that the damage to the protection pier required immediate repair to prevent the risk that another allision would damage the tracks and

---

[1] The complaint named Soo Line Railroad Company, DM&E's corporate parent, as an additional plaintiff and included a second claim relating to a September 7, 2015, allision involving a different bridge owned by Soo Line. That claim was dismissed pursuant to the parties' stipulation prior to trial and no allegations remain relevant to Soo Line.

render the Bridge inoperable. Contractors completed the repairs at a cost of $276,860.85. DM&E brought suit against Ingram to recover these repair costs. {–971–}

Following a bench trial, the district court concluded that no comparative fault could attach to DM&E absent evidence of a breach of a legal duty to expand the Bridge's horizontal clearance, and that the Order to Alter imposed no such duty. It apportioned all of the fault to Ingram and awarded DM&E the full amount of the repair costs plus prejudgment interest.

II

We review findings of a district court's bench trial in admiralty cases, including negligence determinations, under a clearly erroneous standard. *In re MO Barge* [—4—] *Lines, Inc.*, 360 F.3d 885, 889 (8th Cir. 2004). We will overturn a factual finding as clearly erroneous "only if it is not supported by substantial evidence in the record, if it is based on an erroneous view of the law, or if we are left with the definite and firm conviction that an error was made." *Urban Hotel Dev. Co. v. President Dev. Grp., L.C.*, 535 F.3d 874, 879 (8th Cir. 2008) (quoting *Roemmich v. Eagle Eye Dev., LLC*, 526 F.3d 343, 353 (8th Cir. 2008)). "In admiralty as in other contexts, however, we review purely legal determinations de novo." *In re Am. Milling Co.*, 409 F.3d 1005, 1013 (8th Cir. 2005).

As in any negligence case, the plaintiff in a maritime allision suit bears the burden of proof by a preponderance of the evidence. *Zerega Ave. Realty Corp. v. Hornbeck Offshore Transp., LLC*, 571 F.3d 206, 212 (2d Cir. 2009). The plaintiff must prove essentially the same elements as a land-based negligence claim at common law: that the defendant breached a legal duty, causing the injury sustained by the plaintiff. *See In re Cooper/T. Smith*, 929 F.2d 1073, 1077 (5th Cir. 1991) (per curiam); *see also Evergreen Int'l, S.A. v. Norfolk Dredging Co.*, 531 F.3d 302, 308 (4th Cir. 2008). The duty of care owed by a moving vessel to a stationary object such as a bridge is reasonable care under the circumstances. *Fischer v. S/Y NERAIDA*, 508 F.3d 586, 593

(11th Cir. 2007). Experience and common sense counsel that a moving vessel does not ordinarily strike a stationary object unless the vessel is mishandled in some way. *Am. Milling*, 409 F.3d at 1018. As such, the plaintiff in an allision case may invoke the *Oregon* rule, which creates a rebuttable presumption that a moving vessel breached its duty of care when it allides with a stationary object. *Id.* at 1012; *Union Pac. R.R. Co. v. Kirby Inland Marine, Inc. of Miss.*, 296 F.3d 671, 673 (8th Cir. 2002); *see The Oregon*, 158 U.S. 186, 197 (1895). The *Oregon* presumption satisfies the plaintiff's prima facie case, shifting the burden of proof on issues of duty and breach to the defendant. *City of Chicago v. M/V Morgan*, 375 F.3d 563, 572–73 (7th Cir. 2004). [—5—]

To rebut the *Oregon* presumption, the moving vessel may prove one of three things: that "(1) the moving vessel used all reasonable care to avoid the [allision] and was therefore without fault, (2) the stationary object was at fault, or (3) the allision occurred because of an 'inevitable accident.'" *Am. Milling*, 409 F.3d at 1018 (quoting *Bunge Corp. v. M/V Furness Bridge*, 558 F.2d 790, 795 (5th Cir. 1977)). One method of proving that the stationary object was at fault is through the *Pennsylvania* rule. *See The Pennsylvania*, 86 U.S. 125, 136 (1873). Under the *Pennsylvania* rule, "if there is a violation of a statute or regulation designed to prevent collisions, the burden shifts to the violator to prove that the violation was not a contributing cause of the accident." *Am. Milling*, 409 F.3d at 1012. "For the *Pennsylvania* rule to apply, three elements must exist: (1) proof by a preponderance of the evidence of violation of a statute or regulation that imposes a {–972–} *mandatory duty*; (2) the statute or regulation must involve *marine safety* or navigation; and (3) the injury suffered must be of a nature that the statute or regulation was intended to prevent." *Kirby Inland Marine*, 296 F.3d at 674.

Ingram attempts to invoke the *Pennsylvania* rule by relying on the Coast Guard's 1996 Order to Alter. But in *Kirby Inland Marine*, we concluded that an Order to Alter issued by the Coast Guard cannot trigger the *Pennsylvania* rule because the

Truman-Hobbs Act was not drafted to maintain marine safety, impose a specific duty, or prevent a particular sort of injury. 296 F.3d at 674. Instead, the Truman-Hobbs Act is a funding statute, and an Order to Alter is simply a mechanism the Coast Guard can use to make federal funding available for bridge reconstruction. *Id.* at 675. Although bridge alterations may reduce the number of allisions, "this is a collateral consequence and not a direct purpose of the Truman-Hobbs Act." *Id.* An Order to Alter based on the Coast Guard's finding that a bridge is an "unreasonable obstruction to navigation" is "not a direct comment on the safety of the bridge." *Id.* In short, a Truman-Hobbs Act finding does not satisfy the requirements of the *Pennsylvania* rule and therefore does not rebut the *Oregon* presumption. *Id.* at 676–78. [—6—]

Although the Coast Guard's decision to issue an Order to Alter does not automatically rebut the *Oregon* presumption, it is still relevant to the analysis. The Order to Alter may be introduced as "another piece of evidence which the *trier of fact* may consider in determining fault in a negligence action." *Id.* at 677. That is, the vessel operator may still attempt to rebut the presumption through evidence of the stationary object's negligence—including the evidence relied upon by the Coast Guard in making its Truman-Hobbs Act finding. *See id.* at 678 (discussing other evidence of the bridge's obstructive character that may be used to rebut the *Oregon* presumption, including evidence documented by the Coast Guard in the Order to Alter); *I&M Rail Link*, 198 F.3d at 1016 ("If the Coast Guard may find the Sabula Bridge an unreasonable obstruction based on the cost and accident data, then so may the trier of fact in admiralty . . . .").

Relying on *Kirby Inland Marine*, the district court correctly concluded that the 1996 Order to Alter does not, as a matter of law, rebut the *Oregon* presumption through operation of the *Pennsylvania* rule. And it correctly admitted the Order to Alter and the supporting Truman-Hobbs Act reports into evidence. It analyzed the evidence supporting the Coast Guard's decision and concluded that

it was insufficient to rebut the *Oregon* presumption. In other words, Ingram was unable to "exonerate itself from liability" because it could not prove that "the allision was the *sole* fault of the bridge." *M/V Morgan*, 375 F.3d at 574 (emphasis added).

But application of the *Oregon* rule does not end the analysis. The presumption "merely addresses a party's burden of proof and/or burden of persuasion; it is not a rule of ultimate liability." *Id.* at 572; *accord Bessemer & Lake Erie R.R. Co. v. Seaway Marine Transp.*, 596 F.3d 357, 363 (6th Cir. 2010). Furthermore, it is properly limited to the issues of duty and breach; it does not resolve questions of causation or the percentages of fault assigned to the parties adjudged negligent. *Combo Mar., Inc. v. U.S. United Bulk Terminal, LLC*, 615 F.3d 599, 605 (5th Cir. 2010). Under maritime law, liability for an allision is apportioned based upon the [—7—] comparative fault of the parties. *Evergreen Int'l*, 531 F.3d at 308; *see also* {–973–} *United States v. Reliable Transfer Co.*, 421 U.S. 397, 411 (1975). In a comparative fault regime, "[t]he plaintiff's negligence reduces the amount of damages that he can collect, but is not a defense to liability." *Bhd. Shipping Co. v. St. Paul Fire & Marine Ins. Co.*, 985 F.2d 323, 325 (7th Cir. 1993). "Contributory negligence is conduct on the part of the plaintiff which falls below the standard to which he should conform for his own protection, and which is a legally contributing cause co-operating with the negligence of the defendant in bringing about the plaintiff's harm." Restatement (Second) of Torts § 463 (Am. Law Inst. 1965). If the owner of a bridge fails to adhere to the standard of "a reasonable person under like circumstances," and this failure contributes to an allision, the court may reduce the owner's recovery accordingly. *S. C. Loveland, Inc. v. E. W. Towing, Inc.*, 608 F.2d 160, 166 (5th Cir. 1979).

In its comparative fault analysis, the district court concluded that DM&E could not be assigned any share of fault because it had no legal duty to remove or alter the lawfully permitted Bridge. But the owner of a lawful bridge may be found comparatively negligent for an allision even absent an affirmative legal duty to alter the bridge's configuration, as illustrated by the Seventh Circuit's decision in *M/V Morgan*. In that case, the court examined an allision between a tugboat and a bridge that resulted in damage to the bridge's electrical cabling. 375 F.3d at 570. The court concluded that the tugboat operators had failed to rebut the *Oregon* presumption and were liable for negligence. *Id.* at 573–78. Nonetheless, and even though the bridge was in compliance with its permit, the court affirmed the district court's equal apportionment of damages between the parties based on the bridge owner's failure to replace a wooden fender that previously protected the cabling. *Id.* at 578–79. It follows from *M/V Morgan* that a negligent bridge owner may face reduced damages from an allision under admiralty's comparative fault regime, as the Seventh Circuit has held in a previous case dealing with an allision with the Sabula Bridge. *See I&M Rail Link*, 198 F.3d at 1016 (remanding to the district court to determine whether the [—8—] Bridge's design "bear[s] some responsibility" for allision). It also follows that a finding of comparative negligence does not necessarily require the bridge owner to have violated a specific legal duty owed to others imposed by statute or regulation. All that is required is a finding that the bridge owner was negligent and that this "negligence . . . contribute[d] to the loss." 1 *Admiralty & Mar. Law* § 5:7 (6th ed. 2018).

DM&E argues that *California v. Sierra Club*, 451 U.S. 287 (1981), stands for the proposition that a lawfully permitted bridge's obstruction to navigation cannot constitute negligence. We disagree. *Sierra Club* simply concluded that Section 10 of the Rivers and Harbors Appropriation Act, which prohibits the creation of any obstruction to navigable waters not authorized by Congress, did not establish a private right of action. *See id.* at 292–97. This holding does not immunize a bridge from its own comparative fault when an allision occurs. Since *Sierra Club*, we have held that "the trier of fact should determine whether" a lawful bridge's obstruction to navigation is unreasonable and a contributing cause of an allision, *Kirby Inland Marine*, 296 F.3d at 676, as has the Seventh Circuit

specifically with regard to the Sabula Bridge, *I&M Rail Link*, 198 F.3d at 1016. If the district court so concludes, it may reduce the bridge owner's recovery based upon the bridge's comparative fault.

DM&E also argues that the district court independently found that the *Harwell*'s {–974–} crew's negligence was the only "actual cause" of the allision, and that this factual finding was not clearly erroneous. We are dubious that this truly was an independent factual finding. The district court's conclusion that Ingram was solely responsible for the accident came only after it concluded that it could not, as a matter of law, apportion any of the fault to DM&E. And the court acknowledged that the evidence demonstrated that the Bridge "poses a difficult obstacle to barge traffic" due to the narrowness of its channels, which leave "little clearance" for modern barge configurations. It appears that the district court's factual finding apportioning all of [—9—] the fault to Ingram may not have been divorced from its earlier legal error.[2] A factual finding "based on an erroneous view of the law" will not be upheld, even on review for clear error. *Urban Hotel*, 535 F.3d at 879. We express no opinion on whether DM&E in fact was comparatively negligent; we leave that assessment to the district court in the first instance.

In accordance with the above, we vacate the decision of the district court and remand for further proceedings consistent with this opinion.

---

[2] DM&E places great weight on the district court's use of the word "[m]oreover" to separate its legal conclusion that it could not apportion fault to DM&E from its factual finding that Ingram's negligence was the sole cause of the allision. We do not parse the language of the district court's opinion with such granularity. *See Reiter v. Sonotone Corp.*, 442 U.S. 330, 341 (1979). Read in context, the district court's later factual finding may have resulted from its earlier legal analysis.

United States Court of Appeals for the Ninth Circuit

United States Court of Appeals
for the Ninth Circuit

No. 17-35703

CASTRO
VS.
TRI MARINE FISH CO.

Appeal from the United States District Court for the
Western District of Washington

Order and Amended Opinion

Decided: February 27, 2019
Amended: April 15, 2019

Citation: 921 F.3d 766, 7 Adm. R. 424 (9th Cir. 2019) (reh'g
and reh'g en banc denied).

Before **McKEOWN** and **FRIEDLAND,** Circuit Judges,
and **BOLTON,** * District Judge.

* The Honorable Susan R. Bolton, United States District
Judge for the District of Arizona, sitting by designation.

ORDER

The opinion filed on February 27, 2019, and
appearing at 916 F.3d 1191, is amended. On
page 13, <flouted> is replaced with <appears
to have omitted required aspects of>, and
<deviated completely> is replaced with
<appears to have deviated>. An amended
opinion is filed concurrently with this order.

With these amendments, the panel has
voted to deny the petition for panel rehearing.

The full court has been advised of the
petition for rehearing and rehearing en banc
and no judge has requested a vote on whether
to rehear the matter en banc. Fed. R. App. P.
35.

The petition for panel rehearing and
rehearing en banc (Dkt. 36) is denied. The
motion to proceed as amicus (Dkt. 37) is
granted. No further petitions for en banc or
panel rehearing shall be permitted.

OPINION

[—4—] {–770–} McKEOWN, Circuit Judge: {–771–}

Central to the United Nations Convention
on the Recognition and Enforcement of
Foreign Arbitral Awards, June 10, 1958,
21 U.S.T. 2517 ("New York Convention"), and
related federal law is the principle insulating
foreign arbitral awards from second-guessing
by courts. But this appeal involves an even
more fundamental question—whether we are
presented with a foreign arbitral award at all.
In the mine run of cases, the answer is
uncontroversial: when it looks, swims, and
quacks like an arbitral award, it typically is.
Yet, in this unusual appeal, we have an
arbitral award in name only. There was no
dispute to arbitrate, as the parties had fully
settled their claims before approaching an
arbitrator; the purported arbitration consisted
of an impromptu meeting in a building lobby;
and the "proceedings" disregarded the terms
of three arbitration agreements between the
parties and the issuing forum's arbitral rules.
We conclude that the resulting order is not an
arbitral award entitled to enforcement under
the Convention.

BACKGROUND

In late 2012, Michael Castro moved from
the Philippines, where he retains citizenship,
to American Samoa to live with April Castillo,
his fiancé, and her family. Several months
later, Castro was working in a Tri Marine
[—5—] warehouse when Tri Marine offered
him a crew position aboard the *F/V Captain
Vincent Gann* (the "Vessel"), a fishing vessel
with an imminent departure date.[1] He
accepted a position as a deck hand.

The day before departing, Castro visited
Tri Marine's offices to sign employment
paperwork. Castro and Tri Marine dispute
what was signed that day. Tri Marine
contends that Castro signed his employment
agreement, which is consistent with the date

---

[1] Castro sued several entities with alleged
interests in the Vessel. For purposes of this appeal,
there is no relevant distinction between the
entities. We refer to them collectively as Tri
Marine.

typed on the agreement itself. Castro insists that before departing he signed only "a half sheet of paper with a few sentences on it including [a] pay rate of $3.00 per ton [of fish caught], the name of the Vessel[,] and a signature line," and that he did not sign the employment agreement until he appeared before an arbitrator in February 2014. The employment agreement—whenever Castro signed it—contained a mandatory arbitration provision applicable to all disputes or claims arising out of Castro's employment aboard the Vessel. It required arbitration to occur in and subject to the procedural rules of American Samoa.

On July 30, 2013, approximately two weeks into the fishing trip, Castro fell down a set of stairs and severely injured his knee. Castro requested that Tri Marine return him to American Samoa so he could travel to Hawaii for medical care, but Tri Marine instead arranged for Castro's transport to and medical care in the Philippines. In mid-August, Castro underwent surgery for a torn anterior cruciate ligament and a torn meniscus, followed by treatment and [—6—] physical therapy. Tri Marine paid Castro's medical expenses and monthly maintenance.

Several months into Castro's rehabilitation, doctors diagnosed his father with kidney cancer and predicted he would die without surgery. Castro and his family could not afford his father's surgery, so Castro approached Rhodylyn De Torres, a Tri Marine agent in the Philippines, and {–772–} negotiated a settlement of his disability claims. In exchange for an advance of $5,000, Castro reiterated his assent to the employment agreement's arbitration and choice of law clauses. Shortly after, Castro agreed in principle to release fully his claims in exchange for an additional $16,160.[2]

After Tri Marine prepared the settlement paperwork, Castro met De Torres at her office in Manila to finalize the settlement. Castro speaks only rudimentary English—his native tongue is Tagalog—so Castillo, who has a greater proficiency in English, attended the meeting and helped him review the settlement materials. De Torres informed Castro in advance that he would be signing release documents to conclude his case, but not that he would be participating in an arbitration.

De Torres and Castro provide divergent accounts of the meeting. De Torres attests that over the course of two hours, she explained the documents to Castro in "Filipino language" (presumably, Tagalog), Castro indicated that he understood, and Castro signed the release documents. She also indicates that she explained, and Castro agreed, that an [—7—] arbitrator would review and approve the release documents "to make the settlement legal and binding." Castro disputes whether De Torres translated documents into Tagalog, explained that he would be foregoing future legal claims by signing them, or informed him that he would be participating in arbitration. According to Castro, De Torres told him they would go to a different office merely to pick up the settlement check and execute paperwork acknowledging receipt.

Although it is disputed when in the day this happened, Castro executed a release of Tri Marine "from any and all liability or claims . . . arising out of or in any way connected with an illness, incident, and/or incidents aboard the [Vessel] on or about 30 July, 2013." Castro acknowledged and released his right to future maintenance and cure in exchange for the settlement amount. Like Castro's employment agreement (and as he reiterated when accepting his advance payment), the release provided that disputes over its validity and enforceability would be arbitrated in American Samoa.

After the parties had agreed to the terms of the release, a Tri Marine agent ushered Castro and Castillo to an office building that housed the National Conciliation and Mediation Board. De Torres had led Castro to believe that they would merely pick up the settlement disbursement and acknowledge

---

[2] We use variants of the terms "agree" and "settle" for convenience's sake. We do not suggest any conclusion regarding Castro's defenses to formation and enforcement of the purported settlement. Those defenses remain open issues on remand.

receipt. Tri Marine now contends that they went to the Board's office to submit their dispute to arbitration. Gregorio Biares, an accredited maritime voluntary arbitrator, met the parties in the lobby and introduced himself as a neutral arbitrator.

The meeting was Castro's first and only interaction with an arbitrator. Seated at a small table in the public lobby, surrounded by strangers entering and leaving the building, Biares reviewed the settlement paperwork with Castro. [—8—] Biares attests that he explained the implications of the release and confirmed in Tagalog that Castro understood the documents. Castro paints a different picture: Biares "hurriedly flipped through the pages showing [Castro] where to sign," emphasized that the settlement was favorable to Castro, and misled Castro by characterizing the settlement as "just a first payment" and informing Castro that {–773–} he is ineligible for protection under the Jones Act.

Although there was no arbitral case filed, Tri Marine provided Biares a "joint motion to dismiss" pursuant to the parties' settlement, accompanied by the release paperwork that Castro had already signed. The two-page joint motion to dismiss was the first "filing" in the "case," which lacks a case number. Biares signed a one-page document, labeled an "order," which recognized the settlement, stated that Biares found the settlement "not contrary to law, morals, good customs and public policy," and dismissed the "case" with prejudice. The order acknowledges that it is the product of a "Walk In Settlement" and that the release had already been "duly signed by both parties" before meeting with Biares.

Later treatment revealed that Castro's initial surgery had failed to graft his anterior cruciate ligament or address his torn meniscus. Facing additional surgery to repair these mistakes, Castro sued Tri Marine in Washington state court to recover the additional expenses. Invoking the New York Convention, Tri Marine removed the case to federal court and moved to confirm the order as a foreign arbitral award. The district court denied Castro's motion to remand, confirmed the order, and dismissed the case. [—9—]

ANALYSIS

I. The New York Convention

The New York Convention, to which the United States is a party, governs "the recognition and enforcement of *arbitral awards* made in the territory of" a foreign state. New York Convention, art. I(1) (emphasis added). Through the Convention and implementing legislation, the United States sought "to encourage the recognition and enforcement of commercial arbitration agreements in international contracts and to unify the standards by which agreements to arbitrate are observed and arbitral awards are enforced in the signatory countries." *Scherk v. Alberto-Culver Co.*, 417 U.S. 506, 520 n.15 (1974).

The United States codified its Convention obligations in the Convention Act, 9 U.S.C. §§ 201–08. *Rogers v. Royal Caribbean Cruise Line*, 547 F.3d 1148, 1152–53 (9th Cir. 2008). Just as the Federal Arbitration Act ("FAA") affords considerable deference to domestic arbitral awards, the Convention Act does the same for foreign arbitral awards. *Polimaster Ltd. v. RAE Sys., Inc.*, 623 F.3d 832, 836 (9th Cir. 2010). A court must confirm a foreign arbitral award unless the party resisting enforcement meets its "substantial" burden of proving one of seven narrowly interpreted defenses. *Id.*; *see* 9 U.S.C. § 207 (incorporating the Convention's defenses); New York Convention, art. V (listing defenses). The judicial role in this process is circumscribed: "Confirmation under the Convention is a summary proceeding in nature, which is not intended to involve complex factual determinations, other than a determination of the limited statutory conditions for confirmation or grounds for refusal to confirm." *Zeiler v. Deitsch*, 500 F.3d 157, 169 (2d Cir. 2007). [—10—]

Yet, before we employ the Convention's and the Convention Act's substantial protections, the threshold step is, of course, to ensure they apply. This interpretive inquiry requires our de novo review. *CVS Health Corp. v. Vividus, LLC*, 878 F.3d 703, 706 (9th Cir. 2017) (statutes); *Hosaka v. United Airlines, Inc.*, 305

F.3d 989, 993 (9th Cir. 2002) (treaties). The key question here is whether there is an "arbitral award" to consider. Amazingly, that term is not defined in the Convention Act, {–774–} which governs only "arbitral award[s] falling under the Convention." 9 U.S.C. § 207. Congress defined "falling under the Convention," *id.* § 202, but not "arbitral award" or "arbitration." "Arbitration" and "arbitral award" are also undefined in the Convention itself and in the FAA, 9 U.S.C. §§ 1–16. *See Polimaster*, 623 F.3d at 836 ("When interpreting the defenses to confirmation of an arbitration award under the New York Convention, we may look to authority under the FAA.").

We therefore interpret the term by applying its common meaning and common sense. *Green Tree Fin. Corp.-Ala. v. Randolph*, 531 U.S. 79, 86 (2000). We also look to the American Law Institute's recent restatement on international commercial arbitration, which offers helpful guidance and background. *See* Restatement (Third) U.S. Law of Int'l Commercial Arbitration § 1-1 (Am. Law Inst., Tentative Draft No. 2, 2012) ("Restatement TD No. 2").[3] It sets forth several helpful definitions: [—11—]

> An "arbitral award" is a decision in writing by an arbitral tribunal that sets forth the final and binding determination on the merits of a claim, defense, or issue, regardless of whether that decision resolves the entire controversy before the tribunal. . . .
>
> An "arbitral tribunal" is a body consisting of one or more persons designated directly or indirectly by the parties to an arbitration agreement and empowered by them to adjudicate a

dispute that has arisen between or among them.

> "Arbitration" is a dispute resolution method in which the disputing parties empower an arbitral tribunal to decide a dispute in a final and binding manner.

Id. § 1-1(a)–(c).

II. The Purported Arbitral Award

In a superficial sense, the order issued here resembles an arbitral award: it was issued by an arbitrator and purports to award Castro a monetary remedy and dismiss the "case" with prejudice. But labels and appearances are not controlling—we evaluate an award by looking to its essence. *Id.* § 1-1 cmt. a. Several unique aspects of these proceedings lead us to conclude that the order is not an arbitral award within the meaning of the Convention.

To begin, there was no outstanding dispute to arbitrate by the time Castro and Tri Marine sat down with the arbitrator. *Id.* § 1-1(c) ("'Arbitration' is a dispute resolution [—12—] method . . . ."). Integral to the Convention's conception of arbitration is the endeavor to resolve a dispute:

> [T]he tribunal must be dealing with a genuine disagreement to have jurisdiction. Where parties appoint an arbitral tribunal after a settlement to merely record the settlement in the . . . award, there is no "difference" between the parties to resolve; the parties have already settled the dispute. A "difference" is a necessary precondition of an "award" in the sense of the New York Convention.

Yaraslau Kryvoi & Dmitry Davydenko, *Consent Awards in International Arbitration: From Settlement to Enforcement*, 40 Brook. J. Int'l L. 827, 854 (2015); *see also Arbitration*, Black's Law Dictionary (10th ed. 2014) ("A dispute-resolution process in which . . . neutral third parties . . . resolv[e] {–775–} the dispute."); A Decree Instituting a Labor Code Thereby Revising and Consolidating Labor and Social Laws to Afford Protection to Labor,

---

[3] Although the membership has not formally approved the full Restatement (Third) of the U.S. Law of International Commercial Arbitration, the American Law Institute has approved Tentative Draft No. 2, which contains the only sections that we consider here. *See Discussion of Restatement of the Law Third, The U.S. Law of International Commercial Arbitration*, 2012 A.L.I. Proceedings 143 (Am. Law Inst., May 22, 2012).

Promote Employment and Human Resources Development and Insure Industrial Peace Based on Social Justice, Pres. Dec. No. 442 (as amended), art. 262 (1974) (Philippine Labor Code permitting arbitrators to "hear and decide . . . labor disputes"); Revised Procedural Guidelines in the Conduct of Voluntary Arbitration Proceedings, National Conciliation and Mediation Board, Rule II § 1(d) (2005) ("Procedural Guidelines") (Philippine rules of voluntary arbitration defining "Voluntary Arbitration" as a "mode of settling labor-management disputes").

Castro and Tri Marine agreed to settle their dispute, and to terms for doing so, before they ever visited an arbitrator. [—13—] In exchange for a monetary settlement, Castro released Tri Marine "from any and all liability or claims . . . arising out of or in any way connected with" the July 30, 2013 incident. Having settled their dispute, Castro and Tri Marine had nothing to arbitrate. *See* Restatement TD No. 2 § 1-1(c); Kryvoi & Davydenko, 40 Brook. J. Int'l L. at 854.

What's more, the purported arbitration in no way followed the parties' prior agreements to arbitrate. Because "[a]rbitration is consent-based," Restatement TD No. 2 § 1-1 Reporters' Note d, the tribunal "derives its jurisdiction and remedial powers" from the parties' assent, *id*. § 1-1 cmt. b. The employment agreement provided for arbitration in and subject to the procedural rules of American Samoa, the advance payment receipt reiterated the employment agreement's arbitration and choice of law clauses, and even the executed release provided for arbitration in American Samoa. The lobby meeting with Biares was a far cry—in venue and law—from the agreed procedure.

To be sure, parties can waive contractual terms, but Castro's conduct hardly demonstrates an intent to arbitrate his dispute in the Philippines. Castro had no dispute. He simply sought to pick up the settlement check and acknowledge receipt— which Tri Marine led him to believe he was doing. The setting and surroundings of the lobby sit-down suggested a coffee date more than an arbitral proceeding; little wonder,

then, that Castro professed ignorance that the meeting supposedly constituted arbitration. These circumstances scarcely demonstrate that Castro sought to waive or amend his thrice-written agreement to arbitrate disputes in American Samoa. Nor do any of the final documents reference waiver of the parties' repeated commitments to arbitrate in American Samoa. [—14—]

Beyond fidelity to the terms of the arbitration agreement, an "arbitrator[] . . . act[s] pursuant to the arbitration law of the arbitral seat . . . and any procedural rules that the parties may have adopted." Restatement TD No. 2 § 1-1 cmt. c. The parties did not "adopt" any procedural rules apart from those set forth in the three written agreements. The meeting also appears to have omitted required aspects of Philippine arbitral procedure. In the Philippines, voluntary arbitration begins upon receipt of a submission agreement signed by both parties. Procedural Guidelines, Rule IV § 4. No submission agreement was filed here. The submission agreement must list the specific issues to be arbitrated. *Id.*, Rule IV § 5. But no arbitrable issues existed here, as the parties had already resolved their dispute. Other Philippine pre-arbitration procedures, such as an initial conference, joint formulation of ground rules, and pleadings, were conspicuously absent as well. *Id.*, Rule VI §§ 2, 3, 6, 8. In sum, the procedure here appears to have deviated from {–776–} typical Philippine procedures. This divergence confirms our understanding that arbitration did not occur.

We conclude that the parties' free-floating settlement agreement and order did not transform into an arbitral award simply because the parties convened with an arbitrator. Tri Marine may seek to enforce the release as a matter of contract, but the order approving the settlement is not an arbitral award under the Convention.

Importantly, our decision does not encroach on the common practice of reducing settlements reached *during* arbitration into arbitral awards, frequently termed "consent awards." Many international arbitral rules empower arbitrators—upon the parties' request—to enter consent awards. *See* Margaret L. Moses, *The Principles and Practice of International Commercial Arbitration* 205 (3d [—15—] ed. 2017). Consent awards encourage settlement by conferring substantial benefits—including the Convention's protections—upon parties that obtain them. *See* Nigel Blackaby et al., *Redfern and Hunter on International Arbitration* §§ 9.33, 9.34, 9.36 (Student ed. 2009) (noting that several international arbitral bodies embrace consent awards).

Our decision does not disturb this practice for a simple reason: it did not occur here. "Timing is important for a settlement agreement to become an award. Usually a consent award becomes possible after a tribunal has been constituted. . . . Otherwise the tribunal will have no right to render a consent award." Kryvoi & Davydenko, 40 Brook. J. Int'l L. at 842–43.[4] Philippine, American, and broadly applicable international rules impose this temporal limitation on consent awards. Philippine arbitrators may issue a consent award "[i]n the event that the parties finally settle their dispute *during the pendency of the arbitration proceedings*." Procedural Guidelines, Rule VII § 4 (emphasis added). Leading American and international arbitration groups espouse the same limitation. *See* Am. Arbitration Ass'n, *Commercial Arbitration Rules and Mediation Procedures* R-48(a) (2013); United Nations Commission on International Trade Law, *Model Law on International Commercial Arbitration*, art. 30(1) (2006). Even the two cases involving consent awards cited favorably by Tri Marine are consistent with this timing requirement. *See United States v. Sperry Corp.*, 493 U.S. 52, 56–57 (1989) (parties initiated arbitration, then settled, and then obtained a consent award); *Transocean Offshore Gulf of Guinea VII* [—16—] *Ltd. v. Erin Energy Corp.*, No. CV H-17-2623, 2018 WL 1251924, at *1 (S.D. Tex. Mar. 12, 2018) (same). The timing here was backwards— Castro and Tri Marine settled and then

---

[4] The authors characterize their article as "the first major study of the legal regime governing consent awards in international arbitration." Kryvoi & Davydenko, 40 Brook. J. Int'l L. at 828.

sought to arbitrate. The result is not a consent award.

Finally, we emphasize that our decision does not elevate form over function. Tri Marine protests, for instance, that to obtain a proper consent award, it could have simply initiated arbitral proceedings before finalizing the settlement. Perhaps, but not for nothing. An essential aspect of arbitration is each party's inability to unilaterally withdraw from proceedings. Restatement TD No. 2 § 1-1 cmt. c. Other, "[c]ollaborative forms of [alternative dispute resolution]," by contrast, "require the parties' continuing willingness to participate." *Id.* § 1-1 Reporters' Note c. Accordingly, "the weight of decisional authority and international consensus" does not treat collaborative processes, such as mediation, {–777–} as "arbitration" under the Convention. *Id.* Had the arbitrator here balked—for instance, by ordering a hearing on voluntariness or enforcing the venue provision pointing to American Samoa—Tri Marine could have taken its settlement and gone home. Although perhaps a modest hurdle, the modicum of formality required for a proceeding to constitute arbitration is no empty ritual.

III. Remand

Because the district court treated the order as a foreign arbitral award, it proceeded in summary fashion under the Convention. For example, it weighed evidence and resolved genuine disputes of material fact in favor of Tri Marine, thereby rejecting out of hand Castro's coercion defense. In light of our conclusion, the district court's approach was in error. We vacate in full the order confirming the arbitral [—17—] award, including the ruling on the validity of the seaman's release.

At oral argument, Castro suggested for the first time that the absence of an arbitral award calls into question federal jurisdiction. The Convention Act permits removal of cases that "relate[] to an arbitration agreement or award falling under the Convention." 9 U.S.C. § 205. Although the order here is not an arbitral award, the subject matter of the case may nonetheless "relate[] to an arbitration agreement." *Id.*; *see Infuturia Glob. Ltd. v. Sequus Pharm., Inc.*, 631 F.3d 1133, 1138 (9th Cir. 2011) ("The phrase 'relates to' is plainly broad . . . .").

In light of the parties' failure to brief this issue on appeal, we take no position on the ultimate disposition of this jurisdictional question. We remand for the district court to assess jurisdiction and—as appropriate— venue and any defenses to enforcement.

CONCLUSION

We review foreign arbitral awards deferentially, but we do not blind ourselves to reality when presented with an order purporting to be one. To cloak its free-floating settlement agreement in the New York Convention's favorable enforcement regime, Tri Marine asked an arbitrator to wave his wand and transform the settlement into an arbitral award. That is not sufficient to produce an award subject to the Convention.

REVERSED IN PART, VACATED IN PART, AND REMANDED.

Tri Marine shall bear costs on appeal.

United States Court of Appeals
for the Ninth Circuit

No. 17-70415

IOPA

vs.

SALTCHUK-YOUNG BROS., LTD.

On Petition for Review of an Order of the Benefits
Review Board

Decided: March 4, 2019

Citation: 916 F.3d 1298, 7 Adm. R. 431 (9th Cir. 2019).

Before **TALLMAN**, **BYBEE**, and **SMITH**, Circuit Judges.

[—3—] {–1299–} PER CURIAM: {–1300–}

Petitioner Warren Iopa appeals the United States Department of Labor's Benefits Review Board's ("BRB") order affirming an Administrative Law Judge's ("ALJ") decision striking as untimely a petition for payment of his attorney's fees under the Longshore and Harbor Workers' Compensation Act ("Longshore Act"), 33 U.S.C. §§ 901–50, filed more than nine months past the ALJ-ordered deadline. We now consider for the first time in our circuit whether striking an untimely petition for attorney's fees under the Longshore Act is proper only given extreme circumstances, or whether excusable neglect is the proper standard by which to evaluate such petitions. We hold that the excusable neglect analysis is proper and affirm the BRB's decision to uphold the ALJ's dismissal order. [—4—]

I

Following Iopa's successful litigation of claims for temporary disability benefits under the Longshore Act, the ALJ held that he was entitled to reasonable attorney's fees and costs, and that a fee petition had to be filed within 21 days of the award order entered July 31, 2014. *See* 20 C.F.R. § 702.132(a). On June 8, 2015, Iopa's counsel instead improperly filed a fee petition for work done before the Office of Workers' Compensation Programs ("OWCP"). At the request of the ALJ's office, counsel filed a corrected petition with the Office of Administrative Law Judges

("OALJ") on October 27, 2015. The ALJ then issued an order striking the first petition due to his lack of authority to award attorney's fees for work done before the OWCP, and striking the second petition based on a finding of untimeliness without excusable neglect.

II

We have jurisdiction under 33 U.S.C. § 921(c). We review BRB decisions under the Longshore Act "for errors of law and for adherence to the substantial evidence standard." *Gen. Const. Co. v. Castro*, 401 F.3d 963, 965 (9th Cir. 2005) (quoting *Alcala v. Dir., OWCP*, 141 F.3d 942, 944 (9th Cir. 1998)). We conduct de novo review on questions of law, including questions of statutory interpretation, under the Longshore Act. *See Pedroza v. BRB*, 624 F.3d 926, 930 (9th Cir. 2010). "Because the [BRB] is not a policymaking entity, we accord no special deference to its interpretation of the Longshore Act." *Price v. Stevedoring Servs. of Am., Inc.*, 697 F.3d 820, 825 (9th Cir. 2012). [—5—]

III

Iopa's counsel argues that the ALJ did not apply the proper standard in evaluating the circumstances for the untimely fee petition and, alternatively, even if the proper standard was applied, substantial evidence does not support the ALJ's decision to strike fees.

A

Iopa asserts that Longshore Act fee petitions are subject to the relatively lenient standard adopted by the BRB in 1986: "The loss of an attorney's fee is a harsh result and should not be imposed on counsel as a penalty except in the most extreme circumstances." *Paynter v. Dir., OWCP*, 9 Black Lung Rep. (Juris) 1-190, at *1 (Ben. Rev. Bd. 1986). In 2015, however, the Rules of Practice and Procedure for Administrative Hearings Before the OALJ were revised to include, inter alia, the following provision: "When an act may or {–1301–} must be done within a specified time, the judge may, for good cause, extend the time . . . [o]n motion made after the time has expired if the party failed to act because of *excusable neglect.*" 29 C.F.R. § 18.32(b)(2) (emphasis added). This rule applies to claims brought before an ALJ in the Department of Labor, including Longshore Act claims. *See id.* § 18.10(a). While *Paynter* may have previously served as the primary guide in determining whether to strike a fee petition, the 2015 revision of the Rules of Practice and Procedure for Hearings Before the OALJ requiring a showing of "excusable neglect" for untimely claims cannot be ignored. *See id.* § 18.32(b)(2).

In determining whether circumstances constitute excusable neglect, the Supreme Court set forth the following four-factor test in *Pioneer Investment Services Co. v. Brunswick Associates Ltd. Partnership*: "the danger of [—6—] prejudice to the debtor, the length of the delay and its potential impact on judicial proceedings, the reason for the delay, including whether it was within the reasonable control of the movant, and whether the movant acted in good faith." 507 U.S. 380, 395 (1993). We and our sister circuits have adopted the Supreme Court's four-factor test. *See Pincay v. Andrews*, 389 F.3d 853, 855–60 (9th Cir. 2004) (weighing *Pioneer* factors in untimely filing of notice of appeal under Federal Rule of Appellate Procedure 4(a)(1)(A)); *Briones v. Riviera Hotel & Casino*, 116 F.3d 379, 381–82 (9th Cir. 1997) (adopting the *Pioneer* test in evaluating motions for relief under Federal Rule of Civil Procedure 60(b)(1)); *In re O'Brien Envtl. Energy, Inc.*, 188 F.3d 116, 125 n.7 (3d Cir. 1999) (recognizing *Pioneer* as providing "guidance not just with regard to [bankruptcy] Rule 9006, but in other . . . non-bankruptcy contexts discussing the issue of excusable neglect"); *Pratt v. Philbrook*, 109 F.3d 18, 19 (1st Cir. 1997) (explaining that "the *Pioneer* test for 'excusable neglect' was intended to extend beyond the bankruptcy context"). We hold that applying the *Pioneer* factors to the instant case is appropriate and consistent with post-*Pioneer* case law analyzing "excusable neglect" in various regulatory contexts. The ALJ did not, therefore, commit an error of law by applying an improper standard.

B

The ALJ's four-factor *Pioneer* analysis and subsequent conclusion that Iopa's counsel did not establish excusable neglect was supported by substantial evidence. The ALJ found that the first factor—prejudice—weighed against a finding of excusable neglect. The ALJ determined that Respondents demonstrated they would be prejudiced by the delayed filing, because their "memory of the details of the case" and ability "to recall each back and forth between the [—7—] parties for the purpose of contesting the validity or amount of time claimed for a given line item" was affected by the substantial delay. A reasonable factfinder would not be compelled to disagree with this analysis and finding.

The ALJ found that the second factor—the length of delay—weighed strongly against a finding of excusable neglect, because the delay was substantial. That finding is supported by the fact that the petition was filed approximately 280 days past the established deadline of 21 days. The fact that Iopa's lawyer waited another month to correct his petition after being instructed by the ALJ to file the proper petition with the OALJ instead of the OWCP further supports this finding.

The ALJ also found that the third factor—the reasons for delay—weighed against a finding of excusable neglect. The ALJ's determination that "none of [the reasons for delay] are convincing or persuasive" or were beyond the control of {–1302–} counsel is supported by case law. Although Iopa's counsel noted several challenges in managing his caseload, particularly following the departure of the associate who managed this case, the Supreme Court has held that "we give little weight to the fact that counsel was experiencing upheaval in his law practice." *Pioneer*, 507 U.S. at 398; *see also In re Enron Corp.*, 419 F.3d 115, 126–27 (2d Cir. 2005) (holding a party being too busy with negotiations was not excusable neglect); *In re Harlow Fay, Inc.*, 993 F.2d 1351, 1352 (8th Cir. 1993) (holding counsel's relocation to a different state and reduction in staff was not excusable neglect); *cf. Selph v. Council of L.A.*, 593 F.2d 881, 884 (9th Cir. 1979) (explaining that "excusable neglect is not meant to cover the usual excuse that the lawyer is too busy, which can be used, perhaps truthfully, in almost every case") (citation omitted). **[—8—]**

The ALJ found that the fourth factor—good faith—had no weight in this case. Even if the ALJ had found that counsel acted in good faith, that factor does not require a finding of excusable neglect when weighed against the other three factors. *See In re Veritas Software Corp. Sec. Litig.*, 496 F.3d 962, 973 (9th Cir. 2007) (affirming the district court's denial of a fee application as untimely where two factors favored a finding of excusable neglect, stating that an excusable neglect determination is "committed to the discretion of the district court" and "[w]hile the district court would not have abused its discretion in granting [the] fee application, it did not abuse its discretion in denying it"). We affirm the BRB's decision upholding the ALJ's finding of untimeliness absent excusable neglect.

AFFIRMED.

United States Court of Appeals
for the Ninth Circuit

No. 18-15104

GRIMM
vs.
VORTEX MARINE CONSTR.

Appeal from the United States District Court for the
Northern District of California

Decided: April 16, 2019

Citation: 921 F.3d 845, 7 Adm. R. 434 (9th Cir. 2019).

Before **FLETCHER, WATFORD,** and **HURWITZ,** Circuit
Judges.

[—3—] {–846–} **HURWITZ,** Circuit Judge:

The central issue in this case is whether a Department of Labor order requiring payment of a worker's future medical expenses was sufficiently "final" to support a judicial enforcement action under the Longshore and Harbor Workers' Compensation Act ("Longshore Act") and a double damages claim by the worker against the employer under the Medicare Secondary Payer Act ("MSP"). The district court found the order was not final and dismissed the [—4—] worker's complaint. We have jurisdiction over this appeal under 28 U.S.C. § 1291 and affirm.

I

A

Terry Grimm worked 32 years as a pile driver for several employers, including Vortex Marine Construction. After leaving work, Grimm filed a claim against Vortex under the Longshore Act, 33 U.S.C. § 901, *et seq.*, seeking workers' compensation and medical benefits. A Department of Labor administrative law judge ("ALJ") found that Grimm had sustained work-related injuries while employed by Vortex. The ALJ therefore ordered Vortex to "pay or reimburse the Claimant for all medical expenses arising from the Claimant's work-related injuries," and to "provide treatment going forward, including the diagnostic procedures and

therapies his treating physicians judge appropriate." The Benefits Review Board ("BRB") affirmed the ALJ's order. Vortex petitioned this Court for review of the BRB decision, but withdrew the petition.

B

In this action, Grimm alleges that Vortex refused to pay for required medical treatment and he was therefore forced to rely on Medicare to pay his expenses. The operative amended complaint sought to enforce the ALJ's order and also asserted a claim under the MSP, seeking double [—5—] damages for the amounts Medicare paid for the services. *See* 42 U.S.C. § 1395y(b).[1]

The district court granted Vortex's motion to dismiss, finding it lacked jurisdiction {–847–} to enforce the ALJ's order because it was not final and that the MSP claim was premature. This timely appeal followed.

II

A

"The Longshore Act is a worker's compensation plan under which employers subject to the Act are required, within statutory limits, to compensate their employees for job-related injuries or deaths." *Thompson v. Potashnick Constr. Co.,* 812 F.2d 574, 575 (9th Cir. 1987). Compensation claims are "filed with the deputy commissioner in the compensation district in which such injury or death occurred," 33 U.S.C. § 913, and disputes requiring a hearing referred to an ALJ, *id.* § 919(c)–(d). The ALJ can issue a "compensation order," either "rejecting the claim or making the award." *Id.* § 919(e); 20 C.F.R. § 702.348. Appeals from compensation orders go to the BRB. 33 U.S.C. § 921(b)(3). "Final orders of the BRB are reviewable by the United States Courts of Appeals." *Thompson,* 812 F.2d at 576 (citing 33 U.S.C. § 921(c)).

---

[1] The defendants are Vortex; Signal Mutual Indemnity Association, Vortex's insurer; Acclaim Risk Management, Inc., third party administrator for Vortex's Longshore Act claims; an Acclaim insurance adjuster; and two Acclaim officers.

If an employer "fails to comply with a compensation order . . . that has become final," the beneficiary may bring an enforcement action in the district court. 33 U.S.C. [—6—] § 921(d). "Unlike the BRB and court of appeals, the district court has no jurisdiction over the merits of the litigation." *Thompson*, 812 F.2d at 576. A district court accordingly "cannot affirm, modify, suspend or set aside the order." *Id.* Rather, its "jurisdiction extends only to the *enforcement* of compensation orders." *Id.*

The district court dismissed Grimm's enforcement action because it found the ALJ's order not final under § 921(d). We previously have not addressed when an order becomes final under that statute. However, several of our sister Circuits have done so, and we join them in holding that to be "final" for purposes of § 921(d), an order must "at a minimum specify the amount of compensation due or provide a means of calculating the correct amount without resort to extra-record facts which are potentially subject to genuine dispute between the parties." *Severin v. Exxon Corp.*, 910 F.2d 286, 289 (5th Cir. 1990); *see also Stetzer v. Logistec of Conn., Inc.*, 547 F.3d 459, 463–64 (2d Cir. 2008) (adopting *Severin's* analysis).[2] [—7—]

---

[2] Other courts of appeal have also reached identical conclusions in suits under 30 U.S.C. § 932, the Black Lung Benefits Act ("BLBA"). Section 932 expressly incorporates the enforcement scheme in the Longshore Act. *See, e.g., Connors v. Amax Coal Co.*, 858 F.2d 1226, 1228–29 (7th Cir. 1988) ("[A] claimant . . . does not possess a compensation order making an award, that has become final—the ticket to admission to district court under section 921(d)—until that party obtains a final administrative determination resolving any dispute as to whether particular expenses are covered expenses." (internal quotations omitted)); *Connors v. Bethlehem Mines Corp.*, 862 F.2d 461, 463 (3d Cir. 1988) (requiring "the Secretary of Labor to make an initial determination of benefits before the district court has jurisdiction to enforce a final order"); *Connors v. Oglebay Norton Co.*, 848 F.2d 84, 85 (6th Cir. 1988) (holding that a plan could not "proceed directly" in district court to recover BLBA payments made to miners "since it has [—7—] never been determined administratively that the miners are entitled to any specific award").

The Longshore Act does not specify when a "compensation order" becomes "final" under § 921(d). But the Act defines "compensation" as "the money allowance payable to an employee," 33 U.S.C. § 902(12), suggesting that a final order must either specify the "money allowance" or provide a ready method for determining it. And, the governing regulations define "medical care" as that which is "recognized {–848–} as appropriate by the medical profession for the care and treatment of the injury." 20 C.F.R. § 702.401(a). The district court's enforcement power does not extend to determining whether specific medical care is appropriate, or even whether the fees charged by a treating physician are reasonable. *See* 20 C.F.R. § 702.413 (requiring the agency to determine the reasonableness of disputed fees). It thus stands to reason, as *Severin* holds, that a district court's limited jurisdiction over a compensation order extends only to orders whose monetary sweep cannot be disputed.

Under the *Severin* rubric, the district court correctly found that it lacked jurisdiction over Grimm's § 921(d) enforcement claim. The ALJ's order stated "Vortex . . . must pay or reimburse the Claimant for all medical expenses arising from the Claimant's work related injuries." It did not list an amount to be paid or a means of calculating what Vortex owed. *See Severin*, 910 F.2d at 289. Nor did the order specify any specific medical service for which Vortex would be liable. "[A] decision is not final where the extent of damage remains undetermined." *BethEnergy Mines, Inc. v. Dir., Office of Workers' Comp. Programs*, 32 F.3d 843, 849 (3d Cir. 1994) (internal quotations omitted). [—8—]

The relief that Grimm seeks, however justified, would plainly require the district court to insert itself into the "merits of the litigation." *Thompson*, 812 F.2d at 576. The court would be called on to resolve disputes about whether the services Grimm received were for work-related injuries, and perhaps over the charges incurred for those services. Resolution of that dispute plainly turns on "extra-record facts which are potentially subject to genuine dispute between the parties." *Severin*, 910 F.2d at 289. Those disputes must be addressed in the first instance to the agency.[3]

Moreover, the amended complaint improperly requested modification of the ALJ's order. For example, it sought issuance of three LS-1 forms authorizing payment for medical services, as well as an order requiring Vortex to pay timely for future medical care and hold Grimm harmless against claims brought by others. Issuance of these forms would modify, rather than enforce, the ALJ's order and a district court lacks jurisdiction under § 921(d) to "modify" orders. *See Thompson*, 812 F.2d at 576.

Grimm correctly notes that the central purpose of the Longshore Act is "to place the compensation award in the hands of the entitled claimant as soon as possible." *Sea-Land Serv., Inc. v. Barry*, 41 F.3d 903, 907 (3d Cir. 1994). That purpose might be furthered if Congress had seen fit to [—9—] empower district courts to resolve disputes over whether a specific service should be paid for by the employer. But Congress did not do so, instead in § 921(d) limiting the district court to enforcement of final agency orders. The district court therefore did not err in dismissing the enforcement claim for lack of subject matter jurisdiction.

B

The gravamen of Grimm's MSP claim is that Medicare was forced to pay his medical expenses after Vortex wrongfully {–849–} refused to do so. The district court correctly rejected that claim as premature.

"The MSP makes Medicare insurance secondary to any 'primary plan' obligated to pay a Medicare recipient's medical expenses . . .

. ." *Parra v. PacifiCare of Ariz., Inc.*, 715 F.3d 1146, 1152 (9th Cir. 2013) (citing 42 U.S.C. § 1395y(b)(2)(A)). The term "primary plan" includes "workmen's compensation law[s] or plan[s]." 42 U.S.C. § 1395y(b)(2)(A); *see* § 1395y(b)(8)(F); 42 C.F.R. § 411.40(a) (interpreting "primary plan" to include the Longshore Act). The MSP authorizes Medicare to make conditional payment for services if a primary plan "has not made or cannot reasonably be expected to make payment . . . promptly." *Id.* § 1395y(b)(2)(B)(i). Medicare can then seek reimbursement "if it is demonstrated that such primary plan has or had a responsibility to make payment." *Id.* § 1395y(b)(2)(B)(ii).

The MSP's private right of action allows a beneficiary to recover double the amount of Medicare payments made when a plan "fails to provide for primary payment (or appropriate reimbursement)." *Id.* § 1395y(b)(3)(A); *see Parra*, 715 F.3d at 1152. A primary payment includes a "payment [that] has been made, or can reasonably be [—10—] expected to be made" by a primary plan. 42 U.S.C. § 1395y(b)(2)(A).

But, "the defined term 'primary plan' presupposes an existing obligation (whether by statute or contract) to pay for covered items or services." *Humana Med. Plan, Inc. v. W. Heritage Ins. Co.*, 832 F.3d 1229, 1237 (11th Cir. 2016). Grimm's MSP claim would require the district court to determine in the first instance whether Vortex was obliged to pay for the items and services covered by a Medicare conditional payment. Until an ALJ, subject to review by the BRB and court of appeals, has found an employer liable for specific medical expenses, a plaintiff cannot demonstrate the employer's responsibility as required by the MSP. Absent a final compensation order requiring that specific services either be paid for or reimbursed, Grimm has failed to state a claim for recovery under the MSP.

III

For the reasons above, we **AFFIRM** the judgment of the district court.

---

[3] While this appeal was pending, the Office of Workers' Compensation Programs issued a Memorandum of Internal Conference, recommending that Vortex (1) pay or reimburse Grimm for all submitted chiropractic bills; (2) authorize Grimm's medical group to treat him with all appropriate medical care; and (3) review and resolve all outstanding non-chiropractic provider bills within 90 days. We **GRANT** Vortex's motion for judicial notice of the Memorandum.

(Reporter's Note: Concurring Opinion follows
on p. 438).

[—10—] {–849–} **WATFORD,** Circuit Judge, concurring:

I agree that the district court lacks jurisdiction to hear the Longshore Act claim. But while the court casts the jurisdictional issue as one of finality, in my view there is a more basic deficiency. The Longshore Act limits the jurisdiction of the district court to enforcing "compensation orders." 33 U.S.C. § 921(d). What Terry Grimm seeks to enforce here is the portion of an administrative order directing Vortex Marine Construction to pay or reimburse Grimm in the future "for all medical expenses arising from [—11—] [his] work-related injuries." That is not a compensation order within the meaning of the Longshore Act. The Act defines "compensation" as "the money allowance payable to an employee or to his dependents as provided for in this chapter." § 902(12). That definition does not include an employer's obligation to furnish future medical care. *Marshall v. Pletz*, 317 U.S. 383, 390–91 (1943). To obtain an enforceable compensation order, Grimm must first receive the medical care he requires and then seek an additional order directing Vortex to pay for the medical bills he has incurred. *Id.* at 391; *see* 33 U.S.C. § 907(d)(1). The Longshore Act does not permit a district court to issue an injunction under § 921(d) prospectively ordering an employer to pay for future medical {–850–} benefits, no matter how specific the administrative order may be.

United States Court of Appeals
for the Ninth Circuit

No. 16-35314

ADAMSON
vs.
PORT OF BELLINGHAM

Appeal from the United States District Court for the
Western District of Washington

Decided: May 14, 2019

Citation: 923 F.3d 728, 7 Adm. R. 439 (9th Cir. 2019).

Before **GOULD** and **IKUTA,** Circuit Judges, and
TUNHEIM, * District Judge.

* The Honorable John R. Tunheim, United States District
Judge for the District of Minnesota, sitting by
designation.

[—3—] {–728–} PER CURIAM:

We certified two questions to the Washington State Supreme Court. *Adamson v. Port of Bellingham*, 899 F.3d 1047, 6 Adm. R. 370 (9th Cir. 2018). We said that if "the Washington State Supreme Court decides that a priority usage agreement does not absolve a landlord of liability as a possessor of property, we will affirm the district court." *Id.* at 1051, 6 Adm. R. at 372.

The Washington State Supreme Court so decided. "The fact that AMHS was in berth and using the passenger ramp at the time of the incident does not affect the Port's liability as a landowner-lessor. We answer the first certified question in the affirmative." *Adamson v. Port of Bellingham*, 438 P.3d 522, 528 (Wash. 2019). Specifically, it held that "that a priority use provision, an affirmative obligation to maintain and repair, and the ability to lease the property to others together create sufficient control of the property such that a landowner who leases the property is held liable as a premises owner." *Id.* at 525.

We affirm the district court.

AFFIRMED.

United States Court of Appeals
for the Ninth Circuit

No. 15-56775

BATTERTON
vs.
DUTRA GROUP

On Remand from the United States Supreme Court

Decided: August 12, 2019

Citation: 7 Adm. R. 440 (9th Cir. 2019).

Before **THOMAS,** Chief Judge, and **KLEINFELD** and **NGUYEN,** Circuit Judges.

ORDER

In light of the Supreme Court's decision in *The Dutra Grp. v. Batterton*, 139 S. Ct. 2275, 7 Adm. R. 43 (2019), the opinion of this Court dated January 23, 2018, 880 F.3d 1089, 6 Adm. R. 308, is VACATED and judgment is entered REVERSING the district court's order denying Dutra's motion to strike the prayer for punitive damages. We remand this case to the district court for further proceedings consistent with the Supreme Court's opinion.

REVERSED and REMANDED.

United States Court of Appeals
for the Ninth Circuit

No. 18-71216

SECRETARY OF LABOR
vs.
SEWARD SHIP'S DRYDOCK, INC.

On Petition for Review of an Order of the
Occupational Safety & Health Review Commission

Decided: September 11, 2019

Citation: 937 F.3d 1301, 7 Adm. R. 441 (9th Cir. 2019).

Before **TASHIMA, FLETCHER,** and **BERZON,** Circuit Judges.

[—3—] {–1302–} FLETCHER, Circuit Judge:

We are asked to interpret a provision of the Respiratory Protection Standard ("Standard"), promulgated under the Occupational Safety and Health Act of 1970. 29 C.F.R. § 1910.134. Section 1910.134(a)(2) of the Standard provides, "A respirator shall be provided to each employee when such equipment is necessary to protect the health of such employee." The lead sentence of § 1910.134(d) provides, "This paragraph requires the employer to evaluate respiratory hazard(s) in the workplace[.]" Section 1910.134(d)(1)(iii), whose meaning is at issue in this case, provides, "The employer shall identify and evaluate the respiratory hazard(s) in the workplace[.]"

The Secretary of Labor ("Secretary") has consistently interpreted § 1910.134(d)(1)(iii) to require covered employers to evaluate the respiratory hazards at their workplaces whenever there is the "potential" for overexposure of employees to contaminants, in order to determine whether respirators are "necessary to protect the [—4—] health" of employees. In the case now before us, the Occupational Safety and Health Review Commission ("Commission") disagreed with the Secretary. The Commission held that § 1910.134(d)(1)(iii) applies only when respirators have already been determined to be "necessary." In the view of the Commission, the only function of an evaluation under § 1910.134(d)(1)(iii) is to provide guidance as

to which respirator an employer should use once respirators have been determined to be "necessary."

We have jurisdiction under 29 U.S.C. § 660(a). We adopt the Secretary's interpretation of § 1910.134(d)(1)(iii). We accordingly grant the petition for review.

I. Regulatory Framework

We begin with an overview of the Respiratory Protection Standard. The Standard was promulgated under the Occupational Safety and Health Act of 1970, 29 U.S.C. § 651, *et seq.*, pursuant to the Secretary's rulemaking authority. The Standard was first issued in 1971. It applies to industrial facilities in which respiratory hazards are likely to be present. One such facility is a shipyard. 63 Fed. Reg. 1152, 1178–79 (January 8, 1998). The Standard is enforced by the Occupational Safety and Health Administration ("OSHA"). {–1303–}

In its first subsection, the Standard describes its overall purpose. The Standard seeks to "control . . . occupational diseases caused by breathing air contaminated with harmful dusts, fogs, fumes, mists, gases, smokes, sprays, or vapors[.]" 29 C.F.R. § 1910.134(a)(1). The "primary objective" of the Standard is "to prevent atmospheric contamination." *Id.* The [—5—] Standard prescribes the methods by which employers should protect their employees from contamination:

> [Protecting employees from atmospheric contamination] shall be accomplished as far as feasible by accepted engineering control measures (for example, enclosure or confinement of the operation, general and local ventilation, and substitution of less toxic materials). When effective engineering controls are not feasible, or while they are being instituted, appropriate respirators shall be used pursuant to this section.

Id. The Standard provides that respirators must be provided when "necessary":

A respirator shall be provided to each employee *when such equipment is necessary to protect the health of such employee.* The employer shall provide the respirators which are applicable and suitable for the purpose intended. . . .

Id. § 1910.134(a)(2) (emphasis added).

The Standard does not define or describe the conditions under which respirators are "necessary." However, a separate regulation specifies permissible exposure limits ("PELs") for various air contaminants. The regulation requires that "administrative or engineering controls" be implemented to keep exposures below the specified PELs. 29 C.F.R. § 1910.1000(e). If such controls do not achieve "full compliance," "protective equipment or any other protective [—6—] measures shall be used[.]" *Id.* Respirators are "protective equipment." PELs for specific contaminants are set forth in three tables in § 1910.1000.

Section 1910.134(d) of the Standard is titled "Selection of respirators." It begins, "*This paragraph requires the employer to evaluate respiratory hazard(s) in the workplace,* identify relevant workplace and user factors, and base respirator selection on these factors." (Emphasis added.) Section (d)(1), "General requirements," has four subsections. One of them is § 1910.134(d)(1)(iii), the provision whose meaning is at issue in this case. It provides in its entirety:

> *The employer shall identify and evaluate the respiratory hazard(s) in the workplace*; this evaluation shall include a reasonable estimate of employee exposures to respiratory hazard(s) and an identification of the contaminant's chemical state and physical form. Where the employer cannot identify or reasonably estimate the employee exposure, the employer shall consider the atmosphere to be IDLH [immediately dangerous to life or health].

(Emphasis added.)

Section 1910.134(d)(1)(iii) was added to the Standard in 1998. A lengthy "preamble" was published with the revised Standard. The first two sentences addressing the newly added section provide:

> *Section (d)(1)(iii) of the final rule requires the employer to identify and evaluate the [—7—] respiratory hazard(s) in the workplace.* To perform this evaluation, the employer must make a "reasonable estimate" of the employee exposures anticipated to occur as a result of those hazards, including those likely to be encountered in reasonably foreseeable emergency situations, and must also identify the physical state and chemical form of such contaminant(s).

63 Fed. Reg. at 1198 (emphasis added). The preamble goes on to explain that "[m]any of the components of paragraph (d)(1)(iii) of the final standard have been {–1304–} required practice since 1971 because they were included in the selection provisions of the 1969 ANSI [American National Standards Institute] standard incorporated by reference into [the] previous respiratory protection standard." *Id.* Section 1910.134(d)(1)(iii) simply "makes these provisions clearer by stating them explicitly in the regulatory text." *Id.*

An "OSHA Instruction," interpreting the Standard, was issued in 1998. A slightly revised Instruction was issued in 2014. The stated purpose of the Instruction in both versions was (and is) as follows: "This Instruction establishes agency interpretations and enforcement policies, and provides instructions to ensure uniform enforcement of the Respiratory Protection Standard[.]" Inspection Procedures for the Respiratory Protection Standard, CPL 02-00-158, § I (June 26, 2014) ("2014 Instruction"); Inspection Procedures for the Respiratory Protection Standard, CPL 2-0.120, § I (Sept. 25, 1998) ("1998 Instruction"). The 2014 Instruction provides:

> The employer is required to select and provide an appropriate respirator

(NIOSH certified) [—8—] based on the respiratory hazard(s) present in the workplace. The employer must identify hazardous airborne contaminants that employees may inhale and make a reasonable estimate of employee exposures in determining the appropriate respirator for employees to use. The employer must evaluate the respiratory hazards in the workplace where there is a *potential for an employee overexposure.*

2014 Instruction, at § IX(D) (emphasis added). The comparable passage in the 1998 Instruction provided exactly the same, but without the last sentence. 1998 Instruction, at § VII(E) (first two sentences). In a passage one page later, the 1998 Instruction included a roughly equivalent sentence:

> If the employer has not made any effort to assess the respiratory hazards and there is the *potential for an overexposure*, the CSHO should cite section (d)(1)(iii).

Id. at § VII(E)(2) (first sentence) (emphasis added). The critical point is that under both the 1998 and 2014 Instructions, employers were (and are) required to assess respiratory hazards based on the "potential" for overexposure of an employee. That is, an assessment for respiratory hazards is required even if it turns out that respirators are not "necessary to protect the health" of employees. The assessment is required whenever there is a "potential" for overexposure.

With this framework in mind, we turn to the facts giving rise to the present petition. [—9—]

II. Factual Background

In 2009, OSHA issued several citations to respondent Seward Ship's Drydock, Inc. ("Seward") related to working conditions on the *Paula Lee*, a deck barge. Seward was a marine vessel repair business located in Seward, Alaska. It performed both "drydock" repairs, where the vessel is out of the water, and "dockside" repairs, where the vessel is floating in the water. According to the Secretary, respondent Seward no longer conducts repairs but still exists as an employer and would be subject to any penalty assessed. Seward elected not to file an answering brief in this court and did not appear for oral argument.

In February 2009, Seward performed welding work in the voids of the *Paula Lee*. "Voids" are compartments in a deck barge that can be left empty to provide buoyancy or can be filled with water to provide ballast. Prior to beginning repairs, Seward obtained a "Marine Chemist Certificate" from Joseph Graham, a certified marine chemist. Graham inspected the {–1305–} drydocked *Paula Lee*, tested the oxygen levels in each void, and tested for combustible gases and toxic substances. Graham certified the vessel as safe for drydock welding (also known as "hot work") on February 9, 2009. As is customary for purposes of a Marine Chemist Certificate, Graham was not told what types of welding rods Seward planned to use. Graham therefore could not test for fumes that would be produced by welding. Indeed, Graham testified in the administrative hearing, "I don't know how to test for welding fumes."

Seward spent five weeks conducting extensive repairs through "production welding," which involves long, continuous welds of large plates of replacement steel. On [—10—] April 11, 2009, Seward refloated the *Paula Lee* and placed it dockside. A few days later, Seward discovered the need for additional "pick-up" work, which involved spot welding of seams that were not fully closed during production welding.

Seward spent three days performing pick-up work, from April 14 through April 16. Employees spent up to ten hours per day in voids of the *Paula Lee* in order to meet the project's April 17 deadline. The voids were located underneath the main deck and were accessible only through manholes approximately 19 inches wide. Respirators were offered on a voluntary basis, and at least one welder used a respirator.

Each morning before welding began, Larry Williams, the site's superintendent and the designated "shipyard competent person," conducted atmospheric testing in the areas where work would take place. As the shipyard competent person, Williams was responsible for maintaining the conditions described in the Marine Chemist Certificate. Before welding began, Williams tested the voids using a "grab sample," which provides an immediate measurement from a gas meter. His tests determined whether the spaces were "safe for entry" at the time the test was performed.

Williams's pre-welding sampling did not test for the metals found in welding fumes. Welding fumes have different constituent elements depending on the composition of the electrode—or welding rod—used during welding. According to material safety data sheets, the two types of electrodes used on the *Paula Lee* contained iron oxide, manganese, fluorides, and barium compounds. Overexposure to these substances can cause both short- and long-term respiratory difficulties. For example, overexposure to iron [—11—] oxide can cause a condition called "siderosis," commonly known as "iron lung."

Henry "Joe" Hogge and Bruce Whitmore worked as welders on the *Paula Lee*. They testified at the administrative hearing about the conditions they experienced during the pick-up work. Hogge described the air quality within the voids as "extremely poor." He testified that there was "inadequate ventilation" in the void because the fan placed over the manhole cover to provide forced ventilation pulled out fumes only from the top of the void, leaving fumes near the bottom of the void where the welders were working. The void filled "quite quickly" with welding fumes, making it "very smokey . . . to the point where visibility was bad and it was difficult to breathe in." "It was a lot of brown smoke, a lot of welding fumes. . . . [T]he ventilation was so poor that Bruce and I both came in one day and we couldn't hardly even speak. [O]ur—our voices were—were very raspy[,] and I attribute that to the smoke." Whitmore similarly described the "smoke conditions from welding" as "terrible." He testified that

the "air handlers and smoke exhaust fans were not working." The smoke "was very, very thick." "I had lost my voice. Joe had {–1306–} lost his voice. And it was—it was a continuous thing."

On April 14, after welding had begun, Hogge and Whitmore complained about the smoke and lack of effective ventilation. Hogge testified that he "complained about [how] there had been no air monitoring done that day, and we were expected to go into the hole." In response, Williams conducted a "grab sample" by lowering an "air monitor" about six inches into a void. Hogge testified that when Williams put the monitor into the void, there was "an audible alarm." Whitmore asked Williams what it meant. Hogge [—12—] testified that Williams replied, "It's to let you know you're still alive." Whitmore testified similarly: "And he says it meant—it means you're alive, you know, or some derogatory— some kind of statement like that. And I said, 'Well, what does that mean?' And there was no response."

Hogge and Whitmore called OSHA on April 14 to make a complaint. OSHA dispatched two compliance officers, Mathew Pauli and John Casper, to inspect the *Paula Lee*. Pauli and Casper were on site during the evening of April 14 and during the day of April 15.

Pauli and Casper testified that upon arriving the evening of April 14, they observed welders working in a void without adequate ventilation and with visible welding fumes. The following day, Pauli and Casper took two "grab samples" to test for carbon monoxide and fitted two welders with "personal exposure monitoring" devices to test for iron oxide and other possible contaminants. Personal exposure monitoring requires employees to wear a measuring device for a sustained period. The device samples the air and identifies the chemicals and contaminants, and their concentrations, to which an employee is exposed. OSHA considers personal exposure monitoring the "gold standard" of air testing because it is more reliable than other forms of testing such as grab samples. 63 Fed. Reg. at 1199.

The results of the personal exposure monitoring were placed into the record in the administrative hearing for only one of the two employees. As discussed above, respirators are "necessary" if exposure to an air contaminant exceeds OSHA's PEL for that contaminant. OSHA's PELs are based on an eight-hour "time-weighted average," which measures the average concentration of a substance over that time [—13—] period. The PEL for iron oxide is 10 milligrams per cubic meter for eight hours. The personal exposure monitor on the Seward employee measured an exposure of 9.1 milligrams per cubic meter for 6.5 hours.

Following the inspection and testing, OSHA issued a "Citation and Notification of Penalty" alleging thirteen violations of the Occupational Safety and Health Act. A hearing was conducted before an Administrative Law Judge ("ALJ") in March 2011. The ALJ sustained a number of the citations, assessing a total penalty of $34,000. The ALJ vacated the citation at issue in the petition before us—Citation 1, Item 3. That citation alleged as follows:

> 29 C.F.R. § 1910.134(d)(1)(iii): The employer did not identify and evaluate the respiratory hazard(s) in the workplace to include a reasonable estimate of employee exposures to respiratory hazard(s) and an identification of the contaminant's chemical state and physical form . . . : Paula Lee Barge: On or about April 14, 2009 and at times prior thereto, respiratory hazards for welders and helpers working in confined spaces had not been evaluated. This condition exposed employees to inhalation hazards.

Seward argued to the ALJ that it had complied with § 1910.134(d)(1)(iii) because a certified marine chemist had tested the voids in the *Paula Lee* and certified them {–1307–} as safe for hot work. The ALJ agreed. After recounting the testing done by Joseph Graham, the ALJ wrote, "[T]he Marine Certificate on its face indicated an evaluation of respiratory hazards with no conditions which required correction. . . . [—14—]

Therefore, the court concludes that Respondent did evaluate the respiratory hazards on the *Paula Lee*."

The Secretary petitioned the Occupational Safety and Health Review Commission for review of the ALJ's decision to vacate Citation 1, Item 3. In 2012, the parties conducted a full round of briefing on whether Seward had adequately evaluated respiratory hazards in compliance with § 1910.134(d)(1)(iii).

Over a year later, on April 17, 2013, the Commission *sua sponte* asked the parties to submit supplemental briefing on "whether the requirement to 'identify and evaluate the respiratory hazard(s) in the workplace' under § 1910.134(d)(1)(iii) is contingent on the Secretary showing that respirators were 'necessary to protect the health of [Seward's] employee[s]' under § 1910.134(a)(2)." (Second alteration in original.) The parties' prior briefing, as well as the ALJ's decision, had been premised on the understanding that § 1910.134(d)(1)(iii) required employers to evaluate respiratory hazards as an initial matter to determine *whether* respirators are necessary under § 1910.134(a)(2). Neither the parties nor the ALJ had understood § 1910.134(d)(1)(iii) to require evaluation of respiratory hazards only after a determination had been made that respirators were necessary.

More than four years after the conclusion of supplemental briefing, the Commission unanimously concluded that § 1910.134(d)(1)(iii) is unambiguous, and that it requires an evaluation of respiratory hazards only when respirators are "necessary to protect the health" of employees under § 1910.134(a)(2). In the alternative, the Commission held that even if the language is ambiguous, the Secretary's interpretation is unreasonable and not entitled to deference. [—15—]

Two Commissioners concluded that the Secretary had failed to prove that air contaminants were present at levels that made the use of respirators "necessary," and that Seward had therefore not been required to perform an evaluation under

§ 1910.134(d)(1)(iii). The third Commissioner dissented, concluding that the Secretary established that respirators had been "necessary" and that an evaluation under §1910.134(d)(1)(iii) was therefore required.

The Secretary petitioned for review in this court.

III. Meaning of 29 C.F.R. § 1910.134(d)(1)(iii)

"[W]e presume that Congress intended for courts to defer to agencies when they interpret their own ambiguous rules." *Kisor v. Wilkie*, 139 S. Ct. 2400, 2414 (2019). In the case of OSHA regulations like the one at issue here, "a reviewing court may not prefer the reasonable interpretations of the Commission to the reasonable interpretations of the Secretary." *Martin v. Occupational Safety & Health Review Comm'n*, 499 U.S. 144, 158 (1991). But, as the Supreme Court wrote in *Kisor*, "The possibility of deference can arise only if a regulation is genuinely ambiguous[,] . . . even after a court has resorted to all the standard tools of interpretation." 139 S. Ct. at 2414. To determine whether a regulation's meaning is truly ambiguous, courts must "carefully consider the text, structure, history, and purpose of a regulation." *Id.* at 2415 (internal quotation marks omitted). "Doing so will resolve many seeming ambiguities out of the box." *Id.* {–1308–}

We conclude that § 1910.134(d)(1)(iii) is sufficiently clear that it is not "genuinely ambiguous" under *Kisor*. Section 1910.134(d)(1)(iii) requires covered employers to evaluate respiratory hazards that exist in the workplace in [—16—] order to determine *whether* respirators must be provided. There is no threshold requirement that respirators be found "necessary" in order to trigger such an evaluation.

A. Text and Structure of the Regulation

We begin with the text and structure of § 1910.134(d)(1)(iii). "A regulation should be construed to give effect to the natural and plain meaning of its words." *Bayview Hunters Point Cmty. Advocates v. Metro. Transp. Comm'n*, 366 F.3d 692, 698 (9th Cir. 2004)

(quoting *Crown Pacific v. Occupational Safety & Health Review Comm'n*, 197 F.3d 1036, 1038 (9th Cir. 1999)).

Section 1910.134(d)(1)(iii) requires an employer to "identify and evaluate the respiratory hazard(s)" in the workplace. The dictionary defines "hazard" in relevant part to mean "a thing or condition that *might* operate against success or safety: a *possible* source of peril, danger, duress, or difficulty." Webster's Third New International Dictionary Unabridged (1961) (emphases added); *see also* Oxford English Dictionary Online (defining hazard as "a physical object which is regarded as a source of *potential* difficulty or danger") (last visited July 30, 2019) (emphasis added). Consistent with this definition, the Secretary has interpreted § 1910.134(d)(1)(iii) to require evaluation of respiratory hazards whenever there is "potential" for overexposure of employees.

The Commission disagreed with this interpretation of § 1910.134(d)(1)(iii). Under the Commission's interpretation, § 1910.134(d)(1)(iii) is triggered only if a respirator is "necessary to protect the health" of employees under § 1910.134(a)(2). The sole purpose of [—17—] § 1910.134(d)(1)(iii), according to the Commission, is to enable the employer to choose the correct respirator. The Commission wrote, "This requires the Secretary to show there was a significant risk of harm necessitating the use of respirators." *See Weirton Steel Corp.*, 20 BNA OSHC 1255, 1259 (No. 98-0701, 2003). A "significant risk of harm" exists if "a reasonable person familiar with the circumstances surrounding an allegedly hazardous condition . . . would recognize a hazard warranting the use of protective equipment." *See Owens-Corning Fiberglass Corp.*, 7 BNA OSHC 1291, 1295 (No. 76-4990, 1979), *aff'd on other grounds*, 659 F.2d 1285 (5th Cir. 1981). More specifically, as we noted above, respirators are "necessary" under the Secretary's regulations if the exposure level for a specified air contaminant exceeds OSHA's maximum permissible exposure limit for that contaminant. 29 C.F.R. §1910.1000(e).

The Commission gave two reasons for its reading of § 1910.134(d)(1)(iii). Neither is persuasive.

First, the Commission wrote that the word "the" before "respiratory hazard(s)" "plainly presumes that such hazards are present and directs the employer to assess them; the provision does not state that the employer must evaluate the workplace *for* such hazards." (Emphasis in original.) The Commission is not correct that § 1910.134(d)(1)(iii) "presumes that [respiratory] hazards are present." Section 1910.134(d)(1)(iii) requires employers to both "*identify* and evaluate the respiratory hazard(s) in the workplace." (Emphasis added.) The word "identify" indicates that, contrary to the Commission's analysis, the regulation applies even where an employer does not already know of hazards in the {–1309–} workplace. And, the fact that employers must "identify [—18—] … the respiratory hazard(s) in the workplace" indicates that in some circumstances, employers carrying out such duty will identify no such hazards.

In light of the clear meaning expressed by the term "identify," the Commission's dispositive reliance on the regulation's use of the word "the" was improper. Where, as here, there are better indicators of a regulation or statute's meaning, we have rejected excessive reliance on the distinction between definite articles such as "the" and indefinite articles such as "a" and "any." *See, e.g., Ileto v. Glock, Inc.*, 565 F.3d 1126, 1145–46 (9th Cir. 2009); *City of Ketchikan v. Cape Fox Corp.*, 85 F.3d 1381, 1384 (9th Cir. 1996); *see also Hernandez v. Williams, Zinman & Parham PC*, 829 F.3d 1068, 1074 (9th Cir. 2016); *NLRB v. New Vista Nursing & Rehab.*, 719 F.3d 203, 227–28 (3d Cir. 2013).

Second, the Commission placed great weight on the location of § 1910.134(d)(1)(iii) in the subsection titled "Selection of respirators," "alongside provisions that deal exclusively with either respirator selection factors or respirator specifications." To start, "the title of a statute and the heading of a section cannot limit the plain meaning of the text." *Brotherhood of R.R. Trainmen v. Balt. & Ohio R.R. Co.*, 331 U.S. 519, 528–29 (1947). Further, it is not unreasonable to include a provision requiring employers to assess *whether* it is necessary to select a respirator within a subsection on the "selection of respirators."

B. Purpose and History of the Regulation

We thus find little or no ambiguity in the plain text of the regulation. Any ambiguity that might remain is dispelled by the purpose of the Standard and its regulatory history. *See* [—19—] *Kisor*, 139 S. Ct. at 2415 ("[B]efore concluding that a rule is genuinely ambiguous, a court must exhaust all the 'traditional tools' of construction. . . . To make that effort, a court must 'carefully consider[ ]' the text, structure, *history, and purpose* of a regulation[.]" (emphasis added)).

The Standard's "primary objective" is "to prevent atmospheric contamination" in order to prevent employees working in industrial facilities from experiencing "occupational diseases caused by breathing air contaminated with harmful dusts, fogs, fumes, mists, gases, smokes, sprays, or vapors." 29 C.F.R. § 1910.134(a)(1). To achieve this goal, the Standard requires an employer first to put in place engineering control measures, such as ventilation, as feasible. Only if those measures are not feasible or are inadequate is the employer required to use respirators. *See id.* Under the Commission's reading, employers would be required to evaluate respiratory hazards only *after* it becomes clear that employees will be overexposed without a respirator. But such a reading undermines the Standard's goals of *preventing* exposure to atmospheric contamination in the first place. Without an initial evaluation of respiratory hazards, employers would not be able to assess whether the engineering control measures they employ—if any—are sufficiently protective of employee health.

The regulatory history of the Standard also supports our reading. In the preamble to the Standard, the discussion of § 1910.134(d)(1)(iii) begins,

Paragraph (d)(1)(iii) of the final rule requires the employer to identify and evaluate the respiratory hazard(s) in the workplace. To perform this evaluation, the employer must **[—20—]** make a "reasonable estimate" of the employee *exposures anticipated to occur* as a result of those hazards, including those likely to be encountered in reasonably foreseeable **{—1310—}** emergency situations, and must also identify the physical state and chemical form of such contaminant(s).

63 Fed. Reg. at 1198 (emphasis added). The "exposures anticipated to occur" plainly include all exposures, not just those that exceed a contaminant's permissible exposure limit. This text directly contradicts the Commission's understanding that actual or anticipated *over*exposure is a prerequisite to a § 1910.134(d)(1)(iii) evaluation.

The preamble's discussion of the appropriate tools for an evaluation under § 1910.134(d)(1)(iii) reiterates the purpose of that evaluation. The preamble states, "OSHA recognizes that there are many instances in which it may not be possible or necessary to take personal exposure measurements *to determine whether respiratory protection is needed." Id.* at 1199 (emphasis added). The preamble then discusses alternate acceptable methods to estimate exposure, such as data from industry-wide surveys and mathematical analysis. *See id.* The preamble continues that, under certain circumstances, employers may nonetheless "find it easier and less costly to conduct personal exposure monitoring *to evaluate the need for respiratory protection." Id.* (emphasis added). OSHA clearly intended for an evaluation to first determine *whether* a respirator is necessary, and only if a respirator is necessary, to use that evaluation to choose the appropriate type of respirator. **[—21—]**

Enforcement guidance issued contemporaneously with the Standard in 1998 further confirms our reading. As noted above, the 1998 OSHA Instruction stated, "If the employer has not made any effort to assess the respiratory hazards, and there is *potential*

for an overexposure, the [compliance officer] should cite section (d)(1)(iii)." *See* 1998 Instruction, at § VII(E)(2) (emphasis added). The Instruction also recognized the employer's "continuing" obligation under § 1910.134(d)(1)(iii) to "identify hazards as a result of changes in the workplace" and then provide "[a]ppropriate respirators . . . *as necessary." Id.* at § VII(E) (emphasis added). This flatly contradicts the Commission's reading that § 1910.134(d)(1)(iii) operates only when respirators are already necessary.

Conclusion

The text, structure, purpose, and regulatory history of the Standard all point in the same direction. We adopt the Secretary's interpretation of § 1910.134(d)(1)(iii) without resorting to *Auer* deference. Using "all the 'traditional tools' of construction," we conclude that § 1910.134(d)(1)(iii) is not truly ambiguous. *See Kisor*, 139 S. Ct. at 2415. We hold that 29 C.F.R. § 1910.134(d)(1)(iii) requires an evaluation of which, if any, respiratory hazards exist in a workplace where there is a potential for overexposure of employees.

We grant the petition and remand for further proceedings consistent with this opinion.

GRANTED and REMANDED for further proceedings.

United States Court of Appeals
for the Ninth Circuit

No. 13-36165

STURGEON
vs.
FROST

On Remand from the United States Supreme Court

Decided: November 1, 2019

Citation: 941 F.3d 953, 7 Adm. R. 449 (9th Cir. 2019).

Before **FARRIS, NELSON,** and **NGUYEN,** Circuit Judges.

[—2—] {–954–} ORDER

Appellant John Sturgeon's request for action is **GRANTED**. In light of the Supreme Court's decision in *Sturgeon v. Frost*, 139 S. Ct. 1066, 7 Adm. R. 11 (2019), the opinion of this Court dated October 2, 2017, 872 F.3d 927, 5 Adm. R. 418, is **VACATED** and judgment is entered **REVERSING** the district court's judgment. We remand this case to the district court with directions to enter judgment in favor of Sturgeon consistent with the Supreme Court's opinion.

REVERSED and REMANDED.

This page intentionally left blank

United States Court of Appeals for the Eleventh Circuit

United States Court of Appeals
for the Eleventh Circuit

No. 17-13535

UNITED STATES
vs.
VALOIS

Appeal from the United States District Court for the Southern District of Florida

Decided: February 12, 2019

Citation: 915 F.3d 717, 7 Adm. R. 452 (11th Cir. 2019).

Before **JORDAN, GRANT,** and **HULL,** Circuit Judges.

[—1—] {–721–} **HULL,** Circuit Judge:

Henry Vazquez Valois ("Vazquez"), Luis Felipe Valencia ("Valencia"), and Diego Portocarrero Valencia ("Portocarrero") appeal their convictions and [—2—] sentences for trafficking cocaine in international waters, in violation of the Maritime Drug Law Enforcement Act ("MDLEA"). *See* 46 U.S.C. §§ 70501–70508. Broadly speaking, they raise five issues on appeal. After review and with the benefit of oral argument, we conclude that the defendants have shown no error, and we affirm their convictions {–722–} and sentences. We address each issue in turn.

I. MDLEA

All three defendants challenge the district court's exercise of extraterritorial jurisdiction under the MDLEA.[1] Collectively, they argue that the MDLEA is unconstitutional for four reasons: (1) Congress's authority to define and punish felonies on the high seas does not extend to felonies without any connection to the United States; (2) due process prohibits the prosecution of foreign nationals for offenses that lack a nexus to the United States; (3) the MDLEA violates the Fifth and Sixth Amendments by removing the determination of jurisdictional facts from the

---

[1] We review *de novo* a district court's interpretation of a statute. *United States v. Cruickshank,* 837 F.3d 1182, 1187, 4 Adm. R. 472, 472 (11th Cir. 2016). Likewise, we review *de novo* whether a statute is constitutional. *Id.,* 4 Adm. R. at 472.

jury; and (4) the admission of a certification of the Secretary of State to establish extraterritorial jurisdiction violates the Confrontation Clause.

As the defendants concede, each of these arguments is foreclosed by binding precedent. Regarding the defendants' first argument, in *United States v. Campbell,* we held that the MDLEA is a valid exercise of Congress's power under the [—3—] Felonies Clause as applied to offenses without a nexus to the United States. 743 F.3d 802, 810, 2 Adm. R. 543, 548–49 (11th Cir. 2014); *see also United States v. Cruickshank,* 837 F.3d 1182, 1187-88, 4 Adm. R. 472, 473 (11th Cir. 2016) (following *Campbell* and reaching the same holding). In *Campbell,* we recognized that we have upheld extraterritorial convictions under our drug trafficking laws as an exercise of power under the Felonies Clause. 743 F.3d at 810, 2 Adm. R. at 548.

As to the defendants' second contention, in *United States v. Rendon,* we held that the Due Process Clause of the Fifth Amendment does not prohibit the trial and conviction of aliens captured on the high seas while drug trafficking because the MDLEA provides clear notice that all nations prohibit and condemn drug trafficking aboard stateless vessels on the high seas. 354 F.3d 1320, 1326 (11th Cir. 2003). The defendants' MDLEA convictions do not violate their due process rights even if the offenses lack a nexus to the United States. *Campbell,* 743 F.3d at 812, 2 Adm. R. at 550.

Concerning the defendants' third argument, in *United States v. Tinoco,* we held that the MDLEA jurisdictional requirement goes to the subject-matter jurisdiction of courts and is not an essential element of the MDLEA substantive offense, and, therefore, it does not have to be submitted to the jury for proof beyond a reasonable doubt. 304 F.3d 1088, 1109-12 (11th Cir. 2002); *see also Cruickshank,* 837 F.3d at 1192, 4 Adm. R. at 476 (following *Tinoco* and reaching the same holding); [—4—] *Campbell,* 743 F.3d at 809, 2 Adm. R. at 547–48 (following *Tinoco* and *Rendon* and reaching the same holding); *Rendon,* 354 F.3d at 1326-28 (following *Tinoco* and reaching the same holding).

As to the defendants' fourth argument, in *Campbell*, we held that the introduction of a certification of the Secretary of State to establish extraterritorial jurisdiction under the MDLEA does not violate the Confrontation Clause. 743 F.3d at 806-08, 2 Adm. R. at 545–47; *see Cruickshank*, 837 F.3d at 1192, 4 Adm. R. at 476 ("A United States Department of State certification of jurisdiction under the MDLEA does not implicate the Confrontation Clause because it does not affect the guilt or innocence of a defendant."). In *Campbell*, we determined that because the stateless nature of the defendant's vessel was not an element of his MDLEA offense to be proved at trial, the admission of the certification {–723–} did not violate his right to confront the witnesses against him. 743 F.3d at 806, 2 Adm. R. at 545.

Based on our precedent, the district court properly exercised jurisdiction in this case.

II. MOTION FOR MISTRIAL

Next, defendant Valencia argues that the district court abused its discretion when it denied a motion for a mistrial based on the government's reference in [—5—] closing arguments to a separate drug seizure.[2] Vazquez and Portocarrero adopt this argument.

A.

We begin by summarizing the evidentiary context for the prosecutor's comments. Over a 36-hour period in November 2016, the U.S. Coast Guard Cutter *Dependable* interdicted two separate go-fast vessels, each with three individuals onboard, trafficking cocaine in international waters off the coasts of Panama and Costa Rica. The first vessel was seized overnight on November 23 to November 24. The Coast Guard recovered 16 bales of cocaine from the water after the individuals on the first vessel had jettisoned the bales. This group of individuals was indicted and prosecuted for this drug trip independently from this case.

The three defendants in this case were on a second vessel seized during the day on November 25, about 36 hours after the first vessel was seized. The defendants in this group were the only individuals charged in this indictment. At trial, Valencia tried to sow doubt about whether he, Vazquez, and Portocarrero were trafficking cocaine onboard their vessel. There was testimony at trial that on November 25 the defendants here had jettisoned 16 bales of cocaine, which the Coast Guard retrieved from the water. By the time the Coast Guard got to the [—6—] defendants' vessel, no cocaine was found onboard the vessel itself. Valencia therefore attempted to show that the Coast Guard mistakenly attributed the cocaine from the first seizure to the defendants in this case.

To that end, Valencia's defense counsel, over the government's objections, repeatedly cross-examined government witnesses about the prior seizure that had happened 36 hours earlier. The government objected on relevance grounds and because the questions were beyond the scope of direct examination. Vazquez and Portocarrero did not object to this line of questioning from Valencia's defense counsel, and the district court overruled the government's objections.

More specifically, on cross-examination, Valencia's defense counsel asked one government witness about how close in time the prior seizure was, whether he was patrolling in the same area, whether individuals were detained, how many packages were retrieved, and whether and when the packages were tested for cocaine. The witness answered that he was involved in another operation with a go-fast boat overnight on November 23 to November 24, approximately 24 to 36 hours before interdicting the defendants' vessel. He stated that the prior seizure occurred in the same area in the Eastern Pacific that he was patrolling and that he had detained individuals. He stated that there were no drugs on the earlier vessel because the vessel was sinking when the Coast Guard approached. He answered [—7—] that the Coast Guard retrieved 16 bales from the water

---

[2] We review for abuse of discretion the denial of a motion for a mistrial. *United States v. McGarity*, 669 F.3d 1218, 1232 (11th Cir. 2012).

in the earlier case, and he tested those bales for cocaine on November 24 and 26. {–724–}

Valencia's defense counsel also asked another government witness whether he personally was able to find the debris field of packages from the prior seizure on November 23 to November 24. The witness answered that he personally was not able to find the debris field, but that the Coast Guard did find the debris field in the vicinity of where the individuals on the earlier vessel jettisoned the bales. The witness also stated that he saw at least one individual jettisoning the bales off the defendants' vessel in this case.

Valencia's defense counsel asked another government witness whether the packages from the prior seizure were packaged similarly to those from this case and whether 16 packages were recovered from each seizure. The witness answered that the bales from the earlier seizure looked very similar and had similar multicolored packaging to the bales in this case. He stated that there were 16 bales recovered from the earlier seizure on November 23 to November 24 and another 16 bales recovered on November 25 as part of the second seizure.

On redirect, the prosecutor invariably tried to make clear that the witnesses were not mistaken that the cocaine retrieved from the water on November 25 had come from the defendants' vessel in this case. [—8—]

Notably, in addition to not objecting to the cross-examination by Valencia's defense counsel, Vazquez's defense strategy aligned with Valencia's in that Vazquez denied having any cocaine on his boat. Specifically, at trial, Vazquez testified in his defense that he owned the go-fast vessel and that he had hired Valencia and Portocarrero to help him flee Colombia to escape death threats from individuals who had demanded he pay a "tax" on the boat. Vazquez testified that there was never any cocaine on his vessel and that he did not transport cocaine. In other words, the cocaine found in the water came from the first vessel seized.

With this evidentiary context in mind and Valencia's interjection of the first vessel into evidence in the trial, we now turn to the prosecutor's comments in closing arguments. Responding to Vazquez's testimony, the prosecutor referenced the prior seizure and suggested that both go-fast vessels were part of a "concerted effort" that was "being directed by whoever was orchestrating these deliveries to Central America." The prosecutor asserted that the defendants' vessel "followed the exact same procedures as that first boat had done," including attempting to elude the Coast Guard, jettisoning the cargo, and then scuttling the vessel. These activities, according to the prosecutor, showed that the defendants "were following the instructions of the people who hired them and directed their activities," just like the individuals on the other vessel. The prosecutor also argued that the 640 [—9—] kilograms of cocaine recovered from the water by the Coast Guard came from the defendants' vessel and not from the prior seizure the night before.[3]

During the prosecutor's argument, defense counsel for Valencia reserved a motion and, once the prosecutor concluded, moved for a mistrial outside of the presence of the jury. Valencia argued that the government appeared to be trying to tie the defendants to a broader conspiracy and to hold them accountable for the first drug seizure. Defense counsel for Vazquez and Portocarrero did not explicitly object to the prosecutor's comments or join in Valencia's mistrial motion on the record. However, Vazquez's defense counsel did {–725–} assist Valencia's defense counsel with the argument on the motion.

As to Valencia's mistrial argument, the prosecutor responded that he was simply trying to place the other seizure—which Valencia "interjected into this trial" and made "a primary feature of his defense"—in context of the overall scheme.

After hearing from the parties, the district court found that "an appropriate curative instruction would ameliorate any potential harm to any defendant" and that none of the

---

[3] The 16 bales totaled 640 kilograms of cocaine.

defendants "ha[d] been deprived [of] their right to a fair and impartial trial." Valencia's counsel conferred with the other defense counsel and [—10—] prepared a curative instruction. The prosecutor did not object to the instruction. The district court then read the curative instruction to the jury as follows:

> During the trial you heard evidence of acts allegedly done by other individuals on other occasions that may be similar to acts with which the defendants are currently charged. You must not consider any of this evidence to decide whether the defendants engaged in the activity alleged in the indictment.

After the prosecutor's closing argument and the district court's curative instruction, defense counsel gave their closing arguments. Vazquez's defense counsel argued that the Coast Guard did not see the first bale in the water thrown off the defendants' boat, but the Coast Guard immediately attributed it to the defendants' boat. Vazquez's counsel contended that the Coast Guard did not have any video showing any of the 16 bales of cocaine being thrown off the defendants' boat. Vazquez's counsel argued that just because the Coast Guard recovered 640 kilograms of cocaine and Vazquez's boat was in the proximity of where the cocaine was recovered did not put that cocaine on Vazquez's boat or mean that the cocaine was his.

Portocarrero's defense counsel argued that as soon as the Coast Guard saw a bale in the water, the Coast Guard claimed that the defendants were jettisoning the bales from their boat and that the bales belonged to the defendants, even though many of the witnesses did not see bales being tossed off the defendants' boat and the video did not record any jettisoning of bales. Portocarrero's counsel argued [—11—] that the conflicting evidence and lack of details in the case showed without a doubt that nobody was throwing bales off the defendants' boat. Specifically, he argued that the Coast Guard could not state how many bales they saw jettisoned off the defendants' boat or who was jettisoning the bales, even though the bales were brightly colored. Portocarrero's counsel also contended

that the physical evidence showed that the debris field of bales did not trail the defendants' boat. Also, he argued that there was no evidence the defendants had cocaine in their boat, as there was nothing on their boat that could be connected to the cocaine found in the water. Portocarrero's counsel argued that if there was cocaine on the defendants' boat, there would have been evidence of it.

In turn, Valencia's defense counsel argued that the jury could consider that the government witnesses who he questioned about the prior seizure became defensive or unhappy when he asked them about the prior seizure. Valencia's counsel also argued about the similarities between the prior seizure and the instant case, including that 16 bales were also recovered from the prior seizure and they had the same packaging as those in this case. Valencia's counsel argued that the boat from the prior seizure could have carried 16 bales of cocaine, but the boat in this case would have been over maximum load. He argued that the boat from the prior seizure could have carried and jettisoned all 32 bales of {—726—} cocaine, including the 16 bales mistakenly attributed to the defendants. He contended that there was [—12—] reasonable doubt that Valencia, Vazquez, and Portocarrero were transporting 16 bales of cocaine. Once again, Vazquez's and Portocarrero's counsel did not object to the argument of Valencia's counsel that the cocaine in the water came from the first vessel, not the defendants' boat.

In the prosecutor's rebuttal argument, the prosecutor argued that the government witnesses testified that they did not confuse what happened with the prior seizure with the instant case.

B.

The defendants assert that the prosecutor's reference to the earlier seizure amounted to the introduction of improper evidence under Federal Rule of Evidence 404(b), for which no notice had been given. We disagree. For starters, "statements and arguments of counsel are not evidence." *United States v. Lopez*, 590 F.3d 1238, 1256 (11th Cir. 2009) (quotations omitted). More importantly, it was

Valencia who interjected the prior seizure, which involved other individuals, into the trial as part of his defense. Neither Vazquez nor Portocarrero objected to Valencia's introduction of evidence about the prior seizure. Indeed, it was only the government that opposed that effort. Because this evidence was not introduced by the government and did not concern a prior bad act by any of the defendants, Rule 404(b) and its notice requirements did not apply. [—13—]

To the extent the defendants argue more generally that the prosecutor's comments in closing were improper suggestions that the two seizures were connected, they must prove two things: (1) that the remarks were improper; and (2) that the remarks prejudicially affected their substantial rights. *United States v. Reeves*, 742 F.3d 487, 505 (11th Cir. 2014). The prosecutor understandably desired to refute Vazquez's story of no cocaine on his boat and to respond to the considerable testimony Valencia elicited regarding the details of the other seizure and how similarly the cocaine was packaged. Moreover, the prosecutor had objected to the defendants presenting evidence about the prior seizure, but the district court had allowed the evidence, which showed that 16 bales of cocaine similarly packaged had been seized 36 hours earlier. While one possible inference was that the second 16 cocaine bales seized came from the first boat, another possible inference, as the prosecutor argued, was the two vessels were doing the same activity in the same way and were connected. Given the way the trial proceeded, we cannot say the prosecutor's brief comments in closing were improper.

Even if we assume *arguendo* that the prosecutor's comments were somehow improper, the defendants have not proved prejudice to their substantial rights. The district court cured the complained-of remarks through a clear and specific limiting instruction to the jury. *See Lopez*, 590 F.3d at 1256 ("If the district court takes a [—14—] curative measure, we will reverse only if the evidence is so prejudicial as to be incurable by that measure."). The court told the jury that it could not consider the evidence of the other

drug seizure when deciding whether the defendants engaged in the activity of the second vessel alleged in the indictment. "We presume that the jury followed the district court's curative instructions." *Id.* And the defendants "ha[ve] not come close to establishing that the closing argument was so highly prejudicial as to be incurable by the court's instructions." *Reeves*, 742 F.3d at 506. Therefore, the district court did not abuse its discretion {–727–} by denying the defendants' motion for mistrial.

III. CONFLICT OF INTEREST

The third issue, raised by defendant Portocarrero, likewise concerns the two seizures. As noted above, the two groups of three defendants were prosecuted independently. A total of three attorneys were appointed for the six defendants, with each attorney representing one defendant within each group.[4] Portocarrero argues that this defense arrangement violated his Sixth Amendment right to conflict-free counsel because he did not validly waive the conflict and the conflict harmed his defense. Portocarrero says that the conflict prevented his attorney from [—15—] attempting to shift blame to the other group of defendants arrested overnight on November 23 to 24 for the cocaine found in the water on November 25. Vazquez adopts this argument, but Valencia does not raise this claim.

A defendant's right to effective assistance of counsel is violated when the defendant's attorney has an actual conflict of interest that impacts the defendant adversely. *United States v. Rodriguez*, 982 F.2d 474, 477 (11th Cir. 1993). A defendant, however, may in some circumstances waive his right to conflict-free counsel. *United States v. Garcia*, 517 F.2d 272, 277 (5th Cir. 1975).[5] *Garcia* provides that, in

---

[4] Attorney Juan Gonzalez represented Portocarrero in this case and a defendant in the other drug case. Attorney Stewart Abrams represented Vazquez in this case and a defendant in the other drug case. Attorney Martin Feigenbaum represented Valencia in this case and a defendant in the other drug case.

[5] This Court adopted as binding precedent all Fifth Circuit decisions prior to October 1, 1981.

the case of a potential conflict of interest, the court should conduct an inquiry, akin to the plea colloquy under Federal Rule of Criminal Procedure 11, to determine whether a defendant wishes to waive the conflict. *Id.* at 277–78. A defendant may waive an actual conflict of interest if the waiver is "knowing, intelligent, and voluntary." *United States v. Ross*, 33 F.3d 1507, 1524 (11th Cir. 1994).

However, a district court's failure to comply with *Garcia* will not require reversal absent an actual conflict of interest. *United States v. Mers*, 701 F.2d 1321, 1326 (11th Cir. 1983) (holding that a district court's violation of *Garcia* and Federal Rule of Criminal Procedure 44(c) was harmless error because there was no [—16—] actual conflict). "Although joint representation of multiple defendants creates a danger of counsel conflict of interest, the mere fact of joint representation will certainly not show an actual conflict." *Id.* (quotation marks omitted). Rather, an appellant must demonstrate inconsistent interests and show that the attorney chose between courses of action that were "helpful to one client but harmful to the other." *Id.* at 1328 (quotation marks omitted). Actual conflicts must have a basis in fact; hypothetical conflicts are not enough. *Id.*

Here, at the time defense counsel were initially appointed, the government had separately indicted and was prosecuting the seizures of two different go-fast vessels on different days as two independent cases against three different individuals in each case. No party or counsel has pointed to any place in the record before trial where anyone alleged or mentioned that the cocaine found in the water on November 25 came from the boat seizure overnight on November 23 to 24. Rather, all of the testimony until Valencia's counsel {–728–} cross-examined the government's witnesses at trial was that the Coast Guard had seen that cocaine being thrown from the defendants' boat on November 25.

The issue of a potential conflict did not arise until the testimony during the trial.

Thus, we cannot say the district court was required to hold a *Garcia* hearing before the trial began. And before sentencing the district court did hold a *Garcia* hearing. [—17—]

Even if the *Garcia* hearing was timely enough, Portocarrero and Vazquez argue that it was substantively deficient. Although they expressly waived any potential conflict at the *Garcia* hearing, they allege that the district court did not ask all of the questions it should have. We need not reach that issue because Portocarrero and Vazquez have not shown that their attorneys' dual representation of the two groups presented any actual conflict. Despite the prosecutor's brief reference to a broader conspiracy during closing arguments, the government's case against Portocarrero and Vazquez related solely to their own personal acts of transporting cocaine onboard the vessel on which they were found. They were not being tried jointly with or for the same offenses as their attorneys' other clients on the first vessel. Shifting the blame in Portocarrero's and Vazquez's trial to the first vessel would not have been harmful to Portocarrero and Vazquez, or to the defendants on the first vessel who were being tried separately. In fact, as Portocarrero notes, Valencia's attorney attempted to do just that, despite representing a client in the other group of defendants on the first vessel.

Furthermore, Portocarrero's and Vazquez's counsel did not object when Valencia's counsel cross-examined the government witnesses about the similarity of the cocaine packaging and other features of the first and second boat seizures. In fact, Vazquez's and Portocarrero's defense counsel later did implicitly shift the blame to the other clients on the first vessel during their closing arguments. [—18—] Vazquez argued that just because the Coast Guard recovered 640 kilograms of cocaine and Vazquez's boat was in the proximity of where the cocaine was recovered did not put that cocaine on Vazquez's boat or mean that it belonged to him. Portocarrero's counsel argued that nobody was throwing bales off of their boat and there was no evidence that they had cocaine in their boat when the Coast Guard boarded it. Under the particular circumstances here, neither Portocarrero nor

---

Bonner v. City of Prichard, 661 F.2d 1206, 1209 (11th Cir. 1981) (en banc).

Vazquez have demonstrated that there was an actual conflict of interest, and, thus, no reversal is required.[6] *See Mers*, 701 F.2d at 1326. {–729–}

IV. SAFETY-VALVE ISSUES

As to the fourth issue, Valencia challenges the constitutionality of the "safety-valve" provisions of 18 U.S.C. § 3553(f) and U.S.S.G. § 5C1.2. Valencia says that these provisions both unfairly deny benefits to Title 46 defendants, in [—19—] violation of equal-protection guarantees, and violate the Fifth Amendment by requiring a defendant to forfeit his right to silence. Portocarrero adopts these arguments.[7]

---

[6] Portocarrero and Vazquez abandoned any argument that an actual conflict existed relating to any post-trial issues and proceedings. *See United States v. Jernigan*, 341 F.3d 1273, 1283 n.8 (11th Cir. 2003). In any case, there has been no suggestion that Portocarrero or Vazquez knew the other group of defendants or were interested in cooperating with the government against them. Additionally, before sentencing, the district court held a *Garcia* hearing; because there is no claim in this appeal that the three defendants' waivers given for post-trial issues were deficient, we do not evaluate that *Garcia* hearing.

Although affirming in this case, we observe that, in an abundance of caution, the more careful course next time would likely be for the magistrate judge to consider appointing separate counsel for all defendants on each boat where (1) the two go-fast boats with cocaine are interdicted so close in time and geography and (2) two indictments, although separate, were filed on the same day. A conflict could have arisen here if a defendant on one boat decided to cooperate with the government and testify against the defendants on the other boat. *See Ruffin v. Kemp*, 767 F.2d 748, 749-51 (11th Cir. 1985) (concluding an actual conflict of interest existed where the attorney represented both defendants Ruffin and Brown and actually offered the testimony of Brown against Ruffin in exchange for a lesser penalty for Brown).

[7] We ordinarily review *de novo* the constitutionality of a statute, because it presents a question of law, but we review for plain error where a defendant raises his constitutional challenge for the first time on appeal. *United States v. Wright*, 607 F.3d 708, 715 (11th Cir. 2010). The parties debate what was raised in the district court, but we need not decide that issue because the defendants' constitutional claims fail in any event.

When the safety valve applies, the district court may impose a sentence without regard to the statutory minimum sentences that would otherwise limit the court's discretion. 18 U.S.C. § 3553(f); U.S.S.G. § 5C1.2(a). By its plain terms, the safety valve applies only to convictions under five specified statutes: 21 U.S.C. §§ 841, 844, 846, 960, and 963. *United States v. Pertuz-Pertuz*, 679 F.3d 1327, 1328 (11th Cir. 2012). This Court held in *Pertuz-Pertuz* that, because no Title 46 offense appears in the safety valve, defendants convicted under Title 46 are not eligible for safety-valve relief. *Id.* Therefore, defendants convicted of offenses under the MDLEA, which are Title 46 offenses, are not eligible for safety-valve relief. *See id.* at 1328–29. Thus, as a threshold matter, Valencia and Portocarrero are not eligible for safety-valve relief.

As to their equal-protection claim, Valencia and Portocarrero argue that there is no rational basis to exclude Title 46 defendants from the safety valve when it is available to defendants convicted of drug trafficking within the United States. [—20—] However, this Court recently held that the safety valve's exclusion of Title 46 defendants does not violate the equal-protection guarantee of the Fifth Amendment. *United States v. Castillo*, 899 F.3d 1208, 6 Adm. R. 463 (11th Cir.), *cert. denied*, 2019 WL 113114 (Jan. 7, 2019). Applying rational-basis review, we concluded that Congress had "legitimate reasons to craft strict sentences for violations of the [MDLEA]." *Id.* at 1213, 6 Adm. R. at 465. Specifically, "[i]n contrast with domestic drug offenses, international drug trafficking raises pressing concerns about foreign relations and global obligations." *Id.*, 6 Adm. R. at 465. "Moreover, the inherent difficulties of policing drug trafficking on the vast expanses of international waters suggest that Congress could have rationally concluded that harsh penalties are needed to deter would-be offenders." *Id.*, 6 Adm. R. at 465. Thus, based on *Castillo*, we reject Valencia's and Portocarrero's equal-protection challenge to the safety valve.

Valencia and Portocarrero also contend that the safety valve violates Fifth Amendment protections against self-incrimination by requiring defendants to provide the government with all information and evidence that they have concerning the offense. 18 U.S.C. § 3553(f)(5); U.S.S.G. § 5C1.2(a)(5). They note that, while they were not eligible to be sentenced below the mandatory minimum, *see Pertuz-Pertuz*, 679 F.3d at 1328, they could have received a two-level reduction in their offense level {–730–} for meeting the five safety-valve criteria. *See* U.S.S.G. § 2D1.1(b)(17) (2016). [—21—]

Although this Court has not addressed in a published opinion this Fifth Amendment issue as to the safety valve, we have concluded that U.S.S.G. § 3E1.1, the acceptance-of-responsibility provision of the Guidelines, does not violate the Fifth Amendment right against self-incrimination. *United States v. Henry*, 883 F.2d 1010, 1011 (11th Cir. 1989). "Section 3E1.1(a) is not a punishment; rather, the reduction for acceptance of responsibility is a reward for those defendants who express genuine remorse for their criminal conduct." *United States v. Carroll*, 6 F.3d 735, 740 (11th Cir. 1993). Several of our sister circuits have concluded that the same is true for the safety valve in 18 U.S.C. § 3553(f) and U.S.S.G. § 5C1.2(a). *United States v. Cruz*, 156 F.3d 366, 374 (2d Cir. 1998) (conviction under § 841); *United States v. Warren*, 338 F.3d 258, 266-67 (3d Cir. 2003) (conviction under § 846); *United States v. Washman*, 128 F.3d 1305, 1307 (9th Cir. 1997) (conviction under § 841); *United States v. Arrington*, 73 F.3d 144, 149-50 (7th Cir. 1996) (same).

Although the parties briefed the Fifth Amendment issue, we ultimately do not need to address it given our conclusions above that the safety-valve relief is unavailable to all Title 46 MDLEA defendants, such as Valencia and Portocarrero, and that such unavailability does not violate the Equal Protection Clause and is constitutional. Because Valencia and Portocarrero are not eligible for safety-valve relief in the first place, we need not consider whether these defendants otherwise [—22—] meet the substantive requirements of safety-valve relief or the defendants' constitutional claim based on the Fifth Amendment.

V. MINOR-ROLE REDUCTION

Finally, Vazquez argues that at sentencing the district court erred in denying him a minor-role reduction under U.S.S.G. § 3B1.2(b).[8] Valencia and Portocarrero purport to adopt this argument.[9] Unlike § 3553(f) and § 5C1.2(a), MDLEA offenders may seek a minor-role reduction under § 3B1.2(b).

As background, Vazquez's, Portocarrero's, and Valencia's presentence investigation reports ("PSI") assigned each of them a base offense level of 38, pursuant to U.S.S.G. § 2D1.1(a)(5) and (c)(1), because their offenses involved at least 450 kilograms of cocaine, specifically 640 kilograms of cocaine.

Vazquez received a two-point enhancement under § 2D1.1(b)(3)(C) because he was the captain of the vessel and a two-point enhancement for obstruction of justice under § 3C1.1 because he made a series of statements during trial that contradicted the evidence. As a result, Vazquez received a total offense level of [—23—] 42. Portocarrero and Valencia received no enhancements or reductions, and their total offense level remained at 38.

Each defendant received zero criminal history points, placing each of them in criminal history category I. As to Vazquez, with a total offense level of 42 and a {–731–} criminal history category of I, he had an advisory guideline range of 360 months to life imprisonment. As to Portocarrero and Valencia, with a total offense level of 38 and a criminal history category of I, each had an advisory guideline range of 235 to 293 months'

---

[8] We review a district court's denial of a role reduction for clear error. *Cruickshank*, 837 F.3d at 1192, 4 Adm. R. at 476–77.

[9] The government maintains that these adoptions were ineffective because minor-role reductions are too individualized to be raised by adoption. *Cf. United States v. Cooper*, 203 F.3d 1279, 1285 n.4 (11th Cir. 2000) (stating that sufficiency arguments are too individualized to be generally adopted). Valencia's and Portocarrero's general adoptions are likely inadequate to properly raise the issue on appeal, but we need not address that issue because they lack merit in any event.

imprisonment. All three defendants also faced a statutory minimum term of ten years' imprisonment as to their counts.

Each defendant objected to his PSI, arguing that he was entitled to a minor-role reduction. Specifically, Vazquez contended that there was no evidence that he had any ownership interest in the drugs, any decision-making authority, or any role other than transportation. Portocarrero argued that he was not the owner or master of the vessel, was a last-minute addition to the trip, and was the youngest and most inexperienced of the three men on the boat. Valencia asserted that there was no evidence that he had any ownership interest in the cocaine or that he was going to make any money from it.

At the defendants' sentencing hearings, each of them renewed the objection to the lack of a minor-role reduction. Vazquez reiterated that he did not own the drugs or share in the drugs' profits. He contended that he did not participate in [—24—] planning or organizing the criminal activity or exercise decision-making authority, as he merely provided transportation for the drugs. Portocarrero asserted that he was only 20 years old and was a very small part of the operation.

The district court overruled the defendants' objections to the lack of a minor-role reduction because each defendant failed to establish that he was substantially less culpable than the average participant in the offense.

After overruling the objections, the district court determined that Vazquez's offense level was 42, his criminal history category was I, and his advisory guideline range was 360 months to life imprisonment. After hearing arguments and considering the 18 U.S.C. § 3553(a) factors, the district court sentenced Vazquez to 144 months' imprisonment as to both of his counts, to run concurrently, followed by 5 years' supervised release. The district court noted that Vazquez's punishment should be slightly greater than his codefendants based on his enhancements for being captain of the vessel and obstruction of justice.

The district court determined that Portocarrero's and Valencia's total offense level was 38, their criminal history category was I, and their advisory guideline range was 235 to 293 months' imprisonment. Following arguments from the parties, the court sentenced both Portocarrero and Valencia to 120 months' imprisonment as to both counts, to run concurrently, followed by 5 years' supervised release. [—25—]

As to our review of a district court's denial of a role reduction, we will not disturb a district court's findings unless we are left with a definite and firm conviction that a mistake has been made. *Cruickshank*, 837 F.3d at 1192, 4 Adm. R. at 477. The court's choice between two permissible views of the evidence will rarely constitute clear error, so long as the basis of the trial court's decision is supported by the record and the court did not misapply a rule of law. *Id.*, 4 Adm. R. at 477. "The defendant bears the burden of establishing his minor role in the offense by a preponderance of the evidence." *Id.*, 4 Adm. R. at 477.

Under § 3B1.2(b), a defendant is entitled to a two-level decrease in his offense level if he was a minor participant in the criminal activity. U.S.S.G § 3B1.2(b). A minor participant is one "who is less culpable than most other participants in the criminal activity, but whose role could not {–732–} be described as minimal." *Id.* § 3B1.2, cmt. n.5.

When evaluating a defendant's role in the offense, the district court must consider the totality of the circumstances. *Id.* § 3B1.2, cmt. n.3(C). According to § 3B1.2's commentary, the factors courts should consider include "the degree to which the defendant understood the scope and structure of the criminal activity," "the degree to which the defendant participated in planning or organizing the criminal activity," "the degree to which the defendant exercised decision-making authority," "the nature and extent of the defendant's participation in the [—26—] commission of the criminal activity," and "the degree to which the defendant stood to benefit from the criminal activity." *Id.* The court must consider all of these factors to the extent applicable, and it commits "legal error in making a minor role decision based solely on one factor." *United States v. Presendieu*, 880 F.3d 1228, 1249 (11th Cir. 2018).

In *United States v. De Varon*, we established two principles to "guide the determination of whether a defendant played a minor role in the criminal scheme: (1) 'the defendant's role in the relevant conduct for which [he] has been held accountable at sentencing,' and (2) '[his] role as compared to that of other participants in [his] relevant conduct.'" *Presendieu*, 880 F.3d at 1249 (quoting *United States v. De Varon*, 175 F.3d 930, 940 (11th Cir. 1999) (en banc)). "In making the ultimate finding as to role in the offense, the district court should look to each of these principles and measure the discernable facts against them." *De Varon*, 175 F.3d at 945.

Here, the district court did not clearly err in denying the defendants' requests for a minor-role reduction. Under *De Varon*'s first principle, the inquiry is whether the defendant "played a relatively minor role in the conduct for which [he] has already been held accountable—not a minor role in any larger criminal conspiracy." *Id.* at 944. The record shows that all three defendants knowingly participated in the illegal transportation of a large quantity of cocaine, they were [—27—] important to that scheme, and they were held responsible only for that conduct. *See* U.S.S.G. § 3B1.2, cmt. n.3(C); *De Varon*, 175 F.3d at 941-43; *see also United States v. Monzo*, 852 F.3d 1343, 1347 (11th Cir. 2017) (considering, as part of the totality of the circumstances, the facts that the defendant "was responsible only for his direct role in the conspiracy, and that he was important to the scheme"). While these facts do not render the defendants ineligible, they support the court's denial of the role reduction.

Further, under *De Varon*'s second principle, the record supports the district court's finding that none of the defendants were "less culpable than most other participants in the criminal activity." U.S.S.G. § 3B1.2, cmt. n.5. Vazquez was the most

culpable of the three defendants because he was the master of the vessel and, according to his own testimony, he recruited Valencia and Portocarrero to accompany him. While Valencia and Portocarrero appear to have had less of a role than Vazquez, that fact alone does not make them minor participants. "The fact that a defendant's role may be less than that of other participants engaged in the relevant conduct may not be dispositive of role in the offense, since it is possible that none are minor or minimal participants." *De Varon*, 175 F.3d at 944. And the defendants here failed to show how they were less culpable than "most other participants" in the criminal activity. *See* U.S.S.G. § 3B1.2, cmt. n.5. Based on [—28—] the totality of the circumstances, the district {–733–} court did not clearly err in denying the defendants minor-role reductions under § 3B1.2.

Alternatively and as an independent ground for affirmance as to Valencia and Portocarrero, we note that both Valencia and Portocarrero received a substantial sentencing variance from their advisory guideline range of 235 to 293 months' imprisonment to 120 months. The sentencing court did not just mechanically impose the statutory mandatory minimum but did so only after considering the defendants' request for a variance. Nonetheless, 120 months is the statutory mandatory minimum. *See* 21 U.S.C. § 960(b)(1)(B) and 46 U.S.C. § 70506(a). Thus, any error in the guidelines calculation was harmless as both Valencia and Portocarrero received the statutory mandatory minimum sentence and the district court could not have sentenced them to less. *See United States v. Westry*, 524 F.3d 1198, 1221-22 (11th Cir. 2008) (finding no error in district court's application of firearm enhancement and then concluding, in any event, any error in guidelines calculation was harmless where application of enhancement did not affect defendants' overall sentences).

VI. CONCLUSION

For the reasons stated, we reject the defendants' challenges and affirm their convictions and total sentences.

AFFIRMED.

United States Court of Appeals
for the Eleventh Circuit

No. 17-11961

OCEAN MARINE CONSTR., INC.
vs.
CARROLL

Appeal from the United States District Court for the
Middle District of Florida

Decided: March 20, 2019

Citation: 918 F.3d 1323, 7 Adm. R. 463 (11th Cir. 2019).

Before **MARCUS, NEWSOM,** and **ANDERSON,** Circuit
Judges.

[—2—] {–1324–} NEWSOM, Circuit Judge:
{–1325–}

This admiralty appeal requires us to navigate uncharted waters in order to determine what constitutes sufficient notice of a claim under the Shipowner's Limitation of Liability Act, 46 U.S.C. §§ 30501, *et seq.* The Act establishes a procedure by which a shipowner can limit its liability for certain claims involving one of its vessels to the value of the vessel plus its then-pending freight. *Id.* § 30505(a). Importantly here, to invoke the Act's protection, the shipowner must bring a limitation-of-liability action in federal court "within 6 months after a claimant gives the owner written notice of a claim." *Id.* § 30511(a). If the owner meets the six-month statutory deadline, and then creates a qualifying limitation "fund," all related lawsuits against the owner "shall cease," leaving the claimants to pursue their rights in the limitation proceeding. *Id.* § 30511.

In connection with a large bridge-construction project in Florida, Orion Marine Construction used four barges to drive piles into the seabed. After numerous local residents complained that their homes had been damaged by vibrations caused by the barges' pile-driving activities, Orion filed a limitation action under the Act. Claimants Mark and Christine Dawson moved to dismiss Orion's suit, arguing that Orion had received adequate notice of the claims against it more than six months before it filed, that the action was therefore time-barred, [—3—] and, accordingly, that the district court lacked subject matter jurisdiction. The district court agreed and granted the Dawsons' motion to dismiss. We reverse.

This appeal presents several interesting and important questions about the meaning and operation of the Act:

First, does § 30511(a)'s six-month filing deadline erect a jurisdictional barrier to suit, as the Dawsons contend and the district court concluded? We hold that it does not, and that it is instead (like most timely-filing requirements) a non-jurisdictional claim-processing rule.

Second, what constitutes "written notice of a claim" within the meaning of § 30511(a)? We hold that in order to trigger the six-month filing period, a claimant (not someone else) must provide the shipowner or its agent (not someone else) with written (not oral) notice that reveals a "reasonable possibility" that his claim will exceed the value of the vessel(s) at issue.

Third, does a shipowner incur a duty to investigate known or potential claims immediately upon receipt of a claimant's notice, as the district court concluded? We hold that it does not, and that the duty to investigate arises only if the notice reveals the required "reasonable possibility."

Finally, did Orion receive the statutorily required written notice—revealing a reasonable possibility of claims that would exceed the value of its barges—more [—4—] than six months before it filed its limitation action? We hold that it did not, and, accordingly, that its suit was timely filed.

I

A

The pertinent facts here are undisputed. In 2011, Orion—a company specializing in {–1326–} marine construction—contracted with the Florida Department of Transportation (FDOT) to rebuild the Pinellas Bayway Bridge in Pinellas County, Florida. As part of the project, Orion's barges were used to drive concrete piles into the bay floor. Hundreds of local residents complained that the vibrations created by Orion's pile-driving damaged their surrounding properties, and 247 of them eventually filed formal claims in the limitation action that gave rise to this appeal.

Early on, though, the claims trickled in slowly. Between March 2012 and June 2014, only nine residents lodged complaints—typically alleging cracks in their homes, patios, and driveways, or leaks in their pools—with either Orion, FDOT, or Orion's third-party administrator, FARA Insurance. We focus here on these first nine claimants because they (alone among the 247) made their complaints before November 11, 2014—and thus, critically, more than six months before Orion filed suit on May 11, 2015. [—5—]

In response to a few of these early complaints, Orion dispatched an investigator to assess the alleged damage. Some of the cracks that he observed, he reported, were "old," and others were "minor" and "cosmetic." As for one of the reported pool leaks, he found that it was "just a crack in a PVC pipe." Orion installed vibration monitors at two residents' homes; the numbers came back "low" at one and "very, very low" at the other.

According to Orion, around December 2014 or January 2015 it began to receive property-damage claims "in bulk" from a public adjuster, beginning with 11 additional complaints during those two months alone. This flood of new claims, Orion says, prompted it to file its limitation action on May 11, 2015.

B

Mark and Christine Dawson—who lodged one of the original nine complaints—moved to dismiss Orion's action on the ground that it was untimely and, therefore, that the district court lacked subject matter jurisdiction. Orion's action was time-barred, they asserted, because Orion had received "written notice of

a claim" within the meaning of 46 U.S.C. § 30511(a) prior to November 11, 2014—and thus earlier than the statutorily specified six-months mark before it filed. Orion responded that none of the nine original claims provided it with proper notice under the Act because (1) a number of the complaints were not "written," as the Act requires, and (2) in any event, the complaints failed to reveal [—6—] a "reasonable possibility" that the claims would exceed the aggregate value of the four vessels used during the bridge construction.

Because it "lacked sufficient factual information" about which of the original nine claims were made when, to whom, and in what form, the district court denied the Dawsons' motion without prejudice and ordered the parties to conduct limited discovery on the timeliness issue. Discovery revealed a hodge-podge of formal and informal oral and written complaints, which were submitted to various employees at Orion, FDOT, and FARA. When FDOT received complaints, it memorialized them in written summaries or emails, which it then forwarded to Orion. FARA typically responded to the complaints that it received by acknowledging them, disclaiming any assumption of coverage, advising that construction was ongoing, requesting copies of—or that the claimant maintain records of—photos and repair quotes, and agreeing to investigate further. In an effort to impose some order—and to facilitate our own analysis—we will group the complaints into the following categories: {–1327–} (a) oral complaints that were (i) made to and memorialized in writing by Orion or (ii) made to and memorialized in writing by FARA or FDOT and then forwarded to Orion; and (b) written complaints that were (i) made to FARA and then forwarded to Orion or (ii) made to FDOT and then forwarded to Orion. [—7—]

Based on the information obtained during discovery, Orion emphasized that none of the nine original claimants had provided "written notice" to it and that only four had provided written notice to anyone—two to FDOT and two to FARA. Moreover, Orion said, none of the nine presented specific damage computations (in any form) before November 11,

2014. Estimates that Orion received after the completion of the bridge revealed the total amount of claimed damages by written notice to be $164,901.10 and the total from all pre-November 11, 2014 notices (both oral and written) to be $330,046.22.[1] Because neither number exceeds the aggregate value of the four barges used during the construction—$1,258,217.00—Orion contended that the nine original claimants' notices didn't start the six-month clock on its obligation to file a limitation action. Rather, Orion reiterated, "[i]t was not until a public adjuster began signing up claimants in droves in December 2014 . . . that [it] was reasonably on notice the claims may exceed the value of its vessels." Accordingly, Orion argued, its May 11, 2015 filing fell comfortably within the six-month period prescribed by the Act.

C

Following discovery, the Dawsons renewed their motion to dismiss, reiterating that because Orion's action was untimely under § 30511(a), the district [—8—] court lacked subject matter jurisdiction over the case. The district court granted the motion and dismissed Orion's complaint, concluding that "Orion was aware or should have been aware that claims against it would likely exceed the value of the vessel[s] . . . certainly no later than November 11, 2014," and, accordingly, that its limitation action filed on May 11, 2015 was "untimely and must be dismissed for lack of jurisdiction."

In so holding, the district court admitted that it was "[w]ithout any case law directly analogous to the case at hand" and, accordingly, that it had to "extrapolate from the available precedent to determine whether the nine [original] complaints constituted notice." In so doing, it considered all nine pre-November 11, 2014 notices "in the aggregate" and the sufficiency of those communications "as a whole." Significantly, as to the form of notice, the district court concluded "that both the written complaints Orion received directly

from the [c]laimants or by forward from the FDOT, and the memorialized oral complaints Orion received [either directly or from FDOT or FARA] constitute 'written' notice under the Act." The district court further reasoned that the complaints that Orion received before November 11, 2014 triggered a duty—which it found Orion breached—to investigate any "potential" additional claims that might be asserted by owners of other properties in the surrounding area. [—9—]

Orion timely appealed to this Court, arguing that the district court erred in concluding (1) that § 30511(a)'s six-month filing requirement is jurisdictional and (2) that the nine original claimants provided adequate notice under the Act. In support of the latter contention, Orion argued that the district court erred by holding (a) that even oral complaints, if later memorialized, satisfy the Act's "written notice" requirement, {–1328–} (b) that the nine pre-November 11, 2014 notices identified "limitable" claims even though the record revealed no reasonable possibility that the alleged damages (no matter how measured) would exceed the value of the barges used during construction, and (c) that Orion was obligated to investigate the possibility of additional claims immediately upon receipt of the initial complaints.

We consider those issues in turn.

II

We begin, as we must, with jurisdiction. A number of courts—including at least two of our sister circuits—have held, as the district court did here, that § 30511(a)'s six-month time bar constitutes a jurisdictional limitation. *See, e.g., In re Eckstein Marine Serv., L.L.C.*, 672 F.3d 310, 315 (5th Cir. 2012); *Cincinnati Gas & Elec. Co. v. Abel*, 533 F.2d 1001, 1003 (6th Cir. 1976). We disagree.

Not long ago, in *Secretary v. Preston*, 873 F.3d 877 (11th Cir. 2017), we had occasion to survey the Supreme Court's recent precedent outlining the distinction [—10—] between true jurisdictional limitations and non-jurisdictional "claim-processing" rules—and, in particular, concerning the jurisdictional-

---

[1] Orion explained that because two of the claimants never filed claims in the limitation action or made specific demands, their estimated damages remain unknown.

ness of statutory time bars. *See id.* at 881–82. What we said there—about ERISA's six-year statute of repose—applies here pretty much foursquare. As a general matter, we observed that in recent years, "the Supreme Court has set out to impose some discipline on the previously slippery use of the term 'jurisdictional.'" *Id.* at 881. "In so doing," we recounted, "the Court has emphasized—repeatedly—that statutory limitation periods and other filing deadlines 'ordinarily are not jurisdictional' and that a particular time bar should be treated as jurisdictional 'only if Congress has clearly stated that it is.'" *Id.* (quoting *Musacchio v. United States*, 136 S. Ct. 709, 716–17 (2016)). Establishing the required clear statement, we explained, is a tall task—a party must "demonstrat[e] that 'traditional tools of statutory construction . . . plainly show that Congress imbued a procedural bar with jurisdictional consequences.'" *Id.* (quoting *United States v. Kwai Fun Wong*, 135 S. Ct. 1625, 1632 (2015)).

More particularly, the considerations that we emphasized in *Preston* in concluding that ERISA's statute of repose is not jurisdictional lead us to the same conclusion about § 30511(a). First, we observed that the language of the provision there at issue "d[id] not 'speak in jurisdictional terms or refer in any way to the jurisdiction of the district courts.'" *Id.* at 882 (quoting *Arbaugh v. Y & H Corp.*, [—11—] 546 U.S. 500, 515 (2006)). "When," we said, "a statute 'speaks only to a claim's timeliness, not to a court's power,' it should be treated as non-jurisdictional." *Id.* (quoting *Kwai Fun Wong*, 135 S. Ct. at 1632). Just so here. Section 30511(a)'s language— "[t]he action must be brought within 6 months"—does not "plainly show that Congress imbued" the deadline "with jurisdictional consequences." *Kwai Fun Wong*, 135 S. Ct. at 1632. Rather, it "reads like an ordinary, run-of-the-mill statute of limitations, spelling out a litigant's filing obligations without restricting a court's authority." *Id.* at 1633 (internal quotation marks and citation omitted). In short, § 30511(a)'s text reveals a filing deadline of the sort that the Supreme Court has consistently called a "quintessential claim-

processing rule[]." *Henderson v. Shinseki*, 562 U.S. 428, 435 (2011).

Second, and relatedly, we stressed in *Preston* that Congress's "use of mandatory language"—there, "No action may be commenced"—does {–1329–} not alone impart jurisdictional significance. "The Supreme Court," we noted, "has flatly 'rejected the notion that all mandatory prescriptions, however emphatic, are . . . properly typed jurisdictional.'" 873 F.3d at 882 (quoting *Henderson*, 562 U.S. at 439). Not even sweeping proscriptions like "no action shall be brought," *Jones v. Bock*, 549 U.S. 199, 220 (2007), and "shall be forever barred," *Kwai Fun Wong*, 135 S. Ct. at 1633–38, will do the trick. *See Preston*, 873 F.3d at 882. Rather, we summarized, "[u]nder clear Supreme Court precedent, it is only an express [—12—] reference to jurisdiction, not firmness more generally, that counts." *Id.* Section 30511(a)'s mandatory phrasing, therefore—"The action must be brought within 6 months"—provides no basis for inferring a jurisdictional limitation.

Finally, just as in *Preston*, "[s]tatutory context"—and in particular, the location of the time bar within the statute's architecture—confirms § 30511(a)'s "non-jurisdictional character." *Id.* Here, as there, Congress situated the filing period among provisions that describe the standards and procedures that govern the cause of action—and (well) away from those that allocate jurisdiction. Congress, that is, didn't write the six-month bar into 28 U.S.C. § 1333(1), which gives federal district courts original jurisdiction over "any civil case of admiralty or maritime jurisdiction." Instead, it placed the time limit in Chapter 305 of Title 46, which is titled "Exoneration and Limitation of Liability" and which prescribes the mechanics of shipowner suits—liability caps, apportionment, personal-injury and wrongful-death actions, etc. (Tellingly, § 30511(a)'s six-month deadline is repeated in Rule F(1) of the Supplemental Admiralty and Maritime Claims Rules, which are located in an addendum to the Federal Rules of Civil Procedure.) The fact that here—again, just as in *Preston*—Congress "separat[ed]" the filing deadline from the jurisdictional grant fortifies our determination that § 30511(a)'s six-month "time bar is not jurisdictional." *Preston*, 873 F.3d at 882 (quoting *Kwai Fun Wong*, 135 S. Ct. at 1633). [—13—]

"Because we find no clear textual indication" that § 30511(a)'s six-month time bar "was intended to limit courts' subject matter jurisdiction," *id.*—because, in short, it does nothing "special, beyond setting an exception-free deadline," *Kwai Fun Wong*, 135 S. Ct. at 1632—we hold that the provision is an ordinary non-jurisdictional claim-processing rule, and that the district court erred in concluding otherwise.[2] {—1330—}

* * *

Where, you might ask, does that leave us procedurally? Fair question. Given the

---

[2] We are untroubled by the fact that our holding in this respect places us athwart the consensus of courts to address § 30511(a)'s jurisdictional status. Many of the decisions holding—or assuming, really—that § 30511(a) limits courts' subject matter jurisdiction predate the Supreme Court's recent effort to "bring some discipline" to the use of the term "jurisdictional." *Henderson*, 562 U.S. at 435. Moreover, and in any event—and with respect—we think that many of the § 30511(a) decisions represent the sort of "drive-by jurisdictional rulings," *Reed Elsevier, Inc. v. Muchnick*, 559 U.S. 154, 161 (2010), that the Supreme Court has condemned. *See, e.g., Cincinnati Gas*, 533 F.2d at 1003 (relying on a 1939 district court decision for the proposition that if a deadline is a condition precedent then it must be jurisdictional—a mechanical rationale that the Supreme Court has since rejected); *Complaint of Tom-Mac, Inc.*, 76 F.3d 678, 682 (5th Cir. 1996) (assuming that § 30511(a)'s predecessor's filing deadline is jurisdictional without elaboration or citation to authority); *In re Waterfront License Corp.*, 231 F.R.D. 693, 699 (S.D. Fla. 2005) (same); *In re Eckstein*, 672 F.3d at 315 & n.11, n.12 (relying on *Cincinnati Gas, Complaint of Tom-Mac*, and *In re Waterfront License Corp.*, as well as an earlier Fifth Circuit decision holding the Federal Tort Claims Act's statute of limitations is jurisdictional—a decision that the Supreme Court has since expressly abrogated); *In re Complaint of RLB Contracting, Inc.*, 773 F.3d 596, 601 & n.5, 602 & n.14, 2 Adm. R. 378, 380 & n.5, 380 & n.14 (5th Cir. 2014) (relying without analysis on *In re Eckstein*).

peculiarities of this particular case, the proper course, we think, is to evaluate the merits of the parties' contentions—about whether the nine original (*i.e.*, pre-November 11, 2014) claimants gave Orion notice sufficient to commence [—14—] § 30511(a)'s six-month clock—under a summary-judgment standard. For reasons just explained, despite its label, the Dawsons' Rule 12(b)(1) motion to dismiss for lack of subject matter jurisdiction is more accurately considered a Rule 12(b)(6) motion to dismiss for failure to state a claim. Because the district court considered materials outside the pleadings in deciding the Dawsons' motion, though—and indeed, affirmatively directed discovery—that motion may properly be converted into a motion for summary judgment. *See* Fed. R. Civ. P. 12(d). Given that (1) the parties here conducted discovery on the timeliness issue, (2) the Dawsons alternatively framed their motion as one for summary judgment and Orion maintained that it should have been reviewed under a summary-judgment rubric, (3) the parties agree (and have reiterated before us) that there are no disputed material facts, and (4) the parties further agree that the timeliness issue is squarely presented on appeal, we feel confident proceeding to decide the merits under a summary-judgment standard, reviewing the district court's decision de novo. *Cf. Miller v. Herman*, 600 F.3d 726, 731–33 (7th Cir. 2010) (confronting a similar "procedural hiccup" and opting to treat a Rule 12(b)(1) motion as a Rule 12(b)(6) motion, which was properly converted to, and thus reviewed as, a summary-judgment motion). [—15—]

III

Our consideration of the merits comprises several issues, which we will address in turn. First, which of two competing doctrinal tests—which we have acknowledged but have never (until now) had to choose between—governs the determination whether a claimant's notice is sufficient under § 30511(a)? Second, what forms and methods of notice qualify as "written notice" within the meaning of the Act? And third, what does it mean for a claimant's notice to reveal—as we hold it must in order to start the statutory clock and trigger a duty to investigate additional claims—a "reasonable possibility" that his claim will exceed the value of the shipowner's vessel(s)?

A

Because the Act doesn't define "written notice of a claim," courts have been left to formulate tests to determine whether a claimant's notice suffices under § 30511(a). Under one, which originated in the Second Circuit's decision in *Doxsee Sea Clam Co. v. Brown,* "[n]otice will be sufficient if it informs the vessel owner of an actual or potential claim . . . which may exceed the value of the vessel . . . and is subject to limitation." 13 F.3d 550, 554 (2d Cir. 1994) (internal citations omitted). The Seventh Circuit has since adopted the *Doxsee* standard with one important refinement—elaborating on the word "may," that court held that "the written notice of a claim must reveal a 'reasonable possibility' that the claim made [—16—] is one subject to limitation." *In re Complaint of McCarthy Bros. Co./Clark Bridge,* 83 F.3d 821, 829 (7th Cir. 1996) (citing *Complaint of Tom-Mac,* 76 F.3d at 683). The competing test requires only that the claimant's notice (1) demand a right or supposed right, (2) blame the vessel owner {–1331–} for any damage or loss, and (3) call on the vessel owner for anything due. *See Rodriguez Moreira v. Lemay,* 659 F. Supp. 89, 91 (S.D. Fla. 1987).

We have twice noted the existence of these two tests—first in *Paradise Divers, Inc. v. Upmal,* 402 F.3d 1087 (11th Cir. 2005), and then, a year later, in *P.G. Charter Boats, Inc. v. Soles,* 437 F.3d 1140 (11th Cir. 2006). On both occasions, we found it unnecessary to choose between them. The district court here did the same thing, concluding that the claimants' notices satisfied both. But for reasons that we'll explain, the distinction between the two standards actually matters here. Although we have described these two tests as "similar," *Paradise Divers,* 402 F.3d at 1090, there is one crucial difference: What we'll call the "*Doxsee/McCarthy* test" entails an amount/value element that the "*Moreira* test" does not—namely, it requires that the notice reveal a "reasonable possibility" that

the claim will exceed the value of the offending vessel(s). No one—not even Orion—disputes that the claimants' notices would meet the *Moreira* standard. Instead, Orion contends that the claimants' notices fail the *Doxsee/McCarthy* test because the notices (even considered in the aggregate) failed to convey a [—17—] reasonable possibility that the claims' total value would exceed the value of its barges.

With the lines thus drawn—and because we agree that Orion can't win under *Moreira* but has a fighting chance under *Doxsee/McCarthy*—the time has finally come for us to decide which standard to apply. The answer, we think, is clear. For starters, the *Doxsee/McCarthy* test is the most widely-accepted among our sister circuits—in addition to the Second and Seventh Circuits, the Fifth has also embraced it, *see In re Eckstein,* 672 F.3d at 317—and indeed, it has been described as the "most authoritative." *Paradise Divers,* 402 F.3d at 1090 (quoting *McCarthy Bros.,* 83 F.3d at 829). The *Moreira* test, by contrast, while perhaps once "found in many district court cases," *id.,* does not appear to have been adopted by any circuit court, and generally seems to have fallen into desuetude since *Doxsee* was decided.

More substantively, the key distinction between the two tests—namely, that *Doxsee/McCarthy* incorporates an amount/value element (in the form of the "reasonable possibility" showing) that *Moreira* doesn't—underscores the superiority of the former. *Doxsee/McCarthy*'s reasonable-possibility requirement serves the six-month limitation period's purpose by encouraging shipowners to act promptly while at the same time eliminating consideration of small-value cases unlikely to benefit from the Act's protection. In contrast, by requiring a shipowner [—18—] to initiate limitation proceedings regardless of the amount likely at issue, the *Moreira* test would (1) "obligate a shipowner to go to the expense of posting security and taking the other steps necessary to commence a limitation proceeding" even when the claims indicate that doing so would be "wholly unnecessary," (2) "encourage claimants to understate the amount of their damage in the hope that the shipowner would be misled into not filing a timely petition for limitation," and (3) "serve no purpose other than to clog the courts with unneeded petitions and cause great expense to shipowners without in any way benefiting claimants." *Complaint of Morania Barge No. 190, Inc.*, 690 F.2d 32, 34 (2d Cir. 1982).

For all of these reasons, we hold that the *Doxsee/McCarthy* test is the controlling standard for determining the sufficiency of notice under § 30511(a).

B

That leads us to the question whether claimants' notices here satisfied the {–1332–} *Doxsee/McCarthy* standard—which, as we have described it before and adopt it today, requires a claimant to give the shipowner written notice that reveals a "reasonable possibility" of a claim that exceeds the value of the vessel(s). *See P.G. Charter Boats*, 437 F.3d at 1143.

Orion argues that claimants' notices fail this test (1) because some of them were not "written" at all, as § 30511(a) plainly requires, and (2) because, in any event, the notices—even including those made orally—"never demonstrated a [—19—] reasonable possibility of a claim exceeding the value of the vessel, and to this day, even added together, Claimants' filed claims do not." Br. for Appellant at 21. The Dawsons, by contrast, contend that the district court properly determined that the pre-November 11, 2014 claims—when considered in the aggregate and including the oral complaints that were later reduced to writing—provided notice sufficient to allow Orion to evaluate its overall exposure, and thus triggered Orion's duty to investigate and to file suit within six months.

1

First things first: Which of the pre-November 11, 2014 complaints qualify as "written notice" within the meaning of the Act? And more particularly, what of the district court's conclusion "that both the written complaints Orion received directly from the Claimants or by forward from the FDOT, and the memorialized oral complaints Orion received [either directly or from FDOT or FARA] constitute 'written' notice under the Act"? Put simply, in so holding, the district court erred. Section 30511(a) couldn't be clearer about what we have called its "writing" requirement. *See P.G. Charter Boats*, 437 F.3d at 1143. The statute says, in no uncertain terms, that the six-month filing period begins to run when "a claimant gives the owner written notice of a claim." 46 U.S.C. § 30511(a). Broken down into its constituent parts, that straightforward provision requires that the *claimant* [—20—] (not someone else) give the *owner* (not someone else) *written* (not oral) notice of his claim.

As noted earlier, the complaints lodged by the original nine claimants can be grouped into the following categories: (a) oral complaints that were (i) made to and memorialized in writing by Orion or (ii) made to and memorialized by FARA or FDOT and then forwarded to Orion; and (b) written complaints that were (i) made to FARA and forwarded to Orion or (ii) made to FDOT and forwarded to Orion. We will consider each type of complaint in turn.

a

As an initial matter, we think it clear—contrary to the district court's determination—that the memorialized oral complaints don't qualify.

The complaints that were made orally to Orion and that it later reduced to writing—those are easy. No reasonable interpretation of § 30511(a)'s text—requiring that the "claimant give[] the owner written notice"—could include a vessel owner's *own* written notes recording a claimant's oral report. In that circumstance, no "written notice" has been provided at all—by anyone, to anyone. What about the complaints that were made orally to FARA and/or FDOT, which they then memorialized and forwarded to Orion? Closer, but still no cigar. In that circumstance, Orion might have received written notice from someone, but it [—21—] didn't receive written notice from a *claimant*, as § 30511(a) expressly requires.[3] The fact that someone, somewhere has reduced an {–1333–} oral communication to writing doesn't transform an invalid oral notice into a valid written notice under the Act.[4]

b

What, though, about the *written* notices provided by the claimants to FARA and/or FDOT, which were then forwarded to Orion? Much closer. The Second Circuit has held that "[i]t is settled that a notice of claim may be received by an agent of the vessel owner," *Doxsee*, 13 F.3d at 553, and that seems right to us as a matter of hornbook agency law. *See,*

---

[3] The district court suggested that FDOT was a "potential claimant" by way of the indemnification provision in Orion's contract—and therefore, that the oral claims memorialized by FDOT could constitute written notice by a claimant. That is incorrect. The Supreme Court has made clear that contracts entered into by vessel owners are personal and not subject to the Act. *See, e.g., Am. Car & Foundry Co. v. Brassert*, 289 U.S. 261, 264 (1933); *Richardson v. Harmon,* 222 U.S. 96, 106 (1911). Accordingly, no claim made by FDOT against Orion pursuant to their contract would be subject to limitation, and FDOT could never be a "claimant" in a limitation action.

[4] In support of its conclusion that the memorialized oral complaints should be considered, the district court cited only the magistrate's report and recommendation in *Paradise Divers* for the proposition that "although a notice of claim must obviously be in writing, the notice need not take any particular form." Doc. 634 at 16 (quoting *In re Paradise Divers, Inc.,* No. 03-10021 CIV, 2003 WL 25731109, at *4 (S.D. Fla. Nov. 9, 2003)). But that statement doesn't support the district court's position. Rather, the *Paradise Divers* R&R sought only to clarify what other circuits have expressly held—that *informal* written notice, such as a letter sent by a claimant or his attorney, will suffice under the Act in lieu of a formal complaint. *See, e.g., RLB Contracting*, 773 F.3d at 603, 2 Adm. R. at 381; *Doxsee,* 13 F.3d at 554. The Act's plain text still requires that the *claimant* provide *written* notice to the *owner*. 46 U.S.C. § 30511(a). The district court also emphasized that Orion acted on the memorialized oral complaints—and thus, the theory presumably goes, had actual knowledge of them. But even actual knowledge of alleged damage is no substitute for the *written* notice required by the Act. *See, e.g., Moreira*, 659 F. Supp. at 91.

e.g., Restatement (Third) of Agency § 5.03 [–22–] (Am. Law Inst. 2006) (observing that, as a general rule, "[f]or purposes of a principal's legal relations with a third party, notice of a fact that an agent knows or has reason to know is imputed to the principal if knowledge of the fact is material to the agent's duties to the principal"). And for that matter, even Orion admits that "*written* notice provided to an agent might be imputed to the principal." Reply Br. for Appellant at 6. So the sufficiency of the written notices sent to FARA and/or FDOT hinges on whether they were Orion's agents.

It seems reasonably clear to us—and no one here disputes—that FARA was Orion's agent for claims-processing purposes. FARA had at the very least apparent—and probably even actual—authority to act on Orion's behalf; indeed, it was hired specifically to assist Orion with the adjustment of claims. *See* Restatement (Third) of Agency §§ 3.01, 3.03 (describing actual and apparent authority). Accordingly, any claimant who gave written notice to FARA, as Orion's agent, satisfied § 30511(a)'s writing requirement.

Those who gave written notice only to FDOT (which the claimants describe as Orion's "project partner") stand on different footing. So far as we can tell, the record contains no evidence that Orion—as the would-be principal—made any "manifestation" that would have clothed FDOT with either actual or apparent authority to accept claim notices on Orion's behalf. *See id.* §§ 3.01, 3.03 (emphasizing that the "manifestation" that gives rise to an agent's authority must [–23–] emanate from the principal). Perhaps not surprisingly, then, the record demonstrates that when FDOT {–1334–} received complaints, it simply—and consistently— redirected them to Orion rather than attempting to process them.[5] Because FDOT

---

[5] In fairness, the record does reveal one instance in which an FDOT employee sent a copy of a property-damage form to a claimant with instructions that the claimant complete the form and copy her on the submission "so that [she could] make sure Orion receive[d] the documentation." Dispositively, though, that "manifestation"— assuming it was one—wasn't made by Orion, which

(unlike FARA) had no authority to act as Orion's agent for claims-processing purposes, written notice provided to FDOT didn't meet § 30511(a)'s written-notice-to-owner requirement.

* * *

So to sum up, the district court erred in holding that all of the claims—oral and written, and to whomever communicated—constituted "written notice" to the "owner" under § 30511(a). Complaints delivered orally and later reduced to writing (by anyone) don't qualify. Nor do the written complaints submitted to FDOT, which had no authority to act as Orion's claims-processing agent. Only the written complaints submitted in writing to Orion—either directly or through FARA, its agent—satisfy § 30511(a)'s "written notice" requirement.

2

Having said that, even if we were to consider—as the district court erroneously did—the oral and written complaints lodged by all nine of the pre- [—24—] November 11, 2014 claimants, their notices still fail the *Doxsee/McCarthy* test because they don't reveal a "reasonable possibility" that the claims, even considered (as the district court put it) "in the aggregate," would exceed the value of Orion's barges.[6] Here's why.

(as explained in text) agency law requires in order to establish apparent authority.

[6] Although there is nothing in the Act explicitly stating that the value of claims should be considered cumulatively, we will assume for present purposes that it is permissible to do so, as no one here seems to dispute that we may aggregate the value both of individual property owners' claims and of Orion's four barges for purposes of determining whether the claimants' notices reveal the required "reasonable possibility." We do note a distinction between this case and the Fifth Circuit's decision in *RLB Contracting*, on which the district court here relied. In particular, the district court pointed to the Fifth Circuit's statement that § 30511(a)'s "statutory text does not foreclose the possibility of aggregate notice; it only requires the claimant to give 'the owner written notice,' not *a* written notice." 773 F.3d at 603, 2 Adm. R. at 382. To be clear, though, *RLB*

a

It is undisputed that the four Orion barges involved in the pile-driving were valued, collectively, at no less than $1,258,217.00. The question, then, is whether the nine original claimants' notices revealed a reasonable possibility that their claims, collectively, would exceed that amount. It is clear to us that they didn't.

Let's first review the sort of damage that the claimants alleged. In general, the homeowners complained that Orion's pile-driving had caused (1) external cracks in their homes' walls, chimneys, porches, and driveways, (2) internal cracks [—25—] in drywall {–1335–} and around windows, ceilings, and fireplaces, and (3) leaks in their swimming pools and related water lines. The most extensive—and arguably most serious—complaints came from Mary White. After lodging a general complaint about damage in May 2012, she filed a more detailed grievance a year later. There, she said that her home had "sustained substantial damage from the work that is being done building the new Byway bridge." In particular, she complained about "cracking in every room in [her] home (including around the windows and ceilings, and . . . along [her] marble fireplace)," "cracks in [her] new cement driveway," "dropped pavers in [her] patio," "a leak in [her] swimming pool," and "a wet spot in [her] downstairs room." Six months thereafter, White followed up, alleging that she "had additional cracks in all [her] rooms."

Another homeowner, Robert Orsi, lodged a series of complaints, the most descriptive of

---

Contracting was different—the court there sanctioned aggregating multiple notices from a *single* claimant pertaining to a *single* incident, not (as here) multiple notices from *multiple* claimants arising out of *multiple* incidents. And while the Fifth Circuit was correct that the statute does not require *a* written notice, it does require "written notice of *a* claim." 46 U.S.C. § 30511(a) (emphasis added). Even so, we needn't tarry on the aggregate-notice issue here, because, as we explain in text, even if we consider all nine of the original claimants' notices together, they don't reveal a reasonable possibility that the claims would exceed the value of Orion's four barges.

which alleged damage to his "chimney and . . . front entrance," "cracks . . . above [his] door [that] made opening the door all the way difficult," and cracks "at the top of [his] stairs" that he feared suggested "issues with the concrete header over the doorway." Another couple, Mark and Christine Dawson—the appellees here—repeatedly complained about "damage to [their] swimming pool"—in particular, about "damage to [the] lines to [the] swimming pool caused by pile driving vibration." They also alleged, more vaguely, that "[i]n addition to the pool leaks," they had "a list of other issues that have happened, and [—26—] continue to happen." The other homeowners' complaints were similar, albeit less detailed—"leak in [my] pool," "cracking on [my] ceiling," "cracks in [my] home," "a lot of damage," etc.

As already noted, in response to several of the early complaints, Orion sent one of its agents to investigate. He determined that the alleged damage to White's home was "minor" and "cosmetic," that the cracks in Orsi's house were "old" and that the damage was "very minor cosmetic stuff," and that the Dawsons' pool leak was "just a crack in a PVC pipe." Orion installed vibration monitors at White's and Orsi's homes; the numbers registered "low" at Orsi's and "very, very low" at White's.

The question, then, is whether these notices revealed a reasonable possibility that the claims—in the aggregate, we have said we will assume—would exceed the barges' $1,258,217.00 value. We think it clear that they didn't. In explaining why not, it will be useful to compare this case with two recent Fifth Circuit decisions that have unpacked the reasonable-possibility standard. In *Eckstein*, a shipowner contended that a claimant's state-court complaint failed to reveal a reasonable possibility that his claim would exceed a vessel's $750,000 value. In disagreeing, the Fifth Circuit emphasized the seriousness of the claimant's physical injuries, sustained when he became "entangled in a line and was pulled into a mooring bit." 672 F.3d at 313. The claimant's injuries were not only gruesome—according to [—27—] eyewitness testimony, his "foot was hanging off of his leg at . . . a 90 degree angle" and there was "blood

everywhere"—but also "permanent and catastrophic." *Id*. at 317–18. He required "multiple surgeries including debridement, the insertion of hardware to treat his bone fractures, and a skin graft." *Id*. at 318. In his complaint, he sought "compensation for the remainder of his lifetime, including past loss of earning, future loss of earning capacity, past and future disability, past and future disfigurement, past and future medical and hospital expenses, past and future pain and mental anguish, and maintenance and c[u]re." *Id*. at 317. The Fifth Circuit held that the claimant's complaint "alleging catastrophic and permanent injuries raised at least a {–1336–} reasonable possibility that his claim might exceed" the ship's $750,000 value and, accordingly, that "it was [the shipowner's] responsibility to conduct an investigation, and to file a limitation action within six months." *Id*. at 319.

The Fifth Circuit faced the reasonable-possibility issue again in *RLB Contracting*. In that case, a fishing boat carrying a family had collided with a ship's floating dredge pipe; "[a]ll occupants of the fishing boat were thrown overboard, suffering various physical injuries, and [a child] was killed." 773 F.3d at 599, 2 Adm. R. at 378. Following *Eckstein*, the court held that a series of letters sent by the family's lawyer—including one emphasizing "the nature of the injuries, bystander claims, graphic photos, [and] the PTSD claims"—revealed a reasonable possibility [—28—] of a claim exceeding the vessel's $750,000 value. *Id*. at 600, 2 Adm. R. at 379. Put simply, the Fifth Circuit concluded, the shipowner "should have realized that an action involving the death of a child would easily exceed $750,000 in potential damages." *Id*. at 606, 2 Adm. R. at 384.

Needless to say, the nature and severity of the property damage alleged here pale in comparison to the claims for "permanent and catastrophic" personal injuries in *Eckstein* and wrongful death in *RLB Contracting*. And on the other side of the ledger, the value of the vessels here—more than $1.2 million—is significantly higher than in those cases. Even considering the notices provided by all nine of the original claimants, we hold that they failed to reveal a reasonable possibility of claims exceeding the value of Orion's four barges.

b

In concluding otherwise, the district court relied not on an empirical (or even anecdotal) valuation of the pre-November 11, 2014 claims—or a comparison of those claims with the acknowledged value of Orion's barges—but rather on twin determinations (1) that Orion had a duty to investigate both known and potential claims "immediately" upon receiving the homeowners' notices and (2) that it failed to do so. The key passage of the district court's opinion:

> Had Orion fulfilled its obligation to investigate immediately upon knowing of the claims and the uncertainty of their value or if it had simply filed its petition to limit liability in the face of this uncertainty, it would have either discovered that its losses were much greater than the specific claims about which it knew or it would have limited its liability in any event from all claims known or unknown occasioned [—29—] by the alleged injury caused by its pile-driving activity. Instead Orion did nothing, and that inaction is fatal to its Complaint to limit liability.

Doc. 634 at 23. In so concluding, the district court erred, both as a matter of law and as a matter of undisputed fact.

First, as to the law: The district court stated (and restated) that Orion had a legal duty to investigate known and potential property-damage claims "immediately" upon learning of them. For support, the court quoted the Fifth Circuit's decision in *RLB Contracting*, which in turn quoted that court's earlier decision in *Eckstein*:

> The purpose of the reasonable possibility standard is to place the burden of investigating potential claims on the vessel owner:

> The Limitation Act provides generous statutory protection to the vessel owners who reap all of its benefits. When there is uncertainty as to whether a claim will exceed the vessel's value, the reasonable possibility standard places the risk and the burdens associated with that risk on the owner. In other words, if doubt exists as to the {-1337-} total amount of the claims or as to whether they will exceed the value of the ship the owner will not be excused from satisfying the statutory time bar since he may institute a limitation proceeding even when the total amount claimed is uncertain.

Doc. 634 at 20 (quoting *RLB Contracting*, 773 F.3d at 602, 2 Adm. R. at 381 (quoting *Eckstein*, 672 F.3d at 317–18)) (additional internal quotation marks and citations omitted).

The district court, though, prematurely cut short its quotation from *RLB Contracting*. Just two sentences later—and again invoking its earlier decision in [—30—] *Eckstein*—the Fifth Circuit clearly explained when a shipowner's duty to investigate arises: "'*[O]nce a reasonable possibility has been raised*, it becomes the vessel owner's responsibility to initiate a prompt investigation and determine whether to file a limitation action.'" 773 F.3d at 603, 2 Adm. R. at 381 (quoting *Eckstein*, 672 F.3d at 317) (emphasis added). *RLB* does *not* say—as the district court here phrased it—that the shipowner has an "obligation to investigate *immediately* upon knowing of the claims." And in fact, *Eckstein*, which *RLB* followed, flatly *rejects* the district court's investigate-immediately-upon-receipt position: "The Limitation Act's six-month timeline does *not* automatically begin to run when a vessel owner learns a claimant has filed a lawsuit. It is triggered *only* if and when the written notice reveals a 'reasonable possibility' that the claim will exceed the value of the vessel, and therefore that the vessel owner might benefit from the Limitation Act's protection." 672 F.3d at 317 (emphasis added).

We think that the Fifth Circuit has it exactly right. While we agree with the district court that a claimant's notice needn't include a specific demand for damages, and while it's true that the vessel owner bears the burden of "uncertainty" and "doubt" as to the amount of alleged damages, it remains the case that the claimant's notice must reveal a reasonable possibility that the claims may [—31—] exceed the offending vessel's value. It is at that point—but not before—that the shipowner's duty to investigate arises.[7]

Because Orion's duty to investigate didn't arise "automatically" or "immediately" upon the filing of claims, it didn't violate that duty in the way the district court concluded. Indeed, and to the contrary, because (for reasons already explained) the claimants' notices here didn't reveal a reasonable possibility of claims exceeding $1,258,217.00, Orion's duty to investigate never materialized—meaning, by definition, that it couldn't have violated that duty, as the district court held.

Now, briefly, as to the *facts*: It simply isn't accurate, as the district court said, that "Orion did nothing." Doc. 634 at 23. As already explained, the undisputed facts demonstrate that, in response to the first several complaints, Orion sent one of its agents to investigate. That agent visited the White, Orsi, and Dawson residences, observed the alleged damage, and conducted vibration monitoring. He concluded that the problems were either "old," "minor," {–1338–} or "cosmetic"—or perhaps all three—and that the vibration measurements ranged [—32—] from "low" to "very, very low." Thus, faced with claims of uncertain value—and even *without* concluding that the notices underlying those claims revealed the requisite "reasonable possibility"—Orion investigated and determined (in its opinion, with certainty) that the alleged damage was minor.

* * *

In sum, the notices that Orion had received prior to November 11, 2014 didn't reveal a reasonable possibility that the residents' claims would exceed the value of its four barges, and Orion's preliminary investigation confirmed that conclusion. Had Orion bulled ahead with a limitation action at that point—as the district court concluded the law required—it would have "serve[d] no purpose other than to clog the courts with [an] unneeded petition[]." *Morania Barge*, 690 F.2d at 34.

IV

For the foregoing reasons, we hold as follows:

1. The six-month filing deadline specified by 46 U.S.C. § 30511(a) is a non-jurisdictional claim-processing rule, and a shipowner's failure to meet it does not deprive the district court of subject matter jurisdiction but rather provides a basis on which to dismiss the owner's limitation action on the merits.

2. In order to trigger § 30511(a)'s six-month filing period, a claimant (not someone else) must provide the shipowner or its agent (not someone else) [—33—] with a written (not oral) notice that reveals a "reasonable possibility" of a claim that will exceed the value of the vessel(s) at issue.

3. A shipowner's duty to investigate known or potential claims does not arise immediately upon receipt of a claimant's notice, but only if the notice reveals a reasonable possibility that the underlying claim exceeds the value of the vessel(s).

4. The notices provided by the first nine claimants here—*i.e.*, those who lodged

---

[7] And to be clear, the Fifth Circuit is hardly alone in concluding that a shipowner's duty to investigate does not arise "automatically" or "immediately," but rather only if and when a claimant's notice reveals a reasonable possibility of a claim that exceeds the vessel's value. The Second and Seventh Circuits have said the same thing, *see* *McCarthy*, 83 F.3d at 829 ("[T]he written notice of claim must reveal a 'reasonable possibility' that the claim made is one subject to limitation." (emphasis added)); *Doxsee*, 13 F.3d at 554 ("Notice will be sufficient if *it* informs the vessel owner of an actual or potential claim . . . which may exceed the value of the vessel . . . and is subject to limitation." (emphasis added)).

complaints before November 11, 2014—failed to reveal the required reasonable possibility, and thus neither started the six-month clock nor obligated Orion to investigate.

REVERSED AND REMANDED.

United States Court of Appeals
for the Eleventh Circuit

No. 17-14889

GUEVARA
VS.
NCL (BAHAMAS) LTD.

Appeal from the United States District Court for the
Southern District of Florida

Decided: April 1, 2019

Citation: 920 F.3d 710, 7 Adm. R. 476 (11th Cir. 2019).

Before **WILSON, PRYOR,** and **SUTTON,** * Circuit
Judges.

* Honorable Jeffrey S. Sutton, United States Circuit
Judge for the Sixth Circuit, sitting by designation

[—2—] {–714–} WILSON, Circuit Judge:

Pablo Guevara slipped and fell as he stepped down from a landing located on the outer deck of a cruise ship operated by NCL (Bahamas) Ltd. Guevara claimed that he did not perceive the step down because NCL failed to adequately warn him of the change in elevation. Moreover, a lightbulb was out in the area where Guevara fell, making it harder for him to navigate the floor level change at night. Guevara sued NCL, alleging that NCL negligently failed to (1) warn passengers of the step down and (2) maintain and inspect the lighting in the area. The district court granted summary judgment in favor of NCL on both claims, holding that Guevara failed to create a genuine issue of material fact regarding NCL's actual or constructive notice of the allegedly dangerous conditions posed by the step down or the unilluminated light.

Guevara appeals the district court's orders (1) striking his expert's supplemental reports and (2) granting summary judgment in favor of NCL. After careful review and with the benefit of oral argument, we reverse and remand the district court's ruling on Guevara's failure to warn claim. We affirm, however, the [—3—] district court's orders (1) striking Guevara's expert's supplemental reports and (2) granting summary {–715–}

judgment on Guevara's negligent maintenance claim.

I. Factual Background

Guevara was a cruise passenger on the Norwegian *Spirit*, which departed from Barcelona, Spain. On his first night aboard, at approximately 11:30 p.m., Guevara was walking on an outdoor deck near the pool, searching for the ship's cigar lounge. He walked up three steps to a landing. After the landing, there is a single step down, which Guevara claims he did not see.[1] When he stepped down, Guevara slipped on the deck and fell, landing with his arm wedged between the wall and a handrail. As a result, Guevara broke his arm.

After he fell, Guevara noticed a "sheen" of water on the floor where he slipped and that a lightbulb was out in one of the globe lamps at the top of the steps. Directly underneath the unilluminated lamp was a permanently affixed warning sign: "ATTENTION! FOR YOUR OWN SAFETY PLEASE USE THE HANDRAIL. WATCH YOUR STEP." Guevara contends that he could not see the warning sign because the bulb immediately above the sign was out.

II. Procedural History [—4—]

Guevara filed a complaint against NCL in the Southern District of Florida. He alleged that NCL negligently failed to (1) warn passengers of the step down, and (2) maintain and inspect the lighting in the area.

A. Expert Witness Reports

The parties proceeded to discovery. The district court's Scheduling Order set Guevara's expert disclosure deadline for June 18th, NCL's expert disclosure deadline for July 2nd, and the disclosure deadline for any rebuttal expert witness reports for July 16th.

Guevara disclosed Dr. Ronald Zollo as an expert and served a copy of his report on June

---

[1] Guevara claims that the landing appeared flush with the brown deck area below the step.

20th—two days after the expert disclosure deadline.

NCL's human factors and illumination expert, Dr. Joseph B. Sala, opined that there was sufficient lighting on the deck of the *Spirit* for a reasonably alert and attentive person walking in the area to safely navigate the floor level change. Guevara successfully moved for an extension of time to file rebuttal expert reports. He served Dr. Zollo's rebuttal expert report on July 26th. Dr. Zollo's rebuttal report addressed the step's dimensions and the insufficient slip resistance on the flooring.

On August 19th—the Friday before Dr. Zollo's Monday deposition—Guevara served NCL with a copy of a thirteen-page "Addendum to the Preliminary Report" (First Supplemental Report) that supplemented both Dr. Zollo's initial and [—5—] rebuttal expert opinions. The First Supplemental Report contained previously undisclosed opinions and references to authoritative materials. NCL proceeded with Dr. Zollo's deposition notwithstanding its objection to the submission of the First Supplemental Report. Dr. Zollo terminated his deposition after three hours and refused to resume later in the day.

Discovery closed on August 26th.

On September 26th—a month after the close of discovery and three days after the district court's deadline for dispositive and *Daubert* motions—Guevara filed a second, three-page addendum to Dr. Zollo's preliminary {–716–} report (Second Supplemental Report).

NCL moved to strike Dr. Zollo's testimony and reports because of Guevara's untimely disclosure of Dr. Zollo as an expert witness, Dr. Zollo's early termination of his deposition, and the presentation of new arguments in Dr. Zollo's supplemental reports that were not addressed in NCL's expert's report or alleged in the complaint. NCL also filed a *Daubert* motion to exclude Dr. Zollo's opinions, arguing that (1) he was not qualified to offer opinions on the construction of seaworthy vessels or human factors; (2) he did not use a sufficiently reliable methodology; (3) his opinions were based on assumptions and speculation; and (4) his opinions would not assist the trier of fact. [—6—]

The district court did not strike Dr. Zollo's initial expert report as untimely, even though it was filed two days late. In considering Dr. Zollo's First and Second Supplemental Reports, the district court acknowledged that NCL was dilatory in setting the deposition of NCL's corporate representative, which was taken well after the expert discovery deadlines and a week before discovery closed on August 26th. During the corporate representative's deposition, NCL produced for the first time a drawing of the deck area, photographs of the area taken the night of Guevara's fall, and a coefficient of friction (COF)[2] testing report of the deck. The district court found that, given NCL's late production, Dr. Zollo was justified in supplementing his initial report based on the new information obtained during the corporate representative's deposition. Dr. Zollo did not, however, have "*carte blanche* to supplement everything in both his initial and rebuttal expert reports." As such, the district court excluded certain portions of the First Supplemental Report and the entirety of the Second Supplemental Report because Guevara failed to show that their late disclosure was either justified or harmless.

The district court struck the portion of Dr. Zollo's First Supplemental Report listing industry standards on lighting because it was produced too close in time to Dr. Zollo's deposition. In reaching this conclusion, the district court explained that [—7—] none of Dr. Zollo's opinions on lighting in the First Supplemental Report referred to any of the late discovery produced by NCL. The district court found that the late submission of the report was not harmless.

The district court struck the entirety of Dr. Zollo's Second Supplemental Report because

---

[2] Coefficient of friction measures a surface's "degree of slip resistance." *Sorrels v. NCL (Bahamas) Ltd.*, 796 F.3d 1275, 1279, 3 Adm. R. 659, 659 (11th Cir. 2015) (citing *Mihailovich v. Laatsch*, 359 F.3d 892, 896, 921 n.2 (7th Cir. 2004)).

its late disclosure harmed NCL. While Dr. Zollo was justified in supplementing his initial expert reports on account of NCL's late production of the COF report, the court found no justification for Dr. Zollo supplementing his expert opinion more than five weeks after he received the COF report, over a month after the close of discovery, and three days after the district court's dispositive and *Daubert* motions deadline. Guevara did not seek leave to extend discovery, which left NCL with no opportunity to depose Dr. Zollo about his Second Supplemental Report.

B. NCL's Motion for Summary Judgment

NCL moved for summary judgment, arguing that there was no record evidence of a dangerous condition, or evidence of actual or constructive notice of a dangerous condition, in the area where Guevara fell. Guevara opposed NCL's motion, asserting {–717–} two theories of NCL's negligence liability: duty to warn and negligent maintenance. Under the first theory, Guevara argued that NCL failed to adequately warn him of the dangerous condition posed by the step down. Under the negligent maintenance theory, Guevara argued that NCL "permit[ed] the light [—8—] to go out and remain out and [did] not post[] warning signs (or other more effective warnings such as yellow tape) that could have been seen by passengers traveling from the direction that Mr. Guevara was traveling."

The district court granted summary judgment in favor of NCL, holding that Guevara did not create a genuine issue of material fact regarding NCL's actual or constructive notice of the allegedly dangerous condition posed by the step down. The district court rejected Guevara's argument that the presence of the warning sign alone was sufficient to create an issue of fact regarding NCL's notice of the dangerous step.[3] The court reasoned that Guevara offered no evidence that NCL created or affixed the warning sign, and thus failed to create a

---

[3] Guevara conceded that NCL did not design, manufacture, construct, or install the step or decking materials. Guevara also conceded that there had been no prior injuries, accidents, or claims against NCL related to the step.

"logical inference that [NCL] had prior knowledge of the dangerous condition necessitating the warning." *Lipkin v. Norwegian Cruise Line Ltd.*, 93 F. Supp. 3d 1311, 1323 (S.D. Fla. 2015).

Guevara also argued that NCL was on constructive notice that the light had been out because, under NCL's normal practices, the light was checked at 7:00 or 8:00 p.m. The light thus theoretically could have been out for up to four hours before Guevara fell. The district court disagreed. The court reasoned that the possibility that the light *could* have been out for four hours was not evidence of [—9—] when the light *actually* went out. The district court held that Guevara failed to create a genuine dispute of material fact about NCL's notice of the alleged dangerous condition posed by the unilluminated light. Guevara appealed.

III. Discussion

We now consider Guevara's argument that the district court erred in excluding Dr. Zollo's supplemental expert reports and in granting summary judgment to NCL.

A. Exclusion of Supplemental Expert Reports

Guevara challenges the district court's ruling to exclude his expert's supplemental reports, arguing that those reports would have created a genuine dispute of material fact. "We . . . review a district court's exclusion of expert reports for abuse of discretion." *Corwin v. Walt Disney Co.*, 475 F.3d 1239, 1250 (11th Cir. 2007). "A district court abuses its discretion when it makes a clear error of judgment or applies an incorrect legal standard." *Sorrels v. NCL (Bahamas) Ltd.*, 796 F.3d 1275, 1281, 3 Adm. R. 659, 661 (11th Cir. 2015).

Federal Rule of Civil Procedure 26 requires that "[a] party must make [expert witness] disclosures at the times and in the sequence the court orders." Fed. R. Civ. P. 26(a)(2)(D). In order to make a proper disclosure, parties must, by the deadline, disclose the identity of their experts "accompanied by a written report." Fed. R. Civ. P. 26(a)(2)(B). This written report "must contain a complete [—10—] statement of all opinions the witness will express and the basis and reasons for them" and "the facts or data considered by the witness in forming them." Fed. R. Civ. P. 26(a)(2)(B)(i)–(ii). {–718–}

Rule 26(e) imposes a duty on an expert to supplement her report "in a timely manner if the party learns that in some material respect the disclosure . . . is incomplete or incorrect, and if the additional or corrective information has not otherwise been made known to the other parties during the discovery process or in writing." Fed. R. Civ. P. 26(e)(1)(A). But "[a]ny additions or changes to" the expert report "*must* be disclosed by the time the party's pretrial disclosures under Rule 26(a)(3) are due." Fed. R. Civ. P. 26(e)(2) (emphasis added).

If a party violates Rule 26(a) or (e), Rule 37(c) provides for the exclusion of the expert evidence "unless the failure was substantially justified or is harmless." Fed. R. Civ. P. 37(c)(1); *see also OFS Fitel, LLC v. Epstein, Becker and Green, P.C.*, 549 F.3d 1344, 1363 (11th Cir. 2008) ("Under Rule 37(c)(1), a district court clearly has authority to exclude an expert's testimony where a party has failed to comply with Rule 26(a) unless the failure is substantially justified or harmless."). Courts have broad discretion to exclude untimely expert testimony—even when they are designated as "supplemental" reports. *See Corwin*, 475 F.3d at 1252 ("[A] supplemental expert report may be excluded pursuant to Federal Rule of Civil Procedure 37(c) if a party fails to file it prior to the deadline imposed."). [—11—]

Guevara submitted Dr. Zollo's supplemental reports out of time. The district court set deadlines for Guevara to produce initial and rebuttal reports from his experts. But Guevara produced Dr. Zollo's two supplemental reports after these deadlines. The district court set a June 18th deadline for Guevara to identify his expert witnesses and produce their reports. Guevara identified Dr. Zollo as an expert and produced his initial report on June 20th. In his initial report, Dr. Zollo opined that Guevara's fall was caused by

the inadequate design of the stairway landing, insufficient maintenance of the landing and surrounding area (including insufficient lighting), and the use of improper flooring material that was unreasonably slippery when wet. On August 19th, Guevara filed Dr. Zollo's First Supplemental Report, which listed a host of industry standards on lighting. The standards were not included in Dr. Zollo's initial or rebuttal reports and were not produced ahead of his deposition. A month after the close of discovery and three days after the deadline for dispositive and *Daubert* motions, Guevara filed Dr. Zollo's Second Supplemental Report. The Second Supplemental Report largely addressed the COF report disclosed by NCL's corporate representative. The district court excluded certain portions of the First Supplemental Report addressing the industry standards on lighting and the entirety of the Second Supplemental Report because Guevara failed to show that the late disclosure of these reports was [—12—] either justified or harmless. We conclude that the district court did not abuse its discretion.

Guevara argues that the district court erred in excluding portions of the First Supplemental Report because his delay in disclosing these opinions was harmless as NCL had delayed producing documents and responding to discovery. The problem with this argument is that the district court did not strike the opinions in Dr. Zollo's First Supplemental Report that incorporated or relied upon NCL's late discovery. The portions of the First Supplemental Report that the district court excluded made no reference to any of NCL's late discovery. The district court did not abuse its discretion in finding that NCL's late production did not give Dr. Zollo "*carte blanche* to supplement everything in both his initial and rebuttal expert reports." {–719–}

We also cannot say that the district court's conclusion that the late disclosure harmed NCL was an abuse of discretion given the timing of Guevara's disclosure of the First Supplemental Report immediately before Dr. Zollo's deposition. Guevara only produced Dr. Zollo's First Supplemental Report on the eve of Dr. Zollo's deposition, which gave NCL little time to review or prepare questions on the new information. The severity of the harm to NCL increased when Dr. Zollo left his deposition after only three hours without the prior agreement of the [—13—] parties.[4] NCL attempted to object to Dr. Zollo's early departure. In response, Guevara moved for a protective order, claiming that NCL's counsel took an "inordinate amount of time" going through Dr. Zollo's file. But Guevara, not NCL, created the problem by disclosing Dr. Zollo's First Supplemental Report on the eve of Dr. Zollo's deposition.

The First Supplemental Report attempts to bolster Dr. Zollo's preliminary and rebuttal opinions regarding lighting conditions in response to NCL's expert report. But "a party cannot abuse Rule 26(e) to merely bolster a defective or problematic expert witness report." *Companhia Energetica Potiguar v. Caterpillar Inc.*, No. 14-cv-24277, 2016 WL 3102225, at *6 (S.D. Fla. June 2, 2016). Given these facts, we cannot say that the district court abused its discretion when it struck portions of Dr. Zollo's First Supplemental Report.

We also cannot say that the district court abused its discretion in striking Dr. Zollo's Second Supplemental Report in its entirety. The district court acknowledged that NCL was not diligent in producing the COF report, and permitted Dr. Zollo to supplement his initial expert report after receiving the new information. But Guevara unreasonably delayed in filing that supplement. Guevara filed Dr. Zollo's Second Supplemental Report more than *five weeks after* he received the COF report, over *a month after* the close of discovery, and *three* [—14—] *days after* the district court's deadline for dispositive and *Daubert* motions. Guevara did not seek leave of the district court prior to disclosing the Second Supplemental Report, nor did he move to extend discovery.

Our decision in *Reese v. Herbert*, 527 F.3d 1253 (11th Cir. 2008), is instructive. In *Reese*,

a plaintiff filed his expert report almost seven weeks after the close of discovery. 527 F.3d at 1264–65. This late filing harmed the defendants because it "foreclosed the defendants' opportunity to depose [the expert]." *Id.* at 1265. We found that, at a minimum, the plaintiff could have filed a motion to extend discovery to permit a proper disclosure, but he failed to do so. *Id.* at 1266. "Because the expert witness discovery rules are designed to allow both sides in a case to prepare their cases adequately and to prevent surprise," we reasoned, "compliance with the requirements of Rule 26 is not merely aspirational." *Id.* Accordingly, we held that the district court did not abuse its discretion in striking the expert's report in its entirety. *Id.*

Similarly, the district court did not abuse its discretion in striking the Second Supplemental Report, which Guevara unreasonably delayed in filing. By that point, NCL had already filed its motion for summary judgment and *Daubert* motions. As in *Reese*, Guevara never sought leave of the district court for the late filing or moved to extend discovery. [—15—]

We thus conclude that the district court did not abuse its discretion in striking a portion of Dr. Zollo's First Supplemental {–720–} Report and the entirety of his Second Supplemental Report.

B. Summary Judgment

Guevara contends that the district court erred in holding that (1) the warning sign was insufficient to establish NCL's actual or constructive notice of the dangerous condition posed by the step down, and (2) Guevara failed to present evidence of negligent maintenance of the lightbulb.

"We review a district court's grant of summary judgment de novo, viewing all the evidence, and drawing all reasonable factual inferences, in favor of the nonmoving party." *Stephens v. Mid-Continent Cas. Co.*, 749 F.3d 1318, 1321 (11th Cir. 2014). Summary judgment must be granted "if the movant shows that there is no genuine dispute as to

---

[4] Federal Rule of Civil Procedure 30(d)(1) limits a deposition to one day of seven hours.

any material fact and the movant is entitled to judgment as a matter of law." Fed. R. Civ. P. 56(a). Summary judgment is improper, however, "if the evidence is such that a reasonable jury could return a verdict for the nonmoving party." *Anderson v. Liberty Lobby, Inc.*, 477 U.S. 242, 248 (1986).

Maritime law governs actions arising from alleged torts committed aboard a ship sailing in navigable waters. *See Keefe v. Bahama Cruise Line, Inc.*, 867 F.2d 1318, 1320–21 (11th Cir. 1989). "In analyzing a maritime tort case, [we] rely on [—16—] general principles of negligence law." *Chaparro v. Carnival Corp.*, 693 F.3d 1333, 1336 (11th Cir. 2012) (quoting *Daigle v. Point Landing, Inc.*, 616 F.2d 825, 827 (5th Cir. 1980)).

To prevail on a negligence claim, a plaintiff must show that "(1) the defendant had a duty to protect the plaintiff from a particular injury, (2) the defendant breached that duty, (3) the breach actually and proximately caused the plaintiff's injury, and (4) the plaintiff suffered actual harm." *Id*. With respect to the duty element in a maritime context, "a shipowner owes the duty of exercising reasonable care towards those lawfully aboard the vessel who are not members of the crew." *Kermarec v. Compagnie Generale Transatlantique*, 358 U.S. 625, 630 (1959). This standard "requires, as a prerequisite to imposing liability, that the carrier have had actual or constructive notice of [a] risk-creating condition, at least where, as here, the menace is one commonly encountered on land and not clearly linked to nautical adventure." *Keefe*, 867 F.2d at 1322. In this circumstance, a cruise ship operator's liability "hinges on whether it knew or should have known" about the dangerous condition. *Id.*[5]

A maritime plaintiff can establish constructive notice with evidence that the "defective condition exist[ed] for a sufficient period of time to invite corrective [—17—] measures." *Monteleone v. Bahama Cruise*

Line, Inc.*, 838 F.2d 63, 65 (2d Cir. 1988); *see Keefe*, 867 F.2d at 1322; *Rodgers v. Costa Crociere, S.p.A.*, No. 08-60233, 2009 WL 10666976, at *3 (S.D. Fla. July 6, 2009). Alternatively, a plaintiff can establish constructive notice with evidence of substantially similar incidents in which "conditions substantially similar to the occurrence in question must have caused the prior accident." *Jones v. Otis Elevator Co.*, 861 F.2d 655, 661–62 (11th Cir. 1988).

i. Guevara's Failure to Warn Claim

Guevara argues that NCL failed to adequately warn him of the dangerous {–721–} condition posed by the step down. NCL responds that summary judgment is warranted because it lacked prior notice of the dangerous condition and therefore had no duty to warn Guevara of the step down. Guevara points to the warning sign alerting passengers to "watch your step" as evidence that NCL was on actual or constructive notice of the deceptive, and therefore dangerous, nature of the step down.

NCL contends that the mere presence of a warning sign does not automatically establish a cruise line's notice of a potentially dangerous condition. Specifically, NCL asserts that the warning sign at issue was installed by either the original owner or the builder of the *Spirit*, and there is no evidence as to why the [—18—] sign was placed at that location or what specific condition, if any, it was affixed to address.

In analyzing whether the warning sign raises a genuine issue of material fact as to NCL's knowledge, we look to our recent decision in *Sorrels*. In *Sorrels*, a cruise ship passenger slipped and fell on the deck of a Norwegian ship, which was wet from rain. 796 F.3d at 1279, 3 Adm. R. at 659. We held that the cruise ship employees' testimony—that the cruise line regularly placed warning signs advising passengers that the deck was "slippery when wet"—was enough to create a genuine issue of material fact regarding whether the cruise line had actual or constructive knowledge that the deck could be

---

[5] An operator of a cruise ship has a duty to warn only of known dangers that are not open and obvious. *See Thomas v. NCL (Bahamas) Ltd.*, 203 F. Supp. 3d 1189, 1192 (S.D. Fla. 2016).

slippery after precipitation. *Id.* at 1288–89, 3 Adm. R. at 666–67.

Not all warning signs will be evidence of notice; there must also be a connection between the warning and the danger. *See, e.g., Taiariol v. MSC Crociere S.A.*, 677 F. App'x 599 (11th Cir. 2017). The district court cited *Taiariol* in support of its ruling against Guevara, but we find *Taiariol* favors Guevara. In *Taiariol*, the plaintiff slipped on the metal nosing of a step while leaving a theater on a cruise ship. *Id.* at 600. The plaintiff argued that the presence of a "watch your step" sticker affixed to the nosing of the step was evidence that the cruise line had notice of the nosing's slippery condition. *Id.* at 601. We disagreed, holding that "[c]ommon sense dictates that the sticker served to caution persons on the ship that the step was there; that is, it warned passengers that the surface *was not flat.* [—19—] There is no evidence that it was intended to warn passengers that the nosing may be slippery." *Id.* at 602 (emphasis added).

In *Taiariol*, the plaintiff attempted to utilize the "watch your step" sticker as evidence of notice for a different purpose: that the stair's nosing was slippery. By contrast, Guevara argues that the "watch your step" warning sign means precisely what it says, and what this Court interpreted a similar warning to mean in *Taiariol*: "to caution persons on the ship that the step was there." *Id.* Contrary to the district court's application of *Taiariol* against Guevara, we find that the similarity of the signs establishes a sufficient connection between the warning and the danger—the step down.

NCL argues that *Sorrels* does not control here because the cruise line in that case was responsible for creating and placing the warning. But we see no significant distinction between a cruise line placing a warning sign and a cruise line having knowledge of a permanently affixed warning sign that has been present on its ship for years. A warning sign's primary function is to warn of dangers. Whether a cruise line places the warning sign itself or becomes aware of the warning sign after taking ownership is of little

significance.[6] Both situations allow [—20—] for an inference that {–722–} NCL had actual or constructive knowledge that the step down could be deceiving, and therefore dangerous, to cruise passengers. *See Sorrels*, 796 F.3d at 1288, 3 Adm. R. at 666–67.

The district court noted that the language of the warning sign did not demonstrate notice of the dangerous condition posed by the step down because it only "generically advises passengers to 'hold the handrail' and 'watch your step' as they climb the three steps to the landing. It does not warn of a potential danger associated with the small step from the landing to the deck." At the summary judgment stage, however, we must view all evidence and factual inferences in favor of Guevara. *See Stephens*, 749 F.3d at 1321. Contrary to the district court's conclusion, NCL's corporate representative testified that the warning sign was intended to draw passengers' attention to the step down in the area at issue. A reasonable jury could conclude that the warning sign's language applies to the step down, particularly where, as here, the warning sign immediately precedes the very step at issue and expressly warns passengers to "watch your step." Guevara has thus raised a genuine issue of material fact regarding NCL's prior notice of

---

[6] The district court heavily relied on its previous decision in *Lipkin*, in which it held that a warning label affixed to a moving walkway off of the vessel in the port of Miami was insufficient to establish Norwegian's notice because "the undisputed evidence shows that the walkway manufacturer, not Norwegian, affixed the warning labels, and that Miami-Dade County, not Norwegian, was responsible for maintenance of the walkway." 93 F. Supp. 3d at 1322–23. We find *Lipkin* distinguishable on its facts, and therefore unpersuasive. In *Lipkin*, the [—20—] warning in question was affixed to a moving walkway *off of the vessel* in the port of Miami. And it was Miami-Dade County, *not Norwegian*, who was responsible for maintaining the walkway. It is one thing to find that a cruise line cannot be responsible for a sign that is off of the vessel—it is another thing entirely to rule that a cruise line is not responsible for a sign that has been permanently affixed *on the vessel* for years. In further contrast to *Lipkin*, NCL itself was responsible for maintaining the deck area in the present case.

the dangerous condition posed by the step down. [—21—]

NCL contends that by holding that the warning sign here put it on notice of the dangerous condition, we are improperly transforming cruise ship operators into insurers of their passengers' safety. But NCL overstates the effect of our decision. We are merely holding that a cruise ship operator has notice of a condition—and thus a duty to warn—if a sign is posted on a ship warning about the condition. This decision does not mean that a cruise ship operator is automatically liable any time a passenger is injured in the area of the sign. After all, the cruise ship operator may be able to defeat the negligence claim by showing that it did not breach its duty to warn because the sign provided passengers with a sufficient warning about the dangerous condition in the area. In this case, NCL still may argue at trial that it is not liable because it fulfilled its duty to warn through the posted sign.[7]

Accordingly, we reverse and remand the district court's ruling regarding Guevara's failure to warn claim.

ii. Guevara's Negligent Maintenance Claim

Guevara argues that the district court erroneously granted summary judgment {–723–} based on its finding that he failed to present any evidence of NCL's [—22—] negligent maintenance of the unilluminated lightbulb. Guevara asserts that he was not required to present evidence of negligent maintenance because NCL did not present any admissible evidence of its proper maintenance of the lightbulb. We disagree.

---

[7] Guevara contends that he did not see the warning sign alerting him to the change in elevation because the bulb immediately above the sign was out. At trial, the factfinder can decide whether Guevara could see the sign at the time of his fall and, if Guevara could see the sign prior to falling, whether the warning was sufficient to satisfy NCL's duty to warn. *See Outlaw v. Firestone Tire & Rubber*, 770 F.2d 1012, 1014 (11th Cir. 1985) (holding that once a duty to warn is established, the adequacy of the warning is usually a question for the jury).

NCL may carry its burden of showing no genuine issue of material fact by showing "an absence of evidence to support the nonmoving party's case." *Celotex Corp. v. Catrett*, 477 U.S. 317, 325 (1986); *Jeffery v. Sarasota White Sox, Inc.*, 64 F.3d 590, 593 (11th Cir. 1995). In its motion for summary judgment, NCL argued that there was no evidence in the record establishing "a condition requiring maintenance or inspection of the subject deck or light fixtures, that [NCL] failed to maintain or inspect the subject deck or lighting fixtures, or that [NCL's] alleged failure to maintain or inspect the subject deck or lighting fixtures caused [Guevara's] injuries."

Guevara has failed to adduce evidence proving that NCL had actual or constructive notice that the subject lightbulb was out on the night that Guevara fell. Guevara does not point to any prior passenger complaints or reported issues about the ship's lighting that would alert NCL to any potential safety concern. *See Cohen v. Carnival Corp.*, 945 F. Supp. 2d 1351, 1355 (S.D. Fla. 2013) (finding no evidence of notice where plaintiff cannot offer "any accident reports, passenger comment reviews or forms, or reports from safety inspections"); *see also Klein v.* [—23—] *Seven Seas Cruises S. DE R.L.*, No. 16-21981, 2017 WL 3405531, at *4 (S.D. Fla. Aug. 7, 2017). Moreover, the record indicates that NCL retained four electrical engineers who were responsible for inspecting the lighting on the *Spirit* at 8:00 a.m. and 7:00 or 8:00 p.m. each day. Given these routine inspections,[8] and that Guevara cannot identify when the light went out, he has failed to make a sufficient showing that the dangerous condition was "present for a period of time so lengthy as to invite corrective measures." *Keefe*, 867 F.2d at 1322 (citing *Monteleone*, 838 F.2d at 65). Accordingly, the district court did not err in concluding that Guevara failed to create a triable issue of fact on whether NCL had notice of the allegedly dangerous condition posed by the unilluminated lightbulb.

---

[8] NCL's regular inspections weigh against a finding of constructive notice. *See Monteleone*, 838 F.2d at 66.

IV. Conclusion

We affirm in part and reverse in part the district court's ruling granting summary judgment in favor of NCL. We affirm the district court's orders (1) striking Dr. Zollo's supplemental reports and (2) granting summary judgment on Guevara's negligent maintenance claim. But we reverse and vacate the grant of summary judgment on Guevara's failure to warn claim. We remand for further proceedings consistent with this opinion.

AFFIRMED IN PART, REVERSED IN PART, AND REMANDED.

(Reporter's Note: Concurring Opinion follows on p. 485).

[—24—] {–723–} **PRYOR**, Circuit Judge, concurring:

I concur fully in the majority's opinion. I write this special concurrence to respond in more detail to the dissent's argument that our decision today is in tension with the admiralty law of this circuit. {–724–}

Plaintiff Pablo Guevara contends that defendant NCL (Bahamas), Inc. was negligent because it failed to warn him of a hidden step down on its cruise ship, the *Spirit*. To determine whether the district court erred in granting summary judgment to NCL, we must decide whether NCL owed Guevara a duty.

Like the dissent, I begin with the premise that a cruise ship operator "is not liable to passengers as an insurer." *See Keefe v. Bahama Cruise Line, Inc.*, 867 F.2d 1318, 1322 (11th Cir. 1989) (internal quotation marks omitted). But a cruise ship operator remains liable for its negligence and thus must exercise "ordinary reasonable care under the circumstances." *Id.* The reasonable care standard "requires, as a prerequisite to imposing liability, that the carrier have had actual or constructive notice of the risk-creating condition," at least when the menace is commonly encountered on land. *Id.* The dissent accepts that when a cruise ship operator has actual or constructive notice of a dangerous condition, it generally owes a duty to warn its passengers of that condition.

Whether NCL had a duty to warn Guevara of the step down turns on whether it had notice of the dangerous condition. Guevara contends that NCL had [—25—] notice of the dangerous condition based on a sign installed immediately before the step down that cautioned "WATCH YOUR STEP." As an initial matter, the entire panel agrees that a reasonable jury could find that the sign warned about the dangerous condition created by the step down (as opposed to some other dangerous condition). *See* Dissent at 34 (observing that the risk created by the step down "came with a warning").

The dissent nonetheless concludes that NCL had no notice of the dangerous condition because the ship's manufacturer, rather than NCL, installed the sign. But I see no reason to require that NCL must have installed the sign for a factfinder to conclude that NCL had notice. A reasonable jury could infer that NCL understood or at least should have understood from the sign that the step down created a dangerous condition. After all, the dissent acknowledges, "[w]arning signs are meant to be seen," *id.*, and this sign could be seen by the ship's crew and passengers alike.

Instead of allowing this question of fact to be decided by a jury, the dissent would prefer a legal rule that a cruise ship operator can be put on notice of a dangerous condition by a warning sign only if the ship operator installed the warning sign. *See id.* at 35 ("Because the boat came with the warning sign, [NCL] never took any affirmative act in connection with the alleged risk and cannot be held liable for it."). The dissent's bright-line rule would require courts to ignore [—26—] facts establishing that the cruise ship's officers and crew learned or should have learned of the dangerous condition from the sign. Nothing in our precedent establishes such a rule. We have held that a cruise ship operator's affirmative act of warning of a risk is *sufficient* to establish that it had notice of a danger. *See, e.g., Sorrels v. NCL (Bahamas) Ltd.*, 796 F.3d 1275, 1288-89, 3 Adm. R. 659, 666–67 (11th Cir. 2015) (concluding that a cruise ship operator had notice that the ship's pool deck could be slippery after rain from evidence that crew members sometimes posted warning signs on the pool deck after rain). But we have never held that it is *necessary* that a cruise ship operator have taken an affirmative act regarding a risk to establish that it had knowledge of the danger. To the contrary, we have recognized that a cruise ship operator may be put on notice of a danger after the dangerous condition causes an injury, even though the operator has taken no affirmative act. *See* {–725–} *Caron v. NCL (Bahamas), Ltd.*, 910 F.3d 1359, 1370, 6 Adm. R. 471, 477 (11th Cir. 2018) (accepting that that prior reports of similar incidents are sufficient to provide a cruise ship operator with notice of a dangerous condition); *see generally Chimene v. Royal Caribbean Cruises, Ltd.*, No. 16-23775-CV, 2017 WL 8794706, at *4 (S.D. Fla. Nov. 14, 2017) (concluding that cruise ship operator had notice of dangerous condition created by zip line from prior reports of substantially similar incidents).

The dissent contends that our previous decision in *Everett v. Carnival Cruise Lines*, 912 F.2d 1355 (11th Cir. 1990), bars us from concluding that a cruise ship [—27—] operator could receive notice of a dangerous condition from a sign that it did not install. In that case, a cruise ship passenger sustained injuries when she tripped over a metal threshold on the ship. *Id.* at 1357. The passenger argued that the cruise ship operator had knowledge of the dangerous condition because it created and maintained the threshold. *Id.* at 1359. We rejected this argument, explaining that accepting the passenger's argument would effectively "defeat[]" the notice requirement. *Id.* Although we recognized in *Everett* that a cruise ship operator does not have knowledge of a dangerous condition simply because the condition is present on the ship that it maintains, *Everett* did not address whether a *warning* posted on a cruise ship—that is, a posting identifying a condition as dangerous—could put the operator on notice of that dangerous condition.[1]

---

[1] The dissent also relies on our unpublished decision in *Pizzino v. NCL (Bahamas) Ltd.*, 709 F. App'x 563 (11th Cir. 2017) (unpublished). Like *Everett*, *Pizzino* did not address whether a warning sign placed by a third party can put a cruise ship operator on notice. In *Pizzino*, a passenger sued a cruise ship operator for negligence after slipping on the cruise ship's floor. *Id.* at 564. The hazard was created by water that appeared to splash out of a ship employee's bucket. *Id.* at 563-64. After the district court instructed the jury that the passenger had to show that the operator had actual or constructive notice of the dangerous condition, the jury returned a verdict in favor of the cruise ship operator. *Id.* at 564. The passenger appealed, arguing that the cruise ship operator could be held liable on the basis that its employee had created the dangerous condition by spilling water on the floor. *Id.* We affirmed, concluding that the district court had properly instructed the jury that a cruise ship operator must have actual or constructive notice of a dangerous condition, even if it created the danger. *Id.* at 566-67. There was no posted warning in *Pizzino* that arguably put the cruise ship operator on notice of the dangerous condition,

The majority opinion runs afoul of the rule established by *Everett*, the dissent argues, because if the warning sign put NCL on notice, it must have also [—28—] put Guevara on notice, unless NCL's ability to understand the sign differed from Guevara's. And "the only thing that differentiates Guevara from [NCL]," according to the dissent, "is [NCL's] operation of the *Spirit*." Dissent at 36. The dissent glosses over another important difference between NCL and Guevara, however. A reasonable jury could find that NCL received notice before Guevara's fall when the *Spirit's* officers and crew members encountered the area with the sign in daylight or at night time when the sign was lit. In contrast, a reasonable jury could find that Guevara encountered this area just once—the night of the incident when the light above the sign was not lit, which made the sign unreadable.

The dissent also asserts that NCL should not be held liable because it was due only to "bad luck" that the light was out and Guevara could not see the sign. *Id.* at 34. This argument addresses a different issue, though: whether, assuming NCL had a duty to warn, the sign was sufficient to discharge NCL's duty. At trial, the jury could find that the warning sign was visible {–726–} and adequately warned Guevara of the danger, meaning that NCL had discharged its duty to warn. But whether NCL gave an adequate warning, assuming it had a duty to warn, does not tell us whether it had notice and thus owed such a duty. *See Chaparro v. Carnival Corp.*, 693 F.3d 1333, 1336 (11th Cir. 2012) (identifying duty and breach as separate elements of a negligence claim). [—29—]

Returning to where it began, the dissent closes with the concern that our decision will make a cruise ship operator a general insurer liable for every warning any manufacturer places on a ship. To answer that concern, the dissent would adopt a bright-line rule that a cruise ship operator can *never* receive notice of a dangerous condition from a warning sign installed by a manufacturer or other third

---

so *Pizzino* did not decide or address the issue we face here.

party. By eliminating one way in which a cruise ship operator could actually gain knowledge of a danger, the dissent's approach defies common experience and would erode the long-standing principle of admiralty law that a cruise ship operator must warn its passengers of known dangerous conditions. Because questions of fact remain about whether the warning sign installed by the ship's manufacturer put NCL on notice of the danger associated with the step down, I voted with the majority to allow the case to go to a jury.

I want to emphasize that the majority's decision today is narrow. Even assuming the dissent is correct that the decision means a cruise ship operator owes a duty to warn of any danger for which a warning is posted on a ship,[2] only in rare [—30—] cases will a passenger attempting to hold a cruise ship operator liable for a breach of that duty get past summary judgment. To get to trial, the passenger will have to come forward with evidence, not speculation, that the warning was sufficiently visible to put the cruise ship operator on notice yet was not visible to the passenger. Guevara has carried this burden given the cruise ship operator's "bad luck" that the light over the sign went out, but I doubt many operators will be so unlucky.

---

[2] Some warnings posted by third parties on a ship would be insufficient to put a cruise ship operator on notice of the dangerous condition identified by the warning. To take the dissent's example, a sticker placed on a lamp in a cabin stateroom warning that the lamp becomes hot may not give the cruise ship operator actual or constructive notice of the danger. The question of whether such a sticker would put the cruise ship operator on notice could depend on factual issues such as: the access that officers and crew had to the cabin stateroom to see the sticker, the size of the sticker, and the location of the sticker (in this example, the warning could be hidden by the lamp shade). In contrast, here there is ample evidence from which a reasonable jury could infer that the warning sign informed NCL of the danger caused by the step down [—30—] because the warning sign was large and prominently posted in a public area that was accessible to anyone on the ship.

(Reporter's Note: Opinion concurring in part and dissenting in part follows on p. 488).

[—31—] {–726–} SUTTON, Circuit Judge, concurring in part and dissenting in part:

As a visiting judge, I am reluctant to quibble over the meaning of local law. And as a visiting judge from a largely land-locked and exclusively fresh-water circuit, I am especially reluctant to quibble over the meaning of admiralty law with judges from a circuit whose every State touches the sea. In overcoming that hesitation, I take some comfort in the reality that the Miami-based district court judge who handled this case reached the same conclusion I do and the view that one does not have to be a seaworthy judge to see some tension between today's decision and the admiralty law of this circuit.

Eleventh Circuit admiralty law establishes three related propositions when it comes to slip-and-fall accidents at sea. The first is that cruise ships are not general {–727–} insurers of their passengers. *See Keefe v. Bahama Cruise Line, Inc.*, 867 F.2d 1318, 1322 (11th Cir. 1989) (per curiam). The second is that cruise ships may be liable only if they knew or should have known about the danger that caused the accident. *Id.* The third is that such knowledge does not arise from buying and operating a ship with pre-existing signage about pre-existing risks. *See Everett v. Carnival Cruise Lines*, 912 F.2d 1355, 1358–59 (11th Cir. 1990); *see also Malley v. Royal Caribbean Cruises Ltd.*, 713 F. App'x 905, 908 (11th Cir. 2017) (per curiam); *Pizzino v. NCL (Bahamas) Ltd.*, 709 F. App'x 563, 566–67 (11th Cir. [—32—] 2017) (per curiam); *cf. Lipkin v. Norwegian Cruise Line Ltd.*, 93 F. Supp. 3d 1311, 1323 (S.D. Fla. 2015).

Applied here, these principles should make short work of this case. On November 26, 2014, Pablo Guevara and his wife boarded a cruise ship, the *Spirit*, in Barcelona, Spain. Later that first night, at around 11:30 p.m., Guevara left his wife in the casino and went in search of the cigar lounge. The accident occurred on *Spirit*'s pool deck. Here's the scene: Three steps lead up to a small landing, followed by a step down. Two pillars flank the landing. Each pillar has a light and a handrail; one pillar bears a sign warning pedestrians to "please use the handrail" and "watch your step." R. 66-1.

According to Guevara, the light next to the sign was out and the deck was wet. After he ascended the three steps, he didn't notice the step down, tripped, slipped, and broke his arm.

Guevara's negligence complaint against Norwegian targeted three defects: (1) The company "[f]ailed to adequately inspect the lights in the subject area to make sure operational"; (2) the company "[f]ailed to warn plaintiff of the danger of a wet and slippery floor in the subject area"; and (3) the company "failed to warn of the change of level in the area." R. 1 at 3–4.

Each theory does not work. [—33—]

Begin with the broken-light-bulb theory. The unrebutted evidence shows that Norwegian did not notice the spent light bulb, that no one identified any such problem before the accident, and that its employees checked the area (and the light bulbs) twice a day and did not see any problem. On this record, Norwegian did not act negligently. The majority agrees.

Turn to the wet-deck theory. Here too Norwegian did nothing wrong, as it had no notice of any problem. The record does not contain any evidence of prior accidents on this part of the ship due to a wet deck. This thus is not a case in which the cruise ship identified the problem, say by putting orange cones near the hazard, and could be liable if its precautions did not adequately address the risk.

Think by comparison of *Horne v. Carnival Corporation*, 741 F. App'x 607 (11th Cir. 2018) (per curiam). A passenger sued the cruise line after high winds caused a door to slam and chop off part of his finger. *Id.* at 608. The cruise line had previously "put up signs warning of strong winds" but failed to provide notice on the day of the accident. *Id.* at 609. The prior signs, the court reasoned, could show that the cruise line had "notice of the hazardous condition." *Id.*

Nor is this a case in which passengers had slipped on this same wet deck before, placing the cruise ship on notice of the danger. *See Sorrels v. NCL (Bahamas) Ltd.*, 796 F.3d 1275, 1287–88, 3 Adm. R. 659, 666–67 (11th Cir. 2015). No evidence of any such accidents appears in the record. Apparently appreciating these gaps in this [—34—] theory of liability, Guevara does not develop on appeal his claim premised on a wet deck, which explains {–728–} why the court (correctly) does not address it.

That leaves the last theory—that Norwegian did not adequately warn of the risk from the step down. But that's the least plausible theory of the three. It takes up the one risk that night (a drop down in the steps) that came with a warning (a "please use the handrail" and "watch your step" sign). It involves a risk and a warning sign that predated Norwegian's ownership of the cruise ship. And it involves a warning sign that by Guevara's own admission could not be seen given the broken light. For many of the reasons that Judge Kathleen Williams rejected this claim as a matter of law, so would I.

Start with a problem of Guevara's making. By his own account, Guevara could not see the sign "because the bulb immediately above the sign was not functioning." Appellant's Br. 6; *id.* at 36 ("[T]he light on the pedestal just above the warning sign was out."); *see also* Reply Br. 6 ("The sign is clearly visible in daylight, or at night with appropriate lighting."). Warning signs are meant to be seen. Just as arguments are meant to be heard. And briefs and opinions are meant to be read. The law does not hold parties liable for signs that, by a claimant's own account, cannot be seen. I am not aware of any case from any court that holds a property owner liable for posting an inadequate warning sign when the source of the inadequacy—darkness—turned on bad luck, not the negligence of the owner. [—35—] Guevara never acknowledges, much less fills, this yawning gap in his theory of the case.

No less importantly, Norwegian had nothing to do with the sign. It came with the boat. And no evidence shows that the sign did not do its job. The record does not contain any

evidence of prior accidents during the day based on the step down or accidents during the night (whether the light worked or not) based on the step down. Because the boat came with the warning sign, Norwegian never took any affirmative act in connection with the alleged risk and cannot be held liable for it. *See Horne*, 741 F. App'x at 609; *Sorrels*, 796 F.3d at 1287–88, 3 Adm. R. at 666–67.

Last of all, precedent does not allow us to hold that Norwegian knew about the sign and realized that the step was dangerous simply because Norwegian bought and operated the vessel. *See Everett*, 912 F.2d at 1359. That's simply another way of making Norwegian a general insurer—liable for all risks of running a cruise ship and transporting passengers—which is just what this court's decisions foreclose. *See Keefe*, 867 F.2d at 1322.

Everett v. Carnival Cruise Lines illustrates the point. 912 F. App'x 1355 (11th Cir. 1990). A passenger tripped over a metal door threshold. *Id.* at 1357. She argued that she did not need to prove the cruise line knew about the threshold because the cruise line "created the threshold and maintained it. In other words, [the shipowner] should have known that there was a danger of passenger injury [—36—] because it was the owner and operator of the ship." *Id.* at 1359. The court rejected the theory as a matter of law, holding that it would "defeat[]" the point of having a notice requirement and the point of "limit[ing] . . . the shipowner's liability" so that it was not a general insurer of its passengers. *Id.*

Pizzino v. NCL (Bahamas) Ltd. is of a piece. 709 F. App'x 563 (11th Cir. 2017) (per curiam). A crew member spilled water on the deck, and the Eleventh Circuit re-affirmed that operation of a ship alone does not create notice. *Id.* at 564–66. Something more is required—namely that the passenger prove that the shipowner knew about the danger. *Id.* at 565. {–729–}

Size up this aspect of Guevara's argument—that the pre-existing warning sign gave Norwegian notice of this risk—from another direction. If it's fair to say that the warning sign put Norwegian on notice of the danger posed by the step down, the sign also must have made Guevara aware of the danger as well—unless daylight exists between Guevara's ability to understand the sign and Norwegian's. But the only thing that differentiates Guevara from Norwegian is Norwegian's operation of the *Spirit*. And we cannot attribute notice to a shipowner simply because it operates a ship, as case after case from this circuit says. *See supra*.

Any other approach to this case will make shipowners liable for every warning that a manufacturer places on any part of the ship. Imagine a manufacturer who places a sticker on lamps in cabin bedrooms, warning patrons [—37—] that they can become hot to the touch. Or a manufacturer who warns that children might suffocate if they play with the plastic trash bags in cabin bathrooms. Under the majority's rule, the cruise line now possesses constructive notice of these dangers and can become liable to the first passenger who burns himself or the first child who asphyxiates. Cruise ships are floating cities, and these types of scenarios end only when the horizon does.

That Norwegian may argue at trial that this sign fulfilled its duty to warn and thus may still prevail, as the court points out, offers cold comfort to this shipowner and any other. All that means is that in some number of cases juries will not treat shipowners as general insurers and in some number of cases they will. But *never*, not *sometimes*, is the point of the court's steadfast commitment to declining to make shipowners the general insurers of their passengers. That is a rule of law, not a rule of fact.

I respectfully dissent.

United States Court of Appeals
for the Eleventh Circuit

No. 18-10953

CROWLEY MARITIME CORP.
vs.
NATIONAL UNIION FIRE INS. CO. OF PITTSBURGH,
PA

Appeal from the United States District Court for the
Middle District of Florida

Decided: July 23, 2019

Citation: 931 F.3d 1112, 7 Adm. R. 491 (11th Cir. 2019).

Before **CARNES,** Chief Judge, **MARTIN** and
ANDERSON, Circuit Judges.

[—1—] {-1114-} **ANDERSON,** Circuit Judge:
[—2—]

This case involves an unusual and factually complex insurance coverage dispute between two sophisticated parties. It requires us to consider the coverage and reporting requirements in a claims-made executive and organization liability insurance policy that provides, *inter alia*, defense costs coverage for certain directors, officers, and employees of the insured. After obtaining an unfavorable result in an arbitration proceeding, Plaintiff-Appellant Crowley Maritime Corporation ("Crowley Maritime") sued its insurer Defendant-Appellee National Union Fire Insurance Company of Pittsburgh, Pa. ("National Union") in federal court seeking reimbursement of over $2.5 million in legal defense fees paid on behalf of Thomas Farmer ("Farmer"), an employee of Crowley Liner Services, Inc. ("Crowley Liner" and, together with Crowley Maritime, "Crowley"). Jurisdiction is based on diversity.

Relying in part on the res judicata effect of the arbitration proceeding, the district court granted National Union's converted motion for summary judgment on grounds that Crowley failed to timely report the Claim[1] at issue in this appeal to National Union as required by the relevant insurance policy. Crowley insists it timely reported the Claim even though an affidavit evidencing the Claim was under seal until after the relevant Claim reporting periods expired. Although our [—3—] reasoning differs somewhat from the reasoning adopted by the district court, we affirm the district court's grant of National Union's converted motion for summary judgment.

I. BACKGROUND

A. Factual Background.

1. Crowley purchases executive and organization liability insurance policy from National Union.

Crowley Liner is a Jacksonville-based water freight carrier that carries freight {-1115-} between the United States and Puerto Rico. It is a wholly owned subsidiary of Crowley Maritime. National Union is among the largest providers of directors and officers insurance policies. As it relates to this case, Crowley Maritime purchased liability insurance from National Union pursuant to Executive and Organization Liability Insurance Policy No. 061-36-48 (the "Policy"), which provided coverage for an initial Policy Period running from November 1, 2007 through November 1, 2008 and an extended Discovery Period running through November 1, 2013. The Policy provided coverage on a "claims made" basis, meaning that National Union insured Crowley "solely with respect to Claims[2] first [—4—] made against an Insured during the Policy Period or the Discovery Period (if applicable) and reported to the Insurer pursuant to the terms of [the P]olicy."

---

[1] Any capitalized term that is not otherwise defined in this opinion shall have the meaning, if any, given to such term in the Policy.

[2] We note at the outset that in claims-made policies there are two separate "claims" that matter: the first is the "claim" brought by a third party against an insured during the policy period, and the second is the "insurance claim" submitted by the insured to the insurer for payment under the policy. Both concepts are relevant here, and it is important to maintain a distinction between the "Claim" made against an Insured and the "insurance claim" reported to National Union when applying the facts presented in this appeal to the Policy.

As relevant to the issues in this case, the Policy covered Defense Costs resulting from the investigation, adjustment, and defense of a Claim against an Insured (Farmer in this case).

2. Sealed search warrant Affidavit leads to execution of search warrant at Crowley Liner headquarters.

During the initial Policy Period, Crowley Liner and Farmer, Crowley Liner's then-Vice President of Price and Yield Management, attracted the attention of federal law enforcement officers. On April 17, 2008, a search warrant was executed at Crowley Liner's Jacksonville headquarters. The search warrant ordered that certain property be seized from Crowley Liner management, pricing, or sales personnel—including Farmer and three other individuals specifically named in the search warrant—in connection with a joint investigation by the Federal Bureau of Investigation ("FBI") and the Department of Justice ("DOJ") of an alleged price-fixing conspiracy in the Puerto Rican trade lane.

On April 16, 2008, the day before federal law enforcement officers executed the search warrant, an FBI special agent signed and delivered an affidavit supporting the search warrant (the "Affidavit") to a federal magistrate judge in the Middle District of Florida. The Affidavit—which spans forty-eight pages and describes in great detail an ongoing FBI/DOJ antitrust investigation involving **[—5—]** several water freight carriers—asserted that Farmer and others had been involved in communications and agreements to allocate customers and coordinate pricing in violation of the Sherman Act.[3] To protect the ongoing FBI/DOJ investigation, the Affidavit was sealed by court order the day it was presented to the magistrate judge. The search warrant itself noted generally the existence of an affidavit supporting probable cause, but it did not specifically identify the Affidavit, reveal its content, or note that it had been placed under

seal. The detailed descriptions of Farmer's alleged conduct in the sealed Affidavit were not apparent from the face of the search warrant itself. Crowley and Farmer also received **{—1116—}** subpoenas to appear before a grand jury, but Farmer never testified.

3. National Union accepts Crowley's notice of Claim as a notice of circumstances under section 7(c) of the Policy.

A little over a week later, in a letter dated April 25, 2008 (the "April 2008 Notice"), Crowley's insurance broker sent National Union a notice it characterized as a notice of a Claim. An email attached to the April 2008 Notice provided the initial "details of a DOJ/FBI investigation," including a statement that "[t]he charges that may have [led] to the subpoena and search warrant are sealed at this point in time and no indictments have been filed." Crowley also asked National **[—6—]** Union to consent to the retention of defense counsel and the expenditure of Defense Costs by Crowley and Farmer.

National Union responded to the April 2008 Notice in a letter dated May 27, 2008. Although it acknowledged that Crowley had submitted the April 2008 Notice and other related information "as Claims under the Policy," National Union concluded that the Policy did not provide coverage because, in part, no one had been identified in writing as a target of the investigation as required by the Policy. National Union noted that its determination was "preliminary, as it [was] based solely upon the documentation currently available." National Union did, however, accept the April 2008 Notice "as a notice of circumstances that may give rise to a Claim being made against an Insured, pursuant to Clause 7(c) of the Policy." It then invited Crowley to submit additional information in the future that might be relevant to a coverage determination.

Crowley and National Union continued to correspond over roughly the next four years. For its part, Crowley asserted that a Claim existed and had been reported to National Union in April 2008. It also informed National Union of Farmer's mounting legal expenses.

---

[3] Farmer eventually went to trial and a federal jury in Puerto Rico found him not guilty. *See* J. of Acquittal, *United States v. Farmer*, No. 13-0162 (D.P.R. May 8, 2015), ECF No. 460.

National Union acknowledged the existence of circumstances that might eventually result in a Claim against an Insured Person, but it persisted in its denial of coverage. Subject to customary reservation of rights [—7—] language, National Union also encouraged Crowley to send additional information that might be relevant to its coverage determination.

4. Arbitration panel enters decision favoring National Union's position.

Crowley eventually initiated arbitration, and the arbitrators held a hearing in December 2012. The proceeding addressed whether, based on the information provided to National Union at the time of the arbitration hearing, the FBI/DOJ investigation constituted a Claim under the Policy. The arbitration order noted that the evidence of a Claim presented to National Union at that time included only: the search warrant, the Farmer and Crowley subpoenas, several documents relating to a plea agreement entered into by Crowley, and the investigation relating to those documents. National Union encouraged the arbitrators to ignore the Affidavit,[4] and the {—1117—} arbitration order observed that "[t]he [A]ffidavit has remained sealed; therefore, its specific allegations have never been made known to Crowley or its

---

[4] *See* Hr'g Tr., ECF No. 36-9, at 25, 29, 37 ("The search warrant and the subpoena identified [Farmer and others] as people who may have relevant information, but on the face of the document, that is all it says . . . . Now, we know that there must have been an affidavit of some sort issued in order to get the search warrant issued, but we don't have the [A]ffidavit. Nobody here knows what it says. To the extent that [Crowley's expert] is testifying about what he thinks . . . the [A]ffidavit says, he's speculating. He's never seen the [A]ffidavit, and he doesn't know what it says. . . . The issue is whether these specific documents that were submitted to National Union in 2008 qualified. And the answer to that, consistently from National Union, has always been that they do not, because they don't identify . . . a person who may be charged. . . . The problem here is that nobody has seen the [A]ffidavit, and nobody knows what it says. And everybody is guessing what they think it says, but nobody knows what it says. That's the big problem here.").

[—8—] employees." The Affidavit does not appear in the list of documents considered by the arbitrators as evidence of the FBI/DOJ investigation.

A majority of the arbitration panel entered a decision in favor of National Union on January 29, 2013. The arbitration order observed that "the triggering event for a Claim . . . is when the DOJ identifies in writing an Insured Person as one against whom a criminal proceeding may be commenced." It continued, ultimately concluding that "[t]he materials Crowley submitted to National Union did not constitute a Claim for Insured Persons as the term 'Claim' is defined in the Policy. The triggering event specified in the Policy has not yet been presented to National Union."

5. Farmer receives and rejects Plea Offer, is acquitted at trial.

In a letter dated February 11, 2013, the government offered to enter into a plea agreement with Farmer on certain terms and conditions, including acceptance of a recommended sentence (the "Plea Offer"). Crowley notified National Union of the Plea Offer in a letter dated February 15, 2013 (the "February 2013 Notice"). In response to the February 2013 Notice, National Union agreed to treat the FBI/DOJ investigation as a Claim under the Policy as of February 18, 2013 (the date it received the February 2013 Notice). In making this new coverage determination, National Union acknowledged that Crowley submitted the February 2013 Notice within the six-year Discovery Period and that it also "appear[ed] to be [—9—] related to prior correspondence [i.e., the April 2008 Notice] which was acknowledged by [National Union] as a notice of circumstances under Section 7(c) of the Policy." National Union agreed to provide coverage for future Defense Costs relating to the investigation (i.e., those incurred on or after February 18, 2013), but took the position that Crowley was not entitled to reimbursement of its earlier Defense Costs (i.e., those incurred between April 25, 2008 and February 18, 2013 before National Union received notice of Farmer's Plea Offer).

Farmer rejected the Plea Offer and went to trial. Shortly before the end of his trial, on April 24, 2015, the Affidavit was unsealed. A federal jury in Puerto Rico found Farmer not guilty and the United States District Court for the District of Puerto Rico entered a judgment of acquittal on May 8, 2015.[5] In a letter dated July 22, 2015 (the "July 2015 Notice"), Crowley notified National Union that Farmer had been acquitted and that it had received and reviewed a copy of the unsealed Affidavit, which Crowley said made "clear" that a Claim had been "asserted with respect to Mr. Farmer as of the date of filing of the search warrant affidavit in April 2008." It demanded reimbursement of $2,541,346.34 in legal fees Crowley paid on Farmer's behalf (net of the Policy deductible) between the date of the April 2008 Notice and the date of the February 2013 Notice. National Union refused, insisting it was not "obligated under the terms of the Policy to [—10—] reimburse Crowley for the fees." We note that National Union did cover {–1118–} almost $3 million in Defense Costs incurred in connection with Farmer's defense after it received Crowley's February 2013 Notice. These post-Plea Offer Defense Costs are not at issue in this appeal. Rather, the issue in this case involves Farmer's Defense Costs from April 2008 to February 2013.

B. Procedural Background.

Crowley brought a diversity action for breach of contract against National Union in the United States District Court for the Middle District of Florida, claiming it was entitled to be reimbursed for its payment of Farmer's pre-February 2013 (pre-Plea Offer) Defense Costs. Crowley argued that the Claim based on the previously sealed Affidavit (hereafter referred to as the "Claim based on the Affidavit") not only existed all along but also was reported to National Union pursuant to the terms of the Policy. National Union moved to dismiss the complaint on grounds that the prior arbitration was res judicata to Crowley's breach of contract action and that it was also barred by the applicable statute of limitations. The district court converted

National Union's motion to dismiss to a motion for summary judgment. The parties conducted discovery, filed supplemental briefing, and participated in a motion hearing before the district court. [—11—]

In supplemental briefing, National Union repeated its res judicata and statute of limitations arguments, but it also raised a third argument: that Crowley's claim for coverage based on the Affidavit was untimely under the Policy because it was not reported to National Union until July 22, 2015, well after the extended six-year Discovery Period expired on November 1, 2013. In response, Crowley argued that the arbitration was not res judicata to its claim for coverage based on the Affidavit because the arbitration was limited in scope and did not consider the unsealed Affidavit, and that the application of res judicata principles would be inequitable in any event. It also argued that the statute of limitations did not accrue until 2015 when National Union denied coverage after receiving the unsealed Affidavit. Finally, Crowley also argued that it had timely reported the Claim in its April 2008 Notice, and in the alternative, that its July 2015 Notice was timely because it should relate back to the April 2008 Notice under section 7(c) of the Policy.

The district court granted National Union's converted motion for summary judgment and ordered that judgment be entered in favor of National Union. *Crowley Mar. Corp. v. Nat'l Union Fire Ins. Co. of Pittsburgh*, 307 F. Supp. 3d 1286, 1297 (M.D. Fla. 2018). It found that Crowley did not notify National Union of the existence of the unsealed Affidavit until 2015. *Id*. at 1291. As a result, the district court concluded that the December 2012 arbitration proceeding was not res judicata to Crowley's claim for coverage based on the Affidavit because the [—12—] unsealed Affidavit was "like newly discovered evidence." *Id*. at 1291–95 (citation omitted). Framing the issues as a "catch-22 for Crowley," the district court went on to conclude that, even though the limited-scope arbitration did not preclude consideration of the unsealed Affidavit in Crowley's federal lawsuit, Crowley's reporting of the Claim based on the Affidavit in 2015

---

[5] *See* note 3, *supra*.

was still untimely under the Policy because the Discovery Period ended on November 1, 2013. *Id.* at 1291, 1295–97. In the alternative, the district court concluded that if a Claim based on the Affidavit was deemed reported in 2008 (as a result of the relation back provisions in section 7(c) of the Policy or otherwise), then the 2012 arbitration would preclude Crowley from bringing its federal lawsuit on res judicata grounds. *Id.* at 1296–97. In other words, Crowley lost either {–1119–} way. *Id.* The district court expressly declined to address National Union's statute of limitations arguments. *Id.* at 1295.

Crowley appealed to this Court, and we now consider whether the district court erred when it granted National Union's converted motion for summary judgment. Following a close review of the parties' briefs, the Policy, other relevant parts of the record, and applicable law—and with the benefit of oral argument—we affirm the judgment of the district court, albeit on somewhat different grounds. [—13—]

II. ISSUE

As noted above, the issue in this case involves only whether Crowley is entitled to coverage, and thus reimbursement from National Union, of its pre-February 2013 (pre-Plea Offer) Defense Costs, on behalf of the Insured, Farmer. The only relevant new facts revealed after the arbitration are the government's February 2013 Plea Offer and the 2015 unsealing of the Affidavit. On appeal, Crowley relies solely upon the Affidavit. Crowley's challenge to the judgment of the district court relies solely upon the Claim based on the Affidavit. Thus, the issue is: Does Crowley establish that the Claim based on the Affidavit not only existed as of its April 2008 Notice to National Union, but also was reported to National Union as required by the terms of the Policy so as to provide the coverage sought by Crowley?[6]

---

[6] Although Crowley does argue on appeal that its February 2013 Notice also constitutes a qualifying Claim, and that this notice was given to National Union before the expiration of the Discovery Period (November 1, 2013), Crowley does not explain how that fact supports its claim for

III. STANDARD OF REVIEW AND APPLICABLE LAW

This Court reviews *de novo* a district court's grant of summary judgment. *Sierra Club, Inc. v. Leavitt*, 488 F.3d 904, 911 (11th Cir. 2007). We also review *de* [—14—] *novo* decisions applying res judicata rules, *Lobo v. Celebrity Cruises, Inc.*, 704 F.3d 882, 892, 1 Adm. R. 440, 445 (11th Cir. 2013), and decisions interpreting insurance contracts, *Tech. Coating Applicators, Inc. v. U.S. Fid. and Guar. Co.*, 157 F.3d 843, 844 (11th Cir. 1998). Summary judgment is appropriate when, viewing the record in the light most favorable to the non-moving party, there is no genuine issue of material fact and the moving party is entitled to judgment as a matter of law. *Leavitt*, 488 F.3d at 911; *see also* Fed. R. Civ. P. 56(a).

"[I]n a diversity case, a federal court applies the substantive law of the forum state, unless federal constitutional or statutory law is contrary." *HR Acquisition I Corp. v. Twin City Fire Ins. Co.*, 547 F.3d 1309, 1314 (11th Cir. 2008) (citation omitted). In this case, the forum state is Florida. The parties' arguments below,[7] {–1120–} the district court's order, and the parties' arguments before this Court focus exclusively on the application of Florida law to the substantive contract interpretation and

---

coverage of pre-February 2013 (pre-Plea Offer) Defense Costs. As noted above, National Union did recognize a Claim against Farmer pursuant to Crowley's February 2013 Notice, and did provide coverage of Defense Costs for Farmer from and after February 2013, but not before. On appeal, Crowley does not challenge National Union's refusal to provide such retroactive coverage, does not make any argument that its February 2013 Notice should relate back to its April 2008 Notice under the relation back provisions of section 7 of the Policy, and makes no other argument that might warrant coverage of pre-February 2013 (pre-Plea Offer) Defense [—14—] Costs on the basis of its February 2013 Notice. Indeed, Crowley has affirmatively waived reliance on any relation back theory. *See infra*, part IV.B.3.c.

[7] *See* Mot. Hr'g Tr., ECF No. 49, at 28 ("So we have the usual law that we have a contract issued to an insured in Florida. And the usual rules of Florida law would govern that kind of contract. So that's been [National Union's] position here. And I think it's been the position of both parties.").

res judicata issues raised by Crowley's federal lawsuit. We agree and also apply Florida law. [—15—]

IV. ANALYSIS

Our analysis proceeds in two main parts. First, we briefly consider the essence of a claims-made insurance policy. Second, we consider whether the Policy provisions limiting coverage to Claims that are "first made against an Insured" during the Policy Period or the Discovery Period[8] and that also are "reported to the Insurer" pursuant to the terms of the Policy[9] were satisfied in this case. We do not adopt the "catch-22" analysis set forth by the district court. However, for the reasons explained in some detail below, we ultimately affirm the district court's order granting National Union's converted motion for summary judgment because the record supports the conclusion that Crowley failed to timely report the Claim based on the Affidavit as required by the Policy. *See Aaron Private Clinic Mgmt. LLC v. Berry*, 912 F.3d 1330, 1335 (11th Cir. 2019) (noting that "[w]e may affirm on any ground supported by the record, regardless of whether that ground was relied upon or even considered below" (alteration in original) (citation omitted)). With respect to the reporting period between April 16, 2008 and December 31, 2012, Crowley is bound by the arbitration panel's finding that Crowley had not reported a Claim to National Union as required by the Policy at that time.[10] With respect to the reporting period beginning immediately [—16—] after December 31, 2012 and running through the end of the Discovery Period on November 1, 2013, Crowley failed to report the Claim based on the Affidavit as required by section 7(a) of the Policy because it did not report any new information about the Claim based on the Affidavit until after both the Policy Period and the Discovery Period had expired.[11] Also, as discussed in greater detail below, Crowley has waived any arguments that either its February 2013 Notice or its July 2015 Notice should relate

back to the April 2008 Notice under section 7 of the Policy.[12]

A. The Essence of a Claims-Made Policy.

Claims-made policies are common in the professional liability insurance market. *See* Eric M. Holmes, *Appleman on Insurance Law & Practice Archive* § 146.4, LEXIS (database updated 2011). They "differ from traditional 'occurrence'-based policies primarily based upon the scope of the risk against which they insure." Steven Plitt et al., 1 *Couch on Insurance* § 1:5, Westlaw (database updated December 2018). With claims-made policies, coverage is provided only where the act giving rise to coverage "is discovered and brought to the attention of the insurance company during the period of the policy." *Id.* In contrast, coverage is provided under an occurrence-based policy if the act giving [—17—] rise to coverage "occurred during the period of the policy, regardless of the date a claim is actually made against the insured." *Id.* "The essence, then, of a claims-made policy is notice to the carrier within the policy period." *Gulf Ins. Co. v. Dolan, Fertig & Curtis*, 433 So. 2d 512, 514 (Fla. 1983). *See also* {–1121–} Holmes, *supra*, § 130.3 ("Claims-made or discovery policies are essentially reporting policies. If the claim is reported to the insurer during the policy period, then the carrier is legally obligated to pay; if the claim is not reported during the policy period, no liability attaches.").

Insurance companies favor claims-made policies because they allow for a more precise calculation of risks and premiums. *Id.* "This theoretically results in lower premiums for an insured since there is no open-ended 'tail' after the expiration date of the policy." *Gulf Ins. Co.*, 433 So. 2d at 516. With these general principles in mind, we turn our attention to the actual language of the particular insurance contract at issue in this appeal.

---

[8] *See infra*, part IV.B.1–2.
[9] *See infra*, part IV.B.3.
[10] *See infra*, part IV.B.3.a.
[11] *See infra*, part IV.B.3.b.

---

[12] *See infra*, part IV.B.3.c.

B. The Policy expressly limits coverage to Claims that are "first made against an Insured" during the Policy Period or the Discovery Period and that also are "reported to the Insurer" pursuant to the terms of the Policy.

In applying Florida law to the interpretation of an insurance contract, "we begin with the language of the coverage section." *Hyman v. Nationwide Mut. Fire Ins. Co.*, 304 F.3d 1179, 1188 (11th Cir. 2002) (citation omitted). As it relates to this case, section 1 of the Policy (the coverage statement) provides that: [—18—]

> solely with respect to Claims first made against an Insured during the Policy Period or the Discovery Period (if applicable) and reported to the Insurer pursuant to the terms of this [P]olicy, and subject to the other terms, conditions and limitations of this [P]olicy, this [P]olicy affords the following coverage:[13]
>
> ....
>
> ... This [P]olicy shall pay the Loss of an Organization arising from a Claim made against an Insured Person . . . for any Wrongful Act of such Insured Person, but only to the extent that such Organization has indemnified such Insured Person.

The initial Policy Period ran from November 1, 2007 to November 1, 2008, and the Discovery Period extended the Claims reporting timeline through November 1, 2013 because National Union issued a run-off endorsement providing that:

---

[13] The preamble to the Policy, which appears in emphasized text on the first page of the Policy, clearly announces similar limitations: "**THE COVERAGE OF THIS POLICY IS GENERALLY LIMITED TO LIABILITY FOR CLAIMS THAT ARE FIRST MADE AGAINST THE INSUREDS AND CRISIS FIRST OCCURRING DURING THE POLICY PERIOD AND REPORTED IN WRITING TO THE INSURER PURSUANT TO THE TERMS HEREIN.**"

> The Named Entity shall have the right to a period of [6] years following the Effective Date (herein referred to as the Discovery Period) in which to give written notice to the Insurer of any Claim first made against any Insured during said 6 year period for any Wrongful Act occurring on or prior to the Effective Date and otherwise covered by this [P]olicy.

The parties do not dispute that Farmer was an Insured Person under the Policy; that the allegations against Farmer raised in the Affidavit qualified as Wrongful Acts under the Policy; that the Policy Period ended on November 1, 2008; that the [—19—] Discovery Period ended on November 1, 2013; or that Crowley had indemnified Farmer with respect to his Defense Costs.

Accordingly, in resolving whether National Union has breached any contractual obligation to reimburse Crowley for Farmer's pre-February 2013 (pre-Plea Offer) Defense Costs, it is necessary to consider {–1122–} (1) whether the substantive content of the Affidavit—regardless of when it became known to Crowley or National Union—qualified as a Claim under the Policy; (2) whether the sealed Affidavit constituted a Claim that was "first made against" an Insured Person during the Policy Period or the Discovery Period; and (3) if the Affidavit was a Claim that was first made against an Insured Person during the Policy Period or the Discovery Period, whether a Claim based on the Affidavit was timely "reported to the Insurer pursuant to the terms of this [P]olicy." We consider each of these questions in turn, ultimately concluding that, even assuming the Affidavit constituted a Claim that was first made against Farmer during the Policy Period or the Discovery Period, such Claim was not timely reported to National Union as required by the Policy.

1. Did the substantive contents of the Affidavit give rise to a Claim against an Insured Person under the Policy?

In pertinent part, section 2(b) of the Policy defines a Claim as (1) a written demand for relief; (2) a criminal proceeding commenced by return of an indictment, information, or similar charging document or receipt or filing of a [—20—] notice of charges; or (3) a criminal investigation of an Insured Person "once such Insured Person is identified in writing by such investigating authority as a person against whom a proceeding [described in section 2(b)(2)] may be commenced."[14] Crowley argues that, under subpart three of the definition of Claim, the substantive content of the Affidavit clearly identifies Farmer in writing as a person against whom a criminal proceeding may be commenced. National Union's arguments before this Court do not clearly focus on whether the substantive contents of the Affidavit, once known, qualified as Claim under the Policy. And even though National Union denied Crowley's request for admission on this very question in discovery, we note that it also informed the district court during the summary judgment hearing that it was not relying on this argument as the basis for its motion. [—21—]

In any event, under the language of this particular insurance contract, the substantive content of the Affidavit clearly did constitute a Claim. That said, we think it unnecessary to

recount the factual details of the Affidavit here because Farmer was eventually acquitted at trial.[15] Instead, it is sufficient to say that the forty-eight-page Affidavit identified Farmer by name more than fifty times, noted that he held a "position of pricing authority" at Crowley Liner, and otherwise made it clear to us that {–1123–} the Affidavit identified Farmer as a person against whom a criminal proceeding may be commenced.

2. When was a Claim based on the Affidavit "first made against" Farmer?

Having established the substantive content of the Affidavit constituted a Claim under the Policy, we must next consider when that Claim was "first made against" Farmer. We again start with the coverage grant. *Hyman*, 304 F.3d at 1188. With respect to this question—which under this Policy is related to but separate from the question whether the Claim was timely reported to National Union—section 1 of the Policy limits coverage to "Claims first made against an Insured during the Policy Period or the Discovery Period (if applicable)." Subpart three of the definition of Claim defines Claim to include a criminal investigation of an Insured Person "once such Insured Person is identified in writing" as a person [—22—] against whom a criminal proceeding may be commenced. The Policy does not define the phrase "first made against" or the phrase "identified in writing."

Crowley argues that the mere existence of the Affidavit means a Claim was first made against Farmer in April 2008. It points out that the Policy does not require the Insured Person (or anyone else) to have knowledge of the Claim or receive a copy of the writing identifying the Insured Person as a person against whom a criminal proceeding may be brought.

National Union responds that Crowley's "unreasonable interpretation" is neither required nor supported by the Policy language. It also argues that Crowley's interpretation would lead to an "absurd result" because it would potentially place on

---

[14] The full text of section 2(b) of the Policy defines a Claim as:

(1) a written demand for monetary, non-monetary or injunctive relief;

(2) a civil, criminal, administrative, regulatory or arbitration proceeding for monetary, non-monetary or injunctive relief which is commenced by: (i) service of a complaint or similar pleading; (ii) return of an indictment, information or similar document (in the case of a criminal proceeding); or (iii) receipt or filing of a notice of charges; or

(3) a civil, criminal, administrative or regulatory investigation of an Insured Person:

(i) once such Insured Person is identified in writing by such investigating authority as a person against whom a proceeding described in [section 2](b)(2) may be commenced; or

(ii) in the case of an investigation by the SEC or a similar state or foreign government authority, after the service of a subpoena upon such Insured Person.

The term "Claim" shall include any Securities Claim and any Employment Practices Claim.

[15] *See* note 3, *supra*.

insureds the impossible burden of reporting existing Claims of which they are completely unaware. National Union argues that the very nature of a claims-made policy assumes that a claim is not made against the insured until the insured is aware thereof and thus capable of reporting the claim to the insurer. Because Crowley was not aware of the content of the Affidavit until it was unsealed in 2015, National Union's position is that the Claim based on the Affidavit was first made against Farmer in 2015. Of course, as National Union [—23—] points out, Crowley's 2015 report to National Union was after the expiration of the Discovery Period and thus untimely.[16]

The parties suggest only two dates as possible dates on which the Claim based on the Affidavit might first have been made against Farmer: either April 2008 or 2015. Crowley suggests April 2008 when the Affidavit was signed and presented to the magistrate judge; National Union suggests 2015 when the content of the Affidavit was unsealed and first became known. We too see no other feasible alternatives for the date on which the Claim based on the Affidavit might reasonably be deemed to have been first made against Farmer. We need not—and expressly do not—resolve this dispute between the parties for the following reason. Even assuming, *arguendo*, that the Claim was first made against Farmer in April 2008, as Crowley urges, we would still find in favor of National Union because Crowley did not timely report the Claim based on the Affidavit to National Union in the manner required by the Policy, as explained below. {–1124–}

3. Did Crowley timely report a Claim based on the Affidavit as required by the Policy?

Having assumed *arguendo*, and thus determined for purposes of this appeal, that the Claim based on the Affidavit was first

made against Crowley in April [—24—] 2008, we turn to the separate issue of whether Crowley timely reported the Claim to National Union in the manner required by the Policy. As noted above, section 1 of the Policy limits coverage not only to Claims that are first made against an Insured during the Policy Period or the Discovery Period, but also to Claims that are "reported to the Insurer pursuant to the terms of [the Policy]." The reporting provisions of the Policy, at least as they relate to this appeal, are found in section 7 of the Policy.[17] Section 7 provides three

---

[16] We also note that, if the Claim based on the Affidavit were first made against Farmer in 2015, it would not fall within the coverage. Section 1 of the Policy covers only "Claims first made against an Insured during the Policy Period or the Discovery Period," the latter of which expired on November 1, 2013.

[17] Section 7 (the "Notice/Claim Reporting Provisions" of the Policy) provides as follows:

Notice hereunder shall be given in writing to the Insurer named in Item 8 of the Declarations . . . .

(a) An Organization or an Insured shall, as a condition precedent to the obligations of the Insurer under this [P]olicy, give written notice to the Insurer of a Claim made against an Insured or a Crisis as soon as practicable: (i) after the Named Entity's Risk Manager or General Counsel (or equivalent position) first becomes aware of the Claim; or (ii) the Crisis commences, but in all events no later than either:

(1) the end of the Policy Period or the Discovery Period (if applicable); or
(2) within 30 days after the end of the Policy Period or the Discovery Period (if applicable), as long as such Claim was first made against an Insured within the final 30 days of the Policy Period or the Discovery Period (if applicable).

(b) If written notice of a Claim has been given to the Insurer pursuant to Clause 7(a) above, then a Claim which is subsequently made against an Insured and reported to the Insurer alleging, arising out of, based upon or attributable to the facts alleged in the Claim for which such notice has been given, or alleging any Wrongful Act which is the same as or related to any Wrongful Act alleged in the Claim of which such notice has been given, shall be considered related to the first Claim and made at the time such notice was given.

(c) If during the Policy Period or during the Discovery Period (if applicable) an Organization or an Insured shall become aware of any circumstances which may reasonably be expected to give rise to a

different methods pursuant to which an [—25—] Insured may properly report a Claim to the Insurer under the Policy. The first method involves the direct reporting of an existing Claim to the Insurer under section 7(a). This is the focus of Crowley's arguments on appeal. The second method, set forth in section 7(b), involves the reporting of a subsequent Claim that relates to an earlier Claim that was previously reported to the Insurer. Crowley does not argue on appeal that its reporting of the Claim based on the Affidavit could be timely under section 7(b) relation back so as to provide coverage of Defense Costs beginning in April 2008. Section 7(c) provides the third method, which involves the reporting of a Claim that relates to an earlier set of circumstances— circumstances which at the time of reporting had not yet produced a Claim—previously reported to the Insurer. Again, Crowley does not argue on appeal that its reporting of the Claim based on the Affidavit could be timely under section 7(c) relation back. Both section 7(b) and section 7(c) involve what the parties refer {–1125–} to as "relation back" theories or arguments, and we adopt their useful terminology here. Although Crowley presented relation back arguments to the district court, it has waived any relation back argument before this Court.[18] [—26—] Accordingly, Crowley must prevail, if at all, on

---

Claim being made against an Insured and shall give written notice to the Insurer of the circumstances, the Wrongful Act allegations anticipated and the reasons for anticipating such a Claim, with full particulars as to dates, persons and entities involved, then a Claim which is subsequently made against such Insured and [—25—] reported to the Insurer alleging, arising out of, based upon or attributable to such circumstances or alleging any Wrongful Act which is the same as or related to any Wrongful Act alleged or contained in such circumstances, shall be considered made at the time such notice of such circumstances was given.

[18] *See infra*, part IV.B.3.c (concluding that Crowley has waived any relation back argument under section 7 with respect either to the Claim based on the Affidavit or the February 2013 Plea Offer Claim).

the basis of its argument that it did timely report the Claim based on the Affidavit pursuant to section 7(a).

For the reasons described in greater detail below, we conclude that Crowley did not timely report a Claim based on the Affidavit as required by the Policy. Crowley's efforts to establish that it properly notified National Union of a Claim under section 7 must fail for three reasons. First, as we describe in the following subpart (a), Crowley is bound by the arbitration panel's determination that it had not reported a Claim to National Union as of December 31, 2012. Second, in subpart (b), we demonstrate why Crowley's July 2015 Notice describing the unsealed Affidavit was untimely because it came after the November 1, 2013 expiration of the extended Discovery Period. Finally, in subpart (c), we conclude that Crowley has expressly waived any argument that either its February 2013 Notice or its July 2015 Notice should relate back to the April 2008 Notice under section 7 of the Policy.

> (a) The arbitration order precludes Crowley from arguing that it reported a Claim to National Union at any time prior to December 31, 2012.

We begin by considering whether Crowley timely reported a Claim based on the Affidavit under section 7(a) of the Policy, which provides in relevant part that

> An Organization or an Insured shall, as a condition precedent to the obligations of the Insurer under this [P]olicy, give written notice to the Insurer of a Claim made against an Insured . . . as soon as practicable . . . after the Named Entity's Risk Manager or General [—27—] Counsel (or equivalent position) first becomes aware of the Claim . . . but in all events no later than . . . the end of the Policy Period or the Discovery Period (if applicable) . . . .

Thus, as a condition precedent to coverage based on notice under section 7(a), Crowley was required to give National Union written notice of a Claim made against an Insured before November 1, 2008 (the end of the Policy Period) or before November 1, 2013 (the end of the Discovery Period set forth in the run-off endorsement). Crowley argues that it reported a Claim based on the Affidavit in its April 2008 Notice by simply pointing to the sealed Affidavit, even if it could not provide National Union with any details regarding the substantive content of the Affidavit at that time. For its part, National Union argues that Crowley did not report the Claim based on the Affidavit in the April 2008 Notice because no one knew what the Affidavit said until 2015. National Union also argues that the arbitration order is res judicata in this case because the arbitration panel concluded that Crowley had failed to report a Claim to National Union.

National Union's res judicata argument is persuasive, at least with respect to the materials that were before the arbitration panel when it closed the hearing record on December 31, 2012. We are careful to note, as we have before, that res judicata is a term that "has more than one meaning." *Brown v. R.J. Reynolds Tobacco Co.*, 611 F.3d 1324, 1331 (11th Cir. 2010). {-1126-} As Florida's Fourth District Court of Appeal recently observed: [—28—]

Res judicata is a term applied to various forms of preclusion. It is also a term that is applied inconsistently.

In modern times, the preclusive effect of a judgment is defined by claim preclusion and issue preclusion, which are collectively referred to as res judicata. More specifically, res judicata is now recognized as a general term for various different forms of preclusion including claim preclusion, and a separate category of defenses commonly referred to as issue preclusion, collateral estoppel, estoppel by judgment, and direct estoppel.

Philadelphia Fin. Mgmt. of San Francisco, LLC v. DJSP Enters., Inc., 227 So. 3d 612, 617 (Fla. 4th DCA 2017) (citations and internal

quotation marks omitted). This Court sorted through some of these subtleties in Florida preclusion law in *Brown*, raising several important distinctions between the two primary subcategories of res judicata: claim preclusion and issue preclusion. *See Brown*, 611 F.3d at 1331–36. The parties here address the preclusion issues associated with the arbitration order under the general rubric of res judicata, but the district court noted that it preferred to "use the more precise terminology adopted by the Supreme Court: claim preclusion." *Crowley*, 307 F. Supp. 3d at 1290 n.3 (citation omitted). We agree with National Union and the district court that the arbitration proceeding is entitled to some res judicata effect in these proceedings. At the risk of splitting hairs, however, we think the arbitration order in this case properly presents a question of issue preclusion (and not claim preclusion) because the [—29—] arbitration was limited in scope and decided "factual issues and not causes of action."[19] *Brown*, 611 F.3d at 1333.

Generally speaking, issue preclusion operates more narrowly than claim preclusion "to prevent re-litigation of issues that have already been decided between the parties in an earlier lawsuit." *Id.* at 1332 (citation omitted). For issue preclusion to apply under Florida law, "an identical issue must be

---

[19] In reaching this conclusion, we acknowledge some tension in the Florida cases regarding the proper application of claim preclusion and issue preclusion rules within the broader context of current res judicata doctrine. *See, e.g., Philip Morris USA, Inc. v. Douglas*, 110 So. 3d 419, 436–39 (Fla. 2013) (Canady, J., dissenting) (insisting that majority's application of claim preclusion rules instead of issue preclusion rules was "exactly backward"). Even so, this is neither the right court nor the right case for ironing out any wrinkles in Florida preclusion law, and it is plain enough to us that the Florida courts would give some form of "res judicata effect" to matters that were, as here, raised and actually determined in an earlier proceeding involving the same parties. *Douglas*, 110 So. 3d at 432–36. Whether it is properly classified as claim preclusion or issue preclusion, or collateral estoppel or direct estoppel, the arbitration proceeding already answered a common question in a prior proceeding involving the same parties, and we therefore afford that answer "res judicata effect" under Florida law in this case.

presented in a prior proceeding; the issue must have been a critical and necessary part of the prior determination; there must have been a full and fair opportunity to litigate that issue; the parties in the two proceedings must be identical; and the issues must have been actually litigated." *Id.* at 1333 (quoting *Holt v. Brown's Repair Serv., Inc.*, 780 So. 2d 180, 182 (Fla. 2d DCA 2001)). Issue preclusion may be asserted offensively by a plaintiff or defensively by a defendant, in either case for the purpose of preventing the other party from re-litigating an identical issue previously decided against the other party. *Id.* Under Florida law, an arbitration **[—30—]** proceeding may serve as the foundation for the assertion of issue preclusion. {**–1127–**}[20] *See Dadeland Depot, Inc. v. St. Paul Fire and Marine Ins. Co.*, 945 So. 2d 1216, 1235–36 (Fla. 2006) (answering certified question); *see also Dadeland Depot, Inc. v. St. Paul Fire and Marine Ins. Co.*, 483 F.3d 1265, 1279–80 (11th Cir. 2007) (holding, in light of response to certified question from the Florida Supreme Court, that insurer was "collaterally estopped from raising . . . the same defenses that were raised and rejected in [an] earlier arbitration proceeding").

In this case, the arbitration order precludes Crowley from re-litigating the issue of whether it reported a Claim to National Union on or before December 31, 2012. Crowley and National Union were the only parties to the arbitration proceeding, and they are the only parties to this action. The arbitrators received numerous exhibits and also held a hearing over a period of three days. Excerpts of what appears to be a thorough and robust hearing appear in the record before this Court, and it is not apparent to us (nor have the parties argued) that either party was not afforded a

full and fair opportunity to litigate the issue that was then before the arbitrators. **[—31—]**

The arbitrators defined the issue as whether the joint FBI/DOJ investigation, as evidenced by the materials provided to National Union on or before December 31, 2012, was sufficient to constitute a Claim under the Policy. In this appeal, we are called upon to answer an identical question with respect to a slightly broader time period. After defining the issue, the arbitrators went on to conclude that the April 2008 Notice and other materials submitted to National Union on or before December 31, 2012 "did not constitute a Claim for Insured Persons as the term 'Claim' is defined in the Policy" and that "[t]he triggering event specified in the Policy ha[d] not yet been presented to National Union." We construe this to mean the arbitrators found that Crowley had not, based on the information in the hearing record as of December 31, 2012, reported a Claim to National Union as required by the Policy. In making this determination, the arbitrators clearly were aware of the existence of the sealed Affidavit—it was referenced generally in Crowley's April 2008 Notice and discussed at length during the arbitration hearing—but all parties freely admit that no one knew what the Affidavit actually said at the time of the arbitration.

Given this, it is clear that, even if the arbitration panel did not (or really could not) consider the substantive contents of the unsealed Affidavit because they were still under seal and thus unavailable in December 2012, it did consider and reject the idea that Crowley had somehow reported a Claim to National Union by **[—32—]** merely pointing to the existence of the sealed Affidavit. *See* Arb. Decision and Award, ECF No. 16-1, at 7 (observing that the search warrant, which only noted generally the existence of an affidavit supporting probable cause, was "devoid of any identification by the DOJ (or FBI) of any individual as a person against whom a covered proceeding may be commenced" and that the potential of any such proceeding against any individual named in the search warrant arose "only by inference derived from context beyond the four corners

---

[20] In neither the district court nor on appeal has Crowley challenged the application of preclusion principles on the basis that the prior litigation was in an arbitral forum, or on any other basis except Crowley's arguments that the subsequent revelation of the content of the Affidavit is a new fact which was not considered by the arbitration panel and/or that application of preclusion principles would be inequitable. Thus, we decline to consider any other argument against the application of preclusion principles.

of the search warrant"). Thus, we conclude that the question whether Crowley reported {–1128–} a Claim to National Union at any time between April 16, 2008 (the earliest date as of which we could assume the Claim based on the Affidavit was first made against Farmer) and December 31, 2012 (when the arbitration hearing record closed) was both "actually litigated" in and a "critical and necessary part" of the arbitration proceeding. Indeed, that issue appears to have been the sole and limited focus of the arbitration.[21]

Because all requirements for issue preclusion have been satisfied, as explained above, we conclude that Crowley is precluded from challenging the fact [—33—] finding of the arbitrators that the materials submitted by Crowley to National Union on or before December 31, 2012—which materials revealed the existence of a sealed Affidavit but not the content thereof—did not satisfy the requirements of section 7(a) of the Policy for reporting a Claim to the Insurer. The identical issue is now before us (although we also have before us a similar issue with respect to the additional time period after December 31, 2012 up to the November 1, 2013 expiration of the Discovery Period). Crowley has adduced no additional evidence—over and above the evidence before the arbitrators—which is relevant to what was reported to National Union as of December 31, 2012. Although we now know the content of the then-sealed Affidavit, and we now know that the content did satisfy the Policy's requirements for a Claim, there is still no more evidence with respect to a report to National Union as of December 31, 2012 than was presented to the arbitrators.

---

[21] As discussed in greater detail below, we also conclude that the arbitration order necessarily was limited to the materials before the arbitrators at that time and that the question whether Crowley reported a Claim to National Union at any time after December 31, 2012 was not "actually litigated" by the arbitration proceeding. The district court was correct when it observed that "[t]he arbitration panel only determined whether the documentation that Crowley had submitted to National Union at that point in time constituted a Claim under the Policy." *Crowley*, 307 F. Supp. 3d at 1294.

We also summarily reject Crowley's argument that application of preclusion principles in this case would be inequitable. To conclude otherwise would require us to ignore not only the contractual language of this particular Policy, but also the customary nature of claims-made insurance policies, in which "coverage depends on the claim being discovered and reported to the insurer during the policy period." *Country Manors Ass'n, Inc. v. Master Antenna Sys., Inc.*, 534 So. 2d 1187, 1194 (Fla. 4th DCA 1988). We add only that parties worried about the difficulties [—34—] associated with timely discovering or reporting claims under a claims-made policy— as a result of the judicial sealing of a probable cause affidavit or otherwise—could conceivably negotiate special terms or enter into a more costly but less predictable occurrence-based insurance policy, under which coverage would be effective "regardless of the date of discovery or the date the claim is made or asserted." *Gulf Ins. Co.*, 433 So. 2d at 514 (citations omitted).

We conclude that the Florida courts would give preclusive effect to the ruling of the arbitrators. We thus conclude on the basis of issue preclusion that—even though we assume *arguendo* that the Claim based on the Affidavit was first made against Farmer in April 2008—that Claim was not reported to the Insurer on or before December 31, 2012.[22] We turn now to consider whether Crowley reported to National {–1129–} Union the Claim based on the Affidavit at any time after December 31, 2012 and before November 1, 2013—when a report to the Insurer under section 7(a) could have been timely. On appeal, Crowley relies in this regard only upon the Claim based on the Affidavit which, as discussed immediately below, was not reported to National Union until July 2015. [—35—]

---

[22] Because we rely on issue preclusion, we do not address the merits of this issue. We also note that Crowley's counsel confirmed at oral argument that Crowley does not dispute the correctness of the arbitration panel's ruling on this question.

(b) Crowley's July 2015 Notice did not provide timely notice of a Claim based on the Affidavit under section 7(a) because the Discovery Period expired on November 1, 2013.

In relying on its July 2015 Notice to National Union of the Claim based on the Affidavit, Crowley challenges National Union's argument that the arbitration proceeding should preclude consideration of the unsealed Affidavit altogether. In particular, Crowley asserts that the unsealing of the Affidavit in 2015 is a new fact that was not presented to or considered by the arbitration panel, and therefore res judicata principles should not bar its consideration in Crowley's federal lawsuit. We agree.

Under Florida law, issue preclusion extends only to issues that were "actually adjudicated." *Brown*, 611 F.3d at 1334 (citation omitted). We have previously observed that the Florida courts enforce this requirement "with rigor." *Id*. In fact, "if there is any doubt as to whether a litigant has had his day in court such doubt must be resolved in favor of the full consideration of the substantive issues of the litigation." *Id*. (quoting *Hittel v. Rosenhagen*, 492 So. 2d 1086, 1089–90 (Fla. 4th DCA 1986)). In this light, it is obvious that the question whether Crowley reported a Claim to National Union in its July 2015 Notice was not—and indeed could not have been—actually adjudicated during the arbitration proceeding. The arbitration panel closed the hearing record on December 31, 2012 and issued its decision on January 29, 2013, more than two years before Crowley [—36—] delivered its July 2015 Notice to National Union. And by observing that "[t]he triggering event specified in the Policy has not yet been presented to National Union," the arbitration order itself clearly contemplated that it was not intended to be dispositive of all issues relating to Crowley's breach of contract cause of action against National Union. In other words, the arbitrators left open the possibility that circumstances might develop in such a way that Crowley could eventually report a Claim based on the Affidavit to National Union as required by the Policy, even if it had not done

so as of December 31, 2012. We find further support for this conclusion in the fact that the arbitrators were clearly aware of the sealed Affidavit but, at National Union's urging, declined to speculate about what it might say.[23] Because the arbitration findings "may be given effect to the full extent of, but no farther than, what the [arbitrators] found," we find that the arbitration order does not preclude consideration of Crowley's delivery of the July 2015 Notice in this case. *Id*.

But that does not mean that Crowley can prevail. Returning again to section 7(a) of the Policy, we conclude that Crowley failed to timely report the Claim based on the Affidavit at any time after the arbitration. That is, Crowley failed to report the Claim based on the Affidavit before the November 1, 2013 expiration of [—37—] the Discovery Period. In relevant part, section 7(a) required Crowley to give written {–1130–} notice of a Claim to National Union "in all events no later than . . . the end of the Policy Period or the Discovery Period." The Policy Period ended on November 1, 2008, and the Discovery Period ended on November 1, 2013. Thus, to comply with the reporting requirements of section 7(a) for the Claim based on the Affidavit under subpart three of the Policy definition of Claim, Crowley was required to show, on or before November 1, 2013, that Farmer had been identified in writing as a person against whom a criminal proceeding may be commenced. Put another way, Crowley had to do more than simply point to the sealed Affidavit and ask National Union to take its word for it that a Claim in fact existed.[24]

---

[23] *See* Hr'g Tr., ECF No. 36-9, at 30 ("The regrettable thing, in part, about this case is, the damn thing is under seal. If that thing were not under seal, we would be having a very interesting discussion about what it shows, or doesn't show.").

[24] Because the question is not squarely presented by this case, we decline to say exactly how much substantive information Crowley was required to provide National Union to satisfy the reporting requirements of section 7(a) for a Claim based on the Affidavit under subpart three of the Policy definition of Claim. This is partly because the arbitration already answered the question and partly because any later information Crowley provided regarding the substantive content of the Affidavit was untimely in any event. We believe it

Additionally, because of the preclusive nature of the intervening arbitration proceeding, we are concerned in this analysis only with materials submitted to National Union during the period between December 31, 2012 (the day the arbitration hearing record closed) and November 1, 2013 (the end of the Discovery Period). Although Crowley did report Farmer's Plea Offer to National Union [—38—] during this time period (thus triggering undisputed coverage based on that Claim against Farmer as of February 18, 2013),[25] the record does not reveal that Crowley reported any helpful information relating to the substantive contents of the Affidavit before the November 1, 2013 expiration of the Discovery Period. As we now know, Crowley did not—and really could not—do this because the Affidavit did not become available until April 24, 2015. Crowley did not notify National Union that the Affidavit had been unsealed until July 22, 2015, and it would not be able to provide National Union with a copy of the unsealed Affidavit until November 10, 2015. In either case, Crowley's reporting of a Claim based on the Affidavit under section 7(a) of the Policy was more than a year-and-a-half too late.

Finally, the judicial unsealing of the Affidavit in 2015 does nothing to call into question the arbitration panel's conclusion that Crowley had not, based on the information then before the arbitration panel, reported a Claim to National Union. At best, the act of unsealing the Affidavit in 2015 confirmed that a Claim might have been "first made against" Farmer on April 16, 2008; it did nothing to change the fact, as determined by the arbitrators, that Crowley had not reported a Claim to National Union as of December 31, 2012. [—39—]

---

is enough to say that the substantive information relating to the Affidavit that Crowley provided to National Union between December 31, 2012 and November 1, 2013—which really amounted to no new information at all about the Affidavit—was insufficient to timely report a Claim based on the Affidavit to National Union under section 7(a) of the Policy.

[25] *See* note 6, *supra*; *see also infra*, part IV.B.3.c (discussing Crowley's waiver of relation back arguments).

(c) Crowley has expressly waived any argument that either its February 2013 Notice or its July 2015 Notice should relate back to the April 2008 Notice under section 7 of the Policy.

Crowley has expressly waived any argument under Section 7 of the Policy that either of its later notices (either the February 2013 Notice regarding Farmer's Plea Offer or the July 2015 Notice regarding {–1131–} the unsealed Affidavit) should relate back to Crowley's initial April 2008 Notice in a way that would require National Union to reimburse Crowley for Farmer's pre-February 2013 (pre-Plea Offer) Defense Costs. *See United States v. Doyle*, 693 F.3d 769, 771 (7th Cir. 2012) ("Waiver occurs when a defendant or his attorney manifests an intention, or expressly declines, to assert a right."); *see also United States v. Willis*, 649 F.3d 1248, 1254 (11th Cir. 2011) ("[A] party seeking to raise a claim or issue on appeal must plainly and prominently so indicate. This common-sense rule seeks to avoid confusion as to the issues that are in play and those that are not. Where a party fails to abide by this simple requirement, he has waived his right to have the court consider that argument." (alteration in original) (citations and internal quotation marks omitted)); *Cont'l Tech. Servs., Inc. v. Rockwell Intern. Corp.*, 927 F.2d 1198, 1199 (11th Cir. 1991) (noting that "[a]n argument not made is waived" and holding that appellant waived its right to argue that California (rather than Georgia) law should apply because it failed to present reasoned arguments [—40—] supported by citations to relevant law and instead only perfunctorily suggested California law applied).

The case for waiver against Crowley is strong here because Crowley affirmatively manifested an intention to waive its relation back arguments. *See* Appellant's Reply Br. 14 ("As made clear in Crowley's Brief, this is not Crowley's argument. National Union is attempting to rebut a 'relation back' argument that Crowley does not even make. . . . Crowley is not relying on 'relation back' . . . ."); Oral Argument at 5:13, 6:10 (confirming that Crowley was not relying on a notice of circumstances and relation back argument under section 7 and that it was instead relying on the April 2008 Notice to establish that notice of a Claim had been given at that time).[26] Because Crowley has waived reliance on a relation back argument, we express no opinion on whether any such argument might have resulted in coverage for Crowley's pre-February 2013 (pre-Plea Offer) Defense Costs. However, we do conclude that the arguments Crowley does make—especially when paired with the preclusive effect of the arbitration proceeding—fail to [—41—] establish that Crowley reported the Claim based on the Affidavit to National Union as required by the language of this particular claims-made insurance policy.

V. CONCLUSION

In sum, we conclude that the district court did not err when it granted National Union's converted motion for summary judgment. Even assuming that the Claim based on the Affidavit was "first made against" Farmer during the Policy Period or the Discovery Period, Crowley failed to timely report that Claim to National Union as required by section 7(a) of the Policy. With respect to the reporting period between April 16, 2008 and December 31, 2012, Crowley is bound by the arbitration panel's finding that Crowley had not reported {–1132–} a Claim to National Union as required by the Policy at that time. With respect to the reporting period beginning immediately after December 31, 2012 and

running through the end of the Discovery Period on November 1, 2013, we conclude that Crowley failed to report the Claim based on the Affidavit as required by section 7(a) of the Policy because it did not report any new information relating to the Affidavit until after both the Policy Period and the Discovery Period had expired. We also conclude that Crowley has waived any arguments that either its February 2013 Notice or its July 2015 Notice should relate back to the April 2008 Notice under section 7, and we therefore decline to consider whether a relation back theory [—42—] might have afforded coverage for the pre-February 2013 (pre-Plea Offer) Defense Costs which Crowley seeks.

The judgment of the district court is therefore

AFFIRMED.

---

[26] Crowley's initial brief on appeal did not make a straightforward relation back argument supported by citation of authority and provided no discussion or analysis of Policy language in an effort to show that the language might support relation back in this case, but that initial brief probably did not rise to the level of a clear and affirmative waiver of a relation back argument. In other words, there was a waiver for failure to fairly raise and support a relation back argument, *see Cont'l Tech. Servs., Inc.*, 927 F.2d at 1199, although probably not an affirmative waiver. This is true, both with respect to the Claim based on the Affidavit, and Crowley's casual mention of the February 2013 (Plea Offer) Claim. However, in both Crowley's reply brief on appeal and its oral argument, Crowley did clearly and affirmatively waive any reliance on relation back.

United States Court of Appeals
for the Eleventh Circuit

No. 17-14237

K.T.

vs.

ROYAL CARIBBEAN CRUISES, LTD.

Appeal from the United States District Court for the
Southern District of Florida

Decided: July 24, 2019

Citation: 931 F.3d 1041, 7 Adm. R. 507 (11th Cir. 2019).

Before **CARNES**, Chief Judge, **ROSENBAUM**, and **HULL**, Circuit Judges.

[—1—] {–1042–} **CARNES**, Chief Judge:

According to the complaint in this case, on the day after Christmas in 2015, K.T. embarked on a seven-day Royal Caribbean cruise with her two sisters and her [—2—] grandparents. {–1043–} She was a minor at the time.[1] She alleges that on the first night of the cruise, a group of nearly a dozen adult male passengers bought multiple alcoholic beverages for her in a public lounge and other public areas of the ship. They plied her with enough alcohol that she became "highly intoxicated," "obviously drunk, disoriented, and unstable," and "obviously incapacitated." The group of nearly a dozen men then steered her "to a cabin where they brutally assaulted and gang raped her."

She also alleges that everything (other than the assault and gang rape) happened in the view of multiple Royal Caribbean crewmembers, including those responsible for monitoring the ship's security cameras. But Royal Caribbean's crewmembers allegedly did nothing to stop the group of adult male passengers from buying alcohol for K.T., from getting her drunk, or from leading her away to a cabin while she was incapacitated. They allegedly did nothing to protect or help her. [—3—]

K.T. sued Royal Caribbean and the district court dismissed her lawsuit under Rule 12(b)(6) of the Federal Rules of Civil Procedure for failure to state a claim. This is her appeal.

I.

This Court "review[s] *de novo* the district court's grant of a motion to dismiss under 12(b)(6) for failure to state a claim." *Butler v. Sheriff of Palm Beach Cty.*, 685 F.3d 1261, 1265 (11th Cir. 2012) (quotation marks omitted). When doing that, "we accept the factual allegations supporting a claim as true and draw all reasonable inferences in favor of the nonmovant." *Newton v. Duke Energy Fla., LLC*, 895 F.3d 1270, 1275 (11th Cir. 2018). To get past a motion to dismiss, "[t]he plaintiff's [f]actual allegations must be enough to raise a right to relief above the speculative level, on the assumption that all the allegations in the complaint are true (even if doubtful in fact)." *Butler*, 685 F.3d at 1265 (second alteration in original) (quotation marks omitted). Stated a bit differently, "[t]o survive a motion to dismiss, the plaintiff must plead a claim to relief that is plausible on its face." *Id.* (quotation marks omitted).

The operative complaint[2] included more claims, but the only ones relevant to this

---

[1] While the complaint and amended complaints allege that K.T. was a minor when the events took place on December 26, 2015, they do not otherwise specify her age on that date. When she filed her Third Amended Complaint on November 7, 2017, K.T. alleged that she was at least 18 years old by that date, which would mean that she had been 16 or 17 when the events occurred. In various submissions to the district court and in her opening brief to this Court, however, K.T. asserted that she was only 15 on the day in question. In any event, according to all of the relevant allegations and assertions, K.T. was a minor, somewhere between the ages of 15 and 17 at the time of the cruise.

[2] In its order dismissing K.T.'s claims against Royal Caribbean, the district court treated her Second Amended Complaint as the operative one. K.T. filed her Third Amended Complaint [—4—] while this appeal was pending to clear up any doubt about diversity jurisdiction. There is no material difference between the Second and Third Amended Complaints as far as the negligence claims against Royal Caribbean are concerned. We will treat the Third Amended Complaint as the operative one because it is the last one.

appeal are for Royal Caribbean's negligence, both in failing to warn [—4—] passengers and prospective passengers of the danger of sexual assault on a cruise ship, and in failing to take action to prevent the physical assault, including the sexual assault, that K.T. suffered. The district court found that K.T.'s negligence claims against Royal Caribbean failed because they did not sufficiently allege that Royal Caribbean {–1044–} breached its duty of care or that any breach proximately caused her injuries. Reviewing the matter anew, as we must, we conclude otherwise.

II.

"In analyzing a maritime tort case, we rely on general principles of negligence law." *Chaparro v. Carnival Corp.*, 693 F.3d 1333, 1336 (11th Cir. 2012) (quotation marks omitted).[3] "To plead negligence, a plaintiff must allege that (1) the defendant had a duty to protect the plaintiff from a particular injury; (2) the defendant breached that duty; (3) the breach actually and proximately caused the plaintiff's injury; and (4) the plaintiff suffered actual harm." *Id.* "Determination of negligence tends to be a fact-intensive inquiry highly dependent [—5—] upon the given circumstances." *Souran v. Travlers Ins. Co.*, 982 F.2d 1497, 1506 (11th Cir. 1993).

K.T. has sufficiently alleged that she suffered actual harm. And the parties agree that Royal Caribbean owed K.T. a duty of "ordinary reasonable care under the circumstances, a standard which requires, as a prerequisite to imposing liability, that the carrier have had actual or constructive notice of the risk-creating condition, at least where, as here, the menace is one commonly encountered on land and not clearly linked to nautical adventure." *Keefe v. Bahama Cruise*

Line, Inc., 867 F.2d 1318, 1322 (11th Cir. 1989); *see also Kermarec v. Compagnie Generale Transatlantique*, 358 U.S. 625, 630, 79 S. Ct. 406, 409 (1959) ("[A] shipowner owes the duty of exercising reasonable care towards those lawfully aboard the vessel who are not members of the crew."); *Guevara v. NCL (Bahamas) Ltd.*, 920 F.3d 710, 720, 7 Adm. R. 476, 481 (11th Cir. 2019) ("In this circumstance, a cruise ship operator's liability hinges on whether it knew or should have known about the dangerous condition.") (quotation marks omitted). The scope of Royal Caribbean's duty to protect its passengers is informed, if not defined, by its knowledge of the dangers they face onboard. And it allegedly knew a lot.

The allegations are that Royal Caribbean "had experienced and had actual knowledge of . . . assaults and batteries and sexual crimes, and other violence between passengers and between passengers and crew," and "anticipated and [—6—] foresaw that crimes would be perpetrated on passengers aboard its vessels." Not only that but Royal Caribbean also allegedly "had experienced and had actual knowledge of minors wrongfully being provided with or allowed to gain access to alcohol, and then becoming the victim of assaults and batteries and sexual crimes, perpetrated aboard its vessels both by crew and by other passengers." It allegedly "knew or should have known, that the high risk to its passengers of crime and injury aboard the vessels was enhanced by [its] sale of copious quantities of alcohol on its vessels," and "knew or should have known of the need to prevent minors wrongfully being provided with or allowed to gain access to alcohol, both by crew and by other passengers."

Those allegations, which we must accept as true for present purposes, are enough to establish that the danger of sexual assault in general and of sexual assault on minors in particular was foreseeable, and indeed was known, to Royal Caribbean. {–1045–} And that foreseeable and known danger imposed on Royal Caribbean and its crew a duty of ordinary reasonable care, which included the duty to monitor and regulate the behavior of

---

[3] "[F]or federal common law to apply" in a diversity case like this one, the "suit must also be sustainable under the admiralty jurisdiction." *Norfolk. S. Ry. Co. v. Kirby*, 543 U.S. 14, 23, 125 S. Ct. 385, 392–93 (2004) (emphasis omitted). This one is. *See Doe v. Celebrity Cruises, Inc.*, 394 F.3d 891, 900–02 (11th Cir. 2004). So we apply federal admiralty law, which is the law "argued by the parties." *Id.* at 902.

its passengers, especially where minors are involved.

The allegations are that Royal Caribbean and its crew breached that duty by failing to: "adequately monitor the public areas" of its ship; "promulgate and/or enforce adequate policies and/or procedures to prevent alcohol being served to minors"; "promulgate and/or enforce adequate policies and/or procedures to [—7—] prevent sexual assaults on minors aboard [its] ships"; and "intervene to prevent the service of alcohol to a minor and/or to assist an obviously intoxicated minor, when a reasonable and prudent crewmember would have taken action." The complaint alleges that Royal Caribbean already "had experienced and had actual knowledge of minors wrongfully being provided with or allowed to gain access to alcohol, and then becoming the victim of assaults and batteries and sexual crimes, perpetrated aboard its vessels . . . by other passengers." And Royal Caribbean allegedly "knew . . . from previous experience[] that the risk of crime and injury against passengers aboard its vessels tended to be greatest in passenger cabins and in bars."

The complaint also alleges that K.T. was a minor on the day in question, so the duty of ordinary reasonable care under the circumstances required Royal Caribbean's crewmembers to do more than simply refuse to sell alcoholic beverages to her directly; the duty also required that they refuse to sell alcoholic beverages to any adult male passengers they knew were "purchas[ing] multiple alcoholic beverages" for K.T. And it certainly required that crewmembers intervene when they saw a group of nearly a dozen men steering a "highly intoxicated," "obviously drunk, disoriented," "unstable," and "obviously incapacitated" girl to a private cabin. Even though that allegedly happened "[i]n [—8—] view of multiple crewmembers and still under surveillance by the ship's security cameras," no crewmember did anything to help K.T. as she was led away.

In sum, the complaint has sufficiently alleged that because Royal Caribbean's crewmembers did nothing to prevent the large group of men from plying K.T. with enough alcohol to incapacitate her and did nothing to stop those men from leading her away to a private cabin, Royal Caribbean breached the duty of ordinary care it owed her. And it is self-evident from the allegations of the complaint that but for Royal Caribbean's breach of its duties of care to K.T. she would not have been brutalized and gang raped. If the allegations are true, Royal Caribbean proximately caused the alleged injuries. The complaint states a claim against Royal Caribbean.

Royal Caribbean protests that allowing liability for its alleged failures would effectively impose strict liability for harm passengers suffer aboard its ships and would make cruise lines insurers of their passengers. We recognize that "[a] carrier by sea . . . is not liable to passengers as an insurer." *Kornberg v. Carnival Cruise Lines, Inc.*, 741 F.2d 1332, 1334 (11th Cir. 1984). But we are not talking about strict liability. We are talking about negligence in failing to act to prevent a foreseeable or known danger. If K.T. can prove the allegations in her complaint, Royal Caribbean is liable for its negligence and that of its crew. [—9—]

III.

We turn now to K.T.'s second theory of negligence, which is based on the claimed failure of Royal Caribbean to warn K.T. and her grandparents of known dangers. {–1046–} "A defendant's failure to warn [a] plaintiff does not breach" the duty of reasonable care under federal maritime law "unless the resultant harm is reasonably foreseeable." *Daigle v. Point Landing, Inc.*, 616 F.2d 825, 827 (5th Cir. 1980). "Liability for a failure to warn thus arises from foreseeability, or the knowledge that particular conduct will create danger." *Id.*

We have held that a cruise line's duty of "ordinary reasonable care under the circumstances" includes a "duty to warn of known dangers beyond the point of debarkation in places where passengers are invited or reasonably expected to visit." *Chaparro*, 693 F.3d at 1336 (quotation marks omitted). If a cruise line owes its passengers a "duty to warn of known dangers" at excursion destinations, *id.*—areas over which it usually has little (if any) control—a cruise line certainly owes its passengers a "duty to warn of known dangers" aboard its ship. *See Keefe v. Bahama Cruise Line, Inc.*, 867 F.2d 1318, 1322 (11th Cir. 1989).

The allegations in the complaint demonstrate that Royal Caribbean must have known about the dangers of sexual assaults aboard its ships. *See supra* pp. 5–6. They are that Royal Caribbean: "anticipated and foresaw that crimes would be perpetrated on passengers aboard its vessels;" "knew, or should have known, that [—10—] the high risk to its passengers of crime and injury aboard the vessels was enhanced by [its] sale of copious quantities of alcohol on its vessels;" and "knew, or should have known of the need to prevent minors wrongfully being provided with or allowed to gain access to alcohol, both by crew and by other passengers." So Royal Caribbean allegedly had abundant notice and actual knowledge of the dangers that K.T. alleges resulted in the injuries she suffered during the cruise.

In short, the allegations in the complaint are that Royal Caribbean's duty of ordinary care under the circumstances required it to warn K.T. and her grandparents about the dangers of violent sexual crimes aboard its ships, including those committed against minors who have been wrongfully provided with alcohol. And it is alleged that Royal Caribbean breached that duty by not warning its passengers, including K. T. and her grandparents, of those dangers. The complaint also makes the additional (unnecessary but relevant) allegation that "Royal Caribbean willfully chooses not to warn its passengers about rapes and sexual assaults aboard its ships so as not to scare any prospective passengers away."

That leaves the element of causation. The complaint alleges that because of Royal Caribbean's failure to warn K.T. and her family members of the dangers and prevalence of sexual assault on its vessels, including sexual assaults on minors, they were unaware of the need to take any special precautions. It

alleges that K.T. was injured due to Royal Caribbean's failure to warn passengers. More [—11—] specifically, the complaint alleges that "[a]s a direct and proximate result" of Royal Caribbean's negligence and failures, K.T. "was directly and proximately caused to be sexually assaulted and/or physically battered and/or gang raped." The complaint sufficiently alleges that Royal Caribbean's failure to warn was a but-for cause of the harm K.T. suffered.

"A carrier by sea" is liable to its passengers "for its negligence," *Kornberg*, 741 F.2d at 1334, and K.T.'s allegations are "more than a mere recitation of the elements of the cause of action." *Chaparro*, 693 F.3d at 1337. Her allegations "are plausible and raise a reasonable expectation that discovery could supply additional proof of [Royal Caribbean's] liability." *Id.* {–1047–} As a result, "the district court erred in dismissing [the] negligence claim[s]." *Id.*

IV.

On its website, Royal Caribbean Cruises assures all who are thinking of sailing with it that "the safety and security of our guests and crew is our highest priority and fundamental to our operations."[4] It boasts that it "is committed to preventing illegal activity," and "[d]uring each voyage, we remain dedicated to [—12—] safeguarding our guests and crew."[5] And it promises that the ship's Captain "will take appropriate action to ensure the safety, security and wellbeing of our guests."[6] Not if the allegations of the complaint are true.

---

[4] *Safety & Security*, Royal Caribbean Cruises, https://www.royalcaribbean.com/resources/safety-and-security (last visited July 24, 2019). In keeping with Eleventh Circuit Internal Operating Procedure 10, "Citation to Internet Materials in an Opinion," under Federal Rule of Appellate Procedure 36, copies of all of the internet materials cited in this opinion are available at this Court's Clerk's Office.

[5] *Id.*

[6] *Royal Caribbean Guest Conduct Policy*, Royal Caribbean Cruises, https://www.royalcaribbean.com/content/dam/royal/resources/pdf/guest-conduct-policy.pdf (last updated Nov. 12, 2018).

Royal Caribbean's website also proclaims that the cruise line has an "ongoing commitment to innovation and continuous improvement in every aspect of [its] business."[7] Again, if the allegations of the complaint are true, Royal Caribbean's approach to protecting passengers from being sexually assaulted and raped certainly could be improved. One of the purposes of tort law is to spur along such improvements.

REVERSED AND REMANDED

(Reporter's Note: Concurring Opinion follows on p. 512).

---

[7] *Safety & Security, supra* note 4.

[—13—] {–1047–} CARNES, Chief Judge, concurring specially:

Of course, I concur in every word of the Court's opinion. *See United States v. Hough*, 803 F.3d 1181, 1197 (11th Cir. 2015) (Carnes, C.J., concurring) ("Not surprisingly, as the author of the Court's opinion I concur in all of it."). Usually, there is nothing else for the author of a majority opinion to say, but here there is. I write separately to point out that, in addition to K.T.'s allegations, publicly available data (of which we can take judicial notice) reinforces the allegations in the complaint that Royal Caribbean knew or should have known about the danger of sexual assault aboard its cruise ships.

Since 2010 cruise lines have been required to keep records of all complaints about certain crimes—including sexual assault and rape—that occur aboard any of their ships during a cruise "that embarks or disembarks passengers in the United States." 46 U.S.C. § 3507(g)(1)(A); *see id.* § 3507(k)(1). Cruise lines must report those complaints to the FBI and the Department of Transportation. *Id.* § 3507(g)(3)(A)(i), (ii). The DOT has a statutory duty to compile the reports and publish quarterly "statistical compilation[s]" about certain crimes—including sexual assault and rape—that occur on board cruise vessels. *See id.* § 3507(g)(4). Those compilations are called Cruise Line Incident Reports. *Cruise Line Incident Reports*, U.S. Dep't Transp., https://www.transportation.gov/mission/safety/cruise-line-incident-reports (last updated Apr. 17, 2019). **[—14—]**

We may take judicial notice of Cruise Line Incident Reports. *See* Fed. R. Evid. 201(b), (d); *Terrebonne v. Blackburn*, 646 F.2d 997, 1000 n.4 (5th Cir. June 1981) (en banc) ("Absent some reason for mistrust, courts {–1048–} have not hesitated to take judicial notice of agency records and reports."); *In re PEC Sols., Inc. Sec. Litig.*, 418 F.3d 379, 388 & n.7, 390 & n.10 (4th Cir. 2005) (taking judicial notice of information in public documents the parties had filed with a federal agency).

And in ruling on a motion to dismiss courts may supplement the allegations in a complaint with facts contained in judicially noticed materials. *See Tellabs, Inc. v. Makor Issues & Rights, Ltd.*, 551 U.S. 308, 322, 127 S. Ct. 2499, 2509 (2007) ("*[C]ourts must consider the complaint in its entirety, as well as* other sources courts ordinarily examine when ruling on Rule 12(b)(6) motions to dismiss, in particular, documents incorporated into the complaint by reference, and *matters of which a court may take judicial notice.*") (emphasis added); *Lozman v. City of Riviera Beach*, 713 F.3d 1066, 1075 n.9 (11th Cir. 2013) ("Although this matter is before the court on a motion to dismiss, we may take judicial notice of the court documents from the state eviction action."); *Kaspersky Lab, Inc. v. U.S. Dep't of Homeland Sec.*, 909 F.3d 446, 464 (D.C. Cir. 2018) ("Among the information a court may consider on a motion to dismiss are public records subject to judicial notice.") (quotation marks omitted). **[—15—]**

We may take judicial notice of matters that the district court did not. *See* Fed. R. Evid. 201(d) ("The court may take judicial notice at any stage of the proceeding."); *United States v. Greer*, 440 F.3d 1267, 1272 (11th Cir. 2006) (taking judicial notice of a fact even though the district court did not); *Coney v. Smith*, 738 F.2d 1199, 1200 (11th Cir. 1984) (noting that although the matter was "not made a part of the record before the district court, we may take judicial notice of the same").

The attorneys were put on notice at oral argument that we might consider Cruise Line Incident Reports, and Royal Caribbean's counsel agreed that knowledge of those reports could be imputed to Royal Caribbean. *See* Oral Argument at 11:42–14:14.[1] **[—16—]** {–1049–}

---

[1] The relevant exchange with Royal Caribbean's counsel went as follows:

Q: [P]art of the thing that, in my view — and I'm speaking my tentative position to give you an opportunity to convince me to the contrary — part of the thing that does turn it into a cause of action is that it's a sad and often told tale. Sad and repeated facts. This is not the first time this has happened on one of Royal Caribbean's vessels. You're familiar, of course, with the Cruise Vessel Safety and Security Act of 2010 requiring that there be a compilation of incidents, statistical incidents, in which passengers or crew were sexually assaulted, are you not?

A: I am.

Q: And your client, of course, is too.

A: Yes. [—16—]

Q: And according to those reports, even if you exclude all those that are still under investigation, in the five-year period before this assault, 2010 to 2015, there were twenty assaults, actually sexual assaults, on your client's vessels, were there not?

A: I don't know that statistic offhand, but it's possible.

Q: Sounds reasonable, doesn't it?

A: Yes.

Q: Except it's not reasonable to allow that to happen.

A: I would agree.

Q: And on all cruise lines, 64. *So that knowledge is imputed to your client, is it not?*

A: I would agree.

Q: So they were well aware of the risk. And that's what the plaintiff has alleged. In paragraph 11: "knew of the serious risk of crime and injury to its passengers aboard"; "had experienced and had actual knowledge of such crimes and injuries perpetuated aboard its vessels both by crew and by other passengers"; "assault and batteries and sexual crimes and other violence." And so having that knowledge, you'd agree that under just general negligence law they had an obligation to protect their passengers and crew from those kinds of sexual assaults that they knew happen all too frequently, didn't they?

A: Well I do think there is a distinction there, and if I may go into it for a minute, your honor —

For all of those reasons, it is appropriate to take judicial notice of the contents of the Cruise Line Incident Reports. According to the reports covering [—17—] the period from 2010 to September 30, 2015, which was just before the alleged events in this case, cruise lines had reported a total of at least 66 complaints of sexual assault committed by passengers aboard cruises embarking or disembarking passengers in the United States.[2] *See Cruise Line Incident Reports, supra.* And Royal Caribbean itself had reported receiving at least 20 complaints of sexual assaults committed by passengers, which is nearly one-third of the number reported for all cruise lines. *See id.*

Those numbers probably understate the number of complaints of sexual assault Royal Caribbean received because the reports include only matters that were "no longer under investigation" by the FBI at the time of the report. *See* 46 U.S.C. § 3507(g)(4) (2012), *amended by Howard Coble Coast Guard and Maritime Transportation Act of 2014*, Pub. L. No. 113-281, § 321, 128 Stat. 3022, 3054 (2014) (codified at 46 U.S.C. § 3507(g)(4)(A)(i) (2018)). As a congressional staff report explained:

> [W]ith respect to alleged sexual assault crimes, the 13 alleged crimes publicly reported [in the Cruise Line Incident

---

Q: I mean, before you go into it, you're telling me they didn't have an obligation to take reasonable efforts, measures, to protect the passengers from that?

A: Of course. Under the law their obligation is to provide reasonable care under the circumstances, and that applies in this case just as it would in any other negligence case.

Oral Argument at 11:30–14:14, *K.T. v. Royal Caribbean Cruises, Ltd.*, No. 17-14237 (11th Cir. Nov. 7, 2018).

[2] These numbers do not include any of the complaints of sexual assaults by passengers that are contained in the Cruise Line Incident Reports for the fourth quarter of 2015 — the quarter in which K.T. embarked on the cruise in question. I have excluded from the totals those last quarter numbers to ensure that no alleged rapes that occurred after K.T.'s were included.

Reports] in 2011 represented only 31% of the 42 alleged crimes reported to the FBI, and in 2012 the 11 alleged crimes publicly reported represented only 38% of the 28 alleged crimes reported to the FBI. [—18—]

Staff of S. Comm. on Commerce, Science, and Transp., 113 Cong., Cruise Ship Crime: Consumers Have Incomplete Access to Cruise Crime Data 11 (2013).

The reports this Court cited in *Doe v. Princess Cruise Lines, Ltd.*, 657 F.3d 1204 (11th Cir. 2011), also support K.T.'s allegations that Royal Caribbean was on notice a decade before K.T.'s cruise that sexual assaults on cruise ships were a serious problem. In that opinion we stated:

> Unfortunately, if congressional reports are to be believed, sexual assaults and other violent crimes on cruise ships are a serious problem. The House Subcommittee on Coast Guard and Maritime Transportation Staff has reported that:
>
> > At a hearing in March 2006 convened by the Committee on Government Reform, cruise industry executives testified that 178 passengers on North American cruises reported being sexually assaulted between 2003 and 2005. During that same period, 24 people were reported missing and four others reported being robbed.
> >
> > From fiscal year 2000 through June 2005, the FBI opened 305 case files involving "crime on the high seas," {–1050–} and during those five years about 45% of those cases were sexual assaults that occurred on cruise ships.
> >
> > Salvador Hernandez, Deputy Assistant Director of the FBI, testified before Congress in 2007 about sexual and other physical assaults that have taken place on

cruise ships: "Sexual assault and physical assaults on cruise ships were the leading crime reported to and investigated by the FBI on the high seas over the last five years, 55 percent and 22 percent respectively . . . ."

Id. at 1208 n.4 (citations omitted). [—19—]

All of this data supplements the allegations contained in the complaint and reinforces the conclusion that the complaint states a valid claim and adequately pleads that, among other things, Royal Caribbean knew or should have known that there was a serious problem of violent crime, including passenger-on-passenger sexual assaults, on cruise ships including its own. The Cruise Line Incident Reports, after all, are based in part on information Royal Caribbean itself submitted. And it would be absurd to suggest that a multi-billion dollar business like Royal Caribbean was not aware of congressional reports about the problem of sexual assaults aboard its cruise ships.

The allegations of the complaint alone are enough to state a cause of action. If anything else were needed, the reports of which we can take judicial notice would provide it.

United States Court of Appeals for the Eleventh Circuit

No. 18-11815

CVORO
vs.
CARNIVAL CORP.

Appeal from the United States District Court for the Southern District of Florida

Decided: October 17, 2019

Citation: 941 F.3d 487, 7 Adm. R. 515 (11th Cir. 2019).

Before **ROSENBAUM**, **GRANT**, and **HULL**, Circuit Judges.

[—1—] {–490–} HULL, Circuit Judge: [—2—]

Plaintiff Sladjana Cvoro appeals the district court's denial of her petition to "vacate and/or alternatively to deny recognition and enforcement" of the foreign arbitral award in favor of her employer, defendant Carnival Corporation d.b.a. Carnival Cruise Lines ("Carnival"), on Cvoro's claims brought under the Jones Act, 46 U.S.C. § 30104, and U.S. maritime law for injuries related to the carpal tunnel syndrome she developed while working on a Carnival cruise ship. The district court denied Cvoro's petition because, even though the arbitrator did not apply U.S. law during arbitration, enforcing the foreign arbitral award did not violate U.S. public policy. After careful review of the unique factual circumstances of this case and with the benefit of oral argument, we must affirm.

I. FACTUAL BACKGROUND

A. Seafarer's Employment Agreement

In August 2012, Cvoro, who is a citizen and resident of Serbia, signed a seafarer's employment agreement (the "seafarer's agreement") to work for Carnival. Carnival is a Panamanian corporation that operates cruise ships with its principal place of business in Miami, Florida. *Everett v. Carnival Cruise Lines*, 912 F.2d 1355, 1357 (11th Cir. 1990).

In her seafarer's agreement, as a condition of her employment, Cvoro agreed to resolve all legal disputes with Carnival by arbitration. Specifically, Cvoro's seafarer's agreement contains mandatory-arbitration and forum-selection clauses, [—3—] which provide that "[t]he place of arbitration shall be London, England, Monaco, Panama City, Panama or Manila, Philippines whichever is closer to the Seafarer's home country." Her seafarer's agreement also contains a choice-of-law clause designating the governing {–491–} law for disputes as the laws of the flag of the cruise ship on which Cvoro was assigned:

> *Governing Law.* This Agreement shall be governed by, and all disputes arising under or in connection with this Agreement of Seafarer's service on the vessel shall be resolved in accordance with, the laws of the flag of the vessel on which Seafarer is assigned at the time the cause of action accrues, without regard to principles of conflicts of laws thereunder. The parties agree to this governing law notwithstanding any claims for negligence, unseaworthiness, maintenance, cure, failure to provide prompt, proper and adequate medical care, wages, personal injury, or property damage which might be available under the laws of any other jurisdiction.

Cvoro does not dispute that she entered into this seafarer's agreement or what its terms say.

B. Cvoro's Employment on the *Carnival Dream*

Beginning in August 2012, Carnival employed Cvoro as a seaman to work as an assistant waitress aboard the cruise ship *Carnival Dream*, which sails under the flag of Panama. During her employment, Cvoro developed pain and swelling in her left wrist. On March 28, 2013, Cvoro reported to the shipboard medical center, complaining of pain and swelling in her left wrist, and "pins and needles" in her wrist and hand. The ship's physician gave Cvoro a splint and prescribed her prednisone to stop the swelling. [—4—]

The next day, Cvoro returned to the medical center with the same left wrist pain, which was getting worse. This time, the physician prescribed her ketorolac and naproxen to treat the pain. Despite this treatment, Cvoro's condition did not improve. On March 31, 2013, Cvoro went to the medical center a third time for her wrist pain, at which point the ship's physician determined that she could no longer carry out her duties aboard the ship. Cvoro was taken off duty the next day.

On April 1, 2013, Cvoro was examined by an orthopedic specialist ashore in Cozumel, Mexico, who diagnosed her as having carpal tunnel syndrome. Thereafter, Cvoro stopped working on the *Carnival Dream*, and upon her own request, defendant Carnival repatriated her home to Serbia.

To comply with its maintenance and cure obligations under maritime law, Carnival selected shore-side physicians in Serbia to continue treating Cvoro's condition. On May 28, 2013, a doctor selected by Carnival performed surgery on Cvoro for her carpal tunnel syndrome. According to Cvoro, shortly after her surgery, she began experiencing horrific symptoms due to the negligence of the Serbian doctors, and she was eventually diagnosed with complex regional pain syndrome. After further treatment from a variety of specialists in Europe, on June 30, 2014, Cvoro's physicians declared her to have reached maximum medical improvement. But to date, Cvoro suffers from gross motor deficits in her left hand [—5—] and wrist, frozen shoulder, tendonitis of the wrist, and other permanent problems with her left arm.

C. Arbitration in Monaco

Pursuant to her seafarer's agreement, Cvoro filed an arbitration proceeding against Carnival in Monaco—the venue closest to her home country Serbia—in an attempt to recover for her injuries. She asserted two claims based on U.S. law. First, Cvoro brought a claim under the Jones Act, 46 U.S.C. § 30104, asserting that Carnival was vicariously liable for the alleged negligence of the shore-side doctors it selected to treat her

carpal tunnel syndrome. Second, Cvoro asserted a claim {–492–} under general maritime law, that is, the doctrine of maintenance and cure, for Carnival's alleged failure to provide her with medical treatment and to pay for her medical bills and room and board. This second claim was later dropped because Carnival had in fact paid for all of Cvoro's medical bills and expenses for room and board.

D. Panamanian Law Governed Arbitration

As a preliminary matter, the arbitrator determined that Panamanian law governed the arbitration proceeding because, in the choice-of-law clause of the seafarer's agreement, the parties agreed that the law of Panama would apply. Panama is where the *Carnival Dream* is flagged. The arbitrator concluded further that Cvoro did not establish that U.S. law should apply, notwithstanding the [—6—] choice-of-law clause, because there was not a sufficiently close connection between the dispute and the United States. In reaching this conclusion, the arbitrator noted that: (1) Cvoro was in Serbia; (2) Carnival is incorporated in Panama; (3) the *Carnival Dream* was flagged in Panama at all relevant times; (4) the parties chose Panamanian law to govern the dispute; (5) the seat of the arbitration was Monaco; (6) there was no evidence that the *Carnival Dream* was in U.S. territorial waters when the alleged cause of action accrued; and (7) Cvoro did not allege that the United States was the only venue for enforcing an arbitral award against Carnival in the event that she prevailed. In fact, the only connection between the dispute and the United States was that Carnival's principal place of business is in Miami, which the arbitrator deemed insufficient to disregard the parties' valid agreement to apply Panamanian law.

Despite this ruling, Cvoro persisted in arguing that her claim was based solely on U.S. law—that is, a Jones Act claim that Carnival was vicariously liable for the negligence of the shore-side physicians in Serbia that it selected to treat her carpal tunnel syndrome. Cvoro even invited the arbitrator to find in favor of Carnival because, she contended, she had no cause of action under Panamanian law. On that score, it is undisputed that Panamanian law does not recognize a claim based on vicarious liability for shore-side malpractice occurring after a seaman leaves the vessel. [—7—]

As the parties' experts at arbitration generally agreed, Panamanian law recognizes that Cvoro, as a seafarer who was injured aboard a vessel, has a labor (contractual) cause of action and a tort cause of action for negligence against Carnival. The labor claim under Panamanian law is akin to a no-fault maintenance and cure claim under U.S. law. Panamanian law also recognizes a claim related to disability compensation for any occupational injury or illness irrespective of fault, but Cvoro did not pursue this remedy. In addition, Panamanian law recognizes a seafarer's action for the negligence of her employer or the shipowner, such as a claim for Carnival's negligent hiring of the shore-side physicians. But Cvoro did not pursue a direct negligence claim against Carnival either.

E. Arbitrator's Final Award

Even though Cvoro conceded that she had not pursued any cause of action under Panamanian law, in its final award, the arbitrator examined Cvoro's possible claims under Panamanian law, based on both labor and tort law. First, as to a claim for maintenance and cure, the arbitrator found that such a claim failed because Cvoro did not contest that Carnival satisfied its obligations to provide assistance, room and board, and medical care. As to a disability claim, the arbitrator determined that, because Cvoro's claim was based {–493–} solely on the medical negligence of the shore-side physicians in Serbia, which occurred after she signed off the *Carnival Dream*, Carnival had no obligation to pay any disability. [—8—] Moreover, the arbitrator concluded that Cvoro's tort-based claim failed because she did not establish that Carnival was directly negligent in any way. Accordingly, the arbitrator dismissed Cvoro's claims.

II. PROCEDURAL HISTORY

A. District Court Proceedings

In May 2016, Cvoro filed the instant suit in the district court in the United States District Court for the Southern District of Florida, seeking to (1) "vacate and/or alternatively to deny recognition and enforcement" of the arbitral award under Article V of the Convention on the Recognition and Enforcement of Foreign Arbitral Awards (the "New York Convention" or the "Convention")[1] (Count I) and (2) then litigate the merits of her Jones Act claim based on Carnival's alleged vicarious liability for the malpractice of the shore-side doctors it selected to treat her (Count II) and an overlapping claim under general maritime law for damages caused by the doctors' malpractice (Count III).[2] After preliminary motions, the district court bifurcated the proceeding to adjudicate first the threshold and [—9—] potentially dispositive issue of Cvoro's request that the district court refuse to enforce the arbitral award.

In further briefing on the issue, Cvoro argued that the arbitral award was void as being against U.S. public policy because the arbitrator applied Panamanian law, not U.S. law, which deprived her of the opportunity to assert a Jones Act claim against Carnival for vicarious liability. The arbitrator's final award, therefore, refused to give her the Jones Act remedy available in the United States, to which she was entitled as a seafarer. On this basis, Cvoro argued that enforcing the final arbitral award violated U.S. public policy and thus must be vacated under Article V(2)(b) of the New York Convention.

---

[1] The Convention on the Recognition and Enforcement of Foreign Arbitral Awards is commonly known as the New York Convention. *See* New York Convention, June 10, 1958, 21 U.S.T. 2517, 330 U.N.T.S. 38.

[2] Because Cvoro's request to deny recognition and enforcement of the foreign arbitral award under the New York Convention was only ancillary to her Jones Act and general maritime law claims, we need not contemplate, and do not decide, whether the district court would have had subject matter jurisdiction had Cvoro solely moved to vacate the foreign arbitral award.

In response, Carnival contended, *inter alia,* that the district court should deny the petition to vacate the arbitral award because: (1) Cvoro had a meaningful remedy in arbitration under Panamanian law; and (2) Cvoro's arguments did not overcome the clear federal interest in enforcing arbitration awards under the New York Convention.

In April 2018, the district court issued its order denying Cvoro's request that it refuse to enforce the arbitral award and dismissing her claims brought under the Jones Act and general maritime law. In assessing whether the arbitrator's dismissal of Cvoro's Jones Act claim violated U.S. public policy, the district court identified three American public policies that were at play. First, the United States [—10—] has a strong federal policy favoring arbitration, which applies with special force in the field of international commerce. Second, the United States has an explicit, well-defined, and dominant public policy extending "special solicitude" to seamen, who are considered "wards of admiralty." And third, the Supreme Court has rejected the notion that {–494–} all disputes must be resolved under U.S. law, even where foreign law provides a lesser remedy.

The district court then concluded that the distinctions between Panamanian law and U.S. law did not overcome the strong federal presumption to enforce arbitral awards, especially because Cvoro's theory of vicarious liability is not an explicitly "well-defined and dominant" U.S. policy "rooted in basic notions of morality and justice." Of significance, the district court highlighted that Cvoro never attempted to pursue any remedies under Panamanian law, so the court could not say that the remedies during arbitration were so inadequate as to render the proceeding and its result unfair. The district court therefore determined that Cvoro did not establish that enforcing the arbitral award would violate U.S. public policy.

This appeal followed.

B. Monaco Court Confirms Arbitral Award

Meanwhile, after Cvoro initiated this lawsuit in the district court, and while it was still pending there, defendant Carnival instituted a parallel proceeding in the seat of the arbitration, Monaco, seeking confirmation of the arbitral award. On [—11—] March 21, 2019, the court of first instance in Monaco issued final judgment in favor of Carnival confirming the arbitral award because: (1) the seafarer's agreement was valid and enforceable under Monegasque law and the New York Convention; and (2) Cvoro did not provide evidence that the arbitral award was invalid as contrary to Panamanian law or Monaco's international public policy.

III. STANDARD OF REVIEW

In reviewing a district court's decision regarding the enforcement of a foreign arbitral award, we review its "findings of fact for clear error and its legal conclusions *de novo.*" *Inversiones y Procesadora Tropical INPROTSA, S.A. v. Del Monte Int'l GmbH,* 921 F.3d 1291, 1304 n.17 (11th Cir. 2019) (quotation omitted); *see also Indus. Risk Insurers v. M.A.N. Gutehoffnungshutte GmbH,* 141 F.3d 1434, 1443 (11th Cir. 1998) (requiring *de novo* review of whether admission of expert testimony at arbitration violated U.S. public policy).

IV. NEW YORK CONVENTION

A. New York Convention, Generally

We begin with the New York Convention, which Cvoro relies upon in arguing that the district court erred in denying her petition to vacate the arbitral award. In 1958, the United Nations Economic and Social Council adopted the New York Convention. *Lindo v. NCL (Bahamas), Ltd.,* 652 F.3d 1257, 1262 (11th Cir. 2011). In 1970, the United States acceded to the Convention, which was [—12—] implemented that same year by Chapter 2 of the Federal Arbitration Act ("FAA"), 9 U.S.C. § 201 *et seq. See* 9 U.S.C. § 201 ("The Convention on the Recognition and Enforcement of Foreign Arbitral Awards of

June 10, 1958, shall be enforced in United States courts in accordance with this chapter."); *Mitsubishi Motors Corp. v. Soler Chrysler-Plymouth, Inc.*, 473 U.S. 614, 631, 105 S. Ct. 3346, 3356 (1985).

The Convention requires that contracting states, such as the United States, recognize written arbitration agreements concerning subject matter capable of settlement by arbitration:

> Each Contracting State shall recognize an agreement in writing under which the parties undertake to submit to arbitration all or any differences which have arisen or which may arise between them in respect of a defined legal relationship, {–495–} whether contractual or not, concerning a subject matter capable of settlement by arbitration.

New York Convention, art. II(1).

The U.S. Supreme Court has explained that "the principal purpose" behind the adoption of the Convention "was to encourage the recognition and enforcement of commercial arbitration agreements in international contracts and to unify the standards by which agreements to arbitrate are observed and arbitral awards are enforced in the signatory countries." *Scherk v. Alberto–Culver Co.*, 417 U.S. 506, 520 n.15, 94 S. Ct. 2449, 2457 n.15 (1974). By encouraging the recognition and enforcement of international arbitration agreements and awards, the Convention "relieve[s] congestion in the courts and . . . provide[s] parties with an alternative [—13—] method for dispute resolution that [is] speedier and less costly than litigation." *Indus. Risk Insurers*, 141 F.3d at 1440 (quotation omitted) (final alteration in original). In that vein, the Supreme Court has emphasized that the United States has a "federal policy in favor of arbitral dispute resolution" which "appl[ies] with special force in the field of international commerce." *Mitsubishi Motors*, 473 U.S. at 631, 105 S. Ct. at 3356.

To that end and as relevant here, the FAA creates two causes of action in federal court regarding an international arbitration agreement that falls under the New York Convention. First, a party may file a motion to compel that arbitration be held in accordance with an arbitration agreement. 9 U.S.C. § 206; *Suazo v. NCL (Bahamas), Ltd.*, 822 F.3d 543, 546, 4 Adm. R. 446, 447 (11th Cir. 2016). Second, after arbitration is completed, a party may file a motion to confirm the arbitral award, at which time the opposing party may raise a particular set of defenses as to whether the district court should enforce the arbitral award. 9 U.S.C. § 207; *Lindo*, 652 F.3d at 1280 (explaining that defenses to the enforcement of an arbitral award may be raised at the arbitration-award-enforcement stage in actions brought under 9 U.S.C. § 207). This case concerns only the latter cause of action.

At this arbitration-award-enforcement stage, a district court must confirm the arbitral award unless a party "successfully assert[s] one of the seven defenses against enforcement of the award enumerated in Article V of the New York [—14—] Convention." *Indus. Risk Insurers*, 141 F.3d at 1441; *see also* 9 U.S.C. § 207; New York Convention, art. III. Here, Cvoro invoked only one of the seven defenses listed in Article V— that enforcement of the arbitral award would be contrary to the public policy of the United States. The party opposing enforcement of the award, here Cvoro, has the burden of proving that Article V defense discussed below. *Indus. Risk Insurers*, 141 F.3d at 1442; *Imperial Ethiopian Gov't v. Baruch-Foster Corp.*, 535 F.2d 334, 335–36 (5th Cir. 1976).

B. Article V(2)(b): Public-Policy Defense

The New York Convention's public-policy defense, Article V(2)(b), states that enforcement of an arbitral award "may . . . be refused if the competent authority in the country where . . . enforcement is sought finds that . . . recognition or enforcement of the award would be contrary to the public policy of that country." New York Convention, art. V(2)(b); *see also Vimar Seguros y Reaseguros, S.A. v. M/V Sky Reefer*, 515 U.S. 528, 540, 115

S. Ct. 2322, 2330 (1995) ("'A court in the United States need not recognize a judgment of the court of a foreign state if . . . the judgment itself, is repugnant to the public policy of the United States.'" (alteration in original) (quoting 1 {-496-} Restatement (Third) of Foreign Relations Law of the United States § 482(2)(d) (1986))).

"[T]he public-policy defense under the Convention is very narrow" and is likewise to be construed narrowly in light of the presumption favoring enforcement [—15—] of international arbitral awards. *Inversiones y Procesadora*, 921 F.3d at 1306; *Indus. Risk Insurers*, 141 F.3d at 1445. The defense applies to only violations of an "explicit public policy" that is "well-defined and dominant" and is ascertained "by reference to the laws and legal precedents and not from general considerations of supposed public interests." *Indus. Risk Insurers*, 141 F.3d at 1445 (internal quotation marks omitted) (citing *Drummond Coal Co. v. United Mine Workers, Dist. 20*, 748 F.2d 1495, 1499 (11th Cir. 1984)).

Moreover, the public-policy defense "applies only when confirmation or enforcement of a foreign arbitration award would violate the forum state's most basic notions of morality and justice." *Inversiones y Procesadora*, 921 F.3d at 1306 (internal quotation marks omitted) (quoting *Bamberger Rosenheim, Ltd., (Israel) v. OA Dev., Inc., (United States)*, 862 F.3d 1284, 1289 n.4 (11th Cir. 2017). Consequently, "[a]lthough this defense is frequently raised, it 'has rarely been successful.'" *Ministry of Def. & Support for the Armed Forces of the Islamic Republic of Iran v. Cubic Def. Sys., Inc.*, 665 F.3d 1091, 1097 (9th Cir. 2011) (quoting Andrew M. Campbell, Annotation, *Refusal to Enforce Foreign Arbitration Awards on Public Policy Grounds*, 144 A.L.R. Fed. 481 (1998 & supp.)); *see, e.g., Indus. Risk Insurers*, 141 F.3d at 1444–45 (rejecting a party's public-policy defense against enforcement of an arbitral award because the violation alleged—the side-switching of an expert witness during arbitration—was [—16—] not so "well-defined and dominant" to rise to the level of a "public policy of the sort required to sustain a defense

under article V(b)(2) of the New York Convention").

V. DISCUSSION

On appeal, Cvoro argues that the arbitral award should not be enforced because enforcement is contrary to the United States' explicit public policy with respect to the protection of seamen, who have long been treated as wards of admiralty. According to Cvoro, this public policy was articulated by Congress in the expansive protections afforded to seamen as part of the Jones Act, which includes providing seamen with a cause of action against their employer based on the vicarious liability for injuries sustained due to the negligence of their employer's agents. *See* 46 U.S.C. § 30104 (incorporating the provisions of the Federal Employers' Liability Act applicable to railway workers, including 45 U.S.C. § 51, which holds an employer vicariously liable for the negligence of its agents); *Hopson v. Texaco, Inc.*, 383 U.S. 262, 264, 86 S. Ct. 765, 766 (1966). Relying on a footnote in *Mitsubishi Motors*, Cvoro maintains that because she was deprived of this Jones Act remedy during arbitration, the arbitral award violates U.S. public policy, rendering it unenforceable in the United States under Article V(2)(b) of the Convention. *See Mitsubishi Motors*, 473 U.S. at 637 n.19, 105 S. Ct. at 3359 n.19. [—17—]

A. Relevant Caselaw

Our Court has never addressed at this arbitration-award-enforcement stage whether depriving a seaman of a Jones Act remedy violates U.S. public policy for purposes of the Article V(2)(b) defense. However, two of our decisions provide substantial guidance. {-497-}

First, in *Lipcon v. Underwriters at Lloyd's, London*, 148 F.3d 1285 (11th Cir. 1998), we addressed the "question of whether the anti-waiver provisions of the United States securities laws preclude enforcement of certain choice-of-law and forum-selection clauses . . . in international agreements." *Id.* at 1287. Acknowledging that choice clauses "may operate in tandem as a prospective waiver of the statutory remedies for securities violations," this Court nevertheless held that the choice clauses were enforceable and not contrary to public policy. *Id.* at 1287, 1298 (internal quotation omitted). In so ruling, we examined whether the English remedies were inadequate, given that English law contained no direct analogues to the U.S. Securities Act for securities registration violations. *Id.* at 1297. We recognized numerous ways in which English securities law allegedly provided inferior remedies as compared to U.S. law. *Id.* at 1297–98. Despite the fact that "the United States securities laws would provide [appellants] with a greater variety of defendants and a greater chance of success due to lighter scienter [—18—] and causation requirements," we refused to invalidate the choice clauses "simply because the remedies available in the contractually chosen forum are less favorable than those available in the courts of the United States." *Id.* at 1297 (quotation omitted) (alteration in original). "Instead, we will declare unenforceable choice clauses only when the remedies available in the chosen forum are so inadequate that enforcement would be fundamentally unfair." *Id.*

More recently, in *Lindo*, our Court confronted a similar issue as here regarding waiver of a seaman's Jones Act remedy in arbitration, albeit at the earlier arbitration-enforcement stage. In *Lindo*, the seafarer, Harold Lindo, brought a Jones Act claim against his employer, the cruise line operator NCL (Bahamas) Ltd. ("NCL"), in Florida state court, alleging that he had injured his back while lifting trash bags at work. 652 F.3d at 1260–61. The employment agreement between NCL and Lindo required that such claims be arbitrated in Nicaragua (the country where Lindo was a citizen) and that the law of the Bahamas (the law of the vessel) would apply. *Id.* at 1261. NCL removed the case to federal court and then moved to compel arbitration, which the district court granted. *Id.* at 1261–62. Lindo appealed, arguing, *inter alia*, that the application of Bahamian law in the arbitral forum would eliminate his U.S. statutory claim under the Jones Act. *Id.* at 1263–64. Therefore, according to Lindo, compelling arbitration would violate public

policy under the New York Convention. *Id.* [—19—]

This Court affirmed the district court's order compelling arbitration. First, we extensively examined a series of cases where the Supreme Court and this Court enforced forum-selection and choice-of-law clauses in contracts that required application of non-American law in suit or arbitration. *Lindo*, 652 F.3d at 1264–69. For starters, in *M/S Bremen v. Zapata Off-Shore Co.*, 407 U.S. 1, 92 S. Ct. 1907 (1972), the Supreme Court "announced a strong presumption in favor of enforcing such forum-selection clauses, despite the possibility that a markedly different result would be obtained if the case proceeded in English courts as opposed to American Courts." *Lindo*, 652 F.3d at 1264. Two years later, in *Scherk v. Alberto–Culver Co.*, 417 U.S. 506, 94 S. Ct. 2449 (1974), the Supreme Court "recognized that U.S. statutory claims are amenable to arbitral resolution—even U.S. statutory claims containing anti-waiver provisions." *Lindo*, 652 F.3d at 1264–65. After reviewing these cases and others, we distilled from the Supreme Court precedents several overarching themes applicable {–498–} to agreements requiring the application of non-American law in international arbitrations:

> (1) courts should apply a strong presumption in favor of enforcement of arbitration and choice clauses; (2) U.S. statutory claims are arbitrable, unless Congress has specifically legislated otherwise; (3) *choice-of-law clauses may be enforced even if the substantive law applied in arbitration potentially provides reduced remedies (or fewer defenses) than those available under U.S. law*; and (4) even if a contract expressly says that foreign law governs . . . courts should not invalidate an arbitration agreement at the arbitration-enforcement stage on the basis of speculation about what the arbitrator will do, as there will be a later opportunity to review any arbitral award. [—20—]

Id. at 1265-69 (emphasis added). The *Lindo* Court then concluded that Lindo could not raise the public-policy defense under Article V(2)(b) at that time, because that defense "applies only at the arbitral award-enforcement stage and not at the arbitration-enforcement stage." *Id.* at 1280.

Nevertheless, we assumed *arguendo* that Lindo could raise the Article V(2)(b) public-policy defense at the arbitration-enforcement stage, and this Court said that his challenge to the arbitration agreement—that it was void as against public policy because he would be prevented from asserting his Jones Act claim under Bahamian law—would still fail. *Id.* at 1283–84. This is because "(1) Bahamian law itself recognizes negligence actions; and (2) even if, as Lindo claims, U.S. law under the Jones Act has a more relaxed causation standard for negligence claims than Bahamian law, these were precisely the same arguments lodged (and rejected) in *Lipcon*." *Id.* at 1283. Moreover, Lindo did not show that international arbitration under Bahamian negligence law would provide an inadequate remedy such that enforcement of the choice-of-law provision would be "fundamentally unfair." *Id.* at 1283–84. Finally, this Court observed that Lindo's position would effectively eviscerate the mutually binding nature of the New York Convention because every country could refuse to recognize valid, mutually agreed-upon arbitration provisions if they contemplate the application of foreign law. *Id.* at 1284–85. [—21—]

B. Competing Public Policies at Issue

Against this legal framework, we will now consider the competing public policies at issue in this case. First, we agree with Cvoro that the United States has an "explicit public policy that is well-defined and dominant" with respect to the solicitude of seamen. *Indus. Risk Insurers*, 141 F.3d at 1445 (quotations omitted). American courts have long acted to protect the interests of seafarers, including "from the harsh consequences of arbitrary and unscrupulous action of their employers, to which, as a class, they are peculiarly exposed." *Collie v. Fergusson*, 281 U.S. 52, 55, 50 S. Ct. 189, 191 (1930); *see also Aguilar v. Standard*

Oil Co. of N.J., 318 U.S. 724, 727–28, 63 S. Ct. 930, 932–33 (1943) ("[W]ith the combined object of encouraging marine commerce and assuring the well-being of seamen, maritime nations uniformly have imposed broad responsibilities for their health and safety upon the owners of ships. In this country these notions were reflected early, and have since been expanded, in legislation designed to secure the comfort and health of seamen aboard ship[.]"). For instance, when a seaman falls ill or suffers an injury in the service of the ship, maritime law requires her employer or the shipowner to provide "maintenance and cure of the seaman for illness or injury {–499–} during the period of the voyage, and in some cases for a period thereafter." *Cent. Gulf Steamship Corp. v. Sambula*, 405 F.2d 291, 300 (5th Cir. 1968). [—22—]

Second, when assessing whether enforcing an arbitral award violates public policy, we also must consider that the United States has a "federal policy in favor of arbitral dispute resolution" which "applies with special force in the field of international commerce." *Mitsubishi Motors*, 473 U.S. at 631, 105 S. Ct. at 3356. Third, we also recognize that "[t]he Supreme Court has rejected the 'concept that all disputes must be resolved under our laws and in our courts,' even when remedies under foreign law do not comport with American standards of justice." *Asignacion v. Rickmers Genoa Schiffahrtsgesellschaft MBH & CIE KG*, 783 F.3d 1010, 1017, 3 Adm. R. 304, 307 (5th Cir. 2015) (quoting *M/S Bremen*, 407 U.S. at 9, 92 S. Ct. at 1912–13 (1972)). The Supreme Court has admonished: "To determine that 'American standards of fairness' . . . must [apply] . . . demeans the standards of justice elsewhere in the world, and unnecessarily exalts the primacy of United States law over the laws of other countries." *Scherk*, 417 U.S. at 517 n.11, 94 S. Ct. at 2456 n.11. Indeed, as we intimated in *Lindo*, United States public policy does not necessarily disfavor applying foreign law during arbitration, even when the foreign law provides a seaman with reduced or different remedies than those available under U.S. law. *Lindo*, 652 F.3d at 1264–69, 1283–85.

And fourth, we may consider the fact that the Monaco court already has confirmed the arbitral award in this case, which weighs in favor of enforcement here. That is because we take into account "concerns of international comity, [—23—] respect for the capacities of foreign and transnational tribunals, and sensitivity to the need of the international commercial system for predictability in the resolution of disputes[,] . . . even assuming that a contrary result would be forthcoming in a domestic context." *Mitsubishi Motors*, 473 U.S. at 629, 105 S. Ct. at 3355.

C. Analysis of Public-Policy Defense

Weighing the policies at issue and considering the specific unique factual circumstances of this case, we must conclude that Cvoro's Article V(2)(b) defense fails. Cvoro's public-policy defense hinges on the adequacy of remedies under Panamanian law afforded to her as a seaman. We acknowledge that the arbitrator in Monaco dismissed Cvoro's Jones Act claim, awarding her nothing. We also acknowledge that, if Cvoro were to prevail in a suit under United States law based on Carnival's vicarious liability for the negligence of the shore-side physicians who treated her, she may well recover money damages. But that likelihood, in and of itself, does not render the arbitral award unenforceable. Nor does it mean that a U.S. claim must be available. As we have explained, simply because a foreign arbitral award provides for a smaller recovery than may have been available under United States maritime law does not necessarily mean the award violates public policy. *See Lindo*, 652 F.3d at 1283–87.

Cvoro argues that her case is distinguishable from *Lindo* and other similar precedent because she did not receive merely a smaller recovery in arbitration, she [—24—] was awarded no recovery at all. That is not entirely correct. The arbitral award does not represent the sum total of Carnival's obligations to Cvoro, nor is it an accounting of monetary benefits that Cvoro received from Carnival for her carpal tunnel syndrome. To be sure, in the arbitration, Cvoro initially brought a separate claim for maintenance and

cure. But Cvoro later agreed that Carnival had, in fact, {–500–} complied with its maintenance and cure obligations under Panamanian law, including paying for her medical bills, room and board, and living expenses while under medical care. As a result, Cvoro dropped this maintenance and cure claim in her arbitration, as it was no longer necessary or valid.

In this regard, Cvoro obtained many of the benefits to which she would be entitled under U.S. law: Carnival treated Cvoro's carpal tunnel syndrome after it manifested in March 2013, repatriated Cvoro home to Serbia, arranged for continued medical care, and paid for ongoing maintenance and cure during her recovery to the point when her physician declared her to have reached maximum medical improvement in June 2014. As such, Cvoro's contention that Panamanian law did not afford her any remedy for her injuries is unavailing. Although not listed in the final arbitral award, Carnival paid for Cvoro's full maintenance and cure benefits.

Furthermore, Panamanian law itself provides Cvoro, as a seaman, with additional remedies that she never pursued in arbitration. First, Panamanian law [—25—] provides a seafarer who was injured aboard a vessel with an action for the negligence of a shipowner, including for negligently referring a seaman to a physician. Cvoro did not pursue this claim because she "ha[d] no affirmative proof that [Carnival] acted negligently other than simply choosing the physician in this case."

Second, Panamanian law also provides a seafarer who suffers an incapacity or disability with a claim related to disability compensation for any occupational injury or illness irrespective of fault. Cvoro did not pursue this remedy either. We recognize that the arbitrator found that Cvoro would not be entitled to those disability benefits because her claim was based solely on the medical negligence of the shore-side physicians. In particular, the arbitrator reasoned that, under Panamanian law, Carnival would not be obligated to pay disability in connection with this "new" injury sustained after she signed off the ship, as such disability claims must be based on an "occupational hazard" while onboard the *Carnival Dream*. But significantly, Cvoro never sought disability benefits at all, including benefits based on the wrist injuries she developed while working onboard the *Carnival Dream* and before the surgery.

And third, to the extent that Cvoro now argues that she did not reach maximum medical improvement in June 2014 and has unmet medical needs that Carnival should pay for, Cvoro did not advance this position during arbitration [—26—] either. To the contrary, she dropped her maintenance and cure claim, conceding that Carnival had complied with its obligation to pay for her medical bills. Given these potential avenues for recovery under Panamanian law and Cvoro's failure to fully employ them, we cannot say that the remedies available to her were so inadequate as to render the arbitration proceedings and arbitral award fundamentally unfair.

The primary relevant distinction between Panamanian and U.S. law is that Panamanian law does not recognize a claim that Carnival was vicariously liable for the negligence of the shore-side physicians that it selected to treat Cvoro, whereas U.S. law does. Cvoro contends that enforcement of the arbitral award violates the public policy of the United States because the arbitrator deprived her of this Jones Act remedy.

The problem for Cvoro is that the arbitral award here was not so inadequate as to violate this nation's "most basic notions of morality and justice." *See Inversiones y Procesadora*, 921 F.3d at 1306. The record does not show that Carnival took advantage {-501-} of Cvoro in its handling of her injuries or otherwise saddled her with maintenance and cure expenses. Instead, the evidence shows that Carnival promptly treated Cvoro's wrist condition, took her off duty when the treatment did not work, and repatriated her home to Serbia while continuing to provide her with maintenance and cure benefits until she reached maximum [—27—] medical improvement for what was ultimately diagnosed to be carpal tunnel syndrome.

Moreover, Cvoro does not claim that Carnival was negligent in hiring the Serbian doctors who continued to treat her carpal tunnel syndrome and, in fact, admits that Carnival was not negligent in hiring the specific Serbian doctor who performed surgery on her wrist.[3]

At bottom, Cvoro's argument that we must refuse to enforce the award because she was deprived of a statutory remedy against Carnival is precisely the same argument that we rejected in *Lipcon. Lipcon*, 148 F.3d at 1297 ("We have little doubt that the United States securities laws would provide [appellants] with a greater variety of defendants and a greater chance of success due to lighter scienter and causation requirements . . . . We will not invalidate choice clauses, however, simply because the remedies available in the contractually chosen forum are less favorable than those available in the courts of the United States.") (alterations in original) (internal quotations and citations omitted). As in *Lipcon*, here, we may not refuse to enforce the arbitral award simply because the remedies available under Panamanian law are less favorable to Cvoro than the remedies available [—28—] under U.S. law. And, as detailed above, the remedies available to Cvoro under Panamanian law are not "so inadequate that enforcement would be fundamentally unfair." *Id.*

D. *Mitsubishi Motors* Does Not Help Cvoro

Contrary to Cvoro's assertion, the Supreme Court in *Mitsubishi Motors* did not establish that a public policy violation has occurred

[3] Cvoro concedes that claiming that Carnival was negligent in selecting the Serbian doctor who performed her surgery would have been frivolous based on documents produced by Carnival, which establish: (1) the doctor graduated from a major urban medical school in Yugoslavia in 1976; (2) after completing a three-year internship, the doctor passed his specialized exams in plastic and reconstructive surgery, which are the European equivalent to board certification; and (3) the doctor received additional training at a university hospital in Yugoslavia and Germany before returning to Serbia where he was a practicing surgeon for over 20 years prior to the subject incident.

under the Convention when a party is deprived of a federal statutory claim in arbitration. Cvoro's argument is based on dictum from a footnote in *Mitsubishi Motors*, from which the "prospective waiver doctrine" originated.

In *Mitsubishi Motors*, the Supreme Court deemed enforceable an arbitration clause requiring the parties to arbitrate antitrust claims arising from the Sherman Act in Japan. 473 U.S. at 616–24, 628–29, 105 S. Ct. at 3348–52, 3354–55. The Court held that a party is bound by its agreement to arbitrate U.S. statutory claims unless Congress has precluded arbitration as to that subject matter. *Id.* at 627–28, 105 S. Ct. at 3354–55. Even though it was clear in that case that U.S. law would apply to the antitrust claims during arbitration, in a footnote, the Supreme Court noted a willingness to condemn, on "public policy" grounds, an arbitration agreement that has "choice-of-forum and choice-of-law clauses [that] operate[] in tandem as a prospective waiver of a party's right to pursue statutory remedies for antitrust violations." {–502–} *Id.* at 637 n.19, 105 S. Ct. at 3359 n.19. But because the [—29—] arbitral panel had taken under submission the antitrust claims—due to an agreement by the parties that U.S. law would apply—the Supreme Court emphasized that, "at this stage in the proceedings," it had "no occasion to speculate" on whether the arbitration agreement's potential deprivation of a claimant's right to pursue federal remedies may render that agreement unenforceable. *Id.* The Court also declined to consider "the effect of an arbitral tribunal's failure to take cognizance of the statutory cause of action on the claimant's capacity to reinitiate suit in federal court." *Id.*

In subsequent cases, the Supreme Court has asserted the existence of this "prospective waiver" doctrine, but the Court has never invoked it to justify the refusal to enforce an arbitration clause in either the domestic or foreign arbitration context. *See, e.g., Am. Exp. Co. v. Italian Colors Rest.*, 570 U.S. 228, 235, 133 S. Ct. 2304, 2310 (2013); *Sky Reefer*, 515 U.S. at 540, 115 S. Ct. at 2330; *see also Suazo*, 822 F.3d at 548.

The Supreme Court in *Sky Reefer* declined to apply the "prospective waiver" doctrine, noting that it was premature to do so since arbitration had not yet taken place, and it was unclear what law the arbitrator would apply or whether the plaintiff would receive "diminished protection as a result" of the application of that law. *Sky Reefer*, 515 U.S. at 540, 115 S. Ct. at 2329–30. Because, at that point, the respondents sought only to enforce the arbitration agreement, the Court noted [—30—] there would be an opportunity for later review of the arbitral award in federal court. *Id.* In other words, the district court would have the opportunity at the award-enforcement stage to address public policy concerns. *Id.* The *Sky Reefer* Court suggested, "[w]ere there no subsequent opportunity for review and were we persuaded that 'the choice-of-forum and choice-of-law clauses operated in tandem as a prospective waiver of a party's right to pursue statutory remedies,'" the Court could perhaps condemn an arbitration agreement as being void as against public policy. *Id.* at 540, 115 S. Ct. at 2330 (quoting *Mitsubishi Motors*, 473 U.S. at 637 n.19, 105 S. Ct. at 3359 n.19). But because there was an opportunity for review at the award-enforcement stage, it was premature to make findings on whether foreign-law remedies would be inadequate. *See Lindo*, 652 F.3d at 1279.

Of course, here, Cvoro has already engaged in arbitration and the district court had the opportunity to review the foreign arbitral award. So it is not premature at this point to consider Cvoro's prospective-waiver argument.

Importantly though, following its decision in *Sky Reefer*, the Supreme Court limited the import of the "prospective waiver" language in *Mitsubishi Motors* to dicta, making plain that "*Mitsubishi Motors* did not *hold* that federal statutory claims are subject to arbitration so long as the claimant may effectively vindicate his rights in the arbitral forum." *Italian Colors Rest.*, 570 U.S. at 235 n.2, 133 S. Ct. at 2310 n.2 (emphasis added). *Id.* Nonetheless, because the Supreme Court [—31—] has suggested that an arbitral agreement could perhaps contravene public policy if the combination of choice-of-forum and choice-of-law clauses work together as a prospective waiver of a party's rights to pursue statutory remedies, we discuss the issue here. Ultimately, that analysis leads us back to our decisions in *Lipcon* and *Lindo*.

We first assume, without deciding, that Cvoro's Jones Act claim is a statutory remedy, since *Mitsubishi Motors* and its progeny spoke of only the potential prospective waiver of a right to pursue statutory remedies. Next, we consider whether {–503–} the choice-of-forum and choice-of-law clauses in the seafarer's agreement in this case operate together as a prospective waiver of Cvoro's statutory remedy, such that the agreement could perhaps be void as against public policy.

In *Lipcon*, we considered the dicta set forth in *Mitsubishi Motors* and reached the conclusion that the choice-of-forum and choice-of-law clauses did not contravene public policy, even if the clauses may have worked together as a prospective waiver of the party's statutory remedies. *Lipcon*, 148 F.3d at 1298. In doing so, we found significant the fact that English law provided adequate remedies to the appellants. *Id.* at 1298–99. As a result, we agreed with the district court's finding that the choice clauses were enforceable. *Id.* at 1299. **[—32—]**

We recognize, though, that *Lipcon* was not an arbitral-award-enforcement-stage case like this one and therefore was "not subject to the New York Convention's linking of Article V public policy defense to the arbitral award-enforcement stage." *Lindo*, 652 F.3d at 1269. However, this Court in *Lindo* found the decision in *Lipcon* to be "highly relevant to footnote 19 in *Mitsubishi*." *Id.* And while *Lindo*, like *Lipcon*, was also an arbitration-agreement-enforcement-stage case (as opposed to an arbitral-award-enforcement-stage case), we alternatively held that even assuming *arguendo* that Article V's public-policy defense could apply at that earlier stage, *Lindo's* challenge to the arbitration agreement—that it was void as against public policy because he would be prevented from asserting his Jones Act claim under Bahamian law—would still fail. *Id.* at 1283–84.

Indeed, this Court concluded that the fact that *Lindo* asserted a Jones Act claim did "not affect the strong presumption in favor of enforcement of the choice clauses in [the seafarer's agreement]." *Id.* at 1276 (citing *Mitsubishi Motors*, 473 U.S. at 626, 105 S. Ct. at 3354 ("There is no reason to depart from" the strong presumption of enforceability "where a party bound by an arbitration agreement raises claims founded on statutory rights."). And we rejected *Lindo's* challenge to the arbitration agreement as being void as against public policy because he would be prevented from asserting his Jones Act claim under Bahamian law. *Id.* at 1283– **[—33—]** 84. There, we relied on our decision in *Lipcon* and compared the remedies available under Bahamian law and U.S. law, ultimately finding that *Lindo* did not show that international arbitration under Bahamian negligence law would provide an inadequate remedy such that enforcement of the arbitration agreement would be "fundamentally unfair." *Id.*

Applying that reasoning here, we find under our current precedent, the question of prospective waiver of a party's Jones Act claim collapses into our examination of whether choice clauses in arbitration agreements render remedies so inadequate that enforcement of those clauses would be fundamentally unfair. And in making this determination, we compare the remedies available under the law chosen in the arbitration agreement and U.S. law. For the reasons already discussed, we find the remedies available to Cvoro under Panamanian law are not "so inadequate that enforcement would be fundamentally unfair." *See Lipcon*, 148 F.3d at 1297. Accordingly, Cvoro's prospective-waiver argument fails.

Ultimately, at this arbitration-award-enforcement stage, the test for whether a court should refuse to enforce a foreign arbitral award based on public policy is not whether the claimant was provided with all of her statutory rights under U.S. law during arbitration. *Italian Colors Rest.*, 570 U.S. at 235 n.2, 133 S. Ct. at 2310 n.2. Rather, the public-policy defense "applies only when confirmation or enforcement of {–504–} a foreign arbitration award would violate the forum state's most [—34—] basic notions of morality and justice." *Inversiones y Procesadora*, 921 F.3d at 1306. Cvoro has not made that showing here. Under the totality of the specific facts of this case, enforcing the arbitral award does not violate our "most basic notions of morality and justice." *Id.*

VI. CONCLUSION

For the foregoing reasons, despite Cvoro's status as a ward of admiralty, she has not established that the foreign arbitral award in this case offends the United States' "most basic notions of morality and justice." We therefore conclude that the district court did not err in denying Cvoro's request that it refuse to enforce the arbitral award and dismissing her claims brought under the Jones Act and general maritime law.

AFFIRMED.

United States Court of Appeals
for the Eleventh Circuit

No. 18-12105

GEICO MARINE INS. CO.
vs.
SHACKLEFORD

Appeal from the United States District Court for the
Middle District of Florida

Decided: December 17, 2019

Citation: 945 F.3d 1135, 7 Adm. R. 528 (11th Cir. 2019).

Before **PRYOR**, **MARTIN**, and **KATSAS**,* Circuit
Judges.

* Honorable Gregory G. Katsas, United States Circuit
Judge for the District of Columbia Circuit, sitting by
designation.

[—1—] {–1137–} **PRYOR**, Circuit Judge: [—2—]

This appeal requires us to decide whether damage to a yacht was covered under a marine insurance policy. Geico Marine Insurance Company insured James Shackleford's 65-foot sailboat, *Sea the World*. After a storm damaged the vessel in Florida, Geico Marine denied Shackleford's claim under the policy. Geico Marine then filed a declaratory-judgment action against Shackleford. As one ground for relief, Geico Marine sought a declaration that a navigational limit in the policy that required the vessel to be north of Cape Hatteras, North Carolina, during hurricane season barred coverage. After a bench trial, the district court ruled against Geico Marine and declared that the policy covered the loss. Because we agree with Geico Marine that the navigational limit bars coverage, we reverse and remand.

I. BACKGROUND

Shackleford purchased the *Sea the World* in 2009. He paid about $120,000 for the vessel, and at one point he planned to sail her around the world. But those plans never came to pass.

In 2011, lightning struck the vessel. Shackleford took the vessel to Sailor's Wharf, a yacht yard in St. Petersburg, Florida, for repairs. But Sailor's Wharf only made matters worse. It improperly hauled the vessel from the water and improperly "blocked" the vessel while storing it on shore, which caused structural damage to the ship's hull.

Shackleford filed an insurance claim with Continental Insurance Company, [—3—] which insured the *Sea the World* then. In 2014, Continental declared the vessel a constructive total loss, settled Shackleford's claim, and canceled the policy. Continental also waived its subrogation rights and assigned its interest in any claim against Sailor's Wharf to Shackleford. {–1138–}

In 2015, Shackleford sued Sailor's Wharf for breach of its repair contract. *Shackleford v. Sailor's Wharf, Inc.*, No. 8:15-cv-00407-VMC-TBM (M.D. Fla. filed Feb. 26, 2015). As part of discovery in that litigation, Shackleford arranged to have the vessel hauled ashore for inspection by expert witnesses at Taylor Boatworks, a boatyard in Cortez on Florida's west coast. But before Taylor Boatworks would haul the vessel from the water, it required Shackleford to obtain liability insurance on the vessel.

In March 2016, Shackleford obtained a liability-only policy from Geico Marine, which insured several of his other watercraft. The policy did not insure the hull of the vessel against damage but did permit navigation. The General Conditions section provided the following terms of coverage:

Where Covered
Coverage is provided:
A. While the boat is afloat within the navigational area shown on the Declarations Page; and
B. While the boat or its equipment is ashore or being transported by land conveyance in the United States or Canada.

The accompanying declarations page, in turn, included the following navigational limit: [—4—]

CRUISING LIMITS: While afloat, the insured Yacht shall be confined to the waters indicated below:
(There is no coverage outside of this area without the Company's written permission.)
U.S. Atlantic and Gulf Coastal waters and inland waters tributary thereto between Eastport, ME and Brownsville, TX, inclusive and the waters of the Bahamas including the Turks and Caicos, however the boat must be north of Cape Hatteras, NC from June 1 until November 1 annually.

The day after the policy issued, Shackleford asked Geico Marine to change the policy to "Port Risk Ashore." That restriction provides no coverage for navigation; instead, it provides coverage only while the vessel is out of the water. Geico Marine issued an endorsement and updated declarations page adding the restriction that same day. Because coverage now applied only if the vessel was ashore, the updated declarations page removed the original navigational limit that required the vessel to be north of Cape Hatteras during hurricane season if afloat.

With the Port Risk Ashore restriction in place, Taylor Boatworks hauled the vessel ashore so that Shackleford's expert marine surveyor could inspect her in connection with the Sailor's Wharf litigation. Following the inspection, Shackleford concluded that the damage to the vessel's hull was less severe than he originally believed and that the vessel was worth repairing. So he made plans to sail her from Taylor Boatworks on the west coast of Florida to Fort Lauderdale on the east coast, where she would undergo extensive repairs.

In May 2016, Shackleford called Geico Marine to seek removal of the Port [—5—] Risk Ashore restriction so he could sail the vessel to Fort Lauderdale. He also confirmed that the policy now insured the vessel's hull for $264,000 and that the vessel had "full coverage" for the voyage. On May 27, 2016, Geico Marine sent Shackleford an email confirming that it had removed the Port Risk Ashore restriction. Attached to the email was an endorsement removing the restriction and an updated declarations page. The updated declarations page reinstated the original navigational limit that required the vessel "[w]hile afloat" to be "north of Cape Hatteras, NC from June 1 until November 1 annually." Shackleford testified that he never requested or discussed such a navigational {–1139–} limit with Geico Marine and that he does not recall seeing the updated declarations page before departing for Fort Lauderdale.

On May 28, one day after Geico Marine removed the Port Risk Ashore restriction and reinstated the navigational limit, Shackleford set sail from Taylor Boatworks to Fort Lauderdale. After arriving in Fort Lauderdale, Shackleford anchored the vessel in nearby Lake Sylvia. In June 2016, a storm caused the vessel to drag anchor and drove her into a sea wall, leading her to take on water and suffer other damage. Shackleford filed a claim under his insurance policy, but Geico Marine denied coverage.

After denying coverage, Geico Marine filed a declaratory-judgment action against Shackleford, 28 U.S.C. § 2201, and invoked admiralty jurisdiction, *id.* [—6—] § 1333. Geico Marine sought a declaration that the policy was void *ab initio* under the maritime doctrine of *uberrimae fidei*, or utmost good faith, because Shackleford failed to disclose material facts about the vessel when procuring insurance. And it sought a declaration that coverage was barred by the policy's navigational limit, which required the vessel to be north of Cape Hatteras, North Carolina, during hurricane season.

Following a bench trial, the district court ruled against Geico Marine on both counts and declared that the policy covered Shackleford's loss. As to *uberrimae fidei*, the district court ruled that the parties contracted out of the doctrine and that, even if the doctrine applied, Shackleford did not omit any material facts when procuring insurance. As to the navigational limit, it ruled that the policy did not contain a navigational limit at the time of the loss and that, if it did, Geico Marine implicitly waived the limit when it agreed that Shackleford could sail the vessel to Fort Lauderdale in late May. Geico Marine challenges both rulings.

II. STANDARDS OF REVIEW

In an appeal from a judgment following a bench trial, we review the conclusions of law *de novo* and the factual findings for clear error. *U.S. Commodity Futures Trading Comm'n v. S. Tr. Metals, Inc.*, 894 F.3d 1313, 1322 (11th Cir. 2018). "Questions of contract interpretation are pure questions of law," so we review the interpretation of an insurance contract *de novo*. *Tims v. LGE* [—7—] *Cmty. Credit Union*, 935 F.3d 1228, 1237 (11th Cir. 2019).

III. DISCUSSION

Marine insurance contracts qualify as maritime contracts, which fall within the admiralty jurisdiction of the federal courts and are governed by maritime law. *AIG Centennial Ins. Co. v. O'Neill*, 782 F.3d 1296, 1302 & n.6, 3 Adm. R. 643, 646 & n.6 (11th Cir. 2015) (citing U.S. Const. art. III, § 2, cl. 1 and 28 U.S.C. § 1333). Even so, "it does not follow that every term in every maritime contract can only be controlled by some federally defined admiralty rule." *Id.* at 1302, 3 Adm. R. at 646 (alteration adopted) (quoting *Wilburn Boat Co. v. Fireman's Fund Ins. Co.*, 348 U.S. 310, 313 (1955)). "In the absence of a 'judicially established federal admiralty rule,' we rely on state law when addressing questions of marine insurance." *Id.*, 3 Adm. R. at 646 (quoting *Wilburn Boat*, 348 U.S. at 314); *see also* Bryan A. Garner et al., *The Law of Judicial Precedent* § 69, at 570 (2016). The parties agree that Florida law fills any gaps here.

Geico Marine argues that the policy's navigational limit unambiguously conditioned coverage on the vessel being north of Cape Hatteras, North Carolina, from June 1 until November 1 annually if the vessel was afloat. Because Shackleford {–1140–} breached that limit and because maritime law requires absolute enforcement of express navigational limits, Geico Marine contends the navigational limit bars coverage.

Shackleford responds with three reasons why the navigational limit does not [—8—] bar coverage. First, he argues that the policy is ambiguous as to whether it contained a navigational limit at the time of the loss, and Florida law construes ambiguities in insurance contracts against the insurer. Second, he argues that Geico Marine implicitly waived its right to enforce the navigational limit when it agreed that he could sail the vessel to Fort Lauderdale in late May. And third, he argues that any breach of the navigational limit does not bar coverage because Florida law does not strictly enforce express warranties in marine insurance contracts.

We reject Shackleford's arguments and agree with Geico Marine that the navigational limit bars coverage. And because we agree with Geico Marine on this issue, we need not address its argument that Shackleford breached a duty of *uberrimae fidei*. The navigational limit is dispositive.

No established rule of maritime law governs whether a navigational limit is part of a marine insurance contract, so we apply Florida law to determine whether the policy contained a navigational limit. *AIG Centennial*, 782 F.3d at 1302, 3 Adm. R. at 646. Under Florida law, we first look to the text of the policy and construe the policy "in accordance with [its] plain language." *Swire Pac. Holdings, Inc. v. Zurich Ins. Co.*, 845 So. 2d 161, 165 (Fla. 2003). But "if the relevant policy language is susceptible to more than one reasonable interpretation, one providing coverage and the other limiting coverage," the policy is ambiguous and we must construe it in favor of coverage. *Id.* (alterations adopted). That "a provision is complex and requires [—9—] analysis for application" does not "automatically" mean it is ambiguous. *Id.* Before concluding that a provision is ambiguous, we must "read [the] policy as a whole, endeavoring to give every provision its full meaning and operative effect." *Id.* at 166 (citation and internal quotation marks omitted).

Reading the policy as a whole, we readily conclude that it unambiguously contained a navigational limit when the loss occurred. The policy states that "[c]overage is provided . . . [w]hile the boat is afloat within the navigational area shown on the Declarations Page." And the updated declarations page that issued the day before Shackleford sailed for Fort Lauderdale includes the following provision:

CRUISING LIMITS: While afloat, the insured Yacht shall be confined to the waters indicated below: (There is no coverage outside of this area without the Company's written permission.)
U.S. Atlantic and Gulf Coastal waters and inland waters tributary thereto between Eastport, ME and Brownsville, TX, inclusive and the waters of the Bahamas including the Turks and Caicos, however the boat must be north of Cape Hatteras, NC from June 1 until November 1 annually.

Four textual clues lead us to conclude that the "cruising limits" section of the declarations page unambiguously describes the "navigational area" referenced in the policy. First, the policy states that the declarations page will contain a "navigational area." In the maritime context, the term "navigation" means "[t]he act of sailing vessels on water." *Navigation, Black's Law Dictionary* (11th ed. [—10—] 2019). And the declarations page specifies the "area"—specifically, the "waters"—in which the vessel could be sailed. So the declarations page contains a "navigational area" within {–1141–} the ordinary meaning of that term. Second, the policy states that coverage applies "[w]hile the boat is afloat" within the navigational area on the declarations page, and the declarations page likewise explains that its navigational restrictions apply to the vessel "[w]hile afloat." Third, both the policy and the declarations page make clear that "coverage" is conditioned on the vessel remaining within the prescribed navigational area while afloat. And fourth, the "cruising limits" section of the declarations page serves no purpose if not to define the "navigational area" upon which the policy conditions coverage. We must not read the "cruising limits" section out of the policy. *See*

Antonin Scalia & Bryan A. Garner, *Reading Law: The Interpretation of Legal Texts* § 26, at 174 (2012) ("If possible, every word and every provision is to be given effect."); *Swire*, 845 So. 2d at 166 (courts must "endeavor[] to give every provision its full meaning and operative effect" (citation and internal quotation marks omitted)). No other interpretation of the policy would give effect to the "cruising limits" section of the declarations page.

The district court offered two reasons why the policy is ambiguous as to whether it contained a navigational limit at the time of the loss. One concerns a discrepancy between the policy and the declarations page, and the other concerns a [—11—] discrepancy between the declarations page and an endorsement to the policy. But neither reason is persuasive.

First, the district court suggested the policy is ambiguous because it refers to the "navigational area" shown on the declarations page, and the declarations page instead uses the term "cruising limits." But "navigational area" is not a defined term in the policy, so it carries its ordinary meaning. *See Arguelles v. Citizens Prop. Ins. Corp.*, 278 So. 3d 108, 111 (Fla. Dist. Ct. App. 2019). And as explained above, the cruising limits in the declarations page unmistakably identify a "navigational area" under the ordinary meaning of that term.

Second, the district court found ambiguity based on a perceived inconsistency between the endorsement and the declarations page that Geico Marine issued the day before Shackleford sailed for Fort Lauderdale. Unlike the declarations page, the endorsement contained a section titled "Navigation Area," which was left blank. The district court ruled that the blank "Navigation Area" section at the bottom of the endorsement was inconsistent with the "cruising limits" in the declarations page and that a reasonable interpretation of the blank "Navigation Area" section was that the policy contained no navigational limit. But the district court ignored the following language on the endorsement form: "Nothing herein contained shall vary, alter or extend any provision or condition of the Policy other than as stated *above*." The blank "Navigation Area" section of the [—12—] endorsement appeared *below* the preceding language, so it could not alter (or conflict with) any navigational limit the policy imposed.

The district court erred. The policy is not ambiguous about whether it contained a navigational limit when the loss occurred. The plain language of the policy contains a navigational limit. *See Taurus Holdings, Inc. v. U.S. Fid. & Guar. Co.*, 913 So. 2d 528, 532 (Fla. 2005) ("[I]nsurance contracts are interpreted according to the plain language of the policy except when a genuine inconsistency, uncertainty, or ambiguity in meaning remains after resort to the ordinary rules of construction." (citation and internal quotation marks omitted)).

The district court alternatively ruled that Geico Marine "implicitly waived" the navigational limit when it agreed that Shackleford could sail the vessel {–1142–} to Fort Lauderdale for repairs in late May. The district court found that Geico Marine knew on May 27 when it lifted the Port Risk Ashore restriction that the vessel "would be sailed to Fort Lauderdale within a few days for repairs." And it found that a navigational limit "was 'absolutely' not discussed" when Shackleford first inquired about removing the Port Risk Ashore restriction. Even accepting those factual findings, this ruling was legal error.

No established rule of maritime law governs the waiver of a navigational limit, so we apply Florida law to determine whether Geico Marine waived its right to enforce that provision. *AIG Centennial*, 782 F.3d at 1302, 3 Adm. R. at 646. In Florida, implied [—13—] waiver of a contractual right requires "conduct which implies the voluntary and intentional relinquishment of a known right." *Raymond James Fin. Servs., Inc. v. Saldukas*, 896 So. 2d 707, 711 (Fla. 2005). Shackleford's theory of implied waiver appears to be that Geico Marine waived the navigational limit by agreeing to a course of conduct that it knew would make it impossible for Shackleford to comply with the requirement that his vessel

be north of Cape Hatteras by June 1. We are unpersuaded.

Geico Marine's decision to lift the Port Risk Ashore restriction on May 27 knowing that Shackleford would soon sail the vessel to Fort Lauderdale for repairs does not imply waiver of its right to enforce the navigational limit. The navigational limit required the vessel to be north of Cape Hatteras by June 1 only if the vessel was "afloat." The policy provided coverage without regard to geography "[w]hile the boat . . . is ashore . . . in the United States or Canada." Geico Marine knew Shackleford was taking the vessel to Fort Lauderdale for "extensive repairs," and it could reasonably have expected that Shackleford would comply with the navigational limit by having the vessel hauled ashore for repairs in Fort Lauderdale by June 1. The only way Geico Marine's conduct could have suggested it intended to waive the navigational limit is if the voyage to Fort Lauderdale was impossible to complete by June 1. But Shackleford conceded at oral argument that the vessel arrived in Fort Lauderdale by June 1 and that he intended to haul the vessel ashore [—14—] upon arrival, which would have complied with the navigational limit. Oral Arg. Recording at 12:27–12:38, 18:23–18:30 (Dec. 3, 2019). That the vessel arrived in Fort Lauderdale by June 1 shows that it was possible to complete the voyage by June 1. So Geico Marine plainly did not agree to a course of conduct that it knew would make compliance with the navigational limit impossible. Nothing in this record supports the conclusion that Geico Marine voluntarily and intentionally relinquished its right to enforce the navigational limit. The district court erred in ruling otherwise.

Even if Geico Marine did not waive the navigational limit, Shackleford argues that his breach of the navigational limit does not bar coverage because Florida law does not strictly enforce express warranties in marine insurance contracts. As Shackleford acknowledges, federal maritime law requires "strict" or absolute enforcement of express navigational warranties. *Lexington Ins. Co. v. Cooke's Seafood*, 835 F.2d 1364, 1366 (11th Cir. 1988); *see also Strict, Black's Law Dictionary* (11th ed. 2019) ("Absolute;

requiring no showing of fault."). And established federal maritime rules, like the rule requiring absolute enforcement of express navigational warranties, ordinarily control "even in the face of contrary state authority." *AIG Centennial*, 782 F.3d at 1303, 3 Adm. R. at 646 (citation and internal quotation marks omitted). But Shackleford contends that he and Geico Marine {–1143–} contracted out of the federal maritime rule of enforcement and instead selected Florida's more [—15—] forgiving rule.

Shackleford argues that the parties contracted out of the federal maritime rule requiring absolute enforcement of express navigational warranties by including a "Conformity to Law" provision in their policy. The provision states: "Any terms of this policy that conflict with the laws of the state where this policy is issued are considered amended to conform to such laws." Although parties to a marine insurance policy are generally free to contract out of federal maritime law, *King v. Allstate Ins. Co.*, 906 F.2d 1537, 1540–42 (11th Cir. 1990), we are not persuaded that Shackleford and Geico Marine did so.

Shackleford's argument that this provision contracts out of the federal maritime rule has two premises. First, the federal rule of absolute enforcement, as a default rule of maritime law, was one of the "terms of this policy" to which the provision refers. Second, the federal rule of enforcement conflicts with Florida law because Florida allows a marine insurer to avoid coverage based on an insured's breach of warranty only if the breach "increased the hazard by any means within the control of the insured." Fla. Stat. § 627.409(2). Because the federal rule of enforcement, an implied term of the policy, conflicts with Florida's rule, Shackleford argues that this implied "term" must be amended to conform to Florida's more insured-friendly laws.

Shackleford's argument fails because its first premise is false. As used in the [—16—] policy, the phrase "terms of this policy" refers only to the policy's *express* terms, not terms implied by law. Florida gives words in an insurance contract their ordinary meaning, which requires reading the words in context. *Swire*, 845 So. 2d at 165–66. We do not doubt that as a matter of ordinary meaning the "terms" of a contract may include terms implied by law. *See Term, Black's Law Dictionary* (11th ed. 2019) (listing "implied term" as one kind of term). But here context makes clear that the phrase "terms of this policy" refers only to the policy's express terms.

The phrase "terms of this policy" appears in a provision titled "Conformity to Law," and as its name suggests, the provision operates to conform any illegal policy terms to Florida law. Provisions like this one exist to address conflicts between the contract the parties wrote and what the law requires. *See* 16 Samuel Williston & Richard A. Lord, *A Treatise on the Law of Contracts* § 49:24, at 138 (4th ed. 2000) ("Many [insurance] policies have a provision, doubtless superfluous, that in the event of a conflict between the policy's terms and the requirements of a state's insurance law, the latter will control."). Because the provision exists to save the policy the parties *wrote* from invalidity under state law, the phrase "terms of this policy" refers only to the policy's express terms—those *written* by the parties.

Shackleford effectively asks us to transform the policy's *conformity-to*-law provision into a *choice-of*-law provision. By default, federal maritime law [—17—] displaces contrary state law when construing a marine insurance contract. *AIG Centennial*, 782 F.3d at 1302–03, 3 Adm. R. at 646. Shackleford would have us read the conformity-to-law provision as reversing this default rule, so that state law displaces any contrary federal maritime rule. But the provision does no such thing. The parties could have included a choice-of-law provision selecting state law over federal law, but they did not. And we "may not rewrite [the parties'] contract[], add meaning that is not present, or otherwise reach results contrary to the intentions of the parties." *Taurus Holdings*, 913 So. 2d at 532 (citation and internal quotation marks omitted). {–1144–}

Because the parties did not contract out of maritime law, we must apply the federal rule requiring absolute enforcement of express navigational limits. Under that rule, "breach of [an] express [navigational] warranty by the insured releases the insurance company from liability even if compliance with the warranty would not have avoided the loss." *Lexington*, 835 F.2d at 1366. Here, the policy contained a navigational limit that conditioned coverage on the vessel being "north of Cape Hatteras, NC from June 1 until November 1 annually" if the vessel was "afloat." The vessel suffered damage while afloat during a storm in Florida in early June. Because the vessel was outside of the covered navigational area when the loss occurred, the policy does not cover the loss.
[—18—]

IV. CONCLUSION

We **REVERSE** the judgment in favor of Shackleford and **REMAND** with instructions for the district court to enter judgment in favor of Geico Marine.

United States Court of Appeals for the District of Columbia Circuit

United States Court of Appeals
for the District of Columbia Circuit

No. 18-7148

DISTRICT NO. 1, PAC. COAST DIST., MARINE
ENG'RS BENEFICIAL ASS'N
vs.
LIBERTY MARITIME CORP.

Appeal from the United States District Court for the
District of Columbia

Decided: August 9, 2019

Citation: 933 F.3d 751, 7 Adm. R. 536 (D.C. Cir. 2019).

Before **MILLETT**, **KATSAS**, and **RAO**, Circuit Judges.

[—1—] {–754–} **RAO**, Circuit Judge:

Liberty Maritime Corporation (Liberty) is a shipping company that has contracted over the past thirty years with District No. 1, Pacific Coast District, [—2—] Marine Engineers Beneficial Association, AFL-CIO (MEBA), a labor union representing supervisory employees in the maritime industry. This case arises out of an underlying dispute about whether Liberty was contractually required to hire MEBA employees on a new vessel managed by Liberty. MEBA sued in the United States District Court for the District of Columbia, claiming its contract with Liberty required the parties to submit the dispute to arbitration. The district court ruled in favor of the union, granting judgment on the pleadings under Federal Rule of Civil Procedure 12(c) and compelling arbitration. Liberty timely appealed, arguing that the district court lacked subject matter jurisdiction, or in the alternative, erred in its application of the Rule 12(c) standards.

For the reasons explained below, we agree that the district court had jurisdiction over MEBA's claim under Section 301 of the Labor Management Relations Act of 1947 (LMRA), 29 U.S.C. §§ 141 *et seq.*, which provides federal jurisdiction over suits for "violation of contracts between an employer and a labor organization." *Id.* § 185(a). MEBA raised contractual issues regarding the arbitrability of the dispute and thus its claim clearly falls within the district court's statutory jurisdiction. Although Liberty alleges that the dispute primarily raised representational issues and thus should be within the exclusive jurisdiction of the National Labor Relations Board (NLRB) under the doctrine of "*Garmon* preemption," federal courts retain jurisdiction over "hybrid" claims raising both contractual and representational issues. {–755–} *Dist. No. 1, Pac. Coast Dist., Marine Engineers' Beneficial Ass'n, AFL-CIO v. Liberty Mar. Corp.*, 815 F.3d 834, 840, 4 Adm. R. 490, 493 (D.C. Cir. 2016) ("*Liberty Maritime I*"); *see also William E. Arnold Co. v. Carpenters Dist. Council of Jacksonville & Vicinity*, 417 U.S. 12, 18 (1974). [—3—]

Although jurisdiction here was proper, we reverse and remand because material facts remained in dispute regarding the existence of an applicable arbitration clause, and therefore MEBA was not entitled to judgment on the pleadings under Rule 12(c).

I.

Appellant Liberty is a shipping company that transports commodities, vehicles, equipment, and other cargoes on the seagoing vessels it manages. Liberty's clients include the U.S. Government, the United Nations, and commercial entities such as automobile manufacturers. Liberty manages vessels transporting bulk cargo—including dry bulk, break bulk, and bagged commodities—and "roll on/roll-off" vessels, like car and truck carriers configured to transport vehicles that drive on and off the vessel. Many of these vessels are enrolled in the U.S. Maritime Security Program, a federal program that subsidizes shipping companies for national security purposes—namely, to ensure a fleet of vessels is available in the event of a war or national emergency. *See generally* 46 U.S.C. §§ 53101 *et seq.* Appellee MEBA is a labor organization that represents supervisory employees in the U.S. maritime industry at ports throughout the United States and on oceangoing vessels. On car and truck carrier vessels operated by Liberty and enrolled in the U.S. Maritime Security Program, MEBA represents licensed officers and engineers.

The parties' relationship began in 1988 when they signed two agreements: the Tanker Vessels Master Agreement and the Dry Cargo Vessels Master Agreement. Although the authenticity of some of the documents attached to the pleadings is disputed, the documents that purport to be current copies of these Master Agreements provide that "[a]ll disputes relating to the interpretation or performance of this Agreement shall be [—4—] determined in accordance with the provisions of this Section." "[T]his Section" states that grievances will be presented to a licensed personnel board consisting of two persons appointed by the union and two persons appointed by the company; if the licensed personnel board fails to resolve a grievance, an arbitrator will assume jurisdiction over the grievance.

Over the past three decades, the parties have modified their contractual relationship on numerous occasions. At this stage of the proceedings, the record includes only a few of these agreements. Both parties agree, however, they were signatories to a 2012 Memorandum of Understanding (MOU). This MOU identifies numerous prior agreements and states that prior agreements will remain in effect except as expressly modified, but the MOU does not expressly modify any arbitration clause in a manner relevant to this case.

This suit arises out of a dispute between Liberty and MEBA over a ship named the *M/V Liberty Peace*. On July 24, 2017, Liberty sent MEBA a letter stating its intention to commence managing this foreign flagged car and truck carrier vessel and operate it as a U.S. flagged vessel. In the letter, Liberty claimed the *Liberty Peace* would not fall under the parties' collective bargaining agreements and the various contractual modifications of those agreements because the vessel would not be enrolled in the U.S. Maritime Security Program. MEBA disagreed, insisting the existing agreements covered the new vessel. Although the parties met to discuss {–756–} the matter, they did not resolve their dispute. In the meantime, Liberty began managing the *Liberty Peace* as the agent of a third party,

and that third party entered into labor agreements with a different union.

MEBA sent Liberty a grievance letter on August 31, 2017, asserting Liberty was "in violation of the parties' collective [—5—] bargaining agreement by failing to apply the terms and conditions of the parties' labor contract" to the *Liberty Peace*. Liberty did not submit MEBA's grievance to arbitration.

MEBA subsequently filed a "Complaint to Compel Arbitration" in the United States District Court for the District of Columbia. MEBA requested the district court compel Liberty to participate in the arbitration process set forth in the parties' collective bargaining agreement and grant any other appropriate relief, including attorneys' fees and costs. MEBA attached as exhibits several documents purporting to be the two original Master Agreements, the MOU, MEBA's August 31 grievance letter, and some additional correspondence between MEBA and Liberty.

In its answer to MEBA's complaint, Liberty admitted it had signed the Master Agreements and the MOU. Liberty admitted the authenticity of the MOU, but denied the authenticity of the exhibits MEBA claimed were copies of the Master Agreements. Liberty denied that the MOU incorporated the terms of the Master Agreements and that the arbitration clauses covered the *Liberty Peace*. Liberty also denied that any labor contract or arbitration agreement with MEBA covered the *Liberty Peace*. As an affirmative defense, Liberty alleged the district court lacked subject matter jurisdiction because the suit concerned representational rights and therefore was preempted by the jurisdiction of the NLRB under the terms of the National Labor Relations Act (NLRA).

MEBA moved for judgment on the pleadings under Federal Rule of Civil Procedure 12(c), and the district court granted the motion. The district court found that the Master Agreements stated, "[a]ll disputes relating to the interpretation or performance of this Agreement shall be determined in accordance with the provisions of this

Section." Dist. Ct. Op. [—6—] at 3, 13. The district court concluded that this language created a presumption of arbitrability; Liberty failed to rebut the presumption; and no agreement between the parties excluded this sort of dispute from arbitration. *Id.* at 13–14. The district court also rejected Liberty's preemption argument on the grounds that federal courts have jurisdiction over contractual matters and that MEBA's suit "plainly requires deciding a contractual matter: whether the arbitration clause covers the dispute at issue." *Id.* at 10–11 n.7.

Liberty timely appealed, challenging the district court's order on jurisdictional grounds and arguing the district court violated Rule 12(c) by making findings the pleadings did not adequately support.

II.

"The 'first and fundamental question' that we are 'bound to ask and answer' is whether the court has jurisdiction to decide the case." *Bancoult v. McNamara*, 445 F.3d 427, 432 (D.C. Cir. 2006) (quoting *Steel Co. v. Citizens for a Better Env't*, 523 U.S. 83, 94 (1998)). The district court held that federal courts have jurisdiction over contractual matters under Section 301 of the LMRA, which provides:

> Suits for violation of contracts between an employer and a labor organization representing employees in an industry {–757–} affecting commerce as defined in this chapter, . . . may be brought in any district court of the United States having jurisdiction of the parties . . . .

29 U.S.C. § 185(a). Section 301 confers federal court jurisdiction over suits for breach of collective bargaining agreements, which are contractual. "Congress deliberately chose to leave the enforcement of collective agreements to the [—7—] usual processes of the law." *Charles Dowd Box Co. v. Courtney*, 368 U.S. 502, 513 (1962).

Nevertheless, Liberty argues the district court lacked subject matter jurisdiction over this case under the judicially created doctrine known as "*Garmon* preemption." *Washington*

Serv. Contractors Coal. v. Dist. Columbia, 54 F.3d 811, 815 (D.C. Cir. 1995) (citing *San Diego Bldg. Trades Council v. Garmon*, 359 U.S. 236 (1959)). This doctrine holds that "[w]hen an activity is arguably subject to § 7 or § 8 of the [NLRA], . . . the federal courts must defer to the exclusive competence of the [NLRB]." *Garmon*, 359 U.S. at 245. Suits implicating § 7 or § 8 of the NLRA are often described as "representational."

Liberty attempts to rely on this court's decision in a previous suit between Liberty and MEBA, in which Liberty raised and lost a similar jurisdictional argument. Liberty cites this case for the proposition that three categories of legal claims are preempted by the NLRA under *Garmon*: claims over which the NLRB "has already exercised jurisdiction," claims that call for "an initial decision in the representation area," and claims "in which the center of the dispute is a representational question." Appellant Br. 35–36 (quoting *Liberty Maritime I*, 815 F.3d at 841, 4 Adm. R. at 494 (citations and quotation marks omitted)). Liberty urges this court to evaluate whether MEBA's claim is "primarily representational or primarily contractual," as several other circuits do. *See, e.g., United Food & Commercial Workers Union, Local 400 v. Shoppers Food Warehouse Corp.*, 35 F.3d 958, 961 (4th Cir. 1994); *Local Union 204 of Int'l Bhd. of Elec. Workers, AFL-CIO v. Iowa Elec. Light & Power Co.*, 668 F.2d 413, 419 (8th Cir. 1982). Liberty claims such analysis would show this suit may fall into the purported third category of claims preempted under *Garmon*: that the center of the dispute may concern a representational matter, such as whether [—8—] MEBA or another union has representational rights over crewmembers of the *Liberty Peace*. In order to determine the true center of this dispute, Liberty argues the district court should have considered MEBA's grievance letter instead of focusing only on MEBA's complaint. Liberty contends it was legal error for the district court to have concluded that, as a matter of law, it maintained jurisdiction over MEBA's claims.

MEBA responds that Liberty's argument on appeal "conflates the type of claim with the effect of a claim's enforcement." Appellee Br.

26 (quoting *Liberty Maritime I*, 815 F.3d at 843, 4 Adm. R. at 495). While the possible outcome of its suit may touch on representational issues, MEBA argues it has a contract that requires Liberty to arbitrate, and MEBA asked the district court to compel compliance with that contract. MEBA maintains this type of contractual dispute is squarely covered by Section 301 of the LMRA.

The district court properly exercised jurisdiction over MEBA's claim under the plain meaning of Section 301 as well as established Supreme Court and Circuit precedent. Section 301 covers "[s]uits for violations of contracts between an employer and a labor organization." *Liberty Maritime I*, 815 F.3d at 840, 4 Adm. R. at 493 (quoting {–758–} 29 U.S.C. § 185(a)). As the Supreme Court has stated, Section 301 "permits suits for breach of a collective bargaining agreement *regardless of whether the particular breach is also an unfair labor practice within the jurisdiction of the Board*." *Vaca v. Sipes*, 386 U.S. 171, 179–80 (1967) (emphasis added); *see also Carey v. Westinghouse Corp.*, 375 U.S. 261, 267–68 (1964) (holding that Section 301 gives a federal court jurisdiction over a suit to enforce an arbitration clause in a collective bargaining agreement even if the case is "truly a representation case" that could also be heard by the NLRB under Section 9 of the NLRA). Thus, the "*Garmon* doctrine is 'not relevant' to actions within the [—9—] purview of § 301" of the LMRA. *Arnold*, 417 U.S. at 16 (citing *Local 174, Teamsters v. Lucas Flour Co.*, 369 U.S. 95, 101 n.9 (1962)). We held in *Liberty Maritime I* that federal courts and the NLRB have concurrent jurisdiction over claims that are "*both* contractual and representational." 815 F.3d at 840, 4 Adm. R. at 493 (emphasis original) (citing *Arnold*, 417 U.S. at 16, and *Smith v. Evening News Ass'n*, 371 U.S. 195, 197 (1962)).

Thus, if a case is both representational and contractual, it is treated as a "hybrid" claim. *See, e.g., United Parcel Serv., Inc. v. Mitchell*, 451 U.S. 56, 66 (1981) (Stewart, J., concurring in the judgment) (describing "a hybrid '§ 301 and breach of duty suit'"); *DelCostello v. Int'l Bhd. of Teamsters*, 462 U.S. 151, 165 (1983)

(describing "hybrid § 301/fair representation litigation"); *Cephas v. MVM, Inc.*, 520 F.3d 480, 485 (D.C. Cir. 2008) (same). Such "hybrid" claims create concurrent jurisdiction for the federal courts and the NLRB, but they do not divest courts of their statutory jurisdiction. Consistent with Supreme Court precedent, that is precisely what this court has held: "Instead of forcing courts to shoehorn a hybrid claim into one category or the other, the Supreme Court has held that they retain jurisdiction to hear a contractual claim even if the claim is also representational." *Liberty Maritime I*, 815 F.3d at 840, 4 Adm. R. at 493 (citing *Arnold*, 417 U.S. at 16). "[F]ederal courts have independent jurisdiction to decide cases alleging a breach of collective bargaining agreements, even though that very breach may also be an unfair labor practice." *Mullins v. Kaiser Steel Corp.*, 642 F.2d 1302, 1316 (D.C. Cir. 1980), *rev'd on other grounds*, 455 U.S. 72 (1982).

Allowing "hybrid" claims to be brought in federal court reads together the two statutes, the LMRA and the NLRA, giving effect to Congress's provision of federal court jurisdiction for contractual claims and NLRB jurisdiction over representational claims. *See Vaca*, 386 U.S. at 179–80; [—10—] *Wachovia Bank v. Schmidt*, 546 U.S. 303, 315–16 (2006) ("under the *in pari materia* canon of statutory construction, statutes addressing the same subject matter generally should be read as if they were one law") (citations and quotation marks omitted).

Liberty continues to argue that if a case is both representational and contractual, a district court must place those claims on a sliding scale to determine if the case is primarily one or the other. Neither the Supreme Court nor this court have required such an inquiry. In *Liberty Maritime I*, we described and discussed the practice in some circuits, which "examine the major issues to be decided" and "determine whether they can be characterized as primarily representational or primarily {–759–} contractual" in order to dismiss "primarily representational" claims.[1] *Liberty Maritime I*, 815 F.3d at 840, 4 Adm. R. at 493 (alterations, quotation marks, and citation omitted).

Liberty's reliance on the categories recognized by other circuits is misplaced. While the *Liberty Maritime I* court described the approaches from "several of our sister circuits," it did not adopt any of these competing decisions. *Id.* at 841, 4 Adm. R. at 493. Because the categories identified by other circuits were not necessary to the decision, the *Liberty Maritime I* discussion of those cases "does not constitute a precedent to be followed with respect to that issue." *UC Health v. NLRB*, 803 F.3d 669, 682 (D.C. Cir. 2015) (quotation marks and citations omitted). We follow *Liberty Maritime I*, which refused to define the [—11—] "parameters of a claim that is 'primarily representational' as opposed to 'primarily contractual'" and declined "to shoehorn" a given "claim into one category or the other." 815 F.3d at 840–41, 4 Adm. R. at 493.

Liberty also contends that it cannot "be ruled out, based on the pleadings alone, that the major issues to be decided are primarily representational." Appellant Br. 38. MEBA's grievance letter, like its complaint, however, raised numerous contractual issues. *See* MEBA Compl. Exhibit G ("Please be advised that Liberty is in violation of the parties' collective bargaining agreement . . . . Consider this notice of an official grievance for violation of the parties' labor contract . . . . We demand that the parties participate in expedited arbitration to resolve this contractual dispute . . . ."). And Liberty does not argue that the claim here is exclusively representational. *See Liberty Maritime I*, 815 F.3d at 843, 4 Adm. R. at 495 ("*Garmon* preemption is designed to prevent a court from deciding a claim that can

only be characterized as representational.") (emphasis added). At most, then, Liberty has left open the possibility that this case involves a hybrid claim raising both contractual and representational questions. As discussed, however, such hybrid claims are subject to the concurrent jurisdiction of the NLRB and the federal courts. *Id.* at 840, 4 Adm. R. at 493. To hold otherwise "would frustrate rather than serve the congressional policy expressed in [Section 301]." *Smith*, 371 U.S. at 200.

Finally, it may be true, as Liberty stresses, that "a party's mere assertion that a claim is contractual is not an automatic ticket to federal court" under the LMRA. Appellant Br. 35 (quoting *Liberty Maritime I*, 815 F.3d at 840, 4 Adm. R. at 493). A plaintiff must plausibly demonstrate the dispute falls within the terms of Section 301, and is not an "end run around [the NLRA] . . . under the guise of contract interpretation." *Pace*, 227 F.3d at 1157 (citation and alteration omitted); *accord* [—12—] *Paper*, 300 F.3d at 675 ("[S]imply referring to the claim as a 'breach of contract' was insufficient for purposes of § 301 federal courts' jurisdiction."). This proposition, however, goes little further than the axiom that a plaintiff's claim must invoke a proper basis for federal court jurisdiction within a well-pleaded complaint. *Cf. Greenhill v. Spellings*, 482 F.3d 569, 575 (D.C. Cir. 2007) (under the well-pleaded complaint rule, jurisdiction arising under federal law is established by looking to the legal basis of plaintiff's claim) (citing {–760–} *Louisville & Nashville R.R. Co. v. Mottley*, 211 U.S. 149, 152–53 (1908)); *see also* 13D Charles Alan Wright, Arthur R. Miller, Edward H. Cooper, & Richard D. Freer, *Federal Practice and Procedure* § 3566, at 261–62 (3d ed. 2008) ("The well-pleaded complaint rule stands for the proposition that the court, in determining whether the case arises under federal law, will look only to the claim itself.").

Put simply, Congress gave federal courts jurisdiction to hear contractual claims between labor organizations and employers in Section 301 of the LMRA. The existence of representational issues does not divest the federal courts of jurisdiction. Here, MEBA's suit alleges a breach of the parties' labor

---

[1] *Compare Iowa Elec. Light & Power Co.*, 668 F.2d at 419; *Paper, Allied–Indus., Chem. & Energy Workers Int'l Union v. Air Prods. & Chems., Inc.*, 300 F.3d 667, 675 (6th Cir. 2002); *Pace v. Honolulu Disposal Serv., Inc.*, 227 F.3d 1150, 1156 (9th Cir. 2000); *Shoppers*, 35 F.3d at 961; *Copps Food Ctr., Inc. v. United Food & Commercial Workers Union, Local 73–A*, No. 90–1905, 1991 WL 135508, at *2 (7th Cir. July 23, 1991) (unpublished).

contract. The suit requires a judicial determination as to whether an arbitration clause in the agreements between Liberty and MEBA covers the dispute over the *Liberty Peace*. *See Gen. Elec. Co. v. Local 205, United Elec., Radio & Mach. Workers of Am.*, 353 U.S. 547, 548 (1957) (Section "301(a) furnishes a body of federal substantive law for the enforcement of collective bargaining agreements" that provides for suits "to enforce the obligation to arbitrate grievance disputes."); *see also Westinghouse*, 375 U.S. at 267–68. As the dispute includes contractual claims, the district court properly concluded subject matter jurisdiction was established under Section 301 of the LMRA. **[—13—]**

III.

Proceeding to the merits of Liberty's appeal, we consider next whether the district court properly granted MEBA's motion for judgment on the pleadings.

A.

This court reviews a Rule 12(c) judgment on the pleadings de novo. *Judicial Watch, Inc. v. United States Dep't of Homeland Sec.*, 895 F.3d 770, 777 (D.C. Cir. 2018); *Mpoy v. Rhee*, 758 F.3d 285, 287 (D.C. Cir. 2014). Federal Rule of Civil Procedure 12(c) provides, "After the pleadings are closed—but early enough not to delay trial—a party may move for judgment on the pleadings." Pleadings include any "copy of a written instrument that is an exhibit to a pleading," Fed. R. Civ. P. 10(c), such as relevant and authentic documents attached to the complaint. *See, e.g., Philips v. Pitt Cty. Mem'l Hosp.*, 572 F.3d 176, 180 (4th Cir. 2009).

Very few of our precedents discuss Rule 12(c), in part because judgment on the pleadings is rare. As Wright & Miller notes, "Federal Rule 12(c) has its historical roots in common law practice, which permitted either party, at any point in the proceeding, to demur to his opponent's pleading and secure a dismissal or final judgment on the basis of the pleadings." 5C Wright & Miller § 1367, at 205; *see also Patel v. Contemp. Classics of Beverly Hills*, 259 F.3d 123, 126 (2d Cir. 2001) ("[A]

motion for judgment on the pleadings is the direct descendant of that ancient leper of the common law, the 'speaking demurrer.'"); 5C Wright & Miller § 1369, at 265 (noting "the Rule 12(c) motion is little more than a relic of the common law and code eras").

Because Rule 12(c) provides judicial resolution at an early stage of a case, the party seeking judgment on the pleadings **[—14—]** shoulders a heavy burden of justification. A reviewing court "will affirm the district court if the moving party demonstrates that no material fact is in dispute and that it is entitled to judgment as a matter of law." *Peters v. Nat'l R.R. Passenger Corp.*, 966 F.2d 1483, 1485 (D.C. Cir. 1992) (quotation marks omitted). The moving party must demonstrate its entitlement to judgment in its favor, even though {–761–} the "court evaluating the 12(c) motion will accept as true the allegations in the opponent's pleadings, and as false all controverted assertions of the movant." *Haynesworth v. Miller*, 820 F.2d 1245, 1249 n.11 (D.C. Cir. 1987) (collecting cases), *abrogated on other grounds by Hartman v. Moore*, 547 U.S. 250 (2006); *see also Beal v. Missouri Pac. R.R. Corp.*, 312 U.S. 45, 51 (1941) (when the plaintiff moves for judgment on the pleadings, the defendant's "denials and allegations of the answer which are well pleaded must be taken as true"). We must give "all reasonable inferences to the opponent's pleadings" before entering a judgment on the pleadings. *Wager v. Pro*, 575 F.2d 882, 884 (D.C. Cir. 1976).

Under this standard, "a judgment on the pleadings is not appropriate" if there are "issues of fact which if proved would defeat recovery," "even if the trial court is convinced that the party opposing the motion is unlikely to prevail at trial." *Id.* "[I]f material questions of fact are presented by the pleadings, the remedy by motion for judgment on the pleadings under Rule 12(c) is not available." *Noel v. Olds*, 149 F.2d 13, 14 & n.7 (D.C. Cir. 1945) (citing James A. Pike, *Objections to Pleadings Under the New Federal Rules of Civil Procedure*, 47 Yale L.J. 50 (1937)).

B.

Applying these standards, MEBA's pleadings and attachments cannot carry the day. The district court erred in [—15—] granting MEBA's Rule 12(c) motion. The district court found that Liberty and MEBA agreed to arbitrate their disputes in the Master Agreements, which included clauses stating: "All disputes relating to the interpretation or performance of this Agreement shall be determined in accordance with the provisions of this Section." Dist. Ct. Op. at 13. The district court acknowledged that Liberty contested "whether a collective bargaining agreement exists between the parties under which the union can assert its right to arbitrate" and that Liberty argued the absence of such an agreement rendered judgment on the pleadings inappropriate. *Id.* at 9–10 & n.7. But the district court construed Liberty's assertion that no agreement existed as a legal conclusion, not a factual dispute. Because legal conclusions about a collective bargaining agreement are accorded "no special deference," *id.* at n.7 (quoting *Local Union No. 47, Int'l Bhd. Of Elec. Workers v. NLRB*, 927 F.2d 635, 640 (D.C. Cir. 1991)), the district court found no material fact about the contract to be in dispute.

On appeal, Liberty argues that its denial was factual, not legal, and so failure to accept its denial as true was legal error; that the complete contractual terms and scope were not before the district court on the pleadings, as recognized by the district court's opinion and the pleadings; and that without a full contract to interpret, the order to arbitrate was error. Echoing the district court, MEBA simply responds that Liberty's claim that it did not have an agreement with MEBA covering the *Liberty Peace* is a legal conclusion, not a dispute of material fact. MEBA also argues that Liberty never denied the existence of a collective bargaining agreement that contains a broad arbitration clause, nor that those agreements are still in effect. It claims that Liberty's "tactic" is "smoke and mirrors." Appellee Br. 10. MEBA maintains that Liberty contradicted its appellate theory of the case in litigating the case below, claiming that Liberty conceded the

existence of the contract [—16—] and disputed only whether the contract's broad terms covered the *Liberty Peace*. Essentially, MEBA claims that Liberty's {–762–} appeal is rooted in procedural technicalities, rather than a good faith factual dispute over whether an arbitration clause exists in an authentic, extant contract.

Giving all reasonable inferences to Liberty, Liberty raised material issues of fact that rendered judgment on the pleadings inappropriate. *First*, Liberty properly disputed the existence of a contract to arbitrate in this case. Without a contract binding the parties to arbitrate, an order compelling arbitration is improper. "[A]rbitration is a matter of contract and a party cannot be required to submit to arbitration any dispute which he has not agreed so to submit." *AT&T Techs., Inc. v. Commc'ns Workers of Am.*, 475 U.S. 643, 648 (1986) (quotation marks and citation omitted). Such contracts must be "interpreted as a whole." *United States v. Hunt*, 843 F.3d 1022, 1028 (D.C. Cir. 2016) (quoting Restatement (Second) of Contracts § 202(2)). And although "the determination that parties have contractually bound themselves to arbitrate disputes . . . is a legal conclusion[,] . . . the findings upon which that conclusion is based are factual." *Bailey v. Fed. Nat'l Mortg. Ass'n*, 209 F.3d 740, 744 (D.C. Cir. 2000) (quoting *Chelsea Square Textiles, Inc. v. Bombay Dyeing & Mfg. Co.*, 189 F.3d 289, 295 (2d Cir. 1999)); *see also* 11 Williston on Contracts § 30:3 (4th ed.) ("It is generally a question of fact . . . whether or not a contract . . . actually exists.").

The existence of a contract to arbitrate must first be established through a factual determination of what constitutes the parties' full agreement. As such, the district court erred when it based its conclusion of arbitrability on a contract of genuinely disputed authenticity. Liberty denied the authenticity of the copies of the Master Agreements that MEBA attached to its complaint. Specifically, MEBA alleged in its complaint: [—17—]

Liberty first became signatory to a collective bargaining agreement with

MEBA in 1988 when the Company signed on to both the Union's 1986-1990 Tanker Vessels Master Agreement and the 1986-1990 Dry Cargo Vessels Master Agreement. A copy of the 1986-1990 Tanker Vessels Master Agreement and Liberty's signature page is attached hereto as Exhibit A. A copy of the 1986-1990 Dry Cargo Vessels Master Agreement is attached hereto as Exhibit B. These agreements cover all U.S. flagged vessels owned, managed or operated by Liberty.

MEBA Compl. ¶ 8. In its answer, Liberty admitted that Liberty signed the Master Agreements but denied all other allegations in ¶ 8 of the complaint not expressly admitted. This included denying MEBA's allegation that Exhibits A and B were copies of the Master Agreements. Liberty also denied that even the authentic version of these agreements covered all U.S. flagged vessels managed by Liberty.

Accepting Liberty's allegations as true and making all reasonable inferences in Liberty's favor, as the Rule 12(c) standards require, means that Exhibits A and B were not authenticated copies of the two Master Agreements. Without authenticated Master Agreements, the district court lacked adequate factual support for its finding that the language of the agreements contained an extant arbitration clause. This dispute over authenticity created a material issue of fact that should have been enough to defeat MEBA's Rule 12(c) motion. *See Horsley v. Feldt*, 304 F.3d 1125, 1135 (11th Cir. 2002) ("Because the authenticity of the [documents] attached to the amended answer is disputed, . . . they may not be considered in deciding the Rule 12(c) motion for judgment on the {–763–} pleadings."); *see also Philips*, 572 F.3d at 180. **[—18—]**

Second, several disputed contract provisions were not included in the pleadings and attachments. The pleadings showed that, at least in 2012, Liberty and MEBA were parties to "a Memorandum of Understanding dated September 23, 2005, as amended; various Side Letters, dated June 8, 2005, October 28, 2005, and July 14, 2010,

respectively; and Letters of Understanding, dated July 7, 2009, and February 21, 2010, respectively." MEBA Compl. Exhibit C. Liberty conceded the authenticity of the MOU. But Liberty maintained that the six documents referenced in the MOU, but not attached to MEBA's complaint, were relevant to whether any collective bargaining agreement or arbitration clause applied to the new vessel.

Liberty stresses the pre-suit correspondence attached to MEBA's complaint referenced over a dozen other documents, only three of which were attached to the complaint, and only one of which was conceded to be authentic. Liberty also disputed that a contract covered the *Liberty Peace* on the basis that MEBA failed to define "this Agreement" in the arbitration clause. Because the parties' contractual relationship has been modified by numerous agreements over the decades since the Master Agreements were signed, the record does not make clear to what "this Agreement" refers.

The district court, however, assumed these numerous side letters and letters of understanding did not modify the agreement in any meaningful way, accepting that "the grievance and arbitration procedures contained in the Tanker and Dry Cargo Master Agreements remain binding" without having reviewed the "terms and conditions of employment of the [collective bargaining agreements], side letters, and letters of understanding." Dist. Ct. Op. at 3. These assumptions were inappropriate in the face of controverted facts about the Agreements' content. The pleadings and limited attachments **[—19—]** did not support the conclusion that "no material fact is in dispute." *Peters*, 966 F.2d at 1485.

Third, the district court drew improper inferences against Liberty, the opposing party, rather than against MEBA, the moving party. The district court concluded "Liberty failed to point to any evidence to rebut the presumption of arbitrability." Dist. Ct. Op. at 14. Yet at this stage of the proceedings, it was MEBA's burden to demonstrate the existence of an applicable arbitration agreement, not

Liberty's burden to rebut it. *See Beal*, 312 U.S. at 51. Although the district court correctly identified the federal policy in favor of arbitration agreements, *Moses H. Cone Mem'l Hosp. v. Mercury Constr. Corp.*, 460 U.S. 1, 24–25 (1983), that policy becomes a presumption only when the factual existence of a contract for arbitration has been established. *See AT&T*, 475 U.S. at 648; *Bailey*, 209 F.3d at 744. The district court also found that "no agreement between the parties contains language excluding this sort of dispute from arbitration." Dist. Ct. Op. at 14. But because the whole "agreement" was not before the district court, it erred by inferring, in a manner that favored MEBA, that the "cont[ent]" and "language" of the agreement did not exclude the dispute over the *Liberty Peace* from arbitration.

Fourth, the district court erred by refusing to allow discovery over Liberty's objection that there was a material factual dispute about the existence of an agreement to arbitrate issues relating to the *Liberty Peace*. *See* Dec. 14, 2017 Minute Order. Discovery would have required the district {–764–} court to treat MEBA's motion as one for summary judgment. Fed. R. Civ. P. 12(d) ("If, on a motion under Rule 12(b)(6) or 12(c), matters outside the pleadings are presented to and not excluded by the court, the motion must be treated as one for summary judgment under Rule 56. All parties must be given a reasonable opportunity to present all the material that is pertinent to the [—20—] motion."). Granting such discovery would have allowed Liberty to attempt to substantiate, or MEBA to refute, the claim that the complete contractual record, when read as a whole, does not require arbitration of this dispute.

Despite MEBA's claim that Liberty's argument consists of "smoke and mirrors," MEBA has not shown that Liberty lacks a good faith basis for its appeal. Parties are presumed to have a good faith basis for denying allegations, even at the pleading stage. *See Amnesty Am. v. Town of W. Hartford*, 361 F.3d 113, 131 (2d Cir. 2004) ("Because attorneys, as officers of the court, are presumed not to offer in opposition" to dispositive motions "evidence that they have

no good faith basis to believe will be available or admissible at trial, the burden is on the moving party."). For the reasons stated above and in light of the incomplete contractual record, we assume there was a good faith basis for Liberty to challenge judgment on MEBA's pleadings. We expect the parties, on remand, will act in good faith to narrow their dispute and avoid burying the district court with reams of contractual provisions not arguably relevant to the arbitrability issue in this case.

* * *

This case involved disputed issues of material fact that rendered the unusual remedy of judgment on the pleadings inappropriate. Because the district court should have first determined whether Liberty and MEBA had a valid contract for arbitration by looking at their whole agreement, we reverse the judgment on the pleadings and remand the case for further proceedings consistent with this opinion.

So ordered.

United States Court of Appeals for the Federal Circuit

United States Court of Appeals
for the Federal Circuit

No. 18-1698

VIRGIN ISLANDS PORT AUTH.
VS.
UNITED STATES

Appeal from the United States Court of Federal
Claims

Decided: April 26, 2019

Citation: 922 F.3d 1328, 7 Adm. R. 546 (Fed. Cir. 2019).

Before **DYK, MAYER,** and **CLEVENGER**, Circuit Judges.

[—1—] {–1331–} DYK, Circuit Judge: [—2—]

The Virgin Islands Port Authority ("VIPA") appeals from the grant of the United States' motion for summary judgment in the U.S. Court of Federal Claims ("Claims Court"). The Claims Court rejected VIPA's claim that the collection of wharfage and tonnage fees by the U.S. Customs and Border Protection ("Customs") constituted an illegal exaction. We affirm. {–1332–}

BACKGROUND

The dispute between VIPA and the United States centers on the question of whether certain fees were lawfully collected by Customs from users of ports in the U.S. Virgin Islands ("Virgin Islands"). The particular fees at issue are wharfage fees, "the charge assessed for the service or use of the wharf," and tonnage fees, "the fee charged a vessel for entering and using a port of the U.S. Virgin Islands." J.A. 11 & n.1. While Customs is required under statute to collect customs duties, *see* 48 U.S.C. §§ 1406h, 1406i, and 1642a, the government abandoned reliance on those statutes below as authorizing collection of the disputed fees.

The parties agree that the statutory source, if any, of Customs' authorization to collect the disputed fees is 48 U.S.C. § 1469c, which provides in pertinent part:

To the extent practicable, services, facilities, and equipment of agencies and instrumentalities of the United States Government may be made available, on a reimbursable basis, to the governments of the territories and possessions of the United States . . . .

The Claims Court has detailed the history between Customs and the Virgin Islands, so we focus only on the particularly salient portions. The Virgin Islands is a territory of the United States that can set and receive proceeds from duties, and VIPA is "a public corporation and autonomous governmental instrumentality" of the Virgin Islands' government. V.I. Code Ann. tit. 29, § 541(a). VIPA is [—3—] authorized to, *inter alia*, "determine, fix, alter, charge, and collect reasonable rates, fees, rentals, ship's dues and other charges." *Id.* § 543(12). Since its creation in 1968, VIPA has set wharfage and tonnage fees in its Marine Tariff Schedule.

Customs collected the wharfage and tonnage fees from 1969 to 2011, deducted the costs it incurred from providing its services, and remitted any remaining funds to the Virgin Islands Deposit Fund, which the Virgin Islands controls. The funds were then transferred to VIPA. The source of authority for Customs' collection of the fees before 1994 is unclear.

In 1994, the Virgin Islands and Customs entered into a memorandum of agreement ("1994 MOA"), whereby the parties agreed to "the methodology for determining the costs chargeable to [the Virgin Islands] . . . for operating various [Customs] activities in and for the U.S. Virgin Islands." J.A. 345. The 1994 MOA "identif[ied] those activities that are reimbursable," which included Customs' collection of tonnage and wharfage fees from cargo being imported and exported. J.A. 345, 347. Customs further agreed to report on the collection of these fees to the Virgin Islands. The 1994 MOA also included provisions for amending or revoking the agreement. *See* J.A. 353 ("Any change . . . shall be initiated by the requesting party in a written statement setting forth the exact nature and reason for the change."); J.A. 354 ("This MOA may be revoked by either party upon providing written notice to the other party 180 days prior to the proposed revocation date."). One of the statutes cited in the agreement for Customs' authority to enter into the 1994 MOA was 48 U.S.C. § 1469c.

The current dispute arose from Customs' increasing collection costs, which outpaced the collection of the disputed fees starting in 2004. This left VIPA without any proceeds from the disputed fees. In 2006, VIPA removed the instruction in its Marine Tariff Schedule that users should [—4—] pay the disputed fees to Customs.[1] But Customs continued to collect the fees. In {–1333–} 2007, VIPA sent a letter, approved by the Virgin Islands' governor, "appealing to [Customs] so that [VIPA] can start to collect" the disputed fees. J.A. 371. Customs "respectfully denie[d] VIPA's request" based on Customs' position that 48 U.S.C. §§ 1406h, 1406i, and 1642a, required it to collect the disputed fees as customs duties—a position the government abandoned below. J.A. 375–77. Following a series of letters and meetings between VIPA, the Virgin Islands, and Customs, VIPA sent a letter to Customs in February 2011, indicating that VIPA would start to collect the disputed fees on March 1, 2011. Customs thereafter ceased collecting the disputed fees and VIPA started to collect them instead.[2]

In 2012, VIPA sued Customs to recover the approximately $ 10 million in disputed fees that Customs collected from February 2008 to March 1, 2011.[3] The parties filed cross-motions for summary judgment, and the

---

[1] Before the 2006 amendment, the Marine Tariff Schedule instructed "[a]ll vessels using the facilities of the Virgin Islands Port Authority shall pay to the District Director, U.S. Customs" wharfage fees, and ship dues were to be paid to the "District Director of U.S. Customs." J.A. 11. The 2006 amendment, in relevant part, removed those references for users to pay these fees to Customs.

[2] Eventually in 2014, the 1994 MOA was amended by Customs and the Virgin Islands to remove mention of wharfage and tonnage fees.

[3] VIPA's basis for the choice of start date of Customs' unauthorized collection (February 2008) is unclear as it does not seem to be tied to any action VIPA or Customs took with respect to the disputed fees at issue here. VIPA's counsel also did not know why that start date was selected. Oral Arg. at 9:35–9:37.

Claims Court denied VIPA's motion and granted the United States' [—5—] motion. The only issue VIPA has appealed is whether Customs committed an illegal exaction by collecting the disputed fees allegedly without authorization from 2008 to 2011.[4] We have jurisdiction pursuant to 28 U.S.C. § 1295(a)(3).

DISCUSSION

We review the Claims Court's grant of summary judgment de novo, and summary judgment is appropriate if the movant shows that there is no genuine dispute as to any material fact and that the movant is entitled to judgment as a matter of law. *8x8, Inc. v. United States*, 854 F.3d 1376, 1380 (Fed. Cir. 2017).

One way an illegal exaction occurs is when the "plaintiff has paid money over to the Government, directly or in effect, and seeks return of all or part of that sum" that was "improperly paid, exacted, or taken from the claimant in contravention of the Constitution, a statute, or a regulation." *Eastport S.S. Corp. v. United States*, 372 F.2d 1002, 1007 (Ct. Cl. 1967). "The amount [allegedly illegally] exacted and paid may be recovered whether the money was paid directly to the government, or was paid to others at the direction of the government to meet a governmental obligation" in contravention of law. *Aerolineas Argentinas v. United States*, 77 F.3d 1564, 1573 (Fed. Cir. 1996). VIPA argues that Customs committed an illegal exaction when it collected the disputed fees after its authority to do so was revoked in 2007. *See Eastport*, 372 F.2d at 1007–08; *Aerolineas*, 77 F.3d at 1572–74. The government argues that Customs' actions did not constitute an illegal exaction because it neither received money directly from VIPA nor [—6—] required VIPA to pay a third party. *See Aerolineas*, 77 F.3d at 1578; *Camellia Apartments, Inc. v. United States*, 334 F.2d 667, 669 (Ct. Cl. 1964). We need not resolve the issue of whether Customs' collection constitutes an "in effect"

---

[4] VIPA abandoned its contract-based claims at summary judgment, and it did not appeal the Claims Court's grant of summary judgment to the government on the contracts issue and VIPA's takings claim.

{–1334–} illegal exaction because this is a merits issue, not a jurisdictional one. As discussed below, we conclude that VIPA's claim is without merit because Customs was authorized to collect the disputed fees and that this authority was not revoked during the time frame at issue here.

I. Authorization

On its face, 48 U.S.C. § 1469c allows an agency or instrumentality of the United States (for example, Customs) to provide services to the government of a territory (for example, the Virgin Islands) on a reimbursable basis. The government does not suggest that it could provide reimbursable services without authorization by a territory's government under this statute. Instead, the government relies on the 1994 MOA with the Virgin Islands for Customs' authorization to collect the disputed fees. VIPA argues that the 1994 MOA could not be the source of authority because Customs was collecting the disputed fees before 1994. VIPA argues that its Marine Tariff Schedule, which has been in effect since 1968, was what authorized Customs' collection of the disputed fees, at least until 2006 when it was amended.

By its own terms, the 1994 MOA provided a "methodology for determining the costs chargeable to [the Virgin Islands] . . . for operating various [Customs] activities in and for the U.S. Virgin Islands." J.A. 345. It also "identif[ied] those activities that are reimbursable" including "[p]rocessing [imported and exported] cargo," which included collecting the "tonnage [and] wharfage" fees. J.A. 345, 347. Customs also agreed to report on the collection of these fees. One of the sources of authority for these activities cited in the agreement was 48 U.S.C. § 1469c. As VIPA recognized in its 2007 letter to Customs, the 1994 [—7—] MOA was an agreement "for services to be provided" by Customs, including Customs' "collecti[on of] the following on behalf of the Government of the Virgin Islands: . . . tonnage and wharfage [fees]." J.A. 371. "The [1994 MOA] further allowed [Customs], based on a formula, to retain a portion of the funds collected to be compensated for its services." J.A. 371. On its

face, the 1994 MOA provides authorization for Customs to collect the disputed fees and to reimburse itself for costs attendant to that service. Because we conclude that no reasonable fact-finder could conclude that the 1994 MOA did not authorize Customs' collection of the fees, there is no material dispute of fact on this issue.[5]

To the extent VIPA's Marine Tariff Schedule also constituted authorization for Customs to collect the disputed fees, that does not undermine our conclusion. It may be that Customs has had multiple overlapping sources of authorization throughout the years to collect the disputed fees, but the issue in this litigation is whether Customs had authority from February 2008 to March 1, 2011. The 1994 MOA provided authority during that time period, unless that authority was revoked.[6] [—8—] {–1335–}

II. Revocation

VIPA argues that even if the 1994 MOA constitutes authorization for purposes of 48 U.S.C. § 1469c, that authority was revoked in 2007 before Customs collected the disputed fees from 2008 to 2011. The Claims Court stated that "VIPA's 2007 letter was not effective to revoke the 1994 MOA according to the terms of the MOA itself." J.A. 21. Here, principles of agency law provide guidance as to what is required to revoke authorization under 48 U.S.C. § 1469c. "The question [of

---

[5] To the extent VIPA argues that it is entitled to further discovery on this issue, it did not move for such relief pursuant to Rule 56(d) of the Rules of the U.S. Court of Federal Claims.

[6] The government contends that the 1994 MOA is "an agreement between two sovereigns that did not necessarily contemplate a lawsuit for contract damages" but instead merely "provided for a process whereby the parties would either" amend or revoke the agreement. United States, Response Br. at 31. Even if that is the case, the MOA nevertheless provided authorization for Customs to provide a service (collecting the fees) on a reimbursable basis under 48 U.S.C. § 1469c. Moreover, it does not make a difference that VIPA was not party to the 1994 MOA [—8—] because § 1469c requires authorization from the government of a territory, which Customs had from the Virgin Islands' agreement to the 1994 MOA.

authorization] is at least presumptively governed by principles of agency law . . . ." *Fed. Election Comm'n v. NRA Political Victory Fund*, 513 U.S. 88, 98 (1994). "When discussing the contours and scope of the common law, the Supreme Court has instructed that it is appropriate for us to look to the pertinent Restatement . . . ." *Commonwealth Edison Co. v. United States*, 271 F.3d 1327, 1353 (Fed. Cir. 2001) (en banc).

"[An agent's] authority is revoked or renounced by written or spoken words or other conduct which, reasonably interpreted, indicates that the principal no longer consents to have the agent act for him . . . ." Restatement (Second) of Agency § 119 cmt. a (1958). "[T]he meaning that may reasonably be inferred from [a manifestation of revocation] will reflect the context in which the manifestation is made . . . ." Restatement (Third) of Agency § 1.03 cmt. e (2006). "Between particular persons, prior dealings or an ongoing relationship frame the context in which manifestations are made and understood." *Id.* "The principal has power to revoke and the agent has power to renounce, although doing so is in violation of a contract between the [—9—] parties and although the authority is expressed to be irrevocable." Restatement (Second) of Agency § 118 cmt. b.

The Claims Court's conclusion that VIPA could not revoke Customs' authority without revoking or amending the 1994 MOA is inconsistent with settled agency law that a principal may revoke an agent's authority even if such revocation is in violation of an agreement. The question here is whether Customs' authority under the 1994 MOA was revoked.

At the outset we note that the 2006 amendment to VIPA's Marine Tariff Schedule could not have revoked Customs' authority under the 1994 MOA. In 2006, VIPA removed its instructions for users to pay the disputed fees to Customs. The amended Marine Tariff Schedule did not otherwise indicate to whom the fees should be paid, and Customs continued to collect the fees until 2011. Based on Customs' historical practice of collecting the disputed fees, the equivocal meaning of

VIPA's actions, and the separate ongoing vitality of the 1994 MOA, we conclude that this change in the Marine Tariff Schedule could not have reasonably indicated a revocation of authority under the 1994 MOA.[7]

Instead, VIPA relies on its letter sent to Customs in 2007 as revoking Customs' authority. The letter indicated that VIPA was "appealing to [Customs] so that [VIPA] can start to collect port fees and charges as listed in its tariff." J.A. 371. The letter also noted that VIPA "stands ready to submit any additional information [Customs] may require, [—10—] and is willing to meet to discuss this matter." J.A. 372. Customs responded on August 24, 2007, "respectfully den[ying] VIPA's request" {–1336–} because it believed it was required under federal law, specifically identifying 48 U.S.C. §§ 1406h, 1406i, 1642a, to collect the disputed fees as customs duties. J.A. 375–76. It noted that "[i]f VIPA disagrees with [Customs'] position outlined above, VIPA is welcome to provide [Customs] with evidence to the contrary." J.A. 376. The Virgin Islands' governor's signature with VIPA's 2007 letter indicates that the Virgin Islands agreed to VIPA's request.

The 2007 letter cannot reasonably be interpreted as revoking Customs' authority and therefore does not implicate a dispute of material fact. The 2007 letter merely stated that VIPA was *"appealing* to [Customs] so that it can start to collect" wharfage and tonnage fees. J.A. 371 (emphasis added). And VIPA indicated it was "ready to submit any additional information [Customs] may require, and is *willing to meet to discuss* this matter." J.A. 372 (emphasis added). Thus, the letter indicated that VIPA and the Virgin Islands were willing to discuss the issue of whether or not Customs would continue to collect the disputed fees, not that the authority was being revoked. *Compare Gov't Guarantee Fund of Republic of Finland v.*

---

[7] There is also the issue of whether VIPA's actions could be attributable to the government of a territory, i.e., the Virgin Islands, under 48 U.S.C. § 1469c. We need not decide that issue as we conclude that VIPA's change to the tariff schedule did not constitute an effective revocation of authority for Customs to collect the disputed fees.

Hyatt Corp., 95 F.3d 291, 306 (3d Cir. 1996) (concluding that a letter stating the agreement was "void, terminated, and/or expired" and demanding "immediate[] surrender" of the property indicated that the agency relationship was terminated). This conclusion is supported by communications after 2007 between the Virgin Islands and Customs, which focused on amending the 1994 MOA to change the collection of the disputed fees.

Moreover, the 1994 MOA clearly laid out a process by which the Virgin Islands could either revoke or amend the agreement. It provided that "[t]his MOA may be revoked by either party upon providing written notice to the other party 180 days prior to the *proposed revocation date*." J.A. [—11—] 354 (emphasis added). "Any change required by the [parties] . . . in the provisions of this MOA shall be *initiated* by the requesting party in a written statement setting forth the exact nature and reason for the change." J.A. 353 (emphasis added). To be sure, as noted earlier, an agency relationship can be terminated even in violation of an agreement. But absent a clear statement to the contrary, it was reasonable for Customs to assume that if the Virgin Islands wanted to revoke Customs' authority, revocation would be accomplished by invoking the specific revocation provision in the 1994 MOA. VIPA's reliance on the 2007 letter is therefore misplaced, as it cannot be reasonably interpreted as revoking Customs' authority.

Finally, VIPA argues that it was futile for it to attempt to revoke Customs' collection authority under the 1994 MOA because Customs claimed an obligation to collect based on other statutory sources, 48 U.S.C. §§ 1406h, 1406i, 1642a, claims of authority that Customs has since abandoned. VIPA claims that "[h]aving declared that its collection of VIPA's fees would continue with or without VIPA's authorization, [Customs] effectively mooted any effort by VIPA or the USVI Government to amend the 1994 MOA, because under [Customs'] legal position such an amendment would not have stopped [Customs] from collecting and retaining VIPA's fees." VIPA, Open. Br. at 11.

In the regulatory takings context, an erroneous government claim of right does not constitute a taking unless there is "a prohibition or . . . coercive government action." *Dimare Fresh, Inc. v. United States*, 808 F.3d 1301, 1311 (Fed. Cir. 2015). "[G]overnment action devoid of coercion, legal threat, regulatory restriction, or any binding obligation [does not] effect a regulatory taking." *Id.* Coercion of the claimant is of course not typically an {–1337–} element of an illegal exaction claim, though coercion might in the present context excuse action to revoke the government's authority. But, as in the takings context, a mere claim of right is not coercive and here, there was neither a prohibition nor [—12—] coercive government action. Indeed, VIPA disputed Customs' claim that statutes required it to collect the disputed fees, and VIPA never suggested until the lawsuit began it was coerced into foregoing revocation of Customs' authority under the 1994 MOA. The government's claim of statutory compulsion did not prevent VIPA from challenging the government's claim of statutory authority by revoking the government's authority under the 1994 MOA.

CONCLUSION

Because Customs was authorized under 48 U.S.C. § 1469c, in combination with the 1994 MOA, to collect the disputed fees from February 2008 to March 1, 2011, and because that authority was not revoked during that time, we affirm the Claims Court's grant of the United States' motion for summary judgment.

AFFIRMED

COSTS

No costs.

Tables of Authority

This page intentionally left blank

Table of Cases

This page intentionally left blank

TABLE OF CASES¹

---

¹ Cases named solely after ships, *see, e.g., The Pennsylvania*, 86 U.S. (19 Wall.) 125 (1873), are alphabetized under the letter "T." Cases where the United States is the plaintiff are alphabetized by defendant under the letter "U."

B

C

D

E

F

G

H

I

J

K

N

O

P

Q

R

S

T

U

V

W

Y

Z

Table of Statutes and Rules

This page intentionally left blank

TABLE OF STATUTES AND RULES[1]

PAGE

TREATIES/INTERNATIONAL

FEDERAL

CONSTITUTION

MISCELLANEOUS

---

[1] As cited in the opinions reported.

Statutes

RULES

REGULATIONS

STATE

This page intentionally left blank

Index

This page intentionally left blank

INDEX

A

B

C

D

E

F

G

H

I

J

L

M

N

O

P

Q

R

S

T

U

V

W